Fourth Canadian Edition

FINANCIAL INSTITUTIONS

MANAGEMENT

A Risk Management Approach

Anthony Saunders
Stern School of Business
New York University

Marcia Millon Cornett
Southern Illinois University

Patricia A. McGraw
Ted Rogers School of Management
Ryerson University

McGraw-Hill Ryerson
Connect. Learn. Succeed.

Financial Institutions Management: A Risk Management Approach
Fourth Canadian Edition

ISBN-13: 978-0-07-097979-6
ISBN-10: 0-07-097979-0

1 2 3 4 5 6 7 8 9 0 TCP 1 9 8 7 6 5 4 3 2 1 0

Printed and bound in Canada.

Care has been taken to trace ownership of copyright material contained in this text; however, the publisher will welcome any information that enables rectification of any reference or credit for subsequent editions.

Vice-President and Editor-in-Chief: Joanna Cotton
Sponsoring Editors: Kimberley Redhead, Jeremy Guimond
Marketing Manager: Cathie Lefebvre
Developmental Editor: Sarah Fulton
Supervising Editor: Kara Stahl
Editorial Associate: Jennifer Clark
Copy Editor: June Trusty
Production Coordinator: Sheryl MacAdam
Cover and Interior Design: Katherine Strain
Cover Image Credit: © Joel Rogers/Getty Images
Page Layout: Laserwords Private Limited
Printer: Transcontinental Printing Group

Library and Archives Canada Cataloguing in Publication

Saunders, Anthony
    Financial institutions management / Anthony Saunders,
Marcia Millon Cornett, Patricia McGraw. — 4th Canadian ed.

Includes index.
ISBN 978-0-07-097979-6

    1. Financial institutions—Canada—Management—Textbooks.   2. Risk
management—Canada—Textbooks. I. Cornett, Marcia Millon II. McGraw, Patricia
(Patricia Anne), 1951- III. Title.

HG185.C2S29 2010   332.1068   C2009-906967-9

This book is dedicated to Pat, Nicholas, and Emily and to my mother, Evelyn.

Anthony Saunders

To the Millons and the Cornetts, especially Galen.

Marcia Millon Cornett

This book is dedicated to Gary, Bryan, Andrea, Tyler, Lavon, Doreen, Joanna, and Cameron.

Patricia A. McGraw

About the Authors

Anthony Saunders

Anthony Saunders is the John M. Schiff Professor of Finance and Chair of the Department of Finance at the Stern School of Business at New York University. Professor Saunders received his Ph.D. from the London School of Economics and has taught both undergraduate- and graduate-level courses at NYU since 1978. Throughout his academic career, his teaching and research have specialized in financial institutions and international banking. He has served as a visiting professor all over the world, including INSEAD, the Stockholm School of Economics, and the University of Melbourne. He is currently on the Executive Committee of the Salomon Center for the Study of Financial Institutions, NYU.

Professor Saunders holds positions on the Board of Academic Consultants of the Federal Reserve Board of Governors as well as the Council of Research Advisors for the Federal National Mortgage Association. In addition, Dr. Saunders has acted as a visiting scholar at the Comptroller of the Currency and at the Federal Reserve Bank of Philadelphia. He also held a visiting position in the research department of the International Monetary Fund. He is an editor of the *Journal of Banking & Finance* and the *Journal of Financial Markets, Instruments and Institutions*, as well as the associate editor of eight other journals, including *Financial Management* and the *Journal of Money, Credit and Banking*. His research has been published in all the major money and banking and finance journals and in several books. In addition, he has authored or co-authored several professional books, the most recent of which is *Credit Risk Measurement: New Approaches to Value at Risk and Other Paradigms*, 2nd edition, John Wiley and Sons, New York, 2002.

Marcia Millon Cornett

Marcia Millon Cornett is the Rehn Professor of Business at Southern Illinois University at Carbondale. She received her B.S. degree in Economics from Knox College in Galesburg, Illinois, and her M.B.A. and Ph.D. degrees in Finance from Indiana University in Bloomington, Indiana. Dr. Cornett has written and published several articles in the areas of bank performance, bank regulation, and corporate finance. Articles authored by Dr. Cornett have appeared in such academic journals as the *Journal of Finance*, the *Journal of Money, Credit and Banking*, the *Journal of Financial Economics*, *Financial Management*, and the *Journal of Banking & Finance*. She served as an associate editor of *Financial Management* and is currently an associate editor for the *Journal of Banking & Finance*, *Journal of Financial Services Research*, *FMA Online*, the *Multinational Finance Journal* and the *Review of Financial Economics*. Dr. Cornett is currently a member of the Board of Directors, the Executive Committee, and the Finance Committee of the SIU Credit Union. Dr. Cornett has also taught at the University of Colorado, Boston College, and Southern Methodist University. She is a member of the Financial Management Association, the American Finance Association, and the Western Finance Association.

Patricia A. McGraw

Patricia A. McGraw is Associate Professor, Finance, at the Ted Rogers School of Management, Ryerson University. Dr. McGraw holds a B.Sc. degree in Geology and Chemistry from McGill University, an M.Sc. in Geology from Dalhousie University, an M.B.A. in Finance and Accounting from the University of Toronto, and a Ph.D. in Interdisciplinary Studies from Dalhousie University. She has taught undergraduate and graduate finance courses at Dalhousie University and Ryerson University in Canada; at Lincoln University in Christchurch, New Zealand; and at Universiti Tenaga Nasional in Kuala Lumpur, Malaysia.

Dr. McGraw has worked as an exploration geologist and as a corporate banker specializing in lending to resource companies. She has also consulted to the offshore natural gas industry. Her research and publications focus on lender environmental liability, capital market evolution, and capital structure and cost of capital in emerging markets.

Brief Contents

Chapter Appendices

*Available at the Online Learning Centre:
www.mcgrawhill.ca/olc/saunders*

Contents

Chapter Appendices

All appendices are available at the Online
Learning Centre:
  www.mcgrawhill.ca/olc/saunders

Preface to the Fourth Canadian Edition

"For us, of course, things can change so abruptly, so violently, so profoundly, that futures like our grandparents' have insufficient 'now' to stand on. We have no future because our present is too volatile. . . . We have only risk management. The spinning of the given moment's scenarios. Pattern recognition."

William Gibson, *Pattern Recognition*, New York: Berkley Books, p. 57

Financial intermediaries (FIs) have always been in the business of risk management. However, the contracts that they create to manage and to transfer risk have changed significantly in the last 20 years. This has resulted in the development of different methods of "pattern recognition," that is, risk management techniques that an FI uses to protect its customers and its shareholders and, as well, to satisfy regulators in protecting the financial system. Thus, the purpose of this textbook is to identify patterns, to develop scenarios, and to provide information about the risk management techniques used by financial institutions in Canada. However, the global scope of Canada's FIs and the global nature of today's financial markets mean that the pattern recognition must extend beyond the Canadian border.

My purpose in adapting this textbook from the U.S. version is to present a view of the Canadian financial services industry that situates it clearly within the North American market and provides a sense of the global patterns that shape this industry. It is my hope that the readers of this textbook will obtain an understanding of the issues that make these firms so fascinating to study, and will be able to apply the risk management techniques whether as an employee of an FI or as a consumer of the products of FIs.

The global financial system suffered a meltdown in 2007 and 2008 that saw many consumers go bankrupt (U.S. subprime mortgage borrowers), companies go bankrupt (Lehman Brothers), and countries go bankrupt (Iceland). The Canadian financial system and its financial institutions, however, were incredibly stable. This fourth Canadian edition focuses on the response of Canadian financial institutions and their regulators to the global financial crisis and, where appropriate, compares the Canadian experience to that of U.S. and global FIs.

Intended Audience

Financial Institutions Management: A Risk Management Approach is aimed at upper-level undergraduate and M.B.A. audiences. The more technical sections are marked with a footnote: *These sections may be included or dropped from the chapter reading, depending on the rigour of the course, without harming the continuity of the chapters.*

What's New in the Fourth Canadian Edition

A focus of the revision is the effect of the 2007–2009 global financial disruptions on Canadian and international financial institutions. The *Ethical Dilemmas* and *Industry Perspectives* features reflect this issue, and chapters related to the global credit crunch are significantly revised. These include the chapters involving credit risk (Chapters 11, 12, 26, and 27), liquidity risk (Chapters 17 and 18), and capital adequacy (Chapter 20). The emphasis throughout is on the stability of Canadian financial intermediaries relative to U.S. and global financial markets.

Each chapter in this edition has been revised to reflect the most up-to-date information available. End-of-chapter questions and problems have been expanded and updated to provide a complete selection of testing material, and an *Integrated Mini-Case* has been added to several chapters. The following are some of the new features of this edition:

- Chapter 1 introduces the market disruptions of 2007 and 2008 and provides a table summarizing the six types of regulatory response to the financial crisis.
- Chapter 2 considers the impact of the global credit crisis on Canadian banks.
- Chapter 3 contains new material introducing the concept of moral hazard.
- Chapter 4 has new content regarding a national securities regulator in Canada. New *Global Issues* material has been included as well.
- Chapter 5 has an expanded discussion of pension funds, including the Canada Pension Fund Investment Board and its global investing strategy. The chapter also includes new information on hedge funds and their role in the subprime crisis.
- Chapter 6 provides a discussion of government financial entities (sovereign wealth funds) and venture capital sources.
- Chapter 7 contains new Canadian examples and discusses the importance of enterprise risk management, governance, and reputational risk for Canadian FIs.
- Chapter 10 considers the advantages and weaknesses of the value at risk (VaR) measure and provides new examples of how Canadian FIs manage market risk.
- Chapter 13 discusses the impact of off-balance-sheet risks coming back onto the balance sheet of FIs, as in the recent credit crisis.
- The order of Chapters 14 through 16 has been changed so that all client-based risk measures are presented first, followed by risk measures associated with the internal operations of the financial institution.
- Chapter 16 contains new content related to Basel II and operational risk.
- Chapter 17 and Chapter 18 provide updated material related to Basel II and liquidity risk for banks. Liquidity issues for each type of FI are also discussed.
- Chapter 19 has an updated discussion of the Canada Deposit Insurance Corporation (CDIC) and new material on protection programs for credit unions, pensions, and insurance companies.
- Chapter 20 has updated material on market value versus book value and accounting issues (mark to market). There is also new material on ratings agencies and Basel II, their role in the current financial crisis, and the move to regulate them.
- Chapter 21 discusses the conversion of U.S. investment banks into commercial banks as a result of the credit crisis, and provides a comparison with Canada and reasons why the Canadian financial system is sound.
- Chapter 22 has new material on international diversification, with an emphasis on the international nature of Canadian FIs.
- Chapters 23, 24, and 25 contain updated material on futures, forwards, swaps, and options and their role in the credit crisis, as well as new material on plans to regulate over-the-counter derivatives (the Geithner proposal) and credit default swaps.

- Chapter 27 has been expanded to consider collateralized debt obligations (CDOs), collateralized mortgage obligations (CMOs), structured investment vehicles (SIVs), special-purpose entities (SPEs), etc., to put the global financial crisis into perspective. An updated discussion of asset securitization in terms of Canadian FIs and the differences between Canadian, U.S., and global practices has been provided. A discussion of the asset-backed commercial paper (ABCP) freeze in Canada is also included.

Organization

Since the focus is on return and risk and the sources of that return and risk, this book relates ways in which the managers of modern FIs can expand return with a managed level of risk to achieve the best, or most favourable, return-risk outcome for FI owners.

Part 1: Introduction

Chapter 1 introduces the special functions of FIs and takes an analytical look at how financial intermediation benefits the Canadian and the global economies. Chapters 2 through 6 provide an overview describing the key balance sheet and regulatory features of the major sectors of the Canadian financial services industry. Deposit-taking institutions are discussed in Chapter 2; insurance companies in Chapter 3; securities firms and investment banks in Chapter 4; mutual funds, pension funds, and hedge funds in Chapter 5; and finance companies in Chapter 6. Chapter 7 previews the risk measurement and management sections with an overview of the risks facing a modern FI.

Part 2: Risk Measurement

Chapters 8 and 9 start the risk measurement section by investigating the net interest margin as a source of profitability and risk, with a focus on the effects of interest rate volatility and the mismatching of asset and liability durations on FI risk exposure. Chapter 10 analyzes market risk, a risk that results when FIs actively trade bonds, equities, and foreign currencies.

Chapter 11 looks at the measurement of credit risk of individual loans and bonds and how this risk adversely affects an FI's profits through losses and provisions against the loan and debt security portfolio. Chapter 12 looks at the risk of loan (asset) portfolios and the effects of loan concentrations on risk exposure. Modern FIs do more than generate returns and bear risk through traditional maturity mismatching and credit extensions. They also engage in off-balance-sheet activities to generate fee income (Chapter 13), pursue foreign exchange activities and overseas financial investments (Chapter 14), participate in sovereign lending and securities activities (Chapter 15), and make technological investments to reduce costs (Chapter 16). Each of these has implications for the size and variability of an FI's profits and/or revenues. In addition, as a by-product of the provision of their interest rate and credit intermediation services, FIs face liquidity risk. The special nature of this risk is analyzed in Chapter 17.

Part 3: Risk Management

Chapter 18 begins the risk management section by looking at ways in which FIs can insulate themselves from liquidity risk. Chapter 19 looks at the key role that deposit insurance and other guarantee programs play in reducing liquidity risk. At the core of FI risk insulation is the size and adequacy of the owners' capital or equity investment in the FI, which is the focus of Chapter 20. Chapters 21 and 22 analyze how and why product diversification and geographic expansion—both domestic and international—can improve an FI's return-risk performance and the impact of regulation on the diversification opportunity set. Chapters 23 through 27 review various new markets and instruments that have been innovated or engineered to allow FIs to better manage three important types of risk: interest rate risk, credit risk, and foreign exchange risk. These markets and instruments and their strategic use by FIs include futures and forwards (Chapter 23); options, caps, floors, and collars (Chapter 24); swaps (Chapter 25); loan sales (Chapter 26); and securitization (Chapter 27).

Main Features

Throughout the text, special features have been integrated to encourage students' interaction with the text and to aid them in absorbing the material. Some of these features include:

In-chapter examples, which provide numerical demonstrations of the analytics described in various chapters.

> **EXAMPLE 5–1**
>
> *Effect of Capital Appreciation on NAV*
>
> Suppose a mutual fund contains 1,000 shares of Canadian Tire currently trading at $37.75, 2,000 shares of Encana currently trading at $43.70, and 1,500 shares of CIBC currently trading at $46.67. The mutual fund currently has 15,000 shares outstanding held by investors. Thus, today, the NAV of the fund is calculated as
>
> NAV = [(1,000 × $37.75) + (2,000 × $43.70) + (1,500 × $46.67)] ÷ 15,000 = $13.01
>
> If next month Canadian Tire shares increase to $45, Encana shares increase to $48, and CIBC shares increase to $50, the NAV (assuming the same number of shares outstanding) would increase to
>
> NAV = [(1,000 × $45) + (2,000 × $48) + (1,500 × $50)] ÷ 15,000 = $14.40

Ethical Dilemmas **and** *Industry Perspectives* **features,** which demonstrate the application of chapter material to real current events. See page xxii for a complete listing.

> **INDUSTRY PERSPECTIVES**
>
> **ING SELLING MOST OF ITS STAKE IN CANADIAN UNIT**
> Financially stressed Dutch bank ING Groep NV is giving up control of its Canadian unit, ING Canada Inc. for at least $1.75-billion, but it is doing it at a steep discount to the market price.
>
> The parent, which has received a 10-billion euro bailout from the Dutch government and installed a new chief executive officer last week, is selling most of its 70% stake in Canada's largest provider of home, auto and business insurance through a two-part offering.
>
> It will sell a minimum of $850-million of its ING Canada common shares to certain institutional investors in a private placement at a price of $25 a share. As part of the deal, investors are required to hold those shares for four months.
>
> The parent will also sell an additional $900-million of its ING Canada common shares, at a price of $26.35 a share to other investors. Those shares are freely tradeable. The underwriters have been given an option to sell an additional 5.12 million shares.
>
> Charles Brindamour, chief executive of ING Canada, said "thanks to our partnership with ING Group, we have built over the years a world-class organization. Now, with the proposed transactions, for the first time in recent history, a Canadian-listed and con-
>
> This political and regulatory uncertainty is a key reason foreign-based buyers were reluctant to increase their exposure to the Canadian market by buying the unit.
>
> But the main reason ING opted for a heavily discounted sale to insurers appears to have been a strong desire on the part of the parent to liquidate its holdings for cash quickly, as it continues to reel from heavy losses.
>
> Given that the financing is being done on a secondary basis, the Canadian division, which went public in late 2004, will not receive any of the proceeds.
>
> The shares are being offered at prices that are considerably below the recent trading price of common shares of ING Canada, which operates under the ING Canada, Belair Direct and Grey Power banners. When the stock was halted, the shares were trading at $33.79, 21% above the price of the shares it will now be offering to the retail market. And at about $26 a share, the price is almost identical to the $26 a share that ING was able to garner when it went public just over four years back.
>
> The deal will also heighten questions over the future of ING Bank of Canada, which specializes in high-interest online deposits and holds more than $24-billion in assets for more than 1.6-million Canadians.

Bold key terms and marginal glossary, which emphasize the main terms and concepts throughout the chapter and aid in studying.

Global Issues **highlights,** which call out material relating to North American and global issues.

GLOBAL ISSUES

The disruptions in the global capital markets in 2007 and 2008 reshaped the investment banking industry in the United States and globally. As mentioned earlier in the chapter, Canada went through a "Big Bang" in 1987 that resulted in revisions to the Bank Act and the formation of OSFI. The largest securities firms were bought by the Big Six banks, the trust companies were also consolidated, and Canadian financial institutions moved toward universal banking. The model thus saw investment activities supported by merging with a bank funded by a stable source of deposits. By the time of the credit crisis in 2007, Canada had 20 years of experience with this model. The United States, however, didn't replace

Concept Questions, which aid in studying by allowing students to test themselves on the main concepts within each major chapter section.

1. How are liquidity and liability management related?
2. Describe the trade-off faced by an FI manager in structuring the liability side of the balance sheet.

Internet Exercises and references, which guide the student to access the most recent data on the Web.

INTERNET EXERCISE

Go to the Thomson Reuters website (www.thomsonreuters.com) and find the latest information available for top global underwriters of various securities. Click on "Financial" and then on the live link under "League Tables." Click on "Debt & Equity Archive" to access files that contain the most recent information on top underwriters for various securities.

Comprehensive Teaching and Learning Package

We have developed a number of supplements for both teaching and learning to accompany this text:

For Instructors

Instructor's Online Learning Centre

(www.mcgrawhill.ca/olc/saunders)

The Online Learning Centre includes a password-protected website for instructors. The site offers downloadable supplements, including an Instructor's Manual, test bank, and PowerPoint® package, and PageOut, the McGraw-Hill Ryerson course website development centre.

For Students

Student Online Learning Centre

(www.mcgrawhill.ca/olc/saunders)

The Student Online Learning Centre, prepared by Larbi Hammami, McGill University, offers a wealth of learning materials, including online quizzes, appendices, Web links, Standard & Poor's questions, and much more. There is also a link to *Finance Around the World,* a tremendous resource that takes students to important and popular finance websites from around the globe.

Superior Service

Service takes on a whole new meaning with McGraw-Hill Ryerson and *Financial Institutions Management.* More than just bringing you the textbook, we have consistently raised the bar in terms of innovation and educational research—both in finance and in education in general. These investments in learning and the education community have helped us to understand the needs of students and educators across the country, and allowed us to foster the growth of truly innovative, integrated learning.

Integrated Learning

Your Integrated Learning Sales Specialist is a McGraw-Hill Ryerson representative who has the experience, product knowledge, training, and support to help you assess and integrate any of our products, technology, and services into your course for optimum teaching and learning performance. Whether it's helping your students improve their grades, or putting your entire course online, your *i*Learning Sales Specialist is there to help you do it. Contact your *i*Learning Sales Specialist today to learn how to maximize all of McGraw-Hill Ryerson's resources!

*i*Learning Services

McGraw-Hill Ryerson offers a unique services package designed for Canadian faculty. This includes technical support, access to our educational technology conferences, and custom e-courses to name just a few. Please speak to your local *i*Learning Sales Specialist for details.

Create Online

(www.mcgrawhillcreate.com)

McGraw-Hill's Create Online gives you access to the most abundant resource at your fingertips—literally. With a few mouse clicks, you can create customized learning tools simply and affordably. McGraw-Hill Ryerson has included many of our market-leading textbooks within Create Online for e-book and print customization as well as many licensed readings and cases. For more information, go to www.mcgrawhillcreate.com.

Teaching & Learning Conference Series

The educational environment has changed tremendously in recent years and McGraw-Hill Ryerson continues to be committed to helping you acquire the skills you need to succeed in this new milieu. Our innovative Teaching & Learning Conference Series brings faculty together from across Canada with 3M Teaching Excellence award winners to share teaching and learning best practices in a collaborative and stimulating environment. Pre-conference workshops on general topics, such as teaching large classes and technology integration, are also offered. We will also work with you at your own institution to customize workshops that best suit the needs of the faculty at your institution.

Acknowledgements

When considering the efforts of contributors, I am indebted and offer special thanks to the following reviewers, whose constructive suggestions have been incorporated as much as possible into the development of the fourth Canadian edition:

Nalinaksha Bhattacharyya, University of Manitoba

Keith Cheung, University of Windsor

Eldon Gardner, University of Lethbridge

Larbi Hammami, McGill University

Frank Ingold, George Brown College

Maria Pacurar, Dalhousie University

Charles Schell, University of Northern British Columbia

Brian Smith, Wilfrid Laurier University

Lois Tullo, Schulich School of Business, York University

I would also like to thank McGraw-Hill Higher Education and McGraw-Hill Ryerson for their professional contributions, including Kimberley Redhead and Jeremy Guimond, Sponsoring Editions; Sarah Fulton, Developmental Editor; Kara Stahl, Supervising Editor; June Trusty, Copy Editor; Maria Pacurar, Technical Checker; and many others.

Finally, I look forward to teachers' comments, suggestions, and questions. It is my hope that this textbook will make a positive difference in your students' education.

Patricia A. McGraw
Ted Rogers School of Management
Ryerson University

Feature Boxes

Industry Perspectives

Ethical Dilemmas

The Financial Services Industry

Why Are Financial Intermediaries Special?

In this chapter, we look at the specialness of financial institutions (FIs) and discuss

▸ the special functions that FIs provide

▸ how these special functions benefit the economy

▸ what makes some FIs more special than others

▸ how unique and long-lived the special functions of FIs are

INTRODUCTION

Bank Act
Federal legislation in Canada governing deposit-taking financial institutions.

four pillars
A term used to describe the separation of financial intermediation into four functions: banking, trust (fiduciary), insurance, and investment banking (securities).

universal bank
An FI that is permitted by regulators to offer a full range of financial services.

Prior to the revision of the **Bank Act** in 1992, financial institutions (FIs) in Canada were divided by function into **four pillars:** chartered banks, trust companies, insurance companies, and investment dealers. These FIs were prevented from providing services "cross-pillar." For example, prior to 1954, Canadian banks could not offer residential mortgages. In the 1970s and 1980s, new, relatively unregulated financial service industries sprang up (mutual funds, brokerage funds, etc.) that separated financial services functions even further. However, in the 21st century, regulatory barriers, technology, and financial innovations are changing so that, eventually, a full set of financial services may be offered by a single firm or **universal bank.** Not only have the boundaries between traditional industry sectors weakened, but competition has become global as well. As the competitive environment changes, attention to profit and, more than ever, risk, becomes increasingly important. The major themes of this book are the measurement and management of the risks of financial institutions. Financial institutions (e.g., banks, credit unions, insurance companies, and mutual funds) perform the essential function of channelling funds from those with surplus funds (suppliers of funds) to those with shortages of funds (users of funds). At the beginning of 2008, the assets of just the banks in Canada were greater than \$2.6 trillion. By comparison, the market capitalization of the 341 mining companies listed on the Toronto Stock Exchange (TSX) was \$338 billion.

Although we might categorize or group FIs as life insurance companies, banks, finance companies, and so on, they face many common risks. Specifically, all FIs described in this chapter and Chapters 2 through 6 (1) hold some assets that are potentially subject to default or credit risk and (2) tend to mismatch the maturities of their balance sheet assets and liabilities to a greater or lesser extent and are thus exposed to interest rate risk. Moreover, all FIs are exposed to some degree of liability withdrawal or liquidity risk, depending on the type of claims they have sold to liability holders. In addition, most FIs are exposed to some type of underwriting risk, whether through the sale of securities or the issue of various types of credit guarantees on or off the balance sheet. Finally, all FIs are exposed to operating cost risks because the production of financial services requires the use of real resources and back-office support systems (labour and technology combined to provide services).

TABLE 1–1 **Areas of Financial Intermediaries' Specialness in the Provision of Services**

Information costs The aggregation of funds in an FI provides greater incentive to collect information about customers (such as corporations) and to monitor their actions. The relatively large size of the FI allows this collection of information to be accomplished at a lower average cost (so-called economies of scale) than would be the case for individuals.

Liquidity and price risk FIs provide financial claims to household savers with superior liquidity attributes and with lower price risk.

Transaction cost services Similar to economies of scale in information production costs, an FI's size can result in economies of scale in transaction costs.

Maturity intermediation FIs can better bear the risk of mismatching the maturities of their assets and liabilities.

Transmission of monetary supply Deposit-taking institutions are the conduit through which monetary policy actions by the country's central bank (such as the Bank of Canada) affect the rest of the financial system and the economy.

Credit allocation FIs are often viewed as the major, and sometimes only, source of financing for a particular sector of the economy, such as farming, small business, and residential real estate.

Intergenerational wealth transfers FIs, especially life insurance companies and pension funds, provide savers with the ability to transfer wealth from one generation to the next.

Payment services The efficiency with which deposit-taking institutions provide payment services such as cheque clearing directly benefits the economy.

Denomination intermediation FIs, such as mutual funds, allow small investors to overcome constraints to buying assets imposed by large minimum denomination size.

Because of these risks and the special role that FIs play in the financial system, FIs are singled out for special regulatory attention. In this chapter, we first examine questions related to this specialness. In particular, what are the special functions provided by FIs, both deposit-taking institutions (banks, credit unions, and caisses populaires) and non-deposit-taking institutions (insurance companies, securities firms, investment banks, finance companies, and mutual funds)? These special functions are summarized in Table 1–1. How do these functions benefit the economy? Second, we investigate what makes some FIs more special than others. Third, we look at how unique and long-lived the special functions of FIs really are.

FINANCIAL INTERMEDIARIES' SPECIALNESS

To understand the important economic function of FIs, imagine a simple world in which FIs do not exist. In such a world, households generating excess savings by consuming less than they earn would have the basic choice: They could hold cash as an asset or invest in the securities issued by corporations. In general, corporations issue securities to finance their investments in real assets and cover the gap between their investment plans and their internally generated savings such as retained earnings.

As shown in Figure 1–1, in such a world, savings would flow from households to corporations; in return, financial claims (equity and debt securities) would flow from corporations to household savers.

FIGURE 1–1
Flow of Funds in a World without FIs

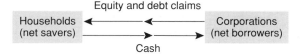

In an economy without FIs, the level of fund flows between household savers and the corporate sector is likely to be quite low. There are several reasons for this. Once they have lent money to a firm by buying its financial claims, households need to monitor, or check, the actions of that firm. They must be sure that the firm's management neither absconds with nor wastes the funds on any projects with low or negative net present values. Such monitoring actions are extremely costly for any given household because they require considerable time and expense to collect sufficiently high-quality information relative to the size of the average household saver's investments. Given this, it is likely that each household would prefer to leave the monitoring to others; in the end, little or no monitoring would be done. The resulting lack of monitoring would reduce the attractiveness and increase the risk of investing in corporate debt and equity.

The relatively long-term nature of corporate equity and debt, and the lack of a secondary market in which households can sell these securities, creates a second disincentive for household investors to hold the direct financial claims issued by corporations. Specifically, given the choice between holding cash and holding long-term securities, households may well choose to hold cash for **liquidity** reasons, especially if they plan to use savings to finance consumption expenditures in the near future.

Finally, even if financial markets existed (without FIs to operate them) to provide liquidity services by allowing households to trade corporate debt and equity securities among themselves, investors also face a **price risk** on sale of securities, and the secondary market trading of securities involves various transaction costs. That is, the price at which household investors can sell securities on secondary markets such as the Toronto Stock Exchange may well differ from the price they initially paid for the securities.

Because of (1) monitoring costs, (2) liquidity costs, and (3) price risk, the average household saver may view direct investment in corporate securities as an unattractive proposition and prefer either not to save or to save in the form of cash.

However, the economy has developed an alternative and indirect way to channel household savings to the corporate sector. This is to channel savings via FIs. Because of costs of monitoring, liquidity, and price risk, as well as for some other reasons, explained later, savers often prefer to hold the financial claims issued by FIs rather than those issued by corporations.

Consider Figure 1–2, which is a closer representation than Figure 1–1 of the world in which we live and the way funds flow in our economy. Notice how financial intermediaries or institutions are standing, or intermediating, between the household and corporate sectors. These intermediaries fulfill two functions; any given FI might specialize in one or the other or might do both simultaneously.

liquidity
The ease of converting an asset into cash.

price risk
The risk that the sale price of an asset will be lower than the purchase price of that asset.

FIGURE 1–2
Flow of Funds in a World with FIs

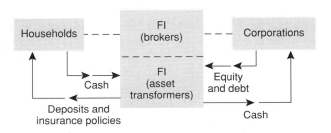

FIs Function as Brokers

The first function is the brokerage function. When acting as a pure broker, an FI acts as an agent for the saver by providing information and transaction services. For example, full-service securities firms (e.g., RBC Dominion Securities) carry out investment research and make investment recommendations for their retail (or household) clients as well as conduct the purchase or sale of securities for commission or fees. Discount brokers (e.g., E*Trade) carry out the purchase or sale of securities at better prices and with greater efficiency than household savers could achieve by trading on their own. This efficiency results in reduced costs of trading, or **economies of scale** (see Chapter 21 for a detailed discussion). Independent insurance brokers identify the best types of insurance policies household savers can buy to fit their savings and retirement plans. In fulfilling a brokerage function, the FI plays an extremely important role by reducing transaction and information costs or imperfections between households and corporations. Thus, the FI encourages a higher rate of savings than would otherwise exist.[1]

FIs Function as Asset Transformers

The second function is the asset-transformation function. In acting as an **asset transformer,** the FI issues financial claims that are far more attractive to household savers than the claims directly issued by corporations. That is, for many households, the financial claims issued by FIs dominate those issued directly by corporations as a result of lower monitoring costs, lower liquidity costs, and lower price risk. In acting as asset transformers, FIs purchase the financial claims issued by corporations—equities, bonds, and other debt claims called **primary securities**—and finance these purchases by selling financial claims to household investors and other sectors in the form of deposits, insurance policies, and so on. The financial claims of FIs may be considered **secondary securities** because these assets are backed by the primary securities issued by commercial corporations that in turn invest in real assets. Specifically, FIs are independent market parties that create financial products whose value added to their clients is the transformation of financial risk.

Simplified balance sheets of a commercial firm and an FI are shown in Table 1–2. Note that in the real world, FIs hold a small proportion of their assets in the form of real assets such as bank branch buildings. These simplified balance sheets reflect a reasonably accurate characterization of the operational differences between commercial firms and FIs.

How can FIs purchase the direct or primary securities issued by corporations and profitably transform them into secondary securities more attractive to household savers? This question strikes at the very heart of what makes FIs special and

economies of scale
The concept that the cost reduction in trading and other transaction services results from increased efficiency when FIs perform these services.

asset transformer
An FI issues financial claims that are more attractive to household savers than the claims directly issued by corporations.

primary securities
Securities issued by corporations and backed by the real assets of those corporations.

secondary securities
Securities issued by FIs and backed by primary securities.

TABLE 1–2
Simplified Balance Sheets for a Commercial Firm and an FI

Commercial Firm		Financial Intermediary	
Assets	**Liabilities**	**Assets**	**Liabilities**
Real assets (plant, machinery)	Primary securities (debt, equity)	Primary securities (debt, equity)	Secondary securities (deposits and insurance policies)

---

[1] With the introduction of new derivative securities markets for financial futures, options, and swaps, financial institutions that participate in the markets may reduce transaction and information costs for firms and consumers wanting to hedge their risks. Thus, FIs may encourage better risk management than otherwise would exist.

important to the economy. The answer lies in the ability of FIs to better resolve the three costs facing a saver who chooses to invest directly in corporate securities.

Information Costs

One problem faced by an average saver directly investing in a commercial firm's financial claims is the high cost of information collection. Household savers must monitor the actions of firms in a timely and complete fashion after purchasing securities. Failure to monitor exposes investors to **agency costs,** that is, the risk that the firm's owners or managers will take actions with the saver's money contrary to the promises contained in the covenants of its securities contracts. Monitoring costs are part of overall agency costs. That is, agency costs arise whenever economic agents enter into contracts in a world of incomplete information and thus costly information collection. The more difficult and costly it is to collect information, the more likely it is that contracts will be broken. In this case the saver (the principal) could be harmed by the actions taken by the borrowing firm (the agent).

agency costs
Costs relating to the risk that the owners and managers of firms that receive savers' funds will take actions with those funds contrary to the best interests of the savers.

FI's Role as Delegated Monitor

One solution to this problem is for a large number of small savers to place their funds with a single FI. This FI groups these funds together and invests in the direct or primary financial claims issued by firms. This agglomeration of funds resolves a number of problems. First, the large FI now has a much greater incentive to collect information and monitor actions of the firm because it has far more at stake than does any small individual household. In a sense, small savers have appointed the FI as a **delegated monitor** to act on their behalf.[2] Not only does the FI have a greater incentive to collect information, the average cost of collecting information is lower. For example, the cost to a small investor of buying a $100 broker's report may seem inordinately high for a $10,000 investment. For an FI with $10 million under management, however, the cost seems trivial. Such economies of scale of information production and collection tend to increase the advantages to savers of using FIs rather than directly investing themselves.

delegated monitor
An economic agent appointed to act on behalf of smaller agents in collecting information and/or investing funds on their behalf.

FI's Role as Information Producer

Second, associated with the greater incentive to monitor and the costs involved in failing to monitor appropriately, FIs may develop new secondary securities that enable them to monitor more effectively. Thus, a richer menu of contracts may improve the monitoring abilities of FIs. Perhaps the classic example of this is the bank loan. Bank loans are generally shorter-term debt contracts than bond contracts. This short-term nature allows the FI to exercise more monitoring power and control over the borrower. In particular, the information the FI generates regarding the firm is frequently updated as its loan renewal decisions are made. When bank loan contracts are sufficiently short term, the banker becomes almost like an insider to the firm regarding informational familiarity with its operations and financial conditions. This more frequent monitoring often replaces the need for the relatively inflexible and hard-to-enforce covenants found in bond contracts. Thus, by acting as a delegated monitor and producing better and more timely

---

[2] For a theoretical modelling of the delegated monitor function, see D. W. Diamond, "Financial Intermediaries and Delegated Monitoring," *Review of Economic Studies* 51 (1984), pp. 393–414; and A. Winton, "Competition among Financial Intermediaries When Diversification Matters," *Journal of Financial Intermediation* 6 (1997), pp. 307–46.

information, FIs reduce the degree of information imperfection and asymmetry between the ultimate suppliers and users of funds in the economy.

Liquidity and Price Risk

In addition to improving the flow and quality of information, FIs provide financial or secondary claims to household and other savers. Often, these claims have superior liquidity attributes compared with those of primary securities such as corporate equity and bonds. For example, banks and other deposit-taking institutions (DTIs) issue transaction account deposit contracts with a fixed principal value (and often a guaranteed interest rate) that can be withdrawn immediately on demand by household savers.[3] Money market mutual funds issue shares to household savers that allow those savers to enjoy almost fixed principal (deposit-like) contracts while often earning interest rates higher than those on bank deposits. Even life insurance companies allow policyholders to borrow against their policies held with the company at very short notice. The real puzzle is how FIs such as deposit-taking institutions can offer highly liquid and low price-risk contracts to savers on the liability side of their balance sheets while investing in relatively illiquid and higher price-risk securities issued by corporations on the asset side. Furthermore, how can FIs be confident enough to guarantee that they can provide liquidity services to investors and savers when they themselves invest in risky asset portfolios? And why should savers and investors believe FIs' promises regarding the liquidity of their investments?

diversify
Reducing risk by holding a number of securities in a portfolio.

The answers to these questions lie in the ability of FIs to **diversify** away some but not all of their portfolio risks. The concept of diversification is familiar to all students of finance: Basically, as long as the returns on different investments are not perfectly *positively* correlated, by exploiting the benefits of size, FIs diversify away significant amounts of portfolio risk—especially the risk specific to the individual firm issuing any given security. Indeed, experiments have shown that equal investments in as few as 15 securities can bring significant diversification benefits to FIs and portfolio managers.[4] Further, as the number of securities in an FI's asset portfolio increases beyond 15 securities, portfolio risk falls, albeit at a diminishing rate. What is really going on here is that FIs exploit the law of large numbers in their investments, achieving a significant amount of diversification, whereas because of their small size, many household savers are constrained to holding relatively undiversified portfolios. This risk diversification allows an FI to predict more accurately its expected return on its asset portfolio. A domestically and globally diversified FI may be able to generate an almost risk-free return on its assets. As a result, it can credibly fulfill its promise to households to supply highly liquid claims with little price or capital value risk. A good example of this is the ability of a bank to offer highly liquid demand deposits—with a fixed principal value—as liabilities, while at the same time investing in risky loans as assets. As long as an FI is sufficiently large to gain from diversification and monitoring, its financial claims are likely to be viewed as liquid and attractive to small savers compared with direct investments in the capital market.

---

[3] Also, the largest commercial banks in the world make markets for swaps, allowing businesses to hedge various risks (such as interest rate risk and foreign exchange risk) on their balance sheets.

[4] For a Canadian perspective, see S. Cleary and D. Copp, "Diversification with Canadian Stocks: How Much Is Enough?" *Canadian Investment Review* 12, Fall 1999, pp. 21–25.

Other Special Services

The preceding discussion has concentrated on three general or special services provided by FIs: reducing household savers' monitoring costs, increasing their liquidity, and reducing their price-risk exposure. Next, we discuss two other special services provided by FIs: reduced transaction costs and maturity intermediation.

Reduced Transaction Costs

Just as FIs provide potential economies of scale in information collection, they also provide potential economies of scale in transaction costs. For example, small retail buyers face higher commission charges or transaction costs than do large wholesale buyers. By grouping their assets in FIs that purchase assets in bulk—such as in mutual funds and pension funds—household savers can reduce the transaction costs of their asset purchases. In addition, bid–ask (buy–sell) spreads are normally lower for assets bought and sold in large quantities.

Maturity Intermediation

An additional dimension of FIs' ability to reduce risk by diversification is that they can better bear the risk of mismatching the maturities of their assets and liabilities than can small household savers. Thus, FIs offer maturity intermediation services to the rest of the economy. Specifically, through maturity mismatching, FIs can produce new types of contracts, such as long-term mortgage loans to households, while still raising funds with short-term liability contracts. Further, while such mismatches can subject an FI to interest rate risk (see Chapters 8 and 9), a large FI is better able to manage this risk through its superior access to markets and instruments for hedging such as loan sales and securitization (Chapters 26 and 27); futures (Chapter 23); swaps (Chapter 25); and options, caps, floors, and collars (Chapter 24).

	1. **What are the three major risks to household savers from direct security purchases?** 2. **What are two major differences between brokers (such as security brokers) and deposit-taking institutions (such as banks)?** 3. **What are primary securities and secondary securities?** 4. **What is the link between asset diversification and the liquidity of deposit contracts?**

OTHER ASPECTS OF SPECIALNESS

The theory of the flow of funds points to three principal reasons for believing that FIs are special, along with two other associated reasons. In reality, academics, policymakers, and regulators identify other areas of specialness relating to certain specific functions of FIs or groups of FIs. We discuss these next.

The Transmission of Monetary Policy

The highly liquid nature of bank and other FI deposits has resulted in their acceptance by the public as the most widely used medium of exchange in the economy. Indeed, at the core of the three most commonly used definitions of the money supply—M1, M2, and M3[5]—lie deposit-taking institutions' deposit contracts.

---

[5] The Bank of Canada defines the money supply as M1: ($207.7 billion outstanding in November 2008) the currency in circulation (bank notes and coins) plus personal chequing accounts and current accounts at banks; M2: ($868.2 billion outstanding in November 2008) equal to M1 plus personal savings accounts and other chequing accounts, term deposits, and non-personal notice deposits; and M3: ($1.303 trillion in November 2008) equal to M1 plus M2 plus bank non-personal term deposits plus foreign currency deposits of residents of Canada.

Because the liabilities of deposit-taking institutions are a significant component of the money supply that influences the rate of inflation, they play a key role in the *transmission of monetary policy* from the central bank to the rest of the economy. That is, chartered banks and other DTIs are the conduit through which monetary policy actions affect the rest of the financial sector and the economy in general. The aim of monetary policy in Canada is to protect the value of the dollar by controlling the level of inflation. The Bank of Canada carries out monetary policy primarily through setting the target overnight rate (the rate at which financial institutions lend money to each other for one day in the overnight inter-bank market). The target overnight rate in turn influences the loan rates and deposit rates offered by the deposit-taking institutions.

www.bankofcanada.ca

Credit Allocation

A further reason FIs are often viewed as special is that they are the major and sometimes the only source of finance for a particular sector of the economy pre-identified as being in special need of finance. Policymakers in Canada, the United States, and a number of other countries, such as the United Kingdom, have identified *residential real estate* as needing special subsidies. For example, Canada Mortgage and Housing Corporation (CMHC) insures residential mortgage loans where the downpayment is less than 25 percent. This has enhanced the specialness of FIs that most commonly service the needs of that sector. In a similar fashion, farming is an especially important area of the economy in terms of the overall social welfare of the population. Farm Credit Canada (FCC) provides loans to the agricultural industry members who are unable to get credit elsewhere.

www.cmhc.ca

www.fcc-fac.ca

Intergenerational Wealth Transfers or Time Intermediation

The ability of savers to transfer wealth between youth and old age and across generations is also of great importance to the social well-being of a country. Because of this, life insurance companies (see Chapter 3) and pension funds (see Chapter 5) are often especially encouraged, via special taxation relief and other subsidy mechanisms, to service and accommodate those needs.

Payment Services

Deposit-taking institutions such as banks, credit unions, and caisses populaires (see Chapter 2) are special in that the efficiency with which they provide payment services directly benefits the economy. Important payment services are cheque-clearing, debit and credit transactions, and wire transfer services. For example, on any given day, billions of dollars' worth of payments are effected through the Large Value Transfer System (LVTS) operated by the Canadian Payments Association (see Chapter 16). Any breakdowns in this system probably would produce gridlock in the payment system with resulting harmful effects to the economy.

Denomination Intermediation

Both money market and debt-equity mutual funds are special because they provide services relating to denomination intermediation (see Chapter 5). Because they are sold in very large denominations, many assets are either out of reach of individual savers or would result in savers holding highly undiversified asset portfolios. For example, the minimum size of a negotiable CD is $100,000 and commercial paper (short-term corporate debt) is often sold in minimum packages of $250,000 or more. Individually, a saver may be unable to purchase such instruments. However, by buying shares in a money market mutual fund along with other small investors, household savers overcome the constraints to buying assets imposed by large minimum denomination sizes. Such indirect access to these markets may allow small savers to generate higher returns on their portfolios as well.

SPECIALNESS AND REGULATION

negative externalities
Action by an economic agent imposing costs on other economic agents.

In the preceding section, FIs were shown to be special because of the various services they provide to sectors of the economy. Failure to provide these services or a breakdown in their efficient provision can be costly to both the ultimate sources (households) and users (firms) of savings. The **negative externalities**[6] affecting firms and households when something goes wrong in the FI sector of the economy make a case for regulation. That is, FIs are regulated to protect against a disruption in the provision of the services discussed above and the costs this would impose on the economy and society at large. For example, bank failures may destroy household savings and at the same time restrict a firm's access to credit. Insurance company failures may leave households totally exposed in old age to catastrophic illnesses and sudden drops in income on retirement. Further, individual FI failures may create doubts in savers' minds regarding the stability and solvency of FIs in general and cause panics and even runs on sound institutions. In addition, racial, sexual, age, or other discrimination—such as mortgage **redlining**—may unfairly exclude some potential financial service consumers from the marketplace.

redlining
The procedure by which a banker refuses to make loans to residents living inside given geographic boundaries.

This type of market failure needs to be corrected by regulation. Although regulation may be socially beneficial, it also imposes private costs, or a regulatory burden, on individual FI owners and managers. For example, regulations prohibit banks from making loans to individual borrowers that exceed more than 25 percent of their total capital even though the loans may have a positive net present value to the bank. Consequently, regulation is an attempt to improve the social welfare benefits and mitigate the social costs of the provision of FI services. The private costs of regulation relative to its private benefits, for the producers of financial services, is called the **net regulatory burden.**[7]

net regulatory burden
The difference between the private costs of regulations and the private benefits for the producers of financial services.

Six types of regulation seek to increase the net social welfare benefits of financial intermediaries' services: (1) safety and soundness regulation, (2) monetary policy regulation, (3) credit allocation regulation, (4) consumer protection regulation, (5) investor protection regulation, and (6) entry and chartering regulation. Regulations are imposed differentially on the various types of FIs. For example, deposit-taking institutions are the most heavily regulated of the FIs. Regulation can also be imposed at the federal or the provincial/territorial level and occasionally at the international level, as in the case of bank capital requirements (see Chapter 20).

Finally, some of these regulations are functional in nature, covering all FIs that carry out certain functions, such as payment services, while others are institution-specific.

---

[6] A good example of a negative externality is the costs faced by small businesses in a one-bank town if the local bank fails. These businesses could find it difficult to get financing elsewhere, and their customers could be similarly disadvantaged. As a result, the failure of the bank may have a negative or contagious effect on the economic prospects of the whole community, resulting in lower sales, production, and employment.

[7] Other regulated firms, such as gas and electric utilities, also face a complex set of regulations imposing a net regulatory burden on their operations.

Safety and Soundness Regulation

To protect depositors and borrowers against the risk of FI failure due, for example, to a lack of diversification in asset portfolios, regulators have developed layers of protective mechanisms. These mechanisms are intended to ensure the safety and soundness of the FI and thus to maintain the credibility of the FI in the eyes of its borrowers and lenders. In the first layer of protection are requirements encouraging FIs to diversify their assets. Thus, banks are required not to make loans exceeding 25 percent of their total equity capital funds to any one company or borrower (see Chapter 11).

The second layer of protection concerns the minimum level of capital or equity funds that the owners of an FI need to contribute to the funding of its operations (see Chapter 20). For example, FI regulation is concerned with the minimum ratio of capital to (risk) assets. The higher the proportion of capital contributed by owners, the greater the protection against insolvency risk to outside liability claimholders such as depositors and insurance policyholders. This is because losses on the asset portfolio due, for example, to the lack of diversification are legally borne by the equity holders first, and only after equity is totally wiped out by outside liability holders.[8] Consequently, by varying the required degree of equity capital, FI regulators can directly affect the degree of risk exposure faced by nonequity claimholders in FIs. (See Chapter 20 for more discussion on the role of capital in FIs.)

www.cdic.ca The third layer of protection is the provision of guaranty funds such as the Canada Deposit Insurance Corporation (CDIC) to meet insolvency losses to small claimholders (see Chapter 19). By protecting FI claimholders, when an FI collapses and owners' equity or net worth is wiped out, these funds create a demand for regulation of the insured institutions to protect the funds' resources (see Chapter 19 for more discussion).

The fourth layer of regulation is monitoring and surveillance itself. Regulators subject all FIs, whether banks, securities firms, or insurance companies, to varying degrees of monitoring and surveillance. This involves on-site examination as well as an FI's production of accounting statements and reports on a timely basis for off-site evaluation. Just as savers appoint FIs as delegated monitors to evaluate the behaviour and actions of ultimate borrowers, society appoints regulators to monitor the behaviour and performance of FIs.

Finally, note that regulation is not without costs for those regulated. For example, society's regulators may require FIs to have more equity capital than private owners believe is in their own best interests. Similarly, producing the information requested by regulators is costly for FIs because it involves the time of managers, lawyers, and accountants. Again, the socially optimal amount of information may differ from an FI's privately optimal amount.[9]

As noted earlier, the differences between the private benefits to an FI from being regulated—such as insurance fund guarantees—and the private costs it faces from adhering to regulation—such as examinations—is called the *net regulatory burden*. The higher the net regulatory burden on FIs, the more inefficiently they produce any given set of financial services from a private (FI) owner's perspective.

---

[8] Thus, equity holders are junior claimants and debt holders are senior claimants to an FI's assets.

[9] Also, a social cost rather than social benefit from regulation is the potential risk-increasing behaviour (often called moral hazard) that results if deposit insurance and other guaranty funds provide coverage to FIs and their liability holders at less than the actuarially fair price (see Chapter 19 for further discussion).

Monetary Policy Regulation

www.bankofcanada.ca

outside money
The part of the money supply directly produced by the government or central bank, such as notes and coin.

inside money
The part of the money supply produced by the private banking system.

Another motivation for regulation concerns the special role banks play in the transmission of monetary policy from the Bank of Canada (the central bank) to the rest of the economy. The problem is that the central bank directly controls only the quantity of notes and coin in the economy—called **outside money**—whereas the bulk of the money supply consists of deposits—called **inside money.** In theory, a central bank can vary the quantity of cash or outside money and directly affect a bank's reserve position as well as the amount of loans and deposits a bank can create without formally regulating the bank's portfolio. In practice, regulators have chosen to impose formal controls.[10] Banks in Canada are not subject to reserve requirements but in many countries, including the United States, regulators commonly impose a minimum level of required cash reserves to be held against deposits (see Chapter 17). Some argue that imposing such reserve requirements makes the control of the money supply and its transmission more predictable. Such reserves also add to an FI's net regulatory burden if they are more than the institution believes are necessary for its own liquidity purposes. In general, whether banks or insurance companies, all FIs would choose to hold some cash reserves—even non-interest-bearing—to meet the liquidity and transaction needs of their customers directly. For well-managed FIs, however, this optimal level is normally low, especially if the central bank (or other regulatory body) does not pay interest on required reserves. As a result, FIs often view required reserves as similar to a tax and as a positive cost of undertaking intermediation.[11]

Credit Allocation Regulation

Credit allocation regulation supports the FI's lending to socially important sectors such as housing and farming. Canada does not have this type of regulation, but in the United States these regulations may require an FI to hold a minimum amount of assets in one particular sector of the economy or to set maximum interest rates, prices, or fees to subsidize certain sectors. Examples of asset restrictions include insurance regulations that set maximums on the amount of foreign or international assets in which insurance companies can invest. Examples of interest rate restrictions are the usury laws on the maximum rates that can be charged on loans. The Canadian Criminal Code defines a criminal rate as an effective annual rate greater than 60 percent.

Such price and quantity restrictions may have justification on social welfare grounds—especially if society has a preference for strong (and subsidized) housing and farming sectors. However, they can also be harmful to FIs that have to bear the private costs of meeting many of these regulations. To the extent that the net private costs of such restrictions are positive, they add to the costs and reduce the efficiency with which FIs undertake intermediation.

---

[10] In classic central banking theory, the quantity of bank deposits *(D)* is determined as the product of 1 over the banking system's required (or desired) ratio of cash reserves to deposits *(r)* times the quantity of bank reserves *(R)* outstanding, where *R* comprises notes and coin plus bank deposits held on reserve at the central bank. $D = (1/r) \times R$. Thus, by varying *R*, given a relatively stable reserve ratio *(r)*, the central bank can directly affect *D*, the quantity of deposits or inside money that, as just noted, is a large component of the money supply. Even if not required to do so by regulation, banks would still tend to hold some cash reserves as a liquidity precaution against the sudden withdrawal of deposits or the sudden arrival of new loan demand.

[11] In the United States, bank reserves held with the central bank (the Federal Reserve, or the Fed) are non-interest-bearing. In some other countries, interest is paid on bank reserves, thereby lowering the "regulatory tax" effect. Canada eliminated bank reserves in 1994.

Consumer Protection Regulation

www.fcac-acfc.gc.ca

In 2001, Bill C-8 was passed by the federal government to reform the financial services industry in Canada. The Financial Consumer Agency of Canada was created to protect consumers of financial services by ensuring that FIs adhered to the consumer protection regulation in Canada. For example, the FCAC provides information for consumers on such services as bank accounts and investment products. The FCAC also examines and imposes fines on FIs who violate the consumer protection laws.

In addition, on July 21, 2003, eight Canadian FIs renewed a public commitment to provide low-cost banking services to Canadians. Thus, it can be argued that consumer protection laws impose a considerable net regulatory burden on FIs, but the offsetting benefit is the provision of equal access to mortgage and lending markets. As deregulation proceeds, it is likely that such laws will be extended beyond banks to other financial services providers such as insurance companies.

Investor Protection Regulation

A considerable number of laws protect investors who use investment banks directly to purchase securities and/or indirectly to access securities markets through investing in mutual or pension funds. Various laws protect investors against abuses such as insider trading, lack of disclosure, outright malfeasance, and breach of fiduciary responsibilities (see Chapter 4). As with consumer protection legislation, compliance with these acts can impose a net regulatory burden on FIs.[12]

Entry Regulation

The entry and activities of FIs are also regulated (e.g., new bank chartering regulations). Increasing or decreasing the cost of entry into a financial sector affects the profitability of firms already competing in that industry. Thus, the industries heavily protected against new entrants by high direct costs (e.g., through required equity or capital contributions) and high indirect costs (e.g., by restricting individuals who can establish FIs) of entry produce bigger profits for existing firms than those in which entry is relatively easy (see Chapters 21 and 22). In addition, regulations (such as the Bank Act) define the scope of permitted activities under a given charter (see Chapter 21). The broader the set of financial service activities permitted under a given charter, the more valuable that charter is likely to be. Thus, barriers to entry and regulations pertaining to the scope of permitted activities affect the *charter value* of an FI and the size of its net regulatory burden.

CONCEPT QUESTIONS	1. Why should more regulation be imposed on FIs than on other types of private corporations? 2. Define the concept of net regulatory burden. 3. What six major types of regulation do FIs face?

---

[12] There have been a number of moves to extend these regulations to hedge funds, which have traditionally been outside regulations and the securities acts as long as they have fewer than 100 "sophisticated" investors. It has been believed that large sophisticated investors do not need such protections. However, scandals and failures relating to hedge funds and their investments—such as the failure of Long-Term Capital Management in 1998 and its subsequent bailout—appear to be changing lawmakers' and regulators' perceptions, as we discuss in Chapter 5.

THE CHANGING DYNAMICS OF SPECIALNESS

At any moment in time, each FI supplies a set of financial services (brokerage-related, asset transformation-related, or both) and is subject to a given net regulatory burden. As the demands for the special features of financial services change as a result of changing preferences and technology, one or more areas of the financial services industry become less profitable. Similarly, changing regulations can increase or decrease the net regulatory burden faced in supplying financial services in any given area. These demand, cost, and regulatory pressures are reflected in changing market shares in different financial service areas as some contract and others expand. Clearly, an FI seeking to survive and prosper must be flexible enough to move to growing financial service areas and away from those that are contracting. If regulatory activity restrictions inhibit or reduce the flexibility with which FIs can alter their product mix, this will reduce their competitive ability and the efficiency with which financial services are delivered. That is, activity barriers within the financial services industry may reduce the ability to diversify and potentially add to the net regulatory burden faced by FIs.

Trends in Canada

Figure 1-3 shows the percentage distribution of the financial sector assets held in Canada in 2007 by banks, mutual fund companies, property and casualty insurance companies, life and health insurers, and credit unions/caisses populaires. The banks are highest at 68 percent, followed by mutual fund companies at 18 percent. The effect of mutual fund companies is understated in Figure 1-3 as the data for the banks, insurance companies, and credit unions/caisses populaires include the assets of their mutual fund subsidiaries. Mutual fund assets have increased from $42.2 billion in 1990 to $700 billion in 2007, almost a 17-fold increase over the 17-year period. The major banks took over the largest independent securities firms (Dominion Securities, McLeod Young Weir, Wood Gundy, among others) in the 1980s. The 1990s saw more consolidation in the financial services sector subsequent to the implementation of the revised Bank Act in 1992 that permitted banks to own trusts. Toronto-Dominion Bank took over Central Guaranty Trust in 1992 and Canada Trust in 2000, which resulted in the virtual elimination of the trust industry as one of the four pillars. The asset allocation by sector has changed very little.[13]

FIGURE 1–3
Financial Services Assets in Canada by Sector, 2007

Sources: Office of the Superintendent of Financial Institutions (OSFI), Mutual Fund Dealers Association of Canada, and Credit Union Central of Canada.

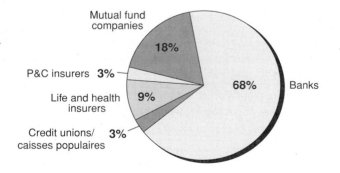

---

[13] The Bank Act determines who may operate as a bank in Canada and specifies which activities are allowed. For a detailed history of the Bank Act and its influence on Canadian financial markets, see P. L. Siklos, *Money, Banking, and Financial Institutions: Canada in the Global Environment,* 5th ed., 2006, Toronto: McGraw-Hill Ryerson, Chapter 18, pp. 350–356. See also M. Babad and C. Mulroney's book, *Pillars: The Coming Crisis in Canada's Financial Industry,* 1993, Toronto: Stoddart Publishing, for an early popular history and predictions of the impact of consolidation on Canada's financial services sector.

Traditional services provided by deposit-taking institutions (payment services, transaction cost services, information costs) have become relatively less significant as a portion of all services provided by FIs. In particular, FIs engaged in securities functions such as the sale of mutual funds and other investment products differ from banks and insurance companies in that they give savers cheaper access to the direct securities markets. They do so by exploiting the comparative advantages of size and diversification, with the transformation of financial claims, such as maturity transformation, a lesser concern. Thus, mutual funds buy stocks, bonds, commercial paper, and Treasury bills directly in financial markets and issue savers shares whose value is linked in a direct pro rata fashion to the value of the mutual fund's asset portfolio. To the extent that these funds efficiently diversify, they also offer price-risk protection and liquidity services.

The maturity and return characteristics of the financial claims issued by mutual funds closely reflect the maturities of the direct equity and debt securities portfolios in which they invest. In contrast, banks, credit unions, and insurance companies have lower correlations between their asset portfolio maturities and the promised maturity of their liabilities. Thus, banks may partially fund a 10-year commercial loan with demand deposits; a credit union may fund 25-year conventional mortgages with three-month term deposits.

To the extent that the financial services market is efficient and these trends reflect the forces of demand and supply, they indicate a current trend: Savers increasingly prefer the denomination intermediation and information services provided by mutual funds. These FIs provide investments that closely mimic diversified investments in the *direct* securities markets over the transformed financial claims offered by traditional FIs. This trend may also indicate that the net regulatory burden on traditional FIs—such as banks and insurance companies—is higher than that on investment companies. As a result, traditional FIs are unable to produce their services as cost efficiently as they could previously. It is increasingly important that FI managers deal with changing trends and reconsider how best to exploit any remaining competitive advantages to keep the net benefit of regulation positive for their FIs.

In addition to a decline in the use of traditional services provided by deposit-taking institutions and insurance companies and an increase in the services provided by investment banks and mutual funds, the early 2000s saw an overall weakening of public trust and confidence in the ethics followed by financial institutions. Specifically, tremendous publicity was generated concerning conflicts of interest in a number of financial institutions between analysts' research recommendations on stocks to buy or not buy and whether these firms played a role in underwriting the securities of the firms the analysts were recommending. As a result, several highly publicized securities violations resulted in criminal cases brought against securities law violators in the United States. Such allegations of securities law violations can reach across the U.S.-Canada border and lead to a loss in public trust and confidence in many sectors of the FI industry.

Future Trends

The growth of mutual funds coupled with the weakening of public trust and confidence (amid a multitude of regulatory investigations into the practices of investment advisors, brokers, and banks), and with investors' recent focus on direct investments in primary securities, may together signal the beginning of a trend away from intermediation as the most efficient mechanism for savers to channel funds to borrowers. While this trend may reflect changed investors' preferences toward risk and return, it may also reflect a decline in the relative costs of direct securities investment versus investment via FIs. This decline in costs has led to many FI products being "commoditized" and sold directly in financial markets; for example, many options initially offered over the counter by FIs eventually migrate to the public option markets as trading volume grows and trading terms become standardized. As Merton has noted, financial markets "tend to be efficient institutional alternatives to intermediaries when the products have standardized terms, can serve a large number of customers and are well-enough understood for transactors to be comfortable in assessing their prices . . . intermediaries are better suited for low volume products."[14]

A dominant issue for Canadian FIs in recent years has been the merger of firms within the financial sector (see Chapter 22). Revisions to the Bank Act in the 1980s and 1990s allowed banks to own brokerage firms as well as trust companies and insurance subsidiaries (banks are still not allowed to sell insurance in their branches). This moved Canada's financial sector closer to universal banking and the creation of larger banks as well as larger insurance firms (Manulife Financial, Sun Life Financial). Some of this growth has come from expansion overseas (Bank of Nova Scotia's purchase of Mexico's Banco Inverlat) and in the United States. (Manulife Financial's merger with John Hancock of Boston). However, the issue of bank–bank mergers as well as cross-pillar mergers of banks and insurance companies within Canada has yet to be resolved. The 1998 MacKay report recognized that the safety and soundness of the financial system, fair and ethical competitive markets, and consumer protection were necessary aims for the regulation of the financial sector. The disallowance in 1998 by the minister of Finance of two proposed mergers (Canadian Imperial Bank of Commerce with Toronto-Dominion Bank, and Royal Bank of Canada with Bank of Montreal) came with a promise of a ruling with respect to mergers that was still awaited in 2009.[15]

Nevertheless, since the late 1980s, Canada's experiment with universal banking has been relatively successful. Canada's 20 years of experience contrasts with that of the United States, where the Financial Services Modernization Act, which allowed the FI industry to consolidate, was not enacted until 1999. As of 2008, the U.S. stand-alone investment banks had been converted to bank holding companies, and the commercial banks were downsizing as a result of the credit and liquidity crises that had begun. See the Industry Perspectives boxed feature relating to Citigroup's universal bank strategy and the Global Issues discussion later in this chapter.

e-trading
Buying and selling shares on the Internet.

Direct financial markets are evolving fast. Because of technological advances, the costs of direct access to financial markets by savers are falling and the relative benefits to individual savers of investing through FIs are narrowing. The ability to reduce transaction costs by **e-trading** on the Internet rather than using a traditional stockbroker and paying brokerage fees has reduced the need for FIs to perform these services. In addition, large FIs such as the Royal Bank of Canada are adapting technology to serve their existing customers across banking and investment services (Chapter 16) as well as to meet the demands placed on FIs for information regarding money laundering and terrorism as a result of the terrorist attacks on the World Trade Center and the Pentagon in September 2001.

---

[14] R. Merton, "A Functional Perspective of Financial Intermediation," *Financial Management,* Summer 1995, p. 26.

[15] The MacKay Task Force, appointed by the minister of Finance in 1996, submitted its report in 1998: *Report of the Task Force on the Future of the Canadian Financial Services Sector,* September 1998.

INDUSTRY PERSPECTIVES

CITIGROUP'S "UNIVERSAL" STRATEGY SUFFERS DEATH BLOW

The world's most ambitious banking experiment is over.

Citigroup Inc., which forged the financial supermarket model and became the planet's biggest bank, took a major step yesterday toward unwinding a decade of history.

Amid speculation that it could announce a $10-billion (U.S.) quarterly operating loss next week, Citigroup agreed to swap Smith Barney, viewed as one of its top businesses and a cash cow, for a 49-per-cent stake in the new Morgan Stanley Smith Barney and a $2.7-billion upfront cash payment.

Now it's reportedly considering a further overhaul to slim down and refocus. The plan, expected to be announced this month, could mark the end of the bank's ambitions to be a one-stop shop for financial services.

The shift in strategy has been quick. As recently as late November, Citigroup chief executive Vikram Pandit was standing by the bank's model, reiterating the goal of being a "truly global universal bank."

But that was days before the U.S. government became the bank's largest shareholder by way of a $45-billion injection.

Citigroup's decision yesterday to put its prized brokerage network into a joint venture with Morgan Stanley marks a "sudden departure from the party line," UBS analysts said in a note to clients. The analysts believe the move is partly being driven by the U.S. government, which might feel selling some key assets should be part of the healing plan.

Yesterday's move appears to be only the beginning, with Citigroup now looking at the sale of some non-core businesses and at narrowing its concentration to two major lines of business.

The private-label credit card business, consumer finance operations and a number of consumer businesses in Japan are among those on the block, while the key business lines going forward will be wholesale banking for large corporate clients and retail banking for customers in selected global markets, *The Wall Street Journal* reported.

Such moves would be a massive retreat for Citigroup, which gave birth to the so-called financial supermarket model in the U.S. with the 1998 merger of Citicorp and Travelers Group. The bank had consumer lending, investment banking, a brokerage and even insurance.

"Citigroup's model was let's get bigger, and that will make us better," said Robert Millen, who helps invest $2.5-billion at Jensen Investment Management in Portland, Ore. "It didn't work that way."

"The problem with Citi is the model, the execution, the management," said William Smith at Smith Asset Management.

"How do you go a decade without integrating?"

The bank has been struggling to raise capital since suffering $20.3-billion in losses in the 12 months up to September.

Its stock price, now about a 10th of what it was two years ago, closed up 5.4 per cent yesterday.

Source: Tara Perkins, *The Globe and Mail*, "Report on Business," January 14, 2009, p. B1. *With files from AP, Reuters.*

GLOBAL ISSUES

deleveraging
A decline in a company's debt-to-equity ratio, either through asset shrinkage or through a decline in debt and an increase in owner's equity.

The turmoil in credit markets started in August 2007 when global financial institutions began to experience losses related to subprime mortgages that originated in the United States. These mortgages had been transformed through securitization and sold to investors (commercial banks, investment banks, hedge funds, pension funds, governments) around the world. However, 2007 was just the beginning. In 2008, financial markets experienced disruptions of credit that resulted in **deleveraging,** a decline of confidence in the markets, runs on financial institutions, and failures of insurance companies and commercial and investment banks worldwide. Stock exchanges around the world experienced declines in value on the order of 40 percent, and financial institutions lost close to US$1 trillion in asset value.

This amount had to be replaced by additional capital in order to meet regulatory requirements. Regulators acted internationally to support the financial system by providing liquidity, guarantees, capital, and purchasing assets. Table 1–3 summarizes the six major measures taken by central banks and regulators in Canada, the United States, the United Kingdom, and the Eurozone during 2008. The largest initiative was the US$700 billion Troubled Assets Relief Program (TARP) passed by the U.S. government in September 2008 after the failure of Lehman Brothers investment bank and the near-failure of the U.S. insurance company American International Group Inc. (AIG). AIG received a separate US$85 million support

TABLE 1–3   Central Banks' and Regulators' Actions to Stabilize the Global Financial System

	Canada	United States	United Kingdom	Eurozone
Liquidity injection *Provision of term funding by central banks*	• Increased size of term PRAs to over $30 billion, and increased frequency to weekly • Introduced new facilities: (i) a money market term PRA that can be accessed by eligible money market participants on an indirect basis; and (ii) a Term Loan Facility (TLF) for LVTS participants, with non-mortgage loan portfolios used as collateral	• Increased size of U.S.-dollar Term Auctions Facility to US$900 billion, and increased frequency to weekly • Increased U.S.-dollar swap agreements with 14 central banks, in some cases to unlimited amounts • Introduced new temporary facilities to support short-term debt markets	• Increased size of weekly injections • Created discount window facility against wide range of collateral • Long-term repo open market operations against broader range of collateral to be introduced • U.S.-dollar swap agreement with Federal Reserve (unlimited amount)	• Enhanced provision of longer-term refinancing (previously announced operations rolled over) • U.S.-dollar swap agreement with Federal Reserve (unlimited amount)
Collateral changes *Broadening the list of assets eligible as collateral for central banks' lending operations*	• Broadened list of securities eligible for term PRAs and accepted ABCP from affiliated dealers on a temporary basis • Accepted general assignment of non-mortgage loan portfolio at standing liquidity facility and TLF on a temporary basis	• Further broadened the range of acceptable collateral to term-lending facilities	• Broadened the range of acceptable collateral for long-term repo operations (term repo)	• Extended eligible collateral for both credit operations and longer-term refinancing operations
Deposit insurance *Increase in the amount of customer deposits insured by the government*	• No change: the Canada Deposit Insurance Corporation (CDIC) insures savings up to $100,000.	• The Federal Deposit Insurance Corporation (FDIC) increased deposit insurance from US$100,000 to US$250,000 per depositor through to 31 December 2009.	• The Financial Services Compensation Scheme increased coverage from £35,000 to £50,000 for each customer (joint accounts thus guaranteed up to £100,000).	• The EU has agreed on an increase in the minimum deposit guarantee to €50,000 with permission to member states to offer higher guarantees up to €100,000.

(continued)

	Canada	United States	United Kingdom	Eurozone
Guarantees of bank liabilities *Introduction of government guarantee on interbank lending, bank debt, and/or other bank liabilities*	• The Canadian Lenders Assurance Facility, available to federally regulated deposit-taking institutions (and provincially regulated institutions when an agreement is reached with the provincial government) insures new issues of certain senior unsecured wholesale debt up to 3 years to a maximum of 125% of wholesale debt or 20% of deposits. A fee of 110 bps, plus 25 bps or 50 bps based on credit rating, applies.	• FDIC's Temporary Liquidity Guarantee Program guarantees new senior debt of: (i) FDIC-insured depository institutions; (ii) bank holding companies; (iii) financial holding companies; and (iv) some savings and loan holding companies. Guarantees up to 125% of debt outstanding as of 30 September 2008 that matures before 30 June 2009. A fee of 75 bps plus 10 bps applies.	• The 2008 Guarantee Scheme guarantees certificates of deposit, commercial paper, and senior unsecured bonds and notes for any U.K. incorporated bank or building society for no longer than 3 years. A fee of 50 bps plus 100% of median 5-year CDS spread applies.	• Numerous European countries, including Germany, Greece, Ireland, the Netherlands, Spain, and Sweden, announced bank debt guarantees. Fees vary across countries. • France will not guarantee bank debt directly but set up a company to lend to banks for up to 5 years (a guarantee was provided to Dexia jointly with Belgium and Luxembourg).
Capital injection *Injection of public funds into the capital of banks or other major financial intermediaries*	• No capital injections announced	• Capital Purchase Program within TARP. Allows financial institutions to apply for non-voting, preferred share investment by Treasury: 5% cumulative dividend for 5 years, 9% thereafter.	• £25 billion to £50 billion recapitalization scheme to provide Tier 1 capital in the form of equity and preference shares at institution's request. All U.K. banks and building societies eligible.	• Many European countries, including Austria, France, Germany, Greece, the Netherlands, Sweden, and Switzerland announced plans to inject capital into financial institutions.
Asset purchases *Purchase of various assets from financial institutions, including impaired assets*	• The federal government will purchase, via auctions, up to $75 billion in insured mortgage pools through the Canada Mortgage and Housing Corporation.	• Mortgage-backed securities and whole loan purchase programs (initially part of TARP) • Commercial Paper Funding Facility to provide liquidity to issuers and finance purchase of unsecured and asset-backed commercial paper • Federal Reserve to buy up to US$200 billion ABS (auto, student, credit card, or small business loans) through the Term Asset-Backed Securities Loan Facility (TALF), up to US$100 billion in GSE obligations, and up to US$500 billion in MBS backed by GSEs.	• The £200 billion Special Liquidity Scheme allows banks to swap temporarily illiquid assets of sufficiently high quality for treasury bills (Gilts).	• Spain created a fund to buy high-quality bank assets on a voluntary basis, at market prices. • Switzerland will purchase US$60 billion in assets from UBS AG.

Source: Bank of Canada, *Financial System Review,* December 2008, p. 13.

package. The TARP was designed to purchase impaired assets in order to remove them from the balance sheets of FIs and allow the FIs to begin lending again. Australia, China, and other countries also brought in their own initiatives to fight their liquidity issues and potential FI failures. These support measures show the importance and the specialness of FIs to the global economy as well as the cost to the global financial system when the market and regulatory systems fail.

Early in 2008, the International Monetary Fund (IMF) published a report that concluded that "Canada's financial system is mature, sophisticated, and well managed.[16] While other countries undertook FI bailouts in 2008, Canada experienced less disruption. Canadian banks claimed losses of only $12 billion in the first three quarters of 2008. There were no failures and no need to bail out any of Canada's major FIs. The situation was much like the Great Depression from 1929 to 1933, when over 5,000 U.S. banks failed but no Canadian banks went under.

CONCEPT QUESTION	**Describe the global challenges facing FIs.**

INTERNET EXERCISE	Go to the website of the Office of the Superintendent of Financial Institutions (OSFI) at www.osfi-bsif.ca and compare the total assets of the different types of FIs that OSFI regulates. Click on "Banks." Scroll down and click on "Financial Data—Banks." Click on "Submit" to download the latest balance sheet for Domestic Banks. Repeat the process for Life Insurance Companies, and Property and Casualty Insurance Companies.

Summary

This chapter described the various factors and forces impacting financial intermediaries and the specialness of the services they provide.

The major theme of this book is the measurement and management of FI risks. In particular, although we might categorize or group FIs and label them as life insurance companies, banks, finance companies, and so on, in fact, they face risks that are more common than different. Specifically, all the FIs described in this and the next five chapters (1) hold some assets that are potentially subject to default or credit risk and (2) tend to mismatch the maturities of their balance sheets to a greater or lesser extent and are thus exposed to interest rate risk. Moreover, all are exposed to some degree of saver withdrawal or liquidity risk depending on the type of claims sold to liability holders. And most are exposed to some type of underwriting risk, whether through the sale of securities or by issuing various types of credit guarantees on or off the balance sheet. Finally, all are exposed to operating cost risks because the production of financial services requires the use of real resources and back-office support systems.

In Chapters 7 through 27 of this textbook, we investigate the ways managers of FIs are measuring and managing this inventory of risks to produce the best return-risk trade-off for shareholders in an increasingly competitive and contestable market environment.

Questions and Problems

1. What are five risks common to financial institutions?
2. Explain how economic transactions between household savers of funds and corporate users of funds would occur in a world without financial intermediaries.
3. Identify and explain three economic disincentives that probably would dampen the flow of funds between household savers of funds and corporate users of funds in an economic world without financial intermediaries.

---

[16] See International Monetary Fund, *Canada: Financial System Stability Assessment—Update,* January 15, 2008, p. 3, available at imf.org/external/pubs/ft/scr/2008/cr0859.pdf.

4. Identify and explain the two functions in which FIs may specialize that would enable the smooth flow of funds from household savers to corporate users.

5. In what sense are the financial claims of FIs considered *secondary securities*, while the financial claims of commercial corporations are considered *primary securities*? How does the transformation process, or intermediation, reduce the risk, or economic disincentives, to savers?

6. Explain how financial institutions act as delegated monitors. What secondary benefits often accrue to the entire financial system because of this monitoring process?

7. What are five general areas of FI specialness that are caused by providing various services to sectors of the economy?

8. How do FIs solve the information and related *agency costs* when household savers invest directly in securities issued by corporations? What are agency costs?

9. What is a benefit to the lenders, borrowers, and financial markets in general of the solution to the information problem provided by large financial institutions?

10. How do FIs alleviate the problem of liquidity risk faced by investors who wish to invest in the securities of corporations?

11. How do financial institutions help individual savers diversify their portfolio risks? Which type of financial institution is best able to achieve this goal?

12. How can financial institutions invest in high-risk assets with funding provided by low-risk liabilities from savers?

13. How can individual savers use financial institutions to reduce the transaction costs of investing in financial assets?

14. What is *maturity intermediation?* What are some of the ways the risks of maturity intermediation are managed by financial intermediaries?

15. What are five areas of institution-specific FI specialness, and which types of institutions are most likely to be the service providers?

16. How do deposit-taking institutions such as commercial banks assist in the implementation and transmission of monetary policy?

17. What is meant by *credit allocation regulation?* What social benefit is this type of regulation intended to provide?

18. Which intermediaries best fulfill the intergenerational wealth transfer function? What is this wealth transfer process?

19. What are two of the most important payment services provided by financial institutions? To what extent do these services efficiently provide benefits to the economy?

20. What is *denomination intermediation?* How do FIs assist in this process?

21. What is *negative externality?* In what ways do the existence of negative externalities justify the extra regulatory attention received by financial institutions?

22. If financial markets operated perfectly and costlessly, would there be a need for financial intermediaries?

23. What is mortgage redlining?

24. Why are FIs among the most regulated sectors in the world? When is the net regulatory burden positive?

25. What forms of protection and regulation do the regulators of FIs impose to ensure their safety and soundness?

26. What legislation has been passed specifically to protect investors who purchase securities? Give some examples of the types of abuses for which protection is provided.

27. How do regulations regarding barriers to entry and the scope of permitted activities affect the *charter value* of financial institutions?

28. What reasons have been given for the growth of mutual funds at the expense of "traditional" banks and insurance companies?

29. What are some of the methods banking organizations have employed to reduce the net regulatory burden? What has been the effect on profitability?

30. What characteristics of financial products are necessary for financial markets to become efficient alternatives to financial intermediaries? Give some examples of the commoditization of products that were previously the sole property of financial institutions.

Web Question

31. Go to the Bank of Canada's website at www.bankofcanada.ca. Find the latest figures for M2 and M3 using the following steps. Click on "Rates and Statistics," scroll down to "Monetary Policy Indicators," and click on "Weekly Financial Statistics." Under "Periodicals," you will see the date of the previous Friday. Click on it to access the available PDF file, and go to BFS Table E1 on page 11. By what percentage have these measures of the money supply grown over the past year?

Deposit-Taking Institutions

In this chapter, we discuss federally regulated deposit-taking financial institutions (banks, trusts, and loan companies) and other deposit-taking FIs (credit unions and caisses populaires) in terms of

- ▶ size, structure, and composition of the industry group
- ▶ balance sheets and recent trends
- ▶ regulation
- ▶ industry performance

INTRODUCTION

The theme of this book is that the products sold and the risks faced by modern financial institutions are becoming increasingly similar, as are the techniques used to measure and manage those risks. To illustrate this, Tables 2–1A and 2–1B contrast the products sold by the financial services industry before the Bank Act revisions of the 1980s with those sold in 2009. In this chapter we begin by describing the major FI groups—banks, trusts and loans, credit unions, and caisses populaires—which are also called deposit-taking institutions (DTIs) because significant amounts of their funds come from customer deposits. In Chapters 3 through 6 other (non-deposit-taking) FIs will be described. We focus on four major characteristics of each group: (1) size, structure, and composition of the industry group, (2) balance sheet and recent trends, (3) regulation, and (4) industry performance. Figure 2–1 presents a very simplified product-based balance sheet for deposit-taking institutions. Notice that deposit-taking institutions offer products to their customers on both sides of their balance sheets (loans on the asset side and deposits on the liability side). This joint-product nature of the deposit-taking institution business creates special challenges for management as they deal with the many risks facing these institutions. These risks will be discussed in Chapters 8 through 27.

Table 2–2 lists the largest Canadian deposit-taking institutions at the beginning of 2009 ranked by asset size. All but two of the ten FIs in Table 2–2 are banks (Desjardins Group, a caisse populaire, and Vancouver City Savings, a credit union), demonstrating the concentration of deposit-taking services in Canada and the dominance of the **Big Six** banks (Bank of Montreal, Bank of Nova Scotia, Canadian Imperial Bank of Commerce, National Bank of Canada, Royal Bank of Canada, and TD Canada Trust). There are nine financial services powerhouses in Canada, that is, what may be called "full-service" FIs. These include the six major banks and the three largest insurance companies, (Manulife Financial, Great-West Life Company, and Sun Life Financial), whose operations will be discussed in greater detail in Chapter 3.

The Big Six
The six largest banks in Canada (Bank of Montreal, Bank of Nova Scotia, Canadian Imperial Bank of Commerce, National Bank of Canada, Royal Bank of Canada, and TD Canada Trust)

TABLE 2–1A Products Sold by the Financial Services Industry, Pre-1985

	Function							
Institution	Payment Services	Savings Products	Fiduciary Services	Lending Business	Consumer	Underwriting Issuance of Equity	Debt	Insurance and Risk Management Products
Deposit-taking institutions	X	X	X	X	X			
Insurance companies		X		*				X
Finance companies				*	X			
Securities firms		X	X			X	X	
Pension funds		X						
Mutual funds		X						

*Minor involvement.

TABLE 2–1B Products Sold by the Financial Services Industry, 2009

	Function							
Institution	Payment Services	Savings Products	Fiduciary Services	Lending Business	Consumer	Underwriting Issuance of Equity	Debt	Insurance and Risk Management Products
Deposit-taking institutions	X	X	X	X	X	X	X	X
Insurance companies	X	X	X	X	X	X	X	X
Finance companies	X	X	X	X	X	†	†	X
Securities firms	X	X	X	X	X	X	X	X
Pension funds		X	X	X				X
Mutual funds	X	X	X					X

†Selective involvement via affiliates.

TABLE 2–2 The Largest Canadian Deposit-Taking Institutions by Asset Size, Year-End 2008 ($ billions)

Source: 2008 Company Annual Reports

Company	Assets
Royal Bank of Canada	$723.9
Toronto-Dominion Bank	563.2
Bank of Nova Scotia	507.6
Bank of Montreal	416.0
Canadian Imperial Bank of Commerce	353.9
Desjardins Group Inc.*	152.3
National Bank of Canada	129.3
HSBC Bank Canada*	72.0
Laurentian Bank Canada	19.6
Vancouver City Savings*	14.5

*As of December 31, 2008; all others as of October 31, 2008.

FIGURE 2–1
A Simple Deposit-Taking Institution Balance Sheet

Deposit-Taking Institution

Assets	Liabilities and Equity
Loans	Deposits
Other assets	Other liabilities and equity

BANKS

bank
A federally regulated deposit-taking financial institution governed by the Bank Act and requiring a charter or letter of patent to operate.

Office of the Superintendent of Financial Institutions (OSFI)
The main regulator of federally chartered FIs in Canada.

Schedule I bank
A domestic Canadian FI, widely held, chartered to conduct business under the Bank Act.

Schedule II bank
A subsidiary, usually closely held, of a foreign bank that is authorized to conduct business in Canada under the Bank Act.

Schedule III bank
A foreign bank branch that is authorized under the Bank Act to accept deposits only in amounts over $150,000.

contagion
Asset withdrawals from FIs because of financial system uncertainty and destabilization resulting from the failure of another FI.

Size, Structure, and Composition of the Industry

FIs that are allowed to operate as **banks** in Canada are governed by the Bank Act and regulated at the federal level by the **Office of the Superintendent of Financial Institutions (OSFI).** OSFI provides a list of all of the banks that are currently allowed to operate in Canada on its website at www.osfi-bsif.gc.ca. Banks are divided into domestic chartered banks (**Schedule I banks,** 21 companies in 2009), and foreign banks whose activities are restricted as follows: (i) subsidiaries of foreign banks (**Schedule II banks,** 26 companies), (ii) foreign bank full-service branches (**Schedule III banks,** 23 companies) that may only accept deposits over $150,000 (wholesale deposits), and (iii) foreign bank lending branches (7 companies) that are only allowed to provide lending services in Canada. In addition, there are 31 foreign bank representative offices that are not allowed to accept deposits and that are primarily focused on facilitating banking business for their clients from their home country. Large Canadian banks (equity > $5 billion) must be widely held; no one person may hold more than 20 percent of the voting shares. A comparison of the assets of Canadian and foreign banks is presented in Table 2–3 where it can be seen that while the balance sheets have similar weights in each category, the Canadian domestic banks represented almost 95 percent of the $2.9 trillion total assets reported at October 31, 2008. The intent of regulators has been to maintain Canadian control of the financial services sector and to provide a safe and sound banking system. This has meant that the largest banks, the Big Six, have dominated the industry in Canada.

Compared to the United States and other countries, the concentration of assets, the payments system, and the coast-to-coast branch banking system have meant that the Canadian banking industry has been remarkably stable. The 1980s saw the first bank failures since the failure of the Home Bank in 1923. The Canadian Commercial Bank and the Northland Bank of Canada, which both operated in Western Canada and which had major exposure to real estate and oil and gas loans, failed in 1985. However, their assets were only 0.75 percent of the total assets of the banking system at the time.[1] When these two banks got into trouble early in 1985, the Big Six banks worked together with the Bank of Canada and the Inspector General of Banks, the regulator at the time, to provide a rescue package, but the Canadian Commercial and Northland banks ultimately failed and "**contagion**" effects resulted in two other smaller banks, the Bank of British Columbia and the Continental Bank of Canada merging their operations with other banks. This stability contrasts with the reorganization and failures in the U.S. banking system, which had a turbulent history. The Savings and Loan (S&L) crisis of the mid-1980s saw the failure of almost 400 commercial banks in 1984 alone. (115 had failed by early November 2009).

At the time of the FI failures in the 1980s, the Canadian and U.S. financial systems were still based on the concept of the "four pillars" (banking, trust or fiduciary functions, investment banking activities, and insurance). Each financial institution was prohibited from offering services outside of its own pillar. In Canada, this changed with the revision of the Bank Act in the 1980s. The shift toward universal banking started with the purchase of almost all of the independent investment dealers by the Big Six by the early 1990s. This was followed by the movement of banks into trust functions when the 1991 Bank Act revisions permitted them

---

[1] See J. F. Dingle, *Planning an Evolution: The Story of the Canadian Payments Association 1980–2002,* The Bank of Canada and the Canadian Payments Association, May 2003, Chapter 5, pp. 25–30, available at www.bankofcanada.ca/en/dingle_book for an account of the bank failures with respect to the stability of the payment system in Canada.

TABLE 2–3 Assets of Canadian and Foreign Banks, October 31, 2008 ($ billions)

Source: OSFI, www.osfi-bsif.ca

Asset Categories	Canadian Banks		Foreign Banks		Canadian & Foreign Banks	
	Amount	%	Amount	%	Total	%
Cash & deposits	$ 126.6	4.6	$ 6.9	4.6	$ 133.5	4.6
Securities	634.8	23.1	25.4	16.7	660.2	22.8
Non-mortgage loans	890.7	32.5	63.9	42.1	954.6	33.0
Mortgages	521.5	19.0	31.8	20.9	553.3	19.1
Insurance-related assets	2.2	0.1	0.0	0.0	2.2	0.1
Other assets	566.9	20.7	23.8	15.7	590.7	20.4
Total assets	2742.6	100.0	151.8	100.0	2,894.4	100.0

Canadian banks as percentage of total = 94.8%

to own trust companies. As a result, the trust pillar was virtually eliminated as a stand-alone function by the end of the 1990s. Banks have been permitted to own insurance subsidiaries since 1991, but they are still not permitted to sell insurance products (property and casualty and life insurance policies) side by side with banking services (e.g., mortgages and chequing accounts) and investment services (e.g., mutual funds) in their branches. However, online insurance sales were permitted by OSFI but vetoed by the Minister of Finance in 2009.

The history of the financial services industry in Canada since the 1980s and the United States since the mid-1990s can thus be viewed as a move to universal banking. In Canada, this has resulted in the creation of the ten large deposit-taking institutions that are listed in Table 2–2. The consolidation of the financial services industry as a whole continues with issues related to banks' selling insurance products in their branches, and the perennial question of whether the Canadian banks should be allowed to merge with each other to create a larger concentration of banking assets in Canada and result in stronger FIs that are better able to operate in the global market place. The question of bank mergers, a political issue as much as an economic one in Canada, is discussed in more detail in Chapter 22.

Canadian banks fund themselves in the national markets and in the international interbank markets and they lend to larger corporations. This means that their **spreads** (i.e., the difference between lending and deposit rates) are subject to both North American market and global market conditions. To the extent that their lending is based on **LIBOR,** the interest rate charged to larger customers represents a market-based **cost of funds.** This has an effect on the return on equity (ROE) and the return on assets (ROAs) as reported along with the average interest rate spread in Table 2–4 for the Big Six banks from 1999–2008. The ROA averages less than 1 percent in every year. However, the ROE is positive in every year and is less than 10 percent only in 2002. As of December 2007, *The Banker* reported that, of the top ten banks in the world ranked by asset size, only Bank of America (ROA of 1.22), and HSBC Holdings (ROA of 1.03) had an average pre-tax return on assets greater than 1 percent. The average interest rate spread for the six Canadian banks has decreased over time from 2.75 percent in 1999 to 2.37 percent in 2008. Appendix 2A shows how a bank's ROE can be decomposed to examine the different underlying sources of profitability. This decomposition is often referred to as DuPont analysis. However, the use of balance sheet items for FI analysis has become less valuable as FIs, particularly banks, have moved more of their assets off of the balance sheet. The current trend by both FIs and their regulators has thus been to a risk-based analysis.

spread
The difference between lending and deposit rates.

LIBOR
London inter-bank offered rate.

cost of funds
The market cost of all sources of capital used as the base rate in pricing loans.

TABLE 2–4   ROA and ROE of the Big Six Canadian Banks, 1999–2008

For the Fiscal Year Ended Oct. 31	Return on Average Assets (%)	Return on Common Shareholders' Equity (%)	Return on Total Shareholders' Equity (%)	AVERAGE INTEREST RATE SPREAD (percentages, all currencies)		
				Earned On Loans	Paid On Deposits	Average Spread
1999	0.71	17.50	15.76	7.03	4.29	2.75
2000	0.72	16.81	15.27	7.64	4.77	2.86
2001	0.66	15.14	13.91	7.13	4.15	2.98
2002	0.44	9.90	9.38	5.36	2.37	2.99
2003	0.69	15.88	14.70	5.24	2.15	3.09
2004	0.79	21.75	20.70	4.85	1.89	2.95
2005	0.67	15.32	14.76	5.01	2.28	2.73
2006	0.96	22.96	21.87	5.78	3.08	2.70
2007	0.55	21.08	19.74	6.01	3.58	2.44
2008	0.55	15.98	14.52	5.39	3.02	2.37

Source: Canadian Bankers Association, www.cba.ca.

Balance Sheet and Recent Trends

Assets

disintermediation
The process by which firms go directly to the financial markets to raise funds without using an FI.

securitization
The removal of assets from the balance sheet by creating a contract that is sold in the financial market place.

Figure 2–2 shows the broad trends over the 1996–2008 period in the four principal earning asset areas of banks: Canadian securities, business loans, mortgages, and personal loans. Over the time period, mortgages have remained relatively steady at 46 percent of the total of these assets, while personal loans have increased only slightly. Canadian securities have increased as an asset source from 9 percent to 17 percent of the total, while business loans have declined from 24 percent to 16 percent over the 13 years. One important long-term influence has been the growth of the commercial paper market, which has become an alternative funding source for major corporations. This is an example of **disintermediation** whereby companies who have their own credit ratings are able to bypass a financial intermediary and go directly to the market to raise funds. Another has been the **securitization** of mortgages—the pooling and packaging of mortgage loans for sale in the form of bonds (see Chapter 27).

Look at the detailed balance sheet for all Canadian banks as of October 31, 2008 (Table 2–5) as reported to OSFI on a monthly basis. As noted previously, loans, personal and business, as well as mortgages make up a major portion of

FIGURE 2–2
Canadian Chartered Banks' Financial Assets, 1996–2008

Source: Bank of Canada, www.bankofcanada.ca.

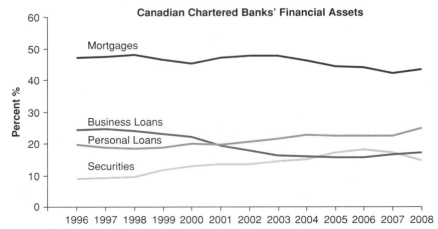

Canadian Chartered Banks' Financial Assets

TABLE 2–5
Balance Sheet of
Canadian Chartered
Banks as of October
31, 2008

Source: OSFI, www.osfi-bsif.
gc.ca.

ASSETS	($ millions)	(%)
Cash assets	$137,336.6	4.60
Securities:		
Government of Canada	198,937.1	6.66
Other	470,296.3	15.74
Loans, net of allowance for impairment:		
Non-mortgage	1,064,616.3	35.62
Mortgage loans	555,310.6	18.58
Land, building, & equipment, net of depreciation	15,049.6	0.50
Insurance-related assets	2,159.2	0.07
Other assets	545,089.2	18.24
Total assets	$2,988,795.0	100.00

LIABILITIES	($ millions)	(%)
Deposits:		
Demand	$392,837.4	13.14
Notice	341,889.3	11.44
Fixed term	1,181,944.0	39.55
Insurance-related liabilities	12,129.6	0.41
Subordinated debt	40,770.3	1.36
Borrowed securities obligations	102,354.6	3.42
Asset repurchase agreement obligations	167,546.9	5.61
Derivative related amounts	372,612.5	12.47
Other liabilities	241,566.4	8.08
Shareholders' equity:		
Preferred shares	13,317.9	0.45
Common shares	45,837.5	1.53
Contributed surplus and retained earnings	75,988.9	2.54
Total liabilities and shareholders' equity	$2,988,795.3	100.00

the assets. Hard assets (i.e., land, building and equipment) make up less than 1 percent of total assets. The securities are composed of those issued or guaranteed by the Canadian federal government, province/territory, or municipality, as well as other debt securities and shares. Foreign assets make up 43 percent of the total assets, an indication of the international nature of the operations. It is notable that insurance-related assets make up only 0.07 percent of the total, an indication that this cross-pillar diversification so far is small for these FIs.

A major inference that we can draw from this asset structure is that, with loans and mortgages at over 50 percent of the assets, credit or default risk exposure is a major risk faced by bank managers (see Chapters 11 and 12). Because banks are highly leveraged and therefore hold little equity (see next section) compared with total assets, even a relatively small number of loan defaults could decrease the equity of a bank, moving it toward insolvency.[2]

Liabilities

Banks have two major sources of funds other than the equity provided by owners: deposits and borrowed or other liability funds. A major difference between banks

---

[2] Losses such as those due to defaults are charged off against the equity (shareholders' stake) in a bank. Loans are carried on the balance sheet net of an allowance for impairment, which is calculated according to criteria set by OSFI. The intent is to cause the bank to recognize potential loan losses on a timely basis and so not overstate the balance sheet position.

demand deposits
Deposits held at an FI that can be withdrawn by the depositor without notice.

notice deposits
Deposits held at an FI that require notification to the FI before withdrawal. If the notice period is not met, the depositor could be denied access to the funds.

fixed-term deposits
Deposits held at an FI that cannot be withdrawn by the depositor prior to the maturity date. Often these deposits may be withdrawn prior to maturity with a penalty being paid by the depositor.

Canada Deposit Insurance Corporation (CDIC)
The corporation that insures eligible deposits of federally regulated deposit-taking FIs in Canada, www.cdic.ca.

and other firms is the banks' high leverage. For example, banks had an average ratio of total shareholders' equity to assets of 4.5 percent in 2008; this implies that 95.5 percent of their assets were funded by debt, either deposits or borrowed funds.

Note in Table 2–5 that deposits amounted to $1,917 billion or 64.1 percent of total liabilities and equity. Subordinated debt and other liabilities represented just 29.0 percent. Note also that **demand deposits** represented only 13.4 percent of liabilities and equity, **notice deposits** 11.44 percent and **fixed-term deposits** represented 39.55 percent. A good portion of these will be accounts insured by **Canada Deposit Insurance Corporation (CDIC),** the deposit insurance company for deposit-taking institutions. Deposit insurance is discussed in greater detail in Chapter 19. Insurance liabilities are negligible at less than 1 percent (0.41 percent) of the total.

Overall, the liability structure of bank balance sheets tends to reflect a shorter maturity structure than does the asset portfolio, with relatively more liquid instruments such as deposits and **inter-bank borrowings** used to fund less liquid assets such as loans. Thus, maturity mismatch or interest rate risk and liquidity risk are key exposure concerns for bank managers (see Chapters 8, 9, 17, and 18).

Equity

Bank equity capital (4.52 percent of total liabilities and shareholders' equity at October 31, 2008), consists mainly of preferred and common shares and retained earnings. Contributed surplus is a minor amount, representing the difference between a share's stated par value and what the original shareholders paid when they bought the newly issued stock. OSFI requires banks to hold a minimum level of equity capital to act as a buffer against losses from their on- and off-balance-sheet activities (see Chapter 20). Because of the relatively low cost of deposit funding, banks may tend to hold equity close to the minimum levels set by regulators. As we discuss in subsequent chapters, this impacts banks' exposures to risk and their ability to grow—both on and off the balance sheet—over time.

INTERNET EXERCISE

Go to the Office of the Superintendent of Financial Institutions' website at www.osfi-bsif.gc.ca and click on "Banks." Scroll down and click on "Financial Data — Banks." Click on "Submit" to view the latest monthly balance sheet for the Canadian banks.

---

inter-bank borrowings
Short-term loans (deposits), usually overnight, received from other FIs.

Off-Balance-Sheet Activities

The balance sheet itself does not reflect the total scope of bank activities. Banks conduct many fee-related activities off the balance sheet. Off-balance-sheet (OBS) activities are becoming increasingly important, in terms of their dollar value and the income they generate for banks. OBS activities include issuing various types of guarantees (such as letters of credit), which often have a strong insurance underwriting element, and making future commitments to lend. Both services generate additional fee income for banks. Off-balance-sheet activities also involve engaging in derivative transactions—futures, forwards, options, and swaps.

Under current accounting standards, such activities are not shown on the current balance sheet. Rather, an item or activity is an **off-balance-sheet asset** if, when a contingent event occurs, the item or activity moves onto the asset side

off-balance-sheet asset

An item that moves onto the asset side of the balance sheet when a contingent event occurs.

off-balance-sheet liability

An item that moves onto the liability side of the balance sheet when a contingent event occurs.

capital adequacy requirements

Levels of equity capital that an FI is required by regulators to maintain in order to be allowed to continue in operation.

of the balance sheet or an income item is realized on the income statement. Conversely, an item or activity is an **off-balance-sheet liability** if, when a contingent event occurs, the item or activity moves onto the liability side of the balance sheet or an expense item is realized on the income statement.

By moving activities off the balance sheet, banks hope to earn additional fee income to complement the margins or spreads on their traditional lending business. At the same time, they can avoid regulatory costs or "taxes" since deposit insurance premiums are not levied on off-balance-sheet activities (see Chapter 13). As well, the **capital adequacy requirements** for on-balance-sheet loans differ from those for off-balance sheet items and in some cases may make the off-balance-sheet activity more profitable (see Chapter 20). Thus the banks have both earnings and regulatory "tax-avoidance" incentives to undertake activities off their balance sheets.

Off-balance-sheet activities, however, can involve risks that add to the overall insolvency exposure of an FI. In 2001, Allied Irish Bank incurred a US$750 million loss from foreign exchange derivative trades by a rogue trader, and in 2004 unauthorized trading of foreign currency options at National Australian Bank resulted in a loss of US$450 million. However, off-balance-sheet activities and instruments have both risk-reducing as well as risk-increasing attributes, and, when used appropriately, they can reduce or hedge an FI's interest rate, credit, and foreign exchange risks.

Table 2–6 shows the notional, or face value of Canadian banks' OBS activities, reported quarterly to OSFI, at January 31, 2009. The OBS notional amount of

TABLE 2–6 **Notional Amount of Derivatives Reported by Canadian Banks at January 31, 2009 ($ thousands)**

	Contracts held for trading purposes	**Notional Amount**			
		Remaining term to maturity			
		Total Contracts	**One year and less**	**Over 1 year to 5 years**	**Over 5 years**
Interest Rate Contracts					
OTC contracts	8,206,275,782	8,952,929,673	3,504,791,267	3,748,138,402	1,700,000,006
Exchange-traded contracts	761,627,471	768,380,006	522,449,563	124,015,474	121,914,970
Foreign Exchange & Gold Contracts					
OTC contracts	2,829,072,388	2,992,934,581	1,983,706,149	670,978,579	338,249,855
Exchange-traded contracts	28,184,224	28,184,224	22,040,285	1,897,727	4,246,212
Credit Derivative Contracts					
OTC contracts	741,490,657	768,570,309	85,312,439	457,365,051	225,892,819
Equity-linked Contracts					
OTC contracts	187,250,357	194,350,059	127,683,227	50,179,506	16,487,326
Exchange-traded contracts	134,775,794	134,912,499	36,571,725	3,555,487	94,785,287
Other					
OTC contracts	145,423,201	145,466,202	90,311,533	49,164,600	5,990,070
Exchange-traded contracts	210,923,364	210,923,365	94,596,764	115,376,555	950,046
Total Derivative Contracts	13,245,023,237	14,196,650,919	6,467,462,946	5,220,671,379	2,508,516,594

Source: OSFI, www.osfi-bsif.gc.ca.

derivative contracts was $14.2 trillion, an amount that is over four times the total on balance sheet assets of $3.0 trillion reported. It should be noted that the notional, or face value of OBS activities does not accurately reflect the risk to the bank undertaking such activities. The potential for the bank to gain or lose is based on the possible change in the market value over the life of the contract rather than the notional, or face value of the contract, normally less than 3 percent of the notional value of an OBS contract. For example, the market value of a swap today is the difference between the present value of the cash flows expected to be received minus the present value of the cash flows expected to be paid.

The growth in the use of derivative securities activities by banks has been a direct response to the increased interest rate risk, credit risk, and foreign exchange risk exposures they have faced, both domestically and internationally. In particular, these contracts offer banks a way to hedge these risks without having to make extensive changes on the balance sheet. However, as shown in Table 2–6, of the total notional amount of derivatives contracts reported, $13.2 trillion or 93.3 percent were held for trading purposes, indicating that this is a profitable source of income for the banks. The exposure is limited since, as shown, 45 percent of the contracts have a maturity of less than one year, and $13.1 trillion of the contracts are over the counter rather than exchange-traded, an indication of the market-making function of the banks as well as a market risk.

Although the simple notional dollar amount of OBS items overestimates their risk exposure amounts, the increase in these activities has been phenomenal and has pushed regulators into imposing capital requirements on such activities to explicitly recognize an FI's solvency risk exposure from pursuing such activities, as described in Chapter 20.

Other Activities

Banks engage in other fee-generating activities that cannot easily be identified from analyzing their on- and off-balance-sheet accounts.

Trust Services

Federally regulated trusts are governed by OSFI under the Trust and Loans Companies Act (47 firms were listed in 2009). There are also some provincially regulated trusts. Trusts offer similar services to banks (i.e., deposit-taking, loans), as well as fiduciary activities such as administering estates, trusts, and pension plans. Since banks are prohibited from providing these fiduciary services directly, the banks offer these types of services through their subsidiaries. For example, TD Waterhouse, the securities arm of TD Canada Trust, the result of a merger of Toronto-Dominion Bank with Canada Trust, offers estate planning, tax planning, and other trust services. TD's banking customers can access TD Waterhouse directly from its website, an advantage of a full-service FI. The largest trust companies are owned by the banks (for example, The Bank of Nova Scotia Trust Company, CIBC Mellon Trust Company, and The Canada Trust Company). The total assets of federally regulated trusts were $121.2 billion at November 30, 2008. In many cases, the deposits of trust companies are covered by deposit insurance from CDIC. The advantage for banks of offering deposit services, investment services, and trust services is the **cross-selling** of services to customers, providing banks with additional revenue. As well, with Internet banking and online access to accounts, a bank client may be less likely to move to another institution because of the difficulty of establishing online accounts with another FI.

cross-selling
The marketing of other services such as mutual funds or insurance to a customer along with traditional banking.

Loan Companies

In addition to operating trust subsidiaries, the banks also participate in loan companies, of which there were 19 listed by OSFI in 2009. A loan company may be federally (falling under the Trust and Loan Companies Act) or provincially regulated, may offer deposit-taking services that are covered by CDIC's deposit insurance, and conduct other activities similar to a bank. The total assets of the loan companies regulated by OSFI were $150.8 billion at November 30, 2008. The 19 loan companies supervised by OSFI primarily represent the mortgage arms of the chartered banks (e.g., Bank of Montreal Mortgage Corporation, TD Mortgage Corporation).

Correspondent Banking

Correspondent banking is the provision of banking services to other banks that do not have the staff resources to perform the services themselves. These services include cheque-clearing and collection, foreign exchange trading, hedging services, and participation in large loan and security issuances. The nature of the Canadian economy means that firms rely heavily on both exporting and importing, which implies a risk of non-payment and also foreign exchange risk. In addition to supplying over-the-counter foreign exchange contracts (forwards), the banks also provide **letters of credit** that allow a seller to be guaranteed that they will be paid in an exporting agreement with an unknown party (Chapter 15).

letters of credit
Letters from a bank to an exporter (importer) stating that it will pay the amount of the contract on the completion of certain conditions.

Regulation

The current regulatory system for banks in Canada dates back to July, 1987, when the government enacted the Financial Institutions and Deposit Insurance Amendment Act and the Office of the Superintendent of Financial Institutions Act. The Department of Insurance and the Office of the Inspector General of Banks joined to form one national regulator, OSFI, to supervise federally regulated deposit-taking institutions. OSFI's role has, since then, been to ensure the safety and soundness of the financial system in Canada under the Bank Act. As a member of global committees that determine capital requirements for international banks (set by the Bank for International Settlements, BIS, and discussed in detail in Chapter 20), OSFI enforces those rules through its reporting requirements and inspection of the FIs under its jurisdiction. As well, OSFI sets rules relating to the safety and soundness of the national and international payments systems (discussed in Chapter 17).

The Bank of Canada is responsible for ensuring the integrity of the financial markets system in Canada, primarily through its monetary policy. As such, the Bank of Canada participates indirectly in the regulation of banks, primarily by producing research on capital markets and identifying global and national trends that may affect different aspects of the financial services industry.

Depositors are protected by the Canada Deposit Insurance Company (CDIC), which insures specified deposits of both federal and provincial deposit-taking institutions. Canadian consumers of banking products are also protected by the **Financial Consumer Agency of Canada (FCAC)**, which was established in 2001 to enforce consumer protection laws related to FIs in Canada. One of the initiatives related to consumers was the commitment of eight Canadian financial institutions to provide low-cost accounts for consumers.[3]

www.fcac-acfg.gc.ca

---

[3] See the Department of Finance website at www.fin.gc.ca for additional details and news related to Canada's financial services sector. See also the FCAC's website at www.fcac-acfc.gc.ca for the list of acts and regulations that the FCAC is responsible for enforcing.

Regulations

www.cdnpay.ca
www.iiac.ca
www.mfda.ca
www.cdic.ca
www.fintrac.gc.ca
www.assuris.ca
www.pacicc.com

Banks are among the most regulated firms in the global economy. Because of the inherent special nature of banking and banking contracts, as discussed in Chapter 1, regulators impose numerous restrictions on their product and geographic activities. In Canada, the division of powers between the federal government and the provinces/territories under the British North America (BNA) Act means that there are additional national, territorial, and provincial regulatory agencies that come into play. The creation of one federal regulator (OSFI) was intended to simplify the regulatory framework and reduce the regulatory burden for FIs, as well as to firmly establish responsibility for the implementation of the BIS capital adequacy regulations (Basel I). In addition, the move cross-pillar to include insurance and securities functions means that, although banks are primarily governed by the Bank Act administered by OSFI at the federal level, the provincial and territorial regulators also have jurisdiction, as shown in Table 2–7. As well, the formation of a national securities regulator is being planned.

Table 2–7 shows the list of federal and provincial regulators of the bank financial groups in Canada and their responsibilities. At the federal level, OSFI is the **prudential regulator,** responsible for monitoring the solvency and risk management of an FI. FCAC is the **market conduct regulator** charged with ensuring that consumers of financial services are treated ethically and fairly. In addition, there are many **self-regulating organizations (SROs)** such as the Canadian Payments Association (CPA), the Investment Industry Association of Canada (IIAC), and the Mutual Fund Dealers Association of Canada (MFDA), which are industry associations that police their members. Other regulators at the federal level are CDIC, which establishes deposit insurance coverage, and the Financial Transactions and Reports Analysis Centre of Canada (FINTRAC), which oversees the reporting of terrorist activities as well as money laundering.[4] In addition to the reporting of insurance activities as required by OSFI and provincial insurance regulators, bank insurance subsidiaries that are members may have their policies covered by Assuris, which protects life insurance policyholders in the event of the failure of a life insurance company, and the Property and Casualty Insurance Compensation Corporation (PACICC), which protects property and casualty (P&C) policyholders.

prudential regulator
The government agency responsible for ensuring compliance with good management practices within an FI to ensure the safety and soundness of the financial system.

market conduct regulator
The government agency responsible for enforcing adherence to regulations regarding FIs behaviour toward consumers of financial services.

self-regulating organizations (SROs)
FI industry groups that regulate the conduct and business practices of their members.

The major source of compliance for banks comes from the monthly and quarterly reporting requirements to OSFI, which include such things as allowance for impairments, average assets and liabilities, capital adequacy and market risk, as well as an income statement, interest rate risk, and details of mortgage loans. OSFI maintains a table of guidelines for all of the FIs that it supervises (banks, foreign bank branches, trust and loan companies, cooperative credit and retail associations, life insurance, and property and casualty insurance) on its website, which covers capital adequacy requirements, prudential limits, and accounting guidelines.

Industry Performance

Table 2–8 presents selected performance ratios for eight members of the Canadian Bankers Association, which represent more than 90 percent of the assets of banks in

---

[4] Money laundering and terrorism have become significant global issues for FIs since the terrorist attacks on the World Trade Center in New York on September 11, 2001. It is estimated by the International Monetary Fund (IMF) that money laundering could range between US$600 billion and US$1.5 trillion per year. OSFI provides a list of known terrorist organizations on its website and is developing the approach that will be applied to Canadian FIs. FINTRAC is charged with ensuring compliance with the Proceeds of Crime (Money Laundering) and Terrorist Financing Act. See N. W. R. Burbidge, "International Anti-Money Laundering and Anti-Terrorist Financing: The Work of the Office of the Superintendent of Financial Institutions in Canada," *Journal of Money Laundering Control*, 7(4), 2004, pp. 320–332, and "A Matter of Compliance," *CGA Magazine*, March/April 2005, 39(2), p. 12.

Canada. The return on assets was below 1 percent in every year, a low amount compared to U.S. banks, which achieved a return on assets higher than 1 percent (ranging from 1.15 in 2001 to 1.40 in 2003). The return on total shareholders' equity exceeded 10 percent in every year except 2002, a year associated with the highest loan loss provision to average total assets, which was equal to 0.56 percent. However, the loan loss provision to average total assets was equal to 0.22 and 0.06 percent in 2003 and 2004, likely reflecting the low interest rate climate. When interest rates start to climb, then the **provision for loan losses** should also be expected to increase as borrowers feel the financial stress and become less able to meet their interest obligations. **Net interest income** as a percentage of average total assets has held relatively steady over the period, but non-interest expense climbed from 2.45 percent in 1999 to 2.71 percent in 2005, tapering off to 1.92 percent of average total assets in 2008. Other income as a percentage of total assets has increased from 1.95 percent to 2.11 percent between 1999 and 2006, likely an indication of the increasing expansion of fee-generating activities of the banks. The low interest rate climate was good for these banks as the average interest rate spread increased from 2.74 percent in 1999 to average 3.08 percent in 2003.

Several explanations have been offered for the strong performance of banks during the early 2000s. First, lower interest rates made debt cheaper to service and kept many households and small firms borrowing. Second, lower interest rates made home purchasing more affordable. Thus, the housing market boomed throughout the period. Third, the development of new financial instruments, such as credit derivatives and mortgage-backed securities helped banks shift credit risk from their balance sheets to financial markets and other FIs such as insurance companies. Finally, improved information technology helped banks manage their risk better.

However, as shown in Table 2–8, in 2007 the effect of the credit crisis was starting to be felt at the Canadian banks. The return on average assets was down, as were ROE and other income. As well, loan loss provisions were up, reflecting the spread of the global recession that carried over into 2008 and 2009. Housing prices started to drop, the global credit crisis had an impact on liquidity, and securitization markets dried up, putting a further strain on banks' balance sheets.

As mentioned in Chapter 1, the early 2000s saw a weakening in the public trust and confidence in the ethics followed by financial institutions. A number of banks continue to deal with ethics-related issues. For example, in 2003, JPMorgan Chase, Citigroup, and CIBC settled with the New York District Attorney over allegations that the banks wrongly helped Enron hide its debt prior to the energy company's filing for bankruptcy in 2001. Also, ethical issues related to the trading of mutual funds in the United States caused the Ontario Securities Commission to review the trading practices of 105 Ontario mutual fund managers from November 2003 to December 2004. The commission's report discussed **late trading** and **market timing** issues and resulted in fines of $205.6 million levied against five fund managers.[5] Related to the ethical issues are conflicts of interest that can arise between the market-oriented trading culture of the securities subsidiaries of the banks and the gatekeeper role of the traditional banker.

Also certain to affect the future performance of banks as well as credit unions and caisses populaires is the extent to which banks adopt the newest technology (Chapter 16), including the extent to which industry participants embrace the Internet and online banking. Early entrants into Internet banking have introduced new technology in markets with demographic and economic characteristics that help ensure customer acceptance. In addition, keeping up to date with advances

provision for loan losses
Bank management's recognition of expected bad loans for the period.

net interest income
Total interest income less total interest expense before provision for credit losses.

late trading
Illegally buying or selling mutual fund securities after the close of trading at the current price rather than at the next day's price as required by law.

market timing
Frequent short-term trading of mutual fund securities by a fund manager to take advantage of changes in price, but that are not in the best interests of the funds' investors.

---

[5] See Ontario Securities Commission, *Report on Mutual Fund Trading Practices Probe*, March 2005, available at www.osc.gov.on.ca.

TABLE 2–7   Who Regulates Bank Financial Groups in Canada?

JURISDICTION	PRUDENTIAL REGULATOR	MARKET CONDUCT REGULATOR	
FEDERAL	OSFI	FCAC	
NATIONAL			
Alberta	Alberta Finance, Financial Institutions	Alberta Ministry of Government Services, Consumer Services Division	
British Columbia	Financial Institutions Commission (British Columbia)	British Columbia Ministry of the Attorney General, Community Justice Branch, Consumer services Division	
Manitoba	Manitoba Consumer and Corporate Affairs	Manitoba Consumer and Corporate Affairs, Consumer Bureau	
New Brunswick	New Brunswick Department of Justice	New Brunswick Department of Justice, Consumer Affairs Branch	
Newfoundland and Labrador	Newfoundland and Labrador, Government Services, Consumer & Commercial Affairs, Financial Services Regulaton	(Same as prudential regulator)	
Nova Scotia	Nova Scotia Department of Environment and Labour, Financial Institutions Section	Nova Scotia Department of Business and Consumer Services	
Ontario	Financial Services Commission of Ontario	Ontario Ministry of Consumer and Business Services, General Enquiries Unit	
Prince Edward Island	Prince Edward Island Ministry of the Attorney General, Consumer, Corporate and Insurance Division	(Same as prudential regulator)	
Québec	Autorité des marchés financières	(Same as prudential regulator)	
Saskatchewan	Saskatchewan Financial Services Commission	(Same as prudential regulator)	
Northwest Territories	Northwest Territories Department of Finance	Northwest Territories, Municipal and Community Affairs, Community Operations Programs, Consumer Services	
Nunavut	Nunavut Department of Justice	Nunavut, Department of Community Government and Transportation	
Yukon	Yukon Department of Justice, orporate Affairs and Registrar of Securities	Yukon Department of Justice, Consumer Services Branch	

Source: Canadian Bankers Association, 2004, and authors' updates.

SECURITIES REGULATOR	INSURANCE REGULATOR	SROs	OTHER
		CPA	FINTRAC, CDIC
		IIROC*, IIAC, MFDA	Assuris, PACICC
Alberta Securities Commission	(See SROs)	Alberta Insurance Council	
British Columbia Securities Commission	(See SROs)	Insurance Council of British Columbia	
Manitoba Securities Commission	(See SROs)	Insurance Council of Manitoba	
Department of Justice Securities Administration	Superintendent of Insurance (Department of Justice, Insurance Branch)		
(Same as prudential regulator)	(Same as prudential regulator)		
Nova Scotia Securities Commission	Superintendent of Insurance, Department of Environment and Labour		
Ontario Securities Commission	(Same as prudential regulator)		
(Same as prudential regulator)	(Same as prudential regulator)		
(Same as prudential regulator)	• Chambre de l'assurance de dommages • Chambre de la sécurité financière		
(Same as prudential regulator)	(See SROs)	Insurance Council of Saskatchewan	
Registrar of Securities, Northwest Territories	Superintendent of Insurance		
Registrar of Securities, Nunavut	Superintendent of Insurance, Department of Finance/Fiscal Policy and Taxation		
(Same as prudential regulator)	Superintendent of Insurance, Department of Justice		

*The Investment Industry Regulatory Organization of Canada (IIROC) was formed in 2008 to replace the Investment Dealers Association (IDA) and Market Regulation Services Inc.

TABLE 2–8   Selected Indicators for Canadian Banks, 1999–2008

	1999	2000	2001	2002	2003	2004	2005	2006	2007	2008
Return on average assets (ROA) (%)	0.71	0.71	0.66	0.44	0.69	0.79	0.67	0.96	0.88	0.50
Return on total shareholders' equity (ROE) (%)	15.89	15.25	13.89	9.34	14.65	16.65	14.64	21.68	19.63	10.80
Net interest income/average total assets (%)	1.83	1.83	1.93	2.01	1.88	1.78	1.67	1.53	1.45	1.52
Other income/average total assets (%)	1.95	2.27	2.11	1.81	1.94	2.04	2.09	2.10	1.88	1.15
Loan loss provision/average total assets (%)	0.23	0.27	0.39	0.56	0.22	0.06	0.09	0.10	0.13	0.22
Non-interest expenses/average total assets	2.45	2.64	2.71	2.62	2.64	2.67	2.71	2.31	2.13	1.93
Average interest rate spread (%)	2.74	2.85	2.98	2.98	3.08	2.97	2.73	2.70	2.44	2.37

Source: Canadian Bankers Association, 2009. Includes data for eight banks (BMO Financial Group, Canadian Western Bank, CIBC, Laurentian Bank of Canada, National Bank of Canada, RBC Financial Group, Scotiabank, and TD Bank Financial Group).

in technology helps FIs to provide better customer service, both for retail customers and for business customers, which ultimately helps FIs to retain customers.[6]

In addition to the development of Internet banking as a complement to the traditional services offered by banks, a new segment of the industry has arisen that consists of Internet-only banks such as ING Bank. So far, Internet-only banks have failed to capture more than a small fraction of the banking market.

CONCEPT QUESTIONS

1. What are the major assets held by banks?
2. What are the major sources of funding for banks?
3. Describe the responsibilities of the regulatory agencies responsible for banks in Canada.
4. What has the trend in ROA and ROE been in the banking industry?

CREDIT UNIONS AND CAISSES POPULAIRES

credit unions (CUs)
Cooperative deposit-taking financial institutions that are owned by their members.

caisses populaires (CPs)
Cooperative deposit-taking financial institutions similar to credit unions that are owned by their members and operate primarily in Quebec.

cooperative financial institutions
Generic term used for FIs owned by their members.

mutual organizations
Savings banks in which the depositors are also the legal owners of the bank.

Credit unions (CUs) and caisses populaires (CPs) (which primarily operate in Quebec) are cooperative financial institutions that are owned by their members (depositors). The shares are covered by share and deposit insurance and the owner of the shares may receive dividends from the CU or CP. These cooperatives are also called mutual organizations. The cooperative credit movement has been important globally as it is based on the principle that a local community can provide banking services.[7] In this respect, cooperatives in Canada have been an alternative to the major banks, which were seen as unfriendly to retail customers and small borrowers by providing low deposit rates paired with high interest rates on loans. Thus universities, labour unions, cultural organizations and even towns formed credit cooperatives to pool the resources of the community. This was particularly important in Quebec and British Columbia where two of these independent FIs (Desjardins Group Inc. and Vancouver City Savings) now rank in the top ten of the deposit-taking Canadian FIs based on asset size (see Table 2–2). CUs and CPs, both large and small, will have a role to play in the issue of bank mergers (see Chapter 22) as they are an integral part of small towns and remote communities in Canada and will continue to provide banking services even if bank mergers result in branch closings.

---

[6] The approach of the Royal Bank of Canada to its technology for its retail and wholesale clients is discussed in "RBC Treads the Integration Path in Its Client-First Strategy," *The Banker*, June 6, 2006, p. 118.

[7] Whereas in developed countries like Canada and the United States credit cooperatives account for a relatively small proportion of the financial services industry, in many less developed countries they play an important role in mobilizing savings at the rural level. One very important credit union-type FI, first developed in Bangladesh and extended to other developing countries, has been the Grameen Bank. Credit cooperatives still provide deposit functions and lending to rural areas of China. These small FIs are part of the regulatory challenge facing China as it modernizes its financial architecture.

The primary objective of financial cooperatives is to satisfy the deposit-taking and lending needs of their members. Credit union and caisse populaire member deposits (shares) are used to provide loans to other members in need of funds. Any earnings from these loans are used to pay higher rates on member deposits, charge lower rates on member loans, and attract new members. Because cooperatives do not issue common stock, the members are legally the owners.

Size, Structure, and Composition of the Industry and Recent Trends

www.cucentral.ca

Credit unions and caisses populaires are the most numerous of the deposit-taking FIs in Canada. However, like other FIs, they have declined in number from over 2,000 in 1999 to 1,008 in 2008. CUs and CPs are mostly regulated at the provincial level, but Credit Union Central of Canada (CUCC), as well as six provincial organizations, are federally regulated and report to OSFI. Table 2–9 presents statistics on the CUs and CPs in Canada for the fourth quarter of 2008. As can be seen from

TABLE 2–9 Statistics for Credit Unions and Caisses Populaires, Fourth Quarter 2008*

($ millions) Province	Total Savings/ Deposits	Total Loans	Total Assets	Total Credit Unions	Total Locations	Total Members
AFFILIATED CREDIT UNIONS & CAISSES POPULAIRES						
Credit Union Central Class						
British Columbia	$39,003	$38,130	$45,451	48	373	1,681,500
Alberta	14,928	13,934	16,487	48	212	642,612
Saskatchewan	11,351	9,496	12,588	66	314	515,683
Manitoba	13,224	12,159	14,432	48	182	553,674
Ontario	17,931	16,970	20,106	145	454	1,222,823
New Brunswick	620	606	768	18	39	78,667
Nova Scotia	1,507	1,220	1,659	31	82	167,573
Prince Edward Island	640	504	699	10	15	64,008
Newfoundland & Labrador	654	563	699	13	40	47,254
SUBTOTAL	$99,858	$93,582	$112,889	427	1,711	4,973,794
Federation Class						
Ontario-L'Alliance	878	831	1,004	13	23	79,178
TOTAL	$100,736	$94,413	$113,893	440	1,734	5,052,972
NON-AFFILIATED CREDIT UNIONS & CAISSES POPULAIRES						
Caisses Populaires						
Ontario-La Federation	$2,731	$2,713	$3,152	21	61	156,629
Manitoba	704	614	774	5	28	31,000
New Brunswick	2,352	1,995	2,626	31	86	207,126
TOTAL CPs (excluding Quebec)	$5,787	$5,322	$6,552	57	175	394,755
Quebec	84,464	85,433	102,075	492	1,338	5,562,733
TOTAL (All)	$90,251	$90,755	$108,627	549	1,513	5,957,488
Credit Unions						
Ontario	$3,368	$2,756	$3,664	19	94	211,816
TOTAL	$93,619	$93,511	$112,291	568	1,607	6,169,304
COMBINED CANADIAN CREDIT UNION & CAISSE POPULAIRE SYSTEM RESULTS						
TOTAL	$194,355	$187,924	$226,184	1,008	3,341	11,222,276

*Above figures do not include affiliated companies of the credit union system, such as Concentra Financial Inc., The CUMIS Group Ltd., The Co-operators Credential Financial Inc., and Northwest and Ethical Investments LP.

Source: Credit Union Central of Canada, www.cucentral.ca.

Table 2–9, the total membership of credit unions and caisses populaires in Canada in 2008 was 11.2 million, roughly 30 percent of the Canadian population. British Columbia and Ontario had the largest number of CU members, but over 50 percent of the members (5.6 million) live in Quebec, a demonstration of the strength of the cooperative movement in Quebec and the source of the success of Desjardins Group Inc. presented in Table 2–2 previously as one of the largest deposit-taking FIs in Canada. In addition, the total assets of $226.1 billion are made up of $187.9 billion in loans (83.1 percent). Total members' deposits of $194.3 billion funded 85.9 percent of assets.

To attract and keep customers, CUs and CPs have expanded their services to compete with banks. For example, CUs and CPs offer products and services ranging from mortgages and auto loans to credit lines and automated teller machines. In addition, CUCC lists other cooperatives operating in Canada such as Agrifinance, which provides agricultural loans; Co-operative Trust Company of Canada, providing fiduciary and trust services; The Co-operators Group Limited, a property and casualty insurance company; as well as Credential Financial Inc., which provides wealth management services; and Ethical Funds, a mutual fund company.

Balance Sheets

Table 2–10 shows the balance sheet of the six cooperatives that report to OSFI (Credit Union 1, Credit Union Central of Nova Scotia, Credit Union Central of Alberta Limited, Credit Union Central of Canada, Co-operative Credit Society of Manitoba Limited, and Credit Union Central of Saskatchewan) for year-end 2008. Of the $19.6 billion assets reported, 19.0 percent represent cash and deposits with federally regulated financial institutions. Securities issued by federal and provincial/territorial governments, municipalities, and school corporations are 10.0 percent. The remaining assets are composed of loans ($6.5 billion, 33 percent) and land, building, and equipment and other assets ($1.1 billion, 5.6 percent). The greatest dollar amount of loans is for residential and non-residential mortgages ($3.3 billion, 16.7 percent). On the liability side, deposits make up $15.9 billion, or 80.7 percent of total liabilities and equity. Members' equity funded 5.1 percent of total assets.

Regulation

With the exception of the seven cooperatives that chose to be regulated federally by OSFI, the regulation of credit unions and caisses populaires is primarily at the provincial/territorial level. The provincial/territorial regulators are charged with ensuring that the CUs and CPs follow sound financial practices and in most provinces and territories, require that external auditors prepare their annual financial statements. In addition, each firm is inspected by the regulator on an annual basis.

Depositors' funds are protected at varying levels by provincial and territorial organizations. These may take the form of deposit insurance, deposit guarantee corporations, stabilization funds, or a central CU or CP.

Industry Performance

Given the mutual-ownership status of this industry, growth in ROA (or profits) is not necessarily the primary goal of CUs and CPs. Rather, as long as capital or equity levels are sufficient to protect a CU or CP against unexpected losses on its credit portfolio as well as other financial and operational risks, this not-for-profit industry has a primary goal of serving the deposit and lending needs of its members. This contrasts with the emphasis placed on profitability by shareholder-owned banks.

TABLE 2–10 Assets and Liabilities of Federally Regulated Cooperative Credit Associations, December 2008 ($ thousands)

ASSETS

	Central 1	Credit Union Central of Nova Scotia	Credit Union Central of Alberta Limited	Credit Union Central of Canada	Co-operative Credit Society of Manitoba Limited	Credit Union Central of Saskatchewan	Total 2008
Cash resources		$ 2	$16,395	$463,284	–$13,577	$2,711	$468,815
Deposits with regulated financial institutions	$2,874,364	295,188	74,843	1,360		15,510	3,261,265
Securities issued or guaranteed by federal and/or provincial governments	1,231,793	28,827	27,775	2,117	266	560,517	1,851,295
Securities issued or guaranteed by Canadian municipalities and/or school corporations	46,450					60,463	106,913
Other Securities							
Debt	1,352,717	47,848	1,404,779	18,829	1,942,547	1,423,662	6,190,382
Shares	59,431	4,838	8,535	4,351	10,027	128,532	215,714
Loans							
To credit unions	2,314,389	11,402	216,462	37,356	268	81,134	2,661,011
To regulated financial institutions		864		4,137			5,001
To Canadian federal governments, provinces, municipal, or school corporations		939				12,701	13,640
To member co-operative associations	20,262	130	23,937	10		48,256	92,595
Lease receivables	3,983					73,724	77,707
To individuals for non-business purposes	872	7,986				157	9,015
Reverse repurchase agreements							0
To individuals and others for business purposes	136,501				21	194,197	330,719
Mortgage Loans Residential							
Insured	376	257,665	838			944,128	1,203,007
Uninsured	117,637	119,900	4,166		386	1,164,202	1,406,291
Non-Residential		72,714	170,796			420,579	664,089
Land, building, and equipment, less accumulated depreciation	15,128	2,834	2,619	419	20,254	16,302	57,556
Other assets	387,681	7,835	51,654	452,811	38,298	94,706	1,032,985
Total Assets	$8,561,584	$858,972	$2,002,799	$984,674	$1,998,490	$5,241,481	$19,648,000

(continued)

TABLE 2–10   Assets and Liabilities of Federally Regulated Cooperative Credit Associations, December 2008 ($ thousands) (concluded)

LIABILITIES AND MEMBERS' EQUITY

	Central 1	Credit Union Central of Nova Scotia	Credit Union Central of Alberta Limited	Credit Union Central of Canada	Co-operative Credit Society of Manitoba Limited	Credit Union Central of Saskatchewan	Total 2008
Deposits							
Credit unions	$6,470,845	$361,042	$1,736,698	$230,691	$1,553,105	$2,281,615	$12,633,996
Others	392,292	415,052		15	31,985	2,390,979	3,230,323
Cheques and other items in transit (net)	70,597			271,277			341,874
Advances from Credit Union Central of Canada or Bank of Canada	193,333		14,984	448,000	241,284		897,601
Liabilities of consolidated subsidiaries, other than deposits						910	910
Other liabilities	946,102	17,034	40,010	2,815	79,153	265,119	1,350,233
Non-controlling interests in subsidiaries		13,987				30,186	44,173
Subordinated debt	50,616	7,102				83,012	140,730
Members' equity							
Common/members shares	162,580	25,245	180,330	27,725	154,629	94,352	644,861
Preferred shares							0
Contributed surplus	87,901						87,901
Other	2						2
Retained earnings	191,260	16,901	28,551	4,151	−61,666	99,635	278,832
Accumulated other comprehensive income (loss)	−3,944	2,609	2,226			−4,327	−3,436
Total Liabilities and Members' Equity	$8,561,584	$858,972	$2,002,799	$984,674	$1,998,490	$5,241,481	$19,648,000

Source: OSFI, www.osfi-bsif.gc.ca.

CONCEPT QUESTIONS

1. How do credit unions and caisses populaires differ from banks?
2. Why have credit unions and caisses populaires prospered in recent years?
3. What is the major asset held by credit unions and caisses populaires?

GLOBAL ISSUES

Table 2–11 lists the top 25 banks in the world, ranked by asset size at year-end 2008. Canadian financial institutions that ranked in the top 150 banks worldwide were Royal Bank of Canada (33), Toronto Dominion Bank (47), Scotiabank (48), Bank of Montreal (53), Canadian Imperial Bank of Commerce (60), National Bank of Canada (116), and Desjardins Group (103). Asset size relative to their global

TABLE 2–11
Top 25 Banks
Worldwide, Ranked
by Assets, 2009
(US$ billions)

Source: *The Banker,* "Top 1000
World Banks 2009," www.
thebanker.com.

Rank	Bank	Assets	Pre-Tax Profit (Loss)	Return on Assets (%)
1	Royal Bank of Scotland (United Kingdom)	$3,500.950	(59.281)	−1.7
2	Deutsche Bank (Germany)	3,065.307	(7.990)	−0.3
3	Barclays Bank (United Kingdom)	2,992.682	8.859	0.3
4	BNP Paribas (France)	2,888.728	5.461	0.2
5	HSBC Holdings (United Kingdom)	2,418.033	9.307	0.4
6	Crédit Agricole Group (France)	2,239.370	5.388	0.2
7	JPMorgan Chase & Co. (USA)	2,175.052	2.773	0.1
8	Mitsubishi UFJ Financial(Japan)	2,025.830	1.173	0.1
9	Citigroup (USA)	1,938.470	(53.055)	−2.7
10	UBS (Switzerland)	1,894.423	(19.636)	−1.0
11	ING Bank (Netherlands)	1,853.393	(2.070)	−0.1
12	Bank of America Corp. (USA)	1,817.943	4.428	0.2
13	Société Générale (France)	1,572.721	5.578	0.4
14	Mizuho Financial Group (Japan)	1,494.960	4.956	0.3
15	Santander Central Hispano (Spain)	1,460.866	15.825	1.1
16	Unicredit (Italy)	1,455.270	6.952	0.5
17	ICBC (China)	1,427.685	21.260	1.5
18	Wells Fargo & Co. (USA)	1,309.639	(47.788)	−3.7
19	Sumitomo Mitsui Financial Group (Japan)	1,219.544	0.301	0.02
20	China Construction Bank (China)	1,105.471	17.520	1.6
21	Credit Suisse Group (Switzerland)	1,100.263	(14.010)	−1.3
22	Agricultural Bank of China (China)	1,026.300	7.659	0.8
23	Bank of China (China)	1,017.718	12.620	1.2
24	HBOS (United Kingdom)	1,005.710	(15.780)	−1.6
25	Dexia (Belgium)	906.063	(5.396)	0.6

competitors is the yardstick used to measure Canadian FIs, and this statistic figures prominently in any discussion of FI mergers in Canada (Chapter 22). As well, cross-border issues are important for foreign FIs operating in Canada (Chapter 2) and for the expansion of FIs into new banking and insurance territory, such as the emerging markets in China and other Asian countries (Chapter 22).

Banks in most regions of the world posted strong performance in the early and mid-2000s. However, net interest margins narrowed, reflecting competitive pressures and flattening yield curves. The growth of interest revenue was driven by rapid loan extension compensating for narrower margins. The return on assets changed little, largely as a result of falling operating costs and minimal provisions for loan losses. Retail business also contributed to banks' strong financial performance. In many countries, mortgages dominated loan growth. In France and Spain, the rapid pace of mortgage lending boosted revenue. In addition, asset management and the sale of pension and insurance products contributed to noninterest income. Finally, the continued expansion of the retail business showed few signs of abating and was expected to advance further in countries where personal indebtedness remained relatively low, such as Italy.

Credit growth increased at various speeds in different countries, conveying a mixed overall picture. The euro area's robust credit growth rate of 11 percent in 2005 included substantial differences among countries. For example, lending in Germany remained almost flat. Diversification across locations and business lines helped banks overcome various challenges including natural disasters, litigation, and the flattening of the yield curve. The number of personal bankruptcies rose worldwide, and with it the arrears and provisions banks recorded for personal loans, including credit cards. But U.K. banks' profitability, cost efficiency, and diversification allowed them to cope with any deterioration.[8]

However, not all countries fared as well. In April 2001, the Japanese government announced plans for a government-backed purchase of ¥11,000 billion (US$90 billion) of shares of Japanese banks as part of an increasingly frantic drive to avert a banking crisis, recover from a 16-year low in the levels of Japanese stock markets, and stem the country's economic decline. This was the third major attempt to bail out the banking system since 1998. Previous attempts had been unsuccessful. For example, in March 2001, Fitch Investors Service (a major international rating agency) put 19 of the biggest Japanese banks on its credit watch list. The purchase of bank shares was intended to offset losses from writing off bad loans (estimated to be as high as ¥32,000 billion (US$260 billion) in bank portfolios. Foreign financial institutions were also solicited in attempts to prevent a complete financial collapse in Japan. For instance, in October 2003, Goldman Sachs set up an investment fund to buy as much as ¥1 trillion (US$9.1 billion) in non-performing loans from the Sumitomo Mitsui Banking Corporation. Earlier, in January 2003, Goldman agreed to buy ¥150.3 billion (US$1.4 billion) of preferred shares from Sumitomo. Merrill Lynch and Deutsche Bank also bought troubled assets from Japanese banks. These efforts, along with a strengthening Japanese economy, appear to have averted a disaster. By the end of 2003, Japanese banks posted their largest earnings in years. Specifically, as of September 2003, Japan's eight biggest banking groups all reported positive six-month net profits.

However, the Bank of Japan ended its five-year policy of keeping short-term interest rates near zero only in July 2006 when it raised its rate target to 0.25 percent and then to 0.50 percent in February 2007. But the low target rate, combined with rising competition, forced Japanese banks to hold down consumer borrowing rates. As a result, Japanese banks reported declines in performance at their core businesses. Mitsubishi UFJ Financial Group Inc., Japan's largest bank by both market capitalization and assets, said its consolidated net business profit in the third quarter of 2006

---

[8] See Bank for International Settlements, *BIS 76th Annual Report,* June 2006, www.bis.org.

dropped 3.8 percent from a year earlier, while Mizuho Financial Group, Japan's second-largest bank, dropped 12 percent. These results show how difficult it is for Japanese banks to boost earnings even after cleaning up the bad loans that dragged them down for years. To increase profitability, Japanese banks tried to reduce their dependency on the traditional lending business, while expanding into more profitable areas such as wealth management, credit cards, and investment banking.

In China, however, the banking industry deteriorated in the early 2000s. China's four state-run banks had about $120 billion in non-performing loans, accounting for about 21 percent of total loans. Private economists put the percentage of non-performing loans closer to 50 percent of total loans. Looking to clean up its troubled banking sector, the China Banking Regulatory Commission unveiled a comprehensive plan to overhaul the country's banking system, one that included a shift by China from restricting overseas competition to allowing it. The plan gives foreign banks greater scope to operate. Measures include raising the ceiling on foreign ownership in Chinese financial institutions from 15 percent to 20 percent for a single investor, expanding the number of cities where foreign branches can do some local currency business and easing capital requirements for branches.

However, as of 2007, foreign banks had not yet been allowed to reach out to retail customers in China. For example, in 2007, Citigroup operated just 13 branches in six Chinese cities. Its growing network of ATMs, including a new one at the Great Wall, existed mainly to dispense cash to foreign visitors and to publicize its brand. Neither Citigroup nor any other non-Chinese bank could take deposits from individuals or make them loans in China's currency, the yuan. Citigroup's own employees, in fact, had to be paid through accounts at Chinese banks.

Also experiencing trouble in the early 2000s were Germany's largest banks, which were experiencing their worst downturn since World War II. German banks' problems were due to mounting bad loans (the result of low growth and high unemployment in Germany for nearly a decade) which resulted in plummeting profits and share prices. Further, smaller local banks increasingly competed for loan business, contributing to a crisis for the country's biggest banks. Backed by government guarantees on their own borrowing, small banks enjoyed high credit ratings and low cost of funds. This resulted in a tradition of low lending rates that left these banks with 67 percent of the small business loan market and 39 percent of all chequing accounts. Without a robust stream of loan income, the large German banks were heavily reliant on trading and fee income from securities business. But that income dried up with the fall in the stock market.

Islamic banking
Banking services based on the Qu'ranic principles banning interest and usury.

An additional issue globally has been **Islamic banking,** which, while not a large feature of the North American banking scene, is prominent in other countries, particularly Pakistan and Malaysia, where traditional banks and Islamic banks co-exist. In some respects Islamic banks share the features of cooperative credit institutions in their community-based approach. However, the growth of Islamic finance has been hindered by the development of regulations to ensure their safety and soundness with respect to the global financial system. For Islamic banks, this means the development of appropriate risk management techniques and capital adequacy measures.[9]

---

[9] See F. Bokhari, "Pakistan—The Outlook for Islamic Banking," *The Banker,* May 1, 2005; Z. Awad, "Islamic Banking Has Global Reach: The Problem Is That There Are Not Industry-Wide Regulations and Practices to Govern It," *Investment Executive,* July 2005, p. 39; and S. Emling, "Islamic Banking Grows More Popular, Even in U.S.," *Cox News Service,* April 21, 2005.

Summary

This chapter provided an overview of the major activities of the deposit-taking institutions in Canada that rely heavily on deposits to fund their activities, although borrowed funds have also been important for the largest institutions. Historically, the four-pillar approach in Canada meant that banks concentrated on business lending and on investing in securities, while trusts, credit unions, and caisses populaires concentrated on mortgage and consumer lending. These differences have been eroded as a result of competitive forces, regulation, and changing financial and business technology, both in Canada and globally.

The creation of large financial service firms operating cross-pillar has meant that competition has been important in Canada and has figured prominently in the debate about mergers of large FIs. The universal bank model, which has been relatively successful in Canada, has been called into question globally, as the largest financial intermediaries have sold assets, raised capital, and taken government bailouts when all else failed as a result of the global financial meltdown. Globally, FIs may write down US$4 trillion. As we will discuss in Chapter 20, the declines in capital that result may make these FIs a greater systemic risk to the global financial system.

Questions and Problems

1. What are the differences between Schedule I, Schedule II, and Schedule III banks?
2. What changes have banks implemented to deal with changes in the financial services environment?
3. What are the major uses of funds for banks in Canada? What are the primary risks to a bank caused by each use of funds? Which of the risks is most critical to the continuing operation of a bank?
4. What are the major sources of funds for banks in Canada? How is the landscape for these funds changing and why?
5. How does the liability maturity structure of a bank's balance sheet compare with the maturity structure of the asset portfolio? What risks are created or intensified by these differences?
6. a. What types of activities are normally classified as off-balance-sheet (OBS) activities?
   b. How does an OBS activity move onto the balance sheet as an asset or liability?
   c. What are the benefits of OBS activities to a bank?
   d. What are the risks of OBS activities to a bank?
7. What factors explain the revitalization of the banking industry during the 1990s? How is Internet banking expected to provide benefits in the future?
8. What factors are given credit for the strong performance of commercial banks in the early 2000s?
9. How does the asset structure of credit unions compare with the asset structure of banks?
10. Compare and contrast the performance of the Canadian deposit-taking institution industry with U.S. and global FIs.

Web Questions

11. Go to OSFI's website at www.osfi-bsif.gc.ca and find the most recent monthly balance sheet for Canadian chartered banks using the following steps. Click on "Banks." Scroll down and click on "Financial Data—Banks." Click on "Submit" to retrieve the latest balance sheet. Repeat the process for foreign banks by selecting "Foreign Bank Branches" and select the most recent balance sheet. Compare the balance sheet of the domestic banks with that of the foreign banks. How have the assets of both changed from Table 2–5? Are foreign subsidiaries increasing or decreasing their share of assets in Canada?
12. Go to Credit Union Central of Canada's website at www.cucentral.ca and download the most recent information on number, assets, and membership in credit unions and caisses populaires using the following steps. Click on "Facts and Figures" and then on "National System Results" for the latest quarterly report. How has the number of CUs and CPs, their size, and membership changed since 2008?

Appendix 2A   **Financial Statement Analysis Using a Return on Equity (ROE) Framework**

Appendix 2B   **Technology in Commercial Banking**

View Appendices 2A and 2B at the Online Learning Centre: www.mcgrawhill.ca/olc/saunders.

Insurance Companies

In this chapter, we discuss the main features of (1) life insurance companies and (2) property and casualty insurance companies by concentrating on

▸ the size, structure and composition of the industry in which they operate

▸ balance sheets and recent trends

▸ regulation

▸ global competition and trends in the industry

INTRODUCTION

The primary function of insurance companies is to protect individuals and corporations (policyholders) from adverse events. By accepting premiums, insurance companies promise policyholders compensation if certain specified events occur. These policies represent financial liabilities to the insurance company. With the premiums collected, insurance companies invest in financial securities such as corporate bonds and stocks. The industry is classified into two major groups: life, and property and casualty (P&C). Life insurance provides protection against the possibility of untimely death, illnesses, and retirement. Property insurance protects against personal injury and liability such as accidents, theft, and fire. However, as will become clear, insurance companies also sell a variety of investment products in a similar fashion to other financial service firms, such as mutual funds (Chapter 5) and deposit-taking institutions (Chapter 2).

LIFE INSURANCE COMPANIES

Size, Structure, and Composition of the Industry

As competition in the insurance industry increased in the late 1990s, many of the largest global insurance firms converted from being mutual companies owned by their policyholders to stockholder-controlled companies, a process called **demutualization.** Figure 3–1 illustrates the difference between a mutual insurer and a stock insurance company. Demutualization allows an insurance firm to gain access to the equity markets in order to raise additional capital for future business expansions and compete with the much larger banking industry. The ability to raise capital is also important from a regulatory standpoint since a mutual company cannot readily raise capital to offset a decline in asset values. Because a mutual company is owned by its policyholders, the existing capital and reserves (equal to accumulated past profits) have to be distributed to the insurer's policyholders.

In 1957, the Canadian and British Insurance Companies Act was amended to allow insurance companies to mutualize in order to prevent U.S. takeovers of Canadian companies. As a result, in the 1960s, Mutual of Canada (a mutual since

demutualization
Conversion from a mutual insurance company owned by policyholders to a stockholder-controlled insurance firm.

FIGURE 3–1
Mutual versus
Stock Insurance
Companies

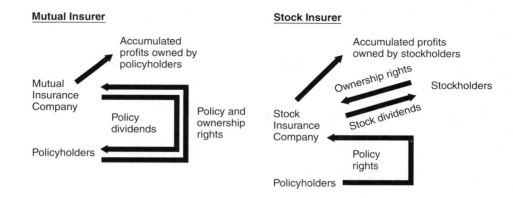

1870) and North American Life Insurance (which mutualized in 1931) were joined by Canada Life, Sun Life, Equitable Life, Confederation Life, and Manufacturers Life as federally regulated mutual companies. Demutualization in Canada (e.g., Manulife and Sun Life), the United States (e.g., Metropolitan Life and Prudential) as well as in other countries (e.g., Australia and the United Kingdom) has set the stage for further global consolidation as well as bank–insurance company mergers that are currently prohibited in Canada.[1]

In Canada, the number of firms declined from 163 firms in 1990 to 102 companies in 2008. In 2009, 88 firms were regulated by the Office of the Superintendent of Financial Services (OSFI), composed of 46 Canadian and 42 foreign life insurance companies. The consolidation has taken the form of Canadian insurers acquiring the assets of other Canadian companies, such as Great-West Life's acquisition of London Life and Canada Life, and Sun Life's acquisition of Clarica Life Insurance in 2002. In addition, Canadian companies have been expanding their operations abroad. The most notable was the US$11 billion merger of Manulife Financial with the U.S. company, John Hancock, that was concluded in April 2004. Maritime Life, based in Halifax as a wholly owned subsidiary of John Hancock, became part of Manulife. Table 3–1 shows the top ten Canadian companies ranked by revenue at December 31, 2008.

www.gwl.ca
www.sunlife.ca

www.manulife.ca

Life insurance allows individuals and their beneficiaries to protect against losses in income through premature death or retirement. By pooling risks, life insurance transfers income-related uncertainties from the insured individual to a group. While life insurance may be the core activity area, modern life insurance companies also sell annuity contracts, manage pension plans, and provide accident and health insurance (Figure 3–2 shows the distribution of premiums written for the various lines of insurance in 2008). We discuss these different activity lines in the following sections.

moral hazard
The loss exposure faced by an insurer when the provision of insurance encourages the insured to take more risks.

adverse selection
The tendency for higher-risk individuals to carry higher levels of insurance, making the overall risk in the insurance pool higher than in the general population.

Two problems that face life insurers and property and casualty insurers are moral hazard and adverse selection. **Moral hazard** occurs when the insured person or company is encouraged to take more risks because the downside risk has been transferred to the insurer. **Adverse selection** is a problem in that customers who apply for insurance policies are more likely to be those most in need of insurance (i.e., someone with chronic health problems is more likely to purchase a life

[1] For background to the insurance industry in Canada see L. B. Mussio, *Sun Ascendant: A History of Sun Life of Canada,* McGill-Queen's University Press, 2005.

TABLE 3–1
Largest Canadian Life Insurance Companies by Revenue, December 2008 ($ billions)

Source: *Financial Post*, "FP500," June 2009.

Company	Revenue	Assets*
Great-West Lifeco Inc.	$33.9	$130.1
Manulife Financial Corp.	33.0	187.5
Sun Life Financial Inc.	15.6	119.8
Industrial Alliance Insurance and Financial Services Inc.	4.5	15.4
Desjardins Financial Security Life Assurance Co.	2.9	13.8
The Standard Life Assurance Company of Canada	1.8	16.4
SSQ, Société d'Assurance-Vie Inc.	1.5	2.3
RBC Life Insurance	1.3	5.2
La Capitale Civil Service Mutual	1.0	3.0
Co-operators Life Insurance Co.	0.7	2.5

*Assets under management.

FIGURE 3–2
Distribution of Premiums Written on Various Life Insurance Lines, 2008

Source: Canadian Life and Health Insurance Association, www.clhia.ca.

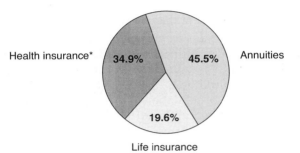

*Includes $8.9 billion (11.6%) premium equivalents for uninsured contracts administered by life insurance companies.

insurance policy than someone in perfect health). Thus, in calculating the probability of having to pay out on an insurance contract and, in turn, determining the insurance premium to charge, insurance companies' use of health (and other) statistics representing the overall population may not be appropriate (since the insurance company's pool of customers is more prone to health problems than the overall population). Insurance companies deal with the adverse selection problem by establishing different pools of the population based on health and related characteristics (such as income). By altering the pool used to determine the probability of losses to a particular customer's health characteristics, the insurance company can more accurately determine the probability of having to pay out on a policy and can adjust the insurance premium accordingly. Such premiums are said to be **actuarially priced.**

actuarially priced insurance premium
Insurance premiums based on the perceived risk of the insured.

As the various types of insurance policies and services offered are described below, notice that some policies (such as universal life policies and annuities) provide not only insurance features but also savings components. For example, universal life policy payouts are a function of the interest earned on the investment of the policyholder's premiums.

Life Insurance

The four basic classes or lines of life insurance are distinguished by the manner in which they are sold or marketed to purchasers. These classes are (1) individual life, (2) group life, (3) industrial life, and (4) credit life. According to the Canadian Life and Health Insurance Association Inc. (CLHIA), of the total life insurance of $306.1 billion that Canadians purchased in 2008, $194.3 billion or 63 percent was for individual life insurance. The remaining $111.8 billion was for group life insurance.

Individual Life   Individual life insurance involves policies marketed on an individual basis, usually in units of $1,000, on which policyholders make periodic premium payments. Despite the enormous variety of contractual forms, there are essentially five basic contractual types. The first three are traditional forms of life insurance, and the last two are newer contracts that originated in the 1970s and 1980s as a result of increased competition for savings from other segments of the financial services industry. The three traditional contractual forms are term life, whole life, and endowment life. The two newer forms are variable life and universal life. The key features of each of these contractual forms are as follows:

- *Term life.* A term life policy is the closest to pure life insurance, with no savings element attached. Essentially, the individual receives a payout contingent on death during the coverage period. The term of coverage can vary from as little as 1 year to 40 years or more.
- *Whole life.* A whole life policy protects the individual over an entire lifetime. In return for periodic or level premiums, the individual's beneficiaries receive the face value of the life insurance contract on death. Thus, there is certainty that if the policyholder continues to make premium payments, the insurance company will make a payment—unlike term insurance. As a result, whole life has a savings element as well as a pure insurance element.
- *Endowment life.* An endowment life policy combines a pure (term) insurance element with a savings element. It guarantees a payout to the beneficiaries of the policy if death occurs during some endowment period (e.g., prior to reaching retirement age). An insured person who lives to the endowment date receives the face amount of the policy.
- *Variable life.* Unlike traditional policies that promise to pay the insured the fixed or face amount of a policy if a contingency arises, variable life insurance invests fixed premium payments in mutual funds of stocks, bonds, and money market instruments. Usually, policyholders can choose mutual fund investments to reflect their risk preferences. Thus, variable life provides an alternative way to build savings compared with the more traditional policies such as whole life because the value of the policy increases or decreases with the asset returns of the mutual fund in which the premiums are invested.
- *Universal life and variable universal life.* Universal life allows both the premium amounts and the maturity of the life contract to be changed by the insured, unlike traditional policies that maintain premiums at a given level over a fixed contract period. In addition, for some contracts, insurers invest premiums in money, equity, or bond mutual funds—as in variable life insurance—so that the savings or investment component of the contract reflects market returns. In this case, the policy is called *variable universal life.*

Group Life   Group life insurance covers a large number of insured persons under a single policy. Usually issued to corporate employers, these policies may be either contributory (where both the employer and employee cover a share of the employee's cost of the insurance) or non-contributory (where the employee does not contribute to the cost of the insurance) for the employees. Cost economies represent the principal advantage of group life over ordinary life policies. Cost economies result from mass administration of plans, lower costs for evaluating individuals through medical screening and other rating systems, and reduced selling and commission costs.

Industrial Life   Industrial life insurance currently represents a very small area of coverage. Industrial life usually involves weekly payments directly collected by representatives of the companies. To a large extent, the growth of group life insurance has led to the demise of industrial life as a major activity class.

Credit Life   Credit life insurance is sold to protect lenders against a borrower's death prior to the repayment of a debt contract such as a mortgage or car loan. Usually, the face amount of the insurance policy reflects the outstanding principal and interest on the loan. Credit life insurance can also be sold by deposit-taking institutions in their branches in Canada.

Other Life Insurer Activities

The other major activities of life insurance companies involve the sale of investment and retirement products (annuities, pension plans, RRSPs, RRIFs) and accident and health insurance.

Investment   Annuities represent the reverse of life insurance activities. Whereas life insurance involves different contractual methods of *building up* a fund, annuities involve different methods of *liquidating* a fund, such as paying out a fund's proceeds. As with life insurance contracts, many different types of annuity contracts have been developed. Specifically, they can be sold to an individual or a group and on a fixed or a variable basis by being linked to the return on some underlying investment portfolio. Individuals can purchase annuities with a single payment or with payments spread over a number of years. The annuity builds up a fund whose returns are tax-deferred; that is, they are not subject to capital gains taxes on their investments. Payments may be structured to start immediately, or they can be deferred (at which time taxes are paid based on the income tax rate of the annuity receiver). These payments may cease on death or continue to be paid to beneficiaries for a number of years after death. Payments received by individuals from annuity contracts are declared as income that may or may not be taxable as determined by the Income Tax Act available from the Canada Revenue Agency (CRA), at www.cra-arc.gc.ca. Annuity sales provided premiums of $34.7 billion in 2008, representing 45.5 percent of the total premium income as shown in Figure 3–2. Although annuities were the largest source of premium income, primarily from the growth in retirement products such as pension plans and **registered retirement savings plans (RRSPs),** premium income from annuities has declined from 47.8 percent of total premium income in 2000.[2] Life insurance has held steady at around 19.6 percent (versus 22.7 percent in 2000), whereas health insurance premium income has increased from 29.5 percent in 2000 to 34.9 percent in 2008.

Annuity premiums include group retirement plans such as private pension plans known as registered pension plans in Canada (pension plans are covered in more detail in Chapter 5). According to the Canadian Life and Health Insurance Association, individual annuities amounted to $16.8 billion in 2008 whereas group annuities were $17.9 billion. Individual premiums come from demand for assets placed in an RRSP, and from **registered retirement income funds (RRIFs).** Individuals in Canada are able to shelter income from tax during their earning

registered retirement savings plan (RRSP)
Retirement savings fund that allows Canadians to shield a portion of their income from tax, but must be converted into a RIFF by age 71.

registered retirement income fund (RRIF)
A fund that is designed to provide a regular income to an individual and allow the individual to defer payment and tax on money withdrawn from an RRSP.

---

[2] As discussed in Chapter 21, life insurers are facing increasingly intense competition from banks in the annuity product market.

years via RRSPs, but must transfer the funds to a RRIF after retirement and pay the tax on withdrawal. Individual and group RRSPs provided 40.8 percent of the life insurance industry's total 2008 annuity premiums.

Accident and Health Insurance   Although life insurance protects against mortality risk, accident and health insurance protect against morbidity, or ill health, risk. Canada's public health system provides coverage for many medical services but health insurance provides additional coverage, often through supplementary health insurance plans provided by employers as benefits to their employees. These include dental plans, travel insurance, disability insurance, and accidental death and dismemberment insurance. At year-end 2008, 22.1 million people in Canada were insured for extended health care, and total health insurance premiums were $26.7 billion, 34.9 percent of total premium income. Life insurers provide over 90 percent of the supplementary health insurance in Canada, and the remainder is provided by property and casualty insurers. In many respects, the loss exposures faced by insurers in health insurance are more similar to those faced under property–casualty insurance than to those faced under traditional life insurance, as discussed below.

Balance Sheet and Recent Trends

Assets

Because of the long-term nature of their liabilities (as a result of the long-term nature of life insurance policyholders' claims) and the need to generate competitive returns on the savings elements of life insurance products, life insurance companies concentrate their asset investments at the longer end of the maturity spectrum (e.g., bonds, equities, and government securities). Look at Table 3–2, where we show the distribution of Canadian life insurance companies' assets.

As you can see, in 2008, for the firms reporting to OSFI, 50.9 percent of life insurance assets were invested in bonds and debentures, 14.6 percent in mortgage

TABLE 3–2   **Distribution of Assets of Canadian Life Insurance Companies, 2001–2008**

	2001	2002	2003	2004	2005	2006	2007	2008
Cash	1.0%	0.9%	1.2%	1.2%	1.7%	1.5%	1.4%	1.4%
Short-Term Investments	4.7%	4.9%	4.5%	5.0%	3.7%	4.8%	4.0%	5.6%
Accrued Investment Income	1.1%	1.1%	1.0%	1.0%	0.9%	0.8%	0.8%	0.8%
Accounts Receivable	1.5%	1.7%	1.6%	1.3%	2.5%	2.8%	2.7%	2.3%
Policy Loans	3.7%	3.8%	3.5%	3.2%	2.9%	2.7%	2.7%	2.9%
Bonds and Debentures	55.5%	57.7%	56.7%	56.2%	54.1%	51.1%	53.9%	50.9%
Mortgage Loans	15.4%	13.8%	14.4%	15.2%	15.4%	14.6%	14.7%	14.6%
Preferred and Common Shares	7.0%	5.7%	5.4%	5.6%	6.2%	7.0%	8.0%	5.6%
Real Estate	3.2%	3.1%	3.1%	3.2%	3.4%	3.4%	3.6%	3.8%
Other Loans and Invested Assets	1.3%	1.6%	1.7%	1.7%	2.8%	2.5%	3.0%	3.4%
Future Income Taxes	0.7%	0.4%	0.5%	0.4%	0.3%	0.4%	0.3%	0.5%
Goodwill and Other Assets	4.9%	5.3%	6.4%	6.1%	6.1%	8.4%	5.1%	8.2%
Total	100.0%	100.0%	100.0%	100.0%	100.0%	100.0%	100.0%	100.0%
Canadian Life Insurers Total Assets ($ billions)	$289.9	$266.7	$287.1	$305.6	$296.0	$331.1	$338.1	$373.3
Foreign Life Insurers Total Assets ($ billions)	25.7	27.6	33.1	19.4	18.4	15.5	15.0	14.9
Total Industry Assets ($ billions)	$315.6	$294.4	$320.2	$325.0	$314.4	$346.6	$353.1	$388.2
Total Assets in Segregated Funds ($ billions)	$186.8	$155.8	$199.4	$231.0	n.a.	n.a.	$311.8	$277.4

Source: Office of Superintendent of Financial Institutions, www.osfi-bsif.gc.ca.

policy loans
Loans made by an insurance company to its policyholders, using their policies as collateral.

loans, 5.6 percent in preferred and common shares, and 5.6 percent in short-term investments, with other assets, including cash, accrued investment income, accounts receivable, **policy loans** (loans made to policyholders using their policies as collateral), real estate, other loans and invested assets, deferred income taxes, and goodwill making up the remainder. The decline in preferred and common shares between 2007 and 2008 can be related to the downturn in the stock market, starting with the collapse of the stock market. The CLHIA reported that, for 2008, life and health insurance companies had Canadian investments totalling $77.6 billion in provincial, municipal and federal bonds, $143.8 billion in corporate securities, and $77.3 billion in mutual funds, a significant participation in Canadian capital markets. While banks are the major issuers of new mortgages (sometimes keeping the mortgages on their books and sometimes selling them to secondary market investors), insurance companies hold mortgages as investment securities. That is, they purchase many mortgages in the secondary markets (see Chapters 26 and 27). Thus, insurance company managers must be able to measure and manage the credit risk, interest rate risk, and other risks associated with these assets.

segregated funds
Investment funds held and managed separately by life and health insurance companies in Canada.

In Canada, life and health insurance companies offer shares in investment funds called **segregated funds** that are similar to the mutual funds offered by other FIs, and that are similarly invested in equities, bonds and money market instruments. These funds have been popular since the early 2000s when many investors saw their retirement savings in stocks and mutual funds reduced by the downturn in the market. Segregated funds must return a minimum percentage (usually 75 percent or more) of the capital invested to the investor at the maturity, reducing the risk of capital loss. Also, segregated funds are a means of **creditor proofing** assets, a feature of interest to small-business owners. Segregated funds must be managed separately from the other assets of the firm, and insurance companies report the market value of their assets held as segregated funds to OSFI separately. Table 3–2 shows that segregated funds have increased from $186.8 billion in 2001 to $277.4 billion in 2008, reflecting the growth of individual and group pension plans.

creditor proofing
The placing of assets in a vehicle that cannot be claimed by creditors in the event of the owners' bankruptcy.

actuarial liabilities
A liability item for insurers that reflects their expected payment commitment on existing policy contracts.

Liabilities

The aggregate balance sheet for the life insurance industry at the end of 2008 is shown in Table 3–3. Looking at the liability side, we see that 68.9 percent represent **actuarial liabilities** under insurance policies and annuity contracts. These are based on actuarial assumptions regarding the insurers' expected future liability commitments to pay out on present contracts, including death benefits, matured endowments (lump sum or otherwise), and the cash **surrender values of policies** (the cash value paid to the policyholder if the policy is surrendered before it matures). Even though the actuarial assumptions underlying policy reserves are normally very conservative, unexpected fluctuations in future required payouts can occur; thus, underwriting life insurance is risky. For example, mortality rates—and life insurance payouts—might unexpectedly increase above those defined by historically based mortality tables as a result of a catastrophic epidemic illness such as AIDS. To meet unexpected future losses, the life insurer holds a capital and surplus reserve fund with which to meet such losses (and reduce insolvency risk). The total of policyholders' and shareholders' equity at year-end 2008 was $52.4 billion, 14.1 percent of the total liabilities and equity. The ratio of total liabilities to equity is thus 6.12. The equity accounts provide a surplus to meet unexpected

surrender value of a policy
The cash value of a policy received from the insurer if a policyholder surrenders the policy before maturity. The cash surrender value is normally only a portion of the contract's face value.

underwriting losses as do the insurer's investment income from its asset portfolio plus any new premium income flows.

TABLE 3–3
Canadian Life Insurance Industry Balance Sheet, December 31, 2008 ($ thousands)

Source: OSFI, www.osfi-bsif. gc.ca.

Assets	Dec. 31, 2008	% of Assets
Cash	$ 5,333,100	1.4
Short-Term Investments	20,926,838	5.6
Accrued Investment Income	3,059,003	0.8
Accounts Receivable	8,438,076	2.3
Policy Loans	10,759,879	2.9
Bonds and Debentures	190,024,150	50.9
Mortgage Loans	54,507,112	14.6
Preferred Shares	1,309,605	0.4
Common Shares	19,462,877	5.2
Real Estate	14,369,442	3.8
Other Equity Investments	934,075	0.3
Other Loans and Invested Assets	12,604,429	3.4
Future Income Taxes	1,701,736	0.5
Goodwill	10,007,925	2.7
Intangible Assets	1,797,439	0.5
Other Assets	18,048,644	4.8
Total Assets	**$373,284,330**	**100.0**

Liabilities		% of Total
Net Actuarial Liabilities	$257,143,040	68.9
Other Insurance Policy and Contract Liabilities	16,309,128	4.4
Trust and Banking Deposits	12,792,298	3.4
Accounts Payable	7,668,186	2.1
Mortgage Loans and Other Real Estate Encumbrances	497,483	0.1
Other Liabilities	14,964,408	4.0
Net Deferred Gains (Losses) on Real Estate		
Backing Liabilities	329,685	0.1
Backing Assets	350,962	0.1
Future Income Taxes	1,713,532	0.5
Subordinated Debt	6,263,706	1.7
Other Debt	2,449,706	0.7
Total Liabilities	**$320,482,134**	**85.9**
Non-Controlling Interests	$ 405,900	0.1
Total Policyholders' Equity	2,885,225	0.8
Shareholders' Equity		
Capital Stock	21,933,646	5.9
Contributed Surplus	3,428,907	0.9
Retained Earnings	27,165,304	7.3
Shareholders' Accumulated Other Comprehensive Income (Loss)	−6,033,572	−1.6
Total Shareholders' Equity	**$ 49,511,071**	**13.3**
Total Liabilities and Equity	**$373,284,330**	**100.0**

Regulation

At the federal level, Canadian health and life insurers and branches of foreign-owned life insurance companies are regulated by OSFI under the Insurance Companies Act. These companies hold more than 95 percent of the industry's assets. Total assets of foreign life insurance companies in Canada were only $14.9 billion compared to the $373.3 billion of the Canadian life insurers. This is a decline from the $23.2 billion reported to OSFI in 2000. However, on a global basis, the foreign insurance companies operating in Canada represent some of the largest life insurers in the world, including the AXA Group of France, Metropolitan Life of the United States, and Prudential Assurance of the United Kingdom. OSFI's regulatory approach is primarily prudential, meaning that its focus is on the safety and soundness of the health and life insurers so that these FIs do not pose a risk to the Canadian financial system. To, this end, OSFI provides guidelines that pertain specifically to health and life insurers on its website. These guidelines include minimum capital and surplus requirements (which will be discussed in detail in Chapter 20) as well as guidelines for innovative instruments, large exposure limits, securities lending, asset securitization, derivatives best practices, money laundering, and outsourcing. As well, accounting guidelines and reporting requirements are specified. Effective February 1998, OSFI issued guidelines with standards for sound business and financial practices specifically for life insurance companies that address capital management, credit risk management, foreign exchange risk management, interest rate risk management, and liquidity management, among others—all of the risks that will be addressed for FIs in subsequent chapters.

Health and life insurers are also regulated at the provincial/territorial level. In each province/territory in which they do business, the insurer must abide by the market conduct regulation and licensing requirements.

www.assuris.ca

The Canadian Life and Health Insurance Compensation Corporation (Assuris) is a private, non-profit corporation that is financed by the life and health insurance companies. Assuris provides a guarantee, subject to limits, of existing life insurance policies, accident and sickness policies, and annuity contracts in the event of the bankruptcy of an insurance company. Assuris insures up to 85 percent of insurance benefits on the bankruptcy of an insurer, and up to $100,000 for deposit-type products. In addition, the OmbudService for Life & Health Insurance (OLHI) provides support for consumers who have concerns about life and health insurance companies.

www.olhi.ca

CONCEPT QUESTIONS

1. What is the difference between a life insurance contract and an annuity contract?
2. Describe the different forms of life insurance.
3. Why do life insurance companies invest in long-term assets?
4. What is the major source of life insurance underwriting risk?
5. Who are the main regulators of the life insurance industry?

PROPERTY AND CASUALTY INSURANCE

Size, Structure, and Composition of the Industry

Table 3–4 lists the gross premiums written in Canada by the leading property and casualty (P&C) companies in 2007 and by life insurance companies in 2006.

TABLE 3–4
Leading P&C and
Life Insurance
Companies in
Canada, Ranked
by Gross Written
Premiums
($ millions)

Source: Insurance Information Institute, *III International
Insurance Fact Book 2009–
2010,* "Country Profiles,"
www.iii.org/assets/docs/
pdf/canada.pdf.

LEADING P&C INSURANCE COMPANIES, 2007	
Company	**Gross Written Premiums**
ING	$4,002.4
Aviva Canada	3,021.0
Co-operators Group	1,938.6
TD Insurance Meloche Monnex	1,836.0
Economical Ins. Group	1,833.0
State Farm Ins. Companies	1,527.6
Royal & SunAlliance	1,503.7
Lloyd's	1,484.7
Wawanesa Mutual	1,466.6
Desjardins General	1,401.8

LEADING LIFE INSURANCE COMPANIES, 2006	
Company	**Gross Written Premiums***
Sun Life Assurance of Canada	$3,281.5
Manulife Canada	2,683.7
London Life	2,027.1
Industrial Alliance	1,726.2
Canada Life Financial	1,338.2
Standard Life	1,065.7
Desjardins Financial Security Life	1,041.2
Great-West Life	844.8
Transamerica Life	475.7
RBC Life	401.5

*Excludes segregated funds.

While the dollar amounts of premiums are similar for the top companies in both categories, the products provided by the two industries are different. The property and casualty insurance industry performs the important function of spreading risk of personal or business loss over many policyholders. The industry is much less concentrated than the life and health insurance industry, and, because it does not have a savings function, it is much smaller in size. However, estimates of the Insurance Bureau of Canada (IBC) place the industry employment at over 100,000 people spread across Canada and divided among primary insurers and reinsurers, brokers, independent adjusters, and appraisers. **Primary insurers** are the originators of a policy, whereas **reinsurance** provides "insurance for insurers" by spreading the risk across many insurers. The major reinsurers are large international companies so that a major catastrophe such as the terrorist attack in New York in 2001, which may result in large insurance claims, could increase property insurance premiums in Canada and globally.

Like the life and health insurance industry, the P&C industry is regulated jointly by provincial bodies with respect to marketing and licensing issues, and by OSFI with respect to solvency issues. In 2009, OSFI listed 188 companies authorized to operate in Canada, 94 Canadian firms and 94 foreign firms. Many of the Canadian firms are subsidiaries of large, global firms such as Allianz, Allstate, ING, Munich Reinsurance, and Swiss RE (see Tables 3–4 and 3–5). Assets of the Canadian firms totalled $83.1 billion at December, 2008. This represented just 2.6 percent of the $3.2 trillion on balance sheet assets of the Canadian banks and 22.2 percent of

primary insurers
Originators of insurance policies.

reinsurance
The payment of a premium to transfer the risk of a part of a claim to another insurer, called a *reinsurer.*

TABLE 3–5
Property and Casualty Insurance Companies Operating in Canada, Ranked by Revenue, December 2008 ($ billions)

Source: *Financial Post,* "FP500," June 2009.

Company	Revenues	Assets
ING Canada Inc.	$4.1	$9.8
Insurance Corp. of British Columbia	3.7	n.a.
Aviva Canada Inc.	3.5	8.2
Co-operators General Insurance Co.	2.2	4.6
The Wawanesa Mutual Insurance Co.	2.0	4.7
The Economical Insurance Group	1.9	n.a.
TD Insurance	1.9	4.3
Royal & Sun Alliance Insurance Co. of Canada	1.9	5.5
State Farm Group	1.8	5.3
Lloyd's Underwriters (Canada)	1.8	3.6

the $373.3 billion assets of the Canadian life insurance companies that OSFI supervises. At the present time, some Canadian banks have insurance subsidiaries who report to OSFI, but they are allowed to sell insurance online, but not through their branch networks, a regulation that has been challenged by the banks but that has so far limited their expansion into this field. This issue will be discussed under product diversification in Chapter 21.

Property and Casualty Insurance

Property insurance covers the loss of real and personal property. Casualty—or, perhaps more accurately, liability—insurance concerns protection against legal liability exposures. However, the distinctions between the two broad areas of property and liability insurance are increasingly becoming blurred. Some insurance lines are marketed to both individuals and commercial firms (e.g., automobile insurance) and other lines are marketed to one specific group (e.g., boiler and machinery insurance). To understand the importance of each line in terms of premium income and losses incurred, look at Figure 3–3, which shows the **net premiums written (NPW)** (the entire amount of premiums on insurance contracts written) for major P&C lines as well as the **claims ratio.** Major insurance lines include the following:

net premiums written (NPW)
The entire amount of premiums on insurance contracts written.

claims ratio
Ratio of premiums written to claims paid out.

- *Property insurance.* Protects personal and commercial property against fire, lightning, and other damage (30.5 percent of net premiums written in 2007; 31.1 percent in 1996).
- *Automobile insurance.* Provides protection against (1) losses resulting from legal liability due to the ownership or use of a vehicle (auto liability) and (2) theft of or damage to vehicles (auto physical damage). Auto insurance represents the

FIGURE 3–3
Net Premiums Written in Canada by Line of Business, 2007 ($000,000)

Source: Insurance Bureau of Canada, *Facts of the General Insurance Industry in Canada 2009,* www.ibc.ca.
* A few general insurance companies sell a small amount of accident and sickness insurance; the majority of such insurance, however, is sold by life and health insurers.

46.4%	$16,758	Auto (including commercial vehicles)
2.3	839	Accident & sickness*
7.5	2,701	Other
13.2	4,766	Liability
13.8	4,997	Commercial property
16.7	6,033	Personal property
	$36,095	Total business

FIGURE 3–4
Net Premiums
and Claims of the
P&C Industry in
Canada, 1986–2006
($ millions)

Source: The Insurance
Bureau of Canada *Fact Book*,
2008, www.ibc.ca.

largest category of premiums of all types of insurance (46.4 percent of net premiums written in 2007 versus 54.0 percent in 1996).

- *Liability insurance (other than auto).* Provides either individuals or commercial firms with protection against non-automobile-related legal liability. For commercial firms, this includes protection against liabilities relating to their business operations (other than personal injury to employees covered by Workers' Compensation insurance) and product liability hazards (13.2 percent in 2007 versus 9.2 percent in 1996).

The claims ratio (net premiums written divided by claims incurred) shows how well premiums cover claims. A higher ratio reflects higher payouts and a smaller surplus from premiums to cover claims and provide a buffer against loss of capital. For example, the claims ratio for automobile insurance for the first quarter of 2009 for Canadian firms reporting to OSFI was 78.45, down from 81.55 for the first quarter of 2008. Figure 3–4 shows net premiums written and claims incurred from 1986 to 2006 for the Canadian P&C industry. Like the spread on a loan, the difference between net premiums written and claims incurred affects the profitability of the industry. Premiums are estimates and if they do not cover claims (e.g., environmental cleanup costs that exceed the original expected loss) then the insurer's capital is affected. However, profitable years always bring calls for government inquiries and controls on high insurance premiums.[3]

Balance Sheet and Recent Trends

The Balance Sheet and Underwriting Risk

The balance sheet of the Canadian P&C firms reporting to OSFI at the end of 2008 is shown in Table 3–6. Similar to life insurance companies, P&C insurers invest

---

[3] Escalating automobile insurance premiums in the early 2000s across the country, but particularly in Ontario, led some consumers of automobile insurance to pay accident costs themselves rather than make a claim and see their insurance premiums escalate or perhaps be denied insurance and be unable to drive their cars. Some provincial governments (e.g., Nova Scotia) froze insurance premiums.

the majority of their assets in long-term securities, thus subjecting them to credit and interest rate risks. Bonds and debentures ($40.9 billion), preferred shares ($2.6 billion), and common shares ($3.9 billion) constituted 57.1 percent of total assets in 2008. P&C insurers, unlike life insurers, have more uncertain payouts on their insurance contracts (i.e., they incur greater levels of liquidity risk). Thus, their asset structure includes many assets with relatively fixed returns that can be liquidated easily and at low cost. Looking at their liabilities, we can see that major components are the unpaid claims and adjustment expenses ($39.7 billion) item, which relates to expected administrative and related costs of adjusting (settling) these claims. This item constitutes 47.8 percent of total liabilities and equity. **Unearned premiums** (a reserve set-aside that contains the portion of a premium that has been paid before insurance coverage has been provided) are also a major liability, representing 20.9 percent of total liabilities and capital.

To understand how and why a loss reserve on the liability side of the balance sheet is established, we need to understand the risks of underwriting P&C insurance. In particular, P&C underwriting risk results when the premiums generated on a given insurance line are insufficient to cover (1) the claims (losses) incurred insuring against the peril and (2) the administrative expenses of providing that insurance (legal expenses, commissions, taxes, etc.) after taking into account (3) the investment income generated between the time premiums are received and the time claims are paid. Thus, underwriting risk may result from (1) unexpected increases in loss rates, (2) unexpected increases in expenses, and/or (3) unexpected decreases in investment yields or returns. Next, we look more carefully at each of these three areas of P&C underwriting risk.

Loss Risk   The key feature of claims loss exposure is the actuarial *predictability* of losses relative to premiums earned. This predictability depends on a number of characteristics or features of the perils insured, specifically:

- *Property versus liability.* In general, the maximum levels of losses are more predictable for property lines than for liability lines. For example, the monetary value of the loss of, or damage to, an auto is relatively easy to calculate, while the upper limit to the losses an insurer might be exposed to in a product liability line—for example, asbestos damage to workers' health under other liability insurance—may be difficult, if not impossible, to estimate.

- *Severity versus frequency.* In general, loss rates are more predictable on low-severity, high-frequency lines than they are on high-severity, low-frequency lines. For example, losses in fire, auto, and homeowners peril lines tend to involve events expected to occur with a high frequency and to be independently distributed across any pool of the insured. Furthermore, the dollar loss on each event in the insured pool tends to be relatively small. Applying the law of large numbers, insurers can estimate the expected loss potential of such lines—the **frequency of loss** times the size of the loss (**severity of loss**)—within quite small probability bounds. Other lines, such as earthquake, hail, and financial guaranty insurance, tend to insure very low-probability (frequency) events. Here the probabilities are not always stationary, the individual risks in the insured pool are not independent, and the severity of the loss could be enormous. This means that estimating expected loss rates (frequency times severity) is extremely difficult in these coverage areas. For example, in the United States, since the September 11 terrorist attacks, coverage for high-profile buildings in big cities, as well as other properties considered potential targets, remains expensive. This higher

unearned premiums
Reserve set-aside that contains the portion of a premium that has been paid before insurance coverage has been provided.

frequency of loss
The probability that a loss will occur.

severity of loss
The size of the loss.

uncertainty of losses forces P&C firms to invest in more short-term assets and hold a larger percentage of capital and reserves than life insurance firms hold.

TABLE 3–6
Balance Sheet for Canadian P&C Companies, December 2008 ($ thousands)

Source: OSFI, www.osfi-bsif. gc.ca.

Assets		% of Total Assets
Cash	$3,472,368	4.2%
Investment Income Due and Accrued	390,064	0.5%
Investments:		
Term Deposits	1,863,383	2.2%
Bonds and Debentures	40,930,475	49.3%
Mortgage Loans	515,717	0.6%
Preferred Shares	2,591,240	3.1%
Common Shares	3,932,932	4.7%
Real Estate	41,932	0.1%
Other Investments	1,003,194	1.2%
Total Investments	**$50,878,873**	**61.3%**
Receivables:		
Instalment Premiums	5,369,180	6.5%
Other Receivables	3,602,435	4.3%
Recoverable from Reinsurers:		
Unearned Premiums	2,324,528	2.8%
Unpaid Claims and Adjustment Expenses	9,315,218	11.2%
Other Recoverables on Unpaid Claims	652,713	0.8%
Investment in Subsidiaries, Affiliates, and Partnerships	2,754,478	3.3%
Real Estate for Insurer's Own Use	129,645	0.2%
Deferred Policy Acquisition Expenses	2,834,341	3.4%
Future Income Taxes	439,325	0.5%
Other Assets	902,806	1.1%
Total Assets	**$83,065,974**	**100.0%**
Liabilities		**% of Total**
Overdrafts, Borrowed Money, and Accrued Interest	$198,386	0.2%
Payables	1,242,155	1.5%
Expenses Due and Accrued	944,648	1.1%
Taxes Due and Accrued	448,197	0.5%
Unearned Premiums	17,330,468	20.9%
Unpaid Claims and Adjustment Expenses	39,694,966	47.8%
Unearned Commissions	464,939	0.6%
Other Liabilities	1,686,402	2.0%
Total Liabilities	**$62,010,161**	**74.7%**
Equity		**% of Total**
Share Capital Issued and Paid	6,840,520	8.2%
Contributed Surplus	2,113,719	2.5%
Other	1,712	0.0%
Retained Earnings	12,918,821	15.6%
Reserves	273,600	0.3%
Accumulated Other Comprehensive Income (Loss)	−1,092,560	−1.3%
Total Equity	**$21,055,812**	**25.3%**
Total Liabilities and Equity	**$83,065,974**	**100.0%**

long-tail loss
A claim that is made some time after a policy was written.

- *Long tail versus short tail.* Some liability lines suffer from a long-tail risk exposure phenomenon that makes the estimation of expected losses difficult. This **long-tail loss** arises in policies in which the insured event occurs during a coverage period but a claim is not filed or reported until many years later. The delay in filing of a claim is in accordance with the terms of the insurance contract and often occurs because the detrimental consequences of the event are not known for a period of time after the event actually occurs. Losses incurred but not reported have caused insurers significant problems in lines such as medical malpractice and other liability insurance where product damage suits (e.g., the Dalkon shield case and asbestos cases) have mushroomed many years after the event occurred and the coverage period expired.[4] For example, in 2002 Halliburton, a major U.S. corporation, agreed to pay US$4 billion in cash and stock, and to seek bankruptcy protection for a subsidiary to settle more than 300,000 asbestos claims. Questions still remain about how much insurance companies will be required to reimburse Halliburton for the cost of asbestos case settlements and when. The company had only US$1.6 billion of expected insurance on its books for asbestos claims.

- *Product inflation versus social inflation.* Loss rates on all P&C property policies are adversely affected by unexpected increases in inflation. Such increases were triggered, for example, by the oil price shocks of 1973 and 1978. However, in addition to a systematic unexpected inflation risk in each line, there may be line-specific inflation risks. The inflation risk of property lines is likely to reflect the approximate underlying inflation risk of the economy. Liability lines may be subject to social inflation, as reflected in the courts' willingness to award punitive and other liability damages at rates far above the underlying rate of inflation. Such social inflation has been particularly prevalent in commercial liability and medical malpractice insurance in the United States.

Reinsurance   An alternative to managing risk on a P&C insurer's balance sheet is to purchase reinsurance from a reinsurance company. *Reinsurance* is essentially insurance for insurance companies. It is a way for primary insurance companies to protect against unforeseen or extraordinary losses. Depending on the contract, reinsurance can enable the insurer to improve its capital position, expand its business, limit losses, and stabilize cash flows, among other things. In addition, the reinsurer, drawing information from many primary insurers, will usually have a far larger pool of data for assessing risks. Reinsurance takes a variety of forms. It may represent a layer of risk, such as losses within certain limits, say, $5 million to $10 million, that will be paid by the reinsurer to the primary insurance company for which a premium is paid, or a sharing of both losses and profits for certain types of business. Reinsurance is an international business. About 75 percent of the reinsurance business that comes from U.S. insurance companies is written by non-U.S. reinsurers such as Munich Re. Some investment banks are now setting up reinsurers as part of a move to develop alternative risk financing deals such as catastrophe bonds. Insurers and reinsurers also typically issue catastrophe bonds. The bonds pay high interest rates and diversify an investor's portfolio because natural disasters occur randomly and are not associated with (independent of) economic factors. Depending on how the bond is structured, if losses reach the

---

[4] In some product liability cases, such as those involving asbestos, the nature of the risk being covered was not fully understood at the time many of the policies were written.

threshold specified in the bond offering, the investor may lose all or part of the principal or interest. For example, a deep-discount or zero-coupon catastrophe bond would pay $100(1 - \alpha)$ on maturity, where α is the loss rate due to the catastrophe. Thus, Munich Re issued a US$250 million catastrophe bond in 2001 where α (the loss rate) reflected losses incurred on all reinsurer policies over a 24-hour period should an event (such as a flood or hurricane) occur and losses exceed a certain threshold. The required yield on these bonds reflected the risk-free rate plus a premium reflecting investors' expectations regarding the probability of the event occurring.

loss (claims) ratio
Ratio that measures losses incurred to premiums earned.

premiums earned
Premiums received and earned on insurance contracts because time has passed with no claim being filed.

Measuring Loss Risk   The **loss ratio** (also called the *claims ratio*) measures the actual losses incurred on a line. It measures the ratio of losses incurred to **premiums earned** (premiums received and earned on insurance contracts because time has passed with no claim being filed). Thus, a loss ratio less than 100 means that premiums earned were sufficient to cover losses incurred on that line. For example, referring back to Figure 3–4, net premiums written by the Canadian P&C industry in 2001 were $21.242 billion and claims incurred were $16.161 billion, resulting in a claims ratio, also called an *earned loss ratio*, of 76 ($16.161/$21.242). For 2006, net premiums written were $34.964 billion and claims incurred were $20.326 billion, resulting in a claims ratio of 58 ($20.326/$34.964). From 2001 to 2006, the claims ratio declined, reflecting an increase in premiums written that was greater than the increase in claims incurred, resulting in an increase in profitability for the insurance companies. However, the earned loss ratio does not tell the whole story, as the expense of providing insurance coverage must also be considered.

Expense Risk   The two major sources of expense risk to P&C insurers are (1) loss adjustment expenses (LAE) and (2) commissions and other expenses. Loss adjustment expenses related to the costs surrounding the loss settlement process. For example, many P&C insurers employ adjusters who determine the liability of the insurer and the size of the adjustment or settlement to be made. The other major area of expense occurs in the commission costs paid to insurance brokers and sales agents, and other expenses related to the acquisition of new business. The underwriting loss/gain is calculated as net premiums written less claims and expenses incurred. Table 3–7 shows the underwriting loss/gain for Canadian P&C insurers for the 21-year period from 1986 to 2006. Despite the claims ratio of 76 in 2001 (see above), P&C insurers experienced their largest underwriting loss ($2.16 billion) over the period, as well as underwriting losses in every year from 1986 to 2002. Clearly, insurance broker commissions and other operating costs can rapidly render an insurance line unprofitable.

combined ratio
Ratio that measures the overall underwriting profitability of a line; it is equal to the loss ratio plus the ratios of loss adjustment expenses to premiums earned and commission and other acquisition costs to premiums written as a proportion of premiums earned.

A common measure of the overall underwriting profitability of a line, which includes both loss and expense experience, is the **combined ratio.** Technically, the combined ratio is equal to the loss ratio plus the ratios of LAE to premiums earned, commissions and other acquisition costs and general expense costs to premiums written. If the combined ratio is less than 100, premiums alone are sufficient to cover both losses and expenses related to the line.

If premiums are insufficient and the combined ratio exceeds 100, the P&C insurer must rely on investment income earned on premiums for overall profitability. As shown in Table 3–7, the underwriting losses from 1986 to 2002 were offset by investment income in each year. The profitability of the industry thus depends on identifying the risks and setting appropriate premiums, as well as on investment skills. Bad years for the investment portfolios shown in Table 3–6 may

TABLE 3–7
P&C Industry
Underwriting
and Investment
Income, 1986–2006
($ millions)

Source: Insurance Bureau of
Canada, based on data from
Statistics Canada, OSFI, A.M.
Best Canada's *Statement File*,
MSA Research, and *Canadian
Insurance*.

Year	Underwriting Loss/Gain	Investment Income	Underwriting Loss as a Proportion of Investment Income
1986	(498)	1,500	(33.2%)
1987	(486)	1,696	(28.6%)
1988	(751)	1,933	(38.9%)
1989	(1,364)	2,310	(59.0%)
1990	(1,234)	2,363	(52.2%)
1991	(1,421)	2,548	(55.8%)
1992	(1,375)	2,505	(54.9%)
1993	(1,351)	2,671	(50.6%)
1994	(1,027)	2,061	(49.9%)
1995	(631)	2,508	(25.2%)
1996	(517)	3,111	(16.6%)
1997	(421)	3,324	(12.7%)
1998	(1,366)	2,864	(47.7%)
1999	(1,027)	2,543	(40.4%)
2000	(1,614)	3,251	(49.6%)
2001	(2,155)	2,762	(78.0%)
2002	(1,390)	2,248	(61.8%)
2003	559	3,020	18.5%
2004	3,072	3,182	96.5%
2005	2,350	3,887	60.5%
2006	3,848	4,302	89.4%

also result in poor profitability for the P&C insurers. Declines in the value of the investment portfolio would be reflected in an erosion of capital. However, Canadian P&C companies have less exposure to equity investments than do U.S. and European firms and, while showing a decline in profitability, did not experience as large an impact on their income statements and balance sheets from the global recession in 2008.[5]

The effects of the global liquidity crisis for property and casualty insurers were felt in Canada by some consolidation of the industry. For example, the Dutch bank ING Group was forced to sell most of its interest in ING Canada. See the Industry Perspectives feature "ING Selling Most of Its Stake in Canadian Unit" later in this chapter.

Investment Yield/Return Risk   As discussed above, when the combined ratio is more than 100, overall profitability can be ensured only by a sufficient investment return on premiums earned. That is, P&C firms invest premiums in assets between the time they are received and the time they are paid out to meet claims. For example, in 2002, net investment income to premiums earned (or the P&C insurers' investment yield) was 8.9 percent. As a result, the overall average profitability (or **operating ratio**) of P&C insurers was 96.9. It was equal to the combined ratio after dividends (105.8) minus the investment yield (8.9). Since the operating ratio was less than 100, P&C insurers were profitable in 2002. However, lower net returns on investments (e.g., 5 percent rather than 8.9 percent) would have meant that underwriting P&C insurance was marginally unprofitable (i.e., the operating

operating ratio
A measure of the
overall profitability
of a P&C insurer; it
equals the combined
ratio minus the
investment yield.

---

[5] See Swiss Re, Economic and Research Consulting, *Implications of the Financial Crisis for the Canadian P&C Industry*, December 2008, www.swissre.com/pws/researchpublications/sigma.

ratio of insurers in this case would have been 100.8). Thus, the effect of interest rates and default rates on P&C insurers' investments is crucial to P&C insurers' overall profitability. That is, measuring and managing credit and interest rate risk are key concerns of P&C managers.

Consider the following example. Suppose an insurance company's projected loss ratio is 79.8 percent and its expense ratio is 27.9 percent. The combined ratio for this insurance company is equal to:

$$\text{Loss ratio} + \text{Expense ratio} = \text{Combined ratio}$$
$$79.8 \quad + \quad 27.9 \quad = \quad 107.7$$

Thus, expected losses on all P&C lines and expenses exceeded premiums earned by 7.7 percent.

If the company's investment portfolio, however, yielded 12 percent, the operating ratio and overall profitability of the P&C insurer would be:

$$\text{Operating ratio} = \text{Combined ratio after dividends} - \text{Investment yield}$$
$$= \quad\quad 107.7 \quad\quad - \quad\quad 12.0$$
$$= \quad\quad 95.7 \text{ percent}$$

and

$$\text{Overall profitability} = 100 - \text{Operating ratio}$$
$$= 100 - 95.7$$
$$= 4.3 \text{ percent}$$

As can be seen, the high investment returns (12 percent) make the P&C insurer profitable overall.

Finally, if losses, expenses, and other costs are higher and investment yields are lower than expected so that operating losses are incurred, P&C insurers carry reserves (0.3 percent of total assets in 2007) to reduce the risk of insolvency.

Recent Trends

Table 3–8 lists the claims and payments for natural disasters for property and automobile insurance in Canada from 1987–2006. The major source for insurance company losses came from storms (hail, flooding, winds, and tornados) across Canada. The ice storm of 1998, which affected southern Quebec (730,169 claims, $1.48 billion) and eastern Ontario (165,562 claims, $165.56 million), was the only incident in Canada where total payouts have exceeded $1 billion. By way of contrast, insurance incidents in the United States regularly exceed US$1 billion. Reinsurance means that large payouts affect global insurance rates and therefore rates in Canada. For example, Hurricane Katrina in 2005 cost insurers over US$35 billion. Manulife's reinsurance losses related to Hurricane Katrina were estimated to be US$135 million.

Although catastrophes may be random, the period 1987–2004 was characterized by a number of catastrophes of historically great severity. A succession of catastrophes meant that, in the terminology of insurers, the global industry was in the trough of an **underwriting cycle,** or underwriting conditions were hard. These cycles are characterized by periods of rising premiums leading to increased profitability. Following a period of solid but not spectacular rates of returns, the industry enters a down phase in which premiums soften as the supply of insurance products increases. Most analysts agree that a cycle that affects all lines simultaneously is unlikely. As an example of how bad things can be in this industry, Lloyd's

underwriting cycle
The tendency of profits in the P&C industry to follow a cyclical pattern.

TABLE 3–8
Natural Disasters in
Canada, 1987–2006

Source: Insurance Bureau of
Canada, *Facts of the General
Insurance Industry in Canada,
2004, 2008,* www.ibc.ca. Used
with permission.

Date and Place		Event	Total Number of Claims	Total Loss ($000)
1987	Edmonton, Alberta	Tornado	58,506	$148,337
1991	Calgary, Alberta	Hail	116,311	342,745
1996	Winnipeg, Manitoba; Calgary	Flooding, hail	93,841	351,138
1998	Southern Quebec, eastern Ontario	Ice storm	792,514	1,641,608
2003	British Columbia	Forest fires	3,385	200,000
2003	Nova Scotia, Prince Edward Island	Hurricane Juan	24,292	139,336
2004	Alberta	Hail, flooding	17,195	187,500
2005	Alberta, Manitoba	Flooding	n.a.	360,000
2005	Ontario	Wind, rainstorm	n.a.	500,000
2006	British Columbia	Storm	14,437	133,086

of London, one of the world's most well-known and respected insurers, posted a £510 million loss in 1991, a result of four years of unprecedented accident claims.

The year 2001 saw yet another blow to the insurance industry and the world with the terrorist attacks on the World Trade Center and the Pentagon. Because of the tremendous impact these attacks had on the health of the U.S. insurance industry, the Bush administration proposed that the U.S. government pay the majority of the losses of the insurance industry due to the attacks. The proposal capped insurers' 2002 liabilities at US$12 billion, 2003 liabilities at US$23 billion, and 2004 liabilities at US$36 billion. Despite this bailout of the industry, many insurers did not survive and those that did were forced to increase premiums significantly.[6]

The traditional reaction to losses or poor profit results has been the exit from the industry—through failure or acquisition—of less profitable firms and a rapid increase in premiums among the remaining firms. As shown in Table 3–7, underwriting finally showed a gain for Canadian P&C insurers in 2003. The decline in the earned loss ratio and the operating expense ratio drew new entrants such as Arch Capital Group, which is Bermuda-based and has operations in the United States and Europe. In addition to general P&C insurance, Arch also provides **directors and officers (D&O) insurance.**[7]

directors and officers (D&O) insurance
Insurance that protects corporate directors and senior managers from legal claims.

In summary, major issues for the P&C industry in Canada are its image with consumers, particularly with respect to automobile insurance and the perceived "gouging" of consumers with high insurance rates. Consumer access to insurance affects the industry's relationship with the federal and provincial/territorial governments and regulators, particularly with the financial sector reform that may see the sale of insurance in the branches of the major banks.

Regulation

Similar to life insurance companies, regulation of the property and casualty insurance industry is shared by the provincial/territorial and federal governments. Property and casualty insurers may be incorporated federally or provincially/territorially. OSFI, the federal regulator, is responsible for over 75 percent of the companies. OSFI provides a *Table of Guidelines* that are specific to property and

---

[6] See "The Risk That Nobody Wants," *The Economist,* November 17, 2001, pp. 66–68.

[7] See R. Marquez, "New P&C Insurer on Canadian Scene," *The Insurance Journal,* June/July 2005.

casualty insurers, including investment concentration limits, securities lending, asset securitization, derivatives best practices, earthquake exposure, outsourcing, impaired loans, and accounting guidelines. Provincial and territorial regulators govern the marketing and licensing of property and casualty insurers.

www.pacicc.ca Canadian property and casualty policyholders are protected from the insolvency of their insurers, up to certain limits, by the Property and Casualty Insurance Compensation Corporation (PACICC), which is industry-run. All Canadian provinces and territories require PACICC coverage prior to licensing. In addition, foreign insurers are required to vest assets in Canada so that their policyholders are protected.

The deterioration of P&C insurers, particularly the decline in capital levels, prompted the Secretary of State for International Financial Institutions to request a report on the P&C insurance industry in Canada. In its report released in 2003, OSFI concluded that the investment portfolios were prudent and returns from these investment portfolios were able to carry the industry despite higher claims and declining premiums.[8] However, OSFI, the Insurance Bureau of Canada, and the Canadian Council of Insurance Regulators are working to bring the *Minimum Capital Test* (MCT, see Chapter 20) in line with life insurers.

CONCEPT QUESTIONS	
	1. Why do P&C insurers hold more capital and reserves than do life insurers?
	2. Why are life insurers' assets, on average, longer in maturity than those of P&C insurers?
	3. Describe the main lines of insurance offered by P&C insurers.
	4. What are the components of the combined ratio?
	5. How does the operating ratio differ from the combined ratio?
	6. Why does the combined ratio tend to behave cyclically?

GLOBAL ISSUES

Like the other sectors of the financial institutions industry, the insurance sector is global. Table 3–9 lists the top ten countries in terms of total premiums written in 2008 (in U.S. dollars) and their percentage share of the world market. Panel A lists the data for life insurance, while panel B lists the data for non-life insurance (called P&C in Canada and the United States). Table 3–10 lists the top ten insurance companies worldwide by total revenues. While North America, Japan, and Western Europe dominate the global market, all regions are engaged in the insurance business and many insurers are engaged internationally.

Globalization has certainly affected the U.S. insurance market. In the early 2000s, insurers headquartered outside the United States accounted for over 10 percent of all premiums written in the United States. Because of lax regulations, such as lower capital regulations, many insurance companies have set up offices in the Cayman Islands and the Bahamas. It has been estimated that 44 percent of the insurance companies selling life insurance in the Caribbean are from outside the region. The pressure of the global economy, the inability of local insurers to serve all domestic customers, and the domestic demand for better economic performance have caused governments around the world to introduce and accelerate insurance market reform. This includes improving insurance and insurance

---

[8] See N. Le Pan, *Report on the Property and Casualty (P&C) Insurance Industry in Canada*, September 19, 2003, at www.osfic-bcif.gc.ca for a detailed analysis of the industry to 2002.

TABLE 3–9
The World's Top
Countries in Terms
of Insurance
Premiums Written,
2008

Source: Swiss Re, *Sigma 3*,
2009.

Panel A: Life Insurance

Rank	Country	Premium Volume (US$ billions)	Share of World Market (%)
1	United States	$ 578.2	23.2
2	Japan	367.1	14.7
3	United Kingdom	342.8	13.8
4	France	181.2	7.3
5	Germany	111.3	4.5
6	PR China	95.8	3.9
7	Italy	82.6	3.3
8	South Korea	66.4	2.7
9	Taiwan	52.7	2.1
10	India	48.7	2.0
	Top 10	**$1,926.8**	**77.4**
11	Canada	47.9	1.9

Panel B: Non-Life Insurance

Rank	Country	Premium Volume (US$ billions)	Share of World Market (%)
1	United States	$ 662.4	37.2
2	Germany	131.8	7.4
3	United Kingdom	107.4	6.0
4	Japan	106.1	6.0
5	France	91.9	5.2
6	Netherlands	73.7	4.0
7	Italy	58.1	3.3
8	Canada	57.3	3.2
9	Spain	47.9	2.7
10	PR China	45.2	2.5
	Top 10	**$1,381.8**	**77.7**

supervision by formulating common principles and practices across nations. One consequence of these changes is that there were a number of mergers of insurance companies across country borders, such as the Dutch ING Group's 2000 acquisition of U.S. Aetna for US$7.75 billion.

However, like the other sectors of the financial services industry, the insurance sector has been impacted by the global financial crisis. Insurance companies can be exposed to the credit crisis on the asset side through holding subprime mortgage-backed securities. On the liability side, insurance companies provide mortgage insurance, financial guarantees such as credit default swaps, and directors and officers insurance. Losses in these areas affect their profitability and result in declines in capital. In September 2008, the world's largest property and casualty insurer, American International Group Inc. (AIG), received a US$85 billion rescue

TABLE 3–10
Top Ten Global
Insurance
Companies
by Revenues,
2008[1](US$ millions)

Source: Insurance Information Institute, *International Insurance Fact Book, 2009–2010*, www.iii.org/international/rankings.

Panel A: Life/Health Insurance

Rank	Company	Revenues[2]	Country
1	Japan Post Holdings	$198,700	Japan
2	Assicurazioni Generali	103,103	Italy
3	AXA	80,257	France
4	Nippon Life Insurance	66,621	Japan
5	MetLife	55,085	U.S.
6	China Life Insurance	54,534	China
7	Dai-ichi Mutual Life Insurance	52,012	Japan
8	CNP Assurances	38,482	France
9	Meiji Yasuda Life Insurance	38,082	Japan
10	Sumitomo Life Insurance	36,308	Japan

[1] Based on an analysis of companies in the *Global Fortune 500*. Includes stock and mutual companies.
[2] Revenues include premium and annuity income, investment income and capital gains or losses, but exclude deposits; includes consolidated subsidiaries, excludes excise taxes.

Panel B: Property and Casualty Insurance

Rank	Company	Revenues[2]	Country
1	Allianz	$142,395	Germany
2	Berkshire Hathaway	107,786	U.S.
3	Munich Re Group	67,515	Germany
4	State Farm Insurance Companies	61,343	U.S.
5	Tokio Marine Holdings	34,870	Japan
6	Zurich Financial Services	32,349	Switzerland
7	Allstate	29,394	U.S.
8	Liberty Mutual Insurance Group	28,855	U.S.
9	Travelers Companies	24,477	U.S.
10	Mapfre Group	23,186	Spain

[1] Based on an analysis of companies in the Global Fortune 500. Includes stock and mutual companies.
[2] Revenues include premium and annuity income, investment income and capital gains or losses, but exclude deposits; includes consolidated subsidiaries, excludes excise taxes.

monoline insurers
Companies that act as guarantors of the debt or equity obligations of other firms.

package and became 79.9 percent owned by the U.S. government. The stress placed on insurance companies globally has resulted in further consolidation of the markets. See the discussion of ING's sale of its property and casualty insurance arm, ING Canada Inc., in the Industry Perspectives feature. As well, the global market disruptions have caused problems for **monoline insurers** that act as guarantors of corporate and municipal debt and other securities. This issue is important as a credit enhancement for off-balance-sheet items.

As with commercial banks, Japanese non-life insurance companies suffered severe losses in the early 2000s. Six of the nine major non-life insurance groups that announced earnings (for the April through December 2003 period) saw their net premiums drop relative to the prior year. The main factor in the decline was the sluggish performance of automobile insurance, which accounts for roughly half of the revenue for these firms. The total net premiums of the nine groups declined

0.5 percent on the year to ¥4.9 trillion (US$46.4 billion). Life insurers did not fare much better. In 2004, many Japanese life insurers took steps to boost reserves and repair their capital bases after two very difficult years. The sector continues to face problems due to asset deflation, low interest rates, and a shrinking market for life insurance products in 2009.

INDUSTRY PERSPECTIVES

ING SELLING MOST OF ITS STAKE IN CANADIAN UNIT

Financially stressed Dutch bank ING Groep NV is giving up control of its Canadian unit, ING Canada Inc., for at least $1.75-billion, but it is doing it at a steep discount to the market price.

The parent, which has received a 10-billion euro bailout from the Dutch government and installed a new chief executive officer last week, is selling most of its 70% stake in Canada's largest provider of home, auto and business insurance through a two-part offering.

It will sell a minimum of $850-million of its ING Canada common shares to certain institutional investors in a private placement at a price of $25 a share. As part of the deal, investors are required to hold those shares for four months.

The parent will also sell an additional $900-million of its ING Canada common shares, at a price of $26.35 a share to other investors. Those shares are freely tradeable. The underwriters have been given an option to sell an additional 5.12 million shares.

Charles Brindamour, chief executive of ING Canada, said "thanks to our partnership with ING Group, we have built over the years a world-class organization. Now, with the proposed transactions, for the first time in recent history, a Canadian-listed and controlled company will assume the leadership position in the Canadian home, auto and business insurance industry."

The change in control comes at a pivotal moment for relations between the property and casualty industry and Ottawa as insurers seek to replace a patchwork of provincial regulations with harmonized federal rules.

In turn, the industry is under pressure to abandon practices that antagonize consumers, such as heavy use of arcane clauses in insurance contracts to deny claims.

Lawmakers are regularly inundated by complaints from constituents who feel they have been treated unfairly, and are prone to advocating for national and provincial probes and crackdowns.

This political and regulatory uncertainty is a key reason foreign-based buyers were reluctant to increase their exposure to the Canadian market by buying the unit.

But the main reason ING opted for a heavily discounted sale to insurers appears to have been a strong desire on the part of the parent to liquidate its holdings for cash quickly, as it continues to reel from heavy losses.

Given that the financing is being done on a secondary basis, the Canadian division, which went public in late 2004, will not receive any of the proceeds.

The shares are being offered at prices that are considerably below the recent trading price of common shares of ING Canada, which operates under the ING Canada, Belair Direct and Grey Power banners. When the stock was halted, the shares were trading at $33.79, 21% above the price of the shares it will now be offering to the retail market. And at about $26 a share, the price is almost identical to the $26 a share that ING was able to garner when it went public just over four years back.

The deal will also heighten questions over the future of ING Bank of Canada, which specializes in high-interest online deposits and holds more than $24-billion in assets for more than 1.6 million Canadians.

The company said Tuesday the deal would "not affect ING Group's ownership of ING Bank of Canada, known as ING Direct, which is a separate and distinct company from ING Canada."

The online bank was downgraded last week by Moody's, the credit ratings agency, which said one of its "primary credit concerns" was "the impact on the bank's liquidity position of a high reliance on Internet-sourced, high-interest deposits."

Moody's downgraded "the long-term deposit ratings of ING Bank of Canada to A2 from A1 following the downgrade of the bank financial strength rating of its ultimate parent [in the Netherlands]."

Source: Barry Critchley and Eoin Callan, *Financial Post*, February 3, 2009, www.financialpost.com.

Summary

This chapter examined the activities and regulation of insurance companies. The first part of the chapter described the various classes of life insurance and recent trends. The second part covered property and casualty companies. The various lines that make up property and casualty insurance are becoming increasingly blurred as multiple activity line coverages are offered. Both life and property and casualty insurers are coming under threat from other financial services firms that offer similar or competitive products.

Questions and Problems

1. What is the primary function of an insurance company? How does this function compare with the primary function of a deposit-taking institution?

2. What is moral hazard?

3. What is the adverse selection problem? How does adverse selection affect the profitable management of an insurance company?

4. What are the similarities and differences among the four basic lines of life insurance products?

5. Explain how annuity activities represent the reverse of life insurance activities.

6. Explain how life insurance and annuity products can be used to create a steady stream of cash disbursements and payments to avoid paying or receiving a single lump-sum cash amount.

7. a. Calculate the annual cash flows of a $1 million, 20-year fixed-payment annuity earning a guaranteed 10 percent per annum if payments are to begin at the end of the current year.

   b. Calculate the annual cash flows of a $1 million, 20-year fixed-payment annuity earning a guaranteed 10 percent per annum if payments are to begin at the end of year 5.

   c. What is the amount of the annuity purchase required if you wish to receive a fixed payment of $200,000 for 20 years? Assume that the annuity will earn 10 percent per annum.

8. You plan to deposit $10,000 annually into a life insurance fund for the next 10 years, after which time you plan to retire.

   a. If the deposits are made at the beginning of the year and earn an interest rate of 8 percent, what will be the amount of retirement funds at the end of year 10?

   b. Instead of a lump sum, you wish to receive annuities for the next 20 years (years 11 through 30). What is the constant annual payment you expect to receive at the beginning of each year if you assume an interest rate of 8 percent during the distribution period?

   c. Repeat parts (a) and (b) above assuming earning rates of 7 percent and 9 percent during the deposit period and earning rates of 7 percent and 9 percent during the distribution period. During which period does the change in the earning rate have the greatest impact?

9. a. Suppose a 65-year-old person wants to purchase an annuity from an insurance company that would pay $20,000 per year until the end of that person's life. The insurance company expects this person to live for 15 more years and would be willing to pay 6 percent on the annuity. How much should the insurance company ask this person to pay for the annuity?

   b. A second 65-year-old person wants the same $20,000 annuity, but this person is much healthier and is expected to live for 20 years. If the same 6 percent interest rate applies, how much should this healthier person be charged for the annuity?

   c. In each case, what is the difference in the purchase price of the annuity if the distribution payments are made at the beginning of the year?

10. Contrast the balance sheet of a life insurance company with the balance sheet of a bank. Explain the balance sheet differences in terms of the differences in the primary functions of the two organizations.

11. Using the data in Table 3–2, how has the composition of assets of Canadian life insurance companies changed over time?

12. How do life insurance companies earn a profit?

13. How would the balance sheet of a life insurance company change if it offered to run a private pension fund for another company?

14. How does the regulation of insurance companies differ from the regulation of deposit-taking institutions?

15. How do guarantee funds for life insurance companies compare with deposit insurance for banks?

16. What are the two major activity lines of property and casualty insurance firms?

17. How have the product lines of property and casualty insurance companies changed over time?

18. Contrast the balance sheet of a property and casualty insurance company with the balance sheet of a bank. Explain the balance sheet differences in terms of the differences in the primary functions of the two organizations.

19. What are the three sources of underwriting risk in the property and casualty insurance industry?

20. How do unexpected increases in inflation affect property and casualty insurers?

21. Identify the four characteristics or features of the perils insured against by property and casualty insurance. Rank the features in terms of actuarial predictability and total loss potential.

22. Insurance companies will charge a higher premium for which of the insurance lines listed below? Why?

    a. Low-severity, high-frequency lines versus high-severity, low-frequency lines.

    b. Long-tail lines versus short-tail lines.

23. What does the loss ratio measure? What has been the long-term trend of the loss ratio? Why?

24. What does the expense ratio measure? Identify and explain the two major sources of expense risk to a property and casualty insurer?

25. How is the combined ratio defined? What does it measure?

26. What is the investment yield on premiums earned? Why has this ratio become so important to property and casualty insurers?

27. How is investment yield related to the interest rate risk and credit risk faced by a property and casualty insurer?

28. An insurance company's projected loss ratio is 77.5 percent, and its loss adjustment expense ratio is 12.9 percent. The company estimates that commission payments will be 16 percent. What must be the minimum yield on investments to achieve a positive operating ratio?

29. a. What is the combined ratio for a property insurer who has a simple loss ratio of 73 percent, a loss adjustment expense of 12.5 percent, and a ratio of commissions and other acquisition expenses of 18 percent?

    b. What is the combined ratio adjusted for investment yield if the company earns an investment yield of 8 percent?

30. An insurance company collected $3.6 million in premiums and disbursed $1.96 million in losses. Loss adjustment expenses amounted to 6.6 percent. The total income generated from the company's investments was $170,000 after all expenses were paid. What is the net profitability in dollars?

Web Questions

31. Go to OSFI's website at www.osfi-bsif.gc.ca. Download the latest balance sheet for the life insurance industry as follows. Click on "Life Insurance Companies & Fraternals." Click on "Financial Data – Life Insurance Companies." Click on "Submit" to see the latest total assets for Canadian life insurers. How has the asset composition changed from Table 3–2? How many life insurance companies are regulated by OSFI? Submit a request for the assets of Manulife, Sunlife, and Great-West Life. How have their total assets changed from Table 3–1?

32. Go to the Insurance Bureau of Canada's website at www.ibc.ca and download the latest version of the *Fact Book of the General Insurance Industry in Canada*. How has the return on equity, earned loss ratio, operating expense ratio, and combined ratio changed since 2007? Have Canadian property and casualty insurers maintained their combined ratio below 100 percent? Have Canadian property and casualty insurers shown an underwriting loss or gain annually since 2007? Calculate the return on investment (net investment income/net premiums earned). Has the return on investment helped the industry?

33. Go to the Insurance Information Institute website at www2.iii.org/international/toc and download the latest version of the *International Insurance Fact Book*. How have the premiums written for (a) life insurance companies and (b) property and casualty companies changed from 2007? Compare the performance of Canadian companies with the performance of international insurance companies over the period of greatest global market disturbances between 2008 and 2010.

Securities Firms and Investment Banks

In this chapter, we present an overview of securities firms and investment banks in terms of

▸ the size, structure, and composition of the industry
▸ balance sheets and recent trends
▸ regulation of the industry
▸ global competition and trends in the industry

INTRODUCTION

broker-dealers
Securities firms that assist in the trading of existing securities.

investment banks
Firms that specialize in originating, underwriting, and distributing issues of new securities.

The securities industry in Canada performs two functions: (1) the raising of debt and equity securities, including the origination, underwriting, and placement of securities in money and capital markets for corporate or government issuers and (2) assistance in the trading of securities in the secondary markets including brokerage services and/or market-making. Firms in the securities industry that specialize in the purchase, sale, and brokerage of existing securities (the retail side of the business) are called **broker-dealers,** whereas firms that specialize in originating, underwriting, and distributing issues of new securities are called **investment banks.**

Investment banking also includes corporate finance activities such as advising on mergers and acquisitions (M&As), as well as advising on the restructuring of existing corporations. Figure 4–1 reports merger activity for Canada for 1998–2007. Merger and acquisition activity on a year-to-year dollar basis increased from just over $150 billion in 1998 to over $350 billion in 2007. Merger activity fell between 2001 and 2003, but the industry picked up again in 2004 led by two large cross-border deals, the acquisition of Banknorth Group Inc. by Toronto-Dominion Bank, the largest deal at $4.97 billion, and the merger of Molson Inc. with Adolph Coors Company, a $4.53 billion deal. Merger activity in Canada parallels that of the United States, which had the same peak in merger and acquisition activity in 2000 but with much larger deals totalling over US$1,800 billion at its peak. Canadian investment banks are in direct competition domestically with the major Wall Street investment firms (Morgan Stanley, JPMorgan, Goldman Sachs, Citigroup, Credit Suisse First Boston), which lead the world in terms of size, experience, research capability, and relationships. In fact, the history of the investment industry since the 1980s can be viewed as one of consolidation within Canada and increasing competition with globally dominant firms.[1]

---

[1] See Department of Finance, Canada, *Canada's Securities Industry,* January 2005 (or the latest version), for a history and summary of the securities industry. See also the most recent *Capital Markets Report* produced by the Financial Markets Division of the Financial Sector Policy Branch available at www.fin.gc.ca. The Investment Industry Association of Canada publishes the *Chartbook: Securities Industry & Capital Markets Developments* annually that is available on its website at www.iiac.ca.

FIGURE 4–1
Mergers and Acquisitions in Canada, 1998–2007

MERGERS AND ACQUISITIONS
Value of Transactions

Source: Material reprinted with the express permission of FPInfomart,
a division of Canwest Publishing Inc.

FIGURE 4–2
Securities Industry Employment in Canada, 2008

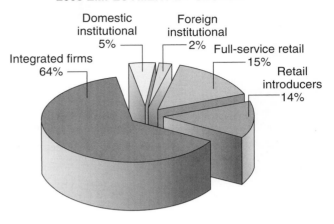

2008 EMPLOYMENT BY SECTOR

Source: Investment Industry Association of Canada, *Chartbook*, "Securities
Industry Performance Q1 09," June 2008, www.iiac.ca.

SIZE, STRUCTURE, AND COMPOSITION OF THE INDUSTRY

integrated firm
A securities firm offering a full range of investment services to retail, institutional, and corporate customers.

underwriting
Assisting in the issue of new securities.

regulatory capital
Capital and margin requirements, including shareholders' equity and subordinated debt, as defined by the Investment Industry Association of Canada for its members.

Investment Industry Association of Canada (IIAC)
The self-regulating organization (SRO) responsible for the regulation of its members in Canada.

The current structure of the securities industry dates back to the mid-to-late 1980s when the federal government changed the Bank Act to allow banks, trust companies, and foreign firms to operate in the industry. This resulted in many securities firms, previously wholly owned and operated as partnerships, being taken over by the major banks, creating the six largest integrated bank-owned firms (BMO Nesbitt Burns, CIBC World Markets, National Bank Financial, RBC Dominion Securities Limited, Scotia Capital, and TD Securities). The global stock market crash of 1987 accelerated the consolidation by making investment dealers cheap to acquire. Table 4–1 shows the investment firms acquired and the year of acquisition for the largest investment dealers in Canada ranked by their revenue in 2007.

As shown in Figure 4–2 and Table 4–2, the Canadian securities industry can be divided into integrated, institutional, and retail firms based on their activities as follows:

1. **integrated firms:** The integrated firms service retail customers (especially in acting as broker-dealers, assisting in the trading of existing securities) and corporate customers (such as **underwriting,** assisting in the issue of new securities), as well as institutional customers (servicing other FIs such as insurance companies, mutual funds, banks, trust companies, and pension funds). The 11 integrated firms generated 67.2 percent of the total operating revenue of the securities industry in 2008 and, as well, represented 63.9 percent of the total shareholders' equity of $13.5 billion and 71.1 percent of the **regulatory capital** (shareholders' equity and subordinated debt as defined by Regulation 100 of the **Investment Industry Association of Canada (IIAC)** for its members) as shown in Table 4–2. They derived 38 percent of their revenue from mutual fund and other commissions. Fee income represented 19.2 percent of their operating revenue in 2008. The integrated firms had the highest return at 17.4 percent.

TABLE 4–1
Canadian Bank
Investment Firm
Acquisitions,
1987–1996

Source: Company websites
and annual reports, 2008.

Firm	2007 Revenue ($ millions)	Company Acquired, Year of Acquisition
1. RBC Capital Markets	$4,389.0	Dominion Securities, 1988
		Pemberton Willoughby Investment Co. 1989
		McNeil Mantha, 1991
		Richardson Greenshields, 1996
2. TD Securities	2,494.0	Marathon Brokerage, 1993
3. Scotia Capital	2,450.0	McLeod, Young, Weir, 1987
4. CIBC World Markets	2,239.0	Wood Gundy Inc., 1988
5. BMO Nesbitt Burns	1,969.0	Nesbitt Thomson, 1987
		Burns Fry, 1994
6. National Bank Financial	1,428.1	Lévesque Beaubien Geoffrion, 1988
		First Marathon Securities, 1993

TABLE 4–2   **Structure and Statistics of the Securities Industry in Canada, 2008 ($ millions)**

	Industry Totals	Integrated Firms	Total Institutional	Full-Service Retail Firms	Retail Introducer Firms
Number of firms	202	11	69	34	88
Number of employees	40,836	25,973	2,926	6,018	5,919
Shareholders' equity	$13,507	$8,637	$3,803	$894	$173
Regulatory capital	27,197	19,334	6,118	1,094	650
Client cash holdings	33,677	28,157	1,326	2,745	1,448
Client margin debt outstanding	8,846	n.a.	n.a.	n.a.	n.a.
Annual return (net profit/shareholders' equity)	13.9%	17.4%	10.0%	−3.2%	12.2%
Revenue					
Commission	$5,592	$3,675	$777	$659	$480
Investment banking:					
New equity issues	1,580	967	438	107	69
New debt issues	483	405	42	27	9
Corporate advisory fees	1,014	502	458	22	32
Fixed-income trading	1,045	782	94	136	34
Equity trading	(11)	106	(61)	(50)	(6)
Net interest	1,894	1,488	212	104	89
Fees	2,624	1,877	79	292	375
Other	371	(1)	174	58	140
Total revenue	$14,593	$9,801	$2,214	$1,356	$1,222
Percentage of industry total	100.0%	67.2%	15.2%	9.3%	8.4%

Source: Investment Industry Association of Canada, *Security Industry Performance 2009*, www.iiac.ca.

institutional firm
A securities firm offering services only to other financial institutions such as insurance companies, mutual funds, banks, trust companies, and pension funds.

retail firm
A securities firm offering investment services only to retail investors, either on a full-service or discount basis.

full-service retail
A securities firm that provides all services to clients, including back-office functions.

retail introducer
A securities firm that contracts with a full-service firm to carry out specified trading functions on its behalf.

discount brokers
Stockbrokers that conduct trades for customers but do not offer investment advice.

www.tsx.com

IPO
An initial, or first-time, public offering of debt or equity by a corporation.

2. **Institutional firms:** They offer investment services primarily to other FIs. These firms may be domestic (e.g., Maison Placements Canada Inc.) or subsidiaries of U.S. or European firms (e.g., Deutsche Bank Securities). As shown in Table 4–2, 69 domestic and foreign institutional firms generated 15.2 percent of the total operating revenue for the industry, but their combined annual return in 2008 was much lower than the integrated firms at 10 percent. The major source of income for these firms came from investment banking activities, particularly new equity issues. Commission fees are also important.

3. **Retail firms:** They act primarily as investment advisors and brokers for retail customers. Retail firms can be divided into **full-service retail** and **retail introducer** firms. They also include specialized **discount brokers** who carry out trades for customers online or offline without offering investment advice or tips and usually charge lower commissions than do full-service retail firms. As shown in Table 4–2, the revenue of retail firms comes from commissions on mutual funds as well as other securities. Retail firms provided 17.7 percent of the revenue of the industry in 2008, ranking behind the integrated firms.

In addition, there are specialized electronic trading securities firms (such as Scotiabank's iTRADE [formerly E*Trade Canada] at https://www.scotiaitrade.com) that provide a platform for customers to trade without the use of a broker. These trades are enacted on a computer via the Internet. Also, venture capital firms pool money from individual investors and other FIs (e.g., hedge funds, pension funds, and insurance companies) to fund relatively small new businesses (e.g., in biotechnology).[2]

Securities firms engage in as many as seven key activity areas. Note that while each activity is available to a firm's customers independently, many of these activities can be and are conducted simultaneously, such as mergers and acquisitions financed by new issues of debt and equity underwritten by the M&A advising firm.

1. Investing

Investing involves managing not only pools of assets such as closed- and open-end mutual funds but also pension funds in competition with life insurance companies. Securities firms can manage such funds either as agents for other investors or as principals for themselves. The objective in funds management is to choose asset allocations to beat some return-risk performance benchmark such as the S&P TSX Composite Index or the S&P 500 index.[3] Since this business generates fees that are based on the size of the pool of assets managed, it tends to produce a more stable flow of income than does either investment banking or trading (discussed next).

2. Investment Banking

Investment banking refers to activities related to underwriting and distributing new issues of debt and equity. New issues can be either primary, the first-time issues of companies (sometimes called **IPOs** [initial public offerings]), or secondary issues (the new issues of seasoned firms whose debt or equity is already trading). In recent years, public confidence in the integrity of the IPO process has eroded significantly. Investigations have revealed that certain underwriters of IPOs have engaged in conduct contrary to the best interests of investors and the markets. Among the most harmful practices that have given rise to public concerns are spinning (in which certain underwriters allocate "hot" IPO issues to directors and/or executives of potential

---

[2] Venture capital firms generally play an active management role in the firms in which they invest, often including a seat on the board of directors, and hold significant equity stakes. This differentiates them from traditional banking and securities firms.

[3] Or the "securities market line" given the fund's "beta."

investment banking clients in exchange for investment banking business) and biased recommendations by research analysts (due to their compensation being tied to the success of their firms' investment banking business). We discuss these issues and some of the legal proceedings resulting from these practices below.[4]

Figure 4–3 shows the dollar value of common equity issues (secondary issues, IPOs, private placements) from 2002 to Q4 2008. Higher levels of the S&P/TSX Composite Index result in higher levels of equity financing and higher levels of operating profit for the industry, with a record profit of $2.771 billion in 2007 (see Table 4–6, discussed later). However, the disruptions in the global capital markets in 2008 resulted in significant declines in common equity financings (Figure 4–3) and the issuance and trading of corporate bonds, as shown in Figure 4–4. This reduced industry operating revenues and profits (Figure 4–6, discussed later). In 2008, equity-related issues dropped almost 50 percent by dollar volume. The most activity came from banks that were raising capital to meet their capital adequacy requirements.

Table 4–3 shows the top underwriters of Canadian equity and debt in 2008. In both cases, the top five positions are occupied by the investment banking subsidiaries of the Big Six Canadian banks. According to these league tables compiled by Thomson Reuters, the top equity underwriters were RBC Capital Markets (28 issues, $4.6 billion), TD Securities (18 issues, $3.5 billion), and CIBC World Markets (23 issues, $3.4 billion).

Securities underwritings can be undertaken through either public offerings or private offerings. In a private offering, the investment banker acts as a **private placement** agent for a fee, placing the securities with one or a few large institutional investors such as life insurance companies. In a public offering, the securities may be underwritten on a best-efforts or a firm commitment basis, and the securities may be offered to the public at large. With best-efforts underwriting,

private placement
A securities issue placed with one or a few large institutional investors.

FIGURE 4–3
Common Equity Financings in Canada, 2002 to Q4 2008

Source: Investment Industry Association of Canada, *IIAC Equity New Issues & Trading Q4 08*, p. 2, www.iiac.ca.

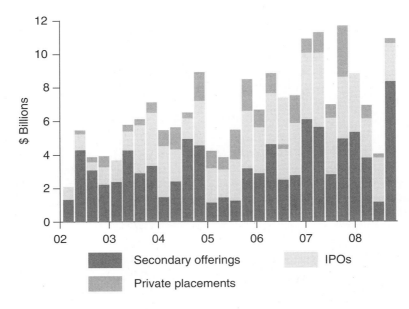

Secondary offerings   **IPOs**

Private placements

[4] R. Aggarwal, N. R. Prabhala, and M. Puri, in "Institutional Allocation in Initial Public Offerings: Empirical Evidence," *The Journal of Finance,* June 2002, pp. 1421–1442, document a positive relationship between institutional allocation and day-one IPO returns. The result is partly explained by the practice of giving institutions more shares in IPOs with strong pre-market demand.

FIGURE 4–4
Corporate Bond Gross Issuance and Trading in Canada, April 2009

Source: Investment Industry Association of Canada, *New Issues & Trading Debt Q4 08*, www.iiac.ca.

TABLE 4–3
Top Underwriters of Canadian Equity and Debt Issues, 2008

Source: Thomson Reuters, 2008, www.thomsonreuters.com.

Panel A: Canadian Equity & Equity-Related				
	1/1/2008 – 12/31/2008			
Bookrunner	Proceeds CDN $m	Rank	Mkt. Share	No. Deals
RBC Capital Markets	4,628.3	1	15.3	28
TD Securities Inc.	3,501.5	2	11.6	18
CIBC World Markets Inc.	3,413.5	3	11.3	23
BMO Capital Markets	3,172.3	4	10.5	19
Scotiabank-Bank of Nova Scotia	2,650.1	5	8.7	9
GMP Capital Corp.	1,797.6	6	5.9	40
Macquarie Group	1,704.5	7	5.6	10
UBS	1,481.6	8	4.9	6
Canaccord Capital Corp.	886.8	9	2.9	35
Genuity Capital Markets	880.8	10	2.9	6
Top Ten Total	24,117.0	–	79.6	194
Industry Total	30,309.7	–	100.0	324
Panel B: Canadian All Debt—Ex-Self-Funded				
	1/1/2008 – 12/31/2008			
Bookrunner	Proceeds CDN $m	Rank	Mkt. Share	No. Deals
RBC Capital Markets	27,312.9	1	23.4	87
TD Securities Inc.	20,839.5	2	17.9	55
BMO Capital Markets	15,839.7	3	13.6	37
Scotia Capital Inc.	14,694.6	4	12.6	34
CIBC World Markets Inc.	14,148.9	5	12.1	49
National Bank Financial Inc.	11,543.5	6	9.9	37
Merrill Lynch	9,369.2	7	8.0	18
Deutsche Bank AG	2,206.6	8	1.9	2
HSBC Holdings PLC	292.0	9	0.3	1
Morgan Stanley	186.3	10	0.2	1
Top Ten Total	116,433.2	–	100.0	321
Industry Total	116,633.1	–	100.0	249

investment bankers act as *agents* on a fee basis related to their success in placing the issue. In firm commitment underwriting, the investment banker acts as a *principal,* purchasing the securities from the issuer at one price and seeking to place them with public investors at a slightly higher price. Finally, in addition to investment banking operations in the corporate securities markets, the investment banker may participate as an underwriter (primary dealer) in government, municipal, and asset-backed securities.

3. Market-Making

Market-making involves creating a secondary market in an asset by a securities firm or investment bank. Thus, in addition to being primary dealers in government securities and underwriters of corporate bonds and equities, investment bankers make a secondary market in these instruments. Market-making can involve either agency or principal transactions. *Agency* transactions are two-way transactions on behalf of *customers,* for example, acting as a *stockbroker* or dealer for a fee or commission. On the TSX, a market maker in a stock may, upon the placement of orders by its customers, buy the stock at $78 from one customer and immediately resell

EXAMPLE 4–1 *Best-Efforts versus Firm Commitment Securities Offering*	An investment banker agrees to underwrite an issue of 20 million shares of stock for Murray Construction Corp. on a firm commitment basis. The investment banker pays $15.50 per share to Murray Construction Corp. for the 20 million shares of stock. It then sells those shares to the public for $16.35 per share. How much money does Murray Construction Corp. receive? What is the profit to the investment banker? If the investment bank can sell the shares for only $14.75, how much money does Murray Construction Corp. receive? What is the profit to the investment banker? If the investment bank sells the stock for $16.35 per share, Murray Construction Corp. receives $15.50 × 20,000,000 shares = $310,000,000. The profit to the investment bank is ($16.35 − $15.50) × 20,000,000 shares = $17,000,000. The stock price of Murray Construction Corp. is $16.35 since that is what the public agrees to pay. From the perspective of Murray Construction Corp., the $17 million represents the commission that it must pay to issue the stock. If the investment bank sells the stock for $14.75 per share, Murray Construction Corp. still receives $15.50 × 20,000,000 shares = $310,000,000. The profit to the investment bank is ($14.75 − $15.50) × 20,000,000 shares = −$15,000,000. The stock price of Murray Construction Corp. is $14.75 since that is what the public agrees to pay. From the perspective of the investment company, the −$15 million represents a loss for the firm commitment it made to Murray Construction Corp. to issue the stock. Suppose, instead, that the investment banker agrees to underwrite the 20 million shares on a best-efforts basis. The investment banker is able to sell 18.4 million shares for $15.50 per share, and it charges Murray Construction Corp. $0.375 per share sold. How much money does Murray Construction Corp. receive? What is the profit to the investment banker? If the investment bank can sell the shares for only $14.75, how much money does Murray Construction Corp. receive? What is the profit to the investment banker? If the investment bank sells the stock for $15.50 per share, Murray Construction Corp. receives ($15.50 − $0.375) × 18,400,000 shares = $278,300,000, the investment banker's profit is $0.375 × 18,400,000 shares = $6,900,000, and the stock price is $15.50 per share since that is what the public pays. If the investment bank sells the stock for $14.75 per share, Murray Construction Corp. receives ($14.75 − $0.375) × 18,400,000 shares = $264,500,000, the investment banker's profit is still $0.375 × 18,400,000 shares = $6,900,000, and the stock price is $14.75 per share since that is what the public pays.

it at $79 to another customer. The $1 difference between the buy and sell price is usually called the bid–ask spread and represents a large portion of the market maker's profit. Many securities firms offer online trading services to their customers as well as direct access to a client representative (stockbroker). Thus, customers may now conduct trading activities from their homes and offices through their accounts at securities firms at a lower cost in terms of fees and commissions. Purely electronic securities trading firms offer investors (day traders) high-speed access to the stock markets. Accordingly, technology risk is an increasingly important issue for these FIs (see Chapter 16).

In *principal* transactions, the market maker seeks to profit on the price movements of securities and takes either long or short inventory positions for its own account. (Or an inventory position may be taken to stabilize the market in the securities.) In the example above, the market maker would buy the stock at $78 and hold it in its own portfolio in expectation of a price increase later on. Normally, market-making can be a fairly profitable business; however, in periods of market stress or high volatility, these profits can rapidly disappear.

INTERNET EXERCISE

Go to the Thomson Reuters website (www.thomsonreuters.com) and find the latest information available for top global underwriters of various securities. Click on "Financial" and then on the live link under "League Tables." Click on "Debt & Equity Archive" to access files that contain the most recent information on top underwriters for various securities.

4. Trading

Trading is closely related to the market-making activities just described, where a trader takes an active net position in an underlying instrument or asset. There are at least four types of trading activities:

1. *Position trading* involves purchasing large blocks of securities on the expectation of a favourable price move. Such positions also facilitate the smooth functioning of the secondary markets in such securities.

2. *Pure arbitrage* entails buying an asset in one market at one price and selling it immediately in another market at a higher price.

3. *Risk arbitrage* involves buying blocks of securities in anticipation of some information release, such as a merger or takeover announcement or an interest rate announcement.[5]

4. *Program trading* is defined as the simultaneous buying and selling of a large portfolio of different stocks using computer programs to initiate such trades. Program trading is often associated with seeking a risk arbitrage between a cash market price and the *futures* market price of that instrument.

As with many activities of securities firms, such trading can be conducted on behalf of a customer as an agent (or broker), or on behalf of the firm as a principal.

5. Cash Management and Banking Services

Retail investment firms offer their customers the ability to invest in shares through a cash account, or to borrow on margin. As shown in Table 4–2, client cash holdings

---

[5] It is termed *risk arbitrage* because if the event does not actually occur—for example, if a merger does not take place or the Bank of Canada does not change interest rates—the trader stands to lose money.

in the industry equalled $33.7 billion and margin debt outstanding, a credit risk for the securities firms, equalled $8.8 billion. The integrated firms owned by the major banks are able to offer their retail, business, and corporate clients online access to banking and investment accounts in addition to services such as investment advice, **private banking** (domestic and global), trust services, investment management, and financial planning.

private banking
The provision of wealth management services for high net worth clients.

6. Mergers and Acquisitions

Investment banks are frequently involved in providing advice or assisting in mergers and acquisitions. For example, they will assist in finding merger partners, underwriting new securities to be issued by the merged firms, assessing the value of target firms, recommending terms of the merger agreement, and even helping target firms prevent a merger (for example, seeing that poison-pill provisions are written into a potential target firm's securities contracts). Table 4–4 lists the top ten financial advisors for Canadian completed mergers and acquisitions in 2008, ranked by market share based on value of transactions (in U.S. dollars for easy comparison with the global rankings) of the deals in which they participated. The total market for M&As in Canada in 2008 was US$160.6 billion and 2,129 deals, a significant decline from 2007. While foreign firms, including the U.S. heavyweights Merrill Lynch, JPMorgan, Goldman Sachs, and Citigroup, rank in the top ten, the five large Canadian bank-owned integrated firms also have a presence in M&A advising, particularly for cross-border deals. However, ranking and market share each year depend on the size and the number of deals in which investment advisors are able to participate. As shown in Table 4–4, Canadian deals are small compared to the worldwide completed mergers and acquisitions of US$2.69 trillion in 2008. The bank-owned integrated firms (e.g., CIBC World Markets) are active participants on Wall Street, providing expertise in resource financing, particularly oil and gas and mining.[6] Worldwide in 2008, the Americas ranked first in mergers and acquisitions with 41.5 percent of the total, followed by Europe at 39.4 percent.

7. Back-Office and Other Service Functions

These functions include custody and escrow services, clearance and settlement services, and research and other advisory services—for example, giving advice on divestitures and asset sales. In performing these functions, a securities firm normally acts as an agent for a fee. As mentioned above, fees charged are often based on the total bundle of services performed for the client by the firm. The portion of the fee or commission allocated to research and advisory services is called *soft dollars*. When one area in the firm, such as an investment advisor, uses client commissions to buy research from another area in the firm, it receives a benefit because it is relieved from the need to produce and pay for the research itself. Thus, the advisor using soft dollars faces a conflict of interest between the need to obtain research and the client's interest in paying the lowest commission rate available.

---

[6] Often, in addition to providing M&A advisory services, an investment banker will be involved in underwriting new securities that help finance an M&A. See L. Allen, J. Jagtiani, S. Peristiani and A. Saunders, "The Role of Financial Advisors in Mergers and Acquisitions," *Journal of Money, Credit, and Banking* 36(2), April 2004, pp. 197–224. A. Saunders and A. Srinivasan, in *Investment Banking Relationships and Merger Fees,* 2002, Working Paper, New York University, investigate the effect of prior investment banking relationships on merger advisory fees paid by acquiring firms. Their findings indicate that acquiring firms perceive benefits of retaining merger advisors with whom they have had a prior relationship (even at a cost of higher fees) and/or they face some other (higher) costs of switching to new bank advisors. Finally, V. Ivashina, V. Nair, A. Saunders, N. Massoud, and R. Stover, in *The Role of Banks in Takeovers,* 2004, Working Paper, New York University, show that banks use the information generated in lending to increase the probability of takeovers.

TABLE 4–4
Ten Largest Merger
and Acquisition
Firms, Ranked by
Value of Completed
Mergers, 2008

Source: Thomson Reuters,
2009, www.thomsonreuters.
com.

Panel A: Mergers Completed in Canada				
	1/1/2008 – 12/31/2008			
Financial Advisor	Rank Value US$m	Rank	Mkt. Share	No. Deals
RBC Capital Markets	$ 58,806.5	1	36.6	44
TD Securities Inc	40,158.4	2	25.0	22
JPMorgan	37,141.9	3	23.1	16
BMO Capital Markets	37,036.4	4	23.1	34
CIBC World Markets Inc	34,463.7	5	21.5	51
Citi	31,988.9	6	19.9	9
Goldman Sachs & Co	26,946.2	7	16.8	11
Merrill Lynch	25,153.1	8	15.7	17
Morgan Stanley	24,112.5	9	15.0	17
UBS	23,659.6	10	14.7	14
Industry Total	$160,634.0	–	100.0	2,129

Panel B: Mergers Completed Worldwide				
	1/1/2008 – 12/31/2008			
Financial Advisor	Rank Value US$m	Rank	Mkt. Share	No. Deals
JPMorgan	$ 898,206.0	1	33.4	353
Goldman Sachs & Co	780,969.0	2	29.1	309
Citi	604,997.3	3	22.5	312
Merrill Lynch	602,966.5	4	22.4	306
Morgan Stanley	598,576.7	5	22.3	298
UBS	578,345.1	6	21.5	305
Credit Suisse	517,346.1	7	19.3	313
Deutsche Bank AG	472,193.1	8	17.6	250
Lazard	312,106.6	9	11.6	202
Barclays Capital	290,848.1	10	10.8	115
Industry Total	$2,688,177.8	–	100.0	28,861

CONCEPT QUESTIONS

1. Describe the difference between brokerage services and underwriting services.
2. What are the key areas of activities for securities firms?
3. Describe the difference between a best-efforts offering and a firm commitment offering.
4. What are the trading activities performed by securities firms?

BALANCE SHEET AND RECENT TRENDS

Recent Trends

In this section, we look at the balance sheet and trends in the securities firm and investment banking industry. Trends in this industry depend heavily on the state of the stock market. For example, a major effect of the 1987 stock market crash was a sharp decline in stock market trading volume and thus in commissions earned by securities firms over the 1987–1991 period. Commission income began to recover only after 1992, with record equity trading volumes being achieved in 1995–2000 when stock market indexes hit new highs. As stock market values declined in 2001 and 2002, so did commission income. The overall level of commissions has declined from 63 percent of total revenues in 1980 to 38 percent in 2008 (Figure 4–5). This reflects the greater competition in the industry for customers, particularly after the banks formed the large integrated firms, whose effect was felt from the early 1990s, as well as the introduction of discount brokers.

Between 1991 and 2001, however, the securities industry generally showed a growth in profitability. For example, investment banking revenue grew from $424 million in 1990 to $3.12 billion in 2004 and after-tax return on equity rose from −20 percent in 1990 to 13 and 21 percent in 1995 and 2000, respectively. The principal reasons for this were improved trading profits and increased growth in new issue underwritings. Corporate debt issues became highly attractive to corporate treasurers because of relatively low long-term interest rates. Another sign of the resurgence in this industry during the 1990s appears in employment figures. Annual employment in the securities industry increased by 97 percent, from 19,986 jobs in 1992 to 39,433 employees in 2000.

As can be seen from Figure 4–6, the investment industry showed a trend of increasing operating revenues and profits from 2003 through to 2007. However, the world economy entered a recession in late 2008, causing industry profits to reach their lowest in three years. The TSX showed an annual decline of 35 percent in 2008, a loss in value of approximately $700 billion. Table 4–5 provides a summary of the operating revenue for the industry from 1987 to 2008, and Table 4–6 provides a summary of statistics for the industry from 1996 to 2008.

Balance Sheet

A fourth-quarter balance sheet for investment services firms, the retail brokers discussed previously (including stockbrokers and investment managers), is shown in Table 4–7. Investments and accounts with affiliates as well as portfolio investments make up 58 percent of total assets. **Reverse repurchase agreements (reverse repos),**

reverse repurchase agreements (reverse repos)
Securities purchased under agreement to resell.

FIGURE 4–5
Commission Income as a Percentage of Total Revenues

Source: Investment Industry Association of Canada, www.iiac.ca.

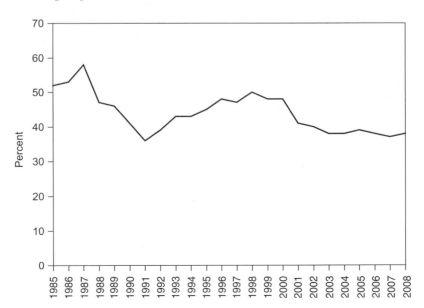

FIGURE 4–6
Securities Industry
Operating Profits
and Revenues,
1990–2008

Source: Investment Investment Industry Association of
Canada, *www.ida.ca*

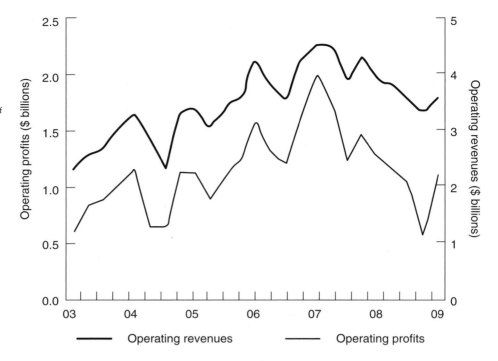

securities purchased under agreement to resell (i.e., the broker gives a short-term
loan to the repurchase agreement reseller) are included in the total assets. Because
of the extent to which this industry's balance sheet consists of financial market securities, the industry is subjected to particularly high levels of market risk (see Chapter 10) and interest rate risk (see Chapters 8 and 9). Further, to the extent that many
of these securities are foreign-issued securities, FI managers must also be concerned
with foreign exchange risk (see Chapter 14) and sovereign risk (see Chapter 15).

TABLE 4–5   **Securities Industry Total Operating Revenue by Source, 1987—2008**

	2008	2007	2006	2005	2004	2003	2002	2001	2000	1995	1990	1987
Total Revenue ($ millions)	$14,593	$17,123	$15,879	$13,485	$12,469	$10,618	$9,805	$10,133	$12,260	$5,139	$2,403	$3,247
Revenue Source												
Commissions	38%	37%	38%	39%	38%	38%	40%	41%	48%	45%	41%	58%
Investment banking	21%	27%	25%	27%	25%	25%	22%	21%	17%	19%	18%	20%
Fixed-income trading	7%	4%	5%	5%	5%	7%	9%	10%	5%	14%	20%	6%
Equity trading	0.1%	3%	5%	4%	5%	6%	3%	4%	9%	5%	−2%	6%
Net interest	13%	10%	10%	9%	8%	10%	10%	11%	10%	10%	15%	6%
Other	21%	19%	17%	16%	18%	13%	16%	13%	10%	8%	7%	5%
Total	**100%**	**100%**	**100%**	**100%**	**100%**	**100%**	**100%**	**100%**	**100%**	**100%**	**100%**	**100%**
Mutual fund commissions as a percentage of total	13%	13%	12%	13%	11%	10%	12%	12%	12%	9%	3%	2%

Source: Investment Industry Association of Canada, www.iiac.ca.

TABLE 4–6 Securities Industry Statistics, 1996–2008 ($ millions unless otherwise noted)

	2008	2007	2006	2005	2004	2003	2002	2001	2000	1999	1998	1997	1996
Highlights													
Number of													
Employees	40,086	42,329	40,919	39,174	37,739	37,262	37,949	37,121	39,433	36,175	34,445	32,990	29,636
Number of Firms	202	203	198	201	205	207	206	198	191	188	186	187	182
Operating													
Revenue	$14,593	$17,123	$15,879	$13,485	$12,469	$10,613	$9,807	$10,133	$12,260	$8,812	$7,725	$8,478	$7,472
Operating													
Expenses	6,528	6,279	5,711	5,279	5,187	4,477	4,666	4,683	4,723	3,990	3,753	3,456	2,815
Operating Profit	3,914	6,382	5,765	4,315	3,934	3,321	2,735	2,793	3,565	1,946	1,345	2,070	2,061
Net Profit (loss)	1,875	2,771	2,515	1,752	1,773	1,484	1,257	1,011	1,183	582	395	769	850
Shareholders'													
Equity	13,507	12,655	11,103	8593	8,372	7,076	6,995	5,681	5,526	4,850	3,745	3,526	3,344
Regulatory Capital	27,197	23,413	19,804	17,430	15,108	13,962	12,968	12,454	10,557	8,667	7,458	8,143	7,158
Client Cash													
Holdings	36,777	28,500	25,281	23,156	22,109	20,615	18,750	21,102	18,501	14,941	14,283	11,500	10,799
Client Margin Debt													
Outstanding	8,846	14,001	11,710	11,580	9,478	7,615	7.019	7,833	10,696	na	na	na	na
Productivity ($000s)													
(annual revenue													
per employee)	367	405	388	347	330	285	258	273	311	244	224	257	252
Annual Return													
(net profit/share-													
holders' equity)	13.9%	21.9%	22.7%	20.3%	21%	21%	18%	18%	21%	12%	11%	22%	25%

Source: Investment Industry Association of Canada, www.iiac.ca.

TABLE 4–7
Balance Sheet for Stockbrokers and Investment Dealers, 2008 ($ millions)

Source: Statistics Canada, www.statcan.gc.ca.

	2008	Percent of Total Assets
Assets	**$280,448**	
Cash and deposits	26,131	9.3
Accounts receivable and accrued revenue	30,724	10.9
Investments and accounts with affiliates	56,611	20.2
Portfolio investments	106,039	37.8
Loans	16,891	6.0
Mortgage	9,306	3.3
Non-mortgage	7,585	2.7
Allowance for losses on investments and loans	−208	
Bank customers' liabilities under acceptances	0	
Net capital assets	19,834	7.1
Other assets	24,425	8.7
Liabilities	**$145,833**	**52**
Deposits	24	0
Accounts payable and accrued liabilities	30,291	10.8
Loans and accounts with affiliates	53,692	19.1
Borrowings	33,481	11.9
Loans and other borrowings	25,777	9.2
Bankers' acceptances and paper	1,208	0.4
Bonds and debentures	4,169	1.5
Mortgages	2,326	0.8
Future income tax	4,569	1.6
Other liabilities	23,775	8.5
Equity	**$134,615**	**48.0**
Share capital	54,006	19.3
Contributed surplus and other	20,397	7.3
Retained earnings	60,211	21.5

With respect to liabilities, loans and accounts with affiliates accounted for 19.1 percent of total liabilities. Other borrowings accounted for 11.9 percent of total liabilities. Equity capital (share capital, contributed surplus, and retained earnings) represented 48.0 percent of total assets. The level of capital maintained by securities firms is governed by the rules of the securities regulators and by the IIAC for its member firms, as noted previously. Capital adequacy will be discussed in Chapter 20.

CONCEPT QUESTIONS	1. Describe the trend in profitability in the securities industry over the last 10 years. 2. What are the major assets held by broker–dealers?

REGULATION

The regulation of the securities industry in Canada is a provincial and territorial responsibility. The securities regulators of Canada's ten provinces and three territories coordinate regulation through the Canadian Securities Administrators (CSA, www.csa-acvm.ca) via a passport system.[7] In 2008, the Investment Dealers Association of Canada and Market Regulation Services Inc. combined to form the Investment Industry Regulatory Organization of Canada (IIROC, www.iiroc.ca). The IIROC is a national **self-regulatory organization (SRO),** the goals of which are market efficiency, integrity, and transparency.

self-regulatory organization (SRO)
Industry-owned organization designated by a provincial securities regulator to regulate its members.

The growth of the securities industry, plus the globalization of securities trading (particularly cross-border issues that arise as a result of company cross-listing on the Canadian and U.S. exchanges) has meant that the securities industry in Canada needs to have consistent regulation across the country. With this in mind, the minister of Finance created the Wise Persons' Committee in 2003, whose report recommended that a single regulator be established to replace the provincial and territorial bodies. In January 2009, the Expert Panel on Securities Regulation, chaired by Thomas Hockin, released its final report, which also recommended the formation of the Canadian Securities Regulator. A transition team was appointed in 2009 to produce a plan for a national securities act. Initially, participation will be voluntary for each province and territory.

Currently, the provincial and territorial regulators establish legislation in their own jurisdictions, but they allow self-regulatory organizations to carry out certain aspects of regulation. For example, the exchanges are SROs, as is the IIROC. Each SRO has a particular role in the regulation of securities firms. The IIROC, as mentioned previously, regulates its member firms for capital adequacy, as well as code of conduct, and provides details of the current regulations at its website. Also, since mutual funds have become such a large source of revenue for securities firms, having grown from 2 percent ($43 million) of commission income in 1988 to 13 percent ($2.3 billion) in 2007, securities dealers are also members of the Mutual Fund Dealers Association of Canada (MFDA), which is an SRO recognized in several provinces.

www.cipf.ca

In addition to the regulators, consumer protection is provided by the Canadian Investor Protection Fund (CIPF), a trust fund organized by the TSX Group, the

---

[7] The passport system allows market participants to issue a prospectus or register in their home province or territory and be recognized by all other jurisdictions in Canada.

www.cfson.org

IIROC, and the Montréal Exchange (MX) to provide investor protection of up to $1 million if a dealer were to become insolvent. Also, the Centre for Financial Services OmbudsNetwork (CFSON) provides dispute resolution for consumers free of charge.

While Canadian regulators are still wrestling with the establishment of a national securities regulator, the primary regulator of the securities industry in the United States, the Securities and Exchange Commission (SEC), spurred on by the corporate governance scandals of Enron, Global Crossings, Tyco, and WorldCom in the early 2000s, moved to limit state regulators' ability to control securities firms. The primary role of the SEC includes administration of securities laws, review and evaluation of registrations of new securities offerings (ensuring that all relevant information is revealed to potential investors), review and evaluation of annual and semiannual reports summarizing the financial status of all publicly held corporations, and the prohibition of any form of security market manipulation.

The SEC has instituted rules requiring Wall Street analysts to vouch that their stock picks are not influenced by investment banking colleagues and that analysts disclose details of their compensation that would alert investors to any possible conflicts. If evidence surfaces that the analysts have falsely attested to the independence of their work, it could be used to bring enforcement actions. Violators could face a wide array of sanctions, including fines and other penalties, such as a suspension or banning from the securities industry. In addition, the SEC proposed that top officials from all public companies sign off on financial statements.

These SEC regulations, the Sarbanes-Oxley Act passed by the U.S. Congress in 2002, and the USA Patriot Act all have potential cross-border impacts on Canadian companies.

In the spring of 2003, an agreement between U.S. regulators and ten of the largest securities firms required the firms to pay a record US$1.4 billion in penalties to settle charges involving investor abuse. The settlement centred on civil charges that securities firms routinely issued overly optimistic stock research to investors in order to gain favour with corporate clients and win their investment banking business. The agreement also settled charges that at least two big firms, Citigroup and Credit Suisse First Boston, improperly allocated shares to corporate executives to win banking business from their firms. The Wall Street firms agreed to the settlement without admitting or denying any wrongdoing. The agreement forced brokerage companies to make structural changes in the way they handle research—for example, preventing analysts from attending certain investment banking meetings with bankers. The agreement also required securities firms to have separate reporting and supervisory structures for their research and banking operations. Additionally, it required that analysts' pay be tied to the quality and accuracy of their research rather than the amount of the investment banking business they generate.

wash trading
Manipulating share prices by related investors buying and selling the same security to give the appearance of a legitimate trade even though there has been no real change in ownership.

Despite the fact that Bernard Ebbers (a Canadian and former chief executive officer of WorldCom) was convicted of fraud in the United States and sentenced to 25 years in prison in 2005 for filing false financial reports in the US$11 billion conspiracy that brought down WorldCom, there have yet to be securities frauds in Canada on the scale of those in the United States. However, in addition to the involvement of Canadian dealers in U.S. scandals (e.g., CIBC World Markets and Enron), there have been some made-in-Canada scandals. For example, in May 2005, four traders at RBC Dominion Securities were accused of **wash trading,** a form of share price manipulation, by buying and selling more than $33 million worth of shares. The distortion in prices is alleged to have cost bystanders $232,000.

That Bernard L. Madoff was running a massive Ponzi scheme wasn't news to many industry professionals who were skeptical of his amazingly consistent returns during inconsistent markets. But what is becoming more apparent is that it shouldn't have been news to the Securities and Exchange Commission (SEC) either.

Bernard L. Madoff Investment Securities LLC (BLMIS) was a registered broker dealer and a registered investment advisor (RIA), giving the SEC access to Madoff's operations. The SEC suggested that move when it found Madoff was acting as an investment advisor to hedge funds and high-net-worth individuals in violation of the Advisors Act. The SEC also found that client disclosure documents didn't adequately reflect Madoff's advisory role and that Madoff misled the SEC about the nature of the strategy implemented in several funds. All of this was brought to light in January 2006, while the SEC was investigating fraud allegations against Madoff. "The Commission has learned that credible and specific allegations regarding Mr. Madoff's financial wrongdoing, going back to at least 1999, were repeatedly brought to the attention of SEC staff, but were never recommended to the Commission for action," noted Christopher Cox, SEC chairman.

In a whitepaper delivered to the SEC dated Nov. 7, 2005, and entitled "The world's largest hedge fund is a fraud," Harry Markopolos, then a competitor of Madoff's, examines the BLMIS corporate structure and debunks the claimed returns of the "split-strike conversion" strategy that Madoff purportedly used. In all, Markopolos lists 29 red flags indicating that BLMIS was either front-running customer order flow or was the world's largest Ponzi scheme.

Madoff founded the firm in 1960 and held numerous executive positions at the Nasdaq Stock Exchange including chairman. The fraud is estimated at as much as $50 billion. In mid-December, the Southern District Court of New York granted the Securities Investor Protection Corporation's application to liquidate the firm's holdings and named a Trustee.

Source: Chris McMahon, *Futures*, February 2009, p. 14.

It is not clear, however, that a national securities regulator like the SEC will prevent securities fraud. The case of Bernard Madoff came to light in late 2008. Madoff was a U.S. investment manager who was found guilty of running a Ponzi scheme that defrauded U.S. and global investors of an estimated US$65 billion; Madoff was sentenced to 150 years in prison. Madoff's case provides an example of the limits of regulation. The relationship between securities firms, investors, and regulators is complex and the potential for conflicts of interest and market failures is shown in the Ethical Dilemmas feature.

Securities firms and banks have historically been strongly supportive of efforts to combat money laundering, and the industry has been subject to laws that impose extensive reporting and record-keeping requirements. However, the USA Patriot Act, passed in response to the September 11 terrorist attacks, included additional provisions that financial services firms operating in the United States must implement. The new rules, which took effect on October 1, 2003, imposed three requirements. First, firms must verify the identity of any person seeking to open an account. Second, firms must maintain records of the information used to verify the person's identity. Third, firms must determine whether a person opening an account appears on any list of known or suspected terrorists or terrorist organizations. The new rules are intended to deter money laundering without imposing undue burdens that would constrain the ability of firms to serve their customers.

Canadian securities firms have been required to identify money laundering since 1993 and, in response to global concerns following September 11, 2001, amendments to the Proceeds of Crime (Money Laundering) and Terrorist Financing Act 2001 require firms to report suspicious transactions, report large cash transactions, and obtain clear identification of their clients. IIROC maintains a section for its members on money laundering on its website similar to that maintained by OSFI for federally regulated banks and insurance companies.

CONCEPT QUESTIONS	1. **How does the regulation of the securities industry differ between Canada and the United States?** 2. **How and why does the regulatory framework differ for deposit-taking institutions, insurance companies, and securities firms?**

GLOBAL ISSUES

The disruptions in the global capital markets in 2007 and 2008 reshaped the investment banking industry in the United States and globally. As mentioned earlier in the chapter, Canada went through a "Big Bang" in 1987 that resulted in revisions to the Bank Act and the formation of OSFI. The largest securities firms were bought by the Big Six banks, the trust companies were also consolidated, and Canadian financial institutions moved toward universal banking. The model thus saw investment activities supported by merging with a bank funded by a stable source of deposits. By the time of the credit crisis in 2007, Canada had 20 years of experience with this model. The United States, however, didn't replace the Glass-Steagall Act (1933) with the Financial Services Modernization Act until 1999, so the U.S. system was ten years behind the Canadian system in consolidating. Markets now are more globally connected and more complex, which makes them more opaque and increases the potential for global systemic risk. At the time of the crisis in 2007, the U.S. investment banks were stand-alone. As well, their high debt levels and reliance on short-term market funding made their model a risky strategy when liquidity dried up in the global capital markets.

Table 4–8 lists the top ten U.S. securities and investment companies by assets based on their year-end 2008 annual statements. In 2007, the top four global investment banks, ranked by revenue, were Goldman Sachs Group, Inc. (2007 revenues of US$88 billion), Morgan Stanley (2007 revenues of US$87.9 billion), Merrill Lynch & Co., Inc. (2007 revenues of US$64.2 billion), and Lehman Brothers Holdings (2007 revenues of US$59 billion). By the end of 2008, Goldman Sachs and Morgan Stanley had converted to bank holding companies, which gave them access to the Federal Reserve's liquidity facilities. Morgan Stanley received US$10 billion from the U.S. Treasury in 2008. Merrill Lynch was acquired by the Bank of America. JPMorgan Chase acquired Bear Stearns. Lehman Brothers filed for bankruptcy and its investment banking and capital markets assets were acquired by Barclays Capital Inc. Despite the problems, Goldman Sachs Group Inc., JPMorgan Chase, and Citigroup Inc. remained the top three advisors in the world on mergers and acquisitions. These FIs provided advice on US$2.28 trillion in takeovers, 44 percent less than the US$3.2 trillion in 2007 (Table 4–4).

Table 4–9 lists the top five global diversified financial companies by revenues in 2008. This industry also suffered upheavals. GE Capital cut its payments to its parent company in 2008 and put its own and its parent's debt rating at risk. Fannie Mae and Freddie Mac, U.S. government-sponsored entities (GSEs) were put into conservatorship by the U.S. government and are now managed by the U.S. federal government. Fannie Mae and Freddie Mac purchased and guaranteed

TABLE 4–8 Top
Ten U.S. Securities
and Investment
Companies by
Assets, 2008
($ millions)

Source: Insurance Information Institute, www.iii.org.

Rank	Company	Assets
1	Goldman Sachs Group, Inc.*	$884,547
2	Merrill Lynch & Co., Inc.	667,543
3	Morgan Stanley*	659,035
4	J.P. Morgan Securities Inc.	399,545
5	Credit Suisse Securities (USA) LLC	326,348
6	Citigroup Global Markets Inc.	286,825
7	UBS Securities LLC	253,420
8	Deutsche Bank Securities Inc.	244,413
9	Barclays Capital Inc.	240,429
10	Mizuho Securities Co. Ltd.	212,944

* Converted to a bank holding company in 2008.

mortgage-backed securities that were sold to investors worldwide. In November 2008, American Express (ranked fourth in 2007) was permitted to become a bank holding company and allowed to participate in the U.S. Treasury's Troubled Asset Relief Fund and sell preferred stock to the Treasury. GMAC (ranked fifth in 2007) also applied to be a bank holding company and received US$5 billion in support from the financial sector rescue funds.

As a result of the global credit crisis, net issuance of international bonds and notes and money market instruments were down in 2007 and 2008 as shown in Figure 4–7. Major declines were announced in international equity issues, which were only US$185.5 through Q3 of 2008 versus a total of US$500.8 for all of 2007.

Although firms in smaller capital markets such as Canada, Australia, and New Zealand, for example, have traditionally listed securities on U.S. exchanges and raised debt overseas when their markets were unable to accommodate their need for capital,[8] the phenomenon of U.S. firms going outside of their country to raise funds has been a relatively new trend, representing a 533 percent increase in all offerings by U.S. issuers between 1995 and 2003. In fact, international offerings by U.S. issuers represented 39 percent of total offerings of US$2,999.0 billion in 2004. At the same time, concerns about U.S. accounting practices as a result of the recent scandals, the burdensome nature of reporting accounting figures using U.S. accounting standards as well as local accounting standards (Sarbanes-Oxley, as discussed above),[9] the decline in the U.S. stock market, and the fall in the value of the U.S. dollar against the euro and yen were all working to weaken the attractiveness of U.S. markets to foreign investors and issuers in the early 2000s. However, Canadian FIs are seasoned participants in the international capital markets and Canadian firms and their investment advisors continued to benefit from improved U.S.–Canadian dollar exchange rates and engaged in cross-border merger and

---

[8] For discussions of U.S. listing for Canadian and Mexican firms, see S. R. Foerster and A. G. Karolyi, "International Listings of Stocks: The Case of Canada and the U.S.," *Journal of International Business Studies,* 1993, 24(4), pp. 763–785 and P. Y. Davis-Friday, T. J. Frecka, and J. M. Rivera, "The Financial Performance, Capital Constraints and Information Environment of Cross-Listed Firms: Evidence from Mexico," *The International Journal of Accounting,* 2005, 40(1), p. 1.

[9] OSFI requires Canadian FIs to apply Canadian generally accepted accounting principles (GAAP) and will require the adoption of international financial reporting standards (IFRS) in 2011 (see Chapter 20). The Securities and Exchange Commission (SEC) requires FIs operating in the United States to report material differences between U.S. GAAP and Canadian GAAP.

TABLE 4–9
Top Five Global Diversified Financial Companies by Revenues, 2008 ($ millions)

Source: Insurance Information Institute, www.iii.org.

Rank	Company	Revenues	Country
1	General Electric	$183,207	U.S.
2	Cie Nationale à Portefeuille	22,656	Belgium
3	Fannie Mae	22,639	U.S.
4	Citic Group	22,229	PR China
5	Hypo Real Estate Holding	21,636	Germany

FIGURE 4–7 **International Debt Securities Net Issuance, 2004–2008 (US$ billions)***

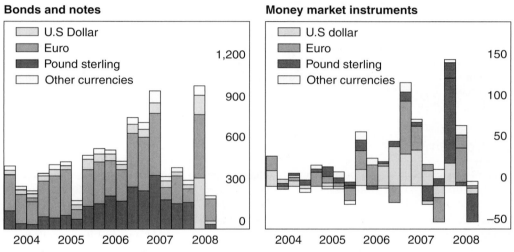

*Bond and note issuance, by nationality.

Source: Bank for International Settlements, *BIS Quarterly Review,* December 2008, www.bis.org

acquisition activity. For example, five of the ten largest deals announced in Canada in 2004 (including the merger of breweries Molson Inc. and Adolph Coors Company, Jean Coutu Group's acquisition of Eckerd Drugstores, and the Toronto-Dominion Bank's acquisition of Banknorth Group Inc.) were cross-border deals. Because of the importance of a strong global financial market to both developed and developing nations, the harmonization of regulations governing securities firms can be expected to continue.

The international credit crisis that started in 2007 had an impact on the issuance of debt securities in the international capital markets. As shown in Figure 4–7, bond and note issuance in most currencies declined in 2007 and again in 2008. Net issuance of money market instruments was negative in the third and fourth quarters of 2007 when the market for asset-backed securities worldwide declined because of concerns about the U.S. subprime mortgages backing these securities. The asset-backed commercial paper (ABCP) market in Canada was caught up in this crisis, and the market of approximately CDN$35 billion was frozen from

August 2007 until a legal solution was found in January 2009. The extreme global liquidity crisis in October and November of 2008 is shown in Figure 4–7 by the net retirements of money market instruments. Investor confidence is seen to play a major part in the role of pricing securities in international markets.

| CONCEPT QUESTION | What were the trends in international securities offerings in 2007 and 2008? |

Summary

This chapter presented an overview of the securities industry in Canada. Firms in this industry assist in getting new issues of debt and equity to the markets, often related to corporate mergers and restructurings, earning fees as financial advisors as well as from the underwriting function. Additionally, this industry facilitates trading and market-making of securities after they are issued. We looked at the structure of the industry and changes over the last decade. We analyzed balance sheet information that highlighted the major assets and liabilities of firms in the industry and discussed the regulation of the industry and the implications of changes both within Canada and globally.

Questions and Problems

1. What are the different types of firms in the securities industry, and how does each type differ from the others?

2. What are the key activity areas for securities firms? How does each activity area assist in the generation of profits, and what are the major risks for each area?

3. What is the difference between an IPO and a secondary issue?

4. What is the difference between a private placement and a public offering?

5. What are the risk implications to an investment banker from underwriting on a best-efforts basis versus a firm commitment basis? If you operated a company issuing stock for the first time, which type of underwriting would you prefer? Why? What factors might cause you to choose the alternative?

6. How do agency transactions differ from principal transactions for market makers?

7. An investment banker agrees to underwrite a $500 million, 10-year, 8 percent semiannual bond issue for KDO Corporation on a firm commitment basis. The investment banker pays KDO on Thursday and plans to begin a public sale on Friday. What type of interest rate movement does the investment bank fear while holding these securities? If interest rates rise 0.05 percent, or 5 basis points, overnight, what will be the impact on the profits of the investment banker? What if the market interest rate falls 5 basis points?

8. An investment banker pays $23.50 per share for 4 million shares of JCN Company. It then sells those shares to the public for $25 per share. How much money does JCN receive? What is the profit to the investment banker? What is the stock price of JCN?

9. XYZ, Inc., has issued 10 million new shares. An investment banker agrees to underwrite these shares on a best-efforts basis. The investment banker is able to sell 8.4 million shares for $27 per share, and it charges XYZ $0.675 per share sold. How much money does XYZ receive? What is the profit to the investment banker? What is the stock price of XYZ?

10. One of the major activity areas of securities firms is trading.
    a. What is the difference between pure arbitrage and risk arbitrage?
    b. What is the difference between position trading and program trading?

11. If an investor observes that the price of a stock trading in one exchange is different from the price in another exchange, what form of arbitrage is applicable, and how can the investor participate in that arbitrage?

12. An investor notices that an ounce of gold is priced at US$318 in London and US$325 in New York.

    a. What action could the investor take to try to profit from the price discrepancy?

    b. Under which of the four trading activities would this action be classified?

    c. If the investor is correct in identifying the discrepancy, what pattern should the two prices take in the short-term future?

    d. What may be some impediments to the success of this transaction?

13. What factors are given credit for the steady decline in brokerage commissions as a percentage of total revenues over the period beginning in 1987 and ending in 1991?

14. What factors are given credit for the resurgence of profitability in the securities industry beginning in 1991? Are firms that trade in fixed-income securities more or less likely to have volatile profits? Why?

15. How do the operating activities, and thus the balance sheet structures, of securities firms differ from the operating activities of deposit-taking institutions such as banks and insurance firms? How are the balance sheet structures of securities firms similar to those of other financial intermediaries?

16. Based on the data in Table 4–7, what were the second-largest single asset and the largest single liability of securities firms in 2008? Are these asset and liability categories related? Exactly how does a repurchase agreement work?

17. Identify the major regulatory organizations that are involved in the daily operations of the securities industry, and explain their role in providing smoothly operating markets.

Web Questions

18. Go to the Thomson Reuters website at www.thomsonreuters.com/business_units/financial and click on the link under "League Tables."

    a. Scroll down to "Canada Debt Capital Markets" and download the latest quarterly report. How has the Canadian debt market behaved in the latest quarter?

    b. Scroll down to "Canada Equity Capital Markets" and download the latest report. How has the Canadian debt market behaved in the latest quarter?

    c. Compare the Canadian debt and equity markets with the global debt and equity capital markets by downloading the results for the latest quarter.

Mutual Funds, Hedge Funds, and Pension Funds

In this chapter, we provide an overview of (1) mutual funds, (2) hedge funds, and (3) pension funds, and highlight their rapid growth over the last decade. We look at

▸ the size, structure, and composition of each industry, highlighting historical trends, the different types, objectives, returns, and costs

▸ the balance sheets and recent trends

▸ the regulations and regulators

▸ global issues

INTRODUCTION

fund
A financial intermediary whose primary purpose is to acquire and manage financial assets for its owners.

mutual fund
An FI that pools the financial resources of individuals and companies and invests in diversified portfolios of assets, targeting a specific level of risk.

hedge fund
An FI that pools the financial resources of sophisticated investors and invests in a diversified pool of assets, usually high risk.

pension fund
A financial intermediary that pools the retirement savings of individuals, invests in a diversified portfolio of assets, and pays an income to its owners after retirement.

When the term "fund" is mentioned, most people automatically add the term "mutual" as an adjective. However, a **fund** can be defined more generally as a financial intermediary whose primary purpose is to acquire and manage financial assets (e.g., bonds, shares, money market securities) for its owners. The types of funds that will be discussed in this chapter are **mutual funds, hedge funds,** and **pension funds.** By pooling the financial resources of individuals and companies and investing in diversified portfolios of assets, funds provide opportunities for small savers to invest in financial securities and to diversify risk. Funds may also be able to generate greater economies of scale by incurring lower transactions costs and commissions than are incurred when individual investors buy securities directly. In this respect, funds are similar to deposit-taking FIs in converting savings into income-earning assets. However, while the 1990s saw savings transferred from banks and other deposit-taking institutions into funds, these funds differ for investors in the increased risk of a loss of capital, a market risk not present with government-insured deposits. Many investors saw their retirement savings devastated by the market downturn of 2001 and again in 2008.

The growth in savings, as a result of an employment benefit (a pension fund, firm-operated or government-operated) or through individual efforts (often within a legal shelter such as a **registered retirement savings plan (RRSP)** or a **registered education savings plan (RESP),** created FIs whose liability side is essentially all owners' equity. The fiduciary nature of pension funds was recognized early and regulations were established to govern them. Mutual funds were left to self-regulating organizations (SROs) for their control, and hedge funds, a product offered to knowledgeable investors, were left unregulated. The history of the last decade is thus one of growth in size and in regulation for these three types of FIs that developed into an industry whose primary service is **wealth management,** the provision of professional asset management to individual investors and companies.

By providing wealth management services, mutual funds, hedge funds, and pension funds are subject to interest rate risk, market risk, foreign exchange risk, and possibly off-balance-sheet risk on the asset side of their balance sheet. With the exception of capital adequacy rules, the risk management of funds parallels that of other FIs.

MUTUAL FUNDS

registered retirement savings plan (RRSP)
A retirement savings plan that allows Canadians to defer tax until retirement.

An open-ended mutual fund (the major type of mutual fund) continuously stands ready to sell new shares to investors and to redeem outstanding shares on demand at their fair market value. As a result of the tremendous increase in the market value of financial assets, such as equities, in the 1990s (for example, the S&P TSX Composite Index saw a return of over 25 percent in 1993, 1996, and 1999) and the relatively low-cost opportunity mutual funds provide to investors (particularly small investors) who want to hold such assets (through either direct mutual fund purchases or contributions to their registered retirement savings plans), the mutual fund industry boomed in size and customers in the 1990s.[1] In 2001, the market correction and a slowdown in the economy brought an end to such a rapid pace of growth. Further, allegations of trading abuses and excessive management fees resulted in a loss of confidence in mutual funds as an investment vehicle. Despite these issues, at the end of 2008, more than 2,000 different mutual companies held total assets of $507 billion.[2]

Size, Structure, and Composition of the Industry

Historical Trends

registered education savings plan (RESP)
A savings plan that allows Canadians to earn income for their children that is not taxed if used for educational purposes when withdrawn.

Figure 5–1 presents information about the growth of the net assets of the mutual fund industry in Canada from 1998 to 2008. The figures are split between short-term money markets funds and long-term funds. These data were collected by the Investment Funds Institute of Canada (IFIC) whose members reported 75 to 80 percent of the assets under management in Canada prior to September 1991 and an average of 85 percent from 1998 to 2008. Figure 5–1 shows that net assets have grown from $303.9 billion at year-end 1998 to $507.0 billion at year-end 2008. Over the same time period, the number of funds of IFIC's members has increased from 1,130 in 1998 to 2,015 in 2008. The number of accounts has ballooned from 32.8 million to over 50 million. According to IFIC's data, net mutual fund assets decreased only in 2002 when the return on the S&P TSX Composite Index was –14 percent and again in 2008 when the index declined by 35 percent.

wealth management
The provision of professional portfolio management, tax planning, and retirement planning services to individuals and companies.

Figure 5–2 shows the dollar value of net new sales of mutual funds from December 1998 to December 2008. The impact of the decline of financial markets is shown in the net sales of only $108 million in 2008. However, comparison of these statistics year over year may be misleading due to changes in the markets. The limit on foreign content in RRSPs was at 10 percent in 1990, 30 percent in 2001, and

---

[1] Shareholder services offered by mutual funds include free exchanges of investments between a mutual fund company's funds, automatic investing, automatic reinvestment of dividends, and automatic withdrawals.

[2] See Investment Funds Institute of Canada, www.ific.ca.

FIGURE 5–1
Mutual Fund Net Assets in Canada, 1998–2008 ($ billions)

Source: The Investment Funds Institute of Canada, www.ific.ca. Funds reported averaged 85 percent of assets under management in Canada.

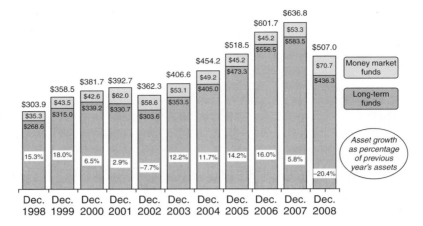

FIGURE 5–2
Mutual Fund Net Sales in Canada, 1998–2008 ($ billions)

Source: The Investment Funds Institute of Canada, www.ific.ca. Funds reported averaged 85 percent of assets under management in Canada.

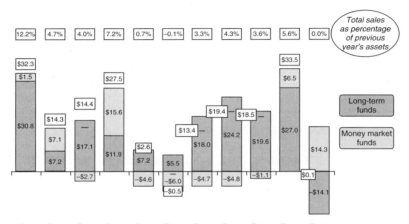

clone fund
A mutual fund that is RRSP-eligible and that creates returns equivalent to a foreign stock portfolio using derivatives.

fund of funds
A mutual fund that invests in other mutual funds.

www.iiac.ca

www.osfi-bsif.ca

was eliminated in 2005. In addition, some foreign **clone funds** have been created, which increase the foreign content of a mutual fund by using derivatives to emulate the returns of a foreign stock portfolio.

Industry participants consist of those who manufacture mutual funds, those who distribute funds, and those who do both, such as banks and credit unions. As well, there are **funds of funds,** which invest in other mutual funds.

Mutual funds represent an investment security and are therefore regulated at the provincial/territorial level in Canada. A provincial/territorial regulator's goal is the protection of the investor by ensuring disclosure of information and market transparency. In order to sell mutual funds, individuals must meet the licensing requirements of their home province or territory, which includes training in the products sold. As well, training in the evaluation of the clients' investment goals, their risk tolerance, and their investment knowledge is included in order to ensure that the funds recommended are appropriate. Each dealer must be a member of a self-regulating organization such as the Investment Industry Association of Canada (IIAC). However, in addition to specific securities laws, the sale of funds by deposit-taking institutions and others regulated by the Office of the Superintendent of Financial Services (OSFI) means that the Bank Act, The Insurance Companies Act, the Trust and Loan Companies Act, and other federal and provincial/territorial statutes may also apply. The majority of Canadian mutual funds are regulated by the Ontario Securities Commission (OSC), which is involved with other provincial/territorial securities regulators in harmonizing the regulations through the Canadian Securities Administrators (CSA).

The number of mutual fund participants in Canada is concentrated and is declining as the industry becomes more consolidated. Table 5–1 lists the net assets and net sales of 15 IFIC members reported at December 2008. With the exception of RBC, Dynamic Funds, Fidelity Investments Canada, and Manulife Investments, all funds showed negative net sales in 2008, reflecting the declines in markets in North America and worldwide. These 15 funds represent 93 percent of the $470 billion mutual fund assets reported to IFIC at December 2008. The Big Six banks are represented, led by RBC. Together, subsidiaries of the Big Six banks have net mutual fund assets of $237 billion, 47 percent of the net mutual fund assets reported to IFIC in 2008. While banks are still prohibited from selling insurance products in their branches, they are able to distribute mutual funds through their branch networks, provided their salespeople have been certified by the appropriate provincial or territorial regulator. In addition, the banks' clients are able to buy and sell mutual funds online from the same website where they conduct their other banking. This gives the banks an advantage in extending their sales of funds.

IGM Financial, part of Power Corporation of Canada, is ranked in second place based on net assets. Power Corporation of Canada is a financial conglomerate whose controlling shareholder is the Desmarais family of Quebec. As shown in Figure 5–3, Power Corporation has expanded into two areas of financial

TABLE 5–1
Mutual Fund Investment Companies in Canada, December 2008 ($000) (Includes only IFIC members)

Source: The Investment Funds Institute of Canada, www.ific.ca.

Company	Net Assets	Net Sales
RBC[1]	$92,462,956	$723,519
IGM Financial Inc.	84,523,377	−287,346
TD Asset Management	46,940,612	−27,248
CIBC Asset Management	41,928,563	−210,781
Fidelity Investments Canada ULC	33,659,009	250,429
BMO Financial Group	29,547,155	−312,952
Invesco Trimark Ltd.[2]	28,659,453	−482,094
AGF Funds Inc.	19,972,547	−104,532
Franklin Templeton	18,402,289	−133,156
Dynamic Funds	16,871,031	76,108
Scotia Securities Inc.	16,788,638	−38,246
MD Management Limited	13,142,203	−55,871
National Bank Securities[3]	9,642,130	−27,190
Fonds Desjardins	9,100,143	−176,036
Manulife Investments	8,328,219	171,484
Total net assets	$469,968,325	−$633,912
Percent of all assets reported to IFIC	93%	

[1] RBC Asset Management Inc. and Phillips, Hager & North Ltd. are now grouped under RBC. RBC completed acquisition of Phillips, Hager & North Investment Management on May 1, 2008.
[2] AIM Trimark Investments has been renamed Invesco Trimark Ltd. (August 11, 2008).
[3] Altamira Investment Services Inc. reporting has now been amalgamated into National Bank Securities (November 2008).

FIGURE 5–3
Ownership
Structure of Power
Corporation of
Canada, September
2008

Source: Power Corporation
of Canada website, www.
powercorporation.com.

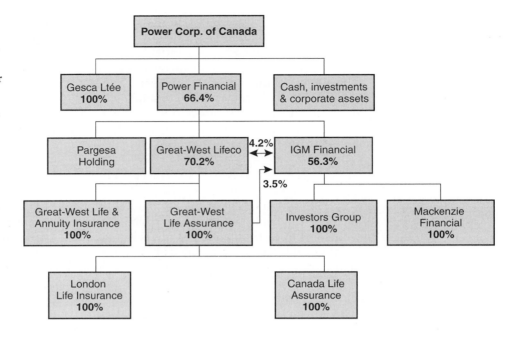

bond funds
Funds that contain fixed-income capital market debt securities.

equity funds
Funds that contain primarily common stock securities.

balanced funds
Funds that contain bond and stock securities.

RRSP-eligible
A mutual fund or other security that meets the criteria of Canada Revenue Agency (CRA) for inclusion in a registered retirement savings plan.

intermediation: Its assets include life insurance (Great-West Life, London Life, Canada Life), as well as mutual funds (IGM Financial, Investors Group, Mackenzie Financial, Counsel Group of Funds). Through its website, IGM Financial Inc. sells mortgages, insurance, and other banking products.

AGF Management is an independent Canadian-owned fund. Three of the funds in Table 5–1 (Invesco Trimark, Fidelity Investments Canada, and Franklin Templeton) are owned by large U.S.-based companies. Fonds Desjardins is owned by a caisse populaire based in Quebec, and Manulife Investments is owned by an insurance company.

Different Types of Mutual Funds

As shown in Figure 5–1 the assets of the mutual fund industry can be divided into two sectors: long-term funds and short-term funds. These are reported on an aggregate basis by the Bank of Canada as money market mutual funds and non-money market mutual funds as part of the money supply. Long-term funds include **bond funds** (composed of fixed-income securities with a maturity over one year), **equity funds** (composed of primarily common stock securities) **balanced funds** (composed of common and preferred shares and bonds), and specialty funds. Short-term funds include money market mutual funds that are invested in short-term paper, usually with maturities of less than six months. Since the goal of most mutual funds is to be **RRSP-eligible,** and since, as noted previously, there have been restrictions on the level of foreign content in RRSPs, mutual funds are further classified as to whether they contain foreign or U.S. common shares, foreign bonds, or foreign money market securities.

As can be seen from Table 5–2, the long-term funds dominate, with the short-term money market funds making up only 14 percent of total assets in 2008. Foreign content has increased over time as government restrictions for maintaining the tax-deferred status of RRSPs have eased. In 2008, domestic equity represented 20.4 percent of the Canadian dollar value of all funds, with U.S. equity at 3 percent

TABLE 5–2
Canadian Mutual Fund Assets by Fund Type, December 31, 2008 ($000) (Includes only data reported to IFIC)

Source: The Investment Funds Institute of Canada, www.ific.ca.

Asset Class	Total Net Assets Month-End	% Market Share	% Change Yr. to Yr.	Year-to-Date Net Sales (Excl. Reinvested Distributions)
Equity Funds				
Domestic Equity	103,327,012	20.4%	−35.5%	(6,683,493)
Global and International Equity	64,383,347	12.7%	−36.5%	(5,570,460)
U.S. Equity	15,104,610	3.0%	−26.3%	(244,280)
Sector Equity	9,464,388	1.9%	−38.1%	314,954
Total Equity Funds	**$192,279,357**	**37.9%**	**−35.3%**	**$(12,183,280)**
Balanced Funds				
Domestic Balanced	114,364,947	22.6%	−20.2%	(3,769,915)
Global Balanced	70,770,918	14.0%	−16.6%	2,643,227
Total Balanced Funds	**$185,135,864**	**36.5%**	**−18.9%**	**$ (1,126,688)**
Bond Funds				
Domestic Fixed Income	46,886,200	9.2%	2.4%	(1,627,715)
Global and High-Yield Fixed Income	6,593,228	1.3%	−8.2%	(140,898)
Total Bond Funds	**$ 53,479,427**	**10.5%**	**1.0%**	**$ (1,768,612)**
Specialty Funds	**5,419,233**	**1.1%**	**8.1%**	**941,231**
Long-Term Funds Total	**$436,313,882**	**86.0%**	**−25.2%**	**$(14,137,348)**
Short-Term/Money Market Funds	**70,745,137**	**14.0%**	**32.7%**	**14,288,530**
All Funds	**$507,059,018**	**100.0%**	**−20.4%**	**$ 151,182**

and global and international equity at 12.7 percent. Markets in 2008 showed historic levels of exchange rate, equity, and credit volatility. As a result, most funds showed a significant decline in total net assets between December 2007 and December 2008. Of interest is the switch from long-term funds (down 25.2 percent) to short-term money market funds (up 32.7 percent). This feature is shown more clearly in Figure 5–2.

INTERNET EXERCISE

Go to the Investment Funds Institute of Canada's website at www.ific.ca. Find the latest figures for the month-end dollar value of mutual fund assets by using the following steps: Click on "Our Industry." Click on "Industry Statistics." Click on "Overview Report by Asset Class." This will open an Excel spreadsheet that can be downloaded to your computer.

Mutual Fund Objectives

Mutual funds are legally required to provide investors with a prospectus that outlines the fund's investment strategy and its costs. In addition, each fund produces an annual report that provides details of its activities, and also maintains a website to provide monthly and quarterly information, and, in some cases, a copy of the fund's prospectus. The goal is to fully inform existing and potential investors of its activities so that they can evaluate the risks and returns. Investment advisors and sellers of mutual funds must meet provincial/territorial requirements, which include a duty to ensure that the investor is informed and that the fund is appropriate for a particular client.

TABLE 5–3   The Largest Mutual Funds Ranked by Assets Held, October 31, 2009

Fund Name	Category	Assets ($ millions) (Oct. 31/09)	NAVPS ($) (Nov. 20/09)	Return (%) 1 Year	Return (%) 3 Year	Load Type	MER (%)
Investors Dividend A	Canadian Equity Balanced	$11,896.3	$20.66	4.8	–2.9	DSC	2.68
RBC Premium Money Market	Canadian Money Market	$11,556.2	$10.00	1.3	3.1	N	0.34
iShares CDN LargeCap 60 Index	Canadian Equity	$9,805.5	—	12.8	–0.3	N	—
RBC Canadian Dividend Series T	Canadian Dividend & Income Equity	$9,145.8	$10.57	9.7	—	N	1.68
RBC Canadian Dividend Series D	Canadian Dividend & Income Equity	$9,145.8	$42.28	10.2	—	N	1.15
RBC Canadian Dividend Advisor	Canadian Dividend & Income Equity	$9,145.8	$42.42	9.6	–1.9	FE, LSC	1.68
RBC Canadian Dividend	Canadian Dividend & Income Equity	$9,145.8	$42.22	9.6	–1.9	N	1.70
TD Canadian Bond - I	Canadian Fixed Income	$8,454.4	$13.37	13.7	4.6	N	1.05
TD Canadian Bond - A	Canadian Fixed Income	$8,454.4	$11.67	13.4	4.3	DSC, FE, LSC	1.31
CI Harbour Growth & Income	Canadian Equity Balanced	$8,262.3	$17.18	10.4	0.0	DSC, FE, LSC	2.31

Note: N = no load; DSC = deferred sales commission; FE = front end; LSC = low sales charge

Source: *Morningstar*, November 23, 2009, www.morningstar.ca.

The choice of the investor is to meet his or her investment objectives (e.g., diversification while satisfying RRSP requirements in order to keep the funds tax-sheltered), and also to minimize the fees paid, as discussed below. Table 5–3 lists the top mutual funds by asset size at October 31, 2009. The end of February marks the deadline for Canadians to contribute to their RRSPs and be able to claim the amount against their income taxes for the previous year. The funds listed are RRSP-eligible, reflecting the emphasis on retirement savings in Canada.

Investor Returns from Mutual Fund Ownership

marked-to-market
Adjusting asset and balance sheet values to reflect current market prices.

net asset value (NAV) *or* **net asset value per share (NAVPS)**
The net asset value of a mutual fund is equal to the market value of the assets in the mutual fund portfolio divided by the number of shares outstanding.

The return an investor gets from investing in mutual fund shares reflects three aspects of the underlying portfolio of mutual fund assets. First, income and dividends are earned on those assets; second, capital gains occur when assets are sold by a mutual fund at prices higher than the purchase price; third, capital appreciation in the underlying values of the assets held in a fund's portfolio add to the value of mutual fund shares. With respect to capital appreciation, mutual fund assets are normally **marked-to-market** daily. This means that the managers of the fund calculate the current value of each mutual fund share by computing the daily market value of the fund's total asset portfolio and then dividing this amount by the number of mutual fund shares outstanding. The resulting value is called the **net asset value (NAV)** or **net asset value per share (NAVPS)** of the fund. This is the price the investor gets when selling shares back to the fund that day or buying any new shares in the fund on that day.

EXAMPLE 5–1

Effect of Capital Appreciation on NAV

Suppose a mutual fund contains 1,000 shares of Canadian Tire currently trading at $37.75, 2,000 shares of Encana currently trading at $43.70, and 1,500 shares of CIBC currently trading at $46.67. The mutual fund currently has 15,000 shares outstanding held by investors. Thus, today, the NAV of the fund is calculated as

$$NAV = [(1,000 \times \$37.75) + (2,000 \times \$43.70) + (1,500 \times \$46.67)] \div 15,000 = \$13.01$$

If next month Canadian Tire shares increase to $45, Encana shares increase to $48, and CIBC shares increase to $50, the NAV (assuming the same number of shares outstanding) would increase to

$$NAV = [(1,000 \times \$45) + (2,000 \times \$48) + (1,500 \times \$50)] \div 15,000 = \$14.40$$

---

open-end mutual fund
The supply of shares in the fund is not fixed but can increase or decrease daily with purchases and redemptions of shares.

Most mutual funds are **open-end** in that the number of shares outstanding fluctuates up and down daily with the amount of share redemptions and new purchases. With open-end mutual funds, investors buy and sell shares from and to the mutual fund company. Thus, the demand for shares determines the number outstanding and the NAV of shares is determined solely by the market value of the underlying securities held in the mutual fund divided by the number of shareholders outstanding.

EXAMPLE 5–2

Effect of Investment Size on NAV

Consider the mutual fund in Example 5–1, but suppose that today 1,000 additional investors buy into the mutual fund at the current NAV of $13.01. This means that the fund manager now has $13,010 in additional funds to invest. Suppose the fund manager decides to use these additional funds to buy additional shares in Canadian Tire. At today's market price, he or she can buy $13,010 ÷ $37.75 = 344 additional shares of Canadian Tire. Thus, the mutual fund's new portfolio of shares would be 1,344 in Canadian Tire, 2,000 in Encana, and 1,500 in CIBC. At the end of the month, the NAV of the portfolio would be

$$NAV = [(1,344 \times \$45) + (2,000 \times \$48) + (1,500 \times \$50)] \div 16,000 = \$14.47$$

given the appreciation in value of all three stocks over the month.

Note that the fund's value changed over the month due to both capital appreciation and investment size. A comparison of the NAV in Example 5–1 with the one in this example indicates that the additional shares alone enabled the fund to gain a slightly higher NAV than if the number of shares had remained static ($14.47 versus $14.40).

---

closed-end investment companies
Specialized investment companies that invest in securities and assets of other firms but have a fixed supply of shares outstanding themselves.

Open-end mutual funds can be compared to most regular corporations traded on stock exchanges and to **closed-end investment companies,** both of which have a fixed number of shares outstanding at any given time. For example, **income trusts** are closed-end funds as are **real estate investment trusts (REITs),** which specialize in investment in real estate company shares and/or in buying mortgages. With closed-end funds, investors must buy and sell the investment company's shares on a stock exchange similar to the trading of corporate stock. Since the number of shares available for purchase at any moment in time is fixed, the NAV of the fund's shares is determined not only by the value of the underlying shares but also by the demand for the investment company's shares themselves. When demand is high, the shares can trade at more than the NAV of the

income trust
An income fund/trust set up to own assets whose earnings (income) are passed on to the unit holders monthly or quarterly and taxed in their hands.

securities held in the fund. In this case, the fund is said to be *trading at a premium*, that is, at more than the fair market value of the securities held. When the value of the closed-end fund's shares are less than the NAV of its assets, its shares are said to be *trading at a discount*, that is, at less than the fair market value of the securities held.

EXAMPLE 5–3

Market Value of Closed-End Mutual Fund Shares

Because of high demand for a closed-end investment company's shares, the 50 shares (N_S) are trading at $20 per share ($P_S$). The market value of the equity-type securities in the fund's asset portfolio, however, is $800, or $16 ($800 ÷ 50), per share. The market value balance sheet of the fund is shown below:

Assets		Liabilities and Equity	
Market value of asset portfolio	$800	Market value of closed-end fund shares ($P_S \times N_S$)	$1,000
Premium	$200		

The fund's shares are trading at a premium of $4 (200 ÷ 50) per share.

Because of low demand for a *second* closed-end fund, the 100 shares outstanding are trading at $25 per share. The market value of the securities in this fund's portfolio is $3,000, or each share has a NAV of $30 per share. The market value balance sheet of this fund is:

Assets		Liabilities and Equity	
Market value of asset portfolio	$3,000	Market value of closed-end fund shares (100 × $25)	$2,500
Discount	−$500		

Mutual fund investors can get information on the performance of mutual funds from several places. For example, for a comprehensive analysis of mutual funds, *The Globe and Mail* and Morningstar, Inc., offer information on over 10,000 open-end and closed-end funds. Neither *The Globe and Mail* nor Morningstar own, operate, or hold an interest in any mutual fund. Thus, they are recognized as leading providers of unbiased data and performance analysis (e.g., of returns) for the industry.

www.globefund.com
www.morningstar.ca

real estate investment trust (REIT)
A closed-end investment company that specializes in investing in mortgages, property, or real estate company shares.

Mutual Fund Costs

Mutual funds charge shareholders a price or fee for the services they provide (i.e., management of a diversified portfolio of financial securities). Two types of fees are incurred by investors: sales loads and fund operating expenses. We discuss these next. The total cost to the shareholder of investing in a mutual fund is the sum of the annualized sales load and other fees charged.

Load versus No-Load Funds

load fund
A mutual fund with an up-front sales or commission charge that has to be paid by the investor.

An investor who buys a mutual fund share may be subject to a sales charge, sometimes as high as 8.5 percent. In this case, the fund is called a **load fund**.[3] Other funds

---

[3] Another kind of load, called a *back-end load*, is sometimes charged when mutual fund shares are sold by investors. Back-end loads, also referred to as *deferred sales charges*, are an alternative way to compensate the fund managers or sales force for their services.

no-load fund
A mutual fund that does not charge up-front fees or commission charges on the sale of mutual fund shares to investors.

that directly market shares to investors do not use sales agents working for commissions and have no up-front commission charges; these are called **no-load funds.**

The argument in favour of load funds is that their managers provide investors with more personal attention and advice than managers of no-load funds. However, the cost of this increased attention may not be worthwhile. It can be seen from Table 5–3 that, with the exception of Investors Dividend-A, which carries a back-end load, and CI Harbour Growth & Income Fund, which gives the investor the option to choose to pay either a front-end or a back-end fee, the top funds in Canada are no-load funds.

Fund Operating Expenses

management fee
The amount paid to an investment manager for operating a mutual fund.

In contrast to one-time up-front load charges on the initial investment in a mutual fund, annual fees are charged to cover all fund-level expenses experienced as a percentage of the fund assets. One type of fee (called a *management fee*) is charged to meet operating costs (such as administration and shareholder services). In addition, mutual funds generally require a small percentage (or fee) of investable funds to meet fund-level marketing and distribution costs.

management expense ratio (MER)
A mutual fund's operating costs expressed as a percentage of its total average assets.

The amount the investor pays to the fund for investment management and administrative costs (excluding brokerage fees) is reported as a **management fee.** As shown in Table 5–3, the level of management fees is expressed as the **management expense ratio (MER),** which is the ratio of all the costs to operate a fund as a percentage of the average total assets in the fund. The quoted returns are net of the MER. The one-year and three-year returns reported in Table 5–3 are net of MER, reflecting the fact that investment managers are paid even in years with large declines in value.

trailer fee
A commission paid monthly or quarterly to the investment advisor who sells a fund. It is payable as a percentage of the assets for as long as the investor owns the fund.

The MER is often increased by the inclusion of a **trailer fee** (also called *a trailer commission*), which is an amount paid monthly or quarterly to the **investment advisor** (i.e., the person who sells the fund to the investor) as long as the investor owns the fund. These fees are controversial as they may amount to 50 basis points or 0.5 percent per year of the amount of assets owned by the investor and, since they are essentially a sales commission, do not relate to the actual management of the funds year to year. The payment of trailer fees is included in the fund's prospectus, but many investors rely on their advisor's recommendations. The advisor has a conflict of interest and could recommend those funds for which he or she would receive a trailer fee.[4]

investment advisor
A person licensed to sell investment products to the public.

INTERNET EXERCISE

Go to *The Globe and Mail*'s Globefund website and obtain data for the top mutual funds by asset size. Go to www.globefund.com. Click on "Fund Filter." Under "Total Assets" set the drop-down menus to "greater than or equal to" on the left and "$5,000 M" on the right. Click on "Get Results." The report listed will show you the top funds. You can change the information displayed by clicking on the "report type" tabs above the chart and selecting "Key Facts." This will show the funds by asset size. Have the rankings of the funds changed since February 2, 2009, as reported in Table 5–3? How have total assets changed?

---

[4] Since mutual fund pricing is done on funds whose values and number of units outstanding may change on a daily basis, calculating the returns can be a difficult exercise, and the results subject to interpretation. See K. Ruckman, "Expense Ratios of North American Mutual Funds," *The Canadian Journal of Economics,* February 2003, 36(1), p.192; A. Mawani, M. Milevsky, and K. Panyagometh, "The Impact of Personal Income Tax on Returns and Rankings of Canadian Equity Mutual Funds," *Canadian Tax Journal,* 2003, 51(2), p. 863; and R. Deaves, "The Comparative Performance of Load and No-Load Mutual Funds in Canada," *Canadian Journal of Administrative Sciences,* December 2004, 21(4), pp. 326–333.

EXAMPLE 5–4	The cost of mutual fund investing to the shareholder includes both the one-time sales load

EXAMPLE 5–4

Caculation of Mutual Fund Costs

The cost of mutual fund investing to the shareholder includes both the one-time sales load and any annual fees charged. Because the sales load is a one-time charge, it must be converted to an annualized payment incurred by the shareholder over the life of his or her investment. With this conversion, the total shareholder cost of investing in a fund is the sum of the annualized sales load plus any annual fees.

For example, suppose an investor purchases fund shares with a 4 percent front-end load and expects to hold the shares for 10 years. The annualized sales load[5] incurred by the investor is

$$4 \text{ percent}/10 \text{years} = 0.4 \text{ percent per year}$$

Further, suppose the fund has a management expense ratio of 1 percent per year. The annual total shareholder cost for this fund is calculated as

$$0.4 \text{ percent} + 1 \text{ percent} = 1.4 \text{ percent per year}$$

CONCEPT QUESTIONS

1. Describe the difference between short-term and long-term mutual funds.
2. What are the three largest mutual fund companies? How have their funds performed in recent years?
3. Describe the difference between open-end and closed-end mutual funds.

Regulation

The mutual fund industry is regulated by the provincial and territorial securities commissions (e.g., The Ontario Securities Commission, OSC) and thus is subject to the rules regarding securities sales and distribution. In addition, each mutual fund is a member of a self-regulating organization (SRO) such as the Investment Industry Association of Canada and the **Mutual Fund Dealers Association of Canada (MFDA).** However, Canadian FIs and investors are globally oriented and integration of the Canadian and the U.S. financial markets means that cross-border issues are important for both Canadian FIs and Canadian regulators. The actions of the U.S. Securities and Exchange Commission (SEC), including the Sarbanes-Oxley Act of 2002, and the prosecution of brokers for insider trading and market timing have implications for Canadian markets and have focused global attention on corporate governance and stable and efficient capital markets.

In the early 2000s, the SEC investigated securities violations by the mutual fund industry. The market for mutual funds was rocked by charges of **market timing, late trading** (also called **backward pricing**), and **directed brokerage fees.**

Market timing involves short-term trading of mutual funds that seeks to take advantage of short-term discrepancies between the price of a mutual fund's shares and out-of-date values on the securities in the fund's portfolio. It is especially common in international funds, as traders can exploit differences in time zones. Typically, market timers hold a fund for only a few days. For example, when Asian markets close with losses but are expected to rebound the following day, market timers can buy a mutual fund, investing in Asian securities after the loss on that day, and then

www.mfda.ca

Mutual Fund Dealers Association of Canada (MFDA) An SRO governing issues related to mutual funds in Canada.

market timing Excessive buying and selling of securities to take advantage of arbitrage opportunities between different markets.

late trading (backward pricing) Illegally buying or selling securities submitted after the closing time at that day's price.

---

[5] Convention in the industry is to annualize the sales load without adjusting for the time value of money.

directed brokerage fees
Fees paid to brokerage firms for promoting a stock or mutual fund.

sell the shares for a profit the next day. This single-day investment dilutes the profits of the fund's long-term investors, while market timers profit without much risk.

The U.S. late trading allegations involved cases in which some investors were able to buy or sell mutual fund shares long after the price had been set at 4:00 p.m. Eastern time each day (i.e., after the close of the exchange). Under existing rules, investors have to place an order with their broker or another FI by 4:00 p.m. If the mutual fund company has not received the order until much later, it legally must be **forward priced,** that is, processed at the next trading day's price. However, because of this time delay, some large U.S. investors had been able to illegally call their broker back after the market closed and alter or cancel their orders. The Canadian system differs in that most orders are processed through the banks (or through a clearing agency, FundSERV Inc.), which automatically time-stamp the order and place it in the queue for next-day pricing. This makes late trading difficult in Canada.

forward pricing
Execution of a security trade received after market hours at the following day's price.

Directed brokerage involves arrangements between mutual fund companies and brokerage houses and whether those agreements improperly influenced which funds brokers recommended to investors. The U.S. investigation examined whether some mutual fund companies agreed to direct orders for stock and bond purchases and sales to brokerage houses that agreed to promote sales of the mutual fund company's products.

The U.S. investigations resulted in some of the largest names in the U.S. securities industry (Bank of America, Charles Schwab, Citigroup, Merrill Lynch) being disciplined, destroying investor confidence in the fairness of the markets. In 2003, in response to the U.S. situation, an investigation in Canada was set up with the securities regulators, the Investment Dealers Association (IDA), and the MFDA. From late 2003–2004, Canadian mutual funds were questioned about market timing (which is not illegal in Canada but is not in the interests of all investors in the funds) and late trading. The report was released in March 2005, and agreements were made with five mutual fund dealers (CI Mutual Funds, $49.3 million; AGF Funds, $29.2 million; IG Investment Management, $19.2 million; and AIC, $58.8 million) to repay $156.5 million to investors harmed by the trading practices.

The result of both the Canadian and the U.S. investigations is the increased and ongoing scrutiny of the industry by investors and the movement toward more regulation in order to ensure a transparent system that is fair for investors and promotes efficient markets. The major proposals include independent committees to review issues of conflicts of interest but there is a trade-off between industry independence and investor protection.[6]

CONCEPT QUESTION	Who regulates mutual funds in Canada?

GLOBAL ISSUES

As discussed throughout the chapter, mutual funds have been a fast-growing sector in the Canadian financial institutions industry throughout the 1990s and into

---

[6] The full report, *Ontario Securities Commission Report on Mutual Fund Trading Practices Probe,* March 2005, available online at www.osc.gov.on.ca, discusses the nature of the investigation as well as proposed policy and regulatory changes. A comparison of the U.S. and Canadian regulation of mutual funds is given in S. G. Kelman, "The Canadian Way," *CA Magazine,* November 2004, 137(9), pp. 36–38. See E. Church, "Watchdogs to Put More Bite in Mutual Fund Conflict Rules," *The Globe and Mail,* May 27, 2005, p. B1 for a summary of the consultation process that is leading toward better governance in the industry and the restoration of investors' confidence in the markets.

the 2000s. Worldwide investment in mutual funds is shown in Table 5–4. While not as striking as the growth in U.S. funds, worldwide investments in mutual funds have increased over 120 percent, from US$11.65 trillion in 2001 to US$26.1 trillion

TABLE 5–4   Woldwide Total Net Assets of Mutual Funds, Year-End 2001–Year-End 2008 (US$ millions)

World	2001	2002	2003	2004	2005	2006	2007	2008
	$11,654,868	$11,324,128	$14,048,311	$16,164,795	$17,771,027	$21,807,505	$26,129,564	$18,974,521
Americas	**7,433,106**	**6,776,289**	**7,969,541**	**8,792,450**	**9,763,921**	**11,469,062**	**13,421,149**	**10,579,430**
Argentina	3,751	1,021	1,916	2,355	3,626	6,153	6,789	3,867
Brazil	148,189	96,729	171,596	220,586	302,927	418,771	615,365	479,321
Canada	267,863	248,979	338,369	413,772	490,518	566,298	698,397	416,031
Chile	5,090	6,705	8,552	12,588	13,969	17,700	24,444	17,587
Costa Rica	1,577	1,738	2,754	1,053	804	1,018	1,203	1,098
Mexico	31,723	30,759	31,953	35,157	47,253	62,614	75,428	60,435
United States	6,974,913	6,390,358	7,414,401	8,106,939	8,904,824	10,396,508	11,999,523	9,601,090
Europe	**3,167,965**	**3,462,999**	**4,682,836**	**5,640,452**	**6,002,261**	**7,803,906**	**8,934,864**	**6,288,138**
Austria	55,211	66,877	87,982	103,709	109,002	128,236	138,709	93,269
Belgium	68,661	74,983	98,724	118,373	115,314	137,291	149,842	105,057
Bulgaria	n.a.	n.a.	n.a.	n.a.	n.a.	n.a.	n.a.	226
Czech Republic	1,778	3,297	4,083	4,860	5,331	6,490	7,595	5,260
Denmark	33,831	40,153	49,533	64,799	75,199	95,620	104,082	65,182
Finland	12,933	16,516	25,601	37,658	45,415	67,804	81,136	48,750
France	713,378	845,147	1,148,446	1,370,954	1,362,671	1,769,258	1,989,690	1,591,082
Germany	213,662	209,168	276,319	295,997	296,787	340,325	372,072	237,986
Greece	23,888	26,621	38,394	43,106	32,011	27,604	29,807	12,189
Hungary	2,260	3,992	3,936	4,966	6,068	8,523	12,577	9,188
Ireland	191,840	250,116	360,425	467,620	546,242	855,011	951,371	720,486
Italy	359,879	378,259	478,734	511,733	450,514	452,798	419,687	263,588
Liechtenstein	n.a.	3,847	8,936	12,543	13,970	17,315	25,103	16,781
Luxembourg	758,720	803,869	1,104,112	1,396,131	1,635,785	2,188,278	2,685,065	1,860,763
Netherlands	79,165	84,211	93,573	102,134	94,357	108,560	113,759	84,568[a]
Norway	14,752	15,471	21,994	29,907	40,122	54,065	74,709	41,157
Poland	2,970	5,468	8,576	12,014	17,652	28,957	45,542	17,782
Portugal	16,618	19,969	26,985	30,514	28,801	31,214	29,732	14,180
Romania	10	27	29	72	109	247	390	326
Russia	297	372	851	1,347	2,417	5,659	7,175	2,026
Slovakia	n.a.	n.a.	1,061	2,168	3,035	3,171	4,762	3,841
Slovenia	n.a.	n.a.	n.a.	n.a.	n.a.	2,484	4,219	2,067
Spain	159,899	179,133	255,344	317,538	316,864	367,918	396,534	270,983
Sweden	65,538	57,992	87,746	107,064	119,059	176,943	194,955	113,331
Switzerland	75,973	82,622	90,772	94,407	116,669	159,515	176,282	165,709
Turkey	n.a.	6,002	14,157	18,112	21,761	15,463	22,609	15,404
United Kingdom	316,702	288,887	396,523	492,726	547,103	755,156	897,460	526,957
Asia and Pacific	**1,039,236**	**1,063,857**	**1,361,473**	**1,677,887**	**1,939,251**	**2,456,511**	**3,678,330**	**2,037,536**
Australia	334,016	356,304	518,411	635,073	700,068	864,254	1,192,992	841,133
China	n.a.	n.a.	n.a.	n.a.	n.a.	n.a.	434,063	276,303
Hong Kong	170,073	164,322	255,811	343,638	460,517	631,055	818,421	n.a.
India	15,284	20,364	29,800	32,846	40,546	58,219	108,582	62,805
Japan	343,907	303,191	349,148	399,462	470,044	578,883	713,998	575,327
Korea, Rep. of	119,439	149,544	121,663	177,417	198,994	251,930	329,979	221,992
New Zealand	6,564	7,505	9,641	11,171	10,332	12,892	14,924	10,612
Pakistan	n.a.	n.a.	n.a.	n.a.	n.a.	2,164	4,956	1,985
Philippines	211	474	792	952	1,449	1,544	2,090	1,263
Taiwan	49,742	62,153	76,205	77,328	57,301	55,571	58,323	46,116
Africa	**14,561**	**20,983**	**34,460**	**54,006**	**65,594**	**78,026**	**95,221**	**69,417**
South Africa	14,561	20,983	34,460	54,006	65,594	78,026	95,221	69,417

Note: Components may not add to total because of rounding. For more worldwide mutual fund statistics, visit the Investment Company Institute's website at www.ici. org/stats/mf/arcglo/index.html.
Source: Investment Company Institute, *ICI Fact Book,* 2009, www.ici.org.

in 2007 but declined to US$18.97 trillion in 2008. In contrast, as this industry developed in countries throughout the world, the number of mutual funds worldwide increased from 53,371 in 2001 to 69,032 in 2008.

As may be expected, the worldwide mutual fund market is most active in those countries with the most sophisticated securities markets (e.g., Japan, France, Australia, and the United Kingdom). However, in the late 1990s and early 2000s, the faltering Japanese economy resulted in a decrease in both the assets invested in and the number of mutual funds. Assets invested in Japanese mutual funds fell from US$502.7 billion in 1999 to US$432.0 billion in 2000 (a drop of 14.1 percent) and the number of funds fell from 3,444 to 2,884 (16.3 percent) over the period. Some U.S. FIs saw this decline in the Japanese market as an opportunity. U.S. FIs such as Paine Webber Group (teaming up with Yasuda Life Insurance Co.) and Merrill Lynch (buying the assets of failed Japanese brokerage firm Yamaichi Securities) entered the Japanese mutual fund market in the late 1990s. The U.S. FIs saw Japan as a profitable market for mutual fund sales, noting that about 60 percent of Japan's savings was in low-yielding bank deposits or government-run institutions.[7] The worldwide economic downturn in 2001–2002 also affected the global mutual fund industry. Assets invested in non-U.S. mutual funds fell from US$4.91 trillion in 1999 to US$4.68 trillion in 2001. As the worldwide economic situation improved in the mid-2000s, so did assets invested in mutual funds, rising to US$10.49 trillion by 2006.

Although Canadian and U.S. mutual fund companies sponsor funds abroad, barriers to entry overseas are typically higher than in Canada and the United States. The mutual fund industry has worked to lower the barriers that prevent mutual fund firms from marketing their services more widely and to improve competition in the often diverse fund markets around the world. The mutual fund industry, for example, has worked to achieve a true cross-border market for mutual fund companies in Europe and to ensure that publicly offered mutual fund companies can be used as funding vehicles in the retirement fund market in Europe and Japan. The industry also has sought to reduce barriers for mutual fund sponsors seeking to offer mutual fund company products in China and other Asian countries.

CONCEPT QUESTION	**What have been the trends in the assets invested in worldwide mutual funds from 2000 to 2007?**

HEDGE FUNDS

History, Size, Structure, and Composition of the Industry

Hedge funds are a type of investment pool that solicits funds from wealthy individuals (also called *high net worth individuals,* whose financial assets exceed $1 million) and other investors (e.g., banks, insurance companies) and invests these funds on their behalf. Hedge funds, however, are not technically mutual funds in that, in many cases, they are subject to virtually no regulatory oversight in Canada, the United States, or globally. The absence of hedge fund regulations is due to the small number of investors permitted in each fund as well as the fact that

---

[7] It might be noted that as many European countries move away from state-sponsored pension plans to privately funded pension plans and retirement vehicles, the rate of growth in mutual funds in these countries is likely to accelerate rapidly.

investors are viewed as being sufficiently sophisticated so as not to need protection. Therefore, hedge funds are usually sold without a prospectus and generally are not required to publish financial statements on the System for Electronic Document Analysis and Retrieval (SEDAR).

Hedge funds are also not subject to the numerous regulations that apply to mutual funds for the protection of individuals, such as regulations requiring a certain degree of liquidity, regulations requiring that mutual fund shares be redeemable at any time, regulations protecting against conflicts of interest, regulations to ensure fairness in the pricing of funds shares, disclosure regulations, and regulations limiting the use of leverage. Further, hedge funds do not have to disclose their activities to third parties. Thus, as well as adopting riskier strategies and higher leverage to earn higher returns, hedge funds offer a high degree of privacy for their investors.

Hedge funds grew in popularity in the 1990s as investors saw returns of over 40 percent after management fees (often more than 25 percent of the fund's profits).[8] They came to the forefront in the news in the late 1990s when one large hedge fund, Long-Term Capital Management (LTCM), nearly collapsed. LTCM's troubles not only hurt its investors, but arguably came close to damaging the world's financial system through the credit risk exposure of other FIs. LTCM had lines of credit from financial institutions such as banks and brokerages that were used to increase the size of its investment pool and to take advantage of arbitrage opportunities. At its peak, LTCM had only approximately US$5 billion in capital supporting US$120 billion in investments, a debt-to-equity ratio of 24 times. To prevent LTCM's collapse, the U.S. Federal Reserve intervened by brokering a US$3.6 billion bailout by a consortium of some of the world's largest financial institutions.

A report on the hedge fund industry by the Investment Dealers Association, the precursor to IIAC, using statistics estimated by Investor Economics, a consulting firm in Toronto, reported 191 Canadian hedge funds with assets of $26.6 billion in 2004. Of this, $14.1 billion represented Canadian-sponsored assets (Table 5–5). Initially, hedge fund managers found mainly wealthy individual investors to invest in their funds, but in the late 1990s, corporate pension plan sponsors, insurance companies, and university endowment funds became important investors such that $10.9 billion hedge fund assets were pension plan assets at June 2004.[9]

Because hedge funds are exempt from many of the rules and regulations governing mutual funds, they can use aggressive strategies that are unavailable to

TABLE 5–5
Canadian Hedge Funds by Fund Size ($ billions)

Source: Investor Economics, *Hedge Funds Report,* Winter 2005.

	No. of Funds	Total Assets ($ billions)	Share (%)
Assets < $25 million	107	0.9	6.7
Assets $25 to $100 million	60	3.5	24.5
Assets > $100 million	24	9.6	68.4
Total	191	14.1	100.0

[8] Although S. J. Brown, in "Hedge Funds: Omniscient or Just Plain Wrong," *Pacific Basin Finance Journal,* 9, 2001, pp. 301–311, found that over the period 1989–1995, hedge funds earned, on average, 3 percent less than the S&P 500 index over the same period. Further, hedge fund risk was below that of the S&P 500 Index. Douglas Cumming, in "Don't Fence Them In: Hedge Fund Regulation and Performance," *Canadian Investment Review,* Winter 2008, pp. 26–33, found that hedge fund regulation tended to reduce risk as well as performance.

[9] See Hedge Fund Working Group, *Regulatory Analysis of Hedge Funds,* May 18, 2005, Investment Dealers Association of Canada. The data for the IDA's analysis was provided by Investor Economics, *Hedge Fund Report,* 2, Winter 2005.

mutual funds, including short selling, leveraging, program trading, arbitrage, and derivatives trading. Further, since as of early 2009, hedge funds are not required to register with a regulator, their actual data cannot be independently tracked. Therefore, hedge fund data are self-reported. It is estimated that global hedge fund assets reached a peak of managed assets estimated at US$1.93 trillion in mid-2008. By the end of 2008, losses (estimated at over 18 percent) and withdrawals reached US$525 billion, leaving the industry total assets under management of US$1.4 trillion. The credit and liquidity crisis so far has weakened this once-flourishing industry, which had begun to attract more conservative investors such as pension plans that were looking for superior returns. Table 5–6 lists the ten largest global managers as of September 30, 2008.

Since 2005, Scotia Capital has produced the *Canadian Hedge Fund Performance Index* that tracks open and closed funds with a minimum of $15 million in assets under management (www.scotiacapital.com/hfpi). Figure 5–4 shows the historical performance as at October 2009.

Some hedge funds take positions (using sophisticated computer models) speculating that some prices will rise faster than others. For example, a hedge fund may buy (take a long position in) a bond expecting that its price will rise. At the same time the fund will borrow (taking a short position) in another bond and sell it, promising to return the borrowed bond in the future. Generally, bond prices tend to move up and down together. Thus, if prices go up as expected, the hedge fund will gain on the bond it purchased while losing money on the bond it borrowed. The hedge fund will make a profit if the gain on the bond it purchased is larger than the loss on the bond it borrowed. If, contrary to expectations, bond prices fall, the hedge fund will make a profit if the gains on the bond it borrowed are greater than the losses on the bond it bought. Thus, regardless of the change in prices, the simultaneous long and short positions in bonds will minimize the risk of overall losses for the hedge fund. The IDA's report classified this strategy as **non-directional** since the direction of market movement is irrelevant and so the market risk exposure for the hedge fund is low.

Despite their name, hedge funds do not always "hedge" their investments to protect the fund and its investors against market price declines and other risks. The IDA's report pointed out that some strategies may be **event-driven** (e.g., potential mergers) and others are **opportunistic**, designed to take advantage of discrepancies in global macroeconomic conditions or markets. For example, although bond prices generally move in the same direction, the risk in hedge funds is that bond prices may unexpectedly move faster in some markets than in others. In 1997

non-directional strategy
An arbitrage position that allows a hedge fund to benefit whether market prices go up or down.

event-driven strategy
A hedge designed to take advantage of a potential occurrence in the market such as purchase of shares of a merger target or an investment in distressed debt.

opportunistic strategy
A hedge designed to take advantage of temporary pricing discrepancies in markets.

TABLE 5–6
Largest Hedge Funds by Assets Managed, at September 30, 2008 (US$ billions)

Source: *Pensions & Investments,* www.pionline.com.

Rank	Manager	Country	Total Assets
1	JPMorgan Chase	United States	$41
2	Bridgewater Associates	United States	38
3	D. E. Shaw Group	United States	36
4	Paulson & Co,	United States	36
5	Och-Ziff	United States	31
6	Farallon Capital Management	United States	30
7	Barclays Global Investors	United Kingdom	27
8	Goldman Sachs	United States	27
9	Brevan Howard Asset Management	United Kingdom	26
10	Man Investments	United Kingdom	25

FIGURE 5–4   Scotia Capital's *Canadian Hedge Fund Performance Index*, Historical Monthly Performance, December 2004–September 2009

Source: Scotia Capital, www.scotiacapital.com/hfpi, October 2009.

and 1998, computer models used by LTCM detected a price discrepancy between U.S. Treasury markets and other bonds (including high-yield corporate bonds, mortgage-backed securities, and European government bonds). LTCM consequently shorted U.S. Treasury securities (betting that their prices would fall) and took long positions in other types of bonds (betting their prices would rise). However, unexpectedly, in 1998 large drops in many foreign stock markets caused money to pour into the U.S. Treasury markets, driving Treasury security prices up and yields down. This drop in U.S. Treasury yields drove rates on mortgages down, which pushed down the prices of many mortgage-backed securities. Further, the flight to U.S. Treasury security markets meant a drop in funds flowing into European bond markets and high-yield corporate bond markets. With all of their positions going wrong, LTCM experienced huge losses.

Types of Hedge Funds

Most hedge funds are highly specialized, relying on the specific expertise of the fund manager(s) to produce a profit. Hedge fund managers follow a variety of investment strategies, some of which use leverage and derivatives, while others use more conservative strategies and involve little or no leverage. Generally, hedge funds are set up with specific parameters so that investors can forecast a risk-return profile. Figure 5–5 shows the general categories of hedge funds by risk classification.

More risky funds are the most aggressive and may produce profits in many types of market environments. Funds in this group are classified by objectives such as aggressive growth, emerging markets, macro, market timing, and short selling. Aggressive growth funds invest in equities expected to experience acceleration in growth of earnings per share. Generally, high price-to-earnings ratio, low or no

FIGURE 5–5 **Clssification of Hedge Funds**

dividend companies are included. These funds hedge by shorting equities where earnings disappointment is expected or by shorting stock indexes. Emerging market funds invest in equity or debt securities of emerging markets, which tend to have higher inflation and volatile growth. Macro funds aim to profit from changes in global economies, typically brought about by shifts in government policy that impact interest rates. These funds include investments in equities, bonds, currencies, and commodities. They use leverage and derivatives to accentuate the impact of market moves. Market timing funds allocate assets among different asset classes depending on the manager's view of the economic or market outlook. Thus, portfolio emphasis may swing widely between asset classes. The unpredictability of market movements and the difficulty of timing entry and exit from markets add significant risk to this strategy. Short-selling funds sell securities in anticipation of being able to buy them back in the future at a lower price based on the manager's assessment of the overvaluation of the securities or in anticipation of earnings disappointments.

Moderate risk funds are more traditional funds, similar to mutual funds, with only a portion of the portfolio being hedged. Funds in this group are classified by objectives such as distressed securities, fund of funds, opportunistic, multistrategy, and special situations. Distressed securities funds buy equity, debt, or trade claims, at deep discounts, of companies in or facing bankruptcy or reorganization. Profit opportunities come from the market's lack of understanding of the true value of these deep-discount securities and from the fact that the majority of institutional investors cannot own below-investment-grade securities. Funds of funds mix hedge funds and other pooled investment vehicles. This blending of different strategies and asset classes aims to provide a more stable long-term investment return than any of the individual funds. Returns and risk can be controlled by the mix of underlying strategies and funds. Capital preservation is generally an important consideration for these funds. Opportunistic funds change their investment strategy as opportunities arise to profit from events such as IPOs, sudden price changes resulting from a disappointing earnings announcement, and hostile takeover bids. These funds may utilize several investing styles at any point in time and are not restricted to any particular investment approach or asset class. Multistrategy funds take a diversified investment approach by implementing various strategies simultaneously to realize short- and long-term gains. This style of investment allows the manager to overweight or underweight different strategies to best capitalize on current investment opportunities. Special-situation funds invest in event-driven situations such as mergers, hostile takeovers, reorganizations, or leveraged buyouts. These funds may undertake the simultaneous purchase of stock in a company being acquired and sale of stock in its bidder, hoping to profit from the spread between the current market price and the final purchase price of the company.

Risk-avoidance funds are more traditional funds, emphasizing consistent but moderate returns while avoiding risk. Funds in this group are classified by objectives such as income, market neutral–arbitrage, market neutral–securities hedging, and value. Income funds invest with the primary focus on yield or current income rather than solely on capital gains. These funds use leverage to buy bonds and some fixed-income derivatives, profiting from principal appreciation and interest income. Market neutral-arbitrage funds attempt to hedge market risk by taking offsetting positions, often in different securities of the same issuer, for example, long convertible bonds and short the firm's equity. Their focus is on obtaining returns with low or no correlation to both equity and bond markets. Market neutral–securities hedging funds invest equally in long and short equity portfolios in particular market sectors. Market risk is reduced, but effective stock analysis is critical to obtaining a profit. These funds use leverage to magnify their returns. They also sometimes use market index futures to hedge systematic risk. Value funds invest in securities perceived to be selling at deep discounts relative to their intrinsic values. Securities include those that may be out of favor or underfollowed by analysts.

Using traditional risk-adjusted measures of performance (such as Sharpe ratios), the performance of hedge funds has been very strong compared to that of traditional financial investments like stocks and bonds.[10] Many hedge funds posted strong returns during the early 2000s even as stock returns were plummeting. Total assets managed by hedge funds increased by almost 6 percent in the last quarter of 2006 and by 22 percent in the first quarter of 2007. Funds of hedge funds grew by 22 percent to US$953 billion, equity-focused hedge funds increased 30 percent to US$743 billion, emerging market equity-focused funds increased by 58 percent, and energy sector funds grew by 52 percent to US$79.3 billion. Note that while mutual fund performance is generally measured by returns relative to some benchmark (and therefore can perform "well" even by losing 10 percent if the benchmark loses 10.5 percent), performance of hedge funds is measured by the growth in total assets managed.

Fees on Hedge Funds

Hedge fund managers generally charge two type of fees: management fees and performance fees. As with mutual funds, the management fee is computed as a percentage of the total assets under management and typically runs between 1.5 and 2.0 percent. Performance fees are unique to hedge funds. Performance fees give the fund manager a share of any positive returns on a hedge fund. The

---

[10] However, data deficiencies in the reporting and collection of hedge fund returns somewhat reduce confidence in all measures of hedge fund performance. Further, the inability to explain returns of individual hedge funds with standard multifactor risk models leaves open the possibility that it is not possible to properly measure the risk associated with at least some hedge fund strategies. If so, risk-adjusted returns earned by hedge funds may be overstated.

average performance fee on hedge funds is approximately 20 percent but varies widely. For example, Steven Cohen's SAC Capital Partners charges a performance fee of 50 percent. Performance fees are paid to the hedge fund manager before returns are paid to the fund investors. Hedge funds often specify a *hurdle rate*, which is a minimum annualized performance benchmark that must be realized before a performance fee can be assessed. Further, a *high-water mark* is usually used for hedge funds in which the manager does not receive a performance fee unless the value of the fund exceeds the highest net asset value it has previously achieved. High-water marks are used to link the fund manager's incentives more closely to those of the fund investors and to reduce the manager's incentive to increase the risk of trades.

Offshore Hedge Funds

Many offshore financial centres encourage hedge funds to locate in their countries. The major centres include the Cayman Islands, Bermuda, Dublin, and Luxembourg. The Cayman Islands are estimated to be the location of approximately 75 percent of all hedge funds. Offshore hedge funds are regulated in that they must obey the rules of the host country. However, the rules in most of these countries are not generally burdensome and provide anonymity to fund investors. Europe has been a growing area for offshore hedge funds, whose assets managed were estimated at US$870 billion in 2009.

When compared to domestic hedge funds, offshore hedge funds have been found to trade more intensely, due to the low or zero capital gains tax for offshore funds. Further, offshore hedge funds tend to engage less often in positive feedback trading (rushing to buy when the market is booming and rushing to sell when the market is declining) than domestic hedge funds. Finally, offshore hedge funds have been found to herd (mimic each other's behaviour when trading while ignoring information about the fundamentals of valuation) less than domestic hedge funds. Many hedge fund managers maintain both domestic and offshore hedge funds. Given the needs of their client investors, hedge fund managers want to have both types of funds to attract all types of investors.

Regulation

While mutual funds are very highly regulated, hedge funds have generally been unregulated. However, their role in global capital markets has come under scrutiny in recent years, particularly in the United States and Europe. During the early 2000s, riskier securities around the globe became popular investments for hedge funds eagerly searching for higher returns in a low interest rate environment. In early 2004, emerging market bond yields started to rise far more rapidly than those on U.S. Treasury bonds, increasing the gap in yields between the two as investors moved out of the riskier emerging-country bond market. As a result, as rising interest rates negatively impacted emerging-market hedge fund investments, many hedge funds saw decreases in returns. Consequently, there are fears that hedge funds may see a repeat of 1998. However, no one fund is likely to pose a systemic risk since, after LTCM, the amount of borrowing that banks extend to any one hedge fund client is far more carefully monitored by bank regulators. But, given the copycat nature of hedge fund management, there is concern that similar fund strategies by many hedge funds are combining to create potential systematic LTCM-type problems. Along with the use of similar investment strategies, many hedge funds are using the same risk models. These models are often historically based and are subject to similar errors in predicting the future.

www.iosco.org

The International Organization of Securities Commissions (IOSCO), whose members represent securities regulators around the world, including Canada and the United States, issued a report in 1999 following LTCM's collapse. The report recommended that regulators require FIs with a "material exposure" to highly leveraged institutions (HLIs) to (1) disclose their relationships to hedge funds and (2) enhance their risk management, particularly the credit risk that arises from lending to hedge funds.[11] In Canada, as hedge funds expand from targeting the sophisticated large investor to the smaller "retail" customer, securities regulators are starting to be concerned, hence the 2005 report by IDA (now IIAC), *Regulatory Analysis of Hedge Funds.* Unlike mutual funds, hedge funds are not required to report their holdings and they are usually organized as limited partnerships and structured to be exempt from securities laws governing their marketing practices, conflicts of interest, and disclosure of financials. Since September 2009, however, they are required to be registered. Discussions about regulating hedge funds have been spurred on by the scandal surrounding Portus Alternative Asset Management Inc., a hedge fund that has caused losses for investors and other FIs who referred investors such as Manulife Securities International Ltd., a unit of Manulife Financial that sells mutual funds. The global impact of hedge funds means that disclosure and regulation of their activities can be expected to increase in the future. (See the Industry Perspectives feature.)

In 2006 regulators found it necessary to examine circumstances surrounding the multibillion-dollar losses of Amaranth Advisors, a Connecticut-based hedge fund. The fund lost US$6.4 billion in September 2006, and its assets were down 65 to 70

INDUSTRY PERSPECTIVES

HEDGE FUNDS WITHER UNDER $152B IN WITHDRAWALS

Hedge funds have seen the best of times and the worst of times in the fourth quarter. In the last quarter of 2007, the industry attracted a record $194 billion from investors. But it's been all downhill from there as the financial crisis handed hedge funds their worst returns in nearly 20 years, according to Hedge Fund Research, prompting a crippling $152 billion in withdrawals in the fourth-quarter 2008.

With hedge funds posting losses of 18.3% last year, investors fled the industry as 2008 came to a close, using the fourth-quarter window—usually the only time hedge funds allow withdrawals—to make their exit. Many funds require a three-month notice from investors who want to exit by year's end, setting a deadline of Sept. 30—known in the industry as "D-Day."

Since then the situation has only worsened as numerous funds—including Bernard Madoff's—have been exposed to Ponzi schemes at the same time that equity and debt markets have wilted. Industry stalwarts like George Soros have predicted that the fallout from the recession and investors' aversion to risk will crush the industry. In November, Soros told Congress that "the bubble has now burst, and hedge funds will be decimated. I would guess that the amount of money they manage will shrink by between 50% and 75%."

Total assets under management for the industry fell to $1.4 trillion at the end of 2008, a decline of $525 billion from the peak of $1.93 trillion at mid-year 2008.

Source: George White, *The Deal Pipeline*, transaction information service, http://pipeline.thedeal.com, January 21, 2009.

---

[11] See Technical Committee of the International Organization of Securities Commissions, *Hedge Funds and Other Highly Leveraged Institutions,* November 1999, at www.iosco.org.

percent for the month and 55 to 60 percent for the year. Amaranth started 2006 with US$7.5 billion and rose to US$9.2 billion before plummeting to less than US$3 billion in October. Amaranth's energy desk, run by a young trader, Brian Hunter, bet aggressively on natural gas. When certain prices fell in September 2006, the fund found itself in positions too big to liquidate. Ultimately, it was forced to sell its energy holdings at a loss of US$560 million when some of its counterparties threatened to cut off its credit. Once this news got to the markets, and faced with large margin calls and no ability to borrow, Amaranth was forced to sell additional positions, resulting in even bigger losses. In October 2006, the fund announced it would close by the end of the year.

Possibly as a result of the trading abuses and scandals, the SEC began scrutinizing the hedge fund industry more closely. Specifically, in 2003 the SEC recommended that large hedge funds register as investment advisors with the SEC, subjecting them to periodic audits and inspections. Only about 25 percent of hedge funds were registered with the SEC at the time. In 2007, after years of examination and reflection, a committee of U.S. financial system regulators concluded that current regulations on hedge funds were sufficient to prevent hedge funds from threatening the financial system's stability. The report, compiled by the heads of the U.S. Treasury, Federal Reserve, SEC, and Commodity Futures Trading Commission (the President's Working Group on Financial Markets), concluded that while hedge funds present challenges for market participants and policymakers, their risks can be maintained through a combination of market discipline and limiting access to the private pools of capital to wealthy investors.

CONCEPT QUESTIONS	1. What is the difference between a mutual fund and a hedge fund?
	2. What are the performance fees charged by hedge funds?
	3. How is the regulatory status of hedge funds changing?

PENSION FUNDS

Size, Structure, and Composition of the Industry

Growth of mutual funds and hedge funds may be driven by retirement savings as previously discussed, but pension funds are directly driven by government regulations regarding retirement savings in Canada, and represent the biggest funds in Canada. Retirement savings in Canada come from:

1. Government-funded or sponsored plans, e.g., the Canada Pension Plan and Quebec Pension Plan

2. Employer-sponsored pension plans, e.g., **trusteed pension funds,** profit-sharing plans, group RRSPs

3. Individual savings, e.g., RRSPs.

trusteed pension funds (employer pension plans)
Registered pension plans (RPPs) usually sponsored by employers for the benefit of their employees and governed by a trust agreement.

The top 100 pension funds in Canada had total assets of $598.6 billion in 2008. The top 25 funds are shown in Table 5–7. The dollar value of pension assets are the next largest source of FI assets after the Big Six banks, but, in 2008, that was equal to only 22 percent of the reported $2.7 trillion assets of the six large Canadian banks. While the focus of hedge funds and mutual funds is the market and returns in order to attract investors, pension funds are focused on return and risk

TABLE 5–7   TOP 25 Pension Funds in Canada by Asset Size, December 31, 2008 ($ millions)

Rank	Organization	Change 2007–08	2008 ($ millions)	2007 ($ millions)
1	Ontario Teachers' Pension Plan Board	▼ 21.2%	$85,101.0	$108,001.0
2	Ontario Municipal Employees Retirement System	▼ 16.7%	$43,477.0	$52,187.0
3	Quebec Government and Public Employees Retirement Plan	▼ 26.7%	$33,793.9	$46,100.0
4	Public Service Pension Plan	▲ 11.3%	$28,294.0	$25,427.0
5	Hospitals of Ontario Pension Plan	▼ 10.7%	$26,800.0	$30,000.0
6	B.C. Municipal Pension Fund	▼ 10.5%	$22,317.2	$24,944.3
7	B.C. Public Service Pension Plan	▼ 11.9%	$15,753.9	$17,873.9
8	B.C. Teachers Pension Fund	▼ 12.4%	$14,416.0	$16,448.1
9	Local Authorities Pension Plan - Alberta	▼ 13.3%	$13,484.6	$15,557.0
10	Canadian National Railways	▼ 11.3%	$13,482.0	$15,208.0
11	Ontario Pension Board	▼ 18.0%	$13,015.0	$15,872.0
12	Canada Post Corp.	▼ 20.5%	$11,617.6	$14,611.3
13	BCE Master Trust Fund	▼ 22.4%	$11,510.0	$14,841.0
14	OPSEU Pension Trust	▼ 18.8%	$11,043.3	$13,601.0
15	Hydro-Quebec	▼ 19.0%	$10,475.0	$12,926.0
16	Quebec Construction Industry	▼ 16.4%	$9,817.0	$11,740.0
17	Air Canada Pension Investments	▼ 17.3%	$9,717.0	$11,747.0
18	Canadian Forces Pension Plan	▲ 11.2%	$7,833.0	$7,043.0
19	Ontario Power Generation Inc.	▼ 18.5%	$7,256.0	$8,900.0
20	Nova Scotia Pension Agency	▼ 19.1%	$6,717.9	$8,300.0
21	General Motors of Canada Ltd.	▼ 27.4%	$6,331.7	$8,717.0
22	Canadian Pacific Railway	▼ 19.6%	$6,083.0	$7,564.0
23	Régime de retraite du personnel d'encadrement	▼ 21.7%	$6,029.0	$7,700.0
24	Province of Newfoundland & Labrador	▼ 23.7%	$5,115.0	$6,705.8
25	Public Service Pension Plan - Alberta	▼ 18.7%	$4,749.5	$5,844.2

Source: Benefits Canada, *Top 100 Pension Funds,* June 2009, www.benefitscanada.com.

vested assets
Contributions to a pension plan that are legally owned by the employee and may be withdrawn prior to retirement and transferred to another registered plan in which the assets are locked in until retirement.

in order to meet their liabilities to their beneficiaries at retirement. With the exception of **vested assets,** which may be withdrawn by an employee and placed into a restricted RRSP, the assets of pension funds are withdrawn only to meet payments to beneficiaries. The risk for pension funds is that their asset growth, which comes from both investment returns and new contributions, will not meet their liabilities to their beneficiaries.

As shown in Table 5–7, the ten largest pension funds in Canada are employer-sponsored by provincial governments for civil servants (e.g., teachers, hospital workers) who usually negotiate a pension plan and its benefits as part of a union contract. Plans may be employer-sponsored, union-sponsored, or jointly sponsored.

defined contribution plan
A pension plan that sets up a separate account for each employee. A certain percentage is contributed each year and is made available to the employee on retirement.

Pensions can be a significant portion of the benefit package of an employee, and may be classified as a **defined contribution plan,** by which an employer contributes a certain percentage each year (e.g., a percentage of profits) for the benefit of the employee whose payments on retirement depend on the amount in the plan, or a **defined benefit plan,** whose payments to employees on retirement are known and employer contributions are determined by actuarial calculations based on factors such as mortality rates and investment returns. A plan's assets are held in trust for the benefit of employees, but **vesting,** which gives the employee the legal right to the funds, may occur after a specified period.

Balance Sheet and Recent Trends

defined benefit plan
A pension plan that pays benefits to retirees based on a formula.

vesting
Granting of a legal right to an employee to receive funds in a pension plan regardless of whether the employee leaves the company or the pension plan is dissolved.

The importance of pension funds as FIs in Canada comes from their ability to hold significant ownership of both corporate debt and corporate equity. This differs from the banks, which are precluded from having significant equity holdings in any one company. Thus, pension funds can be significant lenders to domestic and foreign corporations through investments in corporate bonds. They are also shareholders of domestic and foreign corporations through public share purchases and private placements. The growth of pension funds and their significant contribution to the capital of corporations, both in Canada and the United States, has led to the growth of shareholder activism and the push for pension funds to have representation on companies' boards of directors. Until the limitation was removed in 2005, pension funds could have a maximum of 30 percent foreign assets. Banks had no such limits on their foreign assets.

Figure 5–6 shows how the assets of the top pension funds in Canada changed from 2000 to 2004. Unlike the mutual funds and the hedge funds, the liabilities of the pension funds are easier to forecast. However, liquidity must be balanced with returns to meet their liabilities. The investment in assets also exposes the funds to interest rate risk, market risk, and foreign exchange risk.

The search for returns along with the growth in size of pension fund assets has fuelled professional fund management in Canada. The management styles of pension funds vary from in-house to balanced to specialist. In-house managers accounted for $279.0 billion of the assets, balanced managers for $33.5 billion, and specialist managers for $211.4 billion of the assets of the top 100 pension funds

FIGURE 5–6
Evolving Assets of the Top 100 Pension Funds in Canada, 2000–2004
Source: Benefits Canada, *Pensions Without Borders,* May 2005, p. 21, www.benefitscanada.com.

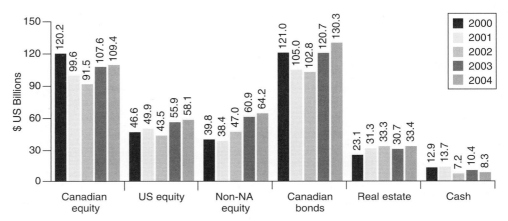

TABLE 5–8   Top 40 Money Managers, 2008

Top 40 Money Managers			As of June 30, 2008 ($ millions)			
			Total Pension Assets		(%)	Total Assets
2008	2007	Company	2008	2007	Change	2008
1	2	Barclays Global Investors Canada Ltd.	51,639.8	51,611.0	0.1%	74,716.1
2	3	TD Asset Management Group	38,746.0	37,692.0	2.8%	149,198.0
3	4	Phillips, Hager & North Investment Management Ltd.	33,894.4	36,091.1	−6.1%	67,277.2
4	5	State Street Global Advisors Ltd.	33,062.3	34,935.6	−5.4%	39,024.8
5	7	Alliance Bernstein Institutional Investments	25,979.0	28,535.0	−9.0%	42,782.0
6	8	McLean Budden Ltd.	25,550.0	27,971.0	−8.7%	37,925.0
7	6	Jarislowsky, Fraser Ltd.	24,089.0	28,783.0	−16.3%	47,791.0
8	9	Greystone Managed Investments Inc.	23,882.1	23,461.0	1.8%	33,116.3
9	11	Addenda Capital Inc.	21,434.0	17,479.0	22.6%	39,323.0
10	10	Connor, Clark & Lunn Financial Group	20,764.0	19,240.2	7.9%	36,469.3
11	13	BNY/Mellon Asset Management Ltd.	15,255.3	14,622.8	4.3%	18,056.0
12	12	Letko, Brosseau & Associates Inc.	14,645.0	14,690.0	−0.3%	24,550.0
13	14	Beutel Goodman & Company Ltd.	14,114.0	14,587.0	−3.2%	15,683.0
14	18	CIBC Global Asset Management	13,543.0	12,288.9	10.2%	65,442.0
15	16	JPMorgan Asset Management	12,446.0	13,137.0	−5.3%	17,029.0
16	22	Bentall	11,461.0	10,128.0	13.2%	17,586.0
17	21	Standard Life Investments Inc.	10,597.0	10,157.0	4.3%	27,852.2
18	17	UBS Global Asset Management Canada	10,556.0	12,604.5	−16.3%	22,978.8
19	19	Franklin Templeton Institutional	10,300.0	11,573.0	−11.0%	17,881.0
20	25	Fidelity Investments Canada ULC	9,085.0	8,557.0	6.2%	53,398.0
21	24	New Brunswick Investment Management Corp.	8,693.8	8,818.9	−1.4%	8,693.8
22	20	Sprucegrove Investment Management Ltd.	8,622.4	11,487.1	−24.9%	10,428.0
23	27	Guardian Capital LP	7,823.5	8,144.2	−3.9%	16,086.3
24	30	Leith Wheeler Investment Counsel Ltd.	7,599.0	7,219.0	5.3%	9,453.0
25	23	Wellington Management Company, LLP	7,441.0	9,565.0	−22.2%	9,929.0
26	29	Fiera Capital Inc.	7,426.3	7,589.1	−2.1%	18,941.8
27	31	Foyston, Gordon & Payne Inc.	6,025.0	7,137.0	−15.6%	13,365.0
28	26	Capital Guardian Trust Co.	5,850.4	8,183.2	−28.5%	7,178.5
29	33	GWL Investment Management Ltd.	5,784.9	6,585.5	−12.2%	16,927.4
30	36	Sceptre Investment Counsel Ltd.	5,683.5	5,493.0	3.5%	9,519.7
31	28	Natcan Investment Management	5,525.0	8,102.0	−31.8%	26,330.0
32	39	Morguard Investments Ltd.	5,381.0	4,727.4	13.8%	7,530.0
33	34	Legg Mason Canada Inc.	5,315.0	6,352.0	−16.3%	10,993.0
34	40	MFC Global Investment Management	5,012.2	4,624.0	8.4%	56,816.3
35	37	Invesco Trimark	4,780.0	5,468.0	−12.6%	40,190.0
36	32	Northwater Capital Management Inc.	4,688.9	6,980.8	−32.8%	5,354.0
37	n/a	Goldman Sachs Asset Management, LP	4,494.0	4,460.0	0.8%	6,888.0
38	n/a	GE Asset Management Canada Company	4,313.3	4,243.2	1.7%	4,386.9
39	35	Brandes Investment Partners, L.P.	4,284.0	6,265.0	−31.6%	11,574.0
40	n/a	Integra Capital Management Corp.	4,126.1	3,143.3	31.3%	4,502.3
		2008 Total:	$ 539,912.2			
		2007 Total:	$ 562,731.7			
		% Variance:	−4.1%			

Notes:

1. As of September 2008, Caisse de dépôt et placement du Québec will no longer be included in the ranking of the Top 40 Money Managers.

2. As of May 2008, Bimoor Inc. will no longer be included in the ranking of the Top 40 Money Managers.

3. Invesco Trimark was formerly listed as AIM Trimark Investments.

4. On April 22, 2008, Addenda Capital Inc. combined its activities with those of Co-operators Investment Counselling Ltd.

5. In addition to assets under management of $7.2 billion, Northwater Capital manages approximately $6.4 billion of beta and currency exposures using swaps and currency forwards where the backing assets are held elsewhere.

Figures in this report are based on responses provided by the survey participants. *Benefits Canada* assumes no responsibility for the accuracy of the data provided.

Source: Carolyn Cakebread, *Top 40 Managers Report: In Sickness and in Wealth,* November 2008, Benefits Canada, www.benefitscanada.com/issuearchive/november2008/top40.pdf.

TABLE 5–9
Revenue and
Expenditures of
Trusteed Pension
Funds over
$10 million in
Canada, 2007
($ billions)

Source: Statistics Canada,
www.statcan.gc.ca.

	2007	Percentage of Revenue
Revenue:		
Employee contributions	$ 11.3	9.1%
Employer contributions	21.4	17.1%
Total contributions	32.8	26.2%
Investment income	38.3	30.7%
Net profit on sale of securities	50.7	40.6%
Miscellaneous	3.1	2.5%
Total non-contributions	92.2	73.8%
Total revenue	$ 124.9	100.0%
Expenditures:		
Pension payments out of funds	$ 33.8	27.1%
Cost of pension purchased	1.0	0.8%
Cash withdrawals	7.2	5.7%
Administration costs	2.8	2.3%
Net loss on sale of securities	1.6	1.3%
Other	3.0	2.4%
Total expenditures	$ 49.4	39.5%

in Canada in 2004. In addition, the assets may be actively or passively managed. Benefits Canada's list of the top 40 money managers in Canada in 2008 is shown in Table 5–8. From the last column, it can be seen that while some managers specialize in pension funds so that their pension assets equal their total assets, most funds manage pensions as well as other funds, earning a return on their investment in employees and their expertise. The largest manager of pension funds is Barclays Global Investors Canada Ltd., which manages $51.6 billion pension assets, 69 percent of the $74.7 billion assets under its management. Other asset managers are a mix of U.S. (e.g., JPMorgan Asset Management) and Canadian (e.g., TD Asset Management Group). The top 40 managers had $539.9 billion assets in 2008, a decline of 4.1 percent from 2007.

Table 5–9 shows the revenue and expenditures of trusteed pension funds in Canada for 2007. Investment income represents 30.7 percent of the total revenue of the funds, a significant source of the long-term growth in assets of the funds. Contributions from employers and employees provided 26.2 percent of revenues. The major expenditures come from cash withdrawals, at 5.7 percent of revenue, and disbursements to pensioners at 27.1 percent. Disbursement to pensioners can be expected to increase over the coming years as the baby boom retires and starts drawing benefits. This demographic shift is of global significance, as it represents a switch from savings to consumption for global capital markets. The funding of the retirement of citizens in developed and developing countries was addressed by the World Bank in 2005, which produced a report recommending a move away from "pay as you go" plans (where current workers pay for the benefits of pensioners) to compulsory contributions of fully funded plans (where workers save part of their earnings). This represents a shift in thinking and the World Bank recommended that, as a significant public policy, countries adopt a five-pillar model of (1) public unfunded savings, (2) private mandatory savings, (3) voluntary savings, (4) a tax-financed safety net, and (5) other supports, primarily non-financial, to ensure that their populations are supported in their retirement.[12]

Regulation

Regulation of pension funds is entirely focused on the best interests of the owners or beneficiaries of the pensions' assets and the regulation, therefore, has not been left to SROs as is the case for mutual funds. Some private pension plans (over 1,000 in 2005) are regulated by and report to OSFI (e.g., Air Canada Pension Plan) and are subject to the Pension Benefits Standards Act of 1985. Others report to provincial or territorial bodies (i.e., Ontario Pension Board). Regulators are concerned with protecting the retirement savings of funds that may be in danger in the event of insolvency or bankruptcy proceedings, such as the reorganization of Air Canada in the early 2000s. OSFI may inspect the funds under its jurisdiction and, as well, provides guidelines for recommended industry practice that focuses on proper governance and accountability, as well as appropriate risk management practices.

CONCEPT QUESTIONS	1. Why are mutual funds and hedge funds primarily self-regulated, whereas pension funds are regulated federally and provincially/territorially?
	2. Compare the investment practices of mutual funds, hedge funds, and pension funds. Why might they differ?

GLOBAL ISSUES

The growth in pension funds worldwide was significant between 2002 and 2007. With an average compound annual growth rate of 22.06 percent, Canada was second only to Australia, which had a growth rate of 27.34 percent. Canada's pension assets in 2007 represented 5.9 percent of the top 300 global pension funds tracked by *Pensions & Investments*/Watson Wyatt as shown in Figure 5–7. Figure 5–8 shows estimates of the relative size of pension funds, mutual funds, insurance companies, official reserves, sovereign wealth funds, and hedge funds globally in 2007. Pension funds at US$22.6 trillion and mutual funds at US$21.8 trillion represent the largest funds. **Sovereign wealth funds,** particularly Abu Dhabi Investment Authority (with assets of US$875 billion in 2007) supplied capital to troubled FIs during the credit crisis in 2008.

sovereign wealth funds
Pools of capital owned by sovereign governments that are managed separately from official reserves.

After growth in total assets at global pension funds of 14.4 percent in 2007, pension funds suffered losses during the credit crisis of 2008. Canadian pension funds showed the worst year on record with assets dropping 15.9 percent for the year. In

---

[12] See *The Economist,* "Second Thoughts on the Third Age," February 19, 2005, pp. 67–68. See also, Robert Holzman and Richard Hinz, *Old-Age Income Support in the 21st Century: The World Bank's Perspective on Pension Systems and Reform,* World Bank, June 2005.

FIGURE 5–7
Percentage of
the Assets of
the *Pensions &*
Investments/Watson
Wyatt World 300
Domiciled in Each
Country

Note: "Other" includes the
following countries: Bel-
gium, Brazil, Chile, China,
Finland, France, India,
Ireland, Malaysia, Mexico,
New Zealand, Portugal, Singapore, South Africa, Spain,
and Thailand.

Source: *Pensions & Invest-*
ments, www.pionline.com.

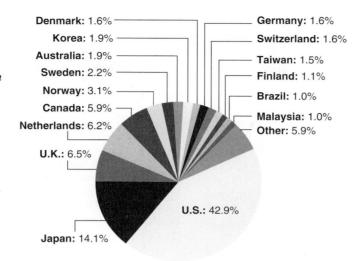

FIGURE 5–8
Relative Sizes of
Funds, 2007

Source: Bank of Canada,
Financial System Review,
December 2008.

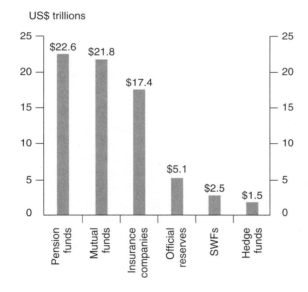

the United States, the top 1,000 funds lost close to US$1 trillion in 2008. Globally, all funds face volatile equity markets and lower interest rates that may hamper their ability to earn sufficient returns on their investments.[13]

---

[13] For information on global and U.S. pension funds, see *Pensions & Investments:* "World's Largest Pension Funds: Global Assets Boom," September 1, 2008, and "Top 1,000 Funds Drop Close to $1 Trillion," January 26, 2009, available at www.pionline.com. For Canadian information, go to the Benefits Canada website at www.benefitscanada.com and see Brooker Smith, *On Guard,* June 1, 2008; Caroline Cakebread, *In Sickness and in Wealth,* November 1, 2008; and Jody White, *Record Losses for Canadian Pension Plans,* January 23, 2009.

Summary

This chapter provided an overview of mutual funds, hedge funds, and pension funds in Canada. Given the growth of savings, particularly retirement savings, in Canada, the amount of assets under administration, and the wealth management provided by FIs to diversify these funds for investors, Canadian and global regulators have focused attention on the activities of these funds and their potential to disrupt global market stability.

Questions and Problems

1. What is a mutual fund? In what sense is it a financial intermediary?

2. What are money market mutual funds? In what assets do these funds typically invest?

3. What are long-term mutual funds? In what assets do these funds usually invest?

4. How might investors' preferences for long-term versus short-term mutual funds have changed since the global market meltdown in 2008?

5. How does the risk of short-term funds differ from the risk of long-term funds?

6. What are the economic reasons for the existence of mutual funds; that is, what benefits do mutual funds provide for investors? Why do individuals rather than corporations hold most mutual funds shares?

7. What are the three possible components reflected in the return an investor receives from a mutual fund?

8. An investor purchases a mutual fund for $60. The fund pays dividends of $1.75, distributes a capital gain of $3, and charges a fee of $3 when the fund is sold one year later for $67.50. What is the net rate of return from this investment?

9. How is the net asset value (NAV) of a mutual fund determined? What is meant by the term *marked-to-market daily?*

10. A mutual fund owns 400 shares of Fiat, currently trading at $7, and 400 shares of Microsoft, currently trading at $70. The fund has 100 shares outstanding.

    a. What is the net asset value (NAV) of the fund?

    b. If investors expect the price of Fiat shares to increase to $9 and the price of Microsoft shares to decrease to $55 by the end of the year, what is the expected NAV at the end of the year?

    c. Assume that the expected price of the Fiat shares is realized at $9. What is the maximum price decrease that can occur to the Microsoft shares to realize an end-of-year NAV equal to the NAV estimated in (a)?

11. What is the difference between open-end and closed-end mutual funds? Which type of fund tends to be more specialized in asset selection? How does a closed-end fund provide another source of return from which an investor may either gain or lose?

12. Open-end Fund A owns 100 shares of Bell valued at $100 each and 50 shares of Toro valued at $50 each. Closed-end Fund B owns 75 shares of Bell and 100 shares of Toro. Each fund has 100 shares of stock outstanding.

    a. What are the NAVs of both funds using these prices?

    b. Assume that in one month the price of Bell stock has increased to $105 and the price of Toro stock has decreased to $45. How do these changes impact the NAV of both funds? If the funds were purchased at the NAV prices in (a) and sold at month end, what would be the realized returns on the investments?

    c. Assume that another 100 shares of Bell are added to Fund A. What is the effect on Fund A's NAV if the stock prices remain unchanged from the original prices?

13. What is the difference between a load fund and a no-load fund?

14. Suppose an individual invests $10,000 in a load mutual fund for two years. The load fee entails an up-front commission charge of 4 percent of the amount invested and is deducted from the original funds invested. In addition, annual fund operating expenses are 0.85 percent. The annual fees are charged on the average net asset value invested in the fund and are recorded at the end of each year. Investments in the fund return 5 percent each year paid on the last day of the year. If the investor reinvests the annual returns paid on the investment, calculate the annual return on the mutual fund over the two-year investment period.

15. Who are the primary regulators of the mutual fund industry in Canada? How do their regulatory goals differ from those of other types of financial institutions?

16. How and why does the regulation of mutual funds, hedge funds, and pension funds differ?

17. What is a hedge fund and how is it different from a mutual fund?

18. What are the different categories of hedge funds?

19. What is the difference between a defined benefit pension plan and a defined contribution pension plan?

20. How are mutual funds, hedge funds, and pension funds different and how does this affect their investment strategies?

Finance Companies

In this chapter, we provide an overview of finance companies, both private and Crown corporations, in terms of

▸ their size, structure, and composition
▸ the services the industry provides
▸ the industry's competitive position
▸ the regulation of the industry
▸ global issues for the industry, including the role of the World Bank

INTRODUCTION

Our discussions so far have moved from highly regulated FIs such as deposit-taking institutions (Chapter 2) to the relatively unregulated hedge funds covered in the last chapter. We now move to finance companies, an industry that, with the exception of the leasing arms of major banks, is unregulated. In addition, since many of the major players are private companies, it is difficult to measure the scope of the industry and its effect on the Canadian and North American economies. However, their role is important for small and medium-sized businesses and in supporting troubled companies. For example, GE Capital provided loans to keep Air Canada flying during its restructuring between 2003 and 2004 and $1.8 billion in refinancing as it came out of bankruptcy, and continued to provide liquidity in 2009.

The primary function of finance companies is to provide consumer lending, business lending, and mortgage financing. Some finance company loans are similar to bank loans, such as consumer and car loans, but others are more specialized, such as aircraft and equipment leasing. The assets of finance companies are subject to credit risk, but this risk is mitigated because their loans are usually backed by collateral. As well, finance companies often lend to customers that banks find too risky. This can lead to losses and even failure if the high risk does not pay off. Since many of their assets are loans for capital expenditures, finance companies are dependent on expansion in the economy for asset growth.

Finance companies differ from banks in that they are not permitted to accept deposits but instead rely on short- and long-term debt (e.g., commercial paper) as a source of funds, often raising these funds in international markets. Their ability to offer loans is therefore affected by their own ability to borrow and, with the right credit conditions, they are able to closely match the maturities of their assets with those of their liabilities, controlling for liquidity risk.

However, the market meltdown in 2008 and the economic slowdown in 2009 resulted in downsizing and reshaping of the industry. The liquidity crisis in 2008 shut off the commercial paper market as a source of funds and many U.S. finance companies converted into bank holding companies, exchanging market liquidity risk for withdrawal risk. Many received funding and guarantees from the U.S.

government. For example, CIT Group, based in New York, was a major lender to small businesses in the United States and to the National Hockey League (Edmonton Oilers, Ottawa Senators), infrastructure projects (roads), and hospitals in Canada. In 2008, CIT became a U.S. bank holding company. As the recession took hold, in 2009, CIT asked the U.S. Federal Deposit Insurance Corporation (FDIC) to guarantee its debt to keep it from having to declare bankruptcy. CIT's request was refused.

Some finance companies suffered as a result of the problems of their parent companies. For example, GMAC Financial, owned by General Motors Corporation and Cerberus Capital Management, is a major provider of car loans and home loans. When credit markets seized up in 2008, GMAC experienced a liquidity crisis, applied for bank status, and received US$6 billion in a bailout from the U.S. government. GMAC Financial now accepts federally insured deposits in the United States and is expected to weather the bankruptcy of GM. On the other hand, GE Capital Corporation, which provides consumer and industrial financing, experienced its own liquidity crisis in 2008, which weakened its parent company, General Electric. GE Capital did not convert into a bank holding company, but received government guarantees. As this book goes to press, it is downsizing and issuing bonds in order to deal with the credit crisis.[1]

SIZE, STRUCTURE, AND COMPOSITION OF THE INDUSTRY

asset-based financing (ABF)/ asset-based lending (ABL)
A loan extended to a borrower based on the assets held as collateral.

structured finance
A unique loan and/or equity financing tailored to meet the specific needs of the borrower.

Crown corporation
A corporation owned by the federal government or by a provincial or territorial government.

Finance companies offer lending services similar to banks, such as mortgages (residential and commercial), loans (e.g., **asset-based financing (ABF)** or **asset-based lending (ABL), structured finance,** consumer loans), equipment leasing (e.g., automobile, aircraft), and credit cards. Finance companies in Canada are dominated by the unregulated institutions that are wholly owned subsidiaries (and therefore private companies) of U.S.-based firms. General Motors Acceptance Corporation of Canada Limited (GMAC Canada) and Ford Motor Credit Company are the financing arms of the automobile manufacturers who provide most of the new car loans in Canada. In addition, there are **Crown corporations** that also offer financing. Both of these types of companies are shown in Table 6–1. In addition, while the major Canadian banks offer some asset-based financing through their commercial lending operations, Canadian Imperial Bank of Commerce (CIBC) formed CIT Business Credit Canada, a joint venture with CIT Group Inc., a large U.S.-based asset-backed lender, in order to compete for the larger deals. There has also been consolidation in the industry. Household Financial, in operation in Canada since 1928, whose assets were in excess of $2 billion (real estate mortgages, private-label credit cards, and personal loans) was taken over by HSBC Financial in 2003. These FIs are much less transparent in their activities, but they are performing more traditional, asset-based lending and providing competition for the large Canadian FIs that were discussed in Chapter 2.

The history of finance companies in North America has been the provision of loans to a clientele that is unable to get credit elsewhere. The first major finance company originated during the Great Depression in the United States when

[1] See Jamie Sturgeon, "Air Canada Boosts Liquidity with $238-Million Loan from GE," *Financial Post,* December 24, 2008, www.financialpost.com. See also Ari Levy, "GMAC Reports Profit on Gains Related to Debt Exchange (Update 2)," *Bloomberg.com,* February 3, 2009, and Rachael Layne, "GE Committed to Keeping Finance Division Intact, Sherin Says," *Bloomberg.com,* July 17, 2009, www.bloomberg.com.

TABLE 6–1
Private and Crown-Owned Finance Companies in Canada, 2008

Source: Company annual reports and websites, and *The Globe and Mail, ROB Magazine,* "The Top 1,000," 2009.

Company	Revenue ($ billions)	Assets ($ billions)
Privately owned:		
CIT Group	n.a.	n.a.
Ford Credit Canada (Dec./08)	$2.598	$11.925
GE Capital Canada*	n.a.	n.a.
GMAC of Canada, Ltd (Dec./08)	3.147	22.522

*GE Capital Solutions reported total assets of US$572.9 billion and revenues of US$71.3 billion globally in 2008.

Bank-owned asset-backed lenders:		
ABN-AMRO a division of ABN-AMRO Bank N.V. based in New York		
CIT Business Credit Canada, a joint venture of CIBC and CIT Group		
Wachovia Asset-Based Lending Group, formerly Congress Financial Corporation of Canada		
HSBC Financial Corporation Limited (formerly Household Financial Corporation), owned by U.K.-based HSBC Bank		
Crown corporations:		
The Business Development Bank of Canada (Mar./08)	$0.863	$11.424
Canada Mortgage and Housing Corp. (Dec./08)	11.985	203.512
Export Development Canada (Dec./08)	1.674	35.256
Farm Credit Canada (Mar./08)	0.972	15.470

www.gmacfs.com

www.fordcredit.ca

www.citgroup.com

www.
gecapitalsolutions.ca

General Electric Corp. created General Electric Capital Corp. (GECC) as a means of financing appliance sales to cash-constrained customers who were unable to get instalment credit from banks. Instalment credit is a loan that is paid back to the lender with periodic payments (instalments) consisting of varying amounts of interest and principal (e.g., car loans and home mortgages). GE Capital has provided loans to Air Canada and airlines worldwide. GE arranges equipment leasing and financing for many other industries, including energy, communications, construction, and real estate.

Because of the attractive rates that finance companies offer on some loans (such as the 0 percent financing offered on new car loans), their willingness to lend to riskier borrowers than banks, their often direct affiliation with manufacturing firms, and the relatively limited amount of regulation imposed on these firms, finance companies have been among the fastest-growing FI groups in North America in recent years. Data collected by the U.S. Federal Reserve show the assets of U.S. finance companies equalled US$2,164.1 billion in 2008 as shown in Table 6–2 and US$104.3 billion in 1977 as shown in Table 6–3, a growth in assets of almost 2000 percent. GMAC Commercial Mortgage Corp. (GMACCM), a subsidiary of General Motors Acceptance Corp. (GMAC) is one of the largest commercial mortgage lenders in the United States, with a mortgage portfolio of over US$370 billion in place. The company announced in the late 1990s that it had plans to expand its product mix to create one of the world's leading "one-stop" commercial finance companies and, in 2002, in line with this global strategy, Mortgage Intelligence, the largest independent **mortgage broker** in Canada, was purchased by GMAC Residential Funding of Canada, a wholly owned subsidiary of GMAC.

mortgage broker
A firm which, for a fee, shops around to other FIs to find the most suitable mortgage at the best rates.

TABLE 6–2
Assets and
Liabilities of U.S.
Finance Companies,
2008

Source: *Federal Reserve Bulletin,* January 2009,
www.federalreserve.gov.

	Billions of U.S. Dollars	Percent of Total Assets
Assets		
Accounts receivable gross	$ 1,740.4	80.4%
Consumer	714.8	33.0
Business	557.0	25.7
Real estate	468.6	21.6
Less reserves for unearned income	(48.7)	(2.3)
Less reserves for losses	(41.0)	(1.9)
Accounts receivable net	1,650.3	76.3%
All other	513.5	23.7
Total assets	$ 2,164.1	100.0%
Liabilities and Capital		
Bank loans	$ 169.2	7.8%
Commercial paper	103.3	4.8
Debt due to parent	326.9	15.1
Debt not elsewhere classified	986.7	45.6
All other liabilities	392.4	18.4
Capital, surplus, and undivided profits	185.7	8.6
Total liabilities and capital	$ 2,164.1	100.0%

TABLE 6–3
Assets and
Liabilities of U.S.
Finance Companies
on December 31,
1977

Source: *Federal Reserve Bulletin,* June 1978, p. A39,
www.federalreserve.gov.

	Billions of U.S. Dollars	Percent of Total Assets
Assets		
Accounts receivable gross	$ 99.2	95.1%
Consumer	44.0	42.2
Business	55.2	52.9
Less reserves for unearned income and losses	(12.7)	(12.2)
Accounts receivable net	86.5	82.9%
Cash and bank deposit	2.6	2.5
Securities	0.9	0.9
All others	14.3	13.7
Total assets	$104.3	100.0%
Liabilities and Capital		
Bank loans	$ 5.9	5.7%
Commercial paper	29.6	28.4
Debt		
Short-term	6.2	5.9
Long-term	36.0	34.5
Other	11.5	11.0
Capital, surplus, and undivided profits	15.1	14.5
Total liabilities and capital	$104.3	100.0%

sales finance institutions
Institutions that specialize in making loans to the customers of a particular retailer or manufacturer.

personal credit institutions
Institutions that specialize in making instalment and other loans to consumers.

business credit institutions
Institutions that specialize in making business loans.

factoring
The process of purchasing accounts receivable from corporations (often at a discount), usually with no recourse to the seller if the receivables go bad.

captive finance company
A finance company that is wholly owned by a parent corporation.

The three major types of finance companies are (1) sales finance institutions, (2) personal credit institutions, and (3) business credit institutions. **Sales finance institutions** (e.g., Ford Motor Credit) specialize in making loans to the customers of a particular retailer or manufacturer. Because sales finance institutions can frequently process loans faster and more conveniently (generally at the location of purchase) than deposit-taking institutions, this sector of the industry competes directly with deposit-taking institutions for consumer loans. **Personal credit institutions** (e.g., HSBC Finance) specialize in making instalment and other loans to consumers. Personal credit institutions will make loans to customers that deposit-taking institutions find too risky to lend to (due to low income or a bad credit history). These institutions compensate for the additional risk by charging higher interest rates than deposit-taking institutions and/or accepting collateral (e.g., used cars) that deposit-taking institutions do not find acceptable. **Business credit institutions** (e.g., CIT Group) are companies that provide financing to corporations, especially through equipment leasing and **factoring,** in which the finance company purchases accounts receivable from corporate customers. These accounts are purchased at a discount from their face value, and the finance company specializes in and assumes the responsibility for collecting the accounts receivable. As a result, the corporate customer no longer has the worry of whether the accounts receivable may or may not be delayed and thus receives cash for sales faster than the time it takes customers to pay their bills. Many finance companies perform more than one of these three services (e.g., GMAC).

The industry is quite concentrated, with the largest 20 firms accounting for more than 65 percent of its assets. In addition, many of the largest finance companies, such as GMAC, tend to be wholly owned or captive subsidiaries of major manufacturing companies. A major role of a **captive finance company** is to provide financing for the purchase of products manufactured by the parent, as GMAC does for cars. In turn, the parent company is often a major source of debt finance for the captive finance company. A benefit of the captive finance company to the parent company is diversification in revenue streams. For example, as the car industry suffered from a lack of sales in the mid-2000s, Ford Motor Credit Company was producing record profits, as much as 80 percent of the overall profits of Ford Motor Corporation. This can also work in reverse. As noted previously, disruptions in the credit markets, particularly the commercial paper markets, stressed the finance subsidiaries as well as the parent company of General Motors and General Electric in 2009.

Table 6–4 lists the top ten U.S. finance companies in terms of total receivables as of 2007. GECC was the largest, with receivables totalling US$496.6 billion. Note that six of the top ten finance companies are subsidiaries of U.S. financial services holding companies. Thus, while banks such as Citibank in the United States and CIBC in Canada cannot make high-risk, high-interest rate loans due to bank regulations that restrict credit risk, banks can indirectly make these loans through a finance subsidiary or joint venture, such as CIBC and CIT Group (refer back to Table 6–1).

In late 2000, Associates First Capital, then the fourth-largest finance company and the largest consumer finance company, was acquired by Citigroup for US$31.1 billion. The acquisition resulted in Citigroup becoming the industry's second-largest receivables financer, with receivables of US$196.8 billion in 2007. A similar bank–finance company consolidation occurred in Canada in 2003 when Household

TABLE 6–4
Largest U.S.
Consumer and
Commercial Finance
Companies, 2007
(US$ millions)[1]

Source: Insurance Information Institute. 2007, www.iii.org.

Rank	Company	Total Managed Receivables[2]
1	General Electric Capital Corporation	$496,634.0
2	Citigroup Inc. (credit card)	196,811.0
3	Bank of America Corporation (credit card)	171,376.0
4	SLM Corporation (Sallie Mae)	165,771.0
5	JPMorgan Chase & Co. (credit card)	157,053.0
6	Ford Motor Credit Co. LLC	148,000.0
7	American Express Company	117,300.0
8	GMAC LLC	100,730.0
9	Capital One Financial Corporation	88,472.6
10	HSBC Finance Corporation	67,513.0

[1] Ranked by total non-mortgage managed receivables. Excludes mortgage and real estate companies.
[2] On-balance-sheet non-mortgage receivables and loans sold that are still serviced and managed.

Financial (which provided consumer loans, credit cards, car finance, and credit insurance) was purchased by the parent of HSBC Bank Canada, HSBC Holdings, a large international bank based in the United Kingdom. As of December 2004, Household Financial changed its name to HSBC Finance Corporation.

CONCEPT QUESTIONS

1. What are the three major types of finance companies? What types of customers does each serve?
2. What is a captive finance company?

BALANCE SHEET AND RECENT TRENDS

Assets

As mentioned above, finance companies provide three basic lending services: customer lending, consumer lending, and business lending. In Table 6–2 we showed the balance sheet of U.S. finance companies in 2008. As you can see, business and consumer loans (called *accounts receivable*) are the major assets held by finance companies, accounting for 58.7 percent of total assets. Comparing the figures in Table 6–2 to those in Table 6–3 for 1977, we see that 95.1 percent of total assets were consumer and business loans in 1977. Since then, finance companies have replaced consumer and business loans with increasing amounts of real estate loans and other assets, although these loans have not become dominant, as is the case with deposit-taking institutions. However, like banks, these activities create credit risk, interest rate risk, and liquidity risk that finance company managers must evaluate and manage.

Table 6–5 shows the breakdown of the industry's loans in the United States from 1995 through 2006 for consumer, real estate, and business lending. In recent years, the fastest-growing areas of asset business have been in the non-consumer finance areas, especially leasing and business lending. In December 2006, consumer loans constituted 40.9 percent of all finance company loans, mortgages represented 30.3 percent, and business loans comprised 28.8 percent.

TABLE 6–5
Finance Company Loans Outstanding, 1995–2006[1] (US$ billions)

Source: Federal Reserve Board, *Flow of Fund Accounts,* various issues, www.federalreserve.gov.

	1995	Percent of Total, 1995	2006	Percent of Total, 2006
Consumer	$ 285.8	41.5%	$ 830.4	40.9%
Motor vehicle loans	81.1	11.8	259.9	12.8
Motor vehicle leases	80.8	11.7	106.0	5.2
Revolving[2]	28.5	4.1	78.2	3.9
Other[3]	42.6	6.2	195.5	9.6
Securitized assets				
Motor vehicle loans	34.8	5.1	118.5	5.8
Motor vehicle leases	3.5	0.5	3.6	0.2
Revolving	n.a.	n.a.	15.9	0.8
Other	14.7	2.1	52.8	2.6
Real estate	72.4	10.5%	616.0	30.3%
One- to four-family	n.a.	n.a.	539.2	26.5
Other	n.a.	n.a.	56.3	2.8
Securitized real estate assets[4]				
One- to four-family	n.a.	n.a.	16.8	0.8
Other	n.a.	n.a.	3.7	0.2
Business	331.2	48.0%	586.0	28.8%
Motor vehicles	66.5	9.6	105.1	5.2
Retail loans	21.8	3.1	17.1	0.8
Wholesale loans[5]	36.6	5.3	55.7	2.8
Leases	8.0	1.2	32.3	1.6
Equipment	188.0	27.3	299.5	14.7
Loans	58.6	8.5	102.4	5.0
Leases	129.4	18.8	197.1	9.7
Other business receivables[6]	47.2	6.8	93.5	4.6
Securitized assets[4]				
Motor vehicles	20.6	3.0	38.0	1.8
Retail loans	1.8	0.3	3.0	0.1
Wholesale loans	18.8	2.7	34.9	1.7
Leases	n.a.	n.a.	0.1	0.0
Equipment	8.1	1.2	15.4	0.8
Loans	5.3	0.8	9.9	0.5
Leases	2.8	0.4	5.5	0.3
Other business receivables[6]	0.8	0.1	34.6	1.7
Total	$ 689.5	100.0%	$2,032.3	100.0%

[1]Owned receivables are those carried on the balance sheet of the institution. Managed receivables are outstanding balances of pools upon which securities have been issued; these balances are no longer carried on the balance sheets of the loan originator.

[2]Excludes revolving credit reported as held by depository institutions that are subsidiaries of finance companies.

[3]Includes personal cash loans, mobile home loans, and loans to purchase other types of consumer goods, such as appliances, apparel, boats, and recreation vehicles.

[4]Outstanding balances of pools on which securities have been issued; these balances are no longer carried on the balance sheets of the loan originator.

[5]Credit arising from transactions between manufacturers and dealers, that is, floor plan financing.

[6]Includes loans on commercial accounts receivable, factored commercial accounts, and receivable dealer capital; small loans used primarily for business or farm purposes; and wholesale and lease paper for mobile homes, campers, and travel trailers.

Consumer Loans

Consumer loans consist of motor vehicle loans and leases, other consumer loans, and securitized loans from each category. Motor vehicle loans and leases are typically the major type of consumer loan. Finance companies generally charge higher rates for automobile loans than do banks. Nevertheless, sometime these rates are lowered dramatically. For example, because new-car sales in the late 1990s and early 2000s were lower than normal, the auto finance companies owned by the major U.S. auto manufacturers slashed interest rates on new-car loans, some to 0.0 percent.

The higher rates finance companies charge for consumer loans are mostly due to the fact that finance companies attract riskier customers than banks. In fact, customers who seek individual (or business) loans from finance companies are often those judged too risky to obtain loans from banks.[2] It is, in fact, possible for individuals to get a loan from a **subprime lender** finance company (a finance company that lends to high-risk customers) even with a bankruptcy on their records. For example, in 1997 Jayhawk Acceptance Corp., one of a group of U.S. finance companies that lent money to used-car buyers with poor or no credit, began marketing loans for tummy tucks, hair transplants, and other procedures. Jayhawk entered into contracts with doctors to lend money to their patients who were seeking cosmetic surgery or some types of dental procedures. Borrowers who paid the loans within a year paid an annual rate of 9.9 percent, but those who repaid within the maximum of two years paid 13.9 percent per year. Left unanswered, however, was what Jayhawk could repossess if a borrower defaulted on a loan. Banks would rarely do this. Most finance companies that offer these types of loans charge rates commensurate with the higher risk, and there are a few **loanshark** companies that prey on desperate consumers, charging exorbitant rates. This has meant that in the past, the industry has had to fight against a reputation for engaging in loansharking and charging usurious rates, a criminal offence in Canada. A class action suit brought against Easyhome Ltd., which sells appliances and furniture on credit, alleged that it charged its customers a **criminal rate** in excess of 60 percent.[3]

Other consumer loans are **payday loans,** which are short-term, small-sum, unsecured loans to people who would not qualify for a bank loan or a bank line of credit. The Canadian Payday Loan Association (CPLA) has a code of ethics and listed 23 companies (e.g., Money Mart) providing loans in Canada in 2009. Its members do not offer Internet services.

Mortgages

Residential and commercial mortgages have become an important component in finance company portfolios. However, since finance companies are not subject to as extensive regulations as are banks, they are often willing to issue mortgages to riskier borrowers than are banks, and they compensate for this additional risk by charging higher interest rates and fees. For example, in 2002, Home Loans Canada (HLC), a subsidiary of CIBC Mortgages Inc., and Household Financial Corporation

---

subprime lender
A finance company that lends to high-risk customers.

loan sharks
Subprime lenders that charge unfairly exorbitant rates to desperate subprime borrowers.

criminal rate
An effective annual rate of interest greater than 60 percent.

www.cpla-acps.ca

payday loans
Short-term, small-sum, unsecured consumer loans.

---

[2] We look at the analysis of borrower (credit) risk in Chapter 11.

[3] Under section 347 of the Criminal Code of Canada, it is unlawful to charge a criminal rate, defined as an effective annual rate of interest that is greater than 60 percent of the amount advanced and including fees, charges, and other expenses. However, recent Canadian court interpretations are modifying this law. See R. Pratt, R. Borins, and D. Salter, "'Unintentionally Usurious' Loans: Canada's Supreme Court Finds a New Way to Put Them Right," *Osler Update,* March 18, 2004, Osler, Hoskin & Harcourt LLP, available at www.osler.com.

high-ratio residential mortgage
A mortgage loan in which the down payment is less than 20 percent.

(now HSBC Financial Corporation Ltd.) provided both first and second mortgages for self-employed entrepreneurs for up to 85 to 90 percent of the value of the home. Because they have an irregular source of income, entrepreneurs have trouble qualifying for a regular or high-ratio mortgage from a deposit-taking institution. Genworth MI Canada Inc. and Canada Mortgage and Housing Corporation (CMHC), a Crown corporation, provide mortgage insurance for **high-ratio residential mortgages;** CMHC also informs consumers about real estate prices, mortgages, and other housing-related issues. FIs (such as banks, credit unions, caisses populaires) that are on the list of CMHC's approved lenders are able to provide mortgages to homebuyers that are insured by CMHC, reducing the default risk for the lender.

lien
A legal charge on real property to secure a loan such as a mortgage loan.

Mortgages include all loans secured by **liens** on any type of real estate. Mortgages can be made directly or as **securitized mortgage assets.** Securitization in mortgages involves the pooling of a group of mortgages with similar characteristics, the removal of these mortgages from the balance sheet, and the subsequent sale of interest in the pool to secondary market investors. Securitization of mortgages results in the creation of mortgage-backed securities (e.g., collateralized mortgage obligations) that can be traded in secondary mortgage markets, as we discuss in more detail in Chapter 27.[4]

securitized mortgage assets
Mortgages packaged and used as assets backing secondary market securities.

Mortgages in the loan portfolio of a finance company can be first mortgages or second mortgages in the form of home equity loans. **Home equity loans** allow customers to borrow on a line of credit secured with a second mortgage on their home.

home equity loans
Loans that let customers borrow on a line of credit secured with a second mortgage on their home.

Business Loans

Business loans represent the largest portion of the loan portfolio of finance companies. Finance companies have several advantages over banks in offering services to small-business customers. First, as mentioned earlier, they are not subject to regulations that restrict the types of products and services they can offer. Second, because finance companies do not accept deposits, they have no bank-type regulators looking directly over their shoulders.[5] Third, being in many cases subsidiaries of corporate-sector holding companies, finance companies often have substantial industry and product expertise. Fourth, as mentioned in regard to consumer loans, finance companies are more willing to accept risky customers than are banks. Fifth, finance companies generally have lower overheads than banks have; for example, they do not need tellers or branches for taking deposits.

The major subcategories of business loans are retail and wholesale motor vehicle loans and leases, equipment loans, other business loans, and securitized business assets. Motor vehicle loans consist of retail loans that assist in transactions between the retail seller of the product and the ultimate consumer (i.e., passenger car fleets and commercial land vehicles for which licences are required). Wholesale loans are loan agreements between parties other than the companies' consumers. For example, GMAC provides wholesale financing to GM dealers for inventory floor plans in which GMAC pays for GM dealers' auto inventory received from GM. GMAC puts a lien on each car on the showroom floor. Although the dealer

---

[4] Mortgage servicing is a fee-related business whereby, after mortgages are securitized, the flow of mortgage repayments (interest and principal) has to be collected and passed on (by the mortgage servicer) to investors in either whole mortgage loan packages or securitization vehicles such as pass-through securities (see Chapter 27). In undertaking this intermediation activity, the servicer charges a fee.

[5] Finance companies do, of course, have market participants looking over their shoulders and monitoring their activities.

pays periodic interest on the floor plan loan, it is not until the car is sold that the dealer pays for the car. These activities extend to retail and wholesale leasing of motor vehicles as well.

Business-lending activities of finance companies also include equipment loans, with the finance company either owning or leasing the equipment directly to its industrial customer or providing the financial backing for a leveraged lease, a working capital loan, or a loan to purchase or remodel the customer's facility. Finance companies often prefer to lease equipment rather than sell and finance the purchase of equipment. One reason for this is that repossession of the equipment in the event of default is less complicated when the finance company retains its title (by leasing). Further, a lease agreement generally requires no down payment, making a lease more attractive to the business customer. Finally, when the finance company retains ownership of the equipment (by leasing), it receives a tax deduction in the form of depreciation expense on the equipment.

www.cfla-acfl.ca

revolver
A credit facility that can be drawn down and repaid over the term of the loan.

term loan
A credit facility that, once it is drawn down, must be repaid according to a schedule set out in the loan agreement.

Companies' Creditors Arrangement Act (CCAA)
Legislation that allows a company that owes its creditors more than $5 million to operate while protected from its creditors while it undergoes restructuring.

The Canadian Finance and Leasing Association (CFLA) estimated that in 2005, the assets of the asset-based financing industry totalled $92.3 billion ($36 billion equipment financing, $14.9 billion business vehicle fleet financing, and $41.4 billion consumer vehicle financing). This means that the industry's assets almost doubled from $50.0 billion in 1996.

Other business loans include loans to finance accounts receivable, factored commercial accounts, small-farm loans, and wholesale and lease paper for mobile homes, campers, and trailers. GMAC Commercial Finance's website also lists credits such as **revolvers** and **term loans,** constructions loans, secured and unsecured credits, and equipment financing. For example, in 2004, GE Commercial Finance, Bank of America, CIT Business Credit Canada Inc., and HSBC Bank Canada arranged a $650 million revolving asset-based facility for Hudson's Bay Company that was secured by the company's merchandise inventory. As well, asset-backed lending and leasing provide a way to extend credit to companies that are in a troubled industry or engaged in bankruptcy proceedings. For example, Stelco, the steelmaker based in Hamilton, Ontario, that entered protection from its creditors under the **Companies' Creditors Arrangement Act (CCAA)** in 2004, was given a $500 million secured loan by Deutsche Bank and CIT Business Credit Canada as part of its 2005 restructuring. (In 2007, Stelco was acquired by U.S. Steel Corp.)

Liabilities and Equity

To finance asset growth, finance companies have relied primarily on short-term commercial paper and other debt (longer-term notes and bonds). Thus, management of liquidity risk is quite different from that in banks that mostly rely on deposits (see Chapter 2). As reported in Table 6–2, in 2008 commercial paper amounted to US$103.3 billion (4.8 percent of total assets), while other debt (debt due to parents and debt not elsewhere classified) totalled US$1,313.6 billion (60.7 percent) and bank loans totalled US$169.2 billion (7.8 percent). Comparing these figures with those for 1977 (in Table 6–3), commercial paper was used more in 1977 (28.4 percent of total liabilities and capital), while other debt (short- and long-term) was less significant as a source of financing (40.4 percent). Finance companies also now rely less on bank loans and commercial paper for financing. In 1977, bank loans accounted for 5.7 percent of total financing. Much of the change in funding sources is due to the strong economy and low interest rates in the U.S. long-term debt markets in the early 2000s. Finally, in 2008, finance companies' capital-to-assets ratio was 8.6 percent, lower than the 14.5 percent in 1977.

To finance assets, finance companies rely on short-term commercial paper, with many having direct sale programs in which commercial paper is sold directly to mutual funds and other institutional investors on a continuous day-by-day basis. For example, in its 2004 annual report, CIT Group Inc. noted that it finances its operations with asset-backed commercial paper in Canada and the United States. As well, it also had bank lines of credit as a backup to the commercial paper borrowings.[6]

Industry Performance

In the early 2000s, the outlook for the industry in North America as a whole was bright. Interest rates were at historical lows. Mortgage refinancing grew, and loan demand among lower- and middle-income consumers was strong. Because many of their potential borrowers had very low savings, no major slowdown in the demand for finance company services was expected. The largest finance companies—those that lend to less risky individual and business customers and with few subprime borrowers (e.g., HSBC Finance)—experienced strong profits and loan growth. (The industry's assets as a whole grew at a rate of almost 8 percent in the early 2000s.) As such, the most successful finance companies became takeover targets for other financial services firms as well as industrial firms. For example, Citigroup acquired Associates First Capital to create the largest full-service financial institution in the United States. In May 2001, American General (the then 13th-largest finance company) was acquired by American International Group (AIG), one of the largest U.S. life insurance companies. Finally, in 2003 Household International was acquired by British commercial bank HSBC Holdings for US$14.9 billion. This acquisition was one of the largest M&As of any kind in 2003. These are just other examples of integration and consolidation among firms in the financial services sector.

Nevertheless, in the mid-2000s, problems for industry participants who specialize in loans to relatively lower-quality customers created large losses in the industry and a very big problem for the U.S. and the global economy. As U.S. home prices fell in 2005 and 2006 and borrowers faced rising interest rates, more people defaulted on their mortgages. At the end of 2006, the percentage of subprime mortgage loans on which payments were at least 60 days late was 14 percent, up from 6 percent in early 2005, and forecasts estimated that 19 percent of subprime mortgages originated in 2005 and 2006 would end in foreclosure. With delinquencies and defaults by borrowers rising, finance companies started a sharp pullback in subprime lending. Originations of subprime mortgages declined 30 to 35 percent in 2007 from 2006, when they totalled approximately US$600 billion, or about one-fifth of the entire U.S. mortgage market. In addition, bank regulators proposed tougher lending standards and regulations. The results were sharply lower values for finance companies. For example, shares of New Century Financial, the number-two subprime lender, plunged nearly 79 percent in early March 2007 after the company said it was facing a criminal probe of its practices by the U.S. Justice Department and its outside auditor said it believed there was substantial doubt about New Century's ability to continue as a going concern. On March 13, 2007,

www.hsbcfinance.ca

---

[6] Lines of credit as a backup for commercial paper became common in Canada in the 1980s when the commercial paper market developed and corporate customers became able to access the capital markets directly. A standby fee is usually charged by the banks to make this facility available to their customers. The freeze in the asset-backed commercial paper markets in 2007 and 2008 required these FIs to switch to another source of short-term financing. See Chapter 27.

the NYSE suspended trading on the company's stock and began steps to delist the company. Fremont General Corp. lost one-third of its value after it announced it would exit the subprime sector due to demands of regulators and market conditions. Other leaders in the subprime mortgage lending market were units of some of the nation's biggest financial services holding companies, including HSBC (the number-one subprime mortgage lender, which took a US$10.6 million charge for bad loans in 2006), General Electric, Wells Fargo, and Washington Mutual.

This crash in the subprime mortgage market, now called the *subprime crisis,* created serious problems in the global economy. The housing boom of the early 2000s held defaults to very low levels because borrowers who fell behind on payments could easily sell their homes or refinance into a loan with easier terms. Further, two-thirds of mortgages were packaged into securities and sold to investors worldwide. That and other innovations made credit cheaper and more available, helping more people to afford a home. But as home prices flattened and dropped, more borrowers fell behind on their mortgage payments. Investors in mortgage-backed securities suffered losses as delinquencies rose. For example, as losses in the subprime mortgage market soared, major banks such as Merrill Lynch and JPMorgan Chase were trying to force mortgage originators to buy back many of the high-risk loans they had bought in 2005 and 2006. The subprime crisis reshaped the global industry. It is discussed in detail in Chapter 27.

CONCEPT QUESTIONS	1. How have the major assets held by finance companies changed over time?
	2. How do subprime lender finance company customers differ from consumer loan customers at banks?
	3. What advantages do finance companies offer over commercial banks to small-business customers?

REGULATION

The U.S. Federal Reserve defines a finance company as a firm (other than a depository institution) whose primary assets are loans to individuals and businesses.[7] Finance companies, like deposit-taking institutions, are financial intermediaries that borrow funds for re-lending, making a profit on the difference between the interest rate on borrowed funds and the rate charged on the loans. Also, like deposit-taking institutions, finance companies are subject to any usury ceilings on the maximum loan rate assigned to any individual customer and are regulated as to the extent to which they can collect on delinquent loans (e.g., legal mechanisms to be followed). However, because finance companies do not accept deposits, they are not subject to extensive oversight by any specific federal or state regulators as are banks—even though they offer services that compete directly with those of deposit-taking institutions (e.g., consumer instalment loans and mortgages). The lack of regulatory oversight for these companies enables them to offer a wide scope of "bank-like" services and yet avoid the expense of regulatory compliance, such as that imposed on banks by the Community Reinvestment Act of 1977, which requires these institutions to keep and file extensive reports showing that they are not discriminating in their lending practices in their local communities.

---

[7] Whereas a bank is defined as an institution that *both* accepts deposits and makes loans.

Further since finance companies are heavy borrowers in the capital markets and do not enjoy the same regulatory "safety net" as banks, they need to signal their solvency and safety to investors.[8] Signals of solvency and safety are usually sent by holding higher equity or capital–asset ratios—and therefore lower leverage ratios—than banks hold. For example, in 2008 the aggregate balance sheet (Table 6–2) shows a capital–assets ratio of 8.6 percent for finance companies. This can be compared to the capital–assets ratio for banks of 4.52 percent reported in Table 2–5 for Canadian banks. Larger, captive finance companies also use default protection guarantees from their parent companies and/or guarantees such as letters of credit or lines of credit purchased for a fee from high-quality commercial or investment banks as additional protection against insolvency risk and as a device to increase their ability to raise additional funds in the capital and money markets. Thus, this group will tend to operate with lower capital-to-asset ratios than smaller finance companies. Given that there is little regulatory oversight of this industry, having sufficient capital and access to financial guarantees are critical to their continued ability to raise funds. Thus, finance companies operate more like non-financial, non-regulated companies than other types of financial institutions examined in this text.

CONCEPT QUESTIONS	1. Since finance companies seem to compete in the same lending markets as banks, why aren't they subject to the same regulations as banks? 2. How do finance companies signal solvency and safety to investors?

GOVERNMENT FINANCING ENTITIES

Crown Corporations in Canada

Additional financing and export-related services to business are provided by the Crown corporations listed in Table 6–1. Crown corporations are government entities that provide complementary services to support business in Canada. None of these firms are large, but they do provide services to areas of the Canadian economy—small and medium-sized businesses, farmers, and home buyers—who may not be served by the other FIs previously discussed, either because they are too small or because they are too risky. Each has a different mandate as discussed below.

Business Development Bank of Canada

www.bdc.ca

venture capital
Business development financing provided in exchange for an equity position and some level of management control.

The Business Development Bank of Canada (BDC) was created in 1944 by an act of Parliament to provide loans to Canadian companies. While its initial focus was on manufacturing, it has evolved over the years into support for small and medium-sized businesses in Canada by providing consulting services, financing, and **venture capital.** In 1995, the Business Development Bank of Canada Act was passed, giving the BDC the mandate to support the development of exporting and technology. For example, during the credit crisis in 2008, the BDC provided additional support and advice for small businesses. Prior to 2008, BDC issued its own short- and long-term debt in the financial markets. This debt was guaranteed by

---

[8] That is, they have no access to the deposit insurance fund or to the central bank discount window (see Chapters 17 and 19). On the other hand, they do not have to pay deposit insurance premiums or meet regulatory imposed minimum capital standards.

the Government of Canada. Since 2008, the BDC has been funded by borrowing directly from the Government of Canada.

Canada Mortgage and Housing Corporation

www.cmhc.ca

The mandate of Canada Mortgage and Housing Corporation (CMHC) is the promotion of housing in Canada. It was formed in 1946 to provide housing for veterans of World War II. Over the years, its mandate has expanded to developing housing programs for low-income housing and first-time homebuyers, as well as support for the quality of housing. CMHC performs a major role by providing mortgage insurance for high-ratio residential mortgages extended by approved lenders under the National Housing Act. CMHC also insures mortgage-backed securities, as discussed in detail in Chapter 27.[9]

Export Development Canada

www.edc.ca

Export Development Canada (EDC) supports companies that are exporting and importing by providing services such as insurance, financing, and bonding, as well as advice on doing business outside of Canada. EDC is different from the other Crown corporations discussed here, as it is self-financing. Its focus is on international business and so it has offices in seven countries that provide local support for Canadian exporters. EDC's business is primarily small and medium-sized exporters, so it provides advice as well as online risk management tools.

Farm Credit Canada

www.fcc-fac.ca

Farm Credit Canada (FCC) completed 50 years in business in 2009. It was created in 1959 to support the agriculture sector in Canada, and reports to the minister of Agriculture. FCC provides services such as loans, life and accident insurance, and venture capital to farmers and others in the agricultural business in Canada, including equipment manufacturers and dealers, sawmills, wholesalers, and processors. Similar to the BDC, as discussed above, FCC came under the Consolidated Borrowing Program in April 2008, which allows it to borrow directly from the Canadian government. Therefore, it no longer issues its own debt.

GLOBAL ISSUES

Because regulations in most foreign countries are not as restrictive as those in North America, finance companies in foreign countries are generally subsidiaries of commercial banks or industrial firms. For those finance companies owned by commercial banks, as the bank goes, so does the finance company. For example, the economic recession in Japan in the late 1990s and early 2000s and the resulting huge volume of non-performing property loans in Japanese commercial banks depleted the banks' capital and restricted their ability to lend to finance company subsidiaries. The result has been some attractive opportunities for others. For example, in January 1999, GE Capital Corporation (GECC) agreed to buy (for US$7 billion) Japan Leasing Corporation (JLC), the Japanese lending unit of Long-Term Credit Bank of Japan, in the biggest acquisition ever involving a Japanese company. GECC bought only the healthy assets of JLC shortly after its parent, Long-Term Credit Bank, was declared insolvent and nationalized because of its huge problems with non-performing property loans. Historically, assets of

---

[9] For an interesting discussion of mortgage insurers and the story of subprime mortgages in Canada, see J. McNish and G. McArthur, "How High-Risk Mortgages Crept North," *The Globe and Mail,* December 12, 2008.

companies such as JLC would never have been acquired by a foreign investor like GECC, but the extreme size of non-performing property loans at Japan's biggest banks restricted their ability to undertake any rescue missions like that of JLC.

An issue related to financial services and global FIs is the development of a sound global financial system, which means sound financial infrastructure, particularly in developing countries. Monetary and technical support for this development is provided by the World Bank Group, an international organization owned by its member countries. The World Bank provides loans, technical assistance, and advice through the International Bank for Reconstruction and Development (IBRD), the International Development Association (IDA), the International Finance Corporation (IFC), the Multilateral Investment Guarantee Agency (MIGA), and the International Centre for Settlement of Investment Disputes (ICSID).

www.worldbank.org

FIs have also recognized that global warming has a potential impact on the value of their financial assets. Institutional investors, including the large global banks and insurance companies, have formed the Carbon Disclosure Project (CDP), which annually requests the FT500 largest companies in the world to respond to a survey regarding their greenhouse gas emissions. Surveys have been completed every year since 2003 and the results made public on the CDP's website: www.cdproject.net.

www.cdproject.net

Summary

This chapter provided an overview of the finance company industry. This industry competes directly with deposit-taking institutions for its high-quality (prime) loan customers by specializing in consumer loans, real estate loans, and business loans. The industry also services subprime (high-risk) borrowers deemed too risky for most deposit-taking institutions. However, because firms in this industry do not accept deposits, they are not regulated to the same extent as are deposit-taking institutions. Because they do not have access to deposits for their funding, finance companies rely heavily on short- and long-term debt, especially commercial paper. Currently, there are concerns about market stability related to the downgrading of GMAC's and Ford Credit's debt, as well as the subprime mortgage crisis and liquidity issues with the commercial paper markets.

Questions and Problems

1. What is the primary function of finance companies? How do finance companies differ from commercial banks?

2. What are the three major types of finance companies? To which market segments do each of these types of companies provide service?

3. What have been the major changes in the accounts receivable balances of finance companies over the 31-year period 1977–2008?

4. What are the major types of consumer loans? Why are the rates charged by consumer finance companies typically higher than those charged by commercial banks?

5. Why have home equity loans become popular? What are securitized mortgage assets?

6. What advantages do finance companies have over commercial banks in offering services to small-business customers? What are the major subcategories of business loans? Which category is the largest?

7. What have been the primary sources of financing for finance companies?

8. How do finance companies make money? What risks does this process entail? How do these risks differ for a finance company versus a commercial bank?

9. How does the amount of equity as a percentage of total assets compare for finance companies and banks? What accounts for this difference?

10. Why do finance companies face less regulation than do banks? How does this advantage translate into performance advantages? What is the major performance disadvantage?

Risks of Financial Intermediation

In this chapter, we introduce the various risks facing FIs that provide the framework for our discussions about the measurement and management of risk in the remaining chapters of the book, including

▸ interest rate risk

▸ market risk

▸ credit risk

▸ off-balance-sheet risk

▸ foreign exchange risk

▸ country or sovereign risk

▸ technology and operational risk

▸ liquidity risk

▸ insolvency risk

INTRODUCTION

"For us, of course, things can change so abruptly, so violently, so profoundly, that futures like our grandparents' have insufficient 'now' to stand on. We have no future because our present is too volatile.... We have only risk management. The spinning of the given moment's scenarios. Pattern recognition."

William Gibson, *Pattern Recognition*[1]

Financial intermediaries are organizations whose job is to find models that will achieve the best risk management, or "pattern recognition," in order to control their future. The pattern recognition takes the form of risk identification and measurement involving the entire organization. For example, the Bank of Montreal has "enterprisewide risk management" that allows it to understand how risks interact. Table 7–1 shows the risks discussed in the financial reports of selected Canadian FIs. The list includes most of those risks identified in the chapter objectives above, as well as additional areas of concern (e.g., environmental risk, reputational risk, regulatory risk). Even though they may not be specifically mentioned, other risks such as off-balance-sheet risk and sovereign risk are considered part of interest rate, liquidity, and foreign exchange risk.

The global issues that we discussed in the first six chapters contribute to the volatile environment for FIs, making it difficult to achieve a major objective of FI management, that is, increasing the returns for the owners. Increased returns often come, however, at the cost of increased risk. By the end of this chapter, you will have a basic understanding of the variety and complexity of risks facing managers of modern FIs. As will become clear throughout the rest of the textbook, the effective management of these risks is central to an FI's performance and, it can be

---

[1] From *Pattern Recognition,* Copyright © 2004 by William Gibson. Used by permission.

TABLE 7–1   Risks Identified by Canadian FIs

	Interest Rate	Market	Credit	Operational	Foreign Exchange	Liquidity	Other
Deposit-Taking Institutions:							
Bank of Montreal	X	X	X	X	X	X	Business, environmental, reputational, strategic
Bank of Nova Scotia	X	X	X	X	X	X	Environmental, reputational
CIBC	X	X	X	X	X	X	Equity, commodity, strategic, reputation and legal, environmental regulatory, model
Desjardins Group		X	X	X	X	X	Insurance
HSBC	X	X	X	X	X	X	Structural, fiduciary
National Bank	X	X	X	X	X	X	Regulatory
Royal Bank of Canada	X	X	X	X	X	X	Insurance
TD Bank	X	X	X	X	X	X	Strategic, regulatory, reputational
Insurance Companies:							
Manulife Financial	X	X	X	X	X	X	Strategic, product
Sun Life Financial	X	X	X	X	X		Insurance, mortality and morbidity

Source: Company annual reports.

argued, the main business of FIs is to manage, not eliminate, risk for themselves and for their customers.[2]

INTEREST RATE RISK

interest rate risk
The risk incurred by an FI when the maturities of its assets and liabilities are mismatched.

Chapter 1 discussed asset transformation as a key special function of FIs. Asset transformation involves an FI buying primary securities or assets and issuing secondary securities or liabilities to fund asset purchases. The primary securities purchased by FIs often have maturity and liquidity characteristics different from those of the secondary securities FIs sell. In mismatching the maturities of assets and liabilities as part of their asset-transformation function, FIs potentially expose themselves to **interest rate risk.**

EXAMPLE 7–1

Effect of an Interest Rate Increase on an FI's Profits When the Maturity of Its Assets Exceeds the Maturity of Its Liabilities

Consider an FI that issues $100 million of liabilities of one-year maturity to finance the purchase of $100 million of assets with a two-year maturity. We show this situation in the following time lines:

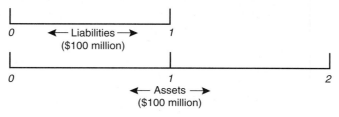

[2] These risks are not necessarily unique to financial institutions. Every global, non-financial corporation faces these risks as well, and managers of these firms must deal with them just as do managers of FIs. The book's website contains an overview of the evaluation of FI performance and risk exposure (Deposit-Taking Institutions' Financial Statements and Analysis). Included are several accounting ratio-based measures of risk. Go to the Online Learning Centre at www. mcgrawhill.ca/olc/saunders.

In these time lines the FI can be viewed as being "short-funded." That is, the maturity of its liabilities is less than the maturity of its assets.

Suppose the cost of funds (liabilities) for an FI is 9 percent per annum and the interest return on an asset is 10 percent per annum. Over the first year the FI can lock in a profit spread of 1 percent (10 percent − 9 percent) times $100 million by borrowing short term (for one year) and lending long term (for two years). Thus, its profit is $1 million (0.01 × $100 million).

However, its profits for the second year are uncertain. If the level of interest rates does not change, the FI can *refinance* its liabilities at 9 percent and lock in a 1 percent, or $1 million, profit for the second year as well. There is always a risk, however, that interest rates will change between years 1 and 2. If interest rates were to rise and the FI can borrow new one-year liabilities only at 11 percent in the second year, its profit spread in the second year would actually be negative; that is, 10 percent − 11 percent = −1 percent, or the FI's loss is $1 million (−0.01 × $100 million). The positive spread earned in the first year by the FI from holding assets with a longer maturity than its liabilities would be offset by a negative spread in the second year. Note that if interest rates were to rise by more than 1 percent in the second year, the FI would stand to take losses over the two-year period as a whole. As a result, when an FI holds longer-term assets relative to liabilities, it potentially exposes itself to **refinancing risk.** This is the risk that the cost of rolling over or reborrowing funds could be more than the return earned on asset investments. During 2008, FIs around the world that had funded their long-term assets with short-term commercial paper or inter-bank funds found that, as the credit crisis intensified, the interest rates on their liabilities increased, reducing their interest rate spreads.

refinancing risk
The risk that the cost of rolling over or reborrowing funds will rise above the returns being earned on asset investments.

EXAMPLE 7–2

Impact of an Interest Rate Decrease When the Maturity of an FI's Liabilities Exceeds the Maturity of Its Assets

An alternative balance sheet structure would have the FI borrowing $100 million for a longer term than the $100 million of assets in which it invests. In the time lines below the FI is "long-funded." The maturity of its liabilities is longer than the maturity of its assets. Using a similar example, suppose the FI borrowed funds at 9 percent per annum for two years and invested the funds in an asset that yields 10 percent for one year. This situation is shown as follows:

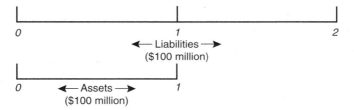

In this case, the FI is also exposed to an interest rate risk: By holding shorter-term assets relative to liabilities, it faces uncertainty about the interest rate at which it can reinvest funds in the second period. As before, the FI locks in a one-year profit spread of 1 percent, or $1 million. At the end of the first year, the asset matures and the funds that have been borrowed for two years have to be reinvested. Suppose interest rates fall between the first and second years so that in the second year the return on $100 million invested in new one-year assets is 8 percent. The FI would face a loss, or negative spread, in the second year of 1 percent (that is, 8 percent asset return minus 9 percent cost of funds), or the FI loses $1 million (−0.01 × $100 million). The positive spread earned in the first year by the FI from holding assets with a shorter maturity than its liabilities is offset by a negative spread in the second year. Thus, the FI is exposed to **reinvestment risk;** by holding shorter-term assets relative to liabilities, it faces uncertainty about the interest rate at which it can reinvest funds borrowed for a longer period. In recent years, good examples of this exposure have been provided by banks that have borrowed fixed-rate deposits while investing in floating-rate loans, that is, loans whose interest rates are changed or adjusted frequently.

reinvestment risk
The risk that the returns on funds to be reinvested will fall below the cost of funds.

In addition to a potential refinancing or reinvestment risk that occurs when interest rates change, an FI faces *market value* risk as well. Remember that the market (or fair) value of an asset or liability is conceptually equal to the present value of current and future cash flows from that asset or liability. Therefore, rising interest rates increase the discount rate on those cash flows and reduce the market value of that asset or liability. Conversely, falling interest rates increase the market values of assets and liabilities. Moreover, mismatching maturities by holding longer-term assets than liabilities means that when interest rates rise, the market value of the FI's assets falls by a greater amount than its liabilities. This exposes the FI to the risk of economic loss and, potentially, the risk of insolvency.

If holding assets and liabilities with mismatched maturities exposes FIs to reinvestment (or refinancing) and market value risks, FIs can seek to hedge, or protect against, interest rate risk by matching the maturity of their assets and liabilities.[3] This has resulted in the general philosophy that matching maturities is somehow the best policy to hedge interest rate risk for FIs that are averse to risk. Note, however, that matching maturities is not necessarily consistent with an active asset-transformation function for FIs. That is, FIs cannot be asset transformers (e.g., transforming short-term deposits into long-term loans) and direct balance sheet matchers or hedgers at the same time. While reducing exposure to interest rate risk, matching maturities may also reduce the FI's profitability because returns from acting as specialized risk-bearing asset transformers are reduced. As a result, some FIs emphasize asset–liability maturity mismatching more than others. For example, banks traditionally hold longer-term assets than liabilities, whereas life insurance companies tend to match the long-term nature of their liabilities with long-term assets. Finally, matching maturities hedges interest rate risk only in a very approximate rather than complete fashion. The reasons for this are technical, relating to the difference between the average life (or duration) and maturity of an asset or liability and whether the FI partly funds its assets with equity capital as well as debt liabilities. In the preceding simple examples, the FI financed its assets completely with borrowed funds. In the real world, FIs use a mix of debt liabilities and shareholders' equity to finance asset purchases. When assets and debt liabilities are not equal, hedging risk (i.e., insulating the FI shareholders' equity values) may be achieved by not exactly matching the maturities (or average lives) of assets and liabilities. We discuss the causes of interest rate risk and methods used to measure interest rate risk in detail in Chapters 8 and 9. We discuss the methods and instruments used to hedge interest rate risk in Chapters 23 through 25.[4]

---

[3] This assumes that FIs can directly "control" the maturities of their assets and liabilities. As interest rates fall, many mortgage borrowers seek to "prepay" their existing loans and refinance at a lower rate. This prepayment risk—which is directly related to interest rate movements—can be viewed as a further interest rate-related risk. Prepayment risk is discussed in detail in Chapter 27.

[4] We assumed in our examples that interest payments are paid only at the end of each year and could be changed only then. In reality, many loan and deposit rates adjust frequently or float as market rates change. For example, suppose a bank makes a one-year loan whose interest rate and interest rate payments are adjusted each quarter while fully funding the loan with a one-year term deposit that pays principal and interest at the end of the year. Even though the maturities of the loan and term deposit are equal to a year, the FI would not be fully hedged in a cash flow sense against interest rate risk since changes in interest rates over the year affect the cash flows (interest payments) on the loan but not those on deposits. In particular, if interest rates were to fall, the FI might lose on the loan in terms of net interest income (interest revenue minus interest expense). The reason for this loss is that the average life of the loan in a cash flow sense is less than that of the deposit because cash flows on the loan are received, on average, earlier than are those paid on the deposit.

<table>
<tr><td>**CONCEPT QUESTIONS**</td><td>
1. What is refinancing risk?
2. Why does a rise in the level of interest rates adversely affect the market value of both assets and liabilities?
3. Explain the concept of maturity matching.
4. Is perfect hedging possible with maturity matching? To what extent is it desirable in view of the asset-transforming function of FIs?
</td></tr>
</table>

MARKET RISK

market risk
The risk incurred in the trading of assets and liabilities due to changes in interest rates, exchange rates, and other asset prices.

Market risk arises when FIs actively trade assets and liabilities (and derivatives) rather than holding them for longer-term investment, funding, or hedging purposes. Market risk is closely related to interest rate, equity return, and foreign exchange risk in that as these risks increase or decrease, the overall risk of the FI is affected. However, market risk adds another dimension resulting from its trading activity. Market risk is the incremental risk incurred by an FI when interest rate, foreign exchange, and equity return risks are combined with an active trading strategy, especially one that involves short trading horizons, such as a day. Conceptually, an FI's trading portfolio can be differentiated from its investment portfolio on the basis of time horizon and secondary market liquidity. The trading portfolio contains assets, liabilities, and derivative contracts that can be quickly bought or sold on organized financial markets. The investment portfolio (banking book) contains assets and liabilities that are relatively illiquid and held for longer holding periods. Table 7–2 shows a hypothetical breakdown between banking book and trading book assets and liabilities. As can be seen, the banking book contains the majority of loans and deposits plus other illiquid assets. The trading book contains long and short positions in instruments such as bonds, commodities, foreign exchange (FX), equities, and derivatives.

With the increasing securitization of bank loans (e.g., mortgages), more and more assets have become liquid and tradable. Of course, with time, every asset and liability can be sold. While bank regulators have normally viewed tradable assets as those being held for horizons of less than one year, private FIs take an even shorter-term view. In particular, FIs are concerned about the fluctuation in value—or value at risk (VaR or VAR)—of their trading account assets and liabilities

TABLE 7–2
The Investment (Banking) Book and Trading Book of a Bank

	Assets	Liabilities
Banking book	Cash	Deposits
	Loans	Capital
	Premises and equipment	
	Other illiquid assets	Other illiquid borrowed funds
Trading book	Bonds (long)	Bonds (short)
	Commodities (long)	Commodities (short)
	Foreign exchange (long)	Foreign exchange (short)
	Equities (long)	Equities (short)
	Derivatives* (long)	Derivatives* (short)

*Derivatives are off-balance-sheet items (as discussed in Chapter 13).

for periods as short as one day—so-called *daily earnings at risk (DEAR)*—especially if such fluctuations pose a threat to their solvency.

To see the type of risk involved in active trading, consider the case of Barings, the 200-year-old British merchant bank that failed in February 1995 as a result of trading losses. In this case, the bank (or, more specifically, one trader, Nick Leeson) was betting that the Japanese Nikkei stock market index would rise by buying futures on that index (some US$8 billion worth). However, for a number of reasons—including the Kobe earthquake—the index actually fell. As a result, over a period of one month, the bank lost over US$1.2 billion on its trading positions, rendering the bank insolvent.[5] That is, the losses on its futures positions exceeded the bank's own equity capital resources. Of course, if the Nikkei Index had actually risen, the bank would have made very large profits and might still be in business.

As the above example illustrates, market, or trading, risk is present whenever an FI takes an open or unhedged long (buy) or short (sell) position in bonds, equities, and foreign exchange (as well as in commodities and derivative products), and prices change in a direction opposite to that expected. As a result, the more volatile are asset prices in the markets in which these instruments trade, the greater are the market risks faced by FIs that adopt open trading positions. This requires FI management (and regulators) to establish controls to limit positions taken by traders as well as to develop models to measure the market risk exposure of an FI on a day-to-day basis. These market risk measurement models are discussed in Chapter 10.

CONCEPT QUESTIONS	1. What is market, or trading, risk? 2. What modern conditions have led to an increase in this particular type of risk for FIs?

CREDIT RISK

credit risk
The risk that the promised cash flows from loans and securities held by FIs may not be paid in full.

Credit risk arises because of the possibility that promised cash flows on financial claims held by FIs, such as loans or bonds, will not be paid in full. Virtually all types of FIs face this risk. However, in general, FIs that make loans or buy bonds with long maturities are more exposed than are FIs that make loans or buy bonds with short maturities. This means, for example, that banks and life insurance companies are more exposed to credit risk than are money market mutual funds and property and casualty insurance companies. If the principal on all financial claims held by FIs was paid in full on maturity and interest payments were made on the promised dates, FIs would always receive back the original principal lent plus an interest return. That is, they would face no credit risk. If a borrower defaults, however, both the principal loaned and the interest payments expected to be received are at risk. As a result, many financial claims issued by corporations and held by FIs promise a limited or fixed upside return (principal and interest payments to the lender) with a high probability and a large downside risk (loss of loan principal and promised interest) with a much smaller probability. Good examples of financial claims issued with these return-risk trade-offs are fixed-income coupon bonds issued by corporations and bank loans. In both cases, an FI holding these claims as assets earns the coupon on the bond or the interest promised on the loan if no borrower default occurs. In the event of default, however, the FI earns zero

---

[5] In 1995 Barings was acquired as a subsidiary of ING, a Dutch bank, and was fully integrated into ING in 2000.

interest on the asset and may lose all or part of the principal lent, depending on its ability to lay claim to some of the borrower's assets through legal bankruptcy and insolvency proceedings. Accordingly, a key role of FIs involves screening and monitoring loan applicants to ensure that FI managers fund the most creditworthy loans (see Chapter 11).

Figure 7–1 presents the probability distribution of dollar returns for an FI investing in risky loans or bonds. The distribution indicates a high probability (but less than 1) of repayment of principal and promised interest in full (point A). Problems with a borrower's cash flows can result in varying degrees of default risk. These range from partial or complete default on interest payments—the range between point A and point B in Figure 7–1—and partial or complete default on the principal lent, the range between point B and point C. Notice, too, that the probability of a complete default on principal and interest (point C) is often small. Nevertheless, because the probability of partial or complete default on bond and loan interest and principal exists, an FI must estimate expected default risk on these assets and demand risk premiums commensurate with the perceived risk exposure. For example, when a business customer applies for a loan, the loan officer must determine whether the default risk is sufficiently low enough to grant the loan and, if so, the interest rate to charge for this risk.

The potential loss an FI can experience from lending suggests that FIs need to monitor and collect information about borrowers whose assets are in their portfolios and to monitor those borrowers over time. Thus, managerial monitoring efficiency and credit risk management strategies directly affect the return and risks of the loan portfolio. Moreover, the credit risk distribution in Figure 7–1 is for an investment in a single asset exposed to default risk. One of the advantages FIs have over individual household investors is the ability to diversify some credit risk away by exploiting the law of large numbers in their asset investment portfolios (see Chapter 1). In the framework of Figure 7–1, diversification across assets, such as loans exposed to credit risk, reduces the overall credit risk in the asset portfolio and thus increases the probability of partial or full repayment of principal and/or interest. That is, the long-tailed downside risk of the return distribution is moderated.

FIs earn the maximum dollar return when all bonds and loans pay off interest and principal in full. In reality, some loans or bonds default on interest payments, principal payments, or both. Thus, the mean return on the asset portfolio would be less than the maximum possible in a risk-free, no-default case. The effect of

FIGURE 7–1

The Probability Distribution of Dollar Returns on Risky Debt (Loans/Bonds)

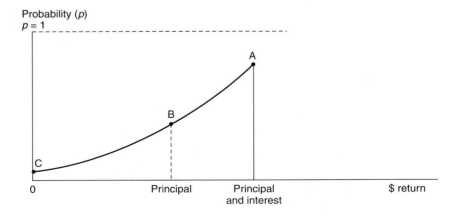

firm-specific credit risk
The risk of default of the borrowing firm associated with the specific types of project risk taken by that firm.

risk diversification is to truncate or limit the probabilities of the bad outcomes in the portfolio. In effect, diversification reduces individual **firm-specific credit risk,** such as the risk specific to holding the bonds or loans of Air Canada, while leaving the FI still exposed to **systematic credit risk,** such as factors that simultaneously increase the default risk of all firms in the economy (e.g., an economic recession). We describe methods to measure the default risk of individual corporate claims such as bonds and loans in Chapter 11. In Chapter 12, we investigate methods of measuring the risk in portfolios of such claims. Chapter 26 discusses various methods—for example, loan sales, reschedulings, and a good bank–bad bank structure—to manage and control credit risk exposures better, while Chapters 23 to 25 discuss the role of the credit derivative markets in hedging credit risk.

CONCEPT QUESTIONS

1. Why does credit risk exist for FIs?
2. How does diversification affect an FI's credit risk exposure?

OFF-BALANCE-SHEET RISK

systematic credit risk
The risk of default associated with general economywide or macroconditions affecting all borrowers.

off-balance-sheet risk
The risk incurred by an FI due to activities related to contingent assets and liabilities.

standby letter of credit (LC or L/C)
An irrevocable credit guarantee that the issuing FI will pay a third party should its customer default on its obligation.

commercial letter of credit
A written undertaking that the issuing FI will pay a third party on the presentation of specified documents evidencing the shipment of goods.

One of the most striking trends for many modern FIs has been the growth in their off-balance-sheet activities and thus their **off-balance-sheet risk.** While all FIs to some extent engage in off-balance-sheet activities, most attention has been drawn to the activities of banks, especially large banks. By contrast, off-balance-sheet activities have been less of a concern to smaller deposit-taking institutions and many insurance companies. An off-balance-sheet activity, by definition, does not appear on an FI's current balance sheet since it does not involve holding a *current primary* claim (asset) or the issuance of a *current secondary* claim (liability). Instead, off-balance-sheet activities affect the *future* shape of an FI's balance sheet in that they involve the creation of contingent assets and liabilities that give rise to their potential (future) placement on the balance sheet. Thus, accountants place them "below the bottom line" of an FI's asset and liability balance sheet. A good example of an off-balance-sheet activity is the issuance of a **standby letter of credit (LC or L/C)** by a bank to support the import activities of one of its customers. For example, the foreign seller of goods to a Canadian importing company may require the importer to provide a standby letter of credit by which the bank guarantees that it will pay for the goods only in the event that its customer defaults. A **commercial letter of credit,** also called a *documentary letter of credit,* requires the bank to pay the foreign seller on presentation of the appropriate documents as specified in the letter of credit. In either case, the bank charges a fee that it includes in its income statement, but does not record the transaction on the balance sheet. Canadian banks show the dollar value of letters of credit in notes to their annual financial statements. The bank will conduct a credit analysis of its customer before issuing the letter of credit but, if the bank pays the commercial letter of credit when the seller of the goods presents the documents and its customer does not pay, the bank may experience a credit loss on the transaction. Thus, a standby letter of credit guarantees payment should a bank's customer face financial problems in paying the promised amount to the supplier. If the customer's cash flow is sufficiently strong so as to pay the supplier directly, the standby letter of credit issued by the FI expires unused. Nothing appears on the FI's balance sheet today or in the future. As a result, the ability to earn fee income while not loading up or expanding the balance sheet has become an important motivation for FIs to pursue off-balance-sheet business. Unfortunately, this activity is not risk-free. If the customer does not pay the supplier, then the contingent liability or guarantee that the FI issued becomes an actual liability that appears on the FI's balance sheet. That is, the FI has to use its own equity to compensate the supplier. Significant losses in off-balance-sheet activities can cause an FI to fail, just as major losses due to balance sheet default and interest rate risks can cause an FI to fail.

Letters of credit are just one example of off-balance-sheet activities. Others include loan commitments and positions in forwards, futures, swaps, and other derivative securities. While some of these activities are structured to reduce an FI's exposure to credit, interest rate, or foreign exchange risks, mismanagement or speculative use of these instruments can result in major losses to FIs. We detail the specific nature of the risks of off-balance-sheet activities more fully in Chapter 13.

CONCEPT QUESTIONS	1. Why are letter of credit guarantees an off-balance-sheet item?
	2. Why are FIs motivated to pursue off-balance-sheet business? What are the risks?

FOREIGN EXCHANGE RISK

Increasingly, FIs have recognized that both direct foreign investment and foreign portfolio investments can extend the operational and financial benefits available from purely domestic investments. For example, the Bank of Nova Scotia invested over $1 billion in Grupo Financiero Inverlat, a Mexican bank, between 1996 and 2004, creating Scotiabank Inverlat. To the extent that the returns on domestic and foreign investments are imperfectly correlated, there are potential gains for an FI that expands its asset holdings and liability funding beyond the domestic border.

The returns on domestic and foreign direct investing and portfolio investments are not perfectly correlated for two reasons. The first is that the underlying technologies of various economies differ, as do the firms in those economies. For example, one economy may be based on agriculture while another is industry-based. Given different economic infrastructures, one economy could be expanding while another is contracting. The second reason is that exchange rate changes are not perfectly correlated across countries. This means the dollar–euro exchange rate may be appreciating while the dollar–yen exchange rate may be falling.

foreign exchange risk
The risk that exchange rate changes can affect the value of an FI's assets and liabilities denominated in foreign currencies.

One potential benefit from an FI's becoming increasingly global in its outlook is an ability to expand abroad directly through branching or acquisitions or by developing a financial asset portfolio that includes foreign securities as well as domestic securities. For example, the removal of the limits on foreign assets in pension funds in 2005 changed the composition of their portfolios and eliminated clone funds and the use of derivatives to circumvent the restriction. Even so, foreign investment exposes an FI to **foreign exchange risk.** Foreign exchange risk is the risk that exchange rate changes can adversely affect the value of an FI's assets and liabilities denominated in foreign currencies.

To understand how foreign exchange risk arises, suppose that an FI makes a loan to a British company in pounds sterling (£). Should the British pound depreciate in value relative to the dollar, the principal and interest payments received by investors would be devalued in dollar terms. If the British pound fell far enough over the investment period, when cash flows were converted back into dollars,

FIGURE 7–2
The Foreign Asset and Liability Position: Net Long Asset Position in Pounds

FIGURE 7–3
The Foreign Asset and Liability Position: Net Short Asset Position in Pounds

the overall return could be negative. That is, on the conversion of principal and interest payments from sterling into dollars, foreign exchange losses can offset the promised value of local currency interest payments at the original exchange rate at which the investment occurred.

In general, an FI can hold assets denominated in a foreign currency and/or issue foreign liabilities. Consider an FI that holds £100 million loans as assets and funds £80 million of them with British pound certificates of deposit. The difference between the £100 million in pound loans and £80 million in pound CDs is funded by dollar CDs (i.e., £20 million worth of dollar CDs). See Figure 7–2. In this case, the FI is *net long* £20 million in British assets; that is, it holds more foreign assets than liabilities. The FI suffers losses if the exchange rate for pounds falls or depreciates against the dollar over this period. In dollar terms, the value of the British pound loan assets falls or decreases in value by more than the British pound CD liabilities do. That is, the FI is exposed to the risk that its net foreign assets may have to be liquidated at an exchange rate lower than the one that existed when the FI entered into the foreign asset–liability position.

Instead, the FI could have £20 million more foreign liabilities than assets; in this case, it would be holding a *net short* position in foreign assets, as shown in Figure 7–3. Under this circumstance, the FI is exposed to foreign exchange risk if the pound appreciates against the dollar over the investment period. This occurs because the value of its British pound liabilities in dollar terms rose faster than the return on its pound assets. Consequently, to be approximately hedged, the FI must match its assets and liabilities in each foreign currency.

Note that the FI is fully hedged only if we assume that it holds foreign assets and liabilities of exactly the same maturity.[6] Consider what happens if the FI matches the size of its foreign currency book (British pound assets = British pound liabilities = £100 million in that currency) but mismatches the maturities so that the pound sterling assets are of six-month maturity and the liabilities are of three-month maturity. The FI would then be exposed to foreign interest rate risk—the risk that British interest rates would rise when it has to roll over its £100 million in CD liabilities at the end of the third month. Consequently, an FI that matches both the size and maturities of its exposure in assets and liabilities of a given currency is hedged, or immunized, against foreign currency and foreign interest rate risk. To the extent that FIs mismatch their portfolio and maturity exposures in different

---

[6] Technically speaking, hedging requires matching the durations (average lives of assets and liabilities) rather than simple maturities (see Chapter 9).

currency assets and liabilities, they face both foreign currency and foreign interest rate risks. As already noted, if foreign exchange rate and interest rate changes are not perfectly correlated across countries, an FI can diversify away part, if not all, of its foreign currency risk. We discuss the measurement and evaluation of an FI's foreign currency risk exposure in depth in Chapter 14.

CONCEPT QUESTIONS	1. Explain why the returns on domestic and foreign portfolio investments are not, in general, perfectly correlated. 2. A bank is net long in European assets. If the euro appreciates against the dollar, will the bank gain or lose? 3. A bank is net short in European assets. If the euro appreciates against the dollar, will the bank gain or lose?

COUNTRY OR SOVEREIGN RISK

country or **sovereign risk**
The risk that repayments from foreign borrowers may be interrupted because of interference from foreign governments.

As we noted in the previous section, a globally oriented FI that mismatches the size and maturities of its foreign assets and liabilities is exposed to foreign currency and foreign interest rate risks. Even beyond these risks, and even when investing in dollars, holding assets in a foreign country can expose an FI to an additional type of foreign investment risk called **country** or **sovereign risk.** Country or sovereign risk is a different type of credit risk that is faced by an FI that purchases assets such as the bonds and loans of foreign corporations. For example, when a domestic corporation is unable or unwilling to repay a loan, an FI usually has recourse to the domestic bankruptcy courts and eventually may recoup at least a portion of its original investment when the assets of the defaulted firm are liquidated or restructured. By comparison, a foreign corporation may be unable to repay the principal or interest on a loan even if it would like to. Most commonly, the government of the country in which the corporation is headquartered may prohibit or limit debt payments because of foreign currency shortages and adverse political reasons.

For example, in 1982, the Mexican and Brazilian governments announced a debt moratorium (i.e., a delay in their debt repayments) to Western creditors. The large global banks had made substantial loans to these countries and their government-owned corporations (such as Pemex, the Mexican state-run oil company). As a result, banks such as the Royal Bank of Canada and the Bank of Nova Scotia eventually had to make additions to their loan loss reserves to meet expected losses on these loans. More recently, Canadian, U.S., European, and Japanese banks had enhanced sovereign risk exposures to countries such as Argentina, Russia, Thailand, South Korea, Malaysia, and Indonesia. Financial support given to these countries by the International Monetary Fund (IMF), the World Bank, and the U.S., Japanese, and European governments enabled the banks to avoid the full extent of the losses that were possible. Nevertheless, Indonesia had to declare a moratorium on some of its debt repayments, and Russia defaulted on payments on its short-term government bonds. In 1999, some banks agreed to settle their claims with the Russian government, receiving less than five cents for every dollar owed them. In 2001, the government of Argentina, which had pegged its peso to the dollar on a one-to-one basis since the early 1990s, had to default on its government debt largely because of an overvalued peso and the adverse effect this had on its exports and foreign currency earnings. In December 2001, Argentina ended up defaulting on US$130 billion in government-issued debt and, in 2002, passed legislation that led to defaults on US$30 billion of corporate debt owed to foreign creditors. Argentina's economic problems continued into 2003; in September 2003 it defaulted on a US$3 billion loan repayment to the IMF.

In the event of such restrictions, reschedulings, or outright prohibitions on the payment of debt obligations by sovereign governments, the FI claimholder has little, if any, recourse to the local bankruptcy courts or an international civil claims court. The major leverage available to an FI to ensure or increase repayment probabilities and amounts is its control over the future supply of loans or funds to the country concerned. However, such leverage may be very weak in the face of a country's collapsing currency and government. Chapter 15 discusses how country or sovereign risk is measured and considers possible financial market solutions to the country risk exposure problems of a globally oriented FI.

| **CONCEPT QUESTIONS** | 1. Can a bank be subject to sovereign risk if it lends only to the highest-quality foreign corporations? |
| | 2. What is one major way an FI can discipline a country that threatens not to repay its loans? |

TECHNOLOGY AND OPERATIONAL RISKS

www.bis.org

Technology and operational risks are closely related and in recent years have caused great concern to FI managers and regulators alike. The Bank for International Settlements (BIS), the principal organization of central banks of the major economies of the world, defines operational risk (inclusive of technological risk) as "the risk of loss resulting from inadequate or failed internal processes, people, and systems or from external events."[7] A number of FIs add reputational risk and strategic risk (e.g., due to a failed merger) as part of a broader definition of operational risk.

Technological innovation has been a major growth area of FIs in recent years. In the 1990s and 2000s, banks, insurance companies, and investment companies all sought to improve operational efficiency with major investments in internal and external communications, computers, and an expanded technological infrastructure. For example, most Canadian FIs provide depositors with the capability to check account balances, transfer funds between accounts, manage finances, pay bills, and perform other functions from their home personal computers. The clearing of both electronic funds and paper-based transactions is conducted through the national clearing and settlement system that is operated by the Canadian Payments Associations (CPA). The Automated Clearing Settlement System (ACSS) clears cheques, wire transfers, direct deposits, pre-authorized debits, bill payments, and point-of-sale transactions, while the Large Value Transfer System (LVTS), the first of its kind in the world, provides real-time transfer of irrevocable payments across Canada.

---

[7] See Basel Committee on Bank Supervision, *Sound Practices for the Management and Supervision of Operational Risk,* July 2002, p. 2, Basel, Switzerland.

economies of scale
The degree to which an FI's average unit costs of producing financial services fall as its outputs of services increase.

economies of scope
The degree to which an FI can generate cost synergies by producing multiple financial service products.

technology risk
The risk incurred by an FI when technological investments do not produce the cost savings anticipated.

operational risk
The risk that existing technology or support systems may malfunction or break down.

The major objectives of technological expansion are to lower operating costs, increase profits, and capture new markets for the FI. In current terminology, the objective is to allow the FI to exploit, to the fullest extent possible, better potential economies of scale and economies of scope in selling its products. **Economies of scale** refer to an FI's ability to lower its average costs of operations by expanding its output of financial services. **Economies of scope** refer to an FI's ability to generate cost synergies by producing more than one output with the same inputs. For example, an FI could use the same information on the quality of customers stored in its computers to expand the sale of both loan products and insurance products. That is, the same information (e.g., age, job, size of family, income) can identify both potential loan and life insurance customers. The attempt to better exploit such economies of scope lies behind mega-mergers such as that of Manulife Financial with John Hancock. In addition to enhancing global competitiveness by increasing their size, economies of scale and economies of scope are given as consideration when potential mergers of financial institutions, particularly among the Big Six banks and also between banks and insurance companies, are discussed in Canada.

Technology risk occurs when technological investments do not produce the anticipated cost savings in the form of either economies of scale or scope. Diseconomies of scale, for example, arise because of excess capacity, redundant technology, and/or organizational and bureaucratic inefficiencies (red tape) that become worse as an FI grows in size. Diseconomies of scope arise when an FI fails to generate perceived synergies or cost savings through major new technology investments. We describe the measurement and evidence of economies of scale and scope in FIs in Chapter 16. Technological risk can result in major losses in the competitive efficiency of an FI and, ultimately, in its long-term failure. Similarly, gains from technological investments can produce performance superior to an FI's rivals as well as allow it to develop new and innovative products, enhancing its long-term survival chances.

Operational risk is partly related to technology risk and can arise whenever existing technology malfunctions or back-office support systems break down. For example, the summer of 2004 saw a string of computer glitches that affected customer accounts and transactions at three major banks. In June, a programming error at the Royal Bank of Canada held up millions of customer transactions from coast to coast for a week. A claims adjuster was hired to sort out the problem. In July, a computer malfunction created duplicate debits and over 60,000 customers at the Canadian Imperial Bank of Commerce overdrew their accounts. At TD Bank, a computer problem made automated teller machines and online banking unavailable to customers for three hours. Even though such computer breakdowns are rare, their occurrence can cause major dislocations in the FIs involved and potentially disrupt the financial system in general.

Operational risk is not exclusively the result of technological failure. For example, employee fraud and errors constitute a type of operational risk that often negatively affects the reputation of an FI (see Chapter 16). For example, human error at the Canadian Imperial Bank of Commerce in 2004 resulted in the much-publicized scandal of confidential customer information being faxed to a scrapyard dealer in the United States. This incident led to an investigation by the Privacy Commissioner. Fraudulent activities and human errors by employees result in an overall loss of reputation and, in turn, loss of business.

CONCEPT QUESTIONS	1. What is the difference between economies of scale and economies of scope?
	2. How is operational risk related to technology risk?
	3. How does technological expansion help an FI better exploit economies of scale and economies of scope? When might technology risk interfere with these goals?

LIQUIDITY RISK

liquidity risk
The risk that a sudden surge in liability withdrawals may leave an FI in a position of having to liquidate assets in a very short period of time and at low prices.

Liquidity risk arises when an FI's liability holders, such as depositors or insurance policyholders, demand immediate cash for the financial claims they hold with an FI or when holders of off-balance-sheet loan commitments (or credit lines) suddenly exercise their right to borrow (draw down their loan commitments). When liability holders demand cash immediacy—that is, "put" their financial claims back to the FI—the FI must either borrow additional funds or sell assets to meet the demand for the withdrawal of funds. The most liquid asset of all is cash, which FIs can use to directly meet liability holders' demands to withdraw funds. Although FIs limit their cash asset holdings because cash earns no interest, low cash holdings are usually not a problem. Day-to-day withdrawals by liability holders are generally predictable, and FIs can normally expect to borrow additional funds to meet any sudden shortfalls of cash on the money and financial markets.

However, there are times when an FI can face a liquidity crisis. Because of a lack of confidence by liability holders in the FI or some unexpected need for cash, liability holders may demand *larger* withdrawals than normal. When all, or many, FIs face abnormally large cash demands, the cost of additional purchased or borrowed funds rises and the supply of such funds becomes restricted. As a consequence, FIs may have to sell some of their less-liquid assets to meet the withdrawal demands of liability holders. This results in a more serious liquidity risk, especially as some assets with "thin" markets generate lower prices when the asset sale is immediate than when the FI has more time to negotiate the sale of an asset. As a result, the liquidation of some assets at low or fire-sale prices (the price an FI receives if an asset must be liquidated immediately at less than its fair market value) could threaten an FI's profitability and solvency. Good examples of such illiquid assets are bank loans to small firms. Such serious liquidity problems may eventually result in a run in which all liability claimholders seek to withdraw their funds simultaneously from the FI because they fear that it will be unable to meet their demands for cash in the near future. This turns the FI's liquidity problem into a solvency problem and can cause it to fail.[8]

We examine the nature of normal, abnormal, and run-type liquidity risks and their impact on banks, insurance companies, and other FIs in more detail in Chapter 17. In addition, we look at ways an FI can better manage liquidity and liability risk exposures in Chapter 18. Chapter 19 discusses the roles of deposit insurance and other liability guarantee schemes in deterring deposit (liability) runs.

---

[8] The 2008 global credit crisis resulted in runs on banks in the United Kingdom (Northern Rock) and the United States (Countrywide Financial) and disrupted money markets, causing hedge funds and other FIs funded with short-term commercial paper to search for other sources of funding. As well, the global inter-bank markets were affected, as FIs lost confidence in each other's stability and refused to lend overnight. The spreads on LIBOR increased as a result. See the Bank of Canada *Financial System Review,* December 2008, and the International Monetary Fund, *Global Financial Stability Report,* October 2008, for discussions of the global financial crisis.

1. Why might an FI face a sudden liquidity crisis?
2. What circumstances might lead an FI to liquidate assets at fire-sale prices?

INSOLVENCY RISK

insolvency risk
The risk that an FI may not have enough capital to offset a sudden decline in the value of its assets relative to its liabilities.

Insolvency risk is a consequence or outcome of one or more of the risks described above: interest rate, market, credit, off-balance-sheet, technology, foreign exchange, sovereign, and liquidity risks. Technically, insolvency occurs when the capital or equity resources of an FI's owners are driven to, or near to, zero because of losses incurred as the result of one or more of the risks described above. Consider the failures of the Canadian Commercial Bank (CCB) and the Northland Bank of Canada (NBC) in 1985. Both concentrated their operations in western Canada, investing in oil and gas, and real estate loans. A decline in the Canadian dollar and increases in interest rates caused the loan portfolios of both banks to deteriorate and led to difficulties in rolling over deposits (liquidity risk). Despite interim support from the other chartered banks and borrowings from the Bank of Canada, the capital of both banks deteriorated (solvency risk) and they eventually were allowed to fail. Similarly, in 1984, a U. S. bank, Continental Illinois National Bank and Trust Company, experienced defaults of its loans to the oil and gas sector and became unable to obtain funding; U.S. federal regulators assumed control.[9]

In 2008 and 2009, liquidity problems resulting from the ongoing credit crisis led to insolvency and caused the failure of U.S. investment banks (e.g., Lehman Brothers). Globally, the threat to global financial stability that would result from the failure of large FIs has led regulators to nationalize banks by purchasing their preferred and common shares. Canadian banks suffered losses in 2008, but the Canadian financial system was remarkably stable throughout 2008. In general, the more equity capital to borrowed funds an FI has—that is, the lower its leverage—the better able it is to withstand losses, whether due to adverse interest rate changes, unexpected credit losses, or other reasons. Thus, both management and regulators of FIs focus on an FI's capital (and adequacy) as a key measure of its ability to remain solvent and grow in the face of a multitude of risk exposures. The issue of what is an adequate level of capital to manage an FI's overall risk exposure is discussed in Chapter 20.

1. When does insolvency risk occur?
2. How is insolvency risk related to the other risks discussed in this chapter?

OTHER RISKS AND THE INTERACTION OF RISKS

In this chapter we have concentrated on ten major risks that continuously impact an FI manager's decision-making process and risk management strategies. These risks were interest rate risk, market risk, credit risk, off-balance-sheet risk, technology

---

[9] See J. F. Dingle, *Planning an Evolution: The Story of the Canadian Payments Association, 1980–2002,* May 2003, The Bank of Canada and The Canadian Payments Association, Chapter 5, and I. Swary, "The Stock Market Reaction to Regulatory Action in the Continental Illinois Crisis," *Journal of Business,* 3, 1986, pp. 451–474.

risk, operational risk, foreign exchange risk, country or sovereign risk, liquidity risk, and insolvency risk. Even though the discussion described each independently, in reality, these risks are often interdependent. For example, when interest rates rise, corporations and consumers find maintaining promised payments on their debt more difficult.[10] Thus, over some range of interest rate movements, credit, interest rate, and off-balance-sheet risks are positively correlated. Furthermore, the FI may have been counting on the funds from promised payments on its loans for liquidity management purposes. Thus, liquidity risk is also correlated with interest rate and credit risks. The inability of a customer to make promised payments also affects the FI's income and profits and, consequently, its equity or capital position. Thus, each risk and its interaction with other risks ultimately affects solvency risk. Similarly, foreign exchange rate changes and interest rate changes are also highly correlated. When the Bank of Canada changes a key interest rate (such as the target overnight rate) through its monetary policy actions, exchange rates are also likely to change.

Various other risks, often of a more discrete or event type, also impact an FI's profitability and risk exposure, although, as noted earlier, many view discrete or event risks as part of operational risks. Discrete risks might include events external to the FI, such as a sudden change in taxation. Such changes can affect the attractiveness of some types of assets over others, as well as the liquidity of an FI's balance sheet.

Changes in regulatory policy constitute another type of external, discrete, or event risk. These include lifting the regulatory barriers to lending or to entry or on products offered (see Chapter 21). Other discrete or event risks involve sudden and unexpected changes in financial market conditions due to war, revolution, or sudden market collapse, such as the 1929 and 1987 stock market crashes or the September 2001 terrorist attacks in the United States. These can have a major impact on an FI's risk exposure. Other event risks include fraud, theft, earthquakes, storms, malfeasance, and breach of fiduciary trust; all of these can ultimately cause an FI to fail or be severely harmed. Yet each is difficult to model and predict.

Finally, more general macroeconomic or systematic risks, such as increased inflation, inflation volatility, and unemployment, can directly and indirectly impact an FI's level of interest rate, credit, and liquidity risk exposure. For example, inflation was very volatile in the 1979–1982 period in Canada and the United States. Interest rates reflected this volatility. During periods in which FIs face high and volatile inflation and interest rates, interest rate risk exposure from mismatching balance sheet maturities tends to rise. Credit risk exposure also rises because borrowing firms with fixed-price product contracts often find it difficult to keep up their loan payments when inflation and interest rates rise abruptly. As well, consumers facing unemployment are more likely to default on their mortgages, consumer loans, and credit card payments.

| **CONCEPT QUESTIONS** | 1. What is meant by the term *event risk*? |
| | 2. What are some examples of event and general macroeconomic risks that impact FIs? |

---

[10] Rising interest rates may also negatively impact derivative contract holders, who may then be inclined to default. This credit risk on derivatives is often called *counterparty risk*.

Summary

This chapter provided an introductory view of ten major risks faced by modern FIs. They face *interest rate risk* when their assets and liabilities maturities are mismatched. They incur *market risk* on their trading assets and liabilities if there are adverse movements in interest rates, exchange rates, or other asset prices. They face *credit risk* or default risk if their clients default on their loans and other obligations. Modern-day FIs also engage in a significant number of off-balance-sheet activities that expose them to *off-balance-sheet risks:* contingent asset and liability risks. The advent of sophisticated technology and automation exposes FIs to both *technological risk* and *operational risk*. If FIs conduct foreign business, they are subject to additional risks, namely *foreign exchange* and *sovereign risks. Liquidity risk* is a result of a serious run on an FI because of excessive withdrawals or problems in refinancing. Finally, *insolvency risk* occurs when an FI's capital is insufficient to withstand a decline in the value of assets relative to liabilities. However, even though we treat these risks at times as stand-alone, risk management for financial institutions involves focusing on enterprisewide risk management. The effective management of risks determines the future success or failure of a modern FI. The chapters that follow analyze each of these risks in greater detail.

Questions and Problems

1. What is the process of *asset transformation* performed by a financial institution? Why does this process often lead to the creation of *interest rate risk?* What is interest rate risk?

2. What is *refinancing risk?* How is refinancing risk part of interest rate risk? If an FI funds long-term assets with short-term liabilities, what will be the impact on earnings of an increase in the rate of interest? A decrease in the rate of interest?

3. What is *reinvestment risk?* How is reinvestment risk part of interest rate risk? If an FI funds short-term assets with long-term liabilities, what will be the impact on earnings of a decrease in the rate of interest? An increase in the rate of interest?

4. The sales literature of a mutual fund claims that the fund has no risk exposure since it invests exclusively in federal government securities that are free of default risk. Is this claim true? Explain why or why not.

5. How can interest rate risk adversely affect the economic or market value of an FI?

6. A financial institution has the following balance sheet structure:

Assets	
Cash	$ 1,000
Bond	10,000
Total assets	$ 11,000
Liabilities and Equity	
Term deposit	$ 10,000
Equity	1,000
Total liabilities and equity	$ 11,000

The bond has a 10-year maturity and a fixed-rate coupon of 10 percent. The term deposit has a 1-year maturity and a 6 percent fixed rate of interest. The FI expects no additional asset growth.

a. What will be the net interest income at the end of the first year? *Note:* Net interest income equals interest income minus interest expense.

b. If at the end of year 1, market interest rates have increased 100 basis points (1 percent), what will be the net interest income for the second year? Is this result caused by reinvestment risk or refinancing risk?

c. Assuming that market interest rates increase 1 percent, the bond will have a value of $9,446 at the end of year 1. What will be the market value of equity for the FI?

d. If market interest rates had decreased 100 basis points by the end of year 1, would the market value of equity be higher or lower than $1,000? Why?

e. What factors have caused the changes in operating performance and market value for this firm?

7. How does the policy of matching the maturities of assets and liabilities work (a) to minimize interest rate risk and (b) against the asset-transformation function of FIs?

8. Corporate bonds usually pay interest semiannually. If a company decided to change from semiannual to annual interest payments, how would this affect the bond's interest rate risk?

9. Two 10-year bonds are being considered for an investment that may have to be liquidated before the maturity of the bonds. The first bond is a 10-year

premium bond with a coupon rate higher than its required rate of return, and the second bond is a zero-coupon bond that pays only a lump-sum payment after 10 years with no interest over its life. Which bond would have more interest rate risk? That is, which bond's price would change by a larger amount for a given change in interest rates? Explain your answer.

10. Consider again the two bonds in problem 9. If the investment goal is to leave the assets untouched until maturity, such as for a child's education or for one's retirement, which of the two bonds has more interest rate risk? What is the source of this risk?

11. A mutual fund bought $1,000,000 of two-year government notes six months ago. During this time, the value of the securities has increased, but for tax reasons the mutual fund wants to postpone any sale for two more months. What type of risk does the mutual fund face for the next two months?

12. A bank invested $50 million in a two-year asset paying 10 percent interest per annum and simultaneously issued a $50 million, one-year liability paying 8 percent interest per annum. What will be the impact on the bank's net interest income if at the end of the first year all interest rates have increased by 1 percent (100 basis points)?

13. What is *market risk?* How does this risk affect the operating performance of financial institutions? What actions can be taken by an FI's management to minimize the effects of this risk?

14. What is *credit risk?* Which types of FIs are more susceptible to this type of risk? Why?

15. What is the difference between *firm-specific credit risk* and *systematic credit risk?* How can an FI alleviate firm-specific credit risk?

16. Many banks and savings institutions that failed in the 1980s in the United States had made loans to oil companies in Louisiana, Texas, and Oklahoma. When oil prices fell, these companies, the regional economy, and the banks and savings institutions all experienced financial problems. What types of risk were inherent in the loans that were made by these banks and savings institutions?

17. What is the nature of an off-balance-sheet activity? How does an FI benefit from such activities? Identify the various risks that these activities generate for an FI, and explain how these risks can create varying degrees of financial stress for the FI at a later time.

18. What two factors provide potential benefits to FIs that expand their asset holdings and liability funding sources beyond their domestic borders?

19. What is *foreign exchange risk?* What does it mean for an FI to be *net long* in foreign assets? What does it mean for an FI to be *net short* in foreign assets? In each case, what must happen to the foreign exchange rate to cause the FI to suffer losses?

20. If the euro is expected to depreciate in the near future, would a Canadian-based FI in Paris prefer to be net long or net short in the euro in its asset positions? Discuss.

21. If international capital markets are well integrated and operate efficiently, will FIs be exposed to foreign exchange risk? What are the sources of foreign exchange risk for FIs?

22. If an FI has the same amount of foreign assets and foreign liabilities in the same currency, has that FI necessarily reduced to zero the risk involved in these international transactions? Explain.

23. An insurance company invests $1 million in a private placement of British bonds. Each bond pays £300 in interest per year for 20 years. If the current exchange rate is £1.7612/$, what is the nature of the insurance company's exchange rate risk? Specifically, what type of exchange rate movement concerns this insurance company?

24. Assume that a bank has assets located in London that are worth £150 million on which it earns an average of 8 percent per year. The bank has £100 million in liabilities on which it pays an average of 6 percent per year. The current spot rate is £1.50/$.

    a. If the exchange rate at the end of the year is £2.00/$, will the dollar have appreciated or depreciated against the pound?

    b. Given the change in the exchange rate, what is the effect in dollars on the net interest income from the foreign assets and liabilities? *Note:* The net interest income is interest income minus interest expense.

    c. What is the effect of the exchange rate change on the value of assets and liabilities in dollars?

25. Six months ago, Qualitybank, Ltd., issued a US$100 million, one-year maturity CD denominated in euros. On the same date, US$60 million was invested in a € denominated loan and US$40 million was invested in a U.S. Treasury bill. The exchange rate on this date was €1.7382/US$. Assume no repayment of principal and an exchange rate today of €1.3905/US$.

    a. What is the current value of the CD principal (in U.S. dollars and euros)?

    b. What is the current value of the euro-denominated loan principal (in dollars and euros)?

c. What is the current value of the U.S. Treasury bill (in U.S. dollars and euros)?

d. What is Qualitybank's profit/loss from this transaction (in U.S. dollars and euros)?

26. Suppose you purchase a 10-year, AAA-rated Swiss bond for par that is paying an annual coupon of 8 percent. The bond has a face value of 1,000 Swiss francs (Sf). The spot rate at the time of purchase is Sf1.50/$. At the end of the year, the bond is downgraded to AA and the yield increases to 10 percent. In addition, the Sf appreciates to Sf1.35/$.

a. What is the loss or gain to a Swiss investor who holds this bond for a year? What portion of this loss or gain is due to foreign exchange risk? What portion is due to interest rate risk?

b. What is the loss or gain to a Canadian investor who holds this bond for a year? What portion of this loss or gain is due to foreign exchange risk? What portion is due to interest rate risk?

27. What is *country or sovereign risk?* What remedy does an FI realistically have in the event of a collapsing country or currency?

28. What is *technology risk?* What is the difference between *economies of scale* and *economies of scope?* How can these economies create benefits for an FI? How can these economies prove harmful to an FI?

29. What is the difference between technology risk and *operational risk?* How does internationalizing the payments system among banks increase operational risk?

30. Characterize the risk exposure(s) of the following FI transactions by choosing one or more of the risk types listed below:

a. Interest rate risk

b. Credit risk

c. Off-balance-sheet risk

d. Technology risk

e. Foreign exchange risk

f. Country or sovereign risk

(1) A bank finances a $10 million, six-year fixed-rate corporate loan by selling one-year certificates of deposit.

(2) An insurance company invests its policy premiums in a long-term government bond portfolio.

(3) A French bank sells two-year fixed-rate notes to finance a two-year fixed-rate loan to a British entrepreneur.

(4) A Japanese bank acquires an Austrian bank to facilitate clearing operations.

(5) A mutual fund completely hedges its interest rate risk exposure by using forward contingent contracts.

(6) A bond dealer uses his own equity to buy Mexican debt on the less-developed country (LDC) bond market.

(7) A securities firm sells a package of mortgage loans as mortgage-backed securities.

31. Consider these four types of risks: credit, foreign exchange, market, and sovereign. These risks can be separated into two pairs of risk types in which each pair consists of two related risk types, with one being a subset of the other. How would you pair off the risk types, and which risk type could be considered a subset of the other type in the pair?

32. What is *liquidity risk?* What routine operating factors allow FIs to deal with this risk in times of normal economic activity? What market reality can create severe financial difficulty for an FI in times of extreme liquidity crises?

33. Why can *insolvency risk* be classified as a consequence or outcome of any or all of the other types of risks?

34. Discuss the interrelationships among the different sources of bank risk exposure. Why would the construction of a bank risk management model to measure and manage only one type of risk be incomplete?

Measuring **Risk**

Interest Rate Risk I

In this chapter, we look at the techniques used by FIs to measure interest rate risk and discuss

▸ monetary policy, a key determinant of interest rate risk

▸ the repricing model for measuring interest rate risk

▸ the maturity model for measuring interest rate risk (Appendix 8A)*

▸ the term structure of interest rates and the shape of the yield curve (Appendix 8B)*

* Appendices 8A and 8B are available at the Online Learning Centre at www.mcgrawhill.ca/olc/saunders.

INTRODUCTION

net worth
The value of an FI to its owners; this is equal to the difference between the market value of assets and that of liabilities.

In Chapter 7 we established that while performing their asset-transformation functions, FIs often mismatch the maturities of their assets and liabilities. In so doing, they expose themselves to interest rate risk. For example, in the 1980s a large number of U.S. savings and loan companies became economically insolvent (i.e., the **net worth** or equity of their owners was eradicated) when interest rates unexpectedly increased. All FIs tend to mismatch their balance sheet maturities to some degree, but excessive interest rate risk can have an impact on the income statement as well as on the balance sheet by squeezing **net interest income (NII),** the difference between an FI's interest income and interest expense. However, measuring interest rate risk exposure by looking only at the size of the maturity mismatch can be misleading. The next two chapters present techniques used by FIs to measure their interest rate risk exposures.

www.bankofcanada.
ca

This chapter begins with a discussion of the Bank of Canada's monetary policy, which is a key determinant of interest rate risk. The chapter also analyzes the simpler method used to measure an FI's interest rate risk: *the repricing model.* The repricing, or funding gap, model concentrates on the impact of interest rate changes on an FI's NII. Because of its simplicity, smaller deposit-taking institutions still use this model as their primary measure of interest rate risk. Appendix 8A, available at the Online Learning Centre (www.mcgrawhill.ca/olc/saunders), compares and contrasts this model with the market value-based maturity model, which includes the impact of interest rate changes on the overall market value of an FI's assets and liabilities and, ultimately, its net worth. Until recently, bank regulators had been content to base their evaluations of bank interest rate risk exposures on the repricing model. As explained later in this chapter, however, the repricing model has some serious weaknesses.

**net interest income
(NII)**
The difference between an FI's interest income and interest expense.

However, although all of the big FIs in Canada report their interest rate gap in their annual reports, most large FIs are adopting more sophisticated value-at-risk (VaR) models, which we will discuss in Chapter 10. For example, the Bank of Montreal uses market value exposure (MVE), earnings volatility (EV), value at risk, simulations, sensitivity analysis, stress testing, and gap analysis to

www.bmo.com

www.osfi-bsif.gc.ca

www.bis.org

understand and manage its interest rate risk.[1] The Office of the Superintendent of Financial Institutions (OSFI) requires gap analysis to be reported quarterly for federally regulated DTIs, but has issued a guideline that supports the Bank for International Settlements (BIS, the organization of the world's major central banks), whose final report issued in 2004 recommends market value accounting and the duration model to be applied by internationally active banks and their regulators to their banking book.[2] Canadian regulators played an important role in developing the principles, and Nicholas Le Pan, the former Superintendent of OSFI, served as the deputy chairman of the Basel Committee on Banking Supervision.[3]

Appendix 8B (available at the Online Learning Centre) looks at the term structure of interest rates that compares the market yields or interest rate on securities, assuming that all characteristics except maturity are the same. This topic is generally covered in introductory finance courses. For students needing a review, Appendix 8B is encouraged introductory reading.

THE LEVEL AND MOVEMENT OF INTEREST RATES

loanable funds theory

A theory of interest rate determination that views equilibrium interest rates in financial markets as a result of the supply and demand for loanable funds.

Given the impact that a change in interest rates has on net income and the market value of the firm, financial institution managers spend much time and effort trying to identify factors that determine the level of interest rates at any moment in time, as well as what causes interest rate movements over time. One model that is commonly used to explain interest rates and interest rate movements is the **loanable funds theory.** The loanable funds theory of interest rate determination views the level of interest rates in financial markets as resulting from factors that affect the supply and demand for loanable funds. This is similar to the way that the prices for goods and services in general are viewed as being the result of the forces of supply and demand for those goods and services. As illustrated in Figure 8–1, the aggregate quantity of funds supplied is positively related to interest rates (supply is higher at i^H than at i^L), while the aggregate quantity of funds demanded is inversely related to interest rates. As long as competitive forces are allowed to operate freely in a financial system, the interest rate that equates the aggregate quantity of loanable funds supplied with the aggregate quantity of loanable funds demanded for a financial security, Q^*, is the equilibrium interest rate for that security, i^*, point E in Figure 8–1.

The equilibrium interest rate (point E in Figure 8–1) is only a temporary equilibrium. Changes in underlying factors that determine the demand and supply of loanable funds can cause continuous shifts in the supply and/or demand curve for loanable funds. Market forces will react to the resulting disequilibrium with a change in the equilibrium interest rate and quantity of funds traded in that market. Figure 8–2(a) shows the effects of an *increase in the supply curve* for loanable funds, from SS to SS'' (and the resulting *decrease in the equilibrium interest rate*, from i^* to $i^{*''}$), while Figure 8–2(b) shows the effects of an *increase in the demand curve* for loanable funds, from DD to DD'' (and the resulting *increase in the equilibrium interest rate*, from i^* to $i^{*''}$).

---

[1] See the Bank of Montreal's *Annual Report 2008,* p. 80, available at www.bmo.com.

[2] In this case, a longer horizon (e.g., one year) would be taken, compared with that used to measure interest rate risk in the trading book (e.g., one day).

[3] See Basel Committee on Banking Supervision. *Principles for the Management and Supervision of Interest Rate Risk,* Bank for International Settlements, Basel, Switzerland, July 2004, and Office of the Superintendent of Financial Institutions, *Guideline B-12: Interest Rate Risk Management,* February 2005.

FIGURE 8–1
Determination
of Equilibrium
Interest Rates

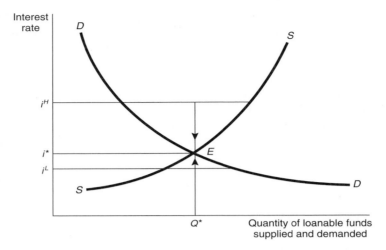

FIGURE 8–2
The Effect on
Interest Rates
from a Shift in the
Demand Curve for
or Supply Curve of
Loanable Funds

(a) Increase in the Supply of Loanable Funds

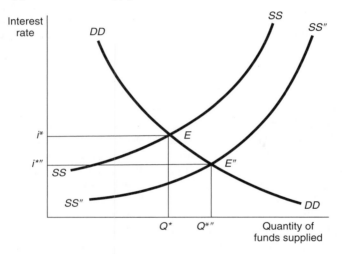

(b) Increase in the Demand for Loanable Funds

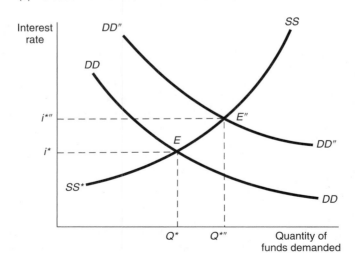

While many factors influence the level and movement of interest rates, it is the central bank's monetary policy strategy that most directly underlies the level and movement of interest rates that, in turn, affect an FI's cost of funds and return on assets.

THE BANK OF CANADA AND INTEREST RATE RISK

overnight rate
The rate that major financial institutions charge on one-day funds borrowed and lent to each other. It is at the middle of the operating band.

bank rate
The rate charged by the Bank of Canada on overnight loans to financial institutions.

operating band
The range (0.5 percent wide) of the overnight rates charged by the Bank of Canada. The bottom of the band is the rate the Bank of Canada will pay on deposits. The top of the band is the rate charged by the Bank of Canada on loans (the bank rate).

federal funds rate
The rate charged by the U.S. Federal Reserve on overnight loans to FIs.

**www.federalreserve.
gov**

Since 1991, Canada's central bank, the Bank of Canada, has followed the practice of setting a target range for inflation (1–3 percent, November 2006 to the end of 2011) and then adjusting the target for the **overnight rate,** the rate that FIs charge each other for one-day funds, to achieve its inflation target (the range midpoint, 2 percent). The **bank rate,** the rate the Bank of Canada charges for one-day loans it makes to FIs, is always the upper limit of the **operating band,** and the overnight rate is at the middle of the band. The lower limit of the operating band is the rate the Bank of Canada will pay on funds deposited with the Bank.

The target overnight rate is the main instrument used by the Bank of Canada to carry out monetary policy. If the Bank of Canada forecasts that production will be below capacity and so it expects that inflation will be below its target rate, it may lower the target overnight rate so that money is cheaper. Companies and consumers will respond by increasing their borrowing and production, and spending in Canada will rise. If the opposite is true and inflation is expected to rise above the target rate, then the bank rate will be set higher, putting pressure on companies and consumers to decrease their spending, bringing inflation levels back into line. The Bank of Canada recognizes that rate changes will not have immediate effects and therefore the Bank forecasts 18 to 24 months into the future. The Bank schedules eight fixed days every year on which it will set the bank rate. In addition, the Bank publishes quarterly monetary policy reports in January, April, July, and October that update its view of the economy and give an indication of where the Bank expects rates to be.

Global financial integration requires the Bank of Canada to pay attention to the actions of other central banks, particularly the central bank in the United States, the Federal Reserve (the Fed). Since 1993, the Federal Reserve has used interest rates—the **federal funds rate**—as its main target variable to guide monetary policy. Under this regime the Fed simply announces after each monthly meeting whether the federal funds rate target has been increased, decreased, or left unchanged. It also should be noted that although Federal Reserve actions are targeted mostly at short-term rates (especially the federal funds rate), changes in short-term rates usually feed through to the whole term structure of interest rates. The linkages between short-term rates and long-term rates and the theories of the term structure of interest rates are discussed in Appendix 8B.

Figure 8–3 shows a comparison of the bank rate with the U.S. federal funds rate for the period from 1965–2009. The rates in both countries vary over time, declining to their lowest levels in 2009. In addition, the bank rate is generally higher than the fed funds rate. This reflects the Bank of Canada's focus on the U.S.–Canadian dollar exchange rate and the flow of funds between the two countries as a result of interest rate differentials. Until 2009, the Canadian government worked to eliminate its deficit, while the U.S. deficit widened. This caused the Canadian dollar, along with the euro and other currencies, to rise in value relative to the U.S. dollar, which is used as a global benchmark for commodities such as metals, oil, and gas. As well, global developments come into play. Of note in

FIGURE 8–3

Comparison of the Canadian Bank Rate and the U.S. Federal Funds Rate, 1965–2009

Source: Bank of Canada, www.bankofcanada.ca

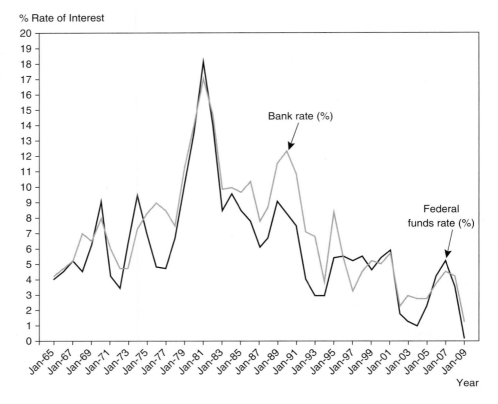

Figure 8–3 is the large decline in the Canadian bank rate from 4.25 percent in January 2008 to 1.25 percent in January 2009. The U.S. federal funds rate fell as well, from 3.50 percent in January 2008 to 0.19 percent in January 2009. These rates reflect the efforts of the central banks to get the credit markets and the economy moving again after the credit meltdowns in September and October of 2008. The global central banks were facing the prospect of deflation in the short term. As a result, interest rates around the world (in the United States, Australia, the United Kingdom, and the Eurozone, for example) reached historically low levels. The Bank of Canada lowered the target overnight rate to 0.25 percent on April 21, 2009, a cumulative decline of 425 basis points (4.25 percent) from December 2007. This set the bank rate at 0.50 percent. At the same time, as noted in Chapter 1, governments around the world were providing liquidity to the markets and running deficits, raising the prospect of higher inflation in the longer term. However, the focus was on stabilizing the global financial system to allow the world to work its way out of a recession. The complex interactions between exchange rates and monetary policy in Canada are discussed in more detail in Chapter 15 when we discuss foreign exchange risk.

Financial market integration increases the speed with which interest rate changes and associated volatility are transmitted among countries. The increased globalization of financial market flows in recent years has made the measurement and management of interest rate risk a prominent concern facing many modern FI managers. For example, investors around the world carefully evaluate the statements made by the chairman of the U.S. Federal Reserve Board of Governors. Even hints of a change in U.S. interest rates may have a major effect on world interest rates, as well as foreign exchange rates and stock prices. This emphasizes that, although we isolate risks in our discussions here, complex FIs engage in enterprisewide risk management that takes into account interactions among risks.

The level and volatility of interest rates and the increase in worldwide financial market integration make the measurement and management of interest rate risk one of the key issues facing FI managers. Further, the Bank for International Settlements has called for regulations that require deposit-taking institutions (DTIs) to have interest rate risk measurement systems that assess the effects of interest rate changes on both earnings and economic value. These systems should provide meaningful measures of a DTI's current levels of interest rate risk exposure and should be capable of identifying any excessive exposures that might arise (see Chapter 20). In this chapter and in Chapter 9, we analyze the different ways an FI might measure the exposure it faces in running a mismatched maturity book (or gap) between its assets and its liabilities in a world of interest rate volatility.

In particular, we concentrate on three ways, or models, of measuring the asset–liability gap exposure of an FI:

1. The repricing (or funding gap) model.
2. The maturity model.
3. The duration model.

INTERNET EXERCISE

The Bank of Canada publishes a *Monetary Policy Report Update* quarterly. Go to the Bank of Canada's website at www.bankofcanada.ca. Click on "Monetary Policy" and then look for the latest *Monetary Policy Report Update*. Download it and then answer the following questions. What is the current inflation target? Does the Bank of Canada expect interest rates to increase or decrease in the next quarter? What are the highlights of the report? What are the major influences that the Bank sees in determining rates in the next three to six months? Are there any issues that would concern an FI that is managing its interest rate risk?

THE REPRICING MODEL

repricing gap
The difference between assets whose interest rates will be repriced or changed over some future period (rate-sensitive assets) and liabilities whose interest rates will be repriced or changed over some future period (rate-sensitive liabilities).

The repricing, or funding gap, model is essentially a book value accounting cash flow analysis of the **repricing gap** between the interest revenue earned on an FI's assets and the interest paid on its liabilities (or its net interest income) over a particular period of time. The assets or liabilities are **rate-sensitive,** that is, the interest rate charged or earned will change (i.e., be repriced) over that period. Consider a bank that has divided its assets and liabilities into the following **maturity buckets:**[4]

---

[4] As of November 1997, OSFI's reporting manual requires FIs to report quarterly and to use 10 maturity buckets for their floating rate assets and liabilities: 1 day to 1 month, 1 month to 3 months, 3 months to 6 months, 6 months to 12 months, 1 year to 2 years, 2 years to 3 years, 3 years to 4 years, 4 years to 5 years, 5 years to 7 years, and greater than 7 years. For illustration purposes, we consider only 6 periods.

rate-sensitive asset or liability
An asset or liability that is repriced at or near current market interest rates within a maturity bucket.

1. One day.
2. More than one day to three months.
3. More than three months to six months.
4. More than 6 months to 12 months.
5. More than one year to five years.
6. More than five years.

maturity bucket
The sum of an FI's rate-sensitive assets or liabilities that are repriced over a particular time period.

Under the repricing gap approach, a bank reports the gaps in each maturity bucket by calculating the rate sensitivity of each asset (RSA) and each liability (RSL) on its balance sheet. *Rate sensitivity* here means that the asset or liability is repriced at or near current market interest rates within a certain time horizon (or maturity bucket). More simply, it means how long the FI manager must wait to change the posted interest rates on any asset or liability. In many cases this occurs on a date prior to maturity.

Table 8–1 shows the asset and liability repricing gaps of an FI, categorized into each of the six previously defined maturity buckets. Although the cumulative repricing gap over the whole balance sheet must, by definition, be zero (see Table 8–1, last column), the advantage of the repricing model lies in its information value and its simplicity in pointing to an FI's *net interest income exposure* (or profit exposure) to interest rate changes in different maturity buckets.[5]

For example, suppose that an FI has a negative $10 million difference between its assets and liabilities being repriced in one day (one-day bucket). Assets and liabilities that are repriced each day are likely to be inter-bank borrowings or repurchase agreements (see Chapter 2). Thus, a negative gap (RSA < RSL) exposes the FI to **refinancing risk,** in that a rise in these short-term rates would lower the FI's *net interest income* since the FI has more rate-sensitive liabilities than assets in this bucket. In other words, assuming equal changes in interest rates on RSAs and RSLs, interest expense will increase by more than interest revenue. Conversely, if the FI has a positive $20 million difference between its assets and liabilities being repriced in 6 months to 12 months, it has a positive gap (RSA > RSL) for this period and is exposed to **reinvestment risk,** in that a drop in rates over this period would lower the FI's net interest income; that is, interest income will decrease by more than interest expense. Specifically, let

refinancing risk
The risk that the cost of rolling over or reborrowing funds will rise above the returns being earned on asset investments.

reinvestment risk
The risk that the returns on funds to be reinvested will fall below the cost of the funds.

ΔNII_i = Change in net interest income in the ith bucket

GAP_i = Dollar size of the gap between the book value of rate-sensitive assets and rate-sensitive liabilities in maturity bucket i

ΔR_i = Change in the level of interest rates impacting assets and liabilities in the ith bucket

Then,

$$\Delta NII_i = (GAP_i) \Delta R_i = (RSA_i - RSL_i) \Delta R_i$$

In this first bucket, if the gap is negative $10 million and short-term interest rates rise 1 percent, the annualized change in the FI's future net interest income is[6]

$$\Delta NII_i = (-\$10 \text{ million}) \times 0.01 = -\$100,000$$

---

[5] If we include equity capital as a long-term (over five years) liability.

[6] One can also calculate an "average" gap. If it is assumed that assets and liabilities reprice on *average* halfway through the period, the one-year gap measure calculated above will be divided by 2.

TABLE 8–1
Repricing Gap
($ millions)

	1	2	3	4
				Cumulative
	Assets	Liabilities	Gaps	Gap
1. One day	$ 20	$ 30	−$10	−$10
2. More than one day–three months	30	40	−10	−20
3. More than three months–six months	70	85	−15	−35
4. More than 6 months–12 months	90	70	+20	−15
5. More than one year–five years	40	30	+10	−5
6. Over five years	10	5	+5	0
	$ 260	$ 260		$ 0

This approach is very simple and intuitive. Remember, however, from Chapter 7 and our overview of interest rate risk that capital or market value losses also occur when rates rise. The capital loss effect that is measured by both the maturity and duration models developed in Appendix 8A (at the Online Learning Centre) and in Chapter 9 is not accounted for in the repricing model. The reason is that in the book value accounting world of the repricing model, assets and liability values are reported at their *historic* values or costs. Thus, interest rate changes affect only current interest income or interest expense—that is, net interest income on the FI's income statement—rather than the market value of assets and liabilities on the balance sheet.[7]

The FI manager can also estimate cumulative gaps (CGAP) over various repricing categories or buckets. A common cumulative gap of interest is the one-year repricing gap estimated from Table 8–1 as

$$CGAP = (-\$10) + (-\$10) + (-\$15) + \$20 = -\$15 \text{ million}$$

If ΔR_i is the average interest rate change affecting assets and liabilities that can be repriced within a year, the cumulative effect on the bank's net interest income is[8]

$$\Delta NII_i = (CGAP) \, \Delta R_i$$
$$= (-\$15 \text{ million})(0.01) = -\$150,000 \qquad (8.1)$$

We can now look at how an FI manager would calculate the cumulative one-year gap from a balance sheet. Remember that the manager asks: Will or can this asset or liability have its interest rate changed within the next year? If the answer is yes, it is a rate-sensitive asset or liability; if the answer is no, it is not rate-sensitive.

Consider the simplified balance sheet facing the FI manager in Table 8–2. Instead of the original maturities, the maturities are those remaining on different assets and liabilities at the time the repricing gap is estimated.

Rate-Sensitive Assets

Looking down the asset side of the balance sheet in Table 8–2, we see the following one-year rate-sensitive assets (RSAs):

---

[7] For example, a 30-year bond purchased 10 years ago when rates were 13 percent would be reported as having the same book (accounting) value as when rates are 7 percent. Using market value, gains and losses to asset and liability values would be reflected in the balance sheet as rates changed.

[8] Note that a change in the dollar value and mix of rate-sensitive assets and liabilities (or a change in CGAP) also affects the FI's net income.

TABLE 8–2
Simple FI Balance Sheet ($ millions)

Assets		Liabilities	
1. Short-term consumer loans (one-year maturity)	$ 50	1. Equity capital (fixed)	$ 20
2. Long-term consumer loans (two-year maturity)	25	2. Demand deposits	40
3. Three-month Treasury bills	30	3. Savings deposits	30
4. Six-month Treasury bills	35	4. Three-month GICs	40
5. Three-year Government of Canada bonds	70	5. Three-month bankers acceptances	20
6. 10-year, fixed-rate mortgages	20	6. Six-month commercial paper	60
7. 25-year, floating-rate mortgages (rate adjusted every six months)	40	7. One-year term deposits	20
		8. Two-year term deposits	40
	$ 270		$ 270

1. *Short-term consumer loans: $50 million.* These are repriced at the end of the year and just make the one-year cutoff.

2. *Three-month T-bills: $30 million.* These are repriced on maturity (rollover) every three months.

3. *Six-month T-bills: $35 million.* These are repriced on maturity (rollover) every six months.

4. *25-year floating-rate mortgages: $40 million.* These are repriced (i.e., the mortgage rate is reset) every six months. Thus, these long-term assets are rate-sensitive assets in the context of the repricing model with a one-year repricing horizon.

Summing these four items produces total one-year rate-sensitive assets (RSAs) of $155 million. The remaining $115 million of assets are not rate-sensitive over the one-year repricing horizon—that is, a change in the level of interest rates will not affect the size of the interest revenue generated by these assets over the next year.[9] Although the $115 million in long-term consumer loans, 3-year Government of Canada bonds, and 10-year fixed-rate mortgages generate interest revenue, the size of revenue generated will not change over the next year, since the interest rates on these assets are not expected to change (i.e., they are fixed over the next year).

Rate-Sensitive Liabilities

Looking down the liability side of the balance sheet in Table 8–2, we see the following liability items clearly fit the one-year rate or repricing sensitivity test:

1. *Three-month GICs $40 million.* These mature in three months and are repriced on rollover.

2. *Three-month bankers' acceptances: $20 million.* These also mature in three months and are repriced on rollover.

3. *Six-month commercial paper: $60 million.* These mature and are repriced every six months.

---

[9] We are assuming that the assets are non-callable over the year and that there will be no prepayments (runoffs, see below) on the mortgages within a year.

4. *One-year term deposits: $20 million.* These are repriced right at the end of the one-year gap horizon.

Summing these four items produces one-year rate-sensitive liabilities (RSLs) of $140 million. The remaining $130 million is not rate-sensitive over the one-year period. The $20 million in equity capital and $40 million in demand deposits (see the following discussion) do not pay interest and are therefore classified as non-interest-paying. The $30 million in savings deposits (see the following discussion) and $40 million in two-year term deposits generate interest expense over the next year, but the level of the interest expense generated will not change if the general level of interest rates changes. Thus, we classify these items as rate-insensitive liabilities.

Note that demand deposits (or transaction accounts in general) were not included as RSLs. We can make strong arguments for and against their inclusion as rate-sensitive liabilities.

Against Inclusion

Although explicit interest is paid on transaction accounts such as chequing/savings accounts, the rates paid by FIs do not fluctuate directly with changes in the general level of interest rates (particularly when the general level of rates is rising). Moreover, many demand deposits act as **core deposits** for FIs, meaning they are a long-term source of funds.

For Inclusion

If interest rates rise, individuals draw down (or run off) their demand deposits, forcing the bank to replace them with higher-yielding, interest-bearing, rate-sensitive funds. This is most likely to occur when the interest rates on alternative instruments are high. In such an environment, the opportunity cost of holding funds in demand deposit accounts is likely to be larger than it is in a low-interest rate environment.

Similar arguments for and against inclusion of retail savings accounts can be made. Banks adjust these rates infrequently. However, savers tend to withdraw funds from these accounts when rates rise, forcing banks into more expensive fund substitutions. The *Interest Rate Risk and Maturities Matching Return* submitted by deposit-taking FIs to OSFI every quarter includes deposits as rate-sensitive assets. In this report, an FI lists deposits under the following categories: personal demand/notice, personal fixed-term, non-personal demand/notice, and non-personal fixed-term deposits.

The four repriced liabilities ($40 + $20 + $60 + $20) sum to $140 million, and the four repriced assets ($50 + $30 + $35 + $40) sum to $155 million. Given this, the cumulative one-year repricing gap (CGAP) for the bank is

$$CGAP = \text{One-year rate-sensitive assets} - \text{one-year rate-sensitive liabilities}$$
$$= RSA - RSL$$
$$= \$155 - \$140 = \$15 \text{ million}$$

Interest rate sensitivity can also be expressed as a percentage of assets (*A*) (typically called the *gap ratio*):

$$\frac{CGAP}{A} = \frac{\$15 \text{ million}}{\$270 \text{ million}} = 0.056 = 5.6\%$$

core deposits
Those deposits that act as an FI's long-term source of funds.

Expressing the repricing gap in this way is useful since it tells us (1) the direction of the interest rate exposure (positive or negative CGAP) and (2) the scale of that exposure as indicated by dividing the gap by the asset size of the institution. In our example the bank has 5.6 percent more RSAs than RSLs in one-year-and-less buckets as a percentage of total assets.

Equal Changes in Rates on RSAs and RSLs

The CGAP provides a measure of an FI's interest rate sensitivity. Table 8–3 highlights the relationship between CGAP and changes in NII when interest rate changes for RSAs are equal to interest rate changes for RSLs. For example, when CGAP (or the gap ratio) is positive (or the FI has more RSAs than RSLs), NII will rise when interest rates rise (row 1, Table 8–3), since interest revenue increases more than interest expense does.

EXAMPLE 8–1

Effect of Rate Changes on Net Interest Income When CGAP Is Positive

Suppose that interest rates rise by 1 percent on both RSAs and RSLs. The CGAP would project the expected annual change in net interest income (ΔNII) of the bank as approximately

$$\Delta NII = CGAP \times \Delta R$$
$$= (\$15 \text{ million}) \times 0.01$$
$$= \$150,000$$

Similarly, if interest rates fall equally for RSAs and RSLs (row 2, Table 8–3), NII will fall when CGAP is positive. As rates fall, interest revenue falls by more than interest expense. Thus, NII falls. Suppose that for our FI, rates fall by 1 percent. The CGAP predicts that NII will fall by approximately

$$\Delta NII = CGAP \times \Delta R$$
$$= (\$15 \text{ million}) \times -0.01$$
$$= -\$150,000$$

It is evident from this equation that the larger the absolute value of CGAP, the larger the expected change in NII (i.e., the larger the increase or decrease in the FI's interest revenue relative to interest expense). In general, when CGAP is positive, the change in NII is positively related to the change in interest rates. Conversely, when CGAP (or the gap ratio) is negative, if interest rates rise by equal amounts for RSAs and RSLs (row 3, Table 8–3), NII will fall (since the FI has more RSLs than RSAs). Thus, an FI would want its CGAP to be positive when interest rates are expected to rise. Similarly, if interest rates fall equally for RSAs and RSLs (row 4, Table 8–3), NII will increase when CGAP is negative. As rates fall, interest expense decreases by more than interest revenue. In general then, when CGAP is negative,

TABLE 8–3
Effect of CGAP on the Relationship between Changes in Interest Rates and Changes in Net Interest Income, Assuming Rate Changes for RSAs Equal Rate Changes for RSLs

Row	CGAP	Change in Interest Rates	Change in Interest Revenue		Change in Interest Expense	Change in NII
1	>0	⇑	⇑	>	⇑	⇑
2	>0	⇓	⇓	>	⇓	⇓
3	<0	⇑	⇑	<	⇑	⇓
4	<0	⇓	⇓	<	⇓	⇑

the change in NII is negatively related to the change in interest rates. Thus, an FI would want its CGAP to be negative when interest rates are expected to fall. We refer to these relationships as **CGAP effects.**

CGAP effects
The relationships between changes in interest rates and changes in net interest income.

Unequal Changes in Rates on RSAs and RSLs

The previous section considered changes in net interest income as interest rates changed, assuming that the change in rates on RSAs was exactly equal to the change in rates on RSLs (in other words, assuming the interest rate spread between rates on RSAs and RSLs remained unchanged). This is not often the case; rather, rate changes on RSAs generally differ from those on RSLs (i.e., the spread between interest rates on assets and liabilities changes along with the levels of these rates). See Figure 8–4, which plots one-year GIC rates (liabilities) and prime lending rates (assets) for the period 1999–2009. Notice that although the rates generally move in the same direction, they are not perfectly correlated. In this case, as we consider the effect of rate changes on NII, we have a spread effect in addition to the CGAP effects.[10]

EXAMPLE 8–2

Influence of Spread Effect on Net Interest Income

To understand spread effect, assume for a moment that RSAs equal RSLs equals $155 million. Suppose that rates rise by 1.2 percent on RSAs and by 1 percent on RSLs (i.e., the spread between the rates on RSAs and RSLs increases by 1.2 percent − 1 percent = 0.2 percent). The resulting change in NII is calculated as

$$\Delta NII = (RSA \times \Delta R_{RSA}) - (RSL \times \Delta R_{RSL})$$
$$= \Delta \text{Interest revenue} - \Delta \text{Interest expense}$$
$$= (\$155 \text{ million} \times 1.2\%) - (\$155 \text{ million} \times 1.0\%)$$
$$= (\$155 \text{ million} (1.2\% - 1.0\%)$$
$$= \$310,000$$

If the spread between the rate on RSAs and RSLs increases, when interest rates rise (fall), interest revenue increases (decreases) by more (less) than interest expense. The result is an increase in NII. Conversely, if the spread between

FIGURE 8–4
One-Year Guaranteed Investment Certificate Rates versus the Prime Business Rate, January 1999– February 2009

Bank of Canada,
www.bankofcanada.ca

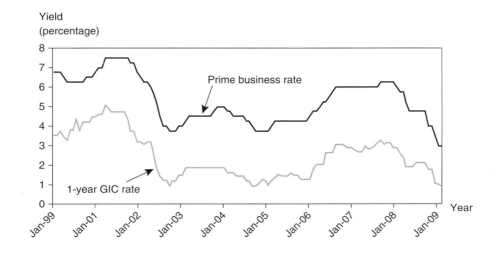

---

[10] The spread effect therefore presents a type of basis risk for the FI. The FI's net interest income varies as the difference (basis) between interest rates on RSAs and interest rates on RSLs varies. We discuss basis risk in detail in Chapter 24.

spread effect
The effect that a change in the spread between rates on RSAs and RSLs has on net interest income as interest rates change.

the rates on RSAs and RSLs decreases, when interest rates rise (fall), interest revenue increases (decreases) less (more) than interest expense, and NII decreases. In general, the **spread effect** is such that, regardless of the direction of the change in interest rates, a positive relationship occurs between changes in the spread (between rates on RSAs and RSLs) and changes in NII. Whenever the spread increases (decreases), NII increases (decreases).

See Table 8–4 for various combinations of CGAP and spread changes and their effects on NII. The first four rows in Table 8–4 consider an FI with a positive CGAP; the last four rows consider an FI with a negative CGAP. Notice in Table 8–4 that both the CGAP and spread effects can have the same effect on NII. For example, in row 6 of Table 8–4, if CGAP is negative and interest rates increase, the CGAP effect says NII will decrease. If, at the same time, the spread between RSAs and RSLs decreases as interest rates increase, the spread effect also says NII will decrease. In these cases, FI managers can accurately predict the direction of the change in NII as interest rates change. When the two work in opposite directions, however, the change in NII cannot be predicted without knowing the size of the CGAP and expected change in the spread. For example, in row 5 of Table 8–4, if CGAP is negative and interest rates increase, the CGAP effect says NII will decrease. If, at the same time, the spread between RSAs and RSLs increases as interest rates increase, the spread effect says NII will decrease.

www.scotiabank.com

The interest rate risk exposure of an FI depends on its size and its view of rates. For example, in its 2008 annual report, Scotiabank reported a cumulative one-year gap on Canadian dollar assets and liabilities of $17.3 billion and on foreign currency assets and liabilities of –$4.5 billion, for a total cumulative gap of $12.8 billion. These figures included off-balance-sheet instruments and an estimate of prepayments on consumer loans, mortgages, and cashable deposits (GICs). The 2008 gap was an increase from $7.7 billion reported at the end of 2007. In 2006, Scotiabank had a negative cumulative one-year gap of –$5.1 billion. Scotiabank estimated that a 100 basis point increase in rates would increase its net income before tax by $133 million, based on its 2008 year-end interest rate position.[11]

The repricing gap is the measure of interest rate risk historically used by FIs, and it is still the main measure of interest rate risk used by small FIs. In contrast to the market value-based models of interest rate risk discussed in Appendix 8A (at the Online Learning Centre) and in Chapter 9, the repricing gap model is conceptually easy to understand and can easily be used to forecast changes in profitability for a given change in interest rates. The repricing gap can be used to allow

TABLE 8–4
Effect of CGAP on the Relationship between Changes in Interest Rates and Changes in Net Interest Income, Allowing for Different Rate Changes for RSAs and RSLs

Row	CGAP	Change in Interest Rates	Change in Spread	NII
1	>0	↑	↑	↑
2	>0	↑	↓	↑↓
3	>0	↓	↑	↑↓
4	>0	↓	↓	↓
5	<0	↑	↑	↑↓
6	<0	↑	↓	↓
7	<0	↓	↑	↑
8	<0	↓	↓	↑↓

---

[11] See *2008 Scotiabank Annual Report*, pp. 69–70, www.scotiabank.com.

an FI to structure its assets and liabilities or to go off the balance sheet to take advantage of a projected interest rate change. However, the repricing gap model has some major weaknesses that have resulted in regulators calling for the use of more comprehensive models (e.g., the duration gap model) to measure interest rate risk. We next discuss some of the major weaknesses of the repricing model.

CONCEPT QUESTIONS

1. Why is it useful to express the repricing gap in terms of a percentage of assets? What specific information does this provide?
2. How can banks change the size and the direction of their repricing gap?

WEAKNESSES OF THE REPRICING MODEL

The repricing model has four major shortcomings: (1) It ignores market value effects of interest rate changes, (2) it is overaggregative, (3) it fails to deal with the problem of rate-insensitive asset and liability runoffs and prepayments, and (4) it ignores cash flows from off-balance-sheet activities. In this section we discuss each of these weaknesses in more detail.

Market Value Effects

As was discussed in the overview of FI risks (Chapter 7), interest rate changes have a market value effect in addition to an income effect on asset and liability values. That is, the present value of the cash flows on assets and liabilities changes, in addition to the immediate interest received or paid on them, as interest rates change. In fact, the present values (and where relevant, the market prices) of virtually all assets and liabilities on an FI's balance sheet change as interest rates change. The repricing model ignores the market value effect—implicitly assuming a book value accounting approach. As such, the repricing gap is only a *partial* measure of the true interest rate exposure of an FI. As we discuss the market value-based measures of interest rate risk (in Appendix 8A on this book's website and in Chapter 9), we will highlight the result of ignoring the market value effect on the ability to accurately measure the overall interest rate risk of an FI.

Overaggregation

The problem of defining buckets over a range of maturities ignores information regarding the distribution of assets and liabilities within those buckets. For example, the dollar values of RSAs and RSLs within any maturity bucket range may be equal; however, on average, liabilities may be repriced toward the end of the bucket's range, while assets may be repriced toward the beginning, in which case a change in interest rates will have an effect on asset and liability cash flows that will not be accurately measured by the repricing gap approach.

Look at the simple example for the three-month to six-month bucket in Figure 8–5. Note that $50 million more RSAs than RSLs are repriced between months 3 and 4, while $50 million more RSLs than RSAs are repriced between months 5 and 6. The bank would show a zero repricing gap for the three-month to six-month bucket [+50 + (–50) = 0]. But as you can easily see, the bank's assets and liabilities are *mismatched* within the bucket. Clearly, the shorter the range over which bucket gaps are calculated, the smaller this problem is. If an FI manager calculated one-day bucket gaps out into the future, this would give a more accurate picture of the net interest income exposure to rate changes. Reportedly, many large banks have

FIGURE 8–5
The Over-Aggregation Problem: The Three-Month to Six-Month Bucket

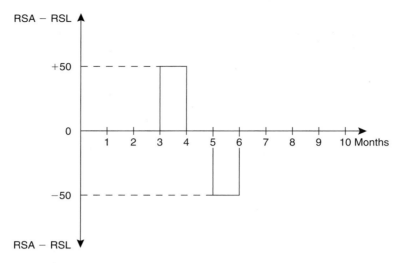

internal systems that indicate their repricing gaps on any given day in the future (252 days' time, 1,329 days' time, etc.). This suggests that although regulators require the reporting of repricing gaps over only relatively wide maturity bucket ranges, FI managers could set in place internal information systems to report the daily future patterns of such gaps.

The Problem of Runoffs

In the simple repricing model discussed above, we assumed that all consumer loans matured in 1 year or that all conventional mortgages matured in 30 years. In reality, the FI continuously originates and retires consumer and mortgage loans as it creates and retires deposits. For example, today, some 30-year original maturity mortgages may have only 1 year left before they mature; that is, they are in their 29th year. In addition, these loans may be listed as 30-year mortgages (and included as not rate-sensitive), yet they will sometimes be prepaid early as mortgage holders refinance their mortgages and/or sell their houses. Thus, the resulting proceeds will be reinvested at current market rates within the year. In addition, even if an asset or liability is rate-insensitive, virtually all assets and liabilities (e.g., long-term mortgages) pay some principal and/or interest back to the FI in any given year. As a result, the FI receives a **runoff** cash flow from its rate-insensitive portfolio that can be reinvested at current market rates; that is, this runoff cash flow component of a rate-insensitive asset or liability is itself rate-sensitive. The FI manager can deal easily with this in the repricing model by identifying for each asset and liability item the estimated dollar cash flow that will run off within the next year and adding these amounts to the value of rate-sensitive assets and liabilities.

runoff
Periodic cash flow of interest and principal amortization payments on long-term assets, such as conventional mortgages, that can be reinvested at market rates.

Cash Flows from Off-Balance-Sheet Activities

The RSAs and RSLs used in the repricing model generally include only the assets and liabilities listed on the balance sheet. Changes in interest rates will affect the cash flows on many off-balance-sheet instruments as well. For example, an FI might have hedged its interest rate risk with an interest rate futures contract (see Chapter 23). As interest rates change, these futures contracts—as part of the marking-to-market process—produce a daily cash flow (either positive or negative) for the FI that may offset any on-balance-sheet gap exposure. These offsetting cash flows from futures contracts are ignored by the simple repricing model and should (and could) be included in the model.

1. **What are four major weaknesses of the repricing model?**
2. **What does *runoff* mean?**

Summary

This chapter introduced a method of measuring an FI's interest rate risk exposure: the repricing model. The repricing model looks at the difference, or gap, between an FI's rate-sensitive assets and rate-sensitive liabilities to measure interest rate risk. The chapter showed that the repricing model has difficulty in accurately measuring the interest rate risk of an FI. In particular, the repricing model ignores the market value effects of interest rate changes. More complete and accurate measures of an FI's exposure are duration and the duration gap, which are explained in the next chapter.

Questions and Problems

1. How do the supply of and demand for loanable funds, together, determine interest rates?

2. How do monetary policy actions made by the Bank of Canada impact interest rates?

3. How has the increased level of financial market integration affected interest rates?

4. What is the repricing gap? In using this model to evaluate interest rate risk, what is meant by *rate sensitivity*? On what financial performance variable does the repricing model focus? Explain.

5. What is a maturity bucket in the repricing model? Why is the length of time selected for repricing assets and liabilities important in using the repricing model?

6. What is the CGAP effect? According to the CGAP effect, what is the relationship between changes in interest rates and changes in net interest income when CGAP is positive? When CGAP is negative?

7. If a bank manager was quite certain that interest rates were going to rise within the next six months, how should the bank manager adjust the bank's six-month repricing gap to take advantage of this anticipated rise? What if the manager believed rates would fall in the next six months?

8. Consider the following balance sheet positions for a financial institution:
   - Rate-sensitive assets = $200 million
     Rate-sensitive liabilities = $100 million
   - Rate-sensitive assets = $100 million
     Rate-sensitive liabilities = $150 million
   - Rate-sensitive assets = $150 million
     Rate-sensitive liabilities = $140 million
   a. Calculate the repricing gap and the impact on net interest income of a 1 percent increase in interest rates for each position.
   b. Calculate the impact on net interest income of each of the above situations, assuming a 1 percent decrease in interest rates.
   c. What conclusion can you draw about the repricing model from these results?

9. What are the reasons for not including demand deposits as rate-sensitive liabilities in the repricing analysis for a commercial bank? What is the subtle but potentially strong reason for including demand deposits in the total of rate-sensitive liabilities?

10. What is the gap ratio? What is the value of this ratio to interest rate risk managers and regulators?

11. Which of the following assets or liabilities fit the one-year rate or repricing sensitivity test?
    a. 3-month Treasury bills
    b. 1-year Government of Canada notes
    c. 20-year Government of Canada bonds
    d. 20-year floating-rate corporate bonds with annual repricing
    e. 30-year floating-rate mortgages with repricing every two years
    f. 30-year floating-rate mortgages with repricing every six months
    g. Overnight fed funds
    h. 9-month fixed-rate GICs

i. 1-year fixed-rate GICs

j. 5-year floating-rate GICs with annual repricing

k. Common stock

12. What is the spread effect?

13. A bank manager is quite certain that interest rates are going to fall within the next six months. How should the bank manager adjust the bank's six-month repricing gap and spread to take advantage of this anticipated rise? What if the manager believed rates would rise in the next six months?

14. Consider the following balance sheet for WatchoverU Savings, Inc. ($ millions):

Assets		Liabilities and Equity	
Floating-rate mortgages (currently 10% annually)	$ 50	1-year term deposits (currently 6% annually)	$ 70
25-year fixed-rate loans (currently 7% annually)	50	3-year term deposits (currently 7% annually)	20
		Equity	10
Total assets	$100	Total liabilities and equity	$100

a. What is WatchoverU's expected net interest income at year-end?

b. What will net interest income be at year-end if interest rates rise 2 percent?

c. Using the cumulative repricing gap model, what is the expected net interest income for a 2 percent increase in interest rates?

d. What will net interest income be at year-end if interest rates on RSAs increase by 2 percent but interest rates on RSLs increase by 1 percent? Is it reasonable for changes in interest rates on RSAs and RSLs to differ? Why?

15. Use the following information about a hypothetical government security dealer named Barclays Merrill Burns Canada. Market yields are in parentheses, and amounts are in millions.

Assets		Liabilities and Equity	
Cash	$ 10	Overnight repos	$170
1-month T-bills (7.05%)	75	Subordinated debt	150
3-month T-bills (7.25%)	75	7-year fixed rate (8.55%)	
2-year Canada bonds (7.50%)	50		
8-year Canada bonds (8.96%)	100		
5-year provincial government debt (floating rate) (8.20% reset every 6 months)	25	Equity	15
Total assets	$335	Total liabilities and equity	$335

a. What is the repricing gap if the planning period is 30 days? 3 months? 2 years? Recall that cash is a non-interest-earning asset.

b. What is the impact over the next 30 days on net interest income if interest rates increase 50 basis points? Decrease 75 basis points?

c. The following one-year runoffs are expected: $10 million for two-year Canada bonds and $20 million for eight-year Canada bonds. What is the one-year repricing gap?

d. If runoffs are considered, what is the effect on net interest income at year-end if interest rates increase 50 basis points? Decrease 75 basis points?

16. A bank has the following balance sheet:

Assets	Avg. Rate	Liabilities/Equity	Avg. Rate
Rate-sensitive $ 550,000	7.75%	Rate-sensitive $ 375,000	6.25%
Fixed rate 755,000	8.75	Fixed rate 805,000	7.50
Non-earning 265,000		Non-paying 390,000	
Total $1,570,000		Total $1,570,000	

Suppose interest rates rise such that the average yield on rate-sensitive assets increases by 45 basis points and the average yield on rate-sensitive liabilities increases by 35 basis points.

a. Calculate the bank's CGAP and gap ratio.

b. Assuming the bank does not change the composition of its balance sheet, calculate the resulting change in the bank's interest income, interest expense, and net interest income.

c. Explain how the CGAP and spread effects influenced this increase in net interest income.

17. A bank has the following balance sheet:

Assets	Avg. Rate	Liabilities/Equity	Avg. Rate
Rate-sensitive $ 550,000	7.75%	Rate-sensitive $ 575,000	6.25%
Fixed rate 755,000	8.75	Fixed rate 605,000	7.50
Non-earning 265,000		Non-paying 390,000	
Total $1,570,000		Total $1,570,000	

Suppose interest rates fall such that the average yield on rate-sensitive assets decreases by 15 basis points and the average yield on rate-sensitive liabilities decreases by 5 basis points.

a. Calculate the bank's CGAP and gap ratio.

b. Assuming the bank does not change the composition of its balance sheet, calculate the resulting change in the bank's interest income, interest expense, and net interest income.

c. The bank's CGAP is negative and interest rates decreased, yet net interest income decreased. Explain how the CGAP and spread effects influenced this decrease in net interest income.

18. The balance sheet of A. G. Fredwards, a government security dealer, is listed below. Market yields are in parentheses, and amounts are in millions.

Assets		Liabilities and Equity	
Cash	$ 20	Overnight repos	$340
1-month T-bills (7.05%)	150	Subordinated debt	
3-month T-bills (7.25%)	150	7-year fixed rate (8.55%)	300
2-year Canada-notes (7.50%)	100		
8-year Canada-notes (8.96%)	200		
5-year municipal notes (floating rate) (8.20% reset every 6 months)	50	Equity	30
Total assets	$670	Total liabilities and equity	$670

a. What is the repricing gap if the planning period is 30 days? 3 months? 2 years?

b. What is the impact over the next three months on net interest income if interest rates on RSAs increase 50 basis points and on RSLs increase 75 basis points?

c. What is the impact over the next two years on net interest income if interest rates on RSAs increase 50 basis points and on RSLs increase 75 basis points?

d. Explain the difference in your answers to parts (b) and (c). Why is one answer a negative change in NII, while the other is positive?

19. A bank has the following balance sheet:

Assets		Avg. Rate	Liabilities/Equity		Avg. Rate
Rate-sensitive	$225,000	6.35%	Rate-sensitive	$300,000	4.25%
Fixed rate	550,000	7.55	Fixed rate	505,000	6.15
Non-earning	120,000		Non-paying	90,000	
Total	$895,000		Total	$895,000	

Suppose interest rates rise such that the average yield on rate-sensitive assets increases by 45 basis points and the average yield on rate-sensitive liabilities increases by 35 basis points.

a. Calculate the bank's repricing GAP.

b. Assuming the bank does not change the composition of its balance sheet, calculate the net interest income for the bank before and after the interest rate changes. What is the resulting change in net interest income?

c. Explain how the CGAP and spread effects influenced this increase in net interest income.

20. What are some of the weaknesses of the repricing model? How have large banks solved the problem of choosing the optimal time period for repricing? What is runoff cash flow, and how does this amount affect the repricing model's analysis?

Integrated Mini-Case:

CALCULATING INTEREST RATES

State Bank's balance sheet is listed below. Market yields are in parentheses, and amounts are in millions.

Assets		Liabilities and Equity	
Cash	$ 20	Demand deposits	$ 250
Overnight Inter-bank deposits (5.05%)	150	Savings accounts (1.5%)	20
3-month T-bills (5.25%)	150	Wholesale deposits (4.5%)	490
2-year Canada bonds (6.50%)	100	3-month GICs (4.2%)	120
8-year Canada bonds (7.50%)	200	6-month GICs (4.3%)	220
5-year provincial government debt (floating rate) (8.20%, repriced @ 6 months)	50	1-year GICs (4.5%)	375
		2-year GICs (5%)	425
6-month consumer loans (6%)	250	4-year GICs (5.5%)	330
1-year consumer loans (5.8%)	300	5-year GICs (6%)	200
5-year car loans (7%)	350	Overnight inter-bank borrowing (5%)	225
7-month business loans (5.8%)	200	Overnight repos (5%)	290
2-year business loans (floating rate) (5.15%, repriced @ 6 months)	275	6-month commercial paper (5.05%)	300
		Subordinate notes:	
15-year variable-rate mortgages (5.8%, repriced @ 6 months)	200	3-year fixed rate (6.55%)	200
		Subordinated debt:	
15-year variable-rate mortgages (6.1%, repriced @ year)	400	7-year fixed rate (7.25%)	100
15-year fixed-rate mortgages (7.85%)	300	Total liabilities	$3,545
25-year variable-rate mortgages (6.3%, repriced @ quarter)	225		
25-year variable-rate mortgages (6.4%, repriced @ month)	355		
25-year fixed-rate mortgages (8.2%)	400		
Premises and equipment	20	Equity	400
Total assets	$3,945	Total liabilities and equity	$3,945

1. What is the repricing gap if the planning period is 30 days? 6 months? 1 year? 2 years? 5 years?
2. What is the impact over the next six months on net interest income if interest rates on RSAs increase 60 basis points and on RSLs increase 40 basis points?
3. What is the impact over the next year on net interest income if interest rates on RSAs increase 60 basis points and on RSLs increase 40 basis points?

Appendix 8A: The Maturity Model

Appendix 8B: Term Structure of Interest Rates

View Appendices 8A and 8B at the Online Learning Centre: www.mcgrawhill.ca/olc/saunders.

CHAPTER 9

Interest Rate Risk II

In this chapter, we present the duration model and duration gap as measures of an FI's interest rate risk. We show

▸ the basic arithmetic needed to calculate the duration of an asset or liability

▸ the economic meaning of *duration*

▸ how duration can be used to immunize an FI's portfolio against interest rate risk

▸ some of the problems in applying the duration measure to real-world FIs' balance sheets

▸ advanced issues relating to duration (see Appendix 9B, at this book's Online Learning Centre at www.mcgrawhill.ca/olc/saunders).

INTRODUCTION

book value accounting
Accounting method in which the assets and liabilities of the FI are recorded at historic values.

As mentioned in Chapter 8, a weakness of the repricing model is its reliance on book values rather than market values of assets and liabilities. Indeed, in most countries, FIs report their balance sheets by using **book value accounting.** This method records the historic values of securities purchased, loans made, and liabilities sold. For example, for banks, investment assets (i.e., those expected to be held to maturity) are recorded at book values, while those assets expected to be used for trading (trading securities or available-for-sale securities) are reported according to market value.[1] The recording of market values means that assets and liabilities are revalued to reflect current market conditions. Thus, if a fixed-coupon bond had been purchased at $100 per $100 of face value in a low-interest rate environment, a rise in current market rates reduces the present value of the cash flows from the bond to the investor. Such a rise also reduces the price—say to $97—at which the bond could be sold in the secondary market today. That is, the **market value accounting** approach reflects economic reality, or the true values of assets and liabilities if the FI's portfolio were to be liquidated at today's securities prices rather than at the prices when the assets and liabilities were originally purchased or sold. This practice of valuing securities at their market value is referred to as **marking to market.** We discuss book value versus market value accounting and the impact that the use of the alternative methods has in measuring the value of an FI in more detail in Chapter 20. Appendix 9A, located at the Online Learning Centre, presents a review of bond pricing and price volatility. This topic is generally covered in introductory finance courses. For students needing a review, Appendix 9A is encouraged reading.

market value accounting
Accounting method in which the assets and liabilities of the FI are revalued according to the current level of interest rates.

marking to market
Valuing securities at their current market price.

---

[1] More accurately, they are reported at the lower of cost or current market value. However, the International Accounting Standards Board, the Canadian Institute of Chartered Accountants Standards Board, and the U.S. Financial Accounting Standards Board are proposing changes that would require held-to-maturity assets to be carried at historical cost and held-for-trading assets to be carried at market values. Currently, bonds held for trading are carried at market price, while loans are not. Canada will adopt International Accounting Standards in 2011.

In this second chapter on measuring interest rate risk, we present a market value-based model of managing interest rate risk: the duration model. We explain the concept of *duration* and see that duration and the duration gap are more accurate measures of an FI's interest rate risk exposure than is the repricing model described in Chapter 8. Unlike the repricing model, duration gap considers market values and the maturity distributions of an FI's assets and liabilities. Further, duration gap considers the degree of leverage on an FI's balance sheet as well as the timing of the payment or arrival of cash flows of assets and liabilities. Thus, duration gap is a more comprehensive measure of an FI's interest rate risk. As a result, regulators are increasingly focusing on this model in determining an appropriate level of capital for an FI exposed to interest rate risk (see Chapter 20).

We begin the chapter by presenting the basic arithmetic needed to calculate the duration of an asset or liability. Then we analyze the economic meaning of the number we calculate for duration. This number, which measures the average life of an asset or liability, also has *economic* meaning as the interest sensitivity (or interest elasticity) of that asset's or liability's value. Next, we show how the duration measure can be used to protect an FI against interest rate risk. Finally, we examine some problems in applying the duration measure to real-world FIs' balance sheets. The more advanced issues associated with these problems are presented in Appendix 9B at the Online Learning Centre.

DURATION: A SIMPLE INTRODUCTION

Duration is a more complete measure of an asset's or liability's interest rate sensitivity than is maturity because duration takes into account the time of arrival (or payment) of all cash flows as well as the asset's (or liability's) maturity. Consider a loan with a 15 percent interest rate and required repayment of half the $100 in principal at the end of six months and the other half at the end of the year. The loan is financed with a one-year Guaranteed Investment Certificate (GIC) paying 15 percent interest per year. The promised cash flows (CF) received by the FI from the loan at the end of one-half year and at the end of the year appear in Figure 9–1.

$CF_{1/2}$ is the $50 promised repayment of principal plus the $7.50 promised interest payment ($100 \times \frac{1}{2} \times 15\%$) received after six months. CF_1 is the promised cash flow at the end of the year and is equal to the second $50 promised principal repayment plus $3.75 promised interest ($50 \times \frac{1}{2} \times 15\%$). To compare the relative sizes of these two cash flows, we should put them in the same dimensions. This is the case because $1 of principal or interest received at the end of a year is worth less to the FI in terms of the time value of money than $1 of principal or interest received at the end of six months. Assuming that the current required interest rates are 15 percent per annum, we calculate the present values (*PV*) of the two cash flows (*CF*) shown in Figure 9–2 as

$$CF_{1/2} = \$57.50 \qquad\qquad PV_{1/2} = \$57.5/(1.075) = \$53.49$$

$$CF_1 = \$53.75 \qquad\qquad PV_1 = \$53.75/(1.075)^2 = \$46.51$$

$$CF_{1/2} + CF_1 = \$111.25 \qquad PV_{1/2} + PV_1 = \$100.00$$

Note that since $CF_{1/2}$, the cash flows received at the end of one-half year, are received earlier, they are discounted at $(1 + \frac{1}{2} R)$, where R is the current annual

FIGURE 9–1
Promised Cash
Flows on the One-
Year Loan

FIGURE 9–2
PV of the Cash
Flows from the
Loan

interest rate on the loan. This is smaller than the discount rate on the cash flow received at the end of the year $(1 + \frac{1}{2} R)^2$.[2] Figure 9–2 summarizes the PVs of the cash flows from the loan.

duration
The weighted-average
time to maturity on
an investment.

Technically speaking, **duration** is the *weighted-average* time to maturity on the loan using the relative present values of the cash flows as weights. On a time value of money basis, duration measures the period of time required to recover the initial investment on the loan. Any cash flows received prior to the loan's duration reflect recovery of the initial investment, while cash flows received after the period of the loan's duration and before its maturity are the profits, or return, earned by the FI. As Figure 9–2 shows, the FI receives some cash flows at one-half year and some at one year. Duration analysis weights the time at which cash flows are received by the relative importance in present value terms of the cash flows arriving at each point in time. In present value terms, the relative importance of the cash flows arriving at time $t = \frac{1}{2}$ year and time $t = 1$ year are as follows:

Time (*t*)	Weight (*X*)			
1/2 year	$X_{1/2} = \dfrac{PV_{1/2}}{PV_{1/2} + PV_1}$	$= \dfrac{53.49}{100.00}$	= 0.5349	= 53.49%
1 year	$X_1 = \dfrac{PV_1}{PV_{1/2} + PV_1}$	$= \dfrac{46.51}{100.00}$	= 0.4651	= 46.51%
			1.0	100%

That is, in present value terms, the FI receives 53.49 percent of cash flows on the loan with the first payment at the end of six months ($t = \frac{1}{2}$) and 46.51 percent with the second payment at the end of the year ($t = 1$). By definition, the sum of the (present value) cash flow weights must equal 1:

$$X_{1/2} + X_1 = 1$$
$$0.5349 + 0.4651 = 1$$

[2] We use here the formula for calculating the present values of cash flows on a security that pays cash flows semiannually. This approach is more accurate, since it reflects the semiannual payment and compounding of interest on the loan. See the Department of Finance's website (www.fin.gc.ca) for a guide to calculating prices on Government of Canada securities.

FIGURE 9–3
PV of the Cash
Flows of the
Deposit

$PV_1 = \$100$

$CF_1 = \$115$

0

1 year

We can now calculate the duration *(D)*, or the weighted-average time to maturity, of the loan using the present value of its cash flows as weights:

$$D_1 = X_{1/2}(^1/_2) + X_1(1)$$

$$= 0.5349(^1/_2) + 0.4651(1) = 0.7326 \text{ years}$$

Thus, while the maturity of the loan is one year, its duration, or average life in a cash flow sense, is only 0.7326 years. On a time value of money basis, the initial investment in the loan is recovered (albeit not realized) after 0.7326 years. After that time the FI earns a profit, or return, on the loan. The duration is less than the maturity of the loan because in present value terms, 53.49 percent of the cash flows are received at the end of one-half year. Note that duration is measured in years since we weight the time (*t*) at which cash flows are received by the relative present value importance of cash flows ($X_{1/2}$, X_1, etc.).

We next calculate the duration of the one-year, $100, 15 percent GIC. The FI promises to make only one cash payment to depositors at the end of the year; that is, $CF_1 = \$115$, which is the promised principal ($100) and interest repayment ($15) to the depositor. Since weights are calculated in present value terms:[3]

$$CF_1 = \$115, \text{ and } PV_1 = \$115/1.15 = \$100$$

We show this in Figure 9–3. Because all cash flows are received in one payment at the end of the year, $X_1 = PV_1/PV_1 = 1$, the duration of the deposit is

$$D_D = X_1 \times (1)$$

$$D_D = 1 \times (1) = 1 \text{ year}$$

Thus, only when all cash flows are limited to one payment at the end of the period with no intervening cash flows does duration equal maturity. This example also illustrates that while the maturities on the loan and the deposit are both one year (and thus the difference or gap in maturities is zero), the duration gap is negative:

$$M_L - M_D = 1 - 1 = 0$$

$$D_L - D_D = 0.7326 - 1 = -0.2674 \text{ years}$$

As will become clearer, to measure and to hedge interest rate risk, the FI needs to manage its duration gap rather than its maturity gap.

CONCEPT
QUESTIONS

1. **Why is duration considered a more complete measure of an asset's or liability's interest rate sensitivity than maturity?**
2. **When is the duration of an asset equal to its maturity?**

---

[3] Since the GIC is like an annual coupon bond, the annual discount rate is $1/(1 + R) = 1/1.15$.

A GENERAL FORMULA FOR DURATION

You can calculate the duration (or Macaulay's duration[4]) for any fixed-income security that pays interest *annually* using the following general formula:

$$D = \frac{\sum_{t=1}^{N} CF_t \times DF_t \times t}{\sum_{t=1}^{N} CF_t \times DF_t} = \frac{\sum_{t=1}^{N} PV_t \times t}{\sum_{t=1}^{N} PV_t} \tag{9.1}$$

where

D = Duration measured in years

CF_t = Cash flow received on the security at end of period t

N = Last period in which the cash flow is received

DF_t = Discount factor = $1/(1 + R)^t$, where R is the annual yield or current level of interest rates in the market

$\sum_{t=1}^{N}$ = Summation sign for addition of all terms from $t = 1$ to $t = N$

PV_t = Present value of the cash flow at the end of the period t, which equals $CF_t \times DF_t$

For bonds that pay interest *semiannually*, the duration equation becomes:[5]

$$D = \frac{\sum_{t=1/2}^{N} \dfrac{CF_t \times t}{(1 + R/2)^{2t}}}{\sum_{t=1/2}^{N} \dfrac{CF_t}{(1 + R/2)^{2t}}} \tag{9.2}$$

where $t = \frac{1}{2}, 1, 1\frac{1}{2}, \ldots, N$.

A key assumption of the simple Macaulay duration model is that the yield curve or the term structure of interest rates is flat and that when rates change, the yield curve shifts in a parallel fashion. Further, the simple duration equation assumes that the issuer of a security or the borrower of a loan pays the interest and principal as promised, that is, the equation assumes no default risk. As we go through the theory and analysis of the duration model and interest rate risk in the body of the chapter, we use the simple Macaulay duration model and these assumptions. In Appendix 9B, we relax these assumptions, allowing for something other than a flat yield curve and default risk. Relaxing these assumptions changes the

---

[4] Named after an economist who was among the first to develop the duration concept.

[5] In general, the duration equation is written as

$$D = \frac{\sum_{t=1/m}^{N} \dfrac{CF_t \times t}{(1 + R/m)^{mt}}}{\sum_{t=1/m}^{N} \dfrac{CF_t}{(1 + R/m)^{mt}}}$$

where m = number of times per year interest is paid.

formulas in the body of the chapter slightly. However, the intuition and general trends remain the same as those seen in the body of the chapter.

Notice that the denominator of the duration equation is the present value of the cash flows on the security (which in an efficient market will be equal to the current market price). The numerator is the present value of each cash flow received on the security multiplied or weighted by the length of time required to receive the cash flow. To help you fully understand this formula, we next look at some examples. Table 9–1 summarizes duration and its features, which we illustrate in the examples.

The Duration of Interest-Bearing Bonds

EXAMPLE 9–1

The Duration of a Six-Year Eurobond

Eurobonds pay coupons *annually.* Suppose the annual coupon is 8 percent, the face value of the bond is $1,000, and the current yield to maturity (*R*) is also 8 percent. We show the calculation of its duration in Table 9–2.

As the calculation indicates, the duration or weighted-average time to maturity on this bond is 4.993 years. In other words, on a time value of money basis, the initial investment of $1,000 is recovered after 4.993 years. Between 4.993 years and maturity (6 years), the bond produces a profit or return to the investor.

TABLE 9–1
Duration:
Definition
and Features

Definition of Duration
1. The weighted-average time to maturity on a security.
2. The interest elasticity of a security's price to small interest rate changes.

Features of Duration
1. Duration increases with the maturity of a fixed-income security, but at a decreasing rate.
2. Duration decreases as the yield on a security increases.
3. Duration decreases as the coupon or interest payment increases.

Risk Management with Duration
1. Duration is equal to the maturity of an immunized security.
2. Duration gap is used by FIs to measure and manage the interest rate risk of an overall balance sheet.

TABLE 9–2
The Duration of a
Six-Year Eurobond
with 8 Percent
Coupon and Yield

t	CF_t	DF_t	$CF_t \times DF_t$	$CF_t \times DF_t \times t$
1	80	0.9259	74.07	74.07
2	80	0.8573	68.59	137.18
3	80	0.7938	63.51	190.53
4	80	0.7350	58.80	235.20
5	80	0.6806	54.45	272.25
6	1,080	0.6302	680.58	4,083.48
			1,000.00	4,992.71

$$D = \frac{4,992.71}{1,000} = 4.993 \text{ years}$$

EXAMPLE 9–2

The Duration of a Two-Year Government of Canada Bond

Government of Canada bonds and U.S. Treasury bonds pay coupon interest semiannually. Suppose the annual coupon rate is 8 percent, the face value is $1,000, and the annual yield to maturity (*R*) is 12 percent. See Table 9–3 for the calculation of the duration of this bond.[6] As the calculation indicates, the duration, or weighted-average time to maturity, on this bond is 1.883 years. Table 9–4 shows that if the annual coupon rate is lowered to 6 percent, duration rises to 1.909 years. Since 6 percent coupon payments are lower than 8 percent, it takes longer to recover the initial investment in the bond. In Table 9–5 duration is calculated for the original 8 percent bond, assuming that the yield to maturity increases to 16 percent. Now duration falls from 1.883 years (in Table 9–3) to 1.878 years. The higher the yield to maturity on the bond, the more the investor earns on reinvested coupons and the shorter the time needed to recover the initial investment. Finally, when the maturity on a bond decreases to 1 year (see Table 9–6), its duration falls to 0.980 years. Thus, the shorter the maturity on the bond, the more quickly the initial investment is recovered.

TABLE 9–3
The Duration of a Two-Year Government of Canada Bond with 8 Percent Coupon and 12 Percent Yield

t	*CF*$_t$	*DF*$_t$	*CF*$_t$ × *DF*$_t$	*CF*$_t$ × *DF*$_t$ × *t*
½	40	0.9434	37.74	18.87
1	40	0.8900	35.60	35.60
1½	40	0.8396	33.58	50.37
2	1,040	0.7921	823.78	1,647.56
			930.70	1,752.40

$$D = \frac{1,752.40}{930.70} = 1.883 \text{ years}$$

TABLE 9–4
Duration of a Two-Year Government of Canada Bond with 6 Percent Coupon and 12 Percent Yield

t	*CF*$_t$	*DF*$_t$	*CF*$_t$ × *DF*$_t$	*CF*$_t$ × *DF*$_t$ × *t*
½	30	0.9434	28.30	14.15
1	30	0.8900	26.70	26.70
1½	30	0.8396	25.19	37.78
2	1,030	0.7921	815.86	1,631.71
			896.05	1,710.34

$$D = \frac{1,710.34}{896.05} = 1.909 \text{ years}$$

TABLE 9–5
Duration of a Two-Year Government of Canada Bond with 8 Percent Coupon and 16 Percent Yield

t	*CF*$_t$	*DF*$_t$	*CF*$_t$ × *DF*$_t$	*CF*$_t$ × *DF*$_t$ × *t*
½	40	0.9259	37.04	18.52
1	40	0.8573	34.29	34.29
1½	40	0.7938	31.75	47.63
2	1,040	0.7350	764.43	1,528.86
			867.51	1,629.30

$$D = \frac{1,629.30}{867.51} = 1.878 \text{ years}$$

---

[6] Here we use the formula for discounting bonds with semiannual coupons: $(1 + R/2)^x$ where *x* is the number of semiannual coupon payments. Thus, at *t* = 1/2, the discount rate is (1.06), at *t* = 1 the discount rate is $(1.06)^2$, and so on.

TABLE 9–6
Duration of a
One-Year
Government of
Canada Bond with 8
Percent Coupon and
12 Percent Yield

t	CF_t	DF_t	$CF_t \times DF_t$	$CF_t \times DF_t \times t$
½	40	0.9434	37.74	18.87
1	1,040	0.8900	925.60	925.60
			963.34	944.47

$$D = \frac{944.47}{963.34} = 0.980 \text{ years}$$

Next, we look at two other types of bonds that are useful in understanding duration.

The Duration of a Zero-Coupon Bond

The Government of Canada and the U.S. Treasury have created zero-coupon bonds that allow securities firms and other investors to strip individual coupons and the principal from regular bonds and sell them to investors as separate securities. Elsewhere, such as in the Eurobond markets, corporations have issued discount or zero-coupon bonds denominated in both Canadian and U.S dollars directly. Canadian and U.S. T-bills and commercial paper usually are issued on a discount basis and are additional examples of discount bonds. These bonds sell at a discount from face value on issue, pay the face value (e.g., $1,000) on maturity, and have no intervening cash flows, such as coupon payments, between issue and maturity. The current price an investor is willing to pay for such a bond is equal to the present value of the single, fixed (face value) payment on the bond that is received on maturity (here, $1,000), or

$$P = \frac{1,000}{(1 + R)^N}$$

where R is the required annually compounded yield to maturity, N is the number of years to maturity, and P is the price. Because there are no intervening cash flows such as coupons between issue and maturity, the following must be true:

$$D_B = M_B$$

That is, the duration of a zero-coupon bond equals its maturity. Note that only for zero-coupon bonds are duration and maturity equal. Indeed, for any bond that pays some cash flows prior to maturity, its duration will always be less than its maturity.

The Duration of a Consol Bond (Perpetuities)

consol bond
A bond that pays a fixed coupon each year forever.

Although consol bonds have yet to be issued in Canada, they are of theoretical interest in exploring the differences between maturity and duration. A **consol bond** pays a fixed coupon each year. The novel feature of this bond is that it *never* matures; that is, it is a perpetuity:

$$M_c = \infty$$

In fact, consol bonds that were issued by the British government in the 1890s to finance the Boer Wars in South Africa are still outstanding. However, while its maturity is theoretically infinity, the formula for the duration of a consol bond is[7]

$$D_c = 1 + \frac{1}{R}$$

where R is the required yield to maturity. Suppose that the yield curve implies $R = 5$ percent annually; then the duration of the consol bond would be

$$D_c = 1 + \frac{1}{0.05} = 21 \text{ years}$$

Thus, while maturity is infinite, duration is finite. Specifically, on the basis of the time value of money, recovery of the initial investment on this perpetual bond takes 21 years. After 21 years, the bond produces profit for the bondholder. Moreover, as interest rates rise, the duration of the consol bond falls. Consider the 1979–1982 period, when some yields rose to around 20 percent on long-term government bonds. Then,

$$D_c = 1 + \frac{1}{0.2} = 6 \text{ years}$$

CONCEPT QUESTIONS

1. What does the denominator of the duration equation measure?
2. What does the numerator of the duration equation measure?
3. Calculate the duration of a one-year, 8 percent coupon, 10 percent yield bond that pays coupons quarterly.
4. What is the duration of a zero-coupon bond?
5. What feature is unique about a consol bond compared with other bonds?

FEATURES OF DURATION

From the preceding examples, we derive three important features of duration relating to the maturity, yield, and coupon interest of the security being analyzed.

Duration and Maturity

A comparison of Tables 9–6, 9–3, and 9–7 indicates that duration *increases* with the maturity of a fixed-income asset or liability, but at a *decreasing* rate:[8]

$$\frac{\partial D}{\partial M} > 0 \qquad \frac{\partial^2 D}{\partial M^2} < 0$$

---

[7] For reasons of space, we do not provide a formal proof here. Interested readers might refer to G. Hawawini, "Controlling the Interest Rate Risk of Bonds: An Introduction to Duration Analysis and Immunization Strategies," *Financial Markets and Portfolio Management* 1 (1986–1987), pp. 8–18.

[8] This is the case for the vast majority of securities. It needs to be noted, however, that for bonds selling below par, duration increases at a decreasing rate up to a point. At long maturities (e.g., 50 years), duration starts to decline. Few bonds in the market have a maturity long enough to see this decline.

TABLE 9–7
Duration of a
Three-Year
Government of
Canada Bond with
8 Percent Coupon
and 12 Percent Yield
(coupon interest
paid semiannually)

t	CF_t	DF_t	$CF_t \times DF_t$	$CF_t \times DF_t \times t$
½	40	0.9434	37.74	18.87
1	40	0.8900	35.60	35.60
1½	40	0.8396	33.58	50.37
2	40	0.7921	31.68	63.36
2½	40	0.7473	29.89	74.72
3	1,040	0.7050	733.16	2,199.48
			901.65	2,442.40

$$D = \frac{2{,}442.40}{901.65} = 2.709 \text{ years}$$

FIGURE 9–4
Duration versus
Maturity

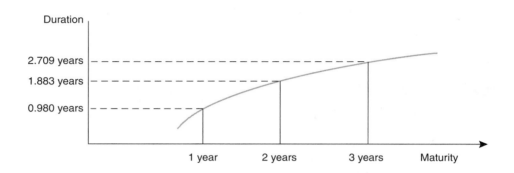

To see this, look at Figure 9–4, where we plot duration against maturity for a three-year, a two-year, and a one-year bond using the *same yield of 12 percent* for all three and assuming an annual coupon of 8 percent (with semiannual payments of 4 percent) on each bond. As the maturity of the bond increases from one year to two years (Tables 9–6 and 9–3), duration increases by 0.903 year, from 0.980 year to 1.883 years. Increasing maturity an additional year, from two years to three years (Tables 9–3 and 9–7), increases duration by 0.826, from 1.883 years to 2.709 years.

Duration and Yield

A comparison of Tables 9–3 and 9–5 indicates that duration decreases as yield increases:

$$\frac{\partial D}{\partial R} < 0$$

As the yield on the bond increased from 12 percent to 16 percent (Tables 9–3 and 9–5), the duration on the bond decreased from 1.883 years to 1.878 years. This makes sense intuitively because higher yields discount later cash flows more heavily and the relative importance, or weights, of those later cash flows decline when compared with earlier cash flows on an asset or liability.

Duration and Coupon Interest

A comparison of Tables 9–4 and 9–3 indicates that the higher the coupon or promised interest payment on the security, the lower its duration:

$$\frac{\partial D}{\partial C} < 0$$

As the coupon rate on the Government of Canada bond increased from 6 percent to 8 percent in Tables 9–4 and 9–3, the duration on the bond decreased from 1.909 years to 1.883 years. This is due to the fact that the larger the coupons or promised interest payments, the more quickly cash flows are received by investors and the higher are the present value weights of those cash flows in the duration calculation. On a time value of money basis, the investor recoups the initial investment faster when coupon payments are larger.

CONCEPT QUESTIONS	1. Which has the longest duration, a 30-year, 8 percent, zero-coupon or discount bond or an 8 percent infinite maturity consol bond? 2. What is the relationship between duration and yield to maturity on a financial security? 3. Do high-coupon bonds have high or low durations?

THE ECONOMIC MEANING OF DURATION

So far we have calculated duration for a number of different fixed-income assets and liabilities. Now we are ready to make the direct link between the number measured in years we call duration and the interest rate sensitivity of an asset or liability or of an FI's entire portfolio.

In addition to being a measure of the average life, in a cash flow sense, of an asset or liability, duration is also a *direct* measure of the interest rate sensitivity, or elasticity, of an asset or liability. In other words, the larger the numerical value of D, the more sensitive the price of that asset or liability is to changes or shocks in interest rates.

Consider the following equation showing that the current price of a bond is equal to the present value of the coupons and principal payment on the bond:

$$P = \frac{C}{(1 + R)} + \frac{C}{(1 + R)^2} + \cdots + \frac{C + F}{(1 + R)^N} \tag{9.3}$$

where

$$P = \text{Price on the bond}$$
$$C = \text{Coupon (annual)}$$
$$R = \text{Yield to maturity}$$
$$N = \text{Number of periods to maturity}$$
$$F = \text{Face value of the bond}$$

We want to find out how the price of the bond (P) changes when yields (R) rise. We know that bond prices fall, but we want to derive a direct measure of the size of this fall (i.e., its degree of price sensitivity).

Taking the derivative of the bond's price (P) with respect to the yield to maturity (R), we can show that[9]

$$\frac{dP}{dR} = -\frac{1}{1+R}[P \times D]$$

By cross-multiplying,

$$\frac{dP}{dR} \times \frac{1+R}{P} = -D$$

or, alternatively, and recognizing that interest rate changes tend to be discrete:[10]

$$\frac{\dfrac{\Delta P}{P}}{\dfrac{\Delta R}{(1+R)}} = -D \qquad (9.4)$$

---

[9] The first derivative of the bond's price in equation 9.3 with respect to the yield to maturity (R) is

$$\frac{dP}{dR} = \frac{-C}{(1+R)^2} + \frac{-2C}{(1+R)^3} + \cdots + \frac{-N(C+F)}{(1+R)^{N+1}}$$

By rearranging, we get

$$\frac{dP}{dR} = -\frac{1}{1+R}\left[\frac{C}{(1+R)} + \frac{2C}{(1+R)^2} + \cdots + \frac{N(C+F)}{(1+R)^N}\right] \qquad (9A)$$

We have shown that duration (D) is the weighted-average time to maturity using the present value of cash flows as weights; that is, by definition,

$$D = \frac{1 \times \dfrac{C}{(1+R)} + 2 \times \dfrac{C}{(1+R)^2} + \cdots + N \times \dfrac{(C+F)}{(1+R)^N}}{\dfrac{C}{(1+R)} + \dfrac{C}{(1+R)^2} + \cdots + \dfrac{(C+F)}{(1+R)^N}}$$

Since the denominator of the duration equation is simply the price (P) of the bond that is equal to the present value of the cash flows on the bond, then,

$$D = \frac{1 \times \dfrac{C}{(1+R)} + 2 \times \dfrac{C}{(1+R)^2} + \cdots + N \times \dfrac{(C+F)}{(1+R)^N}}{P}$$

Multiplying both sides of this equation by P, we get

$$P \times D = 1 \times \frac{C}{(1+R)} + 2 \times \frac{C}{(1+R)^2} + \cdots + N \times \frac{C+F}{(1+R)^N} \qquad (9B)$$

The term on the right side of equation 9B is the same term as that in square brackets in equation 9A. Substituting equation 9B into equation 9A, we get

$$\frac{dP}{dR} = -\frac{1}{1+R}[P \times D]$$

[10] In what follows, we use the Δ (change) notation instead of d (derivative notation) to recognize that interest rate changes tend to be discrete rather than infinitesimally small. For example, in real-world financial markets, the smallest observed rate change is usually one basis point, or 1/100th of 1 percent.

interest elasticity
The percentage change in the price of a bond for any given change in interest rates.

The economic meaning of equation 9.4 is that the number D is the **interest elasticity,** or sensitivity, of the security's price to small interest rate changes. That is, D describes the percentage price fall of the bond ($\Delta P/P$) for any given (present value) increase in required interest rates or yields ($\Delta R/(1 + R)$).

Equation 9.4 can be rearranged in another useful way for interpretation regarding interest sensitivity:

$$\frac{\Delta P}{P} = -D\left[\frac{\Delta R}{1 + R}\right]$$

(9.5)

Equation 9.5 and Figure 9–5, its graphic representation, show that for small changes in interest rates, bond prices move *in an inversely proportional* fashion according to the size of D. Clearly, for any given change in interest rates, long-duration securities suffer a larger capital loss (or receive a higher capital gain) should interest rates rise (fall) than do short-duration securities. By implication, gains and losses under the duration model are *symmetric*. That is, if we repeated the above examples but allowed interest rates to *decrease* by one basis point annually (or 1/2 basis point semiannually), the percentage increase in the price of the bond ($\Delta P/P$) would be proportionate with D. Further, the capital gains would be a mirror image of the capital losses for an equal (small) increase in interest rates.

modified duration
Duration divided by 1 plus the interest rate.

The duration equation can be rearranged, combining D and $(1 + R)$ into a single variable $D/(1 + R)$, to produce what practitioners call **modified duration** (MD). For annual compounding of interest:

$$\frac{\Delta P}{P} = -MD\Delta R$$

where

$$MD = \frac{D}{1 + R}$$

This form is more intuitive because we multiply MD by the simple change in interest rates rather than the discounted change in interest rates as in the general duration equation. Next, we use duration to measure the interest sensitivity of an asset or liability.

FIGURE 9–5
Proportional Relationship between Price Changes and Yield Changes on a Bond Implied by the Duration Model

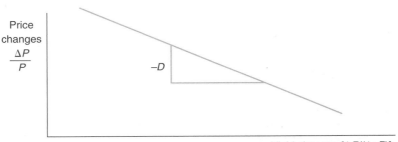

EXAMPLE 9–3

The Six-Year Eurobond

Consider Example 9–1 for the six-year Eurobond with an 8 percent coupon and 8 percent yield. We determined in Table 9–2 that its duration was approximately $D = 4.993$ years. Suppose that yields were to rise by one basis point (1/100th of 1 percent) from 8 to 8.01 percent. Then,

$$\frac{\Delta P}{P} = -(4.993)\left[\frac{0.0001}{1.08}\right]$$

$$= -0.000462$$

$$\text{or } -0.0462\%$$

The bond price had been $1,000, which was the present value of a six-year bond with 8 percent coupons and 8 percent yield. However, the duration model predicts that the price of the bond would fall to $999.538 after the increase in yield by one basis point. That is, the price would fall by 0.0462 percent, or by $0.462.[11]

EXAMPLE 9–4

The Consol Bond

Consider a consol bond with an 8 percent coupon paid annually, an 8 percent yield, and a calculated duration of 13.5 years ($D_c = 1 + 1/0.08 = 13.5$). Thus, for a one basis point change in the yield (from 8 percent to 8.01 percent),

$$\frac{\Delta P}{P} = -(13.5)\left[\frac{0.0001}{1.08}\right]$$

$$= -0.00125$$

$$\text{or } -0.125\%$$

As you can see, for any given change in yields, long-duration securities suffer a greater capital loss or receive a greater capital gain than do short-duration securities.

Semiannual Coupon Bonds

For fixed-income assets or liabilities whose interest payments are received semiannually or more frequently than annually, the formula in equation 9.5 has to be modified slightly. For semiannual payments,

$$\frac{\Delta P}{P} = -D\left[\frac{\Delta R}{1 + \frac{1}{2}R}\right] \tag{9.6}$$

The only difference between equation 9.6 and equation 9.5 is the introduction of a $\frac{1}{2}$ in the discount rate term $1 + \frac{1}{2}R$ to take into account the semiannual payments of interest.

---

[11] To calculate the dollar change in value, we can rewrite the equation as
$\Delta P = (P)(-D)(\Delta R/(1 + R)) = (\$1,000)(-4.993)(0.0001/1.08) = -\$0.462$.

EXAMPLE 9–5

Semiannual Coupon, Two-Year Maturity Treasury Bonds

Recall from Example 9–2 the two-year bond with semiannual coupons whose duration we derived in Table 9–3 as 1.883 years when annual yields were 12 percent. A one-basis-point rise in interest rates would have the following predicted effect on its price:

$$\frac{\Delta P}{P} = -1.883 \left[\frac{0.0001}{1.06}\right]$$

$$= -0.000178$$

or the price of the bond would fall by 0.0178 percent from $930.70 to $930.53. That is, a price fall of 0.0178 percent in this case translates into a dollar fall of $0.17.[12]

CONCEPT QUESTIONS

1. **What is the relationship between the duration of a bond and the interest elasticity of a bond?**
2. **How would the formula in equation 9.6 have to be modified to take into account quarterly coupon payments and monthly coupon payments?**

DURATION AND INTEREST RATE RISK

So far, you have learned how to calculate duration and you understand that the duration measure has economic meaning because it indicates the interest sensitivity, or elasticity, of an asset's or liability's value. For FIs, the major relevance of duration is as a measure for managing interest rate risk exposure. Also important is the role of duration in allowing the FI to immunize its balance sheet or some subset of that balance sheet against interest rate risk. In the following sections we consider two examples of how FIs can use the duration measure for immunization purposes. The first is its use by insurance company and pension fund managers to help meet promised cash flow payments to policyholders or beneficiaries at a particular time in the future. The second is its use to immunize or insulate the whole balance sheet of an FI against interest rate risk.

Duration and Interest Rate Risk Management on a Single Security

Frequently, pension fund and life insurance company managers face the problem of structuring their asset investments so they can pay out a given cash amount to policyholders in some future period. The classic example of this is an insurance policy that pays the holder some lump sum on reaching retirement age. The risk to the life insurance company manager is that interest rates on the funds generated from investing the holder's premiums could fall. Thus, the accumulated returns on the premiums invested could not meet the target or promised amount. In effect, the insurance company would be forced to draw down its reserves and net worth to meet its payout commitments. (See Chapter 3 for a discussion of this risk.)

Suppose that we are in 2010 and the insurer has to make a guaranteed payment to a policyholder in five years, 2015. For simplicity, we assume that this target

---

[12] To calculate the dollar change in value, we can rewrite the equation as
$\Delta P = (P)(-D)(\Delta R/(1 + R/2)) = (\$930.70)(-1.883)(0.0001/1.06) = -\$0.17.$

guaranteed payment is $1,469, a lump-sum policy payout on retirement, equivalent to investing $1,000 at an annually compounded rate of 8 percent over five years. Of course, realistically, this payment would be much larger, but the underlying principles of the example do not change by scaling the payout amount (up or down).

To immunize, or protect, itself against interest rate risk, the insurer needs to determine which investments would produce a cash flow of exactly $1,469 in five years regardless of what happens to interest rates in the immediate future. The FI investing either in a five-year maturity and duration zero-coupon bond or in a coupon bond with a five-year duration would produce a $1,469 cash flow in five years no matter what happened to interest rates in the immediate future. Next, we consider the two strategies: buying five-year maturity (and duration) deep-discount bonds and buying five-year duration coupon bonds.

Buy Five-Year Maturity Discount Bonds

Given a $1,000 face value and an 8 percent yield and assuming annual compounding, the current price per five-year discount bond would be $680.58 per bond:

$$P = 680.58 = \frac{1,000}{(1.08)^5}$$

If the insurer bought 1.469 of these bonds at a total cost of $1,000 in 2010, these investments would produce exactly $1,469 on maturity in five years ($1,000 × (1.08)^5 = $1,469). The reason is that the duration of this bond portfolio exactly matches the target horizon for the insurer's future liability to its policyholder. Intuitively, since no intervening cash flows or coupons are paid by the issuer of the zero-coupon discount bonds, future changes in interest rates have no reinvestment income effect. Thus, the return would be unaffected by intervening interest rate changes.

Suppose no five-year discount bonds exist. Then the portfolio manager may seek to invest in appropriate duration coupon bonds to hedge interest rate risk. In this example the appropriate investment would be in five-year duration coupon-bearing bonds.

Buy a Five-Year Duration Coupon Bond

We demonstrated earlier in Table 9–2 that a six-year maturity Eurobond paying 8 percent coupons with an 8 percent yield to maturity had a duration of 4.993 years, or approximately five years. If we buy this six-year maturity, five-year duration bond in 2010 and hold it for five years, until 2015, the term exactly matches the target horizon of the insurer. The cash flows generated at the end of five years will be $1,469 whether interest rates stay at 8 percent or instantaneously (immediately) rise to 9 percent or fall to 7 percent. Thus, buying a coupon bond whose duration exactly matches the time horizon of the insurer also immunizes the insurer against interest rate changes.

EXAMPLE 9–6

Interest Rates Remain at 8 Percent

The cash flows received by the insurer on the bond if interest rates stay at 8 percent throughout the five years would be

1. Coupons, 5 × $80	$ 400
2. Reinvestment income	69
3. Proceeds from sale of bond at end of fifth year	1,000
	$1,469

We calculate each of the three components of the insurer's income from the bond investment as follows:

1. *Coupons.* The $400 from coupons is simply the annual coupon of $80 received in each of the five years.
2. *Reinvestment income.* Because the coupons are received annually, they can be reinvested at 8 percent as they are received, generating an additional cash flow of $69.[13]
3. *Bond sale proceeds.* The proceeds from the sale are calculated by recognizing that the six-year bond has just one year left to maturity when it is sold by the insurance company at the end of the fifth year. That is

| ↓ *Sell* | *$1,080* |

| *Year 5* | *Year 6* |
| *(2015)* | *(2016)* |

What fair market price can the insurer expect to get when selling the bond at the end of the fifth year with one year left to maturity? A buyer would be willing to pay the present value of the $1,080—final coupon plus face value—to be received at the end of the one remaining year (i.e., in 2016), or

$$P_5 = \frac{1,080}{1.08} = \$1,000$$

Thus, the insurer would be able to sell the one remaining cash flow of $1,080, to be received in the bond's final year, for $1,000.

Next, we show that since this bond has a duration of five years, matching the insurer's target period, even if interest rates were to instantaneously fall to 7 percent or rise to 9 percent, the expected cash flows from the bond would still exactly sum to $1,469. That is, the coupons + reinvestment income + principal at the end of the fifth year would be immunized. In other words, the cash flows on the bond are protected against interest rate changes.

EXAMPLE 9–7

Interest Rates Fall to 7 Percent

In this example with falling interest rates, the cash flows over the five years would be

1. Coupons, 5 × $80	$ 400
2. Reinvestment income	60
3. Bond sale proceeds	1,009
	$1,469

---

[13] Receiving annual coupons of $80 is equivalent to receiving an annuity of $80. There are tables and formulas that help us calculate the value of $1 received each year over a given number of years that can be reinvested at a given interest rate. The appropriate terminal value of receiving $1 a year for five years and reinvesting at 8 percent can be determined from future value of an annuity factor (FVAF) tables, whose general formula is

$$FVAF_{n,R} = \left[\frac{(1 + R)^n - 1}{R}\right]$$

In our example,

$$FVAF_{5,\,8\%} = \left[\frac{(1 + 0.08)^5 - 1}{0.08}\right] = 5.867$$

Thus, the reinvestment income for $80 of coupons per year is

Reinvestment income $= (80 \times 5.867) - 400 = 469 - 400 = 69$

Note that we take away $400 since we have already counted the simple coupon income (5 × $80).

The total proceeds over the five years are unchanged from what they were when interest rates were 8 percent. To see why this occurs, consider what happens to the three parts of the cash flow when rates fall to 7 percent:

1. *Coupons.* Are unchanged since the insurer still gets five annual coupons of $80 = $400.
2. *Reinvestment income.* The coupons can now be reinvested only at the lower rate of 7 percent. Reinvestment income is only $60.[14]
3. *Bond sale proceeds.* When the six-year maturity bond is sold at the end of the fifth year with one cash flow of $1,080 remaining, investors are now willing to pay more:

$$P_5 = \frac{1,080}{1.07} = 1,009$$

That is, the bond can be sold for $9 more than it could have when rates were 8 percent. The reason for this is that investors can get only 7 percent on newly issued bonds, while this older bond was issued with a higher coupon of 8 percent.

A comparison of reinvestment income with bond sale proceeds indicates that the fall in rates has produced a *gain* on the bond sale proceeds of $9. This exactly offsets the loss of reinvestment income of $9 due to reinvesting at a lower interest rate. Thus, total cash flows remain unchanged at $1,469.

EXAMPLE 9–8	In this example with rising interest rates, the proceeds from the bond investment are	
Interest Rates Rise to 9 Percent	1. Coupons, 5 × $80	$ 400
	2. Reinvestment income [(5.985 × 80) − 400]	78
	3. Bond sale proceeds (1,080/1.09)	991
		$1,469

Notice that the rise in interest rates from 8 percent to 9 percent leaves the final terminal cash flow unaffected at $1,469. The rise in rates has generated $9 extra reinvestment income ($78 − $69), but the price at which the bond can be sold at the end of the fifth year has declined from $1,000 to $991, equal to a capital loss of $9. Thus, the gain in reinvestment income is exactly offset by the capital loss on the sale of the bond.

These examples demonstrate that matching the duration of a coupon bond—or any other fixed–interest rate instrument, such as a loan or mortgage—to the FI's target or investment horizon *immunizes* the FI against instantaneous shocks to interest rates. The gains or losses on reinvestment income that result from an interest rate change are exactly offset by losses or gains from the bond proceeds on sale.

Duration and Interest Rate Risk Management on the Whole Balance Sheet of an FI

So far we have looked at the durations of individual instruments and ways to select individual fixed-income securities to protect FIs such as life insurance companies and pensions funds with precommitted liabilities such as future pension plan payouts. The duration model can also evaluate the overall interest rate exposure for an FI, that is, measure the **duration gap** on its balance sheet.

duration gap
A measure of overall interest rate risk exposure for an FI.

---

[14] This reinvestment income is calculated as follows.

$$FVAF_{5,\,7\%} = \left[\frac{(1 + 0.07)5 - 1}{0.07}\right] = 5.751$$

Reinvestment income = (5.751 × 80) − 400 = 60, which is $9 less than it was when rates were 8 percent.

The Duration Gap for a Financial Institution

To estimate the overall duration gap of an FI, we determine first the duration of an FI's asset portfolio (A) and the duration of its liability portfolio (L). These can be calculated as

$$D_A = X_{1A}D_1^A + X_{2A}D_2^A + \cdots + X_{nA}D_n^A$$

and

$$D_L = X_{1L}D_1^L + X_{2L}D_2^L + \cdots + X_{nL}D_n^L$$

where

$$X_{1j} + X_{2j} + \cdots + X_{nj} = 1 \quad \text{and} \quad j = A, L$$

The values of X_{nj} in the equation are equal to the market value proportions of each asset or liability held in the respective asset and liability portfolios. Thus, if new 30-year Government of Canada bonds were 1 percent of a life insurer's portfolio and D_1^A (the duration of those bonds) was equal to 9.25 years, then $X_{1A}D_1^A = 0.01(9.25) = 0.0925$. More simply, the duration of a portfolio of assets or liabilities is a market value weighted average of the individual durations of the assets or liabilities on the FI's balance sheet.[15]

Consider an FI's simplified market value balance sheet:

Assets ($)	Liabilities ($)
A = 100	L = 90
	E = 10
100	100

From the balance sheet,

$$A = L + E$$

and

$$\Delta A = \Delta L + \Delta E$$

or

$$\Delta E = \Delta A - \Delta L$$

That is, when interest rates change, the change in the FI's equity or net worth (E) is equal to the difference between the change in the market values of assets and liabilities on each side of the balance sheet.

Since $\Delta E = \Delta A - \Delta L$, we need to determine how ΔA and ΔL—the changes in the market values of assets and liabilities on the balance sheet—are related to duration.

From the duration model (assuming annual compounding of interest):

$$\frac{\Delta A}{A} = -D_A \frac{\Delta R}{(1 + R)}$$

$$\frac{\Delta L}{L} = -D_L \frac{\Delta R}{(1 + R)}$$

---

[15] This derivation of an FI's duration gap closely follows G. Kaufman, "Measuring and Managing Interest Rate Risk: A Primer," Federal Reserve Bank of Chicago, *Economic Perspectives*, 1984, pp. 16–29.

Here we have simply substituted $\Delta A/A$ or $\Delta L/L$, the percentage change in the market values of assets or liabilities, for $\Delta P/P$, the percentage change in any single bond's price and D_A or D_L, the duration of the FI's asset or liability portfolio, for D_i, the duration on any given bond, deposit, or loan. The term $\Delta R/(1+R)$ reflects the shock to interest rates as before.[16] To show dollar changes, these equations can be rewritten as

$$\Delta A = -D_A \times A \times \frac{\Delta R}{(1+R)} \qquad (9.7)$$

and

$$\Delta L = -D_L \times L \times \frac{\Delta R}{(1+R)} \qquad (9.8)$$

We can substitute these two expressions into the equation $\Delta E = \Delta A - \Delta L$. Rearranging and combining this equation[17] results in a measure of the change in the market value of equity:

$$\Delta E = -[D_A - D_L k] \times A \times \frac{\Delta R}{1+R} \qquad (9.9)$$

where $k = L/A$ is a measure of the FI's leverage, that is, the amount of borrowed funds or liabilities rather than owners' equity used to fund its asset portfolio. The effect of interest rate changes on the market value of an FI's equity or net worth (ΔE) breaks down into three effects:

1. *The leverage adjusted duration gap* $= [D_A - D_L k]$. This gap is measured in years and reflects the degree of duration mismatch in an FI's balance sheet. Specifically, the larger this gap is *in absolute terms*, the more exposed the FI is to interest rate shocks.
2. *The size of the FI.* The term A measures the size of the FI's assets. The larger the scale of the FI, the larger the dollar size of the potential net worth exposure from any given interest rate shock.

---

[16] We assume that the level of rates and the expected shock to interest rates are the same for both assets and liabilities, which means that the FI's spread (the difference between the rate on earning assets and interest-bearing liabilities) is zero. However, as long as the FI has more earning assets than interest-bearing liabilities, it will have a positive level for net interest income. This assumption is standard in Macaulay duration analysis. While restrictive, this assumption can be relaxed. However, if this is done, the duration measure changes, as is discussed in Appendix 9B.

[17] We do this as follows:

$$\Delta E = \left[-D_A \times A \times \frac{\Delta R}{(1+R)} \right] - \left[-D_L \times L \times \frac{\Delta R}{(1+R)} \right]$$

Assuming that the level of rates and the expected shock to interest rates are the same for both assets and liabilities:

$$\Delta E = [-D_A A + D_L L] \frac{\Delta R}{(1+R)}$$

or

$$\Delta E = -[D_A A - D_L L] \frac{\Delta R}{(1+R)}$$

To rearrange the equation in a slightly more intuitive fashion, we multiply and divide both $D_A A$ and $D_L L$ by A (assets):

$$\Delta E = -\left[D_A \frac{A}{A} - D_L \frac{L}{A} \right] \times A \times \frac{\Delta R}{(1+R)}$$

or $$\Delta E = -[D_A - D_L K] \times A \times \frac{\Delta R}{(1+R)}$$

3. *The size of the interest rate shock* $= \Delta R/(1 + R)$. The larger the shock, the greater the FI's exposure.

Given this, we express the exposure of the net worth of the FI as

$$\Delta E = -[\text{Leverage-adjusted duration gap}] \times \text{Asset size} \times \text{Interest rate shock}$$

Interest rate shocks are largely external to the FI and often result from changes in the Bank of Canada's monetary policy (as discussed in the first section of Chapter 8). The size of the duration gap and the size of the FI, however, are under the control of management. A sharp drop in interest rates in 2002 left Fannie Mae, a key U.S. mortgage provider, with a negative duration gap of 14 months on its US$747 billion loan portfolio.[18]

Equation 9.9 and the duration model provide an FI manager with a benchmark measure of the FI's performance for various interest rate changes and therefore the extent to which the FI is exposed to interest rate risk. If, for an expected change in interest rates, managers find the change in equity will be small or negative, the duration model can be used to identify changes needed on or off the FI's balance sheet to reduce or even immunize the FI against interest rate risk. Using an example, the next section explains how a manager can use information on an FI's duration gap to restructure the balance sheet to limit losses in, or even immunize stockholders' net worth against, interest rate risk (i.e., to set the balance sheet up *before* a change in interest rates, so that ΔE is non-negative for an expected change in interest rates). Chapters 23 through 25 look at ways a manager can use the duration gap to take off-balance-sheet positions in derivative securities to reduce or immunize the FI against interest rate risk.

EXAMPLE 9–9

Interest Rates Rise to 9 Percent

Suppose the FI manager calculates that:

$$D_A = 5 \text{ years}$$

$$D_L = 3 \text{ years}$$

Then the manager learns from an economic forecasting unit that rates are expected to rise from 10 to 11 percent in the immediate future; that is:

$$\Delta R = 1\% = 0.01$$

$$1 + R = 1.10$$

The FI's initial balance sheet is assumed to be:

Assets ($ millions)	Liabilities ($ millions)
$A = 100$	$L = 90$
	$E = 10$
100	100

---

[18] We discuss the role of Fannie Mae in the U.S. economy and, specifically, the mortgage markets, in Chapter 26. Fannie Mae and Freddie Mac are U.S. government-sponsored agencies that have been key players in the subprime crisis that has affected FIs and markets globally.

The FI's manager calculates the potential loss to equity holders' net worth (E) if the forecast of rising rates proves true as follows:

$$\Delta E = -(D_A - kD_L) \times A \times \frac{\Delta R}{(1 + R)}$$

$$= -(5 - (0.9)(3)) \times \$100 \text{ million} \times \frac{0.01}{1.1} = -\$2.09 \text{ million}$$

The FI could lose $2.09 million in net worth if rates rise 1 percent. Since the FI started with $10 million in equity, the loss of $2.09 million is almost 21 percent of its initial net worth. The market value balance sheet after the rise in rates by 1 percent would look like this:[19]

Assets ($ millions)	Liabilities ($ millions)
A = 95.45	L = 87.54
	E = 7.91
95.45	95.45

Even though the rise in interest rates would not push the FI into economic insolvency, it reduces the FI's net worth-to-assets ratio from 10 (10/100) to 8.29 percent (7.91/95.45). To counter this effect, the manager might reduce the FI's adjusted duration gap. In an extreme case, the gap might be reduced to zero:

$$\Delta E = -[0] \times A \times \Delta R/(1 + R) = 0$$

To do this, the FI should not directly set $D_A = D_L$, which ignores the fact that the FI's assets (A) do not equal its borrowed liabilities (L) and that k (which reflects the ratio L/A) is not equal to 1. To see the importance of factoring in leverage, suppose the manager increased the duration of the FI's liabilities to five years, the same as D_A. Then,

$$\Delta E = -[5 - (0.9)(5)] \times \$100 \text{ million} \times (0.01/1.1) = -\$0.45 \text{ million}$$

The FI is still exposed to a loss of $0.45 million if rates rise by 1 percent. An appropriate strategy would involve changing D_L until

$$D_A = kD_L = 5 \text{ years}$$

For example,

$$\Delta E = -[5 - (0.9)5.55] \times \$100 \text{ million} \times (0.01/1.1) = 0$$

In this case the FI manager sets $D_L = 5.55$ years, or slightly longer than $D_A = 5$ years, to compensate for the fact that only 90 percent of assets are funded by

---

[19] These values are calculated as follows:

$$\Delta A/A = -5(0.01/1.1) = -0.04545 = -4.545\%$$
$$100 + (-0.04545)100 = 95.45$$

and

$$\Delta L/L = -3(0.01/1.1) = -0.02727 = -2.727\%$$
$$90 + (-0.02727)90 = 87.54$$

borrowed liabilities, with the other 10 percent funded by equity. Note that the FI manager has at least three other ways to reduce the adjusted duration gap to zero:

1. *Reduce D_A.* Reduce D_A from 5 years to 2.7 years (equal to kD_L or (0.9)3) such that

$$[D_A - kD_L] = [2.7 - (0.9)(3)] = 0$$

2. *Reduce D_A and increase D_L.* Shorten the duration of assets and lengthen the duration of liabilities at the same time. One possibility would be to *reduce D_A* to 4 years and to *increase D_L* to 4.44 years such that

$$[D_A - kD_L] = [4 - (0.9)(4.44)] = 0$$

3. *Change k and D_L.* Increase k (leverage) from 0.9 to 0.95 and increase D_L from 3 years to 5.26 years such that

$$[D_A - kD_L] = [5 - (0.95)(5.26)] = 0$$

CONCEPT QUESTIONS

1. Refer to the example of the insurer in Examples 9–6 through 9–8. Suppose rates fell to 6 percent. Would the FI's portfolio still be immunized? What if rates rose to 10 percent?
2. How is the overall duration gap for an FI calculated?
3. How can a manager use information on an FI's duration gap to restructure, and thereby immunize, the balance sheet against interest rate risk?
4. Suppose D_A = 3 years, D_L = 6 years, k = 0.8, and A = $100 million. What is the effect on owners' net worth if $\Delta R/(1 + R)$ rises 1 percent? (ΔE = $1,800,000)

IMMUNIZATION AND REGULATORY CONSIDERATIONS

In the above section we assumed that the FI manager wants to structure the duration of assets and liabilities to immunize the equity or net worth stake (E) of the FI's equity owners from interest rate shocks. However, regulators periodically monitor the solvency or capital position of FIs. As we discuss in greater detail in Chapter 20 on capital adequacy, regulators set minimum target ratios for an FI's capital (or net worth) to assets. The simplest is the ratio of FI capital to its assets, or

$$\frac{E}{A} = \text{Capital (net worth) ratio}$$

Given the regulations imposed on the minimum level of the capital ratio, if an FI's asset levels change significantly through time, FI managers may be most interested in immunizing against changes in the capital ratio [$\Delta(E/A)$] due to interest rate risk rather than changes in the level of capital (ΔE). For example, suppose the FI manager is close to the minimum regulatory required E/A (or capital) ratio and wants to immunize the FI against any fall in this ratio if interest rates rise.[20] That is, the immunization target is no longer ΔE = 0 when rates change but $\Delta(E/A)$ = 0.

---

[20] In actuality, federally regulated deposit-taking institutions (DTIs) in Canada are subject to a risk-based capital adequacy framework that is covered in detail in Chapter 20.

Obviously, immunizing ΔE against interest rate risk cannot result in the same management strategy as immunizing $\Delta(E/A)$. A portfolio constructed to immunize ΔE would have a different duration match from that required to immunize $\Delta(E/A)$. Or, more simply, the manager could satisfy either the FI's stockholders or the regulators *but not both* simultaneously.

More specifically, when the objective is to immunize equity capital against interest rate risk, that is, to set $\Delta E = 0$, the FI manager should structure the balance sheet so that the leverage-adjusted duration gap is zero:

$$\Delta E = 0 = D_A - kD_L$$

or set

$$D_A = kD_L$$

By comparison, to immunize the capital ratio, that is, to set $\Delta(E/A) = 0$ the manager needs to set[21]

$$D_A = D_L$$

In this scenario, the leverage-adjustment effect (k) drops out. If $D_A = 5$, then immunizing the capital ratio would require setting $D_L = 5$.

CONCEPT QUESTION   Is immunizing a bank's net worth the same as immunizing its net worth–assets ratio? If not, why not?

In the next section, we analyze weaknesses of the duration model. Specifically, there are several practical problems in estimating duration and duration gaps for real-world FIs.

DIFFICULTIES IN APPLYING THE DURATION MODEL

www.bis.org

Critics of the duration model have often claimed that it is difficult to apply in real-world situations. However, duration measures and immunization strategies are useful in most real-world situations. In fact, the model proposed by the Bank for International Settlements to monitor bank interest rate risk-taking is based heavily on the duration model. In this section, we look at the various criticisms of the duration model and discuss ways a modern FI manager would deal with them in practice. In Appendix 9B, we present some of the more advanced issues associated with these weaknesses.

Duration Matching Can Be Costly

Critics charge that although in principle an FI manager can change D_A and D_L to immunize the FI against interest rate risk, restructuring the balance sheet of a large and complex FI can be both time-consuming and costly. Although this argument may have been true historically, the growth of purchased funds, asset securitization, and loan sales markets has considerably eased the speed and lowered the transaction costs of major balance sheet restructurings. (See Chapters 26 and 27 for a discussion of these strategies.) Moreover, an FI manager could still manage risk exposure using the duration model by employing techniques other than direct

---

[21] See Kaufman, "Measuring and Managing Interest Rate Risk: A Primer," for a proof.

portfolio rebalancing to immunize against interest rate risk. Managers can get many of the same results of direct duration matching by taking hedging positions in the markets for derivative securities, such as futures and forwards (Chapter 23); options, caps, floors, and collars (Chapter 24); and swaps (Chapter 25).[22]

Immunization Is a Dynamic Problem

Immunization is an aspect of the duration model that is not well understood. Let's go back to the earlier immunization example in which an insurer sought to buy bonds to provide an accumulated cash flow of $1,469 in five years no matter what happened to interest rates. We showed that buying a six-year maturity, 8 percent coupon bond with a five-year duration immunizes the insurer against an instantaneous change in interest rates. The word *instantaneous* is very important here; it means a change in interest rates immediately after purchasing the bond. However, interest rates can change at any time over the holding period. Further, the duration of a bond changes as time passes, that is, as it approaches maturity or the target horizon date. In addition, duration changes at a different rate than does real or calendar time.

To understand this time effect, consider the initially hedged position in which the insurer bought the five-year duration (six-year maturity), 8 percent coupon bond in 2010 to match its cash flow target of $1,469 in 2015. Suppose the FI manager puts the bond in the bottom drawer of a desk and does not think about it for a year, believing that the insurance company's position is fully hedged. After one year has passed (in 2011), suppose interest rates (yields) have fallen from 8 percent to 7 percent and the manager opens the drawer of the desk and finds the bond. Knowing the target date is now only four years away, the manager recalculates the duration of the bond. Imagine the manager's shock on finding that the same 8 percent coupon bond with a 7 percent yield and only five years left to maturity has a duration of 4.33 years. This means the insurance company is no longer hedged; the 4.33-year duration of this bond portfolio *exceeds* the investment horizon of four years. As a result, the manager has to restructure the bond portfolio to remain immunized. One way to do this is to sell some of the five-year bonds (4.33-year duration) and buy some bonds of shorter duration so that the overall duration of the investment portfolio is four years.

For example, suppose the insurer sold 50 percent of the five-year bonds with a 4.33-year duration and invested the proceeds in 3.67-year duration and maturity zero-coupon bonds. Because duration and maturity are the same for discount bonds, the duration of the asset portfolio is

$$D_A = [4.33 \times 0.5] + [3.67 \times 0.5] = 4 \text{ years}$$

This simple example demonstrates that immunization based on duration is a dynamic strategy. In theory, the strategy requires the portfolio manager to rebalance the portfolio continuously to ensure that the duration of the investment portfolio exactly matches the investment horizon (i.e., the duration of liabilities). Because continuous rebalancing may not be easy to do and involves costly transaction fees, most portfolio managers seek to be only approximately dynamically immunized against interest rate changes by rebalancing at discrete intervals, such as quarterly. That is, there is a trade-off between being perfectly immunized and the transaction costs of maintaining an immunized balance sheet dynamically.

---

[22] In particular, instead of direct immunization of a positive duration gap ($D_A > D_L$), an FI manager could sell futures (forwards), take the fixed-rate side of an interest rate swap, buy put options on bonds, and/or buy an interest rate cap.

FIGURE 9–6
Duration versus
True Relationship

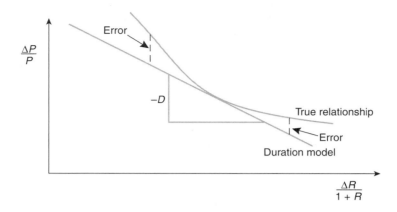

Large Interest Rate Changes and Convexity

Duration accurately measures the price sensitivity of fixed-income securities for small changes in interest rates of the order of one basis point. But suppose interest rate shocks are much larger, of the order of 2 percent, or 200 basis points. Then duration becomes a less accurate predictor of how much the prices of securities will change and therefore a less accurate measure of interest rate sensitivity. Looking at Figure 9–6, you can see the reason for this. Note first the change in a bond's price due to yield changes according to the duration model and second, the true relationship, as calculated directly, using the exact present value calculation for bond valuation.

The duration model predicts that the relationship between interest rate shocks and bond price changes will be proportional to D (duration). However, by precisely calculating the true change in bond prices, we would find that for large interest rate increases, duration overpredicts the *fall* in bond prices, while for large interest rate decreases, it underpredicts the *increase* in bond prices. That is, the duration model predicts symmetric effects for rate increases and decreases on bond prices. As Figure 9–6 shows, in actuality, for rate increases, the *capital loss effect* tends to be smaller than the *capital gain effect* is for rate decreases. This is the result of the bond price–yield relationship exhibiting a property called *convexity* rather than *linearity*, as assumed by the basic duration model.

convexity
The degree of curvature of the price–yield curve around some interest rate level.

Note that **convexity** is a desirable feature for an FI manager to capture in a portfolio of assets. Buying a bond or a portfolio of assets that exhibits a lot of convexity, or curvature, in the price–yield curve relationship is similar to buying partial interest rate risk insurance. Specifically, high convexity means that for equally large changes of interest rates up and down (e.g., plus or minus 2 percent), the capital gain effect of a rate decrease more than offsets the capital loss effect of a rate increase. As we show in Appendix 9B, all fixed-income assets or liabilities exhibit some convexity in their price–yield relationships.[23]

To see the importance of accounting for the effects of convexity in assessing the impact of large rate changes on an FI's portfolio, consider the six-year Eurobond

---

[23] To be more precise, fixed-income securities without special option features such as callable bonds and mortgage-backed securities exhibit convexity. A callable bond tends to exhibit negative convexity (or concavity), as do some mortgage-backed securities.

FIGURE 9–7
The Price–Yield
Curve for the Six-
Year Eurobond

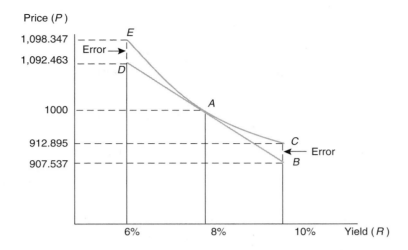

with an 8 percent coupon and yield. According to Table 9–2 (on page 182), its duration is 4.993 years and its current price P_0 is \$1,000 at a yield of 8 percent:

$$P_0 = \frac{80}{(1.08)} + \frac{80}{(1.08)^2} + \frac{80}{(1.08)^3}$$

$$+ \frac{80}{(1.08)^4} + \frac{80}{(1.08)^5} + \frac{1,080}{(1.08)^6} = \$1,000$$

This is point A on the price–yield curve in Figure 9–7.

If rates rise from 8 to 10 percent, the duration model predicts that the bond price will fall by 9.2463 percent; that is

$$\frac{\Delta P}{P} = -4.993 \left[\frac{0.02}{1.08} \right] = -9.2463\%$$

or, from a price of \$1,000 to \$907.537 (see point B in Figure 9–7). However, calculating the exact change in the bond's price after a rise in yield to 10 percent, we find that its true value is

$$P_0 = \frac{80}{(1.1)} + \frac{80}{(1.1)^2} + \frac{80}{(1.1)^3}$$

$$+ \frac{80}{(1.1)^4} + \frac{80}{(1.1)^5} + \frac{1,080}{(1.1)^6} = \$912.895$$

This is point C in Figure 9–7. As you can see, the true or actual fall in price is less than the predicted fall by \$5.358. This means that there is more than a 0.5 percent error using the duration model. The reason for this is the natural convexity to the price–yield curve as yields rise.

Reversing the experiment reveals that the duration model would predict the bond's price to rise by 9.2463 percent if yields fell from 8 to 6 percent, resulting in a predicted price of \$1,092.463 (see point D in Figure 9–7). By comparison, the true or actual change in price can be computed as $1,098.347 by estimating the present value of the bond's coupons and its face value with a 6 percent yield (see point *E* in Figure 9–7). The duration model has underpredicted the bond price increase by $5.884, or by over 0.5 percent of the true price increase.

An important question for the FI manager is whether a 0.5 percent error is big enough to be concerned about. This depends on the size of the interest rate change and the size of the portfolio under management. Clearly, 0.5 percent of a large number will still be a large number!

Summary

This chapter analyzed the duration model approach to measuring interest rate risk. The duration model is superior to the simple repricing model in that it incorporates the timing of cash flows as well as maturity effects into a simple measure of interest rate risk. The duration measure could be used to immunize a particular liability as well as the whole FI balance sheet. How-ever, as the concluding section of the chapter indicates, a number of potential problems exist in applying the duration model in real-world scenarios. Despite these weaknesses, the duration model is fairly robust and can deal with a large number of real-world complexities, such as credit risk, convexity, floating interest rates, and uncertain maturities.

Questions and Problems

1. What are the two different general interpretations of the concept of duration, and what is the technical definition of this term? How does duration differ from maturity?

2. Two bonds are available for purchase in the financial markets. The first bond is a two-year, $1,000 bond that pays an annual coupon of 10 percent. The second bond is a two-year, $1,000 zero-coupon bond.

   a. What is the duration of the coupon bond if the current yield to maturity (YTM) is 8 percent? 10 percent? 12 percent? (*Hint:* You may wish to create a spreadsheet program to assist in the calculations.)

   b. How does the change in the current YTM affect the duration of this coupon bond?

   c. Calculate the duration of the zero-coupon bond with a YTM of 8 percent, 10 percent, and 12 percent.

   d. How does the change in the current YTM affect the duration of the zero-coupon bond?

   e. Why does the change in the YTM affect the coupon bond differently than it affects the zero-coupon bond?

3. A one-year, $100,000 loan carries a market interest rate of 12 percent. The loan requires payment of accrued interest and one-half of the principal at the end of six months. The remaining principal and the accrued interest are due at the end of the year.

   a. What will be the cash flows at the end of six months and at the end of the year?

   b. What is the present value of each cash flow discounted at the market rate? What is the total present value?

   c. What proportion of the total present value of cash flows occurs at the end of six months? What proportion occurs at the end of the year?

   d. What is the duration of this loan?

4. What is the duration of a five-year, $1,000 Government of Canada bond with a 10 percent semi-annual coupon selling at par? Selling with a YTM of 12 percent? 14 percent? What can you conclude about the relationship between duration and yield to maturity? Plot the relationship. Why does this relationship exist?

5. Consider three bonds, each of which has a 10 percent semiannual coupon and trades at par.

   a. Calculate the duration for a bond that has a maturity of four years, three years, and two years.

   b. What conclusions can you reach about the relationship between duration and the time to maturity? Plot the relationship.

6. A six-year, $10,000 GIC pays 6 percent interest annually. What is the duration of the GIC? What would be the duration if interest were paid semiannually? What is the relationship of duration to the relative frequency of interest payments?

7. What is a consol bond? What is the duration of a consol bond that sells at a YTM of 8 percent? 10 percent? 12 percent? Would a consol trading at a YTM of 10 percent have a greater duration than a 20-year zero-coupon bond trading at the same YTM? Why?

8. Maximum Pension Fund is attempting to balance one of the bond portfolios under its management. The fund has identified three bonds that have five-year maturities and trade at a YTM of 9 percent. The bonds differ only in that the coupons are 7 percent, 9 percent, and 11 percent.

   a. What is the duration for each bond?

   b. What is the relationship between duration and the amount of coupon interest that is paid? Plot the relationship.

9. An insurance company is analyzing three bonds and is using duration as the measure of interest rate risk. All three bonds trade at a YTM of 10 percent and have $10,000 par values. The bonds differ only in the amount of annual coupon interest they pay: 8, 10, and 12 percent.

   a. What is the duration for each five-year bond?

   b. What is the relationship between duration and the amount of coupon interest that is paid?

10. You can obtain a loan for $100,000 at a rate of 10 percent for two years. You have a choice of paying the principal at the end of the second year or amortizing the loan, that is, paying interest (10 percent) and principal in equal payments each year. The loan is priced at par.

    a. What is the duration of the loan under both methods of payment?

    b. Explain the difference in the two results.

11. How is duration related to the interest elasticity of a fixed-income security? What is the relationship between duration and the price of the fixed-income security?

12. You have discovered that the price of a bond rose from $975 to $995 when the YTM fell from 9.75 percent to 9.25 percent. What is the duration of the bond?

13. Calculate the duration of a two-year, $1,000 bond that pays an annual coupon of 10 percent and trades at a yield of 14 percent. What is the expected change in the price of the bond if interest rates decline by 0.50 percent (50 basis points)?

14. The duration of an 11-year, $1,000 Government of Canada bond paying a 10 percent semiannual coupon and selling at par has been estimated at 6.9 years.

    a. What is the modified duration of the bond [modified duration = $D/(1 + R)$]?

    b. What will be the estimated price change of the bond if market interest rates increase 0.10 percent (10 basis points)? If rates decrease 0.20 percent (20 basis points)?

    c. What would the actual price of the bond be under each rate change situation in part (b) using the traditional present value bond pricing techniques? What is the amount of error in each case?

15. Suppose you purchase a five-year, 13.76 percent bond that is priced to yield 10 percent.

    a. Show that the duration of this annual payment bond is equal to four years.

    b. Show that if interest rates rise to 11 percent within the next year and your investment horizon is four years from today, you will still earn a 10 percent yield on your investment.

    c. Show that a 10 percent yield also will be earned if interest rates fall next year to 9 percent.

16. Consider the case in which an investor holds a bond for a period of time longer than the duration of the bond, that is, longer than the original investment horizon.

    a. If interest rates rise, will the return that is earned exceed or fall short of the original required rate of return? Explain.

    b. What will happen to the realized return if interest rates decrease? Explain.

    c. Recalculate parts (b) and (c) of problem 15 above, assuming that the bond is held for all five years, to verify your answers to parts (a) and (b) of this problem.

    d. If either calculation in part (c) is greater than the original required rate of return, why would an investor ever try to match the duration of an asset with his or her investment horizon?

17. Two banks are being examined by the regulators to determine the interest rate sensitivity of their balance sheets. Bank A has assets composed solely of a 10-year, 12 percent $1 million loan. The loan is financed with a 10-year, 10 percent $1 million GIC. Bank B has assets composed solely of a 7-year, 12 percent zero-coupon bond with a current (market) value of $894,006.20 and a maturity (principal) value of $1,976,362.88. The bond is financed with a 10-year, 8.275 percent coupon $1,000,000 face value GIC with a YTM of 10 percent. The loan and the GICs pay interest annually, with principal due at maturity.

    a. If interest rates increase 1 percent (100 basis points), how do the market values of the assets and liabilities of each bank change? That is, what will be the net effect on the market value of the equity for each bank?

    b. What accounts for the differences in the changes in the market value of equity between the two banks?

c. Verify your results above by calculating the duration for the assets and liabilities of each bank, and estimate the changes in value for the expected change in interest rates. Summarize your results.

18. If an FI uses only duration to immunize its portfolio, what three factors affect changes in the net worth of the financial institution when interest rates change?

19. An FI has assets of $1 million invested in a 30-year, 10 percent semiannual coupon Government of Canada bond selling at par. The duration of this bond has been estimated at 9.94 years. The assets are financed with equity and a $900,000, two-year, 7.25 percent semiannual coupon capital note selling at par.

a. What is the leverage-adjusted duration gap of the FI?

b. What is the impact on equity value if the relative change in all market interest rates is a decrease of 20 basis points? *Note:* The relative change in interest rates is $\Delta R/(1 + R/2) = -0.0020$.

c. Using the information you calculated in parts (a) and (b), infer a general statement about the desired duration gap for a financial institution if interest rates are expected to increase or decrease.

d. Verify your inference by calculating the change in market value of equity assuming that the relative change in all market interest rates is an increase of 30 basis points.

e. What would the duration of the assets need to be to immunize the equity from changes in market interest rates?

20. The balance sheet for Gotbucks Bank, Inc. (GBI), is presented below ($ millions).

Assets	
Cash	$ 30
Loans (floating)	125
Loans (fixed)	65
Total assets	$ 220

Liabilities and Equity	
Core deposits	$ 20
Euro CDs	180
Equity	20
Total liabilities and equity	$ 220

Notes to the balance sheet: The floating loan rate is LIBOR + 4 percent, and currently LIBOR is 11 percent. Fixed-rate loans have five-year maturities, are priced at par, and pay 12 percent annual interest. Core deposits are fixed rate for two years at 8 percent paid annually. Euros currently yield 9 percent.

a. What is the duration of the fixed-rate loan portfolio of Gotbucks Bank?

b. If the duration of the floating-rate loans is 0.36 year, what is the duration of GBI's assets?

c. What is the duration of the core deposits if they are priced at par?

d. If the duration of the Euro CDs is 0.401 year, what is the duration of GBI's liabilities?

e. What is GBI's duration gap? What is its interest rate risk exposure?

f. What is the impact on the market value of equity if the relative change in all market interest rates is an increase of 1 percent (100 basis points)? Note that the relative change in interest rates is $\Delta R/(1 + R) = 0.01$.

g. What is the impact on the market value of equity if the relative change in all interest rates is a decrease of 0.5 percent ($-$ 50 basis points)?

h. What variables are available to GBI to immunize the bank? How much would each variable need to change to get DGAP to equal zero?

21. Hands Insurance Company issued a $90 million, one-year zero-coupon note at 8 percent add-on annual interest (paying one coupon at the end of the year). The proceeds were used to fund a $100 million, two-year corporate loan at 10 percent annual interest. Immediately after these transactions were simultaneously closed, all market interest rates increased 1.5 percent (150 basis points).

a. What is the true market value of the loan investment and the liability after the change in interest rates?

b. What impact did these changes in market value have on the market value of the FI's equity?

c. What was the duration of the loan investment and the liability at the time of issuance?

d. Use these duration values to calculate the expected change in the value of the loan and the liability for the predicted increase of 1.5 percent in interest rates.

e. What was the duration gap of Hands Insurance Company after the issuance of the asset and note?

f. What was the change in equity value forecasted by this duration gap for the predicted increase in interest rates of 1.5 percent?

g. If the interest rate prediction had been available during the time period in which the loan and the liability were being negotiated, what suggestions would you have offered to reduce the possible effect on the equity of the company? What are the difficulties in implementing your ideas?

22. The following balance sheet information is available (amounts in thousands of dollars and duration in years) for a financial institution:

	Amount	Duration
T-bills	90	0.50
T-notes	55	0.90
Government bonds	176	
Loans	2,724	7.00
Deposits	2,092	1.00
Bank of Canada funds	238	0.01
Equity	715	

The Government of Canada bonds are five-year maturities paying 6 percent semiannually and selling at par.

a. What is the duration of the T-bond portfolio?

b. What is the average duration of all the assets?

c. What is the average duration of all the liabilities?

d. What is the leverage-adjusted duration gap? What is the interest rate risk exposure?

e. What is the forecasted impact on the market value of equity caused by a relative upward shift in the entire yield curve of 0.5 percent [i.e., $\Delta R/(1 + R) = 0.0050$]?

f. If the yield curve shifts downward 0.25 percent (i.e., $\Delta R/(1 + R) = -0.0025$), what is the forecasted impact on the market value of equity?

g. What variables are available to the financial institution to immunize the balance sheet? How much would each variable need to change to get DGAP to equal 0?

23. Assume that a goal of a regulatory agency of a financial institution is to immunize the ratio of equity to total assets, that is, $\Delta(E/A) = 0$. Explain how this goal changes the desired duration gap for the institution. Why does this differ from the duration gap necessary to immunize the total equity? How would your answers to part (h) in problem 20 and part (g) in problem 22 change if immunizing equity to total assets was the goal?

24. Identify and discuss three criticisms of using the duration model to immunize the portfolio of a financial institution.

25. In general, what changes have occurred in the financial markets that would allow financial institutions to restructure their balance sheets more rapidly and efficiently to meet desired goals? Why is it critical for an investment manager who has a portfolio immunized to match a desired investment horizon to rebalance the portfolio periodically? What is convexity? Why is convexity a desirable feature to capture in a portfolio of assets?

26. A financial institution has an investment horizon of two years 9.5 months (or 2.7917 years). The institution has converted all assets into a portfolio of 8 percent, $1,000 three-year bonds that are trading at a YTM of 10 percent. The bonds pay interest annually. The portfolio manager believes that the assets are immunized against interest rate changes.

a. Is the portfolio immunized at the time of the bond purchase? What is the duration of the bonds?

b. Will the portfolio be immunized one year later?

c. Assume that one-year, 8 percent zero-coupon bonds are available in one year. What proportion of the original portfolio should be placed in these bonds to rebalance the portfolio?

Appendix 9A:	**The Basics of Bond Valuation**

Appendix 9B:	**Incorporating Convexity into the Duration Model**

View Appendices 9A and 9B at the Online Learning Centre: www.mcgrawhill.ca/olc/saunders.

Market Risk

In this chapter, we define market risk and discuss the three major approaches that are being used to measure market risk:

1. RiskMetrics (value at risk)
2. historic or back simulation
3. Monte Carlo simulation

and the link between market risk and required capital levels

INTRODUCTION

Over the years, the trading activities of FIs have raised considerable concern among regulators and FI analysts. Some of these trading losses have been spectacular. For example, in 1995, after Barings, the U.K. merchant bank, was forced into insolvency as a result of losses on its trading in Japanese stock index futures in February, a similar incident took place at the New York branch of a leading Japanese FI, Daiwa Bank, in September. The largest trading loss in recent history involving a "rogue trader" occurred in 2008, when Jérôme Kerviel of French bank Société Générale lost US$7.1 billion in trading European stock index futures. The currency market volatility in Eastern Europe and Asia in 1997 continued in 1998 with additional losses on Russian bonds as the ruble fell in value and bond prices collapsed. Major U.S. banks (e.g., Bank of America) were forced to write off hundreds of millions of dollars in losses on their holdings of Russian government securities, and CIBC reported a one-day loss ("negative net trading revenue") of $93 million on August 27, 1998, six days during which trading losses were higher than $20 million, and trading losses on 69 percent of the days in the fourth quarter of 1998.

As markets have become more complex, Canadian and international regulators have worked to create the Basel II capital rules to protect the global financial system. As well, Canadian FIs have been at the cutting edge in developing risk management models, and simulations and scenario testing have evolved from the stand-alone, simplistic models (e.g., gap analysis) discussed in Chapters 8 and 9, to an enterprisewide focus on risk identification and control. The Royal Bank of Canada appointed Suzanne Labarge as one of the first chief risk officers (CROs) in Canada in 1998. She was a deputy superintendent with OSFI prior to her appointment at RBC. Labarge, along with Douglas Brooks, CRO at Sun Life Financial, helped to bring Canadian FIs to the forefront of enterprise risk management for both insurance and banking.[1]

www.osfi-bsif.gc.ca
www.royalbank.com
www.sunlife.ca

principles-based regulation
Regulation of FIs based on generally accepted management principles that must be met.

rules-based regulation
Regulation based on rules applicable to all FIs.

---

[1] Canadian companies are leaders of enterprise risk management (ERM), along with the U.K and Australia (Australian Standard AS-NZ 4360:2004, is called the "bible of risk management"), because of Canada's small size, OSFI's principles-based approach rather than the U.S. regulators' rules-based regulation, and the global nature of the risks that face Canadian FIs. Basel II is an example of **principles-based regulation** in that it allows FIs to use their own internally generated models to report their risk management. The U.S. Sarbanes-Oxley Act is **rules-based regulation** that allows for little individual variation from compliance. See P. Morton, "Risky Business," *CA Magazine*, May 2005, 138(4) pp. 24–29.

As we move through the text, we are developing a framework for understanding the risk exposures of FIs. We now move on from our discussions of interest rate risk in Chapters 8 and 9 to add another layer of complexity—market risk.

MARKET RISK DEFINED

market risk
Risk related to the uncertainty of an FI's earnings on its trading portfolio caused by changes in market conditions.

Market risk can be defined as the risk related to the uncertainty of an FI's earnings on its trading portfolio caused by changes in market conditions such as the price of an asset, interest rates, market volatility, and market liquidity.[2, 3] Thus, risks such as interest rate risk (discussed in the last two chapters) and foreign exchange risk (discussed in Chapter 14) affect market risk. However, market risk emphasizes the risks to FIs that actively trade assets and liabilities (and derivatives) rather than hold them for longer-term investment, funding, or hedging purposes.

Income from trading activities is increasingly replacing income from traditional FI activities of deposit taking and lending. The resulting earnings uncertainty can be measured over periods as short as a day or as long as a year. Moreover, market risk can be defined in absolute terms as a *dollar* exposure amount or as a relative amount against some benchmark. So important is market risk in determining the viability of an FI that since 1999, OSFI has included market risk in determining the required level of capital a federally regulated FI must hold.[4]

Conceptually, an FI's trading portfolio can be differentiated from its investment portfolio on the basis of time horizon and liquidity. The trading portfolio contains assets, liabilities, and derivative contracts that can be quickly bought or sold on organized financial markets (such as long and short positions in bonds, commodities, foreign exchange, equity securities, interest rate swaps, and options). The investment portfolio (or, in the case of banks, the banking book) contains assets and liabilities that are relatively illiquid and held for longer holding periods (such as consumer and business loans, retail deposits, and branches). Table 10–1 shows a breakdown between banking book and trading book assets and liabilities. Note that capital produces a cushion against losses on either the banking or trading books (see Chapter 20).

With the securitization of bank loans (e.g., mortgages), more and more assets have become liquid and tradable (e.g., mortgage-backed securities). Of course, with time, every asset and liability can be sold. Bank regulators have normally viewed tradable assets as those being held for horizons of less than one year, and FIs take an even shorter-term view. In particular, FIs are concerned about the fluctuation in value—or value at risk (VAR or VaR)—of their trading account assets

---

[2] JPMorgan, *Introduction to RiskMetrics* (New York: JPMorgan, October 1994), p. 2. There is an ongoing debate about whether spread risk is a part of market risk or credit risk. JPMorgan includes spread risk as credit risk (and includes it in the CreditMetrics measure [see Chapter 11]) rather than as part of market risk. OSFI defines market risk for capital adequacy purposes as "the risk of losses in on- and off-balance-sheet positions arising from movements in market prices, including interest rates, exchange rates, and equity values." (OSFI, *Capital Adequacy Requirements* A–Part I, January 2001).

[3] Market risk used by FI managers and regulators is not synonymous with systematic market risk analyzed by investors in securities markets. Systematic (market) risk reflects the co-movement of a security with the market portfolio (reflected by the security's beta), although beta is used to measure the market risk of equities, as noted below.

[4] This requirement was introduced in 1996 in the EU and in 1998 in the U.S. OSFI applies the market risk framework to deposit-taking institutions whose trading book assets or trading book liabilities (market value) represent 10 percent of total assets, or are greater than $1 billion.

TABLE 10–1
The Investment (Banking) Book and Trading Book of a Commercial Bank

	Assets	Liabilities
Banking Book	Cash Loans Premises and equipment Other illiquid assets	Deposits Other illiquid borrowed funds Capital
Trading Book	Bonds (long) Commodities (long) FX (long) Equities (long) Mortgage-backed securities (long)	Bonds (short) Commodities (short) FX (short) Equities (short)
	Derivatives* (long)	Derivatives* (short)

*Derivatives are off-balance-sheet (as discussed in Chapter 7).

and liabilities for periods as short as one day (called daily VaR)—especially if such fluctuations pose a threat to their solvency.

Table 10–2 summarizes several benefits of measuring market risk, including providing management with information on the extent of market risk exposure, market risk limits, resource allocation, and performance evaluation, as well as providing regulators with information on how to protect banks and the financial system against failure due to extreme market risk. The sections that follow concentrate on absolute dollar measures of market risk. We look at three major approaches that are being used to measure market risk: RiskMetrics, historic or back simulation, and Monte Carlo simulation. The link between market risk and required capital levels is also discussed in the chapter.

TABLE 10–2
Benefits of Market Risk Measurement (MRM)

1. *Management information.* MRM provides senior management with information on the risk exposure taken by FI traders. Management can then compare this risk exposure to the FI's capital resources.

2. *Setting limits.* MRM considers the market risk of traders' portfolios, which will lead to the establishment of economically logical position limits per trader in each area of trading.

3. *Resource allocation.* MRM involves the comparison of returns to market risks in different areas of trading, which may allow for the identification of areas with the greatest potential return per unit of risk into which more capital and resources can be directed.

4. *Performance evaluation.* MRM, relatedly, considers the return–risk ratio of traders, which may allow a more rational bonus (compensation) system to be put in place. That is, those traders with the highest returns may simply be the ones who have taken the largest risks. It is not clear that they should receive higher compensation than traders with lower returns and lower risk exposures.

5. *Regulation.* With the Bank for International Settlements (BIS) and OSFI currently regulating market risk through capital requirements (discussed later in this chapter), private sector benchmarks are important, since it is possible that regulators will overprice some risks. MRM conducted by the FI can be used to point to potential misallocations of resources as a result of prudential regulation. This is why, in certain cases, regulators are allowing banks to use their own (internal) models to calculate their capital requirements.[5]

---

[5] Since regulators are concerned with the social costs of a failure or insolvency, including contagion effects and other externalities, regulatory models will normally tend to be more conservative than private sector models that are concerned only with the private costs of failure.

CALCULATING MARKET RISK EXPOSURE

Large banks, insurance companies, and mutual funds have all developed market risk models. In the development of these internal models three major approaches have been followed:

- RiskMetrics (or the variance/covariance approach).
- Historic or back simulation.
- Monte Carlo simulation.

We consider RiskMetrics[6] first and then compare it with other internal model approaches, such as historic or back simulation.

THE RISKMETRICS MODEL

The ultimate objective of market risk measurement models can best be seen from the following quote by Dennis Weatherstone, former chairman of JPMorgan (JPM), now JPMorgan Chase: "At close of business each day tell me what the market risks are across all businesses and locations." In a nutshell, the chairman and CEO of JPM wants a single *dollar* number at 4:15 PM New York time that tells him JPM's market risk exposure the next day—especially if that day turns out to be an extremely "bad" day.

This is non-trivial, given the extent of JPM's trading business. When JPM developed its RiskMetrics model in 1994 it had 14 active trading locations with 120 independent units trading fixed-income securities, foreign exchange, commodities, derivatives, emerging-market securities, and proprietary assets, with a total daily volume exceeding US$50 billion. This scale and variety of activities is typical of the major banks, large overseas banks (e.g., Deutsche Bank and Barclays), major insurance companies, and investment banking operations.

Here, we will concentrate on measuring the market risk exposure of a major FI on a daily basis using the RiskMetrics approach. As will be discussed later, measuring the risk exposure for periods longer than a day (e.g., five days) is under certain assumptions a simple transformation of the daily risk exposure number.

Essentially, the FI is concerned with how much it can potentially lose if market conditions move adversely tomorrow; that is

$$\text{Market risk} = \text{Estimated potential loss under adverse circumstances}$$

daily value at risk (daily VaR)
Expected one-day loss at a given confidence level.

More specifically, the market risk is measured in terms of the FI's **daily value at risk (daily VaR)**[7] and has three components:

$$
\begin{array}{ccccc}
\text{Daily value} & & \text{(Dollar market} & \text{(Price} & \text{(Potential} \\
\text{at risk} & = & \text{value of} & \times \text{ sensitivity of } \times & \text{adverse move} \\
& & \text{the position)} & \text{the position)} & \text{in yield)}
\end{array}
$$

---

[6] JPMorgan first developed RiskMetrics in 1994. In 1998 the development group formed a separate company, partly owned by JPM. The material presented in this chapter is an overview of the RiskMetrics model. The details, additional discussion, and examples are found in *Return to RiskMetrics: The Evolution of a Standard,* April 2001, available at the JPMorgan Chase website, www.jpmorganchase.com or www.riskmetrics.com.

[7] Although RiskMetrics calls market risk exposure *daily earnings at risk* (DEAR), we adopt the more common usage, *daily value at risk,* also called *daily VaR, daily VAR,* or often shortened to *VaR* or *VAR.*

Since price sensitivity multiplied by adverse yield move measures the degree of price volatility of an asset, we can also write this equation as

$$
\begin{array}{ccc}
\text{Daily value} & \text{(Dollar market} & \text{(Price} \\
\text{at risk} = & \text{value of} \times & \text{volatility)} \\
& \text{the position)} &
\end{array}
\qquad (10.1)
$$

How price sensitivity and an adverse yield move will be measured depends on the FI and its choice of a price-sensitivity model as well as its view of what exactly is a potentially adverse price (yield) move.

We concentrate on how the RiskMetrics model calculates daily earnings at risk in three trading areas—fixed income, foreign exchange (FX), and equities—and then on how it estimates the aggregate risk of the entire trading portfolio to meet Dennis Weatherstone's objective of a single aggregate dollar exposure measure across the whole bank at 4:15 PM each day.[8]

The Market Risk of Fixed-Income Securities

Suppose an FI has a $1 million market value position in zero-coupon bonds of seven years to maturity with a face value of $1,631,483.[9] Today's yield on these bonds is 7.243 percent per year. These bonds are held as part of the trading portfolio. Thus,

$$
\text{Dollar market value of position} = \$1 \text{ million}
$$

The FI manager wants to know the potential exposure the FI faces should interest rates move against the FI as the result of an adverse or reasonably bad market move the next day. How much the FI will lose depends on the bond's price volatility. From the duration model in Chapter 9 we know that[10]

$$
\begin{aligned}
\text{Daily price volatility} &= (\text{Price sensitivity to a small change in yield}) \\
&\quad \times (\text{Adverse daily yield move}) \\
&= (MD) \times (\text{Adverse daily yield move})
\end{aligned}
\qquad (10.2)
$$

---

[8] It is clear from the above discussion that interest rate risk (see Chapters 8 and 9) is part of market risk. However, in market risk models, we are concerned with the interest rate sensitivity of the fixed-income securities held as part of an FI's active trading portfolio. Many fixed-income securities are held as part of an FI's investment portfolio. While the latter are subject to interest rate risk, they will not be included in a market risk calculation.

[9] The face value of the bonds is $1,631,483—that is, $1,631,483/(1.07243)^7 = $1,000,000 market value. In the original model, prices were determined using a discrete rate of return, R_i. In the 2001 document *Return to RiskMetrics: The Evolution of a Standard,* April 2001, prices are determined using a continuously compounded return, e^{-rt}. The change was implemented because continuous compounding has properties that facilitate mathematical treatment. For example, the logarithmic return on a zero-coupon bond equals the difference of interest rates multiplied by the maturity of the bond. That is

$$
\ln\left(\frac{e^{-\tilde{r}t}}{e^{-rt}}\right) = -(\tilde{r} - r)t
$$

where $\tilde{r}$ is the expected return.

[10] Remember from Chapter 9 that the first derivative of a bond's price with respect to a change in the yield to maturity is

$$
\begin{aligned}
dP/dR &= -[1/(1 + R)] \times P \times D \\
\text{or} \quad dP/P &= -D \times [dR/(1 + R)] \\
\text{and since} \quad MD &= D/(1 + R) \\
\text{then} \quad dP/P &= -MD \times dR
\end{aligned}
$$

The modified duration (MD) of this bond is[11]

$$MD = \frac{D}{1 + R} = \frac{7}{(1.07243)} = 6.527$$

given that the yield on the bond is $R = 7.243$ percent. To estimate price volatility, multiply the bond's MD by the expected adverse daily yield move.

EXAMPLE 10–1	Suppose we define bad yield changes such that there is only a 5 percent chance that the yield changes will exceed this amount in either direction—or, since we are concerned only with bad outcomes, and we are long in bonds, that there is 1 chance in 20 (or a 5 percent chance) that the next day's yield increase (or shock) will exceed this given adverse move.
Daily Value at Risk on Fixed-Income Securities	If we assume that yield changes are normally distributed,[12] we can fit a normal distribution to the histogram of recent past changes in seven-year zero-coupon interest rates (yields) to get an estimate of the size of this adverse rate move. From statistics, we know that (the middle) 90 percent of the area under the normal distribution is to be found within ±1.65 standard deviations (σ) from the mean—that is, 1.65σ—and 10 percent of the area under the normal distribution is found beyond $±1.65\sigma$ (5 percent under each tail, -1.65σ and $+1.65\sigma$, respectively). Suppose that during the last year the mean change in daily yields on seven-year zero-coupon bonds was 0 percent[13] the standard deviation was 10 basis points (or 0.001). Thus, 1.65σ is 16.5 basis points (bp).[14] In other words, over the last year, daily yields on seven-year, zero-coupon bonds have fluctuated (either positively or negatively) by more than 16.5 bp 10 percent of the time. Adverse moves in yields are those that decrease the value of the security (i.e., the yield increases). These occurred 5 percent of the time, or 1 in 20 days. This is shown in Figure 10–1.

We can now calculate the potential daily price volatility on seven-year discount bonds using equation 10.2 as

$$\text{Price volatility} = (MD) \times (\text{Potential adverse move in yield})$$
$$= (6.527) \times (0.00165)$$
$$= 0.01077 \text{ or } 1.077\%$$

Given this price volatility and the initial market value of the seven-year bond portfolio, then equation 10.1 can be used to calculate the daily earnings at risk as[15]

$$\text{Daily value at risk} = (\text{Dollar market value of position}) \times (\text{Price volatility})$$
$$= (\$1,000,000) \times (0.01077)$$
$$= \$10,770$$

That is, the potential daily loss on the $1 million position is $10,770 if the 1 bad day in 20 occurs tomorrow.

---

[11] Assuming annual compounding for simplicity.

[12] In reality, many asset return distributions—such as exchange rates and interest rates—have "fat tails." Thus, the normal distribution will tend to underestimate extreme outcomes. This is a major criticism of the RiskMetrics modelling approach. (See later footnote and references.)

[13] If the mean were non-zero (e.g., −1 basis point), this could be added to the 16.5 bp (i.e., 15.5 bp) to project the yield shock.

[14] RiskMetrics weights more recent observations more highly than past observations (this is called *exponential weighting*). This allows more recent news to be more heavily reflected in the calculation of σ. Regular σ calculations put an equal weight on all past observations.

[15] Since we are calculating loss, we drop the minus sign here.

FIGURE 10–1
Adverse Rate Move,
Seven-Year Rates

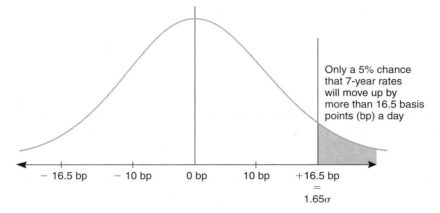

We can extend this analysis to calculate the potential loss over 2, 3, . . . , N days. If we assume that yield shocks are independent and daily volatility is approximately constant,[16] and that the FI is locked in to holding this asset for N number of days, then the N-day market value at risk (VaR) is related to daily value at risk (daily VaR) by

$$VaR = \text{Daily } VaR \times \sqrt{N} \tag{10.3}$$

That is, the earnings the FI has at risk, should interest rate yields move against the FI, are a function of the value or earnings at risk for one day (daily VaR) and the (square root of the) number of days that the FI is forced to hold the securities because of an illiquid market. Specifically, daily VaR assumes that the FI can sell all the bonds tomorrow, even at the new lower price. In reality, it may take many days for the FI to unload its position. This relative illiquidity of a market exposes the FI to magnified losses (measured by the square root of N).[17] If N is five days, then:

$$VaR = \$10,770 \times \sqrt{5} = \$24,082$$

If N is 10 days, then[18]

$$VaR = \$10,770 \times \sqrt{10} = \$34,057$$

---

[16] The assumptions that daily volatility is constant and that there is no autocorrelation in yield shocks are strong assumptions. Much recent literature suggests that shocks are autocorrelated in many asset markets over relatively long horizons. To understand why we take the square root of N, consider a five-day holding period. The σ_5^2, or five-day variance of asset returns, will equal the current one-day variance σ_1^2 times 5 under the assumptions of constant daily variance and no autocorrelation in shocks, or

$$\sigma_5^2 = \sigma_1^2 \times 5$$

The standard deviation of this equation is

$$\sigma_5 = \sigma_1 \times \sqrt{5}$$

or since daily VaR is measured in the same dimensions as a standard deviation (σ), in the terminology of RiskMetrics, the five-day value at risk (VaR_5) is

$$VaR_5 = \text{daily } VaR \times \sqrt{5}$$

[17] In practice, a number of FIs calculate N internally by dividing the position held in a security by the median daily volume of trading of that security over recent days. Thus, if trading volume is low because of a "one-way market," in that most people are seeking to sell rather than buy, then N can rise substantially; that is, N = (\$ position in security/Median daily \$ volume of trading).

[18] Under the BIS 1998 market risk capital requirements, a 10-day holding period ($N = 10$) is assumed to measure exposure. As well, Canadian FIs use a 99 percent confidence level and a minimum holding period of ten days.

In the above calculations, we estimated price sensitivity using modified duration. However, the RiskMetrics model generally prefers using the present value of cash flow changes as the price-sensitivity weights over modified durations. Essentially, each cash flow is discounted by the appropriate zero-coupon rate to generate the daily earnings at risk measure. If we used the direct cash flow calculation in this case, the loss would be $10,771.2.[19] The estimates in this case are very close.

Foreign Exchange

Large FIs actively trade in foreign exchange (FX). Remember that:

$$\text{Daily } VaR = (\text{Dollar value of position}) \times (\text{Price volatility})$$

EXAMPLE 10–2	Suppose the FI had a €1.6 million trading position in spot euros at the close of business on a particular day. The FI wants to calculate the daily value at risk from this position (i.e., the risk exposure on this position should the next day be a bad day in the FX markets with respect to the value of the euro against the dollar).

Daily Value at Risk of Foreign Exchange Contracts

The first step is to calculate the dollar value of the position:

$$\text{Dollar equivalent value of position} = (\text{FX position}) \times (\text{€/\$ spot exchange rate})$$

$$= (\text{€1.6 million}) \times (\text{\$ per unit of foreign currency})$$

Suppose for simplicity that the exchange rate is €1.60/$1 or $0.625/€ at the daily close; then,

$$\text{Dollar value of position} = (\text{€1.6 million}) \times (\text{\$0.625/€})$$

$$= \$1 \text{million}$$

Suppose that, looking back at the daily changes in the €/$ exchange rate over the past year, we find that the volatility, or standard deviation (σ), of daily changes in the spot exchange rate was 56.5 bp. However, suppose that the FI is interested in adverse moves—that is, bad moves that will not occur more than 5 percent of the time, or 1 day in every 20. Statistically speaking, if changes in exchange rates are historically "normally" distributed, the exchange rate must change in the adverse direction by 1.65σ (1.65×56.5 bp) for this change to be viewed as likely to occur only 1 day in every 20 days:[20]

$$\text{FX volatility} = 1.65 \times 56.5 \text{ bp} = 93.2 \text{ bp}$$

In other words, during the last year, the euro declined in value against the dollar by 93.2 bp 5 percent of the time. As a result:

$$\text{Daily } VaR = (\text{Dollar value of position}) \times (\text{FX volatility})$$

$$= (\$1 \text{ million}) \times (0.00932)$$

$$= \$9,320$$

This is the potential daily earnings exposure to adverse euro-to-dollar exchange rate changes for the FI from the €1.6 million spot currency holdings.

---

[19] The initial market value of the seven-year zero was $1,000,000, or $1,631,483/(1.07243)^7$. The (loss) effect on each $1 (market value) invested in the bond of a rise in rates by 1 bp from 7.243 percent to 7.253 percent is 0.0006528. However, the adverse rate move is 16.5 bp. Thus,

$$\text{Daily } VaR = (\$1 \text{ million}) \times (0.0006528) \times (16.5) = \$10,771.2$$

[20] Technically, 90 percent of the area under a normal distribution lies between $\pm 1.65\sigma$ from the mean. This means that 5 percent of the time, daily exchange rate changes will increase by more than 1.65σ, and 5 percent of the time, will decrease by 1.65σ. This case concerns only adverse moves in the exchange rate of euros to dollars (i.e., a depreciation of 1.65σ).

Equities

Many large FIs also take positions in equities. As is well known from the capital asset pricing model (CAPM), there are two types of risk to an equity position in an individual stock i:[21]

$$\text{Total risk} = \text{Systematic risk} + \text{Unsystematic risk}$$

$$(\sigma_{it}^2) = (\beta_i^2 \sigma_{mt}^2) + (\sigma_{eit}^2)$$

beta
Systematic (undiversifiable) risk reflecting the co-movement of the returns on a specific stock with returns on the market portfolio.

Systematic risk reflects the co-movement of that stock with the market portfolio reflected by the stock's **beta** (β_i) and the volatility of the market portfolio (σ_{mt}), whereas unsystematic risk is specific to the firm itself (σ_{eit}).

In a very well-diversified portfolio, unsystematic risk (σ_{eit}^2) can be largely diversified away (i.e., will equal zero), leaving behind systematic (undiversifiable) market risk ($\beta_i^2 \sigma_{mt}^2$). If the FI's trading portfolio follows (replicates) the returns on the stock market index, the β of that portfolio will be 1, since the movement of returns on the FI's portfolio will be one to one with the market,[22] and the standard deviation of the portfolio, σ_{it}, will be equal to the standard deviation of the stock market index, σ_{mt}.

EXAMPLE 10–3 *Daily Value at Risk on Equities*	Suppose the FI holds a $1 million trading position in stocks that reflect a stock market index (e.g., the S&P TSX Composite Index). Then $\beta = 1$ and the daily VaR for equities is: $$\text{Daily VaR} = (\text{Dollar market value of position}) \times (\text{Stock market return volatility})$$ $$= (\$1{,}000{,}000) \times (1.65\ \sigma_m)$$ If, over the last year, the σ_m of the daily returns on the stock market index was 200 bp, then $1.65\ \sigma_m = 330$ bp (i.e., the adverse change or decline in the daily return on the stock market exceeded 330 bp only 5 percent of the time). In this case, $$\text{Daily VaR} = (\$1{,}000{,}000) \times (0.033)$$ $$= \$33{,}000$$ That is, the FI stands to lose at least $33,000 in earnings if adverse stock market returns materialize tomorrow.[23]

In less well-diversified portfolios or portfolios of individual stocks, the effect of unsystematic risk σ_{eit} on the value of the trading position would need to be added. Moreover, if the CAPM does not offer a good explanation of asset pricing compared with, say, multi-index arbitrage pricing theory (APT), a degree of error will be built into the daily VaR calculation.[24]

---

[21] This assumes that systematic and unsystematic risks are independent of each other.

[22] If $\beta \neq 1$, as in the case of most individual stocks, Daily VaR = Dollar value of position $\times \beta_i \times 1.65\ \sigma_m$, where β_i is the systematic risk of the ith stock.

[23] If we consider a single equity security with a beta (β) = 1.25 (i.e., one that is more sensitive than the market, such that as market returns increase [decrease] by 1 percent, the security's return increases [decreases] by 1.25 percent), then with a $1 million investment and the same (assumed) volatility (σ) of 2 percent (such that $1.65 \times 0.02 = 0.033$, or 3.3 percent), the FI would stand to lose at least $41,250 in daily earnings if adverse stock returns materialize (i.e., Daily VaR = $1,000,000 $\times$ 1.25 $\times$ 0.033 = $41,250).

[24] As noted in the introduction, derivatives are also used for trading purposes. In the calculation of its daily VaR, a derivative has to be converted into a position in the underlying asset (e.g., bond, FX, or equity).

Portfolio Aggregation

The preceding sections analyzed the daily values at risk of individual trading positions. The examples considered a seven-year, zero-coupon, fixed-income security ($1 million market value); a position in spot euros ($1 million market value); and a position in the stock market index ($1 million market value). The individual daily VaRs were:

1. Seven-year zero-coupon bonds = $10,770
2. Euro spot = $9,320
3. Equities = $33,000

However, senior management wants to know the aggregate risk of the entire trading position. To calculate this, we *cannot* simply sum the three VaRs—$10,770 + $9,320 + $33,000 = $53,090—because that ignores any degree of offsetting covariance or correlation among the fixed-income, FX, and equity trading positions. In particular, some of these asset shocks (adverse moves) may be negatively correlated. As is well known from portfolio theory, negative correlations and correlations less than one between asset shocks will reduce the degree of portfolio risk.

EXAMPLE 10–4 *Calculation of the Daily VaR of a Portfolio*	Table 10–3 shows a hypothetical correlation matrix between daily seven-year zero-coupon bond yield changes, €/$ spot exchange rate changes, and changes in daily returns on a stock market index. From Table 10–3, the correlation between the seven-year zero-coupon bonds and €/$ exchange rates, $\rho_{z,\epsilon}$, is negative (−0.2), while the seven-year zero-coupon yield changes with stock returns, $\rho_{z,m}$, (0.4) and €/$ shocks, $\rho_{m,\epsilon}$, (0.1) are positively correlated.

Using this correlation matrix along with the individual asset daily VaRs, we can calculate the risk or standard deviation of the whole (three-asset) trading portfolio as[25]

$$\text{Daily VaR portfolio} = \begin{bmatrix} [\text{VaR}_z)^2 + (\text{VaR}_\epsilon)^2 + (\text{VaR}_m)^2 \\ + (2 \times \rho_{z,\epsilon} \times \text{VaR}_z \times \text{VaR}_\epsilon) \\ + (2 \times \rho_{z,m} \times \text{VaR}_z \times \text{VaR}_m) \\ + (2 \times \rho_{m,\epsilon} \times \text{VaR}_m \times \text{VaR}_\epsilon)] \end{bmatrix}^{1/2}$$

This is a direct application of modern portfolio theory (MPT) since daily VaRs are directly similar to standard deviations. Substituting into this equation the calculated individual daily VaRs (in thousands of dollars), we get

$$\text{Daily VaR portfolio} = \begin{bmatrix} [(10.77)^2 + (9.32)^2 + (33)^2 + 2(-0.2)(10.77)(9.32) \\ + 2(0.4)(10.77)(33) + 2(0.1)(9.32)(33)] \end{bmatrix}^{1/2}$$

$$= \$39,969$$

The equation indicates that considering the risk of each trading position as well as the correlation structure among those positions' returns results in a lower measure of portfolio trading risk ($39,969) than when risks of the underlying trading positions (the sum of which was $53,090) are added. A quick check will reveal that had we assumed that all three assets were perfectly positively correlated (i.e., $\rho_{ij} = 1$), daily VaR for the portfolio would have been

---

[25] This is a standard relationship from modern portfolio theory in which the standard deviation or risk of a portfolio of three assets is equal to the square root of the sum of the variances of returns on each of the three assets individually plus two times the covariances among each pair of these assets. With three assets there are three covariances. Here we use the fact that a correlation coefficient times the standard deviations on each pair of assets equals the covariance between each pair of assets. Note that daily VaR is measured in dollars and has the same dimensions as a standard deviation. We discuss modern portfolio theory in more detail in Chapter 12.

$53,090 (i.e., equal to the sum of the three daily VaRs). Clearly, even in abnormal market conditions, assuming that asset returns are perfectly correlated will exaggerate the degree of actual trading risk exposure.

Table 10–4 shows the type of spreadsheet used by FIs to calculate VaR. As you can see, in this example, positions can be taken in 13 different country (currency) bonds in eight different maturity buckets.[26] There is also a column for FX risk (and, if necessary, equity risk) in these different country markets, although in this example, the FI has no FX risk exposure (all the cells are empty).

In the example in Table 10–4, while the FI is holding offsetting long and short positions in both Danish and euro bonds, it is still exposed to trading risks of $48,000 and $27,000, respectively (see the column "Interest VaR"). This happens because the European Union yield curve is more volatile than the Danish and shocks at different maturity buckets are not equal. The VaR figure for a U.S. bond position of long $20 million is $76,000. Adding these three positions yields a VaR

TABLE 10–3
Correlations (ρ_{ij}) among Assets

	Seven-Year Zero	€/$1	Stock Index
Seven-year zero	—	−0.2	0.4
€/$1		—	0.1
Stock index			—

TABLE 10–4 **Portfolio Daily VaR Spreadsheet**

	Interest Rate Risk Notional Amounts (US$ millions equivalents)									FX Risk		Total	
	1 Month	1 Year	2 Years	3 Years	4 Years	5 Years	7 Years	10 Years	Interest VaR	Spot FX	FX VaR	Portfolio Effect	Total VaR
Australia										AUD			
Brazil										BRL			
Canada										CAD			
Denmark	19			−30				11	48	DKK			48
European Union	−19			30				−11	27	EUR			27
Hong Kong										HKD			
Japan										YEN			
Mexico										MXN			
Singapore										SGD			
Sweden										SEK			
Switzerland										CHF			
United Kingdom										GBP			
United States						10		10	76	USD			76
Total						10		10	151				151
Portfolio effect									(62)				(62)
Total VaR ($000s)									89				89

Source: JPMorgan, *RiskMetrics*. New York: JPMorgan, 1994. www.jpmorgan.com, www.riskmetrics.com.

[26] Bonds held with different maturity dates (e.g., six years) are split into two and allocated to the nearest two of the eight maturity buckets (here, five years and seven years) using three criteria: (1) The sum of the current market value of the two resulting cash flows must be identical to the market value of the original cash flow; (2) the market *risk* of the portfolio of two cash flows must be identical to the overall market risk of the original cash flow; and (3) the two cash flows have the same *sign* as the original cash flow. See JPMorgan, *RiskMetrics—Technical Document*, November 1994, and *Return to RiskMetrics: The Evolution of a Standard*, April 2001, www.jpmorganchase.com or www.riskmetrics.com.

of $151,000. However, this ignores the fact that Danish, European Union, and U.S. yield shocks are not perfectly correlated. Allowing for diversification effects (the portfolio effect) results in a total VaR of only $89,000. This would be the number reported to the FI's senior management. Most financial institutions establish limits for value at risk, daily earnings at risk, position limits, and dollar trading loss limits for their trading portfolios. Actual activity compared with these limits is then monitored daily. Should a risk exposure level exceed approved limit levels, management must provide a strategy for bringing risk levels within approved limits. Table 10–5 reports the average, minimum, and maximum daily value at risk reported by five large Canadian banks in 2008 for their trading portfolios. Table 10–6 shows the makeup of the $14.7 million average VaR reported by CIBC for 2008 for its trading portfolio. As can be seen by the table, CIBC calculates interest rate risk and credit spread risk related to trading in Canadian, U.S., and global government and corporate debt and derivatives markets. The equity risk arises from trading primarily U.S., Canadian, and European stocks. Foreign exchange risk represents exposure to the U.S. dollar, the euro, the British pound and the Japanese yen. Commodity risk arises from North American natural gas and oil product indices. Since the risks are correlated, the total is adjusted for the effects of diversification, a reduction from the average VaR of $14.8 million in 2008. The average total VaR has also increased slightly from 2007.[27]

www.bmo.com

www.cibc.com

www.nbc.ca

www.scotiabank.com

TABLE 10–5
Total Daily VaR for the Trading Portfolios of Canadian Banks, 2008* ($ millions)

Source: 2008 annual reports.

Name	Average VaR for the year 2008	Minimum VaR during 2008	Maximum VaR during 2008
Bank of Montreal	25.1	14.5	39.3
CIBC	14.7	8.8	21.1
National Bank	10.2	5.3	17.1
Royal Bank	28	18	50
Scotiabank	16.8	10.8	30.4
TD Bank	42.9	17.9	104.8

*The figures are based on the banks' internal models and may be based on methodologies that differ from RiskMetrics.

TABLE 10–6 VaR by Risk Type for the Trading Portfolios of CIBC, 2008

($ millions, as at or for the year ended October 31)	2008				2007			
	Year-end	Average	High	Low	Year-end	Average	High	Low
Interest rate risk	$ 8.9	$ 7.4	$ 13.9	$ 3.0	$ 7.2	$ 7.1	$ 10.3	$ 4.6
Credit spread risk	8.7	7.5	16.0	3.6	9.6	6.4	15.6	3.0
Equity risk	5.2	5.2	7.6	3.7	6.0	5.5	7.6	3.2
Foreign exchange risk	1.4	0.6	2.1	0.2	0.6	0.5	2.6	0.1
Commodity risk	0.5	0.7	1.4	0.3	1.3	1.3	3.5	0.8
Debt-specific risk[1]	7.1	8.1	13.7	4.0	10.3	9.2	10.5	8.0
Diversification effect[2]	(16.0)	(14.8)	n/m[3]	n/m[3]	(20.3)	(15.4)	n/m[3]	n/m[3]
Total risk	**$ 15.8**	**$ 14.7**	**$ 21.1**	**$ 8.8**	**$ 14.7**	**$ 14.6**	**$ 18.2**	**$ 13.1**

(1) Debt-specific risk for 2007 was computed for the fourth quarter only, as we started reporting this measure in the fourth quarter of 2007.
(2) Aggregate VaR is less than the sum of the VaR of the different market risk types due to risk offsets resulting from portfolio diversification effect.
(3) n/m—Not meaningful. It is not meaningful to compute a diversification effect because the high and low may occur on different days for different risk types.

[27] See *CIBC Annual Accountability Report 2008,* pp. 76–78, www.cibc.com.

As an indication of the complexity of the calculations for a large FI, the number of markets covered by the U.S. bank Citigroup's traders and the number of correlations among those markets require the daily production and updating of over 250,000 volatility estimates (σ) and correlations (ρ). These data are updated daily, requiring a significant investment in computer technology and time.

CONCEPT QUESTIONS	
	1. What is the ultimate objective of market risk measurement models?
	2. Refer to Example 10–1. What is the VaR for this bond if σ is 15 bp?
	3. Refer to Example 10–4. What is the VaR of the portfolio if the returns on the three assets are independent of each other?

HISTORIC (BACK SIMULATION) APPROACH

A major criticism of VaR models is the need to assume a symmetric (normal) distribution for all asset returns.[28] Clearly, for some assets, such as options and short-term securities (bonds), this is highly questionable. For example, the most an investor can lose if he or she buys a call option on an equity is the call premium; however, the investor's potential upside returns are unlimited. In a statistical sense, the returns on call options are non-normal since they exhibit a positive skew.[29]

Because of these and other considerations discussed below, the large majority of FIs (e.g., TD, RBC, CIBC, BNS, BMO, and National Bank) that have developed market risk models have employed a historic or back simulation approach. The advantages of this approach are that (1) it is simple, (2) it does not require that asset returns be normally distributed, and (3) it does not require that the correlations or standard deviations of asset returns be calculated.

The essential idea is to take the current market portfolio of assets (FX, bonds, equities, etc.) and revalue them on the basis of the actual prices (returns) that existed on those assets yesterday, the day before that, and so on. Frequently, the FI

---

[28] Another criticism is that VaR models like RiskMetrics ignore the (risk in the) payments of accrued interest on an FI's debt securities. Thus, VaR models will underestimate the true probability of default and the appropriate level of capital to be held against this risk (see P. Kupiec, "Risk Capital and VAR," *The Journal of Derivatives,* Winter 1999, pp. 41–52). Also, Johansson, Seiles, and Tjarnberg find that because of the distributional assumptions, while RiskMetrics produces reasonable estimates of downside risk for FIs with highly diversified portfolios, FIs with small, undiversified portfolios will significantly underestimate their true risk exposure using RiskMetrics (see, F. Johansson, M. J. Seiles, and M. Tjarnberg, "Measuring Downside Portfolio Risks," *The Journal of Portfolio Management,* Fall 1999, pp. 96–107). Further, a number of authors have argued that many asset distributions have "fat tails" and that RiskMetrics, by assuming the normal distribution, underestimates the risk of extreme losses. See, for example, Salih F. Neftci, "Value at Risk Calculations, Extreme Events and Tail Estimations," *Journal of Derivatives,* Spring 2000, pp. 23–37. One alternative approach to dealing with the "fat-tail" problem is extreme value theory. Simply put, one can view an asset distribution as being explained by two distributions. For example, a normal distribution may explain returns up to the 95 percent threshold, but for losses beyond that threshold another distribution, such as the generalized Pareto distribution, may provide a better explanation of loss outcomes such as the 99 percent level and beyond. In short, the normal distribution is likely to underestimate the importance and size of observations in the tail of the distribution, which is, after all, what value at risk models are meant to be measuring (see also Alexander J. McNeil, *Extreme Value Theory for Risk Managers,* Working Paper, Department of Mathematics, ETH Zentrom, Ch-8092, Zurich, Switzerland, May 17, 1999). Finally, VaR models by definition concern themselves with risk rather than return. It should be noted that minimizing risk may be highly costly in terms of the return the FI gives up. Indeed, there may be many more return–risk combinations preferable to that achieved at the minimum risk point in the trading portfolio. Recent upgrades to RiskMetrics (see the RiskMetrics website at www.riskmetrics.com) allow management to incorporate a return dimension to VaR analysis so that management can evaluate how trading portfolio returns differ as VaR changes.

[29] For a normal distribution, its skew (which is the third moment of a distribution) is zero.

will calculate the market or value risk of its current portfolio on the basis of prices (returns) that existed for those assets on each of the last 500 days. It will then calculate the 5 percent worst case—the portfolio value that has the 25th lowest value out of 500. That is, on only 25 days out of 500, or 5 percent of the time, would the value of the portfolio fall below this number based on recent historic experience of exchange rate changes, equity price changes, interest rate changes, and so on?

Consider the simple example in Table 10–7, where an FI is trading two currencies: the Japanese yen and the Swiss franc. At the close of trade on December 1, 2010, it has a long position in Japanese yen of 500,000,000 and a long position in Swiss francs of 20,000,000. It wants to assess its VaR. That is, if tomorrow is that 1 bad day in 20 (the 5 percent worst case), how much does it stand to lose on its total foreign currency position? As shown in Table 10–7, six steps are required to calculate the VaR of its currency portfolio. It should be noted that the same methodological approach would be followed to calculate the VaR of any asset, liability, or derivative (bonds, options, etc.) as long as market prices were available on those assets over a sufficiently long historic time period.

- *Step 1: Measure exposures.* Convert today's foreign currency positions into dollar equivalents using today's exchange rates. Thus, an evaluation of the FX position of the FI on December 1, 2010, indicates that it has a long position of $3,846,154 in yen and $14,285,714 in Swiss francs.

- *Step 2: Measure sensitivity.* Measure the sensitivity of each FX position by calculating its delta, where delta measures the change in the dollar value of each FX position if the yen or the Swiss franc depreciates (declines in value) by 1 percent against the dollar.[30] As can be seen from Table 10–7, line 6, the delta for the Japanese yen position is −$38,081, and for the Swiss franc position, it is −$141,442.

- *Step 3: Measure risk.* Look at the actual percentage changes in exchange rates, yen/$ and Sf/$, on each of the past 500 days. Thus, on November 30, 2010, the yen declined in value against the dollar over the day by 0.5 percent while the Swiss franc declined in value against the dollar by 0.2 percent. (It might be noted that if the currencies were to appreciate in value against the dollar, the sign against the number in row 7 of Table 10–7 would be negative; that is, it takes fewer units of foreign currency to buy a dollar than it did the day before). As can be seen in row 8, combining the delta and the actual percentage change in each FX rate means a total loss of $47,328.9 if the FI had held the current ¥500,000,000 and Sf 20,000,000 positions on that day (November 30, 2010).

- *Step 4: Repeat Step 3.* Step 4 repeats the same exercise for the yen and Swiss franc positions but uses actual exchange rate changes on November 29, 2010; November 28, 2010; and so on. That is, we calculate the FX losses and/or gains on each of the past 500 trading days, excluding weekends and holidays, when the FX market is closed. This amounts to going back in time over two years. For each of these days the actual change in exchange rates is calculated (row 7) and multiplied by the deltas of each position (the numbers in row 6 of Table 10–7).

---

[30] That is, in the case of FX, delta measures the dollar change in FX holdings for a 1 percent change in the foreign exchange rate. In the case of equities, it would measure the change in the value of those securities for a 1 percent change in price, while for bonds, it measures the change in value for a 1 percent change in the price of the bond (note that delta measures sensitivity of a bond's value to a change in yield, not price).

TABLE 10–7   Hypothetical Example of the Historic, or Back Simulation, Approach Using Two Currencies, as of December 1, 2010

	Yen	Swiss Franc
Step 1. Measure exposures		
1. Closing position on December 1, 2010	500,000,000	20,000,000
2. Exchange rate on December 1, 2010	¥130/$1	Sf 1.4/$1
3. US$ equivalent position on December 1, 2010	3,846,154	14,285,714
Step 2. Measure sensitivity		
4. 1.01 × current exchange rate	¥131.3	Sf 1.414
5. Revalued position in $	3,808,073	14,144,272
6. Delta of position ($) (measure of sensitivity to a 1% adverse change in exchange rate, or row 5 minus row 3)	−38,081	−141,442
Step 3. Measure risk of December 1, 2010, closing position using exchange rates that existed on each of the last 500 days		
November 30, 2010	**Yen**	**Swiss Franc**
7. Change in exchange rate (%) on November 30, 2010	0.5%	0.2%
8. Risk (delta × change in exchange rate)	−19,040.5	−28,288.4
9. Sum of risks = −$47,328.9		

Step 4. Repeat Step 3 for each of the remaining 499 days

November 29, 2010
   ⋮

April 15, 2009
   ⋮

November 30, 2008
   ⋮

Step 5. Rank days by risk from worst to best

Date	Risk ($)
1. May 6, 2009	−105,669
2. Jan 27, 2010	−103,276
3. Dec 1, 2008	−90,939
⋮	⋮
25. Nov 30, 2010	−47,328.9
⋮	⋮
499. April 8, 2010	+98,833
500. July 28, 2009	+108,376

Step 6. VaR (25th worst day out of last 500)

VaR = −47,328.9 (November 30, 2010)

These two numbers are summed to attain total risk measures for each of the past 500 days.

• *Step 5: Rank days by risk from worst to best.* These risk measures can then be ranked from worst to best. Clearly the worst-case loss would have occurred on this position on May 6, 2009, with a total loss of $105,669. Although this worst-case scenario is of interest to FI managers, we are interested in the 5 percent worst case, that is, a loss that does not occur more than 25 days out of the 500 days (25 ÷ 500 equals 5 percent). As can be seen, in our example, the 25th worst loss out of 500 occurred on November 30, 2010. This loss amounted to $47,328.9.

- *Step 6:* VaR. If it is assumed that the recent past distribution of exchange rates is an accurate reflection of the likely distribution of FX rate changes in the future—that exchange rate changes have a stationary distribution—then the $47,328.9 can be viewed as the FX value at risk (VaR) exposure of the FI on December 1, 2010. That is, if tomorrow (in our case, December 2, 2010) is a bad day in the FX markets, and given the FI's position of long yen 500 million and long Swiss francs 20 million, the FI can expect to lose $47,328.9 (or more) with a 5 percent probability. This VaR measure can then be updated every day as the FX position changes and the delta changes. For example, given the nature of FX trading, the positions held on December 5, 2010, could be very different from those held on December 1, 2010.[31]

The Historic (Back Simulation) Model versus RiskMetrics

One obvious benefit of the historic, or back simulation, approach is that we do not need to calculate standard deviations and correlations (or assume normal distributions for asset returns) to calculate the portfolio risk figures in row 9 of Table 10–7.[32] A second advantage is that it directly provides a worst-case scenario number, in our example, a loss of $105,669—see step 5. RiskMetrics, since it assumes asset returns are normally distributed—that returns can go to plus and minus infinity—provides no such worst-case scenario number.[33]

The disadvantage of the back simulation approach is the degree of confidence we have in the 5 percent VaR number based on 500 observations. Statistically speaking, 500 observations are not very many, so there will be a very wide confidence band (or standard error) around the estimated number ($47,328.9 in our example). One possible solution to the problem is to go back in time more than 500 days and estimate the 5 percent VaR based on 1,000 past daily observations (the 50th worst case) or even 10,000 past observations (the 500th worst case). The problem is that as one goes back farther in time, past observations may become decreasingly relevant in predicting VaR in the future. For example, 10,000 observations may require the FI to analyze FX data going back 40 years. Over this period we have moved through many very different FX regimes: from relatively fixed exchange rates in the 1950–1970 period, to relatively floating exchange rates in the 1970s, to more managed floating rates in the 1980s and 1990s, to the abolition of exchange rates and the introduction of the euro in January 2002. Clearly, exchange rate behaviour and risk

---

[31] As in RiskMetrics, an adjustment can be made for illiquidity of the market, in this case, by assuming the FI is locked into longer holding periods. For example, if it is estimated that it will take five days for the FI to sell its FX position, then the FI will be interested in the weekly (i.e., five trading days) changes in FX rates in the past. One immediate problem is that with 500 past trading days, only 100 weekly periods would be available, which reduces the statistical power of the VaR estimate (see below).

[32] The reason is that the historic, or back simulation, approach uses actual exchange rates on each day that explicitly include correlations or co-movements with other exchange rates and asset returns on that day.

[33] The 5 percent number in RiskMetrics tells us that we will lose more than this amount on 5 days out of every 100; it does not tell us the maximum amount we can lose. As noted in the text, theoretically, with a normal distribution, this could be an infinite amount.

in a fixed-exchange rate regime will have little relevance to an FX trader or market risk manager operating and analyzing risk in a floating-exchange rate regime.

This seems to confront the market risk manager with a difficult modelling problem. There are, however, at least two approaches to this problem. The first is to weight past observations in the back simulation unequally, giving a higher weight to the more recent past observations.[34] The second is to use a Monte Carlo simulation approach, which generates additional observations that are consistent with recent historic experience. The latter approach, in effect, amounts to simulating or creating artificial trading days and FX rate changes.

The Monte Carlo Simulation Approach[35]

To overcome the problems imposed by a limited number of actual observations, we can generate additional observations (in our example, FX changes). Normally, the simulation or generation of these additional observations is structured using a Monte Carlo simulation approach so that returns or rates generated reflect the probability with which they have occurred in recent historic time periods. The first step is to calculate the historic variance–covariance matrix (Σ) of FX changes. This matrix is then decomposed into two symmetric matrices, A and A'.[36] This allows the FI to generate scenarios for the FX position by multiplying the A' matrix, which reflects the historic volatilities and correlations among FX rates, by a random number vector z:[37] 10,000 random values of z are drawn for each FX exchange rate.[38] This simulation approach results in realistic FX scenarios being generated as historic volatilities and correlations among FX rates are multiplied by the randomly drawn values of z. The VaR of the current position is then calculated as in Table 10–6, except that in the Monte Carlo approach, the VaR is the 500th worst simulated loss out of 10,000.[39]

CONCEPT QUESTIONS

1. What are the advantages of the historic, or back simulation, approach over RiskMetrics to measure market risk?
2. What are the steps involved with the historic, or back simulation, approach to measuring market risk?
3. What is the Monte Carlo simulation approach to measuring market risk?

REGULATORY MODELS: THE BIS STANDARDIZED FRAMEWORK

The development of internal market risk models was partly in response to proposals by the Bank for International Settlements (BIS) in 1993 to measure and regulate the market risk exposures of banks by imposing capital requirements on their

---

[34] See L. Allen, J. Boudoukh, and A. Saunders, *Understanding Market, Credit and Operational Risk: The Value at Risk Approach.* New York: Blackwell, 2004, Chapters 1–3.

[35] This section, which contains more technical details, may be included in or dropped from the chapter reading, depending on the rigour of the course.

[36] The only difference between A and A' is that the numbers in the rows of A become the numbers in the columns of A'. The technical term for this procedure is the *Cholesky decomposition*, where $\Sigma = AA'$.

[37] Where z is assumed to be normally distributed with a mean of zero and a standard deviation of 1 or $z \sim N(0,1)$.

[38] Technically, let y be an FX scenario; then $y = A'z$. For each FX rate, 10,000 values of z are randomly generated to produce 10,000 values of y. The y values are then used to revalue the FX position and calculate gains and losses.

[39] See, for example, JPMorgan, *RiskMetrics,* Technical Document, 4th ed., 1997.

trading portfolios.[40] As noted in Chapter 7, the BIS is an organization encompassing the largest central banks in the world. After refining these proposals over a number of years, the BIS decided on a final approach to measuring market risk and the capital reserves necessary for an FI to hold to withstand and survive market risk losses. These required levels of capital held to protect against market risk exposure are in addition to the minimum level of capital banks are required to hold for credit risk purposes (see Chapter 20). Since January 1998[41] banks in the countries that are members of the BIS can calculate their market risk exposures in one of two ways. The first is to use a simple standardized framework (to be discussed below). The second, with regulatory approval, is to use their own internal models, which are similar to the models described above. However, if an internal model is approved for use in calculating capital requirements for the FI, it is subject to regulatory audit and certain constraints. Before looking at these constraints, we examine the BIS standardized framework for fixed-income securities, foreign exchange, and equities. Additional details of this model can be found at the BIS website, www.bis.org.

www.bis.org

Fixed Income

We can examine the BIS standardized framework for measuring the market risk on the fixed-income (or debt security) trading portfolio by using the example for a typical FI provided by the BIS (see Table 10–8). Panel A in Table 10–8 lists the security holdings of an FI in its trading account. The FI holds long and short positions in [column (3)] various quality debt issues [column (2)] with maturities ranging from one month to over 20 years [column (1)]. Long positions have positive values; short positions have negative values. To measure the risk of this trading portfolio, the BIS uses two capital charges: (1) a specific risk charge [columns (4) and (5)] and (2) a general market risk charge [columns (6) and (7)].

Specific Risk Charge

specific risk charge
A charge reflecting the risk of a decline in the liquidity or credit risk quality of the trading portfolio.

The **specific risk charge** is meant to measure the risk of a decline in the liquidity or credit risk quality of the trading portfolio over the FI's holding period. As column (4) in panel A of Table 10–8 indicates, Treasuries have a zero risk weight, while junk bonds (e.g., 10- to 15-year non-qualifying "Non Qual" corporate debt) have a risk weight of 8 percent. As shown in Table 10–8, multiplying the absolute dollar values of all the long and short positions in these instruments [column (3)] by the specific risk weights [column (4)] produces a specific risk capital or requirement charge for each position [column (5)]. Summing the individual charges for specific risk gives the total specific risk charge of $229.[42]

General Market Risk Charge

general market risk charges
Charges reflecting the modified duration and interest rate shocks for each maturity.

The **general market risk charges** or weights—column (6) of Table 10–8—reflect the product of the modified durations and interest rate shocks expected for each

---

[40] BIS, Basel Committee on Banking Supervision, *The Supervisory Treatment of Market Risks,* Basel, Switzerland, April 1993; *Proposal to Issue a Supplement to the Basel Accord to Cover Market Risks,* Basel, Switzerland, April 1995; and *The New Basel Capital Accord: Third Consultive Paper,* Basel, Switzerland, April 2003.

[41] The requirements were introduced earlier in 1996 in the European Union.

[42] Note that the risk weights for specific risks are not based on obvious theory, empirical research, or past experience. Rather, the weights are based on regulators' perceptions of what was appropriate when the model was established.

TABLE 10–8   **BIS Market Risk Calculation (Debt Securities, Sample Market Risk Calculation)**

Panel A: FI Holdings and Risk Charges

(1) Time Band	(2) Issuer	(3) Position ($)	Specific Risk		General Market Risk	
			(4) Weight (%)	(5) Charge	(6) Weight (%)	(7) Charge
0–1 month	Government	5,000	0.00	0.00	0.00	0.00
1–3 months	Government	5,000	0.00	0.00	0.20	10.00
3–6 months	Qual Corp	4,000	0.25	10.00	0.40	16.00
6–12 months	Qual Corp	(7,500)	1.00	75.00	0.70	(52.50)
1–2 years	Government	(2,500)	0.00	0.00	1.25	(31.25)
2–3 years	Government	2,500	0.00	0.00	1.75	43.75
3–4 years	Government	2,500	0.00	0.00	2.25	56.25
3–4 years	Qual Corp	(2,000)	1.60	32.00	2.25	(45.00)
4–5 years	Government	1,500	0.00	0.00	2.75	41.25
5–7 years	Qual Corp	(1,000)	1.60	16.00	3.25	(32.50)
7–10 years	Government	(1,500)	0.00	0.00	3.75	(56.25)
10–15 years	Government	(1,500)	0.00	0.00	4.50	(67.50)
10–15 years	Non Qual	1,000	8.00	80.00	4.50	45.00
15–20 years	Government	1,500	0.00	0.00	5.25	78.75
> 20 years	Qual Corp	1,000	1.60	16.00	6.00	60.00
Specific risk				229.00		
Residual general market risk						66.00

Panel B: Calculation of Capital Charge

(1)	(2)	(3)	(4)	(5)	(6)	(7) Charge
1. Specific Risk						229.00
2. Vertical Offsets within Same Time Bands						

Time Band	Longs	Shorts	Residual*	Offset	Disallowance	Charge
3–4 years	56.25	(45.00)	11.25	45.00	10.00%	4.50
10–15 years	45.00	(67.50)	(22.50)	45.00	10.00	4.50

3. Horizontal Offsets within Same Time Zones

Zone 1						
0–1 month	0.00					
1–3 months	10.00					
3–6 months	16.00					
6–12 months		(52.50)				
Total zone 1	26.00	(52.50)	(26.50)	26.00	40.00%	10.40
Zone 2						
1–2 years		(31.25)				
2–3 years	43.75					
3–4 years	11.25					
Total zone 2	55.00	(31.25)	23.75	31.25	30.00%	9.38
Zone 3						
4–5 years	41.25					
5–7 years		(31.50)				
7–10 years		(56.25)				
10–15 years		(22.50)				
15–20 years	78.75					
>20 years	60.00					
Total zone 3	180.00	(111.25)	68.75	111.25	30.00%	33.38

(Continued)

TABLE 10–8 (*Concluded*)

Time Band	Longs	Shorts	Residual*	Offset	Disallowance	Charge
4. Horizontal Offsets between Time Zones						
Zones 1 and 2	23.75	(26.50)	(2.75)	23.75	40.00%	9.50
Zones 1 and 3	68.75	(2.75)	66.00	2.75	150.00%	4.12
5. Total Capital Charge						
Specific risk						229.00
Vertical disallowances						9.00
Horizontal disallowances						
Offsets within same time zones						53.16
Offsets between time zones						13.62
Residual general market risk after all offsets						66.00
Total						370.78

*Residual amount carried forward for additional offsetting as appropriate.
Note: Qual Corp is an investment-grade debt issue (e.g., rated BBB and above). Non Qual is a below-investment-grade debt issue (e.g., rated BB and below), that is, a junk bond.

maturity.[43] The weights in Table 10–8 range from zero for the 0 to 1-month Treasuries to 6 percent for the long-term (longer than 20 years to maturity) quality corporate debt securities. The positive or negative dollar values of the positions in each instrument [column (3)] are multiplied by the general market risk weights [column (6)] to determine the general market risk charges for the individual holdings [column (7)]. Summing these gives the total general market risk charge of $66 for the whole fixed-income portfolio.

Vertical Offsets

The BIS model assumes that long and short positions, in the same maturity bucket but in different instruments, cannot perfectly offset each other. Thus, the $66 general market risk charge tends to underestimate interest rate or price risk exposure. For example, the FI is short $1,500 in 10- to 15-year government securities, producing a market risk charge of $67.50, and is long $1,000 in 10- to 15-year junk bonds (with a risk charge of $45). However, because of basis risk—that is, the fact that the rates on Treasuries and junk bonds do not fluctuate exactly together—we cannot assume that a $45 short position in junk bonds is hedging an equivalent ($45) risk value of government securities of the same maturity. Similarly, the FI is long $2,500 in three- to four-year government securities (with a general market risk charge of $56.25) and short $2,000 in three- to four-year quality corporate bonds (with a risk charge of $45). To account for this, the BIS requires additional capital charges for basis risk, called **vertical offsets** or disallowance factors. We show these calculations in part 2 of panel B in Table 10–8.

In panel B, column (1) lists the time bands for which the bank has both a long and short position. Columns (2) and (3) list the general market risk charges—from

vertical offsets
Additional capital charges assigned because long and short positions in the same maturity bucket but in different instruments cannot perfectly offset each other.

[43] For example, for 15- to 20-year government securities in Table 10–8, the modified duration is assumed to be 8.75 years, and the expected interest rate shock is 0.60 percent. Thus, 8.75 × 0.6 = 5.25, which is the general market risk weight for these securities shown in Table 10–8. Multiplying 5.25 by the $1,500 long position in these securities results in a general market risk charge of $78.75. Note that the shocks assumed for short-term securities, such as three-month T-bills, are larger (at 1 percent) than those assumed for longer-maturity securities. This reflects the fact that short-term rates are more impacted by monetary policy. Finally, note that the standardized model combines unequal rate shocks with estimated modified durations to calculate market risk weights. Technically, this violates the underlying assumptions of the duration model, which assumes parallel yield shifts (see Chapter 9) at each maturity.

column (7) of panel A—resulting from the positions, and column (4) lists the difference (or residual) between the charges. Column (5) reports the smallest value of the risk charges for each time band (or offset). As listed in column (6), the BIS disallows 10 percent[44] of the $45 position in corporate bonds in hedging $45 of the government bond position. This results in an additional capital charge of $4.50 ($45 × 10 percent).[45] The total charge for all vertical offsets is $9.

Horizontal Offsets within Time Zones

horizontal offsets
Additional capital charges required because long and short positions of different maturities do not perfectly hedge each other.

In addition, the debt trading portfolio is divided into three maturity zones: zone 1 (1 month to 12 months), zone 2 (more than 1 year to 4 years), and zone 3 (more than 4 years to 20 years plus). Again because of basis risk (i.e., the imperfect correlation of interest rates on securities of different maturities), short and long positions of different maturities in these zones will not perfectly hedge each other. This results in additional (horizontal) disallowance factors of 40 percent (zone 1), 30 percent (zone 2), and 30 percent (zone 3).[46] Part 3 of the bottom panel in Table 10–8 shows these calculations. The **horizontal offsets** are calculated using the sum of the general market risk charges from the long and short positions in each time zone—columns (2) and (3). As with the vertical offsets, the smallest of these totals is the offset value against which the disallowance is applied. For example, the total zone 1 charges for long positions equal $26.00 and for short positions ($52.50). A disallowance of 40 percent of the offset value (the smaller of these two values), $26.00, is charged, that is, $10.40 ($26 × 40 percent). Repeating this process for each of the three zones produces additional (horizontal offset) charges totalling $53.16.

Horizontal Offsets between Time Zones

Finally, because interest rates on short maturity debt and long maturity debt do not fluctuate exactly together, a residual long or short position in each zone can only partly hedge an offsetting position in another zone. This leads to a final set of offsets, or disallowance factors, between time zones, part 4 of panel B of Table 10–8. Here the BIS model compares the residual charges from zones 1 ($26.50) and 2 ($23.75). The difference, $2.75, is then compared with the residual from zone 3 ($68.75). The smaller of each zone comparison is again used as the offset value against which a disallowance of 40 percent for adjacent zones[47] and 150 percent[48] for non-adjacent zones, respectively, is applied. The additional charges here total $13.62.

Summing the specific risk charges ($229), the general market risk charge ($66), and the basis risk or disallowance charges ($9.00 + $53.16 + $13.62) produces a total capital charge of $370.78 for this fixed-income trading portfolio.[49]

---

[44] Note again that the disallowance factors were set subjectively by regulators.

[45] Intuitively, this implies that long-term government bond rates and long-term junk bond rates are approximately 90 percent correlated. However, in the final plan, it was decided to cut vertical disallowance factors in half. Thus, a 10 percent disallowance factor becomes a 5 percent disallowance factor, and so on.

[46] The zones were also set subjectively by regulators.

[47] For example, zones 1 and 2 are adjacent to each other in terms of maturity. By comparison, zones 1 and 3 are not adjacent to each other.

[48] This adjustment of 150 percent was later reduced to 100 percent.

[49] This number can also be recalculated in risk-adjusted asset terms to compare with risk-adjusted assets on the banking book. Thus, if capital is meant to be a minimum of 8 percent of risk-adjusted assets, then $370.78 × (1/1.08), or $370.78 × 12.5 = $4,634.75 is the equivalent amount of trading book risk-adjusted assets supported by this capital requirement.

Foreign Exchange

The standardized model or framework requires the FI to calculate its net exposure in each foreign currency—yen, euros, and so on—and then convert this into dollars at the current spot exchange rate. As shown in Table 10–9, the FI is net long (million-dollar equivalent) $50 yen, $100 euros, and $150 pounds while being short $20 Australian dollars and $180 Swiss francs. Its total currency long position is $300, and its total short position is $200. The BIS standardized framework imposes a capital requirement equal to 8 percent times the maximum absolute value of the aggregate long or short positions. In this example, 8 percent times $300 million = $24 million. This method of calculating FX exposure assumes some partial, but not complete, offsetting of currency risk by holding opposing long or short positions in different currencies.

Equities

As discussed in the context of the RiskMetrics market value model, the two sources of risk in holding equities are (1) a firm-specific, or unsystematic, risk element and (2) a market, or systematic, risk element. The BIS charges for unsystematic risk by adding the long and short positions in any given stock and applying a 4 percent charge against the gross position in the stock (called the *x*-factor). Suppose stock number 2, in Table 10–10, is Microsoft. The FI has a long $100 million and short $25 million position in that stock. Its gross position that is exposed to unsystematic (firm-specific) risk is $125, which is multiplied by 4 percent to give a capital charge of $5 million.

Market, or systematic, risk is reflected in the net long or short position (the so-called *y*-factor). In the case of Microsoft, this risk is $75 million ($100 long minus $25 short). The capital charge would be 8 percent against the $75 million, or $6 million. The total capital charge (*x*-factor + *y*-factor) is $11 million for this stock.

This approach is very crude, basically assuming the same systematic risk factor (β) for every stock. It also does not fully consider the benefits from portfolio diversification (i.e., that unsystematic risk can be diversified away).

CONCEPT QUESTIONS	1. What is the difference between the BIS specific risk and general market risk in measuring trading portfolio risk?
	2. What methods did the BIS model propose for calculating FX trading exposure?
	3. How are unsystematic and systematic risks in equity holdings by FIs reflected in charges assessed under the BIS model?

TABLE 10–9
Example of the BIS Standardized Framework Measure of Foreign Exchange Risk ($ millions)

Source: BIS, 1993, www.bis.org.

Once a bank has calculated its net position in each foreign currency, it converts each position into its reporting currency and calculates the risk (capital) measure as in the following example, in which the position in the reporting currency (dollars) has been excluded:

Yen*	Euros	GB£	A$	SF
+50	+100	+150	−20	−180
	+300		−200	

The capital charge would be 8 percent of the higher of the longs and shorts (i.e., 300).

*All currencies in $ equivalents.

TABLE 10–10   BIS Capital Requirement for Equities (Illustration of x plus y Methodology)

Under the proposed two-part calculation, there would be separate requirements for the position in each individual equity (i.e., the gross position) and for the net position in the market as a whole. Here we show how the system would work for a range of hypothetical portfolios, assuming a capital charge of 4 percent for the gross positions and 8 percent for the net positions.

Stock	Sum of Long Positions	Sum of Short Positions	x-Factor Gross Position (sum of cols. 2 and 3)	x-Factor 4 Percent of Gross	y-Factor Net Position (difference between cols. 2 and 3)	y-Factor 8 Percent of Net	Capital Required (gross + net)
1	100	0	100	4	100	8	12
2	100	25	125	5	75	6	11
3	100	50	150	6	50	4	10
4	100	75	175	7	25	2	9
5	100	100	200	8	0	0	8
6	75	100	175	7	25	2	9
7	50	100	150	6	50	4	10
8	25	100	125	5	75	6	11
9	0	100	100	4	100	8	12

Source: BIS, 1993, www.bis.org.

THE BIS REGULATIONS AND LARGE BANK INTERNAL MODELS

As discussed above, the BIS capital requirement for market risk exposure introduced in January 1998 allows large banks (subject to regulatory permission) to use their own internal models to calculate market risk instead of the standardized framework. (We examine the initiatives taken by the BIS and the major central banks in controlling bank risk exposure through capital requirements in greater detail in Chapter 20.) However, the required capital calculation has to be relatively conservative compared with that produced internally. A comparison of the BIS requirement for large banks using their internal models with RiskMetrics indicates the following, in particular:

1. In calculating daily VaR, the FI must define an adverse change in rates as being in the 99th percentile rather than in the 95th percentile (multiply σ by 2.33 rather than by 1.65 as under RiskMetrics).
2. The FI must assume the minimum holding period to be 10 days (this means that RiskMetrics' daily VaR would have to be multiplied by $\sqrt{10}$).[50]
3. The FI must use an historical sample of at least one year with data updated at least once each quarter.

The FI must consider its proposed capital charge or requirement as the *higher* of

1. The previous day's VaR (value at risk $\times \sqrt{10}$).
2. The average daily VaR over the previous 60 days times a multiplication factor with a minimum value of 3, i.e., capital charge = (avg. VaR) $\times (\sqrt{10}) \times (3)$. In general, the multiplication factor makes required capital significantly higher than VaR produced from private models.

---

[50] Banks are allowed to vary from the Basel II regulations provided their capital calculations are at least as conservative as Basel II and their regulator is satisfied that the approach is reasonable. See *Revisions to the Basel II Market Risk Framework,* Bank for International Settlements, January 2009.

However, to reduce the burden of capital needs, an additional type of capital can be raised by FIs to meet the capital charge (or requirement). Suppose the portfolio VaR was $10 million using the 1 percent worst case (or 99th percentile).[51] The minimum capital charge would be[52]

$$\text{Capital charge} = (\$10 \text{ million}) \times (\sqrt{10}) \times (3) = \$94.86 \text{ million}$$

As explained in Chapters 7 and 20, capital provides an internal insurance fund to protect an FI, its depositors and other liability holders, and the insurance fund (e.g., CDIC) against losses. The BIS permits three types of capital to be held to meet this capital requirement: Tier 1, Tier 2, and Tier 3. Tier 1 capital is essentially retained earnings and common stock, Tier 2 is essentially long-term subordinated debt (over five years), and Tier 3 is short-term subordinated debt with an original maturity of at least two years. Thus, the $94.86 million in the example above can be raised by any of the three capital types subject to the two following limitations: (1) Tier 3 capital is limited to 250 percent of Tier 1 capital, and (2) Tier 2 capital can be substituted for Tier 3 capital up to the same 250 percent limit. For example, suppose Tier 1 capital was $27.10 million and the FI issued short-term Tier 3 debt of $67.76 million. Then the 250 percent limit would mean that no more Tier 3 (or Tier 2) debt could be issued to meet a target above $94.86 ($27.1 × 2.5 = $67.76) without additional Tier 1 capital being added. This capital charge for market risk would be added to the capital charge for credit risk and operational risk to get the FI's total capital requirement. The different types of capital and capital requirements are discussed in more detail in Chapter 20.

Global banks and their regulators are moving from Basel I to Basel II capital adequacy requirements. Canadian banks regulated by OSFI switched to reporting Basel II capital adequacy requirements for their annual reports in 2008. U.S. banks are expected to adopt Basel II in 2011. The subprime crisis of 2007 and 2008 has pointed out the weaknesses of market risk measures to adequately reflect an FI's exposure, and both the BIS and national regulators are assessing the market risk requirements that are necessary to ensure a stable international financial system.[53]

Table 10–11 shows the dollar amounts of the risk-weighted assets calculated according to Basel II capital adequacy rules that were reported by the major Canadian banks in their 2008 annual reports. Notice how small the market risk-weighted assets are relative to the total risk-weighted assets. In all cases, the largest allowance for risk-weighted assets is for credit risk. For all but the National Bank, operational risk is the next largest category of risk-weighted assets, followed by market risk. Since OSFI requires these six banks to have a minimum

---

[51] Using 2.33σ rather than 1.65σ.

[52] The idea of a minimum multiplication factor of 3 is to create a scheme that is "incentive compatible." Specifically, if FIs using internal models constantly underestimate the amount of capital they need to meet their market risk exposures, regulators can punish those FIs by raising the multiplication factor to as high as 4. Such a response may effectively put the FI out of the trading business. The degree to which the multiplication factor is raised above 3 depends on the number of days an FI's model underestimates its market risk over the preceding year. For example, an underestimation error that occurs on more than 10 days out of the past 250 days will result in the multiplication factor being raised to 4.

[53] *The Turner Review: A Regulatory Response to the Global Banking Crisis* (available at www.fsa.gov.uk), released in March 2009 by the U.K. Financial Services Authority, addresses the causes of the 2007–2008 credit crisis and the weaknesses of market risk models. See also P. Youngman, "Procyclicality and Value at Risk," Bank of Canada *Financial System Review,* June 2009, p. 51. *Principles for Sound Stress Testing Practices and Supervision,* May 2009, www.bis.org, emphasizes stress testing as a complement to risk models.

TABLE 10–11
Risk-Weighted Assets Reported by Canadian FIs under Basel II, 2008 ($ millions)

Source: Company annual reports, 2008.

	Credit Risk	Market Risk	Operational Risk	Total Risk-Weighted Assets
BMO	$163,616	$11,293	$16,699	$191,608
CIBC	95,161	2,928	19,857	117,946
National Bank	45,509	6,623	5,937	58,069
RBC	229,537	17,220	31,822	278,579
Scotiabank	214,500	15,500	20,600	250,600
TD	177,552	9,644	24,554	211,750

Tier 1 capital ratio of 7 percent under Basel II, for its market risk-weighted assets of $11,293,000,000, BMO must have Tier 1 capital of $790,510,000 (Tier 1 capital/Risk-weighted assets = 7 percent) to support its market risk. This represents just 5.9 percent of the total minimum Tier 1 capital of $13,412,560,000 required. BMO's total Tier 1 capital was $23.3 billion at October 31, 2008, giving it a Tier 1 capital ratio of 9.77 percent, well above OSFI's requirement. Chapter 20 covers the Basel II capital adequacy requirements in greater detail.

CONCEPT QUESTIONS

1. What is the BIS standardized framework for measuring market risk?
2. What is the effect of using the 99th percentile (1 percent worst case) rather than the 95th percentile (5 percent worst case) on the measured size of an FI's market risk exposures?

Summary

In this chapter we analyzed the importance of measuring an FI's market risk exposure. This risk is likely to continue to grow in importance as more and more loans and previously illiquid assets become marketable and as the traditional franchises of commercial banks, insurance companies, and investment banks shrink. Given the risks involved, both private FI management and regulators are investing increasing resources in models to measure and track market risk exposures. We analyzed in detail three approaches FIs have used to measure market risk: RiskMetrics, the historic (or back simulation) approach, and the Monte Carlo simulation approach. The three approaches were also compared in terms of simplicity and accuracy. Market risk is also of concern to regulators. Since November 1999, banks in Canada have had to hold a capital requirement against the risk of their trading positions. The novel feature of the regulation of market risk is that large FIs have the option to calculate capital requirements based on their own internal models rather than the regulatory model.

Questions and Problems

1. What is meant by *market risk*?
2. Why is the measurement of market risk important to the manager of a financial institution?
3. What is meant by value at risk (VaR)? What are the three measurable components? What is the price volatility component?
4. Crispin Bank has a $1 million position in a five-year, zero-coupon bond with a face value of $1,402,552. The bond is trading at a yield to maturity of 7.00 percent. The historical mean change in daily yields is 0.0 percent, and the standard deviation is 12 basis points.
   a. What is the modified duration of the bond?
   b. What is the maximum adverse daily yield move given that we desire no more than a 5 percent chance that yield changes will be greater than this maximum?
   c. What is the price volatility of this bond?
   d. What is the daily value at risk for this bond?

5. What would be the VaR for the bond in problem 4 for a 10-day period? What statistical assumption is needed for this calculation? Could this treatment be critical?

6. The daily VaR for a bank is $8,500. What is the VaR for a 10-day period? A 20-day period? Why is the VaR for a 20-day period not twice as much as that for a 10-day period?

7. The mean change in the daily yields of a 15-year, zero-coupon bond has been five basis points (bp) over the past year with a standard deviation of 15 bp. Use these data and assume that the yield changes are normally distributed.

   a. What is the highest yield change expected if a 90 percent confidence limit is required; that is, adverse moves will not occur more than 1 day in 20?

   b. What is the highest yield change expected if a 95 percent confidence limit is required?

8. In what sense is duration a measure of market risk?

9. Bank Alpha has an inventory of AAA-rated, 15-year zero-coupon bonds with a face value of $400 million. The bonds currently are yielding 9.5 percent in the over-the-counter market.

   a. What is the modified duration of these bonds?

   b. What is the price volatility if the potential adverse move in yields is 25 basis points?

   c. What is the daily VaR?

   d. If the price volatility is based on a 90 percent confidence limit and a mean historical change in daily yields of 0.0 percent, what is the implied standard deviation of daily yield changes?

10. Bank Two has a portfolio of bonds with a market value of $200 million. The bonds have an estimated price volatility of 0.95 percent. What are the daily VaR and the 10-day VaR for these bonds?

11. Bank Three has determined that its inventory of 20 million euros (€) and 25 million British pounds (£) is subject to market risk. The spot exchange rates are $0.40/€ and $1.28/£, respectively. The σ values of the spot exchange rates of the € and £, based on the daily changes of spot rates over the past six months, are 65 bp and 45 bp, respectively. Determine the bank's 10-day VaR for both currencies. Use adverse rate changes in the 90th percentile.

12. Bank Four's stock portfolio has a market value of $10,000,000. The beta of the portfolio approximates the market portfolio, whose standard deviation (σ_m) has been estimated at 1.5 percent. What is the five-day VaR of this portfolio using adverse rate changes in the 99th percentile?

13. Jeff Resnick, vice-president of operations of Choice Bank, is estimating the aggregate daily VaR of the bank's portfolio of assets consisting of loans (L), foreign currencies (FX), and common stock (EQ). The individual daily VaRs are $300,700; $274,000; and $126,700, respectively. If the correlation coefficients (ρ_{ij}) between L and FX, L and EQ, and FX and EQ are 0.3, 0.7, and 0.0, respectively, what is the daily VaR of the aggregate portfolio?

14. Calculate the daily VaR for the following portfolio, first with the correlation coefficients and then with perfect positive correlation between the various asset groups.

Assets	Estimated Daily VaR	$(\rho_{S, FX})$	$(\rho_{S, B})$	$(\rho_{FX, B})$
Stocks (S)	$300,000	−0.10	0.75	0.20
Foreign Exchange (FX)	200,000			
Bonds (B)	250,000			

What is the amount of risk reduction resulting from the lack of perfect positive correlation between the various asset groups?

15. What are the advantages of using the back simulation approach to estimate market risk? Explain how this approach would be implemented.

16. Export Bank has a trading position in Japanese yen and Swiss francs. At the close of business on February 4, the bank had ¥300,000,000 and Sf 10,000,000. The exchange rates for the most recent six days are given below.

Exchange Rates per Dollar at the Close of Business

	2/4	2/3	2/2	2/1	1/29	1/28
Japanese yen	112.13	112.84	112.14	115.05	116.35	116.32
Swiss francs	1.4140	1.4175	1.4133	1.4217	1.4157	1.4123

   a. What is the foreign exchange (FX) position in dollar equivalents using the FX rates on February 4?

   b. What is the definition of delta as it relates to the FX position?

   c. What is the sensitivity of each FX position; that is, what is the value of delta for each currency on February 4?

   d. What is the daily percentage change in exchange rates for each currency over the five-day period?

   e. What is the total risk faced by the bank on each day? What is the worst-case day? What is the best-case day?

f. Assume that you have data for the 500 trading days preceding February 4. Explain how you would identify the worst-case scenario with a 95 percent degree of confidence.

g. Explain how the 5 percent value at risk (VaR) position would be interpreted for business on February 5.

h. How would the simulation change at the end of the day on February 5? What variables and/or processes in the analysis may change? What variables and/or processes will not change?

17. What is the primary disadvantage of the back simulation approach in measuring market risk? What effect does the inclusion of more observation days have as a remedy for this disadvantage? What other remedies can be used to deal with the disadvantage?

18. How is Monte Carlo simulation useful in addressing the disadvantages of back simulation? What is the primary statistical assumption underlying its use?

19. In the BIS standardized framework for regulating risk exposure for the fixed-income portfolios of banks, what do the terms *specific risk* and *general market risk* mean? Why does the capital charge for general market risk tend to underestimate the true interest rate or price risk exposure? What additional offsets, or disallowance factors, are included in the analysis?

20. An FI has the following bonds in its portfolio: long 1-year government bills, short 3-year government bonds, long 3-year AAA-rated corporate bonds, and long 12-year B-rated (non-qualifying) bonds worth $40, $10, $25, and $10 million, respectively (market values). Using Table 10–8, determine the following:

a. Charges for specific risk.

b. Charges for general market risk.

c. Charges for basis risk: vertical offsets within same time bands only (i.e., ignoring horizon effects).

d. The total capital charge, using the information from parts (a) through (c).

21. Explain how the capital charge for foreign exchange risk is calculated in the BIS standardized model. If an FI has an $80 million long position in euros, a $40 million short position in British pounds, and a $20 million long position in Swiss francs, what will be the capital charge required against FX market risk?

22. Explain the BIS capital charge calculation for unsystematic and systematic risk for an FI that holds various amounts of equities in its portfolio. What would be the total capital charge required for an FI that holds the following portfolio of stocks? What criticisms can be levied against this treatment of measuring the risk in the equity portfolio?

Company	Long	Short
Encana	$45 million	$25 million
RIM	$55 million	$12 million
CIBC	$20 million	
Air Canada		$15 million

23. What conditions were introduced by BIS to allow large banks to use internally generated models for the measurement of market risk? What types of capital can be held to meet the capital charge requirements?

24. Dark Star Bank has estimated its average daily VaR for the previous 60 days to be $35.5 million. Daily VaR for the previous day was $30.2 million.

a. Under the latest BIS standards, what is the amount of capital required to be held for market risk?

b. Dark Star has $15 million of Tier 1 capital, $37.5 million of Tier 2 capital, and $55 million of Tier 3 capital. Is this amount of capital sufficient? If not, what minimum amount of new capital should be raised? Of what type?

INTERNET EXERCISE

Go to CIBC's website (www.cibc.com) and download the latest annual report. Find the "Management of Risk" section. What methods is CIBC now using to calculate market risk? What was CIBC's maximum daily value at risk on its trading activities? What was its minimum? What components are measured to give the total VaR? How has it changed since the data provided in Table 10–6? Does the annual report give you a good understanding of the market risk of this particular FI?

Credit Risk: Individual Loans

In this chapter, we discuss credit or default risk and look at

▸ the types and charactertistics of loans (business, real estate, consumer, and others) made by Canadian FIs

▸ how interest and fees are incorporated to calculate the return on a loan

▸ how the return on a loan versus the quantity of credit made available for lending is used by FIs to make decisions on business credit versus consumer and residential mortgage lending

▸ the various models used to measure credit risk, including qualitative models, credit scoring models, and newer models of credit risk measurement

▸ the cash flow and financial ratio analysis widely used in the credit analysis process for mortgage, consumer and business loans (see Appendix 11A, available at the Online Learning Centre at www.mcgrawhill.ca/olc/saunders).

INTRODUCTION

As discussed in Chapter 1, financial intermediaries (FIs) are special because of their ability to efficiently transform financial claims of household savers into claims issued to corporations, individuals, and governments. An FI's ability to evaluate information and to control and monitor borrowers allows it to transform these claims at the lowest possible cost to all parties. One of the specific types of financial claim transformation discussed in Chapter 1 is credit allocation. That is, FIs transform claims of household savers (in the form of deposits) into loans issued to corporations, individuals, and governments. The FI accepts the credit risk on these loans in exchange for a fair return sufficient to cover the cost of funding (e.g., covering the costs of borrowing or issuing deposits) to household savers and the credit risk involved in lending.

In this chapter, the first of two chapters on credit risk, we discuss various approaches to analyzing and measuring the credit or default risk on individual loans (and bonds). In the next chapter, we consider methods for evaluating the risk of loan portfolios, or loan concentration risk. Methods for hedging and managing an FI's credit risk are left to Chapters 23 to 27. Measurement of the credit risk on individual loans or bonds is crucial if an FI manager is to (1) price a loan or value a bond correctly and (2) set appropriate limits on the amount of credit extended to any one borrower or the loss exposure it accepts from any particular counterparty. The default of one major borrower can have a significant impact on the value and reputation of many FIs. Thus, managers need to manage the FI's individual loans to protect the FI from the failure of a single borrower. Management of the overall loan portfolio is equally important. For example, Japanese FIs suffered losses from an overconcentration of loans in real estate and in Asia. In the early 2000s, bad loans of the top eight Japanese banks exceeded US$43 billion, and a majority of Japanese banks reported losses as a result of having to write off these loans. In addition, Japanese life insurers were heavily exposed through their over 14 trillion yen (US$129 billion) loan exposure to Japanese banks.

In an economic recession such as the one that developed at the end of 2008 and carried on into 2009, all types of loans become subject to greater scrutiny by FIs as they try to limit their exposure to credit risk. Poor economic conditions can lead to defaults on consumer loans such as lines of credit, mortgages, and credit card debt. Defaults ultimately reduce an FI's operating profits. Thus, it is important to remember that economic conditions have a significant impact on the ability (based on liquidity and capital adequacy) and willingness (based on the assessed credit risk) of FIs to lend to consumers and businesses.

CREDIT QUALITY PROBLEMS

junk bond
A bond rated as speculative or less than investment-grade by bond-rating agencies such as DBRS.

www.dbrs.com
www.moodys.com
www.standardand-poors.com

Over the past two decades the credit quality of many FIs' lending and investment decisions has attracted a great deal of attention. In the 1980s there were tremendous problems with bank loans to less-developed countries (LDCs). In the early 1990s attention switched to the problems of commercial real estate loans (to which banks and insurance companies were all exposed) as well as **junk bonds** (rated as speculative or less than investment-grade securities by bond-rating agencies such as Dominion Bond Rating Service (DBRS), Moody's, or Standard & Poor's). In the late 1990s concerns shifted to the rapid growth in low-quality auto loans and credit cards as well as the declining quality in commercial lending standards as loan delinquencies started to increase. In the late 1990s and early 2000s, attention was focused on problems with telecommunication companies, new technology companies, and a variety of sovereign countries, including at various times Argentina, Brazil, Russia, and South Korea. In 2007 and 2008, FIs started to struggle with the deterioration of credit conditions related to a global economic downturn. All types of assets including subprime loans and credit card receivables had been securitized, as we discuss in detail in Chapter 27. Thus, FIs had distributed the credit risk throughout the global financial system. As well, the ability to securitize assets allowed banks to increase the amount of loans that they originated and earn additional fee income for continuing to service the securitized assets.

The credit quality of the loans of all major Canadian banks has varied over the last two decades. As shown in Figure 11–1A, loan loss provisions as a percentage of income peaked at over 25 percent in 1988 and again in 1992, settling below 10 percent from 1996 to 2002. However, since statistics became available in 1994, non-mortgage business loans have shown much higher impaired rates, ranging from above 10 percent in 1994 to around 4 percent in 2004. These figures reflect the higher credit risk of business loans, but also show that Canadian banks are subject to global conditions such as the high rate of global corporate debt default that peaked in 2002–2003, related to the Enron bankruptcy, among others. For example, in 2002,

www.td.com

Toronto-Dominion Bank reported a net loss of $76 million related to its exposure to telecommunications companies and utilities, and increased its gross impaired loans to $2.5 billion, 2 percent of its loans. Figure 11–1A also shows that Canadian banks' asset quality started to decline again after 2004 as loan loss provisions increased and net non-performing loans[1] as a percentage of Tier 1 capital increased as well.

The Canadian banks' exposure to consumer loans is shown in Figure 11–1B. Personal bankruptcy rates and residential mortgage loans in arrears (three months or more) rise during economic downturns. The impact of residential mortgage

---

[1] Non-performing loans are loans that are 90 days or more past due or are not accruing interest.

FIGURE 11–1A
Asset Quality of Canadian Banks

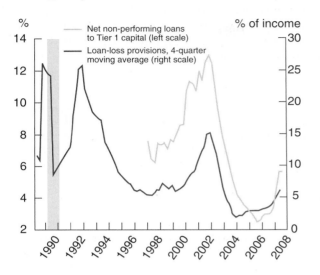

FIGURE 11–1B
Household Sector: Financial Stress Indicators

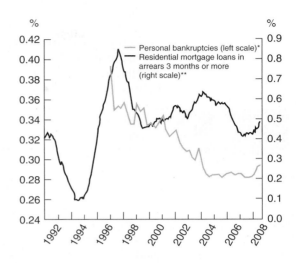

Note: The shaded bar for 1990 indicates a period or recession.

Source: The Bank of Canada, *Financial System Review,* December 2008.

*   As a percentage of population aged 20 and over
** As a percentage of total residential mortgage loans outstanding

loans is not as significant since many of these loans carry mortgage insurance, but defaults on personal loans and credit card debt can have a significant impact on an FI's profitability.

INTERNET EXERCISE

Find the latest information for impaired assets for Canadian banks published by the Office of the Superintendent of Financial Institutions using the following steps. Go to OSFI's website at www.osfi-bsif.gc.ca. Under the heading "Deposit-taking Institutions," click on "Banks." Then click on "Financial Data—Banks." Click on "Quarterly" and from the drop-down menu, click on "Impaired Assets (excluding the memo items)." Click on "Submit" and the table of the most recent quarter's results for all banks reporting to OSFI will appear. Data for individual banks is also available via the drop-down menu.

Credit quality problems, in the worst case, can cause an FI to become insolvent or can result in such a significant drain on capital[2] and net worth that they

_____

[2] Losses drain capital through the income statement item "provision for loan losses." The provision for loan losses is a non-cash, tax-deductible expense representing the FI management's prediction of loans at risk of default for the current period. As credit quality problems arise, the FI recognizes its expected bad loans by recording this expense, which reduces net income and, in turn, the FI's capital. The provision for loan losses is then allocated to the allowance for loan losses listed on the balance sheet. The allowance for loan and lease losses is a cumulative estimate by the FI's management of the percentage of the gross loans (and leases) that will not be repaid to the FI. Although the maximum amount of the provision of loan losses and the reserve for loan losses is influenced by tax laws, the FI's management actually sets the level based on loan growth and recent loan loss experience. The allowance for loan losses is an accumulated reserve that is adjusted each period as management recognizes the possibility of additional bad loans and makes appropriate provisions for such losses. Actual losses are then deducted from, and recoveries are added to (referred to as *net write-offs*), their accumulated loans and lease loss reserve balance. See Appendix 2A, "Financial Statements Analysis Using a Return on Equity Framework" (located at the Online Learning Centre: www.mcgrawhill.ca/olc/saunders) for a more detailed discussion of these items.

adversely affect its growth prospects and ability to compete with other domestic and international FIs.[3]

However, credit risk does not apply only to traditional areas of lending and bond investing. As banks and other FIs have expanded into credit guarantees and other off-balance-sheet activities (see Chapter 13), new types of credit risk exposure have arisen, causing concern among managers and regulators. Thus, credit risk analysis is now important for a whole variety of contractual agreements between FIs and counterparties.[4]

CONCEPT QUESTIONS	
	1. What are some of the credit quality problems faced by FIs over the last two decades?
	2. What are some of the newer, non-traditional activities that create credit risk for today's FIs?

TYPES OF LOANS

Although most FIs make loans, the types of loans made and the characteristics of those loans differ considerably. This section analyzes the major types of loans made by Canadian banks. Remember from Chapters 2 through 6, however, that other FIs, such as trust and mortgage loan companies, life insurance companies, credit unions, and caisses populaires also engage in lending, especially in the real estate area. We also discuss important aspects of other FIs' loan portfolios.

Table 11-1 shows a recent breakdown of the aggregate loan portfolio of Canadian banks into four broad classes: business, mortgages, personal, and all others. We look briefly at each of these loan classes in turn.

Business Loans

The figures in Table 11–1 disguise a great deal of heterogeneity in the business loan portfolio. Business loans can be made for periods as short as a few weeks to

TABLE 11–1
Loans of All Banks Reporting to OSFI as at February 28, 2009: Net of Allowance for Impairment ($ billions)

Source: Office of Superintendent of Financial Institutions Canada, www.osfi-bsif.gc.ca.

	Amount	Percent
Business loans*	$ 631.2	40.6
Mortgages		
Insured	211.1	13.6
Uninsured	268.4	17.3
Non-residential	53.4	3.4
Personal loans	351.7	22.6
Other**	38.4	2.5
Total Loans	**$1,554.1**	**100.0**
Total Assets	**$3,071.0**	
Loans/Total Assets (%)	**50.6**	

*Includes lease receivables and reverse purchase agreements.
**Includes inter-bank loans and loans to domestic and foreign governments.

---

[3] Not only is the book value of the FI's capital affected by credit quality problems in its loan portfolio, but studies have found that returns on banks' common stocks decrease significantly on the announcement of bankruptcy and default by borrowers of their bank. See S. Dahiya, A. Saunders, and A. Srinivasan, "Financial Distress and Bank Lending Relationships," *Journal of Finance,* February 2003, pp. 375–401, and S. V. Jayanti and G. Booth, "The Impact of Latin American Debt Moratoria on Canadian Bank Stocks, *Canadian Journal of Administrative Sciences,* September 1993, 10 (3), pp. 201–212.

[4] This is one of the reasons for bank regulators' setting capital requirements against credit risk and the concern with the ratio of net non-performing loans to Tier 1 capital in Figure 11–1A (see Chapter 20).

as long as eight years or more. Traditionally, short-term business loans (those with an original maturity of one year or less) are used to finance firms' working capital needs and other short-term funding needs, while long-term commercial loans are used to finance credit needs that extend beyond one year, such as the purchase of real assets (machinery), new venture start-up costs, and permanent increases in working capital. They can be made in quite small amounts, such as $100,000, to small businesses or in packages as large as $10 million or more to major corporations. Large loans are often syndicated. A **syndicated loan** is provided by a group of FIs as opposed to a single lender. A syndicated loan is structured by the lead FI (or agent) and the borrower. Once the terms (rates, fees, and covenants) are set, pieces of the loan are sold to other FIs. In addition, business loans can be secured or unsecured. A **secured loan** (or asset-backed loan) is backed by specific assets of the borrower; if the borrower defaults, the lender has a first lien or claim on those assets. In the terminology of finance, secured debt is senior to an **unsecured loan** (or junior debt) that has only a general claim on the assets of the borrower if default occurs. As we explain later in this chapter, there is normally a trade-off between the security or collateral backing of a loan and the loan interest rate or risk premium charged by the lender on a loan.[5]

In addition, loans can be made at either fixed or floating rates of interest. A fixed-rate loan has the rate of interest set at the beginning of the contract period. This rate remains in force over the loan contract period no matter what happens to market rates. Suppose, for example, Encana borrowed $10 million at 10 percent for one year, but the FI's cost of funds rose over the course of the year. Because this is a fixed-rate loan, the FI bears all the interest rate risk. This is why many loans have floating-rate contractual terms. That is, Encana borrows $10 million at a floating rate of LIBOR plus 5 percent for one year. The loan rate can be periodically adjusted according to a formula so that the interest rate risk is transferred in large part from the FI to the borrower. As might be expected, longer-term loans are more likely to be made under floating-rate contracts than are relatively short-term loans.[6]

Finally, loans can be made either spot or under commitment. A **spot loan** is made by the FI, and the borrower uses or takes down the entire loan amount immediately. With a **loan commitment,** or line of credit, the lender makes an amount of credit available, such as $10 million; the borrower has the option to draw down any amount up to the $10 million at any time over the commitment period. In a fixed-rate loan commitment, the interest rate to be paid on any drawdown is established when the loan commitment contract originates. In a floating-rate commitment, the borrower pays the loan rate in force when the loan is actually drawn down. For example, suppose the $10 million Encana loan was made under a one-year loan commitment. When the loan commitment was originated (say, January 2010), Encana borrows nothing. Instead, it waits until six months have passed

syndicated loan
A loan provided by a group of FIs as opposed to a single lender.

secured loan
A loan that is backed by a first claim on certain assets (collateral) of the borrower if default occurs.

unsecured loan
A loan that has only a general claim to the assets of the borrower if default occurs.

spot loan
The loan amount is withdrawn by the borrower immediately.

loan commitment
A credit facility with a maximum size and a maximum period of time over which the borrower can withdraw funds; a line of credit.

[5] The major Canadian banks are active participants in the international syndicated loans market. Details of the North American market are provided in J. Armstrong, "The Syndicated Loan Market: Developments in the North American Context," Bank of Canada *Financial System Review,* June 2003, pp. 69–73. See also N. T Khoury, K. V. Smith, and P. I MacKay, "Comparing Working Capital Practices in Canada, the United States, and Australia: A Note," *Canadian Journal of Administrative Sciences,* March 1999, 16(1), pp. 53–57.

[6] However, floating-rate loans are more credit risky than fixed-rate loans, holding all other contractual features the same. This is because floating-rate loans pass the risk of all interest rate changes on to borrowers. Thus, in rising interest rate environments, floating-rate borrowers may find themselves unable to pay the interest on their loans and may be forced to default. The benefit of floating-rate loans to lenders is that they better enable FIs to hedge the cost of rising interest rates on liabilities (such as deposits). This suggests that controlling interest rate risk may be at the expense of enhanced credit risk.

(say, July 2010) before it draws down the entire $10 million. Encana pays the loan rate in force as of July 2010. We discuss the special features of loan commitments more fully in Chapter 13.

Finally, as we noted in Chapter 2, business loans have declined in importance in bank loan portfolios. The major reason for this has been the rise in non-bank loan substitutes, especially commercial paper. **Commercial paper** is an unsecured short-term debt instrument issued by corporations either directly or via an underwriter to purchasers in the financial markets. By using commercial paper, a corporation can sidestep banks and the loan market to raise funds, often at rates below those that banks charge.

The market for commercial paper in Canada, particularly asset-backed commercial paper (ABCP), grew phenomenally from the 1980s until the freezing of the ABCP market in August 2007.[7] As of October 2004, the Bank of Canada reported $111.4 billion commercial paper outstanding, with $14.4 billion to non-financial corporations. Of that total, $62.8 billion was securitized and provided cheap short-term credit for corporations. Also, $8.363 billion was issued in U.S. dollars, a feature of the Canadian debt market whereby both Canadian non-financial corporations and FIs are able to access the deeper, more liquid U.S. capital markets. At December 2007, according to the Bank of Canada, the market for asset-backed securities totalled $328 billion. This represented $76 billion bank-sponsored ABCP, $32 billion non-bank-sponsored ABCP, $185 billion residential mortgage-backed securities ($160 billion government-guaranteed, $25 billion non-government-guaranteed), and $143 billion other asset-backed securities.[8]

Mortgage Loans

Real estate loans at Canadian FIs are primarily mortgage loans and some revolving home equity loans.[9] Table 11–2 shows the residential (insured and uninsured) and non-residential mortgages for banks, trusts, and loan companies reporting to OSFI. Residential mortgage loans are the largest component of the mortgage portfolio. The characteristics of these loans differ widely, including the size of the loans, the ratio of the loan to the property's price (the loan–price or loan–value ratio), the maturity of the mortgage, and the mortgage interest rate. The mortgage rate differs according to whether the mortgage has a fixed rate or a floating rate, also called a *variable* or *adjustable rate*. **Variable rate mortgages (VRMs)** have their contractual rates periodically adjusted to some underlying index, usually the FI's prime lending rate. The proportion of fixed-rate mortgages to VRMs in FI portfolios varies with the interest rate cycle. In low-interest rate periods, borrowers prefer fixed-rate mortgages. As a result, the proportion of VRM to fixed-rate mortgages can vary considerably over the rate cycle.

commercial paper
Unsecured short-term debt instrument issued by corporations.

variable rate mortgage (VRM)
A mortgage whose interest rate adjusts with movements in an underlying market index interest rate.

---

[7] A discussion of the commercial paper market in Canada is provided by P. Toovey and J. Kiff, "Developments and Issues in the Canadian Market for Asset-Backed Commercial Paper," Bank of Canada *Financial System Review*, June 2003, pp. 43–49. In August 2007, amid concerns about credit risk related to subprime mortgage securitizations in the United States, investors stopped buying commercial paper. Firms were unable to roll over their commercial paper, and banks declined to allow firms to draw down their backup lines of credit for non-bank sponsored securitizations. The Canadian non-bank ABCP market was frozen and investors were unable to redeem the ABCP that they held. The issues related to the frozen ABCP market were not settled until February 2009. See Chapter 27 for details.

[8] See the Bank of Canada *Financial System Review*, June 2008, p. 10, for a summary of the structure of Canadian capital markets at December 2007. A discussion of the Canadian corporate credit market and statistics prior to 2007 is provided by S. Anderson, R. Parker, and A. Spence, "Development of the Canadian Corporate Debt Market: Some Stylized Facts and Issues," Bank of Canada *Financial System Review*, December 2003, pp. 35–41.

[9] Under home equity loans, borrowers use their homes as collateral backing for loans.

Residential mortgages are long-term loans, usually based on an amortization period of 25 years. House prices can fall below the amount of the loan outstanding—that is, the loan-to-value ratio rises—and the residential mortgage portfolio can also be susceptible to default risk. For example, from 1979–1982, a period of volatility in the economy, Canadian five-year mortgage rates varied from 11.05 percent to 21.46 percent, housing prices declined, and mortgage defaults increased as did mortgage foreclosures. As well, following the economic downturn in 2007 and 2008, which led to rising unemployment, housing prices in both Canada and the United States declined significantly in some markets, despite lower interest rates. Mortgage defaults started to increase as well. As shown in Table 11–1, Canadian banks reported mortgage loans of $532.8 billion at February 28, 2009. This represented 34 percent of the total mortgage loans reported. The credit risk of these loans for FIs was reduced since almost 40 percent of the mortgage loans carried mortgage insurance. Table 11–2 shows the trends in total outstanding residential mortgage credit from 2004 to 2008. At December 31, 2008, the total outstanding residential mortgage credit was $863.6 billion, with over 50 percent held by the chartered banks. An additional 12.8 percent was held by credit unions and caisses populaires and 22 percent represented NHA (National Housing Act) mortgage-backed securities.

As we will see in Chapter 27, while the market for mortgage-backed securities in Canada did not grow as fast as the U.S. subprime market, neither did it suffer as steep a decline as did the U.S. mortgage market during the credit crisis in 2007–2008. This is because of the conservative policies of CMHC as well as the limited use of subprime mortgages by lenders in Canada. As shown in Figure 11–2, the subprime mortgage market was still less than 5 percent of mortgage originations in Canada by 2006. U.S. subprime mortgages reached over 20 percent of all mortgages originated in 2005, 2006, and 2007. The U.S. housing policy, which was intended to reduce redlining and to increase the number of lower-income Americans who owned their own homes, encouraged FIs to issue mortgages to higher-risk individuals. A result of this policy was that almost 8 percent of U.S. subprime mortgages were in arrears over 90 days or in foreclosure in 2006. The Canadian experience was much less than 2 percent in the same time period.[10]

TABLE 11–2 **Residential Mortgage Credit in Canada, 2004–2008 ($ millions)**

	2004	2005	2006	2007	2008
Total outstanding balances	$ 570,793	$ 627,063	$ 693,984	$ 772,362	$ 863,600
Chartered banks	352,373	377,998	405,605	442,116	469,576
Trust and mortgage loan companies	6,753	7,877	7,901	8,550	9,802
Life insurance company policy loans	15,383	14,720	14,574	14,790	15,406
Pension funds	**9,621**	**10,604**	**11,740**	**13,238**	**15,105**
National Housing Act mortgage-backed securities	**67,686**	**85,976**	**108,302**	**134,593**	**189,494**
Credit unions and caisses populaires	**76,614**	**84,562**	**93,731**	**102,500**	**110,412**
Special-purpose corporations (securitization)	14,878	16,490	21,147	24,884	22,729

Note: Figures may not add to totals due to rounding.

Source: Statistics Canada, www.statcan.gc.ca.

---

[10] See the Bank of Canada *Financial System Review*, June 2008, p. 6.

FIGURE 11–2
Subprime Share
of Mortgage
Originations in
Canada and the
United States

Source: Bank of Canada
Financial System Review, June
2007, p. 6.

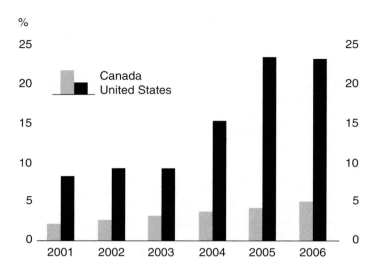

Personal (Consumer) Loans

www.osfi-bsif.gc.ca

Another major type of loan is the individual, or consumer, loan, such as personal loans and car loans. Commercial banks, finance companies, retailers, savings institutions, credit unions, and oil companies also provide consumer loan financing through credit cards, such as Visa, MasterCard, and proprietary credit cards issued by, for example, Sears and Canadian Tire. A typical credit card transaction is illustrated in Figure 11–3. The largest credit card issuers in Canada are Visa and MasterCard, which had 68.2 million cards issued and net retail volume of $266.97 billion in 2008.[11]

personal line of credit
A revolving loan that allows a consumer to borrow and pay back an amount up to the approved credit limit.

Table 11–3 shows the major types of personal, non-mortgage loans at Canadian chartered banks reported for February 2009. **Personal lines of credit,** revolving loans that allow consumers to borrow and repay up to the approved amount or credit limit, are the major source of consumer credit, followed by **personal loan plans** that are generally fixed-rate, fixed-term loans, and then credit cards. Credit cards and lines of credit are revolving loans. With a **revolving loan** the borrower has a credit line on which to draw as well as to repay up to a maximum over the life of the credit contract.

www.cba.ca

personal loan plans
Consumer loans that have a fixed rate, a fixed term, and amortized payments.

The delinquency rate (over 90 days) on Visa and MasterCard year-end outstanding amounts reported by the Canadian Bankers Association (CBA) declined from 0.9 percent to 0.8 percent from 1999 to 2003. The CBA also reported that the percentage of total mortgages in arrears (three or more months) declined from 0.53 percent in 1999 to 0.26 percent in 2004. Consumer credit, excluding mortgages, from chartered banks, trust and mortgage loan companies, life insurance companies, credit unions and caisses populaires grew by 37 percent from 2000 to 2004.

revolving loan
A credit line on which a borrower can both draw and repay many times over the life of the loan contract.

Loss rates on credit cards in Canada have been historically less than 4 percent. However, a survey of credit card issuers in Canada conducted by accounting firm Deloitte found that by October of 2008, delinquencies had jumped and were expected to increase further. The Canadian ratio of debt to disposable income for households reported by the Bank of Canada rose to 137 percent in the second quarter of 2008. Mortgage rules in the United State made it easier for consumers

---

[11] See *Credit Card Statistics—Visa and MasterCard* at the Canadian Bankers Association website at www.cba.ca.

FIGURE 11–3   Payment Flows in a Typical Credit Card Transaction

Source: GAO (1994) (GAO/GGD-94-23), p. 57.

TABLE 11–3
Personal Loans of Chartered Banks, Monthly Average February 2009 ($ millions)

Personal loan plans	$ 48,154	16.3%
Credit cards	51,611	17.4%
Personal lines of credit	175,336	59.2%
Other	20,851	7.1%
Total	$295,952	100%

Source: Bank of Canada, *Monthly Statistics,* April 2009, www.bankofcanada.ca.

to default on their mortgages, forcing FIs to foreclose on houses. In contrast, Canadian consumers were found to default on their credit card debt and car loans first rather than to stop making payments on their homes. The Canadian Bankers Association reported that the number of mortgages in arrears (three or more months) had increased from 9,709 (0.26 percent of the total) in December 2007 to 16,711 (0.42 percent of the total) in July 2009. This is still relatively low, since during the recession of the early nineties, the percentage of mortgages in arrears reached 0.65 percent, the maximum for the period from 1990–2009.[12] As shown in

---

[12] See Deloitte, *Uncharted Waters for Credit Card Issuers,* at www.deloitte.com; Bank of Canada *Financial System Review,* December 2008, at www.bankofcanada.ca; and Canadian Bankers Association, *Number of Residential Mortgages in Arrears,* at www.cba.ca.

Figure 11–4, since 2000, household debt as a percentage of disposable income was on an upward trend in Canada, the United States, the United Kingdom, and the Eurozone. Consumers globally had increased their leverage.

Table 11–4 shows indicative interest rates on car, mortgage, line of credit, and credit card loans in December 2009. These rates differ depending on features such as collateral backing, maturity, default rate experience, and non-interest rate fees. In addition, competitive conditions in each market as well as usury ceilings (60 percent effective annual rate in Canada) all affect the rate structure for consumer loans. Declines in interest rates in 2008–2009 decreased the funding costs for banks and, to the extent that these rates were passed on, helped ease the debt service ratios for businesses and consumers.

Other Loans

The "other" loans category includes secured call loans (also called *demand loans*) and other short-term loans to investment dealers and brokers,[13] loans to the federal and provincial/territorial governments, loans to municipal and school corporations, and loans to foreign (sovereign) governments. Sovereign loans are discussed in Chapter 15.

CONCEPT QUESTIONS

1. What are the major types of loans made by Canadian banks? What are the basic distinguishing characteristics of each type of loan?
2. Will more VRMs be originated in high- or low-interest rate environments? Explain your answer.
3. In Table 11–4, explain why credit card loan rates are much higher than car loan, mortgage, and line of credit rates.

FIGURE 11–4   Household Debt as a Share of Personal Disposable Income

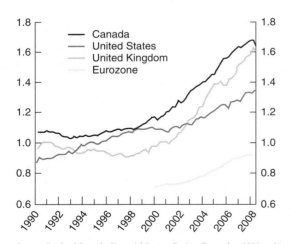

Source: Bank of Canada *Financial System Review*, December 2008, p. 21.

TABLE 11–4   Interest Rates on Consumer Loans, December 2009

48-month car Loan	5.80–14.75%
5-year closed mortgage	4.19–5.19%
Unsecured line of credit	3.25–5.00%
Secured line of credit	3.25–9.75%
Bank credit card	11.50–19.90%

Source: Various financial institutions' websites.

---

[13] A call (demand) loan is a loan contract enabling the lender (e.g., the bank) to request repayment of a loan at any time in the contract period. A non-callable loan leaves the timing of the repayment in the hands of the borrower subject to the limit of the maturity of the loan. For example, most broker loans to investment banks are callable within the day and have to be repaid immediately at the bank lender's request.

CALCULATING THE RETURN ON A LOAN

An important element in the credit management process, once the decision to make a loan has been made, is its pricing. This includes adjustments for the perceived credit risk or default risk of the borrower as well as any fees and collateral backing the loan.[14] This section demonstrates one method used to calculate the return on a loan: the traditional *return on assets approach*. Although we demonstrate the return calculations using examples of business loans, the techniques can be used to calculate the return on other loans (such as credit card or mortgage loans) as well.

The Contractually Promised Return on a Loan

The previous description of loans makes it clear that a number of factors impact the promised return an FI achieves on any given dollar loan (asset) amount. These factors include the following:

1. The interest rate on the loan.
2. Any fees relating to the loan.
3. The credit risk premium on the loan.
4. The collateral backing of the loan.
5. Other non-price terms (especially compensating balances and, in some countries, reserve requirements).

First, let us consider an example of how to calculate the promised return on a business loan. Suppose that an FI makes a spot one-year, $1 million loan. The loan rate is set as follows:

$$\text{Base lending rate } (BR) = 12\%$$
$$+ \text{ Credit risk premium or margin } (m) = \underline{\quad 2\%}$$
$$BR + m = 14\%$$

LIBOR
The London Interbank Offered Rate, which is the rate for inter-bank dollar loans of a given maturity in the offshore or Eurodollar market.

prime lending rate
The base lending rate periodically set by banks.

The base lending rate (*BR*) could reflect the FI's weighted-average cost of capital or its marginal cost of funds, such as the commercial paper rate, or **LIBOR**—the London Interbank Offered Rate, which is the rate for inter-bank dollar loans of a given maturity in the Eurodollar market. The centre of the Eurodollar market is London. Alternatively, it could reflect the **prime lending rate**. The prime rate is most commonly used in pricing longer-term loans, whereas the LIBOR rate is more commonly used in pricing short-term loans. Traditionally, the prime rate has been the rate charged to the FI's lowest-risk customers. Now, it is more of a base rate to which positive or negative risk premiums can be added. In other words, the best and largest borrowers now commonly pay below prime rate to be competitive with the commercial paper market.[15]

---

[14] FIs have also developed relationship pricing programs, which offer discounts on interest rates for customers based on the total amount of fee-based services used and investments held at the FI. Relationship pricing is in contrast to (the more traditional) transaction pricing, in which customers pay a stated rate for a service regardless of the total amount of other (non-loan) business conducted with the FI.

[15] For more information on the prime rate, see P. Nabar, S. Park, and A. Saunders, "Prime Rate Changes: Is There an Advantage in Being First?" *Journal of Business* 66 (1993), pp. 69–92; and L. Mester and A. Saunders, "When Does the Prime Rate Change?" *Journal of Banking and Finance* 19 (1995), pp. 743–64, and P. McGraw, K. Panyagometh, and G. Roberts, "The Evolution of Corporate Borrowers: Prime versus LIBOR," *Research in Finance* 23, A. Chen, ed., 2007, pp. 221–244.

Direct and indirect fees and charges relating to a loan generally fall into three categories:

1. A loan origination fee (*of*) charged to the borrower for processing the application.

2. A compensating balance requirement (*b*) to be held as non-interest-bearing demand deposits. **Compensating balances** are a percentage of a loan that a borrower cannot actively use for expenditures. Instead, these balances must be kept on deposit at the FI. For example, a borrower facing a 10 percent compensating balance requirement on a $100 loan would have to place $10 on deposit (traditionally a demand deposit) with the FI and could use only $90 of the $100 borrowed. This requirement raises the effective cost of loans for the borrower since less than the full loan amount ($90 in this case) can actually be used by the borrower and the deposit rate earned on compensating balances is less than the borrowing rate. Thus, compensating balance requirements act as an additional source of return on lending for an FI.[16]

3. A reserve requirement (*RR*) imposed by the central bank on the FI's demand deposits, including any compensating balances. Currently, the Bank of Canada does not impose reserve requirements on Canadian deposit-taking institutions, but the U.S. Federal Reserve still imposes reserve requirements on banks operating in the United States.

compensating balance
A percentage of a loan that a borrower is required to hold on deposit at the lending institution.

While credit risk may be the most important factor ultimately affecting the return on a loan, these other factors should not be ignored by FI managers in evaluating loan profitability and risk. FIs can compensate for high credit risk in a number of ways other than charging a higher explicit interest rate or risk premium on a loan or restricting the amount of credit available. In particular, higher fees, high compensating balances, and increased collateral backing all offer implicit and indirect methods of compensating an FI for lending risk.

The contractually promised gross return on the loan, *k*, per dollar lent—or ROA per dollar lent—equals[17]

$$1 + k = 1 + \frac{of + (BR + m)}{1 - [b(1 - RR)]}$$

This formula may need some explanation. The numerator is the promised gross cash inflow to the FI per dollar, reflecting direct fees (*of*) plus the loan interest rate (*BR* + *m*). In the denominator, for every $1 in loans the FI lends, it retains *b* as non-interest-bearing compensating balances. Thus, 1 − *b* is the net proceeds of each $1 of loans received by the borrower from the FI, ignoring reserve requirements. However, since *b* (compensating balances) are held by the borrower at the FI as demand deposits, the central bank may require deposit-taking institutions to hold non-interest-bearing reserves at the rate *RR* against these

---

[16] They also create a more stable supply of deposits and thus mitigate liquidity problems. Further, compensating balances are sometimes used as an offset to fees charged on the loan. That is, loans with a compensating balance requirement often have lower fees than loans without a compensating balance. In this case, the additional revenue from the compensating balances is offset by the loss in fee income.

[17] This formula ignores present value aspects that could easily be incorporated. For example, fees are earned in up-front undiscounted dollars while interest payments and risk premiums are normally paid on loan maturity and thus should be discounted by the FI's cost of funds.

compensating balances. Thus, the FI's net benefit from requiring compensating balances must consider the cost of holding additional non-interest-bearing reserve requirements. The net outflow by the FI per \$1 of loans is $1 - [b(1 - RR)]$ or, 1 minus the reserve adjusted compensating balance requirement. With $RR = 0$ in Canada, the denominator reduces to $1 - b$ since Canada eliminated reserve requirements in 1992.

EXAMPLE 11–1

Calculation of ROA on a Loan

Suppose a bank does the following:

1. Sets the loan rate on a prospective loan at 14 percent (where $BR = 12\%$ and $m = 2\%$).
2. Charges a 1/8 percent (or 0.125 percent) loan origination fee to the borrower.
3. Imposes a 10 percent compensating balance requirement to be held as non-interest-bearing demand deposits.
4. Sets aside reserves, at a rate of 10 percent of deposits.

Plugging the numbers from our example into the return formula, we have[18]

$$1 + k = 1 + \frac{0.00125 + (0.12 + 0.02)}{1 - [(0.10)(0.9)]}$$

$$1 + k = 1 + \frac{0.14125}{0.91}$$

$$1 + k = 1.1552 \text{ or } k = 15.52\%$$

This is, of course, greater than the simple promised interest return on the loan, $BR + m = 14\%$.

In the special case where fees (*of*) are zero and the compensating balance (*b*) is zero:

$$of = 0$$

$$b = 0$$

the contractually promised return formula reduces to

$$1 + k = 1 + (BR + m)$$

That is, the credit risk premium or margin (*m*) is the fundamental factor driving the promised return on a loan once the base rate on the loan is set.

Note that as commercial and corporate lending markets have become more competitive, both origination fees (*of*) and compensating balances (*b*) are becoming less important. For example, where compensating balances are still charged, the bank may now allow them to earn interest. As a result, borrowers' opportunity losses from compensating balances have been reduced to the difference between the loan rate and the compensating balance time-deposit rate. Further, compensating balance requirements are very rare on international loans such as Eurodollar

---

[18] If we take into account the present value effects on the fees and the interest payments and assume that the bank's discount rate (*d*) was 12½ percent, then the $BR + m$ term needs to be discounted by $1 + d = 1.125$ while fees (as upfront payments) are undiscounted. In this case, *k* is 13.81 percent.

loans.[19] Finally, note that for a given promised gross return on a loan, k, FI managers can use the pricing formula to find various combinations of fees, compensating balances, and risk premiums they may offer their customers that generate the same returns.

The Expected Return on a Loan

default risk
The risk that the borrower is unable or unwilling to fulfil the terms promised under the loan contract.

The promised return on the loan $(1 + k)$ that the borrower and lender contractually agree on includes both the loan interest rate and non-interest rate features such as fees. The promised return on the loan, however, may well differ from the expected and, indeed, actual return on a loan because of default risk. **Default risk** is the risk that the borrower is unable or unwilling to fulfill the terms promised under the loan contract. Default risk is usually present to some degree in all loans. Thus, at the time the loan is made, the expected return $[E(r)]$ per dollar lent is related to the promised return as follows:

$$1 + E(r) = p(1 + k) + (1 - p)0$$

where p is the probability of complete repayment of the loan (such that the FI receives the principal and interest as promised) and $(1 - p)$ is the probability of default (in which the FI receives nothing, i.e., 0). Rearranging this equation, we get

$$E(r) = p(1 + k) - 1$$

To the extent that p is less than 1, default risk is present. This means the FI manager must (1) set the risk premium (m) sufficiently high to compensate for this risk and (2) recognize that setting high risk premiums as well as high fees and base rates may actually reduce the probability of repayment (p). That is, k and p are not independent. Indeed, over some range, as fees and loan rates increase, the probability that the borrower pays the promised return may decrease (i.e., k and p may be negatively related). As a result, FIs usually have to control for credit risk along two dimensions: the price or promised return dimension $(1 + k)$ and the quantity or credit availability dimension. Further, even after adjusting the loan rate (by increasing the risk premium on the loan) for the default risk of the borrower, there is no guarantee that the FI will actually receive the promised payments. The measurement and pricing approaches discussed in this chapter consider credit risk based on probabilities of receiving promised payments on the loan. The actual payment or default on a loan once it is issued may vary from the probability expected.

In general, compared with business loans, the quantity dimension controls credit risk differences on retail (e.g., consumer) loans more than the price dimension does. We discuss the reasons for this in the next section. That is followed by a section that evaluates various ways FI managers can assess the appropriate size of m, the risk premium on a loan. This is the key to pricing loan risk exposures correctly.

---

[19] For a number of interesting examples using similar formulas, see J. R. Brick, *Commercial Banking: Text and Readings* (Haslett, Mich.: Systems Publications Inc., 1984), Chap. 4. If compensating balances held as deposits paid interest at 8 percent ($r_d = 8$ percent), then the numerator (cash flow) of the bank in the example would be reduced by $b \times r_d$, where $r_d = 0.08$ and $b = 0.1$. In this case, $k = 14.64$ percent. This assumes that the reserve requirement on compensating balances held as time deposits (RR) is 10 percent. However, while currently U.S. reserve requirements on demand deposits are 10 percent, the reserve requirement on time deposits is 0 percent (zero). Recalculating but assuming $RR = 0$ and interest of 8 percent on compensating balances, we find $k = 14.81$ percent. In the Canadian context, reserve requirements are always equal to zero.

1. Calculate the promised return (k) on a loan if the base rate is 13 percent, the risk premium is 2 percent, the compensating balance requirement is 5 percent, fees are ½ percent, and reserve requirements are 10 percent. (16.23%)
2. What is the expected return on this loan if the probability of default is 5 percent? (10.42%)

CONSUMER (RETAIL) VERSUS BUSINESS (WHOLESALE) CREDIT DECISIONS

Consumer (Retail)

Because of the small dollar size of the loans in the context of an FI's overall investment portfolio and the higher costs of collecting information on household borrowers (consumer loans), most loan decisions made at this level tend to be accept or reject decisions. Borrowers who are accepted are often charged the same rate of interest and by implication the same credit risk premium. For example, a wealthy individual borrowing from a credit union to finance the purchase of a Rolls-Royce is likely to be charged the same auto loan rate as a less-wealthy individual borrowing from that credit union to finance the purchase of a Honda. In the terminology of finance, retail customers (consumer loans) are more likely to be sorted or rationed by loan quantity restrictions than by price or interest rate differences.[20]

credit rationing
Restricting the quantity of loans made available to individual borrowers.

That is, at the consumer level, an FI controls its credit risks by **credit rationing** rather than by using a range of interest rates or prices. Thus, the FI may offer the wealthy individual a loan of up to $60,000, while the same FI may offer the less-wealthy individual a loan of up to $10,000, both at the same interest rate. Residential mortgage loans provide another good example. While two borrowers may be accepted for mortgage loans, an FI discriminates between them according to the loan-to-value ratio—the amount the FI is willing to lend relative to the market value of the house being acquired—rather than by setting different mortgage rates.[21]

Business (Wholesale)

In contrast to the retail level, at the business level FIs use both interest rates and credit quantity to control credit risk. Thus, when FIs quote a prime lending rate (BR) to business borrowers, lower-risk borrowers may be charged a lending rate below the prime lending rate. Higher-risk borrowers are charged a markup on the prime rate, or a credit (default) risk premium (m), to compensate the FI for the additional credit risk involved.

As long as they are compensated with sufficiently high interest rates (or credit risk premiums), over some range of credit demand, FIs may be willing to lend funds to high-risk borrowers. However, as discussed earlier, increasing loan interest

---

[20] This does not mean that rates cannot vary across FIs. For example, finance companies associated with car manufacturers (e.g., GMAC) offered 0.0 percent financing on car loans for much of the early 2000s. Unrecognized by many car buyers, the lenders' costs of funds were incorporated into an increased price for the car. Deposit-taking institutions, not able to recover their costs of funds in this manner, offered varying rates in an attempt to compete with finance companies. However, for a given FI, the rate offered on car loans would be the same for all borrowers.

[21] However, as the cost of information falls and comprehensive databases on individual households' credit-worthiness are developed, the size of a loan for which a single interest rate becomes optimal will shrink.

rates (k) may decrease the probability (p) that a borrower will pay the promised return. For example, a borrower who is charged 15 percent for a loan—a prime rate of 10 percent plus a credit risk premium of 5 percent—may be able to make the promised payments on the loan only by using the funds to invest in high-risk investments with some small chance of a big payoff. However, by definition, high-risk projects have relatively high probabilities that they will *fail* to realize the big payoff. If the big payoff does not materialize, the borrower may have to default on the loan. In an extreme case, the FI receives neither the promised interest and fees on the loan nor the original principal lent. This suggests that very high contractual interest rate charges on loans may actually reduce an FI's expected return on loans because high interest rates induce the borrower to invest in risky projects.[22] Alternatively, only borrowers that intend to use the borrowed funds to invest in high-risk projects (high-risk borrowers) may be interested in borrowing from FIs at high interest rates. Low-risk borrowers drop out of the potential borrowing pool at high-rate levels. This lowers the average quality of the pool of potential borrowers. We show these effects in Figure 11–5.

At very low contractually promised interest rates (k), borrowers do not need to take high risks in their use of funds and those with relatively safe investment projects use FI financing. As interest rates increase, borrowers with fairly low-risk, low-return projects no longer think it is profitable to borrow from FIs and drop out of the pool of potential borrowers. Alternatively, borrowers may switch their use of the borrowed funds to high-risk investment projects to have a (small) chance of being able to pay off the loan. In terms of Figure 11–5, when interest rates rise above k^* (8 percent), the additional expected return earned by the FI through higher contractually promised interest rates (k) is increasingly offset by a lower probability of repayment on the loan (p). In other words, because of the potential increase in the probability of default when contractually promised loan rates are high, an FI charging wholesale borrowers loan rates in the 9 to 14 percent region can earn a *lower* expected return than will an FI charging 8 percent.

FIGURE 11–5

Relationship between the Promised Loan Rate and the Expected Return on the Loan

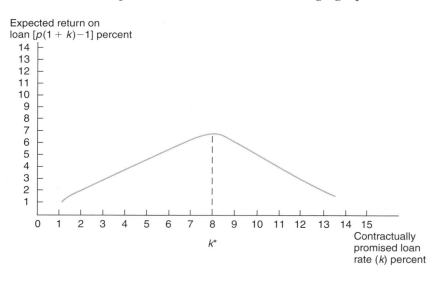

Expected return on loan [$p(1 + k) - 1$] percent

k^*

Contractually promised loan rate (k) percent

---

[22] In the context of the previous section, a high k on the loan reflecting a high base rate (BR) and risk premium (m) can lead to a lower probability of repayment (p) and thus a lower $E(r)$ on the loan, where $E(r) = p(1 + k) - 1$. Indeed, for a very high k, the expected return on the loan can become negative.

This relationship between contractually promised interest rates and the expected returns on loans suggests that beyond some interest rate level, it may be best for the FI to *credit ration* its loans, that is, to not make loans or to make fewer loans. Rather than seeking to ration by price (by charging higher and higher risk premiums to borrowers), the FI can establish an upper ceiling on the amounts it is willing to lend to maximize its expected returns on lending.[23] In the context of Figure 11–5, borrowers may be charged interest rates up to 8 percent, with the most risky borrowers also facing more restrictive limits or ceilings on the amounts they can borrow at any given interest rate.

CONCEPT QUESTIONS	1. Can an FI's return on its loan portfolio increase if it cuts its loan rates?
	2. What might happen to the expected return on a business (wholesale) loan if an FI eliminates its fees and compensating balances in a low-interest rate environment?

MEASUREMENT OF CREDIT RISK

To calibrate the default risk exposure of credit and investment decisions as well as to assess the credit risk exposure in off-balance-sheet contractual arrangements such as loan commitments, an FI manager needs to measure the probability of borrower default. The ability to do this depends largely on the amount of information the FI has about the borrower. At the consumer level, much of the information needs to be collected internally or purchased from external credit agencies. At the business level, these information sources are bolstered by publicly available information, such as certified accounting statements, stock and bond prices, and analysts' reports. Thus, for a publicly traded company, more information is produced and is available to an FI than is available for a small, single-proprietor corner store. The availability of more information, along with the lower average cost of collecting such information, allows FIs to use more sophisticated and usually more quantitative methods in assessing default probabilities for large borrowers compared with small borrowers. However, advances in technology and information collection are making quantitative assessments of even smaller borrowers increasingly feasible and less costly.[24] The simpler details (such as cash flow and ratio analysis) associated with the measurement of credit risk for consumer and business loans are discussed in Appendix 11A, located at the Online Learning Centre: www.mcgrawhill.ca/olc/saunders.

In principle, FIs can use very similar methods and models to assess the probabilities of default on both bonds and loans. Even though loans tend to involve fewer lenders to any single borrower as opposed to multiple bondholders, in essence, both loans and bonds are contracts that promise fixed (or indexed)

---

[23] Indeed, it has been found that the availability of bank credit depends not just on interest rates, but on the borrower's credit quality as well. Specifically, banks sometimes tighten their credit standards (forgoing riskier loans even when higher interest rates can be charged) to maximize their expected return on lending. See C. S. Lown, D. P. Morgan, and S. Rohatgin, "Listening to Loan Officers: The Impact of Commercial Credit Standards on Lending and Output," *FRBNY Economic Policy Review,* July 2000, pp. 1–16. In addition, the degree of competition in the loan market, and hence the price elasticity of demand for loans, will affect the availability of bank credit. That is, as competition for loans increases, the point (interest rate) at which banks switch from risk-based pricing to credit rationing may increase as well, and vice versa.

[24] These advances include database services and software for automating credit assessment provided by companies such as Dun & Bradstreet.

covenants
Restrictions written into bond and loan contracts, either limiting or encouraging the borrower's actions, that affect the probability of repayment.

payments at regular intervals in the future. Loans and bonds stand ahead of the borrowing firm's equity holders in terms of the priority of their claims if things go wrong. Also, bonds, like loans, include **covenants** restricting or encouraging various actions to enhance the probability of repayment. Covenants can include limits on the type and amount of new debt, investments, and asset sales the borrower may undertake while the loan or bonds are outstanding. Financial covenants are also often imposed restricting changes in the borrower's financial ratios such as its leverage ratio or current ratio. For example, a common restrictive covenant included in many bond and loan contracts limits the amount of dividends a firm can pay to its equity holders. Clearly, for any given cash flow, a high dividend payout to stockholders means that less is available for repayments to bondholders and lenders. Moreover, bond yields, like wholesale loan rates, usually reflect risk premiums that vary with the perceived credit quality of the borrower and the collateral or security backing of the debt. Given this, FIs can use many of the following models that analyze default risk probabilities either in making lending decisions or when considering investing in corporate bonds offered either publicly or privately.

CONCEPT QUESTIONS

1. Is it more costly for an FI manager to assess the default risk exposure of a publicly traded company or a small, single-proprietor firm? Explain your answer.
2. How do loan covenants help protect an FI against default risk?

DEFAULT RISK MODELS

Economists, analysts, and FI managers have employed many different models to assess the default risk on loans and bonds. These vary from relatively qualitative to highly quantitative models. Further, these models are not mutually exclusive; an FI manager may use more than one model to reach a credit pricing or loan quantity rationing decision. As will be discussed below in more detail, a great deal of time and effort has recently been expended by FIs in building highly technical credit risk evaluation models. Many of these models use ideas and techniques similar to the market risk models discussed in Chapter 10. We analyze a number of models in three broad groups: qualitative models, credit scoring models, and newer models.

Qualitative Models

In the absence of publicly available information on the quality of borrowers, the FI manager has to assemble information from private sources—such as credit and deposit files—and/or purchase such information from external sources—such as credit rating agencies. This information helps a manager make an informed judgment on the probability of default of the borrower and price the loan or debt correctly.

In general, the amount of information assembled varies with the size of the potential debt exposure and the costs of collection. However, a number of key factors enter into the credit decision. These include (1) *borrower-specific* factors that are idiosyncratic to the individual borrower, and (2) *market-specific* factors, which have an impact on all borrowers at the time of the credit decision. The FI manager then weights these factors subjectively to come to an overall credit decision. Because of their reliance on the subjective judgment of the FI manager, these models are often called *expert systems.* Commonly used borrower-specific and market-specific factors are discussed next.

Borrower-Specific Factors

Reputation The borrower's reputation involves the borrowing–lending history of the credit applicant. If, over time, the borrower has established a reputation for prompt and timely repayment, this enhances the applicant's attractiveness to the FI. A long-term customer relationship between a borrower and lender forms an **implicit contract** regarding borrowing and repayment that extends beyond the formal explicit legal contract on which borrower–lender relationships are based. The importance of reputation, which can be established only over time through repayment and observed behaviour, works to the disadvantage of small, newer borrowers. This is one of the reasons initial public offerings of debt securities by small firms often require higher yields than do offerings of older, more seasoned firms.

implicit contract
Long-term customer relationship between a borrower and lender, based on reputation.

Leverage A borrower's **leverage** or capital structure—the ratio of debt to equity—affects the probability of its default because large amounts of debt, such as bonds and loans, increase the borrower's interest charges and pose a significant claim on its cash flows. As shown in Figure 11–6, relatively low debt–equity ratios may not significantly impact the probability of debt repayment. Yet beyond some point, the risk of bankruptcy increases, as does the probability of some loss of interest or principal for the lender. Thus, highly leveraged firms, such as firms recently engaged in leveraged buyouts (LBOs) financed in part by FIs' provision of junk bonds or below-investment-grade debt, may find it necessary to pay higher risk premiums on their borrowings if they are not rationed in the first place.[25]

leverage
The ratio of a borrower's debt to equity.

Volatility of Earnings As with leverage, a highly volatile earnings stream increases the probability that the borrower cannot meet fixed interest and principal charges for any given capital structure. Consequently, newer firms or firms in high-tech industries with a high earnings variance over time are less attractive credit risks than are those with long and more stable earnings histories.

Collateral As discussed earlier, a key feature in any lending and loan-pricing decision is the degree of collateral, or assets backing the security of the loan. Many loans and bonds are backed by specific assets should a borrower default on repayment obligations. Mortgage bonds give the bondholder first claim to some specific piece of property of the borrower, normally machinery or buildings; debentures give a bondholder a more general and more risky claim to the borrower's assets. Subordinated debentures are

FIGURE 11–6 **Relationship between the Cost of Debt, the Probability of Default, and Leverage**

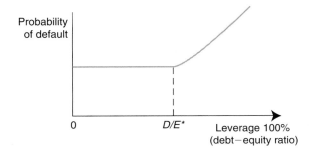

[25] However, S. J. Grossman and O. D. Hart argue that high debt (leverage) may be a signal of managerial efficiency and may in fact lower bankruptcy risk. Similar arguments have been made about the efficiency incentives for managers in junk bond–financed LBOs. That is, firms with a lot of debt have to be "lean and mean" to meet their repayment commitments. See "Corporate Financial Structure and Managerial Incentives," *The Economics of Information and Uncertainty,* J. McCall, ed. (Chicago: Chicago University Press, 1982).

even riskier because their claims to the assets of a defaulting borrower are junior to those of both mortgage bondholders and debenture bondholders. Similarly, loans can be either secured (collateralized) or unsecured (uncollateralized).[26]

Market-Specific Factors

The Business Cycle   The position of the economy in the business cycle phase is enormously important to an FI in assessing the probability of borrower default. For example, during recessions, firms in the consumer durable goods sector that produce autos, refrigerators, or houses do badly compared with those in the non-durable goods sector producing tobacco and foods. People cut back on luxuries during a recession but are less likely to cut back on necessities such as food. Thus, corporate borrowers in the consumer durable goods sector of the economy are especially prone to default risk. For example, the major U.S. car companies of Chrysler (which filed for bankruptcy, in April 2009) and General Motors, as well as Toyota and other international companies, suffered from declines in sales in 2008. The Canadian, U.S., Japanese, and Korean governments were asked to provide support for the car manufacturers. Because of cyclical concerns, FIs are more likely to increase the relative degree of credit rationing in recessionary phases. This has especially adverse consequences for smaller borrowers with limited or no access to alternative credit markets such as the commercial paper market.[27]

www.bankofcanada.ca

The Level of Interest Rates   High interest rates indicate restrictive monetary policy actions by the Bank of Canada. FIs not only find funds to finance their lending decisions scarcer and more expensive but also must recognize that high interest rates are correlated with higher credit risk in general. As discussed earlier, high interest rate levels may encourage borrowers to take excessive risks and/or encourage only the most risky customers to borrow.

So far, we have delineated just a few of the qualitative borrower- and economy-specific factors an FI manager may take into account in deciding on the probability of default on any loan or bond.[28] Rather than letting such factors enter into the decision process in a purely subjective fashion, the FI manager may weight these factors in a more objective or quantitative manner. We discuss quantitative credit scoring models used to measure credit risk next. One frequently used source of much of this information is the Risk Management Association (RMA). RMA has

www.rmahq.org   become a standard reference for thousands of commercial lenders by providing average balance sheet and income data for more than 400 industries, common ratios computed for each size group and industry, five-year trend data, and financial statement data for more than 100,000 commercial borrowers.

---

[26] However, collateralized loans are still subject to some default risk unless these loans are significantly overcollateralized; that is, assets are pledged with market values exceeding the face value of the debt instrument. There is also some controversy as to whether posting collateral signifies a high- or low-risk borrower. Arguably, the best borrowers do not need to post collateral since they are good credit risks, whereas only more risky borrowers need to post collateral. That is, posting collateral may be a signal of more rather than less credit risk.

[27] The Bank of Canada provides a good discussion of the impact of economic conditions on impaired loans and lending in Canada in its semi-yearly publication, *Financial System Review*. See in particular, the *Financial System Review* issues for 2007, 2008, and 2009, downloadable at www.bankofcanada.ca.

[28] More generally, five Cs of credit that should be included in any subjective (qualitative) credit analysis: character (willingness to pay), capacity (cash flow), capital (wealth), collateral (security), and conditions (economic conditions). See Appendix 11A, located at the Online Learning Centre: www.mcgrawhill.ca/olc/saunders.

CONCEPT QUESTIONS	1. Make a list of ten key borrower characteristics you would assess before making a mortgage loan.
	2. How should the risk premium on a loan be affected if there is a reduction in a borrower's leverage?

Credit Scoring Models

credit scoring models
Mathematical models that use observed loan applicant's characteristics either to calculate a score representing the applicant's probability of default or to sort borrowers into different default risk classes.

Credit scoring models are quantitative models that use observed borrower characteristics either to calculate a score representing the applicant's probability of default or to sort borrowers into different default risk classes. By selecting and combining different economic and financial borrower characteristics, an FI manager may be able to

1. Numerically establish which factors are important in explaining default risk.
2. Evaluate the relative degree or importance of these factors.
3. Improve the pricing of default risk.
4. Be better able to screen out bad loan applicants.
5. Be in a better position to calculate any reserves needed to meet expected future loan losses.

The primary benefit from credit scoring is that credit lenders can more accurately predict a borrower's performance without having to use more resources. With commercial loan credit scoring models taking into account all necessary regulatory parameters and posting an 85 percent accuracy rate on average, according to credit scoring experts,[29] using these models means fewer defaults and write-offs for business loan lenders.

To use credit scoring models, the manager must identify objective economic and financial measures of risk for any particular class of borrower. For consumer debt, the objective characteristics in a credit scoring model might include income, assets, age, occupation, and location. For commercial debt, cash flow information and financial ratios such as the debt–equity ratio are usually key factors. After data are identified, a statistical technique quantifies, or scores, the default risk probability or default risk classification.

Credit scoring models include these three broad types: (1) linear probability models, (2) logit models, and (3) linear discriminant analysis. Appendix 11A (located at the Online Learning Centre: www.mcgrawhill.ca/olc/saunders) looks at credit scoring models used to evaluate mortgages and consumer loans. In this section we look at credit scoring models used to evaluate commercial and corporate loans.

Linear Probability Model and Logit Model

The linear probability model uses past data, such as financial ratios, as inputs into a model to explain repayment experience on old loans. The relative importance of the factors used in explaining past repayment performance then forecasts repayment probabilities on new loans. That is, factors explaining past repayment performance can be used for assessing p, the probability of repayment discussed earlier in this chapter (a key input in setting the credit premium on a loan or determining the amount to be lent) and the probability of default (PD).

---

[29] See "Credit Scoring Heats Up," *Collections and Credit Risk,* September 2003, p. 34.

Briefly, we divide old loans (i) into two observational groups: those that defaulted ($PD_i = 1$) and those that did not default ($PD_i = 0$). Then we relate these observations by linear regression to a set of j causal variables (X_{ij}) that reflect quantitative information about the ith borrower, such as leverage or earnings. We estimate the model by linear regression of this form:

$$PD_i = \sum_{j=1}^{n} \beta_j X_{ij} + \text{error}$$

where β_j is the estimated importance of the jth variable (e.g., leverage) in explaining past repayment experience.

If we then take these estimated β_js and multiply them by the observed X_{ij} for a prospective borrower, we can derive an expected value of PD_i for the prospective borrower. That value can be interpreted as the probability of default for the borrower: $E(PD_i) = (1 - p_i) = $ Expected probability of default, where p_i is the probability of repayment on the loan.

EXAMPLE 11–2 *Estimating the Probability of Repayment on a Loan Using Linear Probability Credit Scoring Models*	Suppose there were two factors influencing the past default behaviour of borrowers: the leverage or debt–equity ratio (*D/E*) and the sales–asset ratio (*S/A*). Based on past default (repayment) experience, the linear probability model is estimated as $$PD_i = 0.5(D/E_i) + 0.1(S/A_i)$$ Assume a prospective borrower has a *D/E* = 0.3 and an *S/A* = 2.0. Its expected probability of default (*PD_i*) can then be estimated as $$PD_i = 0.5(0.3) + 0.1(2.0) = 0.35$$

Although this technique is straightforward as long as current information on the X_{ij} is available for the borrower, its major weakness is that the estimated probabilities of default can often lie outside the interval 0 to 1. The logit model overcomes this weakness by restricting the estimated range of default probabilities from the linear regression model to lie between 0 and 1. Essentially this is done by plugging the estimated value of PD_i from the linear probability model (in our example, $PD_i = 0.35$) into the following formula:

$$F(PD_i) = \frac{1}{1 + e^{-PD_i}}$$

where e is exponential (equal to 2.718) and $F(PD_i)$ is the logistically transformed value of PD_i.

Linear Discriminant Models

While linear probability and logit models project a value for the expected probability of default if a loan is made, discriminant models divide borrowers into high or low default risk classes contingent on their observed characteristics (X_j). Similar to these models, however, linear discriminant models use past data as inputs into a model to explain repayment experience on old loans. The relative importance of the factors used in explaining past repayment performance then forecasts whether the loan falls into the high or low default class.

Consider the discriminant analysis model developed by E. I. Altman for publicly traded manufacturing firms in the United States. The indicator variable Z is an overall measure of the default risk classification of a commercial borrower.[30] This in turn depends on the values of various financial ratios of the borrower (X_j) and the weighted importance of these ratios based on the past observed experience of defaulting versus non-defaulting borrowers derived from a discriminant analysis model.[31]

Altman's discriminant function (credit-classification model) takes the form

$$Z = 1.2X_1 + 1.4X_2 + 3.3X_3 + 0.6X_4 + 1.0X_5$$

where

X_1 = Working capital[32]/total assets ratio

X_2 = Retained earnings/total assets ratio

X_3 = Earnings before interest and taxes/total assets ratio

X_4 = Market value of equity/book value of long-term debt ratio

X_5 = Sales/total assets ratio

According to Altman's credit scoring model, any firm with a Z score of less than 1.81 should be considered a high default risk firm; between 1.81 and 2.99, an indeterminant default risk firm; and greater than 2.99, a low default risk firm.

EXAMPLE 11–3 *Calculation of Altman's Z Score*	Suppose that the financial ratios of a potential borrowing firm took the following values: $X_1 = 0.2$ $X_2 = 0$ $X_3 = -0.20$ $X_4 = 0.10$ $X_5 = 2.0$

The ratio X_2 is zero and X_3 is negative, indicating that the firm has had negative earnings or losses in recent periods. Also, X_4 indicates that the borrower is highly leveraged. However, the working capital ratio (X_1) and the sales/assets ratio (X_5) indicate that the firm is reasonably liquid and is maintaining its sales volume. The Z score provides an overall score or indicator of the borrower's credit risk since it combines and weights these five factors according to their past importance in explaining borrower default. For the borrower in question:

$$Z = 1.2(0.2) + 1.4(0) + 3.3(-0.20) + 0.6(0.10) + 1.0(2.0)$$
$$= 0.24 + 0 - 0.66 + 0.06 + 2.0$$
$$= 1.64$$

With a Z score less than 1.81 (i.e., in the high default risk region), the FI should not make a loan to this borrower until it improves its earnings.

There are a number of problems in using the discriminant analysis model to make credit risk evaluations.[33] The first problem is that these models usually discriminate only between two extreme cases of borrower behavior: no default and default. As discussed in Chapter 7, in the real world, various gradations of default

---

[30] The Z score is a default indicator and is not a direct probability of default (*PD*) measure.

[31] E. I. Altman, "Managing the Commercial Lending Process," in *Handbook of Banking Strategy,* R. C. Aspinwall and R. A. Eisenbeis, eds. (New York: John Wiley & Sons, 1985), pp. 473–510.

[32] Working capital is current assets minus current liabilities.

[33] Most of these criticisms also apply to the linear probability and logit models.

exist, from non-payment or delay of interest payments (non-performing assets) to outright default on all promised interest and principal payments. This problem suggests that a more accurate or finely calibrated sorting among borrowers may require defining more classes in the discriminant analysis model.

The second problem is that there is no obvious economic reason to expect that the weights in the discriminant function—or, more generally, the weights in any credit scoring model—will be constant over any but very short periods. The same concern also applies to the variables (X_j). Specifically, because of changing real and financial market conditions, other borrower-specific financial ratios may come to be increasingly relevant in explaining default risk probabilities. Moreover, the linear discriminant model assumes that the X_j variables are independent of one another.[34]

The third problem is that these models ignore important, hard-to-quantify factors that may play a crucial role in the default or no default decision. For example, the reputation of the borrower and the nature of long-term borrower–lender relationships could be important borrower-specific characteristics, as could macro-factors such as the phase of the business cycle. These variables are often ignored in credit scoring models. Moreover, traditional credit scoring models rarely use publicly available information, such as the prices of outstanding public debt and equity of the borrower.[35]

A fourth problem relates to default records kept by FIs. Currently, no centralized database on defaulted business loans for proprietary and other reasons exists. Some task forces set up by consortiums of commercial banks, insurance companies, and consulting firms are currently seeking to construct such databases largely in response to proposed reforms to bank capital requirements (see Chapter 20). However, it may well be many years before they are developed. This constrains the ability of many FIs to use traditional credit scoring models (and quantitative models in general) for larger business loans—although their use for smaller consumer loans, such as credit card loans, where much better centralized databases exist, is well established.

The newer credit risk models use *financial theory* and more widely available *financial market* data to make inferences about default probabilities on debt and loan instruments. Consequently, these models are most relevant in evaluating loans to larger borrowers in the corporate sector. This is the area in which a great deal of current research by FIs is taking place, as noted in Appendixes 12A and 12B (located at the Online Learning Centre). Below we consider a number of these newer approaches or models of credit risk, including

1. Term structure of credit risk approach.[36]
2. Mortality rate approach.

---

[34] Work in non-linear discriminant analysis has sought to relax this assumption. Moreover, work with neural networks, which are complex computer algorithms seeking links or correlations between the X_j variables to improve on Z classifications, shows some promise. See P. K. Coats and L. F. Fant, "Recognizing Financial Distress Patterns: Using a Neural Network Tool," *Financial Management,* Summer 1993, pp. 142–155; and "New Tools for Routine Jobs," *The Financial Times,* September 24, 1994.

[35] For example, S. C. Gilson, K. John, and L. Lang show that three years of low or negative stock returns can usefully predict bankruptcy probabilities. In fact, this market-based approach is supplementary to the market-based information models discussed in later sections of this chapter. See "An Empirical Study of Private Reorganization of Firms in Default," *Journal of Financial Economics,* 1990, pp. 315–353.

[36] They are also called *reduced-form models* (see D. Duffie and K. Singleton "Modeling Term Structure of Defaultable Bonds," *Review of Financial Studies* 12, 1999, pp. 687–720; and R. Jarrow, D. Lando, and S. Turnbull, "A Markov Model for the Term Structure of Credit Risk Spread," *Review of Financial Studies,* 1997, pp. 481–525).

3. Risk-adjusted return on capital (RAROC) models.
4. Option models (including the KMV credit monitor model).[37]

While some of these models focus on different aspects of credit risk, they are all linked by a strong reliance on modern financial theory and financial market data.[38]

CONCEPT QUESTIONS	1. Suppose the estimated linear probability model looked as follows: $Z = 0.3X_1 + 0.1X_2 +$ error, where

$$X_1 = \text{Debt/equity ratio; and } X_2 = \text{Total assets/Working capital ratio}$$

Suppose, for a prospective borrower, $X_1 = 1.5$ and $X_2 = 3.0$. What is the projected probability of default for the borrower? (75%)
2. Suppose $X_3 = 0.5$ in Example 11–3. Show how this would change the default risk classification of the borrower. ($Z = 3.95$)
3. What are two problems in using discriminant analysis to evaluate credit risk?

NEWER MODELS OF CREDIT RISK MEASUREMENT AND PRICING

Term Structure Derivation of Credit Risk

One market-based method of assessing credit risk exposure and default probabilities is to analyze the risk premiums inherent in the current structure of yields on corporate debt or loans to similar risk-rated borrowers. Rating agencies such as Standard & Poor's (S&P) categorize corporate bond issuers into at least seven major classes according to perceived credit quality.[39] The first four quality ratings—AAA, AA, A, and BBB—indicate investment-quality borrowers. Non-investment-grade securities with ratings such as BB, B, and CCC, are known as high-yield or junk bonds. Different quality ratings are reflected in the degree to which corporate bond yields exceed those implied by the Treasury (credit risk-free) yield curve.

www. standardandpoors .com

Look at the spreads shown in Figure 11–7 for zero-coupon corporate (grade B) bonds over similar maturity zero-coupon government debt (called *Treasury strips*). Because **Treasury strips** and **zero-coupon corporate bonds** are single-payment discount bonds, it is possible to extract required credit risk premiums and implied probabilities of default from actual market data on interest rates. That is, the spreads between risk-free discount bonds issued by the Government of Canada and discount bonds issued by corporate borrowers of differing quality reflect

Treasury strips, zero-coupon corporate bonds
Bonds that are created or issued bearing no coupons and only a face value to be paid on maturity. As such, they are issued at a large discount from face value. (Also called *deep-discount bonds*.)

---

[37] These are also called *structural models* since they are based on an economic model of why firms default (see R. C. Merton, "On the Pricing of Corporate Debt," *Journal of Finance* 29, 1974, pp. 449–470).

[38] For further details on these newer models, see A. Saunders and L. Allen, *Credit Risk Measurement: New Approaches to Value at Risk and Other Paradigms,* 2nd ed. (John Wiley and Sons: New York, 2002).

[39] Rating agencies consider several factors in determining and assigning credit ratings on bond issues. For example, a financial analysis is conducted of the issuer's operations and its needs, its position in the industry, and its overall financial strength and ability to pay the required interest and principal on the bonds. Rating agencies analyze the issuer's liquidity, profitability, debt capacity, and corporate governance structure. Then for each particular issue, rating agencies evaluate the nature and provisions of the debt issue (e.g., covenants and callability of the bond) and the protection afforded by, and relative position of, the debt issue in the event of bankruptcy, reorganization, or other arrangements under the laws of bankruptcy and other laws affecting creditors' rights.

FIGURE 11–7
**Corporate and
Government
Discount Bond
Yield Curves**

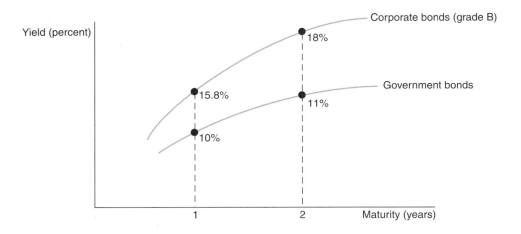

perceived credit risk exposures of corporate borrowers for single payments at different times in the future. FIs can use these credit risk probabilities on existing debt to decide whether or not to issue additional debt to a particular credit risk borrower.

Next, we look at the simplest case of extracting an implied probability of default for an FI considering buying one-year bonds from or making one-year loans to a risky borrower. Then, we consider multi-year loans and bonds. In each case, we show that we can extract a market view of the credit risk—the expected probability of default—of an individual borrower.

Probability of Default on a One-Period Debt Instrument

Assume that the FI requires an expected return on a one-year (zero-coupon) corporate debt security equal to at least the risk-free return on one-year (zero-coupon) Treasury bonds. Let p be the probability that the corporate debt, both principal and interest, will be repaid in full; therefore, $1 - p$ is the probability of default. If the borrower defaults, the FI is (for now) assumed to get nothing (i.e., the recovery rate is zero or the loss given default is 100 percent).[40] By denoting the contractually promised return on the one-year corporate debt security as $1 + k$ and on the credit risk–free one-year Treasury security as $1 + i$, the FI manager would just be indifferent between corporate and Treasury securities when[41]

$$p\,(1 + k) = 1 + i$$

or, the expected return on corporate securities is equal to the risk-free rate.

---

[40] This is a key assumption. If the recovery rate is non-zero (which in reality is true, since in recent years banks have recovered on average up to 40 percent of a defaulted loan and 50 percent of a senior secured bond), then the spread between the corporate bond return and the Treasury bond return will reflect both the probability of default as well as the loss given default (the latter is equal to 1 minus the recovery rate). To disentangle the probability of default from the loss given default, we need to make assumptions about the size of the loss given default (LGD) or the statistical process that either the PD and/or the LGD follow, such as the Poisson process. One simple case assuming that LGD is known is discussed later in this chapter.

[41] This assumes that the FI manager is not risk-averse; that is, this is a risk-neutral valuation method and the probabilities so derived are called *risk-neutral probabilities*. In general these will differ from probabilities estimated from historic data on defaults. See Saunders and Allen, *Credit Risk Management,* Chapter 5.

EXAMPLE 11–4

Calculating the Probability of Default on a One-Year Bond (Loan) Using Term Structure Derivation of Credit Risk

Suppose, as shown in Figure 11–7, the interest rates in the market for one-year zero-coupon government bonds and for one-year zero-coupon grade B corporate bonds are, respectively,

$$i = 10\%$$

and

$$k = 15.8\%$$

This implies that the probability of repayment on the security as perceived by the market is

$$p = \frac{1 + i}{1 + k} = \frac{1.100}{1.158} = 0.95$$

If the probability of repayment is 0.95, this implies a probability of default $(1 - p)$ equal to 0.05. Thus, in this simple one-period framework, a probability of default of 5 percent on the corporate bond (loan) requires the FI to set a risk premium (ϕ) of 5.8 percent.[42]

$$\phi = k - i = 5.8\%$$

Clearly, as the probability of repayment (p) falls and the probability of default $(1 - p)$ increases, the required spread ϕ between k and i increases.

This analysis can easily be extended to the more realistic case in which the FI does not expect to lose all interest and all principal if the corporate borrower defaults. Realistically, the FI lender can expect to receive some partial repayment even if the borrower goes into bankruptcy. For example, Altman and Bana estimated that when firms defaulted on their bonds in 2002, the investor lost on average 74.7 cents on the dollar (i.e., recovered around 25.3 cents on the dollar).[43] Table 11–5 gives recovery rates on defaulted debt by seniority from 1988–2004. As discussed earlier in this chapter, many loans and bonds are secured or collateralized by first liens on various pieces of property or real assets should a borrower default.

Let γ be the proportion of the loan's principal and interest that is collectible on default, where in general γ is positive. The FI manager would set the expected return on the loan to equal the risk-free rate in the following manner:

$$[(1 - p)\,\gamma\,(1 + k)] + [p\,(1 + k)] = 1 + i$$

The new term here is $(1 - p)\,\gamma\,(1 + k)$; this is the payoff the FI expects to get if the borrower defaults.

TABLE 11–5
Recovery Rates (RR) on Defaulted Debt, 1988–2004

Source: E. I. Altman, *The Link between Default and Recovery Rates*, Working paper, New York University Salomon Center, May 2006.

Type of Debt	Recovery Rate	Number of Observations
Bank debt	77.1%	1,023
Senior secured bonds	63.3	259
Senior unsecured bonds	42.7	587
Senior subordinated bonds	31.2	433
Subordinated bonds	30.1	374

[42] In the real world a bank could partially capture this required spread in higher fees and compensating balances rather than only in the risk premium. In this simple example, we are assuming away compensating balances and fees. However, they could easily be built into the model.

[43] E. I. Altman and G. Bana, *Defaults and Returns on High-Yield Bonds: The Year 2002 in Review and the Market Outlook*, Working paper, New York University Salomon Center, February 2003.

As might be expected, if the loan has collateral backing such that $\gamma > 0$, the required risk premium on the loan will be less for any given default risk probability $(1 - p)$. Collateral requirements are a method of controlling default risk; they act as a direct substitute for risk premiums in setting required loan rates. To see this, solve for the risk premium ϕ between k (the required yield on risky corporate debt) and i (the risk-free rate of interest):

$$k - i = \phi = \frac{(1 + i)}{(\gamma + p - p\gamma)} - (1 + i)$$

If $i = 10$ percent and $p = 0.95$ as before but the FI can expect to collect 90 percent of the promised proceeds if default occurs $(\gamma = 0.9)$, then the required risk premium $\phi = 0.6$ percent.[44]

Interestingly, in this simple framework, γ and p are perfect substitutes for each other. That is, a bond or loan with collateral backing of $\gamma = 0.7$ and $p = 0.8$ would have the same required risk premium as one with $\gamma = 0.8$ and $p = 0.7$. An increase in collateral γ is a direct substitute for an increase in default risk (i.e., a decline in p).

Probability of Default on a Multi-Period Debt Instrument

We can extend this type of analysis to derive the credit risk or default probabilities occurring in the market for longer-term loans or bonds (i.e., two-year bonds). To do this, the manager must estimate the probability that the bond will default in the second year conditional on the probability that it does not default in the first year. The probability that a bond will default in any given year is clearly conditional on the fact that the default has not occurred earlier. The probability that a bond will default in any given year, t, is the **marginal default probability** for that year, $1 - p_t$. However, for, say, a two-year loan, the marginal probability of default in the second year $(1 - p_2)$ can differ from the marginal probability of default in the first year $(1 - p_1)$. If we use these marginal default probabilities, the **cumulative default probability** at some time between now and the end of year 2 is

$$Cp = 1 - [(p_1)(p_2)]$$

marginal default probability
The probability that a borrower will default in any given year.

cumulative default probability
The probability that a borrower will default over a specified multi-year period.

EXAMPLE 11–5

Calculating the Probability of Default on a Multi-Period Bond

Suppose the FI manager wanted to find out the probability of default on a two-year bond. For the one-year loan, $1 - p_1 = 0.05$ is the marginal and total or cumulative probability (Cp) of default in year 1. Later in this chapter we discuss ways in which p_2 can be estimated by the FI manager, but for the moment suppose that $1 - p_2 = 0.07$. Then,

$$1 - p_1 = 0.05 = \text{Marginal probability of default in year 1}$$
$$1 - p_2 = 0.07 = \text{Marginal probability of default in year 2}$$

The probability of the borrower surviving—not defaulting at any time between now (time 0) and the end of period 2—is $p_1 \times p_2 = (0.95)(0.93) = 0.8835$.

$$Cp = 1 - [(0.95)(0.93)] = 0.1165$$

There is an 11.65 percent probability of default over this period.

---

[44] For example, the average recovery rate on bonds that were senior secured in 1987 was 90.68 percent (although these bonds recover on average 52.86 percent). Recovery rates are usually calculated in one of two ways: first, by looking at the prices of loans or bonds in the secondary market postdefault or, second (if they are not actively traded), by calculating the net present value of the expected cash flows that are projected to be recovered postdefault.

We have seen how to derive the one-year probability of default from yield spreads on one-year bonds. We now want to derive the probability of default in year 2, year 3, and so on. Refer back to Figure 11–7; as you can see, yield curves are rising for both government issues and corporate bond issues. We want to extract from these yield curves the *market's expectation* of the multi-period default rates for corporate borrowers classified in the grade B rating class.[45]

no arbitrage
The inability to make a profit without taking risk.

Look first at the government yield curve. The condition of efficient markets and thus **no arbitrage** profits by investors requires that the return on buying and holding the two-year government discount bond to maturity just equals the expected return from investing in the current one-year discount government bond and reinvesting the principal and interest in a new one-year discount government bond at the end of the first year at the expected one-year **forward rate**. That is

forward rate
A one-period rate of interest expected on a bond issued at some date in the future.

$$(1 + i_2)^2 = (1 + i_1)(1 + f_1) \tag{11.1}$$

The term on the left side is the return from holding the two-year discount bond to maturity. The term on the right side results from investing in two successive one-year bonds, where i_1 is the current one-year bond rate and f_1 is the expected one-year bond rate or forward rate next year. Since we can observe directly from the government bond yield curve the current required yields on one- and two-year government bonds we can directly infer the market's expectation of the one-year government bond rate next period or the one-year forward rate, f_1:

$$1 + f_1 = \frac{(1 + i_2)^2}{(1 + i_1)} \tag{11.2}$$

We can use the same type of analysis with the corporate bond yield curve to infer the one-year forward rate on corporate bonds (grade B in this example). The one-year rate expected on corporate securities (c_1) one year into the future reflects the market's default risk expectations for this class of borrower as well as the more general time value factors also affecting f_1:

$$1 + c_1 = \frac{(1 + k_2)^2}{(1 + k_1)} \tag{11.3}$$

The expected rates on one-year bonds can generate an estimate of the expected probability of repayment on one-year corporate bonds in one year's time, or what we have called p_2. Since

$$p_2(1 + c_1) = 1 + f_1$$

then

$$p_2 = \left[\frac{1 + f_1}{1 + c_1} \right] \tag{11.4}$$

Thus, the expected probability of default in year 2 is

$$1 - p_2 \tag{11.5}$$

---

[45] To use this model, one has to place borrowers in a rating class. One way to do this for unrated firms would be to use the *Z* score model to calculate a *Z* ratio for this firm. E. I. Altman has shown that there is a high correlation between *Z* scores and Standard & Poor's and Moody's bond ratings. Once a firm is placed in a bond rating group (e.g., B) by the *Z* score model, the term *structure model* can be used to infer the expected (implied) probabilities of default for the borrower at different times in the future.

In a similar fashion, the one-year rates expected in two years' time can be derived from the Treasury and corporate term structures so as to derive p_3, and so on.

EXAMPLE 11–6

Calculating the Probability of Default on a Multi-Period Bond Using Term Structure Derivation of Credit Risk

From the government bond yield curve in Figure 11–7, the current required yields on one- and two-year Treasuries are $i_1 = 10$ percent and $i_2 = 11$ percent, respectively. If we use equation 11.2, the one-year forward rate, f_1, is

$$1 + f_1 = \frac{(1.11)^2}{(1.10)} = 1.12$$

or

$$f_1 = 12\%$$

The expected rise in one-year rates from 10 percent (i_1) this year to 12 percent (f_1) next year reflects investors' perceptions regarding inflation and other factors that directly affect the time value of money.

Further, the current yield curve, in Figure 11–7, indicates that appropriate one-year discount bonds are yielding $k_1 = 15.8$ percent and two-year bonds are yielding $k_2 = 18$ percent. Thus, if we use equation 11.3, the one-year rate expected on corporate securities, c_1, is

$$1 + c_1 = \frac{(1.18)^2}{(1.158)} = 1.202$$

or

$$c_1 = 20.2\%$$

We summarize these calculations in Table 11–6. As you can see, the expected spread between one-year corporate bonds and government bonds in one year's time is higher than the spread for current one-year bonds. Thus, the default risk premium increases with the maturity on the corporate (risky) bond.

From these expected rates on one-year bonds, if we use equations 11.4 and 11.5, the expected probability of repayment on one-year corporate bonds in one year's time, p_2, is

$$p_2 = \frac{[1.12]}{[1.202]} = 0.9318$$

and the expected probability of default in year 2 is

$$1 - p_2 = 1 - 0.9318 = 0.0682$$

or

$$6.82\%$$

The probabilities we have estimated are marginal probabilities conditional on default not occurring in a prior period. We also discussed the concept of the *cumulative probability* of default that would tell the FI the probability of a loan or bond investment defaulting over a particular time period. In the example developed earlier, the cumulative probability that corporate grade B bonds would default over the next two years is

$$Cp = 1 - [(p_1)(p_2)]$$
$$Cp = 1 - [(0.95)(0.9318)] = 11.479\%$$

As with the credit scoring approach, this model creates some potential problems. Its principal advantages are that it is clearly forward-looking and based on

TABLE 11–6
Government and
Corporate Rates and
Rate Spreads

	Current One-Year Rate	Expected One-Year Rate
Government	10.0%	12.0%
Corporate (B)	15.8	20.2
Spread	5.8	8.2

market expectations. Moreover, if there are liquid markets for government and corporate discount bonds—such as Treasury strips and corporate zero-coupon bonds—then we can easily estimate expected future default rates and use them to value and price loans. However, the market for corporate discount bonds is quite small. Although a discount yield curve for corporate bonds could be extracted mathematically from the corporate bond coupon yield curve (see Chapter 25), these bonds often are not very actively traded and prices are not very transparent. Given this, the FI manager might have to consider an alternative way to use bond or loan data to extract default rate probabilities for all but the very largest corporate borrowers. We consider a possible alternative next.

CONCEPT QUESTIONS

1. **What is the difference between the marginal default probability and the cumulative default probability?**
2. **How should the posting of collateral by a borrower affect the risk premium on a loan?**

Mortality Rate Derivation of Credit Risk

Rather than extracting *expected* default rates from the current term structure of interest rates, the FI manager may analyze the *historic* or past default risk experience, the **mortality rates,** of bonds and loans of a similar quality. Consider calculating p_1 and p_2 using the mortality rate model. Here p_1 is the probability of a grade B bond or loan surviving the first year of its issue; thus $1 - p_1$ is the **marginal mortality rate,** or the probability of the bond or loan defaulting in the first year of issue. While p_2 is the probability of the loan surviving in the second year given that default has not occurred during the first year, $1 - p_2$ is the marginal mortality rate for the second year. Thus, for each grade of corporate borrower quality, a marginal mortality rate (MMR) curve can show the historical default rate experience of bonds in any specific quality class in each year after issue on the bond or loan.

Note in Figure 11–8 that as grade B bonds age, their probability of dying increases in each successive year. Of course, in reality, any shape to the mortality curve is possible. It is possible that MMRs can be flat, decline over time, or show a more complex functional form. These marginal mortality rates can be estimated from actual data on bond and loan defaults. Specifically, for grade B quality bonds (loans):

mortality rate
Historic default rate experience of a bond or loan.

marginal mortality rate
The probability of a bond or loan defaulting in any given year after issue.

$$MMR_1 = \frac{\text{Total value of grade B bonds defaulting in year 1 of issue}}{\text{Total value of grade B bonds outstanding in year 1 of issue}}$$

$$MMR_2 = \frac{\text{Total value of grade B bonds defaulting in year 2 of issue}}{\begin{array}{c}\text{Total value of grade B bonds outstanding in year 2 of issue} \\ \text{adjusted for defaults, calls, sinking fund redemptions, and} \\ \text{maturities in the prior year}\end{array}}$$

FIGURE 11–8
Hypothetical
Marginal Mortality
Rate Curve for
Grade B Corporate
Bonds

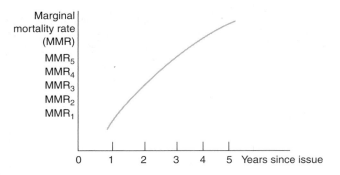

Table 11–7 shows the estimated mortality and cumulative default rates for samples of 1,513 rated corporate bonds over the 1971–2002 period. From Table 11–7 it can be seen that mortality rates are higher the lower the rating of the bond.

The mortality rate approach has a number of conceptual and applicability problems. Probably the most important of these is that, like the credit scoring model, it produces historic, or backward-looking, measures. Also, the estimates of default rates and therefore implied future default probabilities tend to be highly sensitive to the period over which the FI manager calculates the MMRs. For example, WorldCom had an S&P rating of BBB just prior to its defaulting on its debt in 2002. Note in Table 11–7 the second year's marginal mortality rate for BBB bonds (3.42 percent) is much higher than those of years 3 and 4 and is even higher than that of the second year mortality rate for BB bonds. This is primarily due to the default of WorldCom in 2002. In addition, the estimates tend to be sensitive to the number of issues and the relative size of issues in each investment grade.[46]

TABLE 11–7   Mortality Rates by Original Rating—All Rated* Corporate Bonds, 1971–2002

		Years after Issuance									
		1	2	3	4	5	6	7	8	9	10
AAA	Marginal	0.00%	0.00%	0.00%	0.00%	0.03%	0.00%	0.00%	0.00%	0.00%	0.00%
	Cumulative	0.00	0.00	0.00	0.00	0.03	0.03	0.03	0.03	0.03	0.03
AA	Marginal	0.00	0.00	0.33	0.17	0.00	0.00	0.00	0.00	0.03	0.02
	Cumulative	0.00	0.00	0.33	0.50	0.50	0.50	0.50	0.50	0.53	0.55
A	Marginal	0.01	0.10	0.02	0.09	0.04	0.10	0.05	0.20	0.11	0.06
	Cumulative	0.01	0.11	0.13	0.22	0.26	0.36	0.41	0.61	0.72	0.78
BBB	Marginal	0.25	3.42	1.52	1.44	0.92	0.57	0.80	0.26	0.17	0.35
	Cumulative	0.25	3.66	5.13	6.49	7.35	7.88	8.62	8.85	9.01	9.33
BB	Marginal	1.23	2.62	4.53	2.15	2.49	1.14	1.67	0.67	1.76	3.78
	Cumulative	1.23	3.82	8.17	10.15	12.39	13.39	14.83	15.40	16.89	20.03
B	Marginal	3.19	7.14	7.85	8.74	6.22	4.28	3.88	2.39	2.07	0.87
	Cumulative	3.19	10.10	17.16	24.40	29.10	32.14	34.77	36.33	37.65	38.19
CCC	Marginal	6.70	14.57	16.16	11.28	3.36	10.26	5.35	3.25	0.00	4.18
	Cumulative	6.70	20.29	33.17	40.71	42.70	48.58	51.33	52.92	52.92	54.88

*Rated by S&P at issuance.

[46] For example, even though the estimates in Table 11–7 are based on 1,513 observations of bonds, these estimates still have quite wide confidence bands. See Saunders and Allen, *Credit Risk Measurement,* Chapter 8.

1. In Table 11–7, the CMR over three years for CCC-rated corporate bonds is 33.17 percent. Check this calculation using the individual year MMRs.
2. Why would any FI manager buy loans that have a CMR of 33.17 percent? Explain your answer.

RAROC Models

RAROC
Risk-adjusted return on capital.

A popular model used to evaluate (and price) credit risk based on market data is the RAROC model. The **RAROC** (risk-adjusted return on capital) was pioneered by Bankers Trust (acquired by Deutsche Bank in 1998) and has now been adopted by some Canadian banks and virtually all the large banks in the United States and Europe, although with some significant proprietary differences between them.

The essential idea behind RAROC is that rather than evaluating the actual or contractually promised annual ROA on a loan, (that is, net interest and fees divided by the amount lent), the lending officer balances expected interest and fee income less the cost of funds against the loan's expected risk. Thus, the numerator of the RAROC equation is net income (accounting for the cost of funding the loan) on the loan. Further, rather than dividing annual loan income by assets lent, it is divided by some measure of asset (loan) risk or what is often called *capital at risk,* since (unexpected) loan losses have to be written off against an FI's capital:[47]

$$RAROC = \frac{\text{One year net income on a loan}}{\text{Change in loan's market value}}$$

A loan is approved only if RAROC is sufficiently high relative to a benchmark return on capital (ROE) for the FI, where ROE measures the return stockholders require on their equity investment in the FI. The idea here is that a loan should be made only if the risk-adjusted return on the loan adds to the FI's equity value as measured by the ROE required by the FI's stockholders. Thus, for example, if an FI's ROE is 15 percent, a loan should be made only if the estimated RAROC is higher than the 15 percent required by the FI's stockholders as a reward for their investment in the FI. Alternatively, if the RAROC on an existing loan falls below an FI's RAROC benchmark, the lending officer should seek to adjust the loan's terms to make it "profitable" again. Therefore, RAROC serves as both a credit risk measure and a loan pricing tool for the FI manager.

The numerator of the RAROC equation is relatively straightforward to estimate. Specifically,

One year net income on loan = (Spread + Fees)

× Dollar value of the loan outstanding

FIs may deduct any overhead and tax expenses as well to get the one-year net income on the loan. However, a more difficult problem in estimating RAROC is the measurement of loan risk (the denominator in the RAROC equation). Two methods of estimating loan risk involve the use of a duration model and the use of loan default rates.

---

[47] Traditionally, expected loan losses are covered by a bank's loss reserve (or provisions), while unexpected or extreme loan losses are being met by a bank's capital reserves.

Using Duration to Estimate Loan Risk

Chapter 9 on duration showed that the percentage change in the market value of an asset such as a loan ($\Delta LN/LN$) is related to the duration of the loan and the size of the interest rate shock ($\Delta R/(1 + R)$), where R is the base rate, BR, plus the credit risk premium, *m:*

$$\frac{\Delta LN}{LN} = -D_{LN}\frac{\Delta R}{1 + R}$$

The same concept is applied here, except that (assuming that the base rate remains constant) interest rate shocks are the consequence of credit quality (or credit risk premium) shocks (i.e., shocks to *m*). We can thus rewrite the duration equation with the following interpretation to estimate the loan risk or capital at risk on the loan:

$$\Delta LN \quad = \quad -D_{LN} \quad \times \quad LN \quad \times \quad (\Delta R/(1 + R))$$

| (change in loan's market value) | (duration of the loan) | (risk amount or size of loan) | (expected maximum change in the loan rate due to a change in the credit premium (*m*) or risk factor on the loan) |

EXAMPLE 11–7 *Calculation of RAROC on a Loan*	Suppose we want to evaluate the credit risk of a loan to an AAA borrower. Assume there are currently 400 publicly traded bonds in that class (i.e., bonds issued by firms of a rating type similar to that of the borrower). The first step is to evaluate the actual changes in the credit risk premiums ($R_i - R_G$) on each of these bonds for the past year (in this example, the year 2010). These (hypothetical) changes are plotted in the frequency curve of Figure 11–9. They range from a fall in the risk premiums of negative 2 percent to an increase of 3.5 percent. Since the largest increase may be a very extreme (unrepresentative) number, the 99 percent worst-case scenario is chosen (i.e., only 4 bonds out of 400 had risk premium increases exceeding the 99 percent worst case). For the example shown in Figure 11–9 this is equal to 1.1 percent.

The estimate of loan (or capital) risk, assuming that the current average level of rates (R) on AAA bonds is 10 percent, is

$$\Delta LN = -D_{LN} \times LN \times \frac{\Delta R}{1 + R}$$

$$= -(2.7)(\$1\ \text{million})\left(\frac{0.011}{1.1}\right)$$

$$= -\$27,000$$

Thus, while the face value of the loan amount is $1 million, the risk amount, or change in the loan's market value due to a decline in its credit quality, is $27,000.

To determine whether the loan is worth making, the estimated loan risk is compared with the loan's income (spread over the FI's cost of funds plus fees on the loan). Suppose the projected (one-year) spread plus fees is as follows:

$$\text{Spread} = 0.2\% \times \$1\ \text{million} = \$2,000$$

$$\text{Fees} = 0.1\% \times \$1\ \text{million} = \underline{\$1,000}$$

$$\$3,000$$

FIGURE 11–9
Hypothetical
Frequency
Distribution of
Yield Spread
Changes for All
AAA Bonds in 2010

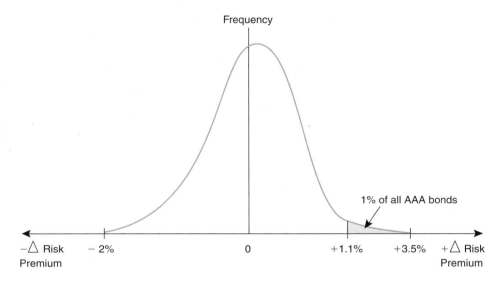

The loan's RAROC is:

$$RAROC = \frac{\text{One-year net income on loan}}{\text{Loan risk (or capital risk)}(\Delta LN)} = \frac{\$3,000}{\$27,000} = 11.1\%$$

Note that RAROC can be either forward-looking, comparing the projected income over the next year on the loan with ΔLN, or backward-looking, comparing the actual income generated on the loan over the past year with ΔLN. If the 11.1 percent exceeds the FI's internal RAROC benchmark (based on its cost of capital, or ROE), the loan will be approved. If it is less, the loan will be rejected outright or the borrower will be asked to pay higher fees and/or a higher spread to increase the RAROC to acceptable levels.

While the loan's duration (say, 2.7 years) and the loan amount (say, $1 million) are easily estimated, it is more difficult to estimate the maximum change in the credit risk premium on the loan over the next year. Since publicly available data on loan risk premiums are scarce, we turn to publicly available corporate bond market data to estimate premiums. First, an S&P credit rating (AAA, AA, A, and so on) is assigned to a borrower. Thereafter, the available risk premium changes of all the bonds traded in that particular rating class over the last year are analyzed. The ΔR in the RAROC equation equals

$$\Delta R = \text{Max}\,[\Delta(R_i - R_G) > 0]$$

where $\Delta(R_i - R_G)$ is the change in the yield spread between corporate bonds of credit rating class i (R_i) and matched duration Treasury bonds (R_G) over the last year. In order to consider only the worst-case scenario, a maximum change in yield spread is chosen, as opposed to the average change. In general, it is common to pick the 1 percent worst case or 99th percentile of credit risk changes.

Using Loan Default Rates to Estimate Loan Risk

Other FIs have adopted different ways of calculating ΔLN in their versions of RAROC. Some FIs, usually the largest ones with very good loan default databases, divide one-year income by the product of an unexpected loss rate and the proportion of the loan lost on default, also called the *loss given default*. Thus,

$$RAROC = \frac{\text{One-year net income per dollar loaned}}{\text{Unexpected default rate} \times \text{Proportion of loan lost on default (loss given default)}}$$

Suppose expected income per dollar lent is 0.3 cents, or 0.003. The 99th percentile historic (extreme case) default rate for borrowers of this type is 4 percent, and the dollar proportion of loans of this type that cannot be recaptured is 80 percent. Then,[48]

$$RAROC = \frac{0.003}{(0.04)(0.8)} = \frac{0.003}{(0.032)} = 9.375\%$$

CONCEPT QUESTION

Describe the basic concept behind RAROC models.

Option Models of Default Risk[49]

Theoretical Framework

Following the pioneering work of Nobel Prize winners Merton, Black, and Scholes, we now recognize that when a firm raises funds by issuing bonds or increasing its bank loans, it holds a very valuable default or repayment option.[50] That is, if a borrower's investment projects fail so that it cannot repay the bondholder or the bank, it has the option of defaulting on its debt repayment and turning any remaining assets over to the debt holder. Because of limited liability for equity holders, the borrower's loss is limited on the downside by the amount of equity invested in the firm.[51] On the other hand, if things go well, the borrower can keep most of the upside returns on asset investments after the promised principal and interest on the debt have been paid. The KMV Corporation (which was purchased by Moody's in 2002) turned this relatively simple idea into a credit monitoring model. Many

www.moodyskmv.com

---

[48] Calculating the unexpected default rate commonly involves calculating the standard derivation (σ) of annual default rates on loans of this type and then multiplying σ by a factor such that 99 percent (or higher) of defaults are covered by capital. For example, if the loss distribution was normally distributed, then the σ of default rates would be multiplied by 2.33 to get the extreme 99 percent default rate. For many FIs, default rates are skewed to the right and have fat tails suggesting a multiplier much larger than 2.33. For example, to get coverage of 99.97 percent of defaults, Bank of America has historically used a multiplier of 6. Finally, the denominator can also be adjusted for the degree of correlation of the loan with the rest of the FI's portfolio. See, for example, Edward Zaik et al., "RAROC at Bank of America: From Theory to Practice," *Journal of Applied Corporate Finance,* Summer 1996, pp. 83–93.

[49] This section, which contains more technical details, may be included in or dropped from the chapter reading depending on the rigour of the course. Students unfamiliar with the basics of options may want to review the section "Basic Features of Options" in Chapter 24 of the text.

[50] R. C. Merton, "On the Pricing of Corporate Debt: The Risk Structure of Interest Rates," *Journal of Finance* 29 (1974), pp. 449–470; and F. Black and M. Scholes, "The Pricing of Options and Corporate Liabilities," *Journal of Political Economy* 81 (1973), pp. 637–659.

[51] Given limits to losses in personal bankruptcy, a similar analysis can be applied to consumer loans.

of the largest FIs are now using this model to determine the expected default risk frequency (EDF) of large corporations.[52] Before we look at the KMV credit monitor model, we will take a closer look at the theory underlying the option approach to default risk estimation. Appendix 11B, located at the Online Learning Centre (www. mcgrawhill.ca/olc/saunders), reviews the Black–Scholes option pricing model.

The Borrower's Payoff from Loans

Look at the payoff function for the borrower in Figure 11–10, where S is the size of the initial equity investment in the firm, B is the value of outstanding bonds or loans (assumed for simplicity to be issued on a discount basis), and A is the market value of the assets of the firm.

If the investments in Figure 11–10 turn out badly such that the firm's assets are valued at point A_1, the limited-liability stockholders–owners of the firm will default on the firm's debt, turn its assets (such as A_1) over to the debt holders, and lose only their initial stake in the firm (S). By contrast, if the firm does well and the assets of the firm are valued highly (A_2), the firm's stockholders will pay off the firm's debt and keep the difference ($A_2 - B$). Clearly, the higher A_2 is relative to B, the better off are the firm's stockholders. Given that borrowers face only a limited downside risk of loss of their equity investment but a very large potential upside return if things turn out well, equity is analogous to buying a call option on the assets of the firm (see also Chapter 24 on options).

The Debt Holder's Payoff from Loans

Consider the same loan or bond issue from the perspective of the FI or bondholder. The maximum amount the FI or bondholder can get back is B, the promised payment. However, the borrower who possesses the default or repayment option would rationally repay the loan only if $A > B$, that is, if the market value of assets exceeds the value of promised debt repayments. A borrower whose asset value falls below B would default and turn over any remaining assets to the debt holders. The payoff function to the debt holder is shown in Figure 11–11.

FIGURE 11–10
Payoff Function to Corporate Borrowers (Stockholders)

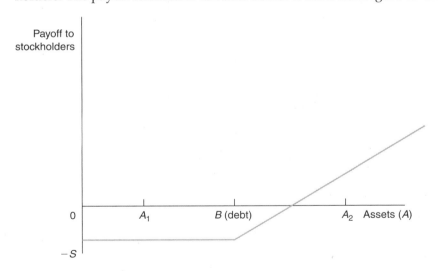

---

[52] See *KMV Corporation Credit Monitor*, KMV Corporation, San Francisco, 1994; and Saunders and Allen, *Credit Risk Measurement*, Chapter 4.

FIGURE 11–11

Payoff Function to the Debt Holder (the FI) from a Loan

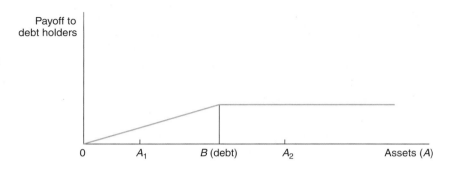

After investment of the borrowed funds has taken place, if the value of the firm's assets lies to the right of B, the face value of the debt—such as A_2—the debt holder or FI will be paid off in full and receive B. On the other hand, if asset values fall in the region to the left of B—such as A_1—the debt holder will receive back only those assets remaining as collateral, thereby losing $B - A_1$. Thus, the value of the loan from the perspective of the lender is always the minimum of B or A, or min $[B, A]$. That is, the payoff function to the debt holder is similar to writing a put option on the value of the borrower's assets with B, the face value of debt, as the *exercise price*. If $A > B$, the loan is repaid and the debt holder earns a small fixed return (similar to the premium on a put option), which is the interest rate implicit in the discount bond. If $A < B$, the borrower defaults and the debt holder stands to lose both interest and principal. In the limit, default for a firm with no assets left results in debt holders' losing all their principal and interest. In actuality, if there are also costs of bankruptcy, the debt holder can potentially lose even more than this.

Applying the Option Valuation Model to the Calculation of Default Risk Premiums

Merton has shown that in the context of the preceding options framework, it is quite straightforward to express the market value of a risky loan made by a lender to a borrower as[53]

$$F(\tau) = Be^{-i\tau}[(1/d)N(h_1) + N(h_2)] \qquad (11.6)$$

where

τ = Length of time remaining to loan maturity; that is, $\tau = T - t$, where T is the maturity date and time t is today.

d = Borrower's leverage ratio measured as $Be^{-i\tau}/A$, where the market value of debt is valued at the rate i, the risk-free rate of interest.

$N(h)$ = Value computed from the standardized normal distribution statistical tables. This value reflects the probability that a deviation exceeding the calculated value of h will occur.

$$h_1 = -\left[\frac{1}{2}\sigma^2\tau - \ln(d)\right]/\sigma\sqrt{\tau}$$

$$h_2 = -\left[\frac{1}{2}\sigma^2\tau + \ln(d)\right]/\sigma\sqrt{\tau}$$

σ^2 = Measures the asset risk of the borrower. Technically, it is the variance of the rate of change in the value of the underlying assets of the borrower.

---

[53] See Merton, "On the Pricing of Corporate Debt."

More important, written in terms of a yield spread, this equation reflects an equilibrium default risk premium that the borrower should be charged:

$$k(\tau) - i = (-1/\tau)\ln[N(h_2) + (1/d)N(h_1)]$$

where

$k(\tau)$ = Required yield on risky debt (the contractually promised return from earlier)

$\ln$ = Natural logarithm

i = Risk-free rate on debt of equivalent maturity (here, one period)

Thus, Merton has shown that the lender should adjust the required risk premium as d and σ^2 change, that is, as leverage and asset risk change.

EXAMPLE 11–8

Calculating the Value of and Interest Rate on a Loan Using the Option Model

Suppose that:

B = $100,000

τ = 1 year

i = 5 percent

d = 90% or 0.9

σ = 12%

That is, suppose we can measure the market value of a firm's assets (and thus $d = Be^{-i\tau}/A$) as well as the volatility of those assets (σ). Then, substituting these values into the equations for h_1 and h_2 and solving for the areas under the standardized normal distribution, we find that

$$N(h_1) = 0.174120$$

$$N(h_2) = 0.793323$$

where

$$h_1 = \frac{-\left[\frac{1}{2}(0.12)^2 - \ln(0.9)\right]}{0.12} = -0.938$$

and

$$h_2 = \frac{-\left[\frac{1}{2}(0.12)^2 - \ln(0.9)\right]}{0.12} = +0.818$$

The current market value of the loan is

$$L(t) = Be^{-i\tau}[N(h_2) + (1/d)N(h_1)]$$

$$= \frac{\$100,000}{1.05127}[0.793323 + (1.1111)(0.17412)]$$

$$= \frac{\$100,000}{1.05127}[0.986788]$$

$$= \$93,866.18$$

and the required risk spread or premium is

$$k(\tau) - i = \left(\frac{-1}{\tau}\right)\ln[N(h_2) + (1/d)N(h_1)]$$

$$= (-1)\ln[0.986788]$$

$$= 1.33\%$$

Thus, the risky loan rate $k(\tau)$ should be set at 6.33 percent when the risk-free rate (i) is 5 percent.

Theoretically, this model is an elegant tool for extracting premiums and default probabilities; it also has important conceptual implications regarding which variables to focus on in credit risk evaluation [e.g., the firm's market value of assets (A) and asset risk (σ^2)]. Even so, this model has a number of real-world implementation problems. Probably the most significant is the fact that neither the market value of a firm's assets (A) nor the volatility of the firm's assets (σ^2) is directly observed.

The KMV Option Model and Expected Default Frequency

www.moodyskmv. com

The KMV model in fact recognizes this problem by using an option pricing model (OPM) approach to extract the implied market value of assets (A) and the asset volatility of a given firm's assets (σ^2). The KMV model uses the value of equity in a firm (from a stockholder's perspective) as equivalent to holding a call option on the assets of the firm (with the amount of debt borrowed acting similarly to the exercise price of the call option). From this approach, and the link between the volatility of the market value of the firm's equity and that of its assets, it is possible to derive the asset volatility (risk) of any given firm (σ) and the market value of the firm's assets (A).[54] Using the implied value of σ for assets and A, the market value of assets, the likely distribution of possible asset values of the firm relative to its current debt obligations can be calculated over the next year. As shown in Figure 11–12, the expected default frequency (EDF) that is calculated reflects the probability that the market value of the firm's assets (A) will fall below the promised repayments on its short-term debt liabilities (B) in one year. If the value of a firm's assets falls below its debt liabilities, it can be viewed as being economically insolvent.

Suppose the value of the firm's assets (A) at the time zero is $100 million and the value of its short-term debt is $80 million. Suppose that the implied volatility (σ) of asset values was estimated at $12.12 million, and it is assumed that asset-value changes are normally distributed. The firm becomes distressed only if the value of its assets falls to $80 million or below (falls by $20 million). Such a fall is equal to 1.65σ, i.e., $1.65 \times \$12.12$ million = $20 million. From statistics, we know that the area of the normal distribution (in each tail) lying $\pm 1.65\sigma$ from the mean is theoretically 5 percent. Thus, the KMV model would suggest a theoretical 5 percent probability of the firm's going into distress over the next year (by time 1). However, KMV calculates empirical EDFs, since we do not know the true distribution of asset values (A) over time. Essentially, it asks this question: In practice, how many firms that started the year with asset values 1.65σ distance from default (see Figure 11–12) actually defaulted at the end of the year? This value may or may not equal 5 percent.

---

[54] More specifically, it does this by using the equity (stock market) value of the firm's shares (E) and the volatility of the value of the firm's shares (σ_E). Since equity can be viewed as a call option on the firm's assets and the volatility of a firm's equity value will reflect the leverage adjusted volatility of its underlying assets, we have in general form:

$$\overline{E} = f(A, \sigma, \overline{B}, \overline{r}, \overline{\tau})$$

and

$$\overline{\sigma}_E = g(\sigma)$$

where the bars denote values that are directly measurable. Since we have two equations and two unknowns (A, σ), we can directly solve for both A and σ and use these, along with the firm's outstanding short-term liabilities or current liabilities, to calculate the EDF (expected default frequency).

FIGURE 11–12
Expected Default Frequency Using the KMV Model

Source: *KMV Corporation Credit Monitor.* Reprinted by permission of KMV Corporation, www.moodyskmv.com.

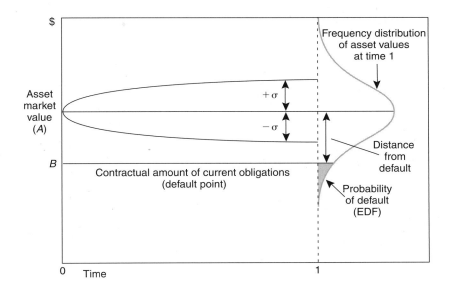

Simulations by KMV have shown that EDF models outperform both Z score-type models and S&P rating changes as predictors of corporate failure and distress.[55]

An example for WorldCom, which filed for Chapter 11 bankruptcy protection in the United States on July 21, 2002, is shown in Figure 11–13. Note that the KMV score (expected default frequency) is rising faster than the rating agencies are downgrading the firm's debt. Indeed, the rating agency ratings are very slow to react to, if not totally insensitive to, the increase in WorldCom's risk. The KMV EDF score starts to rise over a year prior to WorldCom's bankruptcy. Thus, the KMV EDF score gives a better early warning of impending default.[56] In an effort to get control over credit rating firms that give high-quality ratings to high-risk firms such as WorldCom, in September 2006 the Credit Rating Agency Reform Act was passed. This act gave the U.S. Securities and Exchange Commission (SEC) regulatory authority over credit rating firms and was intended to increase competition and oversight of credit rating firms. Credit rating firms came under scrutiny from global regulators for their role in rating securitizations in 2007–2008. We discuss this issue further in Chapter 27.

CONCEPT QUESTIONS	
	1. Which is the only credit risk model discussed in this section that is really forward-looking?
	2. How should the risk premium on a loan be affected if there is a reduction in a borrower's leverage and the underlying volatility of its earnings?
	3. What is the link between the implied volatility of a firm's assets and its expected default frequency?

---

[55] Moody's KMV provides monthly EDFs for over 6,000 U.S. companies and 20,000 companies worldwide.

[56] One reason is that the KMV score is extracted from stock market data that is highly sensitive to new information about a firm's future prospects. Indeed, the acquisition of KMV by Moody's allowed the rating agency to move closer to including market-based information in its rating process. See *Implications of the Acquisition of KMV for Moody's Ratings,* Moody's Investors Service, March 2002.

FIGURE 11–13   KMV and S&P Ratings for WorldCom

Source: KMV Corporation, San Francisco, California, www.moodyskmv.com.

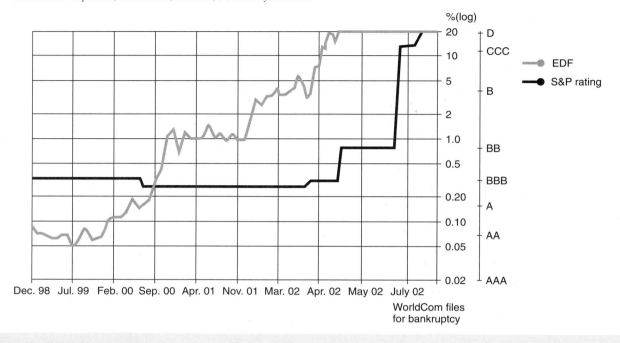

Summary

This chapter discussed different approaches to measuring credit or default risk on individual loans (bonds). The different types of loans made by FIs and some of their basic characteristics were first examined. The expected return on a loan was shown to depend on factors such as origination fees, compensating balances, interest rates, and maturity. The various models to assess default risk include both qualitative and quantitative models. The qualitative models usually contain both firm-specific factors, such as reputation and leverage, and market-specific factors, such as the business cycle and the level of interest rates. Quantitative models, such as the linear probability model, the logit model, and the linear discriminant model, were shown to provide credit scores that can rank or classify loans by expected default risk. The more rigorous of the quantitative models make use of both financial theory and financial data. These include the term structure and mortality rate models as well as the RAROC (risk-adjusted return on capital) and option-based models. In the next chapter we look at methods to evaluate the risk of loan portfolios, or loan concentration risk.

Questions and Problems

1. Why is credit risk analysis an important component of an FI's risk management? What recent activities by FIs have made the task of credit risk assessment more difficult for both FI managers and regulators?

2. Differentiate between a secured loan and an unsecured loan. Who bears most of the risk in a fixed-rate loan? Why would FI managers prefer to charge floating rates, especially for longer-maturity loans?

3. How does a spot loan differ from a loan commitment? What are the advantages and disadvantages of borrowing through a loan commitment?

4. Why did commercial and corporate lending decline in importance in Canada and the United States? What effect did this decline have on overall business lending activities?

5. What are the primary characteristics of residential mortgage loans? Why does the ratio of variable-rate

mortgages to fixed-rate mortgages in the economy vary over the interest rate cycle? When would the ratio be highest?

6. What are the two major classes of consumer loans at Canadian banks? How do revolving loans differ from non-revolving loans?

7. How does the credit card transaction process assist in the credit monitoring function of financial institutions? Which major parties receive a fee in a typical credit card transaction? Do the services provided warrant the payment of these associated fees?

8. What are compensating balances? What is the relationship between the amount of compensating balance requirement and the return on the loan to the FI?

9. Canada Bank offers one-year loans with a stated rate of 9 percent but requires a compensating balance of 10 percent. What is the true cost of this loan to the borrower? How does the cost change if the compensating balance is 15 percent? If the compensating balance is 20 percent?

10. West Coast Bank offers one-year loans with a 9 percent stated or base rate, charges a 0.25 percent loan origination fee and imposes a 10 percent compensating balance requirement. The loans typically are repaid at maturity.

    a. If the risk premium for a given customer is 2.5 percent, what is the simple promised interest return on the loan?

    b. What is the contractually promised gross return on the loan per dollar lent?

    c. Which of the fee items has the greatest impact on the gross return?

11. Why are most consumer loans charged the same rate of interest, implying the same risk premium or class? What is credit rationing? How is it used to control credit risks with respect to loans?

12. Why could a lender's expected return be lower when the risk premium is increased on a loan? In addition to the risk premium, how can a lender increase the expected return on a commercial or corporate loan? A consumer loan?

13. What are covenants in a loan agreement? What are the objectives of covenants? How can these covenants be negative? Positive?

14. Identify and define the borrower-specific and market-specific factors that enter into the credit decision. What is the impact of each type of factor on the risk premium?

    a. Which of these factors is more likely to adversely affect small businesses rather than large businesses in the credit assessment process by lenders?

    b. How does the existence of a high debt ratio typically affect the risk of the borrower? Is it possible that high leverage may reduce the risk of bankruptcy (or the risk of financial distress)? Explain.

    c. Why is the volatility of the earnings stream of a borrower important to a lender?

15. Why is the degree of collateral as specified in the loan agreement of importance to the lender? If the book value of the collateral is greater than or equal to the amount of the loan, is the credit risk of the lender fully covered? Why or why not?

16. Why are FIs consistently interested in the expected level of economic activity in the markets in which they operate? Why is monetary policy of the Bank of Canada important to FIs?

17. What are the purposes of credit scoring models? How could these models possibly assist an FI manager in better administering credit?

18. Suppose the estimated linear probability model is $PD = 0.3X_1 + 0.2X_2 - 0.5X_3 + \text{error}$, where $X_1 = 0.75$ is the borrower's debt–equity ratio, $X_2 = 0.25$ is the volatility of borrower earnings, and $X_3 = 0.10$ is the borrower's profit ratio.

    a. What is the projected probability of default for the borrower?

    b. What is the projected probability of repayment if the debt–equity ratio is 2.5?

    c. What is a major weakness of the linear probability model?

19. Describe how a linear discriminant analysis model works. Identify and discuss the criticisms that have been made regarding the use of this type of model to make credit risk evaluations.

20. MNO, Inc., a publicly traded manufacturing firm, has provided the following financial information in its application for a loan.

Assets	
Cash	$ 20
Accounts receivable	90
Inventory	90
Plant and equipment	500
Total assets	$700

Liabilities and Equity	
Accounts payable	$ 30
Notes payable	90
Accruals	30
Long-term debt	150
Equity	400
Total liabilities and equity	$700

Also assume sales = $500, cost of goods sold = $360, taxes = $56, interest payments = $40, and net income = $44; the dividend payout ratio is 50 percent, and the market value of equity is equal to the book value.

a. What is the Altman discriminant function value for MNO, Inc.? Recall that

Net working capital = Current assets minus current liabilities.

Current assets = Cash + Accounts receivable + Inventories.

Current liabilities = Accounts payable + Accruals + Notes payable.

EBIT = Revenues − Cost of goods sold − Depreciation.

Taxes = (EBIT − Interest) (Tax rate).

Net income = EBIT − Interest − Taxes.

Retained earnings = Net income (1 − Dividend payout ratio).

b. Should you approve MNO, Inc.'s, application to your bank for a $500 capital expansion loan?

c. If sales for MNO were $300, the market value of equity was only half of book value, and the cost of goods sold and interest were unchanged, what would be the net income for MNO? Assume the tax credit can be used to offset other tax liabilities incurred by other divisions of the firm. Would your credit decision change?

d. Would the discriminant function change for firms in different industries? Would the function be different for retail lending in different geographic sections of the country? What are the implications for the use by FIs of these types of models?

21. Consider the coefficients of Altman's Z score. Can you tell by the size of the coefficients which ratio appears most important in assessing credit-worthiness of a loan applicant? Explain.

22. If the rate on one-year T-bills currently is 6 percent, what is the repayment probability for each of the following two securities? Assume that if the loan is defaulted, no payments are expected. What is the market-determined risk premium for the corresponding probability of default for each security?

a. One-year AA-rated bond yielding 9.5 percent.

b. One-year BB-rated bond yielding 13.5 percent.

23. A bank has made a loan charging a base lending rate of 10 percent. It expects a probability of default of 5 percent. If the loan is defaulted, the bank expects to recover 50 percent of its money through the sale of its collateral. What is the expected return on this loan?

24. Assume that a one-year T-bill is currently yielding 5.5 percent and an AAA-rated discount bond with similar maturity is yielding 8.5 percent.

a. If the expected recovery from collateral in the event of default is 50 percent of principal and interest, what is the probability of repayment of the AAA-rated bond? What is the probability of default?

b. What is the probability of repayment of the AAA-rated bond if the expected recovery from collateral in the case of default is 94.47 percent of principal and interest? What is the probability of default?

c. What is the relationship between the probability of default and the proportion of principal and interest that may be recovered in case of default on the loan?

25. What is meant by the phrase *marginal default probability*? How does this term differ from *cumulative default probability*? How are the two terms related?

26. Calculate the term structure of default probabilities over three years using the following spot rates from the Government of Canada and corporate bond (pure discount) yield curves. Be sure to calculate both the annual marginal and the cumulative default probabilities.

	Spot 1 year	Spot 2 year	Spot 3 year
Government bonds	5.0%	6.1%	7.0%
BBB-rated bonds	7.0	8.2	9.3

27. The bond equivalent yields for Government of Canada and A-rated corporate bonds with maturities of 93 and 175 days are given below:

	93 days	175 days
Government	8.07%	8.11%
A-rated corporate	8.42	8.66
Spread	0.35	0.55

a. What are the implied forward rates for both an 82-day Government of Canada and an 82-day A-rated bond beginning in 93 days? Use daily compounding on a 365-day year basis.

b. What is the implied probability of default on A-rated bonds over the next 93 days? Over 175 days?

c. What is the implied default probability on an 82-day A-rated bond to be issued in 93 days?

28. What is the mortality rate of a bond or loan? What are some of the problems with using a mortality rate approach to determine the probability of default of a given bond issue?

29. The following is a schedule of historical defaults (yearly and cumulative) experienced by an FI manager on a portfolio of commercial and mortgage loans.

    a. Complete the blank spaces in the first table below.

    b. What are the probabilities that each type of loan will not be in default after five years?

    c. What is the measured difference between the cumulative default (mortality) rates for commercial and mortgage loans after four years?

30. The second table below shows the dollar amounts of outstanding bonds and corresponding default amounts for every year over the past five years. Note that the default figures are in millions, while those outstanding are in billions. The outstanding figures reflect default amounts and bond redemptions.

    What are the annual and cumulative default rates of the bonds?

31. What is RAROC? How does this model use the concept of duration to measure the risk exposure of a loan? How is the expected change in the credit premium measured? What precisely is ΔLN in the RAROC equation?

32. A bank is planning to make a loan of $5,000,000 to a firm in the steel industry. It expects to charge a servicing fee of 50 basis points. The loan has a maturity of 8 years with a duration of 7.5 years. The cost of funds (the RAROC benchmark) for the bank is 10 percent. Assume the bank has estimated the maximum change in the risk premium on the steel manufacturing sector to be approximately 4.2 percent, based on two years of historical data. The current market interest rate for loans in this sector is 12 percent.

    a. Using the RAROC model, determine whether the bank should make the loan.

    b. What should be the duration in order for this loan to be approved?

    c. Assuming that the duration cannot be changed, how much additional interest and fee income will be necessary to make the loan acceptable?

    d. Given the proposed income stream and the negotiated duration, what adjustment in the loan rate would be necessary to make the loan acceptable?

33. A firm is issuing two-year debt in the amount of $200,000. The current market value of the assets is $300,000. The risk-free rate is 6 percent, and the standard deviation of the rate of change in the underlying assets of the borrower is 10 percent. Using an options framework, determine the following:

    a. The current market value of the loan.

    b. The risk premium to be charged on the loan.

34. A firm has assets of $200,000 and total debts of $175,000. With an option pricing model, the implied volatility of the firm's assets is estimated at $10,730. Under the KMV method, what is the expected default frequency (assuming a normal distribution for assets)?

35. CC Bank (CCB) has a $5,000,000 face value, adjustable-rate loan to a company that has a leverage ratio of 80 percent. The current risk-free rate is 6 percent, and the time to maturity on the loan is exactly 1/2 year. The asset risk of the borrower,

| Loan Type | Years after Issuance | | | | |
	1 Year	2 Years	3 Years	4 Years	5 Years
Commercial:					
Annual default	0.00%	_____	0.50%	_____	0.30%
Cumulative default	_____	0.10%	_____	0.80%	_____
Mortgage:					
Annual default	0.10%	0.25%	0.60%	_____	0.80%
Cumulative default	_____	_____	_____	1.64%	_____

| Loan Type | Years after Issuance | | | | |
	1 Year	2 Years	3 Years	4 Years	5 Years
A-rated: Annual default ($millions)	0	0	0	1	2
Outstanding ($billions)	100	95	93	91	88
B-rated: Annual default ($millions)	0	1	2	3	4
Outstanding ($billions)	100	94	92	89	85
C-rated: Annual default ($millions)	1	3	5	5	6
Outstanding ($billions)	100	97	90	85	79

as measured by the standard deviation of the rate of change in the value of the underlying assets, is 12 percent. The normal density function values are given below.

h	N(h)	h	N(h)
−2.55	0.0054	2.50	0.9938
−2.60	0.0047	2.55	0.9946
−2.65	0.0040	2.60	0.9953
−2.70	0.0035	2.65	0.9960
−2.75	0.0030	2.70	0.9965

a. Use the Merton option valuation model to determine the market value of the loan.
b. What should be the interest rate for the last six months of the loan?

Web Questions

WWW

36. Go to the Bank of Canada's website at www.bankofcanada.ca and find the most recent statistics for Canadian chartered bank loan assets using the following steps. Click on "Rates and Statistics." Click on "Weekly Financial Statistics" Download the most recent report.

a. Find BFS Table C1. What percentage of the total loans is represented by personal loan plans? How much by credit cards? How has the amount of business loans changed over the past 24 months? What percentage of total mortgage loans was residential? What was the percentage change in the total dollar amount of mortgage loans over the last 24 months?

b. From the same file, find BFS Table F1. How do conventional 1-year and 5-year mortgage rates compare to rates in 2009 as reported in Table 11–4? Look at the other financial market statistics in BFS Table F1. How can you relate the change in mortgage rates to the economic climate in Canada (other interest rates, Bank of Canada monetary policy)?

37. Go to the Bank of Canada's website at www.bankofcanada.ca and download the latest version of the *Financial System Review*. How have credit conditions changed since the global crisis of 2007–2008 and the recession of 2009? How has the Bank of Canada's response to global conditions changed from 2009?

Integrated Mini-Case

LOAN ANALYSIS

As a senior loan officer at MC Bancorp, you have the following loan applications waiting for review. The bank uses Altman's Z score, default probabilities, and RAROC to assess loan acceptability. The bank's cost of equity (the RAROC benchmark) is 9 percent. The bank's loan policy states that the maximum probability of default for loans by type is as follows:

Loan Type and Maturity	Maximum Allowable Default Probability
AAA-rated	0.50%
A-rated	1.25

Which of the following loans should be given and which rejected?

1. An AAA-rated, one-year commercial loan from a firm with a liquidity ratio of 2.15, a debt-to-asset ratio of 45 percent, volatility in earnings of 0.13, and a profit margin of 12 percent. MC Bancorp uses a linear probability model to evaluate AAA-rated loans as follows:

$$PD = -0.08X_1 + 0.15X_2 + 1.25X_3 - 0.45X_4$$

where

X_1 = Liquidity ratio
X_2 = Debt-to-asset ratio
X_3 = Volatility in earnings
X_4 = Profit margin

2. An AA-rated, one-year commercial loan from a firm with the following financial statement information (in millions of dollars):

Assets		Liabilities and Equity	
Cash	$ 40	Accounts payable	$ 55
Accounts receivables	120	Notes payable	60
Inventory	210	Accruals	70
		Long-term debt	550
Plant and equipment	1,100	Equity (ret. earnings = $200)	735
Total assets	$1,470	Total liabilities and equity	$1,470

Also assume sales = $1,250, cost of goods sold = $930, taxes = $70, interest payments = $100, and net income = $150; the dividend payout ratio is 50 percent, and the market value of equity is equal to 2.2 times the book value. MC Bancorp uses the Altman's Z score model to evaluate AA-rated loans.

3. An A-rated corporate loan with a maturity of three years. A-rated corporate loans are evaluated using the mortality rate approach. A schedule of historical defaults (yearly and cumulative) experienced by the bank on its A-rated corporate loans is as follows:

	Years after Issuance			
Loan type	1 year	2 years	3 years	4 years
A-rated corporate loans				
Annual default	0.10%	0.25%	0.40%	0.65%
Cumulative default	0.10	0.35	0.75	1.45

4. A $2 million, five-year loan to a BBB-rated corporation in the computer parts industry. MB Bancorp charges a servicing fee of 75 basis points. The duration on the loan is 4.5 years. The cost of funds for the bank is 8 percent. Based on four years of historical data, the bank has estimated the maximum change in the risk premium on the computer parts industry to be approximately 5.5 percent. The current market rate for loans in this industry is 10 percent.

Appendix 11A   Credit Analysis

Appendix 11B   Black–Scholes Option Pricing Model

View Appendices 11A and 11B at the Online Learning Centre: www.mcgrawhill.ca/olc/saunders.

Credit Risk: Loan Portfolios

In this chapter, we examine credit risk in the context of a loan portfolio. We consider

▶ the benefits of loan portfolio diversification

▶ the models used by FI managers to assess the risk of the overall loan portfolio

▶ the potential use of loan portfolio models in setting maximum concentration limits for business or borrowing sectors

▶ the regulatory approach of OSFI to the measurement and control of the default risk of a loan portfolio

INTRODUCTION

www.manulife.ca
www.rbc.com
www.osfi-bsif.gc.ca
www.td.com

The models discussed in the previous chapter describe alternative ways by which an FI manager can measure the default risks of *individual* debt instruments such as loans and bonds. Rather than looking at credit risk one loan at a time, this chapter concentrates on the ability of an FI manager to measure credit risk in a loan (asset) *portfolio context* and the benefit from loan (asset) diversification. The consequences of ignoring portfolio risk can be significant. For example, in 1986, a year after the failures of the Canadian Commercial Bank and Northland Bank of Canada caused by exposure to oil and gas and real estate loans in western Canada, the Royal Bank's (RBC's) senior vice-president and controller Dominic D'Alessandro, and now retired CEO of the insurance conglomerate Manulife Financial, announced loan loss provisions for oil and gas loans of $275 million. The provision reduced RBC's earnings after-tax by $25 million to $30 million. RBC, known as Canada's energy bank, had 7.2 percent of its total assets of $97.53 billion in energy loans. A total of $240 million represented loans to Dome Petroleum, a Calgary oil company that was in trouble because of low prices for oil and gas. Dome's situation was causing concern for Toronto-Dominion Bank, which had loaned $738 million to Dome as well.[1] Thus, while the risk-return characteristics of each loan in its portfolio are a concern for an FI, the risk-return of the overall loan portfolio affects an FI's overall credit exposure. FIs have internal models to analyze this risk and, since 1994, the Office of the Superintendent of Financial Institutions (OSFI) has allowed banks, foreign bank branches, and federal trust and loan companies to self-assess their credit risks and develop their own approaches. However, as long as FIs lend, there will be ups and downs and, in 2002, after trying to buy

---

[1] See A. Freeman, "Big Canada Bank Sees Oil, Gas Loan Loss Provision," *The Wall Street Journal,* June 4, 1986, p. 1. Different regulations influence an FI's income statement and capital. Canadian accounting rules at the time allowed loan losses to be averaged over a five-year period. A change in Canadian GAAP guidelines in 1996 required the discounting of the expected cash flows by the interest rate on the loan at the time of the impairment. See I. Hasan and L. D. Wall, "Determinants of the Loan Loss Allowance: Some Cross-Country Comparisons," *The Financial Review,* 2004, 38, pp. 129–152, for a study of loan loss practices in Canada, the United States, Japan, and 21 other countries.

investment banking business through cheap corporate loans, Canadian banks became overexposed to the U.S. telecommunications industry and re-evaluated their lending practices. More recently, the global economic crisis in 2008 had an impact on bank loan losses as the subprime credit crisis and generally weakening demand for Canadian exports worked its way through the economy.

SIMPLE MODELS OF LOAN CONCENTRATION RISK

migration analysis
A method to measure loan concentration risk by tracking credit ratings of firms in particular sectors or ratings class for unusual declines.

www.dbrs.com
**www.standardand
poors.com**
www.moodys.com

loan migration matrix
A measure of the probability of a loan being upgraded, downgraded, or defaulting over some period.

FIs employ two simple models to measure credit risk concentration in the loan portfolio beyond the purely subjective model of "we have already lent too much to this borrower." The first is **migration analysis,** which tracks the movement (transition) of a loan portfolio from one credit rating to another, based on historical relative frequency. Lending officers track DBRS, S&P, Moody's, or their own internal credit ratings of certain pools of loans or certain sectors, for example, oil and gas. If the credit ratings of a number of firms in a sector or rating class decline faster than has been historically experienced, FIs curtail lending to that sector or rating class.[2]

A **loan migration matrix** (or transition matrix) seeks to reflect the historic experience of a pool of loans in terms of their credit rating migration over time. As such, it can be used as a benchmark against which the credit migration patterns of any new pool of loans can be compared. Table 12–1 shows a hypothetical credit migration matrix, or table, in which loans are assigned to one of three rating classes (most FIs use 10 to 13 rating classes).[3] The rows in Table 12–1 list the S&P rating at which the portfolio of loans began the year, and the columns list the rating at which the portfolio ended the year. The numbers in the table are called *transition probabilities,* reflecting the average experience (proportions) of loans that began the year, say, as rating BBB-B remaining rating BBB-B at the end of the year, being upgraded to an AAA-A, being downgraded to a CCC-C, or defaulting (D).

For example, for loans that began the year at rating BBB-B, historically (on average) 12 percent have been upgraded to AAA-A; 83 percent have remained at BBB-B; 3 percent have been downgraded to CCC-C; and 2 percent have defaulted by the end of the year. Suppose that the FI is evaluating the credit risk of its current portfolio of loans of borrowers rated BBB-B and that over the last few years, a much higher percentage (say, 5 percent) of loans has been downgraded to CCC-C and a higher percentage (say, 3 percent) has defaulted than is implied by the historic transition matrix. The FI may then seek to restrict its supply of lower-quality loans (e.g., those rated BBB-B and CCC-C), concentrating more of its portfolio on grade AAA-A loans.[4] At the very least, the FI should seek higher credit risk

---

[2] For 2008, the Bank of Montreal (BMO) reported using a sixteen-point scale over a one-year time horizon to evaluate credit default risk. BMO assigned an internal rating based on Moody's and Standard & Poor's and tracked the migration of the counterparty between grades. See BMO's most recent annual report at www.bmo.com. As well, see G. N. Gregoriou and C. Hoppe, *The Handbook of Credit Portfolio Management;* (New York: McGraw-Hill, 2008).

[3] A recent survey of credit portfolio management by FIs found the range of credit rating classes to be 5 to 22. See *2002 Survey of Credit Portfolio Management Practices,* International Association of Credit Portfolio Managers, International Swaps and Derivatives Association, and Risk Management Association, October 2002.

[4] The theory underlying the use of the average one-year transition matrix (based on historic data) as a benchmark is that actual transactions will fluctuate randomly around these average transitions. In the terminology of statistics, actual transitions follow a stable Markov (chain) process.

TABLE 12–1
A Hypothetical Rating Migration, or Transition, Matrix

		Risk Rating at End of Year			
		AAA–A	BBB–B	CCC–C	D*
Risk Rating at Beginning of Year	AAA–A	0.85	0.10	0.04	0.01
	BBB–B	0.12	0.83	0.03	0.02
	CCC–C	0.03	0.13	0.80	0.04

* *D* = default.

premiums on lower-quality (rated) loans. Not only is migration analysis used to evaluate commercial loan portfolios, it is widely used to analyze credit card portfolios and consumer loans as well.

The second simple model requires management to set some firm external limit on the maximum amount of loans that will be made to an individual borrower or sector. The FI determines **concentration limits** on the proportion of the loan portfolio that can go to any single customer by assessing the borrower's current portfolio, its operating unit's business plans, its economists' economic projections, and its strategic plans. Typically, FIs set concentration limits to reduce exposures to certain industries and increase exposures to others. When two industry groups' performances are highly correlated, an FI may set an aggregate limit of less than the sum of the two individual industry limits. FIs also typically set geographic limits. They may set aggregate portfolio limits or combinations of industry and geographic limits.

concentration limits
External limits set on the maximum loan size that can be made to an individual borrower.

EXAMPLE 12–1

Calculating Concentration Limits for a Loan Portfolio

Suppose management is unwilling to permit losses exceeding 10 percent of an FI's capital to a particular sector. If management estimates that the amount lost per dollar of defaulted loans in this sector is 40 cents, the maximum loans to a single sector as a percentage of capital, defined as the concentration limit, is

$$\text{Concentration limit} = \text{Maximum loss as a percentage of capital} \times \frac{1}{\text{Loss rate}}$$

$$= 10\% \times [1/0.4]$$
$$= 25\%$$

In recent years, regulators have limited loan concentrations to *individual borrowers* to a certain percentage of the FI's capital, for example, 10 percent. In some countries, such as Chile, limits are mandated by sector or industry. OSFI applies a "prudent person approach," and requires each FI to have written investment and lending policies. Since 1994, OSFI has set **large exposure limits** on credit risk for Canadian banks, federally regulated trust and loan companies, and foreign bank branches. The exposure is limited to a maximum of 25 percent of the FI's total capital as defined in calculating its risk-based capital adequacy ratio. The FI is expected to set lower internal limits and reach the maximum only on an exception basis. Canadian life insurance companies regulated by OSFI are also subject to a maximum exposure of 25 percent of their capital. The aggregate book value of investments of a property and casualty insurance company to an entity or group cannot exceed 5 percent of the company's assets.[5]

large exposure limits
Maximum amount of credit or investment exposure a federally regulated FI may have to a single entity.

---

[5] See *Guideline B-1 (Prudent Person Approach)* and *B-2 (Large Exposure Limits)* for federally regulated FIs at www.osfi-bsif.gc.ca.

FIGURE 12–1
CIBC's Business
and Government
Loans, Including
Acceptances, 2008

Source: CIBC, *2008 Annual Report*, page 160, www.cibc.com.

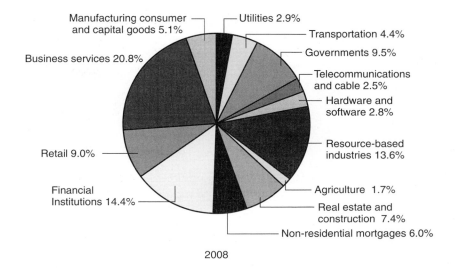

2008

www.cibc.com

In 2008, Canadian Imperial Bank of Commerce (CIBC) set concentration limits for its business and government loan portfolio by geographic location (93 percent of its net loans and acceptances was in Canada and the United States), by individual borrower or related borrower, by product or type of lending, and by industry sector, as shown in Figure 12–1. CIBC's largest exposure was to business services (20.8 percent), followed by financial institutions (14.4 percent), and resource-based industries (13.6 percent). CIBC also controls exposure through loan sales, as discussed in Chapter 26.

CONCEPT QUESTIONS	1. What would the concentration limit be if the loss rate on bad loans is 25 cents on the dollar?
	2. What would the concentration limit be if the maximum loss (as a percentage of capital) is 15 percent instead of 10 percent?

Next we look at the use of more sophisticated portfolio theory–based models to set concentration limits. Although these models have a great deal of potential, data availability and other implementation problems have, until recently, hindered their use. The basic idea is to select the portfolio of loans that maximizes the return on the loan portfolio for any given level of risk (or that minimizes the degree of portfolio risk for any given level of returns).

LOAN PORTFOLIO DIVERSIFICATION AND MODERN PORTFOLIO THEORY

To the extent that an FI manager holds widely traded loans and bonds as assets or, alternatively, can calculate loan or bond returns, portfolio diversification models can be used to measure and control the FI's aggregate credit risk exposure. Suppose the manager can estimate the expected returns of each loan or bond $(\overline{R}_i)$ in the FI's portfolio.

After calculating the individual security return series, the FI manager can compute the expected return $(\overline{R}_p)$ on a portfolio of assets as

$$\overline{R}_p = \sum_{i=1}^{N} X_i \overline{R}_i \tag{12.1}$$

In addition, the variance of returns or risk of the portfolio (σ_i^2) can be calculated as

$$\sigma_p^2 = \sum_{i=1}^{n} X_i^2 \sigma_i^2 + \sum_{i=1}^{n} \sum_{\substack{j=1 \\ i \neq j}}^{n} X_i X_j \sigma_{ij} \qquad (12.2)$$

or

$$\sigma_p^2 = \sum_{i=1}^{n} X_i^2 \sigma_i^2 + \sum_{i=1}^{n} \sum_{\substack{j=1 \\ i \neq j}}^{n} X_i X_j \rho_{ij} \sigma_i \sigma_j \qquad (12.3)$$

where

$\overline{R}_p$ = Expected or mean return on the asset portfolio

Σ = Summation sign

$\overline{R}_i$ = Mean return on the ith asset in the portfolio

X_i = Proportion of the asset portfolio invested in the ith asset (the desired concentration amount)

σ_i^2 = Variance of returns on the ith asset

σ_{ij} = Covariance of returns between the ith and jth assets

ρ_{ij} = Correlation between the returns on the ith and jth assets[6]

The fundamental lesson of modern portfolio theory (MPT) is that by taking advantage of its size, an FI can diversify considerable amounts of credit risk as long as the returns on different assets are imperfectly correlated with respect to their default risk-adjusted returns.[7]

Consider the σ_p^2 in equation 12.2. If many loans have negative covariances or correlations of returns (ρ_{ij} are negative)—that is, when one borrower's loans do badly and another's do well—the sum of the individual credit risks of loans viewed independently overestimates the risk of the whole portfolio. This is what we meant in Chapter 5 when we stated that by pooling funds, FIs can reduce risk by taking advantage of the law of large numbers in their investment decisions.

EXAMPLE 12–2

Calculation of Return and Risk on a Two-Asset Portfolio

Suppose that an FI holds two loans with the following characteristics:[8]

Loan i	X_i	$\overline{R}_i$	σ_i	σ_i^2	
1	0.40	10%	0.0857	0.007344	$\rho_{12} = -0.84$
2	0.60	12	0.0980	0.009604	$\sigma_{12} = -0.007058$

---

[6] The correlation coefficient reflects the joint movement of asset returns or default risks in the case of loans and lies between the values $-1 \leq \rho \leq +1$, where ρ is the correlation coefficient. As can be seen from equations 12.2 and 12.3, the covariance between any two assets (σ_{ij}) is related to the correlation coefficient (ρ_{ij}) by $\sigma_{ij} = \rho_{ij} \sigma_i \sigma_j$.

[7] One objection to using modern portfolio theory for loans is that the returns on individual loans are not normally or symmetrically distributed. In particular, most loans have limited upside returns and long-tail downside risks; see the discussion in Appendix 12A, "CreditMetrics" (available at the Online Learning Centre at www.mcgrawhill.ca/olc/saunders) and Chapter 9 in A. Saunders and L. Allen, *Credit Risk Measurements: New Approaches to Value at Risk and Other Paradigms,* 2nd ed. (New York: John Wiley & Sons, 2002). Also, concerns about maintaining relationships with traditional customers may limit the ability of an FI to diversify. The relationship limit on diversification has been called the "paradox of credit." That is, banks specialize in monitoring and generating information about their key customers (see Chapter 1), yet such monitoring specialization may lead to a highly concentrated loan portfolio. Relationship concerns may inhibit the loan portfolio from being managed like a mutual fund's management of an equity portfolio.

[8] Note that variance (σ^2) is measured in percent squared; standard deviation (σ) is measured in percent.

The return on the loan portfolio is

$$R_p = 0.4(10\%) + 0.6(12\%) = 11.2\%$$

while the risk of the portfolio is

$$\sigma_p^2 = (0.4)^2(0.007344) + (0.6)^2(0.009604) + 2(0.4)(0.6)(-0.84)(0.0857)(0.0980)$$
$$= 0.0012462$$

thus, $\sigma_p = \sqrt{0.0012462} = 0.0353 = 3.53\%$.

Notice that the risk (or standard deviation of returns) of the portfolio, σ_p (3.53 percent), is less than the risk of either individual asset (8.57 percent and 9.8 percent, respectively). The negative correlation between the returns of the two loans (-0.84) results in an overall reduction of risk when they are put together in an FI's portfolio.

To see more generally the advantages of diversification, consider Figure 12–2. Note that *A* is an undiversified portfolio with heavy investment concentration in just a few loans or bonds. By fully exploiting diversification potential with bonds or loans whose returns are negatively correlated or that have a low positive correlation with those in the existing portfolio, the FI manager can lower the credit risk on the portfolio from σ_{pA} to σ_{pB} while earning the same expected return. That is, portfolio *B* is the efficient (lowest-risk) portfolio associated with portfolio return level $\overline{R}_p$. By varying the proportion of the asset portfolio invested in each asset (in other words, by varying the required portfolio return level $\overline{R}_p$ up and down), the manager can identify an entire frontier of efficient portfolio mixes (weights) of loans and bonds. Each portfolio mix is efficient in the sense that it offers the lowest risk level to the FI manager at each possible level of portfolio returns. However, as you can see in Figure 12–2, of all possible efficient portfolios that can be generated, portfolio *B* produces the lowest possible risk level for the FI manager. That is, it maximizes the gains from diversifying across all available loans and bonds so that the manager cannot reduce the risk of the portfolio below σ_{pB}. For this reason, σ_{pB} is usually labelled the **minimum-risk portfolio.**

minimum-risk portfolio

Combination of assts that reduces the variance of portfolio returns to the lowest feasible level.

Even though *B* is clearly the minimum-risk portfolio, it does not generate the highest returns. Consequently, portfolio *B* may be chosen only by the most risk-averse FI managers, whose sole objective is to minimize portfolio risk regardless of the portfolio's return. Most portfolio managers have some desired return-risk trade-off in mind; they are willing to accept more risk if they are compensated with higher expected returns.[9] One such possibility would be portfolio *C* in

---

[9] The point that is chosen depends on the risk aversion of managers and the degree of separation of ownership from control. If the FI is managed by agents who perform the task of maximizing the value of the firm, they act as risk-neutral agents. They would know that stockholders, who are well diversified, could, through homemade diversification, hold the shares of many firms to eliminate borrower-specific risk. Thus, managers would seek to maximize expected return subject to any regulatory constraints on risk-taking behaviour (i.e., they probably would pick a point in region *C* in Figure 12–2). However, if managers are risk-averse because of their human capital invested in the FI and make lending decisions based on their own risk preferences rather than those of the stockholders, they are likely to choose a relatively low-risk portfolio, something closer to the minimum-risk portfolio. Other agency issues such as bonuses to lending officers based on asset growth may also influence lending decisions. Internal controls thus are important for FIs. For more on agency issues and bank risk-taking, see A. Saunders, E. Strock, and N. G., Travlos, "Ownership Structure, Deregulation, and Bank Risk Taking," *Journal of Finance* 45 (1990), pp. 643–654. The trade-off between portfolio return and portfolio risk can now be solved using new methods of optimization called *genetic algorithm-based techniques*. See A. Mukherjee, R. Bisuras, K. Deb, and A. Mathur, "Multi-Objective Evolutionary Algorithms for the Risk-Return Trade-Off in Bank Loan Management," *KanGAL Report Number 200/005*.

FIGURE 12–2
FI Portfolio
Diversification

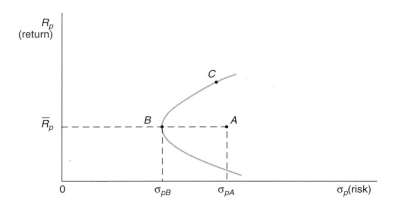

Figure 12–2. This is an efficient portfolio in that the FI manager has selected loan proportions (X_i) to produce a portfolio risk level that is a minimum for that higher expected return level. This portfolio dominates all other portfolios that can produce the same expected return level.[10]

Portfolio theory is a highly attractive tool. Still, over and above the intuitive concept that diversification is generally good, a question arises as to its applicability for banks, insurance companies, and credit unions. These FIs often hold significant amounts of regionally specific non-traded or infrequently traded loans and bonds.

CONCEPT QUESTIONS

1. What is the main point in using MPT for loan portfolio risk?
2. Why would an FI not always choose to operate with a minimum-risk portfolio?

KMV Portfolio Manager Model

www.moodyskmv
.com

KMV Portfolio Manager
A model that applies modern portfolio theory to the loan portfolio.

Despite the non-traded aspect of many loans, a great deal of recent research has gone into developing modern portfolio theory models for loans. Below we look at one approach developed by Moody's KMV Corporation called **Portfolio Manager**.[11]

Any model that seeks to estimate an efficient frontier for loans, as in Figure 12–2, and thus the optimal or best proportions (X_i) in which to hold loans made to different borrowers, needs to determine and measure three things (see equations 12.1, 12.2, and 12.3): the expected return on a loan to borrower i (R_i), the risk of a loan to borrower i (σ_i), and the correlation of default risks between loans made to borrowers i and j (ρ_{ij}). Specifically, in the KMV Portfolio

---

[10] Rather than selecting a point on the loan efficient frontier that reflects managerial risk aversion, as in Figure 12–2 point C (see footnote 9), the FI manager would pick a point that maximizes firm value. This would be the point where the return of the portfolio minus the risk-free rate divided by the standard deviation of portfolio returns is maximized, that is the maximum of [$(R_p - R_f)/\sigma_p$)]. In MPT this is often called the *Sharpe ratio*. Diagrammatically, this is a point on the efficient frontier where a straight line drawn from the vertical axis, from a point equal to R_f, is just tangential to the efficient frontier. At this tangency point, it is impossible to improve upon the risk-return trade-off.

[11] Other portfolio models have been developed, including CreditMetrics, Credit Risk+, and Credit Portfolio View (McKinsey and Company). See Saunders and Allen, *Credit Risk Measurement*. A survey of credit portfolio management by FIs found that 69 percent of the financial institutions that used a credit portfolio model used Portfolio Manager. See *2002 Survey of Credit Portfolio Management Practices*, International Association of Credit Portfolio Managers, International Swaps and Derivatives Association, and Risk Management Association, October 2002.

Manager model, portfolio return and risk are a function of the extent to which loan (exposure) values can change over a one-year horizon and how these value changes move together across different loans in the loan portfolio (correlations). Changes in loan values are determined by changes in the borrower's credit quality (measured as the expected default frequency [EDF], discussed in Chapter 11) and the amount of the loan not recovered (i.e., the loss given default [LGD] on the loan). To calculate correlations, KMV considers the joint impact of 120 different systematic factors, which reflect the global economy, region, industry, and country.

In its simplest model, KMV measures each of these as follows:

$$R_i = AIS_i - E(L_i) = AIS_i - [EDF_i \times LGD_i] \tag{12.4}$$

$$\sigma_i = UL_i = \sigma_{Di} \times LGD_i = \sqrt{EDF_i(1 - EDF_i)} \times LGD_i \tag{12.5}$$

ρ_{ij} = Correlation between the systematic return components of the asset returns of borrower *i* and borrower *j*.

Each of these needs some explanation.

Return on the Loan (R_i)

The return on a loan is measured by the so-called *annual all-in-spread* (AIS), which measures annual fees earned on the loan by the FI plus the annual spread between the loan rate paid by the borrower and the FI's cost of funds. Deducted from this is the expected loss on the loan [$E(L_i)$]. This expected loss is equal to the product of the expected probability of the borrower defaulting over the next year, or its expected default frequency (EDF_i)—as discussed in Chapter 11—times the amount lost by the FI if the borrower defaults [the loss given default, or LGD_i]. Also, if desired, the return on the loan can be expressed in excess return form by deducting the risk-free rate on a security of equivalent maturity.

Risk of the Loan (σ_i)

The risk of the loan reflects the volatility of the loan's default rate (σ_{Di}) around its expected value times the amount lost given default (LGD_i). The product of the volatility of the default rate and the LGD is called the *unexpected loss on the loan* (UL_i) and is a measure of the loan's risk, or σ_i. To measure the volatility of the default rate, assume that loans can either default or repay (no default); then defaults are binomially distributed, and the standard deviation of the default rate for the *i*th borrower (σ_{Di}) is equal to the square root of the probability of default times 1 minus the probability of default [$\sqrt{(EDF)(1 - EDF)}$].

Correlation (ρ_{ij})

To measure the unobservable default risk correlation between any two borrowers, the KMV Portfolio Manager model uses the systematic asset return components of the two borrowers and calculates a correlation that is based on the historical co-movement between those returns. According to KMV, default correlations tend to be low and lie between 0.002 and 0.15. This makes intuitive sense. For example, what is the probability that both IBM and General Motors will go bankrupt at the same time? For both firms, their asset values would have to fall below their debt values at the same time over the next year! The likelihood of this is small except in a very severe or extreme recession or extremely high growth in each firm's short-term debt obligations. The generally low (positive) correlations between the default risks of borrowers is also good news for FI managers in that it implies that by spreading loans across many borrowers, they can reduce portfolio risk significantly.[12]

EXAMPLE 12–3

Calculation of Return and Risk on a Two-Asset Portfolio Using KMV Portfolio Manager

Suppose that an FI holds two loans with the following characteristics:

Loan i	X_i	Annual Spread between Loan Rate and FI's Cost of Funds	Annual Fees	Loss to FI Given Default	Expected Default Frequency	
1	0.60	5%	2%	25%	3%	$\rho_{12} = -0.25$
2	0.40	4.5	1.5	20	2	

The return and risk on loan 1 are

$$R_1 = (0.05 + 0.02) - [0.03 \times 0.25] = 0.0625 \text{ or } 6.25\%$$

$$\sigma_1 = [\sqrt{0.03(0.97)}] \times 0.25 = 0.04265 \text{ or } 4.265\%$$

The return and risk on loan 2 are

$$R_2 = (0.045 + 0.015) - [0.02 \times 0.20] = 0.056 \text{ or } 5.60\%$$

$$\sigma_2 = [\sqrt{0.02(0.98)}] \times 0.20 = 0.028 \text{ or } 2.80\%$$

The return and risk of the portfolio are then

$$R_p = 0.6(6.25\%) + 0.4(5.60\%) = 5.99\%$$

$$\sigma_p^2 = (0.6)^2(0.04265)^2 + (0.4)^2(0.028)^2 + 2(0.6)(0.4)(-0.25)(0.04265)(0.028)$$
$$= 0.0006369$$

thus, $\sigma_p = \sqrt{0.0006369} = 0.0252 = 2.52\%$.

---

[12] The Portfolio Manager model of KMV also can be used to assess the risk of extending more loans to any one borrower. If more loans are extended to one borrower, fewer loans can be made to others (assuming a fixed amount of loans). Technically, since the variance of the loan portfolio is

$$UL_p^2 = \sum_{i=1}^{n} X_i^2 UL_i^2 + \sum_{i=1}^{n} \sum_{i=1}^{n} X_i X_j UL_i UL_j \rho_{ij}$$

The marginal risk contribution of a small amount of additional loans to borrower i can be calculated as

$$\text{Marginal risk contribution} = \frac{dUL_p}{dX_i}$$

where UL_p is the standard deviation (in dollars) of the loan portfolio. Clearly, the marginal risk contribution (dUL_p) of an additional amount of loans to borrower i, (dX_i), will depend not just on the risk of loan i on a stand-alone basis, but also on (1) the correlation of loan i with j other loans, (2) the risk of the j other loans, and (3) where the funds to increase loan i come from. In particular, if $dX_i > 0$, then the sum of the proportion of all remaining loans must decrease unless new funds are raised. Indeed, in the presence of a binding funding constraint $\sum_{i=1}^{n} dx_j$ where $j \neq i$, the key insight is that a loan to a BBB-rated borrower may well be more valuable to an FI (in an MPT sense) if it has a lower correlation with other loans than a loan to an A-rated borrower; that is, it is the loan's marginal risk contribution to total portfolio risk that is important, not its stand-alone risk.

Reportedly, a number of large FIs are using the KMV model (and other similar models) to actively manage their loan portfolios.

<table>
<tr><td>**CONCEPT QUESTIONS**</td><td>1. How does KMV measure the return on a loan?
2. If *EDF* = 0.1 percent and *LGD* = 50 percent, what is the unexpected loss (σ_i) on the loan?
3. How does KMV calculate loan default correlations?</td></tr>
</table>

Partial Applications of Portfolio Theory

Loan Volume-Based Models

As discussed above, direct application of modern portfolio theory is often difficult for FIs lacking information on market prices of assets because many of the assets—such as loans—are not bought and sold in established markets. However, sufficient loan volume data may be available to allow managers to construct a modified or partial application of MPT to analyze the overall concentration or credit risk exposure of the FI. Such loan volume data include:

1. *Bank regulatory reports:* Federally regulated deposit-taking institutions report monthly to the Bank of Canada and classify their loans as business, personal, and residential and non-residential mortgages, as well as those to financial institutions and to domestic and foreign governments. They report geographically for inside and outside of Canada, as well as reporting their impaired assets to OSFI. The information is available on an aggregate basis and can be used to estimate the notional allocation of loans among categories or types.[13]

2. *Data on shared national credits:* A U.S. database on large commercial and industrial loans categorizes loan volume by two-digit Standard Industrial Classification (SIC) codes. For example, loans made to SIC Code 49 are loans to public utilities. Because this database provides a picture of the allocation of large loans across sectors, it is analogous to the market portfolio or basket of commercial and industrial loans and, given the interconnection between the Canadian and U.S. economies, could provide a surrogate database for Canadian lending.

3. *Commercial databases:* Data on 100,000-plus loans by bank and by borrower are provided in the Reuters Loan Pricing Corporation's *DealScan* database. The *DealScan* database provides pricing and details for global corporate loans from 1988 onward. Data on over 1,800 Canadian companies are available.[14]

These data therefore provide *market benchmarks* against which an individual FI can compare its own internal allocations of loans across major lending sectors such as real estate and oil and gas.

---

[13] Some countries, such as Italy, go further and break down a bank's loan portfolio into greater detail including industry and geographic concentrations. In Canada, data is published monthly by the Bank of Canada (www.bankofcanada.ca) on an aggregate basis and quarterly by OSFI (www.osfi-bsif.gc.ca) on an aggregate basis and for the individual deposit-taking institutions under its supervision.

[14] For details regarding the nature of the Canadian borrowers included in *DealScan* see J. Chant, "Corporate Linkages and Bank Lending in Canada: Some First Results," Bank of Canada Conference proceedings (*The Evolving Financial System and Public Policy,* December 2003), www.bankofcanada.ca. See also S. Aintablian and G. S. Roberts, "A Note on Market Response to Corporate Loan Announcements in Canada," *Journal of Banking & Finance,* 24(3), March 2000, pp. 381–393, for an analysis of Canadian loan information in *DealScan. DealScan* also provides data on pricing of new loans. See the discussion in E. Altman, A. Gande, and A. Saunders, *Informational Efficiency of Loans versus Bonds: Evidence from Secondary Market Prices,* Stern School of Business working paper, 2003; and S. Dahiya et al., "Financial Distress and Bank Lending Relationships," *Journal of Finance,* 2003, pp. 375–90. As these databases expand, tests of full MPT models for loans become easier.

TABLE 12–2

Allocation of the Loan Portfolio to Different Sectors (in percentages)

	(1) National	(2) Bank A	(3) Bank B
Real estate	45%	65%	10%
Business	30	20	25
Consumer	15	10	55
Others	10	5	10
	100%	100%	100%

By comparing its own allocation, or the proportions (X_{ij}), of loans in any specific area with the national allocations across borrowers (X_i, where i designates different loan groups), the jth FI can measure the extent to which its loan portfolio deviates from the market portfolio benchmark. This indicates the degree to which the FI has developed *loan concentrations* or relatively undiversified portfolios in various areas.

Consider Table 12–2. In this table we evaluate the first level of the loan asset allocation problem, which is the amount to be lent to each major loan sector or type. Here we show hypothetical numbers for four types of loans: real estate, commercial and industrial, consumer, and others. Column (1) shows the loan allocation proportions at the national level for all banks; this is the market portfolio allocation. Column (2) lists the allocations assumed to be chosen by Bank A, and column (3) shows the allocations chosen by Bank B.

Note that Bank A has concentrated loans more heavily in real estate lending than the national average, while Bank B has concentrated loans more heavily in lending to consumers. To calculate the extent to which each bank deviates from the national benchmark, we use the standard deviation of Bank A's and Bank B's loan allocations from the national benchmark. Of course, the national benchmark may be inappropriate as the relevant market portfolio for a very small bank, insurance company, or credit union. In this case, the FI could construct a regional benchmark.

We calculate the relative measure of loan allocation deviation as[15]

$$\sigma_j = \sqrt{\frac{\sum\limits_{i=1}^{N} (X_{ij} - X_i)^2}{N}} \tag{12.6}$$

where

σ_j = Standard deviation of Bank j's asset allocation proportions from the national benchmark

X_{ij} = Asset allocation proportions of the jth bank

X_i = National asset allocations

N = Number of observations or loan categories, $N = 4$

EXAMPLE 12–4

Calculating Loan Allocation Deviation

Refer again to Table 12–2. Applying equation 12.6 to Bank A's loan portfolio, we get the deviation in its loan portfolio allocation as follows:

$$(X_{1A} - X_1)^2 = (0.65 - 0.45)^2 = 0.0400$$
$$(X_{2A} - X_2)^2 = (0.20 - 0.30)^2 = 0.0100$$

---

[15] For small samples such as this, it is really more appropriate for the divisor of equation 12.6 to be $N - 1$ rather than N.

Regulatory Models

www.federalreserve.gov

As noted in the introduction to this chapter, bank and insurance regulators around the world have also been investigating ways to measure concentration risk. After examining various quantitative approaches, the U.S. Federal Reserve in 1994 issued a final ruling on its proposed measure of credit concentration risk. The method adopted is largely subjective and is based on examiner discretion. The reasons given for rejecting the more technical models were that (1) at the time, the methods for identifying concentration risk were not sufficiently advanced to justify their use and (2) insufficient data were available to estimate more quantitative-type models.

www.osfi-bsif.gc.ca

The board of directors of a Canadian FI has a legal obligation to develop and follow "investment and lending policies, standards and procedures that a reasonable and prudent person would apply in respect of a portfolio of investments and loans to avoid undue risk of loss and obtain a reasonable return."[17] OSFI's B-1 (1993) and B-2 (1994) guidelines for Canadian deposit-taking institutions and federally regulated insurance companies set limits for concentrations as previously noted, allow the FIs to develop in-house models to measure credit risk, and also require them to ensure that the staff assigned to monitor the risks are appropriately trained. In Chapter 20, we look at the details of how credit risk is one component used to determine depository institutions' required level of capital. In June 2006 the Bank for International Settlements released guidance on sound credit risk assessment and valuation for loans. The guidance addresses how common data and processes related to loans may be used for assessing credit risk, accounting for loan impairment, and determining regulatory capital requirements and is structured around ten principles that fall within two broad categories: supervisory expectations concerning sound credit risk assessment and valuation for loans; and supervisory evaluation of credit risk assessment for loans, controls, and capital adequacy.

www.bis.org

CONCEPT QUESTIONS	1. Suppose the returns on different loans were independent. Would there be any gains from loan portfolio diversification?
	2. How would you find the minimum-risk loan portfolio in a modern portfolio theory framework?
	3. Should FI managers select the minimum-risk loan portfolio? Why or why not?
	4. Explain the reasoning behind the U.S. Federal Reserve's 1994 decision to rely more on a subjective rather than a quantitative approach to measuring credit concentration risk. Is that view valid today? How does the U.S. approach differ from OSFI's approach?

---

[17] See *Guideline B-1: Prudent Person Approach* and *Guideline B-2: Large Exposure Limits* for the various federally regulated FIs at www.osfi-bsif.gc.ca.

Summary

This chapter discussed the various approaches available to an FI manager to measure credit portfolio and concentration risk. It showed how portfolio diversification can reduce the loan risk exposure of an FI. Two simple models that allow an FI to monitor and manage its loan concentration risk were also discussed: migration analysis, which relies on rating changes to provide information on desirable and undesirable loan concentrations, and a model that sets concentration limits based on an FI's capital exposure to different lending sectors. The application of the fully fledged MPT model to the credit (loan) concentration issue was also analyzed as was the Moody's KMV Portfolio Manager model. In addition, a model that applies portfolio theory to loan loss ratios in different sectors to determine loan concentrations was discussed. Finally, the approaches of regulators to measuring loan concentrations were described.

Questions and Problems

1. How do loan portfolio risks differ from individual loan risks?

2. What is migration analysis? How do FIs use it to measure credit risk concentration? What are its shortcomings?

3. What does *loan concentration risk* mean?

4. A manager decides not to lend to any firm in sectors that generate losses in excess of 5 percent of equity.

   a. If the average historical losses in the automobile sector total 8 percent, what is the maximum loan a manager can lend to a firm in this sector as a percentage of total capital?

   b. If the average historical losses in the mining sector total 15 percent, what is the maximum loan a manager can make to a firm in this sector as a percentage of total capital?

5. An FI has set a maximum loss of 12 percent of total capital as a basis for setting concentration limits on loans to individual firms. If it has set a concentration limit of 25 percent to a firm, what is the expected loss rate for that firm?

6. Explain how modern portfolio theory can be applied to lower the credit risk of an FI's portfolio.

7. The Bank of Tinytown has two $20,000 loans with the following characteristics: Loan A has an expected return of 10 percent and a standard deviation of returns of 10 percent. The expected return and standard deviation of returns for loan B are 12 percent and 20 percent, respectively.

   a. If the covariance between A and B is 0.015 (1.5 percent), what are the expected return and the standard deviation of this portfolio?

   b. What is the standard deviation of the portfolio if the covariance is −0.015 (−1.5 percent)?

   c. What role does the covariance, or correlation, play in the risk-reduction attributes of modern portfolio theory?

8. Why is it difficult for FIs to measure credit risk using modern portfolio theory?

9. What is the minimum-risk portfolio? Why is this portfolio usually not the portfolio chosen by FIs to optimize the return-risk trade-off?

10. The obvious benefit to holding a diversified portfolio of loans is to spread risk exposures so that a single event does not result in a great loss to the bank. Are there any benefits to not being diversified?

11. A bank vice-president is attempting to rank, in terms of the risk–reward trade-off, the loan portfolios of three loan officers. Information on the portfolios is noted below. How would you rank the three portfolios?

Portfolio	Expected Return	Standard Deviation
A	10%	8%
B	12	9
C	11	10

12. An FI uses Moody's KMV Portfolio Manager model to evaluate the risk-return characteristics of the loans in its portfolio. A specific $10 million loan earns 2 percent per year in fees, and the loan is priced at a 4 percent spread over the cost of funds for the bank. Because of collateral considerations, the loss to the bank if the borrower defaults will be 20 percent of the loan's face value. The expected probability of default is 3 percent. What is the anticipated return on this loan? What is the risk of the loan?

13. What data is available to an FI on loan information? How can they be used to analyze credit concentration risk?

14. Information concerning the allocation of loan portfolios to different market sectors is given below.

Allocation of Loan Portfolios in Different Sectors (%)

Sectors	National	Bank A	Bank B
Corporate & Commercial	30%	50%	10%
Consumer	40	30	40
Real Estate	30	20	50

Bank A and Bank B would like to estimate how much their portfolios deviate from the national average.

   a. Which bank is further away from the national average?

   b. Is a large standard deviation necessarily bad for a bank using this model?

15. Assume that the averages for FIs engaged in mortgage lending have their assets diversified in the following proportions: 20 percent residential, 30 percent commercial, 20 percent international, and 30 percent mortgage-backed securities. A bank has the following ratios: 30 percent residential, 40 percent commercial, and 30 percent international. How does this bank differ from the average?

16. Over the last ten years, a bank has experienced the following loan losses on its business loans, consumer loans, and total loan portfolio.

Year	Business Loans	Consumer Loans	Total Loans
2010	0.0080	0.0165	0.0075
2009	0.0088	0.0183	0.0085
2008	0.0100	0.0210	0.0100
2007	0.0120	0.0255	0.0125
2006	0.0104	0.0219	0.0105
2005	0.0084	0.0174	0.0080
2004	0.0072	0.0147	0.0065
2003	0.0080	0.0165	0.0075
2002	0.0096	0.0201	0.0095
2001	0.0144	0.0309	0.0155

Using regression analysis on these historical loan losses, the bank has estimated the following:

$$X_B = 0.002 + 0.8X_L \quad \text{and} \quad X_h = 0.003 + 1.8X_L$$

where X_B = loss rate in the commercial sector, X_h = loss rate in the consumer (household) sector, and X_L = loss rate for its total loan portfolio.

   a. If the bank's total loan loss rates increase by 10 percent, what are the expected loss rate increases in the business and consumer sectors?

   b. In which sector should the bank limit its loans and why?

17. What guidelines on credit concentrations has OSFI provided for federally regulated FIs?

18. An FI is limited to holding no more than 8 percent of the securities of a single issuer. What is the minimum number of securities it should hold to meet this requirement? What if the requirements are 2 percent, 4 percent, and 7 percent?

Web Question

www

19. Go to the website for a Canadian bank and download the PDF file containing the latest annual report. Search the document using 'credit' or 'credit risk' to find the management's discussion of credit risk. What models does this FI use for evaluating and controlling the risks of its corporate and commercial loans? What models does the FI use for evaluating its consumer loans? Does the FI use other techniques (e.g., loan sales) to reduce its concentration to credit risk?

Appendix 12A   **CreditMetrics**

Appendix 12B   **CreditRisk+**

View Appendices 12A and 12B at the Online Learning Centre: www.mcgrawhill.ca/olc/saunders.

www.mcgrawhill.ca/olc/saunders

Off-Balance-Sheet Risk

This chapter examines the various off-balance-sheet (OBS) activities of FIs. We discuss

- the effect of OBS activities on an FI's risk exposure, return, performance, and solvency
- the different types of OBS activities (credit substitutes, e.g., loan commitments, letters of credit, loans sold; derivative contracts; and other OBS exposure, e.g., when-issued trading, settlement risk, and affiliate risk) and the risks associated with each
- the role of OBS activities in reducing the risk of an FI

INTRODUCTION

contingent assets and liabilities

Assets and liabilities off the balance sheet that potentially can produce positive or negative future cash flows for an FI.

One of the most important choices facing an FI manager is the relative scale of an FI's on- and off-balance-sheet (OBS) activities. Most of us are aware of on-balance-sheet activities because they appear on an FI's published asset and liability balance sheets. For example, an FI's deposits and holdings of bonds and loans are on-balance-sheet activities. By comparison, off-balance-sheet activities are less obvious and often are invisible to all but the best-informed investor or regulator. In accounting terms, *off-balance-sheet items* usually appear "below the bottom line," frequently just as footnotes to financial statements. In economic terms, however, off-balance-sheet items are **contingent assets and liabilities** that affect the future, rather than the current, shape of an FI's balance sheet. As such, they have a direct impact on the FI's future profitability and performance. Consequently, efficient management of these OBS items is central to controlling overall risk exposure in a modern FI.

From a valuation perspective, OBS assets and liabilities have the potential to produce positive or negative *future* cash flows. Fees from OBS activities provide a key source of non-interest income for many FIs, especially the largest and most credit-worthy ones.[1] For example, the notional amount of derivative contracts reported to OSFI by all banks at Quarter 2, 2009, was $14.407 trillion, compared to on-balance-sheet assets of $2.972 trillion. Derivative securities (futures, forwards, options, and swaps) are defined in Table 13–1 and examined in detail in Chapters 23 through 25. Further, FIs use some OBS activities (especially forwards, futures, options, and swaps) to reduce or manage their interest rate risk (see Chapters 8 and 9), foreign exchange risk (see Chapter 14), and credit risk (see Chapters 11 and 12) exposures in a manner superior to what would exist without these activities. However, OBS activities can involve risks that add to an FI's overall risk exposure. As a result, the true value of an FI's capital or net worth is not simply the difference

---

[1] This fee income can have both direct (e.g., a fee from the sale of a letter of credit) and indirect (through improved customer relationships) effects that have a positive income impact in other product areas. In cases where customers feel aggrieved with respect to derivatives purchased from a dealer FI, off-balance-sheet activities can have important negative reputational effects that have an adverse impact on the future flow of fees and other income.

TABLE 13–1   Derivative Securities Held Off the Balance Sheet of FIs

Forward contract   An agreement between a buyer and a seller at time 0 to exchange a non-standardized asset for cash at some future date. The details of the asset and the price to be paid at the forward contract expiration date are set at time 0. The price of the forward contract is fixed over the life of the contract.

Futures contract   An agreement between a buyer and a seller at time 0 to exchange a standardized asset for cash at some future date. Each contract has a standardized expiration, and transactions occur in a centralized market. The price of the futures contract changes daily as the market value of the asset underlying the futures fluctuates.

Option   A contract that gives the holder the right, but not the obligation, to buy or sell the underlying asset at a specified price within a specified period of time.

Swap   An agreement between two parties to exchange assets or a series of cash flows for a specific period of time at a specified interval.

between the market value of assets and liabilities on its balance sheet today, but also reflects the difference between the current market value of its off-balance-sheet or contingent assets and liabilities.

This chapter examines the various OBS activities (listed in Table 13–2) of FIs. We first discuss the effect of OBS activities on an FI's risk exposure, return performance, and solvency. We then describe the different types of OBS activities and the risks associated with each. Because OBS activities create solvency risk exposure, regulators impose capital requirements on these activities. These capital requirements are described in Chapter 20. While the discussion emphasizes that these activities may add to an FI's riskiness, the chapter concludes with a discussion of the role of OBS activities in reducing the risk of an FI.

OFF-BALANCE-SHEET ACTIVITIES AND FI SOLVENCY

off-balance-sheet (OBS) asset
An item or activity that, when a contingent event occurs, moves onto the asset side of the balance sheet.

An item or activity is an **off-balance-sheet asset** if, when a contingent event occurs, the item or activity moves onto the asset side of the balance sheet. Conversely, an item or activity is an **OBS liability** if, when the contingent event occurs, the item or activity moves onto the liability side of the balance sheet. For example, as we discuss in more detail later, FIs sell various performance guarantees, especially guarantees that their customers will not default on their financial and other obligations. Examples of such guarantees include letters of credit and standby letters of credit. Should a customer default occur, the FI's contingent liability (its guaranty)

TABLE 13–2
Major Types of Off-Balance-Sheet Activities

Loan commitment   Contractual commitment to make a loan up to a stated amount at a given interest rate in the future.
Letters of credit   Contingent guarantees sold by an FI to underwrite the performance of the buyer of the guaranty.
Derivative contract   Agreement between two parties to exchange a standard quantity of an asset at a predetermined price at a specified date in the future.
When-issued trading   Trading in securities prior to their actual issue.
Loans sold   Loans originated by an FI and then sold to other investors that (in some cases) can be returned to the originating institution in the future if the credit quality of the loans deteriorates.
Settlement risk   Intraday credit risk, such as that associated with some wire transfer activities.
Affiliate risk   Risk imposed on one holding company affiliate as a result of the potential failure of the other holding company affiliates.

off-balance-sheet liability
An item or activity that, when a contingent event occurs, moves onto the liability side of the balance sheet.

becomes an actual liability and it moves onto the liability side of the balance sheet. FI managers and regulators are just beginning to recognize and measure the risk of OBS activities and their impact on the FI's value. While some part of OBS risk is related to interest rate risk, credit risk, and other risks, these items also introduce unique risks that must be managed by FIs. Indeed, the failure of the U.K. investment bank Barings, the legal problems of Bankers Trust (relating to swap deals involving Procter & Gamble and Gibson Greeting Cards), the US$2.6 billion loss incurred by Sumitomo Corp. (of Japan) from commodity futures trading, and the US$1.5 billion in losses and eventual bankruptcy of Orange County in California have all been linked to FI off-balance-sheet activities in derivatives. For example, in May 1998, Credit Suisse First Boston paid US$52 million to Orange County to settle a lawsuit alleging that it had been in part responsible for that county's investments in risky securities and derivatives transactions.

Prior to 2003, major losses by Canadian FIs were relatively minor. However, the U.S. Securities and Exchange Commission (SEC) investigated Canadian Imperial Bank of Commerce's (CIBC's) structured finance transactions with Enron, the U.S. energy trader that failed in 2001. SEC charged that CIBC took a 3 percent equity holding in 34 structured financing deals (essentially loans carried off the balance sheet) that allowed Enron to treat them as transactions with independent entities, providing US$1 billion in revenues and hiding US$2.5 billion in debt. As a result, in 2003, CIBC paid the SEC a settlement of US$80 million without admitting any wrongdoing and agreed with the Federal Reserve Bank of New York and OSFI to adopt new policies. Subsequently, 10 large FIs (CIBC, Toronto-Dominion Bank, Royal Bank of Canada, Citigroup, JPMorgan, Barclays PLC, Royal Bank of Scotland, Credit Suisse First Boston, Deutsche Bank, and Merrill Lynch & Co.) were sued by Enron in the "MegaClaims lawsuit." In 2005, Royal Bank agreed to pay US$25 million to settle. However, in a separate class action lawsuit led by the University of California, CIBC agreed to pay US$2.4 billion, the largest settlement and one with severe consequences for CIBC. The risks of CIBC's OBS deals with Enron affected the solvency of the FI, bringing its capital ratio to 7.5 percent, close to the 7 percent required by OSFI. The total settlement by FIs related to the class action lawsuit was US$7.12 billion by August 2005, as shown in Table 13–3, along with other large losses by global FIS.

www.cibc.com
www.td.com
www.royalbank.com

Since off-balance-sheet items are contingent assets and liabilities and move onto the balance sheet with a probability less than 1, their valuation is difficult and often highly complex. Because many off-balance-sheet items involve option features, the most common methodology has been to apply contingent claims/option pricing theory models of finance. For example, one relatively simple way to estimate the value of an OBS position in options is by calculating the **delta of an option**—the sensitivity of an option's value to a unit change in the price of the underlying security, which is then multiplied by the notional value of the option's position. (The delta of an option lies between 0 and 1.) Thus, suppose an FI has bought call options on bonds (i.e., it has an OBS asset) with a face or **notional value** of $100 million and the delta is calculated[2] at 0.25. Then the contingent asset value of this option position would be $25 million:

delta of an option
The change in the value of an option for a unit change in the price of the underlying security.

notional value
The face value of an OBS item.

$$d = \text{Delta of an option} = \frac{\text{Change in the option's price}}{\text{Change in price of underlying security}} = \frac{dO}{dS} = 0.25$$

$$F = \text{Notional or face value of options} = \$100 \text{ million}$$

---

[2] A 1-cent change in the price of the bonds underlying the call option leads to a 0.25-cent (or quarter-cent) change in the price of the option.

TABLE 13–3   Some Big Losses on Derivatives

- September–October 1994: Bankers Trust is sued by Gibson Greeting and Procter & Gamble over derivative losses that amounted to US$21 million for Gibson and a US$200 million settlement for Procter & Gamble.

- February 1995: Barings, Britain's oldest investment bank, announces a loss that ultimately totals US$1.38 billion, related to derivatives trading in Singapore by trader Nicholas Leeson.

- December 1996: NatWest Bank finds losses of £77 million caused by mispricing of derivatives in its investment banking arm. Former trader Kyriacos Papouis was blamed for the loss, caused by two years of unauthorized trading by him, but NatWest Markets chief Martin Owen resigned over the incident.

- March 1997: Damian Cope, a former trader at Midland Bank's New York branch, was banned by the Federal Reserve Board over the falsification of books and records relating to his interest rate derivatives trading activities. Midland parent HSBC said the amount of money involved was not significant.

- November 1997: Chase Manhattan was found to have lost up to US$200 million on trading emerging-market debt; part of the problem was reportedly due to debt; part of the problem was reportedly due to exposure to emerging markets through complex derivatives products.

- January 1998: Union Bank of Switzerland was reported to be sitting on unquantified derivatives losses; UBS pledged full disclosure at a later date.

- August–September 1998: Long-Term Capital Management, a hedge fund with an exposure exceeding US$1.25 trillion in derivatives and other securities, had to be rescued by a consortium of commercial and investment banks that infused an additional US$3.65 billion of equity into the fund.

- July 2001: Global banks exposed to losses on credit derivatives issued to a failing Enron.

- December 2001–January 2002: Allied Irish Bank incurs a US$750 million loss from foreign exchange trades by rogue trader John Rusnak.

- September 2006: Amaranth Advisors loses US$6 billion on investments in natural gas futures. Total assets before loss were $9 billion.

- 2008: Rogue trader Jérôme Keviel of the French bank Société Générale lost US$7.1 billion trading European stock index futures.

Source: Dan Atkinson, "UBS Pledged Derivatives Explanation," *Manchester Guardian*, 1998; updated by authors.

The delta equivalent or contingent asset value = delta × face value of option = $0.25 \times \$100$ million = $25 million. Of course, to figure the value of delta for the option, one needs an option pricing model such as Black–Scholes or a binomial model. We provide a review of these models in Appendix 11B, located at the Online Learning Centre at www.mcgrawhill.ca/olc/saunders. In general, the delta of the option varies with the level of the price of the underlying security as it moves in and out of the money;[3] that is, $0 < d < 1$.[4] Note that if the FI sold options, they would be valued as a contingent liability.[5]

Loan commitments and letters of credit are also off-balance-sheet activities that have option features. Specifically, the holder of a loan commitment or credit line

---

[3] For example, for an in-the-money call option, the price of the underlying security exceeds the option's exercise price. For an out-of-the money call option, the price of the underlying security is less than the option's exercise price. In general, the relationship between the value of an option and the underlying value of a security is non-linear. Thus, using the delta method to derive the market value of an option is at best an approximation. To deal with the non-linearity of payoffs on options, some analysts take into account the gamma as well as the delta of the option (gamma measures the change in delta as the underlying security price varies). For example, the standardized model of the BIS used to calculate the market risk of options incorporates an option's delta, its gamma, and its vega (a measure of volatility risk). See Bank for International Settlements, *Standardized Model for Market Risk* (Basel, Switzerland, BIS, 1996). See also JPMorgan, *RiskMetrics,* 4th ed., 1996.

[4] In the context of the Black–Scholes model, the value of the delta on a call option is $d = N(d_1)$, where $N(.)$ is the cumulative normal distribution function and $d_1 = [\ln(S/X) + (r + \sigma^2/(2\tau)]/\sigma \sqrt{T}$.

[5] Note that a cap or a floor is a complex option—that is, a collection of individual options (see Chapter 24).

who decides to draw on that credit line is exercising an *option to borrow*. When the buyer of a guaranty defaults, this buyer is exercising a *default* option. Similarly, when the counterparty to a derivatives transaction is unable or unwilling to meet its obligation to pay (e.g., in a swap), this is considered an exercise of a default option.

With respect to swaps, futures, and forwards, a common approach is to convert these positions into an equivalent value of the underlying assets. For example, a $20 million, 10-year, fixed-floating interest rate swap in which an FI receives 20 semiannual fixed interest rate payments of 8 percent per annum (i.e., 4 percent per half year) and pays floating-rate payments every half year indexed to LIBOR can be viewed as the equivalent, in terms of valuation, of an on-balance-sheet position in two $20 million bonds. That is, the FI can be viewed as being long $20 million (holding an asset) in a 10-year bond with an annual coupon of 8 percent per annum and short $20 million (holding a liability) in a floating-rate bond of 10 years' maturity whose rate is adjusted every six months.[6] The market value of the swap can be viewed as the present value of the difference between the cash flows on the fixed-rate bond and the expected cash flows on the floating-rate bond. This market value is usually a very small percentage of the notional value of the swap. In our example of a $20 million swap, the market value is about 3 percent of this figure,[7] or $600,000.

Given these valuation models, we can calculate, in an approximate sense, the current or market value of each OBS asset and liability and its effect on an FI's solvency. Consider Table 13–4. In panel A of Table 13–4 the value of the FI's net worth (E) is calculated in the traditional way as the difference between the market values of its on-balance-sheet assets (A) and liabilities (L). As we discussed in Chapter 8:

$$E = A - L$$
$$10 = 100 - 90$$

Under this calculation, the market value of the stockholders' equity stake in the FI is 10 and the ratio of the FI's assets to capital (or assets to capital multiple) is 10. Regulators and FIs often use the latter ratio as a simple measure of solvency (see Chapter 20 for more details).

A truer picture of the FI's economic solvency should consider the market value of both its visible on-balance-sheet and off-balance-sheet activities. Specifically, as in panel B of Table 13–4, the FI manager should value contingent or future assets and liability claims as well as current assets and liabilities. In our example, the current market value of the FI's contingent assets (CA) is 50, while the current market value of its contingent liabilities (CL) is 55. Since the market value of contingent liabilities exceeds the market value of contingent assets by 5, this difference is an additional obligation, or claim, on the net worth of the FI. That is, stockholders' true net worth (E) is really

$$E = (A - L) + (CA - CL)$$
$$= (100 - 90) + (50 - 55)$$
$$= 5$$

---

[6] An interest rate swap does not normally involve principal payments on maturity. In the case above, the two principal amounts on the fixed- and floating-rate bonds cancel each other out.

[7] This is based on calculations by J. Kambhu, F. Keane, and C. Benadon, "Price Risk Intermediation in the Over-the-Counter Derivatives Markets: Interpretation of a Global Survey," Federal Reserve Bank of New York, *Economic Policy Review,* April 1996, pp. 1–15.

TABLE 13–4
Valuation of an FI's
Net Worth without
and with Off-
Balance-Sheet Items

Panel A: Traditional Valuation of an FI's Net Worth			
Assets		**Liabilities**	
Market value of assets (A)	$ 100	Market value of liabilities (L)	$ 90
		Net worth (E)	10
	$ 100		$ 100

Panel B: Valuation of an FI's Net Worth with On- and Off-Balance-Sheet Activities Valued			
Assets		**Liabilities**	
Market value of assets (A)	$ 100	Market value of liabilities (L)	$ 90
		Net worth (E)	5
Market value of contingent assets (CA)	50	Market value of contingent liabilities (CL)	55
	$ 150		$ 150

rather than 10, as it was when we ignored off-balance-sheet activities. Thus, economically speaking, contingent assets and liabilities are contractual claims that directly impact the economic value of the FI. Indeed, from both the stockholders' and regulators' perspectives, large increases in the value of OBS liabilities can render an FI economically insolvent just as effectively as can losses due to mismatched interest rate gaps and default or credit losses from on-balance-sheet activities. For example, in 1998, JPMorgan had to recognize US$587 million in currency swaps as non-performing, of which US$489 million were related to currency swaps with SK, a Korean investment company. Two of those swaps involved the exchange of Thai baht for Japanese yen in which SK would benefit if the Thai baht rose in value. As it turned out, soon after the contract was entered into, the baht collapsed and SK disputed the legality of the contract.[8] In 2002, Royal Bank of Canada (RBC) was sued by Cooperatieve Centrale Raiffeisen-Boerenleenbank B.A. (Rabobank) to nullify obligations under a total return swap. RBC carried the receivables due of US$517 million (CDN$805 million) on its books as "Other Assets," but disclosed the amount in a note to the financial statements.[9]

CONCEPT QUESTIONS

1. Define a contingent asset and a contingent liability.
2. Suppose an FI had a market value of assets of $95 and a market value of liabilities of $88. In addition, it had contingent assets valued at $10 and contingent liabilities valued at $7. What is the FI's true net worth position?

RETURNS AND RISKS OF OFF-BALANCE-SHEET ACTIVITIES

In the 1980s, rising losses on loans to less-developed and Eastern European countries, increased interest rate volatility, and squeezed interest margins for on-balance-sheet lending due to non-bank competition induced many large commercial banks to seek profitable OBS activities. By moving activities off the balance sheet, banks hoped to earn more fee income to offset declining margins or spreads

[8] See "J. P. Morgan in Korean Battle on Derivatives," *The New York Times,* February 27, 1998, p. D1.

[9] See Royal Bank of Canada's 2004 annual report, Note 18, p. 92, at www.royalbank.com.

on their traditional lending business. At the same time, they could avoid regulatory costs or taxes, since reserve requirements, deposit insurance premiums, and capital adequacy requirements were not levied on off-balance-sheet activities. Thus, banks had both earnings and regulatory tax-avoidance incentives to move activities off their balance sheets.[10]

www.bis.org

The dramatic growth in OBS activities caused OSFI to introduce a reporting system in 1996 to satisfy the Bank for International Settlements (BIS) capital requirements. In 2008, Canadian banks replaced Basel I with Basel II reporting for off-balance-sheet derivatives, which we discuss in further detail in Chapter 20. Table 13–5 shows the level of OBS activities of Canadian banks, reported quarterly to OSFI at their **notional amount,** which overestimates their current market, or contingent claims value. The results from 1996 to 2007 were reported under Basel I, so a direct comparison with 2008 results is not possible. However, the notional amount of OBS contracts reported has increased by almost 200 percent between Q4 1996 and Q4 2008, a phenomenal growth rate that reflects the global trend toward the provision of and exposure to over-the-counter (OTC) and exchange-traded derivatives contracts by financial intermediaries. In 2008, most of the off-balance-sheet exposure for Canadian banks came from OTC interest rate derivative contracts (59.8 percent of the total notional amount), followed by OTC foreign exchange and gold contracts (22.1 percent). The total notional amount of derivative contracts of $14.98 trillion represents five times the $2.99 trillion on balance sheet assets.[11]

notional amount
The face value of a financial contract.

TABLE 13–5   **Off-Balance-Sheet Items of Canadian Banks (notional amounts, CDN$ billions)**

Off-Balance-Sheet Items	1996	2000	2005	2006	2007	2008*
Interest Rate Contracts						
OTC	2,717.0	4,067.4	5,687.6	7,370.8	7,581.8	8,952.3
Exchange-Traded	339.1	699.6	1,170.3	1,982.1	1,149.0	973.4
Foreign Exchange & Gold Contracts						
OTC	1,938.0	2,234.2	2,403.0	2,508.0	2,760.3	3,315.6
Exchange-Traded	9.3	6.8	24.3	50.3	33.4	35.5
Credit Derivative Contracts						
OTC						835.5
Equity-Linked Contracts						
OTC						225.5
Exchange-Traded						229.8
Other						
OTC	37.2	267.7	700.3	1,015.4	1,083.7	171.8
Exchange-Traded	6.0	90.7	322.1	769.7	798.0	242.8
Total Derivative Contracts	5,046.6	7,366.4	10,307.6	13,696.2	13,406.2	14,982.3
Other Off-Balance-Sheet Items**	487.2	732.5	584.6	645.9	599.0	n.a.
Total OBS Items Reported	5,533.8	8,098.9	10,892.2	14,342.2	14,005.2	n.a.

*2008 results reported under Basel II rules.
** Basel I items including credit commitments and other OBS credit-equivalent amounts reported with credit risk under Basel II for 2008.

Source: OSFI quarterly reports for all banks, www.osfi-bsif.gc.ca.

---

[10] Chapters 26 and 27 go into further details on incentives relating to loan sales and securitizations.

[11] Other off-balance-sheet items (guarantees and standby letters of credit, securities lending, documentary and commercial letters of credit, lease commitments, loan commitments, and loans sold) reported to OSFI under Basel I for 1996–2007 comprised a small notional amount of risk exposure for Canadian banks relative to the notional amounts of derivatives, as we will discuss in Chapter 20. Under Basel II, these amounts are reported with credit risk calculations.

**credit derivative
contract**
A contract that transfers credit risk from one party to another.

**equity-linked
contract**
A contract with an option feature whose value depends in part on a stock, a basket of stocks, or an equity index such as the TSX.

As shown in Table 13–5, OTC **credit derivative contracts** and OTC and exchange-traded **equity-linked contracts** were reported separately for the first time in 2008. This reflects the growth in global markets for credit default swaps and equity-related forwards, swaps, and options. Total OTC derivatives reported to the BIS in June 2008 showed notional amounts of credit default swaps of US\$57.325 trillion and of equity-linked contracts of US\$10.177 trillion. These contracts are largely unregulated and have attracted the attention of regulators for their potential role in the credit crisis in 2007–2008.[12]

The total OBS picture for individual banks can be different since the notional amounts for derivatives overstate an FI's risk. CIBC reported a total notional derivative amount of \$1.17 trillion in its 2008 annual report. When converted for capital adequacy purposes for Basel II as required by OSFI (discussed in Chapter 20), the credit equivalent is only \$16.544 billion and the risk-weighted amount is only \$10.551 billion. In addition to derivatives, CIBC also reports securitizations, guarantees, pledged assets, and credit-related arrangements. Table 13–6 shows a summary of the contract amounts of off-balance-sheet credit-related arrangements reported by CIBC for 2008. These are discussed in the next section.

Other FIs engage in OBS activities as well. For example, Canadian insurance companies provide off-balance-sheet variable annuities as well as guarantees on equities and debt in segregated funds that protect the investor from losses. In 2008, because of the decline in equity markets, Manulife increased its balance

TABLE 13–6   **CIBC's 2008 Off-Balance-Sheet Credit-Related Arrangements (\$ millions, as at October 31)**

	Contract Amounts Expiration Per Period					
	Less than 1 year	1–3 years	3–5 years	Over 5 years	**2008 Total**	2007 Total
Securities lending[(1) (2)]	\$ 49,293	\$ –	\$ –	\$ –	**\$ 49,293**	\$ 69,221
Unutilized credit commitments[(3)]	23,787	4,163	8,927	1,041	**37,918**	4 0,735
Backstop liquidity facilities	9,764	–	–	–	**9,764**	17,278
Standby and performance letters of credit	4,807	516	495	431	**6,249**	6,353
ALM credit derivatives written options[(4)]	–	30	–	–	**30**	103
Documentary and commercial letters of credit	235	–	–	1	**236**	169
Other	394	–	–	–	**394**	353
	\$ 88,280	\$ 4,709	\$ 9,422	\$ 1,473	**\$ 103,884**	\$ 134,212

(1) Includes the full contract amount of custodial client securities totalling \$39.8 billion (2007: \$51.7 billion) lent by CIBC Mellon Global Securities Services Company, which is a 50/50 joint venture between CIBC and The Bank of New York Mellon.
(2) Securities lending of \$6.1 billion (2007: \$4.9 billion) for cash is excluded from the table above because it is reported on the consolidated balance sheet as obligations related to securities lent or sold under repurchase agreements.
(3) Includes irrevocable lines of credit totalling \$28.7 billion (2007: \$30.1 billion), of which \$14.5 billion (2007: \$18.5 billion) will expire in one year or less, and excludes personal lines of credit, home equity lines of credit, and credit card lines.
(4) Represents notional amount of asset/liability management (ALM) credit derivatives written options.

Source: CIBC *Annual Accountability Report 2008*, p. 69.

---

[12] See Bank for International Settlements, *BIS Quarterly Review,* December 2008, Table 19, page A103; and D. Duffie, *Innovations in Credit Risk Transfer: Implications for Financial Stability,* July 2008, BIS Working Paper No. 255, available at www.bis.org.

sheet reserves by $5.78 billion through a charge to operating income and raised additional capital of $4.3 billion in debt and equity.[13]

THE MAJOR TYPES OF OBS ACTIVITIES

The major types of OBS activities for Canadian banks are

- credit instruments: loan commitments, standby letters of credit and letters of credit
- derivatives contracts: futures, forwards, swaps, and options
- other OBS contracts: when-issued securities, loans sold

The next section analyzes these OBS activities in more detail and pays particular attention to the types of risk exposure an FI faces when engaging in such activities. As we discussed earlier, precise market valuation of these contingent assets and liabilities can be extremely difficult because of their complex contingent claim features and option aspects. At a very minimum, FI managers should understand not only the general features of the risk exposure associated with each major OBS asset and liability but also how each one can impact the return and profitability of an FI.

Loan Commitments

loan commitment agreement
A contractual commitment to make a loan up to a stated amount at a given interest rate in the future.

These days, most commercial loans are made by firms that take down (or borrow against) prenegotiated lines of credit or loan commitments rather than borrow spot loans (see Chapter 11's discussion). A **loan commitment agreement** is a contractual commitment by an FI to lend to a firm a certain maximum amount (say, $10 million) at given interest rate terms (say, 12 percent). The loan commitment agreement also defines the length of time over which the borrower has the option to take down this loan. In return for making this loan commitment, the FI may charge an **up-front fee** (or facility fee) of, say, 1/8 percent of the commitment size, or $12,500 in this example. In addition, the FI must stand ready to supply the full $10 million at any time over the commitment period—say, one year. Meanwhile, the borrower has a valuable option to take down any amount between $0 and $10 million. The FI also may charge the borrower a **back-end fee** (or commitment fee) on any unused balances in the commitment line at the end of the period.[14] In this example, if the borrower takes down only $8 million in funds over the year and the fee on *unused* commitments is 1/4 percent, the FI will generate additional revenue of 1/4 percent times $2 million, or $5,000. Figure 13–1 presents a summary of the structure of this loan commitment.

up-front fee
The fee charged for making funds available through a loan commitment.

back-end fee
The fee imposed on the unused balance of a loan commitment.

FIGURE 13–1
Structure of a Loan Commitment

Up-front fee of 1/8% on whole line

Back-end fee of 1/4% on unused portion

0 ←——— 1 year $10 million commitment ———→ 1

---

[13] See the CIBC *Annual Accountability Report,* pp. 125–128 and 141–144, at www.cibc.com for a discussion of a bank's off-balance-sheet items. As well, see Manulife Financial's 2008 annual report at www.manulife.com for a discussion of the types of guarantees provided by an insurance company.

[14] This can be viewed as an excess capacity charge.

EXAMPLE 13–1

*Calculation of
the Promised
Return on a Loan
Commitment*

It is quite easy to show how the unique features of loan commitments affect the promised return $(1 + k)$ on a loan. In Chapter 11 we developed a model for determining $(1 + k)$ on a spot loan. This can be extended by allowing for partial drawdown and the up-front and back-end fees commonly found in loan commitments. For a one-year loan commitment, let

BR = Interest on the loan = 12%

m = Risk premium = 2%

f_1 = Up-front fee on the whole commitment = $\frac{1}{8}$%

f_2 = Back-end fee on the unused commitment = $\frac{1}{4}$%

td = Expected (average) drawdown rate $(0 < td < 1)$ on the loan commitment = 75%

Then the general formula for the promised return $(1 + k)$ of the loan commitment is[15]

$$1 + k = 1 + \frac{f_1 + f_2(1 - td) + (BR + m)td}{td}$$

$$1 + k = 1 + \frac{0.00125 + 0.0025(0.25) + (0.12 + 0.02)0.75}{0.75}$$

$$1 + k = 1 + \frac{0.106875}{0.75} = 1.1425 \text{ or } k = 14.25\%$$

Note that only when the borrower actually draws on the commitment do the loans made under the commitment appear on the balance sheet. Thus, only when the $8 million loan is taken down exactly halfway through the one-year commitment period (i.e., six months later), does the balance sheet show a new $8 million loan being created. When the $10 million commitment is made at time 0, nothing shows on the balance sheet. Nevertheless, the FI must stand ready to make the full $10 million in loans on any day within the one-year commitment period; that is, at time 0 a new contingent claim on the resources of the FI was created.

This raises the question: What contingent risks are created by the loan commitment provision? At least four types of risk are associated with the extension of loan commitments: interest rate risk, drawdown or takedown risk, credit risk, and aggregate funding risk.

Interest Rate Risk

Interest rate risk is a contingent risk emanating from the fact that the FI precommits to make loans available to a borrower over the commitment period at either (1) some fixed interest rate as a fixed-rate loan commitment or (2) some variable rate as a variable-rate loan commitment. Suppose the FI precommits to lend a maximum of $10 million at a fixed rate of 12 percent over the year and its cost of funds rises. The cost of funds may well rise to a level that makes the spread between the 12 percent commitment rate and the FI's cost of funds negative or very small. Moreover, 12 percent may be much less than the rate the customer would have to pay if forced to borrow on the spot loan market under current interest rate conditions. When rates do rise over the commitment period, the FI stands to lose on its

---

[15] This formula closely follows that in John R. Brick, *Commercial Banking: Text and Readings* (Haslett, MI: Systems Publication, Inc., 1984), Chapter 4. Note that for simplicity we have used undiscounted cash flows. Taking into account the time value of money means that we would need to discount both f_2 and $BR + m$ since they are paid at the end of the period. If the discount factor (cost of funds) is $d = 10$ percent, then $k = 12.95$ percent. The calculation can be expanded for multi-year loan commitments by assuming appropriate discount rates and drawdowns.

portfolio of fixed-rate loan commitments as borrowers exercise to the full amount their very valuable options to borrow at below-market rates.[16]

One way the FI can control this risk is by making commitment rates float with spot loan rates, for example, by indexing loan commitments to the prime or LIBOR rate. If the prime rate rises during the commitment period, so does the cost of commitment loans to the borrower—the borrower pays the market rate in effect when the commitment is drawn on. Nevertheless, this fixed formula rate solution does not totally eradicate interest rate risk on loan commitments. For example, suppose that the prime rate rises 1 percent but the cost of funds rises 1.25 percent; the spread between the indexed commitment loan and the cost of funds narrows by 0.25 percent. This spread risk is often called **basis risk**.[17]

basis risk
The variable spread between a lending rate and a borrowing rate or between any two interest rates or prices.

Drawdown or Takedown Risk

Another contingent risk is takedown risk. Specifically, in making the loan commitment, the FI must always stand ready to provide the maximum of the commitment line—$10 million in our example. The borrower has the flexible option to borrow anything between $0 and the $10 million ceiling on any business day in the commitment period, usually with a short notice period of three days. This exposes the FI to a degree of future liquidity risk or uncertainty (see Chapter 17). The FI can never be absolutely sure when, during the commitment period, the borrower will demand the full $10 million or some proportion thereof in cash.[18] For example, in September and October 2008, the severe global liquidity crisis that dried up commercial paper and other short-term money market funds drove borrowers to draw down their credit lines at banks. To some extent, at least, the back-end fee on unused amounts is designed to create incentives for the borrower to take down lines in full to avoid paying this fee. However, in actuality, many lines are only partially drawn upon.[19]

Credit Risk

FIs also face a degree of contingent credit risk in setting the interest or formula rate on a loan commitment. Specifically, the FI often adds a risk premium based on its current assessment of the credit-worthiness of the borrower. For example, the borrower may be judged as an AA credit risk, paying 1 percent above prime rate. However, suppose that over the one-year commitment period the borrowing firm gets into difficulty; its earnings decline so that its credit-worthiness is downgraded to BBB. The FI's problem is that the credit risk premium on the commitment had been preset to the AA level for the one-year commitment period. To avoid being exposed to dramatic declines in borrower credit-worthiness over the commitment period, most FIs include a *material adverse change in conditions clause* by which the FI can cancel or reprice a loan commitment. However, exercising such a clause is really a last resort tactic for an FI because it may put the borrower out of business and result in costly legal claims for breach of contract.[20]

---

[16] In an options sense, the loans are in the money to the borrower.

[17] Basis risk arises because loan rates and deposit rates are not perfectly correlated in their movements over time.

[18] Indeed, the borrower could come to the bank and borrow different amounts over the period ($1 million in month 1, $2 million in month 2, etc.). The only constraint is the $10 million ceiling. We discuss this liquidity risk aspect of loan commitments further in Chapter 17.

[19] See E. Asarnow and J. Marker, "Historical Performance of the U.S. Corporate Loan Market 1988–1993," *Journal of Commercial Lending,* Spring 1995, pp. 13–22. Asarnow and Marker show that the average takedown rates vary widely by borrower credit rating, from a takedown rate of only 0.1 percent by an AAA borrower to 20 percent for BBB and 75 percent for CCC.

[20] Potential damage claims can be enormous if the borrower goes out of business and attributes this to the cancellation of loans under the commitment contract. There are also important reputational costs to take into account in cancelling a commitment to lend.

Aggregate Funding Risk

Many large borrowing firms, such as GM, Ford, and IBM, take out multiple commitment or credit lines with many FIs as insurance against future credit crunches.[21]
In a credit crunch, the supply of spot loans to borrowers is restricted, possibly as a result of restrictive monetary policy actions of the Bank of Canada. Another cause is an FI's increased aversion toward lending, that is, a shift to the left in the loan supply function at all interest rates. In such credit crunches, borrowers with long-standing loan commitments are unlikely to be as credit constrained as those without loan commitments. However, this also implies that borrowers' aggregate demand to take down loan commitments is likely to be greatest when the FI's borrowing and funding conditions are most costly and difficult. In difficult credit conditions, this aggregate commitment takedown effect can increase the cost of funds above normal levels while many FIs scramble for funds to meet their commitments to customers. This is similar to the *externality effect* common in many markets when all participants simultaneously act together and adversely affect the costs of each individual participant.

www.bankofcanada.ca

The four contingent risk effects just identified—interest rate risk, drawdown or takedown risk, credit risk, and aggregate funding risk—appear to imply that loan commitment activities increase the insolvency exposure of FIs that engage in such activities. However, an opposing view holds that loan commitment contracts may make an FI less risky than had it not engaged in them. This view maintains that to be able to charge fees and sell loan commitments or equivalent credit rationing insurance, the FI must convince borrowers that it will still be around to provide the credit needed in the *future*. To convince borrowers that an FI will be around to meet its future commitments, managers may have to adopt *lower*-risk portfolios *today* than would otherwise be the case. By adopting lower-risk portfolios, managers increase the probability that the FI will be able to meet all its long-term on- and off-balance-sheet obligations. Interestingly, empirical studies have confirmed that banks making more loan commitments have lower on-balance-sheet portfolio risk characteristics than those with relatively low levels of commitments; that is, safer banks have a greater tendency to make loan commitments.

Commercial Letters of Credit and Standby Letters of Credit

commercial letters of credit
Contingent guarantees sold by an FI to underwrite the trade or commercial performance of the buyer of the guaranty.

In selling **commercial letters of credit** (LCs) and **standby letters of credit** (SLCs) for fees, FIs add to their contingent future liabilities. Both LCs and SLCs are essentially *guarantees* sold by an FI to underwrite the *performance* of the buyer of the guaranty (such as a corporation). In economic terms, the FI that sells LCs and SLCs is selling insurance against the frequency or severity of some particular future occurrence. Further, similar to the different lines of insurance sold by property and casualty insurers, LC and SLC contracts differ as to the severity and frequency of their risk exposures. We look next at an FI's risk exposure from engaging in LC and SLC off-balance-sheet activities.

standby letters of credit
Guarantees issued to cover contingencies that are potentially more severe and less predictable than contingencies covered under trade-related or commercial letters of credit.

Commercial Letters of Credit

Commercial letters of credit are widely used in both domestic and international trade. For example, they ease the shipment of grain between a farmer in

---

[21] Research by Donald P. Morgan, "The Credit Effects of Monetary Policy: Evidence Using Loan Commitments," *Journal of Money, Credit, and Banking* 30, February 1998, pp. 102–118, has found evidence of this type of insurance effect. Specifically, in credit crunches, spot loans may decline, but loans made under commitment do not.

Saskatchewan and a purchaser in British Columbia or the shipment of goods between a Canadian importer and a foreign exporter. The FI's role is to provide a formal guaranty that payment for goods shipped or sold will be forthcoming regardless of whether the buyer of the goods defaults on payment. We show a very simple LC example in Figure 13–2 for an international transaction between a Canadian importer and a German exporter.

Suppose the importer sent an order for $10 million worth of machinery to a German exporter, as shown by arrow 1 in Figure 13–2. However, the German exporter may be reluctant to send the goods without some assurance or guaranty of being paid once the goods are shipped. The importer may promise to pay for the goods in 90 days, but the German exporter may feel insecure either because it knows little about the credit-worthiness of the importer or because the importer has a low credit rating (say, B or BB). To persuade the German exporter to ship the goods, the importer may have to turn to a large Canadian FI with which it has developed a long-term customer relationship. In its role as a lender and monitor, the FI can better appraise the importer's credit-worthiness. The FI can issue a contingent payment guaranty—that is, an LC to the German exporter on the importer's behalf—in return for an LC fee paid by the importer.[22] In our example, the FI would send to the German exporter an LC guaranteeing payment for the goods in 90 days regardless of whether the importer defaults on its obligation to the German exporter (see arrow 2 in Figure 13–2). Implicitly, the FI is replacing the importer's credit risk with its own credit risk guaranty. For this substitution to work effectively, in guaranteeing payment, the FI must have a higher credit standing or better credit quality reputation than the importer.[23] Once the FI issues the LC and sends it to the German exporter, the exporter ships the goods to the importer, as shown by arrow 3. The probability is very high that in 90 days' time, the importer will pay the German exporter for the goods sent and the FI keeps the LC fee as profit. The fee is, perhaps, 10 basis points of the face value of the letter of credit, or $10,000 in this example.

FIGURE 13–2
Simple Letter of Credit Transaction

---

[22] The FI subsequently notifies the German exporter that, upon meeting the delivery requirements, the exporter is entitled to draw a time draft against the letter of credit at the importer's FI (i.e., withdraw money) for the amount of the transaction. After the export order is shipped, the German exporter presents the time draft and the shipping papers to its own (foreign) FI, who forwards these to the importer's FI. The FI stamps the time draft as accepted and the draft becomes a banker's acceptance listed *on the balance sheet*. At this point, the FI either returns the stamped time draft (now a banker's acceptance) to the German exporter's FI and payment is made on the maturity date (e.g., in 90 days), or the FI immediately pays the foreign FI (and implicitly the exporter) the discounted value of the banker's acceptance. In either case, the foreign FI pays the German exporter for the goods. When the banker's acceptance matures, the importer must pay its FI for the purchases, and the FI sends the importer the shipping papers.

[23] In fact, research has found that, when the market becomes aware that a line of credit is granted, the FI customer experiences a significant increase in its stock price. See M. Mosebach, "Market Response to Banks Granting Lines of Credit," *Journal of Banking & Finance* 23, 1999, pp. 1701–1723, and S. Aintablian and G. S. Roberts, "A Note on Market Response to Corporate Loan Announcements in Canada," *Journal of Banking & Finance*, 24(3), March 2000, pp. 381–393.

A more detailed version of an LC transaction is presented in Appendix 13A, located at the Online Learning Centre: www.mcgrawhill.ca/olc/saunders.

Standby Letters of Credit

Standby letters of credit perform an insurance function similar to that of commercial and trade letters of credit. However, the structure and type of risks covered are different. FIs may issue SLCs to cover contingencies that are potentially more *severe,* less *predictable* or frequent, and not necessarily trade-related. These contingencies include performance bond guarantees whereby an FI may guarantee that a real estate development will be completed in some interval of time. Alternatively, the FI may offer default guarantees to back an issue of commercial paper (CP) to allow issuers to achieve a higher credit rating and a lower funding cost than would otherwise be the case. The $6.249 billion standby and performance letters of credit shown in Table 13–6 for CIBC include loan default commitments or guarantees, also called *credit enhancements.*

Without credit enhancements, for example, many firms would be unable to borrow in the CP market or would have to borrow at a higher funding cost. P1 borrowers, who offer the highest-quality commercial paper, normally pay 40 basis points less than P2 borrowers, the next quality grade. By paying a fee of perhaps 25 basis points to an FI, the FI guarantees to pay CP purchasers' principal and interest on maturity should the issuing firm itself be unable to pay. The SLC backing of CP issues normally results in the paper's placement in the lowest default risk class (P1) and the issuer's savings of up to 15 basis points on issuing costs—40 basis points (the P2–P1 spread) minus the 25-basis-point SLC fee equals 15 basis points.

Note that in selling the SLCs, FIs are competing directly with another of their OBS products, loan commitments. Rather than buying an SLC from an FI to back a CP issue, the issuing firm might pay a fee to an FI to supply a loan commitment. This loan commitment would match the size and maturity of the CP issue, for example, a $100 million ceiling and 45-day maturity. If, on maturity, the CP issuer has insufficient funds to repay the CP holders, the issuer has the right to take down the $100 million loan commitment and to use those funds to meet CP repayments. Often, the up-front fees on such loan commitments are less than those on SLCs; therefore, many CP-issuing firms prefer to use loan commitments.[24]

It needs to be stressed that banks are not the only issuers of SLCs. Not surprisingly, performance bonds and financial guarantees are an important business line of property and casualty insurers. The growth in these lines for property and casualty insurers has come at the expense of banks. Moreover, foreign banks increasingly are taking a share of the U.S. market in SLCs. The reason for the loss in this business line by U.S. banks is that to sell guarantees such as SLCs credibly, the seller must have a better credit rating than the customer. In recent years, few U.S. banks or their parent holding companies have had AA ratings. Other domestic U.S. FIs and Canadian and other foreign banks and insurance companies (e.g., Manulife), on the other hand, have more often had AA ratings. High credit ratings not only make the guarantor more attractive from the buyer's perspective but also make the guarantor more competitive because its cost of funds is lower than that of less credit-worthy FIs.

---

[24] However, it was the refusal of Canadian banks to permit drawdowns under credit lines that supported non-bank commercial paper that led to the freeze in the asset-backed commercial paper market in August 2008. See Chapter 27 for a discussion of this issue related to securitization and the market crises of 2007 and 2008.

Risks Associated with Letters of Credit

The risk to an FI in selling a letter of credit is that the buyer of the LC may fail to perform as promised under a contractual obligation. For example, with the commercial LC described above, there exists a small probability that the Canadian importer will be unable to pay the $10 million in 90 days and will default. Then the FI would be obliged to make good on its guaranty that the contractual obligation will be fulfilled. The cost of such a default would mean that the guaranteeing FI must pay $10 million to the German exporter, although it would have a creditor's claim against the importer's assets to offset this loss. Likewise, for the SLC, there is a small probability that the CP issuer will be unable to pay the CP holders the $100 million as promised at maturity. The FI would then be obliged to pay $100 million to the CP holders (investors) on the issuer's behalf. Clearly, the fee on letters of credit should exceed the expected default risk on the LC or SLC, which is equal to the probability of a default by a counterparty times the expected net payout on the letter of credit, after adjusting for the FI's ability to reclaim assets from the defaulting importer/CP issuer and any monitoring costs.[25]

Derivative Contracts: Futures, Forwards, Swaps, and Options

FIs can be either users of derivative contracts for hedging (see Chapters 23 through 25) and other purposes or dealers that act as counterparties in trades with customers for a fee. Of the notional derivatives amounts reported in Table 13–5 for Q4 2008, RBC and BMO accounted for 36 and 22 percent of the total $14.98 trillion, respectively, followed by TD (19 percent), BNS (10 percent), CIBC (8 percent) and National Bank of Canada (3 percent). OTC contracts are by far the greater portion of OBS exposure for the banks on a notional basis. By comparison, although over 600 U.S. banks were users of derivatives in 2006, the big three dealer banks (JPMorgan Chase, Bank of America, and Citigroup) accounted for 90 percent of the US$119.243 trillion derivatives reported to the U.S. Office of the Comptroller of the Currency.

www.royalbank.com
www.bmo.com
www.td.com
www.scotiabank.ca
www.cibc.com
www.nbc.ca

Contingent credit risk is likely to be present when FIs expand their positions in forwards, futures, swaps, and option contracts. This risk relates to the fact that the counterparty to one of these contracts may default on payment obligations, leaving the FI unhedged and having to replace the contract at today's interest rates, prices, or exchange rates.[26] Further, such defaults are most likely to occur when the counterparty is losing heavily on the contract and the FI is in the money on the contract. This type of default risk is much more serious for forward (and swap) contracts than for futures contracts. This is so because **forward contracts**[27] are non-standard contracts entered into bilaterally by negotiating parties such as two FIs, and all cash flows are required to be paid at one time (on contract maturity). Thus, they are essentially over-the-counter (OTC) arrangements with no external

forward contracts
Non-standard contracts between two parties to deliver and pay for an asset in the future.

---

[25] Hassan finds that stockholders view commercial letter of credit activities by banks as risk-reducing. See M. K. Hassan, "The Market Perception of the Riskiness of Large U.S. Bank Commercial Letters of Credit," *Journal of Financial Services Research* 6 (1992), pp. 207–221.

[26] In fact, J. F. Sinkey, Jr., and D. A. Carter, in "The Reaction of Bank Stock Prices to News of Derivative Losses by Corporate Clients," *Journal of Banking & Finance* 23, 1999, pp. 1725–1743, find that when large non-financial firms announced losses from derivative deals, the FI serving as the derivatives dealer experiences significant stock price declines. Thus, FIs are exposed to OBS risk as a party to a derivatives contract as well as a derivative dealer (acting as a third party, but not a direct party, to the contract).

[27] Conceptually, a swap contract can be viewed as a succession of forward contracts.

guarantees should one or the other party default on the contract. For example, the contract seller might default on a forward foreign exchange contract that promises to deliver £10 million in three months' time at the exchange rate of $1.40 to £1 if the cost to purchase £1 for delivery is $1.60 when the forward contract matures. By contrast, **futures contracts** are standardized contracts guaranteed by organized exchanges such as the Montréal Exchange or the New York Futures Exchange (NYFE), a part of the New York Board of Trade (NYBOT). Futures contracts, like forward contracts, make commitments to deliver foreign exchange (or some other asset) at some future date. If a counterparty defaults on a futures contract, however, the exchange assumes the defaulting party's position and the payment obligations. For example, when Barings, the British merchant bank, was unable to meet its margin calls on Nikkei Index futures traded on the Singapore futures exchange (SIMEX) in 1995, the exchange stood ready to assume Barings' US$8 billion position in futures contracts and ensure that no counterparty lost money. Thus, unless a systematic financial market collapse threatens the exchange itself, futures are essentially default risk-free.[28] In addition, default risk is reduced by the daily marking to market of contracts. This prevents the accumulation of losses and gains that occurs with forward contracts. These differences are discussed in more detail in Chapter 23.

An **option** is a contract that gives the holder the right, but not the obligation, to buy (a call option) or sell (a put option) an underlying asset at a prespecified price for a specified time period. Option contracts can also be purchased or sold by an FI, trading either over the counter (OTC) or bought/sold on organized exchanges. If the options are standardized options traded on exchanges, such as bond options, they are virtually default risk-free.[29] If they are specialized options purchased OTC such as interest rate caps (see Chapter 24), some element of default risk exists.[30]

A **swap** is an agreement between two parties (called *counterparties*) to exchange specified periodic cash flows in the future based on some underlying instrument or price (e.g., a fixed or floating rate on a bond or note). Similar to options, swaps are OTC instruments normally susceptible to counterparty risk (see Chapter 25). If interest rates (or foreign exchange rates) move a lot, one party can be faced with considerable future loss exposure, creating incentives to default.

Credit derivatives (including forwards, options, and swaps) allow FIs to hedge their credit risk. They can be used to hedge the credit risk on individual loans or bonds or portfolios of loans and bonds. The emergence of these new derivatives is important since more FIs fail as a result of credit risk exposures than either interest rate or FX risk exposures. We discuss these derivatives in more detail in Chapters 23 through 25.

Credit Risk Concerns with Derivative Securities

In general, default risk on OTC contracts increases with the time to maturity of the contract and the fluctuation of underlying prices, interest rates, or exchange

futures contracts
Standardized contract guaranteed by organized exchanges to deliver and pay for an asset in the future.

www.nybot.com
www.m-x.ca

option
A contract that gives the holder the right but not the obligation to buy (sell) an asset at a specified price for a specified time period.

swap
An agreement to exchange specified periodic cash flows in the future.

---

[28] More specifically, there are at least four reasons why the default risk of a futures contract is less than that of a forward contract: (1) daily marking to market of futures, (2) margin requirements on futures that act as a security bond, (3) price limits that spread out over extreme price fluctuations, and (4) default guarantees by the futures exchange itself.

[29] Note that the options can still be subject to interest rate risk; see our earlier discussion of the delta on a bond option.

[30] Under an interest rate cap, in return for a fee, the seller promises to compensate the buyer if interest rates rise above a certain level. If rates rise a lot more than expected, the cap seller may have an incentive to default to truncate the losses. Thus, selling a cap is similar to an FI selling interest rate risk insurance (see Chapter 24 for more details).

rates.[31] Most empirical evidence suggests that derivative contracts have generally reduced FI risk or left it unaffected.[32]

Credit risk occurs because of the potential for the counterparty to default on its payment obligations under a derivative contract, a situation that would require the FI to replace the contract at the current market prices and rates, potentially at a loss.[33] This risk is most prevalent in OTC rather than exchange-traded derivative contracts. OTC contracts typically are non-standardized or unique contracts that do not have external guarantees from an organized exchange. Defaults on these contracts usually occur when the FI stands to gain and the counterparty stands to lose.

www.bis.org

The growth of the derivative securities markets was one of the major factors underlying the imposition of the BIS risk-based capital requirements (see Chapter 20). The fear then was that in a long-term derivative security contract, an out-of-the-money counterparty—that is, a counterparty that is currently at a disadvantage in terms of cash flows—would have incentives to default on such contracts to deter current and future losses. Consequently, the BIS imposed a required capital to be held by deposit-taking institutions against their holdings of derivative securities.[34]

Forward Purchases and Sales of When-Issued Securities

when-issued (WI) trading
Trading in securities prior to their actual issue.

Very often banks and other FIs—especially investment banks—enter into commitments to buy and sell securities before issue. This is called **when-issued (WI) trading**. These OBS commitments can expose an FI to future or contingent interest rate risk. FIs often include these securities as a part of their holdings of forward contracts.

www.bankofcanada.ca

An example of a WI commitment is that taken on with new T-bills in the week prior to the announcement of T-bill auction results. The Bank of Canada releases a call for tenders for three-month, six-month, and one-year Government of Canada Treasury bills on Thursday afternoon and the auction is held the following Thursday afternoon, as shown in Figure 13–3. Secondary trading (the "when-issued" market) for these bills occurs until the settlement date, which is the day following the auction of the bills. There are 10 primary dealers for Treasury bills and 12 primary dealers for Government of Canada Bonds that

---

[31] Reputational considerations and the need for future access to markets for hedging deter the incentive to default (see Chapter 25 as well).

[32] See, for example, L. Angbazo, "Commercial Bank Net Interest Margins, Default Risks, Interest Rate Risk and Off-Balance-Sheet Banking," *Journal of Banking & Finance* 21, January 1997, pp. 55–87, who finds no link between interest rate risk and FIs' use of derivatives. N. Y. Naik and P. K. Yadav, "Risk Management with Derivatives by Dealers and Market Quality in Government Bond Markets," *Journal of Finance* 58, 2003, pp. 1873–1904, find that intermediaries use futures contracts to offset or hedge changes in their spot positions. They find that larger intermediaries engage in greater amounts of market risk-taking and hedge their spot exposure to a lesser extent than smaller intermediaries. They do not find that larger intermediaries earn more profit from their selective risk-taking than smaller intermediaries.

[33] For instance, if the new replacement contract has a less favourable price (e.g., the replacement interest rate swap requires the bank to pay a fixed rate of 10 percent to receive a floating-rate payment based on LIBOR rates) than, say, 8 percent before the counterparty (the original floating-rate payer) defaulted. See Chapter 25 on swaps for more details.

[34] Both regulators and market participants have a heightened awareness of credit risk. Merrill Lynch and Salomon Brothers were heavy participants as intermediaries in the derivative securities markets; for example, they acted as counterparty guarantors in most derivative security transactions. To act as counterparty guarantors successfully and to maintain market share, a high—if not the highest—credit rating is required. For example, Merrill Lynch and Salomon Brothers were rated only single A in 1993. To achieve an AAA rating, each established a separately capitalized subsidiary in which to conduct the swap business. Merrill Lynch had to invest US$350 million in its swap subsidiary, and Salomon invested US$175 million in its subsidiary.

FIGURE 13–3
T-Bill Auction Time Line

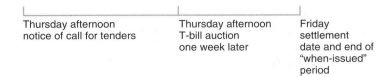

| Thursday afternoon notice of call for tenders | Thursday afternoon T-bill auction one week later | Friday settlement date and end of "when-issued" period |

maintain a market in the securities and 21 government securities distributors that are investment dealers and banks.

Risks Associated with When-Issued Securities

Normally, primary dealers sell the yet-to-be-issued T-bills for forward delivery to customers in the secondary market at a small margin above the price they expect to pay at the primary auction. This can be profitable if the primary dealer gets all the bills needed at the auction at the appropriate price or interest rate to fulfil these forward WI contracts. A primary dealer that makes a mistake regarding the tenor of the auction (i.e., the level of interest rates) faces the risk that the commitments entered into to deliver T-bills in the WI market can be met only at a loss. For example, an overcommitted dealer may have to buy T-bills from other dealers at a loss right after the auction results are announced to meet the WI T-bill delivery commitments made to its customers.[35]

Loans Sold

We discuss in more detail in Chapter 26 the types of loans FIs sell, the FI's incentives to sell, and the way the loans can be sold. Increasingly, banks and other FIs originate loans on their balance sheets, but rather than holding them to maturity, they quickly sell them to outside investors. These outside investors include other banks, insurance companies, mutual funds, and even corporations. In acting as loan originators and loan sellers, FIs are operating more in the fashion of loan brokers than as traditional asset transformers (see Chapter 1).

recourse
The ability to put an asset or loan back to the seller if the credit quality of that asset deteriorates.

When an outside party buys a loan with absolutely no **recourse** to the seller of the loan should the loan eventually go bad, loan sales have no OBS contingent liability implications for FIs. Specifically, *no recourse* means that if the loan the FI sells goes bad, the buyer of the loan must bear the full risk of loss (see arrow 1 in Figure 13–4). In particular, the buyer cannot put the bad loan back to the seller or originating bank.

FIGURE 13–4
Loans Sold with and without Recourse

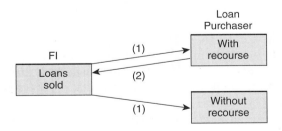

---

[35] This problem occurred when Salomon Brothers cornered or squeezed the market for new two-year U.S. Treasury bonds in 1990. Under the auction rules, no bidder could bid for or attain more than 35 percent of an issue. However, by bidding using customers' names (without their knowledge) in addition to bidding under its own name, Salomon vastly exceeded the 35 percent limit. This put extreme pressure on other dealers, who were unable to meet their selling commitments. The Bank of Canada provides details of the responsibilities of government securities distributors at www.bankofcanada.ca.

Risks Associated with Loan Sales

Suppose the loan is sold with recourse. Then, loan sales represent a long-term contingent credit risk to the seller. Essentially, the buyer of the loan holds a long-term option to put the loan back to the seller (arrow 2 in Figure 13–4), which the buyer can exercise should the credit quality of the purchased loan deteriorate. In reality, the recourse or non-recourse nature of loan sales is often ambiguous. For example, some have argued that FIs generally are willing to repurchase bad non-recourse loans to preserve their reputations with their customers. Obviously, reputational concerns may extend the size of a selling FI's contingent liabilities for OBS activities.

CONCEPT QUESTIONS

1. What are the four risks related to loan commitments?
2. What is the major difference between a commercial letter of credit and a standby letter of credit?
3. What is meant by counterparty risk in a forward contract?
4. Which is more risky for an FI, loan sales with recourse or loan sales without recourse?

OTHER OFF-BALANCE-SHEET RISKS

So far we have looked at five different OBS activities of banks that report to OSFI. Remember that many other FIs engage in these activities as well. Thus, credit unions, insurance companies, and investment banks all engage in futures, forwards, swaps, and options transactions of varying forms. Life insurers are heavily engaged in making loan commitments in commercial mortgages, property and casualty companies underwrite large amounts of financial guarantees, and investment banks engage in when-issued securities trading. Moreover, the five activities just discussed are not the only OBS activities that can create contingent liabilities or risks for an FI. Next, we briefly introduce two other activities that can create them; we discuss the activities at greater length in later chapters.

www.chips.org
www.cdnpay.ca

Settlement Risk

clearing
The exchange and reconciliation of payments in order to transfer funds from one FI to another.

settlement
The adjustment of financial positions of individual FIs at the Bank of Canada.

settlement risk
Intraday credit risk associated with wire transfer activities.

Canadian FIs send their domestic Canadian and U.S. dollar payments via the systems operated by the Canadian Payments Association (CPA), which had 123 member FIs in 2009, of which 12 FIs and the Bank of Canada are direct clearers. The Automated Clearing Settlement System (ACSS) is involved in **clearing** 99 percent of the daily volume of transactions in Canada, but these represent only 12 percent of the total value. The Large Value Transfer System (LVTS) clears 88 percent of the total daily value (CDN$183 billion in 2007) and is used for irrevocable payments. The LVTS is the first of its kind in the world and gives real time **settlement,** eliminating settlement risk for these types of transactions within Canada.

CHIPS is an international and private network owned by approximately 55 participating or member banks. Unlike the ACSS and the LVTS, funds or payment messages sent on the CHIPs network *within* the day are provisional messages that become final and are settled only at the end of the day, giving rise to an intraday, or within-day, **settlement risk** that does not appear on the FI's balance sheet. The balance sheet at best summarizes only the end-of-day-closing position or book of an FI and thus intraday settlement risk represents an additional form of OBS risk for FIs participating on private wholesale wire transfer systems networks. The payments system in Canada is discussed in more detail in Chapter 16.

Affiliate Risk

affiliate risk
The risk imposed on a parent company or holding company due to the potential failure of another unit in the group.

Affiliate risk is the risk imposed on the parent company group or holding company group due to the potential failure of another unit in the group. A **holding company** is a corporation that owns the shares (normally more than 25 percent) of other corporations. Currently, in Canada, federally regulated FIs are permitted to operate with a **parent–subsidiary company structure** where each member of the group is subject to the same regulatory oversight as the parent. However, Bill C-8, passed in June 2001, would allow Canadian FIs to operate in a holding company structure. The regulations have yet to be amended to allow this type of organizational structure. Most developed countries allow bank holding company structures. For example, Citigroup is a one-bank U.S. holding company (OBHC) that owns all the shares of Citibank. Citigroup engages in certain permitted non-bank activities such as data processing through separately capitalized affiliates or companies that it owns. Similarly, a number of other holding companies are multi-bank holding companies (MBHCs) that own shares in a number of different banks. JPMorgan Chase is an MBHC that holds shares in banks throughout the United States. The organizational structures of these two holding companies are presented in Figure 13–5.

holding company
A corporation that owns the shares (normally more than 25 percent) of other corporations.

parent–subsidiary corporate structure
A corporate structure where the subsidiaries are owned and controlled by the parent and subject to the same level of regulatory oversight.

Legally, in the context of OBHCs, the bank and the non-bank affiliate are separate companies, as are Bank 1 and Bank 2 in the context of MBHCs. Thus, in Figure 13–5, the failure of the non-bank affiliate and Bank 2 should have no effect on the financial resources of the bank in the OBHC or on Bank 1 in the MBHC. In reality, the failure of an affiliated firm or bank imposes affiliate risk on another bank in a holding company structure. Both creditors and regulators may look to the holding company (that is, the corporation that owns the shares of the affiliate) for support for a failed affiliate, particularly if they have similar names such as Town Bank and Town Bank Credit Card Company.

special-purpose entity (SPE)
A separate company or trust created for the sale of specific assets.

At the present time, affiliate risk for FIs operating in Canada arises primarily from the use of **special-purpose entities** (SPEs, also called variable-interest entities or VIEs) that are created as vehicles for the securitization of assets. For example, the Royal Bank of Canada securitizes its credit card receivables and the TD Bank securitizes residential mortgage loans, credit card receivables, and commercial mortgage loans by selling them to an SPE. The risk arises when the assets have been removed from the bank's balance sheet but the bank retains an interest in the securitized assets. The mechanisms of securitization will be discussed in greater detail in Chapter 27.

FIGURE 13–5
One-Bank and Multi-Bank Holding Company Structures

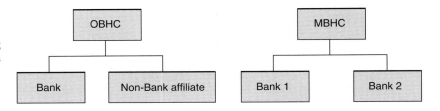

THE ROLE OF OBS ACTIVITIES IN REDUCING RISK

This chapter has emphasized that OBS activities may add to the riskiness of an FI's activities. Indeed, most contingent assets and liabilities have various characteristics that may accentuate an FI's default and/or interest rate risk exposures. Even so, FIs use some OBS instruments—especially forwards, futures, options, and swaps—to reduce or manage their interest rate risk, foreign exchange risk, and credit risk exposures in a manner superior to what would exist in their absence.[36] When used to hedge on-balance-sheet interest rate, foreign exchange, and credit risks, these instruments can actually work to reduce FIs' overall insolvency risk.[37] Although we do not fully describe the role of these instruments as hedging vehicles in reducing an FI's insolvency exposure until Chapters 23 through 25, you can now recognize the inherent danger in the overregulation of OBS activities and instruments. For example, the risk that a counterparty might default on a forward foreign exchange contract risk is very small. It is probably much lower than the insolvency risk an FI faces if it does not use forward contracts to hedge its foreign exchange assets against undesirable fluctuations in exchange rates. (See Chapters 14 and 23 for some examples of this.)

Despite the risk-reducing attributes of OBS derivative securities held by FIs, the expanded use of derivatives has caused many regulators to focus on the risk-increasing attributes of these securities and the possible detrimental effect the risk may have on global financial markets. The result has been an increase in the amount of regulation proposed for these activities. In the wake of the market meltdown in 2008, for example, there have been proposals to move credit default swaps to organized exchanges so that their risk to the global financial system is more transparent and regulated. Despite these rules and regulations, huge losses on derivative securities by FIs such as Bankers Trust (in 1994), Barings (in 1995), and Long-Term Capital Management (in 1998) have resulted in the call for additional regulation. Partially as a result of these concerns, the regulatory costs of hedging have risen (e.g., through the imposition of special capital requirements or restrictions on the use of such instruments [see Chapter 20]). As a result, FIs may have a tendency to underhedge, thereby increasing, rather than decreasing, their insolvency risk.

Finally, fees from OBS activities provide a key source of non-interest income for many FIs, especially the largest and most credit-worthy ones. The importance of non-interest income for large banks is shown in Table 16–1 in Chapter 16. Thus, increased OBS earnings can potentially compensate for increased OBS risk exposure and actually reduce the probability of insolvency for some FIs.[38]

CONCEPT QUESTIONS

1. While recognizing that OBS instruments may add to the riskiness of an FI's activities, explain how they also work to reduce the overall insolvency risk of FIs.
2. Other than hedging and speculation, what reasons do FIs have for engaging in OBS activities?

[36] As we discuss in Chapter 24, there are strong tax disincentives to using derivatives for purposes other than direct hedging.

[37] For example, the London International Financial Futures and Options Exchange (LIFFE) introduced in 2001 a swapnote, which is a futures contract whose settlement price is based on swap market rates. Swapnotes provide an effective mechanism for FIs to hedge interest rate risk with minimal basis risk (see Chapter 25).

[38] In addition, by allowing risk-averse managers to hedge risk, derivatives may induce the managers to follow more value-maximizing investment strategies. That is, derivatives may allow manager–stockholder agency conflicts over the level of risk-taking to be reduced.

Summary

This chapter showed that an FI's net worth or economic value is linked not only to the value of its traditional on-balance-sheet activities but also to the contingent asset and liability values of its off-balance-sheet activities. The risks and returns of several off-balance-sheet items were discussed in detail: loan commitments; commercial and standby letters of credit; derivative contracts such as futures, options, and swaps; forward purchases; and sales of when-issued securities and loans sold. In all cases, it is clear that these instruments have a major impact on the future profitability and risk of an FI. Two other risks associated with off-balance-sheet activities—settlement risk and affiliate risk—were also discussed. The chapter concluded by pointing out that although off-balance-sheet activities can be risk-increasing, they can also be used to hedge on-balance-sheet exposures, resulting in lower risks as well as generating fee income to the FI.

Questions and Problems

1. Classify the following items as (1) on-balance-sheet assets, (2) on-balance-sheet liabilities, (3) off-balance-sheet assets, (4) off-balance-sheet liabilities, or (5) capital account.
   a. Loan commitments.
   b. Loan loss reserves.
   c. Letter of credit.
   d. Bankers' acceptance.
   e. Rediscounted bankers' acceptance.
   f. Loan sales without recourse.
   g. Loan sales with recourse.
   h. Forward contracts to purchase.
   i. Forward contracts to sell.
   j. Swaps.
   k. Loan participations.
   l. Securities borrowed.
   m. Securities lent.
   n. Loss-adjustment expense account (PC insurers).

2. How does one distinguish between an off-balance-sheet asset and an off-balance-sheet liability?

3. Contingent Bank has the following balance sheet in market value terms ($ millions).

Assets		Liabilities	
Cash	$ 20	Deposits	$ 220
Mortgages	220	Equity	20
Total assets	$ 240	Total liabilities and equity	$ 240

   In addition, the bank has contingent assets with $100 million market value and contingent liabilities with $80 million market value. What is the true stockholder net worth? What does the term *contingent* mean?

4. Why are contingent assets and liabilities like options? What is meant by the delta of an option? What is meant by the term *notional value*?

5. An FI has purchased options on bonds with a notional value of $500 million and has sold options on bonds with a notional value of $400 million. The purchased options have a delta of 0.25, and the sold options have a delta of 0.30. What is (a) the contingent asset value of this position, (b) the contingent liability value of this position, and (c) the contingent market value of net worth?

6. What factors explain the growth of off-balance-sheet activities in the 1980s through the early 2000s among FIs?

7. What are the characteristics of a loan commitment that an FI may make to a customer? In what manner and to whom is the commitment an option? What are the various possible pieces of the option premium? When does the option or commitment become an on-balance-sheet item for the FI and the borrower?

8. A FI makes a loan commitment of $2.5 million with an up-front fee of 50 basis points and a back-end fee of 25 basis points on the unused portion of the loan. The takedown on the loan is 50 percent.
   a. What total fees does the FI earn when the loan commitment is negotiated?
   b. What are the total fees earned by the FI at the end of the year, that is, in future value terms? Assume the cost of capital for the FI is 6 percent.

9. An FI has issued a one-year loan commitment of $2 million for an up-front fee of 25 basis points. The back-end fee on the unused portion of the commitment is 10 basis points. The FI's cost of funds is 6 percent, the interest rate on the loan is 10 percent. The customer is expected to draw down 80 percent of the commitment at the beginning of the year.
   a. What is the expected return on the loan without taking future values into consideration?

b. What is the expected return using future values? That is, the net fee and interest income are evaluated at the end of the year when the loan is due.

c. What is the expected return using future values but with the funding of demand deposits replaced by certificates of deposit that have an interest rate of 5.5 percent?

10. Suburb Bank has issued a one-year loan commitment of $10,000,000 for an up-front fee of 50 basis points. The back-end fee on the unused portion of the commitment is 20 basis points. The bank has a cost of funds of 7 percent and will charge an interest rate on the loan of 9 percent. The customer is expected to draw down 60 percent of the commitment.

a. What is the expected return on this loan?

b. What is the expected return per annum on the loan if the drawdown on the commitment does not occur until the end of six months?

11. How is an FI exposed to interest rate risk when it makes loan commitments? In what way can an FI control for this risk? How does basis risk affect the implementation of the control for interest rate risk?

12. How is an FI exposed to credit risk when it makes loan commitments? How is credit risk related to interest rate risk? What control measure is available to an FI for the purpose of protecting against credit risk? What is the realistic opportunity to implement this control feature?

13. How is an FI exposed to takedown risk and aggregate funding risk? How are these two contingent risks related?

14. Do the contingent risks of interest rate, takedown, credit, and aggregate funding tend to increase the insolvency risk of an FI? Why or why not?

15. What is a letter of credit? How is a letter of credit like an insurance contract?

16. A German bank issues a three-month letter of credit on behalf of its customer in Germany, who is planning to import $100,000 worth of goods from Canada. It charges an up-front fee of 100 basis points.

a. What up-front fee does the bank earn?

b. If the exporter decides to discount this letter of credit after it has been accepted by the German bank, how much will the exporter receive, assuming that the interest rate currently is 5 percent and that 90 days remain before maturity? (*Hint:* To discount a security, use the time value of money formula: $PV - FV\ [(1 - (\text{days to maturity}/365)]$.)

c. What risk does the German bank incur by issuing this letter of credit?

17. How do standby letters of credit differ from commercial letters of credit? With what other types of FI products do SLCs compete? What types of FIs can issue SLCs?

18. A corporation is planning to issue $1,000,000 of 270-day commercial paper for an effective annual yield of 5 percent. The corporation expects to save 30 basis points on the interest rate by using either an SLC or a loan commitment as collateral for the issue.

a. What are the net savings to the corporation if a bank agrees to provide a 270-day SLC for an up-front fee of 20 basis points (of the face value of the loan commitment) to back the commercial paper issue?

b. What are the net savings to the corporation if a bank agrees to provide a 270-day loan commitment to back the issue? The bank will charge 10 basis points for an up-front fee and 10 basis points for a back-end fee for any unused portion of the loan. Assume the loan is not needed, and that the fees are on the face value of the loan commitment.

c. Should the corporation be indifferent to the two alternative collateral methods at the time the commercial paper is issued?

19. Explain how the use of derivative contracts such as forwards, futures, swaps, and options creates contingent credit risk for an FI. Why do OTC contracts carry more contingent credit risk than do exchange-traded contracts? How is the default risk of OTC contracts related to the time to maturity and the price and rate volatilities of the underlying assets?

20. What is meant by *when-issued trading*? Explain how forward purchases of when-issued government T-bills can expose FIs to contingent interest rate risk.

21. Distinguish between loan sales with and without recourse. Why would banks want to sell loans with recourse? Explain how loan sales can leave banks exposed to contingent interest rate risks.

22. The manager of Shakey Bank sends a $2 million funds transfer payment message via CHIPS to the Trust Bank at 10 A.M. Trust Bank sends a $2 million funds transfer message via CHIPS to Hope Bank later that same day. What type of risk is inherent in this transaction? How will the risk become reality?

23. Explain how settlement risk is incurred in the interbank payment mechanism and how it is another form of off-balance-sheet risk.

24. What is the difference between a parent–subsidiary structure and a holding company structure? How might Canadian FIs change when the Bank Act is amended to permit holding company structures? Do you expect that the risks will be different for the FIs? How might the failure of an affiliate affect the holding company even if the affiliate were structured separately?

25. Defend the statement that although off-balance-sheet activities expose FIs to several forms of risks, they also can alleviate the risks of FIs.

Web Questions

26. Go to OSFI's website at www.osfi-bsif.gc.ca to update Table 13–5. Click on "Banks." Click on "Financial Data—Banks." Click on "Quarterly" and use the drop-down menu to choose "BCAR Derivative Components." Submit your request and then answer the following questions from the spreadsheet that pops up. What is the notional value increase in total derivatives reported by the banks since Table 13–5 was prepared? Are OTC interest rate derivatives still the largest category? Use the drop-down menu at the top of the page to obtain the results for Royal Bank of Canada and BMO. Are RBC and BMO still the two largest users of derivatives of the six major banks? Click on "Monthly" and find the latest consolidated balance sheet for the banks. How does the growth in reported OBS derivatives compare with the growth in on-balance-sheet assets for the banks over the same time period?

Appendix 13A   A Letter of Credit Transaction

View Appendix 13A at the Online Learning Centre: www.mcgrawhill.ca/olc/saunders.

Foreign Exchange Risk

This chapter looks at how FIs: (1) evaluate, (2) measure, and (3) hedge their foreign exchange risk when

▸ their assets and liabilities are denominated in foreign currencies

▸ they take major positions as traders in the spot and forward foreign currency markets

INTRODUCTION

The globalization of the financial services industry has meant that FIs are increasingly exposed to foreign exchange (FX) risk. FX risk can occur as a result of trading in foreign currencies, making foreign currency loans (such as a loan in sterling to a corporation), buying foreign-issued securities (U.K. sterling-denominated gilt-edged bonds or German euro-government bonds), or issuing foreign currency-denominated debt (sterling certificates of deposit) as a source of funds. Canadian FIs and their business customers may be particularly exposed to exchange rate risk relative to the U.S. dollar both for trade and the pricing of commodities such as oil and gas, metals, and forest products. In particular, exchange rate movements are related to the Bank of Canada's monetary policy and, therefore, interest rate risk (as discussed in Chapters 8 and 9). Exchange rate movements have been particularly important for Canadian FIs as the U.S. dollar has become more volatile relative to other world currencies.

The greater the volatility of foreign exchange rates, the greater the fluctuations in value of an FI's foreign portfolio (see Chapter 10 where we discussed market risk). Extreme foreign exchange risk was evident in 1997 when a currency crisis occurred in Asia. The crisis began July 2 when the Thai baht fell nearly 50 percent in value relative to the U.S. dollar, which led to contagious drops in the value of other Asian currencies and eventually affected currencies other than those in Asia (e.g., the Brazilian real and the Russian rouble). On November 20, 1997, almost five months after the baht's drop in value, the value of the South Korean won dropped by 10 percent relative to the U.S. dollar. As a result of these currency shocks, the earnings of some FIs were adversely impacted. For example, Canadian Imperial Bank of Commerce (CIBC) suffered a trading loss of $70 million in its first quarter (November 1997 to January 1998) related to its Asian exposure and $427 million in the fourth quarter as world markets worried about Asia and Eastern Europe. CIBC's reported total trading revenue declined by $612 million between 1997 and 1998.

www.cibc.com

FOREIGN EXCHANGE RATES AND TRANSACTIONS

Foreign Exchange Rates

A foreign exchange rate is the price at which one currency (e.g., the Canadian dollar) can be exchanged for another currency (e.g., the Swiss franc). Table 14–1 lists the exchange rates between the Canadian dollar and other currencies as of noon,

TABLE 14–1
Foreign Currency
Exchange Rates

Source: Bank of Canada,
www.bankofcanada.ca.

Daily noon foreign exchange rates
Nominal quotations based on official parities or market rates, in terms of U.S. dollars converted into Canadian dollars. Updated at about 12:15 ET the same business day.

	2009/03/17	2009/03/18	2009/03/19
U.S. dollar	1.2718 [0.7863]	1.2720 [0.7862]	1.2325 [0.8114]
Argentine peso	0.3412 [2.9308]	0.3401 [2.9403]	0.3291 [3.0386]
Australian dollar	0.8383 [1.1929]	0.8381 [1.1932]	0.8536 [1.1715]
Bahamian dollar	1.2718 [0.7863]	1.2720 [0.7862]	1.2325 [0.8114]
Brazilian real	0.5577 [1.7931]	0.5522 [1.8109]	0.5473 [1.8272]
Chilean peso	0.002174 [459.9816]	0.002146 [465.9832]	0.002099 [476.4174]
Chinese renminbi	0.1860 [5.3763]	0.1861 [5.3735]	0.1806 [5.5371]
Colombian peso	0.000532 [1,879.6992]	0.000532 [1,879.6992]	0.000527 [1,897.5332]
Croatian kuna	0.2208 [4.5290]	0.2238 [4.4683]	0.2273 [4.3995]
European euro	1.6497 [0.6062]	1.6676 [0.5997]	1.6920 [0.5910]
Hong Kong dollar	0.164057 [6.0954]	0.164078 [6.0947]	0.159008 [6.2890]
Hungarian forint	0.005465 [182.9826]	0.005516 [181.2908]	0.005608 [178.3167]
Icelandic krona	0.01104 [90.5797]	0.01097 [91.1577]	0.01097 [91.1577]
Indian rupee	0.02473 [40.4367]	0.02483 [40.2739]	0.02454 [40.7498]
Indonesian rupiah	0.000106 [9,433.9623]	0.000106 [9,433.9623]	0.000104 [9,615.3847]
Israeli new shekel	0.3078 [3.2489]	0.3076 [3.2510]	0.3058 [3.2701]
Japanese yen	0.012870 [77.7001]	0.012970 [77.1010]	0.013130 [76.1615]
Malaysian ringgit	0.3461 [2.8893]	0.3454 [2.8952]	0.3374 [2.9638]
Mexican peso	0.09061 [11.0363]	0.09000 [11.1111]	0.08760 [11.4155]
New Zealand dollar	0.6718 [1.4885]	0.6723 [1.4874]	0.6912 [1.4468]
Norwegian krone	0.1878 [5.3248]	0.1889 [5.2938]	0.1952 [5.1230]
Pakistan rupee	0.01588 [62.9723]	0.01581 [63.2511]	0.01531 [65.3168]
Panamanian balboa	1.2718 [0.7863]	1.2720 [0.7862]	1.2325 [0.8114]
Peruvian new sol	0.4038 [2.4765]	0.4044 [2.4728]	0.3948 [2.5329]
Philippine peso	0.02633 [37.9795]	0.02635 [37.9507]	0.02552 [39.1850]
Polish zloty	0.3619 [2.7632]	0.3644 [2.7442]	0.3664 [2.7293]
Russian rouble	0.03678 [27.1887]	0.03690 [27.1003]	0.03705 [26.9906]
Singapore dollar	0.8297 [1.2053]	0.8329 [1.2006]	0.8182 [1.2222]
South African rand	0.1274 [7.8493]	0.1280 [7.8125]	0.1277 [7.8309]
South Korean won	0.000897 [1,114.8272]	0.000898 [1,113.5857]	0.000887 [1,127.3957]
Swedish krona	0.1495 [6.6890]	0.1517 [6.5920]	0.1548 [6.4599]
Swiss franc	1.0753 [0.9300]	1.0903 [0.9172]	1.1019 [0.9075]
Taiwanese new dollar	0.03716 [26.9107]	0.03719 [26.8889]	0.03635 [27.5103]
Thai baht	0.03550 [28.1690]	0.03549 [28.1770]	0.03485 [28.6944]
Turkish new lira	0.7419 [1.3479]	0.7391 [1.3530]	0.7210 [1.3870]
U.A.E. dirham	0.3462 [2.8885]	0.3463 [2.8877]	0.3356 [2.9797]
U.K. pound sterling	1.7827 [0.5609]	1.7770 [0.5627]	1.7975 [0.5563]
Venezuelan bolivar fuerte	0.5923 [1.6883]	0.5924 [1.6880]	0.5740 [1.7422]

direct quote
Canadian dollars received for one unit of the foreign currency exchanged.

indirect quote
Foreign currency received for each Canadian dollar exchanged.

Eastern Standard time, on March 17, 18, and 19, 2009. Foreign exchange rates are listed in two ways: Canadian dollars received for one unit of the foreign currency exchanged, or a **direct quote** ("Canadian $ Equivalent"), and foreign currency received for each Canadian dollar exchanged, or an **indirect quote** ("Currency per Canadian $"). For example, the exchange rate of U.S. dollars for Canadian dollars on March 19, 2009, was 0.8114 (US$/CDN$), or US$0.8114 could be received for each Canadian dollar exchanged. Conversely, the exchange rate of Canadian dollars for U.S. dollars was 1.2718 (CDN$/US$), or $1.2718 Canadian dollars could be received for each U.S. dollar exchanged.

Foreign Exchange Transactions

spot foreign exchange transaction
A foreign exchange transaction involving the immediate exchange of currencies at the current (or spot) exchange rate.

There are two basic types of foreign exchange rates and foreign exchange transactions: spot and forward. **Spot foreign exchange transactions** involve the immediate exchange of currencies at the current (or spot) exchange rate—see Figure 14–1. Spot transactions can be conducted through the foreign exchange division of banks or a non-bank foreign currency dealer. For example, a Canadian investor wanting to buy British pounds through a local bank on March 19, 2009, essentially has the dollars transferred from his or her bank account to the dollar account of a pound seller at a rate of $1 per 0.5563 pound (or $1.7975 per pound).[1] Simultaneously, pounds are transferred from the seller's account into an account designated by the Canadian investor. If the dollar depreciates in value relative to the pound (e.g., $1 per 0.5284 pound or $1.8925 per pound), the value of the pound investment, if converted back into Canadian dollars, increases. If the dollar appreciates in value relative to the pound (e.g., $1 per 0.5796 pound or $1.7253 per pound), the value of the pound investment, if converted back into Canadian dollars, decreases.

The appreciation of a country's currency (or a rise in its value relative to other currencies) means that the country's goods are more expensive for foreign buyers and that foreign goods are cheaper for foreign sellers (all else constant). Thus, when a country's currency appreciates, domestic manufacturers find it harder to sell their goods abroad and foreign manufacturers find it easier to sell their goods to domestic purchasers. Conversely, depreciation of a country's currency (or a fall in its value relative to other currencies) means the country's goods become cheaper for foreign buyers and foreign goods become more expensive for foreign sellers.

forward foreign exchange transaction
The exchange of currencies at a specified exchange rate (or forward exchange rate) at some specified date in the future.

A **forward foreign exchange transaction** is the exchange of currencies at a specified exchange rate (or forward exchange rate) at some specified date in the future, as illustrated in Figure 14–1. An example is an agreement today (at time 0) to exchange dollars for pounds at a given (forward) exchange rate three months in the future. Forward contracts are typically written for one-, three-, or six-month periods, but in practice they can be written over any given length of time.

CONCEPT QUESTION

What is the difference between a spot and a forward foreign exchange market transaction?

FIGURE 14–1
Spot versus Forward Foreign Exchange Transaction

[1] In actual practice, settlement—exchange of currencies—occurs normally two days after a transaction.

SOURCES OF FOREIGN EXCHANGE RISK EXPOSURE

The Big Six banks are the major players in foreign currency trading and dealing in Canada. They take significant positions in foreign currency assets and liabilities (see also Chapter 10 on market risk, where we looked at methods of calculating value at risk on foreign exchange contracts). Table 14–2 shows the annual outstanding dollar value of Canadian banks' on-balance-sheet foreign assets and liabilities for the period 2000 to 2008. The 2008 figure for foreign assets (claims) was $1.339 trillion, with foreign liabilities and shareholders' equity of $1.333 trillion, giving a net foreign asset exposure of $6.63 billion. As you can see, Canadian banks reported negative net foreign assets (meaning they are short foreign currency assets, as explained below) in every year except 2008. Foreign assets made up an average of 38 percent of the reporting banks' total on-balance-sheet assets over the time period. In 2008, foreign loans were the highest dollar amount at $476.0 billion, followed by derivative-related amounts at $361.1 billion and securities at $310.6 billion. The reported on-balance-sheet derivative-related amounts more than doubled between 2007 and 2008.

The Bank for International Settlements (BIS) conducts a survey of the foreign exchange and over-the-counter (OTC) derivatives markets activity triennially in April. As well, the Canadian Foreign Exchange Committee (CFEC) conducts a similar survey of the Canadian foreign exchange market semiannually in April and October. The eight banks participating in the CFEC's October 2008 survey were Bank of Nova Scotia, BMO Capital Markets, CIBC World Markets, HSBC Bank Canada, National Bank of Canada, RBC Capital Markets, State Street (Canada), and TD Securities.[2]

TABLE 14–2 **Foreign Currency Assets and Liabilities Reported by Canadian Banks, 2000–2008 ($ millions, as at December 31)**

	2000	2001	2002	2003	2004	2005	2006	2007	2008
Liabilities & Shareholders' Equity	$ 653,562	$ 761,369	$ 770,925	$ 665,470	$ 665,448	$ 740,004	$ 949,927	$ 977,072	$1,332,588
Cash, Equivalents	74,324	78,769	75,074	73,152	67,720	77,723	93,650	100,160	130,132
Securities	168,775	213,760	214,440	237,799	248,143	282,229	342,963	286,142	310,612
Loans	279,236	305,523	278,203	215,156	206,000	240,860	308,675	352,519	476,032
Derivative-Related	76,587	85,688	107,485	73,716	73,121	75,572	46,928	134,667	361,070
Other Assets	28,316	43,187	53,029	39,301	50,454	35,630	132,987	64,112	61,375
Total Foreign Assets	627,240	726,927	728,231	639,123	645,438	712,014	925,203	937,599	1,339,221
Net Foreign Assets	−26,322	−34,442	−42,694	−26,347	−20,010	−27,990	−24,724	−39,473	6,634
Total Assets	1,551,461	1,711,437	1,761,953	1,769,611	1,898,703	2,052,203	2,388,192	2,596,667	3,183,169
Foreign Assets/ Total Assets	40%	42%	41%	36%	34%	35%	39%	36%	42%

Source: Office of Superintendent of Financial Institutions, www.osfi-bsif.gc.ca.

[2] The surveys are available from the Bank of Canada, *Triennial Central Bank Surveys of Foreign Exchange and Over-the-Counter (OTC) Derivatives Markets, Turnover for April 2007 and Amounts Outstanding as at June 30, 2007,* January 4, 2008, at www.bankofcanada.ca, and from the Bank for International Settlements, *Triennial Central Bank Survey: Foreign Exchange and Derivatives Market Activity in 2007,* December 2007, at www.bis.org. The Canadian Foreign Exchange Committee posts its semiannual surveys at www.cfec.ca. See also E. Santor, "Banking Crises, Contagion, and Foreign-Asset Exposures of Canadian Banks," Bank of Canada Conference Proceedings: *The Evolving Financial System and Public Policy,* 2004, available at www.bankofcanada.ca, for a detailed analysis of the exposure of Canadian banks to foreign assets.

Table 14–3 summarizes the foreign currency exchange turnover in Canada as reported to the CFEC's April 2009 survey. The results, by instrument, demonstrate that FX swaps in U.S. dollars against the Canadian dollar constituted the largest amount of foreign exchange transactions in Canada. U.S.–Canadian dollar transactions represent 60.5 percent of the $1.18 trillion total monthly turnover reported for business days covered by the survey. Transactions in Canada of the U.S. dollar against currencies other than the Canadian dollar were the next-largest category. The average daily turnover globally was US$3.2 trillion in April 2007, a growth of 69 percent from April 2004. This compares with an average daily turnover of US$56.4 billion in Canada of traditional FX products for April 2009, a decline of 11.3 percent from October 2008.

spot foreign exchange
Foreign currency traded for immediate delivery.

Table 14–4 gives the categories of foreign currency positions (or investments) of a hypothetical FI in major currencies. Columns (1) and (2) refer to the assets and liabilities denominated in foreign currencies that are held in the portfolios. Columns (3) and (4) refer to foreign currency trading activities (the **spot foreign exchange** and **forward foreign exchange** contracts bought—a long position—and sold—a short position—in each major currency). Foreign currency trading dominates this FI's direct portfolio investments. Even though the aggregate trading positions appear very large—for example, 183,081 million yen—the overall or net exposure position can be relatively small (e.g., the net position in yen was −4,530 million yen).

forward foreign exchange
Foreign currency traded for future delivery.

net exposure
The degree to which an FI is net long (positive) or net short (negative) in a given currency.

An FI's overall FX exposure in any given currency can be measured by the **net position exposure,** which is measured in column (5) of Table 14–4 as

$$\text{Net exposure}_i = (\text{FX assets}_i - \text{FX liabilities}_i) + (\text{FX bought}_i - \text{FX sold}_i)$$

$$= \text{Net foreign assets}_i + \text{Net FX bought}_i$$

where

$$i = i\text{th currency}$$

TABLE 14–3   **Foreign Exchange Turnover in Canada, April 2009 (US$ millions)**

Summary by Instrument	Canadian $ vs. U.S. $	U.S. $ vs. Currencies Other Than Canadian $	Canadian $ vs. Currencies Other Than U.S. $	All Other Currency Pairs	Total All Currencies
Spot	139,903	104,609	11,456	14,021	269,988
Outright forwards	52,169	43,325	16,269	3,766	115,529
FX Swaps	524,182	248,427	21,876	3,085	798,568
Total	716,253	397,360	49,600	20,871	1,184,084

Source: Canadian Foreign Exchange Committee, *Canadian Foreign Exchange Volume Survey,* Table 3, p. 6, April 2009.

TABLE 14–4
Sample FI Positions in Foreign Currencies and Foreign Assets and Liabilities (in currency of denomination)

	(1) Assets	(2) Liabilities	(3) FX Bought*	(4) FX Sold*	(5) Net Position†
U.S. dollars (thousands)	126,812	130,875	367,077	369,335	−6,321
Japanese yen (millions)	43,969	43,869	183,081	187,711	−4,530
Swiss francs (thousands)	52,152	57,423	377,101	384,344	−12,514
British pounds (thousands)	225,987	223,079	519,818	528,657	−5,931
Euros (thousands)	1,113,381	1,072,384	1,848,576	1,867,959	21,614

* Includes spot, future, and forward contracts.
† Net position = (Assets − Liabilities) + (FX bought − FX sold).

Clearly, an FI could match its foreign currency assets to its liabilities in a given currency and match buys and sells in its trading book in that foreign currency to reduce its foreign exchange net exposure to zero and thus avoid FX risk. It could also offset an imbalance in its foreign asset–liability portfolio by an opposing imbalance in its trading book so that its net exposure position in that currency would be zero.

Notice in Table 14–4 that this FI had a positive net FX exposure in one of the five major currencies, euros. A *positive* net exposure position implies the FI is overall **net long in a currency** (i.e., the FI has bought more foreign currency than it has sold) and faces the risk that the foreign currency will fall in value against the dollar, the domestic currency. A *negative* net exposure position implies that the FI is **net short in a foreign currency** (i.e., the FI has sold more foreign currency than it has purchased) and faces the risk that the foreign currency could rise in value against the dollar. Thus, failure to maintain a fully balanced position in any given currency exposes an FI to fluctuations in the FX rate of that currency against the dollar. The greater the volatility of foreign exchange rates given any net exposure position, the greater the fluctuations in value of an FI's foreign exchange portfolio. (See Chapter 10, where we discussed market risk.)

Table 14–2 shows the FX exposures only for Canadian banks, but most non-bank FIs also have some FX exposure either through asset–liability holdings or currency trading, for their own account or for their customers. The absolute sizes of these exposures are smaller for three reasons: smaller asset sizes, prudent person concerns,[3] and regulations. For example, the Canada Pension Plan Investment Board's (CPPIB) annual report states that as at March 31, 2008, 53.0 percent ($65.1 billion) of its assets were invested in Canada. Of the remaining 47 percent, 12.2 percent was invested in North America, excluding Canada; 22.1 percent in the United Kingdom and Europe; 7.5 percent in Japan, Asia, and Australia; and 5.2 percent in other countries. The CPP Fund's investment of $48.2 billion in foreign equities is not hedged in order to take advantage of the diversification and to off-set increases in liabilities from inflation in Canada.[4]

While the levels of claims and positions in foreign currencies held by financial institutions have increased in recent years, the global volume of foreign currency trading declined between 1998 and 2001, and then increased dramatically between 2001 and 2004. The Bank for International Settlements reported that average daily turnover in the foreign exchange markets was US$1,490 trillion in 1996, declining to US$1,200 trillion in 2001, and increasing to US$1,880 trillion in 2004. The increase between 2001 and 2004 was 57 percent at current exchange rates. A report by G. Galati and M. Melvin in the *BIS Quarterly Review* of December 2004 attributed the decline in trading between 1998 and 2001 to the impending introduction of the euro in 2002, growth in electronic brokerages that reduced the number of trading operations, corporate mergers that eliminated the need for foreign exchange transactions, banking consolidations, and the financial events of 1998 that increased global risk aversion and led to lower global liquidity. Between 2001 and 2004, money managers were seeking higher yields and used foreign exchange contracts as an alternative to equity and fixed income assets. Higher volatility in

net long (short) in a currency
Holding more (fewer) assets than liabilities in a given currency.

---

[3] Prudent person concerns are especially important for pension funds.

[4] See the Canada Pension Plan Investment Board's 2008 annual report, pages 4 and 11–12, available at www.cppib.ca. The CPPIB invests Canada Pension Plan contributions on behalf of Canadians. The CPP Fund's assets totalled $108.9 billion at December 31, 2008.

carry trades
The purchase by an investor of a currency in a country with high interest rates funded by borrowing in a currency with low interest rates.

momentum trading
Taking a large position in a currency (or other financial asset) in order to take advantage of long-term increases in exchange rates.

the markets resulted in increased hedging, pushing up the volume of trading. Also, interest rate differentials played a part as **carry trades** were popular, whereby a money manager would buy a higher interest rate currency such as the Australian or New Zealand dollar and fund the trade by borrowing a lower interest rate currency such as the U.S. dollar, the Japanese yen, or the Swiss franc, thus betting that the exchange rate would not change and wipe out the interest rate differential. Since the U.S. dollar depreciated by 30 percent against the Australian dollar and 15 percent against the Canadian dollar and the Japanese yen between April 2001 and early 2004, the carry trade strategy would have been highly profitable in many cases. In addition, traders also engaged in and profited from **momentum trading** by holding long positions in currencies that were experiencing long-run swings in exchange rates.[5]

With the introduction of the euro in January 2002, the cross-trading of member currencies completely disappeared. For example, with the euro in place, cash flows from subsidiaries based in one European country can be put directly into the accounts of a parent company without complicated foreign exchange adjustments. As a result, with the European Monetary Unit (EMU) fully implemented, multinational companies are likely to continue to reduce the number of banking relationships and foreign exchange transactions that they need. Currency unions that have been discussed from time to time for other countries could also act to reduce global foreign exchange transactions in the future. For example, the use of a common dollar between Australia and New Zealand or Canada and the United States has been raised.[6]

The 69 percent increase in daily turnover since 2004 reported by the BIS was a result of changes in the type of counterparty. Between April 2004 and April 2007, foreign currency transactions involving hedge funds, mutual funds, pension funds, and insurance companies more than doubled, as these types of FIs shifted to portfolios that were more diversified. This meant that the inter-bank market fell to 43 percent of the total turnover. As well, trading in OTC foreign exchange derivatives increased by 79 percent. However, the decline of asset values and the failures of hedge funds as a result of the global market crisis in 2008 could mean a decrease in the foreign exchange market globally in future surveys.[7]

Foreign Exchange Rate Volatility and FX Exposure

As Chapter 10 on market risk discussed, we can measure the potential size of an FI's FX exposure by analyzing the asset, liability, and currency trading mismatches on its balance sheet and the underlying volatility of exchange rate movements. Specifically, we can use the following equation:

Dollar loss/gain in currency i = [Net exposure in foreign currency i measured in dollars] $\times$ Shock (volatility) to the $/Foreign currency i exchange rate

[5] See BIS, *Triennial Central Bank Survey,* March 2004. Also, see G. Galati and M. Melvin, "Why Has FX Trading Surged? Explaining the 2004 Triennial Survey," *BIS Quarterly Review,* December 2004, pp. 67–74, and G. Galati, "Why Has Global FX Turnover Declined? Explaining the 2001 Triennial Survey," *BIS Quarterly Review,* December 2001, pp. 39–47, for discussions of the global foreign exchange markets between 1998 and 2004.

[6] See P. Murray and James Powell, "Dollarization in Canada: The Buck Stops There," *Bank of Canada Technical Report No. 90* (2002), as well as J. Powell, *A History of the Canadian Dollar,* Bank of Canada (2003), at www.bankofcanada.ca.

[7] See the Bank for International Settlements, *Triennial Central Bank Survey Foreign Exchange and Derivatives Market Activity in 2007,* December 2007, at www.bis.org.

The larger the FI's net exposure in a foreign currency and the larger the foreign currency's exchange rate volatility,[8] the larger is the potential dollar loss or gain to an FI's earnings (i.e., the greater its daily value at risk). The underlying causes of FX volatility reflect fluctuations in the demand for and supply of a country's currency. That is, conceptually, an FX rate is like the price of any good and will appreciate in value relative to other currencies when demand is high or supply is low and will depreciate in value when demand is low or supply is high. For example, in October 1998 the U.S. dollar fell (depreciated) in value on one day from 121 yen/$ to 112 yen/$, or by over 7 percent. The major reason for this was the purchase of yen by hedge funds and the sale of U.S. dollars to repay Japanese banks for the yen loans they had borrowed at low interest rates earlier in 1998. While not as rapid a decline, in the early 2000s the U.S. dollar fell in value by almost 20 percent relative to the yen (from 134.0 in early 2002 to 107.8 in October 2003), much of which was due to an improving Japanese economy and intervention by Japan's central bank. A final example is the devaluation of the Argentinian peso in 2002. The Bank of Nova Scotia took an after-tax charge to earnings of $540 million in 2002 and sold its subsidiary after 40 years of operating in Argentina. See Chapter 10 for more details on measuring FX exposure.

www.scotiabank.com

CONCEPT QUESTIONS	1. **How is the net foreign currency exposure of an FI measured?** 2. **If a bank is long in British pounds (£), does it gain or lose if the dollar appreciates in value against the pound?** 3. **A bank has £10 million in assets and £7 million in liabilities. It has also bought £52 million in foreign currency trading. What is its net exposure in pounds? (£55 million)**

FOREIGN CURRENCY TRADING

The FX markets of the world have become one of the largest of all financial markets, with trading turnover averaging as high as US$1.8 trillion a day in recent years, 90 times the daily trading volume on the New York Stock Exchange.[9] London continues to be the largest market, followed by New York, Switzerland, and Tokyo.[10] Foreign exchange trading has been called the fairest market in the world because of its immense volume and the fact that no single institution can control the market's direction. Although professionals refer to global foreign exchange trading as a market, it is not really one in the traditional sense of the word. There is no central location where foreign exchange trading takes place. Moreover, the FX market is essentially a 24-hour market, moving among Tokyo, London, and New York throughout the day. Therefore, fluctuations in exchange rates and thus FX

---

[8] In the case of RiskMetrics the shock (or volatility) measure would equal 1.65 times the historic volatility (standard deviation) of the currency's exchange rate with the dollar. This shock, when multiplied by the net exposure in that currency (measured in dollars), provides an estimate of the loss exposure of the FI if tomorrow is that "1 bad day in 20" (see Chapter 10 for more details).

[9] The early 2000s saw a drop in FX trading, with daily volume falling to $1.2 trillion in 2003. Up to 95 percent of all currency trading is now conducted via electronic brokers (resulting in a reduction in the number of people working in the industry).

[10] On a global basis, approximately 34.1 percent of trading in FX occurs in the United Kingdom, 16.6 percent in the United States, and 6.1 percent in Switzerland. Canada's share was 1.5 percent in 2007, eleventh of the 54 countries participating in the *BIS Triennial Central Bank Survey* available at www.bis.org.

trading risk exposure continues into the night even when other FI operations are closed. This clearly adds to the risk from holding mismatched FX positions. Most of the volume is traded among the top international banks, which process currency transactions for everyone from large corporations to governments around the world. Online foreign exchange trading is increasing, and the transnational nature of the electronic exchange of funds makes secure, Internet-based trading an ideal platform. Online trading portals—terminals where currency transactions are being executed—are a low-cost way of conducting spot and forward foreign exchange transactions.

FX Trading Activities

An FI's position in the FX markets generally reflects four trading activities:

1. The purchase and sale of foreign currencies to allow customers to partake in and complete international commercial trade transactions.
2. The purchase and sale of foreign currencies to allow customers (or the FI itself) to take positions in foreign real and financial investments.
3. The purchase and sale of foreign currencies for hedging purposes to offset customer (or FI) exposure in any given currency.
4. The purchase and sale of foreign currencies for speculative purposes through forecasting or anticipating future movements in FX rates.

open position
An unhedged position in a particular currency.

In the first two activities, the FI normally acts as an *agent of* its customers for a fee but does not assume the FX risk itself. Royal Bank of Canada's annual report showed a notional amount of foreign exchange contracts of $1.37 trillion at October 31, 2008. Citigroup is the dominant supplier of FX to retail customers in the United States and worldwide. In the third activity, the FI acts defensively as a hedger to reduce FX exposure. For example, it may take a short (sell) position in the foreign exchange of a country to offset a long (buy) position in the foreign exchange of that same country. Thus, FX risk exposure essentially relates to **open positions** taken as a principal by the FI for speculative purposes, the fourth activity. An FI usually creates an open position by taking an unhedged position in a foreign currency in its FX trading with other FIs. FIs can make speculative trades directly with other FIs or arrange them through specialist FX brokers. Speculative trades can be instituted through a variety of FX instruments. Spot currency trades are the most common, with FIs seeking to make a profit on the difference between buy and sell prices (i.e., on movements in the bid–ask prices over time). However, FIs can also take speculative positions in foreign exchange forward contracts, futures, and options.

The Profitability of Foreign Currency Trading

Remember from the previous section that most profits or losses on foreign trading come from taking an open position or speculating in currencies. Revenues from market making—the bid–ask spread—or from acting as agents for retail or wholesale customers generally provide only a secondary or supplementary revenue source.

www.citigroup.com

www.jpmorganchase.
com

Note the trading income from FX trading for the six large Canadian banks in Table 14–5. As can be seen, total trading revenue is variable, but generally grew for each FI between 2000 and 2008. The level of operations is not large compared to the rest of the banks' operations, and is small relative to the major U.S. banks. For example, Citigroup and JPMorgan Chase, the dominant FX trading banks in

TABLE 14–5 Foreign Exchange Trading Revenue of the Big Six Banks, as Reported for Year-End October 31 ($ millions)

	2000	2001	2002	2003	2004	2005	2006	2007	2008
Bank of Montreal	112	126	69	69	85	89	204	273	379
Bank of Nova Scotia*	152	246	187	201	171	295	301	323	384
CIBC	199	179	152	171	169	169	163	190	264
National Bank	52**	61**	67**	66**	30	28	25	−7	114
Royal Bank*	301	340	264	301	278	235	300	355	584
TD Bank	200	247	217	248	230	248	306	312	481

* Includes precious metals trading.
** Includes all foreign exchange revenue.

Sources: Bank annual reports.

the United States, reported foreign exchange trading income of US$2,277.0 million and US$1,225.0 million, respectively, at December 2004. The decline in the volatility of FX rates among major European countries as well as the increase in volatility in Asian currencies decreased banks' trading profits. The decline in European FX volatility is the result of two forces. The first is the reduction in inflation rates in these countries, and the second is the fixing of exchange rates among European countries as they moved toward full monetary union and the replacement of local currencies with the euro. Specifically, in May 1998, 11 countries in the European Union[11] fixed their exchange rates with each other and on January 1, 1999, all FIs and stock exchanges in these countries began using euros (electronically). On January 1, 2002, the euro went into physical circulation, and on July 1, 2002, local currencies were no longer accepted. While, as noted above, there has been increased FX volatility in many emerging-market countries, such as those of Thailand, Indonesia, and Malaysia,[12] the importance of these currencies in the FX trading activities of major FIs remains relatively small. However, according to the *BIS Triennial Survey,* emerging-markets' share of total turnover had increased to 20 percent in April 2007.

CONCEPT QUESTIONS

1. What are the four major FX trading activities?
2. In which trades do FIs normally act as agents, and in which trades as principals?
3. What is the source of most profits or losses on foreign exchange trading? What foreign currency activities provide a secondary source of revenue?

FOREIGN ASSET AND LIABILITY POSITIONS

The second dimension of an FI's FX exposure results from any mismatches between its foreign financial asset and foreign financial liability portfolios. As discussed earlier, an FI is long a foreign currency if its assets in that currency exceed its liabilities, while it is short a foreign currency if its liabilities in that currency exceed

---

[11] These countries were Austria, Belgium, Finland, France, Germany, Ireland, Italy, Luxemburg, Netherlands, Portugal, and Spain.

[12] For example, in 1997 these currencies fell over 50 percent in value relative to the U.S. dollar. In the fall of 1998 Malaysia introduced capital controls and restrictions on trading in its currency.

its assets. Foreign financial assets might include Swiss franc-denominated bonds, British pound-denominated gilt-edged securities, or peso-denominated Mexican bonds. Foreign financial liabilities might include issuing British pound CDs or a yen-denominated bond in the Euromarkets to raise yen funds. The globalization of financial markets has created an enormous range of possibilities for raising funds in currencies other than the home currency. This is important for FIs that wish to not only diversify their source and use of funds but also exploit imperfections in foreign banking markets that create opportunities for higher returns on assets or lower funding costs.

The Return and Risk of Foreign Investments

This section discusses the extra dimensions of return and risk from adding foreign currency assets and liabilities to an FI's portfolio. Like domestic assets and liabilities, profits (returns) result from the difference between contractual income from or costs paid on a security. With foreign assets and liabilities, however, profits (returns) are also affected by changes in foreign exchange rates.

EXAMPLE 14–1

Calculating the Return of Foreign Exchange Transactions

Suppose that an FI has the following assets and liabilities:

Assets	Liabilities
$100 million loans (one-year) in dollars	$200 million GICs (one-year) in dollars
$100 million equivalent U.K. loans (one-year) (loans made in sterling)	

The FI is raising all of its $200 million liabilities in dollars (one-year GICs) but investing 50 percent in dollar assets (one-year maturity loans) and 50 percent in U.K. pound sterling assets (one-year maturity loans).[13] In this example, the FI has matched the duration of its assets and liabilities ($D_A = D_L = 1$ year) but has mismatched the currency composition of its asset and liability portfolios. Suppose the promised one-year GIC rate is 8 percent, to be paid in dollars at the end of the year, and that one-year, credit risk-free loans in Canada are yielding only 9 percent. The FI would have a positive spread of 1 percent from investing domestically. Suppose, however, that credit risk-free one-year loans are yielding 15 percent in the United Kingdom.

To invest in the United Kingdom, the FI decides to take 50 percent of its $200 million in funds and make one-year maturity U.K. sterling loans while keeping 50 percent of its funds to make dollar loans. To invest $100 million (of the $200 million in GICs issued) in one-year loans in the United Kingdom, the FI engages in the following transactions (illustrated in panel (a) of Figure 14–2).

1. At the beginning of the year, sells $100 million for pounds on the spot currency markets. If the exchange rate is $1.60 to £1, this translates into $100 million/1.6 = £62.5 million.
2. Takes the £62.5 million and makes one-year U.K. loans at a 15 percent interest rate.
3. At the end of the year, sterling revenue from these loans will be £62.5(1.15) = £71.875 million.[14]
4. Repatriates these funds back to Canada at the end of the year. That is, the FI sells the £71.875 million in the foreign exchange market at the spot exchange rate that exists at that time, the end of the year spot rate.

---

[13] For simplicity, we ignore the leverage or net worth aspects of the FI's portfolio.

[14] No default risk is assumed.

FIGURE 14–2
Time Line for a
Foreign Exchange
Transaction

(a) Unhedged Foreign Exchange Transaction

FI lends $100
million for pounds at $1.6/£1

FI receives
£62.5(1.15) for dollars
at $?/£1

|———————————————————————————|
0   1 year

(b) Foreign Exchange Transaction Hedged on the Balance Sheet

FI lends $100
million for pounds at $1.6/£1

FI receives (from a
GIC) $100 million for pounds at $1.6/£1

FI receives
£62.5(1.15) for dollars
at $?/£1

FI pays £62.5(1.11)
with dollars at $?/£1

|———————————————————————————|
0   1 year

(c) Foreign Exchange Transaction Hedged with Forwards

FI lends $100
million for pounds at $1.6/£1

FI sells a one-year pounds for dollars forward
contract with a stated forward rate of $1.55/£1
and nominal value of £62.5 (1.15)

FI receives £62.5(1.15) from borrower and
delivers funds to forward buyer receiving
£62.5 × (1.15) × 1.55 guaranteed.

|———————————————————————————|
0   1 year

Suppose the spot foreign exchange rate has not changed over the year; it remains fixed at $1.60/£1. Then the dollar proceeds from the U.K. investment will be

$$£71.875 \text{ million} \times \$1.60/£1 = \$115 \text{ million}$$

or, as a return,

$$\frac{\$115 \text{ million} - \$100 \text{ million}}{\$100 \text{ million}} = 15\%$$

Given this, the weighted return on the bank's portfolio of investments would be

$$(0.5)(0.09) + (0.5)(0.15) = 0.12 \text{ or } 12\%$$

This exceeds the cost of the FI's GICs by 4 percent (12% − 8%).

Suppose, however, that at the end of the year the British pound had fallen in value relative to the dollar, or the dollar had appreciated in value relative to the pound. The returns on the U.K. loans could be far less than 15 percent even in the absence of interest rate or credit risk. For example, suppose the exchange rate had fallen from $1.60/£1 at the beginning of the year to $1.45/£1 at the end of the year when the FI needed to repatriate the principal and interest on the loan. At an exchange rate of $1.45/£1, the pound loan revenues at the end of the year translate into

$$£71.875 \text{ million} \times \$1.45/£1 = \$104.22 \text{ million}$$

or as a return on the original dollar investment of

$$\frac{\$104.22 - \$100}{\$100} = 0.0422 = 4.22\%$$

The weighted return on the FI's asset portfolio would be

$$(0.5)(0.09) + (0.5)(0.0422) = 0.0661 = 6.61\%$$

In this case, the FI actually has a loss or has a negative interest margin (6.61% − 8% = −1.39%) on its balance sheet investments.

The reason for the loss is that the depreciation of the pound from $1.60 to $1.45 has offset the attractive high yield on British pound sterling loans relative to domestic loans. If the pound had instead appreciated (risen in value) against the dollar over the year—say, to $1.70/£1—then the Canadian FI would have generated a dollar return from its U.K. loans of:

$$£71.875 \times \$1.70 = \$122.188 \text{ million}$$

or a percentage return of 22.188 percent. Then the FI would receive a double benefit from investing in the United Kingdom: a high yield on the domestic British loans plus an appreciation in sterling over the one-year investment period.

Risk and Hedging

Since a manager cannot know in advance what the pound/dollar spot exchange rate will be at the end of the year, a portfolio imbalance or investment strategy in which the FI is *net long* $100 million in pounds (or £62.5 million) is risky. As we discussed, the British loans would generate a return of 22.188 percent if the pound appreciated from $1.60 to $1.70 but would produce a return of only 4.22 percent if the pound depreciated in value against the dollar to $1.45.

In principle, an FI manager can better control the scale of its FX exposure in two major ways: on-balance-sheet hedging and off-balance-sheet hedging. On-balance-sheet hedging involves making changes in the on-balance-sheet assets and liabilities to protect FI profits from FX risk. Off-balance-sheet hedging involves no on-balance-sheet changes but rather involves taking a position in forward or other derivative securities to hedge FX risk.

On-Balance-Sheet Hedging

The following example illustrates how an FI manager can control FX exposure by making changes on the balance sheet.

EXAMPLE 14–2

Hedging on the Balance Sheet

Suppose that instead of funding the $100 million investment in 15 percent British loans with dollar GICs, the FI manager funds the British loans with $100 million equivalent one-year pound sterling GICs at a rate of 11 percent (as illustrated in panel (b) of Figure 14–2). Now the balance sheet of the bank would look like this:

Assets	Liabilities
$100 million Cdn. loans (9%)	$100 million Cdn. GICs (8%)
$100 million U.K. loans (15%) (loans made in sterling)	$100 million U.K. GICs (11%) (deposits raised in sterling)

In this situation, the FI has both a matched maturity and currency foreign asset–liability book. We might now consider the FI's profitability or spreads between the return on assets and the cost of funds under two scenarios: first, when the pound depreciates in value against the dollar over the year from $1.60/£1 to $1.45/£1 and second, when the pound appreciates in value over the year from $1.60/£1 to $1.70/£1.

The Depreciating Pound

When the pound falls in value to $1.45/£1, the return on the British loan portfolio is 4.22 percent. Consider now what happens to the cost of $100 million in pound liabilities in dollar terms:

1. At the beginning of the year, the FI borrows $100 million equivalent in sterling GICs for one year at a promised interest rate of 11 percent. At an exchange rate of $1.60/£, this is a sterling equivalent amount of borrowing of $100 million/1.6 = £62.5 million.
2. At the end of the year, the bank has to pay back the sterling GIC holders their principal and interest, £62.5 million (1.11) = £69.375 million.
3. If the pound had depreciated to $1.45/£ over the year, the repayment in dollar terms would be £69.375 million × $1.45/£1 = $100.59 million, or a dollar cost of funds of 0.59 percent.

Thus, at the end of the year the following occurs:

Average return on assets:

$$(0.5)(0.9) + (0.5)(0.422) = 0.0661 = 6.61\%$$

Canadian asset return + U.K. asset return = Overall return

Average cost of funds:

$$(0.5)(0.08) + (0.5)(0.0059) = 0.04295 = 4.295\%$$

Canadian cost of funds + U.K. cost of funds = Overall cost

Net return:

Average return on assets − Average cost of funds

$$6.61\% - 4.295\% = 2.315\%$$

The Appreciating Pound

When the pound appreciates over the year from $1.60/£1 to $1.70/£1, the return on British loans is equal to 22.188 percent. Now consider the dollar cost of British one-year GICs at the end of the year when the FI has to pay the principal and interest to the GIC holder:

$$£69.375 \text{ million} \times \$1.70/£1 = \$117.9375 \text{ million}$$

or a dollar cost of funds of 17.9375 percent. Thus, at the end of the year:

Average return on assets:

$$(0.5)(0.09) + (0.5)(0.22188) = 0.15594 \text{ or } 15.594\%$$

Average cost of funds:

$$(0.5)(0.08) + (0.5)(0.179375) = 0.12969 \text{ or } 12.969\%$$

Net return:

$$15.594 - 12.969 = 2.625\%$$

Note that even though the FI locked in a positive return when setting the net foreign exchange exposure on the balance sheet to zero, net return is still volatile. Thus, the FI is still exposed to foreign exchange risk. However, by directly matching its foreign asset and liability book, an FI can lock in a positive return or profit spread whichever direction exchange rates change over the investment period. For example, even if domestic banking is a relatively low-profit activity (i.e., there is a low spread between the return on assets and the cost of funds), the FI could be quite profitable overall. Specifically, it could lock in a large positive spread—if it exists—between deposit rates and loan rates in foreign markets. In our example, a 4 percent positive spread existed between British one-year loan rates and deposit rates compared with only a 1 percent spread domestically.

Note that for such imbalances in domestic spreads and foreign spreads to continue over long periods of time, financial service firms would have to face significant barriers to entry in foreign markets. Specifically, if real and financial capital is free to move, FIs would increasingly withdraw from the Canadian market and reorient their operations toward the United Kingdom. Reduced competition would widen loan deposit interest spreads in Canada, and increased competition would contract U.K. spreads, until the profit opportunities from foreign activities disappeared. We discuss FIs' abilities, and limits on their abilities, to engage in cross-border financial and real investments further in Chapter 22.[15]

Hedging with Forwards

Instead of matching its $100 million foreign asset position with $100 million of foreign liabilities, the FI might have chosen to remain unhedged on the balance sheet.[16] As a lower-cost alternative, it could hedge by taking a position in the forward market for foreign currencies—for example, the one-year forward market for selling sterling for dollars. We discuss the nature and use of forward contracts by FI managers more extensively in Chapter 23; however, here we introduce them to show how they can insulate the FX risk of the FI in our example. Any forward position taken would not appear on the balance sheet; it would appear as a contingent off-balance-sheet claim, which we described in Chapter 13 as an item below the bottom line. The role of the forward FX contract is to offset the uncertainty regarding the future spot rate on sterling at the end of the one-year investment horizon. Instead of waiting until the end of the year to transfer sterling back into dollars at an unknown spot rate, the FI can enter into a contract to sell forward its *expected* principal and interest earnings on the loan, at today's known **forward exchange rate** for dollars/pounds, with delivery of sterling funds to the buyer of the forward contract taking place at the end of the year. Essentially, by selling the expected proceeds on the sterling loan forward, at a known (forward FX) exchange rate today, the FI removes the future spot exchange rate uncertainty and thus the uncertainty relating to investment returns on the British loan.

forward exchange rate
The exchange rate agreed to today for future (forward) delivery of a currency.

---

[15] In the background of the previous example was the implicit assumption that the FI was also matching the durations of its foreign assets and liabilities. In our example, it was issuing one-year duration sterling GICs to fund one-year duration sterling loans. Suppose instead that it still had a matched book in size ($100 million) but funded the one-year 15 percent British loans with three-month 11 percent sterling GICs.

$$D_{£A} - D_{£L} = 1 - 0.25 = 0.75 \text{ years}$$

Thus, sterling assets have a longer duration than do sterling liabilities.

If British interest rates were to change over the year, the market value of sterling assets would change by more than the market value of sterling liabilities. This effect should be familiar from Chapter 9. More importantly, the FI would no longer be locking in a fixed return by matching in the size of its foreign currency book since it would have to take into account its potential exposure to capital gains and losses on its sterling assets and liabilities due to shocks to British interest rates. In essence, an FI is hedged against both foreign exchange rate risk and foreign interest rate risk only if it matches both the size and the durations of its foreign assets and liabilities in a specific currency.

[16] An FI could also hedge its on-balance-sheet FX risk by taking off-balance-sheet positions in futures, swaps, and options on foreign currencies. Such strategies are discussed in detail in Chapters 23 through 25.

EXAMPLE 14–3

Hedging with Forwards

Consider the following transactional steps when the FI hedges its FX risk immediately by selling its expected one-year sterling loan proceeds in the forward FX market (illustrated in panel (c) of Figure 14–2).

1. The FI sells $100 million for pounds at the *spot* exchange rate *today* and receives $100 million/1.6 = £62.5 million.

2. The FI then immediately lends the £62.5 million to a British customer at 15 percent for one year.

3. The FI also sells the expected principal and interest proceeds from the sterling loan forward for dollars at today's forward rate for one-year delivery. Let the current forward one-year exchange rate between dollars and pounds stand at $1.55/£1, or at a 5 cent discount to the spot pound; as a percentage discount:

$$(\$1.55 - \$1.60)/\$1.6 = -3.125\%$$

This means that the forward buyer of sterling promises to pay

$$\text{£62.5 million } (1.15) \times \$1.55/\text{£1} = \text{£71.875 million} \times \$1.55/\text{£1} = \$111.406 \text{ million}$$

to the FI (the forward seller) in one year when the FI delivers the £71.875 million proceeds of the loan to the forward buyer.

4. In one year, the British borrower repays the loan to the FI plus interest in sterling (£71.875 million).

5. The FI delivers the £71.875 million to the buyer of the one-year forward contract and receives the promised $111.406 million.

Barring the sterling borrower's default on the loan or the forward buyer's reneging on the forward contract, the FI knows from the very beginning of the investment period that it has locked in a guaranteed return on the British loan of

$$\frac{\$111.406 - \$100}{\$100} = 0.11406 = 11.406\%$$

Specifically, this return is fully hedged against any dollar/pound exchange rate changes over the one-year holding period of the loan investment. Given this return on British loans, *the overall expected return* on the FI's asset portfolio is

$$(0.5)(0.09) + (0.5)(0.11406) = 0.10203 \text{ or } 10.203\%$$

Since the cost of funds for the FI's $200 million GICs is an assumed 8 percent, it has been able to lock in a risk-free return spread over the year of 2.203 percent regardless of spot exchange rate fluctuations between the initial foreign (loan) investment and repatriation of the foreign loan proceeds one year later.

In the preceding example, it is profitable for the FI to increasingly drop domestic loans and invest in hedged foreign U.K. loans, since the hedged dollar return on foreign loans of 11.406 percent is so much higher than 9 percent domestic loans. As the FI seeks to invest more in British loans, it needs to buy more spot sterling. This drives up the spot price of sterling in dollar terms to more than $1.60/£1. In addition, the FI would need to sell more sterling forward (the proceeds of these sterling loans) for dollars, driving the forward rate to below $1.55/£1. The outcome would widen the dollar forward-spot exchange rate spread on sterling, making forward hedged sterling investments less attractive than before. This process would continue until the Canadian cost of FI funds just equals the forward hedged return on British loans. That is, the FI could make no further profits by borrowing in dollars and making forward contract-hedged investments in U.K. loans.

Multicurrency Foreign Asset–Liability Positions

So far, we have used a one-currency example of a matched or mismatched foreign asset–liability portfolio. Many FIs, including banks, mutual funds, and pension funds, hold multicurrency asset–liability positions. As for multicurrency trading portfolios, diversification across many asset and liability markets can potentially reduce the risk of portfolio returns and the cost of funds. To the extent that domestic and foreign interest rates or stock returns for equities do not move closely together over time, potential gains from asset–liability portfolio diversification can offset the risk of mismatching individual currency asset–liability positions.

real interest rate
The difference between a nominal interest rate and the expected rate of inflation.

Theoretically speaking, the one-period nominal interest rate (r_i) on fixed-income securities in any particular country has two major components. First, the **real interest rate** reflects underlying real sector demand and supply for funds in that currency. Second, the *expected inflation rate* reflects an extra amount of interest lenders demand from borrowers to compensate the lenders for the erosion in the principal (or real) value of the funds they lend due to inflation in goods prices expected over the period of the loan. Formally,[17]

$$r_i = rr_i + i_i^e$$

where

r_i = Nominal interest rate in country i

rr_i = Real interest rate in country i

i_i^e = Expected one-period inflation rate in country i

If real savings and investment demand and supply pressures, as well as inflationary expectations, are closely linked or integrated across countries, we expect to find that nominal interest rates are highly correlated across financial markets. For example, if, as the result of a strong demand for investment funds, German real interest rates rise, there may be a capital outflow from other countries toward Germany. This may lead to rising real and nominal interest rates in other countries as policymakers and borrowers try to mitigate the size of their capital outflows. On the other hand, if the world capital market is not very well integrated, quite significant nominal and real interest deviations may exist before equilibrating international flows of funds materialize. Foreign asset or liability returns are likely to be relatively weakly correlated, and significant diversification opportunities exist.

Table 14–6 lists the correlations among the returns on long-term government bonds in major equity and bond markets in the early 2000s. Looking at correlations between foreign bond market returns and U.S. bond market returns, you can see that the correlations across bond markets vary from a high of 0.452 between Canada and the United States to a low of 0.068 between Canada and Germany. Further, these correlations are all positive.[18]

---

[17] This equation is often called the *Fisher equation,* named after Irving Fisher, the economist who first publicized this hypothesized relationship among nominal rates, real rates, and expected inflation. As shown, we ignore the small cross-product term between the real rate and the expected inflation rate.

[18] From the Fisher relationship, high correlations may be due to high correlations of real interest rates over time and/or inflation expectations.

TABLE 14–6
Correlations of Returns on Equity and Bonds in Local Currencies

Source: L. Cappiello, R. F. Engle, and K. Sheppard, *Asymmetric Dynamics in the Correlations of Global Equity and Bond Returns,* Working paper, Stern School of Business, New York University, 2005.

	United States	United Kingdom	Germany	Canada
Equity Markets				
United States	1.000	0.495	0.432	0.692
United Kingdom	0.495	1.000	0.562	0.463
Germany	0.432	0.562	1.000	0.399
Canada	0.692	0.463	0.399	1.000
Bond Markets				
United States	1.000	0.249	0.221	0.452
United Kingdom	0.249	1.000	0.656	0.167
Germany	0.221	0.656	1.000	0.068
Canada	0.452	0.167	0.068	1.000

CONCEPT QUESTIONS

1. The cost of one-year Canadian dollar GICs is 8 percent, one-year Canadian dollar loans yield 10 percent, and U.K. pound loans yield 15 percent. The dollar/pound spot exchange is $1.50/£1, and the one-year forward exchange rate is $1.48/£1. Are one-year Canadian dollar loans more or less attractive than U.K. pound loans?
2. What are two ways an FI manager can control FX exposure?

INTERACTION OF INTEREST RATES, INFLATION, AND EXCHANGE RATES

As global financial markets have become increasingly interlinked, so have interest rates, inflation, and foreign exchange rates. For example, higher domestic interest rates may attract foreign financial investment and impact the value of the domestic currency. In this section, we look at the effect that inflation in one country has on its foreign currency exchange rates—purchasing power parity (PPP). We also examine the links between domestic and foreign interest rates and spot and forward foreign exchange rates—interest rate parity (IRP).

Purchasing Power Parity

One factor affecting a country's foreign currency exchange rate with another country is the relative inflation rate in each country (which, as shown below, is directly related to the relative interest rates in these countries). Specifically,

$$r_{CAN} = i_{CAN} + rr_{CAN}$$

and

$$r_S = i_S + rr_S$$

where

$$
\begin{aligned}
r_{CAN} &= \text{Interest rate in Canada} \\
r_S &= \text{Interest rate in Switzerland (or another foreign country)} \\
i_{CAN} &= \text{Inflation rate in Canada} \\
i_S &= \text{Inflation rate in Switzerland (or another foreign country)} \\
rr_{CAN} &= \text{Real rate of interest in Canada} \\
rr_S &= \text{Real rate of interest in Switzerland (or another foreign country)}
\end{aligned}
$$

Assuming real rates of interest (or rates of time preference) are equal across countries:

$$rr_{CAN} = rr_S$$

Then

$$r_{CAN} - r_S = i_{CAN} - i_S$$

The (nominal) interest rate spread between Canada and Switzerland reflects the difference in inflation rates between the two countries.

As relative inflation rates (and interest rates) change, foreign currency exchange rates that are not constrained by government regulation should also adjust to account for relative differences in the price levels (inflation rates) between the two countries. One theory that explains how this adjustment takes place is the theory of **purchasing power parity (PPP).** According to PPP, foreign currency exchange rates between two countries adjust to reflect changes in each country's price levels (or inflation rates and, implicitly, interest rates) as consumers and importers switch their demands for goods from relatively high inflation (interest) rate countries to low inflation (interest) rate countries. Specifically, the PPP theorem states that the change in the exchange rate between two countries' currencies is proportional to the difference in the inflation rates in the two countries. That is,

$$i_{Domestic} - i_{Foreign} = \Delta S_{Domestic\,/\,Foreign} / S_{Domestic\,/\,Foreign}$$

where

$S_{Domestic\,/\,Foreign}$ = Spot exchange rate of the domestic currency for the foreign currency (e.g., Canadian dollars for Swiss francs)

$\Delta S_{Domestic\,/\,Foreign}$ = Change in the one-period foreign exchange rate

Thus, according to PPP, the most important factor determining exchange rates is the fact that in open economies, differences in prices (and, by implication, price level changes with inflation) drive trade flows and thus demand for and supplies of currencies.

purchasing power parity (PPP)
The theory explaining the change in foreign currency exchange rates as inflation rates in the countries change.

EXAMPLE 14–4

Application of Purchasing Power Parity

Suppose that the current spot exchange rate of Canadian dollars for Russian roubles, $S_{CAN/R}$, is 0.17 (i.e., 0.17 dollar, or 17 cents, can be received for 1 rouble). The price of Russian-produced goods increases by 10 percent (i.e., inflation in Russia, i_R, is 10 percent), and the Canadian price index increases by 4 percent (i.e., inflation in Canada, i_{CAN}, is 4 percent). According to PPP, the 10 percent rise in the price of Russian goods relative to the 4 percent rise in the price of Canadian goods results in a depreciation of the Russian rouble (by 6 percent). Specifically, the exchange rate of Russian roubles to Canadian dollars should fall, so that[19]

Canadian inflation rate − Russian inflation rate

$$= \frac{\text{Change in spot exchange rate of Canadian dollars for Russian roubles}}{\text{Initial spot exchange rate of Canadian dollars for Russian roubles}}$$

or

$$i_{CAN} - i_R = \Delta S_{CAN/R} / S_{CAN/R}$$

---

[19] This is the relative version of the PPP theorem. There are other versions of the theory (such as the absolute PPP and the law of one price). However, the version shown here is the one most commonly used.

Plugging in the inflation and exchange rates, we get

$$0.04 - 0.10 = \Delta S_{CAN/R} / S_{CAN/R} = \Delta S_{CAN/R} / 0.17$$

or

$$-0.06 = \Delta S_{CAN/R} / 0.17$$

and

$$\Delta S_{CAN/R} = -(0.06) \times 0.17 = -0.0102$$

Thus, it costs 1.02 cents less to receive a rouble (i.e., 1 rouble costs 15.98 cents: 17 cents − 1.02 cents), or 0.1598 of $1 can be received for 1 rouble. The Russian rouble depreciates in value by 6 percent against the Canadian dollar as a result of its higher inflation rate.[20]

Interest Rate Parity Theorem

interest rate parity theorem
Relationship in which the discounted spread between domestic and foreign interest rates equals the percentage spread between forward and spot exchange rates.

We discussed earlier that foreign exchange spot market risk can be reduced by entering into forward foreign exchange contracts. In general, spot rates and forward rates for a given currency differ. The forward exchange rate is determined by the spot exchange rate and the interest rate differential between the two countries. The specific relationship that links spot exchange rates, interest rates, and forward exchange rates is described as the **interest rate parity theorem** (IRPT). Intuitively, the IRPT implies that by hedging in the forward exchange rate market, an investor realizes the same returns whether investing domestically or in a foreign country. This is a so-called *no-arbitrage relationship* in the sense that the investor cannot make a risk-free return by taking offsetting positions in the domestic and foreign markets. That is, the hedged dollar return on foreign investments just equals the return on domestic investments. The eventual equality between the cost of domestic funds and the hedged return on foreign assets, or the IRPT, can be expressed as

$$1 + r_t^D = \frac{1}{S_t} \times [1 + r_{ukt}^L] \times F_t$$

Rate on domestic investment = Hedged return on foreign (U.K.) investment

where

$$1 + r_t^D = 1 \text{ plus the interest rate on GICs for the FI at time } t$$
$$S_t = \$/£ \text{ spot exchange rate at time } t$$
$$1 + r_{ukt}^L = 1 \text{ plus the interest rate on U.K. loans at time } t$$
$$F_t = \$/£ \text{ forward exchange at time } t$$

EXAMPLE 14–5

An Application of Interest Rate Parity Theorem

Suppose $r_t^D = 8$ percent and $r_{ukt}^L = 15$ percent, as in our preceding example. As the FI moves into more British loans, suppose the spot exchange rate for buying pounds rises from \$1.60/£1 to \$1.63/£1. In equilibrium, the forward exchange rate would have to fall to \$1.5308/£1 to eliminate completely the attractiveness of British investments to the FI manager. That is,

$$(1.08) = \left(\frac{1}{1.63}\right)[1.15](1.5308)$$

---

[20] A 6 percent fall in the rouble's value translates into a new exchange rate of 0.1598 dollars per rouble if the original exchange rate between dollars and roubles was 0.17.

This is a *no-arbitrage* relationsip in the sense that the hedged dollar return on foreign investments just equals the FI's dollar cost of domestic GICs. Rearranging, the IRPT can be expressed as

$$\frac{r_t^D - r_{ukt}^L}{1 + r_{ukt}^L} \simeq \frac{F_t - S_t}{S_t}$$

$$\frac{0.08 - 0.15}{1.15} \simeq \frac{1.5308 - 1.63}{1.63}$$

$$-0.0609 \simeq -0.0609$$

That is, the discounted spread between domestic and foreign interest rates is, in equilibrium, approximately equal to ($\simeq$) the percentage spread between forward and spot exchange rates.

Suppose that in the preceding example, the annual rate on domestic deposits is 8.1 percent (rather than 8 percent). In this case, it would be profitable for the investor to put excess funds in domestic rather than the U.K. deposits. In fact, the arbitrage opportunity that exists results in a flow of funds out of U.K. time deposits into domestic time deposits. According to the IRPT, this flow of funds would quickly drive up the dollar–British pound exchange rate until the potential profit opportunities from domestic deposits are eliminated. The implication of IRPT is that in a competitive market for deposits, loans, and foreign exchange, the potential profit opportunities from overseas investment for the FI manager are likely to be small and fleeting.[21] Long-term violations of IRPT are likely to occur only if there are major imperfections in international deposit, loan, and other financial markets, including barriers to cross-border financial flows.

CONCEPT QUESTIONS	1. **What is purchasing power parity?** 2. **What is the interest rate parity condition? How does it relate to the existence or non-existence of arbitrage opportunities?**

Summary

This chapter analyzed the sources of FX risk faced by modern FI managers. Such risks arise through mismatching foreign currency trading and/or foreign asset–liability positions in individual currencies. While such mismatches can be profitable if FX forecasts prove correct, unexpected outcomes and volatility can impose significant losses on an FI. They threaten its profitability and, ultimately, its solvency in a fashion similar to interest rate, off-balance-sheet, and credit risks. This chapter discussed possible ways to mitigate such risks, including direct hedging through matched foreign asset–liability books, hedging through forward contracts, and hedging through foreign asset and liability portfolio diversification. The financial crisis of 2008 indicated that settlement risk is also important in global foreign exchange trading. See the Industry Perspectives feature in Chapter 16 for a disscussion of counterparty risk related to foreign exchange transactions.

---

[21] Note that in a fully competitive market for loans and deposits (and free movement of exchange rates), not only would the domestic deposit rate equal the hedged return on U.K. loans (8 percent in our example), but the domestic loan rate (for risk-free loans) would also be driven into equality with the domestic GIC rate, that is, would fall from 9 percent to 8 percent.

Questions and Problems

1. What are the four FX risks faced by FIs?

2. What is the spot market for FX? What is the forward market for FX? What is the position of being net long in a currency?

3. Refer to Table 14–1.

   a. What was the spot exchange rate of Canadian dollars for U.S. dollars as a direct quote on March 17, 2009? As an indirect quote?

   b. What was the spot exchange rate of Canadian dollars for U.K. pound sterling as a direct quote on March 19, 2009? As an indirect quote?

4. Refer to Table 14–1.

   a. On February 19, 2009, Credit Union Jack purchased a U.K. pound-denominated inter-bank certificate of deposit (CD) by converting $1 million into pounds at a rate of 0.5701 pound per Canadian dollar. It is now March 19, 2009. Has the Canadian dollar appreciated or depreciated in value relative to the pound?

   b. Using the information in part (a), what is Credit Union Jack's foreign exchange gain or loss on the investment in the CD? Assume that no interest has been paid on the CD.

5. On March 19, 2009, Olympic Bank converts $500,000 Canadian dollars into U.S. dollars in the spot foreign exchange market and purchases a one-month forward contract to convert U.S. dollars into Canadian dollars. If the forward rate is US$0.8067 per Canadian dollar, how much will Olympic receive in Canadian dollars at the end of the month? Use the data in Table 14–1 for the spot rate.

6. X-IM Bank has ¥14 million in assets and ¥23 million in liabilities and has sold ¥8 million in foreign currency trading. What is the net exposure for X-IM? For what type of exchange rate movement does this exposure put the bank at risk?

7. What two factors directly affect the profitability of an FI's position in a foreign currency?

8. The following are the foreign currency positions of an FI, expressed in dollars.

Currency	Assets	Liabilities	FX Bought	FX Sold
Swiss francs (Sf)	$125,000	$50,000	$10,000	$15,000
British pound (£)	50,000	22,000	15,000	20,000
Japanese yen (¥)	75,000	30,000	12,000	88,000

   a. What is the FI's net exposure in Swiss francs?

   b. What is the FI's net exposure in British pounds?

   c. What is the FI's net exposure in Japanese yen?

   d. What is the expected loss or gain if the Sf exchange rate appreciates by 1 percent?

   e. What is the expected loss or gain if the £ exchange rate appreciates by 1 percent?

   f. What is the expected loss or gain if the ¥ exchange rate appreciates by 2 percent?

9. What are the four FX trading activities undertaken by FIs? How do FIs profit from these activities?

10. CB Bank issued $200 million of one-year GICs in Canada at a rate of 6.50 percent. It invested part of this money, $100 million, in the purchase of a one-year bond issued by a Canadian firm at an annual rate of 7 percent. The remaining $100 million was invested in a one-year Brazilian government bond paying an annual interest rate of 8 percent. The exchange rate at the time of the transactions was Brazilian real 1/$.

    a. What will be the net return on this $200 million investment in bonds if the exchange rate between the Brazilian real and the Canadian dollar remains the same?

    b. What will be the net return on this $200 million investment if the exchange rate changes to real 1.20/$?

    c. What will the net return on this $200 million investment be if the exchange rate changes to real 0.80/$?

11. An FI has purchased a 16 million one-year Swiss franc loan that pays 12 percent interest annually. The spot rate for Swiss franc is Sf1.60/$. Sun Bank has funded this loan by accepting a British pound (£)-denominated deposit for the equivalent amount and maturity at an annual rate of 10 percent. The current spot rate of the British pound is $1.60/£.

    a. What is the net interest income earned in dollars on this one-year transaction if the spot rates at the end of the year are Sf1.70/$ and $1.85/£?

    b. What should be the £ to $ spot rate in order for the bank to earn a net interest margin of 4 percent?

    c. Does your answer to part (b) imply that the dollar should appreciate or depreciate against the pound?

    d. What is the total effect on net interest income and principal of this transaction given the end-of-year spot rates in part (a)?

12. An FI recently made a one-year $10 million loan that pays 10 percent interest annually. The loan was funded with a Swiss francs-denominated one-year deposit at an annual rate of 8 percent. The current spot rate is Sf1.60/$.

   a. What will be the net interest income in dollars on the one-year loan if the spot rate at the end of the year is Sf1.58/$?

   b. What will be the net interest return on assets?

   c. How far can the Sf appreciate before the transaction will result in a loss for the FI?

   d. What is the total effect on net interest income and principal of this transaction given the end-of-year spot rates in part (a)?

13. What motivates FIs to hedge foreign currency exposures? What are the limitations to hedging foreign currency exposures?

14. What are the two primary methods of hedging FX risk for an FI? What two conditions are necessary to achieve a perfect hedge through on-balance-sheet hedging? What are the advantages and disadvantages of off-balance-sheet hedging in comparison to on-balance-sheet hedging?

15. North Bank has been borrowing in the U.S. markets and lending abroad, thus incurring foreign exchange risk. In a recent transaction, it issued a one-year US$2 million GIC at 6 percent and funded a loan in euros at 8 percent. The spot rate for the euro was €1.45/US$ at the time of the transaction.

   a. Information received immediately after the transaction closing indicated that the euro will depreciate to €1.47/US$ by year-end. If the information is correct, what will be the realized spread on the loan? What should have been the bank interest rate on the loan to maintain the 2 percent spread?

   b. The bank had an opportunity to sell one-year forward euros at €1.46. What would have been the spread on the loan if the bank had hedged forward its foreign exchange exposure?

   c. What would have been an appropriate change in loan rates to maintain the 2 percent spread if the bank intended to hedge its exposure using forward contracts?

16. A bank purchases a six-month US$1 million Eurodollar deposit at an annual interest rate of 6.5 percent. It invests the funds in a six-month Swedish krone bond paying 7.5 percent per year. The current spot rate is US$0.18/SK.

   a. The six-month forward rate on the Swedish krone is being quoted at US$0.1810/SK. What is the net spread earned on this investment if the bank covers its foreign exchange exposure using the forward market?

   b. What forward rate will cause the spread to be only 1 percent per year?

   c. Explain how forward and spot rates will both change in response to the increased spread.

   d. Why will a bank still be able to earn a spread of 1 percent knowing that interest rate parity usually eliminates arbitrage opportunities created by differential rates?

17. Explain the concept of interest rate parity. What does this concept imply about the long-run profit opportunities from investing in international markets? What market conditions must prevail for the concept to be valid?

18. Assume that annual interest rates are 8 percent in Canada and 4 percent in Japan. An FI can borrow (by issuing GICs) or lend (by purchasing GICs) at these rates. The spot rate is $0.60/¥.

   a. If the forward rate is $0.64/¥, how could the FI arbitrage using a sum of $1 million? What is the expected spread?

   b. What forward rate will prevent an arbitrage opportunity?

19. How does the lack of perfect correlation of economic returns between international financial markets affect the risk-return opportunities for FIs holding multicurrency assets and liabilities? Refer to Table 14–6. Which country pairings seem to have the highest correlation of returns on long-term government bonds?

20. What is the relationship between the real interest rate, the expected inflation rate, and the nominal interest rate on fixed-income securities in any particular country? Refer to Table 14–6. What factors may be the reasons for the relatively high correlation coefficients?

21. What is economic integration? What impact does the extent of economic integration of international markets have on the investment opportunities for FIs?

22. An FI has $100,000 of net positions outstanding in British pounds (£) and –$30,000 in Swiss francs (Sf). The standard deviation of the net positions as a result of exchange rate changes is 1 percent for the Sf and 1.3 percent for the £. The correlation coefficient between the changes in exchange rates of the £ and the Sf is 0.80.

   a. What is the risk exposure to the FI of fluctuations in the £/$ rate?

b. What is the risk exposure to the FI of fluctuations in the Sf/$ rate?

c. What is the risk exposure if both the £ and the Sf positions are combined?

23. A mutual fund manager is looking for some profitable investment opportunities and observes the following one-year interest rates on government securities and exchange rates: $r_{CAN} = 12\%, r_{UK} = 9\%$, $S = $ CDN$1.50/£, $f = $ CDN$1.6/£, where S is the spot exchange rate and f is the forward exchange rate. Which of the two types of government securities would constitute a better investment?

Web Questions

24. Go to the Royal Bank's website at www.royalbank.com and download RBC's latest annual report. Using the search function in Adobe Acrobat, search the document using the phrase "notional amount of derivatives" and find the table that lists RBC's holdings of derivatives for trading and other purposes. Which derivative had the highest notional amount? Which foreign exchange derivative had the highest notional amount? Search the document using the phrase "trading revenue." How has RBC's trading income from foreign exchange changed in the past year? How does RBC's trading income from foreign exchange compare with its trading income from other sources?

25. The Canadian Foreign Exchange Committee (CFEC) is an organization of the major participants in the foreign exchange market in Canada. Its membership includes the Bank of Canada and the federal Department of Finance. The CFEC publishes monthly statistics on foreign exchange trading in Canada. Go to the CFEC's website at www.cfec.ca and click on "FX Volumes and Rates." Download the latest report on FX volumes. How has the market volume in spot and forward contracts changed over the time period? How have the market volumes of foreign exchange swaps changed? Has the total Canadian dollar foreign exchange market volume increased or decreased over the time period?

Sovereign Risk

In this chapter, we examine sovereign risk, also called *country risk,* and discuss

▸ credit risk versus sovereign risk

▸ country risk evaluation models

▸ sovereign debt markets

INTRODUCTION

www.worldbank.org
www.imf.org

sovereign risk
The risk of a foreign government's limiting or preventing domestic borrowers in its jurisdiction from repaying amounts owed to external lenders.

debt moratorium
Delay in repaying interest and/or principal on a debt.

loan loss provision
An amount deducted from income and used to write off bad loans as the losses are realized.

www.osfi-bsif.gc.ca
www.cibc.com

In the 1970s, major international banks rapidly expanded their loans to Eastern European, Latin American, and other less-developed countries (LDCs). This was largely to meet these countries' demand for funds beyond those provided by the World Bank and the International Monetary Fund (IMF) to aid their development and to allow the international banks to recycle "petrodollar" funds from huge U.S. dollar-holders such as Saudi Arabia, dollars that helped to create the LIBOR market. Making LDC loans resulted in **sovereign risk** for the banks, the risk of a foreign government's limiting or preventing domestic borrowers in its jurisdiction from repaying the principal and interest on debt owed to external lenders. In many cases, these loans appear to have been made with little judgment regarding the credit quality of the sovereign country in which the borrower resided or consideration as to whether that body was a government-sponsored organization (e.g., Pemex, the state-owned Mexican oil company) or a private corporation.

The debt repayment problems of Poland and other Eastern European countries at the beginning of the 1980s and the **debt moratoria** announced by the Mexican and Brazilian governments in the fall of 1982 had a major and long-lasting impact on the banks' balance sheets and profits. In 1987, the newly formed Office of the Superintendent of Financial Institutions (OSFI) required Canadian banks to increase their **loan loss provisions** to 30 to 40 percent of their loans outstanding to 34 countries, including Mexico, Argentina, and Brazil. The Canadian banks made combined provisions of $8.5 billion on loans of $20.5 billion. The net dollar exposure of $12 billion ($20.5 − $8.5 billion) represented 66 percent of the Big Six Canadian banks' common equity. In 1989, Canadian Imperial Bank of Commerce (CIBC), which held $1.17 billion in non-Mexican LDC debt, increased its loan loss provisions by $525 million and took an after-tax charge to its 1989 earnings of $300 million. CIBC also restructured its Mexican debt, which totalled $604 million at the time. By comparison, the U.S. banks' average exposure to LDC debt in 1989 was 120 percent of total equity. Citicorp (now Citigroup) alone set aside US$5 billion in loan loss reserves after Brazil declared a debt moratorium on its US$68 billion commercial bank debt.

Notwithstanding their experience with LDC lending a decade earlier, international FIs began once again to invest considerable amounts in emerging-market countries in the late 1980s to early 1990s. Rather than making loans, however, the FIs concentrated their investments in debt and equity claims.[1] However, with rising trade deficits and declining foreign exchange reserves, as the result of an overvalued peso, Mexico devalued the peso on December 20, 1994.[2] The Mexican devaluation—as with the Mexican loan moratorium 12 years earlier—had devastating short-term repercussions on the Mexican capital markets as well as on other emerging markets. The run on emerging-market debt and equity markets was ameliorated only when U.S. President Clinton, along with the IMF, put together a US$50 billion international aid package, providing loan guarantees over three to five years to help restructure the debt. The IMF and the Bank for International Settlements (BIS) provided loans of US$17.8 billion and $10 billion, respectively. Mexican oil revenues were promised as collateral for the U.S. financial guarantees. By January 1997, the Mexican economy had improved and the Mexican government paid back all of its loans in full to the U.S. government.

Emerging markets in Asia faltered in 1997 when an economic and financial crisis in Thailand, a relatively small country in terms of financial markets, produced worldwide reactions. In early July, the devaluation of the Thai baht resulted in contagious devaluations of currencies throughout Southeast Asia (including those of Indonesia, Singapore, Malaysia, and South Korea) and the devaluations eventually spread to South America and Russia. Hong Kong, which pegged its currency to the U.S. dollar, was forced to take precautionary action by increasing interest rates and using China's foreign currency reserves to stabilize the Hong Kong dollar. In Russia, financial speculation was fuelled in part by the belief that the Russian government would not default on its bonds or let any of its major companies default on theirs.

Possibly as a reaction to the events (losses) experienced with the Latin American countries in the 1980s or to improved sovereign risk assessment techniques, (see later discussion) North American FIs held their exposure in Asia in the mid- and late-1990s to approximately one-third of the investment made by Japanese and European banks. As can be seen in Figure 15–1, in June 1997, foreign banks had US$389 billion in loans and other debt outstanding to emerging-market Asian

FIGURE 15–1
Foreign Banks' Share of Asian Debt in June 1997, excluding Singapore and Hong Kong

Source: Bank for International Settlements, June 1997, www.bis.org.

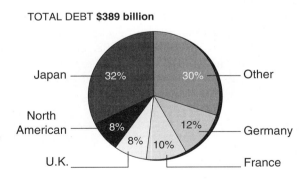

TOTAL DEBT **$389 billion**

Japan 32% — Other 30% — Germany 12% — France 10% — U.K. 8% — North American 8%

---

[1] The Basel I capital regulations came into effect for internationally active banks in the early 1990s, reducing the returns on commercial loans that required 100 percent capital. This is an example of how regulations can influence international financial markets. We discuss Basel I and II in more detail in Chapter 20.

[2] This "tequila crisis" saw Mexico's foreign exchange reserves fall from US$25 billion at the end of 1993 to US$6 billion at the end of 1994.

countries, with 8 percent (US$31.1 billion) to Canadian and U.S. banks. In 1999, North American banks wrote off hundreds of millions of dollars in losses as they accepted a payoff of less than five cents on the dollar for Russian securities.

As Asian currencies collapsed, financial institutions in countries such as Japan and Hong Kong failed or were forced to merge or restructure. Investment bank powerhouses such as Yamaichi Securities, Japan's fourth-largest securities firm, and Peregrine Investment Holding, Ltd., one of Hong Kong's largest investment banks, failed as currency values fell. Commercial banks in Japan and Hong Kong that had lent heavily to other Southeast Asian countries failed in record numbers as well. Estimates of problem loans held by Japanese banks totalled US$577.5 billion in September 1997, compared with US$210 billion in early August 1997. Financial support given to these countries by the International Monetary Fund (IMF) and the U.S., Japanese, and European governments enabled the banks largely to avoid the full extent of the possible losses. Nevertheless, Indonesia had to declare a moratorium on some of its debt repayments, while Russia defaulted on payments on its short-term government bonds.

More recently, in the early 2000s, concerns were raised about the ability of Argentina and Turkey to meet their debt obligations and the effects this would have on other emerging-market countries. For example, in December 2001, Argentina defaulted on US$130 billion in government-issued debt, and in 2002, passed legislation that led to defaults on US$30 billion of corporate debt owed to foreign creditors. The situation continued to deteriorate, and in November 2002 Argentina's government paid only US$79.5 million of an US$805 million repayment (that

www.scotiabank.com

had become more than 30 days delinquent) due to the World Bank. Table 15–1 shows the total external debt outstanding for Argentina as of June 2003 and March 2006. In an attempt to resolve the country's problem and restructure its debt, in January 2004 Argentina's government set up a voluntary register for creditors holding the country's defaulted bonds. However, as Argentina pulled out of its crisis, it was offering debtholders only 25 cents on the dollar for their holdings. In 2002, the Bank of Nova Scotia (BNS) sold its subsidiary in Argentina and left a country where it had done business for 40 years, taking an after-tax charge against earnings of $540 million.

Effective macroeconomic management, focused on the generation of primary fiscal surpluses, played a key role in the recovery of the Argentinian economy. As a result, by the mid-2000s, Argentina experienced rapid recovery from the economic and social crisis of 2001 and 2002. Economic growth in the country averaged 9 percent during 2003–2005 and averaged more than 8 percent in 2006 and 2007. Table 15–1 also shows the amount of external debt outstanding as of

TABLE 15–1

Statistics on External Debt Outstanding, Argentina, June 2003 and March 2006

Source: World Bank, *Joint BIS-IMF-OECD-World Bank Statistics on External Debt,* November 2003 and October 2006, www.worldbank.org.

Type of Debt	Amount Outstanding (US$ millions)	
	2003	2006
Bank loans	$ 25,052	$ 10,470
Debt securities issued abroad	84,740	69,210
Brady bonds	6,846	487
Multilateral claims	30,798	15,273
Total	$147,436	$ 95,440

March 2006. Notice the drop in external debt from US$147,436 million in 2003 to US$95,440 million in 2006.

These recurring experiences confirm the importance of assessing the country or sovereign risk of a borrowing country before making lending or other investment decisions such as buying foreign bonds or equities. We next look at measures of sovereign risk that FI managers can use as screening devices before making loans or other investment decisions. Appendix 15A, available at the Online Learning Centre at www.mcgrawhill.ca/olc/saunders, looks at the ways FIs have managed sovereign risk problems, including entering into **multi-year restructuring agreements (MYRAs)**, debt–equity swaps, loan sales, and **Brady bond** conversions. However, a country's economy can fail with little warning. In October 2008, investors became concerned about the size of Iceland's banking assets relative to the economy and withdrew their funds. Three banks failed, the krona collapsed and the stock market lost 80 percent of its value. Iceland received a US$2.1 billion loan from the IMF.

MYRAs
Multi-year restructuring agreements, the official terminology for a sovereign loan rescheduling.

Brady bonds
Bonds issued by an LDC that are swapped for an outstanding loan to that LDC.

CREDIT RISK VERSUS SOVEREIGN RISK

rescheduling
Changing the contractual terms of a loan, such as its maturity and interest payments.

To understand the difference between the sovereign risk and the credit risk on a loan or a bond, consider what happens to a domestic firm that refuses to repay, or is unable to repay, its loans. The lender would probably seek to work out the loan with the borrower by **rescheduling** its promised interest and principal payments on the loan into the future. Ultimately, continued inability or unwillingness to pay would likely result in bankruptcy proceedings and eventual liquidation of the firm's assets. Consider next a dollar loan made by an FI to a private Indonesian corporation. Suppose that this first-class corporation always maintained its debt repayments in the past; however, the Indonesian economy and the Indonesian government's reserve position are in bad shape. As a result, the Indonesian government refuses to allow any further debt repayment to be made in dollars to outside creditors. This puts the Indonesian borrower automatically into default even though, when viewed on its own, the company is a good credit risk. The Indonesian government's decision is a *sovereign* or *country risk event* in large part independent of the credit standing of the individual loan to the borrower. Further, unlike the situation in Canada, where the lender might seek a legal remedy in the local bankruptcy courts, there is no international bankruptcy court to which the lender can take the Indonesian government. That is, the lender's legal remedies to offset a sovereign country's default or moratoria decisions are very limited.

This situation suggests that making a lending decision to a party residing in a foreign country is a *two-step* decision. First, lenders must assess the underlying *credit quality* of the borrower, as it would do for a normal domestic loan, including setting an appropriate credit risk premium or credit limits (see Chapter 11). Second, lenders must assess the *sovereign risk quality* of the country in which the borrower resides. Should the credit risk or quality of the borrower be assessed as good but the sovereign risk be assessed as bad, the lender should not make the loan. When making international lending or foreign bond investment decisions, an FI manager should consider sovereign risk above considerations of private credit risk.

The World Bank assesses country risk based on several measures. These include political economy risk (the risk that powerful interest groups may undermine reform objectives by blocking implementation, capturing benefits, or reversing reform actions), exogenous risks (the risk of shocks to the external environment, such as a natural disaster or regional economic crisis that might have a bearing on the vulnerability of the poor), and other country risks (the threat of an increase in political instability or social tensions that could undermine effective implementation).[3] As we will see in this chapter, FI managers use many of these measures to assess country risk in their lending practices.

CONCEPT QUESTIONS

1. What is the difference between credit risk and sovereign risk?
2. In deciding to lend to a party residing in a foreign country, what two considerations must an FI weigh?

DEBT REPUDIATION VERSUS DEBT RESCHEDULING

A good deal of misunderstanding exists regarding the nature of a sovereign risk event. In general, a sovereign country's (negative) decisions on its debt obligations or the obligations of its public and private organizations may take two forms: repudiation and rescheduling.

repudiation
Outright cancellation of all current and future debt obligations by a borrower.

www.worldbank.org
www.imf.org

- *Debt repudiation.* **Repudiation** is an outright cancellation of all a borrower's current and future foreign debt and equity obligations. Since World War II, only China (1949), Cuba (1961), and North Korea (1964) have followed this course.[4] The low level of repudiations partly reflects recent international policy toward the poorest countries in the world. Specifically, in the fall of 1996, the World Bank, the International Monetary Fund, and major governments around the world agreed to forgive the external debt of the world's poorest, most heavily indebted poor countries (HIPCs). The HIPC initiative broke new ground by removing debt obligations from countries that pursue economic and social reform targeted at measurable poverty reduction. By 2003, 6 countries had received irrevocable debt relief under the HIPC initiative, and an additional 20 countries had begun to receive interim debt relief. Together, these countries had their outstanding debt reduced by US$40 billion. By March 2009, 35 countries had been approved for debt service relief of US$51 billion (on a year-end 2007 net present value basis). Twenty-nine of these countries are in Africa. Six additional countries are eligible for assistance. Repudiations on debt obligations were far more common before World War II, as we discuss later in this chapter.

- *Debt rescheduling.* Rescheduling has been the most common form of sovereign risk event. Specifically, a country (or a group of creditors in that country) declares a moratorium or delay on its current and future debt obligations and then seeks to ease credit terms through a rescheduling of the contractual terms, such as debt maturity and/or interest rates. Such delays may relate to the principal and/or the interest on the debt (South Korea in January 1998 and Argentina in 2001 are recent examples of debt reschedulings).

One of the interesting questions in the provision of international financial services is why we have generally witnessed international debtor problems (of

---

[3] See *A User's Guide to Poverty and Social Impact Analysis,* World Bank, 2003.

[4] With respect to equity, repudiation can include direct nationalization of private sector assets.

other than the poorest highly indebted countries) being met by reschedulings in the post-World War II period, whereas a large proportion of debt problems were met with repudiations before World War II. A fundamental reason given for this difference in behaviour is that until recently, most postwar international debt has been in *bank loans,* while before the war it was mostly in the form of *foreign bonds.*

International loan rather than bond financing makes rescheduling more likely for reasons related to the inherent nature of international loan versus bond contracts. First, there are generally fewer FIs in any international lending syndicate compared with thousands of geographically dispersed bondholders. The relatively small number of lending parties makes renegotiation or rescheduling easier and less costly than when a borrower or a bond trustee has to get thousands of bondholders to agree to changes in the contractual terms on a bond.[5]

Second, many international loan syndicates comprise the same groups of FIs, which adds to FI cohesiveness in loan renegotiations and increases the probability of consensus being reached. For example, Citigroup was chosen the lead bank negotiator by other banks in five major loan reschedulings in the 1980s, as well as in both the Mexican and South Korean reschedulings. JPMorgan Chase is the lead bank involved in the recent loan reschedulings of Argentina.

Third, many international loan contracts contain cross-default provisions that state that if a country were to default on just one of its loans, all the other loans it has outstanding would automatically be put into default as well. Cross-default clauses prevent a country from selecting a group of weak lenders for special default treatment and make the outcome of any individual loan default decision potentially very costly for the borrower.

A further set of reasons that rescheduling is likely to occur on loans relates to the behaviour of governments and regulators in lending countries. One of the overwhelming public policy goals in recent years has been to prevent large FI failures in countries such as Canada, the United States, Japan, Germany, and the United Kingdom. Thus, government-organized rescue packages for LDCs arranged either directly or indirectly via World Bank/IMF guarantees or the Brady Plan are ways of subsidizing large FIs and/or reducing the incentives for LDCs to default on their loans. To the extent that banks are viewed as special (see Chapter 1), domestic governments may seek political and economic avenues to reduce the probability of foreign sovereign borrowers defaulting on or repudiating their debt contracts. Governments and regulators appear to view the social costs of default on international bonds as less worrisome than those on loans. The reason is that bond defaults are likely to be more geographically and numerically dispersed in their effects, and bondholders do not play a key role in the provision of liquidity services to the domestic and world economy. It should also be noted that the tendency of the IMF/governments to bail out countries and thus, indirectly, FI lenders such as the major North American, Japanese, and European FIs, has not gone without criticism. Specifically, it has been argued that unless FIs and countries are ultimately punished, they will have no incentives to avoid similar risks in the future. This is one reason sovereign debt crises keep recurring.

As part of the aftermath of the 2008 financial crisis and the failure of countries (Iceland) and large systemically important global FIs, (AIG, Lehman Brothers),

---

[5] In January 1998 the rescheduling of South Korean loans required the agreement of just over 100 banks.

central banks and regulators are working to increase regulations on global FIs, including hedge funds. Chapter 20 deals with this issue in more depth.

CONCEPT QUESTIONS

1. **What is the difference between debt repudiation and debt rescheduling?**
2. **Provide four reasons we see sovereign loans being rescheduled rather than repudiated.**

COUNTRY RISK EVALUATION

In evaluating sovereign risk, an FI can use alternative methods, varying from the highly quantitative to the very qualitative. Moreover, as in domestic credit analysis, an FI may rely on outside evaluation services or develop its own internal evaluation or sovereign risk models. Of course, to make a final assessment, an FI may use many models and sources together because different measures of country risk are not mutually exclusive.

We begin by looking at three country risk assessment services available to outside investors and FIs: the *Euromoney Index,* the *Economist Intelligence Unit,* and the *Institutional Investor Index.* We then look at ways an FI manager might make internal risk assessments regarding sovereign risk.

Outside Evaluation Models

The Euromoney Index

LIBOR
The London Inter-bank Offered Rate; the rate charged on prime inter-bank loans on the Euromarket.

When originally published in 1979, the *Euromoney Index* was based on the spread in the Euromarket of the required interest rate on that country's debt over the London Interbank Offered Rate (**LIBOR**), adjusted for the volume and maturity of the issue. More recently, this has been replaced by an index based on a large number of economic and political factors weighted subjectively according to their perceived relative importance in determining country risk problems.

The Economist Intelligence Unit

www.economist.com

A sister firm of *The Economist,* the *Economist Intelligence Unit* (EIU) rates country risk by combining economic and political risk on a 100-point (maximum) scale. The higher the number, the worse the sovereign risk rating of the country. The EIU country risk ratings reported in 2008 are presented in Figure 15–2.

The Institutional Investor Index

Normally published twice a year, this index is based on surveys of the loan officers of major multinational banks. These officers give subjective scores regarding the credit quality of given countries. Originally, the score was based on 10, but since 1980 it has been based on 100, with a score of 0 indicating certainty of default and 100 indicating no possibility of default. The *Institutional Investor* then weighs the scores received from the officers surveyed by the exposure of each bank to the country in question. For a sampling of the *Institutional Investor's* country credit ratings as of March 2009, see Table 15–2. For example, in March 2009, loan officers around the world assessed Switzerland as the country with the least chance of default, while they assessed Zimbabwe as the country with the highest chance of default. In the period from September 2008 to March 2009, all countries listed

FIGURE 15–2
The *Economist Intelligence Unit* Country Risk Ratings

Source: *Economist.com*, October 22, 2008.

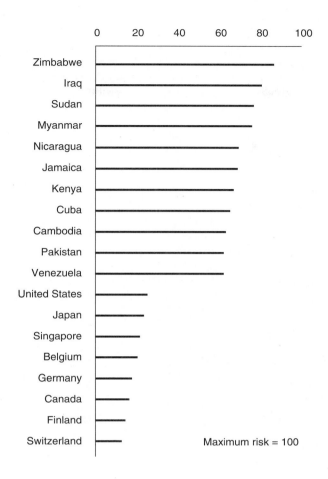

except Slovenia, Sierra Leone, Liberia, and Afghanistan showed a decline in credit rating. This reflects the global increase in credit risk in 2008.

Internal Evaluation Models

Statistical Models

By far, the most common approach to evaluating sovereign country risk among large FIs has been to develop sovereign country risk-scoring models based on key economic ratios for each country, similar to the domestic credit risk-scoring models discussed in Chapter 11.

An FI analyst begins by selecting a set of macro- and microeconomic variables and ratios that might be important in explaining a country's probability of rescheduling. Then the analyst uses past data on rescheduling and non-rescheduling countries to see which variables best discriminate between those countries that rescheduled their debt and those that did not. This helps the analyst identify a set of key variables that best explain rescheduling and a group of weights indicating the relative importance of these variables. For example, domestic credit risk analysis can employ discriminant analysis to calculate a Z score rating of the probability of corporate bankruptcy. Similarly, in sovereign risk analysis we can develop a

TABLE 15–2
*Institutional
Investor's* 2009
**Country Credit
Ratings**

Source: *Institutional Investor,*
April 2009, www.institutiona
linvestor.com.

Global Rank					
March 2009	**Sept. 2008**	**Country**	***Institutional Investor* Credit Rating**	**Six-Month Change**	**One-Year Change**
1	1	Switzerland	94.0	−2.0	−2.4
2	3	Norway	93.8	−1.4	−2.1
3	2	Luxembourg	93.7	−1.7	−2.6
4	4	Germany	92.6	−2.4	−2.2
5	5	Netherlands	92.5	−2.2	−2.5
6	7	Finland	92.3	−2.3	−2.6
7	9	Denmark	92.1	−1.9	−2.6
8	6	Canada	91.6	−3.1	−3.0
9	11	France	91.5	−2.2	−2.6
10	8	Sweden	91.3	−2.8	−3.5
11	10	Austria	90.0	−3.7	−4.6
12	14	Singapore	89.3	−2.6	−3.8
13	12	United Kingdom	88.5	−4.8	−5.5
14	16	Belgium	88.1	−3.2	−3.8
15	13	United States	88.0	−5.0	−5.8
16	18	Australia	86.7	−3.3	−4.5
17	15	Ireland	85.8	−5.8	−7.8
18	17	Japan	85.7	−4.9	−5.7
19	19	Spain	85.4	−3.9	−4.2
20	21	New Zealand	82.8	−3.2	−5.4
21	26	Slovenia	81.5	0.9	0.5
22	22	Hong Kong	81.0	−3.3	−3.1
23	24	Portugal	80.5	−3.1	−4.3
24	23	Italy	79.4	−4.2	−4.7
25	25	Taiwan	78.8	−2.5	−1.6
26*	30	Qatar	76.7	−3.1	−1.5
27*	31	Chile	76.7	−2.4	−0.7
28*	28	Greece	76.7	−3.3	−4.6
29	29	Malta	76.5	−3.4	−1.5
30	20	United Arab Emirates	76.0	−11.1	−4.3
170	169	Sierra Leone	12.2	0.3	1.1
171	170	Sudan	10.8	−0.5	−1.2
172	172	Liberia	10.2	−0.6	0.2
173	174	Afghanistan	9.9	1.2	1.4
174	173	Myanmar	9.7	−0.8	−0.7
175	175	Somalia	7.0	−0.9	−0.8
176	177	North Korea	5.3	−0.3	−1.0
177	176	Zimbabwe	4.6	−3.0	−1.2

*Order determined by results before rounding.

Z score to measure the probability that a country will reschedule (see Chapter 11 for discussion of the Z score model).[6]

The first step in this country risk analysis (CRA) is to pick a set of variables that may be important in explaining rescheduling probabilities. In many cases analysts

---

[6] Alternatively, analysts could employ linear probability, logit, or probit models.

select more than 40 variables. Here we identify the variables most commonly included in sovereign risk probability models.[7]

The Debt Service Ratio (DSR)

$$DSR = \frac{\text{Interest plus amortization on debt}}{\text{Exports}}$$

debt service ratio
The ratio of a country's interest and amortization obligations to the value of its exports.

A country's exports are its primary way of generating hard currencies. The larger the debt repayments in hard currencies are in relation to export revenues, the greater the probability that the country will have to reschedule its debt. Thus, there should be a *positive* relationship between the size of the **debt service ratio** and the probability of rescheduling. Table 15–3 shows the scheduled debt service ratios of various countries. Note that several countries are servicing debt obligations at several times the level of their exports (e.g., Argentina's debt service ratio is 230 percent, Brazil's debt service ratio is 158 percent).

The Import Ratio (IR)

$$IR = \frac{\text{Total imports}}{\text{Total foreign exchange reserves}}$$

Many countries must import manufactured goods since their inadequate infrastructure limits their domestic production. In times of famine, even food becomes a vital import. To pay for imports, the country must run down its stock of hard currencies—its foreign exchange reserves. The greater its need for imports—especially vital imports—the quicker a country can be expected to deplete its foreign exchange

TABLE 15–3
Debt Service Ratio for Various Countries, 2006

Source: *2008 World Development Indicators,* www.worldbank.org.

Country	Debt Service Ratio %
Argentina	230
Brazil	158
Chile	86
China	35
Colombia	143
Costa Rica	66
Ecuador	129
Indonesia	122
Malaysia	31
Philippines	101
Poland	97
Russian Federation	88
Rwanda	58
Thailand	40
Turkey	200
Venezuela	83

---

[7] See, for example, A. Saunders and L. Allen, *Credit Risk Measurement: New Approaches to Value at Risk and Other Paradigms,* 2nd ed. New York: John Wiley and Sons, 2002, and R. Brooks, R. W. Faff, and D. Hillier, "The National Market Impact of Sovereign Rating Changes," *Journal of Banking and Finance* 28, 2004, pp. 233–50.

reserves. For example, Brazil's import ratio was 113 percent in 2003, implying that Brazil imported more goods and services than it had foreign reserves to pay for. Since the first use of reserves is to buy vital imports, the larger the ratio of imports to foreign exchange reserves, the higher the probability that the country will have to reschedule its debt repayments. This is so because these countries generally view repaying foreign debt holders as being less important than supplying vital goods to the domestic population. Thus, the **import ratio** and the probability of rescheduling should be *positively* related.

import ratio
The ratio of a country's imports to its total foreign currency reserves.

Investment Ratio (INVR)

$$INVR = \frac{\text{Real investment}}{\text{GNP}}$$

investment ratio
The ratio of a country's real investment to its GNP.

The **investment ratio** measures the degree to which a country is allocating resources to real investment in factories, machines, and so on, rather than to consumption. The higher this ratio, the more productive the economy should be in the future and the lower the probability that the country would need to reschedule its debt: This implies a *negative* relationship between *INVR* and the probability of rescheduling. An opposing view is that a higher investment ratio allows a country to build up its investment infrastructure. The higher ratio puts it in a stronger bargaining position with external creditors since the country would rely less on funds in the future and would be less concerned about future threats of credit rationing by FIs should it request a rescheduling. This view argues for a *positive* relationship between the investment ratio and the probability of rescheduling, especially if the country invests heavily in import competing industries. Just before the collapse of their economies (in the mid-1990s) investment ratios in Thailand and Malaysia were 34 and 26 percent, respectively, while Brazil's investment ratio was close to zero. The investment ratio in the United Kingdom averaged 17 percent in the mid-2000s.

Variance of Export Revenue (VAREX)

$$VAREX = \sigma_{ER}^2$$

A country's export revenues may be highly variable as a result of two risk factors. *Quantity risk* means that the production of the raw commodities the country sells abroad—for example, coffee or sugar—is subject to periodic gluts and shortages. *Price risk* means that the international dollar prices at which the country can sell its exportable commodities are subject to high volatility as world demand for and supply of a commodity, such as copper, vary. The more volatile a country's export earnings, the less certain creditors can be that at any time in the future it will be able to meet its repayment commitments. That is, there should be a *positive* relationship between σ_{ER}^2 and the probability of rescheduling.

Domestic Money Supply Growth (MG)

$$MG = \frac{\Delta M}{M}$$

The faster the domestic growth rate of a country's money supply $\Delta M/M$, which measures the change in the money supply (ΔM) over its initial level (M), the higher the domestic inflation rate and the weaker that country's currency becomes in domestic and international markets.[8] When a country's currency loses credibility as a medium of exchange, real output is often adversely impacted, and the country must increasingly rely on hard currencies for both domestic and international payments. This happened for Argentina in 2003. These inflation, output, and payment effects suggest a *positive* relationship between domestic money supply growth and the probability of rescheduling.

We can summarize the expected relationships among these five key economic variables and the probability of rescheduling (p) for any country as:

$$p = f\,(DSR, IR, INVR, VAREX, MG \ldots)$$
$$\quad +\ \ +\ + \text{ or } -\quad +\qquad +$$

For example, P is positively related ($+$) to money supply growth (MG). After selecting the key variables, the FI manager normally places countries into two groups or populations:

P_1 = Bad (reschedulers)

P_2 = Good (non-reschedulers)

Then the manager uses a statistical methodology such as discriminant analysis (see Chapter 11) to identify which of these variables best discriminates between the population of rescheduling borrowers and that of non-rescheduling borrowers. Once the key variables and their relative importance or weights have been identified, the discriminant function can classify as good or bad current sovereign loans or sovereign loan applicants using currently observed values for the *DSR*, *IR*, and so on. Again, the methodology is very similar to the credit scoring models discussed in Chapter 11.

Problems with Statistical CRA Models

Even though this methodology has been one of the most common forms of CRA used by FIs, it is fraught with problems. This section discusses six major problems in using traditional CRA models and techniques. We do not imply in any way that these techniques should not be used but instead indicate that FI managers should be aware of the potential pitfalls in using such models.

Measurement of Key Variables   Very often the FI manager's information on a country's *DSR* or *IR* is out of date because of delays in collection of data and errors in measurement. For example, the Bank for International Settlements (BIS) collects aggregate loan volume data for countries; frequently, this information is six months old or more before it is published. This example illustrates the problem: The Bank of Nova Scotia may know today the current amount of its outstanding loans to Indonesia, but it is unlikely to know with any great degree of accuracy Indonesia's total outstanding external loans and debt with every other lender in the world.

www.bis.org

Moreover, these measurement problems are compounded by forecast errors when managers use these statistical models to predict the probabilities of rescheduling with future or projected values of key variables such as *DSR* and *IR*.

---

[8] The purchasing power parity (PPP) theorem argues that high relative inflation rates lead to a country's currency depreciating in value against other currencies.

Population Groups   Usually, analysts seek to find variables that distinguish between only two possible outcomes: reschedulers and non-reschedulers. In actuality, a finer distinction may be necessary—for example, a distinction between those countries announcing a moratorium on only interest payments and those announcing a moratorium on both interest and principal payments. Thus, Peru, which in the early 1980s limited its total debt repayments to a small proportion of its export revenues, should be viewed as a higher-risk country than a country that delayed the interest payments on its debt for a few months because of short-term foreign exchange shortages.

Political Risk Factors   Traditionally, CRA statistical credit scoring models incorporate only economic variables. While there may be a strong correlation between an economic variable such as money supply growth and rescheduling, the model may not capture very well purely political risk events such as *strikes, elections, corruption,* and *revolutions.* For example, the election of a strongly nationalist politician may reduce the probability of repayment and increase the probability of rescheduling. Similarly, a considerable part of the debt repayment and banking crisis problems in Southeast Asia has been attributed to cronyism and corruption.

www.heritage.org   Since 1995, the *Index of Economic Freedom* (compiled by the Heritage Foundation) has provided a measure that summarizes the economic freedom of over 160 countries in the world. The 2009 report covered 183 countries and stated that a "comprehensive definition of economic freedom should *encompass all liberties and rights of production, distribution, or consumption of goods and services. The highest form of economic freedom should provide an absolute right of property ownership; fully realized freedoms of movement for labor, capital, and goods; and an absolute absence of coercion or constraint of economic liberty beyond the extent necessary for citizens to protect and maintain liberty itself.*"[9] The ten categories measured by the index are business freedom, trade freedom, fiscal freedom, government size, monetary freedom, investment freedom, financial freedom, property rights, freedom from corruption, and labour freedom. Each country is assigned a score out of 100 for each of the factors as well as an overall score based on the average of these factors. An index of 100 signifies policies most conducive to economic freedom. The lower a country's score, the lower its economic freedom. Table 15–4 lists the economic freedom index for the highest- and lowest-rated countries based on data as of June 30, 2008. It is interesting to note that the government interventions that were made to support the world's financial system in 2008, particularly in the United States and Europe, may cause the economic freedom scores to be lower in the years to come as the world moves to increase the regulation of FIs.

An alternative quantitative measure of country risk is the *Corruption Perceptions Index* produced by Transparency International. Figure 15–3 shows the corruption index for 18 out of 180 countries covered for 2008. The least-corrupt countries are assigned a score of 10, while the most-corrupt countries are assigned a score of 0.[10]

---

[9] See *2009 Index of Economic Freedom.* Washington, DC: Heritage Foundation, 2009, Chapter 1, p. 11.

[10] J. deHaan and W. J. Kooi, in "Does Central Bank Independence Really Matter? New Evidence for Developing Countries Using a New Indicator," *Journal of Banking and Finance* 24, 2000, pp. 643–64, find that the turnover rate of central bank governors is also an indicator of central bank independence, which in turn is found to affect the economic health (and, consequently, country risk) of the countries examined. C. Pantzalis, D. A. Stangeland, and H. J. Turtle, in "Political Elections and the Resolution of Uncertainty: The International Evidence," *Journal of Banking and Finance* 24, 2000, pp. 1575–1604, find that stock markets react positively in less-free countries when a political election is won by the opposition or lost by the incumbent government.

TABLE 15–4
Economic Freedom Index for Various Countries

Source: The Heritage Foundation website, April 2009, www.heritage.org.

Country	Overall Economic Freedom Index
Hong Kong	90.0
Singapore	87.1
Australia	82.6
Ireland	82.2
New Zealand	82.0
United States	80.7
Canada	80.5
Denmark	79.6
Switzerland	79.4
United Kingdom	79.0
São Tomé & Principe	43.8
Libya	43.5
Comoros	43.3
Democratic Republic of Congo	42.8
Venezuela	39.9
Eritrea	38.5
Burma	37.7
Cuba	27.9
Zimbabwe	22.7
North Korea	2.0

FIGURE 15–3
Corruption Perceptions Index, 2009

Source: Transparency International, November 2009, www.transparency.org.

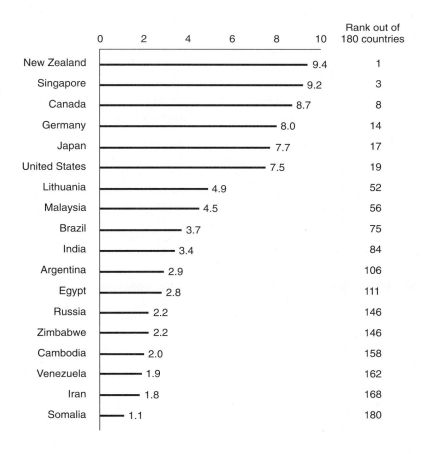

Country	Index	Rank out of 180 countries
New Zealand	9.4	1
Singapore	9.2	3
Canada	8.7	8
Germany	8.0	14
Japan	7.7	17
United States	7.5	19
Lithuania	4.9	52
Malaysia	4.5	56
Brazil	3.7	75
India	3.4	84
Argentina	2.9	106
Egypt	2.8	111
Russia	2.2	146
Zimbabwe	2.2	146
Cambodia	2.0	158
Venezuela	1.9	162
Iran	1.8	168
Somalia	1.1	180

Portfolio Aspects   Traditional CRA considers each country separately. However, many large banks with sovereign risk exposures hold a portfolio of emerging-market loans. In a portfolio context, the risk of holding a well-diversified portfolio of sovereign loans may be smaller than that of having a portfolio heavily concentrated in non-oil-producing emerging-market loans. In particular, the lender may distinguish between those key risk indicator variables having a *systematic* effect on the probability of repayment across a large number of sovereign countries and those variables having an *unsystematic* effect by impacting only one or a few countries.

One way to address this problem is to employ a portfolio framework (such as those discussed in Chapter 12) for sovereign risk analysis. Such an analysis would identify those indicator variables that have a *systematic* impact across all borrowers' probability of repayment and those that tend to be country-specific (or *unsystematic*). The indicator variables that the FI manager should really be concerned with are the *systematic* variables since they cannot be diversified away in a multi-sovereign loan portfolio. By comparison, unsystematic, or country-specific, risks can be diversified away. Consider the following model:

$$X_i = a_i + b_i\overline{X} + e_i$$

where

X_i = Key variable or country risk indicator for country i (e.g., the *DSR* for country i)

$\overline{X}$ = Weighted index of this key risk indicator across all countries to which the lender makes loans (e.g., the *DSR* for each country weighted by the shares of loans for each country in the FI's portfolio)

e_i = Other factors impacting X_i for any given country

Expressing this equation in variance terms, we get:

$$\begin{aligned} VAR(X_i) &= b_i^2 VAR(\overline{X}) + VAR\,(e_i) \\ \text{Total risk} &= \text{Systematic risk} + \text{Unsystematic risk} \end{aligned}$$

From this equation, you can see that the total risk or variability of any given risk indicator for a country, such as the *DSR* for Nigeria, can be divided into a non-diversifiable *systematic* risk element that measures the extent to which that country's *DSR* moves in line with the *DSR*s of all other debtor countries and an unsystematic risk element that impacts the *DSR* for Nigeria independently. The greater the size of the *unsystematic* element relative to the systematic risk element, the less important this variable is to the lender since it can be diversified away by holding a broad array of sovereign loans.

EXAMPLE 15–1

Calculating Sovereign Risk for an FI's Portfolio

The average σ^2_{INVR} (or *INVR* = investment ratio) of a group of countries has been estimated at 20 percent. The individual *INVR*s of two countries in the portfolio, Belgium and Hong Kong, have been estimated at 10 percent and 20 percent, respectively. The regression of individual country *INVR* on average INVR provides the following beta coefficient estimates:

$$\beta_B = \text{Beta of Belgium} = 0.75$$
$$\beta_{HK} = \text{Beta of Hong Kong} = 0.60$$

Based only on the *INVR* estimates, Hong Kong should be charged a higher risk premium because its *INVR* (20 percent) is higher than is Belgium's (10 percent). However, if the FI includes systematic risk in its estimation of risk premiums, the addition of loans to Hong Kong will reduce the overall systematic risk of the FI's foreign loan portfolio. In this case, it benefits the FI to add Hong Kong to its list of countries because its unsystematic risk can be diversified away.

L. S. Goodman found that for the 1970–83 period, the *DSR* had a high systematic element across countries, as did export revenue variance (*VAREX*).[11] This implies that when one country was experiencing a growing debt burden relative to its exports, so were all others. Similarly, when commodity prices or world demand collapsed for one debtor country's commodity exports, the same occurred for other debtor countries as well. A possible reason for the high systematic risk of the *DSR* is the sensitivity of this ratio to rising nominal and real interest rates in the developed (or lending) countries. As we discussed in Chapter 14, international interest rates tend to be positively correlated over time. A possible reason for the high systematic risk of the export variance is the tendency of prices and world demands for commodities to reflect simultaneously economic conditions such as recessions and expansions in developed countries.

By comparison, money supply growth ($\Delta M/M$) and the import ratio appear to have low systematic elements.[12] This is not surprising since control over the money supply and the use of domestic reserves are relatively discretionary variables for governments. Thus, while Argentina may choose a money supply growth rate of 50 percent per annum, the Chilean government may choose a target rate of 10 percent per annum. Similarly, the Argentinean and Chilean economies may have very different demands for imports, and the scale of vital imports may differ quite widely across countries. Using this type of analysis allows an FI manager to focus on relatively few variables such as the *DSR*s and export variances that affect the risk of the sovereign loan portfolio.

In another study[13] of systematic risk versus non-systematic risk, for 54 LDCs over the 1974–1987 period, looking at *Institutional Investor* ratings of a country as the risk indicator variable, it was found that the systematic versus non-systematic risk components varied from 97 percent versus 3 percent for Argentina to 41 percent versus 59 percent for Russia. This would suggest, all else being equal, that an FI should hold more Russian than Argentinean loans—although the experience of FIs in 2002 with Russian defaults and in 2003 with Argentinian defaults may call into question the appropriateness of the portfolio approach and especially, the ability of FIs to diversify away unsystematic sovereign risk in a contagious crisis. More recently, value-at-risk models have been applied to (Dutch) government bond portfolios.[14] Similar to the discussion in Chapter 12, this line of research examines total losses on portfolios of government debt in the worst-case (say, 1 percent) scenario.[15]

---

[11] See L. S. Goodman, "Diversifiable Risks in LDC Lending: A 20/20 Hindsight View," *Studies in Banking and Finance* 3, 1986, pp. 249–62.

[12] Ibid.

[13] See M. Palmer and T. B. Sanders, "A Model for Diversifying International Loan Portfolios," *Journal of Financial Services Research,* 1996, pp. 359–71.

[14] See P. J. G. Vlaar, "Value at Risk Models for Dutch Bond Portfolios," *Journal of Banking and Finance* 24, 2000, pp. 1131–54.

[15] VaR models might also be applied to a country's FX revenues—to evaluate its ability to withstand shocks or crises.

Incentive Aspects   CRA statistical models often identify variables based on rather loose or often non-existent analyses of the borrower's or lender's incentives to reschedule. Rarely are the following questions asked: What are the *incentives* or *net benefits* to a country seeking a rescheduling? What are the incentives or net benefits to an FI that grants a rescheduling? That is, what determines the demand for rescheduling by borrowers and the supply of rescheduling by lenders (FIs)? Presumably, only when the benefits outweigh the costs for both parties does rescheduling occur. Consider the following benefits and costs of rescheduling for borrowers on the one hand and FIs on the other.

Borrowers
Benefits

- By rescheduling its debt, the borrower lowers the present value of its future payments in hard currencies to outside lenders. This allows it to increase its consumption of foreign imports and/or increase the rate of its domestic investment.

Costs

- By rescheduling now, the borrower may close itself out of the market for loans in the future. As a result, even if the borrower encounters high-growth investment opportunities in the future, it may be difficult or impossible to finance them.
- Rescheduling may result in significant interference with the borrower's international trade since it would be difficult to gain access to instruments such as letters of credit, without which trade may be more costly.[16]

Lenders (FIs)
Benefits

- Once a loan has been made, a rescheduling is much better than a borrower default. With a rescheduling, the FI lender may anticipate some present value loss of principal and interest on the loan; with an outright default, the FI stands to lose all its principal and future interest repayments.
- The FI can renegotiate fees and various other collateral and option features into a rescheduled loan.
- There may be tax benefits to an FI's taking a recognized write-down or loss in value on a rescheduled sovereign loan portfolio.[17]

Costs

- Through rescheduling, loans become similar to long-term bonds or even equity, and the FI often becomes locked into a particular loan portfolio structure.
- Those FIs with large amounts of rescheduled loans are subject to greater regulatory attention. For example, in the United States, such FIs may be placed on the regulators' problem list of FIs.[18]

---

[16] See Chapter 13 on letters of credit.

[17] For example, in 1998 Deutsche Bank took a loan loss provision of nearly US$800 million against its Asian loan portfolio.

[18] The problem list singles out banks for special regulatory attention. Normally, examiners rate a problem list bank as 4 or 5 on a rating scale of 1 to 5, where 1 is good and 5 is bad.

All these relevant economic incentive considerations go into the demand for and the supply of rescheduling; however, it is far from clear how the simple statistical models just described incorporate this complex array of incentives. At a very minimum, statistical models should clearly reflect the underlying theory of rescheduling.

Stability   A final problem with simple statistical CRA models is that of stability. The fact that certain key variables may have explained rescheduling in the past does not mean that they will perform or predict well in the future. Over time, new variables and incentives affect rescheduling decisions, and the relative weights on the key variables change. This suggests that the FI manager must continuously update the CRA model to incorporate all currently available information and ensure the best predictive power possible. This is particularly true in today's new global environment of enhanced trade and competition, with major changes in production technology taking place in countries such as China and India.

Using Market Data to Measure Risk: The Secondary Market for Sovereign Debt

Since the mid-1980s, a secondary market for trading distressed sovereign debt has developed among large commercial and investment banks in New York and London. The volume of trading grew dramatically from around US$2 billion per year in 1984 to over US$6 billion today, with trading often taking place in the high-yield (or junk bond) departments of the participating FIs. Trading declined to US$4.2 billion in 1998 after the Russian debt defaults and again in 1999 after Ecuador's failure to pay interest on its Brady bonds (see below). Trading has also been adversely affected by schemes of the more successful emerging-market countries to get investors to swap Brady bonds for domestic government bonds (see below). The early 2000s were characterized by increasing trading activity and growing investor confidence in emerging markets, sparked in large part by Brazil's rapid economic recovery, Mexico's upgraded credit rating to investment grade, and Russia's successful debt restructuring.

These markets provide quoted prices for sovereign loans and other debt instruments that an FI manager can use for CRA. Before we look at how this might be done, we describe the structure and development of the markets for emerging-market loans and related debt instruments, including the determinants of market demand and supply.

The Structure of the Market

This secondary market in distressed sovereign debt has considerably enhanced the liquidity of these loans on bank and other FI balance sheets.[19] The following are the market players that sell and buy distressed loans and debt instruments.

Sellers
- large FIs willing to accept write-downs of loans on their balance sheets
- small FIs wishing to disengage themselves from the sovereign loan market

---

[19] Loans change hands when one creditor assigns the rights to all future interest payments and principal payments to a buyer. In most early market transactions, the buyer had to get the permission of the sovereign debtor country before the loan could be assigned to a new party. The reason for this was that the country might have concerns as to whether the buyer was as committed to any new money deals as part of restructuring agreements as the original lender. Most recent restructuring agreements, however, have removed the right of assignment from the borrower (the sovereign country). This has increased liquidity in the loan market.

- FIs willing to swap one country's debt for another's to rearrange their portfolios of country risk exposures

Buyers
- wealthy investors, hedge funds (see Chapter 5), FIs, and corporations seeking to engage in debt-for-equity swaps or speculative investments
- FIs seeking to rearrange their balance sheets by reorienting their debt concentrations

The Early Market for Sovereign Debt

Consider the quote sheet from Salomon Brothers, in Table 15–5, for May 2, 1988—a relatively early stage of sovereign loan market development. As indicated in Table 15–5, FIs such as investment banks and major commercial banks acted as market makers, quoting two-way bid–ask prices for distressed sovereign debt.[20] Thus, an FI or an investor could have bought US$100 of Peruvian loans from Salomon for US$9 in May 1988, or at a 91 percent discount from face value. However, in selling the same loans to Salomon, the investor would have received only US$7 per US$100, or a 93 percent discount. The bid–ask spreads for certain countries were very large in this period; for example, Sudan's US$2 bid and US$10 ask exemplified a serious lack of market demand for the sovereign loans of many countries.

Developments in the Market for Sovereign Debt

In recent years there have been a large number of changes in the structure of the market. Initially, there were three market segments: Brady bonds, sovereign bonds, and bank loans.

Brady Bonds   The first segment of the market was that for Brady bonds. These reflected programs under which the U.S. and other FIs exchanged their dollar loans for dollar bonds issued by the relevant less-developed countries (LDCs). These bonds had a much longer maturity than that promised on the original loans and a lower promised original coupon (yield) than the interest rate on the original loan. However, the principal was usually collateralized through the issuing country's purchasing U.S. Treasury bonds and holding them in a special-purpose escrow account. Should that country default on its Brady bonds, the buyers of the bonds could access the dollar bonds held as collateral. These loan-for-bond restructuring programs, also called debt-for-debt swaps, were developed under the auspices of the U.S. Treasury's 1989 Brady Plan and international organizations such as the IMF. Once loans were swapped for bonds by banks and other FIs, they could be sold on the secondary market. For example, in March 2002, the 30-year Brazilian discount Brady bonds had a bid price of US$90.75 per US$100 of face value. These bonds had their principal repayments collateralized by U.S. Treasury bonds. As shown in Table 15–6, by 2006, the number of Brady bonds had declined to insignificant amounts, replaced by bank loans and other debt securities, as we discuss below. Mexico retired all of its Brady bonds in 2003 and, by 2007, Colombia, Brazil, Venezuela, and the Philippines had retired their Brady debt as well.

Without the financial crisis in 2008, Brady bonds might be a footnote to the 1980s LDC debt meltdown. However, in 2008, U.S. banks had **toxic assets** related to the subprime mortgage crisis on their balance sheets. The IMF estimated in April 2009 that banks globally would be required to write down assets of US$4.1 trillion.

toxic assets
Illiquid and non-performing assets on an FI's balance sheet, such as mortgage-backed securities and collateralized debt obligations.

---

[20] Major market makers include the Dutch ING bank, as well as Citigroup, JPMorgan, Bankers Trust, and Merrill Lynch.

TABLE 15–5   **Indicative Prices for Less-Developed-Country Bank Loans (US$)**

Country	Indicative Cash Prices		Swap Index		Trading Commentary
	Bid ($)	Offer ($)	Sell	Buy	
Algeria	91.00	93.00	5.22	6.71	Longer-dated paper resurfacing as cash substitute in swaps.
Argentina	29.00	30.00	0.66	0.67	Less volume this period; consolidation exercise slows note trades.
Bolivia	10.00	13.00	0.52	0.54	Minimal current activity.
Brazil	53.00	54.00	1.00	1.02	Rally topping out as supply catches up with auction interest.
Chile	60.50	61.50	1.19	1.22	Market firm and rising as deal calendar fills.
Colombia	67.00	68.00	1.42	1.47	Resurgence of interest as high-quality exit.
Costa Rica	13.00	16.00	0.54	0.56	Market building reserves of patience to deal with this name again.
Dominican Republic	17.00	20.00	0.57	0.59	Trading picks up at lower levels.
Ecuador	31.00	33.00	0.66	0.70	Occasional swaps surfacing.
Honduras	25.00	28.00	0.63	0.65	Viewed as expensive on a relative value basis.
Ivory Coast	30.00	33.00	0.67	0.70	Newly sighted by fee swappers.
Jamaica	33.00	36.00	0.70	0.73	Slow but serious inquiry continues.
Mexico	52.50	53.50	0.99	1.01	Prices continue upward drift on lower, lumpy flow.
Morocco	50.00	51.00	0.94	0.96	Fee swappers oblige sellers by jumping into the wider breach versus Latins.
Nicaragua	3.00	4.00	0.48	0.49	Avoided by the surviving court tasters.
Nigeria	28.50	30.50	0.66	0.68	Retail stonewalls dealer interest.
Panama	20.00	23.00	0.59	0.61	Recent bidding stirs the mud.
Peru	7.00	9.00	0.51	0.52	Debt-for-debt workouts and debt-for-goods deals continue.
Philippines	52.00	53.00	0.98	1.00	Prices drift higher with good interest in non-CB names.
Poland	43.25	44.50	0.83	0.85	Somewhat slower trading this period.
Romania	82.00	84.00	2.61	2.94	Bidding improves on expectations of 1988 principal payments.
Senegal	40.00	45.00	0.78	0.85	Trading talk more serious.
Sudan	2.00	10.00	0.48	0.52	Still on the mat.
Turkey	97.50	99.00	18.80	47.00	CTLDs remain well bid.
Uruguay	59.50	61.50	1.16	1.22	Remains a patience-trying market.
Venezuela	55.00	55.75	1.04	1.06	Trading stronger as uptick in Chile brings swaps back into range.
Yugoslavia	45.50	47.00	0.86	0.89	More frequent trading.
Zaire	19.00	23.00	0.58	0.61	New interest develops.

Source: Salomon Brothers Inc., May 2, 1988.

TABLE 15–6   Brady Bonds and Bank Loans Outstanding, June 2003, 2006, and 2008 (US$ billions)

Country	2003 Brady Bonds Outstanding	2003 Bank Loans Outstanding	2006 Brady Bonds Outstanding	2006 Bank Loans Outstanding	2008 Q4 Debt Securities	2008 Q4 Bank Loans
Argentina	$ 6.8	$ 25.0	$ 0.5	$ 10.5	38.8	37.6
Brazil	17.8	58.2	0.0	57.5	88.6	84.8
Bulgaria	2.4	0.8	0.0	3.9	2.1	20.1
Costa Rica	0.4	3.0	0.1	2.9	1.0	5.3
Côte d'Ivoire	2.2	2.2	2.1	3.8	n.a.	n.a.
Dominican Republic	0.5	2.7	0.4	1.8	n.a.	n.a.
Ecuador	0.0	1.8	0.0	2.2	0	0
Mexico	1.3	45.7	0.0	38.9	116.5	65.3
Nigeria	1.4	2.0	1.3	4.0	n.a.	n.a.
Peru	2.5	4.2	2.3	4.7	7.9	26.4
Philippines	1.2	12.2	0.8	17.2	n.a.	n.a.
Poland	2.8	16.8	1.3	23.4	62.3	85.4
Russian Federation	0.0	35.3	0.0	87.6	27.6	383.2
Uruguay	0.5	2.1	0.1	1.9	7.0	3.3
Venezuela	7.7	11.2	0.0	8.7	n.a.	n.a.

Source: World Bank website, January 2004, November 2006, and January 2009, www.worldbank.org

As in the LDC crisis, the banks did not want to sell these assets at fire sale prices, even though more than 100 fund managers submitted offers to the U.S. Federal Reserve to buy them. However, as long as the assets remain on their balance sheets, it is difficult for banks to resume their regular lending. A proposal by U.S. Secretary of Treasury Timothy Geithner has been compared to Brady bonds. Geithner's proposal, the details of which were still being worked out in early 2009, would provide cheap financing to allow hedge funds and other asset managers to purchase the U.S. banks' toxic assets. This would establish a price for many of the securitization assets and start a market again. In the scenario that is emerging, the new "Brady bonds" are securities of U.S. banks related to the securitization market that we discuss in detail in Chapter 27.

Sovereign Bonds   The second segment of the LDC debt market to develop was that for sovereign bonds. Beginning in May 1996, as the debt position and economies of some LDCs improved, a number started buy-back, or repurchase, programs for their Brady bonds. For example, in April 2003 Mexico sold US$2.5 billion of sovereign bonds to help finance the repurchase of the country's U.S. dollar–denominated Brady bonds. The difference between a Brady bond and a sovereign bond is that a Brady bond's value partly reflects the value of the U.S. Treasury bond collateral underlying the principal and/or interest on the issue. By contrast, sovereign bonds are uncollateralized and their price or value reflects the credit risk rating of the country issuing the bonds. The benefit to the country is the "saving" from not having to pledge U.S. Treasury bonds as collateral. The cost is the higher interest spreads required on such bonds. Thus, the US$2.8 billion June 1997 issue by Brazil of 30-year dollar-denominated bonds (rated BB-grade by Standard & Poor's) was sold at a yield spread of nearly 4 percent over U.S. Treasuries at the time of issue.[21] In July 2001, Argentinian sovereign bonds were trading at spreads of over 15 percent above U.S. Treasury rates, with the JPMorgan *Emerging Market Bond Index* showing a spread of nearly 10 percent over U.S. Treasuries. This reflected the serious economic problems in Argentina and the contagious effects these were having on other sovereign bond markets.

Bank Loans The third category for distressed sovereign debt is bank debt. According to the Bank for International Settlements' *BIS Quarterly Review* for December 2003, outstanding debt for emerging markets was equally divided between bonds and bank loans. This reflects the development of emerging-market debt securities (bonds) as a tradable asset class. As shown in Table 15–6 for Q4 2008, in some countries, debt securities and bank loans were approximately equal in amount (e.g., Argentina and Brazil). However, for others, like Mexico, debt securities outstanding were significantly higher than bank loans, while for the Russian Federation, the opposite was true. Foreign banks increased their share of the total banking assets of developing countries from approximately 20 percent in 1995 to almost 40 percent in 2005 by increasing their bank loans as well as by direct local participation through the purchase of local banks (e.g., Scotiabank's purchase of Inverlat in Mexico). As well, a recent study indicates that foreign bank lending to emerging markets is dependent on economic conditions such as the **TED spread.** It is thought that when the TED spread widens (such as occurred during the credit crisis in 2008), the liquidity in the inter-bank market is tight and therefore loans to emerging markets decline. Thus, while emerging markets were not directly exposed to the toxic assets discussed above in any major way, the tight liquidity in the global financial markets eventually slowed the flow of funds to the emerging-market countries by early 2009.[22]

TED spread
The spread between the three-month U.S. dollar LIBOR and the three-month U.S. Treasury bill rate.

Market Prices and Country Risk Analysis

By combining debt prices with key variables, FI managers can potentially predict future repayment problems. For example, in the markets for which sovereign debt is quite heavily traded, such as Mexico and Brazil, these prices reflect market consensus regarding the current and expected future cash flows on these loans and, implicitly, the probability of rescheduling or repudiation of these loans. Because market prices on LDC loans have been available monthly since 1985, the FI manager might construct a statistical CRA model to analyze which key economic and political variables or factors have driven changes in secondary market prices. Basically, this would involve regressing periodic changes in the prices of LDC debt in the secondary market on a set of key variables such as those described earlier in this section. Table 15–7 presents the results of a study by E. Boehmer and

[21] A. Gande and D. Parsley found that the credit rating on sovereign debt of one country can affect the credit rating and thus the yield spread in other countries' debt. For example, a one-category downgrade (e.g., from BB to B) is associated with a 12-basis-point increase in spreads of sovereign bonds. However, positive rating events have no discernible impact on sovereign bond debt (see "News Spillovers in the Sovereign Debt Market," *Journal of Financial Economics* 75, 2005). Further, D. Duffie, L. H. Pedersen, and K. J. Singleton found that Russian yield spreads in the 1990s and 2000 varied significantly over time (responding to political events) and were negatively correlated with Russian foreign currency reserves and oil prices. Their model suggests that Russian sovereign bonds may have been overpriced in September 1997 (see "Modeling Sovereign Yield Spreads: A Case Study of Russian Debt," *Journal of Finance* 58, February 2003, pp. 119–159).

[22] See P. McGuire and N. Tarashev, "Bank Health and Lending to Emerging Markets," *BIS Quarterly Review,* December 2008, p. 67; "Emerging Markets Join Global Slowdown," *BIS Quarterly Review,* March 2009, p. 15. Both available at www.bis.org. See as well "The Changing Role of International Banking in Development Finance," *Global Development Finance 2008,* World Bank, p. 81, at www.worldbank.org, and H. Kazemi and A. Ogus, "The Determinants of the Secondary Market Price of Less Developed Countries' Debt," *Atlantic Economic Journal* 36, 2008, pp. 153–164.

TABLE 15–7
Variables Affecting Secondary Market Prices

Source: E. Boehmer and W. L. Megginson, "Determinants of Secondary Market Prices for Developing Country Syndicated Loans," *Journal of Finance* 45, 1990, pp. 1517–1540.

The following regression equation is estimated:

$$P_{it} = \beta_1 \times \text{Intercept} + \beta_2 \times \text{TDGNP}_{it} + \beta_3 \times \text{TDEX}_{it} + \beta_4 \times \text{NETDS}_{it} + \beta_5 \times \text{NIRES}_{it}$$
$$+ \beta_6 \times \text{INT}_{it} + \beta_7 \times \text{ARR}_{it} + \beta_8 \times \text{USP}_{it} + \beta_9 \times \text{BDUM}_{it} + \beta_{10} \times \text{PDUM}_{it}$$
$$+ \beta_{11} \times \text{CONVDUM}_{it} + U_{it}$$

where

P =	LDC secondary market loan prices
TDGNP =	Ratio of total long-term debt to GNP
TDEX =	Ratio of total long-term debt to exports
NETDS =	Ratio of net exports to debt service
NIRES =	Ratio of net imports to hard currency reserves
INT =	Monthly London Interbank Offered Rate (a short-term interest rate)
ARR =	Level of incurred payment arrears
USP =	Cumulative developing country-specific loan provisioning by U.S. FIs
BDUM =	Unity for Brazil from January to December of 1987 and zero otherwise to capture the effects of the debt moratorium
PDUM =	Unity for Peru over the whole sampling period and zero otherwise to account for the unilateral limitation of debt service payments
CONVDUM =	Unity for all months in which a country maintained legislation for debt-to-equity conversions

Parameter	Estimate	*t*-Statistic
Intercept	88.51760	13.47
TDGNP	−18.11610	−4.75
TDEX	−0.10437	−3.57
NETDS	−0.30754	−0.50
NIRES	5.79548	1.28
INT	0.22825	0.30
ARR	−0.00574	−2.68
USP	−0.00100	−13.69
BDUM	−10.92820	−6.61
PDUM	−36.07240	−8.31
CONVDUM	−5.43157	−6.75

Degrees of freedom: 309
Adjusted R^2: 0.96

W. L. Megginson of the factors driving the secondary market prices of 10 LDC countries' loans over a 32-month period, July 1985–July 1988.

As you can see, the significant variables affecting LDC loan sale prices (*P*) over this period were a country's debt service ratio (TDGNP and TDEX), its import ratio (NIRES), its accumulated debt in arrears (ARR), and the amount by which FIs had already made loan loss provisions against these LDC loans (USP). Also important were variables that reflect the debt moratoria for Peru and Brazil (PDUM and BDUM) and that indicate whether a debt-for-equity swap program was in place (CONVDUM). Interestingly, debt-for-equity swap programs appear to depress prices. (We discuss these programs in more detail in Appendix 15A on this book's website).

Once managers have estimated a statistical model, they can use the estimate of parameters $\beta_1, \beta_2, \ldots, \beta_n$ along with forecasts for a given country's debt service ratio and other key variables to derive predicted changes in LDC asset prices. That is, this approach might allow the FI manager to come up with another set of forecasts regarding changes in sovereign risk exposure to a number of sovereign debtors.

EXAMPLE 15–2

Calculating Secondary Market Loan Prices

Suppose an FI is considering a loan to a company in Brazil. To estimate country risk, the FI uses the Boehmer and Megginson model to determine secondary market loan prices. Current secondary market prices for Brazilian debt are 65 percent of face value. The FI will make the loan only if prices are expected to rise above 70 percent during the next year. The FI's loan officers have estimated the following macroeconomic data for Brazil over the next year:

Long-term debt to GNP (TDGNP) = 0.87
Long-term debt to exports (TDEX) = 0.50
Net exports to debt service (NETDS) = 0.75
Net imports to hard currency reserves (NIRES) = 1.55
Monthly LIBOR (INT) = 5.50
Level of incurred payments in arrears (ARR) = 0.10
Cumulative loan provisioning of Brazilian loans by U.S. FIs (USP) = 0.50
Dummy variable for Brazil (BDUM) = 1
Dummy variable for Peru (PDUM) = 0
Dummy for debt-to-equity conversion legislation (CONVDUM) = 0

Using these estimates, the FI calculates expected secondary market price on Brazilian debt to be:

$$88.51760 - (18.11610 \times 0.87) - (0.10437 \times 0.50) - (0.30754 \times 0.75) +$$
$$(5.79548 \times 1.55) + (0.22825 \times 5.5) - (0.00574 \times 0.10) - (0.00100 \times 0.50) -$$
$$(10.92820 \times 1) - (36.07240 \times 0) - (5.43157 \times 0) = 71.782848$$

Based on this estimate—that the price of Brazilian debt will be 71.782848 of the face value—the FI would approve this loan.

This approach is subject to many of the same criticisms as the traditional statistical models of country risk prediction. Specifically, the parameters of the model may be unstable; managers can measure variables, such as the *DSR* and the import ratio, only with error; and the sovereign loan market may not be price-efficient.[23] In addition, the link between these key variables and the change in secondary market price is something of a black box in terms of links to the underlying theoretical incentives of borrowers and lenders to engage in future reschedulings or repudiations of their debt obligations.

---

[23] However, in S. H. Lee, H. M. Sung, and J. L. Urrutia, "The Behavior of Secondary Market Prices of LDC Syndicated Loans," *Journal of Banking and Finance* 20, 1996, pp. 537–54, it is shown that returns on LDC loans traded in the secondary market conform to those expected to exist in an efficient market. In fact, more recent research has found that, in general, international and, particularly, emerging markets are becoming increasingly efficient. See B. Eftekhari and S. E. Satchell, "International Investors' Exposure to Risk in Emerging Markets," *Journal of Financial Research*, Spring 1999, pp. 83–106. As noted previously, more recent models have shown that international market conditions and liquidity have an impact on capital flows to and stability of emerging-market debt.

CONCEPT QUESTIONS	1. Are the credit ratings of countries in the *Institutional Investor* rating scheme forward-looking or backward-looking?
	2. What variables are most commonly included in sovereign risk prediction models? What does each one measure?
	3. What are the major problems involved with using traditional CRA models and techniques?
	4. Which sovereign risk indicators are the most important for a large FI, those with a high or those with a low systematic element?
	5. Why did the supply of Brady bonds decline?

Summary

This chapter reviewed the problems FIs face from sovereign or country risk exposures. Sovereign risk is the risk of a foreign government's limiting or preventing domestic borrowers in its jurisdiction from repaying the principal and interest on debt owed to external lenders. In recent years this risk has caused enormous problems for banks lending to LDCs, and Latin American and Asian countries. We reviewed various models for country risk analysis (CRA), including those produced by external monitoring agencies such as Euromoney, the Economist Intelligence Unit, and the Institutional Investor and those that could be constructed by an FI manager for internal evaluation purposes. Such statistical CRA models have problems and pitfalls. An alternative approach using secondary market prices on sovereign loans and bonds was also described. In Appendix 15A at the Online Learning Centre (www.mcgrawhill.ca/olc/saunders), we analyze the advantages and disadvantages of using four alternative mechanisms for dealing with problem sovereign credits from the perspective of the lender: debt–equity swaps, MYRAs, loan sales, and bond-for-loan swaps.

Questions and Problems

1. What risks are incurred in making loans to borrowers based in foreign countries? Explain.

2. What is the difference between debt rescheduling and debt repudiation?

3. Identify and explain at least four reasons that rescheduling debt in the form of loans is easier than rescheduling debt in the form of bonds.

4. What three country risk assessment models are available to investors? How is each model compiled?

5. What types of variables normally are used in a CRA Z score model? Define the following ratios and explain how each is interpreted in assessing the probability of rescheduling.

   a. Debt service ratio.

   b. Import ratio.

   c. Investment ratio.

   d. Variance of export revenue.

   e. Domestic money supply growth.

6. An FI manager has calculated the following values and weights to assess the credit risk and likelihood of having to reschedule the loan. From the Z score calculated from these weights and values, is the manager likely to approve the loan? Validation tests of the Z score model indicated that scores below 0.500 were likely to be non-reschedulers, while scores above 0.700 indicated a likelihood of rescheduling. Scores between 0.500 and 0.700 do not predict well.

Variable	Country Value	Weight
DSR	1.25	0.05
IR	1.60	0.10
INVR	0.60	0.35
VAREX	0.15	0.35
MG	0.02	0.15

7. Countries A and B have exports of US$2 and US$6 billion, respectively. The total interest and amortization on foreign loans for both countries are US$1 and US$2 billion, respectively.

   a. What is the debt service ratio (DSR) for each country?

   b. Based only on this ratio, to which country should lenders charge a higher risk premium?

c. What are the shortcomings of using only these ratios to determine your answer in (b)?

8. What shortcomings are introduced by using traditional CRA models and techniques? In each case, what adjustments are made in the estimation techniques to compensate for the problems?

9. How do price and quantity risks affect the variability of a country's export revenue?

10. The average σ^2_{ER} (or *VAREX* = Variance of export revenue) of a group of countries has been estimated at 20 percent. The individual *VAREX* of two countries in the group, Holland and Singapore, has been estimated at 15 percent and 28 percent, respectively. The regression of individual country *VAREX* on the average *VAREX* provides the following beta (coefficient) estimates:

$$\beta_H = \text{Beta of Holland} = 0.80$$
$$\beta_S = \text{Beta of Singapore} = 0.20$$

a. Based only on the *VAREX* estimates, which country should be charged a higher risk premium? Explain.

b. If FIs include unsystematic risk in their estimation of risk premiums, how would your conclusions to (a) be affected? Explain.

11. Explain the following relationship:

$$p = f(IR, INVR)$$
$$+, + \text{ or } -$$

where

p = Probability of rescheduling

IR = Total imports/Total foreign exchange reserves

$INVR$ = Real investment/GNP

12. What is systematic risk in terms of sovereign risk? Which of the variables often used in statistical models tend to have high systematic risk? Which variables tend to have low systematic risk?

13. What are the benefits and costs of rescheduling to the following?

a. A borrower.

b. A lender.

Web Questions

14. Go to the Heritage Foundation website at www.heritage.org and find the most recent *Economic Freedom Index* for Canada using the following steps. In the site's search window, input "20XX Index of Economic Freedom" and then click on the relevant index. Click on "Visit the Countries." Click on "Canada." What factors led to Canada's rating?

Appendix 15A   Mechanisms for Dealing with Sovereign Risk Exposure

View Appendix 15A at the Online Learning Centre: www.mcgrawhill.ca/olc/saunders.

CHAPTER 16

Technology and Other Operational Risks

This chapter focuses on operational risk and considers

▸ the factors that influence operational returns and risks of FIs (with an emphasis on technology)

▸ the importance of optimal management and control of labour, capital, and other input sources and their costs

▸ how well-managed FIs can use operational cost savings to increase profits and thus reduce the probability of insolvency

▸ how operational risk is addressed at Canadian FIs

▸ how Basel II will change the way operational risk is addressed at Canadian FIs

INTRODUCTION

Chapters 7 through 15 concentrated on the financial risks that arise as FIs perform their asset-transformation and/or brokerage functions on or off the balance sheet. However, financial risk is only one part of a modern FI's risk profile. As with regular corporations, FIs have a real or production side to their operations that results in additional costs and revenues.

Central to FIs' decision-making processes is the cost of inputs, or factors used to produce services both on and off the balance sheet. Two important factors are labour (tellers, credit officers) and capital (buildings, machinery, furniture). Crucial to the efficient management and combination of these inputs (which result in financial outputs at the lowest cost) is technology. Technological innovation has been a major concern of FIs in recent years. Since the 1980s, banks, insurance companies, and other FIs have sought to improve operational efficiency with major investments in internal and external communications, computers, and an expanded technological infrastructure. Internet and wireless communications technologies are having a profound effect on financial services—they are a completely different way of providing financial services. A global financial services firm such as the U.S.-based bank Citigroup has operations in more than 100 countries connected in real time by a proprietary-owned satellite system. Operational risk is partly related to technology risk and can arise when existing technology malfunctions or back-office support systems break down. Further, back-office support systems combine labour and technology to provide clearance, settlement, and other services to back FIs' underlying on- and off-balance-sheet transactions.

According to Hitachi Data Systems, back-office system failures usually occur four times per year in the average firm. Recovery time from system failures averages 12 hours. The terrorist attacks on the World Trade Center and the Pentagon in the United States created back-office system failures of an unforeseen magnitude. For example, over a week after the attacks, Bank of New York was still having trouble with some crucial communications links. The risks of technological

372

malfunctions for FIs were highlighted in June 2004, when the Royal Bank of Canada experienced a programming error that affected its main and backup computer systems. The problem, which lasted for a week, resulted in customers overdrawing their accounts when their paycheques were not deposited on time. This operational risk cost the bank the trust of their clients (**reputational risk**) and increased their non-interest expense by $11 million in 2004.[1]

reputational risk
The potential for an FI's actions to cause a loss of trust of clients, the market, and regulators.

www.bis.org

operational risk
The potential for losses from failed systems, personnel, or external events.

As should already be apparent, technology and operational risks are closely related and in recent years have caused great concern to FI managers and regulators alike. The Bank for International Settlements (BIS), the principal organization of central banks in the major economies of the world, has defined operational risk (inclusive of technological risk) as "the risk of losses resulting from inadequate or failed internal processes, people, and systems or from external events."[2] A number of FIs add reputational risk and strategic risk (e.g., due to a failed merger) as part of a broader definition of **operational risk.** So significant has operational risk become that under Basel II, banks are required to carry a capital cushion against losses from this risk. We discuss this briefly in this chapter and in more detail in Chapter 20.

WHAT ARE THE SOURCES OF OPERATIONAL RISK?

Controlling and reducing operational risks improves the operational efficiency of the FI. As seen in the following section, improvements in operational efficiency lead to increases in net income, return on assets, and other quantitative measures of FI performance.[3] However, as we see throughout the chapter, operational risk is much less tangible and is often hard to quantify. There are at least five sources of operational risk:

1. Technology (e.g., technological failure and deteriorating systems).
2. Employees (e.g., human error and internal fraud).
3. Customer relationships (e.g., contractual disputes).
4. Capital assets (e.g., destruction by fire or other catastrophes).
5. External (e.g., external fraud).

Increasingly important to the profitability and riskiness of modern FIs has been item 1: technology.

---

[1] The Royal Bank's management of operational risk includes self-assessment and control of risk, compilation of a loss event database, and the identification of key risk indicators. See Royal Bank of Canada's 2008 annual report, p. 100, as well as C. Conrath, "Anatomy of a Royal Snafu: A Look Inside RBC's Recent Battle with Its Technology Demons," *ComputerWorld Canada,* June 25, 2004, 20(13). Canadian Imperial Bank of Commerce (CIBC) and TD Canada Trust (TD) also experienced computer problems in the summer of 2004. See F. Sheikh, "Computer Glitches Paralyse CIBC, TD Banking Systems," *Computing Canada,* August 13, 2004, 30(11), pp. 1–2.

[2] See Basel Committee on Bank Supervision, *Overview of the New Basel Capital Accord,* Bank for International Settlements, April 2003, p. 120. Other BIS papers on operational risk are *Working Paper on the Regulatory Treatment of Operational Risk,* September 2001; *Sound Practices for the Management and Supervision of Operational Risk,* February 2003; and *Outsourcing in Financial Services,* February 2005, available at www.bis.org.

[3] J. D. Cummins, C. M. Lewis, and R. Wei find that market value losses significantly exceed the amount of the operational losses reported. See "The Market Value Impact of Operational Loss Events For U.S. Banks and Insurers," *Journal of Banking and Finance* 30, 2006, pp. 2605–34.

TECHNOLOGICAL INNOVATION AND PROFITABILITY

technology
Computers, audio and visual communication systems, and other information systems, which can be applied to an FI's production of services.

Broadly defined, **technology** includes computers, visual and audio communication systems, and other information technology (IT). The Canadian Bankers Association (CBA) reports that, between 1996 and 2008, the six largest Canadian banks spent $48.6 billion, an average of $3.7 billion per year, on technology such as computer hardware and software, capital leases related to computer equipment, data and voice communication equipment, and development expenses related to these items.[4]

An efficient technological base for an FI can result in

www.cba.ca

1. Lower costs, by combining labour and capital in a more efficient mix.
2. Increased revenues, by allowing a wider array of financial services to be produced or innovated and sold to customers.

The importance of an FI's operating costs and the efficient use of technology affecting these costs is clearly demonstrated by this simplified profit function:

$$\text{Earnings or profit before taxes} = (\text{Interest income} - \text{Interest expense})$$
$$+ (\text{Other income} - \text{Non-interest expense}) - (\text{Provision for loan losses})$$

www.osfi-bsif.gc.ca.

Table 16–1 breaks down the profit data for Canadian banks reporting to the Office of the Superintendent of Financial Services (OSFI) over the 1996–2008 period into the different components impacting profits. For example, at the end of quarter four of 2008, year-to-date interest income of $113,562 million and interest expense of $70,289 million produced net interest income of $43,273 million. However, the banks also had total non-interest income of $29,894 million (including service charges on deposits of $4,531) and non-interest expenses of $51,315 million (including salaries, pensions, and employee benefits of $28,056 million and premises and equipment expenses of $9,416 million). Thus, banks' net non-interest income was –$21,421 million ($29,894 – 51,315), reflecting losses on the trading account (–$8,774 million). After considering charges for impaired loans of $7,131 million, non-controlling interest in subsidiaries ($218 million), extra-ordinary items ($290 million), and taxes ($1,145 million), net income was $13,648 million. Underscoring the importance of operating costs is the fact that non-interest expenses amounted to 73 percent of interest expenses ($51,315 ÷ 70,289) and were 3.75 times net income for the four quarters of 2008.

INTERNET EXERCISE

Go to the website for the Office of Superintendent of Financial Services (www.osfi-bsif.gc.ca) and click on "Banks." Then click on "Financial Data—Banks" and then on "Quarterly." On the drop-down menu, select "Summary Income Statement." Click "Submit" to view and print the latest quarterly information.

Technology is important because well-chosen technological investments have the potential to increase both the FI's net interest margin, or the difference between

---

[4] Canadian Bankers Association, *Banks & Consumers,* March 2009, available at the CBA's website, www.cba.ca.

TABLE 16–1   Earnings and Other Data for All Banks Reporting to OSFI ($ millions)*

Financial Data	1996	1999	2002	2004	2006	2008**
Interest income	63,383	76,293	69,592	65,141	95,307	113,562
Interest expense	–40,875	–51,788	–36,091	–31,394	–61,537	–70,289
Net interest income	22,508	24,506	33,501	33,747	33,770	43,273
Charge for impairment	–2,139	–3,177	–9,719	–1,547	–2,538	–7,131
Deposit service charges	2,090	2,455	3,402	3,584	4,045	4,531
Credit & debit card fees	1,432	1,641	2,212	2,371	2,843	3,522
Loan fees	1,056	1,654	1,775	1,522	1,474	1,648
Mutual fund & underwriting fees	3,858	7,599	9,790	10,789	11,559	11,609
Trading account income & gains	1,029	6,192	3,259	4,438	7,664	–8,774
All other	3,836	7,397	10,842	11,621	15,255	17,358
Total non-interest income	13,301	26,938	31,280	34,325	42,840	29,894
Salaries, pensions, & benefits	–12,526	–18,362	–23,826	–24,790	–26,645	–28,056
Premises & equipment	–4,424	–6,366	–7,907	–7,989	–8,134	–9,416
All other	–5,874	–9,357	–12,693	–12,865	–12,522	–13,843
Non-interest expenses	–22,284	–34,085	–44,427	–45,644	–47,301	–51,315
Income taxes	–4,080	–4,542	–2,391	–5,631	–5,679	–1,145
Non-controlling interests in subsidiaries	124	–150	–508	–593	–488	–218
Extraordinary items	0	–9	8	2	107	290
Net income	6,640	9,481	7,745	14,659	20,710	13,648
Total assets ($ billions)	1,014.6	1,367.2	1,688.5	1,816.8	2,265.8	3,183.1
Return on assets (%)	0.65%	0.69%	0.46%	0.81%	0.91%	0.32%

* Year to date as of the end of Quarter 4 of the relevant year.
**As of the third quarter; all other data are for Q4 of the relevant year.
 Source: Office of the Superintendent of Financial Services, www.osfi-bsif.gc.ca.

interest income and interest expense, and other net income. Therefore, technology can directly improve profitability, as the following examples show:

1. *Interest income* can increase if the FI sells a broader array of financial services as a result of technological developments. These may include cross-selling financial products by having the computer identify customers and then having the FI telemarket financial services products directly and over the Internet.

2. *Interest expense* can be reduced if access to markets for liabilities is directly dependent on the FI's technological capability. For example, the wire transfer systems linking domestic and international inter-bank lending markets are based on interlocking computer network systems. Moreover, an FI's ability to originate and sell commercial paper is increasingly computer-driven. Thus, failure to invest in the appropriate technology may lock an FI out of a lower-cost funding market.[5]

3. *Other income* increases when fees for FI services, especially those from off-balance-sheet activities, are linked to the quality of the FI's technology. For example, letters of credit are now commonly originated electronically by customers;

---

[5] Commercial paper has been an important source of funding for Canadian FIs. In 2002, 90 percent of outstanding asset-backed commercial paper (ABCP) was attributed to the major Canadian banks, which were also responsible for US$31.5 million of ABCP issuance in the United States as well as for European U.S. dollar issues totalling US$3.7 billion at September 30, 2002. See P. Toovey and J. Kiff, "Developments and Issues in the Canadian Market for Asset-Backed Commercial Paper," *Bank of Canada Financial System Review,* June 2003, pp. 43–48.

swaps, caps, options, and other complex derivatives are usually traded, tracked, and valued using high-powered computers and algorithms. FIs could not offer innovative derivative products to customers without investments in suitable IT. Further, new technology has resulted in an evolution of the payment systems (see below), which has increased the amount of fee income (non-interest income) as a percentage of total operating income (interest income plus non-interest income) for FIs. For example, referring again to Table 16–1, we see that non-interest income as a percentage of total income was 17.35 percent in 1996 and increased to 31 percent in 2006. With the market disruptions of 2008, non-interest income declined to 20.7 percent of total income in the first three quarters of 2008.

4. *Non-interest expenses* can be reduced if the collection and storage of customer information as well as the processing and settlement of numerous financial products are computer-based rather than paper-based. This is particularly true of security-related back-office activities.

CONCEPT QUESTIONS	1. What are some of the advantages of an efficient technological base for an FI? How can it be used to directly improve profitability?
	2. Looking at Table 16–1, determine if non-interest expenses and non-interest income increased or decreased as a percentage of total bank costs over the 1996–2008 period.

THE EFFECT OF TECHNOLOGY ON WHOLESALE AND RETAIL FINANCIAL SERVICES PRODUCTION

The previous discussion established that modern technology has the potential to directly affect a modern FI's profit-producing areas. The following discussion focuses on some specific technology-based products found in modern retail and wholesale operations of financial institutions.[6] Note that this is far from a complete list.

Wholesale Financial Services

Probably the most important area in which technology has had an impact on wholesale or corporate customer services is an FI's ability to provide cash management or working capital services. Cash management services include collecting, disbursing and transferring funds—on a local, regional, national or international basis—and providing information about the location and status of those funds. Cash management service needs have largely resulted from (1) corporate recognition that excess cash balances result in a significant opportunity cost due to lost or forgone interest and (2) corporate need to know cash or working capital position on a real-time basis. Among the services modern FIs provide to improve the efficiency with which corporate clients manage their financial positions are the following:

1. *Controlled disbursement accounts.* An account feature that establishes in the morning almost all payments to be made by the customer in a given day. The FI informs the corporate client of the total funds it needs to meet disbursements, and the client wire-transfers the amount needed. These chequing accounts are debited early each day so that corporations can obtain an early insight into their net cash positions.

---

[6] A. K. Pennathur, in "'Clicks and Bricks': e-Risk Management for Banks in the Age of the Internet," *Journal of Banking and Finance* 25, 2001, pp. 2103–23, outlines various risks associated with the provision of these services.

float
The interval between the deposit of a cheque and when funds become available for depositor use; that is, the time is takes a cheque to clear at a bank.

2. *Account reconciliation.* A chequing feature that records which of the firm's cheques have been paid by the FI.

3. *Wholesale lockbox.* A centralized collection service for corporate payments to reduce the delay in cheque clearing, or the **float.** In a typical lockbox arrangement, a local FI sets up a lockbox at the post office for a corporate client located outside the area. Local customers mail payments to the lockbox rather than to the out-of-town corporate headquarters. The FI collects these cheques several times per day and deposits them directly into the customer's account. Details of the transaction are wired to the corporate client.

4. *Electronic lockbox.* Same type of service as item 3 but receives online payments for public utilities and similar corporate clients.

5. *Funds concentration.* Redirects funds from accounts in a large number of FIs or branches to a few centralized accounts at one FI.

6. *Electronic funds transfer.* Includes overnight payments, automated payment of payrolls or dividends, and automated transmission of payments messages by SWIFT, an international electronic message service owned and operated by global FIs that instructs FIs to make specific payments.

7. *Cheque deposit services.* Encoding, endorsing, microfilming, and handling customers' cheques.

8. *Electronic initiation of letters of credit.* Allows customers in a network to access FI computers to initiate letters of credit.

9. *Treasury management software.* Allows efficient management of multiple currency and security portfolios for trading and investment purposes.[7]

10. *Electronic data interchange.* A specialized application of electronic mail, allowing businesses to transfer and transact invoices, purchase orders, and shipping notices automatically, using FIs as clearinghouses.

11. *Facilitation of business-to-business e-commerce.* A few of the largest Canadian and U.S. banks offer firms the technology for electronic business-to-business commerce. The banks are essentially undertaking automation of the entire information flow associated with the procurement and distribution of goods and services among businesses.

12. *Electronic billing.* Provides the presentment and collection services for companies that send out substantial volumes of recurring bills. Banks combine the e-mail capability of the Internet to send out bills with their ability to process payments electronically through the inter-bank payment networks.[8]

13. *Verification of identities.* Using encryption technology, banks certify the identities of its own account holders and serve as the intermediary through which its business customers can verify the identities of account holders at other banks.

14. *Assistance to small businesses entering into e-commerce.* Help smaller firms in setting up the infrastructure—interactive website and payment capabilities—for engaging in e-commerce.

---

[7] Computerized pension fund management and advisory services could be added to this list.

[8] Increased speed, tech-savvy consumers, and convenience in online bill payment has resulted in the continuing growth of use of online banking across all age groups in Canada. A survey conducted in June 2008 by the Strategic Counsel for the Canadian Bankers Association indicated that 53 percent of Canadians bank online, and 35 percent use the Internet as their main banking services source. A similar survey conducted in March 2004 had found that only 26 percent of Canadians were using the Internet as their main banking source.

Retail Financial Services

Retail customers have demanded efficiency and flexibility in their financial transactions. Using only cheques or holding cash is often more expensive and time-consuming than using retail-oriented electronic payments technology and, increasingly, the Internet. Further, securities trading is increasingly moving toward electronic platforms not tied to any specific location. Electronic trading networks have lowered the costs of trading and allowed for better price determination. For example, customers of a major bank can obtain information on their account balances, pay their bills online, and trade stocks in their brokerage accounts and their RRSP accounts from one website. Some of the most important retail payment product innovations include:

1. *Automated teller machines (ATMs).* Allow customers 24-hour access to their deposit accounts. They can pay bills as well as withdraw cash from these machines. In addition, if the FI's ATMs are part of a bank network (such as CIRRUS), retail depositors can gain direct nationwide—and in many cases international—access to their deposit accounts by using the ATMs of other banks in the network to draw on their accounts.[9]

2. *Point-of-sale (POS) debit cards.* Allows customers who choose not to use cash, cheques, or credit cards for purchases to buy merchandise using debit card/point-of-sale (POS) terminals. The merchant avoids the cheque float and any delay in payment associated with credit card receivables since the FI offers the debit card/POS service immediately and transfers funds directly from the customer's deposit account into the merchant's deposit account at the time of card use. Unlike cheque or **credit card transactions, debit card transactions** result in an immediate transfer of funds from the customers' account to the merchant's account.[10] Moreover, the customer never runs up a debit to the card issuer as is common with a credit card.

3. *Home banking.* Connects customers to their deposit and brokerage accounts and provides services such as electronic securities trading and bill paying via personal computers.

4. *Preauthorized debits/credits.* Includes direct deposits of payroll cheques into bank accounts as well as direct payments of mortgage and utility bills.

5. *Payment of bills via telephone.* Allows direct transfer of funds from the customer's FI account to outside parties either by voice command or by touch-tone telephone use.

6. *E-mail billing.* Allows customers to receive and pay bills using the Internet, thus saving postage and paper.

7. *Online banking.* Allows customers to conduct retail banking and investment services offered via the Internet.[11] In some cases this involves building a new

---

credit card transaction
An extension of credit to a cardholder and a transfer of payment by the card issuer (e.g., bank, credit union) to the merchant.

debit card transaction
A withdrawal (debit) directly from a customer's account with an FI.

---

[9] Using another bank's ATM usually results in an access fee to the customer that averages $1 but can be as high as $5.

[10] In the case of bank-supplied credit cards, the merchant normally is compensated very quickly but not instantaneously by the credit card issuer (usually one or two days). The bank then holds an account receivable against the card user. However, even a short delay can represent an opportunity cost for the merchant. In 2003, MasterCard and Visa agreed to settle an antitrust suit in the United States consenting to lower fees, modify card policies, and pay over US$3 billion in damages to about 5 million merchants (including Walmart and Sears). The merchants argued that these card associations illegally tied their debit cards to their credit cards, forcing retailers for pay higher fees. The debit transactions are processed on ATM/POS networks.

[11] In addition to cash management services, technology also enhances the ability of FIs to offer security services (e.g., local and global custody and transfer).

www.ingdirect.ca

online Internet-only "bank," such as ING Direct, a virtual bank that has over 1.6 million customers and $24 billion in assets in Canada.

8. *Smart cards (store-value cards).* Allows the customer to store and spend money for various transactions using a card that has a chip storage device, usually in the form of a strip. These have become increasingly popular at universities.[12, 13]

<table>
<tr><td>**CONCEPT QUESTIONS**</td><td>1. Describe some of the wholesale financial services provided to corporate customers that have been improved by technology.
2. Describe some of the automated retail payment products available today. What advantages do these products offer the retail customer?</td></tr>
</table>

THE EFFECT OF TECHNOLOGY ON REVENUES AND COSTS

The previous section presented an extensive list of current products or services being offered by FIs that are built around a strong technological base and, increasingly, the Internet. Technological advances allow an FI to offer such products to its customers and potentially to earn higher profits. The investment of resources in many of these products is risky, however, because product innovations may fail to attract sufficient business relative to the initial cash outlay and the future costs related to these investments once they are in place. In the terminology of finance, a number of technologically based product innovations may turn out to be *negative* net present value projects because of uncertainties over revenues and costs and how quickly rivals will mimic or copy any innovation. Another factor is agency conflicts, in which managers undertake growth-oriented investments to increase an FI's size; such investments may be inconsistent with stockholders' value-maximizing objectives. As a result, losses on technological innovations and new technology could weaken an FI because scarce capital resources were invested in value-decreasing products.

Standard capital budgeting techniques can be applied to technological innovations and new FI products. Let

I_0 = Initial capital outlay for developing an innovation or product at time 0

R_i = Expected net revenues or cash flows from product sales in future years $i, i = 1, \ldots, N$

d = FI's discount rate reflecting its risk-adjusted cost of capital

Thus, a negative net present value (NPV) project would result if

$$I_0 > \frac{R_1}{(1 + d)} + \ldots + \frac{R_N}{(1 + d)^N}$$

identity theft
The theft of electronic identification (debit or credit cards) to gain illegal access to customer accounts.

[12] Dexit is an example of FIs teaming up with communications companies to implement new technology. Dexit is a prepaid service via radio frequency used for small cash purchases that is offered in downtown Toronto in conjunction with Bell Canada, TD Canada, National Bank of Canada, and TELUS Mobility. See www.dexit.com.

[13] Associated with the increased use of electronic transfers is **identity theft,** the use of credit or debit cards illegally to access FIs' customers' accounts. The Bank Act limits credit card users to a maximum liability of $50 if their cards are used illegally, but debit cards are not covered by the same limits on illegal fund withdrawals or transfers. See the latest information on debit card liability at the Office of Consumer Affairs' (OCA) website at www.ic.gc.ca.

Clearly, the profitability of any product innovation is negatively related to the size of the initial setup and development costs (I_0) and the FI's cost of capital (d), and positively related to the size of the stream of expected net cash flows (R_i) from selling the services.

This leads one to consider whether direct or indirect evidence is available that indicates whether technology investments to update the operational structure of FIs have increased revenues or decreased costs. Most of the direct or indirect evidence has concerned the effects of size on financial firms' operating costs, and it is the largest FIs that appear to be investing most in IT and other technological innovations.

We first discuss the evidence on the product revenue side and then discuss the evidence on the operating cost side. However, before looking at these revenue and cost aspects, we should stress that the success of technologically related innovation cannot be evaluated independently from regulation and regulatory changes. For example, while Canadians take their nationwide branch banking for granted, the introduction of full interstate banking in the United States in 1997, as well as the rapid consolidation in the U.S. financial services industry (e.g., as a result of mergers of large banks and the development of national branch systems) have created opportunities for Canadian FIs in the U.S. market. Product and geographic diversification, supported by technological advances, are discussed in more detail in Chapters 21 and 22.

Technology and Revenues

One potential benefit of technology is that it allows an FI to cross-market both new and existing products to customers. Such joint selling does not require the FI to produce all the services sold within the same branch or financial services outlet. For example, a bank may link up with an insurance company to jointly market each other's loan, credit card, and insurance products. This arrangement has proved popular in Germany, where some of the largest banks have developed sophisticated cross-marketing arrangements with large insurance companies. In the United States, Citicorp's merger with Travelers to create Citigroup was explicitly designed to cross-market banking, insurance, and securities products in over 100 countries. However, Citigroup management admitted after the completion of the merger that it could take ten or more years to integrate computer systems to a sufficient degree to achieve this objective.

Although there has been considerable cross-selling of retail banking and brokerage services, Canadian banks are not allowed to offer life insurance products through their branches. A merger of an insurance company and a bank requires the approval of the minister of Finance. The bank–bank mergers and bank–insurance mergers could be addressed by the next review of the Bank Act. This issue is discussed in more detail in Chapters 21 and 22.

The rate of adoption of technology by consumers determines the profitability of the investment. For example, because of large investments in technology globally by FIs, according to the Bank for International Settlements, debit card use in Canada was 104.5 transactions per inhabitant versus 100.1 transactions per inhabitant in the United States in 2007. Table 16–2 shows the volume of transactions by delivery channel for six Canadian banks from 2003 to 2008. The number of transactions by personal computer (PC)/Internet banking for transfers and bill payments both increased by 134.7 percent between 2003 and 2008. The use of automated banking machines (ABMs) for deposits and bill payments decreased, as did cash withdrawals as retail customers increased their usage of debit cards for point of sale (POS) purchases.

Finally, we cannot ignore the issue of service quality and convenience. For example, while ABMs and Internet banking may potentially lower FI operating

TABLE 16–2 Delivery Channels for Canadian Bank Transactions, 2003–2008

DELIVERY CHANNELS	Number of Transactions (in millions) of Six Banks*						
	2008	2007	2006	2005	2004	2003	% change 2008–2007
ABM	**954.7**	**992.8**	**1,026.5**	**1,056.4**	**1,110.1**	**1,120.8**	**–3.8%**
Deposits	230.3	238.8	250.9	258.8	254.6	256.4	–3.5%
Withdrawals	628.3	652.4	672.1	691.8	744.1	761.9	–3.7%
Transfers	41.1	43.7	45.6	46.7	53.3	46.6	–5.9%
Bill payments	55.1	57.9	57.9	59.0	58.1	56.0	–5.0%
DEBIT CARDS	**2,533.2**	**2,351.2**	**2,277.4**	**2,125.4**	**1,997.0**	**1,852.7**	**7.7%**
POS purchases	2,533.2	2,351.2	2,277.4	2,125.4	1,997.0	1,852.7	7.7%
PC/INTERNET BANKING	**445.7**	**393.9**	**347.6**	**297.1**	**238.1**	**189.9**	**13.2%**
Transfers	174.7	146.9	123.2	101.8	78.2	56.6	18.9%
Bill payments	270.9	246.9	224.4	195.4	159.9	133.3	9.7%
TELEPHONE BANKING	**69.3**	**73.6**	**78.3**	**83.1**	**89.1**	**87.0**	**–5.8%**
Transfers	18.8	19.1	19.8	20.3	19.9	18.6	–1.6%
Bill payments	50.5	54.5	58.4	62.8	69.2	68.4	–7.3%

*The six banks were BMO Financial Group, CIBC, National Bank, RBC Financial Group, Scotiabank, and TD Financial Group.

Source: Canadian Bankers Association, www.cba.ca.

costs compared with employing full-service tellers, the inability of machines to address customers' concerns and questions flexibly may drive retail customers away and revenue losses may counteract any cost-savings effects. Customers still want to interact with a person for many transactions. However, a survey of 1,200 consumers in June 2008 indicated that the primary means of bill payment in Canada was through the computer/online. Figure 16–1 summarizes the data of this survey of how Canadians pay their bills. Although 35 percent pay their bills by computer/online, 11 percent still pay at a branch.[14]

Technology and Costs

Traditionally, FIs have considered the major benefits of technological advances to be on the cost side rather than the revenue side. After a theoretical look at how technology favourably or unfavourably affects an FI's costs, we look at the direct and indirect evidence of technology-based cost savings for FIs. In general, technology may favourably affect an FI's cost structure by allowing it to exploit either economies of scale or economies of scope.

Economies of Scale

As financial firms become larger, the potential scale and array of the technology in which they can invest generally expands.[15] As noted above, the largest FIs make

---

[14] See Canadian Bankers Association, *Technology and Banking*, www.cba.ca.

[15] Economies of scale and scope can result from a variety of factors other than technology (e.g., geographic diversification or merger with another FI). In this section, however, we demonstrate these economies using a framework of technological investments.

FIGURE 16–1
How Canadians Pay Bills

Source: Canadian Bankers Association, *Survey: Technology and Canada's Banking Industry, Strategic Counsel,* 2008.

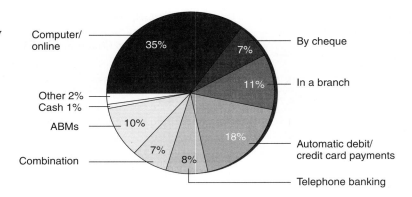

economy of scale

A drop in the average costs of production as the output of an FI increases.

the largest expenditures on technology-related innovations. If improved technology lowers an FI's average costs of financial service production, larger FIs may have an **economy of scale** advantage over smaller financial firms. Economies of scale imply that the unit or average cost of producing FI services in aggregate (or some specific service such as deposits or loans) falls as the size of the FI expands.

Figure 16–2 shows economies of scale for three different-sized FIs. The average cost of producing an FI's output of financial services is measured as

$$AC_i = \frac{TC_i}{S_i}$$

where

AC_i = Average costs of the ith FI
TC_i = Total costs of the ith FI
S_i = Size of the FI measured by assets, deposits, or loans.[16]

The largest FI in Figure 16–2 (of size S_C) has a lower average cost of producing financial services than do smaller firms S_B and S_A. This means that at any given price for financial service firm products, firm S_C can make a bigger profit than either S_B or S_A. Alternatively, firm S_C can undercut S_B and S_A in price and potentially gain a larger market share. For example, Regions Financial and AmSouth Bancorp's US$10 billion merger in 2006 was billed as a cost-saving merger. The

FIGURE 16–2
Economies of Scale in FIs

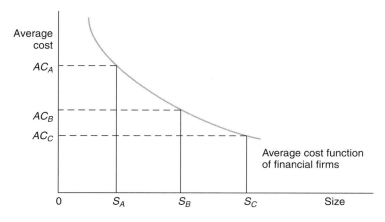

---

[16] It is arguable that the size of a modern FI should be measured by including off-balance-sheet assets (contingent value) as well.

combined company expected to realize US$400 million in annual cost savings (about 10 percent of the combined company's operating expense base) by spring 2008. The banks had headquarter operations across the street from each other, operations centres in the same city, and branches in the same neighbourhoods. Cost-cutting was expected to come mainly from back-office positions in departments such as accounting, public relations, and data processing. In the framework of Figure 16–2, Regions Financial, firm S_A, might be operating at AC_A and AmSouth might be represented as firm S_B operating at AC_B. The consolidation of overlapping activities would lower the average costs for the combined (larger) bank S_C in Figure 16–2, operating at AC_C. The long-run implication of economies of scale on the FI sector is that the larger and most cost-efficient FIs will drive out smaller FIs, leading to increased large-firm dominance and concentration in financial services production. Such an implication is reinforced if time-related operating or technological improvements increasingly benefit larger FIs more than smaller FIs. For example, satellite technology and supercomputers, in which enormous technological advances are being made, may be available to only the largest FIs. The effect of improving technology over time, which is biased toward larger projects, is to shift the AC curve downward over time but with a larger downward shift for large FIs (see Figure 16–3). In Figure 16–3, AC_1 is the hypothetical AC curve prior to cost-reducing technological innovations. AC_2 reflects the cost-lowering effects of technology on FIs of all sizes but with the greatest benefit accruing to those of the largest size.

As noted earlier, technological investments are risky; if their future revenues do not cover their costs of development, they reduce the value of the FI and its net worth to the FI's owners. On the cost side, large-scale investments may result in excess capacity problems and integration problems as well as cost overruns and cost control problems. Then small FIs with simple and easily managed computer systems and/or those leasing time on large FIs' computers (e.g., President's Choice Financial is operated by CIBC) without bearing the fixed costs of installation and maintenance may have an average cost advantage. In this case, technological investments of large-sized FIs result in higher average costs of financial service production, causing the industry to operate under conditions of **diseconomies of scale** (see Figure 16–4). Diseconomies of scale imply that small FIs are more cost-efficient than large FIs and that in a freely competitive environment for financial services, small FIs prosper.

diseconomy of scale
Increase in the average costs of production as the output of an FI increases.

FIGURE 16–3 Effects of Technological Improvement

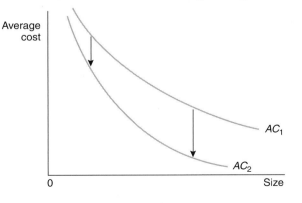

FIGURE 16–4 Diseconomies of Scale

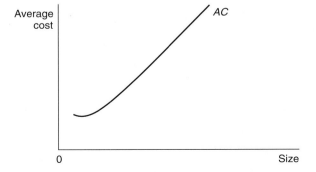

At least two other possible shapes for the *AC* function exist (see Figure 16–5). In panel (a) of Figure 16–5, the financial services industry reflects economies of scale at first and then diseconomies of scale as firms grow larger. This suggests that a best or most efficient size for an FI exists at point S^* and that too much technology investment can be as bad as too little. Panel (b) of Figure 16–5 represents constant returns to scale. Any potential cost-reducing effects of technology are spread evenly over FIs of all sizes. That is, technology investments are neutral rather than favouring one size of FI over another.

Economies of Scope

Although technological investments may have positive or negative effects on FIs in general and these effects may well differ across FIs of different size, technology tends to be applied more in some product areas than in others. That is, FIs are multiproduct firms producing services involving different technological needs. Moreover, technological improvements or investments in one financial service area (such as lending) may have incidental and synergistic benefits in lowering the costs of producing financial services in other areas (such as securities underwriting and brokerage). Specifically, computerization allows the storage and joint use of important information on customers and their needs. The simple *economy of scale* concept ignores these interrelationships among products and the "jointness" in the costs of producing financial products. In particular, FIs' abilities to generate synergistic cost savings through joint use of inputs in producing multiple products is called *economies of scope* as opposed to economies of scale.

Technology may allow two FIs to jointly use their input resources, such as capital and labour, to produce a set of financial services at a lower cost than if financial service products were produced independently of one another. Specifically, let X_1 and X_2 be two financial products; each is produced by one firm as a specialized producer. That is, firm A produces only X_1 and no X_2, and firm B produces only X_2 and no X_1. The average cost functions (*AC*) of these firms are

$$AC_A[X_1, 0] \quad \text{and} \quad AC_B[0, X_2]$$

economies of scope
The ability of FIs to generate synergistic cost savings through joint use of inputs in producing multiple products.

Economies of scope exist if these firms merge and jointly produce X_1 and X_2, resulting in

$$AC_{A+B}[X_1, X_2] < AC_A[X_1, 0] + AC_B[0, X_2]$$

That is, the cost of joint production via cost synergies is less than the separate and independent production of these services.

FIGURE 16–5
Other Average Cost Functions

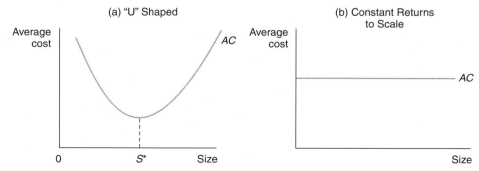

(a) "U" Shaped

(b) Constant Returns to Scale

EXAMPLE 16–1

Calculation of Average Cost

Let TC_B be a bank's total cost of producing lending services to a corporate client. Suppose that the total operating costs of producing these services is $50,000 for a loan volume (L_B) of $10 million. Such costs include information collection and monitoring as well as account maintenance and processing. Thus, the average cost (AC_B) of loan production for the bank is

$$AC_B = \frac{TC_B}{L_B} = \frac{\$50,000}{\$10,000,000} = 0.005 = 0.5\%$$

At the same time, a specialized investment bank is selling commercial paper for the same corporate customer. The investment bank's total cost (TC_S) of running the commercial paper operation is $10,000 for a $1 million issue ($P_S$). These costs include the cost of underwriting the issue as well as placing the issue with outside buyers. Thus,

$$AC_S = \frac{TC_S}{P_S} = \frac{\$10,000}{\$1,000,000} = 0.01 = 1\%$$

Consequently, the total average cost (TAC) of separately producing the loan services through the bank and the commercial paper issuance through the investment bank is

$$TAC = \frac{\$60,000}{\$11,000,000} = 0.54\%$$

Suppose, instead, a single FI produces both $10 million of lending services and $1 million commercial paper issuance services for the same customer (i.e., P_{FS} = $11 million). Loans and commercial paper are substitute sources of funds for corporate customers. For an FI to originate a loan and commercial paper requires very similar expertise both in funding that issue and in credit risk assessment and monitoring. Common technologies in the loan and commercial paper production functions suggest that a single FI simultaneously (or jointly) producing both loan and commercial paper services for the same client at a total cost TC_{FS} should be able to do this at a lower average cost than could the specialized FIs that separately produce these services. That is, the single FI should be able to produce the $11,000,000 ($P_{FS}$) of financial services at a lower cost (say TC_{FS} = $51,000), than should two specialized FIs. Accordingly,

$$AC_{FS} = \frac{TC_{FS}}{P_{FS}} = \frac{\$51,000}{\$11,000,000} = 0.46\% < 0.54\%$$

Formally, if AC_{FS} is the total average cost of a non-specialized financial services firm, then economies of scope imply that

$$AC_{FS} < TAC$$

diseconomies of scope
The costs of joint production of FI services are higher than they would be if they were produced independently.

Nevertheless, **diseconomies of scope** may occur instead; FIs find costs actually higher from joint production of services than if they were produced independently. For example, suppose an FI purchases some very specialized information-based technology to ease the loan production and processing function. The FI could use any excess capacity this system has in other service areas. However, this process could be a relatively inefficient technology for other service areas and could add to the overall costs of production compared with using a specialized technology for each service or product area.

CONCEPT QUESTIONS

1. What are two risk factors involved in an FI's investment of resources in innovative technological products?
2. Does the existence of economies of scale for FIs mean that in the long run, small FIs cannot survive?

3. If there are diseconomies of scope, do specialized FIs have a relative cost advantage or disadvantage over product-diversified FIs?
4. Make a list of the potential economies of scope or cost synergies if two Canadian FIs were allowed to merge. How would the merger of two large Canadian banks differ from the merger of a bank and an insurance company?

TESTING FOR ECONOMIES OF SCALE AND ECONOMIES OF SCOPE

To test for economies of scale and economies of scope, FIs must clearly specify both the inputs to their production process and the cost of those inputs.[17] Basically, the two approaches to analyzing the cost functions of FIs are the production and the intermediation approaches.

The Production Approach

The production approach views FIs' outputs of services as having two underlying inputs: labour and capital. If w = wage costs of labour, r = rental costs of capital, and y = output of services, the total cost function (C) for the FI is

$$C = f(y, w, r)$$

The Intermediation Approach

The intermediation approach views the output of financial services as being produced by labour and capital as well as funds the intermediary uses to produce intermediated services. Thus, deposit costs would be an input in the banking and trust industries, while premiums or reserves would be inputs in the insurance industry, and

$$C = f(y, w, r, k)$$

where k reflects the cost of funds for the FI.

CONCEPT QUESTIONS

1. Describe the basic concept behind the production approach to testing for economies of scale and economies of scope.
2. How does the intermediation approach differ from the production approach?

EMPIRICAL FINDINGS ON COST ECONOMIES OF SCALE AND SCOPE AND IMPLICATIONS FOR TECHNOLOGY EXPENDITURES

A large number of studies have examined economies of scale and scope in different financial services industry sectors.[18] With respect to banks, most of the early studies failed to find economies of scale for any but the smallest banks. More recently,

---

[17] Three major production function forms have been tested: the Cobb–Douglas, the translog, and the Box–Cox flexible functional form.

[18] Good reviews are found in A. Berger, W. C. Hunter, and S. B. Timme, "The Efficiency of Financial Institutions: A Review and Preview of Research Past, Present and Future," *Journal of Banking and Finance* 17, 1993, pp. 221–49; and R. DeYoung, *Learning-by-Doing, Scale Efficiencies, and Financial Performance at Internet-Only Banks,* Federal Reserve Bank of Chicago working paper, June 2002, and A. Berger and R. DeYoung, "Technological Progress and the Geographic Expansion of the Banking Industry," *Journal of Money, Credit, and Banking,* September 2006, pp. 1483–1513.

better data sets and improved methodologies have suggested that economies of scale may exist for banks up to the $10 billion to $25 billion size range. With respect to economies of scope either among deposits, loans, and other traditional banking product areas or between on-balance-sheet products and off-balance-sheet products such as loan sales, the evidence that cost synergies exist is at best very weak. Similarly, the smaller number of studies involving non-bank financial services firms such as savings and loans, co-ops, insurance companies, and securities firms almost always report neither economies of scale nor economies of scope.[19]

Economies of Scale and Scope and X-Inefficiencies

X-inefficiency
The production of less than efficient levels of output from a given level of input.

A number of more recent studies that primarily use data for U.S. FIs have looked at the *dispersion* of costs in any given FI size class rather than the shape of the average cost functions. These efficiency studies find quite dramatic cost differences of 20 percent or more among banks and insurance companies in any given size class ($100 million asset size class, $200 million asset size class, etc.). Moreover, these studies find that only a small part of the cost differences among FIs in any size class can be attributed to economies of scale or scope.[20] This suggests that cost inefficiencies related to managerial performance and other hard-to-quantify factors (so-called ***X-inefficiencies***) may better explain cost differences and operating cost efficiencies among financial firms than technology-related investments per se.[21]

There is little strong, direct evidence that larger multiproduct financial services firms enjoy cost advantages over smaller, more specialized financial firms. Nor do economies of scope and scale explain many of the cost differences among FIs of the same size. These empirical findings raise questions about the benefits of technology investments and technological innovation. While a majority of the studies tested for economies of scope and scale rather than the benefits of technology, these results are consistent with the relatively low payoff from technological innovation. To the extent that large FIs obtain benefits, they may well be on the revenue generation/new product innovation side rather than on the cost side. Indeed, recent studies looking at output and input efficiencies for banks and insurance companies derived from revenue and profit functions found that large FIs tend to be more efficient in revenue generation than smaller FIs and that such efficiencies may well offset scope and scale cost inefficiencies related to size.[22]

---

[19] A. Berger, D. Humphrey, and L. B. Pulley, "Do Consumers Pay for One-Stop Banking? Evidence from an Alternative Revenue Function," *Journal of Banking and Finance* 20, 1996, pp. 1601–21, look at revenue economies of scope (rather than cost economies of scope) between loans and deposits over the 1978–1990 period and find no evidence of revenue economies of scope. J. D. Cummins, S. Tennyson, and M. A. Weiss, "Consolidation and Efficiency in the U.S. Life Insurance Industry," *Journal of Banking and Finance* 23, 1999, pp. 325–57, find that mergers and acquisitions in the insurance industry do produce economies of scale, while efficiency gains are significantly smaller in non-M&A life insurers.

[20] See K. Mukherjee, S. C. Ray, and S. M. Miller, "Productivity Growth in Large U.S. Commercial Banks: The Initial Post-Deregulation Experience," *Journal of Banking and Finance* 25, 2001, pp. 913–39; and A. Akhigbe and J. E. McNulty, "The Profit Efficiency of Small U.S. Commercial Banks," *Journal of Banking and Finance* 27, 2003, pp. 307–25.

[21] See, for example, T. T. Milbourn, A. W. A. Boot, and A. V. Thakor, "Megamergers and Expanded Scope: Theories of Bank Size and Activity Diversity," *Journal of Banking and Finance* 23, 1999, pp. 195–214.

[22] See A. N. Berger and L. J. Mester, "Inside the Black-Box: What Explains Differences in the Efficiencies of Financial Institutions," *Journal of Banking and Finance* 21 (1997), pp. 895–947, for an extensive review of these efficiency studies. See also J. Cummins, S. Tennyson, and M. A. Weiss, "Efficiency, Scale Economies and Consolidation in the U.S. Life Insurance Industry," *Journal of Banking and Finance,* February 1999, pp. 325–57; and R. DeYoung and K. P. Roland, "Product Mix and Earnings Volatility at Commercial Banks: Evidence from a Degree of Total Leverage Model," *Journal of Financial Intermediation* 10, 2001, pp. 54–84. In contrast to the majority of the research, a study of 201 large U.S. commercial banks in the post-deregulation period (after 1984) finds overall productivity growth at a rate of about 4.5 percent per year on average. The growth in productivity reflected adjustments in technology. See Mukherjee et al., "Productivity Growth in Large U.S. Commercial Banks."

Finally, the real benefits of technological innovation may be long term and dynamic, related to the evolution of the Canadian and U.S. payments systems away from cash and cheques and toward electronic means of payment. Such benefits are difficult to obtain in traditional economy of scale and scope studies, which are largely static and ignore the more dynamic aspects of efficiency gains. This dynamic technological evolution not only has affected the fundamental role of FIs in the financial system but also has generated some new and subtle types of risks for FIs and their regulators. In the next section we take a closer look at the effects of technology on the payments system.

CONCEPT QUESTIONS	1. What does the empirical evidence reveal about economies of scale and scope?
	2. What conclusion is suggested by recent studies that have focused on the dispersion of costs across banks of a given asset size?

TECHNOLOGY AND THE EVOLUTION OF THE PAYMENTS SYSTEM

To better understand the changing nature of the payments system, look at Tables 16–3 to 16–5. Non-electronic methods—cheques—accounted for 14.9 percent of non-cash transactions, but this represented 33.5 percent of the dollar *value* of non-cash transactions. By comparison, while electronic methods of payment—credit cards, debit cards, and credit transfer systems and direct debits—accounted for 85.1 percent in volume, they accounted for 66.5 percent in value.

As can be seen from Tables 16–4 and 16–5, the use of electronic methods of payment is higher in other major developed countries than in the United States. For example, in Canada, Germany, and the United Kingdom electronic transactions

TABLE 16–3
Canadian Cashless Payments: Volume, Value, and Average Transaction Amount, 2007

Source: Bank for International Settlements, *Statistics on Payment Systems in Selected Countries*, Basel, Switzerland, March 2009, www.bis.org.

	Volume, (billions)	Percent	Value, ($ billions)	Percent	Transaction Average Value ($)
Cheque	1.3	14.9	$ 4,001.0	33.5	$3,117
Debit card	3.5	40.2	156.8	1.3	46
Credit card	2.2	25.3	240.5	2.0	108
Credit transfers	1.0	11.5	7,025.9	58.7	6,791
Direct debits	0.7	8.0	536.1	4.5	763
	8.7		$11,960.3		

TABLE 16–4
Percentage of Total Volume of Non-Cash Paper and Electronic Transactions, 2007

Source: Bank for International Settlements, *Statistics on Payment Systems in Selected Countries*, Basel, Switzerland, March 2009, www.bis.org.

	Paper (Cheque)	Debit and Credit Cards	Credit Transfers	Direct Debits	Total Electronic
Canada	14.8	65.3	11.9	8.1	85.3
United States	28.6	54.5	6.5	10.4	71.4
Germany	0.6	14.5	36.2	19.9	99.4
United Kingdom	10.7	48.4	21.0	48.3	89.3

TABLE 16–5
Percentage of Total Value of Non-Cash Paper and Electronic Transactions, 2007

Source: Bank for International Settlements, *Statistics on Payment Systems in Selected Countries*, Basel, Switzerland, March 2009, www.bis.org.

	Paper (Cheque)	Debit and Credit Cards	Credit Transfers	Direct Debits	Total Electronic
Canada	33.5	3.3	58.7	4.5	66.5
United States	52.4	4.2	25.1	18.3	47.6
Germany	0.7	0.2	83.0	16.1	99.3
United Kingdom	1.5	0.4	97.3	0.8	98.5

account for over 85 percent of total transactions measured by number of transactions. To some extent, the United States is only now starting to catch up with these countries. Part of the reason for this involves culture and tradition in the United States. For example, cheques have been obsolete in Germany for some time, but in the United States people still prefer to write cheques. As a result, U.S. FIs have been slower in adopting and using online banking and electronic payment methods extensively. The speed with which this electronic payments gap will be closed will in large part depend on two factors: the speed with which the trend toward consolidation and automated banking continues and the degree and speed of technological innovation. Note that in terms of dollar values of transactions completed electronically (Table 16–5), Canada and the United States are lower compared with Germany and the United Kingdom: 47.6 percent in the United States compared with 66.5 percent, 99.3 percent, and 98.5 percent in Canada, Germany, and the United Kingdom, respectively.

Cheque writing lays the foundation of e-money. When a cheque is written and given to a person with an account at a different bank, the banks do not transfer currency. Rather, the banks use an electronic fund transfer. E-money removes the middleman. Instead of requesting that the banks transfer funds, the e-money user transfers the money from his or her bank account to the account of the funds' receiver. The primary function of e-money is to facilitate transactions on the Internet. Many of these transactions may be small in value and would not be cost-efficient through other payment mediums such as credit cards. With e-money, the user can download money into his or her cyber-wallet in any currency desired. A merchant can accept any amount and currency and convert it into local currency when the cyber-cash is uploaded to a bank account. If a user wants e-money offline, all that is necessary is smart card technology. The money is loaded onto the smart card, and electronic wallets are used to offload the money onto other smart cards or directly to an online system. In essence, e-money transfers combine the benefits of other transaction methods. They are similar to debit/credit cards, but allow individuals to conduct transactions directly with each other. Like personal cheques, they are feasible for very small transactions. However, unlike deposits that are insured by CDIC, money stored in e-money accounts and cards is not covered by deposit insurance.

Large Value Transfer System (LVTS)

The payment system operated by the Canadian Payments Association for time-sensitive, large value transactions that are irrevocable.

Automated Clearing Settlement System (ACSS)

The payment system for ordinary transactions operated by the Canadian Payments Association.

Canada has two systems for the clearing of non-cash payments. As noted in Chapter 13, the **Large Value Transfer System (LVTS)** handles time-sensitive, large value transactions. The **Automated Clearing Settlement System (ACSS)** processes regular bill payments (e.g., debit card transactions, cheques, automatic bill payments). The LVTS thus operates essentially as a wholesale type of system while the ACSS is the system for smaller retail transactions.

The payments system has been viewed in Canada as a source of systemic risk to the financial system. For this reason, in 1996, the Payment Clearing and

Settlement Act gave the Bank of Canada responsibility for the payment systems that could put the overall financial system at risk including, since 1999, the LVTS. The focus has been to develop a system that serves Canadians nationally with the best technology and with a view to competition and economies of scale and scope. The additional focus has also been on cross-border transactions within North America, particularly the United States, but with a view to the internationalization of capital flows. Two studies provide details of the current view of the payments system in Canada. The first is James Dingle's history of the Canadian Payments Association from 1980 to 2002. The second is a 2001 BIS study that outlines the future of payment systems from a global perspective.[23]

Another way to see the enormous growth in the use of electronic transfers in Canada is to consider the percentage of electronic versus paper items flowing through the Automated Clearing Settlement System (ACSS) between 1990 and 2008. According to the Canadian Payments Association, the volume of electronic transactions grew from 13.4 per cent in 1990 to 82.08 percent in 2008. On a dollar value basis, electronic transactions increased from 0.6 percent in 1990 to 38.65 percent of the value of the transactions through the ACSS in 2008. Although the value of paper transactions was still 61.35 percent in 2008, the volume of electronic transactions through the ACSS has exceeded the number of paper transactions since 1997. The Canadian Payments Association's systems cleared, on average, 22.7 million items each business day in 2008, an average daily value of $209 billion.

According to the data in Table 16–6, Canada is not the only country in which wholesale wire transfer systems have come to dominate the payment systems. The United States, the United Kingdom, Switzerland, and Japan also have very large wire transfer systems measured as a percentage of local gross domestic product (GDP). In 2001 as a result of the single currency (the euro) and the European Monetary Union, a single wholesale wire transfer system for Europe fully emerged, linking all countries that are members of the European Monetary Union. The transaction system is called TARGET (Trans-European Automated Real-Time Gross-Settlement Express Transfer).

Risks That Arise in an Electronic Transfer Payment System

At least six important risks have arisen along with the growth of wire transfer systems. We mentioned some of these while discussing off-balance-sheet activities in Chapter 13; here, we go into more detail.

Settlement Risk

www.cdnpay.ca

The Canadian Payments Association (CPA) operates the payment systems in Canada. Members of the CPA include the Bank of Canada, all of the domestic banks, and authorized foreign banks. In addition, other deposit-taking institutions (credit unions, caisses populaires, savings and loans) as well as insurance companies, securities dealers, and mutual funds are also eligible for membership. Clearing of accounts is done through the LVTS and the ACSS as mentioned previously,

---

[23] See J. Dingle, *Planning an Evolution: The Story of the Canadian Payments Association, 1980–2002*, May 2003, the Bank of Canada and the Canadian Payments Association, available at www.cdnpay.ca. See also the Bank for International Settlements, Group of Ten, *Report on Consolidation in the Financial Sector, 2001*, Basel, Switzerland, which discusses the payment system in Chapter 6 and is available at www.bis.org. The difference in customs, regulations, and culture between countries, even between close neighbours such as Canada and the United States, is an issue in the globalization of payments systems.

TABLE 16–6
Wholesale Wire Transfer Systems in Selected Countries 2007

Source: Bank for International Settlements, *Statistics on Payment Systems in Selected Countries,* Basel, Switzerland, March 2009, www.bis.org.

	Number of Transactions (millions)	Annual Value of Transactions (US$ billions)	Value of Transactions as % of GDP
Japan			
FXYCS	7.75	$ 47,826	1,092.0%
BOJ-NET	6.76	250,381	5,717.0
Zengin System	1,353.3	22,313	509.5
Tokyo Clearing House	40.71	2,693	61.5
Netherlands			
Equens	3,802.6	2,815	362.8
Top	7.26	54,434	6,885.9
Sweden			
E-RIX	n.a.	2,405	n.a.
K-RIX	1.95	14,839	4.0
Bankgirot	620.0	624	218.2
Dataclearing	90.0	211	69.3
Switzerland			
SIC	356.8	43,570	10,208.9
United Kingdom			
CHAPS-Euro	5.57	n.a.	n.a.
CHAPS-Sterling	35.58	135,836	4,842.4
BACS	2,580.5	7,389	263.4
Cheque/credit	98.4	2,501	89.2
United States			
Fedwire	134.7	670,665	4,857.2
CHIPS	87.3	485,624	3,517.1
European Union			
TARGET	98.91	913,935	—
Euro 1/STEP 1	54.35	79,714	—
Canada			
LVTS	5.3	42,928	3,000.9

www.cls-services.com

continuous linked settlement (CLS)
The method of settling global foreign exchange transactions used by CLS Bank to eliminate settlement risk.

and the settlement of accounts occurs through adjustments to the accounts of approximately 12 financial institutions that have settlement accounts at the Bank of Canada. If an FI is unable to cover its LVTS or ACSS obligations, the Bank of Canada lends funds to the FI on an overnight basis at the upper band of the Bank rate. As a participant in the clearing and settlement system, the Bank of Canada also settles obligations for the Government of Canada.

Since 2002, the LVTS has been used for the settlement of Canadian dollar transfers in foreign exchange transactions through a process called **continuous linked settlement (CLS).** This process occurs between 1 a.m. and 6 a.m., Monday through Friday, resulting in a 24-hour-a-day operation at the CPA, and has virtually eliminated settlement risk on foreign exchange transactions by providing real-time and irrevocable settlement across international time zones. The market turmoil of 2007 and 2008 raised concerns at the Bank of Canada about settlement risk arising on foreign exchange transactions for Canadian banks with international counterparties. While Canadian FIs were remarkably stable during this time period, global FIs (e.g., AIG, Fortis) were experiencing severe liquidity constraints. Canadian banks increased their use of CLS Bank (see Industry Perspectives feature) for forex trades after Lehman Brothers, the U.S. investment bank, collapsed in September

2008. This episode illustrates the interconnection of risks (counterparty, foreign exchange, and operational risks) for major international FIs.[24]

Figure 16–6 illustrates the operations of the LVTS system on a daily basis. The settlement risk is virtually eliminated by the requirement that each direct participant in the LVTS be a member of the CPA, use the SWIFT network for telecommunications, and keep a settlement account at the Bank of Canada. In addition, there are limits on the net amount that each participant is able to owe, and each participant pledges collateral at the Bank of Canada, which provides liquidity to the system if one of the participants defaults. The participants have a choice between Tranche 1 payments, which are covered by the collateral pledged to the Bank of Canada, and Tranche 2 payments, which are bilateral lines of credit granted by each participant to every other participant. These are set daily and can be monitored and adjusted during the day. If the collateral is insufficient to settle the accounts when a participant fails, then the surviving FIs will absorb the losses, and, in the event of more than one participant failing, the Bank of Canada guarantees settlement. Participants with overdrafts at the Bank of Canada at the end of the day, either through their LVTS operations or through the ACSS, borrow overnight at the upper band of the Bank rate.

www.chips.org

The payment systems in the United States (Fedwire, CHIPS) are operated differently and give rise to daylight overdraft risk for those FIs (including Canadian banks) with U.S. operations. Some analysts and regulators view settlement, or daylight, overdraft risk as one of the greatest potential sources of instability in the financial markets today. To understand daylight overdrafts better, look at Figure 16–7. It shows a typical daily pattern of net wire payment transfers—payment messages sent (debits) minus payment messages received (credits)—for a large money centre bank using Fedwire (the Federal Reserve's wire transfer network).

Under the Federal Reserve Act, banks must maintain cash reserves on deposit at the Fed; Fedwire settlement occurs at the end of the banking day at 6:30 p.m. EST. At that time, the Fed adjusts each member bank's reserve account to reflect its net debit (credit) position with other banks.[25] Under current regulations, the

FIGURE 16–6   LVTS Daily Operating Schedule

12:30 a.m. – 11 p.m.	12:30 a.m. – 6 a.m.	6 a.m. – 6 p.m.	6 p.m. – 6:30 p.m.	6:30 p.m. – 7:30 p.m.
CLS participants pledge collateral to the Bank of Canada, set debit caps for Tranche 1 activity and lines of credit for Tranche 2 activity.	CLS transactions. Participants may adjust debit caps, lines of credit, collateral.	Other payments start. Non-CLS participants send debit caps, bilateral lines of credit, and collateral to the Bank of Canada between 7 a.m. and 8 a.m. Participants can track their positions and adjust Tranche 1, Tranche 2, and collateral during the day.	LVTS closes. Transactions between participants occur to reduce the need for overnight borrowing from the Bank of Canada.	The Bank of Canada settles each participant's account irrevocably and releases unused collateral.

Source: Bank of Canada, *LVTS Operating Schedule*, www.bankofcanada.ca.

---

[24] See J. Dingle, *The Elements of the Global Network for Large-Value Funds Transfers,* Bank of Canada Working Paper No. 2–1-1. 2001, pages 14 and 15, for a detailed description of the settlement of a foreign currency transaction involving U.S. dollars and Japanese yen through the international payments systems. See also the website for CLS Group at www.cls-services.com. CLS Bank eliminates the settlement risk of foreign exchange transactions by offsetting each party's account. The Bank of Canada acts as the banker for CLS Bank in Canada. J. Armstrong and G. Caldwell, "Liquidity Risk at Banks: Trends and Lessons Learned from the Recent Turmoil," Bank of Canada, *Financial System Review,* December 2008, pp. 47–52, provides insights into the foreign exchange settlement risk for Canadian banks.

[25] Technically, CHIPS transactions settle on Fedwire by 4:30 p.m. before Fedwire closes.

FIGURE 16–7
Daylight Overdrafts on Fedwire

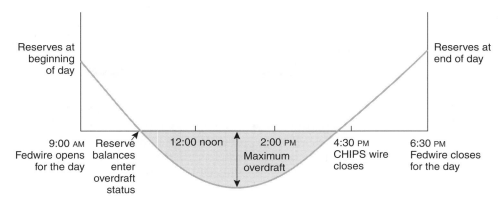

| 9:00 AM | Reserve | 12:00 noon | 2:00 PM | 4:30 PM | 6:30 PM |

Reserves at beginning of day

Reserves at end of day

9:00 AM
Fedwire opens for the day

Reserve balances enter overdraft status

12:00 noon

2:00 PM
Maximum overdraft

4:30 PM
CHIPS wire closes

6:30 PM
Fedwire closes for the day

daylight overdraft
A bank's negative intraday balance in its reserve account at the Fed.

member bank's end-of-day reserve position cannot be negative. However, what is true at the end of the day is not true during the day; that is, the Fed allows banks to run real-time **daylight overdrafts** (or negative intraday balances) on their reserve accounts. These negative reserve balances occur under the current payments system because large banks and their customers often send payment messages repaying overnight loans and making interest payments at the beginning of the banking day and borrow funds and receive payment messages toward the end of the banking day. For periods during the day, banks frequently run daylight overdrafts on their reserve accounts at the Fed by having their payment outflow messages exceed their payment inflow messages (see Figure 16–7).

In effect, the Fed is implicitly lending banks within-day reserves. This process involves two other important institutional factors. First, until 1993, the Fed did not charge banks an explicit interest rate or fee for these daylight overdrafts. As a result, neither banks nor their large corporate customers had any incentive to economize on these transactions. Daylight Fedwire overdrafts were effectively free and therefore oversupplied. The current daylight overdraft fee is 36 basis points, quoted as an annual rate on the basis of a 24-hour day.[26] Second, under Regulation J, the Fed guarantees payment finality for every wire transfer message. Therefore, if the representative bank in Figure 16–7 were to fail at 12:00 noon, the Fed would be liable for all of the bank's Fedwire transactions made that day by that bank until 12 noon. This eliminates any risk that a payment message-receiving bank or its customers would be left short of funds at the end of the day. Essentially, the Fed bears the Fedwire credit risk of bank failures by granting overdrafts without charging a market interest rate.[27]

On CHIPS, net payment flows often reflect a daily pattern similar to that in Figure 16–7 except that, as a privately owned pure net settlement system, the beginning-of-day position must be zero for all banks. As on Fedwire, big banks often run a daylight overdraft, but this is generally larger and more pronounced

---

[26] The annual rate is converted to an effective annual rate by multiplying it by the fraction of the day that Fedwire is scheduled to be open, currently 21.5 hours out of 24, or 21.5/24. Thus, the current effective annual rate charged for overdrafts is 32.25 basis points (36 basis points × 21.5/24 hours). The effective annual rate is converted to an effective daily rate by multiplying it by 1/360. See *Guide to the Federal Reserve's Payments System Risk Policy on Daylight Credit,* Federal Reserve System, January 2006.

[27] M. J. Fleming and K. D. Garbade analyze historical data on trades in U.S. Treasury and other securities that fail to settle as scheduled. They find that surges in fails sometimes result from operational disruptions, but often reflect market participants' insufficient incentive to avoid failing. See "Explaining Settlement Failures," Federal Reserve Bank of New York, *Current Issues in Economics and Finance,* September 2005.

early in the morning than it is on Fedwire. Again, large banks then seek to borrow funds in the afternoon to cover net debit positions created earlier in the day. CHIPS does not charge banks explicit fees for running daylight overdrafts, but it treats a bank's failure to settle at the end of the day differently than does Fedwire. On Fedwire, all payments are in good funds; that is, the Fed guarantees the finality of any wire transfer at the time it is made. By contrast, on CHIPS, US$2.4 billion in funds are made available to cover each day's payment transactions. These idle funds permit some 97 percent of CHIPS payments to be finally settled in real time and released to customers as no net debit is created. The 3 percent of payments that cannot be immediately settled are not released to customers until they are settled at the end of the day. Unlike previous arrangements used by CHIPS, because payments are not now released to receiving banks until adequate funds are in the sending bank's CHIPS account, there is no contractual provision for a payments unwind. However, there can be and has been a refusal of payment request on CHIPS. This last occurred in the wake of the 2001 terrorist attack in New York when some bank payment requests were not made because of insufficient funds (and the payment request was returned to the requesting bank).

Because of these concerns, the FDIC Improvement Act, passed in 1991, required the Federal Reserve to implement Regulation F, under which domestic and foreign banks must develop internal procedures or benchmarks to limit their settlement and other credit exposures to deposit-taking institutions with which they do business (so-called *correspondent banks*). Accordingly, since December 1992, banks have been required to limit their exposure to an individual correspondent to no more than 25 percent of the correspondent bank's capital. However, for adequately capitalized banks, this can be raised to 50 percent, while no set benchmark is required for well-capitalized banks. Thus, it is now easier for the most solvent banks to transact on the wire transfer networks and run daylight overdrafts than for less well-capitalized banks. In addition, as long as the benchmarks are adhered to, regulators' exposure to settlement risk is reduced.

International Technology Transfer Risk

In recent years Canada and the United States have been at the forefront in making technology investments and financial service innovations in the payments system. For example, North American FIs have been pioneers of ATMs, yet such networks have grown relatively slowly in countries such as Sweden and Belgium, often because of prohibitive charges imposed for the use and leasing of domestic telephone lines (see Table 16–7).

This suggests that financial service firms have often been unable to transfer profitably their domestic technological innovations to international markets to gain competitive advantage, at least in the short term.[28] In contrast, foreign financial service firms entering the North American market gain direct access to, and knowledge of, technology-based products at a very low cost.

Crime and Fraud Risk

The increased replacement of cheques and cash by electronic transfers as methods of payment or exchange has resulted in an increase in the efficiency of the

---

[28] Long-term benefits may yet be realized as a result of telecommunications deregulation globally and through better customer recruitment and marketing of products in foreign environments. See S. Claessens, T. Glaessner, and D. Klingebiel, "E-finance in Emerging Markets: Is Leapfrogging Possible?" *Financial Markets Institutions & Instruments,* February 2002, pp. 1–124, for an update on e-banking in emerging markets.

TABLE 16–7
Number of ATMs per 1 Million Inhabitants

Source: The Bank for International Settlements, *Statistics on Payment Systems in Selected Countries*, Basel, Switzerland, March 2009, www.bis.org.

	1991	2001	2004	2007
Belgium	105	669	1,268	1,448
Canada	467	1,142	1,513	1,748
France	284	606	700	821
Germany	161	603	638	831
Italy	204	593	690	817
Japan*	795	918	1,068	1,083
Netherlands	222	445	485	521
Singapore	—	435	386	415
Sweden	258	289	300	307
Switzerland	347	694	723	778
United Kingdom	309	612	909	1,040
United States	331	1,137	1,302	1,375

*At end-March of the following year.

execution of transactions, but it has also resulted in new problems regarding theft, data snooping, and white-collar crime. Because huge sums are transferred across the networks each day and some bank employees have specialized knowledge of personal identification numbers (PINS) and other entry codes, the incentive for white-collar crime appears to have increased. For example, a manager at the Sri Lankan branch of the now-defunct BCCI reportedly stole a computer chip from a telex machine in the bank's Oman branch and used it to transfer $10 million from three banks in the United States and Japan to his own account in Switzerland.

Moreover, considerable security problems exist in trying to develop the Internet as a form of electronic payment system. Internet transactions can be intercepted by third parties. Financial institutions are accordingly concerned about open credit or debit card details on the Internet. Any version of electronic payment via the Internet must not only meet the requirements of recognition and acceptability associated with physical cash but also provide the same high level of security that is demanded of cash payments but which the Internet itself cannot guarantee. After the terrorist attacks on September 11, 2001, the U.S. Congress passed the USA Patriot Act of 2001. The act contains a number of specific amendments to existing criminal laws designed to streamline early detection and investigation of suspected terrorist activity conducted through financial institutions. In December 2005, the Federal Reserve and Treasury Department fined Dutch bank ABN Amro US$80 million for violating U.S. money-laundering laws and sanctions against Iran and Libya. The move came in response to nearly 10 years of violations involving billions of dollars in transactions that passed through the bank's offices in New York and Dubai, United Arab Emirates. The investigation found that bank employees falsified numerous wire transfer records to hide the identities of Iranian and Libyan companies and individuals sending money to the United States.

In the future, greater bank and regulatory resources will have to be spent on surveillance and employee monitoring as well as on developing fail-safe and unbreakable entry codes to wire transfer accounts, especially as a number of countries have passed data privacy laws.

The USA Patriot Act has had unforeseen consequences for Canadian FIs. OSFI keeps an up-to-date list of suspected terrorist organizations on its website, and provides guidelines to deposit-taking institutions regarding the Proceeds of Crime (Money Laundering) and Terrorism Financing Act introduced in 2003. All federally regulated FIs except property and casualty insurance companies are required

INDUSTRY PERSPECTIVES

BANKS FALL IN LINE TO MANAGE RISKS; PRESSURED BY BOC

Bank of Nova Scotia is dropping its resistance to participation in an international system for managing risks in the foreign-exchange market amid pressure from the Bank of Canada.

The largest foreign-exchange dealer in the country has committed to joining the global scheme after the central bank blamed Bay Street's limited participation for worsening the crisis in the banking system, the *Financial Post* has learned.

The move comes as the Bank of Canada takes a more assertive approach to advocating steps that foster financial stability amid a deepening economic crisis.

The central bank is concerned about the threat posed to the country's banking system if a financial institution pays out huge sums in a currency exchange but never gets paid because the other party fails before the trade is settled.

This risk has been a key worry for the world's central bankers for more than a decade and led to the creation of a global clearing house designed to all but eliminate this risk.

"The strategy was motivated by the finding that banks' foreign-exchange settlement exposures to their counter-parties were in many cases extremely large relative to their capital," said a report delivered earlier this year by Timothy Geithner, the central banker chosen by Barack Obama, the U. S. president-elect, as his new Treasury Secretary.

But the Bank of Canada has found Bay Street reluctant to pay the fees required to use the new system, and signalled a new sense of urgency to all the banks last month during a private meeting with top currency dealers.

In a sign of its new bolder approach to public advocacy, the central bank also pointed out last week in a review of the country's financial system that "one major bank does not use [the system] and another settles only a small portion of its foreign exchange transactions through [the scheme]."

It emerged yesterday that Scotiabank is not a participant, while Toronto-Dominion Bank joined Last year.

Barry Wainstein, Scotiabank's head of foreign exchange, said yesterday the bank had made the decision to join the system following a series of collapses on Wall Street. "By the middle of 2009, we will be a fully participating member," he said.

Mr. Wainstein stressed that it was a decision the bank had come to on its own and was not the result of external pressure. "This was a decision that we made," Mr. Wainstein said.

Scotiabank is thought to have resisted paying the fees to join the international scheme because it is not designed to handle swaps of Canadian and U.S. dollars, and is instead geared toward trades across time zones in yen, euros or greenbacks.

But this sticking point has been overshadowed by the earthquake in the banking system and the fear that swept Bay Street after the collapse of Lehman Brothers Holdings Inc., a U.S. investment bank.

Currency traders on Bay Street spent fretful days and weeks wondering if currency trades with Lehman and other wobbly institutions would be honoured, and are now coping with lingering risk aversion.

The Bank of Canada said much of this uncertainty could have been alleviated if Bay Street participated more fully in the global clearing house and is strongly urging all banks to step up their involvement.

Said the central bank: "The Lehman Brothers episode raises questions about the [foreign-exchange settlement risk] management practices of Canadian banks, since a large portion of their foreign exchange transactions are settled outside of the CLS Bank [the clearing bank]."

"Greater use of CLS Bank might have helped to alleviate some of their uncertainty in the wake of the failure of Lehman Brothers. The Bank of Canada encourages Canadian banks to consider using CLS Bank [to manage risks]," the bank added.

Source: Eoin Callan. *Financial Post*, Dec. 19, 2008, p. FP4.

to implement programs to detect and prevent money laundering in order to protect their reputations and the stability of the financial system. OSFI works with the **Financial Transactions and Reports Analysis Centre of Canada** (FINTRAC, www.fintrac.gc.ca) to counteract money laundering and terrorist activities, which come under the Criminal Code of Canada, and the Royal Canadian Mounted Police (RCMP) may subpoena customer account information to investigate a

Financial Transactions and Reports Analysis Centre of Canada (FINTRAC)
A Government of Canada operation that tracks and analyzes money laundering, terrorist activity, and threats to Canadian security.

crime. However, U.S. authorities have much broader powers to search under the Patriot Act and, since both Royal Bank of Canada and CIBC outsource management of their credit card operations to Total Systems Services, a U.S. company, Canadian customers' transactions are open to scrutiny and the FIs are not permitted to let customers know if they are under investigation.[29]

Regulatory Risk

The improvement in FIs' computer and telecommunications networks also enhances the power of FIs' vis-à-vis regulators, effectively aiding regulatory avoidance. Thus, as implied earlier, regulation not only can affect the profitability of technological innovations, but also can spur or hinder the rate and types of innovation.[30] As a result of regulation in Canada and in the United States, banking in the relatively unregulated Cayman Islands has experienced considerable growth. The 500 or more FIs located there do most of their business via public and private telecommunications networks. The use of telecommunications networks and technological improvements has changed, perhaps irreversibly, the balance of power between large multinational FIs and governments—both local and national—in favour of the former. Such a shift in power may create incentives for countries to lower their regulations to attract entrants; that is, the shift may increase the incentives for competitive deregulation. This trend may be potentially destabilizing to the market in financial services, with the weakest regulators attracting the most entrants.[31]

Tax Avoidance

The development of international wire networks as well as international financial service firm networks has enabled FIs to shift funds and profits by using internal pricing mechanisms, thereby minimizing their overall domestic tax burden and maximizing their foreign tax credits. For example, prior to 1986, many large Canadian and U.S. banks paid almost no corporate income taxes, despite large reported profits, by rapidly moving profits and funds across different tax regimes. This raised considerable public policy concerns and was a major reason underlying the 1987 tax reforms in Canada. These reforms changed the rules for issuing preferred shares.[32]

Competition Risk

www.myctfs.com

As financial services become more technologically based, they are increasingly competing with non-traditional financial service suppliers. Also, once established, non-financial firms can easily purchase financial services technology. For example, Canadian Tire Financial Services offers savings accounts, GICs, credit cards, and mortgages. Thus, technology exposes existing FIs to the increased risk of erosion of their franchises as costs of entry fall and the competitive landscape changes.

---

[29] See T. Hamilton, "Prospect of U.S. Patriot Act-Snooping Bothers Canadians. Who's Trustworthy? Canadians, American Disagree," *Toronto Star,* October 11, 2004, p. D01; and S. Laidlaw, "Banks Up Customer Surveillance; U.S.A. Patriot Act's Long Arm Reaching into Canadian Bank, Credit Card Accounts. Bankers Can't Tell Customers They Are Under Investigation," *Toronto Star,* December 29, 2004, p. E01.

[30] A further example of regulatory risk impacts on technology and operating costs in general is the cost of converting European banks' systems from local currencies into the euro. This may cost European banks $150 billion or more. See "A Year before the Millennium Bug, There's the Euro Problem," *New York Times,* March 9, 1998, p. 1.

[31] A closely associated risk for regulators is that increased use of international wire transfer systems weakens the power of central banks to control the domestic money supply.

[32] See I. Fooladi, P. McGraw, and G. Roberts, "Preferred Share Rules Freeze Out the Individual Investor," *CA Magazine,* April 1988, pp. 38–41.

1. Describe the six risks faced by FIs with the growth of wire transfer payment systems.
2. What steps has the Canadian Payments Association taken to lower settlement risk for the LVTS?

OTHER OPERATIONAL RISKS

While technology risk has become increasingly important to the profitability and riskiness of modern FIs, it is not the sole source of operational risk. Indeed, studies have found that the impact of an operational risk crisis (such as embezzlement and loan fraud) on the market value of a firm far exceeds (as much as 12 times) the actual cost.[33] Early in the chapter we listed four other sources of operational risk. These are employees, customer relationships, capital assets, and external risks. For example, employee risk includes employee turnover and fraud, as well as programming errors by employees.

Table 16–8 lists a summary of the problems these sources of operational risk can create, including how the other sources of operational risk interact with technology risk. For example, a survey by the International Swap and Derivatives Association found that only 40 percent of credit derivative contracts are confirmed by electronic means. The average amount of time to confirm the remainder is 12 days. The reasons for the slow confirmation include extreme volume, awaiting data or approval from traders' legal or compliance departments, approval from credit or collateral departments, and systems or technology issues. This could lead to very serious operational risks if there are defaults by corporations.[34] Similarly, the failure of a third-party technology provider to perform as promised, resulting in an FI's online banking services being interrupted, may cause the FI to lose customers.

www.isda.org

Like technology risk, these other sources of operational risk can result in direct costs (e.g., loss of income), indirect costs (e.g., client withdrawals and legal costs), and opportunity costs (e.g., forgone business opportunities) for an FI that reduce profitability and value. To offset these costs, FI managers spend considerable effort and resources to prevent, control, finance, and insulate the FI from losses due to operational risk. These efforts include:

1. *Loss prevention.* Training, development, and review of employees.
2. *Loss control.* Planning, organization, backup (e.g., computer systems).
3. *Loss financing.* External insurance (e.g., catastrophe insurance).
4. *Loss insulation:* FI capital.

Risk management efforts, of course, come at a cost to the FI. As illustrated in Figure 16–8, the greater the commitment of resources to risk management efforts, the lower the costs resulting from operational risks. However, the resources spent in preventing costs of operational risk may, at some point, be greater than the cost of the risk itself. In maximizing profits and value, FIs will invest in these risk management efforts until the costs of such efforts just offset operating losses from not undertaking such efforts (point RME* in Figure 16–8).

---

[33] See R. S. Dunnett, C. B. Levy, and A. P. Simoes, "The Hidden Costs of Operational Risk," *McKinsey on Finance,* Winter 2005, pp. 14–18.

[34] See *ISDA 2005 Operations Benchmarking Survey* and *FpML Use Survey,* International Swaps and Derivatives Association, Inc., 2005.

TABLE 16–8
A Summary of Operational Risks Faced by FIs

Source: C. Marshall, *Measuring and Managing Operational Risks in Financial Institutions: Tools, Techniques and Other Resources*. Singapore: John Wiley and Sons, 2001.

Source of Risk	Specific Problem
Employee risk	Employee turnover
	Key personnel risk
	Fraud risk
	Error
	Rogue trading
	Money laundering
	Confidentiality breach
Technology risk	Programming error
	Model risk
	Mark-to-market error
	Management information
	IT systems outage
	Telecommunications failure
	Technology provider failure
	Contingency planning
Customer risk	Contractual disagreement
	Dissatisfaction
	Default
Capital asset risk	Safety
	Security
	Operating costs
	Fire/flood
External risk	External fraud
	Taxation risk
	Legal risk
	War
	Collapse of markets
	Reputation risk
	Relationship risk

FIGURE 16–8
Optimal Risk Management Effort

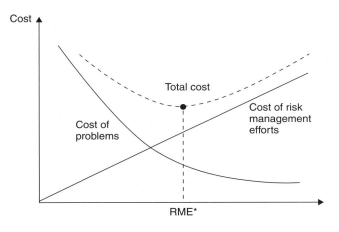

Extent of risk managment efforts

As discussed previously, the Royal Bank of Canada has a three-pronged approach to operational risk (self-assessment and control, a loss event database, and the identification of key risk indicators). Similarly, Bank of Montreal has an "Operational

In Germany, an increasing number of credit institutions outsource loan handling to specialized, unregulated service providers, called "loan factories." These service providers specialize in back-office services concerning loans and mortgages and, in some cases, decide whether to grant a loan.

In 2003 a credit institution wanted to outsource not only the servicing of loans, but also the decision to grant a loan in standard retail lending business and in the non-standard business up to €2.5 m. The result of the assessment by the supervisor was that in the non-standard business, the credit institution was unable to monitor and oversee the loans granted by the loan factory. Although the business is run by the credit institution, which bears the risk emerging from it, the decision on granting the loans had been made by the service provider.

Issues that emerged as part of this scenario included:

- The outsourcing of decisions concerning the incurrence of new exposure is permissible only if it does not impair management's ability to manage risk adequately.
- This aforementioned would be met only if the regulated entity stringently committed the service provider to apply precise and verifiable evaluation and assessment criteria. With the systems currently used by the financial industry, this is possible only in the standardized retail lending business.

Source: Basel Committee on Banking Supervision, The Joint Forum, *Outsourcing in Financial Services,* February 2005, p. 20. Original text available free of charge at www.bis.org.

www.cdic.ca

Risk Framework" that it uses to identify, quantify, and control the risks inherent in its operations, as well as to meet the requirements of OSFI and CDIC.

The Ethical Dilemmas feature presents a case study on German "loan factories" considered by the BIS that presents a regulator's view of the risks inherent in outsourcing for FIs. Thus, while an FI may wish to outsource credit-granting activities for cost and efficiency reasons, all five of the risks listed in Table 16–8 could be relevant in this case.

<table>
<tr><td>

CONCEPT QUESTIONS

</td><td>

1. Using the German loan factory case presented in the Ethical Dilemmas feature, identify how operational risk might arise from employee risk, technology risk, customer risk, capital asset risk, and external risk if an FI were to outsource its credit decisions.
2. What risk management efforts are involved in controlling operational risk?

</td></tr>
</table>

REGULATORY ISSUES AND TECHNOLOGY AND OPERATIONAL RISKS

As stated earlier, operational risk is the risk of direct or indirect loss resulting from inadequate or failed internal processes, people, or systems, and from external events. Certainly, as FIs' use of technology increases, operational risk increases as well. However, little has been done to oversee or regulate these increasing risks. In this section, we look at two areas that have been directly affected by the increase in operational risk.

1. *Operational Risk and FI Insolvency.* Research by Operational Research Inc., an operational risk consultancy firm, estimates that since 1980, FIs have lost over US$200 billion due to operational risk.[35] Regulators have recognized the significance of operational risk for FIs. Specifically, in 1999 the Basel Committee (of the BIS) on Banking Supervision said that operational risks "are sufficiently important for banks to devote necessary resources to quantify the level of such risks and to incorporate them (along with market and credit risk) into their assessment of their

---

[35] See C. Smithson, "Measuring Operational Risk," *Risk,* March 2000, pp. 58–59.

overall capital adequacy."[36] In its follow-up consultative documents released in January 2001 and April 2003, the Basel committee proposed three specific methods by which deposit-taking institutions (DTIs) could calculate the required capital to protect themselves against operational risk. These methods are the basic indicator approach, the standardized approach, and the advanced measurement approach.[37] Banks are encouraged to move along the spectrum of available approaches as they develop more sophisticated operational risk measurement systems and practices. Internationally active banks and banks with significant operational risk exposures (such as specialized processing banks) are expected to use an approach that is more sophisticated than the basic indicator approach and that is appropriate for the risk profile of the institution. A bank can be allowed to use the basic indicator or standardized approach for some parts of its operations and an advanced measurement approach for others provided certain minimum criteria are met. A bank is not allowed to choose to revert to a simpler approach once it has been approved for a more advanced approach without supervisor approval. Research has found that the amount of capital held for operational risk according to these models will often exceed capital held for market risk and that the largest banks could choose to allocate several billion dollars in capital to operational risk.[38] We discuss each of the methods in more detail in Chapter 20.

2. *Consumer Protection.* KPMG *Information Security Survey 2000* reported that business customers hesitate to put their personal and financial information on the Internet for two reasons. First, they are worried about who has access to this information and how it will be used. Second, they worry that credit card or bank account details will be stolen or used fraudulently.[39] The advent of electronic banking is making consumer protection an increasingly important responsibility for regulators of FIs. Global standards and protocols that can be credibly enforced will become increasingly necessary to assure the customer's desired degree of privacy.

With respect to security risk, because Internet transactions involve open systems, they are susceptible to interception and fraud. Cryptographic techniques for ensuring transaction security are rapidly improving and are almost fully secure for consumer transactions. Further, technological developments are soon expected that will provide protection needed for large transactions as well. Availability of these technologies does not ensure that FIs will use them (especially if their costs are high). Consequently, regulators may need to oversee (or even mandate) the implementation of these technologies if FIs are slow to use them operationally.

CONCEPT QUESTIONS

1. What are the three approaches proposed by the Basel Committee on Banking Supervision for measuring capital requirements associated with operational risk?
2. What steps have been or are being taken to ensure privacy and protection against fraud in the use of personal and financial consumer information placed on the Internet?

---

[36] See Basel Committee on Banking Supervision, *A New Capital Adequacy Framework,* Bank for International Settlements, Basel, Switzerland, June 1999, p. 50.

[37] See Basel Committee on Banking Supervision, *The New Basel Capital Accord,* January 2001, and *Overview of The New Basel Capital Accord,* April 2003, Bank for International Settlements, Basel, Switzerland (www.bis.org). The advanced measurement approach offers three alternative methodologies for capital reserve calculations for the most sophisticated and largest banks in the world.

[38] See P. DeFontnouvelle, V. Dejesus-Rueff, J. S. Jordan, and E. S. Rosengren, "Capital and Risk: New Evidence on Implications of Large Operational Losses," *Journal of Money, Credit, and Banking* 38, pp. 1819–46.

[39] See R. Coles, "Safety Net," *The Banker,* September 2000, pp. 7–8; and V. Roth and K. Ritcher, "How to Fend Off Shoulder Surfing," *Journal of Banking and Finance* 30, 2006, pp. 1727–51.

Summary

This chapter analyzed the operating cost side of FIs' activities, including the effects of the growth of technology-based innovations. The impact of technology was first examined separately for wholesale and retail services before an analysis was presented of its effects on cost and revenues. Technology-based investments can potentially result in new product innovations and lower costs, but the evidence for such cost savings is mixed. Moreover, new and different risks appear to have been created by modern technology. These include settlement risk, international technology transfer risk, crime or fraud risk, regulatory avoidance risk, taxation avoidance risk, and competition risk. Nevertheless, although the chapter focuses on the cost and benefits of technology to an FI, a more fundamental issue may not be technology's costs and benefits but the need to invest in technology to survive as a modern full-service FI.

Questions and Problems

1. Explain how technological improvements can increase an FI's interest and non-interest income and reduce interest and non-interest expenses. Use some specific examples.

2. Table 16–1 shows data on earnings, expenses, and assets for banks that report to OSFI. Calculate the annual growth rates in the various income, expense, earnings, and asset categories from 1996 to 2008. If part of the growth rates in assets, earnings, and expenses can be attributed to technological change, in what areas of operating performance has technological change appeared to have the greatest impact? What growth rates are more likely to be caused by economywide economic activity?

3. Compare the effects of technology on an FI's wholesale operations with the effects of technology on an FI's retail operations. Give some specific examples.

4. What are some of the risks inherent in being the first to introduce a financial innovation?

5. The operations department of a major FI is planning to reorganize several of its back-office functions. Its current operating expense is $1,500,000, of which $1,000,000 is for staff expenses. The FI uses a 12 percent cost of capital to evaluate cost-saving projects.

    a. One way of reorganizing is to outsource overseas a portion of its data entry functions. This will require an initial investment of approximately $500,000 after taxes. The FI expects to save $150,000 in annual operating expenses after tax for the next seven years. Should it undertake this project, assuming that this change will lead to permanent savings?

    b. Another option is to automate the entire process by installing new state-of-the-art computers and software. The FI expects to realize more than $500,000 per year in after-tax savings, but the initial investment will be approximately $3,000,000. In addition, the life of this project is limited to seven years, at which time new computers and software will need to be installed. Using this seven-year planning horizon, should the FI invest in this project? What level of after-tax savings would be necessary to make this plan comparable in value creation to the plan in part (a)?

6. City Bank upgrades its computer equipment every five years to keep up with changes in technology. Its next upgrade is two years from today and is budgeted to cost $1,000,000. Management is considering moving up the date by two years to install some new computers with breakthrough software that could generate significant cost savings. The cost for this new equipment also is $1,000,000. What should be the savings per year to justify moving up the planned upgrade by two years? Assume a cost of capital of 15 percent.

7. Identify and discuss three benefits of technology in generating revenue for FIs.

8. Distinguish between economies of scale and economies of scope.

9. What information on the operating costs of FIs does the measurement of economies of scale provide? If economies of scale exist, what implications do they have for regulators?

10. What are diseconomies of scale? What are the risks of large-scale technological investments, especially to large FIs? Why are small FIs willing to outsource production to large FIs against which they are competing? Why are large FIs willing to accept outsourced production from smaller FI competition?

11. What information on the operating costs of FIs is provided by the measurement of economies of scope? What implications do economies of scope have for regulators?

12. Buy Bank had $130 million in assets and $20 million in expenses before the acquisition of Sell Bank, which had assets of $50 million and expenses of $10 million. After the merger, the bank had $180 million in assets and $35 million in costs. Did this acquisition generate either economies of scale or economies of scope?

13. A bank with assets of $2 billion and costs of $200 million has acquired an investment banking firm subsidiary with assets of $40 million and expenses of $15 million. After the acquisition, the costs of the bank are $180 million and the costs of the subsidiary are $20 million. Does the resulting merger reflect economies of scale or economies of scope?

14. What are diseconomies of scope? How could diseconomies of scope occur?

15. A survey of a local market has provided the following average cost data: Mortgage Bank A (MBA) has assets of $3 million and an average cost of 20 percent. Life Insurance Company B (LICB) has assets of $4 million and an average cost of 30 percent. Corporate Pension Fund C (CPFC) has assets of $4 million and an average cost of 25 percent. For each firm, average costs are measured as a proportion of assets. MBA is planning to acquire LICB and CPFC with the expectation of reducing overall average costs by eliminating the duplication of services.

    a. What should be the average cost after acquisition for the bank to justify this merger?

    b. If MBA plans to reduce operating costs by $500,000 after the merger, what will be the average cost of the new firm?

16. What is the difference between the production approach and the intermediation approach to estimating cost functions of FIs?

17. What are some of the conclusions of empirical studies on economies of scale and scope? How important is the impact of cost reductions on total average costs? What are X-inefficiencies? What role do these factors play in explaining cost differences among FIs?

18. Why does the United States lag behind most other industrialized countries in the proportion of annual electronic non-cash transactions per capita? What factors probably will be important in causing the gap to decrease?

19. What are the differences between the LVTS and CHIPS payment systems?

20. What provision has been made by the members of the CPA to reduce the settlement risk problem in the LVTS?

21. Why do FIs in the United States face a higher degree of international technology risk than do the FIs in other countries, especially some European countries?

22. What has been the impact of rapid technological improvements in the electronic payment systems on crime and fraud risk?

23. How does technology create regulatory risk?

24. How has technology altered the competition risk of FIs?

25. What actions has the BIS taken to protect deposit-taking institutions from insolvency due to operational risk?

Web Questions

26. Go to the BIS website at www.bis.org and find the most recent data on the volume and value of payment system transactions in Canada using the following steps. Click on "Statistics," then on "Payment Systems," and then, in the text on that page, click on the word "statistics." Then click on the most recent release of "Statistics on payment and settlement systems in selected countries." To open the PDF file for the Committee on Payment and Settlement Systems (CPSS) Red Book, click on "Full Publication" (you may want to save a copy to your computer). Under "Options" on the left-hand side of the PDF document, click on "Canada" and find Tables 7 and 8 ("Indicators of the use of payment instruments and terminals by non-banks"). How have the volume and value of transactions changed since 2007, as reported in Table 16–3?

27. Using the CPSS Red Book document from Question 26, click on "Comparative Tables" and find Table 7a ("Use of payment instruments by non-banks"). How have the numbers changed since 2007, as reported in Table 16–4?

www.mcgrawhill.ca/olc/saunders

Liquidity Risk

In this chapter, we consider liquidity risk and

▶ identify the causes of liquidity risk on an FI's balance sheet, both on the asset and on the liability side

▶ discuss the methods used to measure an FI's liquidity risk exposure,

▶ discuss the consequences of extreme liquidity risk, including deposit liability drains and bank runs

▶ examine regulatory mechanisms put in place to ease liquidity problems and prevent runs on deposit-taking institutions

▶ examine the reasons for differences in liquidity risk among banks (high exposure), life insurance companies (moderate exposure), and mutual funds, pension funds, and property and casualty insurance companies (low exposure)

INTRODUCTION

liquidity risk
The risk that a sudden surge in liability withdrawals may require an FI to liquidate assets in a very short period of time and at low prices.

As defined in Chapter 7, **liquidity risk** is the risk that a sudden surge in liability withdrawals may require an FI to liquidate assets in a very short period of time and at low prices. For example, in 1998, the hedge fund, Long-Term Capital Management (LTCM), as discussed in Chapter 5, was unable to meet the margin calls (liability withdrawals) on its highly leveraged short positions. When the Russian government defaulted on its debt, the financial markets made a "flight to liquidity" and caught LTCM in its downdraft, driving up the prices of U.S. Treasuries and driving down the values of the securities held by LTCM as it tried to liquidate assets to pay its debt. A US$3.625 billion bailout was organized by the U.S. Federal Reserve Bank of New York, and LTCM's losses on their investments were over US$4.6 billion.[1]

Chapters 8 through 16 examined how the major problems of interest rate risk, market risk, credit risk, off-balance-sheet risk, operational and technology risk, foreign exchange risk, and sovereign risk can threaten the solvency of an FI. This chapter looks at the problems created by liquidity risk. Unlike other risks that threaten the very solvency of an FI, liquidity risk is a normal aspect of the everyday management of an FI. Only in extreme cases do liquidity risk problems develop into solvency risk problems where an FI cannot generate sufficient cash to pay creditors as promised. Moreover, some FIs are more exposed to liquidity risk than others. At one extreme, deposit-taking institutions are highly exposed; in the middle, life insurance companies are moderately exposed; and at the other extreme, mutual funds, hedge funds, pension funds, and property and casualty insurance companies

---

[1] While LTCM's value at risk (VaR) models used to evaluate its strategies were generally correct, LTCM failed to incorporate an adjustment for liquidity. See F. Portnoy, "The Domino Effect," in *Infectious Greed: How Deceit and Risk Corrupted the Financial Markets,* New York: Times Books, Chapter 8, pp. 262–266, for a general discussion of LTCM and its VaR models, as well as a perspective on the effect of unregulated FIs (hedge funds) on the financial system.

generally have relatively low exposure. However, these FIs are certainly exposed to some liquidity risk. For example, in September 2006, Amaranth Advisors, a hedge fund with assets of US$9.2 billion, lost US$6.5 billion when its position in natural gas future contracts became too big to liquidate. When the fund's creditors threatened to cut off credit due to Amaranth's lack of funds, the hedge fund was forced to shut down. As well, the freezing up of money markets, inter-bank lending, and bank loan markets in 2008 led to the insolvency of Lehman Brothers and other highly leveraged investment banks and hedge funds worldwide. We examine the reasons for liquidity risk differences.

CAUSES OF LIQUIDITY RISK

fire-sale price
The price received for an asset that has to be liquidated (sold) immediately.

Liquidity risk arises for two reasons: a liability-side reason and an asset-side reason. The liability-side reason occurs when an FI's liability holders, such as depositors or insurance policyholders, seek to cash in their financial claims immediately. When liability holders demand cash by withdrawing deposits, the FI needs to borrow additional funds or sell assets to meet the withdrawal. The most liquid asset is cash; FIs use this asset to pay claimholders who seek to withdraw funds. However, FIs tend to minimize their holdings of cash reserves as assets because those reserves pay no interest. To generate interest revenues, most FIs invest in less liquid and/or longer-maturity assets. While most assets can be turned into cash eventually, for some assets this can be done only at a high cost when the asset must be liquidated immediately. The price the asset holder must accept for immediate sale may be far less than it would receive with a longer horizon over which to negotiate a sale. Thus, some assets may be liquidated only at low **fire-sale prices,** thus threatening the solvency of the FI. Alternatively, rather than liquidating assets, an FI may seek to purchase or borrow additional funds.

The second cause of liquidity risk is asset-side liquidity risk, such as the ability to fund the exercise of off-balance-sheet loan commitments. As we described in Chapter 13, a loan commitment allows a customer to borrow (draw down) funds from an FI (over a commitment period) on demand. When a borrower draws on its loan commitment, the FI must fund the loan on the balance sheet immediately; this creates a demand for liquidity. As it can with liability withdrawals, an FI can meet such a liquidity need by running down its cash assets, selling off other liquid assets, or borrowing additional funds.

To analyze the differing degrees of importance of liquidity risk across FIs, we next consider liquidity risk problems faced by deposit-taking institutions, insurance companies, and mutual and pension funds.

CONCEPT QUESTIONS

1. What are the sources of liquidity risk?
2. Why is cash more liquid than loans for an FI?

LIQUIDITY RISK AT DEPOSIT-TAKING INSTITUTIONS

Liability-Side Liquidity Risk

As discussed in Chapter 2, a deposit-taking institution's (DTI's) balance sheet typically has a large amount of short-term liabilities, such as demand deposits and other transaction accounts, which fund relatively long-term assets. Demand deposit accounts and other transaction accounts are contracts that give the holders the right to put their claims back to the DTI on any given day and demand immediate repayment of the face value of their deposit claims in cash.[2] Thus, an individual demand deposit account holder with a balance of $10,000 can demand cash to be repaid immediately, as can a corporation with $100 million in its demand deposit account.[3] In theory, at least, a DTI that has 20 percent of its liabilities in demand deposits and other transaction accounts must stand ready to pay out that amount by liquidating an equivalent amount of assets on any banking day. Table 17–1 shows the aggregate balance sheet of the assets and liabilities of Canadian banks and other DTIs. As seen in this table, total deposits are 67.3 percent of total liabilities. By comparison, cash assets are only 1.7 percent of total assets. Also note that borrowed funds are 2.4 percent of total liabilities.

In reality, a deposit-taking institution knows that normally only a small proportion of its deposits will be withdrawn on any given day. Most demand deposits act as consumer **core deposits** on a day-by-day basis, providing a relatively stable or long-term source of savings and time deposit funds for the DTI. Moreover, deposit withdrawals may in part be offset by the inflow of new deposits and income generated from the DTI's on- and off-balance-sheet activities. The DTI manager must monitor the resulting net deposit withdrawals or net deposit drains.[4] Specifically, over time, a DTI manager can normally predict—with a good degree of accuracy—the probability distribution of **net deposit drains** (the difference between deposit withdrawals and deposit additions) on any given normal banking day.[5]

Consider the two possible distributions shown in Figure 17–1. In panel (a) of Figure 17–1, the distribution is assumed to be strongly peaked at the 5 percent net deposit withdrawal level—this DTI expects approximately 5 percent of its net

core deposits
Those deposits that provide a DTI with a long-term funding source.

net deposit drains
The amount by which cash withdrawals exceed additions; a net cash outflow.

TABLE 17–1
Assets and Liabilities of Canadian DTIs, Q4, 2008 ($ billions)

Source: Statistics Canada, www.statcan.gc.ca.

Assets*	$ billions	Percent	Liabilities**	$ billions	Percent
Total cash assets	$ 42.3	1.7%	Total deposits	$1,528.1	67.3%
Total investments	599.8	24.6	Borrowings	54.5	2.4
Total loans	1,398.9	57.3	Other liabilities	687.0	30.3
Other assets	400.9	16.4	Total liabilities	$2,269.6	100.0%
Total assets	$2,441.9	100.0%			

* Includes chartered banks, trust companies, deposit-accepting mortgage companies, credit unions.
** Excludes bank equity capital.

---

[2] Accounts with this type of put option include demand deposits, interest-bearing chequing accounts with minimum balance requirements, and chequing accounts with minimum balance and number-of-cheques-written restrictions. We describe these accounts in more detail in Chapter 18. Deposit-taking institutions typically liquidate deposit account contracts immediately upon request of the customer. Many savings account contracts, however, give a DTI some powers to delay withdrawals by requiring notification of withdrawal a certain number of days before withdrawal or by imposing penalty fees such as loss of interest.

[3] Technology is compounding the risk in these withdrawals. The Internet enables depositors to transfer money between FIs quickly to take advantage of higher rates.

[4] Also a part of liquidity risk (although not as likely to cause an FI to fail) is an unexpected inflow of funds. For example, in the early 2000s as stock prices fell, investors liquidated their mutual fund shares and deposited these funds in their banks and credit unions. With interest rates at historic lows, deposit-taking institutions faced a problem of finding sufficiently attractive (in a return sense) loans and securities in which to invest these funds.

[5] Apart from predictable daily seasonality to deposit flows, there are other seasonal variations, many of which are, to a greater or lesser degree, predictable. For example, many retail DTIs face above-average deposit outflows around the end of the year and in the summer (due to Christmas and the vacation season). Also, the rural branches of many DTIs face a deposit inflow–outflow cycle that closely matches the agricultural cycle of the local crop or crops. In the planting and growing season, deposits tend to fall, while in the harvest season, deposits tend to rise (as crops are sold).

FIGURE 17–1
Distribution of Net Deposit Drains

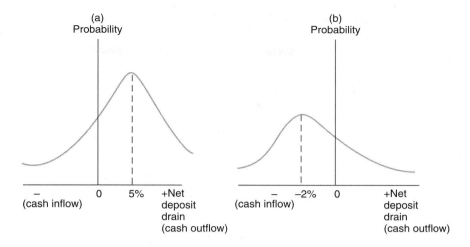

deposit funds to be withdrawn on any given day with the highest probability. In panel (a) a net deposit drain means that the DTI is receiving insufficient additional deposits (and other cash inflows) to offset deposit withdrawals. The DTI in panel (a) has a mean, or expected, net positive drain on deposits, so its new deposit funds and other cash flows are expected to be insufficient to offset deposit withdrawals. The liability side of its balance sheet is contracting. Table 17–2 illustrates an actual 5 percent net drain of deposit accounts (or, in terms of dollars, a drain of $5 million).

For a DTI to be growing, it must have a mean or average deposit drain such that new deposit funds more than offset deposit withdrawals. Thus, the peak of the net deposit drain probability distribution would be at a point to the left of zero. See the −2 percent in panel (b) in Figure 17–1, where the distribution of net deposit drains is peaked at −2 percent, or the FI is receiving net cash inflows with the highest probability.

A DTI can manage a drain on deposits in two major ways: (1) purchased liquidity management and/or (2) stored liquidity management. Traditionally, DTI managers have relied on stored liquidity management as the primary mechanism of

TABLE 17–2
Effect of Net Deposit Drains on the Balance Sheet ($ millions)

Panel A: Balance Sheet Immediately before and after Deposit Drain							
Before the Drain				**After the Drain**			
Assets		**Liabilities**		**Assets**		**Liabilities**	
Assets	100	Deposits	70	Assets	100	Deposits	65
		Borrowed funds	10			Borrowed funds	10
		Other liabilities	20			Other liabilities	20
	100		100		100		95
Panel B: Adjusting to a Deposit Drain through Liability Management							
Assets				**Liabilities**			
Assets		100		Deposits		65	
				Borrowed funds		15	
				Other liabilities		20	
		100				100	

liquidity management. Today, many DTIs—especially the largest banks with access to the money market and other non-deposit markets for funds—rely on purchased liquidity (or liability) management to deal with the risk of cash shortfalls. A more extensive discussion of liability management techniques is left to Chapter 18. Here we briefly discuss the alternative methods of liquidity risk management.

Purchased Liquidity Management

LVTS participant
A member of the Canadian Payments Association who settles directly with the Bank of Canada and participates in the LVTS.

A DTI manager who purchases liquidity may turn to the inter-bank markets for short-term funds. These could be the repurchase agreement markets[6] or via the Large Value Transfer System (LVTS) that allows the major Canadian FIs who are **LVTS participants** to borrow from the Bank of Canada at the Bank rate or from other member FIs who have excess funds.[7]

Alternatively, the DTI manager could issue additional fixed-maturity wholesale certificates of deposit or GICs or even sell some notes and bonds. For example, Table 17–2, panel A shows a DTI's balance sheet immediately before and after a deposit drain of $5 million. As long as the total amount of funds raised equals $5 million, the DTI in Table 17–2 could fully fund its net deposit drain. However, this can be expensive for the DTI since it is paying *market rates* for funds in the wholesale money market to offset net drains on low-interest-bearing deposits.[8] Thus, the higher the cost of purchased funds relative to the rates earned on assets, the less attractive this approach to liquidity management becomes. Further, since most of these funds are not covered by deposit insurance, their availability may be limited should the deposit-taking institution incur insolvency difficulties. Table 17–2, panel B shows the DTI's balance sheet if it responds to deposit drains by using purchased liquidity management techniques.

purchased liquidity management
An adjustment to a deposit drain that occurs on the liability side of the balance sheet.

Note that **purchased liquidity management** has allowed the DTI to maintain its overall balance sheet size of $100 million without disturbing the size and composition of the asset side of its balance sheet—that is, the complete adjustment to the deposit drain occurs on the liability side of the balance sheet. In other words, purchased liquidity management can insulate the asset side of the balance sheet from normal drains on the liability side of the balance sheet. This is one of the reasons for the enormous growth in recent years of FI purchased liquidity management techniques and associated purchased fund markets such as borrowings from the Bank of Canada, repurchase agreements, and wholesale GICs. (We describe and discuss these instruments in more detail in Chapter 18.) Indeed, in the early 2000s regulators expressed concerns about the increased use of these (wholesale) funding sources by DTIs. Regulators noted that during the 1990s, as savers put more into investments (instead of DTI deposit accounts), DTIs were unable to increase deposits as fast as loans (and loan commitments) increased on the asset side of the balance sheet. In the event of a liquidity crunch, additional (wholesale) funds could be hard to obtain. This occurred in the global liquidity crisis in September–October 2008.

---

[6] Securities companies and institutional investors use the repurchase agreement market extensively for liquidity management purposes.

[7] The Bank of Canada plays a role in maintaining the liquidity of the financial system. See the section "Bank Runs, the Bank of Canada, and Deposit Insurance" in this chapter and Chapter 19 for more discussion.

[8] While chequing accounts pay no explicit interest, other transaction accounts do. However, the rates paid are normally sticky, are slow to adjust to changes in market interest rates, and lie below purchased fund rates (see Chapter 18).

Stored Liquidity Management

stored liquidity management
An adjustment to a deposit drain that occurs on the asset side of the balance sheet.

Instead of meeting the net deposit drain by purchasing liquidity in the wholesale money markets, the DTI could use **stored liquidity management.** That is, the FI could liquidate some of its assets, utilizing its stored liquidity. Traditionally, DTIs have held stored cash reserves at the Bank of Canada and in their vaults for this very purpose. Now, Canada and the United Kingdom have no official central bank-designated cash reserve requirements, while the U.S. Federal Reserve sets minimum reserve requirements for the cash reserves that U.S. banks must hold.

www.bankofcanada. ca

Suppose, in our example, that on the asset side of the balance sheet the DTI normally holds $9 million of its assets in cash. We depict the situation before the net drain in liabilities in Table 17–3, panel A. As depositors withdraw $5 million in deposits, the DTI can meet this directly by using the excess cash stored in its vaults or held on deposit at other DTIs or at the Bank of Canada. If the reduction of $5 million in deposit liabilities is met by a $5 million reduction in cash assets held by the DTI, its balance sheet will be as shown in Table 17–3, panel B.

When the DTI uses its cash as the liquidity adjustment mechanism, both sides of its balance sheet contract. In this example, the DTI's total assets and liabilities shrink from $100 to $95 million. The cost to the DTI from using stored liquidity, apart from decreased asset size,[9] is that it must hold excess non-interest-bearing assets in the form of cash on its balance sheet.[10] Thus, the cost of using cash to meet liquidity needs is the forgone return (or opportunity cost) of being unable to invest these funds in loans and other higher-income-earning assets.

Finally, note that while stored liquidity management and purchased liquidity management are alternative strategies for meeting deposit drains, a DTI can combine the two methods by using some purchased liquidity management and some stored liquidity management to meet liquidity needs.

Asset-Side Liquidity Risk

Just as deposit drains can cause a DTI liquidity problems, so can the exercise by borrowers of their loan commitments and other credit lines. During the credit

TABLE 17–3
Composition of the DTI's Balance Sheet ($ millions)

Panel A: Balance Sheet Immediately before Deposit Drain			
Assets		**Liabilities**	
Cash	9	Deposits	70
Other assets	91	Borrowed funds	10
		Other liabilities	20
	100		100
Panel B: Adjusting to a Deposit Drain through Stored Liquidity Management			
Assets		**Liabilities**	
Cash	4	Deposits	65
Other assets	91	Borrowed funds	10
		Other liabilities	20
	95		95

---

[9] It should be noted that there is no empirical evidence showing a significant correlation between a DTI's asset size and profits.

[10] DTIs could hold highly liquid interest-bearing assets such as T-bills, but these are still less liquid than cash and immediate liquidation may result in some small capital value losses.

crisis in 2008, as the money markets and inter-bank markets shut down, many borrowers drew down their credit lines at banks, exacerbating the liquidity problems for many global FIs. Table 17–4, panel A, shows the effect of a $5 million exercise of a loan commitment by a borrower. As a result, the DTI must fund $5 million in additional loans on the balance sheet.[11] Consider panel A in Table 17–4 (the balance sheet before the commitment exercise) and panel B (the balance sheet after the exercise). In particular, the exercise of the loan commitment means that the DTI needs to provide $5 million in loans immediately to the borrower (other assets rise from $91 to $96 million). This can be done either by purchased liquidity management (borrowing an additional $5 million in the money market and lending these funds to the borrower) or by stored liquidity management (decreasing the DTI's excess cash assets from $9 million to $4 million). We present these two policies in Table 17–4, panel B.

Another type of asset-side liquidity risk arises from the FI's investment portfolio. Specifically, unexpected changes in interest rates can cause investment portfolio values to fluctuate significantly. If interest rates increase, the result is that the value of the investment securities portfolio falls and large losses in portfolio value can occur (see Chapter 10 on market risk). Further, there is the risk that liquidity in a particular market will deteriorate because market traders want to sell and no one wants to buy. It has been argued that technological and other developments have led to a steady improvement in the liquidity of financial markets. However, this is questionable in that there is an increasing tendency toward "herd" behaviour, where most traders want to make the same type of trade (such as a sale) at a particular time. During the sell-off, liquidity dries up and investment securities can be sold only at fire-sale prices. The result is a reduction in the value of the investment portfolio and increased liquidity risk for the FI.

In Table 17–5, panel A shows an FI's balance sheet immediately before and after a $5 million decrease in the market value of its investment portfolio. In addition to a loss in equity value, the FI must fund the $5 million loss in value on the balance sheet such that loan requests and deposit withdrawals can be met. The FI must replace the loss in value of the investment portfolio. This can be done either by purchased liquidity management (borrowing an additional $5 million in deposits or purchased funds) or by stored liquidity management (purchasing an additional

TABLE 17–4
Effects of a Loan Commitment Exercise ($ millions)

Panel A: Balance Sheet Immediately before and after Exercise							
(a) Before Exercise				**(b) After Exercise**			
Cash	9	Deposits	70	Cash	9	Deposits	70
Other assets	91	Borrowed funds	10	Other assets	96	Borrowed funds	10
		Other liabilities	20			Other liabilities	20
	100		100		105		100

Panel B: Adjusting the Balance Sheet to a Loan Commitment Exercise							
(a) Purchased Liquidity Management				**(b) Stored Liquidity Management**			
Cash	9	Deposits	70	Cash	4	Deposits	70
Other assets	96	Borrowed funds	15	Other assets	96	Borrowed funds	10
		Other liabilities	20			Other liabilities	20
	105		105		100		100

---

[11] Larger DTIs with more extensive commercial loan portfolios tend to be more susceptible to this type of risk than are smaller retail-oriented or consumer-oriented DTIs such as credit unions.

TABLE 17–5 **Effects of a Drop in the Value of the Investment Securities Portfolio ($ millions)**

Panel A: Balance Sheet Immediately before and after Drop in Portfolio Value							
Before Drop in Value				**After Drop in Value**			
Cash	$ 9	Deposits	$ 60	Cash	$ 9	Deposits	$60
Investment portfolio	40	Borrowed funds	10	Investment portfolio	35	Borrowed funds	10
Other assets	51	Other liabilities	20	Other assets	51	Other liabilities	20
		Equity	10			Equity	5
	$100		$100		$95		$95

Panel B: Adjusting the Balance Sheet for a Drop in Investment Portfolio Value							
(a) Purchased Liquidity Management				**(b) Stored Liquidity Management**			
Cash	$ 9	Deposits	$ 65	Cash	$ 4	Deposits	$60
Investment portfolio	40	Borrowed funds	10	Investment portfolio	40	Borrowed funds	10
Other assets	51	Other liabilities	20	Other assets	51	Other liabilities	20
		Equity	5			Equity	5
	$100		$100		$95		$95

$5 million in assets).[12] Panel B of Table 17–5 shows the effect of these two strategies on the balance sheet. Notice, in both cases, that the FI has lost $5 million in equity.

Measuring a DTI's Liquidity Exposure

Sources and Uses of Liquidity

As discussed above, a DTI's liquidity risk arises from ongoing conduct of business such as a withdrawal of deposits or from new loan demand, and the subsequent need to meet those demands through liquidating assets or borrowing funds. Therefore, a DTI's manager must be able to measure its liquidity position on a daily basis, if possible. A useful tool is a *net liquidity statement* that lists sources and uses of liquidity and thus provides a measure of a DTI's net liquidity position. Such a statement for a hypothetical bank is presented in Table 17–6.

The DTI can obtain liquid funds in three ways. First, it can sell its liquid assets such as T-bills immediately with little price risk and low transaction cost.[13] Second,

TABLE 17–6
Net Liquidity Position ($ millions)

Sources of Liquidity	
1. Total cash-type assets	$ 2,000
2. Maximum borrowed funds limit	12,000
3. Excess cash reserves	500
Total	$14,500
Uses of Liquidity	
1. Funds borrowed	$ 6,000
2. Bank of Canada borrowing	1,000
Total	$ 7,000
Total net liquidity	$ 7,500

---

[12] Note that the FI could raise an additional $5 million in equity, e.g., through a common stock issue. However, this is likely to be more costly than adjusting to the loss via purchased liquidity management or stored liquidity management.

[13] In recent years, as the loan sales and securitization markets have grown, many banks have added to their sources statement loan assets that can be immediately sold or securitized. Chapters 26 and 27 describe the loan sales and securitization markets.

it can borrow funds in the money/purchased funds market up to a maximum amount (this is an *internal* guideline based on the manager's assessment of the credit limits that the purchased or borrowed funds market is likely to impose on the DTI). Third, it can use any excess cash.[14] In Table 17–6 the DTI's *sources* of liquidity total $14,500 million. Compare this with the DTI's *uses* of liquidity, in particular the amount of borrowed or purchased funds it has already utilized and the amount of cash it has already borrowed from the Bank of Canada. These total $7,000 million. As a result, the DTI has a positive net liquidity position of $7,500 million. These liquidity sources and uses can be easily tracked on a day-by-day basis.

The net liquidity position in Table 17–6 lists management's expected sources and uses of liquidity for a hypothetical bank. All FIs report their historical sources and uses of liquidity in their annual and quarterly reports. As an FI manager deals with liquidity risk, historical sources and uses of liquidity statements can assist the manager in determining where future liquidity issues may arise.

Peer Group Ratio Comparisons

Another way to measure a DTI's liquidity exposure is to compare certain key ratios and balance sheet features of the DTI—such as its loans to deposits, borrowed funds to total assets, and commitments to lend to assets ratios—with those of DTIs of a similar size and geographic location. Table 17–7 shows these ratios for the six largest Canadian banks for 2008. A high ratio of loans to deposits (and loans and loan commitments to deposits) means that the DTI relies heavily on the short-term money market rather than on core deposits to fund loans. This could mean future liquidity problems if the DTI is at or near its borrowing limits in the purchased funds market. As noted previously, Canadian banks rely on the commercial paper market for funding. Similarly, a high ratio of loans and loan commitments to assets indicates the need for a high degree of liquidity to fund any unexpected drawdowns of these loans—high commitment DTIs (e.g., BMO, National Bank, and CIBC, from Table 17–7) often face more liquidity risk exposure than do low-commitment FIs (e.g., TD Bank).

www.bmo.com
www.scotiabank.com
www.td.com

TABLE 17–7   **Liquidity Ratios for Canadian Banks, 2008**

	Loans and Acceptances/ Assets	Loans and Credit Commitments/ Assets	Loans and Acceptances/ Deposits	Loans and Credit Commitments/ Deposits	Cash and Securities/ Total Assets	Core Deposits/ Total Deposits
BMO	54.1%	74.5%	83.4%	114.9%	30.5%	46.0%
CIBC	50.9	61.7	77.4	93.7	23.8	38.8
National Bank	61.6	64.7	104.7	110.1	38.5	43.5
RBC	40.0	54.5	66.0	89.9	27.9	n.a.
Scotiabank	56.9	56.9	83.3	83.3	24.7	n.a.
TD Bank	39.0	51.1	58.5	76.7	28.8	n.a.
Average	50.4%	60.6%	78.9%	94.8%	29.0%	42.8%

Source: Authors' calculations from company 2008 annual reports.

---

[14] Some banks add net cash inflows to their sources statement.

Liquidity Index

liquidity index
A measure of the potential losses an FI could suffer as the result of sudden (or fire-sale) disposal of assets.

A third way to measure liquidity risk is to use a **liquidity index.** Developed by Jim Pierce at the U.S. Federal Reserve, this index measures the potential losses an FI could suffer from a sudden or fire-sale disposal of assets compared with the amount it would receive at a fair market value established under normal market (sale) conditions—which might take a lengthy period of time as a result of a careful search and bidding process. The greater the differences between immediate fire-sale asset prices (P_i) and fair market prices (P_i^*), the less liquid is the DTI's portfolio of assets. Define an index I such that

$$I = \sum_{i=1}^{N} [(w_i)(P_i/P_i^*)]$$

where w_i is the percentage of each asset in the FI's portfolio:

$$\sum_{i=1}^{N} w_i = 1$$

EXAMPLE 17–1

Calculation of the Liquidity Index

Suppose that a DTI has two assets: 50 percent in one-month Treasury bills and 50 percent in real estate loans. If the DTI must liquidate its T-bills today (P_1), it receives $99 per $100 of face value; if it can wait to liquidate them on maturity (in one month's time), it will receive $100 per $100 of face value ($P_1^*$). If the DTI has to liquidate its real estate loans today, it receives $85 per $100 of face value ($P_2$); liquidation at the end of one month (closer to maturity) will produce $92 per $100 of face value ($P_2^*$). Thus, the one-month liquidity index value for this DTI's asset portfolio is

$$I = [\tfrac{1}{2}(0.99/1.00)] + [\tfrac{1}{2}(0.85/0.92)]$$

$$= 0.495 + 0.462$$

$$= 0.957$$

Suppose, alternatively, that a slow or thin real estate market caused the DTI to be able to liquidate the real estate loans at only $65 per $100 of face value ($P_2$). The one-month liquidity index for the DTI's asset portfolio is

$$I = [\tfrac{1}{2}(0.99/1.00)] + [\tfrac{1}{2}(0.65/0.92)]$$

$$= 0.495 + 0.353$$

$$= 0.848$$

The value of the one-month liquidity index decreases as a result of the larger discount on the fire-sale price—from the fair (full value) market price of real estate—over the one-month period. The larger the discount from fair value, the smaller the liquidity index or higher the liquidity risk the DTI faces.

The liquidity index will always lie between 0 and 1. The liquidity index for this DTI could also be compared with similar indexes calculated for a peer group of similar DTIs.

Financing Gap and the Financing Requirement

A fourth way to measure liquidity risk exposure is to determine the DTI's financing gap. As we discussed earlier, even though demand depositors can withdraw their funds immediately, they do not do so in normal circumstances. On average, most demand deposits stay at DTIs for quite long periods—often two years or more. Thus, a DTI manager often thinks of the average deposit base, including demand deposits, as a core source of funds that over time can fund a DTI's average amount of loans.

financing gap
The difference between a DTI's average loans and average (core) deposits.

We define a **financing gap** as the difference between a DTI's average loans and average (core) deposits, or

$$\text{Financing gap} = \text{Average loans} - \text{Average deposits}$$

If this financing gap is positive, the DTI must fund it by using its cash and liquid assets and/or borrowing funds in the money market. Thus,

$$\text{Financing gap} = -\text{Liquid assets} + \text{Borrowed funds}$$

We can write this relationship as

$$\text{Financing gap} + \text{Liquid assets} = \text{Financing requirement (borrowed funds)}$$

financing requirement
The financing gap plus a DTI's liquid assets.

As expressed in this fashion, the liquidity and managerial implications of the **financing requirement** (the financing gap plus a DTI's liquid assets) are that the level of core deposits and loans as well as the amount of liquid assets determines the DTI's borrowing or purchased fund needs. In particular, the larger a DTI's financing gap and liquid asset holdings, the larger the amount of funds it needs to borrow in the money markets and the greater is its exposure to liquidity problems from such a reliance.

The balance sheet in Table 17–8 indicates the relationship between the financing gap, liquid assets, and the borrowed fund financing requirement. See also the following equation:

$$\begin{array}{ccc} \text{Financing gap} + \text{Liquid assets} = \text{Financing requirement} \\ (\$5 \text{ million}) \quad (\$5 \text{ million}) \quad (\$10 \text{ million}) \end{array}$$

A widening financing gap can warn of future liquidity problems since it may indicate increased deposit withdrawals (core deposits falling below $20 million in Table 17–8) and increasing loans due to increased exercise of loan commitments (loans rising above $25 million). If the DTI does not reduce its liquid assets—they stay at $5 million—the manager must resort to more money market borrowings. As these borrowings rise, sophisticated lenders in the money market may be concerned about the DTI's credit-worthiness. They may react by imposing higher risk premiums on borrowed funds or establishing stricter credit limits by not rolling over funds lent to the DTI. If the DTI's financing requirements exceed such limits, it may become insolvent. A good example of an excessive financing requirement was Continental Bank of Canada. Following the failure of Canadian Commercial

TABLE 17–8
Financing Requirement of a DTI ($ millions)

Assets		Liabilities	
Loans	$ 25	Core deposits	$ 20
Liquid assets	5	Financing requirement (borrowed funds)	10
Total	$ 30	Total	$ 30
		Financing gap	$ 5

Bank and Northland Bank of Canada in 1985, financial markets in Canada were jittery and short-term wholesale funds moved out of the smaller FIs into larger, safer institutions. This loss of wholesale deposits forced Continental Bank, whose assets were of good quality, to seek a six-month $1.4 billion loan from the Bank of Canada, and then to arrange a $1.5 billion three-month standby line of credit with the other major banks that cost $750,000 in facility fees. Despite these efforts, Continental never regained the confidence of the market, and it ultimately merged with Lloyds Bank International, becoming a Schedule B bank (the equivalent of today's Schedule II banks).[15]

BIS Approach: Maturity Ladder/Scenario Analysis

www.bis.org

In February 2000, recognizing that liquidity is crucial to the ongoing viability of a deposit-taking institution, the Bank for International Settlements (BIS) produced a report on liquidity management for FIs. Subsequent to the market turbulence that started in mid-2007, the BIS became concerned about the stability of the global financial system and those FIs with the potential to be a serious systemic risk. The Basel Committee on Banking Supervision, through its Working Group on Liquidity, conducted further analysis in 2008 that resulted in a framework for liquidity risk management for banks and their supervisors that incorporated 17 principles. These principles cover the governance, measurement and management, disclosure, and the supervisor's role in the liquidity risk of banks.[16] The February 2000 BIS report outlined a maturity laddering method for measuring liquidity risk, and specifically, net funding (financing) requirements. At a minimum, liquidity measurement involves assessing all cash inflows against its outflows, as outlined in Table 17–9. Once identified, a maturity ladder model allows a comparison of cash inflows and outflows on a day-to-day basis and/or over a series of specified time periods. Daily and cumulative net funding requirements can then be determined from the maturity ladder.

For the DTI in Table 17–9, for example, excess cash of $4 million is available over the one-day time horizon. However, a cumulative net cash shortfall of $46 million is expected to exist over the next month. The DTI will need to start planning immediately to obtain additional funding to fill this net funding requirement. Over the six-month period, the DTI has cumulative excess cash of $1,104 million. If these expectations hold true, the DTI will need to find a place to invest these excess funds until they are needed.

---

[15] See "Continental Bank's Care Package." *Financial Post,* November 9, 1985, p. 4, and "Continental Bank Merges with Lloyds," *Toronto Star,* October 2, 1986, p. B1. Other smaller FIs were affected as Morguard Bank of Canada was sold to Security Pacific Bank Canada, and Mercantile Bank of Canada merged with National Bank of Canada. Bank of British Columbia and other FIs in western Canada struggled with higher cost of funds that limited their ability to expand. See S. Horvitch, "Turmoil Persists for Smaller Banks," *Financial Post,* February 1, 1986, p. 4, and A. Toulin, "Banks Face an Uphill Battle in Regaining Lost Confidence," *Toronto Star,* April 3, 1986, p. F1. See also B. Smith and R. W. White, "The Capital Market Impact of Recent Canadian Bank Failures," *Canadian Journal of Administrative Sciences,* June 1990, 7(2), p. 41, which demonstrates the "flight to quality" of deposits from regional to national banks. Around the same time, U.S. FIs experienced similar problems. The large money centre bank, Chicago-based Continental Illinois Bank, failed in 1984 when large money market lenders (such as Japanese banks) failed to roll over their borrowed funds. See L. Wall and D. R. Peterson, "The Effect of Continental Illinois' Failure on the Performance of Other Banks," *Journal of Monetary Economics,* 1990, pp. 77–79.

[16] See Bank for International Settlements, "Sound Practices for Managing Liquidity in Banking Organisations," February 2000; "Liquidity Risk: Management and Supervisory Challenges," February 2008; "Report of the Financial Stability Forum on Enhancing Market and Institutional Resilience," April 7, 2008; and "Principles for Sound Liquidity Risk Management and Supervision," September 2008, available at www.bis.org.

TABLE 17–9
Net Funding Requirement Using the BIS Maturity Laddering Model ($ millions)

	1 Day	1 Month	6 Months
Cash Inflows			
Maturing assets	$ 10	$ 150	$ 1,500
Saleable non-maturing assets	12	250	4,000
Access to deposit liabilities	15	200	2,000
Established credit lines	12	100	750
Ability to securitize	5	50	400
	$ 54	$ 750	$ 8,650
Cash Outflows			
Liabilities falling due	$ 30	$ 490	$ 4,500
Committed lines of credit that can be drawn on and other contingent liabilities	16	300	2,960
Cash outflows from unanticipated events	4	10	40
	$ 50	$ 800	$ 7,500
Net funding requirement	$ 4	$ (50)	$ 1,150
Cumulative net funding requirement	$ 4	$ (46)	$ 1,104

The relevant time frame for active liquidity management is generally quite short, including intraday liquidity. However, the appropriate time frame will depend on the nature of a DTI's business. DTIs that rely on short-term funding concentrate primarily on managing their liquidity in the very short term (e.g., the BIS recommended a five-day horizon). DTIs that are less dependent on short-term funding might actively manage their net funding requirements over a slightly longer period. In addition, DTIs should analyze and monitor their liquidity positions over the longer term. Typically, a DTI may find substantial funding gaps in distant periods and thus need to plan ways to fill these gaps by influencing the maturity of transactions to offset the future funding gap.

While liquidity is typically managed under normal conditions, the BIS cautions that DTIs must also be prepared to manage liquidity under abnormal conditions. Analyzing liquidity thus entails generating and analyzing various what-if scenarios. Under each scenario, the DTI should try to account for any significant positive or negative liquidity swings that could occur. These scenarios should take into account factors both internal (bank-specific) and external (market-related). Under the BIS scenario analysis, a DTI needs to assign a timing of cash flows for each type of asset and liability by assessing the probability of the behaviour of those cash flows under the scenario being examined. Accordingly, the timing of cash inflows and outflows on the maturity ladder can differ among scenarios, and the assumptions may differ quite sharply. For example, a DTI may believe, based on its historical experience, that its ability to control the level and timing of future cash flows from a stock of saleable assets in a DTI-specific funding crisis would deteriorate little from normal conditions. However, in a market crisis, this capacity may fall off sharply if few institutions are willing or able to make cash purchases of less-liquid assets.

The evolution of a DTI's liquidity profile under each scenario can be portrayed graphically, as in Figure 17–2. A stylized liquidity graph enables the evolution of the cumulative net excess or shortages of funds to be compared under the major scenarios (e.g., normal conditions, general market crisis conditions, DTI-specific crisis conditions). The DTI can use this profile to provide additional insights into

FIGURE 17–2
Cumulative Excess or Shortages of Funds for a High-Quality DTI under Various Market Conditions

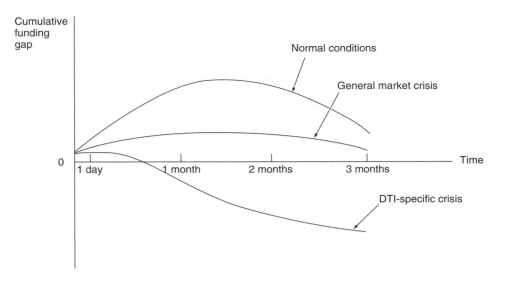

how consistent and realistic the assumptions are for its liquidity. For example, in Figure 17–2, a high-quality bank may look very liquid under normal circumstances and remain so in a general market crisis, but may suffer a liquidity crisis only in a DTI-specific crisis. In contrast, a lower-quality DTI might be equally illiquid in a general and a DTI-specific crisis. Because a DTI's future liquidity position can be affected by factors that cannot always be accurately predicted, it is critical that assumptions used to determine its funding requirements be reviewed and revised frequently.

Liquidity Planning

As implied by the BIS maturity ladder approach, liquidity planning is a key component in measuring (and being able to deal with) liquidity risk and its associated costs. Specifically, liquidity planning allows managers to make important borrowing priority decisions before liquidity problems arise. The BIS (2008) Principle 11 states that "A bank should have a formal contingency funding plan (CFP) that clearly sets out the strategies for addressing liquidity shortfalls in emergency situations."[17] Such planning can lower the cost of funds (by determining an optimal funding mix) and can minimize the amount of excess reserves that a DTI needs to hold.

A liquidity plan has a number of components. The first component is the delineation of managerial details and responsibilities. Responsibilities are assigned to key management personnel should a liquidity crisis occur. The plan identifies those managers responsible for interacting with various government agencies such as the Bank of Canada, CDIC, and OSFI. It also specifies areas of managerial responsibility in disclosing information (BIS Principle 13) to the public—including depositors. The second component of a liquidity plan is a detailed list of fund providers who are most likely to withdraw, as well as the pattern of fund withdrawals. For example, in a crisis, financial institutions such as mutual funds

www.bankofcanada.ca
www.cdic.ca
www.osfi-bsif.gc.ca

---

[17] BIS, "Principles for Sound Liquidity Risk Management and Supervision," September 2008.

and pension funds may be more likely than correspondent banks and small business corporations to withdraw funds quickly from FIs. In turn, correspondent banks and small corporations may be more likely than individual depositors to withdraw funds quickly. This makes liquidity exposure sensitive to the effects of future funding composition changes. Further, DTIs face particularly heavy seasonal withdrawals of deposits in the quarter before Christmas. The third component of liquidity planning is the identification of the size of potential deposit and fund withdrawals over various time horizons in the future (one week, one month, one quarter, etc.) as well as alternative private market funding sources to meet such withdrawals (e.g., emergency loans from other FIs and the Bank of Canada). The fourth component of the plan sets internal limits on separate subsidiaries' and branches' borrowings as well as bounds for acceptable risk premiums to pay in each market. In addition, the plan details a sequencing of assets for disposal in anticipation of various degrees or intensities of deposit/fund withdrawals. Such a plan may evolve from a DTI's asset–liability management committee and may be relayed to various key departments of the DTI (e.g., the money desk and the Treasury department), which play vital day-to-day roles in liability funding.

Consider, for example, Table 17–10. The data are for a DTI that holds $250 million in deposits from mutual funds, pension funds, correspondent banks, small businesses, and individuals. The table includes the average and maximum expected withdrawals over the next one-week, one-month, and one-quarter periods. The liquidity plan for the DTI outlines how to cover expected deposit withdrawals should they materialize. In this case, the DTI will seek to cover expected deposit withdrawals over the next three months, first with new deposits, then with the liquidation of marketable securities in its investment portfolio, then with borrowings from other FIs, and finally, if necessary, with borrowings from the Bank of Canada.

Liquidity Risk, Unexpected Deposit Drains, and Bank Runs

Under normal conditions and with appropriate management planning, neither net deposit withdrawals nor the exercise of loan commitments pose significant liquidity problems for DTIs because borrowed funds availability or excess cash

TABLE 17–10
Deposit
Distributions
and Possible
Withdrawals
Involved in a DTI's
Liquidity Plan
($ millions)

Deposits from	$ 250		
Mutual funds	60		
Pension funds	50		
Correspondent banks	15		
Small businesses	70		
Individuals	55		
Expected Withdrawals	**Average**	**Maximum**	
One week	$ 40	$ 105	
One month	55	140	
Three months	75	200	
Sequence of Deposit Withdrawal Funding	**One Week**	**One Month**	**Three Months**
New deposits	$ 10	$ 35	$ 75
Investment portfolio asset liquidation	50	60	75
Borrowings from other FIs	30	35	45
Borrowings from the Bank of Canada	15	10	5
Total	$ 105	$ 140	$ 200

reserves are adequate to meet anticipated needs. For example, even in December and the summer vacation season, when net deposit withdrawals are high, DTIs anticipate these *seasonal* effects by holding larger than normal excess cash reserves or borrowing more than normal on the wholesale money markets.

Major liquidity problems can arise, however, if deposit drains are *abnormally large* and unexpected. Abnormal deposit drains (shocks) may occur for a number of reasons, including:

1. Concerns about a DTI's solvency relative to that of other DTIs.
2. Failure of a related DTI leading to heightened depositor concerns about the solvency of other DTIs (the contagion effect).
3. Sudden changes in investor preferences regarding holding non-bank financial assets (such as T-bills or mutual fund shares) relative to deposits.

> **bank run**
> A sudden and unexpected increase in deposit withdrawals from a DTI.
>
> **www.scotiabank.com**

In such cases, any sudden and unexpected surges in net deposit withdrawals risk triggering a **bank run** that could eventually force a bank into insolvency. Macroeconomic factors can also trigger a bank run, such as the Bank of Nova Scotia's experience in Argentina. In Argentina, government actions appeared to exacerbate the situation, whereas in Canada, actions by the Bank of Canada and regulators have, in the past, forestalled this type of bank run.[18]

Deposit Drains and Bank Run Liquidity Risk

At the core of bank run liquidity risk is the fundamental and unique nature of the *demand deposit contract.* Specifically, demand deposit contracts are first-come, first-served contracts in the sense that a depositor's place in line determines the amount he or she will be able to withdraw from a DTI. In particular, a depositor either gets paid in full or gets nothing.[19] Because demand deposit contracts pay in full only a certain proportion of depositors when a DTI's assets are valued at less than its deposits—and because depositors realize this—any line outside a DTI encourages other depositors to join the line immediately even if they do not need cash today for normal consumption purposes. Thus, even the DTI's core depositors rationally seek to withdraw their funds immediately when they observe a sudden increase in the lines at their DTI.

---

[18] For more analysis regarding the contagion effects, see A. Kanas, "Pure Contagion Effects in International Banking: The Case of BCCI's failure," *Journal of Applied Economics,* May 2005, 8(1), pp. 101–124. The failure of Bank of Credit and Commerce International (BCCI) in the 1990s was one of the largest bank failures in the world whose story has all the elements of drama, including money laundering, corruption, and terrorist cells. Kanas looks at BCCI's failure in the United Kingdom, the United States, and Canada and finds no evidence of contagion effects in Canada or the United States. S. J. Kamath and J. R. Tilley, "Canadian International Banking and the Debt Crisis," *Columbia Journal of World Business,* Winter 1987, 22(4), pp. 75–87 examines effects from the 1980s LDC debt crisis, and S. V. Jayanti, A. M. Whyte, and A. Quang Do, "Bank Failures and Contagion Effects: Evidence from Britain and Canada," *Journal of Economics and Business,* May 1996, 48(2), pp. 103–116 compares the 1985 Canadian bank failures with the U.K. experience. Jayanti et al. conclude that the actions of regulators determine the market effects, as do L. Kryzanowski and G. S. Roberts, "Capital Forbearance: Depression-Era Experience of Life Insurance Companies," *Canadian Journal of Administrative Sciences,* March 1998, 15(1), pp. 1–16.

[19] We are assuming no deposit insurance exists that guarantees payments of deposits and no borrowing from the Bank of Canada that alters consumers' incentives to engage in a bank run as we describe later in Chapter 19. Bankruptcies of Canadian FIs occurred between 1983–1986 when 15 members of the Canada Deposit Insurance Corporation (CDIC) failed. Two of the failures were banks and the remaining FIs were trust companies. However, there have been no documented occurrences of contagion while deposit insurance has been in place in Canada, even during the market turmoil of 2007 and 2008. Other countries (Northern Rock in the United Kingdom and Countrywide Financial in the United States) did experience bank runs.

As a bank run develops, the demand for net deposit withdrawals grows. The DTI may initially meet this by decreasing its cash reserves, selling off liquid or readily marketable assets such as T-bills and Government of Canada and U.S. government bonds, and seeking to borrow in the money markets. As a bank run increases in intensity, more depositors join the withdrawal line, and a liquidity crisis develops. Specifically, the DTI finds it difficult, if not impossible, to borrow from the money markets at virtually any price. Also, it has sold all its liquid assets, cash, and bonds as well as any saleable loans (see Chapter 26). The DTI is likely to have left only relatively illiquid loans on the asset side of the balance sheet to meet depositor claims for cash. However, these loans can be sold or liquidated only at very large discounts from face value. A DTI needing to liquidate long-term assets at fire-sale prices to meet continuing deposit drains faces the strong possibility that the proceeds from such asset sales are insufficient to meet depositors' cash demands. The DTI's liquidity problem then turns into a solvency problem; that is, the DTI must close its doors.

The incentives for depositors to run first and ask questions later creates a fundamental instability in the banking system in that an otherwise sound DTI can be pushed into insolvency and failure by unexpectedly large depositor drains and liquidity demands. This is especially so in periods of contagious runs, or **bank panics,** when depositors lose faith in the banking system as a whole and engage in a run on all DTIs by not materially discriminating among them according to their asset qualities.

bank panic
A systemic or contagious run on the deposits of the banking industry as a whole.

Bank Runs, the Bank of Canada, and Deposit Insurance

Regulators have recognized the inherent instability of the banking system due to the all-or-nothing payoff features of the deposit contract. As a result, regulatory mechanisms are in place to ease DTIs' liquidity problems and to deter bank runs and panics. The two major liquidity risk insulation devices are *deposit insurance* and *borrowing from the Bank of Canada*. Because of the serious social welfare effects that a contagious run on DTIs could have, government regulators of deposit-taking institutions have established guarantee programs offering deposit holders varying degrees of insurance protection to deter runs. Specifically, if a deposit holder believes a claim is totally secure, even if the DTI is in trouble, the holder has no incentive to run. The deposit holder's place in line no longer affects his or her ability to obtain the funds. Deposit insurance deters runs as well as contagious runs and panics.

lender of last resort (LLR)
The role of a central bank in providing funds to a country's FIs during a liquidity crisis.

In addition to deposit insurance, central banks such as the Bank of Canada have traditionally provided overnight lending facilities to meet DTIs' short-term non-permanent liquidity needs. The Bank of Canada has three roles as **lender of last resort (LLR)** in providing liquidity to the financial system. As previously noted, through the LVTS, the Bank of Canada provides daily and overnight funds to cover temporary shortfalls of an FI. The Bank can also provide emergency lending assistance (ELA) to solvent deposit-taking financial institutions for a longer time period, as it did for Continental Bank of Canada. During extreme conditions, the Bank of Canada can also buy securities issued by financial and non-financial Canadian or foreign firms and government entities. As mentioned in Chapter 1, many central banks, including the Bank of Canada, expanded their programs of providing liquidity to FIs during the credit crisis in 2008.[20]

---

[20] See The Bank of Canada, "Bank of Canada Lender-of-Last-Resort Policies," *Financial System Review,* December 2004, pp. 49–55. See also "Liquidity Risk at Banks. Trends and Lessons Learned from the Recent Turmoil," J. Armstrong and G. Caldwell, Bank of Canada *Financial System Review,* December 2008, pp. 47–52.

1. List two benefits and two costs of using (a) purchased liquidity management and (b) stored liquidity management to meet a deposit drain.
2. What are the three major sources of DTI liquidity? What are the two major uses?
3. What are the measures of liquidity risk used by FIs?

LIQUIDITY RISK AND LIFE INSURANCE COMPANIES

surrender value
The amount received by an insurance policy holder when cashing in a policy early.

Deposit-taking institutions are not the only FIs exposed to liquidity risk or run problems. Like DTIs, life insurance companies hold cash reserves and other liquid assets to meet policy cancellations (surrenders) and other working capital needs that arise in the course of writing insurance. The early cancellation of an insurance policy results in the insurer's having to pay the insured the **surrender value** of that policy.[21] In the normal course of business, premium income and returns on an insurer's asset portfolio are sufficient to meet the cash outflows required when policyholders cash in or surrender their policies early. As with DTIs, the distribution or pattern of premium income minus policyholder liquidations is normally predictable. When premium income is insufficient to meet surrenders, however, a life insurer can sell some of its relatively liquid assets, such as government bonds. In this case, bonds act as a buffer or reserve asset source of liquidity for the insurer.

Nevertheless, concerns about the solvency of an insurer can result in a run in which new premium income dries up and existing policyholders seek to cancel their policies by cashing them in early. To meet exceptional demands for cash, a life insurer could be forced to liquidate the other assets in its portfolio, such as commercial mortgage loans and other securities, potentially at fire-sale prices. As with DTIs, forced asset liquidations can push an insurer into insolvency.[22]

1. What is likely to be a life insurance company's first source of liquidity when premium income is insufficient?
2. Can a life insurance company be subjected to a run? If so, why?

LIQUIDITY RISK AND PROPERTY AND CASUALTY INSURERS

As discussed in Chapter 3, property and casualty (P&C) insurers sell policies insuring against certain contingencies impacting either real property or individuals. Unlike those of life insurers, P&C contingencies (and policy coverages) are relatively short term, often one to three years. With the help of mortality tables, claims on life insurance policies are generally predictable. P&C claims (such as those associated with natural disasters such as the Quebec ice storm and the

---

[21] A surrender value is usually some proportion or percentage less than 100 percent of the face value of the insurance contract. The surrender value continues to grow as funds invested in the policy earn interest (returns). Earnings to the policyholder are taxed if and when the policy is actually surrendered or cashed in before the policy matures. Some insurance companies have faced run problems resulting from their sale of guaranteed investment contracts (GICs). A GIC, similar to a long-term, fixed-rate bank deposit, is a contract between an investor and an insurance company. As market interest rates rose, many investors withdrew their funds early and reinvested elsewhere in higher-return investments. This created both liquidity and refinancing problems for life insurers that supplied such contracts and eventually led to restrictions on withdrawals.

[22] Life insurers also provide loan commitments, especially in the commercial property area. As a result, they face asset-side loan commitment liquidity risk in a fashion similar to that of DTIs.

Winnipeg flood discussed in Chapter 3), however, are virtually impossible to predict. As a result, P&C insurers' assets tend to be shorter term and more liquid than those of life insurers. P&C insurers' contracts and premium-setting intervals are usually relatively short term as well, so problems caused by policy surrenders are less severe. P&C insurers' greatest liquidity exposure occurs when policyholders cancel or fail to renew policies with an insurer because of insolvency risk, pricing, or competitive reasons. This may cause an insurer's premium cash inflow, when added to its investment returns, to be insufficient to meet policyholders' claims. Alternatively, large unexpected claims may materialize and exceed the flow of premium income and income returns from assets, causing severe liquidity crises and failures among smaller P&C insurers.[23]

CONCEPT QUESTIONS	1. **What is the greatest cause of liquidity exposure faced by property and casualty insurers?** 2. **Is the liquidity risk of property and casualty insurers in general greater or less than that of life insurers?**

INVESTMENT FUNDS AND PENSION FUNDS

closed-end fund
An investment fund that sells a fixed number of shares in the fund to outside investors.

open-end fund
An investment fund that sells an elastic or non-fixed number of shares in the fund to outside investors.

net asset value (NAV)
The price at which investment fund shares are sold (or can be redeemed). It equals the total market value of the assets of the fund divided by the number of shares in the funds outstanding.

Investment funds such as mutual funds and hedge funds sell shares as liabilities to investors and invest the proceeds in assets such as bonds and equities. These funds are open-end or closed-end. **Closed-end funds** issue a fixed number of shares as liabilities; unless the issuing fund chooses to repurchase them, the number of outstanding shares does not change. As discussed in Chapter 5, by far the majority of Canadian investment funds are **open-end funds;** that is, they can issue an unlimited supply of shares to investors. Open-end funds must also stand ready to buy back previously issued shares from investors at the current market price for the fund's shares. Thus, at a given market price, P, the supply of open-end fund shares is perfectly elastic. The price at which an open-end investment fund stands ready to sell new shares or redeem existing shares is the **net asset value (NAV)** of the fund. NAV is the current or market value of the fund's assets less any accrued liabilities divided by the number of shares in the fund. An investment fund's willingness to provide instant liquidity to shareholders while it invests funds in equities, bonds, and other long-term instruments could expose it to liquidity problems similar to those banks and life insurance companies face when the number of withdrawals (or fund shares cashed in) rises to abnormally and unexpectedly high levels. Investment funds can be subject to dramatic liquidity runs if investors become nervous about the NAV of the funds' assets.[24] However, the fundamental difference in the way investment fund contracts are valued compared with the valuation of DTI deposit and insurance policy contracts mitigates the incentives for fund shareholders to engage in runs. Specifically, if a fund were to be liquidated, its assets would be distributed to fund shareholders on a pro rata basis rather than the first-come, first-served basis employed under deposit and insurance contracts.

---

[23] Also, claims may arise in long-tail lines where a contingency takes place during the policy period but a claim is not lodged until many years later. As mentioned in Chapter 3, one example is the claims regarding damage caused by asbestos contacts.

[24] For example, this happened to the value of assets held by mutual funds specializing in equities of Asian countries such as Indonesia and Thailand as well as Russia during the emerging-market crisis of 1997–1998.

To illustrate this difference, we can directly compare the incentives for mutual fund and hedge fund investors to engage in a run with those of DTI depositors. Table 17–11 shows a simple balance sheet of an open-end investment fund and a DTI. When they perceive that a DTI's assets are valued below its liabilities, depositors have an incentive to engage in a run on the DTI to be first in line to withdraw. In the example in Table 17–11, only the first 90 bank depositors would receive $1 back for each $1 deposited. The last 10 would receive nothing at all.

Now consider the investment fund with 100 shareholders who invested $1 each for a total of $100, but whose assets are worth $90. If these shareholders tried to cash in their shares, *none* would receive $1. Instead, a fund values its balance sheet liabilities on a market value basis; the price of any share liquidated by an investor is

$$P = \frac{\text{Value of assets}}{\text{Shares outstanding}} = \text{NAV (net asset value)}$$

Thus, unlike deposit contracts that have fixed face values of $1, the value of a fund's shares reflects the changing value of its assets divided by the number of shares outstanding.

In Table 17–11, the value of each shareholder's claim is

$$P = \frac{\$90}{100} = \$0.9$$

That is, each investment fund shareholder participates in the fund's loss of asset value on a *pro rata*, or proportional, basis. Technically, whether first or last in line, each fund shareholder who cashes in shares on any given day receives the same net asset value per share of the fund. In this case, it is 90 cents, representing a loss of 10 cents per share. All fund shareholders realize this and know that investors share asset losses on a pro rata basis; being the first in line to withdraw has no overall advantage as it has at DTIs.

This is not to say that investment funds bear no liquidity risk, but that the incentives for fund shareholders to engage in runs that produce the extreme form of liquidity problems faced by DTIs and life insurance companies are generally absent.[25]

TABLE 17–11
Run Incentives of DTI Depositors versus Mutual Fund Investors

Deposit-Taking Institution		Investment Fund	
Assets	**Liabilities**	**Assets**	**Liabilities**
Assets $90	$100 Deposits (100 depositors with $1 deposits)	Assets $90	$100 Shares (100 shareholders with $1 shares)

[25] A sudden surge of investment fund shareholder redemptions might require a fund manager to sell some of its less marketable bonds and equities at fire-sale prices. Long-Term Capital Management faced severe liquidity problems when trying to unwind large positions in many asset markets at the end of 1998. For example, in 2008, some mortgage-backed securities markets (see Chapter 27) were insufficiently deep to be able to absorb the massive sale of hedge fund assets without major price dislocations. As well, during the liquidity crisis in 2007 and 2008, the requirement of many hedge funds for investors to provide three months' notice before withdrawing their funds helped to mitigate the risk of fire sales of assets. The greatest liquidity risk for hedge funds came from their high levels of short-term debt funding. Hedge funds were forced to sell assets quickly to meet margin calls from their primary dealers as the global financial system underwent deleveraging.

Pension funds differ in that amounts paid out are controlled by the nature of the plan and therefore have been generally insulated from the meltdowns that affected hedge funds and the banks. However, pension funds, as well as mutual funds and hedge funds are subject to the same economywide liquidity risks that affect their returns.[26]

CONCEPT QUESTIONS

1. What would be the impact on their liquidity needs if DTIs offered deposit contracts of an open-end mutual fund type rather than the traditional all-or-nothing demand deposit contract?

2. How do the incentives of investment fund investors to engage in runs compare with the incentives of DTI depositors?

---

[26] T. Anthony, "Avoiding a Run for Your Money," *Canadian Investment Review,* Fall 2004, 17(3), pp. 29–34, discusses adjustments to portfolio management to recognize this type of risk for defined benefit pension plans, particularly with the aging of the Canadian population. Some of the principles can be extended to mutual funds and hedge funds as retirees increase their cash demands as their investment needs decrease.

Summary

Liquidity risk, as a result of heavier-than-anticipated liability withdrawals or loan commitment exercise, is a common problem faced by FI managers. Well-developed policies for holding liquid assets or having access to markets for purchased funds are normally adequate to meet liability withdrawals. However, very large withdrawals can cause asset liquidity problems that can be compounded by incentives for liability claimholders to engage in runs at the first sign of a liquidity problem. These incentives for depositors and life insurance policyholders to engage in runs can push normally sound FIs into insolvency. Investment funds are able to avoid runs because liabilities are marked to market so that losses are shared equally among liability holders. Since such insolvencies have costs to society as well as to private shareholders, regulators have developed mechanisms such as deposit insurance and borrowing from the central bank to alleviate liquidity problems. We discuss these mechanisms in detail in Chapter 19.

Questions and Problems

1. How does the degree of liquidity risk differ for different types of financial institutions?

2. What are the two reasons liquidity risk arises? How does liquidity risk arising from the liability side of the balance sheet differ from liquidity risk arising from the asset side of the balance sheet? What is meant by fire-sale prices?

3. What are core deposits? What role do core deposits play in predicting the probability distribution of net deposit drains?

4. The probability distribution of the net deposit drain of a DTI has been estimated to have a mean of 2 percent and a standard deviation of 1 percent. Is this DTI increasing or decreasing in size? Explain.

5. How is a DTI's distribution pattern of net deposit drains affected by the following?
   a. The holiday season.
   b. Summer vacations.
   c. A severe economic recession.
   d. Double-digit inflation.

6. What are two ways a DTI can offset the liquidity effects of a net deposit drain of funds? How do the two methods differ? What are the operational benefits and costs of each method?

7. What are two ways a DTI can offset the effects of asset-side liquidity risk such as the drawing down of a loan commitment?

8. A DTI with the following balance sheet ($ millions) expects a net deposit drain of $15 million.

Assets		Liabilities and Equity	
Cash	$ 10	Deposits	$ 68
Loans	50	Equity	7
Securities	15		
Total assets	$ 75	Total liabilities and equity	$ 75

Show the DTI's balance sheet if the following conditions occur:

a. The DTI purchases liabilities to offset this expected drain.

b. The stored liquidity management method is used to meet the expected drain.

9. AllStarBank has the following balance sheet ($ millions):

Assets		Liabilities and Equity	
Cash	$ 30	Deposits	$ 110
Loans	90	Borrowed funds	40
Securities	50	Equity	20
Total assets	$ 170	Total liabilities and equity	$ 170

AllStarBank's largest customer decides to exercise a $15 million loan commitment. How will the new balance sheet appear if AllStar uses the following liquidity risk strategies?

a. Stored liquidity management.

b. Purchased liquidity management.

10. A DTI has assets of $10 million consisting of $1 million in cash and $9 million in loans. The DTI has core deposits of $6 million, subordinated debt of $2 million, and equity of $2 million. Increases in interest rates are expected to cause a net drain of $2 million in core deposits over the year.

a. The average cost of deposits is 6 percent, and the average yield on loans is 8 percent. The DTI decides to reduce its loan portfolio to offset this expected decline in deposits. What will be the effect on net interest income and the size of the DTI after the implementation of this strategy?

b. If the interest cost of issuing new short-term debt is expected to be 7.5 percent, what would be the effect on net interest income of offsetting the expected deposit drain with an increase in interest-bearing liabilities?

c. What will be the size of the DTI after the drain if the DTI uses this strategy?

d. What dynamic aspects of DTI management would further support a strategy of replacing the deposit drain with interest-bearing liabilities?

11. Define each of the following four measures of liquidity risk. Explain how each measure would be implemented and utilized by a DTI.

a. Sources and uses of liquidity.

b. Peer group ratio comparisons.

c. Liquidity index.

d. Financing gap and financing requirement.

12. A DTI has $10 million in T-bills and a $5 million line of credit to borrow in the repo market. The DTI currently has borrowed $6 million in inter-bank funds and $2 million from the Bank of Canada to meet seasonal demands.

a. What is the DTI's total available (sources of) liquidity?

b. What is the DTI's current total uses of liquidity?

c. What is the net liquidity of the DTI?

d. What conclusions can you derive from the result?

13. A DTI has the following assets in its portfolio: $20 million in cash reserves with the Bank of Canada, $20 million in T-bills, and $50 million in mortgage loans. If the assets need to be liquidated at short notice, the DTI will receive only 99 percent of the fair market value of the T-bills and 90 percent of the fair market value of the mortgage loans. Estimate the liquidity index using the above information.

14. Conglomerate Corporation has acquired Acme Corporation. To help finance the takeover, Conglomerate will liquidate the overfunded portion of Acme's pension fund. The face values and current and one-year future liquidation values of the assets that will be liquidated are given below.

	Liquidation Values		
Asset	Face Value	$t = 0$	$t = 1$
BCE stock	$10,000	$ 9,900	$10,500
Royal Bank bonds	5,000	4,000	4,500
Government of Canada securities	15,000	13,000	14,000

Calculate the one-year liquidity index of these securities.

15. Plainbank has $10 million in cash and equivalents, $30 million in loans, and $15 million in core deposits.

a. Calculate the financing gap.

b. What is the financing requirement?

c. How can the financing gap be used in the day-to-day liquidity management of the bank?

16. How can an FI's liquidity plan help reduce the effects of liquidity shortages? What are the components of a liquidity plan?

17. What is a bank run? What are some possible withdrawal shocks that could initiate a bank run? What feature of the demand deposit contract provides deposit withdrawal momentum that can result in a bank run?

18. The following is the balance sheet of a DTI ($ millions):

Assets		Liabilities and Equity	
Cash	$ 2	Demand deposits	$ 50
Loans	50		
Plant and equipment	3	Equity	5
Total	$ 55	Total	$ 55

The asset–liability management committee has estimated that the loans, whose average interest rate is 6 percent and whose average life is three years, will have to be discounted at 10 percent if they are to be sold in less than two days. If they can be sold in four days, they will have to be discounted at 8 percent. If they can be sold later than a week, the DTI will receive the full market value. Loans are not amortized; that is, the principal is paid at maturity.

   a. What will be the price received by the DTI for the loans if they have to be sold in two days? In four days?

   b. In a crisis, if depositors all demand payment on the first day, what amount will they receive? What will they receive if they demand to be paid within the week? Assume no deposit insurance.

19. What government safeguards are in place to reduce liquidity risk for DTIs?

20. What are the levels of defence against liquidity risk for a life insurance company? How does liquidity risk for a property and casualty insurer differ from that for a life insurance company?

21. How is the liquidity problem faced by mutual funds different from that faced by DTIs and insurance companies?

22. A mutual fund has the following assets in its portfolio: $40 million in fixed-income securities and $40 million in stocks at current market values. In the event of a liquidity crisis, the fund can sell the assets at 96 percent of market value if they are disposed of in two days. The fund will receive 98 percent if the assets are disposed of in four days. Two shareholders, A and B, own 5 percent and 7 percent of equity (shares), respectively.

   a. Market uncertainty has caused shareholders to sell their shares back to the fund. What will the two shareholders receive if the mutual fund must sell all the assets in two days? In four days?

   b. How does this situation differ from a bank run? How have bank regulators mitigated the problem of bank runs?

23. A mutual fund has $1 million in cash and $9 million invested in securities. It currently has 1 million shares outstanding.

   a. What is the net asset value (NAV) of this fund?

   b. Assume that some of the shareholders decide to cash in their shares of the fund. How many shares at its current NAV can the fund take back without resorting to a sale of assets?

   c. As a result of anticipated heavy withdrawals, the fund sells 10,000 shares of stock currently valued at $40. Unfortunately, it receives only $35 per share. What is the net asset value after the sale? What are the cash assets of the fund after the sale?

   d. Assume that after the sale of stock, 100,000 shares are sold back to the fund. What is the current NAV? Is there a need to sell more securities to meet this redemption?

Web Question

24. Go to the Statistics Canada website at www.statcan.gc.ca. In the Search Box, enter "Banking balance sheet." Click on the first item returned, "Banking—Balance sheet and income statement." Use information in this table to update Table 17–1. How have the assets and liabilities of Canadian banks changed since 2008?

Integrated Mini-Case

MEASURING LIQUIDITY RISK

A DTI has the following balance sheet ($ millions):

Assets		Liabilities and Equity	
Cash	$ 9	Deposits	$ 75
Loans	95	Purchased funds	40
Securities	26	Equity	15
Total assets	$130	Total liabilities and equity	$130

The DTI's securities portfolio includes $16 million in T-bills and $10 million in Government of Canada bonds. The DTI has a $20 million line of credit to borrow in the repo market. The DTI currently has borrowed $22 million in inter-bank funds and $18 million from the Bank of Canada to meet seasonal demands.

1. What are the DTI's total available sources of liquidity?
2. What is the DTI's current total uses of liquidity?
3. What is the net liquidity of the DTI?
4. Calculate the financing gap.
5. What is the financing requirement?

6. The DTI expects a net deposit drain of $20 million. Show the DTI's balance sheet if the following conditions occur:

   a. The DTI purchases liabilities to offset this expected drain.

   b. The stored liquidity management method is used to meet the expected drain (the DTI does not want the cash balance to fall below $5 million, and securities can be sold at their fair value).

7. In the event of an unexpected and severe drain on deposits in the next 3 and 10 days, the DTI will liquidate assets in the following manner:

Liquidation Values ($ millions)			
Asset	Fair Value	$t = 3$	$t = 10$
Cash	$ 9	$ 9	$ 9
Treasury bills	16	14	15.5
Canada bonds	10	8	9
Loans	95	65	75

Calculate the 3-day and 10-day liquidity index for the DTI.

Managing **Risk**

CHAPTER 18

Liability and Liquidity Management

In this chapter, we consider how an FI can manage liquidity risk and discuss

▸ the various liquid assets and liabilities an FI might use to manage liquidity risk

▸ the risk–return trade-offs of using these assets and liabilities to manage liquidity risk

▸ the specific issues associated with liquidity risk management in deposit-taking institutions, insurance companies, and other FIs

▸ the role of central banks and regulators after the liquidity crisis of 2007–2008

INTRODUCTION

Deposit-taking institutions as well as life insurance companies are especially exposed to liquidity risk (see Chapter 17). The essential feature of this risk is that an FI's assets are relatively illiquid when liquid claims are suddenly withdrawn (or not renewed). The classic case is a bank run in which depositors demand cash as they withdraw their claims from a bank and the bank is unable to meet those demands because of the relatively illiquid nature of its assets. For example, the bank could have a large portfolio of non-marketable small business or real estate loans.

To reduce the risk of a liquidity crisis, FIs can insulate their balance sheets from liquidity risk by efficiently managing their liquid asset positions or managing the liability structure of their portfolios. In reality, an FI manager can optimize over both liquid asset and liability structures to insulate the FI against liquidity risk. In addition to ensuring that FIs can meet expected and unexpected liability withdrawals, an additional motive for holding liquid assets is monetary policy implementation.

LIQUID ASSET MANAGEMENT

A liquid asset can be turned into cash quickly and at a low transaction cost with little or no loss in principal value. Specifically, a liquid asset is traded in an active market so that even large transactions in that asset do not move the market price or move it very little. Good examples of liquid assets are newly issued T-bills, and other government debt. The ultimate liquid asset is, of course, cash. While it is obvious that an FI's liquidity risk can be reduced by holding large amounts of assets such as cash, T-bills, and Government of Canada bonds, FIs usually face a return or interest earnings penalty from doing this. Because of their high liquidity and low default risks, such assets often bear low returns that reflect their essentially risk-free nature. By contrast, non-liquid assets often must promise additional returns or liquidity risk premiums to compensate an FI for the relative lack of marketability and often greater default risk of the instrument.

429

Holding relatively small amounts of liquid assets exposes an FI to enhanced illiquidity and risk of a bank run. Excessive illiquidity can result in an FI's inability to meet required payments on liability claims and, at the extreme, in insolvency. It can even lead to contagious effects that negatively impact other FIs (see Chapter 17). Consequently, regulators have often imposed minimum liquid asset reserve requirements that differ in nature and scope for various FIs and according to country. The requirements depend on the liquidity risk exposure perceived for the FI's type and other regulatory objectives. For example, the Federal Reserve Bank of the United States strengthens its monetary policy by setting a minimum ratio of liquid reserve assets to deposits that limits the ability of deposit-taking institutions (DTIs) to expand lending. An increase in the reserve requirement results in a decrease in lending and subsequent decrease in the money supply. Conversely, a decrease in the reserve ratio means that DTIs are able to lend a greater percentage of their deposits, thus increasing credit availability in the economy.[1] As noted in Chapter 17, the Bank of Canada is one of several central banks (another example is the Reserve Bank of New Zealand) that carry out monetary policy to control inflation by setting a target for the overnight rate rather than by imposing reserve requirements. Thus the Bank of Canada has set the reserve requirements for banks at zero since 1994. However, it still stands as the lender of last resort in providing overnight liquidity and emergency lending assistance to deposit-taking institutions in Canada.

www.bankofcanada.ca

CONCEPT QUESTION

Why do regulators set minimum liquid asset requirements for FIs?

THE COMPOSITION OF THE LIQUID ASSET PORTFOLIO

The composition of an FI's liquid asset portfolio, especially among cash and government securities, is determined partly by earnings considerations and partly by the type of minimum liquid asset reserve requirements the central bank imposes. In many countries, such as the United Kingdom, reserve ratios were historically imposed to encompass both cash and liquid government securities such as T-bills.[2] Thus, a 20 percent **liquid assets ratio** requires a DTI to hold $1 of cash plus government securities for every $5 of deposits. Many states in the United States impose liquid asset ratios on life insurance companies that require minimum cash and government securities holdings in their balance sheets. By contrast, the minimum liquid asset requirements on DTIs in the United States have been cash-based and have excluded government securities. As a result, government securities are less useful because they are not counted as part of reserves held by DTIs and at the same time yield lower promised returns than loans. Nevertheless, many DTIs view government securities holdings as performing a useful **secondary** or **buffer reserve** function. In times of a liquidity crisis, when significant drains on cash reserves occur, these securities can be turned into cash quickly and with very little loss of principal value because of the deep nature of the markets in which these assets are traded.

liquid assets ratio
A minimum ratio of liquid assets to total assets set by the central bank.

secondary or buffer reserves
Non-reserve assets that can be quickly turned into cash.

[1] For example, in the United States the Federal Reserve system is divided into 12 districts that are the "operating arms" of the central banking system. Each of the 12 regional banks deals specifically with the liquidity issues in its section of the country.

[2] The United Kingdom no longer imposes minimum reserve requirements on banks.

CONCEPT QUESTION	In general, would it be better to hold three-month T-bills or ten-year government bonds as buffer assets? Explain.

RETURN–RISK TRADE-OFF FOR LIQUID ASSETS

In optimizing its holdings of liquid assets, an FI must trade the benefit of cash immediacy for lower returns. In a jurisdiction that, like Canada and the United Kingdom, does not impose reserve requirements, an FI is able to optimize its liquid asset holdings by matching its assets holdings with the liquidity needs of its short-term liabilities such as deposit withdrawals. A further consideration in the liquid asset mix for large Canadian FIs is the requirement for members of the Large Value Transfer System (LVTS) to provide collateral on a daily basis for the largest transaction that they expect to clear through the payment system. Since LVTS transactions are instantaneous and irrevocable, the collateral acts as a form of co-insurance to protect other LVTS participants and the Bank of Canada should a member experience liquidity difficulties during the day. If an LVTS participant was unable to make its payments, the Bank of Canada would sell the securities held as collateral to meet the FI's obligations. Thus, the collateral is highly liquid and is limited to securities issued or guaranteed by the Government of Canada or provincial governments, deposits held at the Bank of Canada, bankers' acceptances, commercial paper, short-term paper or bonds issued by municipalities, and corporate bonds.[3]

Chapter 17 discussed several models FIs use to measure liquidity risk, including models used to determine the FI's liquid asset needs over a future period of time. However, since cash is a non-earning asset, an FI will hold as little cash as possible to meet its liquid asset needs. The remaining liquid assets are generally stored in the FI's security portfolio (e.g., holding Treasury bills).

Managing the securities portfolio is an integral part of liquidity management for financial institutions. FI managers must determine the optimal combination of lower-yielding, liquid assets versus higher-yielding, less-liquid assets. Short-term marketable securities are held for immediate liquidity needs, and mortgage securities and other longer-term securities are held and can be sold if liquidity needs are larger than expected. Other ways of maintaining liquidity are loan sales and securitization (see Chapters 26 and 27). Briefly, FIs can sell loans (or securitized loans) for liquidity to long-term investors, such as insurance companies. These loan sales provide a stream of liquidity that can be used to fund new loan demand or deposit withdrawals. In addition, if the FI removes loans from its balance sheet, it can use the funds received from the sale of loans to pay off depositors (i.e., shrinking the size of the FI). With fewer assets, the FI's required capital (under capital requirements such as the Tier 1 capital ratio; see Chapter 20) can be reduced.

Liquidity Management as a Knife-Edge Management Problem

The management of a DTI's liquidity position is something of a knife-edge situation because holding too many liquid assets penalizes a DTI's earnings and, thus, its stockholders. A DTI manager who holds excessive amounts of liquid assets is unlikely to survive long. Similarly, a manager who holds too little amounts of

---

[3] See Chapter 16 for a discussion of the Large Value Transfer System (LVTS).

liquid assets faces enhanced risks of liquidity crises and regulatory intervention. Again, such a manager's tenure at the DTI may be relatively short.

LIABILITY MANAGEMENT

Liquidity and liability management are closely related. One aspect of liquidity risk control is the buildup of a prudential level of liquid assets. Another aspect is the management of the DTI's liability structure to reduce the need for large amounts of liquid assets to meet liability withdrawals. However, excessive use of purchased funds in the liability structure can result in a liquidity crisis if investors lose confidence in the DTI and refuse to roll over such funds.

As discussed in Chapter 16, improvements in technology and demand for efficiency and flexibility in the financial transactions of wholesale and retail customers have lowered the costs of holding deposits and changed the way FIs manage liquidity risk. Technologically oriented services (such as online banking) connect customers to their deposit and brokerage accounts via personal computers. These technologies also provide other services such as electronic securities trading and bill-paying via personal computers. Likewise, preauthorized debits of payroll cheques get cash into FIs' deposit accounts faster and with more predictability. In doing so, cheque processing time and handling costs can be reduced significantly for FIs. These types of services have changed the way liquidity management is viewed by FIs.

Funding Risk and Cost

Unfortunately, constructing a low-cost, low-withdrawal-risk liability portfolio is more difficult than it sounds. This is true because those liabilities, or sources of DTI funds, that are the most subject to withdrawal risk are often the least costly to the DTI. That is, a DTI must trade off the benefits of attracting liabilities at a low funding cost with a high chance of withdrawal against liabilities with a high funding cost and low liquidity. For example, demand deposits are relatively low funding cost vehicles for DTIs but can be withdrawn without notice.[4] By contrast, a five-year, fixed-rate **Guaranteed Investment Certificate (GIC)** may have a relatively high funding cost but can be withdrawn before the five-year maturity is up only after the deposit holder pays a substantial interest rate penalty.

Thus, in structuring the liability, or funding, side of the balance sheet, the DTI manager faces a trade-off along the lines suggested in Figure 18–1. That is, funding costs are generally inversely related to the period of time the liability is likely to remain on the DTI's balance sheet (i.e., to funding risk).

Although we have discussed deposit-taking institutions' funding risk, other FIs face a similar trade-off. For example, investment banks can finance through overnight funds (repurchase agreements and brokered deposits) or longer-term sources such as notes and bonds. Finance companies have a choice between commercial paper and longer-term notes and bonds.

In some respects, the management of funding risk and cost is similar to the treasury function of any other large corporation. However, the regulatory climate provides an added dimension to the "treasury" management of a large FI. The

Guaranteed Investment Certificate (GIC)
A fixed-maturity instrument offered to retail clients that is non-redeemable, carries a term from 30 days to 5 years, and pays interest at a specified rate at the end of the term.

---

[4] Depositors do not always exercise this option; therefore, some demand deposits behave like longer-term core deposits. In addition, many DTIs waive monthly fees when a depositor maintains a minimum monthly balance, creating an incentive to leave the funds on deposit.

FIGURE 18–1
Funding Risk versus Cost

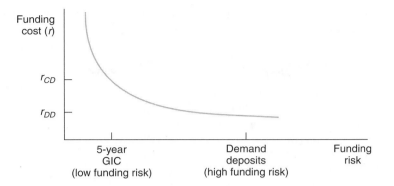

consequences for the FI of undershooting its liquidity needs and, as a result, being unable to settle its payments through the clearing system or meet its customer's deposit withdrawals are a loss of confidence by depositors and regulators, a potential for long-term damage to its reputation and, in a worst case scenario, insolvency. The renewed emphasis by BIS and OSFI on liquidity management for the FIs that they regulate is discussed at the end of the chapter. The next section looks at the spectrum of liabilities available to a DTI manager in seeking to actively impact liquidity risk exposure through the choice of liability structure.

CONCEPT QUESTIONS

1. **How are liquidity and liability management related?**
2. **Describe the trade-off faced by an FI manager in structuring the liability side of the balance sheet.**

CHOICE OF LIABILITY STRUCTURE

This section considers in more detail the withdrawal (or funding) risk and funding cost characteristics of the major liabilities available to a modern DTI manager.

Demand Deposits

Withdrawal Risk

Demand deposits issued by DTIs have a high degree of withdrawal risk. Withdrawals can be instantaneous and largely expected by the DTI manager, such as pre-weekend cash withdrawals, or unexpected, as occur during economic crisis situations (so-called bank runs; see Chapter 17).

Costs

Demand deposits pay the lowest interest rates, making them a low-cost source of funds for DTIs. In addition, DTIs can adjust the levels of interest rates and fees charged in order to partially control for the withdrawal risk associated with these contracts. For example, it is common for deposit accounts at FIs to pay a higher interest rate depending on the amount kept on balance in the account, or to provide no-fee chequing if a minimum monthly balance is maintained. Very few bank deposits in Canada are non-interest-bearing. For example, the Royal Bank's 2008 annual report shows total deposits of $438.6 billion, comprising personal deposits (31.7 percent), business and government deposits (61.6 percent), and bank

www.royalbank.com

deposits (6.7 percent). Of this total, only $43.7 billion of deposits (10 percent) were non-interest bearing.

Competition among DTIs and other FIs has resulted in the payment of implicit interest, or payments of interest in kind, on chequing accounts. Specifically, in providing demand deposits that are chequable accounts, a DTI must provide a whole set of associated services from providing chequebooks, to clearing of cheques, to sending out statements with cleared cheques or cheque images. Because such services absorb real resources of labour and capital, they are costly for DTIs to provide. DTIs can recapture these costs by charging fees, such as 10 cents per cheque cleared. To the extent that these fees do not fully cover the DTI's cost of providing such services, the depositor receives a subsidy or an implicit interest payment.

The payment of implicit interest means that the DTI manager is not absolutely powerless to mitigate deposit withdrawals, especially if rates on competing instruments are rising. In particular, the DTI could lower cheque-clearing fees, which in turn raises implicit interest payments to depositors. Such payments are *payments in kind* or *subsidies* that are not paid in actual dollars and cents as is interest earned on competing instruments. Nevertheless, implicit payments of interest are tax-free to the depositor, but explicit interest payments are taxable.

EXAMPLE 18–1

Calculation of Average Implicit Interest Rate

Suppose a DTI pays 15 cents to clear a cheque but charges a fee of only 10 cents per cheque cleared. The customer receives a 5 cent subsidy per cheque. We can calculate implicit yields for each service, or an average implicit interest rate, for each demand deposit account. For example, an average implicit interest rate for a DTI's demand deposits might be calculated as

$$\begin{array}{c} \text{Average implicit} \\ \text{interest rate} \\ (IIR) \end{array} = \frac{\begin{array}{c}\text{Average management costs} \\ \text{per account per annum}\end{array} - \begin{array}{c}\text{Average fees earned per} \\ \text{account per annum}\end{array}}{\text{Average annual size of account}}$$

Suppose that

$$\text{Average management costs per account per annum} = \$\ \ 150$$
$$\text{Average fees earned per account per annum} = \$\ \ 100$$
$$\text{Average annual size of account} = \$1{,}200$$

Then,

$$IIR = \frac{\$150 - \$100}{\$1{,}200} = 4.166\%$$

Interest-Bearing Chequing Accounts

Withdrawal Risk

Canadian FIs offer chequable deposits that pay interest and are withdrawable on demand. The major distinction between these instruments and traditional demand deposits is that these instruments require the depositor to maintain a minimum account balance to earn interest. If the minimum balance falls below some level, such as $500, the account formally converts to a status equivalent to demand deposits and earns no interest. The payment of explicit interest and the existence of minimum balance requirements make these accounts potentially less prone to withdrawal risk than demand deposits. Nevertheless, they are still highly liquid instruments from the depositor's perspective.

Costs

As with demand deposits, the FI can influence the potential withdrawability of chequing accounts by paying implicit interest or fee subsidies such as not charging the full cost of cheque clearance. However, the manager has two other ways to influence the yield paid to the depositor. The first is by varying the minimum balance requirement. If the minimum balance requirement is lowered—say, from $500 to $250—a larger portion of the account becomes subject to interest payments and thus the explicit return and attractiveness of these accounts increases. The second is to vary the explicit interest rate payment itself, such as increasing it from 2 to $2\frac{1}{4}$ percent. Thus, the FI manager has three pricing mechanisms to increase or decrease the attractiveness, and therefore impact the withdrawal rate, of chequing accounts: implicit interest payments, minimum balance requirements, and explicit interest payments.

EXAMPLE 18–2

Gross Interest Return

Consider a depositor who holds on average $250 per month for the first three months of the year, $500 per month for the next three months, and $1,000 per month for the final six months of the year in a chequing account. The account pays 5 percent per annum if the minimum balance is $500 or more, and it pays no interest if the account falls below $500. The depositor writes an average of 50 cheques per month and pays a service fee of 10 cents for each cheque although it costs the bank 15 cents to process each cheque. The account holder's gross interest return, consisting of implicit plus explicit interest, is

$$\text{Gross interest return} = \text{Explicit interest} + \text{Implicit interest} = \$500(0.05)(0.25)$$
$$+ \$1000(0.05)(0.5) + (\$0.15 - \$0.10)(50)(12)$$
$$= \$6.25 + \$25 + \$30 = \$61.25$$

Suppose the minimum balance was lowered from $500 to $250 and cheque service fees were lowered from 10 cents to 5 cents per cheque. Then,

$$\text{Gross interest return} = \$250(0.05)(0.25) + \$500(0.05)(0.25) + \$1,000(0.05)(0.5)$$
$$+ (\$0.15 - \$0.05)(50)(12)$$
$$= \$3.125 + \$6.25 + \$25 + \$60$$
$$= \$94.375$$

Savings Accounts

Withdrawal Risk

Savings accounts are generally less liquid than demand deposits and chequing accounts for two reasons. First, they are non-chequable and may involve physical presence at the institution for withdrawal. Second, the FI has the legal power to delay payment or withdrawal requests. This is rarely done and FIs normally meet withdrawal requests with immediate cash payment, but they have the legal right to delay, which provides important withdrawal risk control to FI managers.

Costs

Since these accounts are non-chequable, any implicit interest rate payments are likely to be small; thus, the principal costs to the FI are the explicit interest payments on these accounts. In recent years, FIs have normally paid slightly higher explicit rates on savings than on chequing accounts.

Retail Term Deposits and GICs
Withdrawal Risk

retail term deposit

A fixed-maturity instrument offered to retail clients for a term of one to five years with a guaranteed interest payment that is usually semi-annual and carries an interest penalty for early withdrawal.

By contractual design, fixed-term deposits reduce the withdrawal risk to issuers. DTIs in Canada offer **retail term deposits,** which are redeemable prior to maturity subject to an interest penalty, and Guaranteed Investment Certificates (GICs), which are generally not redeemable prior to maturity to retail investors. Term deposits are straightforward deposits whose rates are generally set to be competitive, but fixed over the term of the deposit. The size, maturity, and rate on term deposits are usually standardized. GICs, on the other hand, come in many variations to appeal to retail customers as an alternative to other sources of investment, particularly for registered retirement savings plans (RRSPs) or registered retirement income funds (RRIFs). For example, the rate on GICs may be tied to money market rates (e.g., the FI's rate for bankers' acceptances), or, alternatively, may carry a rate tied to the S&P TSX60 Index or other market indices, which may change over the term of the deposit. In a world of no early withdrawal requests, the DTI knows the exact scheduling of interest and principal payments to depositors holding such deposit claims, since these payments are contractually specified. As such, the FI manager can directly control fund inflows and outflows by varying the maturities of the deposits offered to the public. In addition, since many GICs are held by depositors within an RRSP or RRIF, they may be less subject to withdrawal to another FI on rollover dates.

When depositors wish to withdraw before the maturity of a term deposit, FIs impose penalties on a withdrawing depositor, such as the loss of a certain number of months' interest depending on the maturity of the deposit. Although this does impose a friction or transaction cost on withdrawals, it is unlikely to stop withdrawals of term deposits when the depositor has exceptional liquidity needs. Also, withdrawals may increase if depositors perceive the DTI to be insolvent, despite interest penalties and deposit insurance coverage up to $100,000. Nevertheless, under normal conditions, these instruments have low withdrawal risk compared with chequing accounts and can be used as an important liability management tool to control withdrawal/liquidity risk.

Costs

tax-free savings account (TFSA)

A registered account that allows investors to accumulate and withdraw investment income tax-free on deposits of up to $5,000 per year.

Similar to those of savings accounts, the major costs of these deposits are explicit interest payments. Short-term GICs are often competitive with money market instruments such as T-bills. Note that depositors who buy term deposits and GICs are subject to taxes on their interest payments, although those held within RRSPs are sheltered until withdrawn. As well, the **tax-free savings account (TFSA)** introduced by the Government of Canada in 2009 is registered. TFSAs allow contributions of up to $5,000 per year that can be held in GICs, mutual funds, and other investments such as bonds. The investment income is tax-free, as are withdrawals from the TFSA.[5]

Wholesale Fixed-Term Deposits and CDs
Withdrawal Risk

wholesale CDs

Time deposits with a face value above $100,000.

Wholesale CDs were innovated by U.S. banks in the early 1960s as a contractual mechanism to allow depositors to liquidate their positions in these CDs by selling them in the secondary market rather than settling up with the FI. A depositor can

---

[5] Details of the rules governing tax-free savings accounts are available at the Government of Canada's website at www.tfsa.gc.ca and on the websites of deposit-taking institutions in Canada.

sell a relatively liquid instrument without causing adverse liquidity risk exposure for the FI. Thus, the unique feature of these wholesale CDs is not so much their large minimum denomination size of US$100,000 or more but the fact that they are **negotiable instruments.** That is, they can be resold by title assignment in a secondary market to other investors. This means, for example, that if IBM bought a US$1 million three-month CD from Citibank but for unexpected liquidity reasons needs funds after only one month has passed, it could sell this CD to another outside investor in the secondary market. This does not impose any obligation on Citibank in terms of an early funds withdrawal request. Thus, a depositor can sell a relatively liquid instrument without causing adverse withdrawal risk exposure for the FI. Essentially, the only withdrawal risk (which can be substantial) is that these wholesale CDs are not rolled over and reinvested by the holder of the deposit claim on maturity.[6]

Canadian FIs that operate in the United States are able to take advantage of the CD market. However, a similar active market does not exist in Canada. For Canadian FIs, most core wholesale deposits come from institutional investors (governments, other FIs) and corporate entities with which the FI may have a relationship. These wholesale fixed-term deposits are tailored to meet the cash management requirements of the customer with respect to the term, and the rates are higher than those on retail GICs.[7]

Costs

The rates that FIs pay on these instruments are competitive with other wholesale money market rates, especially those on commercial paper and T-bills. This competitive rate aspect is enhanced by the highly sophisticated nature of investors in CDs, such as money market mutual fund managers, and the fact that these deposits are covered by deposit insurance guarantees only up to the limit per investor, per institution ($100,000). To the extent that these CDs are offered by large FIs perceived as being too big to fail, the required credit risk premium on CDs is less than that required for similar-quality instruments issued by the non-bank private sector (e.g., commercial paper). In addition, required interest yields on CDs reflect investors' perceptions of the depth of the secondary market for CDs. In recent years, the liquidity of the secondary market in CDs appears to have diminished as dealers have withdrawn. This has increased FIs' relative cost of issuing such instruments.[8]

negotiable instrument
An instrument whose ownership can be transferred in the secondary market.

---

[6] Wholesale dollar CDs are also offered in countries other than the United States, in which case they are called Eurodollar CDs. Eurodollar CDs may sell at slightly different rates from domestic CDs because of differences in demand and supply for CDs between the domestic market and the Euromarket and differences in credit risk perceptions of depositors buying a CD from a foreign branch (e.g., Citibank in London) rather than a domestic branch (Citibank in New York). To the extent that it is believed that banks are too big to fail, a guaranty that extends only to domestic branches, a higher risk premium may be required of overseas CDs. Indeed, FDICIA, passed in 1991, has severely restricted the ability of the FDIC to rescue overseas depositors of a failed U.S. bank.

[7] Many FIs rely on asset-backed commercial paper for short-term funding (See Chapter 27 on securitization).

[8] In addition, for all the liability instruments considered so far (with the exception of euro CDs), the U.S.-based FI may have to pay an FDIC insurance premium depending on their perceived riskiness. For example, consider a bank issuing CDs at 3.26 percent, at which rate a depositor might just be indifferent to holding T-bills at 3.00 percent, given a local tax rate of 8 percent. However, the cost to the bank of the CD issue is not 3.26 percent but

$$\text{Effective CD cost} = 3.26\% + \text{Insurance premium} = 3.26\% + 0.27\% = 3.53\%$$

where 27 basis points is the assumed size of the deposit insurance premium. Thus, deposit insurance premiums add to the cost of deposits as a source of funds. However, until 2006, the insurance premium was set by the FDIC at zero for most FIs, with only the very riskiest having to pay 27 basis points.

Inter-Bank Funds

Withdrawal Risk

The liabilities just described are all deposit liabilities, reflecting deposit contracts issued by DTIs in return for cash. However, DTIs not only fund their assets by issuing deposits but also can borrow in various markets for purchased funds. Since the funds generated from these purchases are borrowed funds, not deposits, they are not subject to deposit insurance premium payments to the CDIC (as with all the domestic deposits described earlier).[9] The largest market available for purchased funds is the inter-bank market. While FIs with excess cash reserves can invest some of this excess in interest-earning liquid assets such as T-bills and short-term securities, an alternative is to lend excess cash for short intervals to other FIs seeking increased short-term funding. **Inter-bank funds** are short-term uncollateralized loans made by one FI to another; more than 90 percent of such transactions have maturities of one day. The FI that purchases funds shows them as a liability on its balance sheet, while the FI that sells them shows them as an asset. For example, RBC showed demand deposits of $6.7 trillion from banks on its 2008 annual report.

For the liability-funding FIs, there is no risk that the inter-bank funds they have borrowed can be withdrawn within the day, although there is settlement risk at the end of each day (see Chapter 16). However, there is some risk that funds will not be rolled over by the lending bank the next day if rollover is desired by the borrowing FI. In reality, this has occurred only in periods of extreme crisis. Nevertheless, since inter-bank funds are uncollateralized loans, institutions selling inter-bank funds normally impose maximum bilateral limits or credit caps on borrowing institutions. This may constrain the ability of a bank to expand its inter-bank funds-borrowing position very rapidly if this is part of its overall liability management strategy.

Costs

The cost of inter-bank funds for the purchasing institution is the inter-bank rate. The rate is set by FIs (mostly banks) that trade in the market and can vary considerably both within the day and across days. Another inter-bank source of funding is the London Interbank Offered Rate (LIBOR) market. The LIBOR market normally provides global banks with a low-cost source of funds, often in U.S. dollars, that FIs match with their borrowers who have LIBOR-based loans. The level of liquidity provided by the inter-bank market became evident during the subprime mortgage crisis in 2007 and the liquidity crisis in 2008. Global banks began to doubt each other's solvency after the failure of Bear Stearns in the United States and the bailout of AIG. The cost of LIBOR deposits, that is, the rate banks charge to lend to each other, increased. Market participants watched as the **TED spread,** which measures the difference between the three-month U.S. dollar T-bill rate and the three-month Eurodollar rate, peaked at 465 basis points between September and November 2008. The average TED spread reached 150 to 300 basis points during the economic crisis, up from its normal value of 30 to 50 basis points.

inter-bank funds
Short-term uncollateralized loans made by one FI to another.

TED spread
The difference between the three-month U.S. Treasury bill rate and the three-month Eurodollar rate.

---

[9] Foreign deposits are not subject to deposit insurance premiums.

Repurchase Agreements (Repos)
Withdrawal Risk

repurchase agreements (repos)

Agreements involving the sale of securities by one party (i.e., a DTI) to another with a promise to repurchase the securities at a specified date and price in the future.

Repurchase agreements (RPs or repos) can be viewed as collateralized inter-bank transactions. The FI with excess cash sells overnight funds for one day to the purchasing FI. The next day, the purchasing FI returns the funds plus one day's interest reflecting the Bank of Canada's overnight rate. Since a credit risk exposure exists for the selling FI because the purchasing FI may be unable to repay the funds the next day, the seller may seek collateral backing for the one-day loan. In a repo transaction, the funds-selling FI receives government securities as collateral from the funds-purchasing FI. That is, the funds-purchasing FI temporarily exchanges securities for cash. The next day, this transaction is reversed. The funds-purchasing FI sends back the overnight funds it borrowed plus interest (the repo rate); it receives in return (or repurchases) its securities used as collateral in the transaction.

As with the inter-bank market, the repo market is a highly liquid and flexible source of funds for FIs needing to increase their liabilities and to offset deposit withdrawals. Moreover, these transactions can be rolled over each day. The major liability management flexibility difference between inter-bank funds and repos is that an inter-bank funds transaction can be entered into at any time in the business day. In general, it is difficult to transact a repo borrowing late in the day since the FI sending the funds must be satisfied with the type and quality of the securities collateral proposed by the borrowing institution. This collateral is normally in the form of T-bills, T-notes, T-bonds, and mortgage-backed securities, but their maturities and other features, such as callability and coupons, may be unattractive to the funds seller. Negotiations over the collateral package can delay repo transactions and make them more difficult to arrange than simple uncollateralized loans.[10]

Costs

Because of their collateralized nature, repo rates normally lie below inter-bank rates. Also, repo rates generally show less interday fluctuation than do inter-bank rates. This is partly due to the lesser intraday flexibility of repos relative to inter-bank transactions.

Other Borrowings

While inter-bank funds and repos have been a major sources of borrowed funds, FIs have utilized a host of other borrowing sources to supplement their liability management flexibility. We describe these briefly in the following sections.

Bankers' Acceptances

Banks often convert off-balance-sheet letters of credit into on-balance-sheet bankers' acceptances (BAs) by discounting the letter of credit the holder presents for acceptance (see Chapter 13). Further, these BAs may then be resold to money market investors. Thus, BA sales to the secondary market are an additional funding source.

---

[10] The Bank of Canada also participates in the overnight funds market via purchase and resale agreements (PRAs) in order to enact monetary policy by influencing the overnight rate. When overnight funds are trading below the target rate, the Bank of Canada will offer to sell Government of Canada securities overnight and buy them back at a set price the next day. See the Bank of Canada's website at www.bankofcanada.ca.

Commercial Paper

As noted previously, Canadian FIs are active issuers in the asset-backed commercial paper (ABCP) market. According to P. Toovey and J. Kiff (*Financial System Review,* Bank of Canada, June 2003), Canadian banks issued 90 percent of the $88.2 billion asset-backed securities outstanding in Canada in 2002. As well, Canadian banks are active in the U.S. and the European ABCP markets. ABCP is structured to reduce the credit risk for the purchaser and the cost for the issuer, and carry a credit rating assigned by Dominion Bond Rating Service (DBRS).

Medium-Term and Long-Term Notes

A number of DTIs in search of more stable sources of funds with low withdrawal risk have begun to issue medium-term notes, often in the five- to seven-year range. These notes are additionally attractive because they are not subject to deposit insurance premiums. For example, RBC has two senior deposit notes ($900 million and $999.8 million) included with its business and government deposits in 2008. These notes mature in 2053 and 2017, respectively.

Overnight Loans with the Bank of Canada

As discussed earlier, FIs facing temporary liquidity crunches can borrow from the central bank at the overnight rate. Direct participants in the Large Value Transfer System may borrow directly from the Bank of Canada at the overnight rate through the Standing Liquidity Facility (SLF) as described in detail in Chapter 19.

CONCEPT QUESTIONS

1. Describe the withdrawal risk and funding cost characteristics of some of the major liabilities available to a modern FI manager.
2. Since demand deposits are subject to deposit insurance premiums, whereas inter-bank funds are not, why should an FI not fund all its assets through inter-bank funds? Explain your answer.

LIQUIDITY AND LIABILITY STRUCTURES FOR CANADIAN DEPOSIT-TAKING INSTITUTIONS

We summarize the preceding discussion by considering some balance sheet data for Canadian banks. Table 18–1 shows the liquid asset–nonliquid asset composition of domestic Canadian banks in (March) 2005 and 2009 versus 1996.

Although the level of cash has declined since 1996, total cash plus government securities plus other securities remained relatively stable at 28.4 percent of total assets in 1996, 31.4 percent in 2005, and 29.2 percent in 2009. Loans as a percentage of total on balance sheet assets have declined by almost 16 percent from 1996 to 2009, which could be a reflection of the funding cost, since loans must be supported by capital (see Chapter 20) as well as the sale of loans and the securitization of mortgages (see Chapters 26 and 27).

Table 18–2 presents the liability composition of domestic Canadian banks at March 31 of 1996, 2005, and 2009. The level of demand and notice deposits increased from 24.2 percent in 2005 to 25.8 percent in 2009. There was a shift away from fixed-term deposits over which the FI has some control. Term deposits declined from 53.9 percent in 1996 to 37.3 percent in 2009. This could reflect the decline in interest rates since 2002, which may not have been sufficiently high to encourage depositors to lock up their funds in longer-term instruments.

TABLE 18–1
Liquid Assets versus Non-Liquid Assets for Domestic Canadian Banks, as at March 31, 1996, 2005, and 2009 (in percentages)

Source: Office of the Superintendent of Financial Services, www.osfi-bsif.gc.ca.

Assets	1996	2005	2009
Cash	9.2%	5.2%	4.4%
Government securities	10.3	6.6	10.0
Other securities	8.9	19.6	14.8
Loans	67.4	55.2	51.8
Other assets	4.3	13.4	19.0
	100.0%	100.0%	100.0%

www.bmo.com

www.royalbank.com

www.cibc.com

On an individual basis, the Canadian banks reported that they manage their liquidity risk on an enterprisewide scale. For example, Bank of Montreal (BMO) tracks its liquidity ratio defined as cash and securities as a percentage of total assets over time. BMO reported a liquidity ratio of 29.1 percent in 2008, down from 33.1 percent in 2007. Canadian banks monitor their core deposits, and, as mentioned above, provide incentives such as the waiving of fees or interest rates based on deposit levels to encourage customers to leave their deposits in place. BMO monitors core deposits (customer operating deposits, savings deposits, and fixed deposits under $100,000) and reported an increase in Canadian deposits from $75.9 in 2007 to $85.8 in its 2008 annual report. Royal Bank of Canada (RBC) relies on its core deposits, diversified sources of wholesale funding, and contingency risk planning to determine the impact of market disruptions on its liquidity needs. Similarly, Canadian Imperial Bank of Commerce (CIBC) monitors its core deposits, securitizes assets, and maintains a contingency funding plan.[11]

Finally, it should be noted that too heavy a reliance on borrowed funds can be a risky strategy in itself. Even though withdrawal risk may be reduced if lenders in the market for borrowed funds have confidence in the borrowing FI, perceptions that the FI is risky can lead to sudden non-renewals of inter-bank and repo loans and the non-rollover of wholesale deposits and other purchased funds as they mature. Consequently, excessive reliance on borrowed funds may be as bad an overall liability management strategy as excessive reliance on chequing and savings deposits. Thus, a well-diversified portfolio of liabilities may be the best strategy to balance withdrawal risk and funding cost considerations.

TABLE 18–2
Liability Structure of Domestic Canadian Banks, as at March 31, 1996, 2005, and 2009 (in percentages)

Source: Office of the Superintendent of Financial Services, www.osfi-bsif.gc.ca.

Liabilities	1996	2005	2009
Demand deposits	5.8%	10.6%	25.8%*
Notice deposits	14.4	13.6	—
Fixed-term deposits	53.9	41.5	37.3
Borrowings and other liabilities	21.0	29.6	32.1
Bank capital	4.9	4.7	4.8
	100.0%	100.0%	100.0%

* Includes demand and notice deposits.

---

[11] See Bank of Montreal 2008 annual report, pages 81–82, Royal Bank of Canada's 2008 annual report, pages 109–112, and Canadian Imperial Bank of Commerce's 2008 annual report, pages 80–82, for discussions of specific approaches to liquidity management.

CONCEPT
QUESTIONS

1. Look at Table 18–1. How has the ratio of traditional liquid to illiquid assets changed over the 1996–2009 period?
2. Look at Table 18–2. How has the liability composition of banks changed over the 1996–2009 period?

LIABILITY AND LIQUIDITY RISK MANAGEMENT IN INSURANCE COMPANIES

Insurance companies use a variety of sources to meet liquidity needs. As discussed in Chapters 3 and 17, liquidity is required to meet claims on the insurance policies these FIs have written as well as unexpected surrenders of those policies. These contracts therefore represent a potential future liability to the insurance company. Ideally, liquidity management in insurance companies is conducted so that funds needed to meet claims on insurance contracts written can be met with premiums received on new and existing contracts. However, a high frequency of claims at a single point in time (e.g., an unexpectedly severe hurricane season) could force insurers to liquidate assets at something less than their fair market value.

Insurance companies can reduce their exposure to liquidity risk by diversifying the distribution of risk in the contracts they write. For example, property and casualty insurers can diversify across the types of disasters they cover.

Alternatively, insurance companies can meet liquidity needs by holding relatively marketable assets to cover claim payments. Assets such as government and corporate bonds and corporate stock usually can be liquidated quickly at close to their fair market values in financial markets to pay claims on insurance policies when premium income is insufficient. For example, in the first quarter of 2009, Canadian life insurance companies reporting to OSFI had 51.0 percent of their assets in bonds and debentures and a further 5.3 percent in preferred and common shares. Similarly, Canadian P&C companies had 50.0 percent of their assets in bonds and debentures and 7.8 percent in preferred and common shares.

CONCEPT
QUESTIONS

1. Discuss two strategies insurance companies can use to reduce liquidity risk.
2. Why would property and casualty insurers hold more short-term liquid assets to manage liquidity risk than life insurers hold?

LIABILITY AND LIQUIDITY RISK MANAGEMENT IN OTHER FIs

Other FIs, such as securities firms, investment banks, and finance companies, may experience liquidity risk if they rely on short-term financing (such as commercial paper or bank loans) and investors become reluctant to roll those funds over. Remember from Chapter 4 that the main sources of funding for securities firms are repurchase agreements, bank call loans,[12] and short positions in securities. Liquidity management for these FIs requires the ability to have sufficient cash and other liquid resources at hand to underwrite (purchase) new securities

---

[12] A bank call loan means that a lending bank can call in the loan from an investment bank with very little notice.

from quality issuers before reselling these securities to other investors. Liability management also requires an investment bank or securities firm to be able to act as a market maker, which requires the firm to finance an inventory of securities in its portfolio. As discussed in Chapter 6, finance companies fund assets mainly with commercial paper and long-term debt. Liquidity management for these FIs requires the ability to fund loan requests and loan commitments of sufficient quality without delay.

The experience of Drexel Burnham Lambert in 1989 in the United States is a good example of a securities firm being subjected to a liquidity challenge. Throughout the 1980s, Drexel Burnham Lambert captured the bulk of the junk bond market by promising investors that it would act as a dealer for junk bonds in the secondary market. Investors were, therefore, more willing to purchase these junk securities because Drexel provided an implied guarantee that it would buy them back or find another buyer at market prices should an investor need to sell. However, the junk bond market experienced extreme difficulties in 1989 as its prices fell, reflecting the economy's move into a recession. Serious concerns about the creditworthiness of Drexel's junk bond-laden asset portfolio led creditors to deny Drexel extensions of its vital short-term commercial paper financings. As a result, Drexel declared bankruptcy. Drexel's sudden collapse makes it very clear that access to short-term purchased funds is crucial to the health of securities firms.

| **CONCEPT QUESTIONS** | 1. What is a bank call loan? |
| | 2. Give two reasons an investment bank needs liquidity. |

THE ROLE OF CENTRAL BANKS AND REGULATORS

Lehman Brothers' saga in September 2008 reenacted Drexel's story in 1989: the failure of an investment banking firm that relied on short-term funding. Canadian FIs felt the liquidity crunch through increased inter-bank costs, but their access to term purchase and resale agreements (PRAs) from the Bank of Canada through the LVTS, the expanded acceptable collateral for PRAs, the government guarantees of bank liabilities (the Canadian Lenders Assurance Facility), as well as asset purchases through CMHC, helped to stabilize the Canadian markets. The liquidity crisis of 2008 eliminated the stand-alone investment banks in the United States. Bear Stearns was bought by JPMorgan Chase and Merrill Lynch by Bank of America. Goldman Sachs and Morgan Stanley applied to become bank holding companies in order to gain access to U.S. government funding. American International Group (AIG), an insurance company without access to the Federal Reserve window, was provided with a US$85 billion capital injection. As shown in Table 1–3 in Chapter 1, the central banks in Canada, the United States, the United Kingdom, and the Eurozone injected liquidity, eased collateral requirements for borrowing from the central bank, expanded deposit insurance coverage, guaranteed bank liabilities, injected capital, and purchased assets. These extraordinary measures were intended to deal with and stabilize systemic risk to the domestic and global financial systems.

The severe market turmoil demonstrated the systemic risk to the global financial system posed by unregulated activities of FIs. Governments and regulators became the main providers of liquidity to the global financial system. In some

TABLE 18–3
Summary of BIS Principles for the Management and Supervision of Liquidity Risk

Source: Basel Committee on Banking Supervision, Bank for International Settlements, *Principles for Sound Liquidity Risk Management and Supervision*, September 2008, pages 2–5, www.bis.org.

Fundamental Principle	
Principle 1	A bank is responsible for the sound management of liquidity risk. A bank should establish a robust liquidity risk management framework that ensures it maintains sufficient liquidity, including a cushion of unencumbered, high-quality liquid assets to withstand a range of stress events, including those involving the loss or impairment of both unsecured and secured funding sources. Supervisors should assess the adequacy of both a bank's liquidity risk management framework and its liquidity position.
Governance of Liquidity Risk Management	
Principle 2	Establish a liquidity risk tolerance.
Principle 3	Maintain an adequate level of liquidity, including a cushion of liquid assets.
Principle 4	Allocate liquidity costs, benefits, and risks to all significant business activities.
Measurement and Management of Liquidity Risk	
Principle 5	Identify and measure the full range of liquidity risks, including contingent liquidity risks.
Principle 6	Actively monitor and control risk exposures across business lines and currencies.
Principle 7	Diversify its funding sources and identify factors that affect its ability to raise funds.
Principle 8	Manage intraday liquidity positions to meet payment and settlement obligations.
Principle 9	Manage intraday collateral positions.
Principle 10	Design and use severe stress test scenarios.
Principle 11	Establish a robust and operational contingency funding plan (CFP).
Principle 12	Maintain a cushion of high-quality, unencumbered assets.
Public Disclosure	
Principle 13	Publicly disclose information on a regular basis to enable market participants to make an informed judgment about the soundness of its liquidity risk management and liquidity position.
The Role of Supervisors	
Principle 14	Supervisors regularly perform an assessment of a bank's liquidity management framework and position.
Principle 15	Supervisors supplement their assessments by monitoring internal reports and market information.
Principle 16	Supervisors intervene to address deficiencies.
Principle 17	Supervisors communicate with other supervisors, local and global, in a timely manner.

cases, equity injections (the Troubled Asset Relief Program, TARP, provided to FIs in the United States and the government takeover of Northern Rock in the United Kingdom) resulted in the nationalization of FIs.

The Basel Committee on Banking Supervision (BCBS) revised its principles for liquidity management. As shown in Table 18–3, the 17 BCBS principles proposed in September 2008 put the onus on FIs and their supervisors to recognize, measure, and manage liquidity risk. Under Guideline B-6, OSFI has required liquidity management by Canadian banks since December 1995. OSFI is also releasing a discussion paper that will incorporate the BCBS principles for the domestic and international operations of Canadian FIs. As noted previously, the large Canadian FIs already monitor and manage their liquidity risks. As well, they have contingency plans that incorporate the severe stress to the global financial system in 2007 and 2008 and are updated as required.

Summary

Liquidity and liability management issues are intimately linked for the modern FI. Many factors, both cost and regulatory, influence an FI manager's choice of the amount of liquid assets to hold. An FI's choice of liquidity is something of a knife-edge situation, trading off the costs and benefits of undershooting or overshooting asset targets.

An FI can manage its liabilities in a fashion that affects the overall withdrawal risk of its funding portfolio and therefore the need for liquid assets to meet such withdrawals. However, reducing withdrawal risk often comes at a cost because liability sources that are easier to control from a withdrawal risk perspective are often more costly for the FI to utilize.

Questions and Problems

1. What are the benefits and costs to an FI of holding large amounts of liquid assets? Why are U.S. Treasury and Government of Canada securities considered good examples of liquid assets?

2. How is an FI's liability and liquidity risk management problem related to the maturity of its assets relative to its liabilities?

3. Consider the assets (in millions) of two banks, A and B. Both banks are funded by $120 million in deposits and $20 million in equity. Which bank has the stronger liquidity position? Which bank probably has a higher profit?

Bank A Assets		Bank B Assets	
Cash	$ 10	Cash	$ 20
Govt. securities	40	Consumer loans	30
Commercial loans	90	Commercial loans	90
Total assets	$140	Total assets	$140

4. What concerns motivate regulators to require deposit-taking institutions to hold minimum amounts of liquid assets?

5. Rank these financial assets according to their liquidity: cash, corporate bonds, TSX-traded stocks, and T-bills.

6. What is the relationship between funding cost and funding or withdrawal risk?

7. An FI has estimated the following annual costs for its demand deposits: management cost per account = $140, average account size = $1,500, average number of cheques processed per account per month = 75, cost of clearing a cheque = $0.10, fee charged to customer per cheque = $0.05, and average fee charged per customer per month = $8.

   a. What is the implicit interest cost of demand deposits for the FI?

   b. What should be the per cheque fee charged to customers to reduce the implicit interest cost to 3 percent?

8. A chequing account requires a minimum balance of $750 for interest to be earned at an annual rate of 4 percent. An account holder has maintained an average balance of $500 for the first six months and $1,000 for the remaining six months. She writes an average of 60 cheques per month and pays $0.02 per cheque, although it costs the bank $0.05 to clear a cheque.

   a. What average return does the account holder earn on the account?

   b. What is the average return if the bank lowers the minimum balance to $400?

c. What is the average return if the bank pays interest only on the amount in excess of $400? Assume that the minimum required balance is $400.

d. How much should the bank increase its cheque-clearing fee to ensure that the average interest it pays on this account is 5 percent? Assume that the minimum required balance is $750.

9. Rank the following liabilities with respect, first, to funding risk and, second, to funding cost.

a. Demand deposits.

b. GICs.

c. Inter-bank funds.

d. Bankers' acceptances.

e. Eurodollar deposits.

f. Chequing accounts.

g. Wholesale GICs.

h. Savings accounts.

i. Repos.

j. Commercial paper.

10. How is the withdrawal risk different for inter-bank funds and repurchase agreements?

11. How does the cash balance, or liquidity, of an FI determine the types of repurchase agreements into which it will enter?

12. What characteristics of Bank of Canada funds may constrain a DTI's ability to use these funds to expand its liquidity quickly?

13. What trends have been observed between 1996 and 2009 in regard to liquidity and liability structures of large Canadian banks?

14. What are the primary methods that insurance companies can use to reduce their exposure to liquidity risk?

Deposit Insurance and Other Liability Guarantees

This chapter discusses

▸ deposit insurance for federally regulated deposit-taking institutions, beginning with the history of these funds and including the problems experienced by these funds

▸ the methods available to reduce risk-taking, thus reducing the probability that deposit holders must be paid off with deposit insurance

▸ the Bank of Canada's overnight funds as a (limited) alternative to deposit insurance

▸ other guaranty programs, including those for insurance companies, securities firms, and pension funds

INTRODUCTION

Chapter 17 discussed the liquidity risks faced by FIs and Chapter 18 described ways FIs can better manage that risk. Because of concerns about the asset quality or solvency of an FI, liability holders such as depositors and life insurance policyholders (and to a lesser extent, mutual fund shareholders) have incentives to engage in runs, that is, to withdraw all their funds from an FI. As we discussed in Chapter 17, the incentive to run is accentuated in banks, trusts, and insurance companies by the sequential servicing rule used to meet liability withdrawals. As a result, deposit and liability holders who are first in line to withdraw funds get preference over those last in line.

Although a run on an unhealthy FI is not necessarily a bad thing—it can discipline the performance of managers and owners—there is a risk that runs on bad FIs can become contagious and spread to good or well-run FIs. In contagious run or panic conditions, liability holders do not bother to distinguish between good and bad FIs but instead seek to turn their liabilities into cash or safe securities as quickly as possible. Contagious runs can have a major contractionary effect on the supply of credit as well as the money supply regionally, nationally, or internationally.

Moreover, a contagious run on FIs can have serious social welfare effects. For example, a major run on banks can have an adverse effect on the level of savings in all types of FIs and therefore can inhibit the ability of individuals to transfer wealth through time to protect themselves against major risks such as future ill health and falling income in old age.

Because of such wealth, money supply, and credit supply effects, government regulators of financial service firms have introduced guaranty programs to deter runs by offering liability holders varying degrees of failure protection. Specifically, if a liability holder believes a claim is totally secure even if the FI is in trouble, there is no incentive to run. The liability holder's place in line no longer affects getting his or her funds back. Regulatory guaranty or insurance programs for liability holders deter runs and thus deter contagious runs and panics.

In Canada, insurance protection is provided by the Canada Deposit Insurance Corporation (CDIC) that was created in 1967 for eligible federally regulated deposit-taking institutions (banks, trusts, and savings and loans) and federally regulated cooperative credit associations (interprovincial associations of credit unions). Provincially incorporated credit unions and caisses populaires are covered by provincial stabilization funds or guarantee companies (e.g., Quebec Deposit Insurance Board). Assuris covers life insurance policies, accident and sickness policies, and annuity contracts should an insurance company fail. The Property and Casualty Insurance Compensation Corporation (PACICC) provides coverage in the event of the failure of a property and casualty (P&C) insurance company. As noted in Chapter 4, the Canadian Investor Protection Fund (CIPF) provides coverage for investors through the Investment Industry Regulatory Organization of Canada (IIROC) and the stock exchanges.

In this chapter we look at the Canadian guaranty funds, as well as the experience in the United States with the Federal Deposit Insurance Corporation (FDIC), which has had a longer and more turbulent history since its creation in 1933.

Margin notes:
www.cdic.ca
www.assuris.ca
www.pacicc.ca
www.cipf.ca
www.fdic.gov

The Canadian Experience with Deposit Insurance

Despite the similarities between Canada and the United States, these two North American countries have different histories with respect to deposit insurance. The number of failures of Canadian FIs has been small relative to the experience covered below for the United States. Canada managed to avoid the major bank failures of the Great Depression (which resulted in the creation of U.S. deposit insurance in 1933), the savings and loan failures of the 1980s, and the failures of investment and commercial banks in the subprime and liquidity crises in 2007 and 2008. Thus, Canada Deposit Insurance Corporation (CDIC) was not formed until 1967 as support for the deposits of federally regulated deposit-taking institutions. In fact, no Canadian bank failed from 1923 (the Home Bank) until 1985 (Canadian Commercial Bank and the Northland Bank of Canada). During that time period, when Canadian banks experienced financial difficulties, they were absorbed by other FIs, resulting in the concentrated banking system that Canada has today.

Although CDIC has not had extensive experience with bank failures, it has experienced trust and loan company failures, including Saskatchewan Trust Co. (1991, CDIC's total claim and loans of $64 million), Standard Loan Co./Standard Trust Co. (1991, $1.164 billion), Shoppers Trust Co. (1992, $492 million), Adelaide Capital Corp. (1992, $1.588 billion), Central Guaranty Trust Co. (1992, $500 million), Confederation Trust Co. (1994, $680 million), Income Trust Co. (1995, $193 million), and Security Home Mortgage Corp. (1996, $42 million). The failures in the 1990s were partly caused by a recession in the late 1980s, as well as consolidation in the financial industry as the four pillars (see Chapter 1) broke down. Only 43 members of CDIC have failed and no member has failed since 1996.

However, as we discuss in Chapter 22, Canada's financial system is smaller and more concentrated than that of the United States, which has roughly 100 times the number of deposit-taking institutions. At its largest in 1983, CDIC insured 188 deposit-taking institutions. Of these, 39 (20 percent) have since failed. Nevertheless, the government of the day in the 1980s was sufficiently alarmed by the failures of weaker deposit-taking institutions to form a Royal Commission chaired by W. Z. Estey to review deposit insurance and the regulatory structure. CDIC was

FIGURE 19–1
The Canadian
Regulatory System

Source: CDIC, 2004
annual report, www.cdic.
ca/bin/cdic_ar_e.pdf.

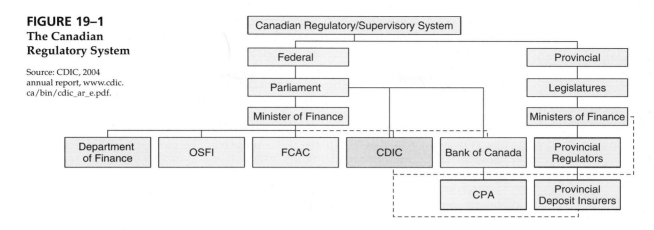

given new risk minimization and early intervention policies. As well, a new regulator, OSFI, was created to supervise federally regulated trusts, insurance companies, and banks.[1] At March 31, 2008, CDIC insured $477 billion in deposits at 80 banks, trust companies, loan companies, cooperative credit associations, and subsidiaries of foreign financial institutions.

www.bankofcanada.ca

www.osfi-bsif.gc.ca

www.fcac-acfc.gc.ca

www.fin.gc.ca

The Canadian regulatory system for financial institutions is shown schematically in Figure 19–1. The Bank of Canada does not directly supervise and audit federally regulated FIs but it does have a mandate to ensure the safety and soundness of the financial system, and therefore its monetary policy affects both OSFI and CDIC, who jointly have powers to regulate FIs.[2] The federal Department of Finance, the Office of the Superintendent of Financial Institutions (OSFI), and the Financial Consumer Agency of Canada (FCAC) report to the minister of Finance. CDIC and the Bank of Canada report to Parliament through the minister of Finance. Under the Bank of Canada Act (amended in 1981) and the Canadian Payments Act (1985, revised in 2007), members of CDIC are eligible to operate in the Large Value Transfer System (see Chapter 17) and to borrow from the Bank of Canada. Banks that accept only wholesale deposits (greater than $150,000) may opt out of CDIC coverage, but remain members of the LVTS and eligible to borrow from the Bank of Canada. As well, the Bank of Canada has responsibility for the Canadian Payments Association (CPA).

Failures of weaker institutions in the 1980s, concerns that the strong were subsidizing the weak, and developments in other jurisdictions, such as the United States, led to CDIC's adoption of risk-based or differential premiums, which is discussed in detail later in the chapter. The stability of the Canadian system was demonstrated during 2007 and 2008. CDIC did not increase its deposit insurance limits, but the

regulatory
forbearance
Regulators' policy of
allowing an FI to
continue to operate
even when it is in
breach of regulations
in hopes that the
situation will correct
itself over time.

[1] The difference in the Canadian and U.S. experiences of FI failures has been of interest to researchers. For example, see L. Kryzanowski and G. S. Roberts, "Canadian Banking Solvency, 1922–1940," *Journal of Money, Credit, and Banking,* August 1993, 25(3), pp. 361–376 for a review of the literature and the proposal that **regulatory forbearance** played a role, along with the Canadian branch banking system in the stability of the Canadian financial system. For a detailed discussion of the bank failures of the 1980s, see W. Z. Estey, *Report of the Inquiry into the Collapse of the CCB and North-land Bank,* 1986, Supply and Services Canada, Ottawa, and also J. F. Dingle, "The Bank Failures of September 1985" in *Planning an Evolution: The Story of the Canadian Payments Association 1980–2002,* 2004, Bank of Canada and the Canadian Payments Association, pp. 25–30.

[2] The powers of OSFI and CDIC to examine, classify, and take action with respect to federally regulated FIs are provided in detail at www.osfi-bsif.gc.ca.

FDIC raised its coverage to US$250,000 (Chapter 1, Table 1–1). The Federal Services Compensation Scheme in the United Kingdom increased its coverage to £50,000, and the European Union increased its deposit insurance coverage to €50,000. CDIC played a lead role in establishing the International Association of Deposit Insurers (IADI) that, along with the BIS, released a report outlining 18 principles for countries to follow regarding deposit insurance.[3] We turn now to the U.S. experience.

www.iadi.org

The U.S. Experience with Bank and Thrift Guaranty Funds

The FDIC was created in 1933 in the wake of the banking panics of 1930–1933, when some 10,000 commercial banks failed. The original level of individual depositor insurance coverage at commercial banks was US$2,500, which was increased to US$100,000 in 1980. Between 1945 and 1980, commercial bank deposit insurance clearly worked; there were no runs or panics, and the number of individual bank failures was very small (see Figure 19–2). Beginning in 1980, however, bank failures accelerated, with more than 1,039 failures in the decade ending in 1990, peaking at 221 in 1988. This number of failures was actually larger than that for the entire 1933–1979 period. Moreover, the costs of each of these failures to the FDIC were often larger than the total costs for the mainly small bank failures in 1933–1979. As the number and costs of these closures mounted in the 1980s, the FDIC fund, built up from premiums paid by banks (and the reinvestment income from those premiums), was rapidly drained. Any insurance fund becomes insolvent if the premiums collected and the reserves built up from investing premiums are insufficient to offset the cost of failure claims. The FDIC's resources were virtually depleted by early 1991, when it was given permission to borrow US$30 billion from the U.S. Treasury.

FIGURE 19–2   **Number of Failed U.S. Banks by Year, 1934–2009**

Source: FDIC annual reports and statistics on banking, www.fdic.gov.

Note: 2009 data for 6 months to June 30.

---

[3] See Basel Committee on Banking Supervision and International Association of Deposit Insurers, *Core Principles for Effective Deposit Insurance Systems*, June 2009, available at www.bis.org.

Even then, it ended 1991 with a deficit of US$7 billion. In response to this crisis, Congress passed the FDIC Improvement Act (FDICIA) in December 1991 to restructure the bank insurance fund and prevent its potential insolvency.

There was a dramatic turnaround in FDIC's finances and a drop in U.S. bank failures after 1991, partly in response to record profit levels in banks. As shown in Figure 19–2, six banks failed in 2000, four in 2001, eleven in 2002, three in 2003, four in 2004, but none in 2005 and 2006. However, as the subprime crisis evolved, three insured FIs were closed in 2007, twenty-five in 2008, and, in the first nine months of 2009, more than a hundred institutions failed. At December 2008, the fund covered only 0.27 percent of insured deposits, a significant decline from the 1.21 percent coverage at the beginning of 2007. As a result, a US$500 billion line of credit was arranged for FDIC by the U.S. Congress in 2009. The FDIC maintains a list of failed banks at www.fdic.gov to provide information for depositors.

INTERNET EXERCISE

Go to the Canada Deposit Insurance Corporation website at www.cdic.ca. Click on "Where Are My Savings Insured by CDIC?" Then, click on "List of CDIC Members" to see the list of member institutions. Historical information about CDIC can be obtained by clicking on "Who Is CDIC?" and then clicking on "Publications, Speeches and Announcements."

CAUSES OF DEPOSIT INSURANCE INSOLVENCY

Deposit insurance provides support for deposit-taking institutions and is therefore intended to contribute to the stability of the financial system. Canada has been fortunate that the impact of economic events in the 1980s and 1990s and in 2007–2009 did not test the deposit insurance fund provided by CDIC beyond its strength, although, as discussed below, Assuris required refunding after the collapse of Confederation Life in 1994. This means, however, that we need to look elsewhere for guidelines to failure. Therefore, the following discussion, although generalized for any deposit insurance system, draws heavily on the U.S. experience for examples and relevant research. There are at least two, not necessarily independent, views as to why deposit insurance funds can become economically insolvent.

The Financial Environment

One view of the cause of insolvency is that a number of external events or shocks can adversely affect DTIs. The dramatic rise in interest rates in the 1979–1982 period had a major negative effect on those FIs funding long-term, fixed-rate mortgages with short-term deposits. The second event was the collapse in oil, real estate, and other commodity prices, which particularly harmed oil, gas, and agricultural loans in the southwestern United States and in western Canada. The third event was increased financial service firm competition at home and abroad, which eroded the value of bank charters during the 1980s.[4] The housing bubble burst in the United States in 2007, causing a decline in the value of the assets supporting subprime mortgage securitizations. As economic conditions declined, overleveraged consumers and

---

[4] The value of a bank charter is the present value of expected profits from operating in the industry. As expected profits fall, so does the value of a bank charter. See A. Saunders and B. Wilson, "An Analysis of Bank Charter Value and Its Risk-Constraining Incentives," *Journal of Financial Services Research,* April/June 2001, pp. 185–196.

businesses defaulted on their loans. The 2007 and 2008 crisis caused a "global flight to quality" and a liquidity crisis. The fallout from these economic effects is responsible for the number of failed banks handled by the FDIC in 2008 and 2009.

Moral Hazard

A second view is that these financial environment effects were catalysts for, rather than the causes of, economic crises. At the heart of the crises was deposit insurance itself, especially some of its contractual features. Although deposit insurance had deterred depositors and other liability holders from engaging in runs prior to 1980, in so doing it had also removed or reduced depositor discipline. Deposit insurance allowed insured FIs to borrow at rates close to the risk-free rate and, if they chose, to undertake high-risk asset investments. The FI owners and managers knew that insured depositors had little incentive to restrict such behaviour, either through fund withdrawals or by requiring risk premiums on deposit rates, since they were fully insured by deposit insurance if the FI failed. Given this scenario, losses on loans in the 1980s and 2007–2009 may be viewed as the outcome of bankers exploiting underpriced or mispriced risk under the deposit insurance contract. The provision of insurance that encourages rather than discourages risk-taking is called **moral hazard**.[5] This is because, with deposit insurance, a highly leveraged bank whose debt holders need not monitor the FI's (borrower's) actions has a strong incentive to undertake excessively risky investment decisions, such as in its loan-generating activities.[6]

moral hazard
The loss exposure faced by an insurer when the provision of insurance encourages the insured to take more risks.

In the absence of depositor discipline (as will be explained below), regulators could have priced risk-taking either through charging explicit deposit insurance premiums linked to the FI's risk-taking or by charging **implicit premiums** through restricting and monitoring the risky activities of FIs. This could potentially have substituted for depositor discipline; those FIs that took more risk would have paid directly or indirectly for this risk-taking behaviour. However, from 1933 until January 1, 1993, U.S. regulators based deposit insurance premiums on a deposit size rather than on risk, as did CDIC in Canada until 1999. The 1980s were a period of deregulation and capital adequacy forbearance rather than stringent activity regulation and tough capital requirements. Even with risk-based premiums and stricter capital adequacy requirements, it can be argued that FIs significantly increased their risks from 2000 to 2006, particularly their market risk exposure through their trading portfolios. Risk-based premiums for deposit insurance and capital adequacy requirements were insufficient to prevent the failure of many U.S. DTIs.

implicit premiums
Deposit insurance premiums or costs imposed on a deposit-taking institution through activity constraints rather than direct monetary charges.

PANIC PREVENTION VERSUS MORAL HAZARD

A great deal of attention focused on the moral hazard reason for the collapse of the U.S. bank and thrift insurance funds in the 1980s and global FIs in 2007–2009. The less FI owners have to lose from taking risks, the greater are their incentives

---

[5] The precise definition of moral hazard is the loss exposure of an insurer (CDIC or FDIC) that results from the character or circumstances of the insured (here, the bank).

[6] Research has shown that explicit deposit insurance tends to be detrimental to bank stability, more so when bank interest rates have been deregulated and moral hazard opportunities are great. In countries in which moral hazard opportunities are limited, regulation and supervision are more effective at offsetting the adverse incentives created by deposit insurance. See A. Demirgüç-Kunt and E. Detragiache, "Does Deposit Insurance Increase Banking System Stability? An Empirical Investigation," *Journal of Monetary Economics*, 2002, pp. 1373–1406.

to take excessively risky asset positions. When asset investment risks or gambles pay off, FI owners make windfall gains in profits. If they fail, however, the insurer bears most of the costs, given that owners—like owners of regular corporations—have limited liability. It's a "heads I win, tails I don't lose (much)" situation.

Note that even without deposit insurance, the limited liability of FI owners or stockholders always creates incentives to take risk at the expense of fixed claimants such as depositors and debt holders.[7] The difference between deposit-taking institutions and other firms is risk-taking incentives induced by mispriced deposit insurance. That is, when risk-taking is not **actuarially fairly priced** in deposit insurance premiums, this adds to the incentives to take additional risks.

actuarially fairly priced insurance
Insurance pricing based on the perceived risk of the insured.

Nevertheless, even though mispriced deposit insurance potentially accentuates risk-taking, deposit insurance effectively deterred panics and runs of the 1930–1933 kind in much of the postwar period (see Figure 19–2). That is, deposit insurance has ensured a good deal of stability in the U.S. and Canadian credit and monetary system.

This suggests that, ideally, regulators should design the deposit insurance contract with the trade-off between moral hazard risk and panic or run risk in mind. For example, by providing 100 percent coverage of all depositors and reducing the probability of runs to zero, the insurer may be encouraging certain deposit-taking institutions to take a significant degree of moral hazard risk-taking behaviour.[8] On the other hand, a very limited degree of deposit insurance coverage might encourage runs and panics, although moral hazard behaviour itself would be less evident.

Extensive insurance coverage for deposit holders and the resulting lack of incentive for deposit holders to monitor and restrict owners' and managers' risk-taking results in small levels of run risk but high levels of moral hazard risk.[9] By restructuring the deposit insurance contract, it may be possible to reduce moral hazard risk quite a bit without a very large increase in run risk.

---

[7] Thus, one possible policy to reduce excessive bank risk-taking would be to eliminate limited liability for bank stockholders. A study by L. J. White found that bank failures in private banking systems with unlimited liability, such as that which existed in 18th-century Scotland, were rare. Indeed, in the United States, double liability existed for bank stockholders prior to the introduction of deposit insurance; that is, on failure, the stockholders would lose their initial equity contribution and be assessed by the receiver an extra amount equal to the par value of their stock, which would be used to pay creditors (over and above the liquidation value of the bank's assets). See L. J. White, "Scottish Banking and Legal Restrictions Theory: A Closer Look," *Journal of Money, Credit and Banking* 22 (1990), pp. 526–536. For a discussion of double liability in pre-1933 United States, see A. Saunders and B. Wilson, "If History Could Be Re-Run: The Provision and Pricing of Deposit Insurance in 1933," *Journal of Financial Intermediation* 4 (1995), pp. 396–413; and J. R. Macey and G. P. Miller, "Double Liability of Bank Shareholders: History and Implications," *Wake Forest Law Review* 27 (1992), pp. 31–62.

[8] Research on deposit insurance schemes in over 60 countries found that explicit deposit insurance tends to be detrimental to banking system stability, particularly when bank interest rates have been deregulated and where the regulatory environment is weak. In particular, deposit insurance encourages FIs to finance high-risk, high-return projects. However, when opportunities for moral hazard are more limited and more effective prudential regulation and supervision exist, the adverse incentives created by deposit insurance are limited. This, in turn, improves banking system stability. See A. Demirgüç-Kunt and E. Detragiache, "Does Deposit Insurance Increase Banking System Stability? An Empirical Investigation," World Bank, *Journal of Monetary Economics* 49(7), October 2002, pp. 1373–1406.

[9] At this point, note that managers may not have the same risk-taking incentives as owners. This is especially true if managers are compensated through wage and salary contracts rather than through shares and share option programs. When managers are on fixed-wage contracts, their preferences in regard to risk lean toward being risk-averse. That is, they are unlikely to exploit the same type of moral hazard incentives that stock owner–controlled banks would. This is because managers have little to gain if their banks do exceptionally well (their salaries are fixed) but probably will lose their jobs and human capital investments in a bank if they fail.

CONTROLLING RISK-TAKING

There are three ways deposit insurance could be structured to reduce moral hazard behaviour:

1. Increase stockholder discipline.
2. Increase depositor discipline.
3. Increase regulator discipline.

Specifically, redesigning the features of the insurance contract can either directly or indirectly impact DTI owners' and stockholders' risk-taking incentives by altering the behaviour of depositors and regulators.

Stockholder Discipline
Insurance Premiums

One approach toward making stockholders' risk-taking more expensive is to link insurance premiums to the risk profile of the deposit-taking institution. Below we look at ways this might be done.

Theory   A major feature of CDIC's deposit insurance contract from 1967–1998 was the flat deposit insurance premium levied on banks. Specifically, each year a bank paid a given sum or premium to the CDIC based on a fixed proportion of its deposits.[10]

To see why a flat or size-based premium schedule does not discipline risk-taking, consider two banks of the same domestic deposit size, as shown in Table 19–1. Banks A and B have domestic deposits of $100 million and (in 1998) would pay the same premium to CDIC (0.00167 × $100 million = $167,000 per annum). However, their risk-taking behaviour is completely different. Bank A is excessively risky, investing all its assets in real estate loans. Bank B is almost risk-free, investing all its assets in government T-bills. We graph the insurance premium rates paid by the two banks compared with their asset risk in Figure 19–3.

TABLE 19–1
Flat Deposit Insurance Premiums and Risk-Taking

Bank A				Bank B			
Assets		**Liabilities**		**Assets**		**Liabilities**	
Real estate loans	100	Domestic deposits	100	T-bills	100	Domestic deposits	100

FIGURE 19–3
Premium Schedules Relative to Risk

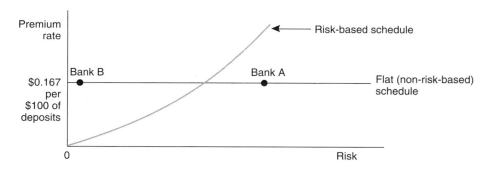

---

[10] The premium was 3.3 basis points (bp.) per dollar of insured deposits from 1967–1985, increased to 10 bp. from 1986–1992 and to 12.5 bp. in 1993 and 16.7 bp. from 1994–1998. See www.cdic.ca.

In Figure 19–3, note that under the flat premium schedule, banks A and B would have been charged the same deposit insurance premium based on a bank's domestic deposit size. Critics of flat premiums argue that a deposit insurance corporation should act more like a private property and casualty insurer. Under normal P&C insurance premium-setting principles, insurers charge those with higher risks higher premiums. That is, low-risk parties (such as Bank B) do not generally subsidize high-risk parties (such as Bank A). If premiums increased as bank risk increased, banks would have reduced incentives to take risks. Therefore, the ultimate goal might be to price risk in an actuarially fair fashion, similar to the process used by a private property and casualty insurer, so that premiums reflect the expected private costs or losses to the insurer from the provision of deposit insurance.

Note that there are arguments against imposing an actuarially fair risk-based premium schedule. If the deposit insurer's mandate is not to act as if it were a private cost-minimizing insurer such as a P&C insurance company because of social welfare considerations, some type of subsidy can be justified. Broader banking market stability concerns and savers' welfare concerns might arguably override private cost-minimizing concerns and require subsidies. Other authors have argued that if an actuarially fair premium is imposed on a banking system that is fully competitive, banking itself cannot be profitable. That is, some subsidy is needed for banks to exist profitably. However, while Canadian banking is competitive, it probably deviates somewhat from the perfectly competitive model.

Calculating the Actuarially Fair Premium[11] Economists have suggested a number of approaches for calculating the fair deposit insurance premium that a cost-minimizing insurer such as the CDIC should charge. One approach would be to set the premium equal to the expected severity of loss times the frequency of losses due to failure plus some load or markup factor.[12] This would exactly mimic the approach toward premium setting in the property and casualty industry. However, the most common approach, the **option pricing model of deposit insurance** (OPM), has been to view the provision of deposit insurance as virtually identical to writing a put option on the assets of the FI that buys the deposit insurance.[13, 14] We depict the conceptual idea underlying the option pricing model approach in Figure 19–4.

In this framework, CDIC charges a premium P to insure the FI's deposits (D). If the FI does well and the market value of the FI's assets is greater than D, its net worth is positive and it can continue in business. CDIC would face no charge

option pricing model of deposit insurance
A model for calculating deposit insurance as a put option on the DTI's assets.

---

[11] This section, which contains more technical topics, may be included in or dropped from the chapter reading, depending on the rigour of the course.

[12] D. Duffie, R. Jarrow, A. Purnanandam, and W. Yang develop a reduced-form model in which fair market deposit insurance rates can be inferred from market pricing of the credit risk in bank debt instruments. They find fair market deposit insurance rates to be much larger than actuarially calculated mean loss rates to the insurer. See "Market Pricing of Deposit Insurance," *Journal of Financial Services Research,* October/December 2003, pp. 93–119.

[13] See, for example, R. C. Merton, "An Analytic Derivation of the Cost of Deposit Insurance and Loan Guarantees: An Application of Modern Option Pricing Theory," *Journal of Banking and Finance* 1, 1977, pp. 3–11.

[14] There is a third approach that views deposit insurance premiums being set as the outcome of an agency conflict among three groups of self-interested parties: bank stockholders, bank managers, and bank regulators. See E. Kane, "Three Paradigms for the Role of Capitalization Requirements in Insured Financial Institutions," *Journal of Banking and Finance* 19, June 1995, pp. 431–460.

FIGURE 19–4

Deposit Insurance
as a Put Option
(D = DTI's deposits;
A = DTI's assets;
P = Premium paid
by DTI)

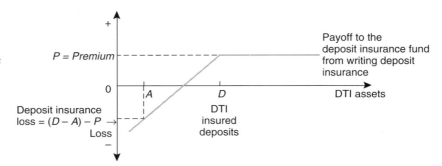

against its resources and would keep the premium paid to it by the FI (P). If the FI is insolvent, possibly because of a bad or risky asset portfolio, such that the value of the assets falls below D (say to A), and its net worth is negative, the owners will "put the bank" back to CDIC. If this happens, CDIC will pay out to the insured depositors an amount D and will liquidate the assets (A). As a result, CDIC bears the cost of the insolvency (or negative net worth) equal to ($D - A$) minus the insurance premiums paid by the FI (P).

When valued in this fashion as a simple European put option, the cost of providing deposit insurance increases with the level of asset risk (σ_A^2) and with the FI's leverage (D/A). That is, the actuarially fair premium (P) is equivalent to the premium on a put option and as such should be positively related to both asset risk (σ_A^2) and leverage risk (D/A). The value of a deposit insurance guaranty is shown to be the same as the Black–Scholes model for a European put option of maturity T, where T is the time period until the next premium assessment:

$$P(T) = De^{-rT}\, \phi(X_2) - A\phi(X_1)$$

where

$$X_1 = \{\log (D/A) - (r + \sigma_A^2/2)T\}/\sigma_A\sqrt{T}$$
$$X_2 = X_1 + \sigma_A\sqrt{T}$$

and ϕ is the standard normal distribution.

Even though the option pricing model is a conceptually and theoretically elegant tool, it is difficult to apply in practice—especially because an FI's asset value (A) and its asset risks (σ_A^2) are not directly observable. However, values of these variables can be extracted from the equity value and the volatility of equity value of the FI (see the discussion on the KMV model in Chapter 11). Even so, the option model framework is useful because it indicates that both leverage and asset quality (or risk) are important elements that should enter into any deposit insurance pricing model.

Next, we look at the risk-based deposit insurance premium scheme introduced by CDIC in 1999.

CONCEPT QUESTIONS

1. Bank A has a ratio of deposits to assets of 90 percent and a variance of asset returns of 10 percent. Bank B has a ratio of deposits to assets of 85 percent and a variance of asset returns of 5 percent. Which bank should pay the higher insurance premium?
2. If deposit insurance is similar to a put option, who exercises that option?

TABLE 19–2
CDIC's Rating
Criteria for Insured
DTIs

Criteria or Factors	Maximum Score
Quantitative:	
Capital Adequacy	20
• Assets to capital multiple	
• Tier 1 risk-based capital ratio	
• Total risk-based capital ratio	
Other Quantitative	
• Return on risk-weighted assets	5
• Mean adjusted net income volatility	5
• Stress-tested net income	5
• Efficiency ratio	5
• Net impaired assets (including net unrealized losses on securities) to total capital	5
• Three-year moving average asset growth ratio	5
• Real estate asset concentration	5
• Aggregate commercial loan concentration ratio	5
Sub-Total: Quantitative Score	60
Qualitative:	
• Examiner's rating	35
• Other information	5
Sub-Total: Qualitative Score	40
Total Score	100

Implementing Risk-Based Premiums

risk-based deposit insurance program
A program that assesses insurance premiums on the basis of capital adequacy and supervisory judgments on FI quality.

As deposit-taking financial institutions were perceived to become more risky in the 1980s and 1990s, the FDIC adopted a **risk-based deposit insurance program** for U.S. FIs in 1993. CDIC established risk-based premiums for Canadian deposit-taking institutions in 1999. The level of premiums charged by CDIC is based on its assessment of the deposit-taking institution's risk. The criteria are both quantitative and qualitative, and include capital adequacy (discussed in detail in Chapter 20) as well as risk-weighted assets, efficiency, impaired assets, asset growth, and loan concentration, as shown in Table 19–2. Based on its score out of 100, the FI is placed into one of four categories, as shown in Table 19–3, and charged the appropriate premium based on its level of insured deposits. For example, an FI with a score greater than or equal to 80 was charged a premium of 1.4 basis points of insured deposits in 2008. So if the deposit-taking institution had $1 billion of insured deposits, it would pay $140,000 ($1,000,000,000 × 0.00014) for deposit insurance. If its score was below 50, it would pay $1,110,000 ($1,000,000,000 × 0.00111). Thus the incentive is to maintain a high score so that the cost to the FI is minimized, since the insurance premium for deposits would be factored into an FI's cost of funds for loans and other services. The rates declined from 2002 to 2009, in line with decreased risk and low claims on the insurance corporation. In 2009/2010, CDIC premium rates increased by one-third over 2008/2009 rates, as shown in Table 19–3. Similar rate increases are proposed in 2010/2011 and 2011/2012, doubling rates over the three years. By comparison, FDIC's proposed

TABLE 19–3   Premium Rates Charged by CDIC for Deposit Insurance, 1999–2010

| | | Premium Categories and Rates | | | | |
| Score | Premium Category | Premium Rate (basis points % of insured deposits) | | | | |
		1999–2001	2001–2002	2002–2005	2005–2009	2009–2010
≥ 80	1 (best rated)	4.2	4.2	2.1	1.4	1.9
≥ 65 but < 80	2	8.3	8.3	4.2	2.8	3.7
≥ 50 but < 65	3	16.7	16.7	8.3	5.6	7.4
< 50	4 (worst rated)	16.7	33.3	16.7	11.1	14.8

Source: Canada Deposit Insurance Corporation, www.cdic.ca.

rates for 2009 are 12 to 14 basis points for the best-rated DTIs, reflecting the higher failure rates. CDIC's "long-term sustainable historical average rate" has been 6 basis points.[15] An insured institution is notified each year of the rate that it will pay, but CDIC does not permit the FI to disclose its risk category, its total score, the examiner's rating, the premium rate that has been assigned, or any other information related to its premiums.[16]

Increased Capital Requirements and Stricter Closure Rules

A second way to reduce stockholders' incentives to take excessive risks is to (1) require higher capital—lower leverage—ratios so that stockholders have more at stake in taking risky investments, and (2) impose stricter closure rules. The moral hazard risk-taking incentives of FI owners increase as their capital or net worth approaches zero and their leverage increases. For those U.S. thrifts allowed to operate in the 1980s with virtually no book equity capital and with negative net worth, the risk-taking incentives of their owners were enormous.

capital forbearance
Regulators' policy of allowing an FI to continue operating even when its capital funds are fully depleted.

By failing to close such FIs, regulators exhibited excessive **capital forbearance.** In the short term, forbearance may save the insurance fund some liquidation costs. In the long run, owners of bad DTIs have continuing incentives to grow and take additional risks in the hope of a large payoff that could turn the institution around. This strategy potentially adds to the future liabilities of the insurance fund and to the costs of liquidation. We now know that huge additional costs were the actual outcome of the regulators' policy of capital forbearance in the U.S. thrift industry in the 1980s.

As we discuss in Chapter 20, a system of risk-based capital requirements mandates that those FIs taking greater on- and off-balance-sheet, market, credit, operating, and interest rate risks must hold more capital. Thus, risk-based capital

---

[15] See CDIC, *Summary of the Corporate Plan, 2009/2010 to 2013/2014,* April 2009, or the most recent report at www.cdic.ca.

[16] Various researchers have examined the issue of moral hazard and the impact of deposit insurance on Canadian FIs. See for example, J. Gueyie and V. Son Lai, "Bank Moral Hazard and the Introduction of Official Deposit Insurance in Canada," *International Review of Economics and Finance* 12 (2003), pp. 247–273; J. So and J. Z. Wei, "Deposit Insurance and Forbearance under Moral Hazard," *Journal of Risk and Insurance,* December 2004, 71(4), pp. 707–736; J. M. Hendrickson and M. W. Nichols, "How Does Regulation Affect the Risk Taking of Banks? A U.S. and Canadian Perspective," *Journal of Comparative Policy Analysis,* June 2003, 3(1), pp. 59–83; and E. J. Kane and B. Wilson, "Regression Evidence of Safety-Net Support in Canada and the U.S., 1893–1992," *The Quarterly Review of Economics and Finance* 42 (2002), pp. 649–671.

supports risk-based deposit insurance premiums by increasing the cost of risk-taking for FI stockholders.[17]

To the extent that the book value of capital approximates true net worth or the market value of capital, this enhances stockholder discipline by imposing additional costs on FI owners for risk-taking. It also increases the degree of co-insurance, in regard to risks taken, between FI owners and regulators such as the CDIC.

| **CONCEPT QUESTIONS** | 1. If you are managing an FI that is technically insolvent but has not yet been closed by the regulators, would you invest in Treasury bonds or real estate development loans? Explain your answer. |
| | 2. Do we need both risk-based capital requirements and risk-based insurance premiums to discipline shareholders? |

Depositor Discipline

An alternative, more indirect route to disciplining riskier FIs is to create conditions for a greater degree of depositor discipline. Depositors could either require higher interest rates and risk premiums on deposits or ration the amount of deposits they are willing to hold in riskier FIs.

Critics argue that under the current deposit insurance regulations, neither insured depositors nor uninsured depositors have sufficient incentives to discipline riskier deposit-taking institutions. To understand these arguments, we consider the risk exposure of both insured and uninsured depositors under the current deposit insurance contract.

Insured Depositors

As noted above, CDIC is a Crown corporation that was created in 1967 to protect deposits held at banks, trust companies, and savings and loans. The level of coverage for a depositor increased from $60,000 to $100,000 effective February 2005. The $100,000 cap applies to a depositor's beneficial interest and ownership of deposited funds that are (1) made with an eligible member of CDIC, (2) are in Canadian dollars payable in Canada, and (3) are repayable within five years from the deposit date. The cap relates to deposits at a single member institution. Tax-free savings accounts (TFSAs) are subject to the same rules as other savings accounts. In actuality, by structuring deposit funds in a CDIC-insured institution in a particular fashion, a depositor can achieve many times the $100,000 cap on deposits. To see this, consider the different categories of deposit fund ownership (defined as savings and chequing accounts, term deposits, debentures issued by loan companies, money orders, drafts, certified cheques, and travellers cheques) available to an individual, shown in Table 19–4. Each of these categories represents a distinct accumulation of funds toward the $100,000 deposit insurance cap, the coverage ceiling per financial institution. We give an example of how depositors can raise the coverage level by adopting certain strategies.

EXAMPLE 19–1   A married couple with one daughter, where both husband and wife have eligible funds in individual RRSPs, could accrue coverage at one CDIC-insured institution of $100,000 each for individual savings or chequing accounts ($300,000 total), $100,000 for each of three joint

---

[17] On the assumption that new equity is more costly to raise than deposits for banks.

chequing accounts ($300,000), $100,000 each for trust deposits ($300,000), and $100,000 each for the husband and wife for five-year GICs in an RRSP ($200,000) for a total coverage cap of $1,100,000 as a family.

---

deposit brokers
Brokers who break up large deposits into smaller units at different banks to ensure full coverage by deposit insurance.

Note that the $100,000 coverage ceiling is per institution, not per branch. Wealthy and institutional investors can spread their funds over many deposit-taking institutions up to the permitted cap insured by CDIC. In this way, all their deposits become explicitly insured. For example, a wealthy individual with $1 million in deposits could split the deposits between ten of the CDIC's members. In the United States, a wealthy individual might use a **deposit broker** such as Merrill Lynch to split US$1 million into parcels of US$100,000 and deposit those funds at ten different banks. During the 1980s, the greatest purchasers of brokered deposits were the most risky banks that had no, or limited, access to the borrowed funds market. These risky banks attracted brokered deposits by offering higher interest rates than did relatively healthy banks. In fact, a high proportion of brokered deposits held by a bank became an early warning signal of its future failure risk. Neither the depositors nor the fund brokers were concerned about the risk of these funds because every parcel, including interest accrued up until the time of failure, was fully insured up to the US$100,000 ceiling.

Uninsured Depositors

The primary intention of deposit insurance is to deter runs and panics. A secondary and related objective has been to protect the smaller, less informed saver against the reduction in wealth that would occur if that person was last in line when an FI fails. Under the current deposit insurance contract, the small, less informed depositor is defined by the $100,000 ceiling. Theoretically

---

TABLE 19–4
CDIC's Deposit Insurance Coverage

Source: Canada Deposit Insurance Corporation, www.cdic.ca.

$100,000 DEPOSIT INSURANCE COVERAGE

What's Covered?

CDIC insures eligible deposits held in each member institution up to a maximum of $100,000 (principal and interest combined) per depositor, for each of the following deposits:
- Savings held in one name
- Savings held in trust for another person
- Savings held in Registered Retirement Savings Plans (RRSPs)
- Savings held in Registered Retirement Income Funds (RRIFs)
- Savings held for paying realty taxes on mortgaged property
- Savings held in more than one name (joint deposits)
- Savings held in Tax-Free Savings Accounts (TFSAs)

Depositors are responsible for ensuring that the member institution's records include all information required for the separate protection of these deposits. (See CDIC's website, www.cdic.ca, for details.)

What's Not Covered?

CDIC deposit insurance does not protect all accounts and financial products. For example, mutual funds, stocks, and foreign currency deposits, including those in U.S. dollars, are not covered by CDIC.

What's an Eligible Deposit?

Eligible deposits include:
- Savings accounts and chequing accounts
- Guaranteed Investment Certificates (GICs) and other term deposits with an original term to maturity of five years or less
- Money orders, travellers' cheques and bank drafts issued by CDIC members, and cheques certified by CDIC members
- Debentures issued by loan companies that are CDIC members

Deposits must be payable in Canada, in Canadian currency.

at least, larger, more informed depositors with more than $100,000 on deposit are at risk if an FI fails. As a result, these large uninsured depositors should be sensitive to risk and seek to discipline more risky FIs by demanding higher interest rates on their deposits or withdrawing their deposits completely. Until recently, the manner in which failures have been resolved meant that both large and small depositors were often fully protected against losses. This was especially so where large banks got into trouble and were viewed as **too big to fail** (TBTF). That is, they were too big to be liquidated by regulators either because of the draining effects on the resources of the insurance fund or for fear of contagious or systemic runs spreading to other major banks. Thus, although uninsured depositors tended to lose in small-bank failures, in large-bank failures the failure resolution methods employed by regulators usually resulted in implicit 100 percent deposit insurance. As a result, for large banks in particular, neither small nor large depositors had sufficient incentives to impose market discipline on riskier banks.

In Canadian banking history, failing institutions have generally been absorbed by other institutions, such as the takeover of Central Guaranty Trust's assets by TD Bank in the early 1990s. In an effort to prevent the failure of the Canadian Commercial Bank and the Northland Bank of Canada in 1985, the federal regulators at the time (the Inspector General of Banks along with the Bank of Canada and the Department of Finance) arranged for support from the six large banks and government to provide liquidity to replace the banks' wholesale deposits that were maturing and not being renewed. In the fallout, Continental Bank of Canada became unable to renew its wholesale deposits, despite being declared solvent by the Big Six banks, who examined its loan portfolio. Continental was subsequently taken over by Hong Kong Bank of Canada. Next we look at three principal methods of failure resolution and their effect on depositors.

too-big-to-fail banks
Banks that are viewed by regulators as being too big to be closed and liquidated without imposing a systemic risk to the banking and financial system.

FDIC'S POLICIES, 2007–2009

In the wake of the FDIC's growing deficit, the FDIC Improvement Act (FDICIA) of 1991 sought to pass more of the costs of insured DTI failures on to uninsured depositors, thereby enhancing their incentives to monitor DTIs and to control risk through requiring higher deposit rates and/or through their deposit placement decisions. The FDICIA required that a **least-cost resolution** (LCR) strategy be put in place by the FDIC. In applying the LCR strategy, the FDIC evaluates failure resolution alternatives on a present value basis and documents their assumptions in deciding which method to use.

However, there was a very important and controversial exemption to using least-cost resolution in all cases. Specifically, a *systemic risk* exemption applies where a large DTI failure could cause a threat to the whole financial system. Then methods that could involve the full protection of uninsured depositors as well as insured depositors could be used. However, the act has restricted the circumstances under which this systemic risk exemption can be used. Such an exemption is allowed only if a two-thirds majority of the boards of the Federal Reserve and the FDIC recommend it to the secretary of the Treasury and if the secretary of the Treasury, in consultation with the president of the United States, agrees. Further, any cost of such a bailout of a big DTI would have to be shared among all other DTIs by charging them an additional deposit insurance premium based on their size as measured by their domestic and foreign deposits as well as their

least-cost resolution
Policy requiring that the lowest-cost method of closure be used for failing DTIs.

borrowed funds, excluding subordinated debt. Because large DTIs have more foreign deposits and borrowed funds, they will have to make bigger contributions (per dollar of assets) than smaller DTIs to any future bailout of a large DTI.

With the growing wave of bank and financial service firm mergers, it was argued that more and more FIs are likely to be covered by TBTF guarantees.[18]

insured depositor transfer
Method of resolution in which uninsured depositors take a loss, or haircut, on failure equal to the difference between their deposit claims and the estimated value of the failed DTI's assets minus insured deposits.

With the exception of the systemic risk exemption, the least-cost resolution strategy requires the FDIC to employ the method that imposes most failure costs on the uninsured depositors. To this end, the FDIC has been increasingly using an **insured depositor transfer** (IDT), or "haircut," method to resolve a number of post-1991 failures. Under the IDT method of resolution, the insured deposits of a closed DTI are usually transferred in full to another local DTI in the community to conduct a direct payoff of the depositors for the FDIC. By contrast, uninsured depositors must file a claim against the receiver of the failed DTI and share with the FDIC in any receivership distributions from the liquidation of the closed DTI's assets. This usually results in a loss for uninsured depositors (a so-called "haircut"). We describe a simplified form of the IDT, or haircut, method next.

EXAMPLE 19–2

Liquidation and Payoff of a Failed Bank Using the Insured Deposit Transfer (IDT) Method

In Table 19–5, the failed bank in panel (a) has only $80 million in good assets to meet the $50 million in deposit claims of insured depositors and the $50 million in claims of the uninsured depositors.[19] Under an IDT, in panel (b), the FDIC would transfer the $80 million in assets to an acquiring bank along with the full $50 million in small insured deposits but only $30 million of the $50 million in uninsured deposits.[20] Notice that the uninsured depositors get protection against losses only up to the difference between the estimated value of the failed bank's assets and its insured deposits. In effect, the uninsured depositors are subject to a "haircut" to their original deposit claims of $20 million (or, as a percentage, 40 percent of the value of their deposit claims on the failed bank). After the IDT, the uninsured depositors own $30 million in deposits in the acquiring bank and $20 million in receivership claims on the bad assets of the failed bank. Only if the FDIC as a receiver can recover some value from the $20 million in bad assets will the loss to the uninsured be less than $20 million.

To summarize the losses of the three parties under the IDT:

Loss ($ millions)		
Insured depositors	=	0
FDIC	=	0
Uninsured depositors	=	$20

---

[18] The Federal Reserve-organized US$3.5 billion bank bailout of the Long-Term Capital Management (LTCM) hedge fund has been described by some as a TBTF bailout because the fund was allowed to continue operations largely on the basis of the size of its exposure both in capital market instruments and in derivatives of over US$1.25 trillion in nominal value. The fear here was that allowing LTCM to liquidate its positions at a massive loss could cause a number of banks that had lent money to the fund to fail or be significantly undercapitalized once losses were written off. Others have argued that this was not really a TBTF bailout in the conventional sense since no government money was directly involved. FDIC's bailouts in 2007, 2008, and 2009 involved the provision of capital ("nationalization") in some cases of large FIs.

purchase and assumption (P&A)
Merger of a failed deposit-taking institution with a healthy FI.

[19] That is, it has $20 million negative net worth.

[20] Unlike in a **purchase and assumption (P&A),** it would not inject cash into the failed bank prior to a merger with the acquiring bank.

TABLE 19–5 Insured Depositor Transfer Resolution ($ millions)

(a) Failed				(b) Insured Depositor Transfer				
Assets		**Liabilities**		**Assets**		**Liabilities**		
Good assets	$80	Insured deposits	$ 50	Good assets	$80	Insured deposits	$50	Merger → with good bank
		Uninsured deposits	50			Uninsured deposits	30	
	$80		$100		$80		$80	

As you can see from this simple example, the uninsured depositors bear all the losses and now have a much stronger incentive than before to monitor and control the actions of FI owners through imposing market discipline via interest rates and the amount of funds deposited.[21]

Regulatory Discipline

In the event that stockholder and deposit holder discipline does not reduce moral hazard-induced risk-taking, regulations can require regulators to act promptly and in a more consistent and predictable fashion to restrain FI risk-taking behaviour by: (1) the frequency and thoroughness of examinations and (2) the forbearance shown to weakly capitalized FIs.

Examinations

As shown in Figure 19–1, the joint oversight by OSFI and CDIC provides the regulatory discipline for federally regulated banks, trusts, and loan companies in Canada. In addition to the monthly and quarterly reporting to OSFI, a federally regulated FI is inspected annually by OSFI, which may also conduct special examinations if desired. As well, CDIC provides oversight for provincially and territorially regulated deposit-taking FIs and may conduct annual or special examinations of these FIs. Since 1987, CDIC has been able to act as a liquidator or receiver in the event of the failure of a CDIC member. In the United States, since 1992, every deposit-taking institution must be examined annually on-site and is also subject to an audit by an independent private accountant. This is similar to the situation in the United Kingdom, where the 1987 Bank Act required an enhanced role for private auditors as a backup for regulatory examiners.

Regulatory Forbearance

OSFI and CDIC jointly follow the *Guide to Intervention for Federal Financial Institutions* in dealing with a troubled FI which, it can be argued, gives them more discretionary powers as opposed to the strict rules-based approach that has been adopted in the United States, which mandates "prompt corrective action" symptomatic of a move toward a regulatory policy based on rules rather than on

---

[21] In September 2008, the largest bank failure by asset size (US$307 billion) in U.S. history occurred when Washington Mutual (Wamu) was acquired by JPMorgan by purchase and assumption for US$1.9 billion. There was no cost to FDIC nor to the uninsured depositors.

discretion. The weakness of such rules is that if a policy is bad, then bad policy becomes more effective.[22]

What additional measures can be taken by regulators to bolster stockholder and depositor discipline?

DEPOSIT INSURANCE SYSTEMS GLOBALLY

The International Association of Deposit Insurers (IADI) was formed in 2002 to encourage cooperation among global deposit insurers. In 2009, the IADI represented 52 insurers, and its website (www.iadi.org) listed 103 countries with some form of explicit deposit insurance. CDIC conducted a survey for IADI of deposit insurance practices in 2008 and, by 2009, had responses from 62 insurers. The survey results were made available on its website at www.cdic.ca.

The BIS and IADI released their report, *Core Principles for Effective Deposit Insurance Systems,* in June 2009. These core principles emphasize moral hazard (Principle 2) and cross-border issues (Principle 6), as well as early detection and timely intervention (Principle 15) and effective resolution processes (Principle 16). After the global turmoil of 2008, regulators have discussed liquidity enhancements (Chapters 17 and 18), deposit insurance issues, and capital adequacy guidelines (Chapter 20). Best practices as well as increased regulatory oversight are on the agenda of policymakers worldwide.

LENDER OF LAST RESORT

Deposit Insurance versus the Central Bank

The previous sections have described how a well-designed deposit insurance system might impose stockholder, depositor, and regulator discipline. Such a system can potentially stop runs and extreme liquidity problems arising in the banking system without introducing significant amounts of moral hazard risk-taking behaviour among insured institutions. However, deposit insurance is not the only mechanism by which regulators mitigate bank liquidity risk. A second mechanism has been the central banks' provision of a lender of last resort facility.

The Bank of Canada's Lender of Last Resort Policies

The Bank of Canada has the role of providing liquidity to the financial system. The Bank of Canada Act allows the Bank to provide loans secured by acceptable collateral (e.g., government securities, bankers' acceptances, and commercial paper) to solvent banks and members of the Canadian Payments Association. These

---

[22] L. Kryzanowski and G. S. Roberts, "Canadian Banking Solvency, 1922–1940," *Journal of Money, Credit, and Banking,* (August 1993) 25(3), pp. 361–376, argue that regulatory forbearance allowed Sun Life to carry its securities at book value rather than at market value, keeping Sun Life from being declared insolvent and forcing the regulators to act to wind it up. J. So and J. Z. Wei, "Deposit Insurance and Forbearance under Moral Hazard," *Journal of Risk and Insurance,* (December 2004), 71(4), pp. 707–735, use a real options model for a bank's assets and conclude that forbearance can help reduce a deposit fund's liability. Similar arguments have been made in the area of monetary policy, where proponents have argued for a rules-based policy around a constant growth rate of the money supply. However, most central bankers prefer discretion in deciding on the timing and size of monetary policy actions such as their open market operations. During the financial crises in 2007 and 2008, central bankers increasingly worked together to prevent a global market meltdown.

functions come under the term "lender of last resort" activities. As a result of foreign bank branches setting up in Canada in 1999 and expansion of the membership of the Canadian Payments Association in 2002, as well as the need of Canadian FIs for foreign liquidity, the Bank reviewed its policies in light of its role in providing stability to the financial system.[23] The Bank provides funds to the payments system in three ways:

1. *The Standing Liquidity Facility (SLF):* The SLF provides overnight, collateralized loans to those FIs that are direct participants in the Large Value Transfer System (LVTS, see Chapter 17) to handle temporary shortfalls in the day-to-day settlement of accounts. The borrowers must be solvent and the collateral limits the amounts that may be borrowed, providing a curb on moral hazard, which would see a troubled FI transfer its risk to the central bank.

2. *Emergency Lending Assistance (ELA):* Through the ELA, the Bank provides longer-term assistance to deposit-taking institutions that are solvent, but are illiquid. That is, they have illiquid assets supported by short-term highly liquid deposits.

3. *Forced LVTS Loans:* In order to protect the payments system from systemic risk that could cause the whole system to fail, the Bank of Canada could be forced to lend to an insolvent deposit-taking institution that failed to make its daily settlement. Since each LVTS participant pledges collateral (effectively co-insurance) in advance to cover its largest single expected daily settlement, the Bank of Canada's position would be protected.

As noted earlier in the chapter, the role of the Bank of Canada interconnects with the roles of OSFI and CDIC to provide a mechanism to ensure the safety and soundness of the Canadian financial system, including the payments system. Thus Canada may be viewed as a stable link in global financial markets that are increasingly connected. During the liquidity crisis in the fall of 2008, the Bank of Canada increased the size of term purchase and resale agreements (PRAs), introduced a money market PRA facility and a term loan facility (TLF), broadened the type of collateral that it would accept, guaranteed bank liabilities through the Canadian Lenders Assurance Facility (CLAF), and agreed to up to $75 billion in asset purchases from CMHC-insured mortgage pools (Chapter 1, Table 1–1). The ability of LVTS participants to borrow from the Bank of Canada was a source of stability during the liquidity crisis of 2008.

The U.S. Federal Reserve

discount window
Central bank lender of last resort facility.

www.federalreserve.gov

Traditionally, the U.S. Federal Reserve has provided a **discount window** facility to meet the short-term, non-permanent liquidity needs of FIs.[24] For example, suppose an FI has an unexpected deposit drain and cannot meet its reserve target. It can seek to borrow from the central bank's discount window facility. Normally, such loans are obtained by discounting short-term high-quality paper such as Treasury

---

[23] For a detailed discussion of the Bank of Canada's role in ensuring the stability of the financial system, see F. Daniel, W. Engert, and D. Maclean, "The Bank of Canada as Lender of Last Resort," *Bank of Canada Review,* Winter 2004–2005, pp. 3–16, as well as "Bank of Canada Lender-of-Last-Resort Policies," Bank of Canada *Financial System Review,* December 2004.

[24] In times of extreme crisis, the discount window can meet the liquidity needs of securities firms as well (as was the case during the stock market crash of October 19, 1987, the terrorist attacks on the United States on September 11, 2001, and the extreme global liquidity crises of September and October 2008).

bills and bankers' acceptances with the central bank. The interest rate at which such securities are discounted is called the *discount rate* and is set by the central bank.

In the wake of the terrorist attacks of September 11, 2001, the Federal Reserve's discount window supplied funds to the banking system in unprecedented amounts. The magnitude of destruction resulting from the attacks caused severe disruptions to the U.S. banking system, particularly in FIs' abilities to send payments. The physical disruptions caused by the attacks included outages of telephone switching equipment in Lower Manhattan's financial district, impaired records processing and communications systems at individual banks, the evacuation of buildings that were the sites for the payment operations of several large FIs, and the suspended delivery of cheques by air couriers. These disruptions left some FIs unable to execute payments to other FIs through the Fed's Fedwire system, which in turn resulted in an unexpected shortfall for other FIs. The Federal Reserve took several steps to address the problems in the payments system on and after September 11, 2001. Around noon on September 11, the Board of Governors of the Fed released a statement saying that the Fed was open and operating, and that the discount window was available to meet liquidity needs of all deposit-taking institutions. The Fed staff also contacted FIs often during the next few days, encouraging them to make payments and to consider the use of the discount window to cover unexpected shortfalls. Thus, the Fed's discount window was a primary tool used to restore payments coordination during this period.

In the United States the central bank has traditionally set the discount rate below market rates, such as the overnight federal funds rates. The volume of outstanding discount loans was ordinarily small, however, because the Fed prohibited deposit-taking institutions from using discount window loans to finance sales of Fed funds or to finance asset expansion. However, in January 2003, the Fed implemented changes to its discount window lending that increased the cost of borrowing but eased the terms. Specifically, three lending programs were offered through the Fed's discount window. *Primary credit* is available to generally sound deposit-taking institutions on a very short-term basis, typically overnight, at a rate above the Federal Open Market Committee's (FOMC) target rate for federal funds. Primary credit may be used for any purpose, including financing the sale of Fed funds. Primary credit may be extended for periods of up to a few weeks to deposit-taking institutions in generally sound financial condition. *Secondary credit* is available to institutions that are not eligible for primary credit. It is extended on a very short-term basis, typically overnight, at a rate that is above the primary credit rate. Secondary credit is available to meet backup liquidity needs when its use is consistent with a timely return to a reliance on market sources of funding or the orderly resolution of a troubled institution. Secondary credit may not be used to fund an expansion of the borrower's assets. *Seasonal credit* is available to institutions that can demonstrate a clear pattern of recurring intra-yearly swings in funding needs. Eligible institutions are usually located in agricultural or tourist areas. These changes also allow healthy banks to borrow from the Fed regardless of the availability of private funds.

Despite the recent changes in the Fed's policy regarding discount window lending, there are a number of reasons why access to the discount window did not deter runs and panics in 2008. The first reason is that to borrow from the discount window, an FI needed high-quality liquid assets to pledge as collateral. Failing, highly illiquid FIs were unlikely to have such assets available to discount (e.g., Lehman Brothers, Bear Stearns). The second reason is that discount window borrowing, unlike deposit insurance coverage, is not automatic. That is, discount window loans are made at the discretion of the central bank. Third, discount window loans are meant to provide temporary liquidity for inherently solvent FIs, not permanent long-term support for otherwise insolvent FIs. Consequently, during the liquidity crisis in the fall of 2008, the U.S. Federal Reserve, the Treasury, and FDIC went to extraordinary lengths to provide liquidity facilities to the market, to increase deposit insurance limits, to guarantee bank liabilities, to inject capital, and to purchase assets (Chapter 1, Table 1–1). The stimulus packages provided by the U.S. government could exceed US$10 trillion.

CONCEPT QUESTION	**Is a deposit-taking institution's access to central bank funds likely to be as effective as deposit insurance in deterring bank runs and panics? Why or why not?**

OTHER GUARANTY PROGRAMS

As discussed in Chapter 17, other FIs are also subject to liquidity crises and liability holder runs. To deter such runs and protect small claimholders, guaranty programs have appeared in other sectors of the financial services industry. We describe these programs and their similarities to and differences from deposit insurance next.

Quebec Deposit Insurance Board (QDIB)

www.radq.gouv.qc.ca

CDIC provides protection for eligible members who are federally regulated (banks, trusts, and loan companies) as well as for eligible provincially and territorially incorporated deposit-taking institutions (trusts and loan companies). The deposits of members of CDIC that are incorporated in the province of Quebec are covered by the Quebec Deposit Insurance Board for deposits in Quebec and by CDIC for deposits made elsewhere in Canada.

Credit Unions and Caisses Populaires

Since credit unions and caisses populaires are regulated at the provincial level in Canada, deposits are protected by the provincial deposit insurance fund or its equivalent. These funds have the ability to monitor their members and may levy premiums based on deposits, gross revenues, total assets, or some other measure. Because credit unions and caisses populaires hold many of their assets in government securities, as well as in residential mortgages and small consumer loans, often for amounts less than $10,000, they have a significant degree of risk diversification, which also lowers their risk of insolvency. Links to the provincial deposit insurers are provided at CDIC's website.

www.cdic.ca

Assuris

Although life insurers, like property and casualty (P&C) insurers, and securities firms, including mutual funds, are subject to regulation, they are not supported by government-run guaranty funds like the CDIC. These industries provide their own funds, supported by levies on their members.

www.assuris.ca

Life insurance companies writing policies in Canada are required to become members of Assuris. If a life insurance company fails, Assuris covers policyholders

TABLE 19–6
Benefits and
Product Coverage
Provided by Assuris

Source: Assuris,
www.assuris.ca.

The following benefits are fully covered by Assuris up to

Monthly Income	$2,000
Death Benefit	$200,000
Health Expense	$60,000
Cash Value	$60,000

If total benefits exceed these amounts, Assuris covers 85% of the promised benefits, but not less than these amounts.

Accumulated value benefits are fully covered by Assuris up to $100,000. If accumulated value benefits are over $100,000, Assuris will ensure receipt of at least $100,000.

Coverage by Product
Assuris coverage applies to the benefits under a variety of products, including:

Individual Products

Life Insurance	Long-Term Care Insurance
Critical Illness	RRIFs
Health Expense Insurance	RRSPs
Disability Income Insurance	Accumulation Annuities
Payout Annuities	Segregated Funds

Group Products

Group Insurance	Group Retirement Plans

for loss of benefits (e.g., health expenses, disability income, RRSPs, RRIFs, and death benefits). Assuris also covers savings benefits from policies. Details of the coverage provided by Assuris are shown in Table 19–6. The products covered reflect the range of consumer services provided by insurance companies in Canada, and is similar in scope to the deposit coverage provided by CDIC.

Assuris's current structure partially reflects a restructuring subsequent to the failure of three insurance companies (Les Coopérants, January 1992, Sovereign Life, December 1992, and Confederation Life, August 1994) in the 1990s, which brought into question the stability of the insurance industry and caused companies with group life and health insurance coverage to reconsider the protection from liability provided by Assuris under these policies. The federal government threatened to create a Crown corporation similar to CDIC for insurance companies, but Assuris increased its borrowing capabilities from members, established an independent board of directors, and put in place a plan for handling restructurings in order to keep control of its members out of government hands. Despite having to call on members for additional funds, Assuris provided 100 percent coverage in the case of Les Coopérants and Confederation Life, costing the industry $175 million and $5 million, respectively. Almost all of Sovereign Life's policyholders (96 percent) were covered 100 percent, with the remainder covered to 90 percent, costing the life insurance industry $25 million in the process. In the insurance company failures in Canada, the industry has worked to transfer policies to other insurers. For example, Confederation Life, which was the fourth-largest group life insurer in 1994, got into trouble by concentrating its investments in commercial real estate. After its failure, many of its policies were eventually taken over by other life insurers (e.g., Manulife, Maritime Life, Canada Life, Sun Life, Empire Life, and others).[25]

Property and Casualty Insurance Compensation Corporation (PACICC)

www.pacicc.ca

Property and casualty insurance companies in Canada have funded and operated a non-profit fund, the Property and Casualty Insurance Compensation Corporation (PACICC) since 1989, which, in the event of the failure of one of its members, will automatically cover policyholders and claims. In order to sell P&C insurance in Canada, a company must be a member of PACICC, so all Canadian insurance policies are automatically covered. Policyholders are covered to a maximum of $250,000 for claims on most P&C policies. The P&C industry, as noted in Chapter 3, relies heavily on investments in bonds and other securities that have suffered lower returns over the past few years. The incentives for insurance policyholders to engage in a run if they perceive that an insurer has asset quality problems or insurance underwriting problems may be quite strong despite the presence of private guaranty funds. However, P&C insurers regulated by OSFI file a "prudent person" investment strategy that provides a measure of comfort that the industry is being monitored.

Canadian Investor Protection Fund (CIPF)

www.cipf.ca

If an investment dealer becomes bankrupt, the Canadian Investor Protection Fund (CIPF), a private insurance fund founded in 1969, will cover the losses of eligible customers of the dealer members of the Investment Industry Regulatory Organization of Canada (IIROC). Since its inception, the fund has had 17 insolvent members for whom it has paid out $37 million. The coverage extends to securities, commodities and futures contracts, segregated insurance funds (the insurance industry's equivalent of mutual funds, as explained in Chapter 3), and cash, up to a total of $1 million per account when a member becomes insolvent and a liquidator is appointed. Coverage is provided for each separate account (e.g., registered retirement plans, registered income plans, trusts), extending the coverage above the $1 million ceiling. Coverage may also exceed this amount if there are additional funds available upon liquidation. Only losses due to insolvency of a member of the CIPF are covered. CIPF had $546 million available at December 31, 2008. None of its members failed during 2008.

| CONCEPT QUESTION | How do industry-sponsored guaranty funds for insurance companies differ from deposit insurance? |

---

[25] See F. Grossi, "Life after Confed Life," *Benefits Canada,* October 1994, 18(9), L. Welsh, "PACIC and the Fall of Confed," *Canadian Underwriter,* November 1994, 61(11), p. 10, and B. Cox, "Canadian Guaranty Fund Revamped," *National Underwriter,* July 10, 1995, 99(28), pp. 2 and 22, as well as Assuris's website at www.assuris.ca.

Summary

A contagious run on FIs can have serious social welfare effects. Because of adverse wealth, money supply, and credit supply effects, regulators of FIs in North America and around the world have introduced guaranty programs to deter runs by offering liability holders varying degrees of failure protection. Mispriced insurance or guarantee programs, however, can lead to moral hazard behaviour by FI owners. That is, since insurance guarantees result in little risk to FI owners with limited liability, they have an incentive to take excessively risky asset positions.

In recent years, deposit insurance and other financial industry guaranty programs have weakened (FDIC in the United States and Assuris in Canada, respectively). This chapter looked at the causes of the deposit insurance fund difficulties, including external economic events and moral hazard behaviour induced by the structure of the insurance plan itself. We discussed the establishment of deposit insurance in Canada and its restructuring in the 1990s, including the introduction of risk-related premiums, risk-based capital, and increased market and regulatory discipline on deposit-taking institutions and liability holders. As a result, the provision and cost of deposit insurance is currently more sensitive to a deposit-taking institution's risk exposure than previously. This chapter also examined liability guaranty programs for other FIs, including credit unions and caisses populaires, life insurance and P&C insurance companies, as well as for investors.

Questions and Problems

1. What is a contagious run? What are some of the potentially serious adverse social welfare effects of a contagious run? Do all types of FIs face the same risk of contagious runs?

2. How does deposit insurance help mitigate the problem of bank runs? What other elements of the safety net are available to FIs in Canada?

3. What is moral hazard?

4. How does a risk-based insurance program solve the moral hazard problem of excessive risk-taking by FIs? Is an actuarially fair premium for deposit insurance always consistent with a competitive banking system?

5. What are three suggested ways a deposit insurance contract could be structured to reduce moral hazard behaviour?

6. What are some ways of imposing stockholder discipline to prevent stockholders from engaging in excessive risk-taking?

7. How is the provision of deposit insurance similar to writing a put option on the assets of an FI that buys the insurance? What two factors drive the premium of the option?

8. What is capital forbearance? How does a policy of forbearance potentially increase the costs of financial distress to the insurance fund as well as the stockholders?

9. Under what conditions may the implementation of minimum capital guidelines, either risk-based or non-risk-based, fail to impose stockholder discipline as desired by regulators?

10. What has happened to the level of deposit insurance premiums since the risk-based program was implemented? Why?

11. Why did the fixed-rate deposit insurance system fail to induce insured and uninsured depositors to impose discipline on risky banks in the 1980s?

   a. How is it possible to structure deposits in an FI to reduce the effects of the insured ceiling?

   b. What has been the effect on FIs in Canada of the deposit insurance ceiling increasing to $100,000?

12. What is the too-big-to-fail doctrine? What factors caused regulators to act in a way that caused this doctrine to evolve?

13. The following is a balance sheet of a commercial bank ($ millions):

Assets		Liabilities and Equity	
Cash	$ 5	Insured deposits	$30
Loans	40	Uninsured deposits	10
		Equity	5
Total assets	$45	Total liabilities and equity	$45

The bank experiences a run on its deposits after it declares that it will write off $10 million of its loans as a result of non-payment. The bank has the option of meeting the withdrawals by first drawing down its cash and then selling off its loans. A fire sale of loans in one day can be accomplished at a 10 percent discount. They can be sold at a 5 percent discount if they are sold in two days. The full market value will be obtained if they are sold after two days.

   a. What is the amount of loss to the insured depositors if a run on the bank occurs on the first day? On the second day?

   b. What amount do the uninsured depositors lose if the CDIC closes the bank immediately? The assets will be sold after the two-day period.

14. A bank with insured deposits of $55 million and uninsured deposits of $45 million has assets valued at only $75 million. What is the cost of failure resolution to insured depositors, uninsured depositors, and CDIC if an insured depositor transfer method is used?

15. A bank has $150 million in assets at book value. The insured and uninsured deposits are valued at $75 and $50 million, respectively, and the book value of equity is $25 million. As a result of loan defaults, the market value of the assets has decreased to $120 million. What is the cost of failure resolution to insured depositors, uninsured depositors, shareholders, and the CDIC if an insured depositor transfer method is used?

16. Match the following policies with their intended consequences:

Policies:

   a. Lower CDIC insurance levels

   b. Stricter reporting standards

   c. Risk-based deposit insurance

Consequences:

   1. Increased stockholder discipline

   2. Increased depositor discipline

   3. Increased regulator discipline

17. Why is access to the discount window of the U.S. Federal Reserve or the Standing Liquidity Facility of the Bank of Canada less of a deterrent to bank runs than deposit insurance?

18. How do insurance guaranty funds differ from deposit insurance? What impact do these differences have on the incentive for insurance policyholders to engage in a contagious run on an insurance company?

Web Question

19. Go to the Bank of Canada's website at www.bankofcanada.ca and click on "Target for the Overnight Rate." What is the percentage increase or decrease in this rate in the past 6 months? 12 months? Go back to the home page and, under "More Rates & Statistics," click on "Interest Rates." Then click on "Selected Historical Interest Rates" and then on "Bank Rate V122530" to display a PDF file with the average monthly bank rate from 1935. In which year(s) was the bank rate the lowest? In which year(s) was the bank rate the highest?

Capital Adequacy

In this chapter, we examine

▸ the different measures of capital used by FI owners, managers, and regulators and the arguments for and against each

▸ the current capital adequacy requirements set by Canadian regulators for deposit-taking institutions, securities firms, and insurance companies

▸ the advanced approaches used to calculate adequate capital according to internal ratings-based models of measuring credit risk (in Appendix 20A, available at the Online Learning Centre at www.mcgrawhill.ca/olc/saunders)

INTRODUCTION

Chapters 7 through 17 examined the major areas of risk exposure facing a modern FI manager. These risks can emanate from both on- and off-balance-sheet (OBS) activities and can be either domestic or international in source. To ensure survival, an FI manager needs to protect the institution against the risk of insolvency, that is, shield it from risks sufficiently large to cause the institution to fail. The primary means of protection against the risk of insolvency and failure is an FI's capital. This leads to the first function of capital, namely:

1. To absorb unanticipated losses with enough margin to inspire confidence and enable the FI to continue as a going concern.

In addition, capital protects non-equity liability holders—especially those uninsured by an external guarantor such as the CDIC—against losses. This leads to the second function of capital:

2. To protect uninsured depositors, bondholders, and creditors in the event of insolvency, and liquidation.

When FIs fail, regulators have to intervene to protect insured claimants (see Chapter 19). The capital of an FI offers protection to insurance funds and ultimately the taxpayers who bear the cost of insurance fund insolvency. This leads to the third function of capital:

3. To protect FI insurance funds and the taxpayers.

By holding capital and reducing the risk of insolvency, an FI protects the industry from larger insurance premiums. Such premiums are paid out of the net profits of the FI. Thus, a fourth function of capital is as follows:

4. To protect the FI owners against increases in insurance premiums.

Finally, just as for any other firm, equity or capital is an important source of financing for an FI. In particular, subject to regulatory constraints, FIs have a choice between debt and equity to finance new projects and business expansion. Thus, the traditional factors that affect a business firm's choice of a capital structure—for instance, the tax deductibility of the interest on debt or the private costs of failure or insolvency—also interpose on the FI's capital decision. This leads to a fifth function of capital:

5. To fund the branch and other real investments necessary to provide financial services.[1]

In the following sections, we focus on the first four functions concerning the role of capital in reducing insolvency risk and in particular the adequacy of capital in attaining these functional objectives.

CAPITAL AND INSOLVENCY RISK

Capital

net worth
A measure of an FI's capital that is equal to the difference between the market value of its assets and the market value of its liabilities.

book value
Historical cost basis for asset and liability values.

To see how capital protects an FI against insolvency risk, we must define *capital* more precisely. The problem is that there are many definitions of capital: An economist's definition of capital may differ from an accountant's definition, which, in turn, may differ from the definition used by regulators. Specifically, the economist's definition of an FI's capital or owners' equity stake in an FI is the difference between the market values of its assets and its liabilities. This is also called the **net worth** of an FI. Although this is the *economic* meaning of capital, regulators have found it necessary to adopt definitions of capital that depart by a greater or lesser degree from economic net worth. The concept of an FI's economic net worth is really a *market value accounting concept*. With the exception of the investment banking industry, regulatory-defined capital and required leverage ratios are based in whole or in part on historical or **book value** accounting concepts.

We begin by looking at the role of economic capital or net worth as an insulation device against two major types of risk: credit risk and interest rate risk. We then compare this market value concept with the book value concept of capital. Because it can actually distort the true solvency position of an FI, the book value of capital concept can be misleading to managers, owners, liability holders, and regulators. We also examine some possible reasons why FI regulators continue to rely on book value concepts in the light of such economic value transparency problems.

The Market Value of Capital

market value or mark-to-market basis
Allowing balance sheet values to reflect current rather than historical prices.

To see how economic net worth or equity insulates an FI against risk, consider the following example. Table 20–1 presents a simple balance sheet where all the assets and liabilities of an FI are valued in **market value** terms at current prices on a **mark-to-market basis** (see Chapter 9). On a mark-to-market or market value basis, the economic value of the FI's equity is $10 million, which is the difference between the market value of its assets and liabilities. On a market value basis, the FI is economically solvent and imposes no failure costs on depositors or regulators if it were liquidated today. Let's consider the impact of two classic types of FI risk on this FI's net worth: credit risk and interest rate risk.

TABLE 20–1
An FI's Market Value Balance Sheet ($ millions)

Assets		Liabilities	
Long-term securities	$ 80	Liabilities (short-term, floating-rate deposits)	$ 90
Long-term loans	20	Net worth	10
	$100		$100

---

[1] A sixth function might be added. This would focus on the role of capital regulation in restraining the rate of asset growth.

Market Value of Capital and Credit Risk

In Table 20–1, an FI has $20 million in long-term loans. (For simplicity, we drop the $ sign and "million" text.) Suppose that, because of a recession, a number of these borrowers get into cash flow problems and are unable to keep up their promised loan repayment schedules. A decline in the current and expected future cash flows on loans lowers the market value of the loan portfolio held by the FI below 20. Suppose that loans are really worth only 12 (the price the FI would receive if it could sell these loans in a secondary market at today's prices). This means the market value of the loan portfolio has fallen from 20 to 12. Look at the revised market value balance sheet in Table 20–2.

The loss of 8 in the market value of loans appears on the liability side of the balance sheet as a loss of 8 to the FI's net worth. That is, the loss of asset value is charged against the equity owners' capital or net worth. As you can see, the liability holders (depositors) are fully protected in that the total market value of their claims is still 90. This is the case because debt holders legally are senior claimants and equity holders are junior claimants to an FI's assets. Consequently, equity holders bear losses on the asset portfolio first. In fact, in our example, liability holders are hurt only when losses on the loan portfolio exceed 10, the original net worth of the FI. Let's consider a larger credit risk shock such that the market value of the loan portfolio plummets from 20 to 8, a loss of 12 (see Table 20–3).

This larger loss renders the FI insolvent; the market value of its assets (88) is now less than the value of its liabilities (90). The owners' net worth stake has been completely wiped out (reduced from 10 to −2), making net worth negative. As a result, liability holders are hurt, but only a bit. Specifically, the first 10 of the 12 loss in value of the loan portfolio is borne by the equity holders. Only after the equity holders are wiped out do the liability holders begin to lose. In this example, the economic value of their claims on the FI has fallen from 90 to 88, or a loss of 2 (a percentage loss of 2.22 percent). After insolvency and the liquidation of the remaining 88 in assets, the depositors would get only 88/90 on the dollar, or 97.77 cents per $1 of deposits. Note here that we are ignoring deposit insurance.[2]

If the FI's net worth had been larger—say 15 rather than 10 in the previous example—the liability holders would have been fully protected against the loss of 12. In this case, the 12 loss reduces net worth to +3. This example clearly demonstrates the concept of net worth or capital as an insurance fund protecting liability holders, such as depositors, against insolvency risk. The larger the FI's net worth relative to the size of its assets, the more insolvency protection or insurance there is for liability holders and liability guarantors such as CDIC. This is why regulators focus on capital requirements such as the ratio of net worth to assets in assessing

TABLE 20–2   An FI's Market Value Balance Sheet after a Decline in the Value of Loans ($ millions)

Assets		Liabilities	
Long-term securities	$80	Liabilities	$90
Long-term loans	12	Net worth	2
	$92		$92

TABLE 20–3   An FI's Balance Sheet after a Major Decline in the Value of the Loan Portfolio ($ millions)

Assets		Liabilities	
Long-term securities	$80	Liabilities	$90
Long-term loans	8	Net worth	−2
	$88		$88

---

[2] In the presence of deposit insurance, the insurer, such as the CDIC, would bear some of the depositors' losses; for details, see Chapter 19.

the insolvency risk exposure of an FI and in setting risk-based deposit insurance premiums (see Chapter 19).

Market Value of Capital and Interest Rate Risk

Consider the market value balance sheet in Table 20–1 after a rise in interest rates. As we discuss in Chapters 8 and 9, rising interest rates reduce the market value of the FI's long-term fixed-income securities and loans whereas floating-rate instruments, if instantaneously repriced, find their market values largely unaffected. Suppose a rise in interest rates reduces the market value of the FI's long-term securities investments from 80 to 75 and the market value of its long-term loans from 20 to 17. Because all deposit liabilities are assumed to be short-term floating-rate deposits, their market values are unchanged at 90.

After the shock to interest rates, the market value balance sheet is represented in Table 20–4. The loss of 8 in the market value of the FI's assets is once again reflected on the liability side of the balance sheet by a fall in FI net worth from 10 to 2. Thus, losses in asset values due to adverse interest rate changes are borne first by the equity holders. Only if the fall in the market value of assets exceeds 10 are the liability holders, as senior claimants to the FI's assets, adversely affected.

These examples show that market valuation of the balance sheet can produce an economically accurate picture of the net worth, and thus, the solvency position of an FI. Credit risk and interest rate risk shocks that result in losses in the market value of assets are borne directly by the equity holders in the sense that such losses are charges against the value of their ownership claims in the FI. As long as the owners' capital or equity stake is adequate, or sufficiently large, liability holders (and, implicitly, regulators that back the claims of liability holders) are protected against insolvency risk. That is, if an FI were closed by regulators before its economic net worth became zero, neither liability holders nor those regulators guaranteeing the claims of liability holders (e.g., CDIC) would stand to lose. Thus, many academics and analysts have advocated the use of market value accounting and market value of capital closure rules for all FIs, especially in light of the subprime crisis of 2007 and 2008.

Canadian generally accepted accounting principles (GAAP) require securities to be classified as trading (the trading book) or other than trading (the banking book). **Trading securities** are carried at their market value and gains and losses recognized in the income statement. Other-than-trading securities are classified as **available-for-sale** and **held-to-maturity securities.** Available-for-sale securities are recorded at market value and unrealized gains and losses charged to **other comprehensive income (OCI)** as part of shareholders' equity. By comparison, no similar market-to-market requirement exists on the liabilities side. In the absence of any contrary ruling by regulators, this would require FI capital (net worth) positions to be adjusted downward if interest rates rose.[3]

trading securities
Securities held for a short time and carried at market value.

available-for-sale securities
Securities carried at fair value whose gains (losses) are charged to the OCI account until sold.

held-to-maturity securities
Securities carried at cost.

other comprehensive income (OCI)
Shareholders' equity account used to record unrealized gains (losses).

TABLE 20–4
An FI's Market Value Balance Sheet after a Rise in Interest Rates ($ millions)

Assets		Liabilities	
Long-term securities	$75	Liabilities	$90
Long-term loans	17	Net worth	2
	$92		$92

[3] Canadian banks prepare financial statements to meet U.S. GAAP. As well, Canadian firms will adopt International Financial Reporting Standards (IFRS) in 2011. U.S. firms are permitted to revalue their liabilities, but it can be misleading. For example, as interest rate spreads on bonds widened in 2008, five U.S. banks reported US$12 billion in revenue by marking their bonds down to market value. See B. Keoun, "Wall Street Says −2 + −2 = 4 as Liabilities Get New Bond Math," *bloomberg.com,* June 1, 2008, www.bloomberg.com.

However, asset valuation can be complex. During 2007 and 2008, markets became illiquid and FIs were unable to fairly value some of their securities (e.g., collateralized debt obligations based on subprime mortgages). Valuations are classified as Level 1 (using a quoted market price), Level 2 (applying observable market inputs to internal models), and Level 3 (internal models used with no market input). During a period of extreme market instability, the lack of market prices for assets greatly increases questions about the solvency of an FI.

The Book Value of Capital

We contrast market value or economic net worth with book value of capital or net worth. As we discuss in later sections, book value capital and capital rules based on book values are most commonly used by FI regulators. In Table 20–5, we use the same initial balance sheet we used in Table 20–1 but assume that assets and liabilities are now valued at their historical book values.

In Table 20–5, the 80 in long-term securities and the 20 in long-term loans reflect the historic or original book values of those assets. That is, they reflect the values when the loans were made and the bonds were purchased, which may have been many years ago. Similarly, on the liability side, the 90 in liabilities reflects their historical cost, and net worth or equity is now the book value of the stockholders' claims rather than the market value of those claims. For example, the book value of capital—the difference between the book values of assets and liabilities—may have the following components for an FI:

1. *Preferred shares:* Preferred shares rank ahead of common shares and may be considered the equivalent of fixed rate debt, but the dividends are not deductible for tax purposes. For regulatory capital, preferred shares may be included provided they meet certain criteria as we discuss later, but for market-to-book ratios, preferred shares are usually considered as debt and therefore are excluded.

2. *Common shares:* The book value of common shares is their issue price times the number of shares issued.

3. *Contributed surplus:* The difference between the price the public paid for common shares when originally offered (e.g., $5/share) and their par values (e.g., $1/share) times the number of shares outstanding. Common shares for the Big Six banks and other FIs are usually issued without a par (face) value.

4. *Retained earnings:* The accumulated value of past profits not yet paid out in dividends to shareholders. Since these earnings could be paid out in dividends, they are part of the equity owners' stake in the FI.

5. *Foreign currency translation adjustments:* These represent unrealized gains (losses) that arise from the translation of investments in foreign operations into Canadian dollars. When a gain (loss) is realized when the investment is sold, the gain (loss) is recorded on the income statement.

Consequently, book value of capital equals the sum of preferred shares plus common shares plus contributed surplus plus retained earnings plus foreign currency translation adjustments.

TABLE 20–5
Book Value of an
FI's Assets and
Liabilities
($ millions)

Assets		Liabilities	
Long-term securities	$ 80	Short-term liabilities	$ 90
Long-term loans	20	Net worth	10
	$100		$100

As the example in Table 20–5 is constructed, the book value of capital equals 10. However, invariably, the *book value of equity does not equal the market value of equity* (the difference between the market value of assets and that of liabilities). This inequality in book and market value of equity can be understood by examining the effects of the same credit and interest rate shocks on the FI's capital position, but assuming book value accounting methods.

Book Value of Capital and Credit Risk

Suppose that some of the 20 in loans are in difficulty regarding repayment schedules. We assumed in Table 20–2 that the revaluation of cash flows leads to an immediate downward adjustment of the loan portfolio's market value from 20 to 12, a market value loss of 8. By contrast, under historic book value accounting methods such as generally accepted accounting principles (GAAP), FIs have greater discretion in reflecting or timing problem loan loss recognition on their balance sheets and can control the impact of such losses on capital. Indeed, FIs may well resist writing down the values of bad assets as long as possible to try to present a more favourable picture to depositors and regulators. Such resistance may be expected if managers believe their jobs could be threatened when they recognize such losses. Only pressure from regulators such as bank or insurance examiners may force loss recognition and write-downs in the values of problem assets.[4] A good international example is the delay shown by Japanese banks in recognizing loan losses incurred over the 1996–2000 period, as a result of the Asian crisis and a domestic economic recession. As of year-end 2000 the collective bad debts of Japanese banks were conservatively estimated to exceed 32 trillion yen, most of which remained on their balance sheets at original book values. Moreover, even when loans are declared substandard by examiners, they may remain on the balance sheet at book value. A problem loan may require a write-down of only 50 percent, whereas only an outright loss requires a full 100 percent charge-off against the FI's equity position.

Suppose that in our example of historical book value accounting, the FI is forced to recognize a loss of 3 rather than 8 on its loan portfolio. Until the actual loan loss occurs, the amount would be recognized in a contra account and the total loans would be reported as "loans less allowance for impairment" on the balance sheet. When the loss is realized, the amount would be recognized on the income statement. The 3 is a charge against the 10 of the stockholders' book equity value. The new book value balance sheet is shown in Table 20–6.

Book Value of Capital and Interest Rate Risk

Although book value accounting systems do recognize credit risk problems, albeit only partially and usually with a long and discretionary time lag, their failure to recognize the impact of interest rate risk is more extreme.

TABLE 20–6
Effect of a Loan Loss Charge-Off against the Book Value of an FI's Equity ($ millions)

Assets		Liabilities	
Long-term securities	$80	Liabilities	$90
Long-term loans net of allowance for impairment	17	Equity (loss of 3 on loan loss allowance)	7
	$97		$97

[4] Canadian federally regulated FIs (banks, cooperatives, property and casualty insurance companies, life insurance companies) are guided by OSFI's Guideline C-1 for impaired loans and Section 3025 of the *Canadian Institute of Chartered Accountants (CICA) Handbook*. See OSFI's website at www.osfi-bsif.gc.ca for the latest version of the guidelines.

In our market value accounting example in Table 20–4, a rise in interest rates lowered the market values of long-term securities and loans by 8 and led to a fall in the market value of net worth from 10 to 2. In a book value accounting world, when all assets and liabilities reflect their original cost of purchase, the rise in interest rates has no effect on the value of assets, liabilities, or the book value of equity. That is, the balance sheet remains unchanged; Table 20–5 reflects the position both before and after the interest rate rise. Consider the U.S. savings and loans companies that, even though interest rates rose dramatically in the early 1980s, continued to report long-term fixed-rate mortgages at historical book values and, therefore, a positive book capital position. Yet, on a market value net worth basis, their mortgages were worth far less than the book values shown on their balance sheets. Indeed, more than half of the firms in the industry were economically insolvent—many massively so.

The Discrepancy between the Market and Book Values of Equity

The degree to which the book value of an FI's capital deviates from its true economic market value depends on a number of factors, especially:

1. *Interest rate volatility.* The higher the interest rate volatility, the greater the discrepancy.
2. *Examination and enforcement.* The more frequent the on-site and off-site examinations and the stiffer the examiner/regulator standards regarding charging off problem loans, the smaller the discrepancy.

In actual practice, for large publicly traded FIs, we can get a good idea of the discrepancy between book values (BV) and market values (MV) of equity even when the FI itself does not mark its balance sheet to market. Specifically, in an efficient capital market, investors can value the shares of an FI by doing an as-if market value calculation of the assets and liabilities of the FI. This valuation is based on the FI's current and expected future net earnings or dividend flows. The stock price of the FI reflects this valuation and thus the market value of its shares outstanding. The market value of equity per share is therefore

$$MV = \frac{\text{Market value of equity ownership shares outstanding}}{\text{Number of shares}}$$

By contrast, the historical or book value of the FI's common equity per share (BV) is equal to

$$BV = \frac{\begin{array}{c}\text{Common} \\ \text{shares}\end{array} + \begin{array}{c}\text{Contributed} \\ \text{surplus}\end{array} + \begin{array}{c}\text{Retained} \\ \text{earnings}\end{array} + \begin{array}{c}\text{Net unrealized foreign} \\ \text{exchange gains (losses)}\end{array}}{\text{Number of common shares outstanding}}$$

market-to-book ratio
Ratio showing the discrepancy between the stock market value of an FI's equity and the book value of its equity.

The ratio MV/BV is often called the **market-to-book ratio** and shows the degree of discrepancy between the market value of an FI's equity capital as perceived by investors in the stock market and the book value of capital on its balance sheet. The lower this ratio, the more the book value of capital *overstates* the true equity or economic net worth position of an FI as perceived by investors in the capital market.

Given such discrepancies, why do regulators and FIs continue to oppose the implementation of market value accounting?

Arguments against Market Value Accounting

The first argument against market value (*MV*) accounting is that it is difficult to implement. This may be especially true for smaller FIs with large amounts of non-traded assets such as small loans on their balance sheets. When it is impossible to determine accurate market prices or values for assets, marking to market may be done only with error. A counterargument to this is that the error resulting from the use of market valuation of non-traded assets is still likely to be less than that resulting from the use of original book or historical valuation since the market value approach does not require all assets and liabilities to be traded. As long as current and expected cash flows on an asset or liability and an appropriate discount rate can be specified, approximate market values can always be imputed (see CreditMetrics, described in Appendix 12A at the Online Learning Centre). Further, with the growth of loan sales and asset securitization (see Chapters 26 and 27), indicative market prices are available on an increasing variety of loans.

The second argument against market value accounting is that it introduces an unnecessary degree of variability into an FI's earnings—and thus net worth—because paper capital gains and losses on assets are passed through the FI's income statement. Critics argue that reporting unrealized capital gains and losses is distortionary if the FI actually plans to hold these assets to maturity. Insurers and FI managers argue that in many cases they do hold loans and other assets to maturity and, therefore, never actually realize capital gains or losses. Further, regulators have argued that they may be forced to close FIs too early—especially during periods of extreme market stress. If an interest rate spike is only temporary, capital losses on securities can be quickly turned into capital gains as rates fall again (e.g., if interest rates are mean reverting, as much empirical evidence shows). The counterargument is that FIs are increasingly trading, selling, and securitizing assets rather than holding them to maturity. Further, the failure to reflect capital gains and losses from interest rate changes means that the FI's equity position fails to reflect its true interest rate risk exposure.

The third argument against market value accounting is that FIs are less willing to accept longer-term asset exposures, such as mortgage loans and business loans, if these assets have to be continuously marked to market to reflect changing credit quality and interest rates. For example, as shown in Chapter 9, long-term assets are more interest rate-sensitive than are short-term assets. The concern is that market value accounting may interfere with FIs' special functions as lenders and monitors (see Chapter 1) and may even result in (or accentuate) a major credit crunch. Of the three arguments against market value accounting, this one is probably the most persuasive to regulators concerned about small-business finance and economic growth.

Having discussed the advantages and disadvantages of book- and market-based measures of an FI's capital, we should note that most FI regulators have chosen some form of book value accounting standard to measure an FI's capital adequacy. The major exception is the U.S. Securities and Exchange Commission (SEC). Along with the NYSE and other major stock exchanges, the SEC imposes on securities firms, retail brokers, and specialists a capital or net worth rule that is, for all intents and purposes, a market value accounting rule.[5]

www.sec.gov

---

[5] The Canadian securities industry is regulated provincially/territorially, but the formation of a national security regulator is under discussion (see Chapter 4) and therefore the regulations for securities firms are not discussed here. The provincial/territorial regulatory bodies and the Investment Industry Regulatory Organization of Canada (IIROC, www.iiroc.ca) require regulatory capital calculations of their members. The 202 member firms reported book value of shareholders' equity to be $13.9 billion compared to regulatory capital of $27.5 billion in Q1, 2009.

Next, we examine the capital adequacy rules imposed in two key FI sectors: (1) deposit-taking institutions and (2) insurance companies. The capital adequacy rules currently differ considerably across these sectors. Nevertheless, there is a clear trend toward similar risk-based capital rules in the banking and insurance (both P&C and life) industries. We discuss this trend in more detail in the remainder of the chapter.

CONCEPT QUESTIONS	1. Why is an FI economically insolvent when its net worth is negative?
	2. What are the major components of an FI's book equity?
	3. Is book value accounting for loan losses backward-looking or forward-looking?
	4. What does a market-to-book ratio that is less than 1 imply about an FI's performance?

CAPITAL ADEQUACY FOR DEPOSIT-TAKING INSTITUTIONS

Actual Capital Rules

Since 1988, Canadian banks and federally regulated trust and loan companies have faced two different capital requirements: an asset to capital multiple and a risk-based capital ratio that is in turn subdivided into a Tier 1 capital risk-based ratio and a total capital (Tier 1 plus Tier 2 capital) risk-based ratio. We describe these in more detail next.

The Assets to Capital Multiple (ACM)

www.osfi-bsif.gc.ca

The assets to capital multiple (ACM) is reported to OSFI by banks and federally regulated trust and loan companies in Canada. It measures the ratio of the book value of assets to the book value of total capital. Total assets include off-balance-sheet items as specified by OSFI. Total capital is the FI's risk-based capital and includes common equity (book value) plus qualifying cumulative perpetual preferred stock plus minority interests in equity accounts of consolidated subsidiaries. The assets to capital multiple is calculated as follows:

$$\text{ACM} = \frac{\text{Total assets (including specified off-balance-sheet items)}}{\text{Total capital}} \leq 20$$

Total assets = All on-balance-sheet assets plus notional amounts of selected off-balance-sheet items (direct credit substitutes such as letters of credit and guarantees, transaction-related contingencies, trade-related contingencies, and sale and repurchase agreements)

Total capital = Net Tier 1 capital + Net Tier 2 capital (described below)

The higher the assets to capital multiple, the greater is the leverage and therefore OSFI requires that the multiple be less than 20, but may set the multiple higher or lower for each deposit-taking institution based on "such factors as operating and management experience, strength of parent, earnings, diversification of assets and appetite for risk."[6] At year-end 2008, the assets to capital multiple for Canadian banks ranged from 16.4 for Bank of Montreal to 20.1 for the Royal Bank, as shown in Table 20–7. An individual FI trades off regulatory requirements for safety and soundness with the cost of holding capital.

---

[6] A table of OSFI guidelines, including the reporting format and the rationale used for the evaluation of the risk-based capital of all federally regulated FIs, is available at OSFI's website at www.osfi-bsif.gc.ca.

TABLE 20–7
Assets to Capital Multiples for Canadian Banks as at October 31, 2008

Source: 2008 annual reports

Name	Assets to Capital Multiple*
Bank of Montreal	16.4
Bank of Nova Scotia	18.0
CIBC	17.9
National Bank	16.7
Royal Bank	20.1
TD Bank	19.3

*Total assets and off-balance-sheet instruments as specified by OSFI, divided by total capital (adjusted net Tier 1 and adjusted Tier 2). Unless otherwise specified by OSFI, total assets can be a maximum of 20 times capital.

Unfortunately, the assets to capital multiple has three problems as a measure of capital adequacy:

1. *Market value.* Even if OSFI closed an FI before its multiple reached an astronomical level, the market value of the FI's assets could have resulted in a negative market value net worth. That is, there is no assurance that depositors and regulators (including taxpayers) are adequately protected against losses. Many U.S. FIs that were closed with low book capital values in the 1980s had negative net worth on a market value basis exceeding 30 percent.

2. *Asset risk.* By taking the numerator of the assets to capital multiple as total assets, the leverage ratio fails to take into account the different credit, interest rate, and other risks of the assets that constitute total assets.

3. *Off-balance-sheet activities.* Despite the massive growth in off-balance-sheet activities, only off-balance-sheet direct credit substitutes are included in the calculation. Thus, even though other derivatives may contribute greatly to an FI's risk, for the purposes of the ACM, no capital is required to be held to meet the potential insolvency risks involved with such contingent assets and liabilities.

Risk-Based Capital Ratios: Basel II

www.bis.org

Basel Agreement
The requirement to impose risk-based capital ratios on banks in major industrialized countries.

In light of the weaknesses of the simple ACM ratio just described, Canadian and U.S. bank regulators formally agreed with other member countries of the Bank for International Settlements (BIS) to implement two new risk-based capital ratios for all commercial banks under their jurisdiction. The BIS phased in and fully implemented these risk-based capital ratios on January 1, 1993, under what has become known as the **Basel** (or Basle) **Agreement** (now called Basel I). The 1993 Basel Agreement explicitly incorporated the different credit risks of assets (both on and off the balance sheet) into capital adequacy measures. This was followed with a revision in 1998 in which market risk was incorporated into risk-based capital in the form of an add-on to the 8 percent (10 percent required by OSFI) ratio for credit risk exposure (see Chapter 11). In 2001, the BIS issued a consultative document, *The New Basel Capital Accord,* that proposed the incorporation of operational risk into capital requirements (see Chapter 16 and below) and updated the credit risk assessments in the 1993 agreement.[7]

---

[7] See Basel Committee on Banking Supervision, *The New Basel Capital Accord,* January 2001; *Potential Modifications to the Committee's Proposals,* November 2001; *The New Basel Capital Accord,* April 2003; and *International Convergence of Capital Measurement and Capital Standards,* June 2004, www.bis.org.

The new Basel Accord or Agreement (Basel II) was adopted by Canadian banks on November 1, 2008. Basel II consists of three mutually reinforcing pillars (illustrated in Figure 20–1), which together contribute to the safety and soundness of the financial system. Pillar 1 covers regulatory minimum capital requirements for credit, market, and operational risk. The measurement of market risk did not change from that adopted in 1998 and is presented in Chapter 10. Basel II allows a range of options for addressing both credit and operational risk. Two options are allowed for the measurement of credit risk. The first is the standardized approach, discussed below, and the second is an internal ratings-based (IRB) approach—see Appendix 20A at the Online Learning Centre. The standardized approach is similar to that of the 1993 agreement, but is more risk-sensitive. Under the IRB approach, banks are allowed to use their internal estimates of borrower credit-worthiness to assess credit risk in their portfolios (using their own internal rating systems and credit scoring models) subject to strict methodological and disclosure standards as well as explicit approval by the bank's supervising regulator (OSFI).[8] Three different approaches are available to measure operational risk: the basic indicator, standardized, and advanced measurement approaches. We discussed these briefly in Chapter 16 and will do so in more detail below.

In Pillar 2, the BIS stresses the importance of the regulatory supervisory review process as a critical complement to minimum capital requirements. Specifically, Basel II provides procedures through which regulators ensure that each bank has sound internal processes in place to assess the adequacy of its capital and set targets for capital that are commensurate with the bank's specific risk profile. Pillar 3 encourages market discipline by developing a set of requirements on the disclosure of capital structure, risk exposures, and capital adequacy. Such disclosure

FIGURE 20–1
Basel II Pillars of
Capital Regulation

Pillar 1	Pillar 2	Pillar 3
Calculation of regulatory minimum capital requirements	Regulatory supervisory review so as to complement and enforce minimum capital requirements calculated under Pillar 1	Requirements on rules for disclosure of capital structure, risk exposures, and capital adequacy so as to increase FI transparency and enhance market/investor discipline
1. Credit risk: On-balance-sheet and off-balance-sheet (standardized vs. internal ratings-based approach)		
2. Market risk (standardized vs. internal ratings-based approach)		
3. Operational risk (basic indicator vs. standardized vs. advanced measurement approach)		

---

[8] Several papers have debated the ability and practicalities of implementing internal bank models. For an application to Canadian banks see M. Illing and G. Paulin, *The New Basel Accord and the Cyclical Behaviour of Bank Capital,* Bank of Canada, Working Paper No. 2004–30, 2004.

requirements allow market participants to assess critical information describing the risk profile and capital adequacy of banks.

OSFI currently enforces the Basel II risk-based capital ratios as well as the ACM in Canada. Unlike the simple assets to capital multiple ratio, the calculation of these risk-based capital adequacy measures is quite complex. Their major innovation is to distinguish among the different credit risks of assets on the balance sheet and to identify the credit risk inherent in instruments off the balance sheet by using **total risk-weighted assets** (RWA) as the denominator in these capital adequacy ratios. In a very rough fashion, these capital ratios mark to market a bank's on- and off-balance-sheet positions to reflect its credit risk. Further, additional capital charges must be held against market risk and operational risk.

In the measurement of a bank's risk-based capital adequacy, its capital is the standard by which each of these risks is measured.

Capital

OSFI requires all banks and federally regulated trust and loan companies to report their components of capital and capital adequacy ratios quarterly. Table 20–8 shows this information for domestic banks, trusts, and loan companies as reported to OSFI at the end of the first quarter of 2009.

Basel II divides capital into Tier 1 and Tier 2. Tier 1 capital is primary or core capital; Tier 2 capital is supplementary capital. The total capital that the FI holds is defined as the sum of Tier 1 and Tier 2 capital, and it is this total capital that is used as the denominator in the assets to capital multiple as well as in the capital adequacy ratios discussed below.

Tier 1 Capital   Tier 1 capital is closely linked to an FI's book value of equity, reflecting the concept of the core capital contribution of an FI's owners. Basically, it includes the book value of common equity, non-cumulative perpetual preferred shares, innovative instruments as defined by OSFI, interests in subsidiaries, and less intangible assets and goodwill. To be included as Tier 1 capital, an item must be intended to be permanent. As can be seen from Table 20–8, the types of Tier 1 capital used by banks, trusts, and loan companies differs.

Tier 2 Capital   Tier 2 capital is a broad array of secondary capital resources that includes non-perpetual preferred shares as well as subordinated debt and non-controlling interests in subsidiaries.

Tier 3 Capital   Tier 3 capital is subordinated debt that can be used only to offset part of the capital requirements for market risk.

In addition, in order to ensure the stability of the capital provided by the FI, limitations are placed on the capital components as follows:

1. Strongly capitalized deposit-taking institutions will have innovative instruments and perpetual preferred shares less than 25 percent of net Tier 1 capital.
2. Innovative instruments will be less than 15 percent of net Tier 1 capital.
3. Tier 2 capital will be less than 100 percent of Tier 1 capital.
4. Limited life instruments will be less than 50 percent of net Tier 1 capital.

We first look at how this capital is used as a cushion against credit risk using the BIS standardized approach for Basel II as applied by OSFI. We also examine the required add-ons to capital under Basel II that cushion a bank against market and operational risk.

---

total risk-weighted assets
On- and off-balance-sheet assets whose values are adjusted for approximate credit, market, and operational risk as defined by OSFI and the BIS.

TABLE 20–8   Components of Capital and Capital Ratios for Domestic Banks, Trusts, and Loan Companies, as at Q1, 2009 ($ thousands)

Capital Elements	Domestic Banks (21 firms)	Trusts (47 firms)	Loans (19 firms)
Tier 1			
Common shares for accounting purposes	$ 46,466,038	$ 4,509,396	$ 3,855,788
Less: Trading in short positions of own shares (gross)	8,823	0	0
Common shares for capital purposes	46,457,215	4,509,396	3,855,788
Contributed surplus	834,658	1,576,936	2,696,340
Retained earnings for accounting purposes	78,334,825	1,437,511	3,199,227
Less: Accumulated net after-tax fair value gains (losses) arising from changes in institution's own credit risk	345,529	2	0
Retained earnings for capital purposes	77,989,296	1,437,509	3,199,227
Accumulated net after-tax foreign currency translation adjustment reported in OCI*	− 1,773,510	0	0
Accumulated net after-tax unrealized holding loss on available-for-sale equities reported in OCI	− 1,292,408	− 38,508	0
For future use	151,838	0	0
Non-cumulative perpetual preferred shares	17,408,593	129,192	55,499
Innovative instruments included in Tier 1 capital	14,637,578	0	0
Non-controlling interests in subsidiaries	1,153,858	20,060	0
Gross Tier 1 capital	**155,567,116**	**7,634,585**	**9,806,854**
Deduct:			
Goodwill	34,073,975	118,847	7,575
Intangible assets in excess of limits	34,561	61,084	0
Net Tier 1 capital	**121,458,579**	**7,454,654**	**9,799,279**
Deduct:			
Gains recorded on securitization	592,880	23,586	113,857
Back-to-back inter-institutional placements of new capital issues	0	0	0
50/50 and other deductions from Tier 1 capital	7,420,242	39,175	77,760
Total deductions from net Tier 1 capital	8,013,122	62,761	191,617
Adjusted net Tier 1 capital	**$ 113,445,457**	**7,391,893**	**9,607,662**
Tier 2A			
Preferred shares	$ 0	$ 63,112	$ 8,000
Subordinated debt (qualifying 99-year debentures)	6,463,013	433,650	96,000
Eligible allowances	2,834,531	58,893	497
Non-controlling interests in subsidiaries (hybrid capital instruments)	0	0	0
Accumulated net after-tax unrealized holding gain on available-for-sale equity securities reported in OCI	5,181	2,710	18
For future use	0	0	0
Total Tier 2A capital	**$ 9,302,726**	**$ 558,365**	**$ 104,515**
Tier 2B			
Instruments qualifying for limited inclusion in Tier 2B	$ 3,024,594	$ 0	$ 0
Book value of:			
Preferred shares	0	148,050	151
Subordinated debt	32,970,208	898,014	734,102
Non-controlling interests in subs (subordinated term instruments)	0	0	0
Less: Accumulated amortization for capital adequacy purposes	482,792	0	0
Total Tier 2B capital	**$ 35,512,010**	**$ 1,046,064**	**$ 734,253**

(Continued)

TABLE 20–8 (*Concluded*)

Total Tier 2 capital	$ 44,814,736	$ 1,604,429	$ 838,768
Deduct:			
Back-to-back inter-institutional placements of new Tier 2 capital issues	0	0	0
50/50 and other deductions from Tier 2 capital	13,074,005	24,304	74,774
Total deductions from Tier 2 capital	13,074,004	24,304	74,774
Adjusted Tier 2 capital	$ 31,740,730	$ 1,580,125	$ 763,994
Total adjusted net Tier 1 and adjusted Tier 2 capital	$ 145,186,188	$ 8,972,017	$10,371,656
Tier 3 capital (for market risk)	$ 0	$ 0	$ 0
Total capital	$ 145,186,188	$ 8,972,017	$10,371,656
Risk-Weighted Assets			
Total Credit Risk	$ 941,049,316	$ 27,379,624	$21,633,485
Market Risk	59,211,147	0	0
Operational Risk	125,523,711	5,725,435	5,210,413
Total risk-weighted assets	1,125,784,175	33,105,056	26,843,898
Adjustment for floor	0	2,652,658	4,595,038
Adjusted risk-weighted assets	$ 1,125,784,175	$ 35,757,712	$31,438,935
Capital ratios:			
Tier 1 ratio	10.08	20.67	30.56
Total ratio	12.90	25.09	32.99
Assets to capital multiple	17.07	13.22	14.67

*OCI = Other comprehensive income

Source: OSFI, www.osfi-bsif.gc.ca.

Minimum Capital Requirements

total risk-based capital ratio
The ratio of the total capital to the risk-weighted assets of an FI.

To be adequately capitalized, a bank must hold a minimum ratio of total capital (Tier 1 core capital plus Tier 2 supplementary capital) to risk-weighted assets of 10 percent; that is, its **total risk-based capital ratio** is calculated as

$$\text{Total risk-based capital ratio} = \frac{\text{Total capital (Tier 1 + Tier 2)}}{\text{Risk-weighted assets}} \geq 10\%$$

Tier 1 (core) capital ratio
The ratio of core capital to the risk-weighted assets of an FI.

In addition, the Tier 1 core capital component of total capital has its own minimum guideline. The **Tier 1 (core) capital ratio** is calculated as

$$\text{Tier 1 (core) capital ratio} = \frac{\text{Core capital (Tier 1)}}{\text{Risk-weighted assets}} \geq 7\%$$

That is, of the 10 percent total risk-based capital ratio, a minimum of 8 percent has to be held in core or primary capital.[9]

For both minimum capital ratios, total risk-weighted assets (RWA) shown in Table 20–8 are calculated as

$$\text{RWA} = \text{Credit RWA} + 12.5 \times \text{Operational risk} + 12.5 \times \text{Market risk}$$

The Tier 1 ratio for the domestic banks in Table 20–8 is therefore calculated as

$$\text{Tier 1 ratio} = \frac{\$113,445,457}{\$1,125,784,175} = 10.08$$

---

[9] Basel II requires Tier 1 ≥ 4, total capital ≥ 8. OSFI sets higher capital ratios for Canadian FIs. See www.osfi-bsif.gc.ca.

Credit RWA using the standardized approach discussed below includes on- and off-balance-sheet risk-weighted assets. The minimum capital requirement for operational risk is calculated using one of the approaches specified by OSFI. The capital charge for market risk is calculated using a standardized model or an FI's internal model that has been approved by OSFI. The operational risk and market risk amounts are multiplied by 12.5, which is the reciprocal of the minimum Basel II total capital requirement of 8 percent (see footnote 9).

Our approach below is intended to give a flavour of the capital requirements for Canadian federally regulated FIs. As shown in Table 20–8, there are many adjustments to capital and risk-weighted assets that make the calculations extremely complex. As well, the regulatory system is evolving since the 2007–2008 market turmoil and the deficiencies identified in Basel II since its implementation. The reader is advised to visit OSFI's website as well as the BIS website for the latest capital rules.

In addition to their use to define adequately capitalized FIs, risk-based capital ratios—along with the assets to capital multiple—also define the adequacy of capital in OSFI's assessment criteria. OSFI rates the adequacy of an FI's capital in four categories from "Strong" to "Weak" as summarized in Table 20–9. In applying these criteria, OSFI also looks at the specific institution and whether its capital management policies are appropriate

www.osfi-bsif.gc.ca

www.bis.org

TABLE 20–9   OSFI's Assessment Criteria for Rating Capital Adequacy

ROLE OF CAPITAL

Capital is a source of financial support to protect an institution against unexpected losses, and is, therefore, a key contributor to its safety and soundness. Capital management is the ongoing process of raising and maintaining capital at levels sufficient to support planned operations. For complex institutions, it also involves allocation of capital to recognize the level of risk in its various activities. The assessment is made in the context of the nature, scope, complexity, and risk profile of an institution.

ADEQUACY OF CAPITAL

The following statements describe the rating categories used in assessing capital adequacy and capital management policies and practices of an institution. Capital adequacy includes both the level and quality of capital. The assessment is made in the context of the nature, scope, complexity, and risk profile of an institution.

Strong

Capital adequacy is strong for the nature, scope, complexity, and risk profile of the institution, and meets OSFI's target levels. The trend in capital adequacy over the next 12 months is expected to remain positive. Capital management policies and practices are superior to generally accepted industry practices.

Acceptable

Capital adequacy is appropriate for the nature, scope, complexity, and risk profile of the institution and meets OSFI's target levels. The trend in capital adequacy over the next 12 months is expected to remain positive. Capital management policies and practices meet generally accepted industry practices.

Needs Improvement

Capital adequacy is not always appropriate for the nature, scope, complexity, and risk profile of the institution and, although meeting minimum regulatory requirements, may not meet, or is trending below, OSFI's target levels. The trend in capital adequacy over the next 12 months is expected to remain uncertain. Capital management policies and practices may not meet generally accepted industry practices.

Weak

Capital adequacy is inappropriate for the nature, scope, complexity, and risk profile of the institution and does not meet, or marginally meets, minimum regulatory requirements. The trend in capital adequacy over the next 12 months is expected to remain negative. Capital management policies and practices do not meet generally accepted industry practices.

Source: OSFI, www.osfi-bsif.gc.ca.

and have sufficient senior management and board of directors oversight. OSFI's examination of the management of capital would short-circuit the incentive for an FI to increase its risk under certain circumstances, as has been suggested by some research.[10]

Calculating Risk-Based Capital Ratios

Credit Risk-Weighted Assets (RWA)

Under Basel II capital adequacy rules, risk-weighted (RWA) assets represent the denominator of the risk-based capital ratio. Two components make up credit risk-weighted assets: (1) credit risk-weighted on-balance-sheet assets, and (2) credit risk-weighted off-balance-sheet assets.

Credit Risk-Weighted On-Balance-Sheet Assets under Basel II

A major criticism of the original Basel Agreement was that individual risk weights depend on the broad categories of borrowers (i.e., sovereigns, banks, or corporates). For example, under Basel I all corporate loans had a risk weight of 100 percent regardless of the borrowing firm's credit risk. The Basel II standardized approach aligns regulatory capital requirements more closely with the key elements of banking risk by introducing a wider differentiation of credit risk weights. Accordingly, compared with Basel I, the standardized approach of Basel II attempts to produce capital ratios more in line with the actual economic risks that FIs are facing.

Under the standardized approach of Basel II, each bank assigns its assets to one of seven categories of credit risk exposure: 0 percent, 20 percent, 35 percent, 50 percent, 75 percent, 100 percent, or 150 percent. Table 20–10 lists the key categories and assets in these categories. The main features are that cash and claims on governments with a high credit rating (S&P rating AAA to AA− or an equivalent rating from another rating agency) attract a 0 percent risk weight. The risk weights increase as the credit rating declines. So, for example, a loan to a corporation with an A+ to A− rating is given a 50 percent risk weighting, while a loan to a firm with a credit rating below BB− attracts a 150 percent risk weighting, making it costlier for the FI. However, the appropriateness of using rating agency credit ratings in assigning risk weights has been criticized since the subprime crisis. See Basel Committee on Banking Supervision, *Stocktaking on the Use of Credit Ratings,* June 2009.

To calculate the credit risk-weighted assets of the bank, we multiply the dollar amount of assets it has in each category by the appropriate risk weight.

EXAMPLE 20–1

Calculation of On-Balance-Sheet Credit Risk-Weighted Assets under Basel II

Consider the bank's balance sheet in Table 20–11, categorized according to the risk weights of Basel II. Under Basel II, the credit risk-weighted value of the bank's on-balance-sheet assets would be

$$\begin{aligned}\text{Credit risk-weighted on-balance-sheet assets} = &\ 0(8\,\text{m} + 13\,\text{m} + 60\,\text{m} + 50\,\text{m} + 42\,\text{m} \\ &+ 10\,\text{m}) + 0.2(10\,\text{m} + 10\,\text{m} + 20\,\text{m} + 55\,\text{m}) \\ &+ 0.35\,(342) + 0.5\,(75\,\text{m}) \\ &+ 1(390\,\text{m} + 108\,\text{m} + 22\,\text{m}) + 1.5(10\,\text{m}) = 711.2\ \text{million}\end{aligned}$$

The simple book value of on-balance-sheet assets is $1,225 million, its credit risk-weighted value under Basel II is $711.2 million.

---

[10] It has been argued that capital adequacy rules may induce a DTI to make portfolio choices that actually increase the risk of the FI. The intuition behind the result is that under binding capital requirements, an additional unit of equity tomorrow is more valuable to an FI. If issuing new equity is excessively costly, the only possibility to increase equity tomorrow is to increase risk today in the hope that high-risk investments produce higher returns and thus boost the retained earnings component of equity tomorrow. Thus, some view higher minimum capital requirements as inducing a greater, not lesser, risk of FI insolvency (e.g., if the high-risk investments result in significant losses rather than profits).

TABLE 20–10   Summary of the Risk-Based Capital Standards for On-Balance-Sheet Items under Basel II

Risk Categories	
Weight	**Details**
0%	Cash, gold bullion
	Claims on (or claims guaranteed by) sovereign governments and central banks with an external (e.g., S&P) credit rating of AAA to AA−
	Claims on provincial and territorial governments
	Claims on specified multilateral development banks (MDBs)
	NHA-insured residential mortgages and NHA mortgage-backed securities guaranteed by CMHC
20%	Claims on countries with credit ratings of A+ to A−
	Claims on banks and securities firms of countries with external credit ratings of AAA to AA−
	Claims on multilateral development banks and corporate entities with external credit ratings of AAA to AA−
	Cheques and cash items in transit
35%	Residential mortgages (uninsured, maximum loan-to-value ratio of 80%)
	Mortgage-backed securities secured against qualifying residential mortgages
50%	Claims on countries with credit ratings of BBB+ to BBB−
	Claims on banks and securities firms of countries with credit ratings of A+ to A−
	Claims on MDBs with credit ratings from A+ to BBB−
	Claims on corporate entities with credit ratings of A+ to A−
75%	Claims on retail customers and small businesses
	Uninsured residential mortgages with a loan-to-value ratio > 80%
100%	Claims on countries with credit ratings of BB+ to B−
	Claims on banks and securities firms of countries with credit ratings of BBB+ to B−
	Claims on MDBs with credit ratings from BB+ to B−
	Claims on corporate customers with credit ratings of BBB+ to BB−
	Claims on governments, banks, securities firms, and corporate entities that are not rated
	Premises, plant, equipment, other fixed assets, real estate
	Future income taxes, prepaid expenses
150%	Claims on countries, multilateral development banks, banks and securities firms below B− and corporate entities with credit ratings below BB−

Note: Claims on public sector entities (PSEs) (e.g., school boards, hospitals, universities, municipalities) are ranked one category above the sovereign risk weight.

Source: OSFI, *Capital Adequacy Requirement (CAR)—Simpler Approaches.* Effective November 2007, www.osfi-bsif.gc.ca.

Credit Risk-Weighted Off-Balance-Sheet Activities

The credit risk-weighted value of on-balance-sheet assets is only one component of the capital ratio denominator; the other is the credit risk-weighted value of the bank's off-balance-sheet (OBS) activities. These OBS activities represent contingent rather than actual claims against deposit-taking institutions (see Chapter 13). Thus, regulations require that capital be held not against the full face value of these items, but against an amount equivalent to any eventual on-balance-sheet credit risk these securities might create for a deposit-taking institution. Therefore, in calculating the credit risk-weighted asset values of these OBS items we must first convert them into **credit-equivalent amounts**—amounts equivalent to an on-balance-sheet item. Further, the calculation of the credit risk-weighted values of the off-balance-sheet activities involves some initial segregation of these activities. In particular, the calculation of the credit risk exposure or the credit risk-weighted asset amounts of contingent or guaranty contracts such as letters of credit differs from the calculation of the credit risk-weighted asset amounts for foreign exchange and interest rate forward, option, and swap contracts. We consider the

credit-equivalent amount

The on-balance-sheet equivalent credit risk exposure of an off-balance-sheet item.

TABLE 20–11   **Bank's Balance Sheet under Basel II ($ millions)**

Weight	Assets		Liabilities/Equity		Capital Class
0%	Cash, gold bullion	$ 8	Demand deposits	$ 150	
	Deposits with the Bank of Canada	13	Notice deposits	500	
	Securities issued or guaranteed by the Government of Canada	60	Fixed-term deposits	400	
	Securities issued or guaranteed by a Canadian province or territory or agents of the federal, provincial, or territorial governments	50	Advances from the Bank of Canada	80	
	CMHC mortgage-backed securities	42			
	Goodwill and intangibles	10			
20	Cheques and items in transit	10	Non-controlling interests in subsidiaries (subordinated)	15	Tier 2
	Loan to multilateral development banks, AA− rated	10	Subordinated debt	15	Tier 2
	Securities issued or guaranteed by a Canadian municipal or school corporation	20	Preferred shares, non-perpetual	5	Tier 2
	Corporate loans, AAA− rated	55			
35	Residential one- to four-family mortgages (uninsured)	342	Common shares	30	Tier 1
			Contributed surplus	0	Tier 1
50	Corporate loans, A rated	75	Retained earnings	30	Tier 1
100	Corporate loans, BB+ rated	390	Non-cumulative perpetual preferred shares	10	Tier 1
	Loans to non-OECD countries, B+ rated	108	Non-controlling Tier 1 interests in subsidiaries	0	Tier 1
	Premises, equipment	22			
150	Corporate loans, CCC+ rated	10		$1225	
	Total assets	$1225			

Off-Balance-Sheet Items

	$80 m in two-year loan commitments to a large BB+ rated Canadian corporation
100%	$10 m direct credit substitute standby letters of credit issued to a BBB− rated Canadian corporation
	$50 million in commercial letters of credit issued to a BBB− rated Canadian corporation
50%	One fixed-floating interest rate swap for 4 years with notional dollar value of $100 m and replacement cost of $3 m
	One two-year Euro$ contract for $40 m with a replacement cost of −$1 m

credit risk-weighted asset value of OBS guarantee-type contracts and contingent contracts and then derivative or market contracts.

The Credit Risk-Weighted Asset Value of Off-Balance-Sheet Contingent Guarantee Contracts

Consider the appropriate conversion factors in Table 20–12.[11] Note that under Basel II, direct credit substitute standby letter of credit (SLC) guarantees issued by banks have a 100 percent conversion factor rating or credit-equivalent amount.

---

[11] "Appropriate" here means those factors used by the regulators and required to be used by banks rather than being equal to conversion factors that might be calculated from a contingent asset valuation (option) model. Indeed, regulators used no such valuation model in deriving the conversion factors in Table 20–12.

TABLE 20–12   **Credit Conversion Factors for Off-Balance-Sheet Contingent or Guarantee Contracts, Basel II**

Conversion Factor	
100%	Direct credit substitutes (general guarantees of indebtedness and guarantee-type instruments, including standby letters of credit serving as financial guarantees for, or supporting, loans and securities)
	Acquisitions of risk participation in bankers' acceptances and participation in direct credit substitutes (for example, standby letters of credit)
	Sale and repurchase agreements
	Forward agreements (contractual obligations) to purchase assets, including financing facilities with certain drawdown
	Written put options on specified assets with the characteristics of a credit enhancement[*]
50%	Transaction-related contingencies (e.g., bid bonds, performance bonds, warranties, and standby letters of credit related to a particular transaction)
	Commitments with an original maturity exceeding one year, including underwriting commitments and commercial credit lines
	Revolving underwriting facilities (RUFs), note issuance facilities (NIFs) and other similar arrangements
20%	Short-term, self-liquidating trade-related contingencies, including commercial/documentary letters of credit (Note: A 20% CCF is applied to both issuing and confirming banks)
	Commitments with an original maturity of one year or less
0%	Commitments that are unconditionally cancellable at any time without prior notice.

[*]Written put options (where premiums are paid up front) expressed in terms of market rates for currencies or financial instruments bearing no credit or equity risk are excluded from the framework.

Source: OSFI, www.osfi-bsif.gc.ca.

Similarly, sale and repurchase agreements and assets sold with recourse are also given a 100 percent conversion factor rating. Future performance-related SLCs and unused loan commitments of more than one year have a 50 percent conversion factor. Other loan commitments, those with one year or less to maturity, have a 20 percent credit conversion factor. Standard trade-related commercial letters of credit and bankers' acceptances sold have a 20 percent conversion factor.

Under Basel II, risk weights assigned to OBS contingent guarantee contracts are the same as if the bank had entered into the transactions as a principal. Thus, the credit ratings used to assign a credit risk weight for on-balance-sheet assets (listed in Table 20–10) are also used to assign credit risk weights on these OBS activities (e.g., issuing a commercial letter of credit to a CCC-rated counterparty would result in a risk weight of 150 percent).

EXAMPLE 20-2

Calculating Off-Balance-Sheet Contingent or Guarantee Contracts' Credit Risk-Weighted Assets

To see how OBS activities are incorporated into the risk-based ratio, we can extend Example 20–1 for the bank in Table 20–11. Assume that in addition to having $711.2 million in credit risk-weighted assets on its balance sheet, the bank also has the following off-balance-sheet contingencies or guarantees:

1. $80 million two-year loan commitments to a large BB+ rated Canadian corporation
2. $10 million direct credit substitute standby letters of credit issued to a BBB rated Canadian corporation
3. $50 million commercial letters of credit issued to a BBB− rated Canadian corporation

To find the risk-weighted asset value for these OBS items, we follow a two-step process.

Step 1. Convert OBS Values into On-Balance-Sheet Credit-Equivalent Amounts

In the first step we multiply the dollar amount outstanding of these items to derive the credit-equivalent amounts using the conversion factors (CF) listed in Table 20–12.

OBS Item	Face Value		Conversion Factor		Credit-Equivalent Amount
Two-year loan commitment	$80 m	×	0.5	=	$40 m
Standby letter of credit	10 m	×	1.0	=	10 m
Commercial letter of credit	50 m	×	0.2	=	10 m

Thus, the credit equivalent amounts of loan commitments, standby letters of credit, and commercial letters of credit are, respectively, $40, $10, and $10 million. These conversion factors convert an OBS item into an equivalent credit or on-balance-sheet item.

Step 2. Assign the OBS Credit-Equivalent Amount to a Risk Category

In the second step we multiply these credit-equivalent amounts by their appropriate risk weights. The appropriate risk weight in each case depends on the underlying counterparty to the OBS activity, such as a municipality, a government, or a corporation. In our example, because each of the contingent guarantee contracts involves a Canadian corporation with a credit rating between BBB+ and BB–, each is assigned a risk weight of 100 percent.

OBS Item	Credit-Equivalent Amount		Risk Weight (w_i)		Risk-Weighted Asset Amount
Two-year loan commitment	$40 m	×	1.0	=	$40 m
Standby letter of credit	10 m	×	1.0	=	10 m
Commercial letter of credit	10 m	×	1.0	=	10 m
					$60 m

The bank's credit risk-weighted asset value of its OBS contingencies and guarantees is $60 million.

The Credit Risk-Weighted Asset Value of Off-Balance-Sheet Market Contracts or Derivative Instruments   In addition to having OBS contingencies and guarantees, modern FIs engage heavily in buying and selling OBS futures, options, forwards, swaps, caps, and other derivative securities contracts for interest rate and foreign exchange management and hedging reasons, as well as buying and selling such products on behalf of their customers (see Chapter 13). Each of these positions potentially exposes FIs to **counterparty credit risk,** that is, the risk that the counterparty (or other side of a contract) will default when suffering large actual or potential losses on its position. Such defaults mean that an FI would have to go back to the market to replace such contracts at (potentially) less favourable terms.

counterparty credit risk
The risk that the other side of a contract will default on payment obligations.

Under the risk-based capital ratio rules, a major distinction is made between exchange-traded derivative security contracts (e.g., the Montréal Exchange's exchange-traded options) and over-the-counter-traded instruments (e.g., forwards, swaps, caps, and floors). The credit or default risk of exchange-traded derivatives is approximately zero because when a counterparty defaults on its obligations, the exchange itself adopts the counterparty's obligations in full. However, no such guarantees exist for bilaterally agreed, over-the-counter contracts originated and traded outside organized exchanges. Hence, most OBS futures and options positions have no capital requirements for a bank while most forwards, swaps, caps, and floors do.[12]

As with contingent or guarantee contracts, the calculation of the risk-weighted asset values of OBS market contracts requires a two-step approach (under both Basel I and Basel II). First, we calculate a conversion factor to create credit-equivalent amounts. Second, we multiply the credit-equivalent amounts by the appropriate risk weights.

Step 1. Convert OBS Values into On-Balance-Sheet Credit-Equivalent Amounts.
We first convert the notional or face values of all non-exchange-traded swap, forward, and other derivative contracts into credit-equivalent amounts. The credit-equivalent amount itself is divided into a *potential exposure* element and a *current exposure* element. That is

$$\begin{array}{l} \text{Credit-equivalent amount} \\ \quad \text{of OBS derivative} \\ \quad \text{security items (\$)} \end{array} = \text{Potential exposure (\$)} + \text{Current exposure (\$)}$$

potential exposure
The risk that a counterparty to a derivative securities contract will default in the future.

The **potential exposure** component reflects the credit risk if the counterparty to the contract defaults in the *future*. The probability of such an occurrence depends on the future volatility of either interest rates for an interest rate contract or exchange rates for an exchange rate contract. The Bank of England and the Federal Reserve carried out an enormous number of simulations and found that FX rates were far more volatile than interest rates.[13] Thus, the potential exposure conversion factors in Table 20–13 are larger for foreign exchange contracts than for interest rate contracts. Also, note the larger potential exposure credit risk for longer-term contracts of all types.

current exposure
The cost of replacing a derivative securities contract at today's prices.

In addition to calculating the potential exposure of an OBS market instrument, a bank must calculate its **current exposure** with the instrument. This reflects the cost of replacing a contract if a counterparty defaults *today*. The bank calculates this *replacement cost* or *current exposure* by replacing the rate or price initially in the contract with the current rate or price for a similar contract and recalculates all

TABLE 20–13   Add-on Factors for Calculating Potential Future Credit Exposure Using the Current Exposure Method

Add-On Factors					
Residual Maturity	**Interest Rate Contracts**	**Foreign Exchange Rate and Gold Contracts**	**Equity**	**Precious Metals Except Gold**	**Other Commodities**
One year or less	0.0%	1.0%	6.0%	7.0%	10.0%
Over one year to five years	0.5%	5.0%	8.0%	7.0%	12.0%
Over five years	1.5%	7.5%	10.0%	8.0%	15.0%

Source: OSFI, *Capital Adequacy Requirements (CAR)—Simpler Approaches,* November 2007, www.osfi-bsif.gc.ca.

---

[12] This may create some degree of preference among banks for using exchange-traded hedging instruments rather than over-the-counter instruments, because using the former may save a bank costly capital resources. However, as we see in Chapters 23, 24, and 25, Canadian FIs trade mainly OTC contracts.

[13] The Bank of England and the Federal Reserve employed a Monte Carlo simulation approach in deciding on the size of the appropriate conversion factors. See C. W. Smith, C. W. Smithson, and D. S. Wilford, *Managing Financial Risk* (New York: Ballinger, 1990), pp. 225–256.

the current and future cash flows that would have been generated under current rate or price terms.[14] The bank discounts any future cash flows to give a current present value measure of the contract's replacement cost. If the contract's replacement cost is negative (i.e., the bank profits on the replacement of the contract if the counterparty defaults), regulations require the replacement cost (current exposure) to be set to zero. If the replacement cost is positive (i.e., the bank loses on the replacement of the contract if the counterparty defaults), this value is used as the measure of current exposure. Since each swap or forward is in some sense unique, calculating current exposure involves a considerable computer processing task for the bank's management information systems. Indeed, specialized service firms are likely to perform this task for smaller banks.[15]

Step 2. Assign the OBS Credit-Equivalent Amount to a Risk Category.   Once the current and potential exposure amounts are summed to produce the credit-equivalent amount for each contract, we multiply this dollar number by a risk weight to produce the final credit risk-weighted asset amount for OBS market contracts.

Under Basel II the appropriate risk weight is generally 1.0, or 100 percent. That is

$$\begin{array}{l} \text{Credit risk-weighted} \\ \text{value of OBS} \\ \text{market contracts} \end{array} = \text{Total credit-equivalent amount} \times 1.0 \text{ (risk weight)}$$

EXAMPLE 20–3

Calculating Off-Balance-Sheet Market Contract Credit Risk-Weighted Assets

Suppose the bank in Examples 20–1 and 20–2 had taken one interest rate hedging position in the fixed-floating interest rate swap market for four years with a notional dollar amount of $100 million and one two-year forward foreign exchange contract for $40 million (see Table 20–11).

Step 1

We calculate the credit-equivalent amount for each item or contract as follows:

			Potential Exposure + Current Exposure				
Type of Contract (remaining maturity)	**Notional Principal**	**×**	**Potential Exposure Conversion Factor**	**= Potential Exposure**	**Replacement Cost**	**Current Exposure**	**= Credit Equivalent Amount**
Four-year fixed–floating interest rate swap	$100 m	×	0.005	= **$0.5 m**	$3 m	**$3 m**	**$3.5 m**
Two-year forward foreign exchange contract	$ 40 m	×	0.050	= **$2 m**	−$1 m	**$0**	**$2 m**

For the four-year fixed-floating interest rate swap, the notional value (contract face value) of the swap is $100 million. Since this is a long-term (one to five years to maturity) interest rate

---

[14] For example, suppose a two-year forward foreign exchange contract was entered into in January 2010 at $1.55/£. In January 2011, the bank has to evaluate the credit risk of the contract, which now has one year remaining. To do this, it replaces the agreed forward rate $1.55/£ with the forward rate on current one-year forward contracts, $1.65/£. It then recalculates its net gain or loss on the contract if it had to be replaced at this price. This is the contract's replacement cost.

[15] One large New York money centre bank has to calculate, on average, the replacement cost of more than 6,000 different forward contracts alone.

market contract, its face value is multiplied by 0.005 to get a potential exposure or credit risk equivalent value of $0.5 million (see row 1 of Table 20–13). We add this potential exposure to the replacement cost (current exposure) of this contract to the bank. The replacement cost reflects the cost of having to enter into a new four-year fixed-floating swap agreement at today's interest rates for the remaining life of the swap should the counterparty default. Assuming that interest rates today are less favourable, on a present value basis, the cost of replacing the existing contract for its remaining life would be $3 million. Thus, the total credit equivalent amount—current plus potential exposures—for the interest rate swap is $3.5 million.

Next, look at the foreign exchange two-year forward contract of $40 million face value. Since this is a foreign exchange contract with a maturity of one to five years, the potential (future) credit risk is $40 million $\times$ 0.05, or $2 million (see row 2 in Table 20–13). However, its replacement cost is *minus* $1 million. That is, in this example our bank actually stands to gain if the counterparty defaults. Exactly why the counterparty would do this when it is in the money is unclear. However, regulators cannot permit a bank to gain from a default by a counterparty since this might produce all types of perverse risk-taking incentives. Consequently, as in our example, current exposure has to be set equal to zero (as shown). Thus, the sum of potential exposure ($2 million) and current exposure ($0) produces a total credit equivalent amount of $2 million for this contract. Since the bank has just two OBS derivative contracts, summing the two credit-equivalent amounts produces a total credit-equivalent amount of $3.5 m + $2 m = $5.5 million for the bank's OBS market contracts.

Step 2

The next step is to multiply this credit-equivalent amount by the appropriate risk weight. Specifically, to calculate the risk-weighted asset value for the bank's OBS derivative or market contracts, we multiply the credit-equivalent amount by the appropriate risk weight, which is generally 1.0 or 100 percent:

$$\begin{matrix} \text{Credit risk-weighted} & = & \$5.5 \text{ million} & \times & 1.0 & = \$5.5 \text{ million} \\ \text{asset value of} & & (\text{credit-equivalent} & & (\text{risk weight}) & \\ \text{OBS derivatives} & & \text{amount}) & & & \end{matrix}$$

Total Credit Risk-Weighted Assets under Basel II

Under Basel II, the total credit risk-weighted assets are $776.7 million ($711.2 million from on-balance-sheet activities, plus $60 million for the risk-weighted value of OBS contingencies and guarantees, plus $5.5 million for the risk-weighted value of OBS derivatives).

Netting under Basel II[16]

One criticism of the above method is that it ignores the netting of exposures. In response, OSFI has adopted a proposal put forward by the BIS that allows netting of off-balance-sheet derivative contracts as long as the bank has a bilateral netting contract that clearly establishes a legal obligation by the counterparty to pay or receive a single net amount on the different contracts.[17] Provided that such written contracts (Master Netting Agreements) are clearly documented by the bank, the new rules require the estimation of *net current exposure* and *net potential exposure* of those positions included in the bilateral netting contract. The sum of the net current exposure and the net potential exposure equals the total credit-equivalent amount.

---

[16] This section, which involves more technical material, may be included in or dropped from the chapter reading depending on the rigour of the course without harming the continuity of the chapter.

[17] See OSFI, *Capital Adequacy Requirements (CAR)—Simpler Approaches.* Effective November 2007, pp. 44–47.

The rules define net current exposure as the net sum of all positive and negative replacement costs (or mark-to-market values of the individual derivative contracts). If the sum of the replacement costs is positive, then the net current exposure equals the sum. If it is negative, the net current exposure is zero. The net potential exposure is defined by a formula that adjusts the gross potential exposure estimated earlier:

$$A_{net} = (0.4 \times A_{gross}) + (0.6 \times NPR \times A_{gross})$$

where A_{net} is the net potential exposure (or adjusted sum of potential future credit exposures), A_{gross} is the sum of the potential exposures of each contract, and NPR is the ratio of net current exposure or net replacement cost (NR) to gross current exposure. The 0.6 is the amount of potential exposure that is reduced as a result of netting.

The same example used in the previous section (without netting) will be used to show the effect of netting on the total credit-equivalent amount. *Here we assume that both contracts are with the same counterparty.*

$$A_{gross} = \$2.5 \text{ m} \quad \text{Net current exposure} = \$2 \text{ m} \quad \text{Current exposure} = \$3 \text{ m}$$

The net current exposure is the sum of the positive and negative replacement costs—that is, +$3 m and –$1 m = $2 m. The gross potential exposure (A_{gross}) is the sum of the individual potential exposures = $2.5 m. To determine the net potential exposure, the following formula is used:

$$A_{net} = (0.4 \times A_{gross}) + (0.6 \times NPR \times A_{gross})$$

$$NPR = \text{Net current exposure/Current exposure} = 2/3$$

$$A_{net} = (0.4 \times 2.5 \text{ m}) + (0.6 \times 2/3 \times 2.5 \text{ m})$$

$$= \$2 \text{ million}$$

$$\text{Total credit equivalent} = \text{Net potential exposure} + \text{Net current exposure}$$

$$= 2 \text{ m} + 2 \text{ m} = \$4 \text{ million}$$

$$\frac{\text{Risk-weighted asset value}}{\text{of OBS market contracts}} = \text{Total credit equivalent amount} \times 1.0 \text{(risk weight)}$$

$$= 4 \text{ m} \times 1.0 = \$4 \text{ million}$$

As can be seen, netting reduces the credit risk-weighted asset value from $5.5 million to $4 million.

Calculating the Overall Risk-Based Capital Position

After calculating the risk-weighted assets for a deposit-taking institution, the final step is to calculate the Tier 1 and total risk–based capital ratios.

EXAMPLE 20–4

Calculating the Overall Risk-Based Capital Position of a Bank

From Table 20–11, the bank's Tier 1 capital (common shares, retained earnings, non-cumulative perpetual preferred shares) less goodwill and intangible assets ($10 million) totals $60 million. Tier 2 capital (subordinated non-controlling interests in subsidiaries, subordinated debt, non-perpetual preferred shares) totals $35 million. The resulting total Tier 1 and Tier 2 capital is, therefore, $95 million.

We can now calculate our bank's overall capital adequacy Basel II risk-based capital requirements as

$$\text{Tier I (core) capital} = \frac{\$60 \text{ m}}{\$776.7 \text{ m}} = 7.72\%$$

and

$$\text{Total risk–based capital ratio} = \frac{\$95 \text{ m}}{\$776.7 \text{ m}} = 12.23\%$$

If the minimum Tier I capital ratio set by OSFI for this FI is 7 percent and the minimum total risk-based capital ratio required is 10 percent, the bank in our example has adequate capital considering only credit risk. However, we need to calculate the market risk and operational risk components as well.[18]

Interest Rate Risk, Market Risk, and Risk-Based Capital

From a regulatory perspective, a credit risk-based capital ratio is adequate only as long as a deposit-taking institution is not exposed to undue interest rate or market risk. The reason is that the risk-based capital ratio takes into account only the adequacy of a bank's capital to meet both its on- and off-balance-sheet credit risks. Not explicitly accounted for is the insolvency risk emanating from interest rate risk (duration mismatches) and market (trading) risk.

www.bis.org   To meet these criticisms, in 1993 the Bank for International Settlements developed additional capital requirements for interest rate risk (see Chapter 9) and market risk (see Chapter 10). As is discussed in Chapter 10, since 1998 DTIs have had to calculate an add-on to the 8 percent risk-based capital ratio to reflect their exposure to market risk. There are two approaches available to DTIs to calculate the size of this add-on: (1) the standardized model proposed by regulators and (2) the DTI's own internal market risk model. To date, no formal add-on has been required for interest rate risk.

Basel II states that banks should have interest rate risk measurement systems that assess the effects of interest rate changes on both earnings and economic value. These systems should provide meaningful measures of a bank's current levels of interest rate risk exposure, and should be capable of identifying any excessive exposures that might arise.[19]

Operational Risk and Risk-Based Capital

Basel II implemented an additional add-on to capital for operational risk. Prior to this proposal, the BIS had argued that the operational risk exposures of banks were adequately taken care of by the 8 percent credit risk-weighted ratio. But increased visibility of operational risks in recent years (see Chapter 16) has induced regulators

---

[18] With netting, the total credit risk–weighted assets ratio would have been $95 m/$775.2 m, or 12.25 percent under Basel II. Basel II distinguishes between performing and non-performing (impaired loans). Unsecured non-mortgage loans that are more than 90 days past due will be given a risk weight of 150 percent if specific loan loss provisions are less than 20 percent and 100 percent when specific provisions are more than 20 percent. Uninsured residential mortgages that are more than 90 days past due will be given a 100 percent risk weight. These requirements entail FIs to recognize and allow for impaired loans each reporting period.

[19] See Basel Committee on Banking Supervision, *Principles for the Management and Supervision of Interest Rate Risk*, July 2004, www.bis.org, and OSFI, *Guideline B-12, Interest Rate Risk Management-Sound Business and Financial Practices*, February 2005, www.osfi-bsif.gc.ca See also *Principles for Sound Stress Testing Practices and Supervision*, May 2009, www.bis.org.

to propose a separate capital requirement for operational risks. As noted above, the BIS now believes that operational risks are sufficiently important for deposit-taking institutions to devote resources to quantify such risks and to incorporate them separately into their assessment of their overall capital adequacy. In its 2001 and 2003 *Consultative Documents* the Basel committee outlined three specific methods by which deposit-taking institutions can calculate capital to protect against operational risk: the basic indicator approach, the standardized approach, and the advanced measurement approaches.[20]

The basic indicator approach is structured so that banks, on average, will hold 12 percent of their total regulatory capital for operational risk. This 12 percent target was based on a widespread survey conducted internationally of current practices by large banks.[21] To achieve this target, the basic indicator approach focuses on the gross income of the bank, that is, its net profits, or what is often called *value added*. This equals a bank's net interest income plus net non-interest income:

$$\text{Gross income} = \text{Net interest income} + \text{Net non-interest income}$$

According to BIS calculations, a bank that holds a fraction (alpha, α) of its gross income for operational risk capital, where alpha (α) is set at 15 percent, will generate enough capital for operational risk such that this amount will be 12 percent of its total regulatory capital holdings against all risks (i.e., credit, market, and operational risks). For example, under the basic indicator approach:

$$\text{Operational capital} = \alpha \times \text{Gross income}$$

or

$$= 0.15 \times \text{Gross income}$$

The problem with the basic indicator approach is that it is too aggregative, or "top–down," and does not differentiate at all among different areas in which operational risks may differ (e.g., Payment and Settlement may have a very different operational risk profile from Retail Brokerage).[22]

The standardized approach attemps to provide a finer differentiation of operational risks in a bank across different activity lines while still retaining a basically top–down approach. This second method, the standardized approach, divides activities into eight major business units and lines (shown in Table 20–14). Within each business line, there is a specified broad indicator (defined as beta, β) that reflects the scale or volume of a deposit-taking institution's activities in that area. The indicator relates to the gross income reported for a particular line of business. It serves as a rough proxy for the amount of operational risk within each of these lines. A capital charge is calculated by multiplying the β for each line by the indicator

---

[20] See Basel Committee on Banking Supervision, *International Convergence of Capital Measurement and Capital Standards,* June 2006, www.bis.org, and OSFI, *Capital Adequacy Requirements—Simpler Approaches,* Chapter 6, November 2007, February 2003, www.osfi-bsif.gc.ca.

[21] Research has found that the amount of capital held for operational risk according to these models will often exceed capital held for market risk and that the largest banks could choose to allocate several billion dollars in capital to operational risk. See P. DeFontnouvelle, V. Dejesus-Rueff, J. S. Jordan, and E. S. Rosengren, "Capital and Risk: New Evidence on Implications of Large Operational Losses," *Journal of Money, Credit, and Banking,* 38, 2006, pp. 1819–1846.

[22] A second issue is that the α term implies operational risk that is proportional to gross income. This ignores possible economies-of-scale effects that would make this relationship non-linear (non-proportional); that is, α might fall as bank profits and/or size grow.

TABLE 20–14
BIS Standardized Approach Business Units and Lines

Source: OSFI, *Capital Adequacy Requirements (CAR)—Simpler Approaches*, November 2007, Chapter 6, p. 131, www.osfi-bsif.gc.ca.

Business Line	Indicator	Capital Factors
Corporate finance	Gross income*	$\beta_1 = 18\%$
Trading and sales	Gross income	$\beta_2 = 18\%$
Retail banking	Gross income	$\beta_3 = 12\%$
Commercial banking	Gross income	$\beta_4 = 15\%$
Payment and settlement	Gross income	$\beta_5 = 18\%$
Agency services	Gross income	$\beta_6 = 15\%$
Asset management	Gross income	$\beta_7 = 12\%$
Retail brokerage	Gross income	$\beta_8 = 12\%$

*The indicator relates to gross income reported for the particular line of business.

assigned to the line and then summing these components. The βs reflect the importance of each activity in the average bank. The βs are set by regulators and are calculated from average industry figures from a selected sample of banks.

Suppose the industry β for corporate finance is 18 percent and gross income from the corporate finance line of business (the activity indicator) is $30 million for the bank. Then, the regulatory capital charge for this line for this year is

$$\text{Capital}_{\text{Corporate Finance}} = \beta \times \text{Gross income from the corporate finance line of}$$
$$\text{business for the bank}$$
$$= 18\% \times \$30 \text{ million}$$
$$= \$5,400,000$$

The total capital charge is calculated as the three-year average of the simple summation of the regulatory capital charge across each of the eight business lines.[23]

The third method, the advanced measurement approach, allows individual banks to rely on internal data for regulatory capital purposes subject to supervisory approval. Under the advanced measurement approach, supervisors require the bank to calculate its regulatory capital requirement as the sum of the expected loss (EL) and unexpected loss (UL) for each event type, as listed in Table 20–15. Internally generated operational risk measures used for regulatory capital purposes must be based on a minimum three-year observation period of internal loss data, whether the internal loss data are used directly to build the loss measure or to validate it. A bank's internal loss data must be comprehensive in that the data capture all material activities and exposures from all appropriate subsystems and geographic locations. Risk measures for different operational risk estimates are added for purposes of calculating the regulatory minimum capital requirement.[24]

Criticisms of the Risk-Based Capital Ratio

The risk-based capital requirement seeks to improve on the simple assets to capital multiple by (1) incorporating credit, market, and operational risks into the determination of capital adequacy; (2) more systematically accounting for credit risk differences among assets; (3) incorporating off-balance-sheet risk exposures; and

---

[23] The Basel Committee's *Loss Data Collection Exercise for Operational Risk* (March 2003), based on data provided by 89 banks from 19 countries, revealed that about 61 percent of operational loss events occurred in the retail area, with an average loss of $79,300. Also, only 0.9 percent of operational loss events occurred in the corporate finance area, but with an average loss of $646,600.

[24] See OSFI, *Guideline A-1, Capital Adequacy Requirements (CAR),* November 2007. FIs need OSFI's permission to use advanced measurement approaches. They also must conduct stress testing as outlined in Chapter 9, p. 358 of *Guideline A-1*.

TABLE 20–15
Operational Risk
Loss Event Types

Internal fraud   Losses due to acts of a type intended to defraud, misappropriate property, or circumvent regulations, the law, or company policy, excluding diversity/discrimination events, which involve at least one internal party.

External fraud   Losses due to third-party acts of a type intended to defraud, misappropriate property, or circumvent the law.

Employment practices and workplace safety   Losses arising from acts inconsistent with employment, health, or safety laws or agreements, from payment of personal injury claims, or from diversity/discrimination events.

Clients, products, and business practices   Losses arising from an unintentional or negligent failure to meet a professional obligation to specific clients (including fiduciary and suitability requirements) or from the nature or design of a product.

Damage to physical assets   Losses arising from loss or damage to physical assets from natural disaster or other events.

Business disruption and system failures   Losses arising from disruption of business or system failures.

Execution, delivery, and process management   Losses from failed transaction processing or process management or from relations with trade counterparties and vendors.

(4) applying a similar capital requirement across all the major deposit-taking institutions (and banking centres) in the world. Unfortunately, the requirements have a number of conceptual and applicability weaknesses in achieving these objectives:

1. *Risk weights.* It is unclear how closely the risk weight categories in Basel II reflect true credit risk. For example, corporate loans have risk weights between 20 and 150 percent under Basel II. Taken literally, these relative weights imply that some corporate loans are exactly four and a half times as risky as other loans.

2. *Risk weights based on external credit rating agencies.* While Basel II proposed reforms to improve on Basel I in measuring credit risk, that is, by replacing the single 100 percent risk weight for sovereign, bank, and corporate loans with different risk weights, depending on the loan's credit rating, it is unclear whether the risk weights accurately measure the relative (or absolute) risk exposures of individual borrowers. Moreover, Standard & Poor's and Moody's ratings are often accused of lagging behind rather than leading the business cycle. As a result, required capital may peak during a recession, when banks are least able to meet the requirements.[25]

3. *Portfolio aspects.* The BIS plans largely ignore credit risk portfolio diversification opportunities. As we discuss in Chapter 12, when returns on assets have negative or less than perfectly positive correlations, an FI may lower its portfolio risk through diversification. As constructed, the Basel II (standardized model) capital adequacy plan is essentially a linear risk measure that ignores correlations or covariances among assets and asset group credit risks—such as between

---

[25] E. I. Altman, S. T. Bharath, and A. Saunders, in "Credit Ratings and the BIS Reform Agenda," *Journal of Banking and Finance,* 2002, pp. 909–922, find that although the new BIS guidelines are an improvement over the original ones, several of the rating categories carry underweighted capital requirements, and that banks will continue to be motivated to skew their portfolios toward lower-rated loans. Moreover, relying on rating agencies to determine a borrower's credit risk questions the specialness of banks as monitors—see Chapter 1. Since the financial disruptions of 2007–2008, the procyclicality of bank capital is important to regulators. See Bank of Canada, *Financial System Review,* June 2009, pp. 31–63, for a discussion of this issue.

residential mortgages and corporate loans.[26] That is, the FI manager weights each asset separately by the appropriate risk weight and then sums those numbers to get an overall measure of credit risk. No account is taken of the covariances among asset risks between different counterparties (or risk weights).[27]

4. *FI specialness.* Giving private sector moderate- and high-risk corporate loans the highest credit risk weighting may reduce the incentive for deposit-taking institutions to make such loans relative to holding other assets. This may reduce the amount of loans to these businesses, as well as the degree of monitoring, and may have associated negative externality effects on the economy. That is, one aspect of banks' special functions—bank lending—may be muted.[28] This effect has been of great concern and controversy. Indeed, the high-risk weight given to loans relative to securities has been blamed in part for inducing a credit crunch and a reorientation of bank portfolios away from loans toward securities in the early 1990s.

5. *Excessive complexity.* Basel II raises the cost of regulation by adding new levels of complexity. The cost of developing and implementing new risk management systems is significant, and the benefits may turn out to be small. Initial calculations suggest that most banks using the IRB approach for operational risk will end up with a higher capital charge than those using the standardized approach. In other words, not only is the most advanced approach extremely complex, it may also not deliver all the benefits that are generally expected. The U.S. Comptroller of the Currency said the "mind-numbing" complexity of the proposed accords underscores a number of voices that are uncomfortable with adopting Basel II.

6. *Other risks.* While market risk exposure was integrated into the risk-based capital requirements in 1998 and operational risk in 2008, the BIS plan does not yet account for other risks, such as interest rate and liquidity risk in the banking book, although these risks are accounted for in the market or trading book. A more complete risk-based capital requirement would include these risks.

7. *Impact on capital requirements.* A study of Canadian banks concluded that Basel II could cause the minimum required capital for exposure to corporate entities to be more volatile, depending on the method chosen by the FI for the internal ratings approach (IRB, see Appendix 20A at the Online Learning Centre) and could have an impact on lending. In December 2003, the U.S. Federal Deposit Insurance Corporation issued a study making the case that the new rules would water down capital in place for U.S. banks instead of providing more protection against losses. However, in the first year of Basel II reporting, the 2008 annual report of Bank of Montreal noted that the Tier 1 capital ratio was 9.77. Under Basel I rules, the ratio would have been 9.41.[29]

---

[26] In a portfolio context, it assumes that asset and OBS risks are independent of each other.

[27] However, the more advanced internal ratings–based approach (IRB—see Appendix 20A at the Online Learning Centre) assumes a correlation among all loans of either 10 or 20 percent. Currently, it is estimated that only the biggest banks will use the IRB approach. Moreover, private sector models, such as KMV and CreditMetrics (see Chapter 12), generally find correlations of less than 10 percent. Most commonly, they find correlations in the 0 to 5 percent range—indicating a greater degree of diversification potential than implied by the IRB.

[28] In addition, since many emerging-market countries have low credit ratings, under the Basel II plan, banks may have to hold considerably more capital against such loans. This may adversely affect the flow of bank financing to these less-developed countries—with major adverse effects on their economies. For example, as FIs, firms, and consumers in the developed world deleveraged, capital flows and the ability of the World Bank to help emerging markets declined in 2007 and 2008.

[29] See M. Illing and G. Paulin, "Basel II and Required Bank Capital," Bank of Canada, *Financial System Review,* December 2004, pp. 61–65. See also the 2008 Bank of Montreal annual report, p. 60.

8. *Competition.* In Canada, OSFI applies Basel II to the Big Six banks and other federally regulated FIs. The U.S. Federal Reserve initially applied the new rules to approximately 20 U.S. banks. Further, in the United States, Basel II will not apply to securities firms or investment banks. In Europe, Basel II is to be incorporated into European Union law and applied to all banks and investment firms, not just internationally active banks. Thus, different standards will apply to Canadian, U.S., and European banks. In addition, as a result of tax and accounting differences across banking systems and in safety net coverages, the 8 percent risk-based capital requirement may not create a level competitive playing field across banks. This is different from what proponents of the scheme claim. In particular, Japan and the United States have very different accounting, tax, and safety net rules that significantly affect the comparability of U.S. and Japanese bank risk-based capital ratios.

9. *Pillar 2 may ask too much of regulators.* Pillar 2 of Basel II requires many very sensitive judgment calls from regulators who may be ill-equipped to make them. This will particularly be a problem for developing-country regulators. If Pillar 2 is taken seriously, supervisors may be exposed to a lot of criticism that most would rather avoid. However, in the wake of the financial meltdown of 2007 and 2008, the role of regulators is seen as central to financial stability as BIS guidelines for liquidity and capital are enhanced.

CONCEPT QUESTIONS

1. What are the major strengths of the risk-based capital ratios?
2. You are a manager of a deposit-taking institution with a total risk-based capital ratio of 6 percent. Discuss four strategies to meet OSFI's required 7 percent ratio in a short period of time without raising new capital.
3. Why isn't a capital ratio levied on exchange-traded derivative contracts?
4. What are three problems with the simple assets to capital multiple measure of capital adequacy?
5. What is the difference between Tier 1 capital and Tier 2 capital?
6. Identify one asset in each of the credit risk weight categories for Basel II.

CAPITAL REQUIREMENTS FOR OTHER FIs

Securities Firms

Canadian securities firms are governed by provincial and territorial governments, as well as self-regulatory organizations (SROs) such as the Investment Industry Association of Canada (IIAC) and the stock exchanges (e.g., the TSX and the Montréal Exchange). The implementation of a single national regulator, which is currently under discussion, would provide a standard calculation of regulatory capital across Canada.

Life Insurance Companies

minimum continuing capital and surplus requirement (MCCSR)
The minimum capital required by OSFI for life insurance companies operating in Canada.

Federally regulated life insurance companies (including branches of foreign life insurance companies operating in Canada) are required to maintain adequate levels of capital under the Insurance Companies Act (ICA). OSFI provides guidelines for the **minimum continuing capital and surplus requirements (MCCSR)** for life insurance companies that is risk-based, and uses the concepts of Tier 1 (core) and Tier 2 (supplementary) capital as for federally regulated deposit-taking institutions. Two MCCSR ratios apply. The Tier 1 ratio is calculated as

$$\text{Tier 1} = \text{Net Tier 1 capital/Total capital required} > 60 \text{ percent}$$

The total capital ratio is calculated as

Total capital ratio = Total capital available/Total capital required > 120 percent

Table 20–16 shows the components and the calculations of the MCCSR ratios for Canadian life insurance companies as reported to OSFI at Quarter 1, 2009. Canadian life insurance companies regulated by OSFI are seen to be well above the minimum MCCSR ratios for Tier 1 and total capital.

As for the banks under its jurisdiction, OSFI requires an estimate of risk-weighted assets that encompass (1) default (credit) and market risk, (2) insurance risks, (3) interest rate risk, and (4) other risks. Default and market risk are similar to the credit

TABLE 20–16
Minimum Continuing Capital and Surplus Requirements (MCCSR) for Canadian Life Insurance Companies as at Quarter 1, 2009 ($ thousands)

Source: Office of the Superintendent of Financial Institutions, www.osfi-bsif.gc.ca.

Capital Available:		
Tier 1 Capital		
Common shares		$20,401,076
Contributed surplus		4,064,187
Retained earnings		25,925,887
Less: Accumulated after-tax fair value gains (losses) arising from changes in institution's own credit risk		0
Future use: Fair value option		0
Non-cumulative perpetual preferred shares		900,501
Qualifying non-controlling interests		386,294
Innovative instruments		2,893,097
Non-participating account (mutual companies)		191,730
Adjusted net deferred gains/losses on real estate that have not been taken into account in the valuation of policy liabilities		262,432
Accumulated net after-tax foreign currency translation adjustment reported in other comprehensive income (OCI)		−1,475,186
Accumulated net after-tax unrealized loss on available-for-sale equity securities reported in OCI		−872,405
Gross Tier 1 Capital		55,390,691
Less: Deductions for net Tier 1 capital		19,342,502
Net Tier 1 Capital	A	36,048,189
Less: Additional deductions for adjusted net Tier 1 capital		1,662,247
Adjusted Net Tier 1 Capital		$34,385,942
Tier 2 Capital		
Tier 2A		869,826
Tier 2B allowed		5,256,047
Tier 2C		9,094,025
Total Tier 2 Capital Allowed		12,890,889
Total Tier 1 and Tier 2 Capital		0
Less Deductions/Adjustments		0
Total Capital Available	B	$47,276,831
Capital Required:		
Assets Default & Market Risk		11,034,016
Insurance Risks		6,965,340
Changes in Interest Environment (C-3) Risk		3,038,232
Other		3,000
Total Capital Required	C	$21,161,358
MCCSR Ratios:		
Tier 1	(A/C) × 100	170.35
Total	(B/C) × 100	223.41

mortality risk
The risk of death.

morbidity risk
The risk of ill health.

risk-weighted asset calculations for deposit-taking institutions. Insurance risk captures the risk of adverse changes in **mortality risk** and **morbidity risk.** Interest rate risk in part reflects the liquidity of liabilities and their probability or ease of withdrawal as interest rates change.[30] Since 2007, representatives of OSFI, Assuris, and the Autorité des marchés financiers (AMF) have been working to update the MCCSR standard framework. Canadian and global regulators are concerned about the increasing complexity of insurance assets, as well as their exposure to market, credit, insurance, and operational risk. Life insurance companies' liabilities from exposure to segregated funds (discussed in Chapter 3) were of considerable concern to regulators during the 2008 market disruptions (see the Industry Perspectives feature).

Property and Casualty Insurance Companies

minimum capital test (MCT)
The ratio of total capital available to minimum capital required for P&C companies regulated by OSFI in Canada.

Since 2003, federally regulated property and casualty (P&C) companies have been required to meet a **minimum capital test (MCT),** which is defined as

Total capital available/Minimum capital required > 100 percent

The minimum ratio is 100 percent, but P&C companies are expected to maintain capital at or above 150 percent, the supervisory target, in order to provide a buffer to deal with market volatility and other risks. Table 20–17 shows the MCT calculation for all Canadian federally regulated P&C companies as reported to OSFI as at Quarter 1, 2009. It can be seen that the ratio is simpler than that required under

TABLE 20–17
Minimum Capital Test (MCT) for Canadian Property and Casualty Insurance Companies as at Quarter 1, 2009 ($ thousands)

Source: Office of the Superintendent of Financial Institutions, **www.osfi-bsif.gc.ca.**

Capital Available	
Total equity less accumulated other comprehensive income	$22,056,579
Subordinated indebtedness and redeemable preferred shares	229,630
Accumulated other comprehensive income (loss)on:	
Available-for-sale equity securities	−909,108
Available-for-sale debt securities	194,599
Foreign currency (net of hedging activities)	−1,481
Included in capital available of regulated FI subsidiaries	−65,932
Other	−15,523
Capital available reported by regulated FI subsidiaries	1,836,777
Less: Accumulated net after-tax fair value gains (losses) arising from changes in the company's own credit risk	0
Less: Other	202,396
Less: Balance sheet value of investments in regulated FI subsidiaries	2,037,275
Less: Assets with a capital requirement of 100%	1,689,776
Total Capital Available	**$19,396,094**
Capital Required	
Balance sheet assets	2,313,448
Unearned premiums/unpaid claims/premium deficiencies	5,457,795
Catastrophes	221,800
Reinsurance ceded to unregistered insurers	38,309
Capital required reported by regulated FI subsidiaries	622,732
Structured settlements, letters of credit, derivatives and other exposures	15,008
Minimum Capital Required	**$ 8,669,092**
Excess Capital Available Over Capital Required	**$10,727,002**
Total Capital Available as a % of Minimum Capital Required	**223.74**

[30] For complete details, see Office of the Superintendent of Financial Institutions, *Minimum Continuing Capital And Surplus Requirements (MCCSR) for Life Insurance Companies—A,* December 2008, www.osfi-bsif.gc.ca.

Basel II for the internationally active banks, but does consider some of the same components for capital that can be included in the numerator of the MCT. The denominator of the MCT establishes the minimum capital required for on- and off-balance-sheet assets, policy liabilities, and accident and sickness insurance, as well as for catastrophes, unearned premiums and unearned claims, and reinsurance. As seen in Table 20–17, the ratio of 223.74 for Canadian P&C companies is well above the 150 percent for individual companies. OSFI may set different targets based on the risk profile of the individual institution. P&C companies must notify OSFI if they expect to fall below their target ratio, and must also provide a plan for returning above their minimum.[31]

CONCEPT QUESTIONS

1. How do the capital requirements for life insurance firms differ from the capital rules employed by OSFI for deposit-taking institutions?
2. What types of risks are included in estimating the MCCSR of life insurance firms?
3. How does the MCT for P&C companies differ from the MCCSR for life insurance companies?

INDUSTRY PERSPECTIVES

FINANCIAL FIRMS NEED HISTORIANS: OSFI HEAD

Julie Dickson, the head of Canada's banking and insurance watchdog, advised financial institutions to hire financial historians so they don't repeat the mistakes they have made in the current credit crunch.

In the dark days of last fall when the financial system seemed on the verge of failure, many industry insiders insisted the situation was unprecedented and that no one could have foreseen it.

But they were mistaken, Ms. Dickson said in a speech to life insurance industry executives in Toronto. The same events have happened before, she said.

"Stock markets have plummeted, banking systems have collapsed and you do not need to go back as far as 1929 to see this," Ms. Dickson said.

Ms. Dickson, the Superintendent of Financial Institutions, said chief risk officers at banks and insurance companies "should think about" hiring a financial historian as a way to broaden their awareness of the potential challenges they face.

By taking into account what has happened in past decades, players will be better able to anticipate consequences of current business decisions.

One area of particular concern is the segregated fund businesses of many life insurance companies, she said.

During the equity market collapse last year, companies had to scramble into damage control mode as liabilities soared, forcing them to put aside more capital.

Indeed, after lobbying by the industry, OSFI last year changed the rules on capital requirements to make it easier for players to comply.

"Many life insurance companies misunderstood the risk associated with segregated fund guarantees," she said.

With life insurance, players can mitigate the risk of losses by simply selling more policies, but with segregated funds the opposite is true, since more sales only bring more exposure to the same risk.

Ms. Dickson said insurance companies should consider slowing the growth of their segregated fund businesses.

Source: John Greenwood. *Financial Post,* June 9, 2009.

---

[31] For complete details, see Office of the Superintendent of Financial Institutions, *Minimum Capital Test (MCT) for Federally Regulated Property and Casualty Insurance Companies—A,* March 2008, www.osfi-bsif.gc.ca.

Summary

This chapter reviewed the role of an FI's capital in insulating it against credit, interest rate, and other risks. According to economic theory, capital or net worth should be measured on a market value basis as the difference between the market values of assets and liabilities. In actuality, regulators use book value accounting rules. While a book value capital adequacy rule accounts for credit risk exposure in a rough fashion, it overlooks the effects of interest rate changes and interest rate exposure on net worth. We analyzed the specific capital rules adopted by the regulators of federally regulated banks, trust and loan companies, and insurance companies, and discussed their problems and weaknesses. In particular, we looked at how regulators are now adjusting book value-based capital rules to account for different types of risk as part of their imposition of risk-based capital adequacy ratios. As a result, actual capital requirements are moving closer to market value-based net worth.

Questions and Problems

1. Identify and briefly discuss the importance of the five functions of an FI's capital.

2. Why are regulators concerned with the levels of capital held by an FI compared with those held by a non-financial institution?

3. What are the differences between the economic definition of capital and the book value definition of capital?

   a. How does economic value accounting recognize the adverse effects of credit and interest rate risk?

   b. How does book value accounting recognize the adverse effects of credit and interest rate risk?

4. A financial intermediary has the following balance sheet ($ millions) with all assets and liabilities in market values:

   Assets

6 percent semiannual four-year notes (par value $12)	$10
7 percent annual three-year AA-rated bonds (par value $15)	15
9 percent annual five-year BBB-rated bonds (par value $15)	15
Total assets	$40

   Liabilities and Equity

5 percent two-year subordinated debt (par value $25)	$20
Equity capital	20
Total liabilities and equity	$40

   a. What would be the effect on equity capital (net worth) if interest rates increased by 30 basis points? The notes are held for trading purposes; the rest are all classified as held to maturity.

   b. How are the changes in the market value of assets adjusted in the income statements and balance sheets of FIs?

5. Why is the market value of equity a better measure of an FI's ability to absorb losses than book value of equity?

6. Provincial Bank has the following year-end balance sheet ($ millions):

   Assets

Cash	$ 10
Loans	90
Total assets	$100

   Liabilities and Equity

Deposits	$ 90
Equity	10
Total liabilities and equity	$100

   The loans primarily are fixed-rate, medium-term loans, while the deposits are either short-term or variable-rate deposits. Rising interest rates have caused the failure of a key industrial company, and as a result, 3 percent of the loans are considered uncollectable and thus have no economic value. One-third of these uncollectable loans will be charged off. Further, the increase in interest rates has caused a 5 percent decrease in the market value of the remaining loans.

   a. What is the impact on the balance sheet after the necessary adjustments are made according to book value accounting? According to market value accounting?

   b. What is the new market to book value ratio if Provincial Bank has 1 million shares outstanding?

7. What are the arguments for and against the use of market value accounting for FIs?

8. How is the assets to capital multiple (ACM) for an FI defined?

9. Identify and discuss the weaknesses of the assets to capital multiple as a measure of capital adequacy.

10. What is the *Basel Capital Accord?*

11. What is the major feature in the estimation of credit risk under Basel II capital requirements?

12. What is the total risk-based capital ratio?

13. What are the definitional differences between Tier 1 and Tier 2 capital?

14. What components are used in the calculation of risk-weighted assets?

15. Explain the process of calculating risk-weighted on-balance-sheet assets.

    a. What assets are included in the categories of credit risk exposure under Basel II?

    b. What are the appropriate risk weights for each category?

16. Halifax Bank has the following balance sheet ($ millions) and has no off-balance-sheet activities:

Assets	
Cash	$ 20
Treasury bills	40
Residential mortgages	600
Other loans	430
Total assets	$1,090

Liabilities and Equity	
Deposits	$ 980
Subordinated debentures	40
Common stock	40
Retained earnings	30
Total liabilities and equity	$1,090

    a. What is the assets to capital multiple?

    b. What is the Tier 1 capital ratio?

    c. What is the total risk-based capital ratio?

    d. How would OSFI categorize this bank's capital? (Table 20–9)

17. Onshore Bank has $20 million in assets, with risk-weighted assets of $10 million. Tier 1 capital is $500,000, and Tier 2 capital is $400,000. How will each of the following transactions affect the value of the Tier 1 and total capital ratios? What will the new values of each ratio be?

    a. The bank repurchases $100,000 of common stock.

    b. The bank issues $2,000,000 of fixed-term deposits and uses the proceeds for uninsured residential mortgages.

    c. The bank receives $500,000 in deposits and invests them in T-bills.

    d. The bank issues $800,000 in common stock and lends it to help finance a new shopping mall. The developer has an A+ credit rating.

    e. The bank issues $1,000,000 in non-qualifying perpetual preferred stock and purchases provincial bonds.

    f. Homeowners pay back $4,000,000 of uninsured residential mortgages, and the bank uses the proceeds to build new ATMs.

18. Explain the process of calculating risk-weighted off-balance-sheet contingent guarantee contracts.

    a. What is the basis for differentiating the credit-equivalent amounts of contingent guarantee contracts?

    b. On what basis are the risk weights for the credit-equivalent amounts differentiated?

19. Explain how off-balance-sheet market contracts, or derivative instruments, differ from contingent guarantee contracts.

    a. What is counterparty credit risk?

    b. Why do exchange-traded derivative contracts have no capital requirements?

    c. What is the difference between the potential exposure and the current exposure of over-the-counter derivative contracts?

    d. Why are the credit conversion factors for the potential exposure of foreign exchange contracts greater than they are for interest rate contracts?

    e. Why do regulators not allow banks to benefit from positive current exposure values?

20. What is the process of netting off-balance-sheet derivative contracts under Basel II?

21. How does the risk-based capital measure attempt to compensate for the limitations of the static assets to capital multiple?

22. Identify and discuss the problems in the risk-based capital approach to measuring capital adequacy.

23. What is the contribution to the credit risk-weighted asset base of the following items under the Basel II requirements?

    a. $10 million cash.

    b. $50 million 91-day Treasury bills.

    c. $25 million cash items in the process of collection.

    d. $5 million U.K. government bonds, AAA rated.

    e. $5 million Australian short-term government bonds, A− rated.

    f. $1 million provincial government bonds.

    g. $40 million repurchase agreements.

    h. $500 million one-to-four family home mortgages.

    i. $500 million corporate loans, BBB− rated.

    j. $100,000 performance-related standby letters of credit to an AAA rated corporation.

    k. $100,000 performance-related standby letters of credit to a Canadian municipality issuing bonds.

    l. $7 million commercial letter of credit to a foreign, A rated corporation.

m. $3 million five-year loan commitment to an OECD government.

n. $8 million bankers' acceptance conveyed to a Canadian, AA– rated corporation.

o. $17 million three-year loan commitment to a private agent.

p. $17 million three-month loan commitment to a private agent.

q. $30 million standby letter of credit to back an A rated corporate issue of commercial paper.

r. $4 million five-year interest rate swap with no current exposure (the counterparty is a private agent).

s. $4 million five-year interest rate swap with no current exposure (the counterparty is a municipality).

t. $6 million two-year currency swap with $500,000 current exposure (the counterparty is a low credit risk entity).

24. Third Bank has the following balance sheet ($ millions) with the risk weights in parentheses:

Assets

Cash (0%)	$ 20
OECD inter-bank deposits (20%)	25
Mortgage loans (50%)	70
Consumer loans (100%)	70
Total assets	$185

Liabilities and Equity

Deposits	$175
Subordinated debt (5 years)	3
Cumulative preferred stock	5
Equity	2
Total liabilities and equity	$185

The cumulative preferred stock is qualifying and perpetual. In addition, the bank has $30 million in performance-related standby letters of credit (SLCs), $40 million in two-year forward FX contracts that are currently in the money by $1 million, and $300 million in six-year interest rate swaps that

are currently out of the money by $2 million. Credit conversion factors follow:

Performance-related standby LCs	50%
1- to 5-year foreign exchange contracts	5%
1- to 5-year interest rate swaps	0.5%
5- to 10-year interest rate swaps	1.5%

a. What are the risk-weighted on-balance-sheet assets of the bank as defined under the Basel Accord?

b. What is the total capital required for both off- and on-balance-sheet assets?

c. Does the bank have enough capital to meet the Basel requirements? If not, what minimum Tier 1 or total capital does it need to meet the requirement?

25. Fifth Bank has the following balance sheet ($ millions) with the risk weights in parentheses:

Assets

Cash (0%)	$ 20
Mortgage loans (35%)	50
Consumer loans (75%)	70
Total assets	$140

Liabilities and Equity

Deposits	$130
Subordinated debt (>5 years)	5
Equity	5
Total liabilities and equity	$140

In addition, the bank has $20 million in commercial standby letters of credit (AA rated) and $40 million in 10-year FX forward contracts that are in the money by $1 million.

a. What are the risk-weighted on-balance-sheet assets of the bank as defined under the Basel II Accord?

b. What is the total capital required for both off- and on-balance-sheet assets?

c. Does the bank have sufficient capital to meet the Basel II requirements? How much in excess? How much short?

Web Questions

WWW

26. Go to the website of the Bank for International Settlements at www.bis.org. Under "Basel Committee on Banking Supervision," click on "Basel II." This page contains information on amendments to the Basel II June 2006 comprehensive document. What types of amendments have been made since 2006?

27. Go to the website of the Office of the Superintendent of Financial Institutions at www.osfi-bsif.gc.ca. Click on "Banks." Click on "Table of OSFI Guidelines." Are all of the FIs under OSFI supervision subject to the same requirements? Why might the regulatory approach differ? Under the heading "Supervisory Practices" click on "Guide to Intervention." Compare the supervisory roles of OSFI and CDIC if an FI is rated No Problem/Normal Activities, Stage 1, Stage 2, Stage 3, and Stage 4.

Integrated Mini-Case

CAPITAL ADEQUACY ANALYSIS

Bank balance sheet information is listed below.

1. What is the bank's risk-weighted asset base under Basel II?

2. What are the bank's Tier 1 and total risk–based capital requirements under Basel II?

3. Using the assets to capital multiple requirement, what is the minimum regulatory capital required to keep the bank in the well-capitalized zone (ACM below 20%)?

4. What is the bank's capital adequacy level under Basel II if the par value of its equity is $225,000, the surplus value of equity is $200,000, and the qualifying perpetual preferred stock is $50,000? Does the bank meet Basel (Tier 1) capital standards?

On-Balance-Sheet Items	Risk Weight (%)	Face Value
Cash	0%	$ 121,600
Short-term government securities (<92 days)	0	5,400
Long-term government securities (>92 days)	0	414,400
Bank of Canada deposits	0	9,800
Repos secured by federal agencies	20	159,000
Claims on Canadian deposit-taking institutions	20	937,900
Short-term (<1 year) claims on foreign banks	20	1,640,000
Municipal bonds	20	170,000
Claims on or guaranteed by federal agencies	20	26,500
Municipal revenue bonds	20	112,900
Corporate loans, BB+ rated	100	6,645,700
Claims on foreign banks (>1 year)	100	5,800

Off-Balance-Sheet Items	Conversion Factor (%)	Face Value
Canadian government counterparty		
Loan commitments, AAA rated:		
<1 year	20%	$ 300
1–5 years	50	1,140
Standby letters of credit, AA rated:		
Performance-related	50	200
Direct credit substitute	100	100
Canadian deposit-taking institution counterparty		
(risk weight category 20%)		
Loan commitments, BBB+ rated:		
<1 year	0	1,000
>1 year	50	3,000
Standby letters of credit, AA− rated:		
Performance-related	50	200
Direct credit substitute	100	56,400
Commercial letters of credit, BBB+ rated	20	400
Provincial government counterparty		
(risk weight category 20%)		
Loan commitments, BBB− rated:		
>1 year	50	100
Standby letters of credit, AAA rated:		
Performance-related	50	135,400
Corporate customer counterparty		
Loan commitments, CCC rated:		
<1 year	20	2,980,000
>1 year	50	3,046,278
Standby letters of credit, BBB rated:		
Performance-related	50	101,543
Direct credit substitute	100	485,000
Commercial letters of credit, AA− rated	20	78,978
Note issuance facilities	50	20,154
Forward agreements	100	5,900
Interest rate market contracts (Current exposure assumed to be zero)		
<1 year (notional amount)	0	2,000
>1–5 years (notional amount)	0.5	5,000

Appendix **20A**	**Internal Ratings-Based Approach to Measuring Credit Risk-Weighted Assets**

View Appendix 20A at the Online Learning Centre: www.mcgrawhill.ca/olc/saunders.

CHAPTER 21

Product Diversification

This chapter examines the issue of product diversification for FIs:

▸ First, we analyze the problems and risks that can arise, and have arisen histori-cally, for FIs constrained to limited financial service sectors or franchises, as well as the potential benefits from greater product expansion.

▸ Second, we analyze the laws and regulations that have restricted prod-uct expansions for banks, insurance companies, and securities firms in North America and elsewhere, as well as the recent modifications of many of these laws and regulations.

▸ Third, we look at barriers to product expansion between the financial sector and the real or commercial sector of the economy.

▸ Fourth, we evaluate the advantages and disadvantages of allowing FIs to adopt more universal franchises.

INTRODUCTION

As we discovered in Chapter 20, an FI's capital, in particular, its Tier 1 capital as defined by regulators, is extremely important to a financial institution and to the stability of the global financial system. Our concepts of what an FI should do, that is, what products it should offer, are tied in with the regulatory capital required to undertake each activity. As a result, the investment decisions that drive the capital structure, dividend, and short-term financing decisions of an FI are motivated by profit as for any other company, but the risk of the activity is paramount. Since each product line undertaken by an FI has a risk component associated with it, domes-tic and global regulations are the starting point for an FI's strategy with respect to product diversification (discussed in this chapter) and geographic expansion (the topic of Chapter 22). The 2008 financial meltdown stands as a watershed for FIs, their customers, their regulators, and their shareholders.

PRODUCT SEGMENTATION

universal FI
An FI that can engage in a broad range of financial service activities.

The Canadian and U.S. financial systems were traditionally structured along segmented product lines. Regulatory barriers and restrictions have often inhib-ited the ability of an FI operating in one area of the financial services industry to expand its product set into other areas. This can be compared with FIs operating in Germany, where a more **universal FI** structure has traditionally allowed individual financial services organizations to offer a far broader range of banking, insurance, securities, and other financial services products. In the late 1980s, both Canada and the United Kingdom underwent "big bangs" that revamped their regulatory systems and moved both countries toward universal banks. The revisions of the Bank Act in the 1980s and 1990s resulted in the Canadian banks absorbing and ultimately dominating the securities industry in Canada and eliminating the trust industry as a stand-alone function. The Canadian issues that remain to be resolved are cross-pillar mergers with insurance companies, as well as mergers within the banking pillar itself, which we discuss in Chapter 22.[1]

commercial banking
Banking activity of deposit taking and lending.

investment banking
Banking activity of underwriting, issuing, and distributing securities.

From 1933 to 1998, the United States was delayed in starting toward universal banking by the Glass–Steagall Act, which separated the functions of **commercial banking** and **investment banking.** After implementation of the Financial Services Modernization Act of 1999, U.S. FIs swiftly caught up; a large number of mergers and acquisitions took place between 1997 and 2000, most notably the bank–insurance company merger between Citicorp and Travelers to create Citigroup. Citigroup was the second-largest universal bank in the world in 2004, as U.S. regulatory barriers receded and the globalization of financial services continued to move forward. However, the market meltdown in 2008 was particularly devastating to Citicorp, bringing its model of a universal bank into question, as we saw in the Industry Perspectives feature in Chapter 1. As well, the model of a large, stand-alone investment bank funded by short-term money market borrowing was eliminated in 2008, with only Goldman Sachs and Morgan Stanley left in the United States after the merger of Bear Stearns with JPMorgan, Merrill Lynch with Bank of America, and the failure of Lehman Brothers. Goldman Sachs and Morgan Stanley both became bank holding companies, which are subject to stricter regulatory oversight. In most cases, global competition has been reduced by the failure or takeover of financial institutions in 2008, as shown in the Industry Perspectives feature in this chapter. But, as in most market disruptions, there are winners and losers. The global market share has shifted to the strongest FIs, as clients look for safer counterparties.

The barriers to product expansion and financial conglomeration are handled differently around the globe. Appendix 21A, available at the Online Learning Centre (www.mcgrawhill.ca/olc/saunders) compares the range of product activities permitted for banks in other major industrialized countries and financial centres. Figure 21–1 shows the highly diversified product structure of the Swiss universal bank Credit Suisse First Boston. Universal banks offer not just investment banking services, but also commercial lending, foreign exchange, and custody and cash management services. We now analyze the advantages and disadvantages of increased product line diversification in more detail.

ISSUES INVOLVED IN THE DIVERSIFICATION OF PRODUCT OFFERINGS

The economic value of narrowly defined bank franchises may decline over time. Product line restrictions can inhibit an FI's ability to optimize the set of financial services it offers, potentially forcing it to adopt a more risky set of activities than it would adopt if it could fully diversify. Product restrictions also limit the ability

---

[1] Canadian banks are permitted to sell some insurance products (e.g., travel insurance and credit life insurance to support mortgages and loans) but since 2001, have been unable to provide information about property and casualty (P&C) insurance or referrals in their branches. This is primarily because of concerns about consumer privacy and protection and the potential for tied selling. In 2009, OSFI permitted banks to sell insurance products online but the Finance minister asked them to remove these links from their websites. Canadian life insurance companies expanded from annuity-type offerings into a full range of mutual fund and investment offerings related to RRSPs, RRIFs, and pensions, as well as segregated funds.

FIGURE 21–1   **The Structure of a Universal Bank: Credit Suisse Holding Group**

CREDIT SUISSE GROUP

Credit Suisse Financial Services
is a leading provider of comprehensive financial services in Europe and other selected markets. Under the brands Credit Suisse and Winterthur, it offers investment products, private banking, and financial advisory services, including insurance and pension solutions, for private and corporate clients.

Private Banking	Life & Pensions
Corporate & Retail Banking	Insurance

Credit Suisse First Boston
is a leading global investment bank serving institutional, corporate, government, and high-net-worth clients. Its businesses include securities underwriting, sales and trading, investment banking, private equity, financial advisory services, investment research, venture capital, and asset management.

Institutional Securities	CSFB Financial Services

Credit Suisse Legal entity	Winterthur Legal entity	Credit Suisse First Boston Legal entity	
Subsidiaries	**Subsidiaries**	**Subsidiaries**	**Subsidiaries**
Bank Leu AG*	Winterthur Life	Credit Suisse First Boston (USA), Inc.	Credit Suisse Asset Management, LLC
Clariden Bank*	DBV-Winterthur Versicherung AG, Germany	Credit Suisse First Boston International	Credit Suisse Trust & Banking Co Ltd.
Bank Hofmann*			
Neue Aargauer Bank* (98.6%)	Winterthur Assicurazioni S. p. A., Italy	Credit Suisse First Boston, LLC	Credit Suisse Asset Management (Australia) Limited
BGP Banca di Gestione Patrimoniale*		Credit Suisse First Boston (Europe) Limited	Credit Suisse Asset Management, Limited
JO Hambro Investment Management Limited			
Frye-Louis Capital Management, Inc.			
Credit Suisse Trust*			
Credit Suisse Fides*			

* Direct holding of Credit Suisse Group.

Source: Credit Suisse Group website, www.credit-suisse.com.

of FI managers to adjust flexibly to shifts in the demand for financial products by consumers and to shifts in costs due to technology and related innovations.

Whether the debate concerns existing activities or expansion into securities, insurance, or commerce, similar issues arise. These include

1. Safety and soundness issues.
2. Economy of scale and scope issues.
3. Conflict of interest issues.
4. Deposit insurance issues.
5. Regulatory oversight issues.
6. Competition issues.

INDUSTRY PERSPECTIVES

RADICAL SHIFT IN THE BANKING POWER BASE

It is barely nine months since the collapse of Lehman Brothers ushered in one of the worst financial crises since the Great Depression. But for the strongest banks, the second quarter of 2009, which closed on Tuesday, has confirmed the upbeat trends of the first quarter.

While banks such as Citigroup, Merrill Lynch, Royal Bank of Scotland and UBS continue to find life difficult, thriving rivals—JPMorgan, Goldman Sachs, Morgan Stanley, Barclays, Deutsche Bank and Credit Suisse—are talking privately of a record second quarter.

They have benefited from lively markets for commodity and foreign exchange trading, at profit margins that are between two and eight times higher than before the height of the financial crisis last autumn. At the same time, companies have been rushing to issue new debt and equity.

More fundamentally and sustainably there have been clear shifts in market share between the banks—in everything from U.K. mortgages to U.S. Treasury bill issuance—as aggressive groups have taken advantage of opportunities left by weakened rivals.

One investment banker says: "There used to be 15 banks competing. Now there are six. This is a phenomenal environment. I've never seen anything like this in 20 years in the business."

Prime brokerage—the business of providing financing services to the world's hedge funds—is not an obvious place to make money, given the troubles that the sector has suffered in recent months, as investors have lost large sums and demanded back much of what was left. But for the banks providing the financing, the market still promises to be lucrative.

The likes of Credit Suisse, Deutsche Bank and JPMorgan, and to an extent Barclays and BNP Paribas, have been challenging the traditional dominance of Goldman and Morgan Stanley, which once held an estimated 80 percent of the market between them.

Market participants estimate that the big two now have barely half the market, with Credit Suisse and Deutsche on about 15 percent apiece. The change was driven from both sides—hedge funds wanted to rely less on a single counterparty for their financial affairs, while Goldman and Morgan Stanley have been shrinking their balance sheets.

Even with hedge fund assets at an estimated 50 percent of previous levels, the most successful banks reckon they are on track to make just as much money this year as in a boom year, though with lower ratios of lending to collateral and higher prices.

"We're putting less balance sheet at risk," says one senior banker. "But we are making the same bottom line."

The trade credit market has similarly been "dislocated", as bankers like to say, by the financial crisis. While much of the market used to be in the hands of Fortis, Citi and RBS, the combination of near-collapse (for the former) and balance sheet shrinkage (for the other two), has left a larger share of the market for a handful of others, such as HSBC, Deutsche Bank, BNP and Standard Chartered.

For them, the market—though shrunken by the turmoil in trade flows over the past year—has been lucrative, reflecting a less competitive market and higher perceived risk. Stuart Nivison, HSBC's head of trade in Europe, says: "Pricing typically doubled towards the end of last year."

Probably the most visible, though still hard to measure, change in market share has been in mortgages, and nowhere more so than in the U.K. where a large swath of traditional lenders simply does not have the funding to maintain mortgage lending.

In a market set to grant net new lending of close to zero this year, it is the big groups—with the deposit base to fund their mortgages—that are dominant, regardless of past troubles.

RBS's mortgage lending rose 9 percent year-on-year in the three months to March to [£]76.1bn, as it strove to meet a government commitment to make [£]9bn of extra mortgage finance available—a quid pro quo for its state bail-out. Santander lent about [£]800m for new mortgages in the first quarter.

RBS, Santander and Barclays recorded net new lending. Ray Boulger, at Charcol mortgage advisers, says the U.K. market is dominated by RBS, Santander and Barclays, plus to a lesser extent Nationwide, Lloyds and HSBC—a far cry from a couple of years ago when there were 165 mortgage providers and tens of thousands of mortgage deals.

There have been other shifts—in private banking, for example, where UBS's problems have unsettled some clients and sent them towards small-scale Swiss competitors.

But for the most part, the new world order is simply a matter of one set of big banks giving way to another set of big banks, with the benefit of higher prices.

Kian Abouhossein, analyst at JPMorgan, says the message is simple. "What clients want today is better, larger counterparties."

Source: Patrick Jenkins and Jane Croft, *Financial Times* [London], June 30, 2009. *Copyright Financial Times Ltd. 2009. All rights reserved.*

Canadian banks have dominated the investment banking and securities industry in Canada since their takeover of the independent securities firms in the late 1980s and early 1990s, as discussed in Chapter 4. However, the regulation of banking functions is carried out by the Office of the Superintendent of Financial Institutions (OSFI), whereas securities regulation remains is in the hands of the provincial and territorial regulators until the establishment of a national securities regulator. The six issues listed above are evaluated in the context of banks and securities firms, but can be extended to consider the last cross-pillar issue: the merger of banks and insurance companies.

www.osfi-bsif.gc.ca

Consider the three alternative organizational structures for linking banking and securities activities in Figure 21–2. In this figure, panel (a) shows the fully integrated universal bank, where banking and securities activities are conducted in different departments of a single organization. This is typical of the way in which large banks in Germany, such as Deutsche Bank, engage in securities activities. Panel (b) shows the universal subsidiary model where a bank engages in securities activities through a separately owned securities affiliate. This is typical of the way in which banks in Canada and in the United Kingdom conduct their securities activities. This is also the model adopted to allow U.S. nationally chartered banks to expand their non-bank activities.

Note that the degree of bank–non-bank integration is much less with the financial services holding company model [panel (c)] than with either the full or subsidiary universal banking model.[2] For example, in the universal subsidiary model, the bank holds a direct ownership stake in the securities subsidiary. By comparison, in the financial services holding company model, the bank and securities subsidiary are separate companies with their own equity capital; the link is that their equity is held by the same parent company, the financial services holding company.[3]

FIGURE 21–2   **Alternative Organizational Forms for Non-Bank Product Expansions of Banking Organizations**

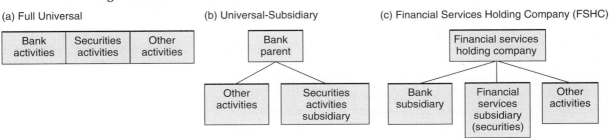

(a) Full Universal

| Bank activities | Securities activities | Other activities |

(b) Universal-Subsidiary

Bank parent
— Other activities
— Securities activities subsidiary

(c) Financial Services Holding Company (FSHC)

Financial services holding company
— Bank subsidiary
— Financial services subsidiary (securities)
— Other activities

---

[2] For a comparative analysis of these three models, see A. Saunders and I. Walter, *Universal Banking in the United States: What Could We Gain? What Could We Lose?* (New York: Oxford University Press, 1994).

[3] In general, the advantages of the full universal model is greater resource flexibility and integration of commercial bank and investment bank product lines. Its perceived disadvantages include greater monopoly power and greater potential conflicts of interest.

Safety and Soundness Concerns

With respect to the securities activities of commercial banks and the possible effects on their safety and soundness, two key questions arise: How risky is securities underwriting? And if losses occur for a securities subsidiary, can this cause the affiliated bank to fail?

The Risk of Securities Underwriting

firm commitment offering
Securities offered from the issuing firm, purchased by an underwriter.

To understand the risk of securities underwriting, you must understand the mechanics of firm commitment securities offerings. In a **firm commitment offering,** the underwriter purchases securities directly from the issuing firm (say, at $99 per share) and then reoffers them to the public or the market at large at a slightly higher price, say, $99.50. The difference between the underwriter's buy price ($99) and the public offer price ($99.50) is the spread that compensates the underwriter for accepting the principal risk of placing the securities with outside investors as well as any administrative and distribution costs associated with the underwriting. In our simple example of a $0.50 spread, the maximum revenue the underwriter can gain from underwriting the issue is $0.50 times the number of shares issued. Thus, if 1 million shares were offered, the maximum gross revenue for the underwriting would be $0.50 times 1,000,000, or $500,000. Note that once the public offering has been made and the price specified in the prospectus, the underwriter cannot raise the price over the offering period. In this example, the underwriter could not raise the price above $99.50 even after determining that the market valued the shares more highly.[4]

The upside return from underwriting is normally capped, but the downside risk is not and can be very large. The downside risk arises if the underwriter overprices the public offering, setting the public offer price higher than outside investors' valuations. As a result, the underwriter will be unable to sell the shares during the public offering period and will have to lower the price to get rid of the inventory of unsold shares, especially because this inventory is often financed through issuing commercial paper or repurchase agreements. In our example, if the underwriter has to lower the offering price to $99, the gross revenue from the underwriting will be zero, since this is the price paid to the issuing firm. Any price less than $99 generates a loss. For example, suppose that the issue can be placed only at $97; the underwriter's losses will be $2 times 1,000,000 shares, or $2 million.

There are a number of possible reasons why an underwriter may take a big loss or big hit on an underwriting. The first is simply overestimating the market's demand for the shares. The second is that in the short period between setting the public offering price and seeking to sell the securities to the public, there may be a major drop in security values in general.

If Underwriting Losses Occur for the Securities Affiliate, Can This Cause a Bank to Fail?

Proponents of allowing banking organizations to expand their securities activities argue that the answer to this question is no, as long as the bank subsidiary is sufficiently insulated from the risk problems of the securities affiliate. As noted earlier, in a financial services holding company structure, the bank is legally a separate

---

[4] The offering period is usually a maximum of ten business days.

FIGURE 21–3 **The Role of Firewalls in Protecting Banks**

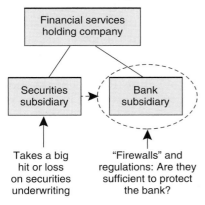

Takes a big hit or loss on securities underwriting

"Firewalls" and regulations: Are they sufficient to protect the bank?

corporation from the securities affiliate. As shown in Figure 21–3, its only link to its securities affiliate is indirect, through the holding company that owns a controlling equity stake in both the bank and securities affiliate. However, even this indirect link raises the concern that the effects of losses by the securities affiliate could threaten the safety of the bank unless firewalls or regulatory barriers are introduced to insulate the bank against such losses (see Figure 21–3).

There are at least three ways a bank could be harmed by losses of a securities affiliate in a holding company structure. First, a holding company might be tempted to drain capital and funds from the bank by requiring excessive dividends and fees from the bank (this is called *upstreaming*). The holding company could then *downstream* these funds to protect the failing securities affiliate from insolvency. As a result, the bank would be weakened at the expense (or because) of the securities affiliate.

A second way in which a bank could be harmed is through interaffiliate loans. For example, the holding company may induce the bank to extend loans to the securities affiliate to keep it afloat even though such loans are excessively risky.

The third way in which a bank may be affected is through a contagious confidence problem. Specifically, difficulty of a securities firm subsidiary may result in a negative information signal to financial service consumers and investors regarding the quality of the management of the holding company and its bank affiliate. Such negative information can create incentives for large depositors and investors to withdraw their money from the bank in the manner described in Chapter 19. This bank run possibility seems more likely to occur if the bank and its securities affiliate share similar names and logos, which in general they do.

Obviously, a big hit taken by the securities subsidiary can potentially threaten the safety and solvency of the affiliated bank, especially through the confidence effect.[5] However, at least two countervailing risk-reducing effects may enhance the safety and soundness of a bank indirectly linked to a securities subsidiary in a holding company framework. The first effect is a **product diversification benefit.** A well-diversified financial services firm (financial services holding company) potentially enjoys a far more stable earnings and profit stream over time than does a product-specialized bank. As demand and cost shifts reduce earnings in one activity area, such as banking, offsetting demand and cost shifts may take place in other activity areas, such as securities or insurance, increasing the holding company's earnings. Advocates argue that a more stable and diversified earnings stream for the holding company enables it to act as a source of strength in keeping the affiliated bank well capitalized.

product diversification benefit
Stabilization of earnings and profits resulting from a well-diversified financial services holding company.

[5] For example, the investment banking activities of CIBC World Markets in New York in providing "loans" to special-purpose entities (SPEs) of Enron led to CIBC agreeing to pay US$2.4 to settle an Enron shareholders' class action lawsuit and an additional US$250 million to Enron in August 2005, amounts that represented one-tenth of CIBC's market capitalization at the time. This seriously weakened its balance sheet, affecting future growth. Analysts downgraded the company's ratings and CIBC's shares dropped from $80.64 to $74.55 in one day. Although CIBC admitted no wrongdoing, the damage was done to its reputation, creating a difficult first day for its new chairman, Gerry McCaughey, who took over from John Hunkin 24 hours before the announcement. See "A Tough Lesson Learned," *Canadian Business*, August 15–August 28, 2005, 78(16), p. 76, and K. Macklem, "A Bank's Enron Bomb," *Maclean's*, August 15, 2005, 118(33), p. 39.

In the academic literature, a number of empirical studies have evaluated the gains from bank activity diversification by looking at the correlations of accounting earnings for segmented financial firms or industries and analyzing correlations between firms' stock market returns. Essentially, the lower these correlations, the greater the potential gains from activity diversification and the lower the coefficient of variation (COV)—the standard deviation divided by the mean—of a banking organization's earnings flows. Other studies have sought to evaluate the potential effects of activity diversification on the risk of failure (ROF) of banks and simulate the effects of bank–non-bank mergers (MS) on bank risk. The majority of the studies find that a financial services holding company's risk could be reduced by diversification. However, the optimal proportion of investment in individual non-bank product lines often falls in the 5 to 25 percent range. This suggests that excessive product expansion in some non-bank lines could actually increase the total risk exposure of a banking organization.[6]

Economies of Scale and Scope

A second issue concerning the expansion of banks into securities and other non-bank activities is the potential for additional economies of scale and scope. As financial firms become larger, the potential scale can lower an FI's average costs of financial services production. Thus, larger financial services holding companies may have an economy of scale advantage over smaller financial firms. Further, financial services holding companies' abilities to generate synergistic cost savings through joint use of inputs in producing multiple financial products create economies of scope.

For example, suppose the average cost of producing an FI's output of financial services is measured as

$$AC_i = \frac{TC_i}{S_i}$$

where

AC_i = Average cost of the ith FI
TC_i = Total cost of the ith FI
S_i = Size of the FI measured by assets, deposits, or loans

As an FI expands its operations, the consolidation of overlapping activities would lower the average costs for the combined (larger) financial services holding company to point C in Figure 21–4, operating at AC_c. The average cost to the largest FI in Figure 21–4 (size S_c) to produce financial services is lower than the cost to smaller firms B, operating at AC_B, and A, operating at AC_A. This means that at any given price for financial service firm products, firm C, the financial services holding company, can make a higher profit than either FI B or A.

Similarly, let X_1 and X_2 be two financial products; each is produced by one firm as a specialized producer. That is, firm A produces only X_1, but no X_2, and firm B produces only X_2, but no X_1. The average cost (AC) functions of these firms are

$$AC_A(X_1, 0) \qquad AC_B(0, X_2)$$

[6] For a review of the literature and its implications for the Canadian financial system, see C. A. Northcott, "Competition in Banking: A Review of the Literature," *Bank of Canada Working Paper 2004–24.*

FIGURE 21–4
Economies of Scale in FIs

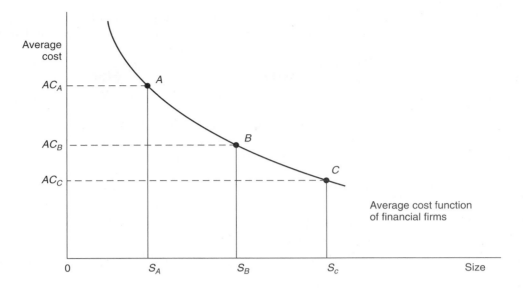

Economies of scope exist if these firms merge and jointly produce X_1 and X_2, resulting in

$$AC_{A+B}(X_1, X_2) < AC_A(X_1, 0) + AC_B(0, X_2)$$

That is, the cost of joint production via cost synergies is less than the separate and independent production of these services. Formally, if AC_{FS} is the total average cost of a non-specialized financial services firm, and TAC is the total average cost of an integrated (universal) FI, economies of scope would imply that

$$AC_{FS} < TAC$$

That is, the average cost to jointly produce many financial services may be less than the average cost to produce these products separately.

As we discussed in Chapter 16, there appear to be economy of scale opportunities for financial firms up to $25 billion in asset size. However, most studies find cost-based economies of scope are negligible, although revenue-based economies of scope may arise for the largest FIs.

Conflicts of Interest

A third issue—the potential for conflicts of interest—lies at the very heart of opposition to an expansion of banking powers into other financial service areas. The two principal questions that arise are (1) the potential conflicts of interest arising from the expansion of banks' securities activities and (2) the type of incentive structures that change *potential* conflicts into *actual* conflicts.

Six Potential Conflicts of Interest

Conflicts of interest that arise when commercial banks, investment banks, and insurance companies combine operations have been prominent in financial markets. In this section, we discuss the six most common potential conflicts of interest identified by regulators and academics.

Salesperson's Incentives   Critics argue that when banks have the power to sell non-bank products, bank employees no longer dispense dispassionate advice to their customers about which product to buy. Instead, they have a salesperson's stake in pushing the bank's own products, often to the disadvantage of the customer. For example, in 2002, Citigroup was under investigation from securities regulators, who were investigating whether Citigroup's stock research was tainted and whether its transactions with corporations and top corporate executives illegally helped the firm win lucrative underwriting contracts. Since the 2008 market meltdown, regulators and the public are increasingly interested in the bonuses paid to top performers at financial institutions during bad times. The issue of corporate governance and other ethical issues for FIs have arisen, particularly for investment advisors who continue to be paid large bonuses even when their clients have suffered huge losses in their retirement accounts and pension funds.

Stuffing Fiduciary Accounts   Suppose a bank is acting as a securities underwriter and is unable to place these securities in a public offering. To avoid being exposed to potential losses, the bank may "stuff" these unwanted securities into accounts managed by its own trust department and over which it has discretionary investment powers. For example, a U.S. judge threw money manager Alan Bond, CIO of Albriond Capital, in jail after he was convicted on charges of allocating winning trades to his own brokerage account and saddling his clients' accounts with losers.

Bankruptcy Risk Transference   Assume that a bank has a loan outstanding to a firm whose credit or bankruptcy risk has increased to the private knowledge of the banker. With this private knowledge, the banker may have an incentive to induce the firm to issue bonds underwritten by the bank's securities affiliate to an unsuspecting public. The proceeds of this bond issue could then be used to pay down the bank loan. As a result, the bank would have transferred the borrowing firm's credit risk from itself to less-informed outside investors, while the securities affiliate also earned an underwriting fee. For example, in 2002, CIBC, JPMorgan Chase, and Citigroup faced several investor lawsuits over funding deals for high-profile bankruptcies such as Enron. Investors say that because of their lending relationships, the banks knew or should have known of the problems at these companies.

Third-Party Loans   To ensure that an underwriting goes well, a bank may make cheap loans to third-party investors on the implicit condition that this loan is used to purchase securities underwritten by its securities affiliate.

Tie-Ins   A bank may use its lending powers to coerce or "tie in" a customer to the products sold by its securities affiliate. For example, the bank may threaten to credit ration unless the customer agrees to let the bank's securities affiliate do its securities underwritings. In the early 2000s, CIBC's "loans" to Enron were in anticipation of other services the company might send its way.

Information Transfer   In acting as a lender, the bank may become privy to certain inside information about its customers or rivals that it can use to set the prices or help the distribution of securities offerings by its affiliate. This information could also flow from the securities affiliate to the bank. Such conflicts are potentially present when M&A activity is involved along with new security issues and loan originations. Such was the case with JPMorgan Chase and Citigroup, FIs involved as lead advisors *and* lead bankers in Enron's failed merger attempt with Dynegy in 2001. The two FIs had large balance sheets and boasted of their ability to provide both loans and advice in the merger. However, the FIs lost their bragging rights for pulling off a difficult deal as Dynegy pulled out of the merger, stating it was deprived of sufficient information on the deal and then learning that Enron had been hiding billions of dollars in debt and had been reporting exaggerated profits for years. Enron ended up declaring bankruptcy in December 2001 and JPMorgan Chase and Citigroup ended up losing between US$800 million and US$900 million each on loans to Enron.

Potential Conflicts of Interest and Their Actual Exploitation

On their own these conflicts appear to be extremely troublesome. Remember, however, that specific and general checks and balances limit their exploitation. Many of these conflicts are likely to remain potential rather than become actual conflicts of interest. Specifically, many of these conflicts, such as tie-ins and third-party loans, breach existing bank regulations and laws. Also, internal barriers or **Chinese walls** in most banks prohibit internal information transfers when they potentially conflict with the best interests of the customer. Further, sales of debt issues to a less-informed public to pay down bank loans may result in future lawsuits against the underwriter once investors discover their losses.[7]

More generally, conflicts of interest are exploitable only under three conditions. First, markets for bank services are uncompetitive so that banks have monopoly power over their customers, for example, in making loans. Second, information flows between the customer and the bank are imperfect or asymmetric so that the bank possesses an information advantage over its customers. Third, the bank places a relatively low value on its reputation. The discovery of having exploited a client can result in considerable market and regulatory penalties.[8]

Chinese wall
An internally imposed barrier within an organization that limits the flow of confidential client information among departments or areas.

Deposit Insurance

A traditional argument against expanded powers is that the explicit and implicit protection given to banks by deposit insurance coverage give banks a competitive advantage over other financial service firms (see Chapter 19). For example, because bank deposits up to $100,000 are covered by explicit deposit insurance, banks are able to raise funds at subsidized, lower-cost rates than are available to traditional securities firms. This may allow them to pass on these lower costs in cheaper loans to their affiliates. This advantage may result if bank regulators regard certain large banking organizations as being too-big-to-fail (TBTF), thereby encouraging these institutions to take excessive risks such as placing aggressive underwriting bids for new issues.

Regulatory Oversight

The regulation of integrated FIs in Canada is complex, involving both federal and provincial/territorial bodies as discussed in Chapter 2 and illustrated by Table 2–7. OSFI has been created as the primary prudential regulator for large federally regulated FIs (banks, savings and loans, life insurance, property and casualty

---

[7] In particular, the underwriter may be accused of lack of due diligence in not disclosing information in the new issue's prospectus.

[8] *The Banker* looked at the top 500 banking brands in 2009. By surveying investors, financial providers, customers, staff, suppliers, and business partners and also looking at business lines (retail, commercial, wholesale, and credit cards), Brand Finance, a U.K.-based valuation firm, found that the market collapse caused a decline in brand value of about one-third in 2008. See "Top 500 Banking Brands," *The Banker,* February 2, 2009, at www.thebanker.com.

insurance), but the regulation of securities activities is handled provincially and territorially. The creation of a national regulatory body for securities firms such as the U.S. Securities and Exchange Commission is under discussion. As well, the regulatory issues regarding the deregulation of FI activities in individual countries are finding their way into the transnational regulations proposed by Basel II for internationally active banks, as discussed in Chapter 20. CIBC's Enron payouts, with their impact on CIBC's Tier 1 capital and thus the safety and soundness of the Canadian financial system, triggered discussions of securities operations risks for integrated banks even though the impact came from operations within the ambit of the U.S. SEC.

www.sec.gov

Competition

The final issue concerns the effects of bank activity expansions on competition in investment banking product lines. Since the Bank Act revisions of the 1980s, banks have come to dominate investment banking activities in Canada, as we discussed in Chapter 4. It could be argued that the banks have had greater monopoly power over capital markets in Canada, but this has been mitigated by the globalization of the investment banking industry, which allows Canadian companies to access international markets through cross-listing of shares on U.S. markets. In addition, large U.S. investment banking firms entered the Canadian market, providing

Increased capital market access for large and small Canadian firms;[9]

Lowered commissions and fees as both Canadian bank-owned firms and international investment bankers compete for large securities issues such as TD Canada Trust's acquisition of BankNorth and the Molson and Coors breweries merger in 2004;

A reduction in the degree of underpricing of new issues.

IPO (initial public offering)
A corporate equity or debt security offered to the public for the first time through an underwriter.

The greatest risk to the underwriter is to price a new issue too high relative to the market's valuation of that security. That is, underwriters stand to lose when they overprice new issues. Given this, underwriters have an incentive to underprice new issues by setting the public offer price (*OP*) below the price established for the security in the secondary market once trading begins (*P*). The investment banker stands to gain by underpricing as it increases the probability of selling out the issue without affecting the fixed underwriting spread. That is, a spread of $0.50 at a bid-offer price spread of $93 and $93.50 produces the same gross revenue (spread) of $0.50 per share to the underwriter as a bid–offer price spread of $97 and $97.50. The major difference is that a lower offer price (i.e., $93 rather than $97) increases the demand for the shares by investors and the probability of selling the whole issue to the public very quickly. Both the underwriter and the outside investor may benefit from underpricing; the loser is the firm issuing the securities because it obtains lower proceeds than if the offer price had been set at a higher price reflecting a more accurate market valuation. In this example, the issuer receives only $93 per share rather than $97. Consequently, underpricing new issues is an additional cost of securities issuance borne by issuing firms. Most empirical research on the underpricing of U.S. new issues, or **initial public offerings (IPOs),** has found that they are underpriced in the range of 8 to 48 percent

---

[9] See G. M. Hebb and D. R. Fraser, "Conflict of Interest in Commercial Bank Security Underwriting: Canadian Evidence," *Journal of Banking and Finance,* 2002, pp. 1935–1949.

secondary issues
A new issue of equity or debt of firms whose securities are already traded in the market.

depending on the sample and time period chosen. In contrast, **secondary issues** tend to be underpriced by less than 3 percent.

If a major cause of IPO underpricing is a lack of competition among existing investment banks, then bank entry and competition should lower the degree of underpricing and increase the new issue proceeds for firms. Nevertheless, many economists argue that monopoly power is not the primary reason for the underpricing of new issues; in their view, underpricing reflects a risk premium that must be paid to investors and investment bankers for information imperfections. That is, underpricing is a risk premium for the information advantage possessed by issuers who better know the true quality of their firm's securities and its assets. If this is so, bank entry into securities underwriting may reduce the degree of underpricing only to the extent that it reduces the degree of information imperfection among issuers and investors. This might reasonably be expected, given the specialized role of banks as delegated monitors (see Chapter 1).

Anticompetitive Effects

With the revision of the Bank Act, the biggest Canadian banking organizations, measured by either capital or assets, were many times larger than the biggest securities firms. The Big Six Canadian banks, aided by the stock market crash of 1987, which weakened securities firms, particularly those that had underwritten the IPO of British Petroleum, absorbed the independent securities firms. The banks thus assumed quasi-oligopoly positions, causing market concentration to rise and perhaps long-run prices for investment banking services to rise also.[10]

Cross-Pillar Mergers: Banks and Insurance Companies

A cross-pillar issue in Canada that has yet to be resolved is the merger of banks and insurance companies. Banks and insurance companies have presented briefs to the federal government since the MacKay Commission report in 1998, and a review of the financial services legislation in Canada is conducted every five years, most recently in October 2005. The six issues discussed with respect to banks and securities mergers are relevant to the insurance discussion and are discussed briefly below:

Safety and Soundness Issues   Both the banks and federally regulated life insurance companies and property and casualty (P&C) insurance companies in Canada are already regulated by OSFI. It can be argued that the regulations for these FIs are converging since OSFI provides guidelines on capital adequacy, large exposure limits, and risk management for all of the FIs under its jurisdiction. Therefore, unlike the securities industry, which is governed by self-regulatory organizations (SROs) such as the exchanges and the Investment Industry Association of Canada (IIAC), the regulatory oversight is already in place for cross-pillar mergers of insurance companies and banks and the safety and soundness of the financial system will not be threatened.

www.iiac.ca

---

[10] One possible reason for the slow development of the German corporate bond market is that German universal banks wish to preserve their monopoly power over corporate debt. This may best be done by encouraging corporate loans rather than bond issues. This may be ascribed to the structure of the financial system in Germany, which historically did not have the strict separation of banking and securities functions found in Canada, the United Kingdom, and the United States. For a discussion of the historical differences in the financial system structures in different countries and their effect on banking and corporate financing, see M. Roe, *Strong Managers, Weak Owners: The Political Roots of American Corporate Finance*, Princeton, NJ: Princeton University Press, 1996.

Economy of Scale and Scope Issues   The banks already possess a branch network that gives them the ability to sell mutual fund and other investment products in their branches. Therefore, the availability of insurance products, along with the banks' experience in creating innovative savings products, could allow them to offer insurance products at a competitive price to existing customers and to generate more profits for their investment in branches, savings that could be passed on to the consumer. If the Finance minister allowed insurance products to be offered through existing bank websites, there could be additional cost savings for online consumers.[11]

Conflict of Interest Issues   Both banks and insurance companies already sell mutual fund and mutual fund-type (segregated funds) products by employees licensed to sell such products. The issue of tied product selling and other legal and ethical issues are already addressed by such organizations as the Mutual Fund Dealers Association of Canada (MFDA).

www.mfda.ca

Deposit Insurance Issues   To the extent that insurance companies would accept deposits similar to other deposit-taking FIs, they would be eligible for membership in the Canada Deposit Insurance Corporation and able to pay the risk-based premiums. This would add another layer of regulation to insurance-based companies and could increase their costs along with the additional annual regulatory evaluation that CDIC conducts to establish the insurance premiums (see Chapter 19).

www.cdic.ca

Regulatory Oversight Issues   Regulation of insurance companies as part of a bank–insurance conglomerate should not be an issue for OSFI since banks already report their assets based on banking, trading, and insurance. No doubt there would be more discussion of the regulation of financial conglomerates, particularly those holding companies outside of the banking sphere, such as Power Financial, which controls significant Canadian insurance (Great West Life, London Life, Canada Life) and mutual fund assets (IGM Financial that includes Investors Group and Mackenzie Financial, see Chapter 5, Figure 5–3).

Competition Issues   The biggest barrier to bank–insurance mergers is the issue of competition in Canada. The banks held in excess of $2.9 trillion on-balance-sheet assets in Canada in 2009, and dwarfed the remaining FIs, including the insurance companies, even with the $7.3 billion merger of Sun Life and Clarica Life Insurance in 2003 and the Manulife and John Hancock of Boston $11 billion deal completed in 2004. There were rumours that Manulife was to merge with CIBC in 2003, but the federal Department of Finance was not open to that possibility. Since the template for bank–insurance mergers has not been established, it is difficult to speculate as to whether a cross-pillar merger would reduce competition and services for consumers. For example, sale of insurance products in bank branches and online might still be prohibited in order to protect the small insurance brokers. Similarly, banks could be required to keep branches open and staff levels up as a condition of mergers, either cross-pillar or bank–bank. Since 2001, and particularly throughout 2004 and 2005, various FIs filed briefs with the federal Department of Finance outlining their positions on competition in the financial services industry. The final report of the Competition Policy Review Panel, filed in June 2008,

---

[11] B. Amoako-Adu and B. F. Smith, "The Wealth Effects of Deregulation of Canadian Financial Institutions," *Journal of Banking & Finance* 19 (1995), pp. 1211–1236, studied the early deregulation and Canadian FIs for the period from 1984 to 1991 and found that there was a significant gain for insurance companies but no evidence to support the transfer of wealth among institutions.

concluded that the "widely held" rule controls the potential for self-dealing and poor corporate governance. The report thus recommended that the minister of Finance allow cross-pillar mergers of large financial institutions that would be overseen by OSFI and the Competition Bureau.[12] The financial markets upheaval in 2008 allowed the Bank of Montreal to expand its insurance presence by acquiring the insurance assets of the U.S. insurer AIG in Canada. As well, the Dutch bank ING Groep NV acted to sell control of its Canadian assets in Canada as shown in the Industry Perspectives feature in Chapter 3. As we will see next in Chapter 22, the large FIs in Canada appear to have adopted different strategies that, because of their strong capital positions, allow them to acquire assets domestically and internationally.

CONCEPT QUESTIONS

1. What are some of the issues that arise in response to bank expansion into securities, insurance, and commercial activities?
2. Explain how firm commitment underwriting of securities is similar to writing put options on assets.
3. Describe ways in which the losses of a securities affiliate in a holding company structure could be transmitted to a bank.
4. In addition to the potential conflicts of interest discussed in this section, can you think of any additional possible conflicts that might arise when commercial banks are allowed to expand their investment banking or insurance activities?

Summary

Traditionally, the financial systems of Canada, the United Kingdom, and the United States have been structured on segmented product lines. These restrictions on product or activity expansion have had some significant costs. Most important has been the loss of potential risk-reducing gains that arise from product diversification, as well as gains from the potential generation of cost and revenue synergies. However, a set of important public policy or social welfare concerns relate to conflicts of interest, safety and soundness, competition, and regulation. Although Canada and the United Kingdom started deregulating in the early 1990s, the United States lagged behind. Nevertheless, in recent years, there has been a dramatic breakdown in many of the regulatory barriers to financial service conglomeration in the United States, culminating with the Financial Services Modernization Act of 1999. The act allowed the creation of a financial services holding company that could engage in banking activities *and* securities underwriting and insurance. As a result, the Canadian and the U.S. financial systems converged toward a "universal banking" system. In such a system, bank, insurance, and securities products were increasingly cross-sold by large conglomerate (universal) financial services firms with the objective of maximizing revenue and cost synergies and reducing risk through diversification.

Questions and Problems

1. How does product segmentation reduce the risks of FIs? How does it increase the risks of FIs?

2. In what ways have other FIs taken advantage of the restrictions on product diversification imposed on commercial banks?

---

[12] The full report of the Competition Policy Review Panel, *Compete to Win,* is available at www.ic.gc.ca.

www.mcgrawhill.ca/olc/saunders

3. How does product segmentation reduce the profitability of FIs? How does product segmentation increase the profitability of FIs?

4. What are the differences in the risk implications of a firm commitment securities offering versus a best-efforts offering?

5. An FI is underwriting the sales of 1 million shares of Ultrasonics, Inc., and is quoting a bid–ask price of $6.00–$6.50.

   a. What are the fees earned by the FI if a firm commitment method is used to underwrite the securities?

   b. What are the fees if it uses the best-efforts method and a commission of 50 basis points is charged?

   c. How would your answer be affected if it manages to sell the shares only at $5.50 using the firm commitment method? The commission for best efforts is still 50 basis points.

6. What is the maximum possible underwriter's fee on both the best-efforts and firm commitment underwriting contracts on an issue of 12 million shares at a bid price of $12.45 and an offer price of $12.60? What is the maximum possible loss? The best-efforts underwriting commission is 75 basis points.

7. The investment arm of a large Canadian bank agrees to underwrite a debt issue for one of its clients. It has suggested a firm commitment offering for issuing 100,000 shares of stock. The bank quotes a bid–ask spread of $97.00–$97.50 to its customers on the issue date.

   a. What are the total underwriting fees generated if all the issue is sold? If only 60 percent is sold?

   b. Instead of taking a chance that only 60 percent of the shares will be sold on the issue date, a bank suggests a price of $95 to the issuing firm. It expects to quote a bid–ask spread of $95.00–$95.40 and sell 100 percent of the issue.

From the FI's perspective, which price is better if it expects to sell the remaining 40 percent at the bid price of $97 under the first quote?

8. What are the reasons why the upside returns from firm commitment securities offerings are not symmetrical in regard to the downside risk?

9. How could the failure of a securities affiliate organizational form negatively affect a bank?

10. What are two operational strategies to reduce the risk to the safety and soundness of a bank resulting from the failure of a securities affiliate or many other types of financial distress?

11. What do empirical studies reveal about the effect of activity diversification on the risk of failure of banks?

12. What role does bank activity diversification play in the ability of a bank to exploit economies of scale and scope? What remains as the limitation to creating potentially greater benefits?

13. What conflicts of interest have been identified as potential roadblocks to the expansion of banking powers into the financial services area?

14. What are some of the legal, institutional, and market conditions that lessen the likelihood that an FI can exploit conflicts of interest from the expansion of commercial banks into other financial service areas?

15. Under what circumstances could the existence of deposit insurance provide an advantage to banks in competing with other traditional securities firms?

16. In what ways does the current regulatory structure argue against providing additional insurance powers to the banking industry? Does this issue just concern banks?

17. What are the potential positive effects of allowing banks to enter more fully into insurance sales and underwriting? What is the anticompetitive argument or position?

Web Question

18. Go to the Board of Governors of the Federal Reserve System website at www.federalreserve.gov. Locate the organizational structure of the largest U.S. commercial bank holding companies using the following steps. Click on "Banking Information and Regulation." Click on "Banking Structure" and then on "National Information Center." Click on "Top 50 BHCs." Click on the top listed (largest) bank holding company. Click on "Organization Hierarchy." Click on "Submit." Repeat these steps for the listed Canadian bank holding companies (TD Banknorth Inc., Harris Financial Corp., RBC Bancorporation). Compare the organizational structure of the institutions.

Appendix 21A EU and G-10 Countries: Regulatory Treatment of the Mixing of Banking, Securities, and Insurance Activities and the Mixing of Banking and Commerce

View Appendix 21A at the Online Learning Centre: www.mcgrawhill.ca/olc/saunders.

Geographic Expansion

This chapter examines the issue of geographic diversification, both international and domestic, for FIs and

▶ traces the potential benefits and costs to the risk management strategies considered by FI managers from geographic expansion, especially from mergers and acquisitions

▶ discusses the reasons underlying the pressure for mergers among financial services firms that dramatically changed and consolidated the structure of the North American and global financial systems

▶ presents some evidence on the cost and revenue synergies as well as other market and firm-specific factors affecting geographic expansion

INTRODUCTION

Just as product expansion (see Chapter 21) may enable an FI to reduce risk and increase returns, so may geographic expansion. Geographic expansions can have a number of dimensions. In particular, expansions can be either domestic or international. For example, Sun Life acquired Celestica in 2002, a domestic insurance firm, whereas Manulife merged with John Hancock of Boston, an "international" expansion, in 2003. Expansions also occur through opening a new office or branch or by acquiring another FI through a merger or acquisition. Insurance companies are able to merge with each other, as noted in Chapter 21, but cross-pillar mergers of banks and insurance companies have yet to occur. Bank–bank mergers are permitted by existing legislation, but are subject to the approval of the minister of Finance. However, since the proposed mergers of Canadian Imperial Bank of Commerce (CIBC) with Toronto-Dominion Bank (TD), and Royal Bank of Canada (RBC) with Bank of Montreal (BMO) were disallowed in 1998, the minister of Finance has yet to provide the promised guidelines on bank mergers.[1] However, after the market turmoil of 2008, Canadian FIs are looking outside of Canada for opportunities (see the Industry Perspectives feature). We now look at expansions in Canada and the United States and then discuss the new global landscape for FIs.

www.cibc.com
www.td.com
www.royalbank.com
www.bmo.com

DOMESTIC EXPANSIONS: CANADA AND THE UNITED STATES

Historically, the ability of FIs to expand domestically has been constrained by regulation. By comparison, no special regulations have inhibited the ability of commercial firms such as General Motors, IBM, and Sears from establishing new or **de novo offices,** factories, or branches anywhere in the country. Nor have

de novo office
A newly established office.

---

[1] The election of a minority federal government in 2004 caused Ralph Goodale, the minister of Finance, to defer a decision on this highly political issue.

INDUSTRY PERSPECTIVES

TOP CANADIAN BANKS EYE DEALS

Sitting on a pile of capital and looking to expand, Canadian banks agree on two things: acquisition opportunities abound, and time is on their side.

But in-depth interviews with the chief executives of the nation's four largest banks suggest each has its own strategy for growth—and each its own degree of caution.

Indeed, the Canadian penchant for prudence is a common thread linking Bank of Montreal, Royal Bank of Canada, Toronto-Dominion Bank and Bank of Nova Scotia as they eye acquisitions from atop the global banking heap.

"Just because a financial institution is sitting there for sale at an attractive price doesn't mean our banks are going to swoop in and pick something up. They're doing their due diligence," said Janet Ecker, a former Ontario finance minister and now head of the Toronto Financial Services Alliance.

Regulators say the caution is well-placed on the part of the banks, all of which are well-regulated, prudent institutions that boast capital levels near 10%.

"I think (caution) is the right stance to take," said Julie Dickson, head of Canada's federal regulator, the Office of the Superintendent of Financial Institutions.

"They will be looking at opportunities and our role is to try to ensure . . . they appreciate the challenges of expanding further. Timing is everything."

Here are the views from the CEOs of the four big players in the market in recent interviews with Reuters:

Royal Bank of Canada

Canada's largest, has targeted organic growth of its capital markets unit and a broadening of U.S. and U.K. banking.

"We're way overcapitalized right now. We know we're overcapitalized, the market knows we're overcapitalized, but that's not going to change in the short term because we want to continue to run a very conservative organization," said Gordon Nixon, the head of Royal Bank.

That's not to say Royal, which built its presence in the U.S. Southeast with a 2001 purchase of North Carolina-based Centura, doesn't have an expansion plan. Nixon aims to invest in Royal's capital markets unit and is looking for ways to build private banking and wealth management.

"In terms of acquisition opportunities, outside of Canada, we've said that our priorities would be either banking or wealth management," said Nixon, 52, pointing to RBC Dexia, its joint venture with Belgian-based Dexia group, as a model.

"I think there are opportunities for consolidation in that industry, largely because a lot of banks have restructured and are looking to shift their business mix," Nixon said.

"I would emphasize we're in no rush. We're not going to run out and buy an asset manager simply because they're available. . . . [Opportunities] are going to increase in number, not shrink in number over the next year."

Toronto-Dominion Bank

A big retail player in the U.S. Northeast, TD Bank wants to expand southwards and is eyeing deals that will help it push down the U.S. East Coast in urban centers. Its boast is a retail brand of extended hours and convenience.

But chief executive Ed Clark admits there is every chance that Canada's banks could miss the boat on acquisitions simply because none is desperate to take over the world.

"I think there's a real possibility that we could be excessively cautious here," said Clark, noting that he has no intention of attempting unfriendly deals. "We're not having to do those to mark out our place in the world."

"I think now is the time to go in the South, the deposits are still there and the assets are now rightly valued," Clark said. "We have really no desire to go to the Midwest or the West. We think that market is well taken."

Bank of Nova Scotia

Canada's third-largest bank is taking a different tack by continuing its slow but steady creep into less developed countries in Latin American, the Caribbean and Asia.

Scotiabank is already the most international of Canada's banks, and has resisted opportunities to ease into the U.S. market. It deployed Chief Executive Rick Waugh last year to "mystery shop" an Ohio bank before deciding against the buy.

"The first check, even though it was a small one, could have been the most expensive. Look what has happened to the American institutions who have made an acquisition there in the last two years," Waugh said.

Scotiabank is inclined to stick to its pattern of buying a small stake in an emerging market, where there are relatively few banks and growth prospects are huge. Invest $50-million or $100-million, and history shows Scotia emerges as a big regional player.

"The difference with us is the bets were small, and we stayed diversified," Waugh said. "Because the U.S. is such a big market, the bets are not small."

Bank of Montreal

BMO, which recently snapped up the Canadian life insurance business of American International Group Inc., and is looking to build its franchise in the U.S. Midwest, where its Harris brand is already strong.

"This is not one of those situations where [opportunities] are going fast," said chief executive Bill Downe.

"The ability to acquire properties at a price that will allow you to earn returns today is significantly better than it was 24 months ago."

Source: Andrea Hopkins, *Financial Post,* June 22, 2009 (Reuters). © 2009 The National Post Company.

---

commercial firms been prohibited from acquiring other firms—as long as they are not banks. Although securities firms and insurance companies have faced relatively few restrictions in expanding their business domestically, other FIs, especially banks, have faced a complex and changing network of rules and regulations. Such regulations may inhibit expansions, but they also create potential opportunities to increase an FI's returns. In particular, regulations may create locally uncompetitive markets with monopoly economic rents that new entrants can potentially exploit. Thus, for the most innovative FIs, regulation can provide profit opportunities as well as costs. As a result, regulation both inhibits and creates incentives to engage in geographic expansions.[2] It is rare that we see a hostile takeover or unfriendly merger in banking. Unlike the case of a merger or acquisition of commercial firms, the extensive review by regulators virtually forces the two parties in a bank merger to work together so that they can get through the review process successfully.

In addition, the economic factors that affect commercial firm expansion and acquisition decisions are likely to influence the decisions of FIs as well. Two major groups of factors are cost and revenue synergies and firm/market-specific attractions, such as the specialized skills of an acquired firm's employees and the markets of the firm to be acquired. Thus, the attractiveness of a geographic expansion, whether through acquisition, branching, or opening a new office, depends on a broad set of factors encompassing

1. Regulation and the regulatory framework.
2. Cost and revenue synergies.
3. Firm- or market-specific factors.

We start by considering how the first factor—regulation—influences an FI's geographic expansion decision.

CONCEPT QUESTIONS

1. Explain why regulation both inhibits and provides incentives to an FI to engage in geographic expansion.
2. What three basic factors influence the attractiveness of geographic expansion to an FI?

---

[2] E. Kane has called this interaction between regulation and incentives the regulatory dialectic. See "Accelerating Inflation, Technological Innovation, and the Decreasing Effectiveness of Banking Regulation," *Journal of Finance* 36 (1981), pp. 335–367. Expansions that are geographic market extensions involving firms in the same product areas are part of a broader set of horizontal mergers.

REGULATORY FACTORS IMPACTING GEOGRAPHIC EXPANSION

Insurance Companies

As discussed in Chapter 3, with the exception of the federally regulated life and property and casualty (P&C) companies, insurance companies are regulated by the provinces and territories. By establishing a subsidiary in one province or territory, an insurance company normally has the opportunity to sell insurance anywhere in that jurisdiction and often to market the product nationally by telemarketing and direct sales. To deliver a financial service effectively, however, it is often necessary to establish a physical presence in a local market. To do this, insurance companies establish offices in other provinces and territories. Thus, most large insurance companies have a physical presence in virtually every Canadian province and territory.

Banks

Canadian banks can only be chartered federally and thus the industry is controlled by one federal regulator. This means that Canadian banks and Canadian consumers take the "sea-to-sea" nature of their banking system for granted. It can be argued that the absence of branching restrictions for domestic banks accelerated the introduction of the technology for interbranch banking and, as well, facilitated the development of the Large Value Transfer System (LVTS) for payments settlements (see Chapters 17 and 20). In a Canadian market that is roughly one-tenth the size of the U.S. market, the major considerations for a domestic expansion are cost and revenue synergies, as discussed below. Regulatory restrictions on branches have been applied to Schedule II and Schedule III banks, as discussed in Chapter 2, in an effort to protect the Canadian control of financial services.

U.S. Commercial Banks

The United States market has provided many opportunities for growth and expansion for Canadian banks (e.g., Bank of Montreal's acquisition of Harris Bank of Chicago in the 1990s and Toronto Dominion's acquisition of Banknorth in 2004). We next consider the U.S. situation in order to provide a North American perspective on the merger wave that has been ongoing since the passage of the Riegle–Neal Interstate Branching and Efficiency Act of 1994.

U.S. Restrictions on Intrastate Banking

unit bank
A bank with a single office.

At the beginning of the century most U.S. banks were **unit banks** with a single office. Improving communications and customer needs resulted in a rush to branching in the first two decades of the 20th century. Increasingly, this movement ran into opposition from the smallest unit banks and the largest money centre banks. The smallest unit banks perceived a competitive threat to their retail business from the larger branching banks; money centre banks feared a loss of valuable correspondent business such as cheque-clearing and other payment services. As a result, several states restricted the ability of banks to branch within the state.

U.S. Restrictions on Interstate Banking

The defining piece of legislation affecting interstate branching until 1997 was the McFadden Act, passed in 1927 and amended in 1933. The McFadden Act and its amendments restricted nationally chartered banks' branching abilities to the same extent allowed to state-chartered banks. Because states prohibit interstate banking for state-chartered banks in general, nationally chartered banks were similarly prohibited.

multi-bank holding company (MBHC)
A parent banking organization that owns a number of individual bank subsidiaries.

Between 1927 and 1997, bank organizations expanding across state lines largely relied on establishing subsidiaries rather than branches. Some of the biggest banking organizations established **multi-bank holding companies** for that purpose. A multi-bank holding company (MBHC) is a parent company that acquires more than one bank as a direct subsidiary. While MBHCs had been around in the early part of the 20th century, the 1927 restrictions on interstate branching gave the bank acquisition movement an added impetus.

Riegle–Neal Interstate Banking and Branching Efficiency Act of 1994   It had long been recognized that nationwide banking expansion through multi-bank holding companies was potentially far more expensive than through branching. Separate corporations and boards of directors must be established for each bank in an MBHC, and it is hard to achieve the same level of economic and financial integration as with branches. Moreover, most major banking countries, such as Canada, Japan, Germany, France, and the United Kingdom, have nationwide branching.

In the fall of 1994, the U.S. Congress passed an interstate banking law that allows U.S. and non-domestic banks to branch interstate by consolidating out-of-state bank subsidiaries into a branch network and/or acquiring banks or individual branches of banks by merger and acquisition. The effective date for these new branching powers was June 1, 1997. The implication of the Riegle–Neal Act is that full interstate banking—with the exception of de novo branching—became a reality in the United States in 1997. The relaxation of the branching restrictions, along with recognition of the potential cost, revenue, and risk benefits from geographic expansions (discussed next), set off a wave of consolidation in the U.S. banking system. This consolidation trend was particularly evident among the largest U.S. banks in a wave of **megamergers,** which reshaped the U.S. banking industry into a nationwide banking system along Canadian and European lines.

megamerger
The merger of two large banks.

The 2008 global market crisis weakened some of the larger U.S. FIs, such as AIG and Citicorp. However, it sparked another reorganization of U.S. banking assets and provided opportunities for further expansion for the strongest, as the Federal Deposit Insurance Corporation looked for purchasers for failing FIs. For example, JPMorgan purchased Washington Mutual's (WaMu's) bad loans and deposits from regulators in September 2008 for US$1.9 billion. WaMu was the largest bank failure in U.S. history. Wells Fargo purchased Wachovia's assets for US$12.7 billion in October 2008 and moved from 123rd to 6th place in *The Banker's* "Top 1000 World Banks" for 2009 (see Table 22–7 on page 550). Bank of America purchased Countrywide, a subprime lender in July 2008 and also acquired Merrill Lynch's assets in September 2008. Many of these purchases proved to be strategic and profitable in 2009.[3]

Canadian FIs expanded by purchasing assets in the United States between 1997 and 2006. Table 22–1 shows the domestic, U.S., and other international assets of the five major Canadian banks at year-end 2008. Bank of Montreal has the highest concentration of U.S. assets with $129.3 billion, 32.5 percent of its total on-balance-sheet assets. However, these asset exposures are dwarfed by the largest 25 banks in the world in 2009 that are listed in Table 22–7. JPMorgan's total assets at year-end 2008 were over US$2 trillion and Germany's Deutsche Bank's assets were over US$3 trillion. This compares with Royal Bank's assets at US$575.2 billion (CDN$724 billion).

---

[3] See A. Levy and E. Hester, "JPMorgan's WaMu Windfall Turns Bad Loans Into Income (Update 2)," *Bloomberg.com*, www.bloomberg.com, May 26, 2009.

TABLE 22–1 Canadian Banks' Domestic, U.S., and International Income and Assets, 2008, for Year Ended October 31 (CDN$ millions)

	Canada	United States	Other Countries	Total
Bank of Montreal:				
Net Interest Income	$ 3,662	$ 1,110	$ 315	$ 5,087
Non-Interest Income	3,951	1,181	(14)	5,118
Net Income	2,008	(184)	154	1,978
Average Assets	236,495	129,262	31,854	397,609
Bank of Nova Scotia:				
Net Interest Income	$ 4,471	$ 236	$ 3,530	$ 8,239
Non-Interest Income	2,614	(202)	1,615	4,027
Net Income	2,038	(84)	1,534	3,488
Average Assets	293,000	30,000	122,000	445,000
CIBC:				
Net Interest Income	$ 3,886	$ 187	$ 1,134	$ 5,207
Non-Interest Income	5,108	(102)	(6,499)	(1,493)
Net Income	1,445	320	(3,825)	(2,060)
Average Assets	252,235	25,727	66,903	344,865
Royal Bank of Canada:				
Net Interest Income	$ 6,929	$ 1,132	$ 1,299	$ 6,402
Non-Interest Income	8,220	2,521	1,481	12,222
Net Income	3,987	152	416	4,555
Average Assets	317,900	135,100	128,000	581,000
Toronto Dominion Bank:				
Net Income	$ 2,486	$ 487	$ 860	$ 3,833
Average Assets	352,418	154,418	56,378	563,214

Source: 2008 Annual Reports

COST AND REVENUE SYNERGIES INFLUENCING GEOGRAPHIC EXPANSION BY MERGER AND ACQUISITION

One reason for an FI deciding to expand (or not to expand) geographically by acquisition relates to the regulations defining its merger opportunities. Other reasons relate to the exploitation of potential cost and revenue synergies from merging (as well as the associated diversification of risk benefits). We look at these potential gains next.

Cost Synergies

X efficiency
Cost savings due to the greater managerial efficiency of the acquiring bank.

A common reason given for bank mergers is the potential cost synergies that may result from economies of scale, economies of scope, or managerial efficiency sources (often called **X efficiencies**[4] because they are difficult to pin down in a quantitative fashion). For example, in 1996, Chase Manhattan and Chemical Bank merged, creating the (then) largest banking organization in the United States, with assets of US$300 billion. It was estimated that annual cost savings from the merger

---

[4] X efficiencies are those cost savings not directly due to economies of scope or economies of scale. As such, they are usually attributed to superior management skills and other difficult-to-measure managerial factors. To date, the explicit identification of what composes these efficiencies remains to be established in the empirical banking literature.

would be US$1.5 billion, to be achieved by consolidating certain operations and eliminating redundant costs, including the elimination of some 12,000 positions from a combined staff of 75,000 in 39 states and 51 countries.

This megamerger was essentially a merger in the same or closely related banking markets. By comparison, an example of a market extension megamerger that has both geographic and cost synergy dimensions was Bank of America's acquisition of FleetBoston. By acquiring FleetBoston for US$43 billion, Bank of America added nearly 1,500 branches and 3,400 ATM machines in the New England area. The combined banks projected annual cost savings to be US$1.1 billion, including consolidation of redundant technology systems. This was followed in 2004 by JPMorgan Chase's US$60 billion merger with Bank One to form the second-largest bank in the United States. With this merger JPMorgan Chase (which had been operating in only four states) acquired Bank One's First USA credit card operations and a massive retail network of about 1,800 branches concentrated in the midwest. Together the merged bank would hold about US$125 billion in credit card balances, giving the combined company an almost 20 percent share of the credit card market. Further, the combined bank was projecting before-tax savings of US$2.2 billion in the three years after the merger, with job cuts estimated to total 10,000 of a combined 140,000 workers.

In a comprehensive study, Berger and Humphrey[5] used data from 1981 to 1989 to analyze the cost savings from megamergers, which they defined as a merger in which the acquirer's and the target bank's assets combined exceeded US$1 billion. They could find very little evidence of potential gains from economies of scale and scope. Indeed, the cost savings they could find were related to improved managerial efficiency (X efficiency). Their study had three major findings. First, the managerial efficiency of the acquirer tended to be superior to that of the acquired bank. Second, the 57 megamergers analyzed produced small but significant X-efficiency gains. Third (and perhaps surprisingly), the degree of cost savings in market overlap mergers (e.g., as in the Chase/Chemical case) was apparently no greater than for geographic extension mergers (as in the Bank of America/FleetBoston case). Overall, Berger and Humphrey could not find the sizable cost synergies of 30 percent or so that are often given as the motivational forces behind such mergers.

In a more recent study of nine megamergers by Rhoades (seven of the nine occurring since 1990), large cost savings were found. Specifically, four of the nine mergers showed significant cost efficiency gains relative to a peer group of non-merged banks and seven of the nine showed a significant improvement in their return on assets. Interestingly, where cost efficiency gains were *not* realized, the major problems came from integrating data processing and operating systems. Houston, James, and Ryngaert examined large bank mergers over the period 1985 through 1996. They found that cost savings represented the primary source of gains in the large majority of recent mergers and that managerial cost savings projections have significant capital market credibility.[6]

---

[5] A. Berger and D. B. Humphrey, "Megamergers in Banking and the Use of Cost Efficiency as an Antitrust Defense," *The Antitrust Bulletin* 37 (1992), pp. 541–600.

[6] S. A. Rhoades, "The Efficiency Effects of Bank Mergers: An Overview of Case Studies of Nine Mergers," *Journal of Banking and Finance* 22(3) (1998), pp. 273–292; and J. F. Houston, C. M. James, and M. D. Ryngaert, "Where Do Merger Gains Come From? Bank Mergers from the Perspective of Insiders and Outsiders," *Journal of Financial Economics* 60 (2001), pp. 285–331.

Revenue Synergies

The revenue synergies argument has three dimensions. First, revenues may be enhanced by acquiring a bank in a growing market. For example, although the 2000 merger of JPMorgan and Chase Manhattan to form JPMorgan Chase was estimated to produce a cost savings of US$1.5 billion, the CEOs of both companies stated that the success of the merger was pinned on revenue growth. The merger combined JPMorgan's greater array of products with Chase's broad client base. The merger added substantially to many businesses (such as equity underwriting, equity derivatives, and asset management) that Chase had been trying to build on its own through smaller deals and gave it a bigger presence in Europe where investment and corporate banking were fast-growing businesses. When JPMorgan Chase then acquired Bank One, analysts praised the combination as one that offered revenue growth potential, the result of the combination of two different business models as well as expense reduction.

Second, the acquiring bank's revenue stream may become more stable if the asset and liability portfolio of the target institution exhibits different credit, interest rate, and liquidity risk characteristics from the acquirer. For example, U.S. real estate loan portfolios showed very strong regional cycles in the 1980s and again in the 2006–2008 period. Specifically, U.S. real estate declined in value in the southwest and then in California. Thus, a geographically diversified real estate portfolio may be far less risky than one in which both acquirer and target specialize in a single region.[7] Studies confirm risk diversification gains from geographic expansions.

Third, there is an opportunity for revenue enhancement by expanding into markets that are less than fully competitive. That is, banks may be able to identify and expand geographically into those markets where *economic rents* potentially exist, but where such entry will not be viewed as being potentially anticompetitive by regulators. Arguably, one of the great potential benefits of the JPMorgan Chase and Bank One merger was the potential for enhanced revenue diversification due to the lack of overlap of the branch networks of the two systems due to the merger.

Merger Guidelines

To the extent that geographic expansions are viewed as enhancing the monopoly power of an FI, regulators and governments may act to prevent a merger unless it produces potential efficiency gains that cannot be reasonably achieved by other means. In Canada, mergers of large FIs require the approval of the minister of Finance. In 1998, Royal Bank of Canada and Bank of Montreal were set to merge, as were Canadian Imperial Bank of Commerce and Toronto-Dominion Bank, but the mergers were not approved. Shortly after, the federal government started public consultations regarding large bank mergers in Canada and accepted submissions until December 31, 2003. As mentioned in Chapter 21, the Competition Bureau's 2008 policy review paper recommended that bank mergers and cross-pillar mergers be allowed in Canada. However, the poor performance of many of the large global FIs has changed the appetite of many FIs and their regulators for consolidation of financial institutions except to prevent the failure of an FI that poses a

www.fin.gc.ca

---

[7] As a result, the potential revenue diversification gains for more geographically concentrated mergers are likely to be relatively low. As noted in Chapter 20, the failures of the Canadian Commercial Bank and the Northland Bank of Canada in 1985 were related to their undiversified loan portfolios that concentrated on oil and gas and real estate loans in western Canada.

systemic risk. Global sentiment has changed from "too big to fail" to "too big to bail."[8]

www.usdoj.gov

**Herfindahl–
Hirschman
Index (HHI)**
An index or measure
of market concen-
tration based on
the squared market
shares of market
participants.

The U.S. Department of Justice has laid down guidelines regarding the acceptability or unacceptability of acquisitions based on the potential increase in concentration in the market in which an acquisition takes place.[9] These merger guidelines are based on a measure of market concentration called the **Herfindahl–Hirschman Index (HHI).** This index is created by taking the percentage market shares of each firm in a market, squaring them, and then adding these squared shares. Thus, in a market where a single firm had a 100 percent market share, the HHI would be

$$HHI = (100)^2 = 10,000$$

Alternatively, in a market in which there were an infinitely large number of firms of equal size, then

$$HHI = 0$$

Thus, the HHI must lie between 0 and 10,000.

Whether a merger will be challenged under the U.S. Department of Justice guidelines depends on the postmerger HHI level. As you can see in Table 22–2, the U.S. Department of Justice defines a *concentrated* market as having a postmerger HHI ratio of 1,800, a moderately concentrated market as having a ratio of 1,000 to 1,800, and an unconcentrated market as having a ratio of less than 1,000. In either

TABLE 22–2
1982 U.S.
Department of
Justice Horizontal
Merger Guidelines

Source: Department of Justice, *Merger Guidelines*, 1982.

Postmerger Market Concentration	Level of Herfindahl-Hirschman Index	Percentage Change in Herfindahl-Hirschman Index and Likelihood of a Challenged Merger
Highly concentrated	Greater than 1,800	Greater than 100—likely to be challenged 50 to 100—depends on other factors* Less than 50—unlikely to be challenged
Moderately concentrated	1,000–1,800	Greater than 100—likely to be challenged; other factors considered* Less than or equal to 100—unlikely to be challenged
Unconcentrated	Less than 1,000	Any increase—unlikely to be challenged

*In addition to the postmerger concentration of the market and the size of the resulting increase in concentration, the department will consider the presence of the following factors in deciding whether to challenge a merger: ease of entry; the nature of the product and its terms of sale; market information about specific transactions; buyer market characteristics; conduct of firms in the market; and market performance. [For a detailed explanation of these factors see Sections III(B) and III(C) of the 1982 Department of Justice *Merger Guidelines*.]

---

[8] The public responses to the 2003 consultation on bank mergers are available at the Department of Finance website at www.fin.gc.ca. The report of the Competition Policy Review Panel, "Compete to Win," is available at www.ic.gc.ca. See also P. Jordan, "Canadian Finance: World Crisis Puts Bank Mergers Out of Mind," July 3, 2009, at www.reuters.com. Jordan suggests that the world of 1998, where bank mergers were necessary for Canadian FIs to compete globally, is gone forever.

[9] The Federal Reserve also has the power to approve or disapprove mergers among state member banks and bank holding companies. The Comptroller of the Currency has similar powers over nationally chartered banks. The Federal Reserve's criteria are similar to those of the Department of Justice in that they take into account the HHI (market concentration index). However, it also evaluates the risk effects of the merger. The Department of Justice has powers to review the decisions made by the bank regulatory agencies. For example, in 1990 and 1991, the Department of Justice successfully challenged two mergers approved by the Federal Reserve Board. These two mergers eventually went ahead only after the acquiring bank had divested some branches and offices.

a concentrated or a moderately concentrated market, postmerger HHI increases of 100 or more may be challenged.[10]

EXAMPLE 22–1 *Calculation of Change in the HHI Associated with a Merger*	Consider a market that has three banks with the following market shares: Bank A = 50% Bank B = 46% Bank C = 4%

The premerger HHI for the market is

$$HHI = (50)^2 + (46)^2 + (4)^2 = 2{,}500 + 2{,}116 + 16 = 4{,}632$$

Thus, the market is highly concentrated according to the Department of Justice guidelines.

Suppose Bank A wants to acquire Bank C so that the postacquisition market would exhibit the following shares:[11]

$$A + C = 54\%$$
$$B = 46\%$$

The postmerger HHI would be

$$HHI = (54)^2 + (46)^2 = 2{,}916 + 2{,}116 = 5{,}032$$

Thus, the increase or change in the HHI (ΔHHI) postmerger is

$$\Delta HHI = 5{,}032 - 4{,}632 = 400$$

Since the increase is 400, which is more than the 100 benchmark defined in the Department of Justice guidelines, the market is heavily concentrated and the merger could be challenged.

There are two problems of interpretation of the HHI in the context of banking and financial services. First, what is the relevant geographic scope of the market for financial services—national, regional, or city? Second, once that market is defined, do we view banks, credit unions, savings and loan companies, and insurance companies as separate or unique lines of business, or are they competing in the same financial market? That is, what defines the institutional scope of the market? In the case of financial services, it has been traditional to define markets on functional, or line of business, criteria, so that commercial banking is a separate market from retail banking and other financial services. Further, the relevant market area has usually been defined as highly localized: the standard metropolitan statistical areas (SMSAs) or rural areas (non-SMSAs). Unfortunately, such definitions become increasingly irrelevant in a world of greater geographic and product expansions. Indeed, the use of HHIs should increasingly be based on regional national market lines and include a broad financial service firm definition of marketplace.

---

[10] In practice, it is only when the change exceeds 200 in banking that a challenge may occur. This is the case banking is generally viewed as being more competitive than most industries. See U.S. Department of Justice *Merger Guidelines.* Systemic risk ("too big to fail") issues were more important to regulators than monop ations during 2008–2009.

[11] Here we consider the effect on the HHI of a within-market acquisition; similar calculations can be ca between-market acquisitions.

TABLE 22–3   **H-Statistic Measures of Concentration for Selected Countries**

	H-Statistic	Number of Banks
Australia	0.94	26
Canada	0.83	49
Germany	0.65	2,226
France	0.81	355
Japan	0.53	44
Switzerland	0.74	227
United Kingdom	0.78	106
United States	0.47	1135

Source: S. Claessens and L. Laeven, 2003, www.worldbank.org/research/interest/confs/042003/papers042003.htm

S. Claessens and L. Laeven evaluated the concentration of banking assets for 50 different countries using an H-statistic that has a value from 0 to 1, with 1 being the highest level of concentration. Table 22–3 summarizes H-statistic data for eight countries from their sample for the period from 1994–2001. As can be seen, Canada's H-statistic was 0.83 while the U.S. had the lowest H-statistic at 0.47, an indication of the difference in the level of banking concentration between Canada and its closest neighbour.[12]

A 2009 study prepared by Celent found that, despite the consolidation in the U.S. system in 2008, the United States and Germany each had an HHI below 500, indicating low bank concentration. Canada and Russia were highly concentrated, with an HHI above 1500. The problems with the Russian banking system versus the stability of the Canadian financial and regulatory system during the global meltdown make it clear that other criteria are needed to assess the stability of a country's financial system (See Chapter 20).[13]

CONCEPT QUESTIONS

1. What recent bank mergers have been motivated by cost synergies?
2. What are the three dimensions of revenue synergy gains?
3. Suppose each of five firms in a banking market has a 20 percent share. What is the HHI?
4. What factors might sway Canada's minister of Finance to allow large bank mergers?

OTHER MARKET- AND FIRM-SPECIFIC FACTORS IMPACTING GEOGRAPHIC EXPANSION DECISIONS

In addition to regulation and cost and revenue synergies, other factors may impact an acquisition decision. For example, an acquiring FI may be concerned about the solvency and asset quality of a potential target FI. Thus, important factors influencing the acquisition decision may include the target FI's leverage or capital ratio, and the amount of non-performing loans in its portfolio.

In a review of a number of U.S. studies that analyzed the determinants of **merger bid premiums** (the ratio of the purchase price of a target bank's equity to its book value), Darius Palia found that premiums are higher (1) in states with the most restrictive regulations and (2) for target banks with high-quality loan portfolios. Palia also concludes that the growth rate of the target bank has little effect

bid

the
ce of a
equity
e.

[12] For details of the calculation of the H-statistic, see S. Claessens and L. Laeven, "What Drives Bank Competition? Some International Evidence, 2003," available at www.worldbank.org. C. A. Northcott, *Competition in Banking: A Review of the Literature,* 2004, Bank of Canada Working Paper 2004–24, available at www.bankofcanada.ca. compares and summarizes this study with others from a Canadian perspective on competition. S. Shaffer, "A Test of Competition in Canadian Banking," 1993, *Journal of Money, Credit, and Banking* 25(1), pp. 49–61, studied the Canadian banking system between 1965–1989 and concluded that the Canadian banking system was concentrated, but still competitive over that time.

[13] See B. Narter, "Too Big to Bail? Bank Concentration in the Developed World," *Celent,* June 22, 2009, at www.celent.com/124_2079.htm.

on bid premiums, while the results for the effects on bid premiums of target bank profitability and capital adequacy are rather mixed. Brewer, Jackson, Jagtiani, and Nguyen found that, in the 1990s, higher-performing targets (as measured by both return on equity and return on assets) receive higher bids; the lower the capital-to-deposit ratio, the larger the bid the acquiring bank is willing to offer; larger targets' loan-to-assets ratios and bank size are positively related to bid premiums, and higher prices occurred in the post-Riegle–Neal environment.[14]

CONCEPT QUESTIONS	1. **Suppose you are a manager of an FI looking at another FI as a target for acquisition. What three characteristics of the target FI would most attract you?**
	2. **Given the same scenario as in question 1, what three characteristics would most discourage you?**

THE SUCCESS OF GEOGRAPHIC EXPANSIONS

A variety of regulatory and economic factors affect the attractiveness of geographic expansions to an FI manager. This section evaluates some of the empirical evidence on the success of market extension mergers. There are at least two levels at which such an evaluation can be done: First, how do investors react when a bank merger is announced? Second, once bank mergers have taken place, do they produce, in aggregate, the expected gains in efficiency and profitability? Both the announcement effect studies and the postmerger performance studies generally support the existence of gains from domestic geographic expansions by U.S. commercial banks.

Investor Reaction

An event study of the 1998 failed Canadian bank mergers (Royal Bank and Bank of Montreal; Canadian Imperial Bank of Commerce and Toronto-Dominion Bank) by Baltazar and Santos found that market power rather than scale, scope, or X-efficiency economies was important to shareholders and that event studies would be useful to regulators in discerning societal benefits. Ng found that investors do not necessarily react positively to the news of an acquisition or merger between financial institutions.[15] Researchers have conducted a number of studies on both non-bank and bank mergers, looking at the announcement effects of mergers on both bidding and target firms' share values. The studies measure the announcement effect by the reaction of investors in the stock market to the news of a merger event. In particular, economists have been interested in whether a merger announcement generates positive **abnormal returns**—risk-adjusted stock returns above normal levels—for the bidding and/or target firms. Unlike the situation with commercial firms, where the typical study finds that only target firms' shareholders gain from merger announcements through significantly positive abnormal

abnormal returns
Risk-adjusted stock returns above expected levels.

---

[14] D. Palia, "Recent Evidence of Bank Mergers," *Financial Markets, Instruments, and Institutions* 3(5), 1994, pp. 36–59; and E. Brewer II, W. E. Jackson III, J. A. Jagtiani, and T. Nguyen, "The Price of Bank Mergers in the 1990s," Federal Reserve Bank of Chicago, *Economic Perspectives* 24(1), 2000, pp. 2–24.

[15] See R. Baltazar and M. Santos, "The Benefits of Banking Mega-Mergers: Event Study Evidence from the 1998 Failed Mega-Merger Attempts in Canada," *Canadian Journal of Administrative Sciences* 20(2), September 2003, pp. 196–208, and A. Ng, "Wealth Effects of Canadian Financial Services Takeovers: Consolidation, Diversification and Foreign Evidence," *American Journal of Finance and Accounting* 1(2), pp. 194–212.

returns, studies in banking find that occasionally both the acquiring bank and the target bank gain.[16] Kane examined bank megamergers in the mid-1990s. He found that large bank bidders gain value when a target is large and when the large target is headquartered in the same state as the bidder. The gain is likely due to the fact that megamergers are more likely to create a bank that regulators would find too big to fail. Nevertheless, other studies find negative returns for bidding banks.[17]

Postmerger Performance

Even though the expectation, on announcement, might be favourable for enhanced profitability and performance as a result of geographic expansion, are such mergers actually proving successful in the postmerger period? For example, after its acquisition of First Chicago, profits of Bank One fell from US$3.45 per share in 1999 to US$2.77 in 2002. Studies of the postacquisition performance of large U.S. bank mergers between 1982 and 1987 and again from 1990 through 2000 have found that merged banks tended to outperform the banking industry. Further, superior performance resulted from improvements in these banks' ability to (1) attract loans and deposits, (2) increase employee productivity, and (3) enhance asset growth. For 1990 through 2000, large bank mergers produced greater performance gains than small bank mergers, activity-focusing mergers produced greater performance gains than diversifying mergers, geographically focusing mergers produced greater performance gains than geographically diversifying mergers, and performance gains were larger after the implementation of nationwide banking in 1997. Finally, the improved performance of a merged bank is the result of both revenue enhancements and cost-reduction activities. However, revenue enhancements are most significant in those mergers that also experience reduced costs. These U.S. banking studies find that the announcement period abnormal stock returns are significantly related to the changes in operating performance after the merger.[18]

A study of small bank mergers (with combined total deposits less than US$400 million) from 1989 through 1991 found that 1989 mergers saw large ROA increases, 1991 mergers resulted in decreases, and 1990 mergers had results somewhere in the middle. However, for all years the merged banks outperformed the banking industry.[19, 20]

---

[16] M. M. Cornett and S. De, "Common Stock Returns in Corporate Takeover Bids: Evidence of Interstate Bank Mergers," *Journal of Banking and Finance* 15, 1991, pp. 273–295.

[17] See E. J. Kane, "Incentives for Banking Megamergers: What Motives Might Regulators Infer from Event-Study Evidence?" *Journal of Money, Credit, and Banking*, 2000, pp. 671–701.

[18] M. M. Cornett and H. Tehranian, "Changes in Corporate Performance Associated with Bank Acquisitions," *Journal of Financial Economics* 31, 1992, pp. 211–234; K. J. Stiroh and P. E. Strahan, "Competitive Dynamics of Deregulation: Evidence from U. S. Banking, "*Journal of Money, Credit, and Banking* 35(5), 2003, pp. 801–828; and M. M. Cornett, J. J. McNutt, and H. Tehranian, "Performance Changes Around Bank Mergers: Revenue Enhancements versus Cost Reductions," *Journal of Money, Credit, and Banking*, 2006, pp. 1013–1050.

[19] J. D. Boyd and S. L. Graham, "Consolidation in U.S. Banking: Implications for Efficiency and Competitive Risk," *Bank Mergers and Acquisitions*, eds. T. Amihud and G. Miller (Amsterdam: Kluwer, 1998).

[20] While most research has found bank acquisitions improve financial performance of the combined bank, results to the contrary have been found in some papers. See B. G. Baradwaj, D. A. Dubofsky, and D. R. Fraser, "Bidder Returns in Interstate and Intrastate Bank Acquisitions," *Journal of Financial Services Research* 5, 1992, pp. 261–273; D. Palia, "Recent Evidence of Bank Mergers," *Financial Markets, Instruments, and Institutions* 3(5), 1994, pp. 36–59; G. Hawawini and I. Swary, *Mergers and Acquisitions in the U.S. Banking Industry* (New York: Elsevier Science, 1990); and M. F. Toyne and J. D. Tripp, "Interstate Bank Mergers and Their Impact on Shareholder Return: Evidence from the 1990s," *Quarterly Journal of Business and Economics* 37(4), 1998, pp. 48–58.

<table>
<tr><td>

CONCEPT QUESTIONS

</td><td>

1. If the abnormal returns for target banks are usually positive, does this mean that managers of acquiring banks tend to overpay the shareholders of the target bank?
2. In general, what do studies of the announcement effect and postmerger performance conclude?

</td></tr>
</table>

GLOBAL AND INTERNATIONAL EXPANSIONS

Many FIs can diversify domestically, but only the very largest can aspire to diversify beyond national frontiers. This section analyzes recent trends toward the globalization of FI franchises and examines the potential return-risk advantages and disadvantages of such expansions. While FIs from some countries are currently seeking to expand internationally, others are contracting their international operations. The extent to which an FI expands internationally is thus part of the overall risk management of the FI.

There are at least three ways an FI can establish a global or international presence: (1) selling financial services from its domestic offices to foreign customers, such as a loan originating in the Toronto office of the Bank of Nova Scotia (BNS) made to a Mexican manufacturer; (2) selling financial services through a branch, agency, or representative office established in the foreign customer's country, such as making a loan to the Mexican customer through BNS's branch in Mexico; and (3) selling financial services to a foreign customer through subsidiary companies in the foreign customer's country, such as BNS buying a Mexican bank and using that wholly owned bank to make loans to the Mexican customer. Note that these three methods of global activity expansion are not mutually exclusive; an FI could use all three simultaneously to expand the scale and scope of its operations.

Canadian and U.S. banks, insurance companies, and securities firms have expanded abroad in recent years, often through branches and subsidiaries; this has been reciprocated by the entrance and growth until recently of foreign FIs in Canadian and U.S. financial service markets. The next section concentrates on the growth of global banking. It begins with Canadian and U.S. bank expansions into foreign countries and the factors motivating these expansions and then discusses foreign bank expansions into Canada and the United States.

Canadian and U.S. Banks Abroad

Serving an exporting nation, particularly in the resource sector, Canadian banks have a long history of international activities, maintaining representative offices for their Canadian clients abroad and networks of correspondent banks to support their exports. As well, Canadian banks are major participants in the global loan syndication markets (see Chapters 12, 14, and 26). However, the level of international diversification varies among the largest banks, ranging from CIBC with just 26.9 percent of its total earning assets outside of Canada to the Royal Bank of Canada with 45.3 percent in 2008. As well as billing itself as "a local bank in 50+ countries" in its 1997 annual report, Bank of Nova Scotia owned 10 percent of Mexico's Grupo Financiero Inverlat, increased the stake to 97.3 percent by 2004, and changed the name of the bank to Scotiabank Inverlat. Table 22–1 shows the foreign income and assets of Canadian banks in 2008. As can be seen, a significant portion of the foreign assets of Canadian banks are located in the United States. This is particularly true for Bank of Montreal, with Harris Bank in Chicago, and CIBC World Capital Markets, with a strong presence in New York.

While some U.S. banks, such as JPMorgan Chase, have had offices abroad since the beginning of the 20th century, the major phase of growth began in the early 1960s after the passage of the Overseas Direct Investment Control Act of 1964. This law restricted domestic U.S. banks' ability to lend to U.S. corporations that wanted to make foreign investments. The law was eventually repealed, but it created incentives for U.S. banks to establish foreign offices to service the funding and other business needs of their U.S. clients in other countries. This offshore funding and lending in dollars created the beginning of a market we now call the *Eurodollar market.* The term **Eurocurrency transaction** denotes any transaction in a currency that takes place outside of the country of origin. For example, a banking transaction booked externally to the boundaries of the United States, often through an overseas branch or subsidiary, is called a **Eurodollar transaction.**[21]

Eurocurrency transaction
Any transaction in a currency that takes place outside of the country of origin.

Eurodollar transaction
Any transaction involving U.S. dollars that takes place outside the United States.

Table 22–4 shows the aggregate size of U.S. bank activities abroad between 1980 and 2006 as well as the different types of loan activities those subsidiaries engage in. As reported in Table 22–4, assets in U.S. bank foreign offices increased from US$353.8 billion in 1980 to US$1,215.4 billion in 2006. However, as a percentage of these banks' total assets, assets in foreign offices fell from 32.4 percent in 1980 to 18.1 percent in 2006. The same trend is found for much of the loan portfolio. The majority of loans (in dollar terms) in foreign offices of U.S. banks are commercial and industrial (C&I) loans, US$158.5 billion in 2006. In 1980, 38.6 percent of these banks' C&I loans were in foreign offices, compared to 20.1 percent in 2006. In 1980, 5.8 percent of these banks' real estate loans were in foreign offices, compared to 3.0 percent in 2006. In contrast to C&I and mortgage loans, in 1980, 8.7 percent of the loans to individuals in these banks were in foreign offices, compared to 15.9 percent in 2006.

U.S. Bank Expansions Abroad

While regulation of foreign lending was the original impetus for the early growth of the Eurodollar market and the associated establishment of U.S. branches and subsidiaries outside the United States, other regulatory and economic factors also have impacted the growth of U.S. offshore banking. These factors are discussed next.

The U.S. Dollar as an International Medium of Exchange   The growth of international trade after World War II and the use of the dollar as an international medium

TABLE 22–4   Assets of U.S. Banks with Foreign Offices, 1980–2006 (US$ billions)

	1980	1990	1995	2000	2005	2006
Total assets	$1,091.4	$1,901.5	$2,530.1	$4,311.4	$6,101.0	$6,726.1
Domestic assets	768.7	1,559.3	1,962.8	3,576.3	5,088.0	5,510.7
Foreign assets	353.8	410.7	666.3	735.1	1,013.0	1,215.4
C&I loans (domestic)*	173.8	326.1	356.8	647.2	564.4	630.6
C&I loans (foreign)	109.4	103.6	125.5	189.8	131.1	158.5
Real estate loans (domestic)	108.9	387.2	486.1	955.5	1,652.0	1,810.0
Real estate loans (foreign)	6.7	26.6	27.2	32.0	48.0	55.4
Individual loans (domestic)	67.1	151.9	207.0	302.1	471.7	483.2
Individual loans (foreign)	6.4	17.2	30.6	44.3	80.8	91.1

*Commercial and industrial loans.

Source: *Federal Reserve Bulletin,* various issues, Table 4–20.

---

[21] That is, the definition of a Eurodollar transaction is more general than "a transaction booked in Europe." In fact, any deposit in dollars taken externally to the United States normally qualifies that transaction as a Eurodollar transaction. The definition may be generalized to all currencies (e.g., Euroyen, etc.).

of exchange encouraged foreign corporations and investors to demand dollars. A convenient way to do this was by using U.S. banks' foreign offices to intermediate such fund flows between the United States and foreigners wishing to hold dollars. Today, trade-related transactions underlie much of the activity in the Eurodollar market. However, with the creation of the new euro currency in January 2002, the importance of the dollar as the "international medium of exchange" has declined. There have been calls for a new international medium of exchange recently.

Political Risk Concerns   Political risk concerns among savers in emerging-market countries have led to enormous outflows of dollars from those countries, often to U.S. branches and subsidiaries in the Cayman Islands and the Bahamas, where there are very stringent bank secrecy rules. Because of the secrecy rules in some foreign countries and the possibility that these rules may result in money laundering and the financing of terrorist activities, the U.S. government enacted the USA Patriot Act of 2001. The act prohibits U.S. banks from providing banking services to foreign banks that have no physical presence in any country (so-called *shell banks*). The bill also added foreign corruption offences to the list of crimes that can trigger a U.S. money-laundering prosecution. Also, U.S. federal authorities have the power to subpoena the records of a foreign bank's U.S. correspondent account. Further, the bill makes a depositor's funds in a foreign bank's U.S. correspondent account subject to the same civil forfeiture rules that apply to depositors' funds in other U.S. accounts. Finally, the act requires U.S. banks to improve their due diligence reviews in order to guard against money laundering. In Canada, the Office of the Superintendent of Financial Institutions (OSFI) maintains a list of suspected terrorist organizations and, under the United Nations Suppression of Terrorism Regulations (UNSTR), requires all Canadian banks and foreign bank subsidiaries to provide reports of accounts held for suspect individuals. Under the Proceeds of Crime (Money Laundering) and Terrorist Financing Act, reports must be sent to the Financial Transactions and Reports Analysis Centre of Canada (FINTRAC).

www.osfi-bsif.gc.ca

www.fintrac.gc.ca

Violations of the USA Patriot Act have resulted in large fines and actions taken against violating banks. For example, in 2004 Hudson United Bank agreed to pay US$5 million to settle a probe into whether a branch failed to monitor accounts in its correspondent banking business. Investigators discovered that more than US$1 billion flowed through suspicious accounts used by customers from South America and the Caribbean at a Hudson United Bank branch over a 16-month period ending in November 2003, when the bank shut down the correspondent business dealing with international customers. The branch was not following required "know your customer" rules set out in the Patriot Act.

Under the Patriot Act, the United States can designate banks or entire countries as being a primary money-laundering concern. It can then take special measures against them. For example, in September 2005, the U.S. Treasury Department said Banco Delta Asia was a "willing pawn" of North Korea, helping the country place counterfeit U.S. currency into circulation and facilitating the criminal activities of the North Korean government and North Korean companies. In the case of Banco Delta Asia, the Treasury Department was seeking to prohibit all U.S. financial institutions from maintaining correspondent accounts for the bank, effectively cutting it off from access to the U.S. financial system.

Domestic Regulatory Restrictions/Foreign Regulatory Relaxations   As discussed in Chapter 21, prior to the 1999 Financial Services Modernization Act, U.S. banks faced considerable activity restrictions at home regarding their securities, insurance, and commercial activities. However, with certain exceptions, Federal Reserve regulations have allowed U.S. banking offices in other countries to engage in the permitted banking activities of the foreign country even if such activities were not permitted in the United States. For example, U.S. banks setting up foreign subsidiaries can lease real property, act as general insurance agents, and underwrite and deal in foreign corporate securities (up to a maximum commitment of US$2 million). Foreign activity regulations also encourage U. S. bank expansion abroad. For example, in late 2003 the Chinese Banking Regulatory Commission signalled a shift in policy away from restricting overseas competition to one of cautiously embracing it when it announced a comprehensive plan to overhaul the country's shaky banking system. The plan gave foreign banks greater scope to operate in China, including increasing the ceiling on foreign ownership in Chinese financial institutions from 15 percent to 20 percent for a single investor, expanding the number of cities where foreign branches could do local currency business, and easing capital requirements for foreign branches.

Technology and Communications Improvements   The improvements in telecommunications and other communications technologies such as CHIPS (the international payment system, see Chapter 16) and the development of proprietary communication networks by large FIs have allowed FIs to extend and maintain real-time control over their foreign operations at a decreasing cost. The decreasing operating costs of such expansions have made it feasible to locate offices in an even wider array of international locations.

Factors Deterring Expansions Abroad

A number of potential factors deter international expansion, as discussed next.

Capital Constraints   The Basel II reforms of the Bank for International Settlements (BIS) capital requirements raised the required capital needed to back loans to sovereign countries outside of the Organisation for Economic Co-operation and Development (OECD) rated below B– as well as any loans to OECD countries that are rated below AA– (i.e., it is only the OECD countries rated above AA– that have zero risk weight; see Chapter 20).

Emerging Market Problems

The problems of other emerging-market countries such as Korea, Thailand, and Indonesia in 1997 and 1998 and in the early 2000s in Argentina have made many Canadian and U.S. banks more cautious in expanding outside traditional foreign markets.[22] This is despite the existence of increasingly favourable regulatory environments. For example, the 1994 **NAFTA** agreement has given U.S. and Canadian banks greater powers to expand into Mexico. See Table 22–5 for details on the NAFTA agreement. The December 1997 agreement by 100 countries, reached under the auspices of the World Trade Organization (WTO), was also an important step toward dismantling the regulatory barriers inhibiting the entry of North American FIs into emerging-market countries.

Competition   During the 1990s, global banks faced extensive competition from Japanese banks for overseas business. Aiding the Japanese banks was

NAFTA
The North American
Free Trade Agreement.

---

[22] Notable exceptions are Bank of Nova Scotia, as previously noted, and Citigroup. Citigroup purchased Mexico's second largest bank, Grupo Financiero Banamex-Accival in 2000. Citing Citigroup's faith in the recovery of Mexico's economy and banking system, the company hoped to use the Banamex brand name to serve the fast-growing Hispanic population in the United States as well.

TABLE 22–5
The NAFTA Agreement and Banks

Source: Institute of International Bankers, *1994 Global Survey of Regulatory and Market Developments in Banking, Securities and Insurance,* September 1994, p. 17.

- Any bank chartered in Canada or the United States, including Canadian or U.S. banks owned by non-domestic banks, may establish a bank subsidiary in Mexico that may expand in Mexico without geographic restriction. Canadian and U.S. banks, however, may not branch directly into Mexico.
- Banks from Mexico and Canada may establish direct branches and subsidiaries in the United States subject to the same geographic restrictions imposed on direct branches of other non-domestic banks and on other U.S. chartered banks, respectively.
- Banks from the United States and Mexico that are not controlled by investors from other countries may establish Schedule II bank subsidiaries in Canada, which subsidiaries enjoy nationwide branching powers. Mexican and U.S. banks may not branch directly into Canada.

Notes:
1. Non-domestic banks cannot open branches but are allowed to establish Schedule II subsidiary banks in Canada. Schedule II subsidiary banks owned by banks from the United States or Mexico have the same nationwide branching privileges as domestic Canadian banks. Schedule II banks owned by banks from other countries must seek government approval to open additional branches. This geographic restriction on Schedule II subsidiaries will be eliminated when the latest round of GATT comes into effect.
2. Mexico does not permit non-domestic banks to establish domestic branches. However, non-domestic banks can establish representative offices and offshore branches and take minority interests in local banking institutions. In addition, under NAFTA, banks from the United States and Canada, including U.S. and Canadian banks owned by banks from other countries, are allowed to establish bank subsidiaries with the same nationwide branching privileges as Mexican banks.

their access to a large domestic savings base at a relatively low funding cost, the relatively slow pace of deregulation in the Japanese domestic financial markets, and their size. For example, for most of the 1990s, Japan had nine of the ten largest banks, measured by asset size, in the world. Though large size does not necessarily mean high profits, it gives a bank a greater ability to diversify across borders (and products) and to attract business by aggressively cutting fees and spreads in selected areas. However, in the late 1990s and early 2000s, as the Japanese economy moved into recession and the bad debts of Japanese banks mounted, the main competitive threat to U.S. banks came from European banks.

Aiding the competitive position of European banks has been the passage of the European Community (EC) Second Banking Directive, which created a single banking market in Europe as well as the introduction of a single currency for much of Europe (the euro). Under the Directive, European banks are allowed to branch and acquire banks throughout the European Union—that is, they have a single EC passport.[23] Although the Second Banking Directive did not come fully into effect until the end of 1992, it was announced as early as 1988. As a result, there was a cross-border merger wave among European banks that paralleled the U.S. domestic merger and acquisition wave.[24] In addition, a number of European banks formed strategic alliances that enabled retail bank customers to open new accounts, access account information, and make payments to third parties through any of the branches of the member banks in the alliance. This greater consolidation in European banking created more intense competition for Canadian and other foreign banks in European wholesale markets and made it more difficult for them to penetrate European retail markets.

---

[23] Direct branching by non-EC banks into member states was not governed by the Second Banking Directive but by the laws of each member state. Currently, all EC countries allow foreign banks to branch.

[24] See P. Angelini and N. Citorellis, "The Effects of Regulatory Reform on Competition in the Banking Industry," *Journal of Money, Credit, and Banking,* October 2003, pp. 663–684.

Foreign Banks in North America

As shown in Table 22–5 and also discussed in Chapter 2, foreign banks in Canada are called Schedule II banks, are regulated by OSFI, and are subsidiaries of international FIs such as Citibank, the U.K.'s HSBC, and Germany's Deutsche Bank. OSFI lists 26 foreign bank branches in Canada in 2009, with total assets of $73.2 billion at August 31, 2009. Canadian banks, as shown in Table 22–1, hold many of their assets in the United States. Just as U.S. banks can profitably expand into foreign markets, Canadian and foreign banks have historically viewed the United States as an attractive market for entry (see the Industry Perspectives feature). The following sections discuss foreign banks in the United States.

Organizational Form

Foreign banks use five primary forms of entry into the U.S. market. The choice of which organizational form to use is a function of regulations in the bank's home country as well as the risk management strategies followed by the bank.

Subsidiary   A foreign bank subsidiary has its own capital and charter; it operates in the same way as any U.S. domestic bank, with access to both retail and wholesale markets.

Branch   A branch bank is a direct expansion of the parent bank into a foreign or U.S. banking market. As such, it is reliant on its parent bank, such as Sumitomo Mitsui Banking Corporation in Japan, for capital support; normally, it has access to both wholesale and retail deposit and funding markets in the United States.

Agency   An agency is a restricted form of entry; this organizational form restricts access of funds to those funds borrowed on the wholesale and money markets (i.e., an agency cannot accept deposits).

Edge Act Corporation
Specialized organizational form open to U.S. domestic and foreign banks that specialize in international trade-related banking transactions or investments.

Edge Act Corporation   An **Edge Act Corporation** is a specialized organizational form open to U.S. domestic banks since 1919 and to foreign banks since 1978. These banks specialize in international trade-related banking transactions or investments.

Representative Office   Even though a representative office books neither loans nor deposits in the United States, it acts as a loan production office, generating loan business for its parent bank at home. This is the most limited organizational form for a foreign bank entering the United States.[25]

Trends and Growth

Table 22–6 shows the expansion of foreign banks in the United States between 1980 and 2006. In 1980, foreign banks had US$166.7 billion in assets (10.8 percent of the size of total U.S. bank assets). This activity grew through 1992, when foreign banks had US$514.3 billion in assets (16.4 percent of the size of U.S. assets). In the mid-1990s, there was a modest retrenchment in the asset share of foreign banks in the United States. In 1994, their U.S. assets totalled US$471.1 billion (13.8 percent of the size of U.S. assets). This retrenchment reflected a number of factors, including the highly competitive market for wholesale banking in the United States, a decline in average U.S. loan quality, capital constraints on Japanese banks at home

---

[25] Also note the existence of international banking facilities (IBF) in the United States since 1981. These are specialized vehicles that are allowed to take deposits from and make loans to foreign (non-U.S.) customers only. As such, they are essentially offshore banking units that operate onshore. Most are located in New York, Illinois, and California and are generally free of U.S. bank regulation and taxes.

TABLE 22–6
U.S. and Foreign
Bank Assets,
1980–2006

Source: *Assets and Liabilities of Commercial Banks in the United States,* Federal Reserve Board website, various dates, www.federalreserve.gov.

| | Bank Assets Held in United States (US$ billions) | |
	U.S.-Owned	Foreign-Owned
1980	$1,537.0	$ 166.7
1985	2,284.8	175.5
1990	3,010.3	389.6
1992	3,138.4	514.3
1994	3,409.9	471.1
1995	3,660.6	530.1
2000	5,366.0	863.9
2005	7,738.1	938.5
2006	8,542.1	1,080.1

and their poor lending performance at home, and the introduction of the Foreign Bank Supervision and Enhancement Act (FBSEA) of 1991, which tightened regulations on foreign banks in the United States (discussed below). However, as foreign banks adjusted to these developments and because of the strong U.S. economy in the late 1990s, activity of foreign banks in the United States grew, reaching 16.1 percent in 2000. The worldwide economic recession in the early 2000s again depressed the level of international activity in the United States. For example, in 2006, the percentage of foreign bank assets in the United States was just 12.6 percent.

Regulation of Foreign Banks in the United States

Before 1978, foreign branches and agencies entering the United States were licensed mostly at the state level. As such, their entry, regulation, and oversight were almost totally confined to the state level. Beginning in 1978 with the passage of the International Banking Act (IBA) and the more recent passage of the Foreign Bank Supervision Enhancement Act (FBSEA), Title II of the FDICIA of December 1991, federal regulators have exerted increasing control over foreign banks operating in the United States.

The International Banking Act of 1978

Pre-IBA. Before the passage in 1978 of the IBA, foreign agencies and branches entering the United States with state licences had some competitive advantages and disadvantages relative to most domestic banks. On the one hand, as state-licensed organizations, they were not subject to the Federal Reserve's reserve requirements, audits, and exams; interstate branching restrictions (the McFadden Act); or restrictions on corporate securities underwriting activities (the Glass–Steagall Act). However, they had no access to the Federal Reserve's discount window (i.e., lender of last resort); no direct access to Fedwire, and, thus, the fed funds market; and no access to FDIC deposit insurance.

www.fdic.gov

Their inability to gain access to deposit insurance effectively precluded them from the U.S. retail banking market and its deposit base. As a result, prior to 1978, foreign banks in the United States largely concentrated on wholesale banking.

www.federalreserve.gov

Post-IBA. The unequal treatment of domestic and foreign banks regarding federal regulation and lobbying by domestic banks regarding the unfairness of this situation provided the impetus for Congress to pass the International Banking Act in 1978. The fundamental regulatory philosophy underlying the IBA was one of

national treatment
Regulating foreign
banks in the same
fashion as domestic
banks or creating a
level playing field.

national treatment, a philosophy that attempted to create a level playing field for both domestic and foreign banks in U.S. banking markets. As a result of this act, foreign banks were required to hold Federal Reserve-specified reserve requirements if their worldwide assets exceeded US$1 billion, were subjected to Federal Reserve examinations, and were subjected to both the McFadden and Glass–Steagall Acts. With respect to the latter, an important grandfather provision in the act allowed foreign banks established in the United States prior to 1978 to keep their "illegal" interstate branches and securities activity operations. That is, interstate and security activity restrictions were applied only to new foreign banks entering the United States after 1978.[26]

The passage of the IBA accelerated the expansion of foreign bank activities in the United States. A major reason for this was that for the first time, the IBA gave foreign banks access to the Federal Reserve's discount window, Fedwire, and FDIC insurance. In particular, access to FDIC insurance allowed entry into retail banking. For example, in 1979 alone, foreign banks acquired four large U.S. banks. In addition, in the early 1980s, the Bank of Tokyo, Mitsubishi Bank, and Sanwa Bank invested US$1.3 billion in California bank acquisitions. Overall, Japanese banks owned over 25 percent of California bank assets at the end of the 1980s. (By the end of the 1990s, many of these Japanese-owned California bank assets were up for sale.)

The Foreign Bank Supervision Enhancement Act (FBSEA) of 1991 Along with the growth of foreign bank assets in the United States came concerns about foreign banks' rapidly increasing share of U.S. banking markets as well as about the weakness of regulatory oversight of many of these institutions. Three events focused attention on the weaknesses of foreign bank regulation. The first event was the collapse of the Bank of Credit and Commerce International (BCCI), which had a highly complex international organizational structure based in the Middle East, the Cayman Islands, and Luxembourg and had undisclosed ownership stakes in two large U.S. banks. BCCI was not subject to any consolidated supervision by a home-country regulator; this quickly became apparent after its collapse, when massive fraud, insider lending abuses, and money-laundering operations were discovered. The second event was the issuance of more than US$1 billion in unauthorized letters of credit to Saddam Hussein's Iraq by the Atlanta agency of the Italian Banca Nazionale del Lavoro. The third event was the unauthorized taking of deposit funds by the U.S. representative office of the Greek National Mortgage Bank of New York.

These events and related concerns led to the passage of the FBSEA of 1991. The objective of this act was to extend U.S. federal regulatory authority over foreign banking organizations in the United States, especially where these organizations entered using state licences. The act's five main features have significantly enhanced the powers of federal bank regulators over foreign banks in the United States.

1. *Entry.* Under FBSEA, a foreign banking organization must now have the Fed's approval to establish a subsidiary, branch, agency, or representative office in the United States. The approval applies to both a new entry and an entry by acquisition. To get Fed approval, the organization must meet a number of standards, two of which are mandatory. First, the foreign bank must be subject to comprehensive supervision on a consolidated basis by a home-country regulator. Second, that regulator must furnish all the information needed by the Federal Reserve to

---

[26] For example, in 1978, some 60 foreign banks had branches in at least three states. As noted earlier, the McFadden Act prevented domestic banks from engaging in interstate branching.

evaluate the application. Both standards are aimed at avoiding the lack of disclosure and lack of centralized supervision associated with BCCI's failure.

2. *Closure.* The act also gives the Federal Reserve authority to close a foreign bank if its home-country supervision is inadequate, if it has violated U.S. laws, or if it is engaged in unsound and unsafe banking practices.

3. *Examination.* The Federal Reserve has the authority to examine each office of a foreign bank, including its representative offices. Further, each branch or agency must be examined at least once a year.

4. *Deposit taking.* Only foreign subsidiaries with access to FDIC insurance can take retail deposits under US$100,000. This effectively rolls back the provision of the IBA that gave foreign branches and agencies access to FDIC insurance.

5. *Activity powers.* Beginning on December 19, 1992, state-licensed branches and agencies of foreign banks could not engage in any activity that was not permitted to a federal branch.

Overall, the FBSEA considerably increased the Federal Reserve's authority over foreign banks and added to the regulatory burden or costs of entry into the United States. Indeed, in the two years after the passage of the FBSEA, federal bank supervisors issued 40 formal enforcement actions against foreign banks operating in the United States. In the most serious case, the Japanese Daiwa bank was ordered to cease its U.S. banking operations. Underlying its forced closure were losses by a single bond trader that had been concealed by Daiwa's management from U.S. regulators for over six weeks, and that amounted to over US$1 billion. In January 1996, Daiwa's U.S. bank assets were sold to Sumitomo Bank of Japan, and in February 1996, Daiwa paid a fine of US$340 million to the U.S. authorities for settlement of charges against the bank. This sent a strong signal regarding the willingness of the authorities to take a tough stand against errant foreign banks.

CONCEPT QUESTIONS	1. What regulatory and economic factors have encouraged the growth of offshore banking? What factors have deterred offshore banking?
	2. What were the major policy changes pertaining to bank expansion introduced by NAFTA?
	3. What are the primary forms of entry by foreign banks into the U.S. market?
	4. What impact did the passage of the International Banking Act of 1978 have on foreign bank activities in the United States?

ADVANTAGES AND DISADVANTAGES OF INTERNATIONAL EXPANSION

Historical and recent trends affecting the geographic expansion of FIs both into and outside North America have been discussed above. Here we summarize the advantages and disadvantages of international expansions to the individual FI seeking to generate additional returns or better diversify its risk.

Advantages

Below are the six major advantages of international expansion.

Revenue and Risk Diversification

As with domestic geographic expansions, an FI's international activities potentially enhance its opportunity to diversify the risk of its revenue flows. Often, domestic revenue flows from financial services are strongly linked to the state of that economy. Therefore, the less integrated the economies of the world are, the greater is the potential for revenue diversification through international expansions. For example, Citigroup's goal during the early 2000s was to aggressively expand its consumer banking presence outside the United States to boost profits and to leave behind rival U.S. banks who were just starting to take steps to combine corporate and consumer banking as a strategy. International expansions can reduce risk if the FI can undertake activities that are not permitted domestically but that have a low, or negative, correlation with domestic activities.

Economies of Scale

To the extent that economies of scale exist, an FI can potentially lower its average operating costs by expanding its activities beyond domestic boundaries.

Innovations

An FI can generate extra returns from new product innovations if it can sell such services internationally rather than just domestically. For example, consider complex financial innovations, such as securitization, caps, floors, and options, that FIs have innovated in North America and sold to new foreign markets with few domestic competitors. It has been argued that the dominance of foreign securities firms in Japan is attributable to their comparative advantage and knowledge of risk management techniques and the use of derivatives compared to domestic Japanese securities firms.[27]

Funds Source

International expansion allows an FI to search for the cheapest and most available sources of funds. This is extremely important given the very thin profit margins in domestic and international wholesale banking. Also, it reduces the risk of fund shortages (credit rationing) in any one market.

Customer Relationships

International expansions also allow an FI to maintain contact with and service the needs of domestic multinational corporations. Indeed, one of the fundamental factors determining the growth of FIs in foreign countries has been the parallel growth of foreign direct investment and foreign trade by globally oriented multinational corporations from the FI's home country.[28]

Regulatory Avoidance

To the extent that domestic regulations such as activity restrictions and reserve requirements impose constraints or taxes on the operations of an FI, seeking out low regulatory tax countries can allow an FI to lower its net regulatory burden and to increase its potential net profitability.

Disadvantages

Below are the three major disadvantages of international expansion.

---

[27] In 1998, Merrill Lynch absorbed 30 branches and 2,000 employees of the defunct Yamaichi Securities (traditionally the fourth-largest domestic securities firm in Japan). In the same year Travelers (and its Salomon Securities subsidiary) bought a 25 percent share in Nikko Securities (traditionally the third-largest securities firm in Japan).

[28] B. Williams, in "The Defensive Expansion Approach to Multinational Banking: Evidence to Date," *Financial Markets, Institutions, and Instruments,* May 2002, pp. 127–203, concludes that defensive expansion (in which banks follow their customers abroad) increases multinational bank size but has little impact on these banks' profit.

Information/Monitoring Costs

Although global expansions give an FI the potential to better diversify its geographic risk, the absolute level of exposure in certain areas such as lending can be high, especially if the FI fails to diversify in an optimal fashion. For example, the FI may fail to choose a loan portfolio combination on the efficient lending frontier (see Chapter 12). Foreign activities may also be riskier for the simple reason that monitoring and information collection costs are often higher in foreign markets. For example, Canadian firms will not adopt international accounting standards until 2011. In addition, language, legal, and cultural issues can impose additional transaction costs on international activities. Finally, because the regulatory environment is controlled locally and regulation imposes a different array of net costs in each market, a truly global FI must master the various rules and regulations in each market.[29]

Nationalization/Expropriation

To the extent that an FI expands by establishing a local presence through investing in fixed assets such as branches or subsidiaries, it faces the political risk that a change in government may lead to the nationalization of those fixed assets.[30] Further, if foreign FI depositors take losses following a nationalization, they may seek legal recourse from the FI in North American courts rather than from the nationalizing government. For example it took many years to resolve the outstanding claims of depositors in Citicorp's branches in Vietnam following the Communist takeover and expropriation of those branches.

Fixed Costs

The fixed costs of establishing foreign organizations may be extremely high. For example, a Canadian FI seeking an organizational presence in the Tokyo banking market faces real estate prices significantly higher than those in Toronto, Vancouver, or New York. Such relative costs can be even higher if an FI chooses to enter by buying an existing bank rather than establishing a new operation. These relative cost considerations become even more important if there is uncertainty about the expected volume of business to be generated.

CONCEPT QUESTIONS

1. What are the major advantages of international expansion to an FI?
2. What are the major disadvantages of international expansion to an FI?

GLOBAL TRENDS: THE IMPACT OF THE 2008 MARKET MELTDOWN

The year 2008 was an important marker for global financial institutions. A change in the global financial order started in 2007 with the rise of some emerging-market banks, and accelerated into 2009. Table 22–7 shows *The Banker*'s list of the top 25 global banks in 2009 based on their Tier 1 capital. In previous years, banks were

---

[29] C. M. Buch and G. DeLong find that high information costs, as proxied by distance and common cultural factors (measured by geographic distance and language differences), tend to hold back merger activity. Moreover, information costs have larger effects on the number of bank mergers than regulatory variables. See *Cross-Border Bank Mergers: What Lures the Rare Animal?* Working Paper, Baruch College, The City University of New York, 2003.

[30] Such nationalizations have occurred with some frequency in African countries.

TABLE 22–7   The World's Largest Banks Ranked by Tier 1 Capital (US$ billions)

	Bank	Tier 1* with Gov't. Support	Tier 1 minus Gov't. Support	Market Capital	Assets	Pre-Tax Profit (Loss)
1	JPMorgan Chase & Co. (U.S.)	$136.104	$111.104	$127.811	$2,175.052	$ 2.773
2	Bank of America Corp. (U.S.)	120.014	105.814	85.351	1,817.943	4.428
3	Citigroup (U.S.)	118.758	73.758	n.a.	1,938.470	−53.055
4	Royal Bank of Scotland (U.K.)	101.818	71.923	34.901	3,500.950	−59.281
5	HSBC Holdings (U.K.)	95.336	95.336	149.920	2,418.033	9.307
6	Wells Fargo & Co. (U.S.)	86.397	61.397	105.360	1,309.639	−47.788
7	Mitsubishi UFJ Financial (Japan)	77.218	77.218	75.005	2,025.830	1.173
8	ICBC (China)	74.701	74.701	56.046	1,427.865	21.260
9	Crédit Agricole Group (France)	71.681	67.521	n.a.	2,239.370	5.388
10	Santander Central Hispano (Spain)	65.267	65.267	88.568	1,460.866	15.825
11	Bank of China (China)	64.961	64.961	36.193	1,017.718	12.620
12	China Construction Bank (China)	63.113	63.113	163.215	1,106.471	17.520
13	Goldman Sachs (U.S.)	62.637	52.637	n.a.	884.547	2.336
14	BNP Paribas (France)	58.175	54.539	70.585	2,888.728	5.461
15	Barclays Bank (U.K.)	54.300	54.300	38.215	2,992.682	8.859
16	Mizuho Financial Group (Japan)	48.752	48.752	n.a.	1,494.960	4.956
17	Morgan Stanley (U.S.)	40.085	38.085	n.a.	297.422	1.707
18	Unicredit (Italy)	47.529	47.529	44.334	1,455.270	6.952
19	Sumitomo Mitsui Financial Group (Japan)	46.425	46.425	n.a.	1,219.544	0.301
20	ING Bank (Netherlands)	44.564	44.564	n.a.	1,853.393	−2.070
21	Deutsche Bank (Germany)	43.276	43.276	38.273	3,065.307	−7.990
22	Rabobank Group (Netherlands)	42.252	42.252	n.a.	851.942	1.655
23	Société Générale (France)	42.203	39.845	n.a.	1,572.721	5.578
24	Agricultural Bank of China	39.998	39.998	n.a.	1,026.300	7.659
25	Intesa Sanpaulo (Italy)	37.681	37.681	39.301	885.363	1.471

* Tier 1 = Common stock, disclosed reserves, and retained earnings.

Source: *The Banker*, "Top 1000 World Banks, 2009," www.thebanker.com.

ranked by total assets. The numbers in this table tell the story of the events of 2008. Some of the pertinent points to note are given below.

Tier 1 Capital

Tier 1 capital in this table is defined by *The Banker* to be common shares, disclosed reserves, and retained earnings. This is a conservative measure since allowable preferred shares are excluded (see Chapter 20). Wells Fargo is ranked sixth because of its merger with Wachovia bank. Goldman Sachs and Morgan Stanley are the remaining large U.S. investment banks that converted to commercial bank holding companies in September 2008. The Chinese banks are included in the table as well, examples of an emerging financial market. In the top 100 of the ranking were RBC (34), BNS (40), TD (46), BMO (52), and CIBC (71).

Government Capital

Table 22–7 also shows the amount of government capital that was provided by central banks to support and partially nationalize those FIs deemed too big to fail. In some cases, (Citigroup, Royal Bank of Scotland) it is questionable whether the bank would have survived without an injection of government capital. Some FIs started to repay the government bailout money in 2009.

Market Capitalization

When ranked by Tier 1 capital, none of the Canadian banks placed in the top 25. However, based on market capitalization, Royal Bank of Canada (US$56.21 billion), TD Bank (US$42.78 billion), and the Bank of Nova Scotia (US$35.96 billion) ranked 9, 16, and 23, respectively, in the world. As we have noted, the Canadian banks did not and are not expected to suffer the level of losses of other FIs. This means that, as shown in the Industry Perspectives feature, the Canadian banks' strategies are to expand by acquiring the operations of other FIs, both domestically and internationally. For example, in 2009, BMO paid $375 million for AIG Life Insurance of Canada. Other FIs are in a position to expand their operations. For example, for investment banking services, Goldman Sachs was on target to have its largest year ever in 2009 as competition was decimated (6 firms versus 20 or so per deal). While the number of deals was down, the fees for services were up because of the flight to quality. Market participants were looking to reduce their risk by working only with top-quality counterparties. As well, consumers, firms, and FIs deleveraged. Many companies looked to reestablish relationships with their bankers as a source of short- and long-term funding. This was a partial reversal of the disintermediation process and the recognition of the specialness of banks and other FIs in monitoring credit risk.

Asset Size

In previous years, banks have been ranked by asset size. The significance of the changes to the industry meant that *The Banker* saw fit to rank them by Tier 1 capital, which is the great leveller for all global banks. The issue of capital and therefore size is the focus for regulators as well as the determinant of which products FIs will be able to offer and how they will be able to offer them.

Pre-Tax Profits

Some of the largest banks did not make a profit in 2008. Of particular note is Royal Bank of Scotland, which received a considerable amount of capital from the U.K. government and showed the largest loss of all the global banks in 2008. Since 2007, the International Monetary Fund (IMF) has increased its estimates of total global losses by FIs to US$4.1 trillion. Most of the losses to the end of 2008 were to U.S. banks. However, the European banks lagged, and their losses were expected to increase in 2009 and 2010. Total profit at US$115 billion for *The Banker*'s top 1000 was a decline of 85.3 percent from 2007. Return on equity was under 3 percent, compared to 20 percent in 2007.

Northcott argues that competition in the banking sector is complex and cannot be judged only by traditional factors, such as the size and number of banks. It will be interesting to see how the global financial system evolves.[31]

---

[31] See C. A. Northcott, "Competition in Banking," Bank of Canada, *Financial System Review*, June 2004, pp. 75–77, and C. A. Northcott, *Competition in Banking: A Review of the Literature*, Bank of Canada, Working Paper 2004-24. See also R. Baltazar and M. Santos, "The Benefits of Banking Mega-Mergers: Event Study Evidence from the 1998 Failed Mega-Merger Attempts in Canada," *Canadian Journal of Administrative Sciences* 20(3), September 2003, pp. 196–208, who argue that the benefit expected to accrue to Canadian bank shareholders from the announcement of bank megamergers was market power rather than economies of scale.

Summary

Domestic expansions are one way in which an FI can improve its return-risk performance. Additionally, there are potential return-risk advantages and disadvantages to FIs from international geographic expansions.

Although regulatory considerations and costs are fundamental to international expansion decisions, several other economic factors play an important role in the net return or benefit–cost analysis for any given FI. For example, considerations such as earnings diversifi-

cation, economies of scale and scope, extension of customer relationships, and better exploiting of financial service innovations add to the potential benefits from international geographic expansions. However, there are also costs or risks of such expansions such as monitoring costs, expropriation of assets, and the fixed costs of market entry. Managers need to carefully weigh each of these factors before making a geographic expansion decision, whether international or domestic.

Questions and Problems

1. How do limitations on geographic diversification affect an FI's profitability?

2. Bank mergers often produce hard-to-quantify benefits called *X efficiencies* and costs called *X inefficiencies*. Give an example of each.

3. What does the Berger and Humphrey study reveal about the cost savings from bank mergers? What differing results are revealed by the Rhoades study?

4. What are the three revenue synergies that may be obtained by an FI from expanding geographically?

5. What is the *Herfindahl–Hirschman Index?* How is it calculated and interpreted?

6. City Bank currently has a 60 percent market share in banking services, followed by Nations Bank with 20 percent and State Bank with 20 percent.

   a. What is the concentration ratio as measured by the *Herfindahl–Hirschman Index* (HHI)?

   b. If City Bank acquires State Bank, what will be the new HHI?

   c. Assume that the government will allow mergers as long as the changes in HHI do not exceed 1,400. What is the minimum amount of assets that City Bank will have to divest after it merges with State Bank?

7. The government has been asked to review a merger request for a market with the following four FIs:

Bank	Assets
A	$ 12 million
B	25 million
C	102 million
D	3 million

   a. What is the HHI for the existing market?

   b. If Bank A acquires Bank D, what will be the effect on the market's level of concentration?

   c. If Bank C acquires Bank D, what will be the effect on the market's level of concentration?

   d. What is likely to be the government's response to the two merger applications?

8. A government measures market concentration using the HHI of market share. What problems does this measure have for (a) multiproduct FIs and (b) FIs with global operations?

9. What factors other than market concentration should a government consider in determining the acceptability of a merger?

10. According to empirical studies, what factors have the highest impact on merger premiums as defined by the ratio of a target bank's purchase price to book value?

11. What are the results of studies that have examined the mergers of banks, including postmerger performance? How do they differ from the studies examining mergers of non-banks?

12. What are some of the important firm-specific financial factors that influence the acquisition of an FI?

13. How has the performance of merged banks compared to that of bank industry averages?

14. What are some of the benefits for banks engaging in geographic expansion?

15. What are three ways in which an FI can establish a global or international presence?

16. What is a Eurodollar transaction? What are Eurodollars?

17. Identify and explain the impact of at least four factors that encourage global bank expansion.

18. What is the expected impact of the implementation of the revised BIS risk-based capital requirements on the international activities of major banks?

19. What effect have the emerging-market economies had on the global expansion of traditional banking activities?

20. What are the advantages of size in a competitive market? Does size necessarily imply high profitability?

21. What is the European Community (EC) Second Banking Directive? What impact has the Second Banking Directive had on the competitive banking environment in Europe?

22. Identify and discuss the various ways in which foreign banks can enter the U.S. market. What are international banking facilities?

23. What are the major advantages of international expansion to FIs? Explain how each advantage can affect the operating performance of FIs.

24. What are the difficulties of expanding globally? How can each of these difficulties create negative effects on the operating performance of FIs?

25. The Canadian minister of Finance has asked you to provide a recommendation regarding the merger of large financial institutions in Canada and to answer the following questions:

   a. What factors should be considered in evaluating the benefits of a merger?

   b. Should bank–bank and bank–insurance mergers be allowed in Canada?

   c. How would your response differ if you were preparing this report for the board of directors of a large Canadian bank or insurance company?

Futures and Forwards

In this chapter, we look at the role that futures and forward contracts play in managing an FI's risk and

▸ compare futures and forward contracts to spot contracts

▸ examine how futures and forward contracts can be used to hedge an FI's

   ▸ interest rate risk

   ▸ foreign exchange (FX) risk

   ▸ credit risk

   ▸ catastrophe risk

INTRODUCTION

notional value of an OBS item
The face value of an off-balance-sheet contract.

Chapter 13 describes the growth in FIs' off-balance-sheet activities. A major component of this growth has been in futures and forward contracts. Although a significant amount of derivatives reflects the trading activity of large banks, FIs of all sizes have used these instruments to hedge their asset–liability risk exposures and thus reduce the value of their net worth at risk due to adverse events. As will be discussed in this chapter, derivative contracts—such as futures and forwards—potentially allow an FI to manage (or hedge) its interest rate, foreign exchange (FX), and credit risk exposures, and even its exposure to catastrophes such as hurricanes.

Table 23–1 lists the derivative holdings of the six major Canadian banks at October 31, 2008. Table 23–2 provides similar data for U.S. commercial banks at December 31, 2008 (in U.S. dollars). The tables show the breakdown of the derivatives positions into futures and forwards, swaps, options, and credit derivatives. The tables show that the **notional value** (dollar) contract volumes for the Canadian banks was equal to CDN\$14.378 trillion, whereas the total for the top ten U.S. banks, reflecting the size of the broader North American market for derivatives, was in excess of US\$198 trillion. As can be seen, both in Canada and in the United States, swaps dominate, representing 57.4 and 65.8 percent, respectively, of the total notional amount. Futures and forwards are in second place in Canada (22 percent) but options are the second-largest notional amount for U.S. banks (15.1 percent). The replacement cost of these derivative contracts (bilaterally netted current exposure) for the Canadian banks is CDN\$117.6 billion and the credit equivalent amount is CDN\$202.2 billion compared with US\$800.0 and US\$782.0 billion for the U.S. banks.[1]

Not only do FIs hold these contracts to hedge their own risk (interest rate, credit, etc.), but FIs also serve as the counterparty (for a fee) in these contracts for other (financial and non-financial) firms wanting to hedge risks on their balance sheets.

---

[1] See Chapter 20 for a discussion of how the credit exposure of derivatives is calculated for regulatory reporting.

TABLE 23–1 Derivative Contracts: Notional Amount, Credit Equivalent Amount, and Risk-Weighted Amount of the Six Major Canadian Banks, October 31, 2008 (CDN$ billions)

Bank	Total Assets	Notional Amount of Derivative Contracts						Replacement Cost of All Contracts	Credit Equivalent Amount	Risk-Weighted Amount
		Futures & Forwards	Total Swaps	Total Options	Credit Derivatives	Other Contracts	Total Derivatives			
BMO	$ 416.1	$ 546.9	$1,680.5	$ 632.0	$150.2	$ 40.9	$ 3,050.5	$ 17.7	$ 35.5	$14.9
BNS	507.6	394.3	868.7	145.7	120.4	32.9	1,561.9	20.7	28.5	9.7
CIBC	353.9	205.6	679.3	122.7	88.2	61.5	1,157.3	10.3	16.5	10.6
National	129.3	38.2	272.0	65.0	n.a.	18.6	393.8	2.4	5.3	2.9
RBC	723.9	1,336.4	3,129.4	376.6	275.8	301.6	5,419.9	53.6	82.2	25.9
TD Bank	563.2	650.5	1,626.8	198.1	230.3	88.9	2,794.6	12.8	34.2	8.2
Total	$2,694.0	$3,171.9	$8,256.7	$1,540.0	$865.0	$544.5	$14,378.1	$117.6	$202.2	$72.1
% of total derivatives		22.1%	57.4%	10.7%	6.0%	3.8%	100.0%			

Note: Replacement cost of all contracts, credit equivalent amount, and risk-weighted amounts reported after master netting agreements.
Source: Bank annual reports, 2008.

TABLE 23–2   Derivative Contracts: Notional Amount, Current Credit Exposure, Potential Future Exposure, Total Credit Exposure, and Credit Exposure to Capital Ratio of U.S. Commercial Banks and Trusts, December 31, 2008 (US$ billions)

| Bank | Total Assets | Notional Amount of Derivative Contracts | | | | | Bilaterally Netted Current Credit Exposure* | Potential Future Exposure** | Total Credit Exposure from All Contracts*** | Credit Exposure to Capital Ratio |
		Forwards & Futures	Total Swaps	Total Options	Credit Derivatives	Total Derivatives				
JPMorgan Chase Bank NA	$ 1,746.2	$ 9,546.7	$ 56,434.8	$12,989.5	$ 8,391.6	$ 87,362.7	$241.2	$308.8	$ 550.0	$382.3
Bank of America NA	1,471.6	4,998.8	27,133.2	4,122.0	2,050.6	38,304.6	80.5	137.4	217.9	179.4
Citibank National Assn.	1,231.2	4,074.7	18,787.2	6,295.6	2,730.4	31,887.9	140.3	161.2	301.5	278.3
Goldman Sachs Bank USA	162.5	589.7	22,940.0	5,303.0	1,396.9	30,229.6	121.9	70.3	192.2	1,056.4
HSBC Bank USA National Assn.	181.6	666.8	1,806.2	280.6	959.4	3,713.1	61.2	34.4	95.6	550.3
Wachovia Bank National Assn.	635.5	408.3	2,487.2	468.0	301.3	3,664.8	26.3	36.1	62.5	113.1
Wells Fargo Bank NA	539.0	692.4	621.1	179.6	1.5	1,494.7	37.7	9.0	46.7	95.1
Bank of New York Mellon	195.6	353.1	418.4	353.1	1.3	1,125.9	26.2	6.4	32.5	223.1
State Street Bank & Trust Co.	171.2	669.4	17.0	39.6	5.1	731.2	12.0	5.5	17.4	120.4
Suntrust Bank	186.0	54.9	150.3	48.8	2.0	255.9	7.0	1.7	8.7	50.2
Total for top 10 commercial banks & trusts	$ 6,520.3	$22,054.8	$130,795.5	$30,079.8	$15,840.3	$198,770.4	$754.3	$770.7	$1,524.9	
Other 910 commercial banks & trusts	4,294.6	457.2	910.2	727.5	56.4	2,061.2	45.7	11.3	57.1	
Total for all banks	$10,814.9	$22,512.0	$131,705.7	$30,807.2	$15,896.7	$200,831.6	$800.0	$782.0	$1,582.0	
% of total derivatives		11.1%	65.8%	15.1%	8.0%	100.0%				

*Approximately equal to the replacement cost reported by Canadian banks in Table 23–1.
**Approximately equal to the credit equivalent amount reported by Canadian banks in Table 23–1.
***Bilaterally netted current credit exposure + Potential future exposure.

Source: U.S. Office of the Comptroller of the Currency, fourth quarter, 2008, www.occ.treas.gov.

The rapid growth of derivatives use by both FIs and non-financial firms has been controversial. Critics charge that derivatives contracts contain potential losses that can materialize to haunt their holders, particularly banks and insurance companies that deal heavily in these instruments. As will be discussed in this chapter and the following two chapters, when employed appropriately, derivatives can be used to hedge (or reduce) an FI's risk.[2] However, when misused, derivatives can increase the risk of an FI's insolvency. A number of scandals involving FIs, firms, and municipalities (such as Bankers Trust and the Allied Irish Bank) led to a tightening of the accounting (reporting) requirements for derivative contracts. Specifically, beginning in 2000, the Financial Accounting Standards Board (FASB) in the United States required all derivatives to be marked to market and mandated that losses and gains be immediately transparent on FIs' and other firms' financial statements.

www.fasb.org

www.acsb.canada.org

In Canada, the Accounting Standards Board (AcSB), aware of the experience with derivative losses elsewhere in the world, produced new regulations for derivative instruments that combined U.S. generally accepted accounting principles (GAAP) and international accounting standards. These new regulations became mandatory for all companies, including FIs, who use derivative products after November 1, 2006.

www.bmo.com

www.scotiabank.com

The use of derivatives for trading as opposed to hedging dominates the derivatives activities of FIs. For example, Bank of Montreal (BMO) reports that of a total notional amount of derivatives contracts of $3,050.5 billion in 2008, just $50.6 billion, or 1.7 percent was used for hedging. The type of risk hedged, as well as the type of contract used to hedge a specific risk, varies across FIs. For example, Bank of Nova Scotia (BNS) notes in its 2008 annual report that it uses spot and forward transactions, swaps, and options as hedging instruments for foreign currency risk, but BMO hedges foreign currency risk using swaps.

FORWARD AND FUTURES CONTRACTS

To understand the essential nature and characteristics of forward and futures contracts, we can compare them with spot contracts. We show appropriate time lines for each of the three contracts using a bond as the underlying financial security to the derivative contract in Figure 23–1.

Spot Contracts

spot contract
An agreement involving the immediate exchange of an asset for cash.

A **spot contract** is an agreement between a buyer and a seller at time 0, when the seller of the asset agrees to deliver it immediately and the buyer of the asset agrees to pay for that asset immediately.[3] Thus, the unique feature of a spot market contract is the immediate and simultaneous exchange of cash for securities, or what is often called *delivery versus payment*. A spot bond quote of $97 for a 20-year

---

[2] E. Brewer III, B. A. Minton, and J. T. Moser, in "Interest-Rate Derivatives and Bank Lending," *Journal of Banking and Finance* 24, 2000, pp. 353–379, find that U.S. banks using interest rate derivatives experience greater growth in their commercial and industrial loan portfolios than banks that do not use these financial instruments. Their results suggest that FIs' use of derivatives enables increased reliance on their comparative advantage as delegated monitors (see Chapter 1).

[3] Technically, physical settlement and delivery may take place one or two days after the contractual spot agreement in bond markets. In equity markets, delivery and cash settlement normally occur three business days after the spot contract agreement.

FIGURE 23–1
Contract Time Lines

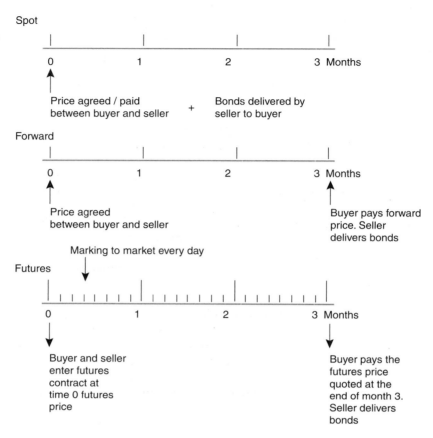

maturity bond is the price the buyer must pay the seller, per $100 of face value, for immediate (time 0) delivery of the 20-year bond.

Forward Contracts

forward contract
An agreement involving the exchange of an asset for cash at a fixed price in the future.

A **forward contract** is a contractual agreement between a buyer and a seller at time 0 to exchange a prespecified asset for cash at a later date. For example, in a three-month forward contract to deliver 20-year bonds, the buyer and seller agree on a price and quantity today (time 0) but the delivery (or exchange) of the 20-year bond for cash does not occur until three months hence. If the forward price agreed to at time 0 was $97 per $100 of face value, in three months' time the seller delivers $100 of 20-year bonds and receives $97 from the buyer. This is the price the buyer must pay and the seller must accept no matter what happened to the spot price of 20-year bonds during the three months between the time the contract was entered into and the time the bonds are delivered for payment.

Futures Contracts

futures contract
An agreement involving the future exchange of an asset for cash at a price that is determined daily.

A **futures contract** is normally arranged through an organized exchange (in Canada, the Montréal Exchange, www.m-x.ca). It is an agreement between a buyer and a seller at time 0 to exchange a standardized, prespecified asset for cash at a later date. As such, a futures contract is very similar to a forward contract. The difference relates to the price, which in a forward contract is fixed over the life of the

marked to market
The process by which the prices on outstanding futures contracts are adjusted each day to reflect current futures market conditions.

contract ($97 per $100 of face value for three months), but in a futures contract is **marked to market** daily. This means the contract's price is adjusted each day as the futures price for the contract changes. Therefore, actual daily cash settlements occur between the buyer and seller in response to this marking-to-market process. This can be compared to a forward contract, where the whole cash payment from buyer to seller occurs at the end of the contract period.[4]

The Montréal Exchange and TSX Group Inc. joined together in 2008 to create the TMX Group. The Montréal Exchange provides futures and options trading in Canada for interest rate, index, and equity contracts. The Canadian Derivatives Clearing Corporation (CDCC) is a self-regulating organization that is wholly owned by the Bourse de Montréal Inc. CDCC issues, clears, and guarantees the contracts traded on the Montréal Exchange.

www.cbot.com
www.cme.com

Canadian FIs also trade futures on U.S. exchanges—for example, the Chicago Board of Trade (CBOT) and the Chicago Mercantile Exchange (CME). Financial futures market trading was introduced in the United States in 1972 with the establishment of foreign exchange future contracts on the International Money Market (IMM). By the mid-1990s, five major exchanges existed in the United States,[5] and several exchanges existed outside of the United States.[6] The terms of futures contracts (e.g., contract size, delivery month, trading hours, minimum price fluctuation, daily price limits, and process used for delivery) traded in the United States are set by the exchange and are subject to the approval of the Commodity Futures Trading Commission (CFTC), the principal U.S. regulator of futures markets. In recent years, "off-market" trading systems have sprung up in which institutional investors and money managers can continue to trade during, as well as after, futures exchange operating hours. Indeed, it is estimated that trading volume in off-market currencies, interest rate swaps, and Eurodollars has grown three to ten times faster than trading volume on futures exchanges.

www.cftc.gov

CONCEPT QUESTIONS

1. What is the difference between a futures contract and a forward contract?
2. What are the major differences between a spot contract and a forward contract?

FORWARD CONTRACTS AND HEDGING INTEREST RATE RISK

naive hedge
When a cash asset is hedged on a direct dollar-for-dollar basis with a forward or futures contract.

To see the usefulness of forward contracts in hedging the interest rate risk of an FI, consider a simple example of a **naive hedge** (the hedge of a cash asset on a direct dollar-for-dollar basis with a forward or futures contract). Suppose an FI portfolio manager holds a 20-year, $1 million face value bond on the balance sheet. At time 0, these bonds are valued by the market at $97 per $100 face value, or $970,000 in total. Assume the manager receives a forecast that interest rates are expected to rise by 2 percent from their current level of 8 to 10 percent over the next three months.

---

[4] Aside from the marking-to-market process, the two major differences between forwards and futures are that (1) forwards are tailor-made contracts whereas futures are standardized contracts and (2) forward contracts are bilateral contracts subject to counterparty default risk, whereas the default risk on futures is significantly reduced by the futures exchange guaranteeing to indemnify counterparties against credit or default risk.

[5] These include the Chicago Board of Trade, the Chicago Mercantile Exchange, the New York Futures Exchange, the MidAmerica Commodity Exchange, and the Kansas City Board of Trade.

[6] These include the London International Financial Futures Exchange (LIFFE), the Singapore International Monetary Exchange (SIMEX), the Marché à Terme International de France (MATIF), and the Montréal Exchange.

Knowing that rising interest rates mean that bond prices will fall, the manager stands to make a capital loss on the bond portfolio. Having read Chapters 8 and 9, the manager is an expert in duration and has calculated the 20-year maturity bonds' duration to be exactly 9 years. Thus, the manager can predict a capital loss, or change in bond values (ΔP) from the duration equation of Chapter 9:[7]

$$\frac{\Delta P}{P} = -D \times \frac{\Delta R}{1 + R}$$

where

ΔP = Capital loss on bonds = ?

P = Initial value of bond position = \$970,000

D = Duration of the bonds = 9 years

ΔR = Change in forecast yield = 0.02

$1 + R$ = 1 plus the current yield on 20-year bonds = 1.08

$$\frac{\Delta P}{\$970,000} = -9 \times \left[\frac{0.02}{1.08}\right]$$

$$\Delta P = -9 \times \$970,000 \times \left[\frac{0.02}{1.08}\right] = -\$161,666.67$$

As a result, the FI portfolio manager expects to incur a capital loss on the bond portfolio of \$161,666.67 (as a percentage loss ($\Delta P/P$) = 16.67%) or as a drop in price from \$97 per \$100 face value to \$80.833 per \$100 face value. To offset this loss—in fact, to reduce the risk of capital loss to zero—the manager may hedge this position by taking an off-balance-sheet hedge, such as selling \$1 million face value of 20-year bonds for forward delivery in three months' time.[8] Suppose at time 0 the portfolio manager can find a buyer willing to pay \$97 for every \$100 of 20-year bonds delivered in three months' time.

Now consider what happens to the FI portfolio manager if the gloomy forecast of a 2 percent rise in interest rates proves to be true. The portfolio manager's bond position has fallen in value by 16.67 percent, equal to a capital loss of \$161,667. After the rise in interest rates, the manager can buy \$1 million face value of 20-year bonds in the spot market at \$80.833 per \$100 of face value, a total cost of \$808,333, and deliver these bonds to the forward contract buyer. Remember that the forward contract buyer agreed to pay \$97 per \$100 of face value for the \$1 million of face value bonds delivered, or \$970,000. As a result, the portfolio manager makes a profit on the forward transaction of

\$970,000	−	\$808,333	=	\$161,667
(price paid by forward buyer to forward seller)		(cost of purchasing bonds in the spot market at t = month 3 for delivery to the forward buyer)		

---

[7] For simplicity, we ignore issues relating to convexity here.

[8] Since a forward contract involves delivery of bonds in a future time period, it does not appear on the balance sheet, which records only current and past transactions. Thus, forwards are one example of off-balance-sheet items (see Chapter 13).

As you can see, the on-balance-sheet loss of $161,667 is exactly offset by the off-balance-sheet gain of $161,667 from selling the forward contract. In fact, for any change in interest rates, a loss (gain) on the balance sheet is offset by a gain (loss) on the forward contract. Indeed, the success of a hedge does not hinge on the manager's ability to accurately forecast interest rates. Rather, the reason for the hedge is the lack of ability to perfectly predict interest rate changes. The hedge allows the FI manager to protect against interest rate changes even if they are unpredictable. Thus, the FI's net interest rate exposure is zero; in the parlance of finance, it has **immunized** its assets against interest rate risk.

immunized
Describes an FI that is fully hedged or protected against adverse movements in interest rates (or other asset prices).

1. Explain how a naive hedge works.
2. What does it mean to say that an FI has immunized its portfolio against a particular risk?

HEDGING INTEREST RATE RISK WITH FUTURES CONTRACTS

Even though some hedging of interest rate risk does take place using forward contracts—such as forward rate agreements commonly used by insurance companies and banks prior to mortgage loan originations—many FIs hedge interest rate risk either at the micro level (called *microhedging*) or at the macro level (called *macrohedging*) using futures contracts. Before looking at futures contracts, we explain the difference between microhedging and macrohedging and between routine hedging and selective hedging.

Microhedging

microhedging
Using a futures (forward) contract to hedge a specific asset or liability.

An FI is **microhedging** when it employs a futures or a forward contract to hedge a particular asset or liability risk. For example, earlier we considered a simple example of microhedging asset-side portfolio risk, where an FI manager wanted to insulate the value of the institution's bond portfolio fully against a rise in interest rates. An example of microhedging on the liability side of the balance sheet occurs when an FI, attempting to lock in a cost of funds to protect itself against a possible rise in short-term interest rates, takes a short (sell) position in futures contracts on U.S. Treasury bonds. In microhedging, the FI manager often tries to pick a futures or forward contract whose underlying deliverable asset is closely matched to the asset (or liability) position being hedged. The earlier example, where we had an exact matching of the asset in the portfolio with the deliverable security underlying the forward contract (20-year bonds) was unrealistic. Such exact matching cannot be achieved often, and this produces a residual unhedgable risk termed **basis risk.** We discuss basis risk in detail later in this chapter; it arises mainly because the prices of the assets or liabilities that an FI wishes to hedge are imperfectly correlated over time with the prices on the futures or forward contract used to hedge risk.

basis risk
A residual risk that arises because the movement in a spot (cash) asset's price is not perfectly correlated with the movement in the price of the asset delivered under a futures or forward contract.

Macrohedging

macrohedging
Hedging the entire duration gap of an FI.

Macrohedging occurs when an FI manager uses futures or other derivative securities to hedge the entire balance sheet duration gap. This contrasts to microhedging, where an FI manager identifies specific assets and liabilities and seeks individual futures and other derivative contracts to hedge those individual risks. Note that macrohedging and microhedging can lead to quite different hedging strategies and results. In particular, a macrohedge takes a whole portfolio view and allows for individual asset and liability interest rate sensitivities or durations to net each other out. This can result in a very different aggregate futures position than when an FI manager disregards this netting or portfolio effect and hedges individual asset and liability positions on a one-to-one basis.[9]

Also, to dynamically hedge the entire portfolio, the assets must be marked-to-market on a daily basis, and the portfolio rebalanced. The futures and forwards markets may not be sufficiently liquid to permit this or a Canadian FI may resort to using U.S. contracts to achieve its goal of being fully hedged.

Routine Hedging versus Selective Hedging

routine hedging
Seeking to hedge all interest rate risk exposure.

Routine hedging occurs when an FI reduces its interest rate or other risk exposure to the lowest possible level by selling sufficient futures to offset the interest rate risk exposure of its whole balance sheet or cash positions in each asset and liability. For example, this might be achieved by macrohedging the duration gap, as described next. However, since reducing risk also reduces expected return and thus shareholder wealth, not all FI managers seek to do this. Indeed, a manager would follow this strategy only if the direction and size of interest rate changes are extremely unpredictable to the extent that the manager is willing to forgo return to hedge this risk. Figure 23–2 shows the trade-off between expected return and risk and the minimum-risk fully hedged portfolio.[10]

hedging selectively
Only partially hedging the gap or individual assets and liabilities.

Rather than a fully hedged position, most FIs choose to bear some interest rate risk as well as credit and FX risks because of their comparative advantage as FIs (see Chapter 1). One possibility is that an FI may choose to **hedge selectively** its portfolio. For example, an FI manager may generate expectations regarding future interest rates before deciding on a futures position. As a result, the manager may selectively hedge only a proportion of its balance sheet position. Alternatively, the FI manager may decide to remain unhedged or even to overhedge by selling more futures than required by the cash position, although regulators may view this as speculative. Thus, the fully hedged position—and the minimum risk portfolio—becomes one of several choices depending, in part, on managerial interest rate expectations, managerial objectives, and the nature of the return-risk trade-off from hedging. Finally, an FI may selectively hedge in an attempt to arbitrage profits between a spot asset's price movements and movements in a futures price.

Macrohedging with Futures

The number of futures contracts that an FI should buy or sell in a macrohedge depends on the size and direction of its interest rate risk exposure and the return-risk trade-off from fully or selectively hedging that risk.

FIGURE 23–2
The Effects of Hedging on Risk and Expected Return

[9] P. H. Munter, D. K. Clancy, and C. T. Moores found that macrohedges provided better hedge performance than microhedges in a number of different interest rate environments. See "Accounting for Financial Futures: A Question of Risk Reduction," *Advances in Accounting* 3, 1986, pp. 51–70. See also R. Stoebe, "Macrohedging Bank Investment Portfolios," *Bankers Magazine,* November–December 1994, pp. 45–48.

[10] The minimum-risk portfolio is not shown as zero here because of basis risk that prevents perfect hedging. In the absence of basis risk, a zero-risk position becomes possible.

Chapter 9 showed that an FI's net worth exposure to interest rate shocks was directly related to its leverage-adjusted duration gap as well as its asset size. Again, this is

$$\Delta E = -(D_A - kD_L) \times A \times \frac{\Delta R}{1 + R}$$

where
ΔE = Change in an FI's net worth
D_A = Duration of its asset portfolio
D_L = Duration of its liability portfolio
k = Ratio of an FI's liabilities to assets (L/A)
A = Size of an FI's asset portfolio

$\dfrac{\Delta R}{1 + R}$ = Shock to interest rates

EXAMPLE 23–1

Calculation of Change in FI Net Worth as Interest Rates Rise

To see how futures might fully hedge a positive or negative portfolio duration gap, consider the following FI where

$$D_A = 5 \text{ years}$$
$$D_L = 3 \text{ years}$$

Suppose the FI manager receives information from an economic forecasting unit that interest rates are expected to rise from 10 to 11 percent over the next year. That is,

$$\Delta R = 1\% = 0.01$$
$$1 + R = 1.10$$

The FI's initial balance sheet is

Assets ($ millions)	Liabilities ($ millions)
A = $100	L = $ 90
	E = 10
$100	$100

so that k equals L/A equals 90/100 equals 0.9.

The FI manager wants to calculate the potential loss to the FI's net worth (E) if the forecast of rising rates proves to be true. As we showed in Chapter 9,

$$\Delta E = -(D_A - kD_L) \times A \times \frac{\Delta R}{1 + R}$$

so that

$$\Delta E = -[5 - (0.9)(3)] \times \$100 \times \frac{0.01}{1.1} = -\$2.091 \text{ million}$$

The FI could expect to lose $2.091 million in net worth if the interest rate forecast turns out to be correct. Since the FI started with a net worth of $10 million, the loss of $2.091 million is almost 21 percent of its initial net worth position. Clearly, as this example illustrates, the effect of the rise in interest rates could be quite threatening to the FI and its insolvency risk exposure.

The Risk-Minimizing Futures Position

The FI manager's objective to fully hedge the balance sheet exposure would be fulfilled by constructing a futures position such that if interest rates do rise by 1 percent to 11 percent, as in the prior example, the FI will make a gain on the futures position that just offsets the loss of balance sheet net worth of $2.091 million.

When interest rates rise, the price of a futures contract falls since its price reflects the value of the underlying bond that is deliverable against the contract. The amount by which a bond price falls when interest rates rise depends on its duration. Thus, we expect the price of the 20-year T-bond futures contract to be more sensitive to interest rate changes than the price of the 3-month T-bill futures contract since the former futures price reflects the price of the 20-year T-bond deliverable on contract maturity. Thus, the sensitivity of the price of a futures contract depends on the duration of the deliverable bond underlying the contract, or

$$\frac{\Delta F}{F} = -D_F \frac{\Delta R}{1 + R}$$

where

ΔF = Change in dollar value of futures contracts

F = Dollar value of the initial futures contracts

D_F = Duration of the bond to be delivered against the futures contracts such as a 20-year, 8 percent coupon T-bond

ΔR = Expected shock to interest rates

$1 + R$ = 1 plus the current level of interest rates

This can be rewritten as

$$\Delta F = -D_F \times F \times \frac{\Delta R}{1 + R}$$

The left side of this expression (ΔF) shows the dollar gain or loss on a futures position when interest rates change.

To see this dollar gain or loss more clearly, we can decompose the initial dollar value position in futures contracts, F, into its two component parts:

$$F = N_F \times P_F$$

The dollar value of the outstanding futures position depends on the number of contracts bought or sold (N_F) and the price of each contract (P_F). N_F is positive when the futures contracts are bought and is assigned a negative value when contracts are sold.

Futures contracts are homogeneous in size. Thus, futures exchanges sell U.S. T-bond futures in minimum units of $100,000 of face value; that is, one T-bond future ($N_F = 1$) equals US$100,000. U.S. T-bill futures are sold in larger minimum units: One T-bill future ($N_F = 1$) equals US$1,000,000. The quote for each contract reported is the price per $100 of face value for delivering the underlying bond. *The Wall Street Journal Online* reports end-of-day information for those futures contracts that are nearest to maturity (see Figure 23–3) and the most recent quotes for the longer maturity contracts for each type of interest rate futures contract as well. Looking at Figure 23–3, a price quote of $122^{30.5}/_{32}$ on Thursday, May 21, 2009, for the T-bond futures contract maturing in June 2009 means that the buyer locks in a

FIGURE 23–3   **U.S. Futures Contracts on Interest Rates**

Contract	Month	Last	Chg	Open	High	Low	Volume	OpenInt	Exchange
U.S. T-Bonds Comp. - CBOT									
U.S. Treasury Bond	Jun '09	122'30.5	0'16.0	122'16.0	123'10.0	122'07.5	61463	624389	CBT
U.S. Treasury Bond	Sep '09	121'20.0	0'16.5	121'07.0	121'31.0	120'29.0	771	110786	CBT
U.S. Treasury Bond	Dec '09	119'31.5y					0	237	CBT
U.S. Treasury Bond	Mar '10	119'06.5y					0	44	CBT
U.S. Treasury Bond	Jun '10	118'06.5y					0	0	CBT
U.S.10-Yr. T-Notes Comp. - CBOT									
10-Yr. Note	Jun '09	121'05.0	0'06.5	120'30.0	121'11.0	120'25.0	228788	1053189	CBT
10-Yr. Note	Sep '09	119'20.5	0'06.5	119'15.5	119'26.0	119'09.0	1203	108738	CBT
10-Yr. Note	Dec '09	118'21.5y					0	5	CBT
10-Yr. Note	Mar '10	117'21.5y					0	0	CBT
10-Yr. Note	Jun '10	116'21.5y					0	0	CBT
U.S.2-Yr. T-Notes Comp. - CBOT									
2-Yr. Note	Jun '09	108'30.7	-0'00.2	108'31.0	109'00.2	108'29.7	46640	495045	CBT
2-Yr. Note	Sep '09	108'14.2	-0'00.7	108'13.7	108'16.0	108'13.7	5580	71180	CBT
2-Yr. Note	Dec '09	107'30.5y					0	0	CBT
U.S. Fed Funds Comp. - CBOT									
Fed Funds 30-Day	May '09	99.815	0.0000	99.8175	99.8175	99.8175	1323	71373	CBT
Fed Funds 30-Day	Jun '09	99.810	0.0050	99.8000	99.8100	99.8000	446	51334	CBT
Fed Funds 30-Day	Jul '09	99.790	0.0050	99.7900	99.8000	99.7900	873	40504	CBT
Libor 1 Mo. Comp. - CME									
Libor 1 Month	Jun '09	99.6900	0.0100	99.6900	99.6900	99.6900	1	8767	CME
Libor 1 Month	Jul '09	99.6475	-0.0075	99.6650	99.6650	99.6475	513	3878	CME
EuroDollar 3 Mo. Comp. - CME									
Eurodollar 3-Month	Jun '09	99.3925	-0.0025	99.4000	99.4425	99.3900	130864	887595	CME
Eurodollar 3-Month	Jul '09	99.3800	-0.0100	99.4100	99.4200	99.3800	1205	54599	CME
Eurodollar 3-Month	Aug '09	99.3900	0.0150	99.4150	99.4150	99.3900	102	3867	CME

Source: *The Wall Street Journal Online*, May 21, 2009.

FIGURE 23–4
Profit or Loss on a Futures Position in Treasury Bonds Taken on May 21, 2009

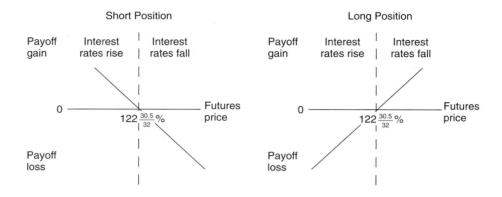

purchase price for the underlying T-bonds of $122,953.125 for one contract. That is, at maturity (in June 2009), the futures buyer would pay $122,953.125 to the futures seller and the futures seller would deliver one $100,000, 20-year, 8 percent T-bond to the futures buyer.[11] The subsequent profit or loss from a position in the June 2009 T-bond taken on May 21, 2009, is graphically described in Figure 23–4. A short position in the futures contract will produce a profit when interest rates rise (meaning that the value of the underlying T-bond decreases). Therefore, a short position in the futures market is the appropriate hedge when the FI stands to lose on the balance sheet if interest rates are expected to rise (e.g., the FI has a positive duration gap). A long position in the futures market produces a profit when interest rates fall (meaning that the value of the underlying T-bond increases).[12] Therefore, a long position is the appropriate hedge when the FI stands to lose on the balance sheet if interest rates are expected to fall (e.g., has a negative duration gap).

In actuality, the seller of the futures contract has a number of alternatives other than an 8 percent coupon, 30-year bond that can be delivered against the T-bond futures contract. If only one type of bond could be delivered, a shortage or squeeze might develop, making it very hard for the short side or seller to deliver. In fact, the seller has quite flexible delivery options; apart from delivering the 30-year, 8 percent coupon bond, the seller can deliver bonds that range in maturity from 15 years upward. Often, up to 25 different bonds may qualify for delivery. As the Industry Perspectives feature describes, however, as futures markets grow, a shortage of deliverable bonds can occur. When a bond other than the 30-year benchmark bond is delivered, the buyer pays a different invoice price for the futures contract based on a **conversion factor** that calculates the price of the deliverable bond if it were to yield 8 percent divided by face value. Suppose $100,000 worth of 18-year, 6 percent semiannual coupon Treasury bonds were valued at a yield of 5.5 percent. This would produce a fair present value of the bond of approximately $105,667. The conversion factor for the bond would be 1.057 (or $105,667/$100,000). This means the buyer would have to pay the seller the

conversion factor
A factor used to figure the invoice price on a futures contract when a bond other than the benchmark bond is delivered to the buyer.

---

[11] In practice, the futures price changes day to day and gains or losses would be generated for the seller/buyer over the period between when the contract is entered into and when it matures. See our later discussion of this unique marking-to-market feature. Note that the FI could sell contracts in T-bonds maturing at later dates. However, while contracts exist for up to two years into the future, longer-term contracts tend to be infrequently traded and therefore relatively illiquid.

[12] Notice that if rates move in an opposite direction from that expected, losses are incurred on the futures position. That is, if rates rise and futures prices drop, the long hedger loses. Similarly, if rates fall and futures prices rise, the short hedger loses. However, such losses are offset by gains on their cash market positions. Thus, the hedger is still protected.

INDUSTRY PERSPECTIVES

SHORT-BOND SHORTAGE ISN'T OVER

In June, one of the world's largest bond-fund managers, Pacific Investment Management Co., set into motion a chain of events that some traders contend cost them and investors hundreds of millions of dollars. And more money may yet be lost. . . . The problem, as in June, boils down to a shortage of bonds to satisfy the futures contract, which represents a promise to deliver or receive bonds at a certain date. The resulting battle for scarce securities could be ugly—and expensive for those who end up on the wrong side of trades. . . .

Lately, the market for futures on 10-year Treasury notes has faced an increasing imbalance. The dollar volume of contracts has boomed, exceeding $200 billion as of Aug. 2, compared with about $62 billion five years earlier. Meanwhile, the amount of bonds available to deliver against those contracts has decreased, in part because the Treasury has instead been issuing more shorter-dated bonds to finance U.S. budget deficits. In addition, more foreign investors are buying the bonds, and they tend to hold them for long periods. Futures contracts specify a number of different bond issues that are acceptable for delivery, but problems can arise when one of the deliverable bonds is a lot cheaper than the others, because people who must deliver face a battle to get those scarce "cheapest-to-deliver" bonds. Certainly, there can be winners in this scenario: someone holding the cheapest-to-deliver bonds could sell them into the futures market and profit. The result is a lot more clamoring for bonds that are needed to close out 10-year futures contacts. . . .

The matter came to a head in June, when market participants noticed a serious mismatch: only about $10 billion to $13 billion of cheapest-to-deliver 10-year Treasury notes were available for September futures contracts, on which the total value of bets was as much as $170 billion. That caused the price of the September contract to rise sharply, as market players bet those on the wrong side of the futures trade would have to deliver more-expensive bonds. . . . But the perceived demand for the cheapest-to-deliver bonds for the June contracts . . . turned into real demand as parties to futures contracts, expecting deliveries, scrambled to get the bond. . . . The inaccessibility of the cheapest-to-deliver bond caused the price of the June futures contract to rise, because the market expected more-expensive bonds to be delivered. This created an unusual arbitrage opportunity for anyone who was holding the cheapest-to-deliver bond and could deliver it at the higher futures price. . . .

On June 29, in an effort to avoid large deliveries in the future, the CBOT issued a new rule saying no single entity could demand delivery of bonds on more than a limited number of contracts—50,000 in the case of the 10-year Treasury note. . . .

Source: Mark Whitehouse, Aaron Lucchetti, and Peter A. McKay, *The Wall Street Journal*, August 11, 2005, p. C1. Reprinted by permission of *The Wall Street Journal*. © 2005 Dow Jones & Company. All Rights Reserved Worldwide, www.wsj.com.

conversion factor of 1.057 times the published futures price of $122,953.125. That is, the futures price would be $129,961.45.[13]

We can now solve for the number of futures contracts to buy or sell to fully macrohedge an FI's on-balance-sheet interest rate risk exposure. We have shown that

1. *Loss on balance sheet.* The loss of net worth for an FI when rates rise is equal to

$$\Delta E = -(D_A - kD_L)A\frac{\Delta R}{1 + R}$$

2. *Gain off balance sheet on futures.* The gain off balance sheet from selling futures is equal to[14]

---

[13] In practice, the seller exploits the delivery option by choosing the cheapest bond to deliver, that is, bonds whose conversion factor is most favourable (being based on an 8 percent yield) relative to the true price of the bond to be delivered (which reflects the actual level of yields).

[14] When futures prices fall, the buyer of the contract compensates the seller, here the FI. Thus, the FI gains when the prices of futures fall.

$$\Delta F = -D_F(N_F \times P_F)\frac{\Delta R}{1 + R}$$

Fully hedging can be defined as buying or selling a sufficient number of futures contracts (N_F) so that the loss of net worth on the balance sheet (ΔE) when interest rates change is just offset by the gain from off-balance-sheet buying or selling of futures (ΔF), or

$$\Delta F = \Delta E$$

Substituting in the appropriate expressions for each,

$$-D_F(N_F \times P_F)\frac{\Delta R}{1 + R} = -(D_A - kD_L)A\frac{\Delta R}{1 + R}$$

Cancelling $\Delta R/(1 + R)$ on both sides[15],

$$D_F(N_F \times P_F) = (D_A - kD_L)A$$

Solving for N_F (the number of futures to sell),

$$N_F = \frac{(D_A - kD_L)A}{D_F \times P_F}$$

Appendix 23A (located at the Online Learning Centre: www.mcgrawhill.ca/olc/saunders) derives the equation and provides an example for the number of futures contracts to buy or sell for a microhedge.

Short Hedge

An FI takes a short position in a futures contract when rates are expected to rise; that is, the FI loses net worth on its balance sheet if rates rise, so it seeks to hedge the value of its net worth by selling an appropriate number of futures contracts.

EXAMPLE 23–2

Macrohedge of Interest Rate Risk Using a Short Hedge

From the equation for N_F, we can now solve for the correct number of futures positions to sell (N_F) in the context of Example 23–1, where the FI was exposed to a balance sheet loss of net worth (ΔE) amounting to $2.091 million when interest rates rose. In that example,

$$D_A = 5 \text{ years}$$
$$D_L = 3 \text{ years}$$
$$k = 0.9$$
$$A = \$100 \text{ million}$$

Suppose the current futures price quote is $97 per $100 of face value for the benchmark 20-year, 8 percent coupon bond underlying the nearby futures contract, the minimum contract size is $100,000, and the duration of the deliverable bond is 9.5 years. That is,

$$D_F = 9.5 \text{ years}$$
$$P_F = \$97,000$$

Inserting these numbers into the expression for N_F, we can now solve for the number of futures to sell:[16]

---

[15] This amounts to assuming that the interest changes of the cash asset position match those of the futures position; that is, there is no basis risk. This assumption is relaxed later.

[16] Also note that if the FI intends to deliver any bond other than the 20-year benchmark bond, the P_F has to be multiplied by the appropriate conversion factor (c). If $c = 1.19$, then $P_F = 97 \times 1.19 = \$115.43$ per $100 of face value and the invoice price per contract would be $115,430.

$$N_F = \frac{[5 - (0.9)(3)] \times \$100 \text{ million}}{9.5 \times \$97,000}$$

$$= \frac{\$230,000,000}{\$921,500}$$

$$= 249.59 \text{ contracts to be sold}$$

Since the FI cannot sell a part of a contract, the number of contracts should be rounded down to the nearest whole number, or 249 contracts.[17]

Next, we verify that selling 249 T-bond futures contracts will indeed hedge the FI against a sudden increase in interest rates from 10 to 11 percent, or a 1 percent interest rate shock.

On Balance Sheet

As shown above, when interest rates rise by 1 percent, the FI loses $2.091 million in net worth (ΔE) on the balance sheet:

$$\Delta E = -(D_A - kD_L)A\frac{\Delta R}{1 + R}$$

$$-\$2.091 \text{ million} = -[5 - (0.9)(3)] \times \$100 \text{ million} \times \left(\frac{0.01}{1.1}\right)$$

Off Balance Sheet

When interest rates rise by 1 percent, the change in the value of the futures position is

$$\Delta F = -D_F(N_F \times P_F)\frac{\Delta R}{1 + R}$$

$$= -9.5(-249 \times \$97,000)\left(\frac{0.01}{1.1}\right)$$

$$= \$2.086 \text{ million}$$

The value of the off-balance-sheet futures position (ΔF) falls by $2.086 million when the FI sells 249 futures contracts in the T-bond futures market. Such a fall in value of the futures contracts means a positive cash flow to the futures seller as the buyer compensates the seller for a lower futures price through the marking-to-market process. This requires a cash flow from the buyer's margin account to the seller's margin account as the price of a futures contract falls.[18] Thus, as the seller of the futures, the FI makes a gain of $2.086 million. As a result, the net gain/loss on and off the balance sheet is

$$\Delta E + \Delta F = -\$2.091 \text{ m} + \$2.086 \text{ m} = -\$0.005 \text{ million}$$

This small remaining net loss of $0.005 million to equity or net worth reflects the fact that the FI could not achieve the perfect hedge—even in the absence of basis risk—as it needed to round down the number of futures to the nearest whole contract from 249.59 to 249

(Continued)

---

[17] The reason for rounding down rather than rounding up is technical. The target number of contracts to sell is that which minimizes interest rate risk exposure. By slightly underhedging rather than overhedging, the FI can generate the same risk exposure level but the underhedging policy produces a slightly higher return (see Figure 23–2).

[18] An example of marking to market might clarify how the seller gains when the price of the futures contract falls. Suppose on day 1 the seller entered into a 90-day contract to deliver 20-year T-bonds at $P = \$97$. The next day, because of a rise in interest rates, the futures contract, which now has 89 days to maturity, is trading at $96 when the market closes. Marking to market requires the prices on all contracts entered into on the previous day(s) to be marked to market at each night's closing (settlement) price. As a result, the price of the contract is lowered to $96 per $100 of face value, but in return for this lowering of the price from $97 to $96, the buyer has to compensate the seller to the tune of $1 per $100 of face value. Thus, given a $100,000 contract, there is a cash flow payment of $1,000 on that day from the buyer to the seller. Note that if the price had risen to $98, the seller would have had to compensate the buyer $1,000. The marking-to-market process goes on until the futures contract matures. If, over the period, futures prices have mostly fallen, then the seller accumulates positive cash flows on the futures position. It is this accumulation of cash flows that can be set off against losses in net worth on the balance sheet.

TABLE 23–3   On- and Off-Balance-Sheet Effects of a Microhedge Hedge

	On Balance Sheet	Off Balance Sheet
Begin hedge t = 0	Equity value of $10 million exposed to impact of rise in interest rates.	Sell 249.59 T-bond futures contracts at $97,000. Underlying T-bond coupon rate is 8%.
End hedge t = 1 day	Interest rates rise on assets and liabilities by 1%	Buy 249.59 T-bond futures (closes out futures position)

Opportunity loss on balance sheet:

$$\Delta E = [5 - 0.9(3)] \times \$100m \times \frac{0.01}{1.1}$$

$$= -\$2.091 \text{ million}$$

Real gain on futures hedge:

$$\Delta F = 9.5 \times (-249.59 \times \$97,000) \times \frac{0.01^*}{1.1}$$

$$= \$2.091 \text{ million}$$

*Assuming no basis risk and no contract "rounding."

contracts. Table 23–3 summarizes the key features of the hedge (assuming no rounding of futures contracts).

Suppose instead of using the 20-year T-bond futures to hedge, it had used the three-month Eurodollar futures.[19] We can use the same formula to solve for N_F in the case of Eurodollar futures:

$$N_F = \frac{(D_A - kD_L)A}{D_F \times P_F}$$

$$= \frac{[5 - (0.9)(3)]\,\$100 \text{ million}}{D_F \times P_F}$$

Assume that $P_F = \$97$ per $100 of face value or $970,000 per contract (the minimum contract size of a Eurodollar future is $1,000,000) and $D_F = 0.25$ (the duration of a three-month Eurodollar deposit that is the discount instrument deliverable under the contract).[20] Then,

$$N_F = \frac{[5 - (0.9)(3)]\,\$100 \text{ million}}{0.25 \times \$970,000} = \frac{\$230,000,000}{\$242,500}$$

$$N_F = 948.45 \text{ contracts to be sold}$$

Rounding down to the nearest whole contract, $N_F = 948$.

As this example illustrates, we can hedge an FI's on-balance-sheet interest rate risk when its $D_A > kD_L$ by shorting or selling either T-bond or Eurodollar futures. In general, fewer T-bond than Eurodollar contracts need to be sold—in our case, 948 Eurodollar versus 249 T-bond contracts. This suggests that on a simple transaction cost basis, the FI might normally prefer to use T-bond futures. However, other considerations can be important, especially if the FI holds the futures contracts until the delivery date. The FI needs to be concerned about the availability

[19] Three-month Eurodollar futures are an alternative interest rate futures contract to the long-term bond futures contract.

[20] We assume the same futures price ($97) here for purposes of comparison. Of course, the actual prices of the two futures contracts are very different.

of the deliverable set of securities and any possible supply shortages or squeezes. Such liquidity concerns may favour Eurodollars.[21]

The Problem of Basis Risk

Because spot bonds and futures on bonds are traded in different markets, the shift in yields, $\Delta R/(1 + R)$, affecting the values of the on-balance-sheet cash portfolio may differ from the shift in yields, $\Delta R_F/(1 + R_F)$, affecting the value of the underlying bond in the futures contract; that is, changes in spot and futures prices or values are not perfectly correlated. This lack of perfect correlation is called *basis risk*. In the previous section, we assumed a simple world of no basis risk in which $\Delta R/(1 + R) = \Delta R_F/(1 + R_F)$.

Basis risk occurs for two reasons. First, the balance sheet asset or liability being hedged is not the same as the underlying security on the futures contract. For instance, in Example 23–2 we hedged interest rate changes on the FI's entire balance sheet with T-bond futures contracts written on 20-year maturity bonds with a duration of 9.5 years. The interest rates on the various assets and liabilities on the FI's balance sheet and the interest rates on 20-year T-bonds do not move in a perfectly correlated (or one-to-one) manner. The second source of basis risk comes from the difference in movements in spot rates versus futures rates. Because spot securities (e.g., government bonds) and futures contracts (e.g., on the same bonds) are traded in different markets, the shift in spot rates may differ from the shift in futures rates (i.e., they are not perfectly correlated).

To solve for the risk-minimizing number of futures contracts to buy or sell, N_F, while accounting for greater or less rate volatility and hence price volatility in the futures market relative to the spot or cash market, we look again at the FI's on-balance-sheet interest rate exposure:

$$\Delta E = -(D_A - kD_L) \times A \times \Delta R/(1 + R)$$

and its off-balance-sheet futures position:

$$\Delta F = -D_F(N_F \times P_F) \times \Delta R_F/(1 + R_F)$$

Setting

$$\Delta E = \Delta F$$

and solving for N_F, we have

$$N_F = \frac{(D_A - kD_L) \times A \times \Delta R/(1 + R)}{D_F \times P_F \times \Delta R_F/(1 + R_F)}$$

Let *br* reflect the relative sensitivity of rates underlying the bond in the futures market relative to interest rates on assets and liabilities in the spot market, that is, $br = [\Delta R_F/(1 + R_F)]/[\Delta R/(1 + R)]$. Then the number of futures contracts to buy or sell is

---

[21] However, when rates change, the loss of net worth on the balance sheet and the gain on selling the futures are instantaneous; therefore, delivery need not be a concern. Indeed, because of the daily marking-to-market process, an FI manager can close out a futures position by taking an exactly offsetting position. That is, a manager who had originally sold 100 futures contracts could close out a position on any day by buying 100 contracts. Because of the unique marking-to-market feature, the marked-to-market price of the contracts sold equals the price of any new contracts bought on that day.

$$N_F = \frac{(D_A - kD_L)A}{D_F \times P_F \times br}$$

The only difference between this and the previous formula is an adjustment for basis risk (*br*), which measures the degree to which the futures price (yield) moves more or less than spot bond price (yield).

EXAMPLE 23–3

Macrohedging Interest Rate Risk When Basis Risk Exists

From Example 23–2, let *br* = 1.1. This means that for every 1 percent change in discounted spot rates [$\Delta R/(1 + R)$], the implied rate on the deliverable bond in the futures market moves by 1.1 percent. That is, futures prices are more sensitive to interest rate shocks than are spot market prices. Solving for N_F we have

$$N_F = \frac{[5 - (0.9)(3)]\, \$100 \text{ million}}{9.5 \times \$97,000 \times 1.1}$$

$$= 226.9 \text{ contracts}$$

or 226 contracts, rounding down. This compares to 249 when we assumed equal rate shocks in both the cash and futures markets [$\Delta R/(1 + R) = \Delta R_F/(1 + R_F)$]. Here we need fewer futures contracts than was the case when we ignored basis risk because futures rates and prices are more volatile, so that selling fewer futures would be sufficient to provide the same change in ΔF (the value of the futures position) than before when we implicitly assumed *br* = 1. Note that if futures rates or prices had been less volatile than spot rates or prices, we would have had to sell more than 249 contracts to get the same dollar gain in the futures position as was lost in net worth on the balance sheet so that $\Delta E = \Delta F$.

An important issue FIs must deal with in hedging interest rate and other risks is how to estimate the basis risk adjustment in the preceding formula. One method is to look at the ratio between $\Delta R/(1 + R)$ and $\Delta R_F/(1 + R_F)$ today. Since this is only one observation, the FI might better analyze the relationship between the two interest rates by investigating their relative behaviour in the recent past. We can do this by running an ordinary least-squares linear regression of implied futures rate changes on spot rate changes with the slope coefficient of this regression giving an estimate of the degree of comovement of the two rates over time. We discuss this regression procedure in greater detail next in connection with calculating basis risk when hedging with FX futures.[22]

CONCEPT QUESTIONS

1. What is the difference between microhedging and macrohedging and between routine hedging and selective hedging?
2. In Example 23–2, suppose the FI had the reverse duration gap; that is, the duration of its assets was shorter ($D_A = 3$) than the duration of its liabilities ($D_L = 5$). (This might be the case of a bank that borrows with long-term notes or time deposits to finance floating-rate loans.) How should it hedge using futures?
3. In Example 23–3, how many futures contracts should have been sold using the 20-year bond and 3-month Eurodollar contracts, if the basis risk measured *br* = 0.8?

---

[22] Another problem with the simple duration gap approach to determining N_F is that it is assumed that yield curves are flat. This could be relaxed by using duration measures that allow for non-flat yield curves (see Chapter 9).

HEDGING FOREIGN EXCHANGE RISK

Just as forwards and futures can hedge an FI against losses due to interest rate changes, they also can hedge against foreign exchange risk.

Forwards

Chapter 14 analyzed how an FI uses forward contracts to reduce the risks due to FX fluctuations when it mismatches the sizes of its foreign asset and liability portfolios. That chapter considered the simple case of an FI that raised all its liabilities in dollars while investing half of its assets in British pound sterling-denominated loans and the other half in dollar-denominated loans. Its balance sheet looks as follows.

Assets	Liabilities
CDN loans ($) $100 million U.K. loans (£) $100 million	CDN GICs $200 million

All assets and liabilities are of a one-year maturity and duration. Because the FI is net long in pound sterling assets, it faces the risk that over the period of the loan, the pound will depreciate against the dollar so that the proceeds of the pound loan (along with the dollar loan) will be insufficient to meet the required payments on the maturing dollar GICs. Then the FI will have to meet such losses out of its net worth; that is, its insolvency risk will increase.

Chapter 14 showed that by selling both the pound loan principal and interest forward one year at the known forward exchange rate at the beginning of the year, the FI could hedge itself against losses on its pound loan position due to changes in the dollar/pound exchange rate over the succeeding year. Note the strategy for hedging (£100 million) of British pound sterling loans with forwards in Figure 23–5.

Futures

Instead of using FX forward contracts to hedge foreign exchange risk, the FI could use FX futures contracts. Consider an FI wishing to hedge a one-year British pound loan of £100 million principal plus £15 million interest (or £115 million) against the risk of the pound falling in value against the dollar over the succeeding year. Suppose the FI wished to hedge this loan position on May 19, 2010, via the futures markets. How many futures should it sell? The answer to this question is that it should sell the amount that produces a sufficient profit on the pound futures contracts to

FIGURE 23–5
Hedging a Long Position in Pound Assets through Sale of Pound Forwards

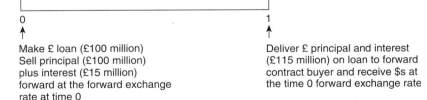

0

Make £ loan (£100 million)
Sell principal (£100 million)
plus interest (£15 million)
forward at the forward exchange
rate at time 0

1

Deliver £ principal and interest
(£115 million) on loan to forward
contract buyer and receive $s at
the time 0 forward exchange rate

just offset any exchange rate losses on the pound loan portfolio should the pound fall in value relative to the dollar. There are two cases to consider:

1. The futures dollar/pound price is expected to change in exactly the same fashion as the spot dollar/pound price over the course of the year. That is, futures and spot price changes are perfectly correlated; there is no basis risk.
2. Futures and spot prices, though expected to change in the same direction, are not perfectly correlated (there is basis risk).

EXAMPLE 23–4
 	
Hedging Foreign Exchange Risk Assuming Perfect Correlation between Spot and Futures Prices
	Suppose on May 19, 2010,
	
	S_t = Spot exchange rate ($/£): $1.9483 per £1
	
	f_t = Futures price ($/£) for the contract
	    expiring in May 2011 (in one year):
	    $1.9468 per £1
	
	Suppose the FI made a £100 million loan at 15 percent interest and wished to hedge fully the risk that the dollar value of the proceeds would be eroded by a declining British pound sterling over the year. Also suppose that the FI manager receives a forecast that in one year's time the spot and futures will be
	
	S_{t+1} = $1.8983 per £1
	f_{t+1} = $1.8968 per £1
	
	so that over the year,
	
	ΔS_t = −5 cents
	Δf_t = −5 cents

For a manager who believes this forecast of a depreciating pound against the dollar, the correct full-hedge strategy is to cover the £115 million of expected earnings on the British loan by selling, or shorting, £115 million of British pound futures contracts on May 19, 2010. We assume here that the FI manager continuously rolls over the futures position into new futures contracts and will get out of futures on May 19, 2011.

The size of each British pound futures contract is £62,500. Therefore, the number (N_F) of futures to be sold is

$$N_F = \frac{£115,000,000}{£62,500} = \frac{\text{Size of long position}}{\text{Size of a pound futures contract}}$$

$$= 1,840 \text{ contracts to be sold}$$

Next, we consider whether losses on the long asset position (the British loan) would just offset gains on the futures should the FI sell 1,840 British pound futures contracts if spot and futures prices change in the direction and amount expected.

Loss on British Pound Loan

The loss on the British pound loan in dollars would be

$$[£ \text{ Principal} + \text{Interest}] \times \Delta S_t$$

$$[£115 \text{ million}] \times [\$1.9483/£ - \$1.8983/£] = \$5.75 \text{ million}$$

That is, the dollar value of the British pound loan proceeds would be $5.75 million less should the pound depreciate from $1.9483/£ to $1.8938/£ in the spot market over the year.

Gain on Futures Contracts

The gain on the futures contracts would be

$$[N_F \times £62{,}500] \times \Delta f_t$$

$$[1{,}840 \times £62{,}500] \times [\$1.9468/£ - \$1.8968/£] = \$5.75 \text{ million}$$

By selling 1,840 futures contracts of 62,500 each, the seller makes \$5.75 million as the futures price falls from \$1.9468/£ at the contract initiation on May 19, 2010, to \$1.8968/£ at the futures position termination on May 19, 2011. This cash flow of \$5.75 million results from the marking to market of the futures contract. As the futures price falls, due to the daily marking to market, the pound futures contract buyer has the contract repriced to a lower level in dollars to be paid per pound. But the seller must be compensated from the buyer's margin account for the difference between the original contract price and the new lower marked-to-market contract price. Thus, over the one year, the buyer compensates the seller by a net of 5 cents per £1 of futures purchased: that is, \$1.9468/£1 minus \$1.8968/£1 as the futures price falls, or a total of 5 cents × the number of contracts (1,840) × the pound size of each contract (62,500). Note that on May 19, 2011, when the principal and interest on the pound loan are paid by the borrower, the FI seller of the pound futures terminates its position in 1,840 short contracts by taking an opposing position of 1,840 long in the same contract. This effectively ends any net cash flow implications from futures positions beyond this date.

---

tail the hedge
Reducing the number of futures contracts that are needed to hedge a cash position because of the interest income that is generated from reinvesting the marked-to-market cash flows generated by the futures contract.

Finally, in this example, we have ignored the interest income effects of marking to market. In reality, the \$5.75 million from the futures position would be received by the FI seller over the course of the year. As a result, this cash flow can be reinvested at the current short-term dollar interest rate to generate a cash flow of more than \$5.75 million. Given this, an FI hedger can sell slightly fewer contracts in anticipation of this interest income. The number of futures that could be sold, below the 1,840 suggested, would depend on the level and pattern of short-term rates over the hedging horizon as well as the precise expected pattern of cash flows from marking to market. In general, the higher the level of short-term interest, the more an FI manager could **tail the hedge** in this fashion.[23]

EXAMPLE 23–5

Hedging Foreign Exchange Risk Assuming Imperfect Correlation between Spot and Futures Prices (Basis Risk)

Suppose, instead, the FI manager did not believe that the spot exchange rate and futures price on the dollar/pound contract would fall by exactly the same amount. Instead, let the forecast for one year's time be

$$S_{t+1} = 1.8983/£1$$
$$f_{t+1} = \$1.9168/£1$$

Thus, in expectation, over the succeeding year,

$$\Delta S_t = -5 \text{ cents}$$
$$\Delta f_t = -3 \text{ cents}$$

This means that the dollar/pound futures price is expected to depreciate less than the spot dollar/pound. This basis risk arises because spot and futures contracts are traded in different markets with different demand and supply functions. Given this, even though futures and spot prices are normally highly correlated, this correlation is often less than 1.

(Continued)

---

[23] One way to do this is to discount the calculated hedge ratio (the optimal number of futures to sell per \$1 of cash position) by a short-term interest rate such as the Bank of Canada's overnight rate.

Because futures prices and spot prices do not always move exactly together, this can create a problem for an FI manager seeking to hedge the long position of £115 million with pound futures. Suppose the FI manager ignored the fact that the spot pound is expected to depreciate faster against the dollar than the futures price for pounds and continued to believe that selling 1,840 contracts would be the best hedge. That manager could be in for a big (and nasty) surprise in one year's time. To see this, consider the loss on the cash asset position and the gain on the futures position under a new scenario where the dollar/pound spot rate falls by 2 cents more than dollar/pound futures over the year.

Loss on British Pound Loan

The expected fall in the spot value of the pound by 5 cents over the year results in a loss of

$$[£115 \text{ million}] \times [\$1.9483/£ - \$1.8983/£] = \$5.75 \text{ million}$$

Gain on Futures Position

The expected gain on the futures position is

$$[1,840 \times £62,500] \times [\$1.9468/£ - \$1.9168/£] = \$3.45 \text{ million}$$

Thus, the net loss to the FI is

Net loss = Loss on British pound loan − Gain on British pound futures
Net loss = \$5.75 − \$3.45
Net loss = \$2.3 million

Such a loss would have to be charged against the FI's profits and implicitly its net worth or equity. As a result, the FI manager needs to take into account the lower sensitivity of futures prices relative to spot exchange rate changes by selling more than 1,840 futures contracts to hedge fully the British pound loan risk.

To see how many more contracts are required, we need to know how much more sensitive spot exchange rates are relative to futures prices. Let h be the ratio of ΔS_t to Δf_t:

$$h = \frac{\Delta S_t}{\Delta f_t}$$

Then, in our example,

$$h = \frac{\$0.05}{\$0.03} = 1.66$$

hedge ratio
The dollar value of futures contracts that should be sold per $ of cash position exposure.

That is, spot rates are 66 percent more sensitive than futures prices, or—put slightly differently—for every 1 percent change in futures prices, spot rates change by 1.66 percent.[24] An FI manager could use this ratio, h, as a **hedge ratio** to solve the question of how many futures should be sold to hedge the long position in the British pound when the spot and futures prices are imperfectly correlated. Specifically, the value of h means that for every £1 in the long asset position, £1.66 futures contracts should be sold. To see this, look at the FI's losses on its long asset position in pound loans relative to the gains on its selling pound futures.

Loss on British Pound Loans

As before, its losses are

$$[£115 \text{ million}] \times [\$1.9483/£ - \$1.8983/£] = \$5.75 \text{ million}$$

---

[24] Of course, this can always be expressed the other way around: A 1 percent change in spot prices leads, on average, to only a 0.6 percent change in futures prices.

Gains on British Pound Futures Position

Taking into account the degree to which spot exchange rates are more sensitive than futures prices—the hedge ratio (*h*)— we can solve for the number of futures (*N~F~*) to sell as

$$N_F = \frac{\text{Long asset position} \times h}{\text{Size of one futures contract}}$$

$$N_F = \frac{£115 \text{ million} \times 1.66}{£62,500} = 3,054.4 \text{ contracts}$$

or, rounding down to the nearest whole contract, 3,054 contracts. Selling 3,054 British pound futures results in expected profits of

$$[3,054 \times £62,500] \times [\$1.9468/£ - \$1.9168/£] = \$5.73 \text{ million}$$

The difference of $0.02 million between the loss on British pound loans and the gain on the pound futures is due to rounding.

Estimating the Hedge Ratio[25]

The previous example showed that the number of FX futures that should be sold to hedge fully foreign exchange rate risk exposure depends crucially on expectations regarding the correlation between the change in the dollar/pound spot rate (ΔS_t) and the change in its futures price (Δf_t). When

$$h = \frac{\Delta S_t}{\Delta f_t} = \frac{\$0.05}{\$0.05} = 1$$

there is no basis risk. Both the spot and futures are expected to change together by the same absolute amount, and the FX risk of the cash position should be hedged dollar for dollar by selling FX futures. When basis risk is present, the spot and future exchange rates are expected to move imperfectly together:

$$h = \frac{\Delta S_t}{\Delta f_t} = \frac{\$0.05}{\$0.03} = 1.66$$

The FI must sell a greater number of futures than it has to when basis risk is absent.

Unfortunately, without perfect foresight, we cannot know exactly how exchange rates and futures prices will change over some future time period. If we did, we would have no need to hedge in the first place! Thus, a common method to calculate *h* is to look at the behaviour of ΔS_t relative to Δf_t over the *recent past* and to use this past behaviour as a prediction of the appropriate value of *h* in the future. One way to estimate this past relationship is to run an ordinary least-squares regression of recent changes in spot prices on recent changes in futures prices.[26]

Consider Figure 23–6, where we plot hypothetical monthly changes in the spot pound/dollar exchange rate (ΔS_t) against monthly changes in the futures pound/

---

[25] The material in this section is more technical in nature. It may be included or dropped from the chapter reading, depending on the rigour of the course, without harming the continuity of the chapter.

[26] When we calculate *h* (the hedge ratio), we could use the ratio of the most recent spot and futures price changes. However, this would amount to basing our hedge ratio estimate on one observation of the change in S_t and f_t. This is why the regression model, which uses many past observations, is usually preferred by market participants.

FIGURE 23–6
Monthly Changes
in ΔS_t and Δf_t in
200X

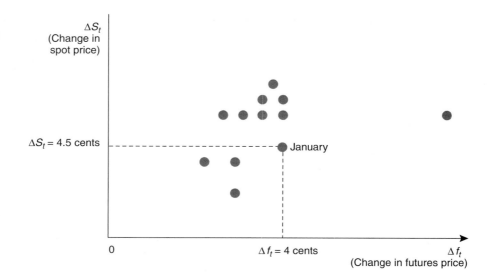

dollar price (Δf_t) for the year 200X. Thus, we have 12 observations from January through December. For information purposes, the first observation (January) is labelled in Figure 23–6. In January, the dollar/pound spot rate rose by 4.5 cents and the dollar/pound futures price rose by 4 cents. Thus, the pound appreciated in value over the month of January but the spot exchange rate rose by more than the futures price did. In some other months, as implied by the scatter of points in Figure 23–6, the futures price rose by more than the spot rate did.

An ordinary least-squares (OLS) regression fits a line of best fit to these monthly observations such that the sum of the squared deviations between the observed values of ΔS_t and its predicted values (as given by the line of best fit) is minimized. This line of best fit reflects an intercept term α and a slope coefficient β. That is,

$$\Delta S_t = \alpha + \beta \, \Delta f_t + u_t$$

where the u_t are the regression's residuals (the differences between actual values of ΔS_t and its predicted values based on the line of best fit).

Definitionally, β, or the slope coefficient, of the regression equation is equal to

$$\beta = \frac{\text{Cov}(\Delta S_t, \Delta f_t)}{\text{Var}(\Delta f_t)}$$

that is, the covariance between the change in spot rates and change in futures prices divided by the variance of the change in futures prices. Suppose ΔS_t and Δf_t moved perfectly together over time. Then,

$$\text{Cov}(\Delta S_t, \Delta f_t) = \text{Var}(\Delta f_t)$$
$$\text{and } \beta = 1$$

If spot rate changes are greater than futures price changes, then $\text{Cov}(\Delta S_t, \Delta f_t) > \text{Var}(\Delta f_t)$ and $\beta > 1$. Conversely, if spot rate changes are less sensitive than futures price changes over time, then $\text{Cov}(\Delta S_t, \Delta f_t) < \text{Var}(\Delta f_t)$ and $\beta < 1$.

Moreover, the value of β, or the estimated slope of the regression line, has theoretical meaning as the hedge ratio (h) that minimizes the risk of a portfolio of spot assets and futures contracts.[27] Put more simply, we can use the estimate of β from the regression model as the appropriate measure of h (the hedge ratio) to be used by the FI manager. For example, suppose we used the 12 observations on ΔS_t and Δf_t in 200X to estimate an OLS regression equation (the equation of the line of best fit in Figure 23–6). This regression equation takes the form

$$\Delta S_t = 0.15 + 1.2\, \Delta f_t$$

Thus,

$$\alpha = 0.15$$
$$\beta = 1.2$$

Using $\beta = 1.2$ as the appropriate risk-minimizing hedge ratio h for the portfolio manager, we can solve our earlier problem of determining the number of futures contracts to sell to protect the FI from FX losses on its £115 million loan:

$$N_F = \frac{\text{Long position in £ assets} \times \beta \; (\text{estimated value of the hedge ratio } h \text{ using past data})}{\text{Size of one £ futures contract}}$$

$$N_F = \frac{\pounds 115 \text{ million} \times 1.2}{\pounds 62{,}500} = 2{,}208 \text{ contracts}$$

Thus, using the past relationship between ΔS_t and Δf_t as the best predictor of their future relationship over the succeeding year dictates that the FI manager sell 2,208 contracts.

The degree of confidence the FI manager may have in using such a method to determine the appropriate hedge ratio depends on how well the regression line fits the scatter of observations. The standard measure of the goodness of fit of a regression line is the R^2 value of the equation, where the R^2 is the square of the correlation coefficient between ΔS_t and Δf_t:

$$R^2 = \rho^2 = \left\{ \frac{[\text{Cov}(\Delta S_t, \Delta f_t)]}{\sigma_{\Delta S_t} \times \sigma_{\Delta f_t}} \right\}^2$$

The term in curly brackets is the statistical definition of a correlation coefficient. If changes in the spot rate (ΔS_t) and changes in the futures price (Δf_t) are perfectly correlated, then

$$R^2 = \rho^2 = (1)^2 = 1$$

and all observations between ΔS_t and Δf_t lie on a straight line. By comparison, an $R^2 = 0$ indicates that there is no statistical association at all between ΔS_t and Δf_t.

Since we are using futures contracts to hedge the risk of loss on spot asset positions, the R^2 value of the regression measures the degree of **hedging effectiveness** of the futures contract. A low R^2 means that we might have little confidence that the slope coefficient β from the regression is actually the true hedge ratio. As the value of R^2 approaches 1, the degree of confidence increases in the use of

hedging effectiveness
The (squared) correlation between past changes in spot asset prices and futures prices.

---

[27] For proof of this, see L. H. Ederington, "The Hedging Performance of the New Futures Markets," *Journal of Finance* 34, 1979, pp. 157–170.

futures contracts, with a given hedge ratio (h) estimate, to hedge our cash asset-risk position.

CONCEPT QUESTIONS

1. Circle an observation in Figure 23–6 that shows futures price changes exceeding spot price changes.
2. Suppose that $R^2 = 0$ in a regression of ΔS_t on Δf_t. Would you still use futures contracts to hedge? Explain your answer.
3. In running a regression of ΔS_t on Δf_t, the regression equation is $\Delta S_t = 0.51 + 0.95\Delta f_t$ and $R^2 = 0.72$. What is the hedge ratio? What is the measure of hedging effectiveness?

HEDGING CREDIT RISK WITH FUTURES AND FORWARDS

Chapter 12 demonstrated that by diversifying their loan portfolios across different borrowers, sectors, and regions, FIs can diversify away much of the borrower-specific or unsystematic risk of the loan portfolio. Of course, the ability of an FI manager to diversify sufficiently depends in part on the size of the loan portfolio under management. Thus, the potential ability to diversify away borrower-specific risk increases with the size of the FI.

In recent years, however, new types of derivative instruments have been developed (including forwards, options, and swaps) to better allow FIs to hedge their credit risk. Credit derivatives can be used to hedge the credit risk on individual loans or bonds or on portfolios of loans and bonds. The credit derivative market, while still relatively young, has already gained a reputation as an early warning signal for spotting corporate debt problems. As shown in Table 23–1, at October 31, 2008, the notional amount of credit derivatives reported by the Big Six Canadian banks was equal to $865.0 billion, 6.0 percent of the total notional amount of $14,378.1 billion reported. As shown in Table 23–2, U.S. banks had US$15,896.7 billion of notional value in credit derivatives outstanding in December 2008 and estimated to be in excess of US$50 trillion worldwide. The emergence of these new derivatives is important since more FIs fail due to credit risk exposure (e.g., Canadian Commercial Bank, Northlands Bank in 1985) than to either interest rate or FX risk exposures. We discuss credit forward contracts below. In Chapter 24, we discuss credit options and in Chapter 25, we discuss credit swaps.

Credit Forward Contracts and Credit Risk Hedging

credit forward
An agreement that hedges against an increase in default risk on a loan after the loan terms have been determined and the loan has been issued.

A **credit forward** is a forward agreement that hedges against an increase in default risk on a loan (a decline in the credit quality of a borrower) after the loan rate is determined and the loan is issued. Common buyers of credit forwards are insurance companies and common sellers are banks. The credit forward agreement specifies a credit spread (a risk premium above the risk-free rate to compensate for default risk) on a benchmark bond issued by an FI borrower. For example, suppose the benchmark bond of a bank borrower was rated BBB at the time a loan was originated. Further, at the time the loan was issued, the benchmark bonds had a 2 percent interest rate or credit spread (representing default risk on the BBB bonds) over a government security (bond) of the same maturity. To hedge against an increase in the credit risk of the borrower, the bank enters into (sells) a credit forward contract when the loan is issued. We define CS_F as the credit spread over the government security (bond) rate on which the credit forward contract is written (equals 2 percent in this example). Table 23–4 illustrates the payment pattern resulting from this credit forward. In Table 23–4, CS_T is the actual credit spread on the bond when the credit forward matures, for example, one year after the loan was originated and the credit forward contract was entered into, MD is the modified duration on the benchmark BBB bond, and A is the principal amount of the forward agreement.

From the payment pattern established in the credit forward agreement, Table 23–4 shows that the credit forward buyer (an insurance company) bears the risk of an increase in default risk on the benchmark bond of the borrowing firm, while the credit forward seller (the bank lender) hedges itself against an increase in the borrower's default risk. That is, if the borrower's default risk increases so that when the forward agreement matures the market requires a higher credit spread on the borrower's benchmark bond, CS_T, than that originally agreed to in the forward contract, CS_F, (i.e., $CS_T > CS_F$), the credit forward buyer pays the credit forward seller, which is the bank, $(CS_T - CS_F) \times MD \times A$. For example, suppose the credit spread between BBB bonds and government bonds widened to 3 percent from 2 percent over the year, the modified duration (MD) of the benchmark BBB bond was five years, and the size of the forward contract A was $10,000,000. Then the gain on the credit forward contract to the seller (the bank) would be $500,000 [$(3\% - 2\%) \times 5 \times \$10,000,000$]. This amount could be used to offset the loss in market value of the loan due to the rise in the borrower's default risk. However, if the borrower's default risk and credit spread decrease over the year, the credit forward seller pays the credit forward buyer $(CS_F - CS_T) \times MD \times A$. [However, the maximum loss on the forward contract (to the bank seller) is limited, as will be explained below.]

Figure 23–7 illustrates the effect on the bank of hedging the loan. If the default risk on the loan increases, the market or present value of the loan falls below its value at the beginning of the hedge period. However, the bank hedged the change in default risk by selling a credit forward contract. Assuming the credit spread on the borrower's benchmark bond also increases (so that $CS_T > CS_F$), the bank receives $(CS_T - CS_F) \times MD \times A$ on the forward contract. If the characteristics of the benchmark bond (i.e., change in credit spread, modified duration, and principal value) are the same as those of the bank's loan to the borrower, the loss on the balance sheet is offset completely by the gain (off the balance sheet) from the credit forward (i.e., in our example, a $500,000 market value loss on the loan would be offset by a $500,000 gain from selling the credit forward contract).

If the default risk does not increase or decreases (so that $CS_T < CS_F$), the bank selling the forward contract will pay $(CS_F - CS_T) \times MD \times A$ to the credit forward buyer (the insurance company). However, importantly, this payout by the bank is

TABLE 23–4
Payment Pattern on a Credit Forward

Credit Spread at End of Forward Agreement	Credit Spread Seller (Bank)	Credit Spread Buyer (Counterparty)
$CS_T > CS_F$	Receives $(CS_T - CS_F) \times MD \times A$	Pays $(CS_T - CS_F) \times MD \times A$
$CS_F > CS_T$	Pays $(CS_F - CS_T) \times MD \times A$	Receives $(CS_F - CS_T) \times MD \times A$

FIGURE 23–7

Effect on a Bank of Hedging a Loan with a Credit Forward Contract

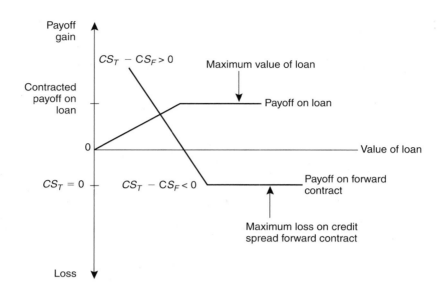

limited to a maximum. This is when CS_T falls to zero, that is, the default spread on BBB bonds falls to zero or the original BBB bonds of the borrower are viewed as having the same default risk as government bonds (in other words, the credit spread or rate on the benchmark bond cannot fall below the risk-free rate). In this case, the maximum loss on the credit forward $[CS_F - (0)] \times MD \times A$ mirrors (offsets) the maximum and limited upside gain (return) on the loan. Anyone familiar with options will recognize that (as was discussed in Chapter 11) when the bank makes a loan, it is similar to writing a put option. In selling a credit forward, the payoff is similar to buying a put option (see Chapter 24 as well).

EXAMPLE 23–6

Hedging Credit Risk with Credit Spread Forward Contract

A bank issues a $5 million loan to a firm with an A− credit rating. The modified duration on the loan is 4.5 years. At the time of issue, the credit spread between A− bonds and government bonds is 2 percent (CS_F). The bank believes that the borrower's credit rating may fall during the period of the loan. To hedge this credit risk, the bank enters (or sells) a $5 million credit spread forward contract. Subsequently, at the end of the forward period, the borrower's credit rating does indeed drop, to BB (CS_T). The credit spread between BB rated bonds and government bonds is 5 percent (or $CS_T > CS_F$). Thus, the change in the market value of the loan to the bank, from the duration model, is

$$\Delta L = L \times D \times [\Delta R_L/(1 + R_L)] = L \times D/(1 + R_L) \times \Delta R_L = L \times MD \times \Delta R_L$$

or

$$\Delta L = \$5,000,000 \times 4.5 \times (0.03) = \$675,000$$

However, the bank hedged this risk with a credit spread forward and receives, from the credit spread buyer,

$$(5\% - 2\%) \times 4.5 \times \$5,000,000 = \$675,000$$

Thus, the loss in the value of the loan due to a drop in the credit rating of the borrower is completely offset with the gain from the credit spread forward contract.

Futures Contracts and Catastrophe Risk

www.cbot.com

In recent years, the Chicago Board of Trade (CBOT) has introduced futures and options for catastrophe insurance. This chapter discusses catastrophe insurance futures, and the next chapter discusses catastrophe insurance options. The essential idea of catastrophe futures is to allow property and casualty insurers to hedge the extreme losses that occur after major hurricanes, such as the series of hurricanes that hit Florida in September 2004 that resulted in damage of over US$25 billion to the properties directly affected or Hurricane Katrina in 2005, which resulted in losses exceeding US$200 billion. Since in a catastrophe the ratio of insured losses to premiums rises (i.e., the so-called loss ratio increases), the payoff on a catastrophe futures contract is directly linked to the loss ratio. Specifically, on settlement, the payoff to the buyer of the futures is equal to the nominal value of the futures contract (which is US$25,000) times the actual loss ratio incurred by insurers. Suppose that on maturity of the futures contract the loss ratio was 1.5. This means that the payoff to the insurance company futures hedger would be 1.5 × US$25,000 = US$37,500. Also suppose that three months earlier (before the catastrophe occurred) the market expected the loss ratio to be only 0.8. Thus, the insurer would have been able to pay 0.8 × US$25,000 = US$20,000 to buy the futures contract. Because actual losses exceeded expected losses, the insurer makes a profit of US$37,500 − $20,000 = US$17,500 on each contract. These profits on futures contracts can be used to help offset the huge payouts on hurricane insurance contracts.[28]

Futures and Forward Regulation

www.m-x.ca

In Canada, derivatives contracts are traded on the Montréal Exchange (ME), which is responsible for the regulation of trading. The ME determines which contracts will trade as well as who may trade. The ME also establishes other rules regarding futures contracts such as price reporting requirements, anti-manipulation regulations, position limits, audit trail requirements, and margin requirements.

www.osfi-bsif.gc.ca

The Office of the Superintendent of Financial Services (OSFI) requires federally regulated financial institutions (domestic and foreign banks, trust and loans, co-operatives, life insurance companies, and property and casualty insurance companies) to follow its *Derivatives Best Practices Guideline B-7*, effective since May 1995. Banks are required to report on their derivatives positions quarterly as well as to follow the guidelines for best practices regarding capital adequacy, innovative instruments, large exposure limits, and derivative best practices, as well as specific guidelines with respect to interest rate risk, and accounting guidelines regarding the disclosure of derivative positions. Overall, the policy of OSFI is to encourage appropriate risk management practices at the FIs under its jurisdiction.

www.acsbcanada.org

As noted previously, as of October 1, 2006, the main regulator of accounting standards, the AcSB required all FIs (and non-financial firms) to reflect the marked-to-market value of their derivative positions in their financial statements.

[28] For more details on catastrophe insurance, see K. K. Aase, "A Markov Model for the Pricing of Catastrophe Insurance Futures and Spreads," *Journal of Risk and Insurance,* March 2001, pp. 25–49; and G. Zanjani, "Pricing and Capital Allocation in Catastrophe Insurance," *Journal of Financial Economics,* August 2002, pp. 283–305.

In the United States, derivatives contracts are subject to three levels of institutional regulation. First, regulators of derivatives specify "permissible activities" that institutions may engage in. Second, once permissible activities have been specified, institutions engaging in those activities are subjected to supervisory oversight. Third, regulators attempt to judge the overall integrity of each institution engaging in derivative activities by assessing the capital adequacy of the institutions and by enforcing regulations to ensure compliance with those capital requirements. The Securities and Exchange Commission (SEC) and the Commodities Futures Trading Commission (CFTC) are often viewed as "functional" regulators. The SEC regulates all securities traded on national securities exchanges, including several exchange-traded derivatives. The CFTC has exclusive jurisdiction over all exchange-traded derivative securities. It therefore regulates all national futures exchanges, as well as all futures and options on futures. This means that U.S. FIs must immediately recognize all gains and losses on such contracts and disclose those gains and losses to shareholders and regulators. Further, firms must show whether they are using derivatives to hedge risks connected to their business or whether they are just taking an open (risky) position.

www.sec.gov
www.cftc.gov

Finally, as noted in Chapter 20, exchange-traded futures contracts are not subject to risk-based capital requirements; by contrast, OTC forward contracts are potentially subject to capital requirements. Other things being equal, the risk-based capital requirements favour the use of futures over forwards.

| CONCEPT QUESTIONS | 1. Why are credit forwards useful for hedging the credit risk of an FI's portfolio? |
| | 2. Manulife Financial Corporation estimated after-tax losses of US$165 million on reinsurance contracts related to Hurricane Katrina that devastated New Orleans (see J. Partridge, "Manulife to Take $165-Million Charge Because of Katrina," *The Globe and Mail*, Tuesday, September 20, 2005, p. B5). What are some of the practical problems an FI manager may face when using catastrophe futures to hedge losses on insurance lines? |

Summary

This chapter analyzed the risk management role of futures and forwards. We saw that although they are close substitutes, they are not perfect substitutes. A number of characteristics, such as maturity, liquidity, flexibility, marking to market, and capital requirements, differentiate these products and make one or the other more attractive to any given FI manager. These products might be used to partially or fully hedge at least four types of risk commonly faced by an FI: interest rate risk, foreign exchange risk, credit risk, and catastrophe risk. An FI can engage in microhedging or macrohedging as well as engage in selective or routine hedging. In all cases, perfect hedging is shown to be difficult because of basis risk. Finally, accounting rules require FIs to disclose the market values of their (off-balance-sheet) derivatives positions.

Questions and Problems

1. What are derivative contracts? What is the value of derivative contracts to the managers of FIs? Which type of derivative contracts had the highest value among Canadian banks as of October 2008?

2. What has been the regulatory result of some of the misuses by FIs of derivative products?

3. What are some of the major differences between futures and forward contracts? How do these contracts differ from spot contracts?

4. What is a naive hedge? How does a naive hedge protect an FI from risk?

5. An FI holds a 15-year, par value, $10,000,000 bond that is priced at 104 with a yield to maturity of 7 percent. The bond has a duration of eight years, and the FI plans to sell it after two months. The FI's market analyst predicts that interest rates will be 8 percent at the time of the desired sale. Because most other analysts are predicting no change in rates, two-month forward contracts for 15-year bonds are available at 104. The FI would like to hedge against the expected change in interest rates with an appropriate position in a forward contract. What will this position be? Show that if rates rise 1 percent as forecast, the hedge will protect the FI from loss.

6. Contrast the position of being short with that of being long in futures contracts.

7. Suppose an FI purchases a bond futures contract at 95.

    a. What is the FI's obligation at the time the futures contract is purchased?

    b. If an FI purchases this contract, in what kind of hedge is it engaged?

    c. Assume that the bond futures price falls to 94. What is the loss or gain?

    d. Assume that the bond futures price rises to 97. Mark to market the position.

8. Long Bank has assets that consist mostly of 25-year mortgages and liabilities that are short-term time and demand deposits. Will an interest rate futures contract the bank buys add to or subtract from the bank's risk?

9. In each of the following cases, indicate whether it would be appropriate for an FI to buy or sell a forward contract to hedge the appropriate risk.

    a. A bank plans to issue GICs in three months.

    b. An insurance company plans to buy bonds in two months.

    c. A credit union is going to sell Government of Canada securities next month.

    d. A Canadian bank lends to a French company: The loan is payable in euros.

    e. A finance company has assets with a duration of 6 years and liabilities with a duration of 13 years.

10. The duration of a 20-year, 8 percent coupon government bond selling at par is 10.292 years. The bond's interest is paid semiannually, and the bond qualifies for delivery against a government bond futures contract.

    a. What is the modified duration of this bond?

    b. What is the effect on the bond price if market interest rates increase 50 basis points?

    c. If you sold a bond futures contract at 95 and interest rates rose 50 basis points, what would be the change in the value of your futures position?

    d. If you purchased the bond at par and sold the futures contract, what would be the net value of your hedge after the increase in interest rates?

11. What are the differences between a microhedge and a macrohedge for an FI? Why is it generally more efficient for FIs to employ a macrohedge than a series of microhedges?

12. What are the reasons why an FI may choose to selectively hedge its portfolio?

13. Hedge Row Bank has the following balance sheet ($ millions):

Assets	$150	Liabilities	$ 135
		Equity	$ 15
Total	$150	Total	$ 150

The duration of the assets is six years, and the duration of the liabilities is four years. The bank is expecting interest rates to fall from 10 percent to 9 percent over the next year.

    a. What is the duration gap for Hedge Row Bank?

    b. What is the expected change in net worth for Hedge Row Bank if the forecast is accurate?

    c. What will be the effect on net worth if interest rates increase 100 basis points?

    d. If the existing interest rate on the liabilities is 6 percent, what will be the effect on net worth of a 1 percent increase in interest rates?

14. For a given change in interest rates, why is the sensitivity of the price of a government bond futures contract greater than the sensitivity of the price of a government T-bill futures contract?

15. What is the meaning of the government bond futures price quote 101–13?

16. What is meant by fully hedging the balance sheet of an FI?

17. Tree Row Bank has assets of $150 million, liabilities of $135 million, and equity of $15 million. The asset duration is six years, and the duration of the liabilities is four years. Market interest rates are 10 percent. Tree Row Bank wishes to hedge the balance sheet with government bond futures contracts, which currently have a price quote of $95 per $100 face value for the benchmark 20-year, 8 percent coupon bond underlying the contract.

    a. Should the bank go short or long on the futures contracts to establish the correct macrohedge?

    b. How many contracts are necessary to fully hedge the bank?

    c. Verify that the change in the futures position will offset the change in the cash balance sheet position for a change in market interest rates of plus 100 basis points and minus 50 basis points.

    d. If the bank had hedged with Treasury bill futures contracts that had a market value of $98 per $100 of face value, how many futures contracts would have been necessary to fully hedge the balance sheet?

    e. What additional issues should be considered by the bank in choosing between T-bond and T-bill futures contracts?

18. Reconsider Tree Row Bank in problem 17 but assume that the cost rate on the liabilities is 6 percent.

    a. How many contracts are necessary to fully hedge the bank?

    b. Verify that the change in the futures position will offset the change in the cash balance sheet position for a change in market interest rates of plus 100 basis points and minus 50 basis points.

    c. If the bank had hedged with Treasury bill futures contracts that had a market value of $98 per $100 of face value, how many futures contracts would have been necessary to fully hedge the balance sheet?

19. What is basis risk? What are the sources of basis risk?

20. How would your answers for part (b) in problem 17 change if the relationship of the price sensitivity of futures contracts to the price sensitivity of underlying bonds was $br = 0.92$?

21. A mutual fund plans to purchase $500,000 of 30-year government bonds in four months. These bonds have a duration of 12 years and are priced at 96–08 (32nds). The mutual fund is concerned about interest rates changing over the next four months and is considering a hedge with government bond futures contracts that mature in six months. The bond futures contracts are selling for 98–24 (32nds) and have a duration of 8.5 years.

    a. If interest rate changes in the spot market exactly match those in the futures market, what type of futures position should the mutual fund create?

    b. How many contracts should be used?

    c. If the implied rate on the deliverable bond in the futures market moves 12 percent more than the change in the discounted spot rate, how many futures contracts should be used to hedge the portfolio?

    d. What causes futures contracts to have a different price sensitivity than assets in the spot markets?

22. Consider the following balance sheet ($ millions) for an FI:

Assets		Liabilities	
Duration = 10 years	$950	Duration = 2 years	$860
		Equity	90

    a. What is the FI's duration gap?

    b. What is the FI's interest rate risk exposure?

    c. How can the FI use futures and forward contracts to put on a macrohedge?

    d. What is the impact on the FI's equity value if the relative change in interest rates is an increase of 1 percent? That is $\Delta R/(1 + R) = 0.01$.

    e. Suppose that the FI in part (c) macrohedges using government bond futures that are currently priced at 96. What is the impact on the FI's futures position if the relative change in all interest rates is an increase of 1 percent? That is, $\Delta R/(1 + R) = 0.01$. Assume that the deliverable government bond has a duration of nine years.

    f. If the FI wants a perfect macrohedge, how many government bond futures contracts does it need?

23. Refer again to problem 22. How does consideration of basis risk change your answers to problem 22?

    a. Compute the number of futures contracts required to construct a perfect macrohedge if

    $$[\Delta R_f/(1 + R_f)/\Delta R/(1 + R)] = br = 0.90$$

    b. Explain what is meant by $br = 0.90$.

    c. If $br = 0.90$, what information does this provide on the number of futures contracts needed to construct a perfect macrohedge?

24. An FI is planning to hedge its US$100 million bond instruments with a cross hedge using Eurodollar interest rate futures. How would the FI estimate

    $$br = [\Delta R_f/(1 + R_f)/\Delta R/(1 + R)]$$

    to determine the exact number of Eurodollar futures contracts to hedge?

25. Village Bank has $240 million worth of assets with a duration of 14 years and liabilities worth $210 million with a duration of 4 years. In the interest of hedging interest rate risk, Village Bank is contemplating a macrohedge with interest rate futures contracts now selling for 102–21 (32nds). The T-bond underlying the futures contract has a duration of nine years. If the spot and futures interest rates move together, how many futures contracts must Village Bank sell to fully hedge the balance sheet?

26. Assume that an FI has assets of $250 million and liabilities of $200 million. The duration of the assets is six years, and the duration of the liabilities is three years. The price of the futures contract is $115,000, and its duration is 5.5 years.

    a. What number of futures contracts is needed to construct a perfect hedge if $br = 1.10$?

    b. If $\Delta R_f/(1 + R_f) = 0.0990$, what is the expected $\Delta R/(1 + R)$?

27. Suppose an FI purchases a US$1 million 91-day Eurodollar futures contract trading at 98.50.

    a. If the contract is reversed two days later by purchasing the contract at 98.60, what is the net profit?

    b. What is the loss or gain if the price at reversal is 98.40?

28. An FI has an asset investment in euros. The FI expects the exchange rate of $/€ to increase by the maturity of the asset.

    a. Is the dollar appreciating or depreciating against the euro?

    b. To fully hedge the investment, should the FI buy or sell euro futures contracts?

    c. If there is perfect correlation between changes in the spot and futures contracts, how should the FI determine the number of contracts necessary to hedge the investment fully?

29. What is meant by tailing the hedge? What factors allow an FI manager to tail the hedge effectively?

30. What does the hedge ratio measure? Under what conditions is this ratio valuable in determining the number of futures contracts necessary to hedge fully an investment in another currency? How is the hedge ratio related to basis risk?

31. What technique is commonly used to estimate the hedge ratio? What statistical measure is an indicator of the confidence that should be placed in the estimated hedge ratio? What is the interpretation if the estimated hedge ratio is greater than one? Less than one?

32. An FI has assets denominated in British pounds sterling of $125 million and sterling liabilities of $100 million.

    a. What is the FI's net exposure?

    b. Is the FI exposed to a dollar appreciation or depreciation?

    c. How can the FI use futures or forward contracts to hedge its FX rate risk?

    d. If a futures contract is currently trading at $1.55/£, what is the number of futures contracts that must be utilized to fully hedge the FI's currency risk exposure? Assume the contract size on the British pound futures contract is £62,500.

    e. If the British pound falls from $1.60/£ to $1.50/£, what will be the impact on the FI's cash position?

    f. If the British pound futures price falls from $1.55/£ to $1.45/£, what will be the impact on the FI's futures position?

    g. Using the information in parts (e) and (f), what can you conclude about basis risk?

33. An FI is planning to hedge its one-year 100 million Swiss francs (Sf)-denominated loan against exchange rate risk. The current spot rate is $0.60/Sf. A one-year Sf futures contract is currently trading at $0.58/Sf. Sf futures are sold in standardized units of Sf125,000.

    a. Should the FI be worried about the Sf appreciating or depreciating?

    b. Should it buy or sell futures to hedge against exchange rate exposure?

    c. How many futures contracts should it buy or sell if a regression of past changes in spot prices on changes in future prices generates an estimated slope of 1.4?

d. Show exactly how the FI is hedged if it repatriates its principal of Sf100 million at year-end, the spot price of Sf at year-end is $0.55/Sf, and the forward price is $0.5443/Sf.

34. An FI has made a loan commitment of Sf10 million that is likely to be drawn down in six months. The current spot rate is $0.60/Sf.

   a. Is the FI exposed to the dollar's depreciating or appreciating? Why?

   b. If the spot rate six months from today is $0.64/Sf, what dollar amount is needed if the loan is drawn down and the FI is unhedged?

   c. If it decides to hedge using Sf futures, should the FI buy or sell Sf futures?

   d. A six-month Sf futures contract is available for $0.61/Sf. What net amount would be needed to fund the loan at the end of six months if the FI had hedged using the Sf10 million futures contract? Assume that futures prices are equal to spot prices at the time of payment (i.e., at maturity).

35. An FI has assets denominated in Swiss francs (Sf) of 75 million and liabilities of 125 million. The spot rate is $0.6667/Sf, and one-year futures are available for $0.6579/Sf.

   a. What is the FI's net exposure?

   b. Is the FI exposed to dollar appreciation or depreciation?

   c. If the Sf spot rate changes from $0.6667/Sf to $0.6897/Sf, how will this affect the FI's currency exposure? Assume no hedging.

   d. What is the number of futures contracts necessary to fully hedge the currency risk exposure of the FI? The contract size is Sf125,000 per contract.

   e. If the Sf futures price falls from $0.6579/Sf to $0.6349/Sf, what will be the effect on the FI's futures position?

36. What is a credit forward? How is it structured?

37. What is the gain on the purchase of a $20,000,000 credit forward contract with a modified duration of seven years if the credit spread between a benchmark government bond and a borrowing firm's debt decreases 50 basis points?

38. How is selling a credit forward similar to buying a put option?

39. A property and casualty (P&C) insurance company purchased catastrophe futures contracts to hedge against loss during the hurricane season. At the time of purchase, the market expected a loss ratio of 0.75. After processing claims from a severe hurricane, the P&C actually incurred a loss ratio of 1.35. What amount of profit did the P&C make on each $25,000 futures contract?

40. What is the primary goal of regulators in regard to the use of futures by FIs? What guidelines have regulators given to banks for trading in futures and forwards?

Web Questions

41. Go to the website of any one of the six major banks in Canada and download the latest version of the annual report. Use the search function in Adobe Acrobat to find the term "notional amount." How have the notional amounts of each type of derivative contract changed since the results reported in Table 23–1 for October 31, 2008? Conduct a second search using the term "hedging." Does this FI report the amount of derivatives held for trading and the amount held for hedging? Repeat the process for a second bank. How does the use of derivatives used for hedging and trading differ between the two FIs?

42. Go to the Office of the U.S. Comptroller of the Currency website at www.occ.treas.gov. Find the most recent levels of futures, forwards, options, swaps, and credit derivatives using the following steps. Click on "Publications." From there click on "Qrtrly. Derivative Fact Sheet." Click on the most recent date to access the relevant data. The tables containing the data are at the bottom of this document. How have these values increased since December 2008 (as reported in Table 23–2)?

Appendix 23A   **Microhedging with Futures**

View Appendix 23A at the Online Learning Centre: www.mcgrawhill.ca/olc/saunders.

Options, Caps, Floors, and Collars

In this chapter, we
- review the four basic options strategies:
  - buying a call
  - writing a call
  - buying a put
  - writing a put[1]
- look at economic and regulatory reasons FIs choose to buy versus write (sell) options
- discuss the use of fixed-income or interest rate options to hedge interest rate risk
- discuss the role of options in hedging:
  - foreign exchange risk
  - credit risk
  - catastrophe risk
- conclude with an examination of caps, floors, and collars

INTRODUCTION

Just as a wide variety of forward and futures contracts are available for an FI to use in hedging, there is an even wider array of option products, including exchange-traded options, over-the-counter options, options embedded in securities, and caps, collars, and floors. As we saw with futures contracts (in Chapter 23), the use of options can protect an FI against a loss of net worth due to unexpected changes in interest rates, credit risk, foreign exchange risk, and so forth. Not only has the range of option products increased in recent years, but the use of options has increased as well. However, options can also lead to huge losses for FIs (see the Ethical Dilemmas feature).

As with futures and forwards, discussed in Chapter 23, options, caps, floors, and collars are held by FIs not only to hedge their own risk, but also to serve as counterparties (for a fee) for other financial and non-financial firms wanting to hedge risk on their own balance sheets.

BASIC FEATURES OF OPTIONS

option
A contract that gives the holder the right but not the obligation to buy or sell the underlying asset at a specified price within a specified period of time.

An **option** is a contract that gives the holder the right, but not the obligation, to buy or sell an underlying asset at a prespecified price for a specified time period. Options are classified as either call options or put options. We discuss both of these below, highlighting their profits in terms of price movements on the underlying asset. The

---

[1] There are two basic option contracts: puts and calls. However, an FI could potentially be a buyer or seller (writer) of each.

Chicago Board of Options Exchange (CBOE), opened in 1973, was the first exchange devoted solely to the trading of stock options. In 1982, financial futures options contracts (options on financial futures contracts, e.g., Treasury bond futures contracts) started trading. Options markets have grown rapidly since the mid-1980s.

The trading process for options is the same as that for futures contracts. An FI desiring to take an option position places an order to buy or sell a stated number of call or put option contracts with a stated expiration date and exercise price. The order is directed to a representative on the appropriate exchange for execution. Trading on the largest exchanges such as the CBOE takes place in trading pits, where traders for each delivery date on an option contract informally group together. As with futures contracts, options trading can occur electronically or by open-outcry auction method. Once an option price is agreed on in a trading pit, the two parties send the details of the trade to the option clearinghouse (the Options Clearing Corporation), which breaks up trades into buy and sell transactions and takes the opposite side of each transaction—becoming the seller for every option contract buyer and the buyer for every option contract seller. The broker on the floor of the options exchange confirms the transaction with the investor's broker.

In the early 2000s, the CBOE increased the speed at which orders can be placed, executed, and filled by equipping floor brokers with hand-held touch-screen computers that allow them to route and execute orders more easily and efficiently. For example, when a broker selects an order from the workstation, an electronic trading card appears on his or her computer screen. The electronic card allows the broker to work the order and enter necessary trade information (e.g., volume, price, opposing market makers). When the card (details of the transaction) is complete, the broker can execute the trade with the touch of a finger. Once the broker has submitted the trade, the system simultaneously sends a "fill" report to the customer and instantaneously transmits this data to traders worldwide.

While the CBOE is the biggest options exchange, Canadian FIs are able to buy and sell options on the Montréal Exchange. As noted in Chapter 23, the Montréal Exchange, part of the TMX Group since 2008, provides options trading in Canada for interest rate, index, and equity contracts. The Canadian Derivatives Clearing Corporation (CDCC), a self-regulating organization wholly owned by the Bourse de Montréal Inc., issues, clears, and guarantees the contracts traded on the Montréal Exchange. The Montréal Exchange offers index options (e.g., S&P/TSX 60 Index Options), **exchange-traded funds (ETFs)** (e.g., Horizons BetaPro S&P/TSX 60 Bear Plus Fund), equity options (e.g., Suncor Energy Inc.), and U.S. dollar currency options.

In describing the features of the four basic option strategies FIs might employ to hedge interest rate risk, we discuss their return payoffs in terms of interest rate movements. Specifically, we consider bond options whose payoff values are inversely linked to interest rate movements in a manner similar to bond prices and interest rates in general (see Chapter 8).

Buying a Call Option on a Bond

The first strategy of buying (or taking a long position in) a call option on a bond is shown in Figure 24–1. A **call option** gives the purchaser the right (but not the obligation) to buy the underlying security—a bond—at a prespecified *exercise* or *strike price* (X). In return, the buyer of the call option must pay the writer or seller an up-front fee known as a *call premium* (C). This premium is an immediate negative cash flow for the buyer of the call, who potentially stands to make a profit if the underlying bond's price rises above the exercise price by an amount

---

exchange-traded funds (ETFs)
Funds that track a specific index or basket of shares and trade like shares on a stock exchange. They can be bought and sold at any time during a trading day.

call option
Gives a purchaser the right (but not the obligation) to buy the underlying security from the writer of the option at a prespecified exercise price on a prespecified date.

Do you dream of writing your memoirs from a white-collar prison cell? David Parkinson offers tips on how to join the banking villains—a group whose number appears to have grown by one this week.

So you want to be a rogue trader? Want to deal in the high-powered world of billions of losses, flying under the radar of your supposedly intelligent and vigilant bosses?

Look no further. Five Things hereby presents five useful tips for anyone wanting to join the rogue's gallery of banking villains—a group whose number looks to have grown by one this week with news of Jérôme Kerviel's $7.2 billion trading disaster at French banking giant Société Générale SA.

1. Trade in Derivatives

Many of the biggest and best-known rogue trader incidents in the past two decades have involved derivatives trading. Nick Leeson of Britain's Barings Bank lost $1.4 billion trading in Asian stock market options; Yasuo Hamanaka lost $2.6 billion for Japan's Sumitomo Corp. speculating in copper futures; Calgary energy trader Brian Hunter lost $6 billion on bad bets on natural gas futures for hedge fund Amaranth LLC. Mr. Kerviel's derivatives of choice were European stock index futures.

"[Derivatives] have an extremely high degree of leverage," said Louis Gagnon, associate professor at Queen's School of Business. "With very little money, you can take on a very large position."

2. Long on Ego, Short on Skill

Invariably, rogue traders didn't start out trying to run up billions of dollars in trading losses. They were trying to make money. They were just really, really bad at it—making an entirely wrong bet on the market's direction, then compounding the error by going double-or-nothing in hopes of being rescued by a miraculous market reversal.

But what these traders lack in market insight, they make up for in nerve and blind ambition. "If they aren't already stars, they're aspiring to be stars," Mr. Gagnon said.

3. Know a Thing or Two About Computers

Understanding and manipulating the computer systems that oversee your company's trading operations give even the most incompetent trader a leg up in hiding trading debacles.

Mr. Kerviel worked in SocGen's trading back office before he made the unusual move up to the front lines. As a result, he knew passwords that would give him access to systems and accounts.

Joseph Jett, the rogue bond trader whose phony trading profits cost Kidder Peabody & Co. $210 million in the 1990s, pulled off the deception through a glitch in a computer program that assigned profits to what were essentially phantom trades. It remains a bone of contention whether Mr. Jett knowingly manipulated trades to take advantage of the glitch.

4. Find an Employer Who Is Napping

Mr. Gagnon said many of the biggest frauds take place at companies that have failed to provide even some of the most basic oversight and security measures to protect themselves. In SocGen's case, he argued, something as simple as password changes could have protected them from a trader getting access to back office functions that could be used to obscure huge trading losses.

"Rule Number One is, you segregate duties. You make sure one person can't have access to both sides," he said.

5. Consider Commercial Banking

Despite the high profile afforded frauds in the jet setter world of investment banking, big-time scams may be more common among staff at those frumpy, boring old commercial banks. A 2005 study by J. David Cummins and Ran Wei of the University of Pennsylvania's Wharton School, which tracked large-scale (more than $50-million U.S.) fraud events in the U.S. financial services community since 1978, found that such frauds are 30 per cent more frequent at commercial banks. Still, the investment banking frauds are typically bigger: The median loss to the bank in such frauds was $207 million for investment banks, versus $89 million for commercial.

Source: David Parkinson, *The Globe and Mail,* January 26, 2008, pg. B2. 2008 CTVglobemedia Publishing Inc. All Rights Reserved.

exceeding the premium. If the price of the bond never rises above X, the buyer of the call never exercises the option (i.e., buying the bond at X when its market value is less than X). In this case, the option matures unexercised. The call buyer incurs a cost, C, for the option, and no other cash flows result.

FIGURE 24–1

Payoff Function for the Buyer of a Call Option on a Bond

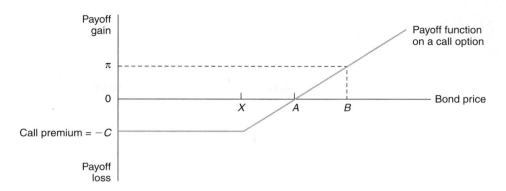

As shown in Figure 24–1, if the price of the bond underlying the option rises to price B, the buyer makes a profit of π, which is the difference between the bond price (B) and the exercise price of the option (X) minus the call premium (C). If the bond price rises to A, the buyer of the call has broken even in that the profit from exercising the call ($A - X$) just equals the premium payment for the call (C).

Notice two important things about bond call options in Figure 24–1:

1. As interest rates fall, bond prices rise and the call option buyer has a large profit potential; the more that rates fall, the higher bond prices rise and the larger the profit on the exercise of the option.

2. As interest rates rise, bond prices fall and the potential for a negative payoff (loss) for the buyer of the call option increases. If rates rise so that bond prices fall below the exercise price X, the call buyer is not obliged to exercise the option. Thus, the losses of the buyer are truncated by the amount of the up-front premium payment (C) made to purchase the call option.

Thus, buying a call option is a strategy to take when interest rates are expected to fall. Notice that unlike interest rate futures, whose prices and payoffs move symmetrically with changes in the level of rates, the payoffs on bond call options move asymmetrically with interest rates (see Chapter 23).

Writing a Call Option on a Bond

The second strategy is writing (or taking a short position in) a call option on a bond. In writing a call option on a bond, the writer or seller receives an up-front fee or premium (C) and must stand ready to sell the underlying bond to the purchaser of the option at the exercise price, X. Note the payoff from writing a call option on a bond in Figure 24–2.

FIGURE 24–2

Payoff Function for the Writer of a Call Option on a Bond

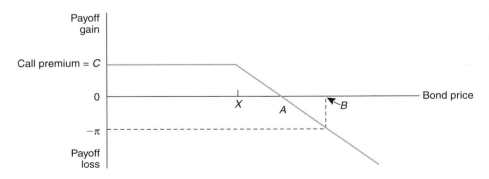

There are two important things to notice about this payoff function:

1. When interest rates rise and bond prices fall, there is an increased potential for the writer of the call to receive a positive payoff or profit. The call buyer is less likely to exercise the option, which would force the option writer to sell the underlying bond at the exercise price. However, this profit has a maximum equal to the call premium (C) charged up front to the buyer of the option.

2. When interest rates fall and bond prices rise, the writer has an increased potential to take a loss. The call buyer will exercise the option, forcing the option writer to sell the underlying bonds. Since bond prices are theoretically unbounded in the upward direction, although they must return to par at maturity, these losses could be very large.

Thus, writing a call option is a strategy to take when interest rates are expected to rise. Caution is warranted, however, because profits are limited but losses are potentially large if rates fall. In Figure 24–2, a fall in interest rates and a rise in bond prices to B results in the writer of the option losing π.

Buying a Put Option on a Bond

put option
Gives a purchaser the right (but not the obligation) to sell the underlying security to the writer of the option at a prespecified exercise price on a prespecified date.

The third strategy is buying (or taking a long position in) a put option on a bond. The buyer of a **put option** on a bond has the right (but not the obligation) to sell the underlying bond to the writer of the option at the agreed exercise price (X). In return for this option, the buyer of the put option pays a premium to the writer (P). We show the potential payoffs to the buyer of the put option in Figure 24–3. Note that

1. When interest rates rise and bond prices fall, the buyer of the put has an increased probability of making a profit from exercising the option. Thus, if bond prices fall to D, the buyer of the put option can purchase bonds in the bond market at that price and put them (sell them) back to the writer of the put at the higher exercise price (X). As a result, the buyer makes a profit, after deducting the cost of the put premium (P), of πp in Figure 24–3.

2. When interest rates fall and bond prices rise, the probability that the buyer of a put will lose increases. If rates fall so that bond prices rise above the exercise price X, the put buyer does not have to exercise the option. Thus, the maximum loss is limited to the size of the up-front put premium (P).

Thus, buying a put option is a strategy to take when interest rates are expected to rise.

FIGURE 24–3
Payoff Function for the Buyer of a Put Option on a Bond

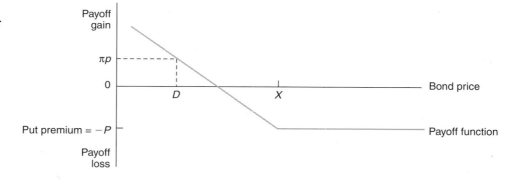

Writing a Put Option on a Bond

The fourth strategy is writing (or taking a short position in) a put option on a bond. In writing a put option on a bond, the writer or seller receives a fee or premium (P) in return for standing ready to buy bonds at the exercise price (X) if the buyer of the put chooses to exercise the option to sell. See the payoff function for writing a put option on a bond in Figure 24–4. Note that

1. If interest rates fall and bond prices rise, the writer has an enhanced probability of making a profit. The put buyer is less likely to exercise the option, which would force the option writer to buy the underlying bond. However, the writer's maximum profit is constrained to be equal to the put premium (P).
2. If interest rates rise and bond prices fall, the writer of the put is exposed to potentially large losses (e.g., $-\pi p$, if bond prices fall to D in Figure 24–4).

Thus, writing a put option is a strategy to take when interest rates are expected to fall. However, profits are limited and losses are potentially unlimited.

CONCEPT QUESTIONS	1. How do interest rate increases affect the payoff from buying a call option on a bond? How do they affect the payoff from writing a call option on a bond?
	2. How do interest rate increases affect the payoff from buying a put option on a bond? How do they affect the payoff from writing a put option on a bond?

WRITING VERSUS BUYING OPTIONS

Many small FIs are restricted to buying rather than writing options. There are two reasons for this, one economic and the other regulatory. However, as we note later, large FIs often both write and buy options including caps, floors, and collars, which are complex forms of interest rate options.

Economic Reasons for Not Writing Options

In writing an option, the upside profit potential is truncated, but the downside losses are not. While such risks may be offset by writing a large number of options at different exercise prices and/or hedging an underlying portfolio of bonds, the downside risk exposure of the writer may still be significant. To see this, look at Figure 24–5, where an FI is long in a bond in its portfolio and seeks to hedge the interest rate risk on that bond by writing a bond call option.

FIGURE 24–4
Payoff Function for the Writer of a Put Option on a Bond

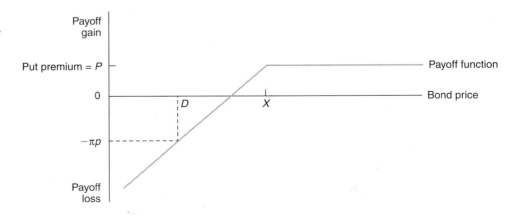

FIGURE 24–5
Writing a Call Option to Hedge the Interest Rate Risk on a Bond

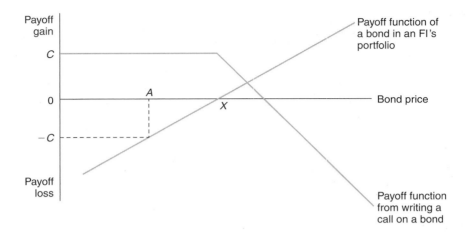

Figure 24–6 shows the net profit, or the difference between the bond and option payoff. Note that writing the call may hedge the FI when rates fall and bond prices rise; that is, the increase in the value of the bond is offset by losses on the written call. When the reverse occurs and interest rates rise, the FI's profits from writing the call may be insufficient to offset the loss on its bonds. This occurs because the upside profit (per call written) is truncated and is equal to the premium income (C). If the decrease in the bond value is larger than the premium income (to the left of point A in Figure 24–5), the FI is unable to offset the associated capital value loss on the bond with profits from writing options.

By contrast, hedging the FI's risk by buying a put option on a bond offers the manager a much more attractive alternative. Figure 24–7 shows the gross payoff of the bond and the payoff from buying a put option on a bond. In this case, any losses on the bond (as rates rise and bond values fall) are offset with profits from the put option that was bought (points to the left of point X in Figure 24–7). If rates fall, the bond value increases, yet the accompanying losses on the purchased put option positions are limited to the option premiums paid (points to the right of point X). Figure 24–8 shows the net payoff or the difference between the bond and option payoff.

FIGURE 24–6
Profit from Writing a Call Option and Investing in a Bond

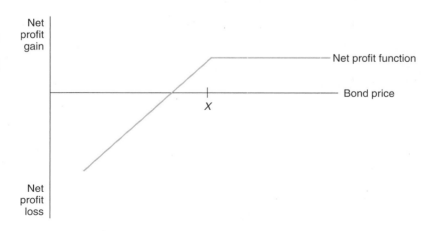

FIGURE 24–7
Buying a Put Option to Hedge the Interest Rate Risk on a Bond

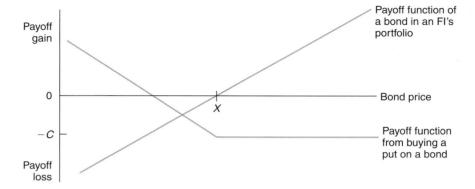

FIGURE 24–8
Net Payoff of Buying a Bond Put and Investing in a Bond

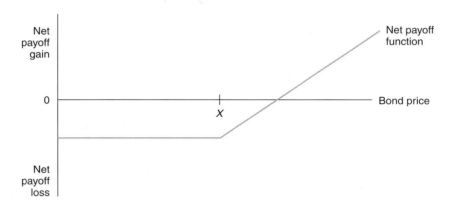

Note that

1. Buying a put option truncates the downside losses on the bond following inter-est rate rises to some maximum amount and scales down the upside profits by the cost of bond price risk insurance—the put premium—leaving some positive upside profit potential.
2. The combination of being long in the bond and buying a put option on a bond mimics the payoff function of buying a call option (compare Figures 24–1 and 24–8).

Regulatory Reasons

naked options
Option positions that do not identifiably hedge an underlying asset or liability.

There are also regulatory reasons why FIs buy options rather than write options. Regulators view writing options, especially **naked options** that do not identifiably hedge an underlying asset or liability position, to be risky because of the large loss potential. Indeed, in some countries, bank regulators prohibit banks from writing puts or calls in certain areas of risk management.

Futures versus Options Hedging

To understand the differences between using futures versus options contracts to hedge interest rate risk, compare the payoff gains illustrated in Figure 24–9 (for futures contracts) with those in Figure 24–7 (for buying put option contracts). A hedge with futures contracts reduces volatility in payoff gains on both the upside and downside of interest rate movements. That is, if the FI in Figure 24–9 loses

FIGURE 24–9
Buying a Futures Contract to Hedge the Interest Rate Risk on a Bond

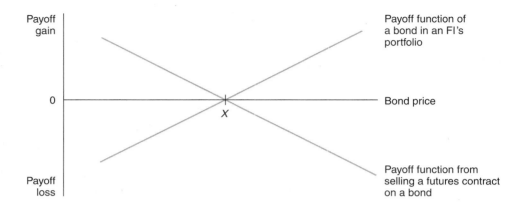

value on the bond resulting from an interest rate increase (to the left of point X), a gain on the futures contract offsets the loss. If the FI gains value on the bond due to an interest rate decrease (to the right of point X), however, a loss on the futures contract offsets the gain.

In comparison, the hedge with the put option contract completely offsets losses but only partly offsets gains. That is, in Figure 24–7, if the FI loses value on the bond due to an interest rate increase (to the left of point X), a gain on the put option contract offsets the loss. However, if the FI gains value on the bond due to an interest rate decrease (to the right of point X), the gain is offset only to the extent that the FI loses the put option premium (because it never exercises the option). Thus, the put option hedge protects the FI against value losses when interest rates move against the on-balance-sheet securities but, unlike futures hedging, does not reduce value when interest rates move in favour of on-balance-sheet securities.

CONCEPT QUESTIONS

1. What are some of the economic reasons for an FI not to write options?
2. What are some regulatory reasons why an FI might choose to buy options rather than write options?

THE MECHANICS OF HEDGING A BOND OR BOND PORTFOLIO[2]

You have seen how buying a put option on a bond can potentially hedge the interest rate risk exposure of an FI that holds bonds as part of its investment portfolio. In this section, we use a simple example to demonstrate the mechanics of buying a put option as a hedging device and how an FI manager can calculate the fair premium value for a put option on a bond.

In calculating the fair value of an option, two alternative models can be used: the binomial model and the Black–Scholes model. The Black–Scholes model produces a closed-form solution to the valuation of call and put options. Appendix 24A to this chapter (located at the Online Learning Centre: www.mcgrawhill.ca/olc/saunders) shows how to calculate the value of an option using the Black–Scholes model. Although it works well for stocks, the Black–Scholes model has two major

---

[2] The material in this section is more technical in nature. It may be included or dropped from the chapter reading depending on the rigour of the course without harming the continuity of the chapter.

problems when employed to value bond options. First, it assumes that short-term interest rates are constant, which they generally are not. Second, it assumes a constant variance of returns on the underlying asset.[3] The application of the Black–Scholes formula to bonds is problematic because of the way bond prices behave between issuance and maturity.[4] This is shown in Figure 24–10, where a bond is issued at par, that is, the price of the bond is 100 percent times its face value at time of issue. If interest rates fall, its price may rise above 100 percent, and if interest rates rise, its price may fall below 100 percent. However, as the bond approaches maturity, all price paths must lead to 100 percent of the face value of the bond or principal paid by the issuer on maturity. Because of this **pull-to-par,** the variance of bond prices is non-constant over time, rising at first and then falling as the bond approaches maturity. We evaluate the mechanics of hedging using bond put options in a simple binomial framework next.

pull-to-par
The tendency of the variance of a bond's price or return to decrease as maturity approaches.

Hedging with Bond Options Using the Binomial Model

Suppose that an FI manager has purchased a $100 zero-coupon bond with exactly two years to maturity. A zero-coupon bond, if held to maturity, pays its face value

FIGURE 24–10
The Variance of a Bond's Price

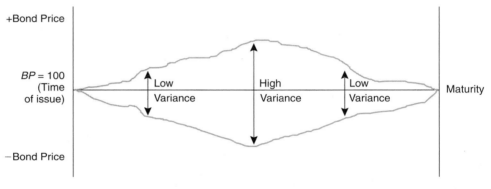

---

[3] The Black–Scholes formulas for a put and a call are

$$P = Xe^{-rT}N[-D + \sigma\sqrt{T}] - SN[-D]$$
$$C = SN[D] - Xe^{-rT}N[D - \sigma\sqrt{T}]$$

where

S = Price of the underlying asset
X = Exercise price
T = Time to option expiration
r = Instantaneous riskless interest rate

$$D = \frac{ln(S/X) + (r + \sigma^2/2)T}{\sigma\sqrt{T}}$$

$ln[\,.\,]$ = Natural logarithm
σ = Volatility of the underlying asset
$N[\,.\,]$ = Cumulative normal distribution function, that is, the probability of observing a value less than the value in brackets when drawing randomly from a standardized normal distribution

[4] There are models that modify Black–Scholes to allow for non-constant variance. These include Merton, who allows variance to be time-dependent; Ball and Tourous, who allow bond prices to change as a stochastic process with a variance that first increases and then decreases (the Brownian bridge process); and the Schaefer–Schwartz model, which assumes that the standard deviation of returns is proportional to a bond's duration. See R. C. Merton, "On the Pricing of Corporate Debt: The Risk Structure of Interest Rates," *Journal of Finance* 29, 1974, pp. 449–470; C. Ball and W. N. Tourous, "Bond Price Dynamics and Options," *Journal of Financial and Quantitative Analysis* 18, 1983, pp. 517–531; and S. Schaefer and E. S. Schwartz, "Time Dependent Variance and the Pricing of Bond Options," *Journal of Finance* 42, 1987, pp. 1113–1128.

of $100 on maturity in two years. Assume that the FI manager pays $80.45 per $100 of face value for this zero-coupon bond. This means that if held to maturity, the FI's annual yield to maturity (R_2) from this investment would be

$$BP_2 = \frac{100}{(1 + R_2)^2}$$

$$80.45 = \frac{100}{(1 + R_2)^2}$$

$$(1 + R_2)^2 = \frac{100}{80.45}$$

$$1 + R_2 = \sqrt{\frac{100}{80.45}}$$

$$R_2 = \sqrt{\frac{100}{80.45}} - 1 = 0.115 = 11.5\%$$

Suppose also that, at the end of the first year, interest rates rise unexpectedly. As a result, depositors, seeking higher returns on their funds, withdraw deposits. To meet these unexpected deposit withdrawals, the FI manager is forced to liquidate (sell) the two-year bond before maturity, at the end of year 1. As we discuss in Chapter 17, government securities are important liquidity sources for an FI. Because of the unexpected rise in interest rates at the end of year 1, the FI manager must sell the bond at a low price.

Assume when the bond is purchased, the current yield on one-year discount bonds (R_1) is $R_1 = 10$ percent. Also, assume that at the end of year 1, the one-year interest rate (r_1) is forecasted to rise to either 13.82 percent or 12.18 percent. If one-year interest rates rise from $R_1 = 10$ percent when the bond is purchased to $r_1 = 13.82$ percent at the end of year 1, the FI manager will be able to sell the zero-coupon bond with one year remaining to maturity for a bond price, BP, of

$$BP_1 = \frac{100}{(1 + r_1)} = \frac{100}{(1.1382)} = \$87.86$$

If, on the other hand, one-year interest rates rise to 12.18 percent, the manager can sell the bond with one year remaining to maturity for

$$BP_1 = \frac{100}{(1 + r_1)} = \frac{100}{(1.1218)} = \$89.14$$

In these equations, r_1 stands for the two possible one-year rates that might arise one year into the future.[5] That is,

---

[5] If one-year bond rates next year equalled the one-year bond rate this year, $R_1 = r_1 = 10$ percent, then the bond could be sold for $BP_1 = \$90.91$.

Assume the manager believes that one-year rates (r_1) one year from today will be 13.82 percent or 12.18 percent with an equal probability. This means that the expected one-year rate one year from today would be

$$[E(r_1)] = 0.5(0.1382) + 0.5(0.1218) = 0.13 = 13\%$$

Thus, the expected price if the bond has to be sold at the end of the first year is[6]

$$E(P_1) = \frac{100}{(1.13)} = \$88.5$$

Assume that the FI manager wants to ensure that the bond sale produces at least \$88.5 per \$100; otherwise the FI has to find alternative and very costly sources of liquidity (for example, the FI might have to borrow from the central bank's discount window and incur the direct and indirect penalty costs involved, see Chapter 19). One way for the FI to ensure that it receives at least \$88.5 on selling the bond at the end of the year is to buy a put option on the bond at time 0 with an exercise price of \$88.5 at time (year) 1. If the bond is trading below \$88.5 at the end of the year—say, at \$87.86—the FI can exercise its option and put the bond back to the writer of the option, who will have to pay the FI \$88.5. If, however, the bond is trading above \$88.5—say, at \$89.14—the FI does not have to exercise its option and instead can sell the bond in the open market for \$89.14.

The FI manager will want to recalculate the fair premium to pay for buying this put option or bond insurance at time 0. Figure 24–11 shows the possible paths (i.e., the binomial tree or lattice) of the zero-coupon bond's price from purchase to maturity over the two-year period. The FI manager purchased the bond at \$80.45

FIGURE 24–11
Binomial Model of Bond Prices: Two-Year Zero-Coupon Bond

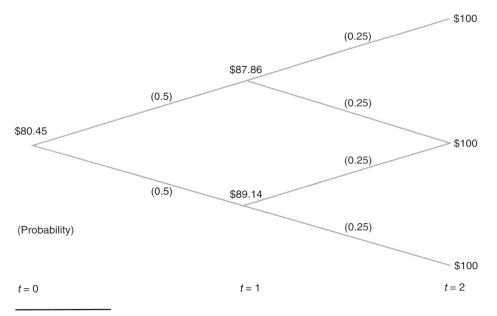

[6] The interest rates assumed in this example are consistent with arbitrage-free pricing under current term structure conditions. That is, the expectations theory of interest rates implies that the following relationship must hold:

$$(1 + R_2)^2 = (1 + R_1) \times [1 + E(r_1)]$$

As you can easily see, when the interest rates from our example are inserted, $R_1 = 10\%$, $R_2 = 11.5\%$, $E(r_1) = 13\%$, this equation holds. Also, the two interest rates (prices) imply that the current volatility of one-year interest rates is 6.3 percent. That is, from the binomial model, $\sigma = 1/2 ln[r_u/r_d]$, such that $\sigma = 1/2 ln[13.82/12.18] = 0.063$ or 6.3%.

with two years to maturity. Given expectations of rising rates, there is a 50 percent probability that the bond with one year left to maturity will trade at $87.86 and a 50 percent probability that it will trade at $89.14. Note that between $t = 1$, or one year left to maturity, and maturity ($t = 2$), there must be a pull-to-par on the bond; that is, all paths must lead to a price of $100 on maturity.

The value of the option is shown in Figure 24–12. The option in Figure 24–12 can be exercised only at the end of year 1 ($t = 1$). If the zero-coupon bond with one year left to maturity trades at $87.86, the option is worth $88.50 − $87.86 in time 1 dollars, or $0.64. If the bond trades at $89.14, the option has no value since the bond could be sold at a higher value than the exercise price of $88.50 on the open market. This suggests that in time 1 dollars, the option is worth

$$0.5(0.64) + 0.5(0) = \$0.32$$

However, the FI is evaluating the option and paying the put premium at time $t = 0$, that is, one year before the date when the option might be exercised. Thus, the fair value of the put premium (P) the FI manager should be willing to pay is the discounted present value of the expected payoff from buying the option. Since one-year interest rates (R_1) are currently 10 percent, this implies

$$P = \frac{\$0.32}{1 + R_1} = \frac{\$0.32}{(1.1)} = \$0.29$$

or a premium, P, of approximately 29 cents per $100 bond option purchased.

Further, as you can easily see, the option becomes increasingly valuable as the variability of interest rates increases. Conceptually, the branches of the binomial tree diagram become more widely dispersed as variability increases. For example, suppose one-year interest rates on the upper branch were expected to be 14.82 percent instead of 13.82 percent. Then, the price on a one-year, zero-coupon bond associated with a one-year yield of 14.82 percent is $87.09 and the option is worth $88.50 − $87.09 in time 1 dollars, or $1.41. Thus, the value of the put option (P) with the same exercise price of $88.50 is

$$P = \frac{0.5(1.41) + 0.5(0)}{1.1}$$

$$= 64 \text{ cents}$$

FIGURE 24–12
The Value of a Put Option on the Two-Year Zero-Coupon Bond

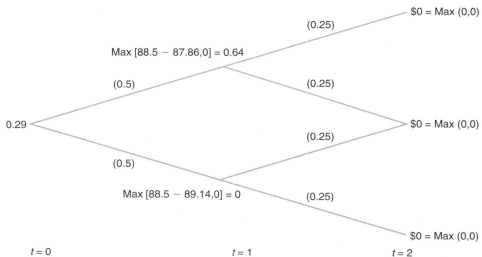

Max [88.5 − 87.86,0] = 0.64

(0.5)

0.29

(0.5)

Max [88.5 − 89.14,0] = 0

(0.25)

(0.25)

(0.25)

(0.25)

(0.25)

(0.25)

$0 = Max (0,0)

$0 = Max (0,0)

$0 = Max (0,0)

$t = 0$ $t = 1$ $t = 2$

Notice the familiar result from option pricing theory holds

$$\frac{\delta P}{\delta \sigma} > 0$$

That is, the value of the put option increases with an increase in underlying variance of asset returns.

CONCEPT QUESTIONS	1. **What are two common models used to calculate the fair value of a bond option? Which is preferable, and why?** 2. **In the example above, calculate the value of the option if the exercise price (X) = $88. ($P$ = $0.064)**

ACTUAL BOND OPTIONS

www.m-x.ca

www.cboe.com

open interest
The outstanding stock of put or call contracts.

futures option
An option contract that, when exercised, results in the delivery of a futures contract as the underlying asset.

We have presented a simple example of how FIs may use bond options to hedge exposure to liability withdrawal and forced liquidation of assets in a world of interest rate variability. In actuality, FIs have a wide variety of over-the-counter (OTC) and exchange-traded options available. Interest rate options are listed on the Montréal Exchange in Canada and on the Chicago Board Options Exchange (CBOE). However, these contracts are rarely traded and the **open interest** (the outstanding stock of put or call contracts) in short-term interest rate options is small. In actual practice, most pure bond options trade over the counter. This is not because interest rate or bond options are not used, although the open interest is relatively small, but because the preferred method of hedging is an option on an interest rate futures contract.

A **futures option** is a contract in which the underlying asset is a futures contract (e.g., $100,000 Treasury bond futures). The buyer of a call (put) option on a futures contract has the right to buy (sell) the underlying futures contract before expiration (i.e., an American option). The seller of a call (put) option on a futures contract creates the obligation to sell (buy) the underlying futures contract on exercise by the option buyer. If exercised, a call (put) option holder can buy (sell) the underlying futures contract at the exercise price. Options on futures can be more attractive to FIs than options on an underlying asset when it is cheaper or more convenient to deliver futures contracts on the asset rather than the actual asset. For example, trading options on T-bond futures contracts rather than options on T-bonds ensures that a highly liquid asset will be delivered and that problems associated with accrued interest and the determination of which long-term bond to deliver are avoided. Another advantage is that price information about futures contracts (the underlying asset on the option) is generally more readily available than price information on the T-bonds themselves (T-bond price information can be obtained only by surveying bond dealers).

Finally, bond or interest rate futures options are generally preferred to options on the underlying bond because they combine the favourable liquidity, credit risk, homogeneity, and marking-to-market features of futures with the same asymmetric payoff functions as regular puts and calls (see Chapter 23). Futures options (i.e., an option contract that, when exercised, results in the delivery of a futures contract as the underlying asset) on bonds are listed in Figure 24–13 for trading on Wednesday, May 20, 2009.

FIGURE 24–13
Futures Options on Interest Rates and Currencies, May 20, 2009

Source: *The Wall Street Journal Online,* May 20, 2009, online.wsj.com. Reprinted by permission of *The Wall Street Journal.* All prices are settlement prices. Volume and open interest are from the previous trading day.

Interest Futures Options

U.S. Treasury Bonds (CBOT)
$100,000, pts & 64ths of 100 pct

Strike Price	CALLS Jun	CALLS Jul	CALLS Sep	PUTS Jun	PUTS Jul	PUTS Sep
11000	12-30	11-14	11-48	0-01	0-08	0-43
11100	11-30	10-17	10-57	0-01	0-11	0-51
11200	10-30	9-20	10-02	0-01	0-14	0-60
11300	9-30	8-26	9-13	0-01	0-19	1-07
11400	8-30	7-33	8-26	0-01	0-26	1-20
11500	7-30	6-41	7-40	0-01	0-34	1-34
11600	6-30	5-52	6-57	0-01	0-45	1-51
11700	5-30	5-02	6-12	0-01	0-59	2-06
11800	4-30	4-19	5-34	0-01	1-12	2-27
11900	3-30	3-39	4-57	0-01	1-32	2-50
12000	2-33	2-63	4-19	0-04	1-56	3-12

Volume calls 20,874 puts 10,063
Op int calls 286,330 Puts 148,423

Eurodollars (CME)
$1 million, pts of 100 pct

Strike Price	CALLS May	CALLS Jun	CALLS Sep	PUTS May	PUTS Jun	PUTS Sep
977500	-	164.50	161.75	-	-	1.00
978750	-	152.00	149.25	-	-	1.00
980000	-	139.50	136.75	-	-	1.00
981250	-	127.00	124.25	-	-	1.00
982500	-	114.50	112.00	-	0.25	1.25
983750	-	102.00	99.75	-	0.25	1.50
985000	-	89.75	87.75	-	0.25	1.75
986250	-	77.25	75.50	-	0.25	2.00
987500	-	64.75	63.50	-	0.25	2.50
988750	-	52.50	51.75	-	0.25	3.25

Volume calls 3,627 puts 1,973
Op int calls 6,938,826 Puts 4,040,426

10-Yr. Treasury (CBOT)
$100,000, prin, pts & 64ths of 100 pct

Strike Price	Jun	Jul	Sep	Jun	Jul	Sep
11700	13-62	12-28	12-33	0-01	0-01	0-06
11750	13-30	11-60	12-02	0-01	0-01	0-07
11800	12-62	11-28	11-35	0-01	0-01	0-08
11850	12-30	10-60	11-03	0-01	0-01	0-09
11900	11-62	10-28	10-37	0-01	0-01	0-10
11950	11-30	9-60	10-06	0-01	0-01	0-11
11000	10-62	9-29	9-40	0-01	0-02	0-13
11050	10-30	8-61	9-10	0-01	0-02	0-15
11100	9-62	8-31	8-44	0-01	0-03	0-17
11150	9-30	7-63	8-14	0-01	0-03	0-19
11200	8-62	7-32	7-48	0-01	0-04	0-21

Volume calls 132,366 puts 70,692
Op int calls 1,115,495 Puts 817,515

Currency Futures Options

Japanese Yen (CME)
12,500,000 yen, cents per 100 yen

Strike Price	Jun	Jul	Sep	Jun	Jul	Sep
950	10.36	10.46	10.57	-	0.02	0.15
955	9.86	9.97	10.10	-	0.03	0.18
960	9.36	9.47	9.64	0.01	0.04	0.22
965	8.86	8.98	9.19	0.01	0.05	0.27
970	8.36	8.49	8.74	-	0.06	0.32
975	7.87	8.01	8.31	0.01	0.08	0.39
980	7.37	7.53	7.88	0.01	0.10	0.46
985	6.88	7.06	7.46	0.02	0.13	0.54
990	6.39	6.60	7.06	0.03	0.17	0.64
995	5.90	6.14	6.67	0.04	0.21	0.75

Volume calls 737 puts 431
Op int calls 23,335 Puts 37,914

Swiss Franc (CME)
125,000 francs, cents per franc

Strike Price	Jun	Jul	Sep	Jun	Jul	Sep
840	6.97	7.13	7.45	0.01	0.09	0.42
845	6.47	6.65	7.01	0.01	0.11	0.48
850	5.98	6.17	6.58	0.02	0.13	0.55
855	5.48	5.70	6.16	0.02	0.16	0.62
860	4.99	5.23	5.75	0.03	0.19	0.71
865	4.50	4.79	5.36	0.04	0.24	0.82
870	4.02	4.35	4.97	0.06	0.30	0.93
875	3.55	3.93	4.60	0.09	0.38	1.06

Volume calls 18 puts 37
Op int calls 6,924 Puts 9.251

Canadian Dollar (CME)
100,000 dollars, cents per dollar

Strike Price	Jun	Jul	Sep	Jun	Jul	Sep
845	3.64	4.15	4.97	0.16	0.62	1.45
850	3.20	3.78	4.63	0.22	0.75	1.61
855	2.78	3.42	4.31	0.30	0.89	1.79
860	2.39	3.08	4.01	0.41	1.05	1.99
865	2.03	2.76	3.73	0.55	1.23	2.20
870	1.70	2.47	3.46	0.72	1.44	2.43
875	1.41	2.19	3.20	0.93	1.66	2.67
880	1.16	1.94	2.95	1.18	1.91	2.92

Volume calls 1,190 puts 335
Op int calls 15,309 Puts 9,436

Euro (CME)
125,000 euros, cents per euro

Strike Price	Jun	Jul	Sep	Jun	Jul	Sep
12450	13.500	13.430	13.860	0.005	0.070	0.520
12500	13.000	12.940	13.400	0.005	0.080	0.560
12550	12.500	12.450	12.950	0.005	0.090	0.610
12600	12.000	11.970	12.500	0.005	0.110	0.660
12650	11.500	11.490	12.060	0.005	0.130	0.720
12700	11.000	11.010	11.620	0.005	0.150	0.780
12750	10.510	10.530	11.190	0.010	0.170	0.850
12800	10.010	10.060	10.780	0.015	0.200	0.930

Volume calls 3,617 puts 1,948
Op int calls 43,310 Puts 26,113

British Pound (CME)
62,500 pounds, cents per pound

Strike Price	Jun	Jul	Sep	Jun	Jul	Sep
1490	8.84	9.20	10.31	0.08	0.53	1.65
1500	7.88	8.33	9.54	0.12	0.66	1.88
1510	6.94	7.49	8.80	0.18	0.82	2.14
1520	6.02	6.69	8.09	0.26	1.02	2.43
1530	5.14	5.93	7.43	0.38	1.26	2.76
1540	4.30	5.22	6.78	0.54	1.54	3.11
1550	3.54	4.55	6.17	0.78	1.87	3.50
1560	2.85	3.94	5.60	1.09	2.26	3.92
1570	2.25	3.38	5.06	1.49	2.70	4.38

Volume calls 967 puts 950
Op int calls 14,544 Puts 11,838

When the FI hedges by buying put options on bond futures, if interest rates rise and bond prices fall, the exercise of the put causes the FI to deliver a bond futures contract to the writer at an exercise price higher than the cost of the bond future currently trading on the futures exchange. The futures price itself reflects the price of the underlying deliverable bond such as a 20-year, 8 percent coupon T-bond; see Figure 24–13. As a result, a profit on futures options may be made to offset the loss on the market value of bonds held directly in the FI's portfolio. If interest rates fall and bond and futures prices rise, the buyer of the futures option will not exercise the put, and the losses on the futures put option are limited to the put premium. Thus, if on May 20, 2009, the FI had bought one US$100,000 July 2009 T-bond futures put option at a strike price of US$119 but did not exercise the option, the FI's loss equals the put premium of $1\,^{32}/_{64}$ per US$100, or US$1,500 per US$100,000 contract. Offsetting these losses, however, would be an increase in the market value of the FI's underlying bond portfolio. Unlike futures positions in Chapter 23, an upside profit potential remains when interest rates fall and FIs use put options on futures to hedge interest rate risk. We show this in the next section.

CONCEPT QUESTIONS	1. **Why are bond or interest rate futures options generally preferred to options on the underlying bond?**
	2. **If an FI hedges by buying put options on futures and interest rates rise (i.e., bond prices fall), what is the outcome?**

USING OPTIONS TO HEDGE INTEREST RATE RISK ON THE BALANCE SHEET

Our previous simple example showed how a bond option could hedge the interest rate risk on an underlying bond position in the asset portfolio. Next, we determine the put option position that can hedge the interest rate risk of the overall balance sheet; that is, we analyze macrohedging rather than microhedging.

Chapter 9 showed that an FI's net worth exposure to an interest rate shock could be represented as

$$\Delta E = -(D_A - kD_L) \times A \times \frac{\Delta R}{1 + R}$$

where

$$\Delta E = \text{Change in the FI's net worth}$$
$$(D_A - kD_L) = \text{FI's leverage-adjusted duration gap}$$
$$A = \text{Size of the FI's assets}$$
$$\frac{\Delta R}{1 + R} = \text{Size of the interest rate shock}$$
$$k = \text{FI's leverage ratio } (L/A)$$

Suppose the FI manager wishes to determine the optimal number of put options to buy to insulate the FI against rising rates. An FI with a positive duration gap (see Figure 24–14) would lose on-balance-sheet net worth when interest rates rise. In this case, the FI manager would buy put options.[7] That is, the FI manager wants

---

[7] Conversely, an FI with a negative duration gap would lose on-balance-sheet net worth when interest rates fall. In this case, the FI manager wants to buy call options to generate profits to offset the loss in net worth due to an interest rate shock.

FIGURE 24–14
**Buying Put Options
to Hedge the
Interest Rate Risk
Exposure of the FI**

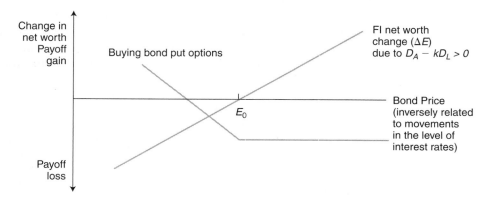

to adopt a put option position to generate profits that just offset the loss in net worth due to an interest rate shock (where E_0 is the FI's initial equity (net worth) position in Figure 24–14).

Let ΔP be the total change in the value of the put option position in T-bonds. This can be decomposed into

$$\Delta P = (N_p \times \Delta p) \qquad (24.1)$$

where N_p is the number of $100,000 put options on T-bond contracts to be purchased (the number for which we are solving) and Δp is the change in the dollar value for each $100,000 face value T-bond put option contract.

The change in the dollar value of each contract (Δp) can be further decomposed into

$$\Delta p = \frac{dp}{dB} \times \frac{dB}{dR} \times \Delta R \qquad (24.2)$$

This decomposition needs some explanation. The first term (dp/dB) shows the change in the value of a put option for each $1 change in the underlying bond. This is called the *delta of an option* (δ) and lies between 0 and 1. For put options, the delta has a negative sign since the value of the put option falls when bond prices rise.[8] The second term (dB/dR) shows how the market value of a bond changes if interest rates rise by one basis point. This value of one basis point term can be linked to duration. Specifically, we know from Chapter 9 that

$$\frac{dB}{B} = -MD \times dR \qquad (24.3)$$

That is, the percentage change in the bond's price for a small change in interest rates is proportional to the bond's modified duration (*MD*). Equation 24.3 can be rearranged by cross-multiplying as

$$\frac{dB}{dR} = -MD \times B \qquad (24.4)$$

---

[8] For call options, the delta has a positive sign since the value of the call rises when bond prices rise. As we proceed with the derivation, we examine only the case of a hedge using a put option contract (i.e., the FI has a positive duration gap and expects interest rates to rise). For a hedge with a call option contract (i.e., the FI has a negative duration gap), the derivation below changes only in that the sign on the delta is reversed (from negative to positive).

Thus, the term dB/dR is equal to minus the modified duration on the bond (MD) times the current market value of the T-bond (B) underlying the put option contract. As a result, we can rewrite equation 24.2 as

$$\Delta p = [(-\delta) \times (-MD) \times B \times \Delta R] \qquad (24.5)$$

where ΔR is the shock to interest rates (i.e., the number of basis points by which rates change). Since from Chapter 9 we know that $MD = D/(1 + R)$, we can rewrite equation 24.5 as

$$\Delta p = \left[(-\delta) \times (-D) \times B \times \frac{\Delta R}{1 + R} \right] \qquad (24.6)$$

Thus, the change in the total value of a put position[9] (ΔP) is

$$\Delta P = N_p \times \left[\delta \times D \times B \times \frac{\Delta R}{1 + R} \right] \qquad (24.7)$$

The term in brackets is the change in the value of one \$100,000 face-value T-bond put option as rates change, and N_p is the number of put option contracts.

To hedge net worth exposure, we require the profit on the off-balance-sheet put options (ΔP) to just offset the loss of on-balance-sheet net worth ($-\Delta E$) when interest rates rise (and thus, bond prices fall). That is,[10]

$$\Delta P = -\Delta E$$

$$N_p \times \left[\delta \times D \times B \times \frac{\Delta R}{1 + R} \right] = [D_A - kD_L] \times A \times \frac{\Delta R}{1 + R}$$

Cancelling $\Delta R/(1 + R)$ on both sides, we get

$$N_p \times [\delta \times D \times B] = [D_A - kD_L] \times A$$

Solving for N_p—the number of put options to buy—we have[11]

$$N_P = \frac{[D_A - kD_L] \times A}{[\delta \times D \times B]} \qquad (24.8)$$

Appendix 24B (located at the Online Learning Centre: www.mcgrawhill.ca/olc/saunders) derives the equation for the number of option contracts to buy or sell for a microhedge.[12]

---

[9] Note that since both the delta and D values of the put option and bond have negative signs, their product will be positive. Thus, these negative signs are not shown in the equation to calculate N_p.

[10] Note that $\quad \Delta E = -(D_A - kD_L) \times A \times \dfrac{\Delta R}{1 + R}$

Thus: $\quad -\Delta E = +(D_A - kD_L) \times A \times \dfrac{\Delta R}{1 + R}$

[11] For a hedge involving a call option, the formula is

$$N_C = \frac{[D_A - kD_L] \times A}{-[\delta \times D \times B]}$$

[12] For a microhedge, this equation becomes

$$N_O = \frac{D \times P}{\delta \times D \times B}$$

where P is the price of the asset or liability being hedged and D is its duration.

EXAMPLE 24–1

Macrohedge of Interest Rate Risk Using a Put Option

Suppose, as in Chapter 23, an FI's balance sheet is such that $D_A = 5$, $D_L = 3$, $k = 0.9$, and $A = \$100$ million. Rates are expected to rise from 10 to 11 percent over the next six months, which would result in a $2.09 million loss in net worth to the FI. Suppose also that δ of the put option is 0.5, which indicates that the option is close to being in the money, $D = 8.82$ for the bond underlying the put option contract, and the current market value of $100,000 face value of long-term Treasury bonds underlying the option contract, B, equals $97,000. Solving for N_p, the number of put option contracts to buy is

$$N_p = \frac{\$230,000,000}{[0.5 \times 8.82 \times \$97,000]} = \frac{\$230,000,000}{\$427,770}$$

$$= 537.672 \text{ contracts}$$

If the FI slightly underhedges, this will be rounded down to 537 contracts. If rates increase from 10 to 11 percent, the value of the FI's put options will change by

$$\Delta P = 537 \times \left[0.5 \times 8.82 \times \$97,000 \times \frac{0.01}{1.1} \right] = \$2.09 \text{ million}$$

just offsetting the loss in net worth on the balance sheet.

The total premium cost to the FI of buying these puts is the price (premium) of each put times the number of puts:

$$\text{Cost} = N_p \times \text{Put premium per contract}$$

Suppose that T-bond put option premiums are quoted at $2½ per $100 of face value for the nearby contract or $2,500 per $100,000 put contract; then the cost of macrohedging the gap with put options will be

$$\text{Cost} = 537 \times \$2,500 = \$1,342,500$$

or just over $1.3 million. Remember, the total assets of the FI were assumed to be $100 million.

Figure 24–15 summarizes the change in the FI's overall value from a 1 percent increase in interest rates and the offsetting change in value from the hedge in the put option market. If rates increase as predicted, the FI's gap exposure results in a

FIGURE 24–15   **Buying Put Options to Hedge an FI's Interest Rate Gap Risk Exposure**

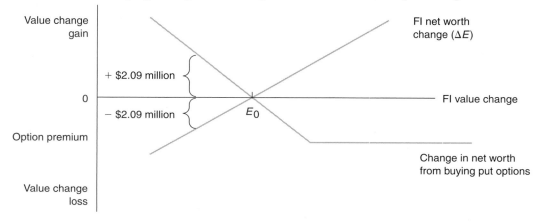

decrease in net worth of $2.09 million. This decrease is offset with a $2.09 million gain on the put option position held by the FI. Should rates decrease, however, the resulting increase in net worth is not offset by a decrease in an out-of-the-money put option.

Appendix 24B to this chapter (located at the Online Learning Centre: www.mcgrawhill.ca/olc/saunders) illustrates how these options can be used to micro-hedge a specific asset or liability on an FI's balance sheet against interest rate risk.

Basis Risk

It is again important to recognize that in the previous examples, the FI hedged interest rate risk exposure perfectly because basis risk was assumed to be zero. That is, we assumed the change in interest rates on the balance sheet is equal to the change in the interest rate on the bond underlying the option contract [i.e., $\Delta R/(1 + R) = \Delta R_b/(1 + R_b)$]. As discussed in Chapter 23, the introduction of basis risk means that the FI must adjust the number of option contracts it holds to account for the degree to which the rate on the option's underlying security (i.e., T-bond) moves relative to the spot rate on the asset or liability the FI is hedging.

Allowing basis risk to exist, the equation used to determine the number of put options to buy to hedge interest rate risk becomes

$$N_p = \frac{(D_A - kD_L) \times A}{\delta \times D \times B \times br}$$

where *br* is a measure of the volatility of interest rates (R_b) on the bond underlying the options contract relative to the interest rate that impacts the bond on the FI's balance sheet (R). That is,

$$br = \frac{\dfrac{\Delta R_b}{1 + R_b}}{\dfrac{\Delta R}{1 + R}}$$

EXAMPLE 24–2

Put Option Macrohedge with Basis Risk

Refer to Example 24–1. Suppose that basis risk, *br*, is 0.92 (i.e., the rate on the option's underlying bond changes by 92 percent of the spot rate change on the balance sheet being hedged). In Example 24–1, with no basis risk, the number of options needed to hedge interest rate risk on the bond position is 537.672 put option contracts. Introducing basis risk, *br* = 0.92:

$$N_p = \frac{\$230,000,000}{0.5 \times 8.82 \text{ years} \times \$97,000 \times 0.92} = 584.4262 \text{ put option contracts}$$

Additional put option contracts are needed to hedge interest rate risk because interest rates on the bond underlying the option contract do not move as much as interest rates on the bond held as an asset on the balance sheet.

As described in Chapter 23, the FI can analyze the relationship between interest rates on the security underlying the futures option contract (e.g., T-bond) and the security being hedged on the FI's balance sheet by investigating their relative behaviour in the recent past. This can be done by running an ordinary least-squares linear regression of T-bond rate changes on spot rate changes with the slope coefficient of this regression giving an estimate of the degree of comovement of the two rates over time, or basis risk.

CONCEPT QUESTIONS

1. If interest rates fall, are you better off purchasing call or put options on bonds, and why?
2. In the example above, what number of put options should you purchase if $\delta = 0.25$ and $D = 6$? ($N_p = 1,718.213$)

USING OPTIONS TO HEDGE FOREIGN EXCHANGE RISK

Just as an FI can hedge a long position in bonds against interest rate risk through bond options or futures options on bonds, a similar opportunity is available to microhedge long or short positions in a foreign currency asset against foreign exchange rate risk. To see this, suppose that a U.S.-based FI bought, or is long in, a Canadian dollar (CDN$) asset in May 2009. This CDN$ asset is a one-month T-bill paying CDN$100 million in June 2009. Since the FI's liabilities are in U.S. dollars, it may wish to hedge the FX risk that the Canadian dollar will depreciate over the forthcoming month. Suppose that if the CDN$ were to fall from the current exchange rate of US$0.8639/CDN$1, the FI would make a loss on its Canadian T-bill investment when measured in U.S. dollar terms. For example, if the CDN$ depreciated from US$0.8639/CDN$ in May 2009 to US$0.8459/CDN$1 in June 2009, the C$100 million asset would be worth only US$84.59 million on maturity instead of the expected US$86.39 million when it was purchased in May. If the foreign exchange rate depreciation is sufficiently severe, the FI might be unable to meet its dollar liability commitments used to fund the T-bill purchase. To offset this exposure, the FI may buy one-month put options on Canadian dollars at an exercise price of US$0.860/CDN1$. Thus, if the exchange rate does fall to US$0.8459/CDN$1 at the end of the month, the FI manager can put the CDN$100 million proceeds from the T-bill on maturity to the writer of the option. Then the FI receives US$86 million instead of the US$84.59 million if the Canadian dollars were sold at the open market spot exchange rate at the end of the month. If the CDN$ actually appreciates in value, or does not depreciate below US$0.86/CDN$1, the option expires unexercised and the proceeds of the CDN$100 million asset will be realized by the FI manager by a sale of Canadian dollars for U.S. dollars in the spot foreign exchange market one month into the future (see Figure 24–16).

As with bonds, the FI can buy put options on foreign currency futures contracts to hedge this currency risk. The futures option contracts for foreign currencies traded on the Chicago Mercantile Exchange (CME) are shown in Figure 24–13.

www.cme.com

FIGURE 24–16
Hedging FX Risk by Buying a Put Option on Canadian Dollars

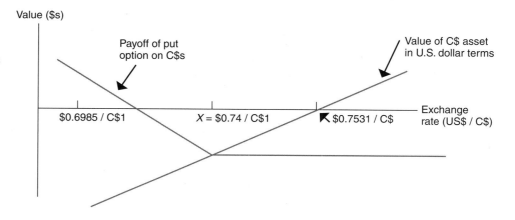

A put position in one foreign currency futures contract with expiration in June 2009 and exercise price of US$0.86/CDN$1 would have cost the FI a premium of US$0.0041 per CDN$1 on May 20, 2009. Since each Canadian dollar futures option contract is CDN$100,000 in size, the cost would have been US$410 per contract. If we ignore the question of basis risk—that is, the imperfect correlation between the U.S.$/CDN$ exchange rate on the spot and futures in options markets—the optimal number of futures options purchased would be

$$\frac{C\$100,000,000}{C\$100,000} = 1,000 \text{ contracts}$$

with a total premium cost of US$410,000.

CONCEPT QUESTIONS

1. What is the difference between options on foreign currency and options on foreign currency futures?
2. If an FI has to hedge a US$5,000,000 liability exposure in Swiss francs (Sf), what options should it purchase to hedge this position? Using Figure 24–13, how many contracts of Swiss franc futures options should it purchase (assuming no basis risk) if it wants to hedge against the Sf falling in value against the dollar given a current exchange rate of US$0.8185/Sf1 (or 1.2217 Sf/US$1). (Buy 48.810 call options on Sf futures)

HEDGING CREDIT RISK WITH OPTIONS

Options also have a potential use in hedging the credit risk of an FI. Relative to their use in hedging interest rate risk, option use to hedge credit risk is a relatively new phenomenon. Although FIs are always likely to be willing to bear some credit risk as part of the intermediation process (i.e., exploit their comparative advantage to bear such risk), options may allow them to modify that level of exposure selectively. In Chapter 23 we stated that an FI could seek an appropriate credit risk hedge by selling credit forward contracts. Rather than using credit forwards to hedge, an FI has at least two alternative credit option derivatives with which it can hedge its on-balance-sheet credit risk.

credit spread call option
A call option whose payoff increases as a yield spread increases above some stated exercise spread.

A **credit spread call option** is a call option whose payoff increases as the (default) risk premium or yield spread on a specified benchmark bond of the borrower increases above some exercise spread, *S*. An FI concerned that the risk on a loan to that borrower will increase can purchase a credit spread call option to hedge the increased credit risk.

Figure 24–17 illustrates the change in the FI's capital value and its payoffs from the credit spread call option as a function of the credit spread. As the credit spread

FIGURE 24–17
Buying Credit Spread Call Options to Hedge Credit Risk

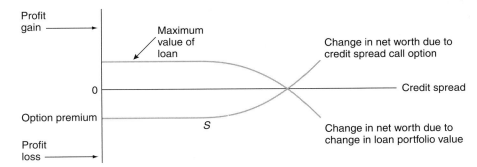

increases on an FI's loan to a borrower, the value of the loan, and consequently the FI's net worth, decreases. However, if the credit risk characteristics of the benchmark bond (i.e., change in credit spread) are the same as those on the FI's loan, the loss of net worth on the balance sheet is offset with a gain from the credit spread call option. If the required credit spread on the FI's loan decreases (perhaps because the credit quality of the borrower improves over the loan period), the value of the FI's loan and net worth increases (up to some maximum value), but the credit spread call option will expire out of the money. As a result, the FI will suffer a maximum loss equal to the required (call) premium on the credit option, which will be offset by the market value gain of the loan in the portfolio (which is reflected in a positive increase in the FI's net worth).

digital default option
An option that pays the par value of a loan in the event of default.

A **digital default option** is an option that pays a stated amount in the event of a loan default (the extreme case of increased credit risk). As shown in Figure 24–18, the FI can purchase a default option covering the par value of a loan (or loans) in its portfolio. In the event of a loan default, the option writer pays the FI the par value of the defaulted loans. If the loans are paid off in accordance with the loan agreement, however, the default option expires unexercised. As a result, the FI will suffer a maximum loss on the option equal to the premium (cost) of buying the default option from the writer (seller).

HEDGING CATASTROPHE RISK WITH CALL SPREAD OPTIONS

catastrophe (CAT) call spread
A call option on the loss ratio incurred in writing catastrophe insurance with a capped (or maximum) payout.

www.cbot.com

In 1993 the Chicago Board of Trade (CBOT) introduced **catastrophe (CAT) call spread** options to hedge the risk of unexpectedly high losses being incurred by property and casualty insurers as a result of catastrophes such as hurricanes. The basic idea can be seen in Figure 24–19. For an option premium, the insurer can hedge a range of loss ratios that may occur (remember that the loss ratio is the ratio of losses incurred divided by premiums written). In Figure 24–19, the insurer buys a call spread to hedge the risk that the loss ratio on its catastrophe insurance may be anywhere between 50 percent and 80 percent. If the loss ratio ends up below 50 percent (perhaps because of a mild hurricane season), the insurance company loses the option premium. For loss ratios between 50 percent and 80 percent, it receives an increasingly positive payoff. For loss ratios above 80 percent, the amount paid by the writers of the option to the buyer (the insurer) is capped at the 80 percent level. Cummins, Lalonde, and Phillips examined catastrophe loss index options in hedging hurricane losses in Florida. Using data from 255 of 264

FIGURE 24–18
Buying a Digital Default Option to Hedge Credit Risk

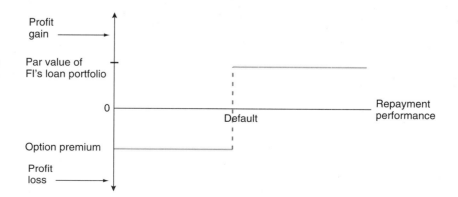

FIGURE 24–19
Catastrophe Call
Spread Options

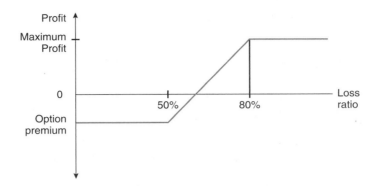

property insurers operating in Florida in 1998, they found that these options can be used effectively by insurers to hedge catastrophe risk.[13]

CONCEPT QUESTIONS

1. What is the difference between a credit spread call option and a digital default option?
2. What is the difference between the profit on the catastrophe call spread option in Figure 24–19 and the profit of a standard call option on a stock?

CAPS, FLOORS, AND COLLARS

cap
A call option on interest rates, often with multiple exercise dates.

floor
A put option on interest rates, often with multiple exercise dates.

collar
A position taken simultaneously in a cap and a floor.

Caps, floors, and collars are derivative securities that have many uses, especially in helping an FI hedge interest rate risk exposure as well as risk unique to its individual customers. Buying a **cap** means buying a call option or a succession of call options on interest rates. Specifically, if interest rates rise above the cap rate, the seller of the cap—usually a bank—compensates the buyer—for example, another FI—in return for an up-front premium. As a result, buying an interest rate cap is like buying insurance against an (excessive) increase in interest rates. A cap agreement can have one or many exercise dates.

Buying a **floor** means buying a put option on interest rates. If interest rates fall below the floor rate, the seller of the floor compensates the buyer in return for an up-front premium. As with caps, floor agreements can have one or many exercise dates.

A **collar** occurs when an FI takes a simultaneous position in a cap and a floor, such as buying a cap and selling a floor. The idea here is that the FI wants to hedge itself against rising rates but wants to finance the cost of the cap. One way to do this is to sell a floor and use the premiums on the floor to pay the premium on the purchase of the cap. Thus, these three over-the-counter instruments are special cases of options; FI managers use them like bond options and bond futures options to hedge the interest rate risk of an FI's portfolios.

In general, FIs purchase interest rate caps if they are exposed to losses when interest rates rise. Usually, this happens if they are funding assets with floating-rate liabilities such as notes indexed to LIBOR (or some other cost of funds) and they have fixed-rate assets or they are net long in bonds, or—in a macrohedging context—their duration gap is $D_A - kD_L > 0$. By contrast, FIs purchase floors

---

[13] See J. D. Cummins, D. Lalonde, and R. D. Phillips, "The Basis Risk of Catastrophe-Loss Index Securities," *Journal of Financial Economics*, January 2004, pp. 77–111.

when they have fixed costs of debt and have variable rates (returns) on assets, are net short in bonds, or $D_A - kD_L < 0$. Finally, FIs purchase collars when they are concerned about excessive volatility of interest rates and to finance cap or floor positions.

Caps

Under a cap agreement, in return for paying an up-front premium, the seller of the cap stands ready to compensate the buying FI whenever the interest rate index defined under the agreement is above the cap rate on the dates specified under the cap agreement. This effectively converts the cost of the FI's floating-rate liabilities into fixed-rate liabilities.

EXAMPLE 24–3	Assume that an FI buys a 9 percent cap at time 0 from another FI with a notional face value of $100 million. The cap agreement specifies exercise dates at the end of the first year and the end of the second year. That is, the cap has a three-year maturity from initiation until the final exercise dates, with exercise dates at the end of year 1 and year 2.[14]

Illustration of a Cap Used to Hedge Interest Rate Risk

Thus, the buyer of the cap would demand two cash payments from the seller of the cap if rates lie above 9 percent at the end of the first year and at the end of the second year on the cap exercise dates. In practice, cap exercise dates usually closely correspond to payment dates on liabilities, for example, coupon dates on floating-rate notes. Consider one possible scenario in Figure 24–20.

In Figure 24–20, the seller of the cap has to pay the buyer of the cap the amount shown in Table 24–1. In this scenario, the cap-buying FI would receive $3 million (undiscounted) over the life of the cap to offset any rise in the cost of liability funding or market value losses on

FIGURE 24–20
Hypothetical Path of Interest Rates

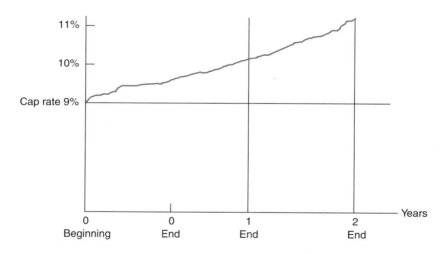

TABLE 24–1
Payments under the Cap

End of Year	Cap Rate	Actual Interest Rate	Interest Differential	Payment by Seller to Buyer
1	9%	10%	1%	$1 million
2	9	11	2	$2 million
Total				$3 million

---

[14] There is no point exercising the option at the end of year 0 (i.e., having three exercise dates) since interest rates for year 0 are set at the beginning of that year and are contractually set throughout. As a result, the FI does not bear interest rate uncertainty until the end of year 0 (i.e., interest uncertainty exists only in years 1 and 2).

its bond/asset portfolio. However, the interest rates in Figure 24–20 are only one possible scenario. Consider the possible path to interest rates in Figure 24–21. In this interest scenario, rates fall below 9 percent at the end of the first year to 8 percent and at the end of the second year to 7 percent on the cap exercise dates. Thus, the cap seller makes no payments.

This example makes it clear that buying a cap is similar to buying a call option on interest rates in that when the option expires out of the money, because the interest rate is below the cap level, the cap seller makes no payments to the buyer. Conceptually, buying this cap is like buying a complex call option on an interest rate or a put option on a bond price with a single exercise price or interest rate and two exercise dates: the end of year 1 and the end of year 2.

The problem for the FI manager is to calculate the fair value of this 9 percent cap in the face of interest rate uncertainty. In particular, the FI manager does not know whether interest rates will be 10 percent at the end of year 1 or 8 percent. Similarly, the manager does not know whether interest rates will be 11 percent or 7 percent at the end of year 2. Nevertheless, to buy interest rate risk insurance in the form of a cap, the manager has to pay an up-front fee or premium to the seller of the cap. Next, we solve for the fair value of the cap premium in the framework of the binomial model introduced earlier to calculate the premium on a bond option.

Consider Figure 24–22, the binomial tree for the cap contract entered into at the beginning of year 0. The cap can be exercised at the end of the first year and the end of the second year.[15] The current (time 0) value of the cap or the fair cap

FIGURE 24–21
Hypothetical Path of Interest Rates

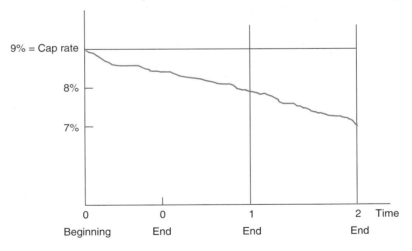

FIGURE 24–22
Interest Rate Cap with a 9 Percent Cap Rate

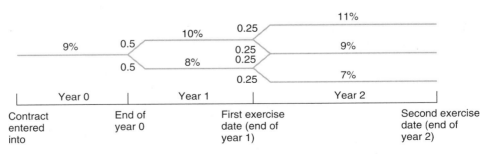

---

[15] Interest rates are normally set at the *beginning* of each period and paid at the *end* of each period.

premium is the sum of the present value of the cap option exercised at the end of year 1 plus the present value of the cap option exercised at the end of year 2:

$$\text{Fair premium} = P = PV \text{ of year 1 option} + PV \text{ of year 2 option}$$

EXAMPLE 24–4 *Calculating the Premium on an Interest Rate Cap*	***PV of Year 2 Option*** At the end of year 2, there are three possible interest rate scenarios: 11 percent, 9 percent, and 7 percent. With a cap exercise price of 9 percent and the 9 percent or 7 percent scenarios realized, the cap would have no value to the buyer. In other words, it would expire out of the money. The only interest rate scenario where the cap has exercise value to the buyer at the end of the second year is if rates rise to 11 percent. With rates at 11 percent, the interest differential would be 11 percent minus 9 percent, or 2 percent. But since there is only a 25 percent probability that interest rates will rise to 11 percent at the end of the second year, the expected value of this interest differential is

$$0.25 \times 2\% = 0.5\%$$

With a $100 million cap, therefore, the expected cash payment at the end of year 2 would be $0.5 million. However, to calculate the fair value of the cap premium in current dollars, the expected cash flow at the end of year 2 has to be discounted back to the present (time 0):

$$PV_2 = \frac{0.5}{(1.09)(1.1)(1.11)} = 0.3757$$

where 9 percent, 10 percent, and 11 percent are the appropriate one-year discount rates for payments in years 0, 1, and 2. Thus, the fair present value of the option at the end of year 2 is 0.3757, or $375,700, given the $100 million face value of the cap.

PV of Year 1 Option

At the end of year 1, there are two interest rate scenarios: Interest rates could rise to 10 percent or fall to 8 percent. If rates fall to 8 percent, the 9 percent cap has no value to the buyer. However, if rates rise to 10 percent, this results in a positive interest differential of 1 percent at the end of year 1. However, the expected interest differential is only 0.5 of 1 percent since this is the probability that rates will rise from 9 percent to 10 percent between the beginning of year 0 and end of year 1:

$$0.5 \times 1\% = 0.5\%$$

In dollar terms, with a $100 million cap, the expected value of the cap at the end of year 1 is $0.5 million. To evaluate the time 0 or present value of a cap exercised at the end of time period 1, this expected cash flow has to be discounted back to the beginning of time 0 using the appropriate one-year discount rates. That is,

$$PV_1 = \frac{0.5}{(1.09)(1.1)} = 0.417$$

or $417,000, given the $100 million face value of the cap. As a result, the fair value of the premium the FI should be willing to pay for this cap is

$$\text{Cap premium} = PV_1 + PV_2$$
$$= \$417,000 + \$375,700$$
$$= \$792,700$$

That is, under the interest rate scenarios implied by this simple binomial model, the FI should pay no more than $792,700, or 0.7927 percent of notional face value, in buying the cap from the seller.

Floors

A floor is a put option or a collection of put options on interest rates. Here the FI manager who buys a floor is concerned about falling interest rates. Perhaps the FI is funding liabilities at fixed rates and has floating-rate assets, or maybe it is short in some bond position and will lose if it has to cover the position with higher-priced bonds after interest rates fall. In a macrohedging sense, the FI could face a duration gap where the duration of assets is less than the leverage-adjusted duration of liabilities ($D_A - kD_L < 0$).

EXAMPLE 24–5	Consider the profit from buying a floor depicted in Figure 24–23. In this simple example, the floor is set at 4 percent and the buyer pays an up-front premium to the seller of the floor.
Illustration of a Floor Used to Hedge Interest Rate Risk	While caps can be viewed as buying a complex call option on interest rates, a floor can be viewed as buying a complex put option on interest rates. In our example, the floor has two exercise dates: the end of year 1 and the end of year 2.
	If the interest scenario in Figure 24–23 is the actual interest rate path, the payments from the seller to the buyer would be as shown in Table 24–2.

Since the buyer of the floor is uncertain about the actual path of interest rates—rates could rise and not fall—such profits are only probabilistic. That is, the buyer would have to use a model similar to the binomial model for caps to calculate the fair up-front premium to be paid for the floor at time 0.

Collars

FI managers who are very risk-averse and overly concerned about the exposure of their portfolios to increased interest rate volatility may seek to protect the FI

FIGURE 24–23
Interest Rate Floor with a 4 Percent Floor

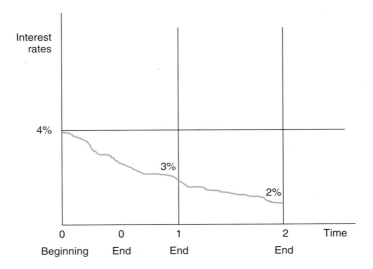

TABLE 24–2
Hypothetical Floor Payments

End of Year	Cap Rate	Actual Interest Rate	Interest Differential	Payment by Seller to Buyer
1	4%	3%	1%	$1 million
2	4	2	2	$2 million
Total				$3 million

against such increases. One method of hedging this risk is through buying a cap and a floor together. This is usually called a collar. Figure 24–24 illustrates the essential risk-protection features of a collar when an FI buys a 9 percent cap and a 4 percent floor.

The shaded areas in Figure 24–24 show the interest rate payment regions (>9 percent or <4 percent) where the cap or floor is in the money and the buyer potentially receives either a cap or a floor payment from the seller. If interest rates stay in the 4 through 9 percent range, the buyer of the collar receives no compensation from the seller. In addition, the buyer has to pay two up-front premiums: one for the cap and one for the floor to the cap and floor sellers. As is clear, buying a collar is similar to simultaneously buying a complex put and call bond option, or straddle.

An alternative and more common use of a collar is to finance the cost of purchasing a cap. In our earlier example of the $100 million cap, the fair cap premium (*pc*) was $792,700, or 0.7927 percent of the notional face value (NV_c) of the cap. That is, the cost (*C*) of the cap is

$$C = NV_c \times pc$$
$$= \$100 \text{ million} \times 0.007927$$
$$= \$792,700$$

To purchase the cap, the FI must pay this premium to the cap seller in up-front dollars.

Many large FIs, more exposed to rising interest rates than falling interest rates—perhaps because they are heavily reliant on interest-sensitive sources of liabilities—seek to finance a cap by selling a floor at the same time.[16] In so doing, they generate up-front revenues; this floor premium can finance the cost of the cap purchase or the cap premium. Nevertheless, they give up potential profits if rates fall rather than rise. Indeed, when rates fall, the floor is more likely to be triggered and the FI must compensate the buyer of the floor.

FIGURE 24–24
Payoffs from a Collar

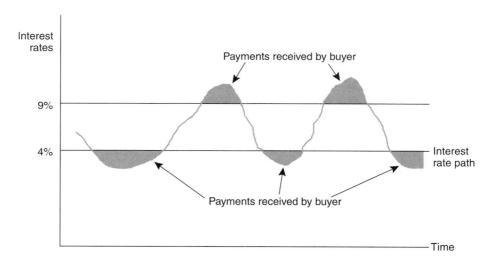

_____

[16] In this context, the sale of the floor is like the sale of any revenue-generating product.

After an FI buys a cap and sells a floor, its net cost of the cap is

$$C = (NV_c \times pc) - (NV_f \times pf)$$

$$C = \text{Cost of cap} - \text{Revenue on floor}$$

where

$$NV_f = \text{Notional principal of the floor}$$
$$pf = \text{Premium rate on the floor}$$

EXAMPLE 24–6

Calculating the Cost of a Collar

Suppose that, in Example 24–3, while buying the cap the FI sold a two-year $100 million notional face value floor at a premium of 0.75 percent. The net up-front cost of purchasing the cap is reduced to

$$C = (\$100,000,000 \times 0.007927) - (\$100,000,000 \times 0.0075) = \$42,700$$

Note that if the FI is willing to raise the floor exercise interest rate, thereby exposing itself to increasing losses if rates fall, it can generate higher premiums on the floor it sells. Like any option, as the exercise price or rate moves from being out of the money, when current rates are above the floor, to being in the money, when current rates are below the floor, the floor buyer would be willing to pay a higher premium to the writer (the FI). Given this, the buyer of the cap could set the floor rate with notional face values of $100 million each so that the floor premium earned by the FI just equals the cap premium paid:

$$C = (\$100,000,000 \times 0.007927) - (\$100,000,000 \times 0.007927)$$
$$= 0$$

When $pc = pf$, the cap buyer–floor seller can reduce the cap's net cost of purchase to zero. Indeed, if the cap buyer bought a very out-of-the-money cap and sold a very in-the-money floor, as shown in Figure 24–25, the net cost of the cap purchase could actually be negative. In Figure 24–25, the current interest rate is 7 percent while the cap rate is 10 percent. Thus, rates would have to rise at least 3 percent for the cap buyer to receive a payment at the end of year 1. By contrast, the 8 percent floor is already 1 percent above the current 7 percent rate. If rates stay at 7 percent until the end of year 1, the FI seller of the floor is already exposed to a 1 percent notional face value loss in writing the floor.

If the out-of-the-money cap can be bought at a premium of 0.7927 percent, but the in-the-money floor is sold at a premium of 0.95 percent, the (net) cost of the cap purchase is

$$C = (NV_c \times pc) - (NV_f \times pf)$$
$$= \$792,700 - \$950,000$$
$$= -\$157,300$$

FIGURE 24–25
In-the-Money Floor and Out-of-the-Money Cap

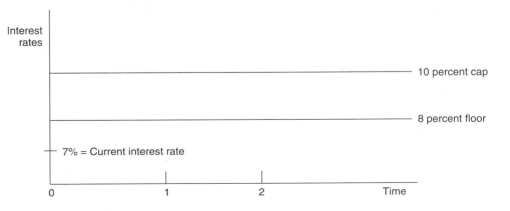

Raising the floor exercise rate and thus the floor premium also can be combined with mismatching the notional principal amounts of the cap and the floor to produce a zero net cost financing for the cap. That is, there is no reason why both the floor and cap agreements have to be written against the same notional face values ($NV_c = NV_f = \$100$ million).

Suppose the out-of-the-money cap can be bought at a premium of 0.7927 percent and the in-the-money floor can be sold at a 0.95 percent premium. An FI manager might want to know what notional principal on the floor (or contract size) is necessary to finance a $100 million cap purchase at zero net up-front cost. That is,

$$C = (NV_c \times pc) - (NV_f \times pf) = 0$$

$$= (\$100 \text{ million} \times 0.007927) - (NV_f \times 0.0095) = 0$$

Solving for NV_f:

$$NV_f = \frac{(\$100 \text{ million} \times 0.007927)}{0.0095} = \frac{(NV_c \times pc)}{pf}$$

$$= \$83.44 \text{ million}$$

Clearly, the higher premium rate on the floor requires a lower notional face value floor amount to generate sufficient premium income up front to finance the cap's purchase. In general, to fund fully the cap purchase ($C = 0$), the relationship between premium rates and notional value should be[17]

$$\frac{NV_f}{NV_c} = \frac{pc}{pf}$$

Caps, Floors, Collars, and Credit Risk

One important feature of buying caps, collars, and floors for hedging purposes is the implied credit risk exposure involved that is absent for exchange-traded futures and options. Since these are multiple exercise over-the-counter contracts, the buyer of these instruments faces a degree of counterparty credit risk. To see this, consider the cap example just discussed. Suppose the writer of the cap defaulted on the $1 million due at the end of the first year if interest rates rose to 10 percent. The buyer not only would fail to collect on this in-the-money option but also would lose a potential payment at the end of year 2. In general, a default in year 1 would mean that the cap buyer would have to find a replacement contract for year 2 (and any succeeding years thereafter) at the cap rate terms or premiums prevailing at the end of year 1 rather than at the beginning of year 0. These cap rates

---

[17] As shown earlier in this chapter, it is possible to macrohedge a gap position of an FI using put options. A cap is economically equivalent to a call option on an interest rate or a put option on a bond. However, the major difference is that the cap is a complex option in that there are multiple exercise dates. For example, in our simple model of the determination of the fair cap premium, there were two exercise dates: the end of year 1 and the end of year 2. However, we showed that we could decompose the value of the cap as a whole into the value of the (end of) year 1 option and the value of the (end of) year 2 option. Both of these options would have their own deltas (δ) because of the different maturity of these options. Thus, the change in the total value of the cap (ΔC) position would equal

$$\Delta C = N_c \times \{[\delta_1 \times (D_1 \times B)] + [\delta_2 \times (D_2 \times B)]\} \times \Delta R/(1 + R)$$

where N_c—the number of $100,000 cap contracts—is calculated by solving

$$N_C = \frac{[D_A - kD_L] \times S}{\{[\delta_1 \times (D_1 \times B)] + [\delta_2 \times (D_2 \times B)]\}}$$

may be far less favourable than those under the original cap contract (reflecting the higher interest rate levels of time 1). In addition, the buyer could incur further transaction and contracting costs in replacing the original contract. Because of the often long-term nature of cap agreements, occasionally extending up to ten years, only FIs that are the most credit-worthy are likely to be able to write and run a large cap/floor book without the backing of external guarantees such as standby letters of credit. As we discuss in the next chapter, swaps have similar credit risk exposures due to their long-run contractual nature and their OTC origination.

CONCEPT QUESTIONS	
	1. In Example 24–4, suppose that in year 2 the highest and lowest rates were 12 percent and 6 percent instead of 11 percent and 7 percent. Calculate the fair premium on the cap. ($980,500)
	2. Assume two exercise dates at the end of year 1 and the end of year 2. Suppose the FI buys a floor of 4 percent at time 0. The binomial tree suggests that rates at the end of year 1 could be 3 percent ($p = 0.5$) or 5 percent ($p = 0.5$) and at the end of year 2 rates could be 2 percent ($p = 0.25$), 4 percent ($p = 0.5$), or 6 percent ($p = 0.25$). Calculate the fair value of the floor premium. Assume the one-year discount rates for payments in years 0, 1, and 2 are 9 percent, 10 percent, and 11 percent, respectively. ($792,700)
	3. An FI buys a $100 million cap at a premium of 0.75 percent and sells a floor at a 0.85 percent premium. What size floor should be sold so that the net cost of the cap purchase is zero? ($88,235,394)
	4. Why are only the most credit-worthy FIs able to write a large cap/floor book without external guarantees?

Summary

In this chapter we evaluated a wide range of option-type contracts that are available to FI managers to hedge the risk exposures of individual assets, portfolios of assets, and the balance sheet gap itself. We illustrated how these options—some of which are exchange-traded and some of which are sold OTC—can hedge the interest rate, credit, FX, and catastrophe risks of FIs. In particular, we described how the unique nature of the asymmetric payoff function of option-type contracts often makes them more attractive to FIs than other hedging instruments, such as forwards and futures.

However, the hedging of on-balance-sheet exposures is a small portion of the risk management activities of FIs. As their expertise has increased in the area of derivatives, FIs have expanded their risk transference expertise to trading, creating complex contracts that enhance the traditional asset transformation function of FIs to accomplish global risk transference. The focus of regulators such as the Office of the Superintendent of Financial Institutions on the risk management activities of FIs has also expanded to ensure the safety and soundness of the financial system and to capture the increased focus of FIs on trading activities rather than hedging activities.

Questions and Problems

1. How does using options differ from using forward or futures contracts?

2. What is a call option?

3. What must happen to interest rates for the purchaser of a call option on a bond to make money? How does the writer of the call option make money?

4. What is a put option?

5. What must happen to interest rates for the purchaser of a put option on a bond to make money? How does the writer of the put option make money?

6. Consider the following:
   a. What are the two ways to use call and put options on government bonds to generate positive cash flows when interest rates decline? Verify your answer with a diagram.

www.mcgrawhill.ca/olc/saunders

b. Under what balance sheet conditions can an FI use options on government bonds to hedge its assets and/or liabilities against interest rate declines?

c. Is it more appropriate for FIs to hedge against a decline in interest rates with long calls or short puts?

7. In each of the following cases, identify what risk the manager of an FI faces and whether that risk should be hedged by buying a put or a call option.

a. A commercial bank plans to issue GICs in three months.

b. An insurance company plans to buy bonds in two months.

c. A credit union plans to sell Government of Canada securities next month.

d. A U.S. bank lends to a French company with a loan payable in euros.

e. A mutual fund plans to sell its holding of stock in a British company.

f. A finance company has assets with a duration of 6 years and liabilities with a duration of 13 years.

8. Consider an FI that wishes to use bond options to hedge the interest rate risk in the bond portfolio.

a. How does writing call options hedge the risk when interest rates decrease?

b. Will writing call options fully hedge the risk when interest rates increase? Explain.

c. How does buying a put option reduce the losses on the bond portfolio when interest rates rise?

d. Diagram the purchase of a bond call option against the combination of a bond investment and the purchase of a bond put option.

9. What are the regulatory reasons why FIs seldom write options?

10. What are the problems of using the Black–Scholes option pricing model to value bond options? What is meant by the term *pull-to-par*?

11. An FI has purchased a two-year, $1,000 par value zero-coupon bond for $867.43. The FI will hold the bond to maturity unless it needs to sell the bond at the end of one year for liquidity purposes. The current one-year interest rate is 7 percent, and the one-year rate in one year is forecast to be either 8.04 percent or 7.44 percent with equal likelihood. The FI wishes to buy a put option to protect itself against a capital loss if the bond needs to be sold in one year.

a. What was the yield on the bond at the time of purchase?

b. What is the market-determined, implied one-year rate one year before maturity?

c. What is the expected sale price if the bond has to be sold at the end of one year?

d. Diagram the bond prices over the two-year horizon.

e. If the FI buys a put option with an exercise price equal to your answer in part (c), what will be its value at the end of one year?

f. What should be the premium on the put option today?

g. Diagram the values of the put option on the two-year, zero-coupon bond.

h. What would have been the premium on the option if the one-year interest rates at the end of one year were expected to be 8.14 percent and 7.34 percent?

12. A pension fund manager anticipates the purchase of a 20-year, 8 percent coupon U.S. Treasury bond at the end of two years. Interest rates are assumed to change only once every year at year-end, with an equal probability of a 1 percent increase or a 1 percent decrease. The Treasury bond, when purchased in two years, will pay interest semiannually. Currently the Treasury bond is selling at par.

a. What is the pension fund manager's interest rate risk exposure?

b. How can the pension fund manager use options to hedge that interest rate risk exposure?

c. What prices are possible on the 20-year T-bonds at the end of year 1 and year 2?

d. Diagram the prices over the two-year period.

e. If options on US$100,000, 20-year, 8 percent coupon Treasury bonds (both puts and calls) have a strike price of 101, what are the possible (intrinsic) values of the option position at the end of year 1 and year 2?

f. Diagram the possible option values.

g. What is the option premium? (Use an 8 percent discount factor.)

13. Why are options on interest rate futures contracts preferred to options on cash instruments in hedging interest rate risk?

14. Consider Figure 24–13. What are the prices paid for the following futures option?

a. June T-bond calls at 116.

b. June 10-year T-note puts at 109.

c. June Eurodollar calls at 985000 (98.50).

15. Consider Figure 24–13 again. What happens to the price of the following?

a. A call when the exercise price increases.

b. A call when the time until expiration increases.

c. A put when the exercise price increases.

d. A put when the time to expiration increases.

16. An FI manager writes a call option on a T-bond futures contract with an exercise price of 114 at a quoted price of 0–55.

 a. What type of opportunities or obligations does the manager have?

 b. In what direction must interest rates move to encourage the call buyer to exercise the option?

17. What is the delta of an option (δ)?

18. An FI has a US$100 million portfolio of six-year Eurodollar bonds that have an 8 percent coupon. The bonds are trading at par and have a duration of five years. The FI wishes to hedge the portfolio with T-bond options that have a delta of −0.625. The underlying long-term Treasury bonds for the option have a duration of 10.1 years and trade at a market value of US$96,157 per US$100,000 of par value. Each put option has a premium of US$3.25.

 a. How many bond put options are necessary to hedge the bond portfolio?

 b. If interest rates increase 100 basis points, what is the expected gain or loss on the put option hedge?

 c. What is the expected change in market value on the bond portfolio?

 d. What is the total cost of placing the hedge?

 e. Diagram the payoff possibilities.

 f. How far must interest rates move before the payoff on the hedge will exactly offset the cost of placing the hedge?

 g. How far must interest rates move before the gain on the bond portfolio will exactly offset the cost of placing the hedge?

 h. Summarize the gain, loss, and cost conditions of the hedge on the bond portfolio in terms of changes in interest rates.

19. Corporate Bank has US$840 million of assets with a duration of 12 years and liabilities worth US$720 million with a duration of 7 years. The bank is concerned about preserving the value of its equity in the event of an increase in interest rates and is contemplating a macrohedge with interest rate options. The call and put options have a delta (δ) value of 0.4 and −0.4, respectively. The price of an underlying T-bond is (104^{17}/$_{32}$), its duration is 8.17 years, and its yield to maturity is 7.56 percent.

 a. What type of option should Corporate Bank use for the macrohedge?

 b. How many options should be purchased?

 c. What is the effect on the economic value of the equity if interest rates rise 50 basis points?

 d. What will be the effect on the hedge if interest rates rise 50 basis points?

 e. What will be the cost of the hedge if each option has a premium of US$0.875?

 f. Diagram the economic conditions of the hedge.

 g. How much must interest rates move against the hedge for the increased value of the bank to offset the cost of the hedge?

 h. How much must interest rates move in favour of the hedge, or against the balance sheet, before the payoff from the hedge will exactly cover the cost of the hedge?

 i. Formulate a management decision rule regarding the implementation of the hedge.

20. An FI has a US$200 million asset portfolio that has an average duration of 6.5 years. The average duration of its US$160 million in liabilities is 4.5 years. The FI uses put options on T-bonds to hedge against unexpected interest rate increases. The average delta (δ) value of the put options has been estimated at −0.3, and the average duration of the T-bonds is 7 years. The current market value of the T-bonds is US$96,000.

 a. What is the modified duration of the T-bonds if the current level of interest rates is 10 percent?

 b. How many put option contracts should it purchase to hedge its exposure against rising interest rates? The face value of the T-bonds is US$100,000.

 c. If interest rates increase 50 basis points, what will be the change in value of the equity of the FI?

 d. What will be the change in value of the T-bond option hedge position?

 e. If put options on T-bonds are selling at a premium of US$1.25 per face value of US$100, what is the total cost of hedging using options on T-bonds?

 f. Diagram the spot market conditions of the equity and the option hedge.

 g. What must be the change in interest rates before the change in value of the balance sheet (equity) will offset the cost of placing the hedge?

 h. How much must interest rates change before the payoff of the hedge will exactly cover the cost of placing the hedge?

 i. Given your answer in part (g), what will be the net gain or loss to the FI?

21. A mutual fund plans to purchase US$10,000,000 of 20-year T-bonds in two months. These bonds have

a duration of 11 years. The mutual fund is concerned about interest rates changing over the next four months and is considering a hedge with a two-month option on a T-bond futures contract. Two-month calls with a strike price of 105 are priced at 1–25, and puts of the same maturity and exercise price are quoted at 2–09. The delta of the call is 0.5 and the delta of the put is −0.7. The current price of a deliverable T-bond is US$103 − 08 per US$100 of face value, its duration is nine years, and its yield to maturity is 7.68 percent.

a. What type of option should the mutual fund purchase?

b. How many options should it purchase?

c. What is the cost of those options?

d. If rates change +/− 50 basis points, what will be the effect on the price of the desired T-bonds?

e. What will be the effect on the value of the hedge if rates change +/− 50 basis points?

f. Diagram the effects of the hedge and the spot market value of the desired T-bonds.

g. What must be the change in interest rates to cause the change in value of the hedge to exactly offset the change in value of the T-bonds?

22. An FI must make a single payment of 500,000 Swiss francs in six months at the maturity of a CD. The FI's in-house analyst expects the spot price of the franc to remain stable at the current $0.80/Sf. But as a precaution, the analyst is concerned that it could rise as high as $0.85/Sf or fall as low as $0.75/Sf. Because of this uncertainty, the analyst recommends that the FI hedge the CD payment using either options or futures. Six-month call and put options on the Swiss franc with an exercise price of $0.80/Sf are trading at 4 cents and 2 cents, respectively. A six-month futures contract on the Swiss franc is trading at $0.80/Sf.

a. Should the analysts be worried about the dollar depreciating or appreciating?

b. If the FI decides to hedge using options, should the FI buy put or call options to hedge the CD payment? Why?

c. If futures are used to hedge, should the FI buy or sell Swiss franc futures to hedge the payment? Why?

d. What will be the net payment on the CD if the selected call or put options are used to hedge the payment? Assume the following three scenarios: the spot price in six months will be $0.75, $0.80, or $0.85/Sf. Also assume that the options will be exercised.

e. What will be the net payment if futures had been used to hedge the CD payment? Use the same three scenarios as in part (a).

f. Which method of hedging is preferable after the fact?

23. An American insurance company issued $10 million of one-year, zero-coupon GICs (guaranteed investment contracts) denominated in Swiss francs at a rate of 5 percent. The insurance company holds no Sf-denominated assets and has neither bought nor sold francs in the foreign exchange market.

a. What is the insurance company's net exposure in Swiss francs?

b. What is the insurance company's risk exposure to foreign exchange rate fluctuations?

c. How can the insurance company use futures to hedge the risk exposure in part (b)? How can it use options to hedge?

d. If the strike price is US$0.6667/Sf and the spot price is US$0.6452/Sf, what is the intrinsic value (on expiration) of a call option on Swiss francs? What is the intrinsic value (on expiration) of a Swiss franc put option? (*Note:* Swiss franc futures options traded on the Chicago Mercantile Exchange are set at Sf125,000 per contract.)

e. If the June delivery call option premium is US0.32 cent per franc and the June delivery put option is US10.7 cents per franc, what is the dollar premium cost per contract? Assume that today's date is April 15.

f. Why is the call option premium lower than the put option premium?

24. An FI has made a loan commitment of Sf10 million that is likely to be drawn down in six months. The current spot rate is $0.60/Sf.

a. Is the FI exposed to the dollar depreciating or the dollar appreciating? Why?

b. If it decides to hedge using Sf futures, should it buy or sell Sf futures?

c. If the spot rate six months from today is $0.64/Sf, what dollar amount is needed in six months if the loan is drawn?

d. A six-month Sf futures contract is available for $0.61/Sf. What is the net amount needed at the end of six months if the FI has hedged using the Sf10 million of futures contracts? Assume that futures prices are equal to spot prices at the time of payment, that is, at maturity.

e. If it decides to use options to hedge, should it purchase call or put options?

f. Call and put options with an exercise price of $0.61/Sf are selling for $0.02 and $0.03, respectively. What would be the net amount needed by the FI at the end of six months if it had used options instead of futures to hedge this exposure?

25. What is a credit spread call option?

26. What is a digital default option?

27. How do the cash flows to the lender differ for a credit spread call option hedge from the cash flows for a digital default option?

28. What is a catastrophe call option? How do the cash flows of this option affect the buyer of the option?

29. What are caps? Under what circumstances would the buyer of a cap receive a payoff?

30. What are floors? Under what circumstances would the buyer of a floor receive a payoff?

31. What are collars? Under what circumstances would an FI use a collar?

32. How is buying a cap similar to buying a call option on interest rates?

33. Under what balance sheet circumstances would it be desirable to sell a floor to help finance a cap? When would it be desirable to sell a cap to help finance a floor?

34. Use the following information to price a three-year collar by purchasing an in-the-money cap and writing an out-of-the-money floor. Assume a binomial options pricing model with an equal probability of interest rates increasing 2 percent or decreasing 2 percent per annum. Current rates are 7 percent, the cap rate is 7 percent, and the floor rate is 4 percent. The notional value is $1 million. All interest payments are annual payments as a percent of notional value, and all payments are made at the end of year 1 and the end of year 2.

35. Use the following information to price a three-year collar by purchasing an out-of-the-money cap and writing an in-the-money floor. Assume a binomial options pricing model with an equal probability of interest rates increasing 2 percent or decreasing 2 percent per annum. Current rates are 4 percent, the cap rate is 7 percent, and the floor rate is 4 percent. The notional value is $1 million. All interest payments are annual payments as a percentage of notional value, and all payments are made at the end of year 1 and the end of year 2.

36. Contrast the total cash flows associated with the collar position in question 34 against the collar in question 35. Do the goals of FIs that utilize the collar in question 34 differ from those that put on the collar in question 35? If so, how?

37. An FI has purchased a $200 million cap (i.e., call options on interest rates) of 9 percent at a premium of 0.65 percent of face value. A $200 million floor (i.e., put options on interest rates) of 4 percent is also available at a premium of 0.69 percent of face value.

   a. If interest rates rise to 10 percent, what is the amount received by the FI? What are the net savings after deducting the premium?

   b. If the FI also purchases a floor, what are the net savings if interest rates rise to 11 percent? What are the net savings if interest rates fall to 3 percent?

   c. If, instead, the FI sells (writes) the floor, what are the net savings if interest rates rise to 11 percent? What if they fall to 3 percent?

   d. What amount of floors should it sell to compensate for its purchase of caps, given the above premiums?

38. What credit risk exposure is involved in buying caps, floors, and collars for hedging purposes?

Web Question

WWW

39. Go to the Chicago Board Options Exchange website at www.cboe.com. Find the most recent data on 10-Year Treasury Yield Options (TNX) by clicking on "CBOE Daily Market Statistics" under "Data." Clicking on the current date on the calendar at the top of the page will allow the user to retrieve data on any particular day. What is the reported Volume, Open Interest, and Level of trading for calls and puts on these options? What is the percentage change in the most recent data from that of one year earlier?

Integrated Mini-Case

HEDGING INTEREST RATE RISK WITH FUTURES VERSUS OPTIONS

On January 4, 2010, an FI has the following balance sheet (rates = 10 percent):

Assets			Liabilities/Equity		
A	200 m	$D_A = 6$ years	L	170 m	$D_L = 4$ years
			E	30 m	

$$\text{DGAP} = [6 - (170/200)4] = 2.6 \text{ years} > 0$$

The FI manager thinks rates will increase by 0.75 percent in the next three months. If this happens, the equity value will change by

$$\Delta E = -[6 - \frac{170}{200}(4)]200 \text{ m}\frac{0.0075}{1.10} = -\$3,545,455$$

The FI manager will hedge this interest rate risk with either futures contracts or option contracts.

If the FI uses futures, it will select June T-bonds to hedge. The duration on the T-bonds underlying the contract is 14.5 years, and the T-bonds are selling at a price of 114–11 per $100,000 m or $114,343.75. T-bond futures rates, currently 9 percent, are expected to increase by 1.25 percent over the next three months.

If the FI uses options, it will buy puts on 15-year T-bonds with a June maturity, an exercise price of 113,

and an option premium of $1\,^{36}/_{64}$ percent. The spot price on the T-bond underlying the option is $135\,^{23}/_{32}$ percent. The duration on the T-bonds underlying the options is 14.5 years, and the delta of the put options is -0.75. Managers expect these T-bond rates to increase by 1.24 percent from 7.875 percent in the next three months.

If by April 4, 2010, balance sheet rates increase by 0.8 percent, futures rates by 1.4 percent, and T-bond rates underlying the option contract by 0.95 percent, would the FI have been better off using the futures contract or the option contract as its hedge instrument?

If by April 4, 2010, balance sheet rates actually fall by 0.75 percent, futures rates fall by 1.05 percent, and T-bond rates underlying the option contract fall by 1.24 percent, would the FI have been better off using the futures contract or the option contract as its hedge instrument?

Appendix **24A**	**Black–Scholes Option Pricing Model**

Appendix **24B**	**Microhedging with Options**

View Appendices 24A and 24B at the Online Learning Centre: www.mcgrawhill.ca/olc/saunders.

Swaps

In this chapter, we discuss three types of swaps:

▸ interest rate swaps

▸ currency swaps

▸ credit swaps

and conclude with a discussion of credit risk concerns related to swaps.

INTRODUCTION

swap
An agreement between two parties to exchange assets or a series of cash flows for a specified period of time at a specified interval.

A **swap** is an agreement between two parties (called *counterparties*) to exchange specified periodic cash flows in the future based on some underlying instrument or price (e.g., a fixed or floating rate on a bond or note). Like forward, futures, and option contracts, swaps allow firms to better manage their interest rate, foreign exchange, and credit risks. While the instrument underlying the swap may change, the basic principle of a swap agreement is the same in that there is a restructuring of asset or liability cash flows in a preferred direction by the transacting parties.

Swaps were first introduced in the late 1970s, and the global market for swaps has grown enormously since then, driven by five generic types of swaps: interest rate swaps, currency swaps, credit swaps, commodity swaps, and equity swaps.[1] The notional amount of over-the-counter (OTC) interest rate swaps reported by the Bank for International Settlements (BIS) globally was US$57.2 trillion at the end of June 2001. As shown in Table 25–1, the notional amount of interest rate swaps, which represent the largest percentage of all swap contracts (79.4 percent notional, 64 percent gross market value at December 2008), grew to US$229.7 trillion in December 2006 and to US$328.1 trillion in December 2008. At December 2008, swap contracts represented 70 percent of the notional amount of all OTC derivatives reported by the G-10 banks, and 76.4 percent of the gross market value. Since the gross market value is an estimate of the cost of replacing these OTC contracts, it gives a better idea of the market risk. As shown in Chapter 23, Table 23–1, for the six large Canadian banks, swap contracts represented 57.4 percent of the notional amount of all derivative contracts reported at October 31, 2008. The notional amount of swap contracts was CDN$8.3 trillion, the replacement cost CDN$117.6 billion.

The massive growth of the swap market has raised regulatory concerns regarding the credit risk exposures of FIs engaging in this market. This growth was one of the motivations behind the introduction of BIS-sponsored risk-based capital adequacy reforms described in Chapter 20. As well, the US$592 trillion notional amount of derivatives at December 2008 as shown in Table 25–1 represented a contraction of 13.4 percent from June 2008 as the credit crisis continued to unsettle global financial markets. In particular, credit default swaps (CDS) contracted 26.9

---

[1] There are also *swaptions*, which are options to enter into a swap agreement at some pre-agreed contract terms (e.g., a fixed rate of 10 percent) at some time in the future in return for the payment of an up-front premium.

TABLE 25–1
Notional Amounts and Gross Market Value of OTC Swap Contracts Outstanding, December 2006 and 2008 (US$ billions)

Source: Bank for International Settlements, *BIS Quarterly Review,* June 2009.

Type of Swap	Notional Amounts Outstanding		Gross Market Value	
	December 2006	December 2008	December 2006	December 2008
Forwards and forex swaps	$ 19,882	$ 24,562	$ 469	$ 1,732
Currency swaps	10,792	14,725	601	1,588
Interest rate swaps	229,693	328,114	4,163	16,573
Equity-linked forwards and swaps	1,767	1,632	166	338
Commodity forwards and swaps	2,813	2,471	n.a.	n.a.
Credit default swaps	28,650	41,868	470	5,652
Total swaps contracts	**$293,597**	**$413,372**	**$5,869**	25,883
Total OTC contracts	**$418,131**	**$591,963**	**$9,791**	**$33,889**
Swaps/OTC contracts	70.2%	69.8%	59.9%	76.4%

shadow banking system
Financial intermediaries (e.g., hedge funds) and over-the-counter contracts (e.g., credit default swaps) that are essentially unregulated.

percent between June and December 2008. Government officials such as Britain's Prime Minister Gordon Brown have expressed concerns about the **shadow banking system** and OTC derivative contracts. There have been many discussions about how to deal with the potential for systemic risk to the global banking system. See the Industry Perspectives feature for an analysis of U.S. Treasury Secretary Timothy Geithner's proposal for dealing with OTC contracts, particularly credit default swaps.

INDUSTRY PERSPECTIVES

GEITHNER'S PLAN FOR DERIVATIVES: THE DEVIL IS IN THE DETAILS

The over-the-counter (OTC) derivatives market is massive in size, largely unregulated and has been heavily implicated in the meltdown that continues to bedevil the global financial system. Designed to provide efficient ways to manage various kinds of risk, derivatives have themselves become a key source of the systemic risk to which we are exposed today.

Just as derivatives provide an easy way to hedge risk, they also provide an efficient way to take risk. So when markets overshoot and bubbles form, derivatives tend to be in the thick of things—so much so that Warren Buffet has famously tagged some of them as "financial weapons of mass destruction."

Indeed, markets for derivatives have their own kinds of fragility that have no doubt exacerbated the financial crisis. Last week [U.S.] Treasury Secretary Tim Geithner offered a sensible plan for dealing with some of this fragility.

As of June 2008, the notional value of all OTC derivative contracts outstanding exceeded [US]$683 trillion ([US]$20.4 trillion of gross market value), more than doubling over two years. Two-thirds of

all outstanding derivatives were interest rate contracts (swapping fixed for floating interest rates, or vice versa, for example), 9% were foreign exchange contracts and only 8% were the credit default swaps (CDS) embroiled in the current crisis.

The counterparty exposures (that one party to a contract could fail to deliver on a commitment) incorporated in the CDS market became a key part of the systemic risk facing the global financial system and propelling its meltdown beginning with the threatened bankruptcy of Bear Stearns and later AIG. So it's no surprise that the Treasury has been working for several months to come up with a plan to regulate derivatives trading, which was announced last week.

Nor are there any real surprises in the Treasury plan—its principal feature being to require clearing of OTC contracts through "regulated central counterparties" (CCPs). This will create much greater transparency and more effective systemic risk management with respect to derivative trading, although it requires dealers to give up proprietary information and reduces flexibility and trading spreads.

Nevertheless, industry participants should accept the Treasury's plan as necessary, timely and protective of their own interests. The market will become more stable and robust at a small sacrifice in creativity and profitability. No pain, no gain.

But as always, the devil is in the details. So the key questions center around how the CCPs will actually operate.

OTC contracts are often idiosyncratic. The Treasury's plan suggests that all derivatives will be standardized into common traded units. But the greater the degree of standardization, the greater will be the "basis risk" that hedgers will encounter when their risks don't exactly fit the standard of the exchange-traded instruments. So there will be pressure to continue substantial OTC business. Moreover, the plan applies to all U.S. derivatives dealers. So a hedger seeking a customized solution could presumably find it in a derivatives market in Europe or Asia, at least until the Treasury plan is adopted by regulators abroad as well.

One way to resolve these issues is for derivatives that are important—but not sufficiently standardized to be traded on an exchange or to attract sufficient transactions volume—to be set up in bilateral negotiations, tailoring them to the specific needs of the counterparties. They would then be registered with a CCP, which in turn would take over managing the margins and would become the actual counterparty to each of the original transactions. Data on individual firm exposures could be collected from the CCP, made available to regulators and published in a suitable form to assure market transparency.

Another detail to be settled is how margining would work on CDSs. A CDS is very different from a future or an option. But most of the discussion we have heard so far suggests that CDS margin requirements are expected to be handled on the same kind of mark-to-market (MTM) basis as other derivative contracts. The protection seller for a CDS receives a regular insurance-like premium in return for promising to make the protection buyer whole if there is a default.

MTM margins track the daily fluctuations in the price of the credit derivative and require the loser each day to put up enough collateral to cover the amount that has already been lost (on an MTM basis) plus an additional amount that is expected to cover a few days of normal fluctuations in that derivative's market price if things go against the trader.

The problem with CDSs is that when there is a credit event, the potential loss immediately jumps from a couple of days of mark-to-market losses if the market moves against the trader's position to up to 100% of the notional principal covered by the contract. This means that, in pretty much every case, when there is a credit event the CCP will not have enough margin on deposit from the protection sellers to cover the loss. With MTM margining, the CDS CCP will bear counterparty default risk in a way that other derivatives clearing houses do not.

It's clear that the CDS market could not exist if protection sellers had to post 100% margins on all of their positions. We suggest that they should be obligated instead to post 100% margin on their biggest position, and only MTM margins on everything else. That way, as long as there is no more than one big default in a single day, the CCP will always be covered. This is essential, because a key function of the CCP is to remove concerns about counterparty credit risk from the market.

It's reasonable to assume that one of the reasons the Geithner announcement lacked details is to encourage derivatives dealers and others to come forward with suggestions such as these before casting the rules into stone. That would be a good and timely idea too.

The authors are professors of finance at the Stern School of Business at New York University. They are contributors to a new book on the financial crisis entitled Restoring Financial Stability *(Wiley, 2009).*

Source: Stephen Figlewski, Roy C. Smith, and Ingo Walter, *Forbes Commentary,* May 18, 2009, www.forbes.com.

SWAP MARKETS

Commercial banks and investment banks are major participants in the market as dealers, traders, and users for proprietary hedging purposes. Insurance companies have only recently adopted hedging strategies using swaps, but their interest in this market has grown quickly. A swap dealer can act as an intermediary or third party by putting a swap together and/or creating an over-the-counter (OTC) secondary market for swaps for a fee. Swap transactions are generally heterogeneous in terms of maturities, indexes used to determine payments, and timing of payments—there is no standardized contract. Swap dealers exist to serve the function of taking the opposite side of each transaction in order to keep the swap market liquid by locating or matching counterparties or, in many cases, taking one side of the swap themselves. In a direct swap between two counterparties, each party must find another party having a mirror image financing requirement—for example, a financial institution in need of swapping fixed-rate payments (for floating-rate payments) made quarterly for the next 10 years on $25 million in liabilities must find a counterparty in need of swapping $25 million in floating-rate payments (for fixed-rate payments) made quarterly for the next 10 years. Without swap dealers, the search costs of finding such counterparties to a swap can be significant.

A further advantage of swap dealers is that they generally guarantee swap payments over the life of the contract. If one of the counterparties defaults on a direct swap, the other counterparty is no longer adequately hedged against risk and may have to replace the defaulted swap with a new swap at less favourable terms (so-called *replacement risk*). By booking or engaging in a swap through a swap dealer as the intermediary, a default by one counterparty will not affect the other counterparty since the swap dealer incurs any costs associated with the default by replacing the defaulting party on the same terms as the original swap.[2] Commercial and investment banks have evolved as the major swap dealers, mainly because of their close ties to the financial markets and their specialized skills in assessing credit risk. Each swap market dealer manages a portfolio of swaps and, as a result, can diversify some of the swap risk exposure away.

INTEREST RATE SWAPS

interest rate swap
An exchange of fixed interest payments for floating interest payments by two counterparties.

By far the largest segment of the global swap market is composed of **interest rate swaps.** Conceptually, an interest rate swap is a succession of forward contracts on interest rates arranged by two parties.[3] As such, it allows an FI to put in place a long-term hedge, sometimes for as long as 15 years. This hedge reduces the need to roll over contracts if reliance had been placed on futures or forward contracts to achieve such long-term hedges.

swap buyer
By convention, makes the fixed-rate payments in an interest rate swap transaction.

In a swap, the **swap buyer** agrees to make a number of fixed interest rate payments on periodic settlement dates to the **swap seller.** The seller of the swap in turn agrees to make floating-rate payments to the swap buyer on the same periodic settlement dates. The fixed-rate side—by convention, the swap buyer—generally has a comparative advantage in making fixed-rate payments, whereas the floating-rate side—by convention, the swap seller—generally has a comparative advantage in making variable or floating-rate payments. In undertaking this transaction, the FI that is the fixed-rate payer is seeking to transform the variable-rate nature of its liabilities into fixed-rate liabilities to better match the fixed returns earned on its assets. Meanwhile, the FI that is the variable-rate payer seeks

swap seller
By convention, makes the floating-rate payments in an interest rate swap transaction.

---

[2] The fee or spread charged by the swap dealer to each party in a swap incorporates this credit risk.

[3] For example, a four-year swap with annual swap dates involves four net cash flows between the parties to a swap. This is essentially similar to arranging four forward contracts: a one-year, a two-year, a three-year, and a four-year contract.

to turn its fixed-rate liabilities into variable-rate liabilities to better match the variable returns on its assets.[4]

To explain the role of a swap transaction in hedging FI interest rate risk, we use a simple example. Consider two FIs: The first is a bank that has raised $100 million of its funds by issuing four-year, medium-term notes with 10 percent annual fixed coupons rather than relying on short-term deposits to raise funds (see Panel A of Table 25–2). On the asset side of its portfolio, the bank makes business loans whose rates are indexed to annual changes in the London Interbank Offered Rate (LIBOR). As we discussed in Chapter 11, banks currently index most large business loans to LIBOR.

As a result of having floating-rate loans and fixed-rate liabilities in its asset–liability structure, the bank has a negative duration gap; the duration of its assets is shorter than that of its liabilities:

$$D_A - kD_L < 0$$

One way for the bank to hedge this exposure is to shorten the duration or interest rate sensitivity of its liabilities by transforming them into short-term floating-rate liabilities that better match the duration characteristics of its asset portfolio. The bank can make changes either on or off the balance sheet. On the balance sheet, the bank could attract an additional $100 million in short-term deposits that are indexed to the LIBOR rate (say, LIBOR plus 2.5 percent) in a manner similar to its loans. The proceeds of these deposits can be used to pay off the medium-term notes. This reduces the duration gap between the bank's assets and liabilities. Alternatively, the bank could go off the balance sheet and sell an interest rate swap—that is, enter into a swap agreement to make the floating-rate payment side of a swap agreement.

The second party in the swap is a credit union that has invested $100 million in fixed-rate residential mortgages of long duration. To finance this residential mortgage portfolio, the credit union has had to rely on short-term guaranteed income certificates (GICs) with an average duration of one year (see Panel B of Table 25–2). On maturity, these GICs have to be rolled over at the current market rate.

Consequently, the credit union's asset–liability balance sheet structure is the reverse of the bank's; that is,

$$D_A - kD_L > 0$$

The credit union could hedge its interest rate risk exposure by transforming the short-term floating-rate nature of its liabilities into fixed-rate liabilities that better

TABLE 25–2
Balance Sheets of Swap Participants

Assets		Liabilities	
Panel A: Bank's Balance Sheet (Swap Seller)			
Business loans (rate indexed to LIBOR) =	$100 million	Medium-term notes (coupons fixed) =	$100 million
Panel B: Credit Union's Balance Sheet (Swap Buyer)			
Fixed-rate mortgages =	$100 million	Short-term GICs (one year) =	$100 million

---

[4] In the early 2000s, record low interest rates and depressed equity values reduced the value of many defined benefit pension plan surpluses. To protect their surplus values from declining further, many pension plans entered into interest rate swaps that protected them from further falls in interest rates.

match the long-term maturity/duration structure of its assets. On the balance sheet, the credit union could issue long-term notes with a maturity equal or close to that on the mortgages (at, say, 12 percent). The proceeds of the sale of the notes can be used to pay off the GICs and reduce the duration gap. Alternatively, the credit union can buy a swap—take the fixed-payment side of a swap agreement.

The opposing balance sheet and interest rate risk exposures of the bank and the credit union provide the necessary conditions for an interest rate swap agreement between the two parties. This swap agreement can be arranged directly between the parties. However, it is likely that an FI—another bank or an investment bank— would act as either a broker or an agent, receiving a fee for bringing the two parties together or intermediating fully by accepting the credit risk exposure and guaranteeing the cash flows underlying the swap contract. By acting as a principal as well as an agent, the FI can add a credit risk premium to the fee. However, the credit risk exposure of a swap to an FI is somewhat less than that on a loan (this is discussed later in this chapter). Conceptually, when a third-party FI fully intermediates the swap, that FI is really entering into two separate swap agreements: one with the bank and one with the credit union.

plain vanilla
Standard agreement without any special features.

For simplicity, we consider a **plain vanilla** fixed–floating rate swap where a third-party intermediary acts as a simple broker or agent by bringing together two FIs with opposing interest rate risk exposures to enter into a swap agreement or contract.

EXAMPLE 25–1

Expected Cash Flows on an Interest Rate Swap

Suppose the notional value of a swap is $100 million—equal to the assumed size of the bank's medium-term note issue—and the maturity of four years is equal to the maturity of the bank's note liabilities. The annual coupon cost of these note liabilities is 10 percent, and the bank's problem is that the variable return on its assets may be insufficient to cover the cost of meeting these coupon payments if market interest rates, and therefore asset returns, *fall*. By comparison, the fixed returns on the credit union's mortgage asset portfolio may be insufficient to cover the interest cost of its GICs if market rates *rise*. As a result, a feasible swap agreement might dictate that the credit union send fixed payments of 10 percent per annum of the notional $100 million value of the swap to the bank to allow the bank to cover fully the coupon interest payments on its note issue. In return, the bank sends annual payments indexed to one-year LIBOR to help the credit union cover the cost of refinancing its one-year renewable GICs. Suppose that one-year LIBOR is currently 8 percent and the bank agrees to send annual payments at the end of each year equal to one-year LIBOR plus 2 percent to the credit union.[5] We depict this fixed–floating rate swap transaction in Figure 25–1; the expected net financing costs for the FIs are listed in Table 25–3.

As a result of the swap, the bank has transformed its four-year, fixed-rate interest payments into variable-rate payments, matching the variability of returns on its assets. Further, through the interest rate swap, the bank effectively pays LIBOR plus 2 percent for its financing. Had it gone to the debt market, we assumed that the bank would pay LIBOR plus 2.5 percent (a savings of 0.5 percent with the swap). Further, the credit union has transformed its variable-rate interest payments into fixed-rate payments, plus a "small" variable component (GIC rate − LIBOR), similar to those received on its assets. Had it gone to the debt market, we assumed that the credit union would pay 12 percent (a savings of 4 percent + GIC rate − LIBOR with the swap).

---

[5] These rates implicitly assume that this is the cheapest way each party can hedge its interest rate exposure. For example, LIBOR + 2 percent is the lowest-cost way in which the bank can transform its fixed-rate liabilities into floating-rate liabilities.

FIGURE 25–1
Fixed–Floating Rate Swap

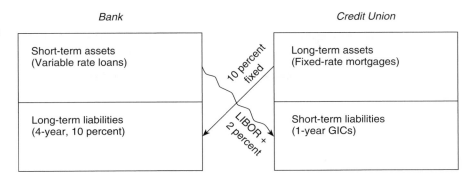

TABLE 25–3
Financing Cost Resulting from Interest Rate Swap ($ millions)

	Bank	Credit Union
Cash outflows from balance sheet financing	−10% × $100	−(GIC) × $100
Cash inflows from swap	10% × $100	(LIBOR + 2%) × $100
Cash outflows from swap	−(LIBOR + 2%) × $100	−10% × $100
Net cash flows	−(LIBOR + 2%) × $100	−(8% + GIC Rate − LIBOR) × $100
Rate available on:		
Variable-rate debt	LIBOR + 2½%	
Fixed-rate debt		12%

Note in Example 25–1 that in the absence of default/credit risk, only the bank is really fully hedged. This happens because the annual 10 percent payments it receives from the credit union at the end of each year allow it to meet the promised 10 percent coupon rate payments to its note holders regardless of the return it receives on its variable-rate assets. By contrast, the credit union receives variable-rate payments based on LIBOR plus 2 percent. However, it is quite possible that the GIC rate the credit union has to pay on its deposit liabilities does not exactly track the LIBOR-indexed payments sent by the bank. That is, the credit union is subject to basis risk exposure on the swap contract. There are two possible sources of this basis risk. First, GIC rates do not exactly match the movements of LIBOR rates over time since the former are determined in the domestic money market and the latter in the Eurodollar market. Second, the credit/default risk premium on the credit union's GICs may increase over time; thus, the +2 percent add-on to LIBOR may be insufficient to hedge the credit union's cost of funds. The credit union might be better hedged by requiring the bank to send it floating payments based on domestic GIC rates rather than LIBOR. To do this, the bank would probably require additional compensation since it would then be bearing basis risk. Its asset returns would be sensitive to LIBOR movements while its swap payments were indexed to GIC rates.

In analyzing this swap, one has to distinguish between how it should be priced at time 0 (now) [that is, how the exchange rate of fixed (10 percent) for floating (LIBOR + 2 percent) is set when the swap agreement is initiated] and the actual realized cash flows on the swap. As we discuss in Appendix 25A (at the Online Learning Centre: www.mcgrawhill.ca/olc/saunders), the fixed and floating rates set on initiation of the swap depend on the market's expectations of future short-term rates, while realized cash flows on the swap depend on the actual market rates (here, LIBOR) that materialized over the life of the swap contract.

Realized Cash Flows on an Interest Rate Swap

EXAMPLE 25–2

Calculation of Realized Cash Flows

We assume that the realized or actual path of interest rates (LIBOR) over the four-year life of the contract would be

End of Year	LIBOR
1	9%
2	9
3	7
4	6

The bank's variable payments to the credit union were indexed to these rates by the formula

$$(\text{LIBOR} + 2\%) \times \$100 \text{ million}$$

By contrast, the fixed annual payments that the credit union made to the bank were the same each year: 10% × $100 million. We summarize the actual or realized cash flows among the two parties over the four years in Table 25–4. The credit union's net gains from the swap in years 1 and 2 are $1 million per year. The enhanced cash flow offsets the increased cost of refinancing its GICs in a higher interest rate environment—that is, the credit union is hedged against rising rates. By contrast, the bank makes net gains on the swap in years 3 and 4 when rates fall; thus, it is hedged against falling rates. The positive cash flow from the swap offsets the decline in the variable returns on the bank's asset portfolio. Overall, the bank made a net dollar gain of $1 million in nominal dollars; its true realized gain would be the present value of this amount.

off-market swaps
Swaps that have non-standard terms that require one party to compensate another.

fully amortized mortgages
Mortgage portfolio cash flows that have a constant payment.

Swaps can always be moulded or tailored to the needs of the transacting parties as long as one party is willing to compensate the other party for accepting non-standard terms or **off-market swap** arrangements, usually in the form of an up-front fee or payments. Relaxing a standardized swap can include special interest rate terms and indexes as well as allowing for varying notional values underlying the swap.

For example, in the case we just considered, the notional value of the swap was fixed at $100 million for each of the four annual swap dates. However, swap notional values can be allowed either to decrease or to increase over a swap contract's life. This flexibility is useful when one of the parties has heavy investments in mortgages (in our example, the credit union) and the mortgages are **fully amortized,** meaning that the annual and monthly cash flows on the mortgage portfolio reflect repayments of both principal and interest such that the periodic payment is kept constant (see Chapter 27). Fixed-rate mortgages normally have larger payments of interest than principal in the early years, with the interest component falling as mortgages approach maturity. One possibility is for the credit union to enter into a mortgage swap to hedge the amortizing nature of the mortgage portfolio or alternatively to allow the notional value of the swap to decline at a rate similar to the decline in the principal component of the mortgage portfolio.

TABLE 25–4
Realized Cash Flows on the Swap Agreement ($ millions)

End of Year	One-Year LIBOR	One-Year LIBOR +2 percent	Cash Payment by Bank	Cash Payment by Credit Union	Net Payment Made by Bank
1	9%	11%	$11	$10	$+1
2	9	11	11	10	+1
3	7	9	9	10	−1
4	6	8	8	10	−2
Total			$39	$40	$−1

Another example of a special type of interest rate swap is the inverse floater swap, which was engineered by major FIs as part of structured note financing deals to lower the cost of financing to various government agencies. Such arrangements have resulted in enormous problems in the United States for investor groups such as municipal authorities and corporations that are part of the overall swap deal.

A structured note–inverse floater swap arrangement is shown in Figure 25–2. In this arrangement, a government agency issues notes (say, $100 million) to investors with a coupon that is equal to 7 percent minus LIBOR—that is, an (inverse) floating coupon. The novel feature of this coupon is that when market rates fall (and thus LIBOR is low), the coupon received by the investor is large. The government agency then converts this spread liability (7 percent − LIBOR) into a LIBOR liability by entering into a swap with an FI dealer (e.g., a bank). In effect, the cost of the $100 million note issue is LIBOR to the agency plus any fees relating to the swap.

The risk of these notes to the investor is very clear. If LIBOR is 2 percent, then the investor will receive coupons of 7 percent − 2 percent = 5 percent, which is an excellent spread return if the investor can borrow at close to LIBOR (or 2 percent in this case). However, consider what happens if interest rates rise. If LIBOR rises from 2 to 8 percent, the promised coupon becomes 7 percent − 8 percent = −1 percent. Since negative coupons cannot be paid, the actual coupon paid to the investor is 0 percent. However, if the investor borrowed funds to buy the notes at LIBOR, the cost of funds is 8 percent in this case. Thus, the investor is facing an extremely large negative spread and loss.

Macrohedging with Swaps

The duration model shown in Chapters 23 and 24 to estimate the optimal number of futures and options contracts to hedge an FI's duration gap also can be applied to estimate the optimal number of swap contracts. For example, an FI manager might wish to know how many 10-year (or 5-year) swap contracts are needed to hedge its overall risk exposure. The optimal notional value of swap contracts should be set so that the gain on swap contracts entered into off the balance sheet just offsets any loss in net worth on the balance sheet when interest rates change.

Assume that an FI has a positive duration gap so that it has positive net worth exposure to rising interest rates:

$$\Delta E = -(D_A - kD_L)A\frac{\Delta R}{1 + R} > 0$$

As discussed above, the FI can seek to hedge by paying fixed and receiving floating payments through an interest rate swap. However, many different maturity swaps are available. As will be shown below, the size of the notional value of the interest rate swaps entered into will depend on the maturity (duration) of the swap contract. Suppose the FI manager chooses to hedge with 10-year swaps.

In terms of valuation, a 10-year swap arrangement can be considered in terms of bond equivalent valuation. That is, the fixed-rate payments on a 10-year swap are formally equivalent to the fixed payments on a 10-year government bond. Similarly, the floating-rate payments on a 10-year swap with *annual* payments can be viewed as equivalent to floating coupons on a bond where coupons are repriced

FIGURE 25–2

Inverse Floater Swap–Structured Note

(to LIBOR) every year. That is, the change in the value of the swap (ΔS) when interest rates $[\Delta R/(1 + R)]$ rise will depend on the relative interest sensitivity of 10-year bonds to 1-year bonds, or in duration terms, $(D_{10} - D_1)$.[6] In general,

$$\Delta S = -(D_{fixed} - D_{float}) \times N_S \times \frac{\Delta R}{1 + R}$$

where

$$\Delta S = \text{Change in the market value of the swap contract}$$

$(D_{fixed} - D_{float}) = $ Difference in durations between a government bond that has the same maturity and coupon as the fixed-payment side of the swap and a government bond that has the same duration as the swap-payment interval (e.g., annual floating payments)

$$N_S = \text{Notional value of swap contracts}$$

$$\frac{\Delta R}{1 + R} = \text{Shock to interest rates}$$

Note that as long as $D_{fixed} > D_{float}$, when interest rates rise, the market (present) value of fixed-rate payments will fall by more than the market (present) value of floating-rate payments; in market (or present) value terms, the fixed-rate payers gain when rates rise and lose when rates fall.

To solve for the optimal notional value of swap contracts,[7] we set

$$\Delta S = \Delta E$$

The gain on swap contracts entered into off the balance sheet just offsets the loss in net worth on the balance sheet when rates rise. Substituting values for ΔS and ΔE:

$$-(D_{fixed} - D_{float}) \times N_S \times \frac{\Delta R}{1 + R} = -(D_A - kD_L) \times A \times \frac{\Delta R}{1 + R}$$

Cancelling out the common terms:

$$(D_{fixed} - D_{float}) \times N_S = (D_A - kD_L) \times A$$

Solving for N_S:

$$N_S = \frac{(D_A - kD_L) \times A}{D_{fixed} - D_{float}}$$

EXAMPLE 25–3	Suppose $D_A = 5$, $D_L = 3$, $k = 0.9$, and $A = \$100$ million. Also, assume the duration of a current 10-year, fixed-rate government bond with the same coupon as the fixed rate on the swap is seven years, while the duration of a floating-rate bond that reprices annually is one year:[8]
Calculating the Notional Value of Swaps in a Macrohedge	$$D_{fixed} = 7 \quad \text{and} \quad D_{float} = 1$$ Then: $$N_S = \frac{(D_A - kD_L) \times A}{D_{fixed} - D_{float}} = \frac{\$230,000,000}{(7 - 1)} = \$38,333,333$$

---

[6] Although principal payments on bonds are not swapped on maturity, this does not matter since the theoretical payment and receipt of principal values cancel each other out.

[7] Note that the FI wants to enter swaps to protect itself against rising rates. Thus, it will pay fixed and receive floating. In the context of swap transactions, when an FI pays fixed, it is said to be "buying swaps." Thus, we are solving for the optimal number of swaps contracts the FI should buy in this example.

[8] See Chapter 9 for a discussion of the duration on floating-rate bonds.

If each swap contract is $100,000 in size,[9] the number of swap contracts into which the FI should enter will be $38,333,333/$100,000 = 383.33, or 383 contracts, rounding down. Table 25–5 summarizes the key features of the hedge assuming that the initial rate on the T-bond is 10 percent and is expected to rise by 1 percent. As shown in Table 25–5, the loss of $2.09 million in net worth on the balance sheet is exactly offset by a gain off the balance sheet on the swap hedge.

If the FI engaged in a longer-term swap—for example, 15 years—such that $D_{fixed} = 9$ and $D_{float} = 1$, then the notional value of swap contracts would fall to $230,000,000/(9 − 1) = $28,750,000. If each swap contract is $100,000 in size, the FI should enter into 287 swap contracts.

While it may seem logical that fewer contracts are preferable in the sense of saving on fees and other related costs of hedging, this advantage is offset by the fact that longer-term swaps have greater counterparty default or credit risk (discussed later in this chapter).

CONCEPT QUESTIONS

1. **In Example 25–2, which of the two FIs has its liability costs fully hedged and which is only partially hedged? Explain your answer.**
2. **What are some non-standard terms that might be encountered in an off-market swap?**
3. **In Example 25–3, what is the notional size of swap contracts if $D_{fixed} = 5$ and swap contracts require payment every six months? ($N_s = $51,111,111$)**

CURRENCY SWAPS

currency swap
A swap used to hedge against exchange rate risk from mismatched currencies on assets and liabilities.

Just as swaps are long-term contracts that can hedge interest rate risk exposure, they can also be used to hedge currency risk exposures of FIs. The following section considers a simple, plain vanilla example of how **currency swaps** can immunize FIs against exchange rate risk when they mismatch the currencies of their assets and liabilities.

Fixed-Fixed Currency Swaps

Consider the Canadian FI in Panel A of Table 25–6 with all of its fixed-rate assets denominated in dollars. Assume that the dollar–pound exchange rate is fixed at $2/£1. It is financing part of its asset portfolio with a £50 million issue of four-year, medium-term British pound notes that have a fixed annual coupon of 10 percent. By comparison, the U.K. FI in Panel B of Table 25–6 has all its assets denominated

TABLE 25–5
On- and Off-Balance-Sheet Effects of a Swap Hedge

	On Balance Sheet	Off Balance Sheet
Begin hedge, $t = 0$	Equity exposed to impact of rise in interest rates	Sell interest rate swap
End hedge, $t = 1$	Interest rates rise on assets and liabilities by 1%	Buy interest rate swap
Opportunity loss on balance sheet: $\Delta E = -[5 - 0.9(3) \times \$100m \times (0.01/(1.1)]$ $= -\$2.09$ million		Gain on interest rate swap: $\Delta S = [(7 - 1) \times \$38,333,333 \times (0.01/(1.1)]$ $= -\$2.09$ million

[9] The notional value of swap contracts can take virtually any size since they are individually tailored OTC contracts.

TABLE 25–6
Balance Sheets of Currency Swap Participants

Assets	Liabilities
Panel A: Canadian FI	
$100 million Canadian loans (4-year) in dollars, 11%	£50 million U.K. GICs or CDs (4-year) in pounds, 10%
Panel B: U.K. FI	
£50 million U.K. loans (4-year) in pounds, 11%	$100 million Canadian notes (4-year) in dollars, 10%

in pounds; it is partly funding those assets with a $100 million issue of four-year, medium-term dollar notes with a fixed annual coupon of 10 percent.

These two FIs are exposed to opposing currency risks. The Canadian FI is exposed to the risk that the dollar will depreciate against the pound over the next four years, making it more costly to cover the annual coupon interest payments and the principal repayment on its pound-denominated notes. On the other hand, the U.K. FI is exposed to the dollar appreciating against the pound, making it more difficult to cover the dollar coupon and principal payments on its four-year $100 million note issue out of the sterling cash flows on its assets.

The FIs can hedge the exposures either on or off the balance sheet. On the balance sheet, the Canadian FI can issue $100 million in four-year, medium-term dollar notes (at, say, 10.5 percent). The proceeds of the sale can be used to pay off the £50 million of four-year, medium-term sterling notes. Similarly, the U.K. FI can issue £50 million in four-year, medium-term sterling notes (at, say, 10.5 percent), using the proceeds to pay off the $100 million of four-year, medium-term dollar notes. Both FIs have taken actions on the balance sheet so that they are no longer exposed to movements in the exchange rate between the two currencies.

EXAMPLE 25–4

Expected Cash Flows on Fixed-Fixed Currency Swap.

Rather than make changes on the balance sheet, a feasible currency swap in which the U.K. and Canadian FIs can enter is one under which the U.K. FI sends annual payments in pounds to cover the coupon and principal repayments of the Canadian FI's pound sterling note issue, and the Canadian FI sends annual dollar payments to the U.K. FI to cover the interest and principal payments on its dollar note issue.[10] We summarize the currency swap in Figure 25–3 and Table 25–7. As a result of the swap, the U.K. FI transforms fixed-rate dollar payments into fixed-rate sterling payments that better match the sterling fixed-rate cash flows from its asset portfolio. Similarly, the Canadian FI transforms fixed-rate sterling payments into fixed-rate dollar payments that better match the fixed-rate dollar cash flows from its asset portfolio. Further, both FIs transform the pattern of their payments at a lower rate than if they had made changes on the balance sheet. Both FIs effectively obtain financing at 10 percent while hedging against exchange rate risk. Had they gone to the market, we assumed above that they would have paid 10.5 percent to do this. In undertaking this exchange of cash flows, the two parties normally agree on a fixed exchange rate for the cash flows at the beginning of the period.[11] In this example, the fixed exchange rate would be $2/£1.

---

[10] In a currency swap, it is usual to include both principal and interest payments as part of the swap agreement. For interest rate swaps, it is usual to include just interest rate payments. The reason for this is that both principal and interest are exposed to FX risk.

[11] As with interest rate swaps, this exchange rate reflects the contracting parties' expectations in regard to future exchange rate movements.

FIGURE 25–3
Fixed-Fixed Pound/Dollar Currency Swap

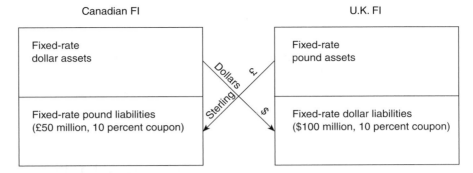

TABLE 25–7
Financing Costs Resulting from the Fixed-Fixed Currency Swap Agreement ($ and £ millions)

	Canadian FI	U.K. FI
Cash outflows from balance sheet financing	$-10\% \times$ £50	$-10\% \times$ \$100
Cash inflows from swap	$10\% \times$ £50	$10\% \times$ \$100
Cash outflows from swap	$-10\% \times$ \$100	$-10\% \times$ £50
Net cash flows	$-10\% \times$ \$100	$-10\% \times$ £50
Rate available on		
Dollar-denominated notes	10.5%	
Pound-denominated notes		10.5%

In this example, both liabilities bear a fixed 10 percent interest rate. This is not a necessary requirement for the fixed-fixed currency swap agreement. For example, suppose that the Canadian FI's note coupons were 5 percent per annum, while the U.K. FI's note coupons were 10 percent. The swap dollar payments of the Canadian FI would remain unchanged, but the U.K. FI's sterling payments would be reduced by £2.5 million (or $5 million) in each of the four years. This difference could be met either by some up-front payment by the U.K. FI to the Canadian FI, reflecting the difference in the present value of the two fixed cash flows, or by annual payments that result in zero net present value differences among the fixed-fixed currency swap participants' payments. Also note that if the exchange rate changed from the rate agreed in the swap ($2/£1), either one or the other side would be losing in the sense that a new swap might be entered into at an exchange rate more favourable to one party. Specifically, if the dollar were to appreciate (rise in value) against the pound over the life of the swap, the agreement would become more costly for the Canadian FI. If, however, the dollar were to depreciate (fall in value), the U.K. FI would find the agreement increasingly costly over the swap's life.

By combining an interest rate swap of the fixed-floating type described earlier with a currency swap, we can also produce a fixed-floating currency swap that is a hybrid of the two plain vanilla swaps we have considered so far.

Fixed-Floating Currency Swaps

EXAMPLE 25–5

Financing Costs Associated with a Fixed-Floating Currency Swap

Consider a Canadian FI that primarily holds floating-rate, short-term, dollar-denominated assets. It has partly financed this asset portfolio with a £50 million, four-year note issue with fixed 10 percent annual coupons denominated in sterling. By comparison, a U.K. FI that primarily holds long-term, fixed-rate assets denominated in sterling has partly financed this portfolio with $100 million, short-term, dollar-denominated Euro CDs whose rates reflect changes in one-year LIBOR plus a 2 percent premium. As a result, the Canadian FI is faced with both an interest rate risk and a foreign exchange risk. Specifically, if dollar short-term rates fall and the dollar depreciates against the pound, the FI may face a problem in covering its promised fixed-coupon and principal payments on the pound-denominated note. Consequently, it may wish to transform its fixed-rate, pound-denominated liabilities into variable-rate, dollar-denominated liabilities. The U.K. FI also faces interest rate and foreign exchange rate risk exposures. If Canadian interest rates rise and the dollar appreciates against the pound, the U.K. FI will find it more difficult to cover its promised coupon and principal payments on its dollar-denominated CDs out of the cash flows from its fixed-rate pound asset portfolio. Consequently, it may wish to transform its floating-rate, short-term, dollar-denominated liabilities into fixed-rate pound liabilities.

Both FIs can make changes on the balance sheet to hedge the interest rate and foreign exchange rate risk exposure. The Canadian FI can issue $100 million, dollar-dominated, floating-rate, short-term debt (at, say, LIBOR plus 2.5 percent), the proceeds of which can be used to pay off the existing £50 million four-year note. The U.K. FI can issue £50 million in four-year notes (at, say, 11 percent) and use the proceeds to pay off the $100 million in short-term Euro CDs. Both FIs, by changing the financing used on the balance sheet, hedge both the interest rate and foreign exchange rate risk. We again assume that the dollar/pound exchange rate is $2/£1.

Alternatively, each FI can achieve its objective of liability transformation by engaging in a fixed-floating currency swap. A feasible swap would be one in which each year, the two FIs swap payments at some prearranged dollar/pound exchange rate, assumed to be $2/£1. The U.K. FI sends fixed payments in pounds to cover the cost of the Canadian FI's pound-denominated note issue, while the Canadian FI sends floating payments in dollars to cover the U.K. FI's floating-rate dollar CD costs. The resulting expected financing costs are calculated in Table 25–8. As a result of the fixed-floating currency swap, both FIs have hedged interest rate and foreign exchange rate risk and have done so at a rate below what they could have achieved by making on-balance-sheet changes. The Canadian FI's net financing cost is LIBOR plus 2 percent with the swap, compared to LIBOR plus 2.5 percent in the debt market. The U.K. FI's financing cost is 10 percent with the swap, compared to 11 percent had it refinanced on the balance sheet.

TABLE 25–8   Financing Costs Resulting from the Fixed-Floating Currency Swap ($ and £ millions)

	Canadian FI	U.K. FI
Cash outflows from balance sheet financing	$-10\% \times £50$	$-(\text{LIBOR} + 2\%) \times \$100$
Cash inflows from swap	$10\% \times £50$	$(\text{LIBOR} + 2\%) \times \$100$
Cash outflows from swap	$-(\text{LIBOR} + 2\%) \times \$100$	$-10\% \times £50$
Net cash outflows	$-(\text{LIBOR} + 2\%) \times \$100$	$-10\% \times £50$
Rate available on		
Dollar-denominated variable-rate debt	LIBOR + 2½%	
Pound-denominated fixed-rate debt		11%

TABLE 25–9
Realized Cash Flows on a Fixed-Floating Currency Swap ($ and £ millions)

Year	LIBOR	LIBOR + 2 percent	Floating Rate Payment by Canadian Bank ($)	Fixed Rate Payment by U.K. FI (£s)	Fixed Rate Payment by U.K. FI ($ at $2/£1)	Net Payment by Canadian FI ($s)
1	9%	11%	$ 11	£5	$ 10	$+1
2	7	9	9	5	10	−1
3	8	10	10	5	10	0
4	10	12	112	55	110	+2
Total net payment						$+2

Given the realized LIBOR rates in column (2), we show the relevant payments among the contracting parties in Table 25–9. The realized cash flows from the swap result in a net nominal payment of $2 million by the Canadian FI to the U.K. FI over the life of the swap.

1. Referring to the fixed-fixed currency swap in Table 25–7, if the net cash flows on the swap are zero, why does either FI enter into the swap agreement?
2. Referring to Table 25–9, suppose that the Canadian FI had agreed to make floating payments of LIBOR + 1 percent instead of LIBOR + 2 percent. What would its net payment have been to the U.K. FI over the four-year swap agreement?

CREDIT SWAPS

In recent years the fastest-growing types of swaps have been those developed to better allow FIs to hedge their credit risk, so-called *credit swaps* or *credit default swaps*. In 2001, the total notional principal for outstanding credit derivative contracts reported to the BIS was US$698 billion. As shown in Table 25–1, by December 2008, this amount had risen to US$41.9 trillion. Credit swaps are important for two reasons. First, credit risk is still more likely to cause an FI to fail than is either interest rate risk or FX risk. Second, credit swaps allow FIs to maintain long-term customer lending relationships without bearing the full credit risk exposure from those relationships. Indeed, then Federal Reserve Board Chairman Alan Greenspan has credited this market with helping the banking system maintain its strength through the economic recession in the early 2000s. He argued that credit swaps were effectively used to shift a significant part of banks' risk from their corporate loan portfolios.[12] For example, significant exposures to telecommunication firms were hedged by banks through credit swaps. However, the Fed chairman also commented that these derivative securities are prone to induce speculative excesses that need to be contained through regulation, supervision, and private sector action, a statement that seemed prophetic and ironic in the midst of the 2007–2008 credit crisis. While banks have been buyers of credit risk protection through credit default swaps, insurance companies, (such as AIG) and reinsurance companies (such as Munich Re) have been net sellers of credit risk protection. Thus, they have been more willing than banks to bear credit risk. The result is that the FI bearing the credit risk of a loan (a bank) is often different from the FI that issued the loan. In 2007 and 2008, insurance companies suffered large losses as buyers of credit risk and, as shown in the Industry Perspectives feature, the U.S. government has proposed regulatory changes to control the systemic risk.

The buyer of a credit swap makes periodic payments to the seller until the end of the life of the swap or until the credit event specified in the contract occurs. These payments are typically made every quarter, six months, or year. The settlement of the swap in the event of a default involves either physical delivery of the bonds (or loans) or a cash payment. Generally, a credit swap specifies that a number of different bonds (loans) can be delivered in the event of a default. The bonds (loans) typically have the same seniority, but they may not sell for the same

---

[12] Much of this risk exposure was absorbed by domestic and foreign insurance and reinsurance companies.

percentage of face value immediately after a default. This gives the holder of a credit swap a cheapest-to-deliver option. When a default happens, the buyer of protection will review alternative deliverable bonds (or loans) and choose the one that can be purchased most cheaply for delivery.

Total Return Swaps

total return swap
A swap involving an obligation to pay interest at a specified fixed or floating rate for payments representing the total return on a specified amount.

Although FIs spend significant resources attempting to evaluate and price expected changes in a borrower's credit risk over the life of a loan, a borrower's credit situation (credit quality) sometimes deteriorates unexpectedly after the loan terms are determined and the loan is issued. A lender can use a total return swap to hedge this possible change in credit risk exposure. A **total return swap** involves swapping an obligation to pay interest at a specified fixed or floating rate for payments representing the total return on a loan or a bond (interest and principal value changes) of a specified amount.

EXAMPLE 25–6

Calculation of Cash Flows on a Total Return Swap

Suppose that an FI lends US$100 million to a Brazilian manufacturing firm at a fixed rate of 10 percent. If the firm's credit risk increases unexpectedly over the life of the loan, the market value of the loan and consequently the FI's net worth will fall. The FI can hedge an unexpected increase in the borrower's credit risk by entering into a total return swap in which it agrees to pay a total return based on an annual fixed rate (f) plus changes in the market value of Brazilian (U.S. dollar-denominated) government debt (changes in the value of these bonds reflect the political and economic events in the firm's home country and thus will be correlated with the credit risk of the Brazilian borrowing firm). Also, the bonds are in the same currency (U.S. dollars) as the loans. In return, the FI receives a variable market rate payment of interest annually (e.g., one-year LIBOR rate). Figure 25–4 and Table 25–10 illustrate the cash flows associated with the typical total return swap for the FI.

Using the total return swap, the FI agrees to pay a fixed rate of interest annually and the capital gain or loss on the market value of the Brazilian (U.S. dollar) bond over the period of the hedge. In Figure 25–4, P_0 denotes the market value of the bond at the beginning of the swap period and P_T represents the market value of the bond at the end of the swap period. If the Brazilian bond decreases in value over the period of the hedge ($P_0 > P_T$), the FI pays a relatively small (possibly negative) amount to the counterparty equal to the fixed payment on the swap minus the capital loss[13] on the bond. For example, suppose the Brazilian (U.S. dollar) bond was priced at par ($P_0 = 100$) at the beginning of the swap period. At the end of the swap period or the payment date, the Brazilian bond had a secondary market value of 90 ($P_T = 90$) due to an increase in Brazilian country risk. Suppose that the fixed-rate payment ($\bar{f}$) as part of the total return swap was 12 percent; then the FI would send to the swap counterparty the fixed rate of 12 percent minus 10 percent (the capital loss on the Brazilian bond), or a total of 2 percent, and would receive in return a floating payment (e.g., LIBOR = 11 percent) from the counterparty to the swap. Thus, the net profit on the swap to the FI lender is 9 percent (11 percent minus 2 percent) times the notional amount of the swap contract. This gain can be used to offset the loss of market value on the loan to the Brazilian firm. This example is illustrated in Table 25–10.

Thus, the FI benefits from the total return swap if the Brazilian bond value deteriorates as a result of a political or economic shock. Assuming that the Brazilian firm's credit risk deteriorates along with the local economy, the FI will offset some of this loss of the Brazilian loan on its balance sheet with a gain from the total return swap.

---

[13] Total return swaps are typically structured so that the capital gain or loss is paid at the end of the swap. However, an alternative structure does exist in which the capital gain or loss is paid at the end of each interest period during the swap.

FIGURE 25–4
Cash Flows on a
Total Return Swap

TABLE 25–10 Cash Flows on a Total Return Swap

	Annual Cash Flow for Year 1 through Final Year	Additional Payment by FI	Total Return
Cash inflow on swap to FI lender	1-year LIBOR (11%)	—	1-year LIBOR (11%)
Cash outflow on swap to other FI	Fixed rate ($\bar{f}$) (12%)	$P_T - P_0$ (90 2 100)	$\left[\bar{f} + \dfrac{P_T - P_0}{P_0}\right]$
			$\left(12\% + \dfrac{90 - 100}{100} = 12\% - 10\% = 2\%\right)$
		Net profit	9%

Note that hedging credit risk in this fashion allows the FI to maintain its customer relationship with the Brazilian firm (and perhaps earn fees from selling other financial services to that firm) without bearing a large amount of credit risk exposure. Moreover, since the Brazilian loan remains on the FI's balance sheet, the Brazilian firm may not even know its loan is being hedged. This would not be the case if the FI sought to reduce its risk by selling all or part of the loan (see Chapter 26). Finally, the swap does not completely hedge credit risk in this case. Specifically, basis risk is present to the extent that the credit risk of the Brazilian firm's dollar loan is imperfectly correlated with Brazilian country risk reflected in the price of the Brazilian (U.S. dollar) bonds.[14]

Pure Credit Swaps

Total return swaps can be used to hedge credit risk exposure, but they contain an element of interest rate risk as well as credit risk. For example, in Table 25–10, if the LIBOR rate changes due to changes in monetary policy, the *net* cash flows on the total return swap also will change—even though the credit risks of the underlying loans (and bonds) have not changed.

pure credit swap
A swap by which an FI receives the par value of the loan on default in return for paying a periodic swap fee.

To strip out the "interest rate"-sensitive element of total return swaps, an alternative swap has been developed called a **"pure" credit swap.** In this case, as shown in Figure 25–5, the FI lender will send (each swap period) a fixed fee or payment (like an insurance premium) to the FI counterparty. If the FI lender's loan or loans do not default, it will receive nothing back from the FI counterparty.

---

[14] In many swaps, the total return on a loan (rather than a bond as in this example) is swapped for a floating payment such as LIBOR. In this case, $\bar{f}$ would equal any fees paid for loan origination and $[(P_T - P_0)/P_0]$ would reflect the estimated change in market value of the loan as perceived by brokers/traders in the secondary market for loan sales. The secondary market for loans is described in Chapter 26.

FIGURE 25–5
A Pure Credit Swap

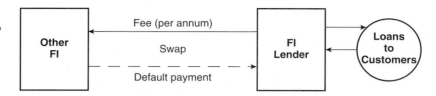

However, if the loan or loans default, the FI counterparty will cover the default loss by making a default payment that is often equal to the par value of the original loan (e.g., $P_0 = \$100$) minus the secondary market value of the defaulted loan (e.g., $P_T = \$40$); that is, the FI counterparty will pay $P_0 - P_T$ (or \$60, in this example).[15] Thus, a pure credit swap is like buying credit insurance and/or a multi-period credit option.

SWAPS AND CREDIT RISK CONCERNS

The growth of the over-the-counter (OTC) swap market was one of the major motivating factors underlying the imposition of the BIS risk-based capital requirements in January 1993 (see Chapter 20). The fear was that in a long-term OTC swap-type contract, the out-of-the-money counterparty would have incentives to default to deter future and current losses. Consequently, the BIS requirements imposed a required capital ratio for deposit-taking institutions against their holdings of both interest rate and currency swaps (and, more recently, other types of swaps, including credit swaps). Many analysts have argued that these capital requirements work against the growth of the swap market since they can be viewed as a cost or tax on market participants.

www.bis.org

In contrast to futures and options markets, swap markets are governed by very little regulation—there is no central governing body overseeing swap market operations. Indeed, it is not entirely clear who the proper regulator of the swap market is. The International Swaps and Derivatives Association (ISDA) is a global trade association with over 830 members (including most of the world's major financial institutions) from some 58 countries on six continents that sets codes and standards for swap markets. Established in 1985, the ISDA establishes, reviews, and updates the code of standards (the language and provisions) for swap documentation. The ISDA also acts as the spokesgroup for the industry on regulatory changes and issues, promotes the development of risk management practices for swap dealers (for example, the ISDA was instrumental in helping to develop the guidelines set by the Basel committee on capital adequacy in financial institutions—see Chapter 20), provides a forum for informing and educating swap market participants about relevant issues, and sets standards of commercial conduct for its members. Further, because commercial banks are the major swap dealers, the swap markets are subject, indirectly, to regulations imposed by the bank regulatory agencies charged with monitoring bank risk. For example, commercial banks must include swap risk exposure when calculating risk-based capital requirements (see Chapter 20). To the extent that swap activity is part of a bank's overall

www.isda.org

www.federalreserve.gov

www.fdic.gov

---

[15] While a pure credit swap is like a default option (e.g., the digital default option in Chapter 24), a key difference is that the fee (or premium) payments on the swap are paid over the life of the swap, whereas for a default option the whole fee (premium) is paid up front.

business, swap markets are monitored for abuses. Investment banks and insurance companies have recently become bigger players in the swap markets, however, and these dealers are subject to few regulations on their swap dealings. As well, many hedge funds and investment banks with questionable credit ratings participated in the CDS markets by 2007 and 2008. This increased the counterparty risk and the systemic risk to the global financial system.

It is critical that both regulators and market participants have a heightened awareness of credit risks. If the transaction is not structured carefully, it may pass along unintended risks to participants, exposing them to higher frequency and severity of losses than if they had held an equivalent cash position. As defined by Moody's Investors Service, default risk on swaps comes from three sources: (1) any missed or delayed payment of interest and/or principal; (2) bankruptcy or receivership; and (3) distressed exchange, where the borrower offers debt holders a new security that amounts to a diminished financial obligation, or the swap dealer has the apparent purpose of helping the borrower avoid default. Both Merrill Lynch (now part of Bank of America) and JPMorgan Chase are heavy participants as intermediaries in the swap market; for example, they act as counterparty guarantors to both the fixed and floating sides in swaps. To do this successfully and to maintain market share, a high if not the highest credit rating is increasingly required.

www.moodys.com

This raises a question: Is credit or default risk on swaps the same as or different from the credit or default risk on loans? In fact, there are three major differences between the credit risk on swaps and the credit risk on loans. As a result, the credit risk on a swap is generally considered to be much less than that on a loan.[16] We discuss these differences next.

Netting and Swaps

One factor that mitigates the credit risk on swaps is the netting of swap payments. On each swap payment date, a fixed payment is made by one party and a floating payment is made by the other. However, in general, each party calculates the net difference between the two payments, and a single payment for the net difference is made by one party to the other. This netting of payments implies that the default exposure of the in-the-money party is limited to the net payment rather than either the total fixed or floating payment. Further, when two parties have large numbers of contracts outstanding against each other, they tend to net across contracts. This process, called *netting by novation*—often formalized through a master netting agreement—further reduces the potential risk of loss if some contracts are in the money and others are out of the money to the same counterparty.[17] However, note that netting by novation has not been fully tested in all international courts of law. For example, in the 1990s a number of U.K. municipal authorities engaged in swaps with U.S. and U.K. banks and investment banks. These municipal authorities, after taking major losses on some swap contracts, defaulted on further payments. The U.K. High Court supported the municipal authorities' right to default

---

[16] As with loans, swap participants deal with the credit risk of counterparties by setting bilateral limits on the notional amount of swaps entered into (similar to credit rationing on loans) as well as adjusting the fixed and/or floating rates by including credit risk premiums. For example, a low-credit-quality fixed-rate payer may have to pay an additional spread to a high-credit-quality floating-rate payer. During the market turmoil of 2007 and 2008, it became apparent that many market participants had considerably underpriced the credit risk of CDSs.

[17] Since 1995, the BIS has allowed banks to use bilateral netting of swap contracts in calculating their risk-based capital requirements (see Chapter 20). It is estimated that this reduces banks' capital requirements against swaps by up to 40 percent.

by stating that their entering into such swaps had been outside their powers of authority in the first place. This still did not stop these municipal authorities from seeking to collect on in-the-money swaps.

Payment Flows Are Interest and Not Principal

While currency swaps involve swaps of interest and principal, interest rate swaps involve swaps of interest payments only measured against some notional principal value. This suggests that the default risk on such swaps is less than that on a regular loan, where both interest and principal are exposed to credit risk.

Standby Letters of Credit

In cases where swaps are made between parties of different credit standing, such that one party perceives a significant risk of default by the other party, the poor-quality credit risk party may be required to buy a standby letter of credit (or another form of performance guaranty) from a third-party high-quality (AA) FI such that if default occurs, the standby letter of credit will provide the swap payments in lieu of the defaulting party. Further, low-quality counterparties are increasingly required to post collateral in lieu of default. This collateral is an incentive mechanism working to deter swap defaults.[18]

CONCEPT QUESTIONS	1. What is the link between preserving "customer relationships" and credit derivatives such as total return swaps? 2. Is there any difference between a digital default option (see Chapter 24) and a pure credit swap? 3. Are swaps as risky as equivalent-sized loans?

EFFECT OF DERIVATIVES ON AN FI'S BALANCE SHEET

As we conclude our three chapters on derivatives-type contracts, it is useful to look at the impact of derivatives on FIs' balance sheets and the actual use of derivatives by Canadian FIs. In Chapter 20, we discussed the effects of market and book value of assets and liabilities on the balance sheets of FIs and noted that in the current economic crisis, the carrying value of toxic assets by global FIs has been an issue for regulators, auditors, and the FIs themselves. As noted in Chapter 20, a write-down in value or a trading loss on these assets has an impact on the capital adequacy of FIs. As noted in Chapter 22, the level of participation of an FI in the derivatives markets depends on the particular financial intermediary. The large Canadian FIs provide risk management services to their clients, including over-the-counter (OTC) foreign exchange, commodity, equity, and interest rate derivatives, and as well are active traders. As shown in Table 25–11, summarized from Bank of Montreal's 2008 annual report, the total notional amount of derivatives contracts held was $3.05 trillion, but only 1.7 percent ($50.55 billion) was held for hedging purposes. This emphasizes the fact that, while we discuss the use of futures, forwards, options, and swaps in the context of hedging for an FI, in fact, Canadian banks use very few derivatives to hedge. Note also that most of the trading contracts are over the

---

[18] One solution being considered by market participants (such as the International Swap Dealers Association) is to use collateral to mark to market a swap contract in a way similar to that in which futures are marked to market to prevent credit risk building up over time. Remember, a swap contract is like a succession of forwards.

TABLE 25–11
Bank of Montreal's 2008 Notional Amounts of Derivatives Contracts for Trading and Hedging (CDN$ millions)

Source: BMO, 2008 annual report, p. 125, www2.bmo.com/ar2008.

	Trading	Hedging	Total
Interest Rate Contracts			
Over the counter:			
Swaps	$ 1,434,047	$50,551	
Forward rate agreements	217,072		
Purchased options	83,497		
Written options	103,492		
Exchange-traded:			
Futures	76,215		
Purchased options	70,356		
Written options	58,288		
Total Interest Rate Contracts	$ 2,042,967	$50,551	$2,093,518
Foreign Exchange Contracts			
Over the counter:			
Cross-currency swaps	$ 13,681		
Cross-currency interest rate swaps	136,219		
Forward foreign exchange contracts	212,927		
Purchased options	8,477		
Written options	10,715		
Exchange-traded:			
Futures	835		
Purchased options	6,806		
Written options	3,073		
Total Foreign Exchange Contracts			$ 392,733
Commodity Contracts			
Over the counter:			
Swaps	45,988		
Purchased options	35,749		
Written options	33,871		
Exchange-traded:			
Futures	39,840		
Purchased options	108,337		
Written options	109,359		
Total Commodity Contracts			$ 373,144
Equity Contracts			
Over the counter	$ 21,809		
Exchange-traded	19,129		
Total Equity Contracts			$ 40,938
Credit Default Swaps			
Over the counter:			
Purchased	$ 78,320		
Written	71,977		
Total Credit Default Swaps			$ 150,207
Total Derivatives Notional Amount	$ 2,999,989	$50,551	$3,050,540

counter rather than exchange-traded. This indicates that BMO is directly exposed to the counterparty risk that would be assumed by an organized exchange.

As well, it is not apparent from a casual glance what impact derivative products have on an FI's balance sheet. The credit crisis of 2007–2008 focused attention on derivative products, in particular, credit default swaps. As can be seen from Table 25–12, the fair value, or market value of BMO's derivatives is significantly different from the notional values reported in Table 25–11. For example, BMO's credit default swaps represent a notional value of $150.207 billion (Table 25–11). However, the fair value of the purchased contracts (assets) is $6.435 billion and the fair value of the written contracts is $5.828 billion (liabilities); these are the amounts that are carried on the balance sheet (Table 25–12). Similarly, for all of the derivative contracts, once a fair value has been calculated, the $3 trillion in notional amount becomes just $65.586 billion on balance sheet assets and $60.048 on balance sheet liabilities. BMO's total on balance sheet assets at October 31, 2008, were $416.1 billion. The value reported for derivatives is subject to the accounting

TABLE 25–12
Bank of Montreal's 2008 Fair Values of Derivative Instruments for Trading and Hedging (CDN$ millions)

Source: BMO, 2008 annual report, p. 124, www2.bmo.com/ar2008.

	Gross Assets	Gross Liabilities	Net
Trading			
Interest rate contracts:			
Swaps	$ 25,925	$(26,243)	$ (318)
Forward rate agreements	165	(166)	(1)
Futures	19	(12)	7
Purchased options	1,804	—	1,804
Written options	—	(1,643)	(1,643)
Foreign exchange contracts:			
Cross-currency swaps	1,212	(1,346)	(134)
Cross-currency interest rate swaps	7,867	(7,259)	608
Forward foreign exchange contracts	8,383	(7,913)	470
Purchased options	566	—	566
Written options	—	(774)	(774)
Commodity contracts:			
Swaps	2,336	(3,102)	(766)
Purchased options	3,953	—	3,953
Written options	—	(3,497)	(3,497)
Equity Contracts	5,606	(2,019)	3,587
Credit Default Swaps			
Purchased	6,435	—	6,435
Written	—	(5,828)	(5,828)
Total fair value—trading derivatives	$ 64,271	$(59,802)	$4,469
Average fair value (1)	$ 43,917	$(40,456)	$3,461
Hedging			
Interest rate contracts			
Cash flow hedges-swaps	$752	$ (187)	$ 565
Fair value hedged-swaps	563	(59)	504
Total swaps	$ 1,315	$ (246)	$1,069
Total fair value-hedging derivatives (2)	$ 1,315	$ (246)	$1,069
Average fair value (1)	$ 540	$ (257)	$ 283
Total fair value—trading and hedging	$ 65,586	$(60,048)	$5,538
Less: Impact of master netting agreements	$(41,748)	$ 41,748	—
Total	$ 23,838	$(18,300)	$5,538
Balance sheet values:			
Fair value of derivative assets	$ 65,586		
Fair value of derivative liabilities	$ 60,048		

(1) Average fair value amounts are calculated using a five-quarter rolling average.
(2) The fair values of hedging derivatives wholly or partially offset the changes in fair values of the related on-balance sheet financial instruments or future cash flows.

standards applied and the regulatory requirements as demonstrated in the following Industry Perspectives feature. Since many of these contracts are contingent, and also subject to market forces, their effect on the systemic risk in the financial system can be difficult to determine.

INDUSTRY PERSPECTIVES

BMO'S USE OF DERIVATIVES: EXCERPTS FROM THE 2008 ANNUAL REPORT

Fair Value

Fair value represents point-in-time estimates that may change in subsequent reporting periods due to market conditions or other factors. Fair value for exchange-traded derivatives is considered to be the price quoted on derivatives exchanges. Fair value for over-the-counter derivatives is determined using multi-contributor prices or zero-coupon valuation techniques further adjusted for credit, model, and liquidity risks, as well as administration costs. Zero-coupon curves are created using generally accepted valuation techniques from underlying instruments such as cash, bonds, and futures observable in the market. Option-implied volatilities, an input into the valuation model, are either obtained directly from market sources or calculated from market prices.

Notional Amount

The notional amounts of our derivatives represent the amount to which a rate or price is applied in order to calculate the amount of cash that must be exchanged under the contract. Notional amounts do not represent assets or liabilities and therefore are not recorded in our Consolidated Balance Sheet.

(a) Fair Value Option

Effective November 1, 2006, we adopted a new Canadian accounting standard that allows us to elect to measure financial instruments that would not otherwise be accounted for at fair value as trading instruments, with changes in fair value recorded in income provided they meet certain criteria. Financial instruments must have been designated on November 1, 2006, when the standard was adopted, or when new financial instruments were acquired, and the designation is irrevocable. Effective November 1, 2007, we adopted the new United States accounting standard, which allows us to elect to report selected financial assets and liabilities at fair value. The new standard eliminated a difference between Canadian and United States GAAP.

(c) Derivatives

Under both Canadian and United States GAAP, hedging derivatives are recorded at fair value in our Consolidated Balance Sheet. Changes in the fair value of hedging derivatives are either offset in our Consolidated Statement of Income against the change in the fair value of the hedged asset, liability, or firm commitment, or are recorded in Accumulated Other Comprehensive Income until the hedged item is recorded in our Consolidated Statement of Income. If the change in the fair value of the derivative is not completely offset by the change in the fair value of the item it is hedging, the difference is recorded immediately in our Consolidated Statement of Income.

Derivative-Related Credit Risk

Over-the-counter derivative instruments are subject to credit risk. Credit risk arises from the possibility that counterparties may default on their obligations. The credit risk associated with derivatives is normally a small fraction of the notional amount of the derivative instrument. Derivative contracts generally expose us to potential credit loss if changes in market rates affect a counterparty's position unfavourably and the counterparty defaults on payment. The credit risk is represented by the positive fair value of the derivative instrument. We strive to limit credit risk by dealing with counterparties that we believe are credit-worthy, and we manage our credit risk for derivatives using the same credit risk process that is applied to loans and other credit assets. We also pursue opportunities to reduce our exposure to credit losses on derivative instruments, including entering into master netting agreements with counterparties. The credit risk associated with favourable contracts is eliminated by master netting agreements to the extent that unfavourable contracts with the same counterparty cannot be settled before favourable contracts. Exchange-traded derivatives have no potential for credit exposure as they are settled net with each exchange.

Derivative-Related Market Risk

Derivative instruments are subject to market risk. Market risk arises from the potential for a negative impact on the balance sheet and/or income statement resulting from adverse changes in the value of derivative instruments as a result of changes in certain market variables. These variables include interest rates, foreign exchange rates, equity and commodity prices and their implied volatilities, as well as credit spreads, credit migration and default. We strive to limit market risk by employing comprehensive governance and management processes for all market risk-taking activities.

Terms used in the credit risk table [Table 25–13] are as follows:

Replacement cost represents the cost of replacing all contracts that have a positive fair value, using current market rates. It represents in effect the unrealized gains on our derivative instruments. Replacement

costs disclosed below represent the net of the asset and liability to a specific counterparty where we have a legally enforceable right to offset the amount owed to us with the amount owed by us and we intend either to settle on a net basis or to realize the asset and settle the liability simultaneously.

Credit equivalent amount represents the total replacement cost plus an amount representing the potential future credit exposure, as outlined in OSFI's *Capital Adequacy Guideline.*

Risk-weighted balance represents the credit risk equivalent, weighted based on the credit-worthiness of the counterparty, as prescribed by OSFI.

Source: Bank of Montreal's annual report, 2008, www2. bmo.com/ar2008.

TABLE 25–13
Comparison of Bank of Montreal's 2008 Replacement Cost, Credit Equivalent Amount, and Risk-Weighted Balance for Trading Derivatives (CDN$ millions)

Source: BMO, 2008 annual report, p. 126, www2.bmo.com/ar2008.

	Replacement Cost	Credit Equivalent Amount	Risk-Weighted Balance*
Interest Rate Contracts			
Swaps	$27,240	$34,264	$ —
Forward rate agreements	165	180	—
Purchased options	1,714	2,057	—
Foreign Exchange Contracts			
Cross-currency swaps	1,212	2,017	—
Cross-currency interest rate swaps	7,867	14,551	
Forward foreign exchange contracts	8,383	9,928	—
Purchased options	398	576	—
Commodity Contracts			
Swaps	2,336	8,242	—
Purchased options	1,670	7,037	—
Equity Contracts	1,996	3,264	907
Credit Default Swaps			
Purchased	6,435	7,564	4,750
Written	—	—	—
Total Derivatives	$59,416	$89,680	$14,897
Impact of master netting agreements	(41,748)	(54,223)	—
Total	$17,668	$35,457	$14,897

*Risk-weighted balance based on Basel II in 2008 and Basel I in 2007.

Summary

This chapter evaluated the role of swaps as risk management vehicles for FIs. We analyzed the major types of swaps: interest rate and currency swaps as well as credit swaps. Swaps have special features of long maturity, flexibility, and liquidity that make them attractive alternatives relative to shorter-term hedging vehicles such as the futures, forwards, options, and caps discussed in Chapters 23 and 24. However, even though the credit risk of swaps is less than that of loans, because of their OTC nature and long maturities, their credit risk is still generally greater than that for other OTC derivative instruments such as floors and caps. Also, the credit risk on swaps compares unfavourably with that on exchange-traded futures and options, whose credit risk is approximately zero.

Questions and Problems

1. Explain the similarity between a swap and a forward contract.

2. Forwards, futures, and options contracts had been used by FIs to hedge risk for many years before swaps were invented. If FIs already had these hedging instruments, why did they need swaps?

3. Distinguish between a swap buyer and a swap seller. In which markets does each have the comparative advantage?

4. An insurance company owns $50 million of floating-rate bonds yielding LIBOR plus 1 percent. These loans are financed by $50 million of fixed-rate guaranteed investment certificates (GICs) costing 10 percent. A finance company has $50 million of car loans with a fixed rate of 14 percent. The loans are financed by $50 million in GICs at a variable rate of LIBOR plus 4 percent.

   a. What is the risk exposure of the insurance company?

   b. What is the risk exposure of the finance company?

   c. What would be the cash flow goals of each company if they were to enter into a swap arrangement?

   d. Which company would be the buyer and which company would be the seller in the swap?

   e. Diagram the direction of the relevant cash flows for the swap arrangement.

   f. What are reasonable cash flow amounts, or relative interest rates, for each of the payment streams?

5. In a swap arrangement, the variable-rate swap cash flow streams often do not fully hedge the variable-rate cash flow streams from the balance sheet due to basis risk.

   a. What are the possible sources of basis risk in an interest rate swap?

   b. How could the failure to achieve a perfect hedge be realized by the swap buyer?

   c. How could the failure to achieve a perfect hedge be realized by the swap seller?

6. A bank has $200 million of floating-rate loans yielding the T-bill rate plus 2 percent. These loans are financed by $200 million of fixed-rate deposits costing 9 percent. A credit union has $200 million of mortgages with a fixed rate of 13 percent. They are financed by $200 million in GICs with a variable rate of the T-bill rate plus 3 percent.

   a. Discuss the type of interest rate risk each FI faces.

   b. Propose a swap that would result in each FI having the same type of asset and liability cash flows.

   c. Show that this swap would be acceptable to both parties.

   d. What are some of the practical difficulties in arranging this swap?

7. Bank 1 can issue five-year GICs at an annual rate of 11 percent fixed or at a variable rate of LIBOR plus 2 percent. Bank 2 can issue five-year GICs at an annual rate of 13 percent fixed or at a variable rate of LIBOR plus 3 percent.

   a. Is a mutually beneficial swap possible between the two banks?

   b. Where is the comparative advantage of the two banks?

   c. What is the net quality spread?

   d. What is an example of a feasible swap?

8. First Bank can issue one-year floating-rate GICs at prime plus 1 percent or fixed-rate GICs at 12.5 percent. Second Bank can issue one-year floating-rate GICs at prime plus 0.5 percent or fixed-rate GICs at 11 percent.

   a. What is a feasible swap with all the benefits going to First Bank?

   b. What is a feasible swap with all the benefits going to Second Bank?

c. Diagram each situation.

d. What factors will determine the final swap arrangement?

9. Two multinational FIs enter their respective debt markets to issue $100 million of two-year notes. FI A can borrow at a fixed annual rate of 11 percent or a floating rate of LIBOR plus 50 basis points, repriced at the end of the year. FI B can borrow at a fixed annual rate of 10 percent or a floating rate of LIBOR, repriced at the end of the year.

a. If FI A is a positive duration gap insurance company and FI B is a money market mutual fund, in what market(s) should each firm borrow to reduce its interest rate risk exposure?

b. In which debt market does FI A have a comparative advantage over FI B?

c. Although FI A is riskier than FI B and therefore must pay a higher rate in both the fixed-rate and floating-rate markets, there are possible gains to trade. Set up a swap to exploit FI A's comparative advantage over FI B. What are the total gains from the swap trade? Assume a swap intermediary fee of 10 basis points.

d. The gains from the swap trade can be apportioned between FI A and FI B through negotiation. What terms of trade would give all the gains to FI A? What terms of trade would give all the gains to FI B?

e. Assume swap pricing that allocates all the gains from the swap to FI A. If A buys the swap from B and pays the swap intermediary's fee, what are the end-of-year net cash flows if LIBOR is 8.25 percent?

f. If A buys the swap in part (e) from B and pays the swap intermediary's fee, what are the end-of-year net cash flows if LIBOR is 11 percent? Be sure to net swap payments against cash market payments for both firms.

g. If all barriers to entry and pricing inefficiencies between FI A's debt markets and FI B's debt markets were eliminated, how would that affect the swap transaction?

10. What are off-market swap arrangements? How are these arrangements negotiated?

11. Describe how an inverse floater works to the advantage of an investor who receives coupon payments of 10 percent minus LIBOR if LIBOR is currently at 4 percent. When is it a disadvantage to the investor? Does the issuing party bear any risk?

12. An FI has $500 million of assets with a duration of nine years and $450 million of liabilities with a duration of three years. The FI wants to hedge its duration gap with a swap that has fixed-rate payments with a duration of six years and floating-rate payments with a duration of two years. What is the optimal amount of the swap to effectively macrohedge against the adverse effect of a change in interest rates on the value of the FI's equity?

13. A Swiss bank issues a $100 million, three-year Eurodollar CD at a fixed annual rate of 7 percent. The proceeds of the CD are lent to a Swiss company for three years at a fixed rate of 9 percent. The spot exchange rate is Sf1.50/$.

a. Is this expected to be a profitable transaction?

b. What are the cash flows if exchange rates are unchanged over the next three years?

c. What is the risk exposure of the bank's underlying cash position?

d. How can the Swiss bank reduce that risk exposure?

e. If the dollar is expected to appreciate against the Sf to Sf1.65/$, Sf1.815/$, and Sf2.00/$ over the next three years, what will be the cash flows on this transaction?

f. If the Swiss bank swaps dollar payments for Sf payments at the current spot exchange rate, what are the cash flows on the swap? What are the cash flows on the entire hedged position? Assume that the dollar appreciates at the rates in part (e).

g. What are the cash flows on the swap and the hedged position if actual spot exchange rates are as follows:

End of year 1: Sf1.55/$

End of year 2: Sf1.47/$

End of year 3: Sf1.48/$

h. What would be the bank's risk exposure if the fixed-rate Swiss loan was financed with a floating-rate $100 million, three-year Eurodollar CD?

i. What type(s) of hedge is appropriate if the Swiss bank in part (h) wants to reduce its risk exposure?

j. If the annual Eurodollar CD rate is set at LIBOR and LIBOR at the end of years 1, 2, and 3 is expected to be 7 percent, 8 percent, and 9 percent, respectively, what will be the cash flows on the bank's unhedged cash position? Assume no change in exchange rates.

k. What are the cash flows on the bank's unhedged cash position if exchange rates are as follows:

End of year 1: Sf1.55/$

End of year 2: Sf1.47/$

End of year 3: Sf1.48/$

l. What are both the swap and the total hedged position cash flows if the bank swaps out its floating rate dollar CD payments in exchange for 7.75 percent fixed-rate Sf payments at the current spot exchange rate of Sf1.50/$?

m. If forecasted annual interest rates are 7 percent, 10.14 percent, and 10.83 percent over the next three years, respectively, and exchange rates over the next years are those in part (k), calculate the cash flows on an 8.75 percent fixed–floating-rate swap of dollars to Swiss francs at Sf1.50/$.

14. Use the following balance sheet information ($ millions) to construct a swap hedge against interest rate risk exposure.

Assets	
Rate-sensitive assets	$ 50
Fixed-rate assets	150
Total assets	$200
Liabilities and Equity	
Rate-sensitive liabilities	$ 75
Fixed-rate liabilities	100
Net worth	25
Total liabilities and equity	$200

Rate-sensitive assets are repriced quarterly at the 91-day Treasury bill rate plus 150 basis points. Fixed-rate assets have five years until maturity and are paying 9 percent annually. Rate-sensitive liabilities are repriced quarterly at the 91-day Treasury bill rate plus 100 basis points. Fixed-rate liabilities have two years until maturity and are paying 7 percent annually. Currently, the 91-day Treasury bill rate is 6.25 percent.

a. What is the bank's current net interest income? If Treasury bill rates increase 150 basis points, what will be the change in the bank's net interest income?

b. What is the bank's repricing or funding gap? Use the repricing model to calculate the change in the bank's net interest income if interest rates increase 150 basis points.

c. How can swaps be used as an interest rate hedge in this example?

15. Use the following information to construct a swap of asset cash flows for the bank in problem 14. The bank is a price taker in both the fixed-rate market at 9 percent and the rate-sensitive market at the T-bill rate plus 1.5 percent. A securities dealer has a large portfolio of rate-sensitive assets funded with fixed-rate liabilities. The dealer is a price taker in a fixed-rate asset market paying 8.5 percent and a floating-rate asset market paying the 91-day T-bill rate plus 1.25 percent. All interest is paid annually.

a. What is the interest rate risk exposure to the securities dealer?

b. How can the bank and the securities dealer use a swap to hedge their respective interest rate risk exposures?

c. What are the total potential gains to the swap trade?

d. Consider the following two-year swap of asset cash flows: An annual fixed-rate asset cash flow of 8.6 percent in exchange for a floating-rate asset cash flow of T-bill plus 125 basis points. The total swap intermediary fee is 5 basis points. How are the swap gains apportioned between the bank and the securities dealer if they each hedge their interest rate risk exposures using this swap?

e. What are the swap net cash flows if T-bill rates at the end of the first year are 7.75 percent and at the end of the second year, 5.5 percent? Assume that the notional value is $107.14 million.

f. What are the sources of the swap gains to trade?

g. What are the implications for the efficiency of cash markets?

16. Consider the following currency swap of coupon interest on the following assets:

5 percent (annual coupon) fixed-rate $1 million bond

5 percent (annual coupon) fixed-rate bond denominated in Swiss francs (Sf)

Spot exchange rates: Sf1.5/$

a. What is the face value of the Sf bond if the investments are equivalent at spot rates?

b. What are the realized cash flows, assuming no change in spot exchange rates? What are the net cash flows on the swap?

c. What are the cash flows if the spot exchange rate falls to Sf0.50/$? What are the net cash flows on the swap?

d. What are the cash flows if spot exchange rate rises to Sf2.25/$? What are the net cash flows on the swap?

e. Describe the underlying cash position that would prompt the FI to hedge by swapping dollars for Swiss francs.

17. Consider the following fixed–floating rate currency swap of assets: 5 percent (annual coupon) fixed-rate $1 million bond and floating-rate Sf1.5 million bond set at LIBOR annually. Currently LIBOR is 4 percent. The face value of the swap is Sf1.5 million. Spot exchange rate: Sf1.5/$.

a. What are the realized cash flows assuming no change in the spot exchange rate? What are the realized cash flows on the swap at the spot exchange rate?

b. If the 1-year forward rate is Sf1.538 per $, what are the end-of-year net cash flows on the swap? Assume LIBOR is unchanged.

c. If LIBOR increases to 6 percent, what are the end-of-year net cash flows on the swap? Evaluate at the forward rate.

18. What is a total return swap?

19. Give two reasons why credit swaps have been the fastest-growing form of swaps in recent years.

20. How does a pure credit swap differ from a total return swap? How does it differ from a digital default option?

21. Why is the credit risk on a swap lower than the credit risk on a loan?

22. What is netting by novation?

23. A Canadian FI has most of its assets in the form of Swiss franc-denominated floating-rate loans. Its liabilities consist mostly of fixed-rate dollar-denominated CDs. What type of currency risk and interest rate risk does this FI face? How might it use a swap to eliminate some of those risks?

The following problem refers to material in Appendix 25A, available at the Online Learning Centre.

24. The following information is available on a three-year swap contract. One-year maturity notes are currently priced at par and pay a coupon rate of 5 percent annually. Two-year maturity notes are currently priced at par and pay a coupon rate of 5.5 percent annually. Three-year maturity notes are currently priced at par and pay a coupon rate of 5.75 percent annually. The terms of a three-year swap of $100 million notional value are 5.45 percent annual fixed-rate payments in exchange for floating-rate payments tied to the annual discount yield.

a. If an insurance company buys this swap, what can you conclude about the interest rate risk exposure of the company's underlying cash position?

b. What are the realized cash flows expected over the three-year life of the swap?

c. What are the realized cash flows that occur over the three-year life of the swap if $d_2 = 4.95$ percent and $d_3 = 6.1$ percent?

Appendix 25A   Setting Rates on an Interest Rate Swap

View Appendix 25A at the Online Learning Centre: www.mcgrawhill.ca/olc/saunders.

CHAPTER 26

Loan Sales

In this chapter, we consider the role of loan sales in managing credit risk and

- ▸ provide an overview of the loan sales market
- ▸ define and look at types of loan sales
- ▸ summarize who are the buyers and sellers of loans
- ▸ discuss why banks and other FIs would sell loans
- ▸ evaluate the factors that deter and encourage loan sales

INTRODUCTION

Traditionally, banks and other FIs have relied on a number of contractual mechanisms to control the credit risks of lending. These have included (1) requiring higher interest rate spreads and fees on loans to more risky borrowers, (2) restricting or rationing loans to more risky borrowers, (3) requiring enhanced seniority (collateral) for the bank over the assets of risky borrowers, (4) diversifying across different types of risky borrowers, and (5) placing more restrictive covenants on risky borrowers' actions, such as restrictions on the use of proceeds from asset sales, new debt issues, and dividend payments. These traditional mechanisms for controlling or managing credit risk were described in Chapters 11 and 12.

Additionally, in Chapters 23 through 25 we discussed the increasing use of credit derivatives in the forward, options, and swaps markets to manage credit risk—for example, the use of digital put options to control the credit risk of an individual loan or portfolio of loans. In addition, FIs may require borrowers to hedge their own risks, especially when the FI makes floating-rate loans to borrowers. When interest rates rise, the borrower of a floating-rate loan may have greater difficulty meeting interest rate payments. However, if the borrower has hedged the risk of rising rates in the derivatives market (e.g., by selling interest rate futures or receiving floating payments—paying fixed payments in an interest rate swap), the borrower is in a far better position to meet its contractual payments to the FI. As a result, the credit risk exposure of the FI is reduced.[1]

This and the following chapter on securitization describe the growing role of loan sales and other newer types of techniques (such as the good bank–bad bank structure) increasingly used by FI managers to control credit risk. Although loan sales have been in existence for many years, the use of loan sales (by removing existing loans from the balance sheet) was recognized as a valuable additional tool in an FI manager's portfolio of credit risk management techniques (see the Industry Perspectives feature). However, as we discuss later in the chapter, the credit crisis of 2007–2008 caused FIs and their regulators to re-think the role of credit risk transfer mechanisms.

---

[1] In addition, the floating-rate loans may enable the FI to better hedge its own duration gap exposure.

655

INDUSTRY PERSPECTIVES

SUDDENLY, BANKS ARE ACTING A LOT LIKE BOND MARKETS

When numerous companies suddenly found investors unwilling to buy their debt this year [2002], amid a rocky economy and accounting scandals, many turned to their lenders of last resort, their banks. They discovered banking has changed a lot. And some discovered that loans cost them a good deal more. Banks traditionally have been the institutions that take a long-term view of a company's prospects, management and ability to repay a debt. By contrast, the fast-paced, fickle bond market can change its mind in an instant about a company's creditworthiness and how much to charge. But many borrowers are finding that banks' loan business had come to look a lot like the markets. . . .

Scarred by their early-1990s experience, they often don't hold onto loans, especially those to lower quality companies. Increasingly, banks sell pieces of their loans to other banks, to specialized investment funds, insurance companies or to other institutional investors. As a result, the loans are subject to all the pricing and other tactics of the markets. And the banks are acting less like lenders and more like middlemen between borrowers and investors.

Although this shift means painfully high interest rates for some, it has benefits to the overall economy in making credit available. Even if a bank considers a particular borrower too risky, it can usually find someone willing to share the risk. And the capital markets help it find out what interest rate is needed to compensate for the risk. "The actual creditworthiness of borrowers had come down," Fed Chairman Alan Greenspan observed earlier this year. "There has, however, been no evidence of anything remotely resembling the credit crunch that we had a decade ago, where you just could not get a loan out of a commercial bank no matter what your creditworthiness was, at least in some cases." . . .

Bank loans and pieces of them now change hands in an increasingly active secondary market. Its daily turnover of about $500 million is puny next to the stock and bond markets but up 15-fold from a decade earlier, according to Credit Suisse First Boston. When a company sets out to borrow now, its lenders can see how this secondary market is valuing its old loans, and adjust terms of this new borrowing accordingly. Initially, many companies weren't happy that banks were selling off their loans. "Today everyone accepts that if you want a noninvestment-grade loan, it's very similar to a bond deal," says Scott Page, co-manager of senior debt portfolios at Eaton Vance Management in Boston. "You're not doing a handshake deal on the golf course with a handful of banks. But ultimately you have a more reliable source of capital." . . .

Source: Greg Ip, *The Wall Street Journal*, September 17, 2002, p. A1, www.wsj.com.

THE BANK LOAN SALES MARKET

Definition of a Loan Sale

Credit derivatives (such as credit swaps) discussed in Chapters 23 through 25 allow FIs to reduce credit risk without physically removing assets from their balance sheet. Loan sales allow FIs to reduce credit risk completely by removing the loan from the balance sheet. Specifically, a **bank loan sale** occurs when an FI originates a loan and sells it either with or without recourse to an outside buyer. Many loan agreements contain a clause that allows an FI to sell the loan to another buyer, sometimes without having to notify the borrower of the sale. This facilitates the legal transfer of ownership of the financial asset and provides increased flexibility for an FI to adjust its balance sheet.

If a loan is sold without recourse, not only is it removed from the FI's balance sheet but the FI has no explicit liability if the loan eventually goes bad. Panel A of Table 26–1 shows an FI's balance sheet before and after a $20 million loan sale. The buyer (and not the FI that originated the loan) bears all the credit risk. If, however, the loan is sold with **recourse,** under certain conditions the buyer can put the

bank loan sale
Sale of a loan originated by an FI with or without recourse to an outside buyer.

recourse
The ability of a loan buyer to sell the loan back to the originator if it goes bad.

TABLE 26–1 FI Balance Sheet Before and After a $20 Million Loan Sale ($ millions)

Panel A: Loan Sale without Recourse

Before Loan Sale				After Loan Sale			
Assets		**Liabilities/Equity**		**Assets**		**Liabilities/Equity**	
Cash assets	$ 10	Deposit	$ 90	Cash assets	$ 10	Deposits	$ 90
				Loans	70		
Loans	90	Equity	10	New investments	20	Equity	10
	$100		$100		$100		$100

Panel B: Loan Sale with Recourse

Before Loan Sale				After Loan Sale			
Assets		**Liabilities/Equity**		**Assets**		**Liabilities/Equity**	
Cash assets	$ 10	Deposit	$ 90	Cash assets	$ 10	Deposits	$ 90
				Loans	70		
Loans	90	Equity	10	New investments	20	Equity	10
	$100		$100		$100		$100
				Off balance sheet: Loan sale (contingent liability)			$ 20

loan back to the selling FI; therefore, the FI retains a contingent credit risk liability. Panel B of Table 26–1 shows the FI's balance sheet, including the contingent liability from the loan sale held off the balance sheet. In practice, most loans are sold without recourse because a loan sale is technically removed from the balance sheet only when the buyer has no future credit risk claim on the FI. Importantly, loan sales involve no creation of new types of securities such as the pass-throughs, CMOs, and MBSs described in Chapter 27. As such, loan sales are a primitive form of securitization in that loan selling creates a secondary market for loans in which ownership of the loan is simply transferred to the loan buyer.

Types of Loan Sales

The loan sales market has three segments: Two involve the sale and trading of domestic loans, while the third involves emerging-market loan sales and trading. Since we described emerging-market loan sales in Chapter 15 on sovereign risk, we concentrate on the North American loan sales market here.

Traditional Short Term

In the traditional short-term segment of the market, FIs sell loans with short maturities, often one to three months. This market has characteristics similar to those of the market for commercial paper issued by corporations in that loan sales have similar maturities and issue size. Loan sales, however, usually have yields that are 1 to 10 basis points above those of commercial paper of a similar rating. In particular, the loan sales market in which an FI originates and sells a short-term loan of a corporation is a close substitute for the issuance of commercial paper. The key characteristics of the short-term loan sales market are

- Secured by assets of the borrowing firm.
- Made to investment-grade borrowers or better.

- Issued for a short term (90 days or less).
- Has yields closely tied to the commercial paper rate.
- Sold in units of $1 million and up.

highly leveraged transaction (HLT) loan
A loan made to finance a merger and acquisition: A leveraged buyout results in a high leverage ratio for the borrower.

Until 1984 and the emergence of the **highly leveraged transactions (HLTs)** and emerging-market loan markets, traditional short-term loan sales dominated the loan sales market. The growth of the commercial paper market, as well as the increased ability of banks to underwrite commercial paper (see Chapter 21), also has reduced the importance of this market segment.

HLT Loan Sales

www.loanpricing.com

With the growth in mergers and acquisitions (M&As) and leveraged buyouts (LBOs) via highly leveraged transactions especially during the period of 1985–1989, a new segment in the loan sales market appeared. One measure of the increase in HLTs is that between January 1987 and September 1994, the Loan Pricing Corporation reported 4,122 M&A deals with a combined dollar amount of new-issue HLT loans estimated at US$593.5 billion.

What constitutes an HLT loan has often caused dispute. However, in October 1989 the three U.S. federal bank regulators adopted a definition of an HLT loan as one that (1) involves a buyout, acquisition, or recapitalization and (2) doubles the company's liabilities and results in a leverage ratio higher than 50 percent, results in a leverage ratio higher than 75 percent, or is designated as an HLT by a syndication agent. HLT loans mainly differ according to whether they are non-distressed (bid price exceeds 90 cents per $1 of loans) or distressed (bid price is less than 90 cents per $1 of loans or the borrower is in default).

Virtually all HLT loans have the following characteristics:

- They are term loans (TLs).
- They are secured by assets of the borrowing firm (usually given senior secured status).
- They have a long maturity (often three- to six-year maturities).
- They have floating rates tied to LIBOR, the prime rate, or a CD rate (normally 200 to 275 basis points above these rates).
- They have strong covenant protection.

financial distress
A period when a borrower is unable to meet a payment obligation to lenders and other creditors.

Nevertheless, HLTs tend to be quite heterogeneous with respect to the size of the issue, the interest payment date, interest indexing, and prepayment features. After origination, some HLT borrowers, such as Macy's and El Paso Electric, suffered periods of **financial distress.** As a result, a distinction is usually made between the markets for distressed and non-distressed HLTs. Spreads on HLT loans behave more like investment-grade bonds than like high-yield bonds. A possible reason for this is that HLT loans tend to be more senior in bankruptcy and to have greater collateral backing than do high-yield bonds.

Approximately 100 banks and securities firms make a market in this debt either as brokers or (less commonly) as broker–dealers, including Bear Stearns (now a division of JPMorgan Chase), CIBC, Prudential Securities, and Goldman Sachs. Most of these FIs view trading in this debt as similar to trading in junk bonds.

Types of Loan Sales Contracts

There are two basic types of loan sale contracts or mechanisms by which loans can be transferred between seller and buyer: participations and assignments. Currently, assignments comprise the bulk of loan sales trading.

Participations

participation in a loan
Buying a share in a loan syndication with limited contractual control and rights over the borrower.

The unique features of **participations in loans** are

- The holder (buyer) is not a party to the underlying credit agreement so that the initial contract between loan seller and borrower remains in place after the sale.
- The loan buyer can exercise only partial control over changes in the loan contract's terms. The holder can vote only on material changes to the loan contract, such as the interest rate or collateral backing.

The economic implication of these features is that the buyer of the loan participation has a double risk exposure: a risk exposure to the borrower and a risk exposure to the loan-selling FI. Specifically, if the selling FI fails, the loan participation bought by an outside party may be characterized as an unsecured obligation of the FI rather than as a true sale if there are grounds for believing that some explicit or implicit recourse existed between the loan seller and the loan buyer. Alternatively, the borrower's claims against a failed selling FI may be set off against its loans from that FI, reducing the amount of loans outstanding and adversely impacting the buyer of a participation in those loans. As a result of these exposures, the buyer bears a double monitoring cost as well.

Assignments

assignment
Buying a share in a loan syndication with some contractual control and rights over the borrower.

Because of the monitoring costs and risks involved in participations, loans are sold on an assignment basis in more than 90 percent of the cases on the North American market. The key features of an **assignment** are

- All rights are transferred on sale, meaning the loan buyer now holds a direct claim on the borrower.
- Transfer is normally associated with legal proof that a change of ownership has occurred.

Although ownership rights are generally much clearer in a loan sale by assignment, frequently contractual terms limit the seller's scope regarding to whom the loan can be sold. In particular, the loan contract may require either the FI agent or the borrower to agree to the sale. The loan contract may also restrict the sale to a certain class of institutions, such as those that meet certain net worth/net asset size conditions. (An *FI agent* is an FI that distributes interest and principal payments to lenders in loan syndications with multiple lenders.) Assignments are common in loan syndications, discussed in Chapter 12. In a syndicated loan, two or more banks agree to jointly make a loan to a borrower. The syndicate is formed around the arrangers, which generally include the borrower's relationship banks, who retain a portion of the loan and look for junior participants (e.g., smaller banks).

accrued interest
The loan seller's claim to part of the next interest payment on the loan.

Currently, the trend appears to be toward loan contracts being originated with very limited assignment restrictions. This is true in both the North American domestic and the emerging-market loan sales markets. The most tradable loans are those that can be assigned without buyer restrictions. Even so, one has to distinguish between floating-rate and fixed-rate assignment loans. For floating-rate loans, most loan sales by assignment occur on the loan's repricing date (which may be two or four times a year), due to complexities for the agent FI in calculating and transferring accrued interest—especially given the heterogeneous nature of floating-rate loan indexes such as LIBOR. In addition, the non-standardization of **accrued interest** payments in fixed-rate loan assignments (trade date, assignment date, coupon payment date) adds complexity and friction to this market.

Moreover, while the FI agent may have a full record of the initial owners of the loans, it does not always have an up-to-date record of loan ownership changes and related transfers following trades. This means that great difficulties often occur for the borrower, FI agent, and loan buyer in ensuring that the current holder of the loan receives the interest and principal payments due. Finally, the buyer of the loan often needs to verify the original loan contract and establish the full implications of the purchase regarding the buyer's rights to collateral if the borrower defaults.

Because of these contractual problems, trading frictions, and costs, some loan sales take as long as three months to complete; reportedly, up to 50 percent eventually fail to be completed at all. In many cases, the incentive to renege on a contract arises because market prices move away from those originally agreed so that the counterparty finds reasons to delay the completion of a loan sale and/or eventually refuses to complete the transaction.[2]

TRENDS IN LOAN SALES

correspondent banking
A relationship entered into between a small bank and a big bank in which the big bank provides a number of deposit, lending, and other services.

Banks and other FIs have sold loans among themselves for over 100 years. In fact, a large part of **correspondent banking** involves small banks making loans that are too big for them to hold on their balance sheets—for lending concentration, risk, or capital adequacy reasons—and selling parts of these loans to large banks with which they have a long-term deposit-lending correspondent relationship. In turn, the large banks often sell parts of their loans called *participations* to smaller banks. Even though this market has existed for many years, it grew slowly until the early 1980s, when it entered a period of spectacular growth, largely due to expansion in **project finance loans** as well as highly leveraged transaction loans to finance leveraged buyouts and mergers and acquisitions. Specifically, the volume of loans sold by North American banks grew from less than US$20 billion in 1980 to US$285 billion in 1989. Between 1990 and 1994 the volume of loan sales fell almost equally dramatically, along with the decline in LBOs and M&As as a result of the credit crunch associated with the 1990–1991 recession. In 1994, the volume of loan sales had fallen to approximately US$20 billion.

project finance loan
A loan made to a single-purpose entity where principal and interest are paid from the cash flows of the project.

Due to an expanding economy and a resurgence in M&As, Loan Pricing Corporation reported that secondary loan trading volume reached US$101.97 billion in 2000 (see Figure 26–1). Triggered by an economic downturn, distressed loan sales (loans trading below 90 cents on the dollar) jumped from 11.3 percent of total loan sales in 1999 to 42.3 percent in 2002. From 2006 to 2008, the percentage of distressed loan sales fell to less than 20 percent, but liquidity needs and capital constraints drove secondary sales of par loans to a record US$310.20 billion in 2007. Total secondary loan sales were greater than US$300 billion in 2007, 2008, and 2009, reflecting the impact of the global market turmoil on FIs.

Many of these loans are syndicated, involving many sponsoring banks. For example, in 2008 the Loan Pricing Corporation reported that JPMorgan Chase was the leading loan syndicator in the worldwide secondary loan market, sponsoring 415 deals worth US$198 billion. JPMorgan Chase, Citigroup (US$116 billion), Bank of America (US$137 billion), Deutsche Bank (US$35 billion), and

---

[2] However, in recent years, completion of a trade within 10 days (or $T + 10$) has become an increasing convention.

FIGURE 26–1
U.S. Secondary
Loan Market
Volume, Trading
1991–2009 Q2
(US$ billions)

Source: Loan Pricing Corporation, May 2009,
www.loanpricing.com.

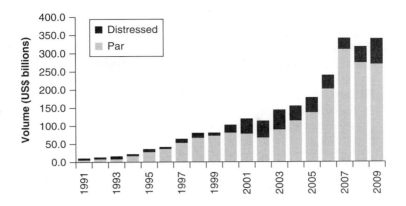

Wachovia Securities (US$28 billion) were the top five secondary-market loan syndicators in 2008.

The Canadian debt market, dominated by the top five banks, plays a very small role in loan sales in North America. Recent figures estimate that $100 million (Canadian) bad debt loans were sold in 2000 and only $300 to $400 million were forecast to be sold in 2005. In 2001, Canadian Imperial Bank of Commerce (CIBC) sold $848 million in U.S. corporate loans to Ark II LLC, a U.S.-based firm, in order to reduce its exposure to credit risk. More recently, Bank of Nova Scotia (BNS) sold some of its US$825 million bridge financing to Masonite to U.S. hedge funds. However, when loan defaults are low and banks have sufficient capital, there is little need for a bank to sell its loans. The major Canadian banks consider loan sales to be a credit management technique and part of their risk management strategy. U.S. companies such as Allied Interstate Inc., Cerberus Capital Management LP (which purchased Air Canada debt during its restructuring in 2003), Portfolio Management Canada Inc., and Portfolio Recovery Associates operate in Canada, but concerns about privacy issues related to the USA Patriot Act and banks' concerns about their reputation appear to have so far limited sales of loans extended to Canadian customers to U.S. buyers. However, Basel II and the 2007–2008 market turmoil provided opportunities for loan sales as global banks readjusted their capital levels (Chapter 20).[3]

www.cibc.com

www.scotiabank.com

The Buyers and the Sellers
The Buyers
Of the wide array of potential buyers, some are concerned with only a certain segment of the market for regulatory and strategic reasons. In particular, an increasingly specialized group of buyers of distressed HLT loans includes investment banks, **vulture funds,** and other banks.

vulture fund
A specialized hedge fund that invests in distressed loans.

---

[3] For more discussion on the secondary market for loans, see A. Gande and A. Saunders, *Are Banks Still Special When There Is a Secondary Market for Loans?* New York University working paper, October 2006; and E. Altman, A. Gande, and A. Saunders, *Informational Efficiency of Loans versus Bonds: Evidence from Secondary Market Prices,* NYU Working Paper No. S-FI-04-02, December 2008.

Investment Banks   Investment banks are predominantly buyers of HLT loans because (1) analysis of these loans utilizes investment skills similar to those used in junk bond trading and (2) investment banks were often closely associated with the HLT distressed borrower in underwriting the original junk bond/HLT deals. As such, large investment banking operations—for example, Credit Suisse First Boston, Merrill Lynch, and Goldman Sachs—are relatively more informed agents in this market, either by acting as market makers or in taking short-term positions on movements in the discount from par.

Vulture Funds   Vulture funds are specialized hedge funds established to invest in distressed loans, often with an agenda that may not include helping the distressed firm to survive (see Chapter 5 for a discussion of hedge funds). They include funds run by entrepreneurs such as George Soros. These investments can be active, especially for those seeking to use the loans purchased for bargaining in a restructuring deal; this generates restructuring returns that strongly favour the loan purchaser. Alternatively, such loans may be held as passive investments, such as high-yield securities in a well-diversified portfolio of distressed securities. Many vulture funds are in fact managed by investment banking firms.

The common perception of vulture funds is that after picking up distressed loans at a discount, they force firms to restructure or are quick to realize the breakup value of the firm: turning their 50-cent-on-the-dollar investment into a fast 70-cent-on-the-dollar profit. Thus, a vulture fund's reputation is often not a congenial one. A possible reason for this adverse reputation is that while banks are looking for a return of loan principal in a restructuring, vulture funds are looking for a return on capital invested. That is, vulture funds are transaction-driven, not relationship-based. Unlike banks, vulture funds are far less interested in making decisions based on developing and maintaining long-term relationships with the corporation in question. Nevertheless, they provide an exit strategy for investors and creditors, and enable assets to be liquidated in an orderly manner. As well, loan purchasers who also hold credit default swaps (CDSs) may have more incentive to see the borrower default than to restructure the loan.

For the non-distressed HLT market and the traditional loan sales market, the major buyers are other domestic or foreign banks, insurance companies and pension funds, closed-end bank loan mutual funds, and non-financial corporations.

Other Banks   Inter-bank loan sales are at the core of the traditional market and have historically revolved around correspondent banking relationships and, in the United States, regional banking/branching restrictions. Restrictions on nationwide banking have often led U.S. banks to originate regionally undiversified and borrower-undiversified loan portfolios. Small U.S. banks often sell loan participations to their large correspondents to improve regional/borrower diversification and to avoid regulatory-imposed, single-borrower loan concentration ceilings. In Canada, FIs (banks, authorized foreign banks, and trust and loan companies) regulated by the Office of the Superintendent of Financial Services (OSFI) are subject to the "prudent person approach" and so must have written internal policies regarding large exposures to any one customer, country, or other FI. These FIs are limited to 25 percent of capital to any one entity and, in the normal course of business, are expected to be below this limit. Thus large loans may be originated with the intention of syndication to other banks. Foreign bank subsidiaries are limited to 100 percent of their total capital to any one entity, and so may be both buyers and sellers of loans. Foreign banks thus are able to diversify their North American

www.osfi-bsif.gc.ca

downsizing
Shrinking the asset size of an FI.

loan portfolios without having a banking network in either Canada or the United States and so, in recent years, purchased over 40 percent of the loans sold in the United States However, asset **downsizing,** as a result of the global financial market turmoil in 2008, has caused this source of demand for loan sales to contract.

Insurance Companies and Pension Funds   Subject to meeting liquidity and quality or investment-grade regulatory restrictions, insurance companies (such as Aetna) and pension funds are important buyers of long-term maturity loans.

Closed- and Open-End Bank Loan Mutual Funds   First established in the United States in 1988, these leveraged mutual funds, such as Merrill Lynch Prime Fund, invest in domestic U.S. bank loans. While they purchase loans on the secondary market, such as loan resales, the largest funds also have moved into primary loan syndications because of the attractive fee income available. That is, these mutual funds participate in funding loans originated by commercial banks. The mutual fund, in turn, receives a fee or part of the interest payment. Indeed, some money centre banks, such as JPMorgan Chase, have actively encouraged closed-end fund participation in primary loan syndications.

There is no track record for this type of loan purchaser in Canada since the first bank loan mutual fund (Trimark Floating Rate Income Fund) was created by AIM Trimark in 2005. However, First Trust/Highland Capital Floating Rate Income Fund was forced to suspend its cash distributions in May 2009 due to a decline in its loan portfolio credit rating and higher default rates. It is estimated that U.S.-based bank loan mutual funds (e.g., Eaton Vance Floating Rate, Fidelity Floating Rate Income) have total assets of US$38.5 billion.[4]

Non-Financial Corporations   There are some corporations that buy loans, but this activity is limited mostly to the financial services arms of the very largest U.S. and European companies (e.g., GE Capital and ITT Finance) and amounts to no more than 5 percent of total U.S. domestic loan sales.[5]

The Sellers

The sellers of domestic loans and HLT loans are major banks, foreign banks, investment banks, and governments and their agencies (e.g., FDIC, CDIC).

Major Banks   In the United States, loan selling has been dominated by the largest money centre banks. In recent years, market concentration on the loan-selling side has been accentuated by the growth of HLTs (and the important role major money centre banks have played in originating loans in HLT deals) as well as the growth in real estate loan sales. Large U.S. money centre banks have engaged in large (real estate) loan sales directly or have formalized such sales through the mechanism of a "good bank–bad bank" structure.

Good Bank–Bad Bank   Bad banks are special-purpose vehicles organized to liquidate portfolios of non-performing loans. The principal objective in their creation is to maximize asset values by separating good loans (in the "good bank") from bad loans (in the "bad bank"). Past examples of bad banks include Grant Street National Bank (established by Mellon Bank), National Loan Bank (established by

---

[4] See Rudy Luukko, *AIM Trimark Becomes Pioneer of Bank-Loan Funds in Canada,* Morningstar Research Inc., February 8, 2005, www.morningstar.ca, and CNW Group Ltd., www.newswire.ca, May 21, 2009.

[5] Non-financial corporations are bigger buyers in the emerging-market loan sales market as part of debt–equity swaps (see Chapter 15).

Chemical Bank), and National Asset Bank (established by First Interstate).[6] For example, Mellon Bank wrote down the face value of US$941 million in real estate loans and sold them to a specially created bad bank subsidiary—Grant Street National Bank—for US$577 million. This special-purpose bad bank was funded by bond issues and common and preferred stock. Managers of the bad bank were given equity (junior preferred stock) as an incentive mechanism to generate maximum values in liquidating the loans purchased from Mellon (i.e., achieving a market resale value greater than US$577 million).

Table 26–2 illustrates the sale of non-performing loans from a good bank to a subsidiary bad bank. In panel A of Table 26–2, the good bank has $950 million of non-performing loans along with $2,500 million in performing loans and $500 million in cash assets on its balance sheet before the loan sale. The assets are financed with $2,500 million in deposits, $750 million in purchased funds, and $700 million in equity. If the bad bank, in panel B, buys the non-performing loans (with the proceeds of a bond, preferred stock, and common stock financing) for $580 million, the good bank gets these loans off of its balance sheet, incurring a $370 million loss in equity (i.e., $950 million face value of loans minus $580 million received in their purchase). The proceeds of the loan sale are then used to pay off purchased funds, bringing their balance down to $170 million, or $750 million minus $580 million.

TABLE 26–2 Good Bank–Bad Bank Balance Sheets Before and After a Loan Sale ($ millions)

Panel A: Good Bank

		Before Loan Sale					After Loan Sale	
Assets			**Liabilities/Equity**		**Assets**			**Liabilities/Equity**
Cash assets	$ 500		Deposits	$2,500	Cash assets	$ 500	Deposits	$2,500
Loans			Purchased		Loans		Purchased	
Performing	2,500		funds	750	Performing	2,500	funds	170
Non-performing	950		Equity	700	Non-performing	0	Equity	330
	$3,950			$3,950		$3,000		$3,000

Panel B: Bad Bank

		Before Loan Sale					After Loan Sale	
Assets			**Liabilities/Equity**		**Assets**			**Liabilities/Equity**
Cash assets	$ 600		Bonds	$300	Cash assets	$ 20	Bonds	$300
Loans	0		Preferred		Loans	580	Preferred	
			stock	100			stock	100
			Common				Common	
			stock	200			stock	200
	$ 600			$600		$600		$600

[6] This technique also has been used outside the United States. For example, in 1998 the good bank–bad bank structure was adopted by the Indonesian government as a way of resolving the bad debt crisis in the domestic banking industry. In the early 2000s, this format was adopted in Japan as a way to separate non-performing loans from other bank assets. It is also the mechanism proposed for cleaning up the FIs carrying toxic assets in 2008 and 2009. In recent cleanups, governments became the owners of the bad assets.

The bad bank now has the $950 million face value loans (for which it paid $580 million) on its balance sheet. These loans can be restructured or disposed of. If the loans realize more than $580 million, additional returns can be passed through to the bad bank common stockholders in dividends or used to repurchase bonds or preferred stock.

There are at least five reasons for believing that loan sales through a bad bank vehicle will be value-enhancing compared to the originating bank itself retaining (and eventually selling) these loans:

1. The bad bank enables bad assets to be managed by loan workout specialists.
2. The good bank's reputation and access to deposit and funding markets tend to be improved once bad loans are removed from the balance sheet.
3. Because the bad bank does not have any short-term deposits (i.e., is a self-liquidating entity), it can follow an optimal disposition strategy for bad assets, as it is not overly concerned with liquidity needs.
4. As in the case of Mellon's bad bank, contracts for managers can be created to maximize their incentives to generate enhanced values from loan sales.
5. The good bank–bad bank structure reduces information asymmetries about the value of the good bank's assets (the so-called *lemons problem*), thus potentially increasing its attractiveness to risk-averse investors.

The good bank–bad bank solution is relatively new and, given the stability of the banking system, has not been employed in Canada as yet. The major banks in Canada use loan sales along with credit derivatives to manage their credit exposure. For example, in the second quarter of 2009, Bank of Montreal reported that it sold or securitized mortgages with low margins to concentrate on loans with higher margins (e.g., credit card loans). The five largest banks (BMO, BNS, CIBC, RBC, and TD) reported an increase of $1.2 billion over Q2, 2008, of the amounts set aside for impaired loans.

www.bmo.com

Foreign Banks   To the extent that foreign banks are sellers rather than buyers of loans, these loans come out of branch networks such as Japanese-owned banks in California or through their market-making activities selling loans originated in their home country in the North American loan sales markets. One of the major market makers in the North American loan sales market (especially the HLT market) is the Dutch FI, ING Bank. Barclays Bank, BNP Paribas, Deutsche Bank, and Royal Bank of Scotland also participate in this market.

Investment Banks   Investment banks, such as Goldman Sachs and Bear Stearns have also acted as loan sellers either as part of their market-making function (selling loans they have originated) or as active traders. Again, these loan sales are generally confined to large HLT transactions.

The U.S. Government and Its Agencies.   In the recent credit crisis, the U.S. government and its agencies have shown an increased willingness to engage in loan sales. This has been aided by the passage of the 1996 Federal Debt Collection Improvements Act, which authorizes federal agencies to sell delinquent and defaulted loan assets. The U.S. Department of Housing and Urban Development also has been an increasingly large seller of mortgage loans on multi-family apartment properties. However, prior to the credit crisis and the extensive U.S. government intervention in 2008 and 2009, the largest loan sales by a government agency to date were made by the Resolution Trust Corporation (RTC). Established in 1989 and

www.fdic.gov
www.hud.gov

disbanded at the end of 1995, the RTC had to resolve more than 700 problem savings institutions through merger, closure, or conservatorship. With respect to the U.S. commercial and industrial loan sale market, RTC dispositions had a relatively moderate supply-side effect, largely because the bulk of RTC's asset sales were real estate assets (such as multi-family mortgages). The tendency of the RTC was to combine good and bad loans into loan packages and sell them at auction to bidders. For example, in an April 21, 1995, auction, it offered the highest bidder a package of 29 different commercial assets for sale—located in New Jersey, New York, and Pennsylvania—with aggregate estimated market values of US$7.5 million. Bidders had only four days to enter bids on this asset package.

In 2009, the FDIC and U.S. Treasury began operating the Legacy Loans Program to remove distressed loans from FIs' balance sheets through public–private investment funds (PPIFs). Canadian FIs have so far not required this type of government support.

CONCEPT QUESTIONS	1. Which loans should have the highest yields: (a) loans sold with recourse or (b) loans sold without recourse? 2. Which have higher yields, junk bonds or HLT loans? Explain your answer. 3. Describe the two basic types of loan sale contracts by which loans can be transferred between seller and buyer. 4. What institutions are the major buyers in the traditional North American loan sales market? What institutions are the major sellers in this market?

WHY BANKS AND OTHER FIs SELL LOANS

The introduction to this chapter stated that one reason that FIs sell loans is to manage their credit risk better. Loan sales remove assets (and credit risk) from the balance sheet and allow an FI to achieve better asset diversification. However, other than credit risk management, there are a number of economic and regulatory reasons that encourage FIs to sell loans. These are discussed below.

Fee Income

An FI can often report any fee income earned from originating (and then selling) loans as current income, whereas interest earned on direct lending can be accrued (as income) only over time. As a result, originating and quickly selling loans can boost an FI's reported income under current accounting rules.

Capital Costs

Like reserve requirements, the capital adequacy requirements imposed on FIs are a burden as long as required capital exceeds the amount the FI believes to be privately beneficial. For tax reasons, debt is a cheaper source of funds than equity capital. Thus, FIs struggling to meet a required assets (A) to capital (K) ratio can reduce this ratio by reducing assets (A) rather than boosting capital (K) (see Chapter 20). One way to downsize or reduce A and reduce the A/K ratio is through loan sales.

Liquidity Risk

In addition to credit risk and interest rate risk, holding loans on the balance sheet can increase the overall illiquidity of an FI's assets. This illiquidity is a problem because FI liabilities tend to be highly liquid. Asset illiquidity can expose an FI to harmful liquidity squeezes whenever liability holders unexpectedly liquidate their claims. To mitigate a liquidity problem, an FI's management can sell some of its loans to outside investors. Thus, the loan sales market has created a secondary market in loans that has significantly reduced the illiquidity of FI loans held as assets on the balance sheet.

CONCEPT QUESTIONS	1. What are some of the economic and regulatory reasons why FIs choose to sell loans? 2. How can an FI use its loans to mitigate a liquidity problem?

FACTORS AFFECTING LOAN SALES GROWTH

The loan sales market has gone through a number of up and down phases in recent years (as discussed above). However, notwithstanding the value of loan sales as a credit risk management tool, there remain a number of factors that will both spur and deter the market's growth and development in future years. We first discuss factors that may deter the market's growth.

Access to the Commercial Paper Market

More and more smaller middle market firms are gaining direct access to the commercial paper market. As a result, they have less need to rely on bank loans to finance their short-term expenditures.

Customer Relationship Effects

As the financial institutions industry consolidates and expands the range of financial services sold, customer relationships are likely to become even more important than they are today. To the extent that a loan customer (borrower) views the sale of its loan by its FI as an adverse statement about the customer's value to the FI,[7] loan sales can harm revenues generated by the FI as current and potential future customers take their business elsewhere.

Legal Concerns

fraudulent conveyance
When a transaction such as a sale of securities or transference of assets to a particular party is ruled illegal.

A number of legal concerns hamper the loan sale market's growth, especially for distressed HLT loans. In particular, while banks are normally secured creditors, this status may be attacked by other creditors if the firm enters bankruptcy. For example, **fraudulent conveyance** proceedings have been brought in the United States against the secured lenders to Revco, Circle K, Allied Stores, and RJR Nabisco. If such legal moves are upheld, then the sale of loans to a particular party may be found to be illegal. Such legal suits represent one of the factors that have slowed the growth of the distressed loan market. Indeed, in many of the most recent HLT sales, loan buyers have demanded a put option feature that allows them to put the loan back to the seller at the purchase price if a transaction is proved to be fraudulent under the Uniform Fraudulent Conveyance Act. Further, a second type

[7] S. Dahiya, M. Puri, and A. Saunders, in "Bank Borrowers and Loan Sales: New Evidence on the Uniqueness of Bank Loans," *Journal of Business*, 2003, pp. 563–582, find that stock returns of borrowers are significantly negatively impacted in the period surrounding the announcement of a loan sale. Further, the post-loan sale period is also marked by a large incidence of bankruptcy filings by those borrowers whose loans are sold. The results support the hypothesis that news of a bank loan sale has a negative certification impact.

of distressed-firm risk may result if, in the process of a loan workout, the FI lender acts more like an equity owner than an outside debtor. For example, the FI may get involved in the day-to-day running of the firm and make strategic investment and asset sales decisions. This could open up claims that the FI's loans should be treated like equity rather than secured debt. That is, the FI's loans may be subordinated in the claims priority ranking or be subject to lender liability.[8]

At least five factors point to an increasing volume of loan sales in the future. These are in addition to the credit risk "hedging" value of loan sales and government sales of the assets of failed FIs.

BIS Capital Requirements

www.bis.org

The Bank for International Settlements (BIS) risk-based capital rules and the proposed reforms to those rules (see Chapter 20) mean that bankers will continue to have strong incentives to sell commercial loans to other FIs and investors to downsize their balance sheets and boost bank capital ratios.

Market Value Accounting

www.sec.gov
www.fasb.org

The U.S. Securities and Exchange Commission (SEC) and the Financial Accounting Standards Board (FASB) have advocated the replacement of book value accounting with market value accounting for financial services firms (see Chapter 20). In addition, capital requirements for interest rate risk and market risk have moved banks toward a market value accounting framework (see Chapter 10). The trend toward the marking to market of assets will make bank loans look more like securities and thus make them easier to sell and/or trade.

Asset Brokerage and Loan Trading

The increased emphasis of large banks as well as investment banks on trading and trading income suggests that significant attention will still be paid to those segments of the loan sales market where price volatility is high and thus potential trading profits can be made. Most HLT loans have floating rates so that their underlying values are in large part insulated from swings in the level of interest rates (unlike fixed-income securities such as government bonds). Nevertheless, the low credit quality of many of these loans and their long maturities create an enhanced potential for credit risk volatility. As a result, a short-term, three-month secured loan to an AAA-rated company is unlikely to show significant future credit risk volatility compared to an eight-year HLT loan to a distressed company. This suggests that trading in loans to below-investment-grade companies will always be attractive for FIs that use their specialized credit monitoring skills as asset traders rather than as asset transformers in participating in the market.

Credit Ratings

There is a growing trend toward the "credit rating" of loans offered for sale. Unlike bonds, a loan credit rating reflects more than the financial soundness of the underlying borrowing corporation. In particular, the value of the underlying collateral can change a loan's credit rating up to one full category above a standard bond

---

[8] See C. James, "When Do Banks Take Equity in Debt Restructurings?" *Review of Financial Studies,* 1995, pp. 1209–1234. See also P. McGraw and G. Roberts, "Lender Liability as a Contract Alteration," *Banking and Finance Law Review,* 12(1), 1996, pp. 1–14.

rating. As more loans are rated, their attractiveness to secondary market buyers is likely to increase.

Purchase and Sale of Foreign Bank Loans

With over US$1,200 billion in doubtful and troubled loans on their books in the early 2000s, Japanese banks presented a huge potential market for the sale of distressed loans. A number of commercial and investment banks established funds to buy up some of the bad loans. For example, in 2003 Goldman Sachs announced a US$9.3 billion fund to buy troubled loans from Japan's second largest bank, SMFG. This fund represented the first transfer of a bad-loan package of this size to a non-government-affiliated entity in Japan. This deal provided banks with a way of removing bad loans from their balance sheets while still retaining control over the corporate restructuring process.[9] This mechanism is useful for FIs restructuring after 2008–2009, as shown below.

THE GLOBAL CREDIT AND LIQUIDITY CRISIS, 2008–2009

As shown in Figure 26–1, the secondary loan market has been impacted by the credit and liquidity crisis that hit global financial markets in 2007 and 2008. There was a decline in trading volume for both distressed and non-distressed loans. Loan Pricing Corporation reported that total loan issuance in the United States declined by 55 percent from US$1.7 trillion in 2007 to US$764 billion in 2008. FIs globally were burdened with toxic assets, non-performing loans, and a global liquidity crisis that shut down the inter-bank market as well as the money markets in the third and fourth quarters of 2008. This meant that borrowers were looking to replace commercial paper and other short-term market funds with bank loans at a time when banks were writing off loans and therefore in need of raising capital or selling assets in order to meet their regulatory capital requirements. The inability to remove loans, both performing and non-performing, from an FI's balance sheet, either through loan sales or securitization (see Chapter 27), resulted in government programs to provide liquidity and to purchase assets as we discussed here and in Chapter 1.

A comparison of Greg Ip's 2002 article in *The Wall Street Journal* (see the Industry Perspectives feature near the beginning of this chapter) with Barry Critchley's 2008 article in the *Financial Post* (see the following Industry Perspectives feature) illustrates the change in our view of global financial markets. In 2002, loan sales were seen as a valid risk management technique likely to pose a minor systemic risk to the markets and, according to Alan Greenspan, the Federal Reserve chairman, there was "no evidence of anything remotely resembling the credit crunch we had a decade ago, where you just could not get a loan out of a commercial bank no matter what your creditworthiness. . . . " Greenspan's statement was prophetic as, by September 2008, credit markets were disrupted and it was difficult for even a highly credit-worthy borrower to draw down existing loan commitments or to increase its credit facilities. The deleveraging process of FIs, non-financial firms, and consumers in 2008 and 2009 resulted in a slowdown in the global economy. The "originate-to-distribute model" that drove the loan sales and securitization

---

[9] See "SMFG Links with Goldman to Tackle Bad Loans," *Financial Times*, October 9, 2003, p. 32.

INDUSTRY PERSPECTIVES

PUSH FOR LIMITS ON LOAN SALES

It's a mouthful of a title—Moral hazard and adverse selection in the originate-to-distribute model of bank credit—and is a little daunting, but the material contained in the 17-page article makes it a worthwhile read.

And what's more, the study is topical given the ongoing problems caused by subprime mortgages, which are loans originated by a lender, onsold to a packager (normally an investment bank) and sold again to investors. Along the way, there are lots of fees.

The paper is written by Antje Berndt, who is from the Tepper School of Business at Carnegie Mellon University, and Anurag Gupta, who is from the Weatherhead School of Management at Case Western Reserve University. The study uses data supplied by Loan Pricing Corp. and the Loan Syndication and Trading Association. The study focuses on those loan transactions originated by a bank and then onsold (for a fee) to investors that want such exposure. The paper is said to be the first to examine the long-term performance of borrowers that have a secondary market for their loans and those that don't.

Here are the key conclusions:

- Borrowers whose loans are sold in the secondary market underperform other bank borrowers by between 8% and 14% per year on a risk-adjusted basis over the three-year period following the sale of the loan;

- And those borrowers suffer a value destruction of about 15% compared with their peers over the same period.

The authors proffer two explanations for those results:

- Banks are originating and selling bad loans based on unobservable private information. In short, they are keeping the good loans and selling the lemons, a practice that's not sustainable in a perfect market; or:

- The severance of the bank–borrower relationship allows the borrowers to undertake suboptimal investing and operating decisions, in the absence of the discipline of bank monitoring. The moral-hazard argument kicks in because banks have diminished incentives to monitor their borrowers once the lending relationship is severed.

The research generates another conclusion: Borrowers whose loans are not sold in the secondary market do not underperform their peers, "reinforcing the inference that bank loan financing is indeed special, except for borrowers whose loans are sold."

What to make of all this? The authors conclude that the originate-to-distribute may not be entirely "socially desirable. We propose regulatory restrictions on loan sales, increased disclosure and a loan trading exchange with a clearinghouse as mechanisms to alleviate these problems."

Source: Barry Critchley, *Financial Post,* December 1, 2008.

markets was being questioned and the future of loan sales, other than syndications, was not clear.

CONCEPT QUESTIONS

1. What are some of the factors that are likely to deter the growth of the loan sales market in the future?
2. What are some specific legal concerns that have hampered the growth of the loan sales market?
3. What are some of the factors that are likely to encourage loan sales growth in the future?
4. Why have the FASB and the SEC advocated that financial services firms replace book value accounting with market value accounting?

Summary

Loan sales provide a primitive alternative to the full securitization of loans through bond packages. In particular, they provide a valuable off-balance-sheet tool to an FI that wishes to manage its credit risk exposure better. The new loan sales market grew rapidly in the 1980s and allowed FIs to sell off short-term and long-term loans of both high and low credit quality. There are a number of important factors that suggest that the loan sales market will continue to grow.

Questions and Problems

1. What is the difference between loans sold with recourse and loans sold without recourse from the perspective of both sellers and buyers?

2. A bank has made a three-year, $10 million loan that pays annual interest of 8 percent. The principal is due at the end of the third year.

   a. The bank is willing to sell this loan with recourse at an interest rate of 8.5 percent. What price should it receive for this loan?

   b. The bank has the option to sell this loan without recourse at a discount rate of 8.75 percent. What price should it receive for this loan?

   c. If the bank expects a 0.5 percent probability of default on this loan, is it better to sell this loan with or without recourse? It expects to receive no interest payments or principal if the loan is defaulted.

3. What are some of the key features of short-term loan sales?

4. Why are yields higher on loan sales than on commercial paper issues with similar maturity and issue size?

5. What are highly leveraged transactions? What constitutes the regulatory definition of an HLT?

6. How do the characteristics of an HLT loan differ from those of a short-term loan that is sold?

7. What is a possible reason why the spreads on HLT loans perform differently than do the spreads on junk bonds?

8. City Bank has made a 10-year, $2 million HLT loan that pays an annual interest of 10 percent. The principal is expected to be paid at maturity.

   a. What should City Bank expect to receive from the sale of this loan if the current market interest rate on loans of this risk is 12 percent?

   b. The price of loans of this risk is currently being quoted in the secondary market at bid–offer prices of 88–89 cents (on each dollar). Translate these quotes into actual prices for the above loan.

   c. Do these prices reflect a distressed or non-distressed loan? Explain.

9. What is the difference between loan participations and loan assignments?

10. What are the difficulties in completing a loan assignment?

11. Who are the buyers of loans, and why do they participate in this activity?

    a. What are vulture funds?

    b. What are three reasons why the inter-bank market has been shrinking?

    c. What are reasons why a small FI would be interested in participating in a loan syndication?

12. Who are the sellers of loans, and why do they participate in this activity?

    a. What is the purpose of a bad bank?

    b. What are the reasons why loan sales through a bad bank will be value-enhancing?

    c. What impact has the 1996 U.S. Federal Debt Collection Improvements Act had on the North American loan sale market?

13. In addition to managing credit risk, what are some other reasons for the sale of loans by FIs?

14. What are factors that may deter the growth of the loan sales market in the future? Discuss.

15. An FI is planning the purchase of a $5 million loan to raise the existing average duration of its assets from 3.5 years to 5 years. It currently has total assets worth $20 million, $5 million in cash (0 duration) and $15 million in loans. All the loans are fairly priced.

    a. Assuming it uses the cash to purchase the loan, should it purchase the loan if its duration is seven years?

    b. What asset duration loans should it purchase to raise its average duration to five years?

16. In addition to hedging credit risk, what are the factors that are expected to encourage loan sales in the future? Discuss the effect of each factor.

Securitization

In this chapter, we consider the growing role of securitization in improving the risk-return trade-off for FIs and

▸ provide an overview of the Canadian market for asset-backed securities (ABS)

▸ describe the major forms, or vehicles, used for asset securitization

▸ analyze the characteristics of asset-backed securities

▸ discuss how the techniques have been applied to loans other than mortgages such as credit card loans, car loans, and business loans

INTRODUCTION

asset securitization
The packaging and selling of loans and other assets as securities.

Along with futures, forwards, options, swaps, and loan sales, **asset securitization**—the packaging and selling of loans and other assets backed by securities—is a mechanism that FIs use to hedge their interest rate exposure gaps. In addition, the process of securitization allows FI asset portfolios to become more liquid, provides an important source of fee income (with FIs acting as servicing agents for the assets sold), and helps reduce the effects of regulatory "taxes" such as capital requirements and deposit insurance premiums.

The Canadian and U.S. securitization markets have evolved differently. Thus, while mortgage-backed securities became a big market in the United States, a small amount of Canadian residential mortgages were securitized. In Canada, short-term commercial borrowing dominates the market, led by credit card receivables.[1] We first discuss the market for asset-backed commercial paper and asset-backed term notes in Canada, followed by a discussion of mortgage-backed securities in a global context.

THE CANADIAN MARKET FOR ASSET-BACKED SECURITIES (ABS)

asset-backed commercial paper (ABCP)
Short-term debt issued by commercial firms that is backed by collateral such as inventory and account receivables.

Through securitization, credit risk is transferred from the balance sheets of FIs into financial markets. This unmonitored credit risk was a major cause of disruption during the financial turmoil that hit global markets in mid-2007. In particular, U.S. subprime mortgage loans were the source of instability that started the global deleveraging process and led to the liquidity and credit crisis that brought down many global FIs. However, Canadian markets and their financial intermediaries were remarkably stable during this time period, with the exception of one portion of the markets: the market for **asset-backed commercial paper (ABCP)**.

---

[1] See C. Freedman and W. Engert, "Financial Developments in Canada: Past Trends and Future Challenges," *The Bank of Canada Review,* Summer 2003, pp. 3–16 for an analysis of the difference between the Canadian and U.S. securitization history. In addition to attributing Canadian market development to FIs who were more risk-averse, the authors cite "luck" as one of the reasons why the Canadian market had only 11 percent of Canadian residential mortgages securitized in 2003.

capital markets
The market for all short-term and long-term financial securities.

money market
The market for short-term financial securities with maturities of less than one year.

Capital markets include both short- and long-term financial securities. The **money market** refers to the part of the capital markets composed of short-term instruments with a maturity of less than one year. As shown in the Industry Perspectives feature on pages 676–677, in December 2007, Canadian capital markets totalled $6.3 trillion, with the money market making up $363 billion (5.8 percent) of this amount. The money markets provided $76 billion in ABCP sponsored by banks and $32 billion sponsored by non-banks.

ABCP Market Freeze: August 2007

When global investors lost confidence in the markets starting in June 2007, the fear spread to Canada. Borrowers became unable to roll over their ABCP. The bank-sponsored ABCP was supported by backup lines of credit that the issuers were able to draw down. However, under the market disruption clause of the contracts, non-bank issuers of ABCP were unable to draw down their backup credit lines. In August 2007, under the Montréal Accord, investors and issuers of ABCP in Canada agreed to a freeze on the approximately $32 billion non-bank commercial paper representing 22 **conduits.** The freeze lasted until early 2009, when the Pan-Canadian ABCP Committee Restructuring Plan allowed small investors to receive some of their capital back and large investors to convert to longer-term notes.[2]

conduit
A trust created to purchase assets from FIs and corporations and issue asset-backed securities to investors.

Credit rating agencies assign a rating to securitizations that helps to determine their price and marketability. DBRS rates the asset-backed securities issued for sale in Canada. After the market freeze, DBRS reviewed its procedures and acted to provide more details and transparency with respect to the methodologies that it employs. Other ratings agencies (Standard & Poor's, Moody's) are being examined for their role in the global market meltdown.[3]

www.dbrs.com

The Securitization Market: 2008–2009

Figure 27–1 shows the total dollar amount of asset-backed securities outstanding in Canada at year-end 2008. The amounts are divided into two types: term asset-backed securities for longer maturities, and asset-backed commercial paper for shorter maturities. As can be seen from this figure, total ABS market outstandings grew from less than $70 billion in January 2000 to $137.6 billion at December 31, 2008, a decline from $164.0 billion at year-end 2007. The market for commercial paper worldwide declined following Lehman Brothers' failure in September 2008 and the freezing of some segments of the money markets. As shown in Figure 27–2, the type of assets securitized in the Canadian ABCP market was dominated by credit cards (25.2 percent), followed by commercial mortgages (17.8 percent) and auto leases (10.9 percent). Residential mortgages totalled 16.3 percent (conventional mortgages at 10.2 percent, insured mortgages at 3.1 percent, and non-conventional mortgages at 3.0 percent).

Canadian banks have been active in securitizing their own credit card receivables as a means of managing their capital and as a source of funding. In addition, Canadian Tire Corporation formed Canadian Tire Bank and Sears Canada Inc.

---

[2] For a detailed discussion of the ABCP freeze in Canada, see the Investment Industry Regulatory Organization of Canada's report, *Regulatory Study, Review and Recommendations Concerning the Manufacture and Distribution by IIROC Member Firms of Third-Party Asset-Backed Commercial Paper in Canada,* October 2008, available at www.iiroc.ca.

[3] See *DBRS Canada Newsletter,* 1(2), April 22, 2009, and recent newsletters available at the DBRS website: www.dbrs.com. The website also contains details of DBRS's ratings methodologies.

FIGURE 27–1   **Asset-Backed Commercial Paper and Term Asset-Backed Securities Outstanding in Canada, January 2000 to December 2008***

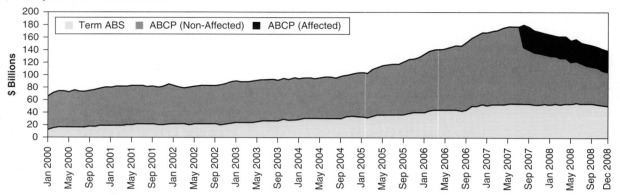

*Floating rate notes (FRNs, term-matched) included but not visible in Figure 27–1 are: June 2008: $0.550 billion; July 2008: $0.8700 billion; August 2008: $0.8700 billion; September 2008: $0.8677 billion; October 2008: $0.8677 billion; November 2008: $0.8542 billion; and December 2008: $0.8542 billion.

Source: DBRS, 2009, www.dbrs.com.

FIGURE 27–2

Asset Composition of the ABS Market in Canada, December 31, 2008

Source: DBRS, 2009, www.dbrs.com.

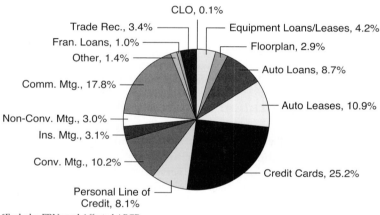

2008 Term ABS and ABCP*
($104.2 billion as of Dec 31, 2008)

*Excludes FRNs and Affected ABCP

created Sears Canada Bank, both of which are regulated by OSFI; the purpose of both is to manage these retail firms' credit card receivables via securitization vehicles. In addition, Canadian banks manage the securitizations of the trade receivables, credit cards, and mortgages of other firms via special-purpose entities (SPEs) or variable-interest entities (VIEs) and receive a fee to administer them. Along with residential mortgage-backed securities (RMBS), Canadian FIs also create commercial mortgage-backed securities (CMBS).

As they developed, the North American and the global markets for securitizations have undergone a convergence in regulations in order to increase the transparency of the deals for investors and, through standardization of these transactions, to reduce the costs for FIs who originate these securities. As noted in Chapter 20, global regulators are concerned with credit risk transfer mechanisms and their effects on the stability of global capital markets, particularly in light of fears about market systemic risk from unregulated FIs and securities in 2007 and 2008.

The harmonization of regulations is important for the major Canadian dealers since in addition to being the major source of ABS, mortgage- and non-mortgage-backed securities (as shown in Table 27–1), Canadian bank-owned dealers

TABLE 27–1
Outstanding
Canadian Asset-
Backed Securities,
August 2009

Source: DBRS, *Canadian
Securitization Market Overview, August 2009*, Octo-
ber 23, 2009, www.dbrs.
com/research/230406.

Total Asset-Backed Securities (excl. Private Placements)		
Dealer/Administrator	**Outstanding Amount**	**Market Share**
TD Securities Inc.	24,338,221,482	22.0%
BlackRock (Institutional) Canada	23,226,891,295	21.0%
BMO Capital Markets	17,899,684,182	16.2%
RBC Capital Markets Inc.	16,225,212,303	14.7%
CIBC World Markets Inc.	12,528,595,566	11.3%
Merril Lynch Canada Inc.	8,684,943,929	7.8%
Scotia Capital Inc.	4,598,665,211	4.2%
National Bank Financial Inc.	1,735,025,730	1.6%
Credit Suisse	594,084,127	0.5%
Dundee Securities Corporation	550,000,000	0.5%
HSBS Securities (Canada) Inc.	266,256,858	0.2%
Canadian Tire Bank	62,813,280	0.1%
Total	**$110,710,393,962**	**100.0%**

Note: Outstanding Amount in the Market Share section includes publicly rated issues only. It may be different from the total market size mentioned elsewhere, which includes both publicly rated and privately rated issues.

generate additional fee income as active participants in the U.S. markets. For example, Bank of Montreal Financial Group, which ranked third with a 16.2 percent market share of outstanding securitizations in Canada in August 2009, maintains a Securitization Group at its U.S. subsidiary, Harris Nesbitt Corp. Thus, while securitization serves as a risk-transfer technique for Canadian FIs, it is also a source of new product development and fee income.

THE PASS-THROUGH SECURITY

FIs frequently pool mortgages and other assets they originate and offer investors an interest in the pool in the form of *pass-through securities*. Pass-through mortgage securities "pass through" promised payments by households of principal and interest on pools of mortgages created by financial institutions to secondary market investors (mortgage-backed security bondholders) holding an interest in these pools. After a financial institution accepts mortgages, it pools them and sells interests in these pools to pass-through security holders. Each pass-through mortgage security represents a fractional ownership share in a mortgage pool. Thus, a 1 percent owner of a pass-through mortgage security issue is entitled to a 1 percent share of the principal and interest payments made over the life of the mortgages underlying the pool of securities. The originating financial institutions (e.g., bank or mortgage company) or third-party servicer receives principal and interest payments from the mortgage holder and passes these payments (minus a servicing fee) through to the pass-through security holders.

While many different types of loans and assets on FIs' balance sheets can be securitized, the original use of securitization is a result of government-sponsored programs to enhance the liquidity of the residential mortgage market. These programs indirectly subsidize the growth of home ownership in Canada and the United States. Given this, we begin by analyzing the government-sponsored securitization of residential mortgage loans. Four government agencies or government-sponsored enterprises are directly involved in the creation of mortgage-backed, pass-through securities in North America. They are Canada Mortgage and Housing Corporation (CMHC), Ginnie Mae (GNMA), Fannie Mae (FNMA), and Freddie Mac (FHLMC).

CMHC

www.cmhc.ca

Most of the residential MBS in Canada are sold by Canada Mortgage and Housing Corporation, a Crown corporation. In addition to being fully insured, CMHC guarantees all payments to the security holders under the National Housing Act (NHA), and so an NHA MBS is the equivalent of a Government of Canada bond that is also secured by residential property. These securities are thus default-free for the purchasers and have, in recent years, with the decrease in the issuance of Canadian government securities, served as substitutes for fixed-income securities. As well, they are eligible for the registered retirement savings plans (RRSPs) and registered retirement income funds (RRIFs) of individual investors and so are sold by Canadian banks and trusts for this purpose. Issuers of NHA MBS are FIs who are approved lenders of NHA-insured mortgages. These include insurance companies, banks, trust and loan companies, credit unions, and caisses populaires, as well as investment dealers who are not originators of mortgages, but who may be approved by CMHC. The issuer pays a fee for the NHA guarantee and generally lists the security in the name of the issuer, or "street name" so that they are liquid and may be sold by the investor at any time.

The markets for mortgage-backed securities have developed differently in the United States and Canada. In the United States, savings and loan companies (S&Ls) were the chief supplier of mortgages that, in the 1980s, were based on fixed rate,

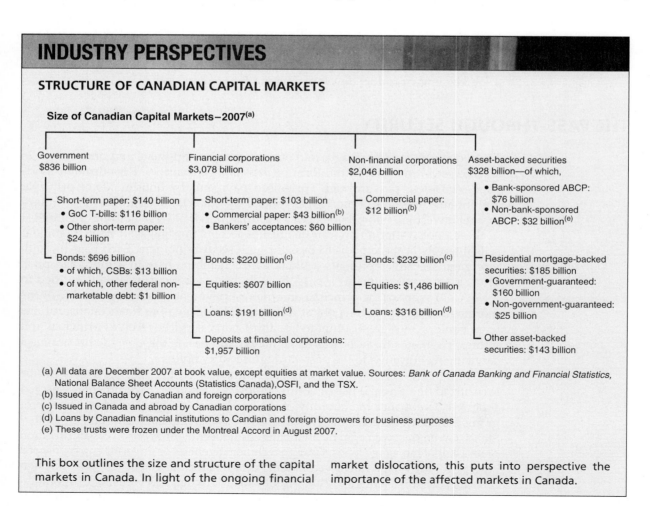

INDUSTRY PERSPECTIVES

STRUCTURE OF CANADIAN CAPITAL MARKETS

Size of Canadian Capital Markets—2007[a]

Government
$836 billion

- Short-term paper: $140 billion
  - GoC T-bills: $116 billion
  - Other short-term paper: $24 billion
- Bonds: $696 billion
  - of which, CSBs: $13 billion
  - of which, other federal non-marketable debt: $1 billion

Financial corporations
$3,078 billion

- Short-term paper: $103 billion
  - Commercial paper: $43 billion[b]
  - Bankers' acceptances: $60 billion
- Bonds: $220 billion[c]
- Equities: $607 billion
- Loans: $191 billion[d]
- Deposits at financial corporations: $1,957 billion

Non-financial corporations
$2,046 billion

- Commercial paper: $12 billion[b]
- Bonds: $232 billion[c]
- Equities: $1,486 billion
- Loans: $316 billion[d]

Asset-backed securities
$328 billion—of which,

- Bank-sponsored ABCP: $76 billion
- Non-bank-sponsored ABCP: $32 billion[e]
- Residential mortgage-backed securities: $185 billion
  - Government-guaranteed: $160 billion
  - Non-government-guaranteed: $25 billion
- Other asset-backed securities: $143 billion

(a) All data are December 2007 at book value, except equities at market value. Sources: *Bank of Canada Banking and Financial Statistics,* National Balance Sheet Accounts (Statistics Canada),OSFI, and the TSX.
(b) Issued in Canada by Canadian and foreign corporations
(c) Issued in Canada and abroad by Canadian corporations
(d) Loans by Canadian financial institutions to Candian and foreign borrowers for business purposes
(e) These trusts were frozen under the Montreal Accord in August 2007.

This box outlines the size and structure of the capital markets in Canada. In light of the ongoing financial market dislocations, this puts into perspective the importance of the affected markets in Canada.

25- or 30-year terms. Because of ceilings on the rates that the S&Ls could pay on their deposits, these FIs mismatched their long-term mortgage assets with short-term deposits. The creation of MBS resolved this issue and, in the process, created three large government agencies, to provide funding for the housing industry. These three organizations provide residential mortgage-backed securities in the United States. They have grown so that Fannie Mae was the third-largest FI by asset size in the United States. The same level of MBS market development did not occur in Canada because by the 1960s, Canadian fixed-rate mortgages, while amortized over 25-year periods, had their rates re-set every five years or less and so could be matched more easily with five-year deposits. Nevertheless, in 2009 there were approximately $563 billion NHA mortgage-backed securities outstanding. Canada Mortgage Bonds, whose first issue by CMHC in June 2001 was $1.5 billion, had over $140 billion outstanding in February 2009.

GNMA

www.ginniemae.gov

The Government National Mortgage Association (GNMA), or "Ginnie Mae," began in 1968 when it split off from the FNMA. GNMA is a government-owned

As in other mature capital markets, corporate equities represent the largest source of corporate financing in Canada, accounting for about one-third of the overall securities market.[1] The relative importance of corporate securities is somewhat higher in Canada and the United States than in the United Kingdom and the euro area, where firms have traditionally relied more heavily on bank loans.[2] This suggests that Canadian and U.S. corporations may be somewhat more directly affected by a deterioration in financial market conditions than firms in the United Kingdom or the euro area. The balance sheet leverage of Canadian firms has improved significantly in recent years relative to those in the United States and the United Kingdom, however, which would suggest that Canadian firms are better positioned to confront economic and financial shocks.

In the United States and Europe, the issuance of structured financial products increased exponentially between 2000 and July 2007, when the financial crisis began.[3] Over the same period, the asset-backed security (ABS) segment in Canada nearly tripled in size; ABS represents a slightly smaller share of the Canadian securities market (5 percent) than of global markets (7 percent). As it has elsewhere, the erosion of investor confidence in structured products has seriously impaired the functioning of the Canadian ABS market since July 2007. Mortgage securitization in Canada is still possible, however, under the NHA MBS Program, which benefits from an explicit government guarantee. This program accounts for close to 90 percent of total outstanding residential mortgage-backed securities in Canada, and recent growth has been strong. It should also be noted, however, that less than a quarter of total outstanding residential mortgages in Canada are securitized, compared with almost 60 percent in the United States.

Nonetheless, exposure to U.S subprime mortgages and CDOs has led to a crisis of investor confidence in Canada's ABCP market, particularly in non-bank-sponsored ABCP, the segment of Canada's securities market that has been most affected by the market turmoil. Since last August, non-bank-sponsored ABCP has been frozen under the terms of the Montreal Accord, as interested parties work to reach an agreement for restructuring the ABCP into longer-term instruments. ABCP has been an important source of short-term financing for Canadian firms over the past several years. Including non-bank-sponsored ABCP, it represents about 33 percent of the Canadian ABS market and nearly 50 percent of privately issued short-term paper.

[1] Global comparisons as of 2006. See McKinsey & Company, *Global Institute, Mapping Global Capital Markets: Fourth Annual Report* (2008) and the Bank of England's *Financial Stability Report* (October 2007). In Canada, the relative shares of the major components changed very little from 2006 to 2007.

[2] For further details, see D. Côté and C. Graham, *Corporate Balance Sheets in Developed Economies: Implications for Investment.* Working Paper No. 2007-24, Bank of Canada, 2007.

[3] The IMF 2008 *Global Financial Stability Report* (April), p. 56, notes that issuance of CDOs, ABS, and MBS in the United States and Europe grew from US$500 billion in 2000 to US$2.6 trillion in 2007.

Source: Bank of Canada, *Financial System Review,* June 2008, pp. 10–11.

timing insurance
A service provided by a sponsor of pass-through securities (such as GNMA) guaranteeing the bondholder interest and principal payments at the calendar date promised.

www.fanniemae.com

agency with two major functions. The first is sponsoring mortgage-backed securities programs by FIs such as banks, thrifts (savings and loans), and mortgage bankers. The second is acting as a guarantor to investors in mortgage-backed securities regarding the timely pass-through of principal and interest payments on their sponsored bonds. In other words, GNMA provides **timing insurance.**

FNMA

Originally created in 1938, the Federal National Mortgage Association (FNMA), or "Fannie Mae," is the oldest of the three mortgage-backed security sponsoring agencies. FNMA creates mortgage-backed securities by purchasing packages of mortgage loans from banks and thrifts; it finances such purchases by selling MBSs to outside investors such as life insurers and pension funds. In addition, FNMA engages in swap transactions whereby it swaps MBSs with an FI for original mortgages. Since FNMA guarantees securities as to the full and timely payment of interest and principal, the FI receiving the MBSs can then resell them on the capital market or hold them in its portfolio.

FHLMC

www.freddiemac.com

The Federal Home Loan Mortgage Corporation (FHLMC), or "Freddie Mac," performs a function similar to that of FNMA except that its major securitization role has historically involved savings institutions. Like FNMA, FHLMC is a stockholder-owned corporation with a line of credit from the U.S. Treasury. Further, like FNMA, it buys mortgage loan pools from FIs and swaps MBSs for loans. FHLMC sponsors conventional loan pools as well as pools of government-sponsored mortage loans, and guarantees timely payment of interest and ultimate payment of principal on the securities it issues.

Together FNMA and FHLC represent a huge presence in the U.S. financial system, owning or providing guarantees for approximately 50 percent of the US$12 trillion mortgage market in 2008. In the early 2000s, their credit losses increased, as did their debt-to-equity ratios, and then Federal Reserve chairman Alan Greenspan stated that Fannie Mae and Freddie Mac posed very serious risks to the U.S. financial system. The potential for "spillover effects" on Canadian markets of a failure of either Fannie Mae or Freddie Mac, while deemed "highly unlikely," was raised in the Bank of Canada's *Financial System Review* in both June and December 2004. With the collapse of the U.S. housing market and the subprime crisis, the highly unlikely occurred and these government-sponsored entities (GSEs) were taken into conservatorship by the U.S. Federal Housing Finance Agency in September 2008. In contrast, CMHC and the Canadian housing market have been relatively stable. CMHC continued to provide Canada Mortgage Bonds, a source of cheap mortgage funding for Canadian FIs, and offered a bond with a ten-year maturity in 2008.

The Incentives and Mechanics of Pass-Through Security Creation

In order to analyze the securitization process, we trace through the mechanics of an NHA MBS securitization to provide insights into the risk-return benefits of this process to the originating FI in enhancing ROE, as well as the attractiveness of these securities to investors. The focus for an FI in creating an ABS is to forecast the projected cash flow that determines the yield and depends on the prepayment model assumed. For an MBS security, contraction risk arises when mortgage rates decline and borrowers speed up their prepayments. Similarly, extension risk arises when mortgage rates rise and prepayments slow down, leading to a decline in market price of the security. This instability in the cash flows makes pass-through securities unsuitable as an investment vehicle for asset–liability management for certain FIs such as pension funds, which have long-term liabilities. Thus, our discussion focuses on the prepayment models used to structure an ABS, followed by a discussion of collateralized mortgage obligations (CMOs) and other innovations in securitization.[4]

Suppose a bank has just originated 1,000 new residential mortgages (box 1 in Figure 27–3). The average size of each mortgage is $100,000. Thus, the total size of the new mortgage pool is

$$1,000 \times \$100,000 = \$100 \text{ million}$$

Half of the mortgages ($50 million) are insured by CMHC mortgage insurance (box 1(a) in Figure 27–3). In addition, each of these new mortgages has an initial stated maturity of 25 years and a mortgage rate—often called the mortgage coupon—of 12 percent per annum. Suppose the bank originating these loans relies mostly on liabilities such as demand deposits as well as its own capital or equity to finance its assets. Under current capital adequacy requirements, each $1 of new uninsured

FIGURE 27–3
Summary of an NHA MBS

---

[4] We assume CMHC mortgage insurance in the discussion that follows, but it is not required. By law, all high-ratio mortgages in Canada (loan to value greater than 80 percent) must carry CMHC mortgage insurance. Low-ratio mortgages are not required to carry mortgage insurance but on April 22, 2005, CMHC announced that it was eliminating application fees and that it would provide portfolio Insurance for three categories of low-ratio mortgages (loan to value less than 75 percent) in order to facilitate securitization for the FI and to make the NHA MBS essentially risk-free for the investor. Insurance fees range from 0.25 percent to 0.45 percent. Private insurance may also be provided. See www.cmhc.ca for up-to-date regulations. See also *Standard Terminology and Calculations for MBS* at CMHC's website for sample calculations on prices and prepayment assumptions for Canadian MBS adopted by Canadian securities dealers. Non-NHA MBS securitizations are rated by a bond rating agency such as DBRS, so other mechanisms may be put in place to improve the quality of the credit to make it marketable and to protect the investor from default.

residential mortgage loans has to be backed by some capital. Since uninsured residential mortgages fall into 35 percent risk weight in the Basel II risk-based capital standards (see Chapter 20), and we assume the risk-based capital requirement is 7 percent, the bank capital needed to back the $100 million mortgage portfolio would be

$$\text{Capital requirement} = \$100 \text{ million} \times 0.35 \times 0.07 = \$2.450 \text{ million}$$

We assume that the remaining $97.550 million needed to fund the mortgages comes from the issuance of demand deposits.

Given these considerations, the bank's initial postmortgage balance sheet may look like that in Table 27–2. In addition to the capital requirement, the bank has to pay an annual insurance premium to CDIC based on the risk of the bank. Assuming a deposit insurance premium of 14.8 basis points (for the lowest-quality FI), the fee would be[5]

$$\$97.550 \text{ million} \times 0.00148 = \$144,374$$

Although the bank is earning a 12 percent mortgage coupon on its mortgage portfolio, it is facing two levels of regulatory costs:

1. Capital requirements.
2. CDIC insurance premiums.

Thus, one incentive to securitize is to reduce the regulatory burden on the FI to increase its after-tax return.[6] In addition to facing regulatory costs on its residential mortgage portfolio earnings, the bank in Table 27–2 has two risk exposure problems.

Gap Exposure or $D_A > kD_L$

The FI funds the 25-year mortgage portfolio with short-term demand deposits; thus, it has a duration mismatch.[7] This is true even if the mortgage assets have been funded with short-term GICs, time deposits, or other purchased funds.

Illiquidity Exposure

The bank is holding a very illiquid asset portfolio of long-term mortgages and no excess cash; as a result, it is exposed to the potential liquidity shortages discussed in Chapter 17, including the risk of having to conduct mortgage asset fire sales to meet large unexpected demand deposit withdrawals.

One possible solution to these duration mismatch and illiquidity risk problems is to lengthen the bank's on-balance-sheet liabilities by issuing longer-term deposits

TABLE 27–2
Bank Balance Sheet ($ millions)

Assets		Liabilities	
Cash	$ 0.00	Demand deposits	$ 97.550
Long-term mortgages	100.00	Capital	2.450
	$100.00		$100.00

---

[5] In 2009, the deposit insurance premium was 1.9 basis points for the highest-quality banks (see Chapter 19).

[6] Other reasons for securitization include greater geographic diversification of the loan portfolio. Specifically, many FIs originate mortgages from the local community; the ability to securitize facilitates replacing them with MBSs based on mortgages from other cities and regions.

[7] As we discuss in Chapters 8 and 9, core demand deposits usually have a duration of less than three years. Depending on prepayment assumptions, mortgages normally have durations of at least 4.5 years.

or other liability claims, such as medium-term notes. Another solution is to engage in interest rate swaps to transform the bank's liabilities into those of a long-term, fixed-rate nature (see Chapter 25). These techniques do not resolve the problem of regulatory costs and the burden they impose on the FI's returns.

By contrast, creating NHA pass-through securities can largely resolve the duration and illiquidity risk problems on the one hand and reduce the burden of regulatory costs on the other. This requires the bank to securitize the $100 million in residential mortgages by issuing NHA pass-through securities. In our example, the bank can do this since the 1,000 underlying mortgages each has the same stated mortgage maturity of 25 years and coupons of 12 percent. Therefore, they are eligible for securitization under the NHA program if the bank is an approved lender (which we assume it is).

The bank begins the securitization process by packaging the $100 million in mortgage loans and removing them from the balance sheet by placing them with a third-party trustee in a special-purpose vehicle (SPV) off the balance sheet. This third-party trustee may be another bank of high credit-worthiness or a legal trustee.[8] Next, the bank determines that (1) CMHC will guarantee, for a fee, the timing of interest and principal payments on the securities issued to back the mortgage pool and (2) the bank itself will continue to service the pool of mortgages for a fee, even after they are placed in trust. Then CMHC issues pass-through securities backed by the underlying $100 million pool of mortgages. These NHA CMHC mortgage-based securities are sold to outside investors in the capital market and the proceeds (net of any underwriting fees) go to the originating bank. Large purchasers of these securities include insurance companies and pension funds.

Before we examine the mechanics of the repayment on a pass-through security, we consider the attractiveness of these bonds to investors. In particular, investors in these bonds are protected against two levels or types of default risk.

Default Risk by the Mortgagees

Suppose that because of rapidly falling house prices, a homeowner walked away from a mortgage, leaving behind a low-valued house to be foreclosed at a price below the outstanding mortgage. This might expose the MBS to losses unless there are external guarantors. Through CMHC housing insurance, government agencies bear the risk of default, thereby protecting the NHA MBS holders against such losses.

Default Risk by Bank/Trustee

Suppose the bank that had originated the mortgages went bankrupt or the trustee absconded with the mortgage interest and principal due to the MBS holders. Because it guaranteed the prompt timing of interest and principal payments on NHA CMHC securities, CMHC would bear the cost of making the promised payments in full and on time to MBS holders.

Given this default protection, the returns for Canada Mortgage Bond holders (or investors) from holding these securities would be the monthly repayments of interest and principal on the 1,000 mortgages in the pool, after the deduction of a mortgage-servicing fee by the mortgage-originating bank and a monthly timing insurance fee to be paid to CMHC. If we assume that the total of these fees is around 50 basis points, or ½ percent, the stated coupons on the NHA MBS bonds

---

[8] For Canada Mortgage Bonds, which are AAA-rated, the trustee is Canada Housing Trust.

would be set at approximately ½ percent below the coupon rate on the underlying mortgages. In our example:

Mortgage coupon rate	=	12.00%
minus		
Servicing fee	=	0.50
NHA MBS coupon	=	11.50%

Suppose that CMHC issues $100 million face value NHA MBS at par to back the pool of mortgage loans. The minimum size of a single MBS is $5,000; each investor gets a pro rata monthly share of all the interest and principal received by the bank minus servicing costs and insurance fees. Thus, if a life insurance company bought 25 percent of the NHA MBS issue (or 1,000 bonds × $5,000 each = $5 million), it would get a 25 percent share of the 300 promised monthly payments from the mortgages comprising the mortgage pool.

Every month, each mortgagee makes a payment to the bank. The bank aggregates these payments and passes the funds through to NHA MBS investors via the trustee net of servicing fee. To make things easy, most fixed-rate mortgages are **fully amortized** over the mortgage's life. This means that as long as the mortgagee does not seek to prepay the mortgage early within the 25-year period, either to buy a new house or to refinance the mortgage should interest rates fall, investors can expect to receive a constant stream of payments each month analogous to the stream of income on other fixed-coupon, fixed-income bonds. In reality, however, mortgagees do not act in such a predictable fashion. For a variety of reasons, they relocate (sell their house) or refinance their mortgages (especially when current mortgage rates are below mortgage coupon rates). This propensity to **prepay** early, before a mortgage matures, and then refinance with a new mortgage means that *realized* coupons/cash flows on pass-through securities can often deviate substantially from the stated or expected coupon flows in a no-prepayment world. This unique prepayment risk provides the attraction of pass-throughs to some investors but leads other, more risk-averse, investors to avoid these instruments. Before we analyze in greater detail the unique nature of prepayment risk, we summarize the steps followed in the creation of a pass-through in Figure 27–3. Then we analyze how this securitization has helped solve the duration, illiquidity, and regulatory cost problems of the FI manager.

In the previous discussion we traced the securitization process, the origination of mortgages on the balance sheet (Figure 27–3, box 1) through to the sale of NHA MBS to outside investors (box 4). To close the securitization process, the cash proceeds of the sale of NHA MBS (box 5) net of any underwriting fees go to the originating bank. As a result, the bank has substituted cash for long-term mortgages by using the securitization mechanism. Abstracting from the various fees and underwriting costs in the securitization process, the balance sheet of the bank might look like the one in Table 27–3 immediately after the securitization has taken place.

There has been a dramatic change in the balance sheet exposure of the bank. First, $100 million illiquid mortgage loans have been replaced by $100 million cash. Second, the duration mismatch has been reduced since both D_A and D_L are now low. Third, the bank has an enhanced ability to deal with and reduce its regulatory costs. Specifically, it can reduce its capital since capital standards require none be held against cash on the balance sheet compared to uninsured residential

---

fully amortized
An equal periodic repayment on a loan that reflects part interest and part principal over the life of the loan.

prepay
A borrower pays back a loan before maturity to the FI that originated the loan.

TABLE 27–3
The Bank's Balance Sheet after Securitization ($ millions)

Assets		Liabilities	
Cash (proceeds from mortgage securitization)	$100.00	Demand deposits	$ 97.550
Mortgages	0.00	Capital	2.450
	$100.00		$100.00

mortgages. Deposit insurance premiums are also reduced if the bank uses part of the cash proceeds from the NHA MBS sale to pay off or retire demand deposits and downsize its balance sheet.

Of course, keeping a highly liquid asset portfolio and/or downsizing is a way to reduce regulatory costs, but these strategies are hardly likely to enhance an FI's profits. The real logic of securitization is that the cash proceeds from the mortgage/NHA MBS sale can be reused to create or originate new mortgages, which in turn can be securitized. In so doing, the FI is acting more like an asset (mortgage) broker than a traditional asset transformer, as we discussed in Chapter 1. The advantage of being an asset broker is that the FI profits from mortgage pool servicing fees plus up-front fees from mortgage origination. At the same time, the FI no longer has to bear the illiquidity and duration mismatch risks and regulatory costs that arise when it acts as an asset transformer and holds mortgages to maturity on its balance sheet. Put more simply, the FI's profitability becomes more fee-dependent than interest rate spread-dependent.

The limits of this securitization process clearly depend on the supply of mortgages (and other assets such as credit card receivables, car loans, business loans, etc.) that can be securitized and the demand by investors for pass-through securities. As was noted earlier, the unique feature of pass-through securities from the demand-side perspective of investors is prepayment risk. To understand the unique nature of this risk and why it might deter or limit investments by other FIs and investors, we next analyze the characteristics of pass-through securities more formally.

CONCEPT QUESTIONS

1. What is a pass-through security?
2. Should an FI with $D_A > kD_L$ seek to securitize its assets? Why or why not?

Prepayment Risk on Pass-Through Securities

To understand the effects of prepayments on pass-through security returns, it is necessary to understand the nature of the cash flows received by investors from the underlying portfolio of mortgages. Most conventional mortgages are fully amortized. This means that the mortgagee pays back to the mortgage lender (mortgagor) a constant amount each month that contains some principal and some interest. While the total monthly promised payment remains unchanged, the interest component declines throughout the life of the mortgage contract and the principal component increases.

The problem for the FI is to figure a constant monthly payment that exactly pays off the mortgage loan at maturity. This constant payment is formally equivalent to a monthly "annuity" paid by the mortgagee. Consider our example of 1,000 mortgages comprising a $100 million mortgage pool that is to be paid off monthly over 300 months at an annual mortgage coupon rate of 12 percent.

Size of pool = $\$100,000,000$
Maturity = 25 years ($n = 25$)
Number of monthly payments = 12 ($m = 12$)
r = Annual mortgage coupon rate = 12 percent
PMT = Constant monthly payment to pay off the mortgage over its life

Thus, we solve for PMT from the following equation:

$$\$100,000,000 = \left[PMT\left(1 + \frac{r}{m}\right)^{-1} + PMT\left(1 + \frac{r}{m}\right)^{-2} \right.$$
$$\left. + \cdots + PMT\left(1 + \frac{r}{m}\right)^{-300} \right]$$
$$= PMT\left[\left(1 + \frac{r}{m}\right)^{-1} + \left(1 + \frac{r}{m}\right)^{-2} + \cdots + \left(1 + \frac{r}{m}\right)^{-300}\right]$$

The term in square brackets is a geometric expansion that in the limit equals

$$100,000,000 = \left[\frac{1 - \dfrac{1}{\left(1 + \dfrac{r}{m}\right)^{mn}}}{\dfrac{r}{m}} \right] \times PMT$$

The new term in brackets is the present value of the annuity factor, *PVAF*, or $100,000,000 = PMT[PVAF]$. Rearranging to solve for *PMT*, the required equal monthly payment on the mortgages, we have

$$PMT = \frac{100,000,000}{PVAF}$$

$$= \frac{100,000,000}{\left[\dfrac{1 - \dfrac{1}{(1 + \dfrac{r}{m})^{mn}}}{\dfrac{r}{m}} \right]}$$

$$= \frac{100,000,000}{\left[\dfrac{1 - \dfrac{1}{(1 + \dfrac{0.12}{12})^{300}}}{\dfrac{0.12}{12}} \right]} = \$1,053,224$$

As a result, $PMT = \$1,053,224$, or, given 1,000 individual mortgages, \$1,053.22 per mortgage rounding to the nearest cent. Thus, payments by the 1,000 mortgagees of an average monthly mortgage payment of $1,053.22 will pay off the mortgages outstanding over 25 years, assuming no prepayments.

The aggregate monthly payments of $1,053,224 comprise different amounts of principal and interest each month.[9] Table 27–4 breaks down the aggregate monthly amortized mortgage payments of $PMT = \$1,053,220$ into their interest and principal components. In month 1, the interest component is 12 percent divided by 12 (or 1 percent) times the outstanding balance on the mortgage pool ($100 million). This comes to $1,000,000, meaning that the remainder of the aggregate monthly payment, or $53,224, can be used to pay off outstanding principal on the pool. At the end of month 1, the outstanding principal balance on the mortgages has been reduced by $53,224 to $99,946,776. In month 2 and thereafter, the interest component declines and the principal component increases, but the two still sum to $1,053,22. Thus, in month 2, the interest component has declined to $999,468 (or 1 percent of the outstanding principal at the beginning of month 2) and the principal component of the payment has increased to $53,752.

Although 12 percent is the coupon or interest rate the house buyers pay on the mortgages, the rate passed through to NHA MBS investors is 11½ percent, reflecting an average 50-basis-point fee paid to the originating bank. The servicing fees are normally paid monthly rather than as lump-sum single payments up front to create the appropriate collection/servicing incentives over the life of the mortgage for the originating bank. For example, the bank's incentive to act as an efficient collection/servicing agent over 300 months would probably decline if it received a single large up-front fee in month 1 and nothing thereafter. The effect of the ½ percent fee is to reduce the cash flows passed through to the MBS investors from $1,053,224 ($100,000,000 amortized at 12 percent) to $1,016,469 (11.5 percent amortization).

As we have shown so far, the cash flows on the pass-through directly reflect the interest and principal cash flows on the underlying mortgages minus service fees. However, over time, mortgage rates change. Let Y be the current annual mortgage coupon rate, which could be higher or lower than 12 percent, and let y be the yield on newly issued par value NHA MBS. With no prepayments, the market value of the 12 percent mortgage coupon pool (11½ percent actual coupons) could be calculated as

$$V = \frac{\$1,016,469}{\left(1 + \dfrac{y}{12}\right)^1} + \frac{\$1,016,469}{\left(1 + \dfrac{y}{12}\right)^2} + \cdots + \frac{\$1,016,469}{\left(1 + \dfrac{y}{12}\right)^{300}}$$

TABLE 27–4
Fully Amortized Mortgages

Month	Outstanding Balance Payment	Fixed Monthly (PMT)	Interest Component	Principal Component	Principal Remaining
1	$100,000,000	$1,053,220	$1,000,000	$53,220	$99,946,780
2	99,946,780	1,053,220	999,468	53,752	99,893,028
.	.	.	.	.	.
.	.	.	.	.	.
.	.	.	.	.	.
.	.	.	.	.	.
300	.	.	.	.	.

---

[9] Because of the rounding of each monthly payment to the nearest cent, we assume that aggregate monthly cash flows are 1,000 × $1,053.22 = $1,053,220. As well, in Canada, the annual percentage rate (APR) is based on semiannual compounding.

If y is less than 11½ percent, the market value of the pool will be greater than its original value; if y is greater than 11½ percent, the pool will decrease in value. However, valuation is more complex than this since we have ignored the prepayment behaviour of the 1,000 mortgages. In effect, prepayment risk has two principal sources: refinancing and housing turnover.

Refinancing

As coupon rates on new mortgages fall, there is an increased incentive for individuals in the pool to pay off old, high-cost mortgages and refinance at lower rates. However, refinancing involves transaction costs and recontracting costs. Many FIs charge prepayment penalty fees on the outstanding mortgage balance prepaid. In addition, there are often origination costs for new mortgages to consider along with the cost of appraisals and credit checks. As a result, mortgage rates may have to fall by some amount below the current coupon rate before there is a significant increase in prepayments in the pool.[10]

Housing Turnover

The other factor that affects prepayments is the propensity of the mortgagees in the pool to move before their mortgages reach maturity. The decision to move or turn over a house may be due to a complex set of factors, such as the level of house prices, the size of the underlying mortgage, the general health of the economy, and even the season (e.g., spring is a good time to move). In addition, if the existing mortgage is an **assumable mortgage,** the buyer of the house takes over the outstanding mortgage's payments. Thus, the sale of a house in a pool does not necessarily imply that the mortgage has to be prepaid. By contrast, non-assumability means a one-to-one correspondence between sale of a house and mortgage prepayment.

assumable mortgage
The mortgage contract is transferred from the seller to the buyer of a house.

Figure 27–4 plots the prepayment frequency of a pool of mortgages in relation to the spread between the current mortgage coupon rate (Y) and the mortgage coupon rate (r) in the existing pool (12 percent in our example). Notice when the current mortgage rate (Y) is above the rate in the pool ($Y > r$), mortgage prepayments are small, reflecting monthly forced turnover as people have to relocate because of jobs, divorces, marriages, and other considerations. Even when the

FIGURE 27–4
The Prepayment Relationship

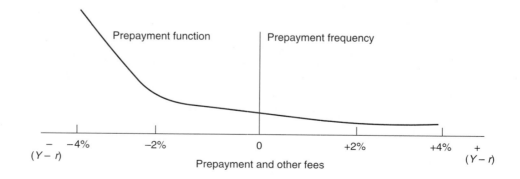

[10] J. R. Follian and D. Tzang, in "The Interest Rate Differential and Refinancing a Home Mortgage," *Appraisal Journal* 56(2), 1988, pp. 243–251, found that only when the mortgage rate fell below the coupon rate by 60 basis points was there an incentive to refinance a mortgage with an average of ten years left to maturity. As might be expected, this required differential declined as the holding period increased.

current mortgage rate falls below r, those remaining in the mortgage pool do not rush to prepay because up-front refinancing, contracting, and penalty costs are likely to outweigh any present value savings from lower mortgage rates. However, as current mortgage rates continue to fall, the propensity for mortgage holders to prepay increases significantly. Conceptually, mortgage holders have a very valuable call option on the mortgage when this option is in the money.[11] That is, when current mortgage rates fall sufficiently low so that the present value savings of refinancing outweigh the exercise price (the cost of prepayment penalties and other fees and costs), the mortgage will be called.

Since the bank has sold the mortgage cash flows to investors and must by law pass through all payments received (minus servicing fees), investors' cash flows directly reflect the rate of prepayment. As a result, instead of receiving an equal monthly cash flow, PMT, as is done under a no-prepayment scenario, the actual cash flows (CF) received on these securities by investors fluctuate monthly with the rate of prepayments (see Figure 27–5).

In a no-prepayment world, each month's cash flows are the same: $PMT_1 = PMT_2 = \ldots = PMT_{300}$. However, in a world with prepayments, each month's realized cash flows from the mortgage pool can differ. In Figure 27–5 we show a rising level of cash flows from month 2 onward, peaking in month 60, reflecting the effects of early prepayments by some of the 1,000 mortgagees in the pool. This leaves less outstanding principal and interest to be paid in later years. For example, if 300 mortgagees fully prepay by month 60, only 700 mortgagees will remain in the pool at that date. The effect of prepayments is to lower dramatically the principal and interest cash flows received in the later months of the pool's life. For instance, in Figure 27–5, the cash flow received by MBS holders in month 300 is very small relative to month 60 and even months 1 and 2. This reflects the decline in the pool's outstanding principal.

The lowering of current mortgage interest rates and faster prepayments have some good news and bad news effects on the current market valuation of the 12 percent mortgage pool, that is, the 11½ percent NHA MBS.

Good News Effects   First, lower market yields reduce the discount rate on any mortgage cash flow and increase the present value of any given stream of cash flows. This would also happen for any fixed-income security. Second, lower yields lead to faster prepayment of the mortgage pool's principal. As a result, instead of principal payments being skewed toward the end of the pool's life, the principal is received (paid back) much faster.

Bad News Effects   First, with early prepayment comes fewer interest payments in absolute terms. Thus, instead of receiving scheduled interest payments over

FIGURE 27–5
The Effects of Prepayments on Pass-Through Bondholders' Cash Flows

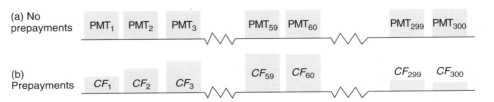

(a) No prepayments PMT_1 PMT_2 PMT_3 PMT_{59} PMT_{60} PMT_{299} PMT_{300}

(b) Prepayments CF_1 CF_2 CF_3 CF_{59} CF_{60} CF_{299} CF_{300}

[11] The option is a call option on the value of the mortgage since falling rates increase the value of calling the old mortgage and refinancing a new mortgage at lower rates for the owner of the call option, who is the mortgagee. This option also can be viewed as a put option on interest rates.

300 months, some of these payments are irrevocably lost as principal outstanding is paid early; that is, mortgage holders are not going to pay interest on mortgage loans they no longer have outstanding. Second, faster cash flow due to prepayments induced by interest rate falls can be reinvested only at lower interest rates when they are received. That is, instead of reinvesting monthly cash flows at 12 percent, investors may reinvest only at lower rates such as 8 percent.

CONCEPT QUESTIONS	1. **What are the two sources of cash flows on a pass-through security?** 2. **What two factors can cause prepayments on the mortgages underlying pass-through securities?**

Prepayment Models

Clearly, managers running FI investment portfolios need to factor in assumptions about the prepayment behaviour of mortgages before they can assess the fair value and risk of their MBS portfolios. Next, we consider three alternative ways to model prepayment effects using the Public Securities Association (PSA) prepayment model, other empirical models, and option valuation models.

www.psa.com

To begin, we look carefully at the results of one prepayment model. The weighted-average life of an MBS reflects an assumed prepayment schedule. This weighted-average life is not the same as duration, which measures the weighted-average time to maturity based on the relative present values of cash flows as weights. Instead, it is a significant simplification of the duration measure seeking to concentrate on the expected timing of payments of principal. Technically, **weighted-average life (WAL)** is measured by

weighted-average life (WAL)
The sum of the products of the time when principal payments are received and the amount of principal received all divided by total principal outstanding.

$$WAL = \frac{\sum (\text{Time} \times \text{Expected principal received})}{\text{Total principal outstanding}}$$

For example, consider a loan with two years to maturity and $100 million in principal. Investors expect $40 million of the principal to be repaid at the end of year 1 and the remaining $60 million to be repaid at maturity.

Time	Expected Principal Payments	Time × Principal
1	$ 40	$ 40
2	60	120
	$100	$160

$$WAL = \frac{160}{100} = 1.6 \text{ years}$$

PSA Model

The prepayment model developed by the Public Securities Association is an empirically based model that reflects an average rate of prepayment based on past experience. Essentially, the PSA model assumes that the prepayment rate starts at 0.2 percent (per annum) in the first month, increasing by 0.2 percent per month for the first 30 months, until the annualized prepayment rate reaches 6 percent. This model assumes that the prepayment rate then levels off at a 6 percent annualized rate for the remaining life of the pool[12] (see Figure 27–6). Issuers or investors who

---

[12] Or, after month 30, prepayments are made at approximately ½ percent per *month*.

FIGURE 27–6
PSA Prepayment
Model

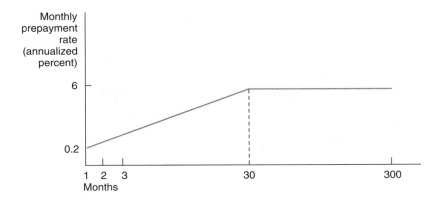

assume that their mortgage pool prepayments exactly match this pattern are said to assume 100 percent PSA behaviour. Realistically, the actual prepayment rate on any specific mortgage pool backing a specific pass-through security may differ from PSA's assumed pattern for general and economic reasons, including

1. The level of the pool's coupon relative to the current mortgage coupon rate (the weighted-average coupon).
2. The age of the mortgage pool.
3. Whether the payments are fully amortized.
4. Assumability of mortgages in the pool.
5. Size of the pool.
6. Conventional or non-conventional mortgages.
7. Geographic location.
8. Age and job status of mortgagees in the pool.

One approach would be to approximately control for these factors by assuming some fixed deviation of any specific pool from PSA's assumed average or benchmark pattern. For example, one pool may be assumed to be 75 percent PSA, and another 125 percent PSA. The former has a slower prepayment rate than historically experienced; the latter, a faster rate. Note these values in Figure 27–7 relative to 100 percent PSA.

Other Empirical Models

FIs that are trading, dealing, and issuing pass-throughs have also developed their own proprietary empirical models of prepayment behaviour to get a pricing edge

FIGURE 27–7
Deviations from
100 Percent PSA

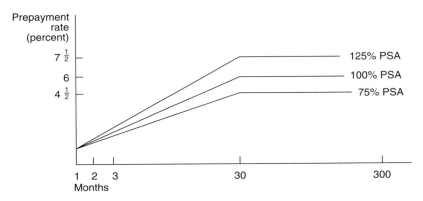

on other issuers/investors. Clearly, the FI that can develop the best, most accurate prepayment model stands to make large profits either in originating and issuing such securities or in trading such instruments in the secondary market. As a wide variety of empirical models have been developed, we briefly look at the types of methodology followed.

Specifically, most empirical models are proprietary versions of the PSA model in which FIs make their own estimates of the pattern of monthly prepayments. From this modelling exercise, an FI can estimate either the fair price or the fair yield on the pass-through. Of course, those FIs that make the most profits from buying and selling pass-throughs over time are the ones that have most accurately predicted actual prepayment behaviour.

In constructing an empirical valuation model, FIs begin by estimating a prepayment function from observing the experience of mortgage holders prepaying during any particular period on mortgage pools similar to the one to be valued. This is conditional, of course, on the mortgages not having been prepaid prior to that period. These conditional prepayment rates in month i (p_i) for similar pools would be modelled as functions of the important economic variables driving prepayment—for example, $p_i = f$ (mortgage rate spread, age, collateral, geographic factors, **burn-out factor**).[13] This modelling should take into account the idiosyncratic factors affecting this specific pool, such as its age and burn-out factor, as well as market factors affecting prepayments in general, such as the mortgage rate spread. Once the p_i frequency distribution is estimated, as shown in Figure 27–8, the FI can calculate the expected cash flows on the mortgage pool under consideration and estimate its fair yield given the current market price of the pool.

burn-out factor
The aggregate percent of the mortgage pool that has been prepaid prior to the month under consideration.

Option Models[14]

The third class of models uses option pricing theory to figure the fair yield on pass-throughs. These so-called option-adjusted spread (OAS) models focus on the prepayment risk of pass-throughs as the essential determinant of the required yield spread of pass-through bonds over Treasuries. As such, they are open to the criticism that they fail to properly include non-refinancing incentives to prepay

FIGURE 27–8
Estimated Prepayment Function for a Given Pool

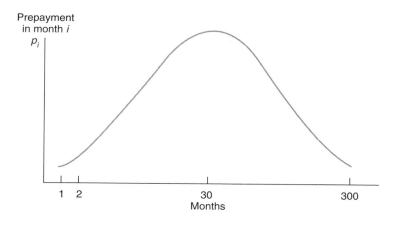

---

[13] A burn-out factor is a summary measure of a pool's prepayments in total prior to month i. As such, it is meant to capture heterogeneity of prepayment behaviour within any given pool rather than between pools.

[14] This section contains material that is relatively technical. It may be included or dropped from the chapter reading depending on the rigour of the course without harming the continuity of the chapter.

and the variety of transaction costs and recontracting costs involved in refinancing. Recent research has tried to integrate the option model approach with the empirical model approach.[15]

Stripped to its basics, the option model views the fair price on a pass-through such as an MBS as being decomposable into two parts:

$$P_{MBS} = P_{TBOND} - P_{PREPAYMENT\ OPTION}$$

That is, the value of an MBS to an investor (P_{MBS}) is equal to the value of a standard non-callable Treasury bond of the same duration (P_{TBOND}) minus the value of the mortgage holder's prepayment call option ($P_{PREPAYMENT\ OPTION}$). Specifically, the ability of the mortgage holder to prepay is equivalent to the bond investor writing a call option on the bond and the mortgagee owning or buying the option. If interest rates fall, the option becomes more valuable as it moves into the money and more mortgages are prepaid early by having the bond called or the prepayment option exercised. This relationship can also be thought of in the yield dimension:

$$Y_{MBS} = Y_{TBOND} + Y_{OPTION}$$

The investors' required yield on an MBS should equal the yield on a similar duration T-bond plus an additional yield for writing the valuable call option. That is, the fair yield spread or **option-adjusted spread (OAS)** between MBS and T-bonds should reflect the value of this option.

To gain further insight into the option model approach and the OAS, we can develop an example along the lines of S. D. Smith, showing how to calculate the value of the option-adjusted spread on MBS.[16] To do this, we make a number of simplifying assumptions indicative of the restrictive nature of many of these models:

1. The only reasons for prepayment are due to refinancing mortgages at lower rates; there is no prepayment for turnover reasons.
2. The current discount (zero-coupon) yield curve for T-bonds is flat (this could be relaxed).
3. The mortgage coupon rate is 10 percent on an outstanding pool of mortgages with an outstanding principal balance of $1,000,000.
4. The mortgages have a three-year maturity and pay principal and interest only once at the end of each year. Of course, real-world models would have 15- or 25-year maturities and pay interest and principal monthly. These assumptions are made for simplification purposes only.
5. Mortgage loans are fully amortized, and there is no servicing fee (again, this could be relaxed). Thus, the annual fully amortized payment under no prepayment conditions is

$$PMT = \frac{1,000,000}{\left[\dfrac{1 - \dfrac{1}{(1 + 0.10)^3}}{0.1}\right]} = \frac{1,000,000}{2.48685} = \$402,114$$

option-adjusted spread (OAS)
The required interest spread of a pass-through security over a Treasury when prepayment risk is taken into account.

[15] See W. Archer and D. C. Ling, *Pricing Mortgage-Backed Securities: Should Contingent-Claim Models Be Abandoned for Empirical Models of Prepayments?* Paper presented at the AFA Conference, Anaheim, California, January 1993.

[16] S. D. Smith, "Analyzing Risk and Return for Mortgage-Backed Securities," Federal Reserve Bank of Atlanta, *Economic Review,* January–February 1991, pp. 2–11.

In a world without prepayments, no default risk, and current mortgage rates (y) of 9 percent, we would have the MBS selling at a premium over par:

$$P_{MBS} = \frac{PMT}{(1 + y)} + \frac{PMT}{(1 + y)^2} + \frac{PMT}{(1 + y)^3}$$

$$P_{MBS} = \frac{\$402{,}114}{(1.09)} + \frac{\$402{,}114}{(1.09)^2} + \frac{\$402{,}114}{(1.09)^3}$$

$$P_{MBS} = \$1{,}017{,}869$$

6. Because of prepayment penalties and other refinancing costs, mortgagees do not begin to prepay until mortgage rates, in any year, fall 3 percent or more below the mortgage coupon rate for the pool (the mortgage coupon rate is 10 percent in this example).

7. Interest rate movements over time change a maximum of 1 percent up or down each year. The time path of interest rates follows a binomial process.

8. With prepayments present, cash flows in any year can be the promised payment $PMT = \$402{,}114$, the promised payment ($PMT$) plus repayment of any outstanding principal, or zero if all mortgages have been prepaid or paid off in the previous year.

In Figure 27–9 we show the assumed time path of interest rates over the three years with associated probabilities (p).

End of Year 1   Since rates can change up or down by only 1 percent per annum, the farthest they can be expected to fall in the first year is to 8 percent. At this level, no mortgage holder would prepay since any mortgage rate savings would be offset by the penalty costs of prepayment, that is, by the assumption it is worth prepaying only when the mortgage rate falls at least 3 percent below its 10 percent coupon rate. As a result, the MBS pass-through investor could expect to receive $PMT = \$402{,}114$ with certainty. Thus, $CF_1 = \$402{,}114$.

End of Year 2   In year 2, there are three possible mortgage interest rate scenarios. However, the only one that triggers prepayment is when mortgage rates fall to

FIGURE 27–9
Mortgage Rate Changes: Assumed Time Path

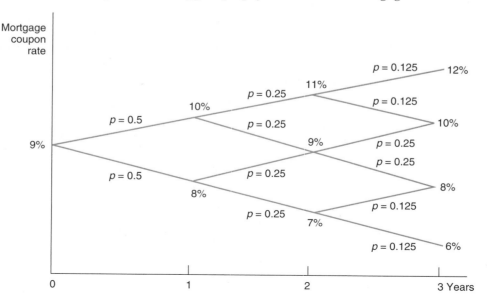

7 percent (3 percent below the 10 percent mortgage coupon rate of the pool). According to Figure 27–9, this occurs with only a 25 percent probability. If prepayment does not occur with 75 percent probability, the investor receives $PMT = \$402,114$. If prepayment occurs with 25 percent probability, the investor receives

$$PMT + \text{Principal balance remaining at end of year 2}$$

We can calculate the principal balance remaining at the end of year 2 as follows. At the end of the first year, we divide the amortized payment, $PMT = \$402,114$, into a payment of interest and a payment of principal. With a 10 percent mortgage coupon rate, the payment of interest component would be $0.10 \times \$1,000,000 = \$100,000$, and the repayment of principal component $= \$402,114 - \$100,000 = \$302,114$. Thus, at the beginning of the second year, there would be $\$1,000,000 - \$302,114 = \$697,886$ principal outstanding. At the end of the second year, the promised amortized payment of $PMT = \$402,114$ can be broken down to an interest component of 10 percent $\times \$697,886 = \$69,788.6$, and a principal component amount of $\$402,114 - \$69,788.6 = \$332,325.4$, leaving a principal balance at the end of year 2 of $\$1,000,000 - \$302,114 - \$332,325.4 = \$365,560.6$.

Consequently, if yields fall to 7 percent, the cash flow received by the investor in year 2 would be

$$PMT + \text{Principal balance outstanding at end of year 2}$$
$$= \$402,114 + \$365,560.6 = \$767,674.6$$

Thus, expected cash flows at the end of year 2 would be

$$CF_2 = 0.25(\$767,674.6) + 0.75(\$402,114)$$
$$= \$191,918.64 + \$301,585.5$$
$$= \$493,504.15$$

End of Year 3 Since there is a 25 percent probability that mortgages will be prepaid in year 2, there must be a 25 percent probability that the investor will receive no cash flows at the end of year 3 since mortgage holders owe nothing in this year if all mortgages have already been paid off early in year 2. However, there is also a 75 percent probability that mortgages will not be prepaid at the end of year 2. Thus, at the end of year 3 (maturity), the investor has a 75 percent probability of receiving the promised amortized payment $PMT = \$402,114$. The expected cash flow in year 3 is

$$CF_3 = 0.25(0) + 0.75(\$402,114) = \$301,585.5$$

Derivation of the Option-Adjusted Spread As just discussed, we conceptually divide the required yield on an MBS, or other pass-throughs, with prepayment risk, into the required yield on T-bonds plus a required spread for the prepayment call option given to the mortgage holders:

$$P = \frac{E(CF_1)}{(1 + d_1 + O_s)} + \frac{E(CF_2)}{(1 + d_2 + O_s)^2} + \frac{E(CF_3)}{(1 + d_3 + O_s)^3}$$

where
  P = Price of MBS
  d_1 = Discount rate on one-year, zero-coupon Treasury bonds

d_2 = Discount rate on two-year, zero-coupon Treasury bonds

d_3 = Discount rate on three-year, zero-coupon Treasury bonds

O_S = Option-adjusted spread on MBS

Assume that the T-bond yield curve is flat, so that

$$d_1 = d_2 = d_3 = 8\%$$

We can now solve for O_S:

$$1,017,869 = \frac{\$402,114}{(1 + 0.08 + O_s)} + \frac{\$493,504.15}{(1 + 0.08 + O_s)^2} + \frac{\$301,185.5}{(1 + 0.08 + O_s)^3}$$

Solving for O_S, we find that

$$O_S = 0.96\% \text{ (to two decimal places)}$$

$$Y_{MBS} = Y_{TBOND} + O_S$$

$$= 8\% + 0.96\%$$

$$= 8.96\%$$

Notice that when prepayment risk is present, the expected cash flow yield at 8.96 percent is 4 basis points less than the required 9 percent yield on the MBS when no prepayment occurs. The slightly lower yield results because the positive effects of early prepayment (such as earlier payment of principal) dominate the negative effects (such as loss of interest payments). Note, however, that this result might well be reversed if we altered our assumptions by allowing a wider dispersion of possible interest rate changes and having heavier penalties for prepayment.

Nevertheless, the option-adjusted spread approach is useful for FI managers in that they can place lower bounds on the yields they are willing to accept on MBS and other pass-through securities before they place them in their portfolios. Realistically, some account has to be taken of non-refinancing prepayment behaviour and patterns; otherwise significant mispricing may occur.

CONCEPT QUESTIONS

1. Should an FI with $D_A < kD_L$ seek to securitize its assets? Why or why not?
2. In general terms, discuss the three approaches developed by analysts to model prepayment behaviour.
3. In the context of the option model approach, list three ways in which transaction and other contracting costs are likely to interfere with the accuracy of its predictions regarding the fair price or interest spread on a pass-through security.

NHA Mortgage-Backed Securities Pools

All NHA MBS issues are pooled according to mortgage type and prepayment provisions of the original mortgages. Table 27–5 lists the numbers and the definition of some of the pool types available. New pools have been created to allow for the types of mortgages that are issued in Canada and the conditions that they must meet in order to be eligible for mortgage insurance. For example, the 970 pool type allows for prepayments up to the third anniversary of the mortgage and the 975 type up to the fifth anniversary. As can be seen in Table 27–6, which shows the percentage share of the market by pool type outstanding in May 2009, the largest pools dollar-wise and in total are the 975 and 980 types, which are single-family mortgages issued according to the standard NHA mortgage provisions. The 966 and 990 pools are backed by non-repayable mortgages and make up less than 5 percent of the total MBS outstanding.

TABLE 27–5
NHA MBS
Mortgage Pool
Classifications

a) Homeowner:

964—Exclusive homeowner mortgage pools, which are classified as prepayable because the borrowers within this type of pool have the option to prepay their mortgage (often at a penalty) in accordance with the specific terms of the mortgage. The appropriate penalty interest payment (PIP) is passed through to the investors.

967—Exclusive homeowner mortgage pools, which are classified as prepayable because the borrowers within this type of pool have the option to prepay their mortgage. However, the PIP is not passed through to the investor.

970—Offers investors an indemnity where mortgages are renegotiated during the closed period of the loan. Penalty interest payments are retained by the issuer. For all prepayments in circumstances other than those permitted in the *Information Circular,* an indemnity is passed through.

b) Multiples:

966—Multi-family pool type, which is comprised exclusively of multiple family loans, and are not prepayable.

c) Social housing:

These NHA-insured mortgages are issued to finance low-cost housing for senior citizens, the disabled, and the economically disadvantaged. Typically, such housing is sponsored by government housing agencies, other social service organizations and private non-profit organizations.

99—Special category of NHA MBS pool created to allow exclusive pools of "social housing mortgages." The key feature of social housing pools is the absence of prepayment at the option of the borrower on the underlying mortgages; this makes them more attractive to investors who seek predictable cash flow.

d) Mixed

965—Mixed pools, which are composed of a combination of homeowner, multiple, or social housing mortgages. These also consist of prepayable multi-family pools.

Other:

975—Similar to 970 but with prepayments allowed up to five years; introduced December 29, 2000.

985—Backed by variable rate mortgages; introduced November 26, 2004.

980—Backed by adjustable rate mortgages with a one-month interest rate reset; introduced May 31, 2005.

987—Backed by floating-rate mortgages with a coupon rate that is a weighted-average of the pooled mortgages; introduced September 1, 2005.

990—Non-repayable mortgages.

The NHA MBS provide a cheaper source of funds for FIs and the benefits are passed on to homebuyers in lower mortgage rates. There are different issuers, including trust companies (Equitable Trust, Home Trust), credit unions and caisses populaires (Vancouver City Savings, Caisse centrale Desjardins du Québec) and investment firms (Merrill Lynch Canada Inc.). As might be expected, the largest issuers of these types of securities are the major banks.

THE COLLATERALIZED MORTGAGE OBLIGATION (CMO)

While pass-throughs are still the primary mechanism for securitization, the CMO is a second and growing vehicle for securitizing FI assets. Innovated in 1983 by the U.S. FHLMC and First Boston, the CMO is a device for making mortgage-backed

TABLE 27–6
NHA MBS Pools Outstanding, May 29, 2009.

Pool Type	Number of Pools	Issued Amount	% of Total
867	43	$ 4,284,026,555.74	0.8%
880	10	102,252,890.27	0.0
964	1,606	21,767,026,924.48	3.9
965	460	11,031,595,641.53	2.0
966	242	4,421,910,762.14	0.8
967	244	2,296,096,018.71	0.4
970	1,004	71,847,337,738.11	12.8
975	4,014	307,664,791,342.67	54.7
980	381	13,999,091,035.08	2.5
985	719	92,716,156,459.21	16.5
987	374	13,836,956,003.93	2.5
990	958	18,330,318,993.51	3.3
Grand Total	**10,055**	**$562,297,560,365.38**	**100.0%**

securities more attractive to investors. The CMO does this by repackaging the cash flows from mortgages and pass-through securities in a different fashion to attract different types of investors. While a pass-through security gives each investor a pro rata share of any promised and prepaid cash flows on a mortgage pool, the CMO is a multiclass pass-through with a number of different investor classes or tranches. Unlike a pass-through, each class has a different guaranteed coupon just like a regular T-bond; but more importantly, the allocation of early cash flows due to mortgage prepayments is such that at any one time, all prepayments go to retiring the principal outstanding of only one class of bondholders at a time, leaving the other classes' prepayment protected for a period of time. Thus, a CMO serves as a way to mitigate or reduce prepayment risk.

Creation of CMOs

CMO (collateralized mortgage obligation)
A mortgage-backed bond issued in multiple classes or tranches.

CMOs can be created either by packaging and securitizing whole mortgage loans or, more usually, by placing existing pass-throughs in a trust off the balance sheet. The trust or third-party FI holds the pass-through as collateral against issues of new CMO securities. The trust issues these CMOs in three or more different classes. We show a three-class or tranche CMO in Figure 27–10.

Issuing CMOs is often equivalent to double securitization. Mortgages are packaged, and a pass-through is issued. An investment bank or a savings institution may buy this whole issue or a large part of the issue and would then place these MBSs as collateral with a trust and issue three new classes of bonds backed by the MBSs as collateral. As a result, the investors in each CMO class have a sole claim to the MBS collateral if the issuer fails. The investment bank or other issuer creates the CMO to make a profit by repackaging the cash flows from the single-class MBS pass-through into cash flows more attractive to different groups of investors. The sum of the prices at which the three CMO bond classes can be sold normally exceeds that of the original pass-through:

$$\sum_{i=1}^{3} P_{i,CMO} > P_{MBS}$$

To understand the gains from repackaging, it is necessary to understand how CMOs restructure prepayment risk to make it more attractive to different classes of investors. We explain this in the following simple example.

FIGURE 27–10
The Creation of a CMO

EXAMPLE 27–1	
The Value Additivity of CMOs	

Suppose an investment bank buys a $150 million issue of MBS and places them in trust as collateral. It then issues a CMO with these three classes:

> Class A: Annual fixed coupon 7 percent, class size $50 million
> Class B: Annual fixed coupon 8 percent, class size $50 million
> Class C: Annual fixed coupon 9 percent, class size $50 million

Under the CMO, each class has a guaranteed or fixed coupon.[17] By restructuring the MBS as a CMO, the investment bank can offer investors who buy bond Class C a higher degree of mortgage prepayment protection compared to a pass-through. Those who buy bond Class B receive an average degree of prepayment protection, and those who take Class A receive virtually no prepayment protection.

Each month, mortgagees in the pool pay principal and interest on their mortgages; each payment includes the promised amortized amount (*PMT*) plus any additional payments as some of the mortgage holders prepay principal to refinance their mortgages or because they have sold their houses and are relocating. These cash flows are passed through to the owner of the MBS. The CMO issuer uses the cash flows to pay promised coupon interest to the three classes of CMO bondholders. Suppose that in month 1 the promised amortized cash flows (PMT) on the mortgages underlying the pass-through collateral are $1 million, but an additional $1.5 million cash flow results from early mortgage prepayments. Thus, the cash flows in the first month available to pay promised coupons to the three classes of investors would be

$$PMT + \text{Prepayments} = \$1 \text{ million} + \$1.5 \text{ million} = \$2.5 \text{ million}$$

This cash flow is available to the trustee, who uses it in the following fashion:

1. *Coupon payments.* Each month (or more commonly, each quarter or half year), the trustee pays out the guaranteed coupons to the three classes of investors at annualized coupon rates of 7 percent, 8 percent, and 9 percent, respectively. Given the stated principal of $50 million for each class, the Class A (7 percent coupon) investors receive approximately $291,667 in coupon payments in month 1, the Class B (8 percent coupon) receive approximately $333,333 in month 1, and the Class C (9 percent coupon) receive approximately $375,000 in month 1. Thus, the total promised coupon payments to the three classes amount to $1,000,000 (equal to *PMT,* the no-prepayment cash flows in the pool).

2. *Principal payments.* The trustee has $2.5 million available to pay out as a result of promised mortgage payments plus early prepayments, but the total payment of coupon interest amounts to $1 million. The remaining $1.5 million has to be paid out to the CMO investors. The unique feature of the CMO is that the trustee would pay this remaining $1.5 million only to Class A investors to retire these investors' principal. This retires early some of these investors' principal outstanding. At the end of month 1, only $48.5 million ($50 million − $1.5 million) of Class A bonds remains outstanding, compared to $50 million Class B and $50 million Class C. These payment flows are shown graphically in Figure 27–11.

Let's suppose that in month 2 the same thing happens. The cash flows from the mortgage pool exceed the promised coupon payments to the three classes of bondholders. Again, the trustee uses any excess cash flows to pay off or retire the principal of Class A bondholders. If the excess cash flows again amount to $1.5 million, at the end of month 2 there will be only $47 million ($48.5 million—$1.5 million) of Class A bonds outstanding.

---

[17] In some cases, coupons are paid monthly, in others quarterly, and in still others semiannually.

Given any positive flow of prepayments, it is clear that within a few years the Class A bonds will be fully retired. In practice, this often occurs between 1.5 and 3 years after issue. After the trustee retires Class A, only Classes B and C remain.

As before, out of any cash flows received from the mortgage pool, the trustee pays the bondholders their guaranteed coupons, $C_B = \$333,333$ and $C_C = \$375,000$ for a total of $708,333. Suppose that total cash flows received by the trustee are $1,208,333 in the first month after the total retirement of Class A bonds, reflecting amortized mortgage payments by the remaining mortgagees in the pool plus any new prepayments. The excess cash flows of $500,000 ($1,208,333 − $708,333) then go to retire the principal outstanding of CMO bond Class B. At the end of that month, there are only $49.5 million Class B bonds outstanding. This is shown graphically in Figure 27–12.

FIGURE 27–11 **Allocation of Cash Flows to Owners of CMO Tranches**

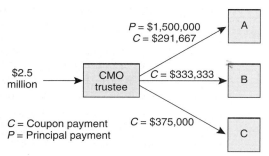

C = Coupon payment
P = Principal payment

FIGURE 27–12 **Allocation of Cash Flows to Remaining Tranches of CMO Bonds**

As the months pass, the trustee will use any excess cash flows over and above the promised coupons to investors of Class B and C bonds to retire bond Class B's principal. Eventually, all of the $50 million principal on Class B bonds will be retired—in practice, five to seven years after the CMO issue. After Class B bonds are retired, all remaining cash flows will be dedicated to paying the promised coupon of investors of Class C bonds and retiring the $50 million principal on Class C bonds. In practice, Class C bonds can have an average life as long as 20 years.

Class A, B, and C Bond Buyers

Class A

These bonds have the shortest average life with a minimum of prepayment protection. They are, therefore, of great interest to investors seeking short-duration mortgage-backed assets to reduce the duration of their mortgage-related asset portfolios.

Class B

These bonds have some prepayment protection and expected durations of five to seven years depending on the level of interest rates. Pension funds and life insurance companies would purchase these bonds, although some deposit-taking institutions would buy this bond class as well.

Class C

Because of their long expected duration, Class C bonds are highly attractive to insurance companies and pension funds seeking long-term duration assets to match their long-term duration liabilities. Indeed, because of their failure to offer prepayment protection, regular pass-throughs may not be very attractive to these institutions. Class C CMOs, with their high but imperfect degree of prepayment protection, may be of greater interest to the FI managers of these institutions.

In summary, by splitting bondholders into different classes and by restructuring cash flows into forms more valued by different investor clienteles, the CMO issuer stands to make a profit.

Other CMO Classes

CMOs can always have more than the three classes described in the previous example. Indeed, issues of up to 17 different classes have been made. Clearly, the 17th-class bondholders would have an enormous degree of prepayment protection since the first 16 classes would have had their bonds retired before the principal outstanding on this bond class would be affected by early prepayments. In addition, trustees have created other special types of classes as products to attract investor interest; we discuss these classes next.

Class Z

Z class
An accrual class of a CMO that makes a payment to bondholders only when preceding CMO classes have been retired.

Frequently, CMO issues contain a **Z class** as the last regular class. The Z implicitly stands for zero, but these are not really zero-coupon bonds. This class has a stated coupon, such as 10 percent, and accrues interest for the bondholder on a monthly basis at this rate. The trustee does not pay this interest, however, until all other classes of bonds are fully retired. When the other classes have been retired, the Z-class bondholder receives the promised coupon and principal payments plus accrued interest payments. Thus, the Z class has characteristics of both a zero-coupon bond (no coupon payments for a long period) and a regular bond.

Class R

R class
The residual class of a CMO giving the owner the right to any remaining collateral in the trust after all other bond classes have been retired plus any reinvestment income earned by the trust.

In placing the MBS collateral with the trustee, the CMO issuer normally uses very conservative prepayment assumptions. If prepayments are slower than expected, there is often excess collateral left over in the pool when all regular classes have been retired. Further, trustees often reinvest funds or cash flows received from the underlying instrument (MBS) in the period prior to paying interest on the CMOs. In general, the size of any excess collateral and interest on interest gets bigger when rates are high and the timing of coupon intervals is semiannual rather than monthly. This residual **R class** or "garbage class" is a high-risk investment class that gives the investor the rights to the overcollateralization and reinvestment income on the cash flows in the CMO trust. Because the value of the returns in this bond class increases when interest rates increase, while normal bond values fall with interest rate increases, Class R often has a negative duration. Thus, it is potentially attractive to deposit-taking institutions seeking to hedge their regular bond and fixed-income portfolios.[18]

Consider the example of a CMO with Classes A, B, C, Z, and R in Table 27–7. From Table 27–7, you can see that the underlying pass-through bond held as collateral is an MBS 9.99 percent coupon bond with an original maturity of 30 years, an issue size of $500 million, and a prepayment rate assumed to be twice the size assumed by the PSA model (200 percent PSA). The five CMO bond classes are issued in different amounts, with the largest class being B. Note that the principal amounts of the five classes sum to $500 million.

---

[18] Negative duration implies that bond prices increase with interest rates; that is, the price–yield curve is positively sloped.

TABLE 27–7   CMO with Five Bond Classes ($ millions)

	Collateral				
Type	Coupon	Amount	Original Term	Remaining Average Term	Assumed Prepayment Rate
MBS	9.99%	$500	360 months	349 months	200% PSA

	Bonds				
Class	A	B	C	Z	R
Amount	$150.9	$238.6	$85.5	$24.0	$1.0
Bond type	Fixed	Fixed	Fixed	Accrual	Residual
Coupon (percent)	7.95	9.35	9.60	9.99	503.88
Price (percent)	99.8099	99.3083	N/A	89.4978	1445.1121
Yield (bond equivalent)	7.85	9.55	N/A	10.86	10.30
Weighted-average life (years)	1.6	5.9	11.2	18.4	3.6
Benchmark Treasury (years)	2	5	N/A	20	N/A
Spread over Treasury (basis points)	15	125	N/A	180	N/A

CONCEPT QUESTIONS

1. Would insurance companies prefer Z-class CMOs? Explain your answer.
2. Are Z-class CMOs exactly the same as T-bond strips? If not, why not?
3. In our example, the coupon on the Class C bonds was assumed to be higher than that on the Class B bonds and the coupon on Class B bonds was assumed to be higher than that on Class A bonds. Under what term structure conditions might this not be the case?

THE MORTGAGE-BACKED (COVERED) BOND (MBB)

mortgage (asset)-backed (covered) bonds
Bonds collateralized by a pool of assets.

Mortgage (asset)-backed bonds (MBBs) (called *covered bonds* in Canada and Europe) are the third asset-securitization vehicle. These bonds differ from pass-throughs and CMOs in two key dimensions. First, while pass-throughs and CMOs help deposit-taking institutions remove mortgages from their balance sheets as forms of off-balance-sheet securitization, MBBs normally remain on the balance sheet. Second, pass-throughs and CMOs have a direct link between the cash flows on the underlying mortgages and the cash flows on the bond vehicles. By contrast, the relationship for MBBs is one of collateralization—there is no direct link between the cash flow on the mortgages backing the bond and the interest and principal payments on the MBB.

An FI issues an MBB to reduce risk to the MBB bondholders, who have a first claim to a segment of the FI's mortgage assets. Practically speaking, the FI segregates a group of mortgage assets on its balance sheet and pledges this group as collateral against the MBB issue. A trustee normally monitors the segregation of assets and makes sure that the market value of the collateral exceeds the principal owed to MBB holders. That is, FIs back most MBB issues by excess collateral. This excess collateral backing of the bond, in addition to the priority rights of the bond-holders, generally ensures that these bonds can be sold with a high credit rating, such as AAA. In contrast, the FI, when evaluated as a whole, could be rated BBB or even lower. A high credit rating results in lower coupon payments than would be required if significant default risk had lowered the credit rating (see Chapter 11). To explain the potential benefits and the sources of any gains to an FI from issuing MBBs, we examine the following simple example.

EXAMPLE 27–2

Gains to an FI from Issuing MBBs

Consider an FI with $20 million in long-term mortgages as assets. It is financing these mortgages with $10 million in short-term uninsured deposits (e.g., wholesale deposits over $100,000) and $10 million in insured deposits (e.g., retail deposits of $100,000 or less). In this example, we ignore the issues of capital and reserve requirements. Look at the balance sheet structure in Table 27–8.

This balance sheet poses problems for the FI manager. First, the FI has a positive duration gap $(D_A > kD_L)$. Second, because of this interest rate risk and the potential default and prepayment risk on the FI's mortgage assets, uninsured depositors are likely to require a positive and potentially significant risk premium to be paid on their deposits. By contrast, the insured depositors may require approximately the risk-free rate on their deposits as they are fully insured by CDIC (see Chapter 19).

To reduce its duration gap exposure and lower its funding costs, the FI can segregate $12 million of the mortgages on the asset side of its balance sheet and pledge them as collateral backing a $10 million long-term MBB issue. Because of this overcollateralization, the mortgage-backed bond issued by the FI may cost less to issue, in terms of required yield, than uninsured deposits; that is, it may well be rated AAA while uninsured deposits might be rated BBB. The FI can therefore use the proceeds of the $10 million bond issue to retire the $10 million of uninsured deposits.

Consider the FI's balance sheet after the issue of the MBBs in Table 27–9. It might seem that the FI has miraculously engineered a restructuring of its balance sheet that has resulted in a better matching of D_A to D_L and a lowering of funding costs. The bond issue has lengthened the average duration of liabilities by replacing short-term deposits with long-term MBBs and lowered funding costs because AAA-rated bond coupon rates are below BBB-rated uninsured funding costs. However, this outcome occurs only because the insured depositors do not worry about risk exposure since they are 100 percent insured by CDIC. The result of the MBB issue and the segregation of $12 million of assets as collateral backing the $10 million bond issue is that the $10 million insured deposits are now backed only by $8 million in free or unpledged assets. If smaller depositors were not insured by CDIC, they would surely demand very high risk premiums to hold these risky deposits. The implication of this is that the FI gains only because CDIC is willing to bear enhanced credit risk through its insurance guarantees to depositors.[19] As a result, the FI is actually gaining at the expense of CDIC. Consequently, it is not surprising that CDIC and OSFI are concerned about the growing use of this form of securitization by risky deposit-taking institutions.

TABLE 27–8
Balance Sheet of Potential MBB Issuer ($ millions)

Assets		Liabilities	
Long-term mortgages	$20	Insured deposits	$10
		Uninsured deposits	10
	$20		$20

TABLE 27–9
FI's Balance Sheet after MBB Issue ($ millions)

Assets		Liabilities	
Collateral = (market value of segregated mortgages)	$12	MBB issue	$10
Other mortgages	8	Insured deposits	10
	$20		$20

[19] And does not make the risk-based deposit insurance premium to banks and other deposit-taking FIs sufficiently large to reflect this risk.

The transfer of risk from the deposit-taking institution to CDIC was considered by OSFI when it allowed Canadian FIs to issue limited amounts of covered bonds in June 2007. The issue of covered bonds by Canadian DTIs is limited to 4 percent of the total assets of the DTI, where *total assets* is defined as the numerator of the asset-to-capital multiple (see Chapter 20). Although the market for covered bonds has been used extensively by German and Danish FIs, it is still in its early stages in Canada. In 2008, RBC had two covered bond issues for a total of €4.5 billion, BMO issued €1.0 billion, and CIBC had two issues totalling €2.32 billion. CIBC's issues were backed by residential mortgages insured by CMHC. Covered bond issues in Canadian dollars are called **Maple covered bonds,** and have been issued by Depfa Bank and Dexia Municipal Agency, among others. Globally, gross issuance of mortgage-backed bonds exceeded US$300 billion in quarter 4 of 2008, as European countries including the United Kingdom, Spain, Germany, Italy and Belgium attempted to deal with the financial crisis following the failure of Lehman Brothers in September 2008. Gross issuance of MBB exceeded 50 percent of all bond issues in Belgium, Spain, and Italy.[20]

Other than regulatory discouragement and the risk of regulatory intervention, there are private return reasons why an FI might prefer the pass-through/CMO forms of securitization to issuing MBBs. First, MBBs tie up mortgages on the FI's balance sheet for a long time. This increases the illiquidity of the asset portfolio. Second, the amount of mortgages tied up is enhanced by the need to overcollateralize to ensure a high-quality credit risk rating for the bond issue; in our example, the overcollateralization was $2 million. Third, by keeping mortgages on the balance sheet, the FI continues to be liable for capital adequacy requirement. Because of these problems, MBBs are the least used of the three basic vehicles of securitization.

Maple covered bonds	Collateralized bonds issued in Canadian dollars.

Would an AAA FI ever issue mortgage-backed bonds? Explain your answer.

INNOVATIONS IN SECURITIZATION

We now turn our attention to the growing innovations in FIs' asset securitization. We discuss two major innovations and their use in return-risk management by FIs: mortgage pass-through strips and the extension of the securitization concept to other assets.

Mortgage Pass-Through Strips

The mortgage pass-through strip is a special type of a CMO with only two classes. The fully amortized nature of mortgages means that any given monthly payment, PMT, contains an interest component and a principal component. Beginning in 1987, investment banks and other FI issuers stripped out the interest component from the principal component and sold each payment stream separately to different bond class investors. They sold an interest only (IO) class and a principal only (PO) class; these two bond classes have very special cash flow characteristics,

FIGURE 27–13
IO/PO Strips

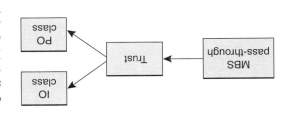

especially regarding the interest rate sensitivity of these bonds. We show this stripping of the cash flows in Figure 27–13 and consider the effects of interest rate changes on the value of each of these stripped instruments below.

IO Strips

IO strip
A bond sold to investors whose cash flows reflect the monthly interest payments received from a pool of mortgages.

The owner of an **IO strip** has a claim to the present value of interest payments made by the mortgage holders in the pool—that is, to the IO segments of each month's cash flow received from the underlying mortgage pool:

$$P_{IO} = \frac{IO_1}{\left(1+\dfrac{y}{12}\right)^1} + \frac{IO_2}{\left(1+\dfrac{y}{12}\right)^2} + \frac{IO_3}{\left(1+\dfrac{y}{12}\right)^3} + \cdots + \frac{IO_{300}}{\left(1+\dfrac{y}{12}\right)^{300}}$$

When interest rates change, they affect the cash flows received on mortgages. We concentrate on two effects: the discount effect and the prepayment effect on the price or value of IOs, denoted by P_{IO}.

Discount Effect As interest rates (y) fall, the present value of any cash flows received on the strip—the IO payments—rises, increasing the value (P_{IO}) of the bond.

Prepayment Effect As interest rates fall, mortgagees prepay their mortgages. In absolute terms, the number of IO payments the investor receives is likely to shrink. For example, the investor might receive only 100 monthly IO payments instead of the expected 300 in a no-prepayment world. The shrinkage in the size and value of the IO payments reduces the value (P_{IO}) of the bond.

Specifically, one can expect that as interest rates continue to fall below the mortgage coupon rate of the bonds in the pool, the prepayment effect gradually dominates the discount effect, so that over some range the price or value of the IO bond falls as interest rates fall. Note the price–yield curve in Figure 27–14 for an IO strip

FIGURE 27–14
Price–Yield Curve of an IO Strip

on a pass-through bond with 10 percent mortgage coupon rates. The price–yield curve slopes upward in the interest rate range below 10 percent. This means that as current interest rates rise or fall, IO values or prices rise or fall. As a result, the IO is a rare example of a **negative duration** asset that is very valuable as a portfolio-hedging device for an FI manager when included with regular bonds whose price–yield curves show the normal inverse relationship. That is, even though as interest rates rise the value of the regular bond portfolio falls, the value of an IO portfolio may rise. Note in Figure 27–14 that at rates above the pool's mortgage coupon of 10 percent, the price–yield curve changes shape and tends to perform like any regular bond. In recent years, FIs have purchased IOs to hedge the interest rate risk on the mortgages and other bonds held as assets in their portfolios. We depict the hedging power of IOs in Figure 27–15.

negative duration
Relationship in which the price of a bond increases or decreases as yields increase or decrease.

PO Strips

The value of the **PO strip** (P_{PO}) is defined by

PO strip
A bond whose cash flows to investors reflect the monthly principal payments received from a pool of mortgages.

$$P_{PO} = \frac{PO_1}{\left(1 + \dfrac{y}{12}\right)^1} + \frac{PO_2}{\left(1 + \dfrac{y}{12}\right)^2} + \frac{PO_3}{\left(1 + \dfrac{y}{12}\right)^3} + \cdots + \frac{PO_{300}}{\left(1 + \dfrac{y}{12}\right)^{300}}$$

where the PO_i ($i = 1$ to 300) represents the mortgage principal components of each monthly payment by the mortgage holders. This includes both the monthly amortized payment component of PMT that is principal and any early prepayments of principal by the mortgagees. Again, we consider the effects on a PO's value (P_{PO}) of a change in interest rates.

Discount Effect As yields (y) fall, the present value of any principal payments must increase and the value of the PO strip rises.

Prepayment Effect As yields fall, the mortgage holders pay off principal early. Consequently, the PO bondholder receives the fixed principal balance outstanding on the pool of mortgages earlier than stated. Thus, this prepayment effect must also work to increase the value of the PO strip.

As interest rates fall, both the discount and prepayment effects point to a rise in the value of the PO strip. The price–yield curve reflects an inverse relationship, but with a steeper slope than for normal bonds; that is, PO strip bond values are very interest rate-sensitive, especially for yields below the stated mortgage coupon rate. We show this in Figure 27–16 for a 10 percent PO strip. (Note that a regular coupon bond is affected only by the discount effect.) As you can see, when

FIGURE 27–15 Hedging with IOs

(a)

Prices / values

Yields

10%

IO strips

Regular bond / mortgage portfolio

(b)

Net portfolio value of bonds, mortgages, and IOs

Yields

10%

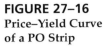

FIGURE 27–16
Price–Yield Curve
of a PO Strip

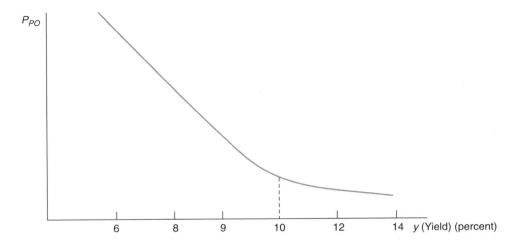

yields fall below 10 percent, the market value or price of the PO strip can increase very quickly. At rates above 10 percent, it tends to behave like a regular bond (as the incentive to prepay disappears).

The IO–PO strip is a classic example of financial engineering. From a given pass-through bond, two new bonds have been created: the first with an upward-sloping price–yield curve over some range and the second with a steeply downward-sloping price–yield curve over some range. Each class is attractive to different investors and investor segments. The IO is attractive to deposit-taking institutions as an on-balance-sheet hedging vehicle. The PO is attractive to FIs that wish to increase the interest rate-sensitivity of their portfolios and to investors or traders who wish to take a naked or speculative position regarding the future course of interest rates. This high and complex interest sensitivity has resulted in major traders such as JPMorgan Chase and Merrill Lynch, as well as many investors such as hedge funds, suffering considerable losses on their investments in these instruments when interest rates have moved unexpectedly against them.

Securitization of Other Assets

Although a major use of securitization vehicles has been for packaging residential mortgages, the techniques have been adapted and used for FIs' other assets such as automobile loans and leases, credit card receivables, commercial mortgages, equipment leases and loans, lines of credit, trade receivables, and corporate loans (Figure 27–2).

In addition to securitizing their residential mortgages, Canadian banks as well as retail stores Canadian Tire (Canadian Tire Bank) and Sears Canada (Sears Canada Bank) have been active in securitizing their credit card receivables. Credit card securitization is very similar in technology to pass-through mortgage securities. As shown in Figure 27–17, the credit card receivables are sold to a trust company or variable-interest entity (VIE) and then asset-backed securities are issued in the form of notes, which are rated and are tradable. Notice from the figure that this securitization of credit card receivables is very similar in technology to the pass-through mortgage bond.

FIGURE 27–17
**The Structure
of a Credit Card
Securitization**

**variable-interest
entities (VIEs)/
multi-seller
conduits**
Special-purpose entities
created by FIs for the
securitization and sale
of customer's assets.

FIs have also implemented the securitization technology for their customers for a fee. These third-party assets are securitized by creating **variable-interest entities (VIEs)** (also called **multi-seller conduits**) that create asset-backed commercial paper (ABCP) that is rated and then sold in the capital markets. Table 27–10 shows the top seven ABCP administrators and their share of the ABCP for August 2009.

CAN ALL ASSETS BE SECURITIZED?

The extension of securitization technology to other assets raises questions about the limits of securitization and whether all assets and loans can be securitized. Conceptually the answer is that they can, as long as it is profitable to do so or the benefits to the FI from securitization outweigh the costs of securitization. In Table 27–11, we summarize the benefits versus the costs of securitization.

From Table 27–11, given any set of benefits, the more costly and difficult it is to find asset packages of sufficient size and homogeneity, the more difficult and expensive it is to securitize. For example, corporate loans have maturities running from a few months up to eight years; further, they have varying interest rate terms (fixed, LIBOR floating, prime rate floating) and fees. In addition, they contain differing

TABLE 27–10
**Asset-Backed
Commercial Paper
in Canada, August
2009**

Source: DBRS, *Canadian
Securitization Market Overview, August 2009*, Octo-
ber 23, 2009, www.dbrs.
com/research/230406.

	Total ABCP	
Administrator	**Outstanding Amount**	**Market Share**
TD Securities Inc.	$13,401,813,500	36.5%
BMO Capital Markets	10,654,375,598	29.0%
RBC Capital Markets Inc.	5,282,885,768	14.4%
CIBC World Markets Inc.	4,940,573,418	13.5%
Scotia Capital Inc.	1,826,899,295	5.0%
National Bank Financial Inc.	511,743,730	1.4%
Canadian Tire Bank	62,813,280	0.2%
Total	**$36,681,104,589**	**100.0%**

TABLE 27–11
**Benefits
versus Costs of
Securitization**

Benefits	Costs
1. New funding source (bonds versus deposits)	1. Cost of public/private credit risk insurance and guarantees
2. Increased liquidity of FI loans	2. Cost of overcollateralization
3. Enhanced ability to manage the duration gap of $(D_A - kD_L)$	3. Valuation and packaging costs (the cost of asset heterogeneity)
4. If off balance sheet, the issuer saves on deposit insurance premiums and capital adequacy requirements	

covenants and are made to firms in a wide variety of industries. Despite this, FIs have still been able to issue securitization packages called CLOs (collateralized loan obligations) containing high-quality, low-default-risk loans and CDOs (collateralized debt obligations) containing a diversified collection of loans and other assets. The interest and principal payments on a CDO are linked to the timing of default losses and repayments on a pool of underlying loans or bonds. The riskiest of the CDOs, sometimes called *toxic waste,* pay out only if everything goes right. The best CDOs will pay out unless the entire portfolio defaults. Generally, it should be much harder to securitize low-quality loans into CDOs. Specifically, the harder it is to value a loan or asset pool, the greater the costs of securitization due to the need for overcollateralization or credit risk insurance. The economic recession of the early 2000s saw some large defaults and frauds at once highly rated companies (such as Enron and WorldCom), and many CDO debt pools suffered large value losses.

The global market turmoil of 2007 and 2008 demonstrated just how far securitization technology had been stretched. CDOs and CDO-squareds (CDOs whose underlying assets were CDOs) carrying high credit ratings from respected ratings agencies had been offered to investors who did not understand or were unable to properly analyze the level of risk. As well, the methodologies, particularly the default assumptions, were found to be unrealistic in a market meltdown, and many formerly highly rated securitized assets became toxic waste. As the global economy slowed down, house prices declined and default rates climbed, particularly on the subprime mortgages securitized by many U.S. FIs and sold to investors around the world. U.S. prime mortgage default rates were over 3.5 percent and subprime mortgage default rates were over 20 percent by December 2008. Canadian prime mortgage default rates were still less than 0.5 percent and subprime default rates less than 5 percent by December 2008.

By mid-2009, regulators were looking at Basel II, domestic and international accounting standards, and the role and responsibilities of credit agencies for ways to better understand and to control the risks of securitization. Global FIs and their regulators were acting to prevent a repeat of the market disruptions experienced in 2008. The question asked is now more along the lines of: *Should* all assets be securitized? The potential boundary to securitization may well be defined by the relative degree of heterogeneity and credit quality of an asset type or group. It is not surprising that fixed-rate residential mortgages were the first assets to be securitized since they are the most homogeneous of all assets on FI balance sheets. For example, the existence of secondary markets for houses provides price information that allows reasonably accurate market valuations of the underlying asset to be made, and extensive data are available on mortgage default rates by locality.

CONCEPT QUESTION

Can all assets and loans be securitized? Explain your answer.

Summary

In Chapter 1 we distinguished between FIs that are asset transformers and those that are asset brokers. By becoming increasingly reliant on securitization, banks moved away from being asset transformers that originate and hold assets to maturity; they became asset brokers more reliant on servicing and other fees. This makes banks look more similar to securities firms. Thus, over time, the traditional financial technology differences between commercial banking and investment banking diminished, as more loans and assets were securitized. The major forms of securitization—pass-through securities, collateralized mortgage obligations (CMOs)—were discussed. Also, the impact of prepayment behaviour on MBS valuation was discussed. Finally, recent innovations in securitization were described and a summary of the Canadian ABS market provided. Securitization markets will evolve as FIs and their regulators recover from the 2007–2008 market turmoil.

Questions and Problems

1. What has been the effect of securitization on the asset portfolios of financial institutions?

2. What regulatory costs do FIs face when making loans? How does securitization reduce the levels of cost?

3. An FI is planning to issue $100 million in BB-rated commercial loans. The FI will finance the loans by issuing demand deposits.

   a. What is the minimum amount of capital required by the Basel Accord?

   b. What is the amount of demand deposits needed to fund this loan, assuming there are no reserve requirements on demand deposits?

   c. Show a simple balance sheet with total assets, total liabilities, and equity if this is the only project funded by the bank.

4. Consider the FI in problem 3.

   a. What additional risk-exposure problems does the FI face?

   b. What are some possible solutions to the duration mismatch and the illiquidity problems?

   c. What advantages does securitization have in dealing with the FI's risk-exposure problems?

5. How are investors in pass-through securities protected against default risk?

6. What specific changes occur on the balance sheet at the completion of the securitization process? What adjustments occur to the risk profile of the FI?

7. Consider a mortgage pool with principal of $20 million. The maturity is 25 years with a monthly mortgage payment of 10 percent per annum. Assume no prepayments.

   a. What is the monthly mortgage payment (100 percent amortizing) on the pool of mortgages?

   b. If the servicing fee is 45 basis points, what is the yield on the MBS pass-through?

   c. What is the monthly payment on the MBS in part (b)?

   d. Calculate the first monthly servicing fee paid to the originating FIs.

8. Calculate the value of (a) the mortgage pool and (b) the MBS pass-through in question 7 if market interest rates increase 50 basis points. Assume no prepayments.

9. What would be the impact on MBS pricing if the pass-through was not fully amortized? What is the present value of a $10 million pool of 15-year mortgages with an 8.5 percent per annum monthly mortgage coupon if market rates are 5 percent? The FI servicing fee is 44 basis points.

   a. Assume that the MBS is fully amortized.

   b. Assume that the MBS is only half amortized. There is a lump-sum payment at the maturity of the MBS that equals 50 percent of the mortgage pool's face value.

10. What is prepayment risk? How does prepayment risk affect the cash flow stream on a fully amortized mortgage loan? What are the two primary factors that cause early payment?

11. Under what conditions do mortgage holders have a call option on their mortgages? When is the call option in the money?

12. What are the benefits of market yields that are less than the average rate in the NHA MBS mortgage pool? What are the disadvantages of this rate inversion? To whom do the good news and the bad news accrue?

13. What is the weighted-average life (WAL) of a mortgage pool supporting pass-through securities? How does WAL differ from duration?

14. If 150 $200,000 mortgages are expected to be prepaid in three years and the remaining 150 $200,000 mortgages in a $60 million 15-year mortgage pool are to be prepaid in four years, what is the weighted-average life of the mortgage pool? Mortgages are fully amortized, with mortgage coupon rates set at 10 percent to be paid annually.

15. An FI originates a pool of 500 25-year mortgages, each averaging $150,000 with an annual mortgage coupon rate of 8 percent. Assume that the FI's servicing fee is 55 basis points.

    a. What is the present value of the mortgage pool?
    b. What is the monthly mortgage payment?
    c. For the first two payments, what portion is interest and what portion is principal repayment?
    d. What are the expected monthly cash flows to each MBS investor?
    e. What is the present value of the MBS? Assume that the risk-adjusted market annual rate of return is 8 percent compounded monthly.
    f. Would actual cash flows to MBS investors deviate from expected cash flows as in part (d)? Why or why not?
    g. What are the expected monthly cash flows for the FI?
    h. If all the mortgages in the pool are completely prepaid at the end of the second month, what is the pool's weighted-average life? *Hint:* Use your answer to part (c).
    i. What is the price of the pass-through security if its weighted-average life is equal to your solution for part (h)? Assume no change in market interest rates.
    j. What is the price of the MBS with a weighted-average life equal to your solution for part (h) if market yields decline 50 basis points?

16. What is the difference between the yield spread to average life and the option-adjusted spread on mortgage-backed securities?

17. What factors may cause the actual prepayment pattern to differ from the assumed pattern? How would an FI adjust for the presumed occurrence of some of these factors?

18. What is the burnout factor? How is it used in modelling prepayment behaviour? What other factors may be helpful in modelling the prepayment behaviour of a given mortgage pool?

19. What is the goal of prepayment models that use option pricing theory? How do these models differ from the PSA or empirical models? What criticisms often are directed toward these models?

20. How does the price on an MBS relate to the yield on an MBS option from the perspective of the investor? What is the option-adjusted spread (OAS)?

21. Use the options prepayment model to calculate the yield on a $30 million three-year fully amortized mortgage pass-through where the mortgage coupon rate is 6 percent paid annually. Market yields are 6.4 percent paid annually. Assume that there is no servicing or guarantee fee.

    a. What is the annual payment on the MBS?
    b. What is the present value of the MBS?
    c. Interest rate movements over time are assumed to change a maximum of 0.5 percent per year. Both an increase of 0.5 percent and a decrease of 0.5 percent in interest rates are equally probable. If interest rates fall 1.0 percent below the current mortgage coupon rates, all of the mortgages in the pool will be completely prepaid. Diagram the interest rate tree and indicate the probabilities of each node in the tree.
    d. What are the expected annual cash flows for each possible situation over the three-year period?
    e. The Treasury yield curve is flat at a discount yield of 6 percent. What is the option-adjusted spread on the MBS?

22. Use the options prepayment model to calculate the yield on a $12 million, five-year, fully amortized mortgage pass-through where the mortgage coupon rate is 7 percent paid annually. Market yields are 8 percent paid annually. Assume that there is no servicing or guarantee fee.

    a. What is the annual payment on the MBS?
    b. What is the present value of the MBS?
    c. Interest rate movements over time are assumed to change a maximum of 1 percent per year. Both an increase of 1 percent and a decrease of 1 percent in interest rates are equally probable. If interest rates fall 3 percent below the current mortgage coupon rates, all mortgages in the pool will be completely prepaid. Diagram the interest rate tree and indicate the probabilities of each node in the tree.
    d. What are the expected annual cash flows for each possible situation over the five-year period?
    e. The Treasury yield curve is flat at a discount yield of 6 percent. What is the option-adjusted spread on the MBS?

23. What conditions would cause the yield on pass-through securities with prepayment risk to be less than the yield on pass-through securities without prepayment risk?

24. What is a collateralized mortgage obligation (CMO)? How is it similar to a pass-through security? How does it differ? In what way does the creation of a CMO use market segmentation to redistribute prepayment risk?

25. Consider $200 million of 25-year mortgages with a coupon of 10 percent per annum paid quarterly.

    a. What is the quarterly mortgage payment?

b. What are the interest repayments over the first year of life of the mortgages? What are the principal repayments?

c. Construct a 25-year CMO using this mortgage pool as collateral. The pool has three tranches, where Tranche A offers the least protection against prepayment and Tranche C offers the most protection against prepayment. Tranche A of $50 million receives quarterly payments at 9 percent per annum, Tranche B of $100 million receives quarterly payments at 10 percent per annum, and Tranche C of $50 million receives quarterly payments at 11 percent per annum. Diagram the CMO structure.

d. Assume non-amortization of principal and no prepayments. What are the total promised coupon payments to the three classes? What are the principal payments to each of the three classes for the first year?

e. If, over the first year, the trustee receives quarterly prepayments of $10 million on the mortgage pool, how are these funds distributed?

f. How are the cash flows distributed if prepayments in the first half of the second year are $20 million quarterly?

g. How can the CMO issuer earn a positive spread on the CMO?

26. How does a Class Z tranche of a CMO differ from a Class R tranche? What causes a Z class to have characteristics of both a zero-coupon bond and a regular bond? What factors can cause an R class to have a negative duration?

27. Why would buyers of Class C tranches of collateralized mortgage obligations (CMOs) be willing to accept a lower return than purchasers of Class A tranches?

28. What are mortgage-backed (covered) bonds (MBBs)? How do MBBs differ from pass-through securities and CMOs?

29. From the perspective of risk management, how does the use of MBBs by an FI assist the FI in managing credit and interest rate risk?

30. What are four reasons why an FI may prefer the use of either pass-through securities or CMOs to the use of MBBs?

31. What is an interest-only (IO) strip? How do the discount effect and the prepayment effect of an IO create a negative duration asset? What macroeconomic effect is required for this negative duration effect to be possible?

32. What is a principal-only (PO) strip? What causes the price–yield profile of a PO strip to have a steeper slope than a normal bond?

33. An FI originates a pool of short-term real estate loans worth $20 million with maturities of five years and paying interest rates of 9 percent per annum.

a. What is the average payment received by the FI, including both principal and interest, if no prepayment is expected over the life of the loan?

b. If the loans are converted into pass-through certificates and the FI charges a servicing fee of 50 basis points, what is the payment amount expected by the holders of the pass-through securities if no prepayment is expected?

c. Assume that the payments are separated into interest-only (IO) and principal-only (PO) payments, that prepayments of 5 percent occur at the end of years 3 and 4, and that the payment of the remaining principal occurs at the end of year 5. What are the expected annual payments for each instrument? Assume discount rates of 9 percent.

d. What is the market value of IOs and POs if the market interest rates for instruments of similar risk decline to 8 percent?

34. What are the factors that, in general, allow assets to be securitized? What are the costs involved in the securitization process?

35. How does an FI use loan sales and securitization to manage interest rate, credit, and liquidity risks? Summarize how each of the possible methods of securitization affects the balance sheet and profitability of an FI in the management of these risks.

Web Question

36. Go to the Bank of Canada's website at www.bankofcanada.ca. Click on "Publications and Research" and then on "Financial System Review." Download the latest copy of the publication. Using the Search feature in Adobe Acrobat, search for "U.S." What are the cross-border issues currently of concern to the Bank of Canada? What short-term and long-term effects are they expected to have on Canadian financial markets? Search the document using the term "global." What current global financial market issues are of concern to the Bank of Canada?

Index